ESSENTIALS OF MARKETING

A Marketing Strategy Planning Approach

ELEVENTH EDITION

ESSENTIALS OF MARKETING

A Marketing Strategy Planning Approach

William D. Perreault, Jr., Ph.D.

UNIVERSITY OF NORTH CAROLINA

Joseph P. Cannon, Ph.D.

COLORADO STATE UNIVERSITY

E. Jerome McCarthy, Ph.D.

MICHIGAN STATE UNIVERSITY

Boston   Burr Ridge, IL   Dubuque, IA   New York   San Francisco   St. Louis
Bangkok   Bogotá   Caracas   Kuala Lumpur   Lisbon   London   Madrid   Mexico City
Milan   Montreal   New Delhi   Santiago   Seoul   Singapore   Sydney   Taipei   Toronto

ESSENTIALS OF MARKETING: A MARKETING STRATEGY PLANNING APPROACH

Published by McGraw-Hill/Irwin, a business unit of The McGraw-Hill Companies, Inc., 1221 Avenue of the Americas, New York, NY, 10020. Copyright © 2008, 2006, 2003, 2000, 1997, 1994, 1991, 1988, 1985, 1982, 1979 by The McGraw-Hill Companies, Inc. All rights reserved. No part of this publication may be reproduced or distributed in any form or by any means, or stored in a database or retrieval system, without the prior written consent of The McGraw-Hill Companies, Inc., including, but not limited to, in any network or other electronic storage or transmission, or broadcast for distance learning.

Some ancillaries, including electronic and print components, may not be available to customers outside the United States.

This book is printed on acid-free paper.

1 2 3 4 5 6 7 8 9 0 DOW/DOW 0 9 8 7

ISBN   978-0-07-340471-4
MHID   0-07-340471-3

Publisher: Paul Ducham
Executive editor: Doug Hughes
Managing developmental editor: Nancy Barbour
Editorial assistant: Devon Raemisch
Marketing manager: Trent Whatcott
Media producer: Lynn M. Bluhm
Lead project manager: Christine A. Vaughan
Senior manager, EDP: Heather D. Burbridge
Lead designer: Matthew Baldwin
Senior photo research coordinator: Jeremy Cheshareck
Photo researcher: Mike Hruby
Cover photos: AP Photo/Chris O'Meara; ©The Procter & Gamble Company. Used by permission; PhotoLink/Getty Images; Photo by Tim Boyle/Getty Images; Courtesy Brendan Mattingly Photography, Inc; Courtesy of Alcoa; Courtesy Michael Coburn/Electric Rentals, Inc; Redux Pictures/Mark Leong.
Typeface: 10.5/12 Goudy
Compositor: Aptara
Printer: R. R. Donnelley

Library of Congress Cataloging-in-Publication Data

Perreault, William D.
    Essentials of marketing : a marketing strategy planning approach / William D.
Perreault, Jr., Joseph P. Cannon, E. Jerome McCarthy. — 11th ed.
        p. cm.
    Includes index.
    ISBN-13: 978-0-07-340471-4 (alk. paper)
    ISBN-10: 0-07-340471-3 (alk. paper)
    1. Marketing. I. Cannon, Joseph P., Ph. D. II. McCarthy, E. Jerome (Edmund
Jerome) III. Title.
HF5415.M378 2008
658.8—dc22

2007027229

www.mhhe.com

About the Authors of *Essentials of Marketing*, 11/e

William D. Perreault, Jr.

William D. Perreault, Jr., is Kenan Professor of Business at the University of North Carolina. Dr. Perreault is the recipient of the two most prestigious awards in his field: the American Marketing Association Distinguished Educator Award and the Academy of Marketing Science Outstanding Educator Award. He also was selected for the Churchill Award, which honors career impact on marketing research. He was editor of the *Journal of Marketing Research* and has been on the review board of the *Journal of Marketing* and other journals.

The Decision Sciences Institute has recognized Dr. Perreault for innovations in marketing education, and at UNC he has received several awards for teaching excellence. His books include two other widely used texts: *Basic Marketing* and *The Marketing Game!*

Dr. Perreault is a past president of the American Marketing Association Academic Council and served as chair of an advisory committee to the U.S. Bureau of the Census and as a trustee of the Marketing Science Institute. He has also worked as a consultant to organizations that range from GE and IBM to the Federal Trade Commission and Venezuelan Ministry of Education.

Joseph P. Cannon

Joseph P. Cannon is associate professor of marketing at Colorado State University. He has also taught at the University of North Carolina at Chapel Hill, Emory University, Instituto de Empresa, INSEAD, and Thammasat University. He has received several teaching awards and honors.

Dr. Cannon's research has been published in the *Journal of Marketing, Journal of Marketing Research, Journal of the Academy of Marketing Science, Journal of Personal Selling and Sales Management, Journal of Public Policy and Marketing,* and the *Academy of Management Review,* among others. He received the 2006 Louis W. Stern Award for his 1999 article, "Buyer-Seller Relationships in Business Markets." He has written many teaching cases. He serves on the editorial review boards of the *Journal of Marketing,* where he received a distinguished reviewer award, and the *Journal of the Academy of Marketing Science.* For three years he served as chair of the American Marketing Association's Interorganizational Special Interest Group (IOSIG). Before entering academics, Dr. Cannon worked for six years in sales and marketing for Eastman Kodak Company.

E. Jerome McCarthy

E. Jerome McCarthy received his Ph.D. from the University of Minnesota and was a Ford Foundation Fellow at the Harvard Business School. He has taught at the Universities of Oregon, Notre Dame, and Michigan State. He was honored with the American Marketing Association's Trailblazer Award in 1987, and he was voted one of the "top five" leaders in marketing thought by marketing educators.

Besides publishing various articles, he is the author of books on data processing and social issues in marketing. He has been a frequent presenter at marketing conferences in the United States and internationally.

In addition to his academic interests, Dr. McCarthy has been involved in guiding the growth of organizations in the United States and overseas—both as a consultant and as a director. He has also been active in executive education. However, throughout his career, his primary interests have been in (1) "converting" students to marketing and effective marketing strategy planning and (2) preparing teaching materials to help others do the same. This is why he has spent a large part of his career developing and improving marketing texts to reflect the most current thinking in the field.

Preface

Essentials of Marketing is designed to satisfy your needs

This book is about marketing and marketing strategy planning. And, at its essence, marketing strategy planning is about figuring out how to do a superior job of satisfying customers. We take that point of view seriously and believe in practicing what we preach. So you can trust that this new edition of *Essentials of Marketing*—and all of the other teaching and learning materials that accompany it—will satisfy *your* needs. We're excited about this 11th edition of *Essentials of Marketing*, and we hope that you will be as well.

In developing this edition we've made hundreds of big and small additions, changes, and improvements in the text and all of the supporting materials that accompany it. We'll highlight some of those changes in this preface, but first it's useful to put this newest edition in a longer-term perspective.

Welcoming a new coauthor

We are excited to have a new coauthor, Joe Cannon. Joe joined us with this edition and has been a great contributor. Before becoming an academic, Joe worked in sales and marketing for Eastman Kodak Company. He has taught at universities in the United States, Europe, and Asia. He has consulted for large companies, including IBM, Kodak, Waterpik Technologies, and smaller companies and nonprofit organizations. Drawing on these experiences, Joe brings a new perspective to *Essentials of Marketing*, and his thinking and ideas are spread throughout this edition of the book and its related teaching and learning materials.

A shorter text—for flexibility and a crisp pace

Essentials of Marketing is a shortened version of our *Basic Marketing*, the most widely used text in the field. Our basic objectives in preparing a shorter text have always been

- To make it easy, interesting, and fast for students to grasp the essential concepts of marketing.
- To provide a flexible text and choices from comprehensive support materials so that instructors can accomplish their objectives for their students even though the time available for the course may be limited.

Accessibility is a key goal. In the whole text—and in all of the supplements, ranging from the new multimedia PowerPoints to the new edition of the *Learning Aid*—we spent much time and effort carefully defining terms and finding the right words, illustrations, and examples to speed understanding and motivate learning.

Building on pioneering strengths

Essentials of Marketing and *Basic Marketing* pioneered an innovative structure—using the "four Ps" with a managerial approach—for the introductory marketing course. They quickly became two of the most widely used business textbooks ever published because they organized the best ideas about marketing so that readers could both understand and apply them. The unifying focus of these ideas was on how to make the marketing decisions that a manager must make in deciding what customers to focus on and how best to meet their needs.

Over many editions of *Essentials of Marketing* there has been constant change in marketing management and the marketing environment. Some of the changes have been dramatic, and others have been subtle. As a result, we have made ongoing changes to the text to reflect marketing's best practices and ideas. Throughout all of these changes, *Essentials of Marketing* and the supporting materials that accompany it have been more widely used than any other teaching materials for introductory marketing. It is gratifying that the four Ps has proved to be an organizing structure that has worked well for millions of students and teachers.

Continuous innovation and improvement

The success of *Essentials of Marketing* is not the result of a single strength—or one long-lasting innovation. Rather, the text's four Ps framework, managerial orientation, and strategy planning focus have proved to be foundation pillars that are remarkably robust for supporting new developments in the field and innovations in the text and package. Thus, with each new edition of *Essentials of Marketing* we have continued to innovate to better meet the needs of students and faculty. In fact, we have made ongoing changes in how we develop the logic of the four Ps and the marketing strategy planning process. As always, though, our objective is to provide a flexible, high-quality text and choices from comprehensive and reliable support materials—so that instructors and students can accomplish their learning objectives. For example, included with the other innovations and improvements for this new edition are

- The *Marketing Strategy Planning Process model,* which enhances the clarity of the organization of the content. The model shows how each chapter's material fits into the "big picture." This and other integrative graphics enhance learning and speed student comprehension and reading.
- Expanded emphasis on customer equity and customer service. These concepts are introduced early in the book and are integrated throughout to emphasize their role in modern marketing.
- Interesting, integrated, and updated coverage of marketing practice. This edition includes hundreds of updated concepts, examples, and best practices—across a broad variety of business and nonprofit organizations. The examples are chosen to be interesting to students and to demonstrate best practices.
- High-involvement, in-chapter *Ethics Questions.* These provocative scenario-based exercises place students in real-world situations faced by today's marketing managers. The questions encourage students to take a stand and think more deeply about the dilemmas facing marketing managers. The flexible format allows instructors to create written assignments, discuss the questions in class, or simply encourage student reflection.
- The new *Marketing Plan Coach* software (on the Student CD) and end-of-chapter *Creating Marketing Plans* questions provide a new set of flexible teaching and learning materials that demonstrate how concepts from the book are applied by marketing managers. The author-developed *Coach* connects concepts from the book with a real marketing plan. The *Coach* helps students understand marketing strategy planning, builds their self-confidence, and prepares them for the business world.
- New and updated cases allow students to apply concepts in real organizations. For example, some topics include market selection and customer equity questions at a soccer academy, customer service problems at an online retailer, recruiting new firefighters to a volunteer fire department, and the challenges of marketing a life-saving innovation in a developing country.
- A sharper focus throughout the text on how the strategy planning process should lead to decisions about a target market and marketing mix that represents the best opportunity and competitive advantage for the firm and superior value for customers.
- Changed, revised, and updated *Internet Exercises.*
- An updated and expanded archive of PowerPoint electronic lecture-support slides.
- The *Instructor CD to Accompany Essentials of Marketing* that offers all of the text's teaching support materials in easy-to-use and electronic form and that

features a refined new user interface to make it even faster to access materials.
- Interesting new video cases and teaching videos that focus on current marketing issues.
- A new collection of short video clips carefully selected from *BusinessWeek* and *MSNBC* news stories to provide lively, real-world examples and foster class discussion.
- *Online Applications in Essentials of Marketing,* which offers links to articles from the popular press as well as some great video clips and podcasts.

We believe in continuous quality improvement

As authors, we're committed to ongoing improvements—and we're proud that we were implementing continuous quality improvements in preparing *Essentials of Marketing* long before the idea became popular in the world of business. We work to be creative in our coverage and approaches—because creativity is at the heart of the marketing spirit. The most creative teaching innovations are ones that meet students' needs and instructors' objectives. That's also why our first priority has always been, and always will be, producing quality materials that really work well for students and teachers. Students take the first marketing course only once. It is an investment and opportunity from which there should be a solid return. So we take it as a serious personal responsibility to support that investment with materials that are interesting and motivating—and that really build the skills and ideas that students need in their lives and careers.

Our belief that attention to continuous quality improvement in every aspect of the text and support materials *does make a difference* is consistently reaffirmed by the enthusiastic response of students and teachers alike to each new edition.

Leading technology innovations for teaching and learning

We take seriously our opportunity and responsibility to lead the marketing discipline in developing new, breakthrough approaches for teaching and learning in the first marketing course. Our thrust over the past two decades has been to use technology to provide better and easier options for teaching and richer and more interesting approaches for learning. Along with other innovations, we were the first to develop and offer spreadsheet-based computer-aided problems, custom-produced videos, a computerized test bank, a PC-based marketing simulation, a hypertext reference, CD-based interactive versions of the text, PowerPoint presentation slides with linking by objectives, CD multimedia archives and presentation software for instructors, multimedia case support, and the multimedia CD for students. With this edition we continue these traditions of innovation with a redesigned *Student CD to Accompany Essentials of Marketing,* an even easier-to-use and more comprehensive *Instructor CD to Accompany Essentials of Marketing,* and a host of new and improved teaching and learning materials available at the *Essentials of Marketing* website at www.mhhe.com/fourps.

Critically revised, updated, and rewritten

This new edition of *Essentials of Marketing* is the highest-quality teaching and learning resource ever published for the introductory marketing course. The whole text and all of the supporting materials have been critically revised, updated, and rewritten. As in past editions, clear and interesting communication has been a priority. *Essentials of Marketing* is designed to make it easy, interesting, and fast for students to grasp the key concepts of marketing. Careful explanations provide a crisp focus on the important "basics" of marketing strategy planning. At the same time, we have thoroughly

- Researched and incorporated new concepts.
- Integrated hundreds of new examples that bring the concepts alive.
- Illustrated marketing ideas and "best practices" in a rich variety of contexts.

We have deliberately used marketing examples from a host of different contexts. Examples span large and small firms, profit and nonprofit organizations, organizations that have moved to e-commerce and those that have found other ways to innovate, domestic and international settings, purchases by organizations as well as by final consumers, services and ideas or "causes" as well as physical goods, and established products as well as new technologies—because this variety reinforces the point that effective marketing is critical to all organizations.

Clear focus on changes in today's dynamic markets

This edition focuses special attention on changes taking place in today's dynamic markets. Throughout every chapter of the text we have integrated discussion and examples of

- Lifetime customer value and customer equity.
- Best practices in marketing, and how to avoid the mistakes of death-wish marketing (including errors and omissions all too common among many failed dot-com operators).
- Effective e-commerce innovations and changes in marketing over the Internet.
- Relationship building in marketing.
- Customer service and customer retention.
- Social impacts of marketing and macro-marketing.
- The importance of providing superior customer value as the means to achieve customer satisfaction and competitive advantage.
- International perspectives, including the challenges and opportunities in developing countries.

- Ethical issues and social impacts of marketing.

Similarly, we've also integrated new material on many important and fast-evolving topics. The following are but a sampling:

- The growing uses of technology in organizational buying—from spend management systems to different forms of online exchange.
- Low-cost methods for conducting marketing research and the use of specialized search engines.
- The increasing emphasis on design in product development.
- The circumstances when using direct channels of distribution make sense—and how to manage channel conflict that might come about when direct and indirect channels are used in combination.
- Successful strategies that have emerged as retailing over the Internet matures.
- Promotional campaigns that use viral communications to generate "buzz" among consumers.
- The use of blogs as a way for companies to interact with their customers.
- The growing importance of customer service in retaining customers and generating future sales.
- New and emerging forms of advertising on the Internet.

Driving home competitive advantage

Throughout the 11th edition we've continued to put more emphasis on the *process* of marketing strategy planning. In today's dynamic markets it's not enough to simply figure out an attractive opportunity and an effective marketing mix. The real challenge is to quickly but logically zero in on the target market and marketing mix that is really best for the firm, while recognizing that strategies need to be refined and improved as market conditions change. This highlights the need for breakthrough opportunities, the problems with me-too imitation, and the crucial role of competitive advantage in providing customers with superior value. In other words, we sharpen the focus on how to figure out the best blend of the four Ps and crush the mistaken view fostered by some texts that the marketing job is just coming up with *some* marketing mix.

Coupled with this, you'll learn how breakthroughs in information technology are driving changes in all aspects of marketing—whether it's e-commerce ordering, getting marketing information, preparing salespeople to interact with customers, or analyzing the "fire-hydrant" flow of data on sales and costs. We'll also highlight the many ways that relationships among marketing partners are changing—ranging from coordination of logistics to alliances among firms focused on the same market opportunity. You'll see how intense competition, both in the United States and around the world, is affecting marketing strategy planning. You'll see what it takes to transform an effective new-product development process into a profitable business.

Some other marketing texts are attempting to describe such changes. But that's not adequate. What sets *Essentials of Marketing* apart is that the explanations and examples equip students to see *why* these changes are taking place and what changes to expect in the future. That is an important distinction—because marketing is dynamic. Our objective is to prepare students to analyze marketing situations and develop exceptional marketing strategies—not just recite endless sets of lists.

A fresh design—to make important concepts even clearer

Along with the new content, we've given the text a fresh design. The changes range from the new cover to hundreds of new photographs, ads, web pages, and illustrations. An exhibit introduces and clearly organizes each chapter's content, highlights specific strategy decision areas, and shows how the material fits into the marketing strategy planning process. We've created many new exhibits—conceptual organizers, charts, and tables—and updated proven pieces from past editions, all with a fresh new design.

The aim of all this revising, refining, editing, and illustrating is to make important concepts and points even clearer to students. We want to make sure that each student really does get a good feel for a market-directed system and how he or she can help it—and some company—run better. We believe marketing is important and interesting—and we want every student who reads *Essentials of Marketing* to share our enthusiasm.

Eighteen chapters—with an emphasis on marketing strategy planning

The emphasis of *Essentials of Marketing* is on marketing strategy planning. Eighteen chapters introduce the important concepts in marketing management and help the student see marketing through the eyes of the marketing manager. The organization of the chapters and topics is carefully planned. But we took special care in writing so that

- It is possible to rearrange and use the chapters in many different sequences—to fit different needs.
- All of the topics and chapters fit together into a clear, overall framework for the marketing strategy planning process.

Broadly speaking, the chapters fall into two groupings. The first seven chapters introduce marketing and a broad view of the marketing strategy planning process. They cover topics such as segmentation, differentiation, the marketing environment, and buyer behavior, as well as how marketing information systems and research provide information about these forces to improve marketing decisions. The second

half of the text goes into the details of planning the four Ps, with specific attention to the key strategy decisions in each area. Then we conclude with an integrative review and an assessment of marketing's challenges and opportunities.

The first chapter deals with the important role of marketing—focusing not only on how a marketing orientation guides a business or nonprofit organization in the process of providing superior value to customers but also on the role of macro-marketing and how a market-directed economy shapes choices and quality of life for consumers. Chapter 2 builds on these ideas with a focus on the marketing strategy planning process and why it involves narrowing down to selection of a specific target market and blending the four Ps into a marketing mix to meet the needs of those customers. With that foundation in place, the chapter introduces an integrative model of the marketing strategy planning process that serves as an organizing framework for the rest of the text.

Chapter 3 shows how analysis of the market and external market environment relate to segmentation and differentiation decisions as well as the criteria for narrowing down to a specific target market and marketing mix. This strategic view alerts students to the importance of evaluating opportunities in the external environments affecting marketing—and these are discussed in Chapter 4. This chapter also highlights the critical role of screening criteria for narrowing down from possible opportunities to those that the firm will pursue.

You have to understand customers to understand marketing and segment markets and satisfy target market needs. So the next two chapters take a closer look at *customers*. Chapter 5 studies the behavioral aspects of the final consumer market. Chapter 6 looks at how business and organizational customers—like manufacturers, channel members, and government purchasers—are using e-commerce and how they are similar to and different from final consumers.

Chapter 7 is a contemporary view of getting information—from marketing information systems and marketing research—for marketing management planning. This chapter includes discussion of how information technology—ranging from intranets to speedy collection of market research data—is transforming the marketing manager's job. This sets the stage for discussions in later chapters about how research and marketing information improve each area of marketing strategy planning.

The next group of chapters—Chapters 8 to 17—is concerned with developing a marketing mix out of the four Ps: Product, Place (involving channels of distribution, logistics, and distribution customer service), Promotion, and Price. These chapters are concerned with developing the "right" Product and making it available at the "right" Place with the "right" Promotion and the "right" Price—to satisfy target customers and still meet the objectives of the business. These chapters are presented in an integrated, analytical way—as part of the overall framework for the marketing strategy planning process—so students' thinking about planning marketing strategies develops logically.

Chapters 8 and 9 focus on product planning for goods and services as well as new-product development and the different strategy decisions that are required at different stages of the product life cycle. We emphasize the value of an organized new-product development process for developing really new products that propel a firm to profitable growth. This chapter also details how quality management approaches can improve goods and services.

Chapters 10 through 12 focus on Place. Chapter 10 introduces decisions a manager must make about using direct distribution (for example, selling from the firm's own website) or working with other firms in a channel of distribution. We put special emphasis on the need for channel members to cooperate and coordinate to better meet the needs of customers. Chapter 11 focuses on the fast-changing arena of logistics and the strides that firms are making in using e-commerce to reduce the costs of storing, transporting, and handling products while improving the distribution service they provide customers. Chapter 12 provides a clear picture of retailers, wholesalers, and their strategy planning, including exchanges taking place via the Internet. This composite chapter helps students see why the big changes taking place in retailing are reshaping the channel systems for many consumer products.

Chapters 13 to 15 deal with Promotion. These chapters build on the concepts of integrated marketing communications, direct-response promotion, and customer-initiated digital communication, which are introduced in Chapter 13. Chapter 14 deals with the roles of personal selling, customer service, and sales technology in the promotion blend. Chapter 15 covers advertising and sales promotion, including the ways that managers are taking advantage of the Internet and other highly targeted media to communicate more effectively and efficiently.

Chapters 16 and 17 deal with Price. Chapter 16 focuses on pricing objectives and policies, including use of information technology to implement flexible pricing, pricing in the channel, and the use of discounts, allowances, and other variations from a list price. Chapter 17 covers cost-oriented and demand-oriented pricing approaches and how they fit in today's competitive environments. The careful coverage of marketing costs helps equip students to deal with the renewed cost-consciousness of the firms they will join.

The final chapter considers how efficient the marketing process is. Here we evaluate the effectiveness of both micro- and macro-marketing—and we consider the competitive, technological, ethical, and social challenges facing marketing managers now and in the future. Chapter 18 also reinforces the integrative nature of marketing management

and reviews the marketing strategy planning process that leads to creative marketing plans. After this chapter, many students want to look at Appendix C—which is about career opportunities in marketing.

Careful integration of special topics

Some textbooks treat "special" topics—like e-commerce, relationship marketing, international marketing, services marketing, marketing over the Internet, marketing for nonprofit organizations, marketing ethics, social issues, and business-to-business marketing—in separate chapters. We deliberately avoid doing that because we are convinced that treating such topics separately leads to an unfortunate compartmentalization of ideas. We think they are too important to be isolated in that way. For example, to simply tack on a new chapter on e-commerce or marketing applications on the Internet completely ignores the reality that these are not just isolated topics but rather must be considered broadly across the whole fabric of marketing decisions. In fact, the huge losses piled up by the collapse of thousands of dot-com firms at the end of the last decade are evidence of what happens when managers fail to understand the need to integrate marketing strategy planning decisions and don't come to grips with issues such as competitor analysis, customer value, and the marketing concept. Conversely, there is virtually no area of marketing decision making where it's safe to ignore the impact of e-commerce, the Internet, or information technology. The same is true with other topics. So they are interwoven and illustrated throughout the text to emphasize that marketing thinking is crucial in all aspects of our society and economy. This text is again packaged with a grid that shows, in detail, how and where specific topics are integrated throughout the text. Talk is cheap, especially when it comes to the hype from some publishers about how important topics are treated in a new text. But the grid offers proof that in *Essentials of Marketing* we have delivered on the promise of integrated treatment.

Students get "how-to-do-it" skill and confidence

Really understanding marketing and how to plan marketing strategies can build self-confidence—and it can help prepare a student to take an active part in the business world. To move students in this direction, we deliberately include a variety of frameworks, models, classification systems, cases, and "how-to-do-it" techniques that relate to our overall framework for marketing strategy planning. Similarly, the *Marketing Plan Coach* on the Student CD helps students see how to create marketing plans. Taken together, all of these items speed the development of "marketing sense" and enable the student to analyze marketing situations and develop marketing plans in a confident and meaningful way. They are practical and they work. In addition, because they are interesting and understandable, they motivate students to see marketing as the challenging and rewarding area it is.

Essentials of Marketing motivates high-involvement learning

After the opening case in each chapter, we provide a set of specific learning objectives and an exhibit that clearly organizes the chapter topics and helps the student see what is coming. And to speed student understanding, important new terms are shown in red and defined immediately. Further, a glossary of these terms is presented at the end of the book. Within chapters, major section headings and second-level headings (placed in the margin for clarity) immediately show how the material is organized *and* summarize key points in the text. Further, we have placed annotated photos and ads near the concepts they illustrate to provide a visual reminder of the ideas and to show vividly how they apply in the current business world. In each chapter we have integrated Internet exercises related to the concepts being developed. The focus of these exercises is on important marketing issues, not just on "surfing the Net." Each chapter also includes an ethics question that encourages students to evaluate an ethical dilemma that real marketers face.

All of these aids help the student understand important concepts and speed review before exams. End-of-chapter questions and problems offer additional opportunities. They can encourage students to investigate the marketing process and develop their own ways of thinking about it. They can be used for independent study or as a basis for written assignments or class discussion.

Varied types of cases

Understanding of the text material can be deepened by analysis and discussion of specific cases. *Essentials of Marketing* features several different types of cases. Each chapter starts with an in-depth case study developed specifically to highlight that chapter's teaching objectives and the specific marketing decision areas covered in that chapter. Students are encouraged to reread the chapter-opening case after finishing the chapter—when they have a deeper understanding of the issues involved. In addition, each chapter features a special case report in a highlighted box. These thought-provoking cases illustrate how companies handle topics covered in that chapter. All of these cases provide an excellent basis for critical evaluation and discussion. And we've included relevant Internet addresses so that it is easy for students to quickly get updated information about the companies and topics covered in the cases. Of course, website addresses referenced in the cases may change. Some companies change their websites to get a fresh look, to take advantage of new web capabilities, or just to update the information that's available. However, when that occurs, our *Essentials of Marketing* website at www.mhhe.com/fourps provides up-to-date links relevant to the chapters in the text. Our CDs also include links to the website so you can bookmark the site in your Internet browser.

In addition, there are several suggested cases at the end of each chapter. These suggested cases have been selected from the set of 35 cases that appear at the end of the book. The focus of these cases is on problem solving. They encourage students to apply, and really get involved with, the concepts developed in the text.

Each of the first 17 chapters also features a computer-aided problem. These case-based exercises stimulate a problem-solving approach to marketing strategy planning and give students hands-on experience that shows how logical analysis of alternative strategies can lead to improved decision making. For the convenience of students and faculty alike, printed versions of the cases for the computer-aided problems are incorporated in the book itself. Further, the award-winning spreadsheet software we developed specifically for use with these problems is integrated with the other applications on the Student CD that comes with the text.

New multimedia video cases are integrative

In recent editions we've included a custom-produced set of exciting video cases. The response to them has been great. Each of the cases combines a written case with an accompanying video. These 8 video cases are a bit longer than the 35 text-only cases and open up the opportunity for students to analyze an organization's whole marketing program in more depth and with even greater integration. The videos reinforce real content while bringing a high-involvement multimedia dimension to the learning experience. And to assure consistency with all of the other *Essentials of Marketing* materials, we've carefully edited and coordinated the whole effort. These cases were developed so that they focus on different areas of the text, and thus they deal with a variety of issues:

- See the factors influencing the development of Chick-fil-A's successful marketing strategy.
- Examine how new shopping malls are adapting to changes in consumer buying behavior.
- View the efforts and thinking behind Celestial Seasonings' successful marketing strategy, which has won profits and customer loyalty with a marketing mix carefully matched to the needs of its customer market.
- Look into the new-product development process that led to the innovative and highly successful Toyota Prius hybrid vehicle.
- See how a marketing strategy used by entrepreneurial sandwich shop Potbelly Sandwich Works is helping the company differentiate and grow in a mature market.
- See how the marketing strategy planning process is being used by a major nonprofit organization, the Girl Scouts of America.

xii

- Get insights into the thinking behind the promotional and branding campaign GM employed to bring the HUMMER SUV to market.
- Explore the evolution of the marketing strategy for Segway's unique personal transporter.

We designed these cases so that students can analyze them before or after seeing the video, or even without seeing the video at all. They can be used in a variety of ways, either for class discussion or individual assignments.

Comprehensive, current references for independent study

Some professors and students want to follow up on text readings. Each chapter is supplemented with detailed references—to both classic articles and current readings in business publications. These can guide more detailed study of the topics covered in a chapter.

Instructor creates a system—with *Essentials of Marketing's* P.L.U.S.

Essentials of Marketing can be studied and used in many ways—the *Essentials of Marketing* text material is only the central component of our *Professional Learning Units Systems* (*P.L.U.S.*) for students and teachers. Instructors (and students) can select from our units to develop their own personalized systems. Many combinations of units are possible, depending on course objectives. As a quick overview, in addition to the *Essentials of Marketing* text, the *P.L.U.S.* package includes a variety of new and updated supplements:

- A redesigned and updated *Student CD to Accompany Essentials of Marketing*, which includes a database of ads and annotations that illustrate key concepts for each chapter, our computer-aided problems (CAP) spreadsheet software, self-test quizzes (with two levels of questions), and narrated self-study electronic slide shows, to introduce students to what's ahead. The CD also includes our new *Marketing Plan Coach*, which shows how marketing concepts fit together and are applied to create marketing plans.
- Our Online Learning Center (www.mhhe.com/fourps) includes sections for instructors and students. The instructor section includes download files for the *Instructor's Manual*, PowerPoint slides, video clips, and other resources. The student section has video clips, *Online Applications in Essentials of Marketing*, multimedia content, and study materials for each chapter, including flash cards, practices quizzes, chapter summaries, and more.
- A new and updated set of Interactive PowerPoint lecture slides, incorporating full-motion video clips, photos, ads, and interactive exercises to support the professor.
- An improved *Instructor's CD to Accompany Essentials of Marketing*, which includes all of the instructor

resources available for *Essentials of Marketing* in electronic form and a redesigned interface that makes it even easier to access the specific items the instructor wants to use.

In addition, we've completely revised and updated

- The *Multimedia Lecture Support Package*.
- The *Learning Aid* workbook.
- *Instructor's Manual*.
- Author-prepared *Manual of Tests*, accompanied by the EZ-Test test-generator software.
- A complete set of new and updated *teaching videos* and eight great video cases (all supported with a specially prepared *Instructor's Manual to Accompany the Teaching Videos*).
- A Windows version of *The Marketing Game!* (and instructor's manual) that offers password-protected digital plan and report files and supports working over the Internet.

We've been busy. You may not want to use all of this. Some people don't want any of it. But whatever you elect to use—and in whatever medium you like to work—the teaching and learning materials work well together. We've designed them that way.

Learning Aid—deepens understanding

There are more components to *P.L.U.S.* A separate *Learning Aid* provides several more units and offers further opportunities to obtain a deeper understanding of the material. The *Learning Aid* can be used by the student alone or with teacher direction. Portions of the *Learning Aid* help students to review what they have studied. For example, there is a brief introduction to each chapter, a list of the important new terms (with page numbers for easy reference), true-false questions (with answers and page numbers) that cover all the important terms and concepts, and multiple-choice questions (with answers) that illustrate the kinds of questions that may appear in examinations. In addition, the *Learning Aid* has cases, exercises, and problems—with clear instructions and worksheets for the student to complete. The *Learning Aid* also features computer-aided problems that build on the computer-aided cases in the text. The *Learning Aid* exercises can be used as classwork or homework—to drill on certain topics and to deepen understanding of others by motivating application and then discussion. In fact, reading *Essentials of Marketing* and working with the *Learning Aid* can be the basic activity of the course.

Compete and learn—with *The Marketing Game!*, 3rd edition

Another valuable resource is *The Marketing Game!*, a PC-based competitive simulation. It was developed specifically to reinforce the target marketing and marketing strategy planning ideas discussed in *Essentials of Marketing*. Students make marketing management decisions—blending the four Ps to compete for the business of different possible target markets. The innovative design of *The Marketing Game!* allows the instructor to increase the number of decision areas involved as students learn more about marketing. In fact, many instructors use the advanced levels of the game as the basis for a second course. *The Marketing Game!* is widely heralded as the best marketing strategy simulation available—and this edition widens its lead over the others available. Competitors don't even need to be on the same continent. It works great with password-protected decisions submitted by e-mail and reports returned the same way.

Multimedia support for preparation, lectures, and discussion

Essentials of Marketing and all of our accompanying materials have been developed to promote student learning and get students involved in the excitement and challenges of marketing management. Additional elements of *P.L.U.S.* have been specifically developed to help an instructor offer a truly professional course that meets the objectives he or she sets for students. Complete instructor's manuals accompany all of the *P.L.U.S.* components.

Electronic presentation slides with many uses

Essentials of Marketing is supported with a large variety of high-quality PowerPoint electronic slide presentations. This flexible package features a large number of PowerPoint graphics developed for every chapter in the text. Presentations can be based on composite slides, or the points on a slide can "build up" one point at a time.

Because we provide the native-format PowerPoint files, instructors can modify or delete any slide or add other slides by using their own copy of PowerPoint. And, of course, if electronic projection equipment isn't available, the instructor can print out the images to customized color acetates or black and white transparencies.

While these slides are intended mainly for instructor use in class discussions and lectures, they are easy to use and can be placed on the Internet, on the school's computer network, or in a computer lab as a supplement for independent review by students.

Complete multimedia lecture support

With the PowerPoint electronic slide presentations we also provide detailed lecture notes, as well as lecture outlines. The PowerPoint slide show includes small versions of the slides for class handouts. All of these materials are packaged in our *Multimedia Lecture Support Package*. This supplement is also available in an electronic form on the *Instructor's CD*, and that makes it even more convenient to use. It gives instructors a great deal of flexibility and saves time that can be spent on other teaching activities.

In addition, the *Multimedia Lecture Support Package* is accompanied by a high-quality selection of ads, graphics, and photos—all organized in easy-to-use PowerPoint format for each chapter. The manual provides detailed suggestions about ways to use them. All of these items are also available on the CD.

Exciting new videos—created by marketing experts

The newly revised *Essentials of Marketing Videos* are also available to all schools that adopt *Essentials of Marketing*. We've developed a number of new video segments for this edition—all carefully linked to key topics in the text. In addition, several of the most popular video modules from the previous edition—the ones instructors and students said they most wanted to keep—have been thoroughly revised and updated. These new videos are really great, but it doesn't stop there! As we noted earlier, there are also eight great videos to accompany the video cases.

Testing that works for faculty and students

In addition, thousands of objective test questions—*written by the authors* to really work with the text—give instructors a high-quality resource. The EZ-Test program allows the instructor to select from any of these questions, change them as desired, or add new questions—and quickly print out a finished test customized to the instructor's course.

The responsibilities of leadership

In closing, we return to a point raised at the beginning of this preface. *Essentials of Marketing* has been a leading textbook in marketing since its first edition. We take the responsibilities of that leadership seriously. We know that you want and deserve the very best teaching and learning materials possible. It is our commitment to bring you those materials—today with this edition and in the future with subsequent editions.

We recognize that fulfilling this commitment requires a process of continuous improvement. Improvements, changes, and development of new elements must be ongoing—because needs change. You are an important part of this evolution, of this leadership. We encourage your feedback. The most efficient way to get in touch with us is to send an e-mail message to Bill_Perreault@unc.edu or Joe.Cannon@colostate.edu. There's also a comment form built into the book's website, and if you prefer the traditional approach, send a letter to 2104 N. Lakeshore Dr., Chapel Hill, NC, 27514. Thoughtful criticisms and suggestions from students and teachers alike have helped to make *Essentials of Marketing* what it is. We hope that you will help make it what it will be in the future.

William D. Perreault, Jr.
Joseph P. Cannon
E. Jerome McCarthy

Walkthrough

ESSENTIALS OF MARKETING HELPS YOU LEARN ABOUT MARKETING AND MARKETING STRATEGY PLANNING.

At its essence, marketing strategy planning is about figuring out how to do a superior job of satisfying customers. With that in mind, the 11th edition of *Essentials of Marketing* was developed to satisfy your desire for knowledge and add value to your course experience. Not only will this text teach you about marketing and marketing strategy planning, but its design, pedagogy, and supplementary learning aids were developed to work well with the text and a variety of study situations.

Each person has a different approach to studying. Some may focus on reading that is covered during class, others prefer to prepare outside of the classroom and rely heavily on in-class interaction, and still others prefer more independence from the classroom. Some are more visual or more "hands on" in the way they learn, and others just want clear and interesting explanations. To address a variety of needs and course situations, many hours went into creating the materials highlighted in this section. When used in combination with the text, these tools will elevate your understanding of marketing.

Take a moment now to learn more about all of the resources available to help you best prepare for this course—and for your future career.

ESSENTIALS OF MARKETING: AN INNOVATIVE MARKETING EXPERIENCE.

With 18 chapters that introduce the important concepts in marketing management, you will see all aspects of marketing through the eyes of the marketing manager. The first seven chapters introduce marketing and give you a framework for understanding marketing strategy planning in any type of organization, and then the second half of the text takes you into planning the four Ps of marketing (Product, Place, Promotion, and Price) with specific attention to the key strategy decisions in each area.

Basic Marketing and *Essentials of Marketing* pioneered the "four Ps" approach to organize and describe managerial marketing for introductory marketing courses. This new edition of *Essentials of Marketing* covers the dynamic changes taking place in marketing management and the marketing environment. Some of these changes have been dramatic, and others have been subtle. But the 11th edition helps you understand the changes taking place and reflects today's best marketing practices and ideas.

CHAPTER NINE

Product Management and New-Product Development

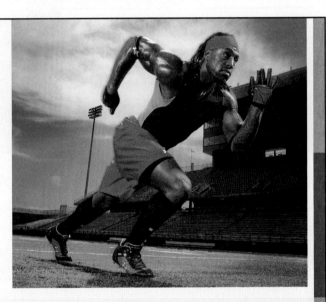

Kevin Plank was a business major and football player at the University of Maryland when he spotted an opportunity. He and his teammates wore cotton T-shirts under their football pads, but the T-shirts quickly became sweat-soaked, heavy, and uncomfortable during practices and games. When Plank began looking for a product that would perform better than a T-shirt, he learned about new types of fabrics and performance clothing for bicyclists and hikers. But he realized a shirt that would meet the needs of football players was a really new idea, not just a minor variation on existing clothing.

In New York City's garment district, Plank learned about a polyester-Lycra blend fabric that didn't trap moisture. He worked with a tailor to develop several prototype shirts and then asked friends who were players in the National Football League, like Vernon Davis of the San Francisco 49ers, to try them. The players really liked the skintight, compression shirts. They fit comfortably under football gear and wicked away sweat—keeping the players cooler, drier, and lighter. When Plank's friends clamored for more shirts, he knew he had a good start. However, he couldn't afford a big ad campaign to tout the benefits of his product, and he didn't have relationships with retailers who could help build demand with final consumers. So Plank moved to commercialization with a focus on a target market he knew: college football teams.

Plank went back to New York and ordered 500 shirts, the first products with the Under Armour brand name and the start of what became the Heat-Gear warm weather product line. Then he loaded his shirts in his SUV and traveled to colleges across the Southeast. He tried to persuade coaches, players, and equipment managers about the benefits of his unique shirts. Many were not initially convinced of the value—especially since the price was 3 to 5 times the price of a T-shirt. But its advantage was clear after a player would try one for a football practice—and praise for the product spread quickly.

Success with college and professional athletes helped the company build credibility. It also led to relationships with specialty-sports retailers who could reach the larger and more profitable consumer market. Sports retailers provided attractive displays and promoted the brand because they liked having a profitable new offering that was not available at lower-service local discount or department stores.

As the market for sports-performance clothes grew, Nike, Adidas, and other firms came out with competing products. To fight back, Under Armour put more emphasis on creative promotion to build customer preference for the Under Armour brand. For example, Under Armour got a prominent product placement in the football movie *Any Given Sunday.* Similarly, Under Armour ran TV and print ads featuring professional athletes, like Dallas Cowboys football player (and former Plank teammate) Eric Ogbogu. When the muscular Ogbogu barked the firm's tag line, "Protect This House," it instantly became a part of popular sports culture. It was the rallying cry of players, fans, and banners in football stadiums across the country.

Of course, the firm continued to look for growth through new product ideas. One successful idea came from a coach who wanted a cold weather version of the shirt that would keep players warm as well as dry. Under Armour responded with the first products in its ColdGear line. New products for a variety of other athletic markets have followed, including leggings that are popular with skiers and polo shirts that are a hit with golfers.

It's tough to quickly steal away a large share of the customers in a mature product-market, but that is just what Under Armour accomplished with its new design for football cleats. The new-product development team researched playing surfaces, player movements, and body types to design cleats that were more durable, lighter, and more

Each chapter begins with an in-depth case study developed specifically to motivate your interest and highlight real-life examples of the learning objectives and specific marketing decision areas covered in that chapter. Each case study is accompanied by a list of learning objectives that will help you understand and identify important terms and concepts covered in the chapter.

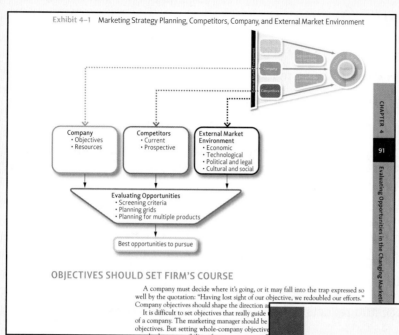

Exhibit 4–1   Marketing Strategy Planning, Competitors, Company, and External Market Environment

xvi

OBJECTIVES SHOULD SET FIRM'S COURSE

A company must decide where it's going, or it may fall into the trap expressed so well by the quotation: "Having lost sight of our objective, we redoubled our efforts." Company objectives should shape the direction a

It is difficult to set objectives that really guide t of a company. The marketing manager should be objectives. But setting whole-company objective

After introducing the Marketing Strategy Planning Process model in Chapter 2, each chapter includes an exhibit that clearly organizes the chapter's content. The exhibit also shows how these concepts fit into the marketing strategy planning process.

Each chapter features a special case report in a highlighted box that illustrates how companies handle a topic of special interest covered in that chapter.

Marketers Are Wading into the Blogosphere

Many marketers are adding a new dimension to their promotion blend by using blogs. A *blog*, short for *web log*, is a website that provides a running stream of messages, links, and comments. Blogs are usually created by an individual to express personal opinions about some topic. But many marketers like the first-person, conversational style that is typical of blogs. As with other types of personal communication, including personal selling, blogs can help make a connection with customers and enhance the relationship with them, but at a low cost.

Lego uses a blog (www.bricksonthebrain.com) to build a sense of community for its small but influential adult hobbyist segment. These Lego fanatics account for only 5 percent of sales, but their huge Lego displays often get media coverage and help to generate buzz. Lego's blog provides a way for these hobbyists to share ideas, photos, and suggestions. Similarly, yogurt maker Stonyfield Farm uses blogs to reinforce the healthy and wholesome positioning of its foods. Its "Baby Babble" blog targets new parents and "The Bovine Bugle" tells about daily activities at a farm that supplies Stonyfield with milk.

Most blogs rely on and reflect the passions of their creators. Ed Brill is a global sales executive for IBM's Lotus Notes software. Each day about 13,000 Lotus users check what he's thinking at his blog (www.edbrill.com).

One reason is that Brill provides important news fast. For example, when the general manager of Lotus was replaced, Brill posted the news within hours and explained what it would mean for customers. But Brill's site isn't strictly business. It includes photos of Brill and his friends and comments on personal matters, like the fancy watch he received as a Valentine's gift. IBM is a big company and Lotus is a huge brand, but Brill's personal blog helps to humanize them and build relationships with customers.

Marketers for GourmetStation, a Web-based retailer of high-end food, wanted to generate a little buzz. They thought a blog "written" by the website's fictional connoisseur of fine food and wine, T. Alexander, would be just the ticket. Soon Alexander was blogging away, recommending foods and wines. However, some bloggers are very protective of "their" media—and don't like the idea of any blog that appears too commercial. Some of these critics quickly blogged their criticism of GourmetStation's blog for not being authentic—and one gave it a "Beyond Lame Award." In this case, the criticisms didn't seem to matter to customers—and instead all the attention generated more hits for the website. However, marketers need to be aware that creative promotion on the Web can draw critics. Still, firms that keep their focus on the target market are likely to win in the long run.[22]

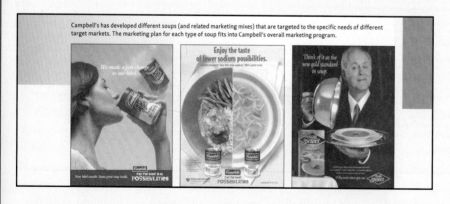

Campbell's has developed different soups (and related marketing mixes) that are targeted to the specific needs of different target markets. The marketing plan for each type of soup fits into Campbell's overall marketing program.

Full-color photos and current ads are carefully placed in every chapter and annotated—to provide a visual emphasis on key concepts and ideas discussed in the text. These illustrations vividly show how companies apply marketing concepts in the modern business world.

Exhibit 2–9
Customer Equity Increases as Firm Attracts Customers, Retains Them, and Increases Earnings from Business with Them

Earnings from initial target customers

Growth in earnings from retained customers

Customer equity from whole marketing program grows over time

firm

Earnings from new target customers

Business enters market

time

A variety of interesting exhibits—"conceptual organizers," charts, and tables—illustrate each chapter and focus your attention on key frameworks and ideas.

Internet exercises are integrated with the discussion of important ideas as they are developed—to help you learn about marketing while you surf interesting websites.

Internet EXERCISE

Marketing Intelligence Service, Ltd, is a U.S.-based firm that tracks new consumer packaged-goods—both successes and failures. Enter its website (**www.productscan.com**) and click on the *What's New* button, then review its selections for new product innovations of the year. Do you think that these products offer customers superior value, or are they just me-too imitations?

a failed effort may not be as high, but it can have a devastating long-term effect if dissatisfied consumers turn elsewhere for help.[17]

A new product may fail for many reasons. Most often, companies fail to offer a unique benefit or underestimate the competition. Sometimes the idea is good but the company has design problems—or the product costs much more to produce than was expected. Some companies rush to get a product on the market without developing a complete marketing plan.[18]

But moving too slowly can be a problem too. With the fast pace of change for many products, speedy entry into the market can be a key to competitive advantage. Marketing managers at Xerox learned this the hard way. Japanese competitors were taking market share with innovative new models of copiers. It turned out that the competitors were developing new models twice as fast as Xerox and at half the cost. For Xerox to compete, it had to slash its five-year product development cycle.[19]

The longer new-product development takes, the more likely it is that customer needs will be different when the product is actually introduced. Back in 2003, consumer interest in trucks and SUVs was high. General Motors expected that popularity to continue when planning new models. But by the time those vehicles were on the market in 2006, gasoline prices had skyrocketed—and consumer preferences were switching to smaller cars. In contrast, Honda's new-product planning had focused on more fuel efficiency, and its new 2006 models were in hot demand.

To move quickly and also avoid expensive new-product failures, companies should follow an organized new-product development process. The following pages describe such a process, which moves logically through five steps: (1) idea generation, (2) screening, (3) idea evaluation, (4) development (of product and marketing mix), and (5) commercialization.[20] See Exhibit 9–4.

The general process is similar for both consumer and business markets—and for both goods and services. There are some significant differences, but we will emphasize the similarities in the following discussion.

Process tries to kill new ideas—economically

An important element in the new-product development process is continued evaluation of a new idea's likely profitability and return on investment. The hypothesis tested is that the new idea will *not* be profitable. This puts the burden on the new

Generating innovative and profitable new products requires an understanding of customer needs—and an organized new-product development process.

234

CREATING MARKETING PLANS

The Marketing Plan Coach software on the Student CD includes a sample marketing plan for Hillside Veterinary Clinic. Look through the "Marketing Strategy" section.

a. Hillside offers many different products. Identify several of these products and indicate where you think each of them is in its product life cycle.

b. Exhibit 9-3 summarizes some marketing mix characteristics based on where a product fits in the product life cycle. Is Hillside's marketing plan consistent with what this exhibit suggests? Why or why not?

The Student CD-ROM includes a sample marketing plan for Hillside Veterinary Clinic. Exercises at the end of each chapter show how concepts from the chapter are used in developing a marketing plan.

THE *LEARNING AID.*

The *Learning Aid* helps you review and test yourself on material from each chapter—while also providing opportunities for you to obtain a deeper understanding of the material. The *Learning Aid* offers a hands-on way to develop a better understanding of the basics of marketing.

Chapter 6

Business and organizational customers and their buying behavior

What This Chapter Is About

Chapter 6 discusses the buying behavior of the important business and organizational customers who buy for resale or for use in their own businesses. They buy more goods and services than final customers! There are many opportunities in marketing to producers, to intermediaries, to government, and to nonprofit organizations--and it is important to understand how these organizational customers buy.

Organizations tend to be much more economic in their buying behavior than final consumers. Further, some must follow pre-set bidding and bargaining processes. Yet, they too have emotional needs. And sometimes a number of different people may influence the final purchase decision. Keep in mind that business and organizational customers are problem solvers too. Many of the ideas in Chapter 5 carry over, but with some adaptation.

This chapter deserves careful study because your past experience as a consumer is not as helpful here as it was in the last few chapters. Organizational customers are much less numerous. In some cases it is possible to create a separate marketing mix for each individual customer. Understanding these customers is necessary to plan marketing strategies for them. Try to see how they are both similar and different from final customers.

Important Terms

business and organizational customers, p. 142
purchasing specifications, p. 144
ISO 9000, p. 145
purchasing managers, p. 145
multiple buying influence, p. 145
buying center, p. 146
vendor analysis, p. 147
requisition, p. 148
new-task buying, p. 149
straight rebuy, p. 149

modified rebuy, p. 149
just-in-time delivery, p. 152
negotiated contract buying, p. 153
outsource, p. 153
competitive bids, p. 155
North American Industry Classification System (NAICS) codes, p. 159
open to buy, p. 163
resident buyers, p. 163
Foreign Corrupt Practices Act, p. 165

The *Learning Aid* provides a brief introduction to each chapter, a list of the important new terms (with page numbers for easy reference), true–false questions (with answers and page numbers) that cover all the important terms and concepts, and multiple-choice questions (with answers) that illustrate the kinds of questions that may appear in examinations.

___ 36. In international markets, it is legal to make small grease money payments--if they are customary in that country.

Answers to True-False Questions

1. F, p. 142	13. F, p. 150	25. T, p. 159
2. T, p. 144	14. F, p. 152	26. T, p. 161
3. T, p. 144	15. F, p. 153	27. F, p. 162
4. T, p. 145	16. T, p. 153	28. T, p. 162
5. T, p. 145	17. F, p. 154	29. T, p. 162-63
6. T, p. 146	18. T, p. 155	30. F, p. 163
7. F, p. 146	19. F, p. 155	31. F, p. 163
8. T, p. 147	20. T, p. 155	32. T, p. 163-64
9. T, p. 147	21. T, p. 156	33. F, p. 164
10. T, p. 148	22. T, p. 157	34. F, p. 164
11. T, p. 149	23. T, p. 158	35. F, p. 164
12. F, p. 149	24. T, p. 158	36. T, p. 165

Multiple-Choice Questions (Circle the correct response)

1. Which of the following is a business or organizational customer?
   a. producers of goods and services.
   b. a retailer.
   c. a wholesaler.
   d. a government agency.
   e. All of the above are business and organizational customers.

2. In comparison to the buying of final consumers, the purchasing of organizational buyers:
   a. is strictly economic and not at all emotional.
   b. is always based on competitive bids from multiple suppliers.
   c. leans basically toward economy, quality, and dependability.
   d. is even less predictable.
   e. Both a and c are true statements.

3. Today, many agricultural commodities and manufactured items are subject to rigid control or grading. As a result, organizational buyers often buy on the basis of:
   a. purchasing specifications.
   b. negotiated contracts.
   c. competitive bids.

4. In a buying center, multiple buying influences can include:
   a. users.
   b. buyers.
   c. gatekeepers.
   d. deciders.
   e. all of the above.

Name: _____   Course & Section: _____

Exercise 6-3

Vendor analysis

This exercise is based on computer-aided problem number 6--Vendor Analysis. A complete description of the problem appears on page 167 of *Essentials of Marketing*, 11th edition.

1. Supplier 2 is thinking about adding U.S. wholesalers to its channel of distribution. The supplier would ship in large, economical quantities to the wholesaler and the wholesaler would keep a stock of chips on hand. The wholesaler would charge CompuTech a higher price--$1.90 a chip. But with the chips available from a reliable wholesaler CompuTech's inventory cost as a percent of its total order would only be 2 percent. In addition, the cost of transportation would only be $.01 per chip. Assuming CompuTech planned to buy 84,500 chips, what would its total costs be with and without the wholesaler? Should CompuTech encourage the supplier to add a wholesaler to the channel?

    Total Costs for Vendor Supplier 2, buying direct   _____

    Total Costs for Vendor Supplier 2, using wholesaler   _____

    _____

    _____

    _____

2. Supplier 2 has explored the idea of adding wholesalers to the channel, but has found that it will take at least another year to find suitable wholesalers and develop relationships. As a result, if CompuTech deals with Supplier 2 its inventory cost as a percent of the total order would remain at 5.4 percent, and transportation cost would remain at $.03 per chip. But the supplier is still interested in improving its marketing mix now--so it can develop a strong relationship with CompuTech. Based on an analysis of CompuTech's needs, Supplier 2 has developed a new design for the electronic memory chips.

    The redesigned chips would have a built-in connector, so CompuTech would not have to buy separate connectors. In addition, the new design would make it faster and easier to replace a defective chip. The supplier estimates that with the new design it would cost CompuTech only $1.00 to replace a bad chip.

    The supplier has not yet priced the new chip, but it would cost the supplier an additional $.06 to produce each chip. If the supplier set the price of the chip at $1.93 each (the old price of $1.87 plus the additional $.06), how much would the new design cost CompuTech on an order of 84,500 chips. (Hint: compute CompuTech's total cost for the current design based on an order quantity of 84,500 chips, and then compute the total cost assuming the new price, the reduced cost of replacing a defective chip, and no cost for a connector.)

The *Learning Aid* also incorporates cases, problems, and exercises, including ones that build on the end-of-chapter computer-aided problems—with clear instructions and worksheets for you to complete for additional practice.

THE MARKETING GAME!

The Marketing Game! is a competitive marketing strategy simulation that allows you the opportunity to apply your marketing knowledge in a fun and interesting way. *The Marketing Game!* is applicable for all areas of marketing and all levels because the game is not based on just one simulation. Rather it is based on several simulations with one integrated framework. *The Marketing Game!* is based on realistic marketing and realistic marketing relationships and allows for maximum flexibility.

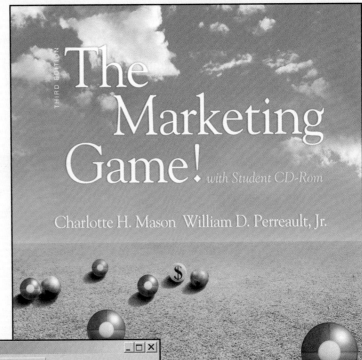

FREE MULTIMEDIA STUDENT CD-ROM.

Each new copy of this book includes a custom-developed multimedia Student CD. Loaded with interesting and interactive tools, programs, videos, graphics, and illustrations, this CD will help you review and apply concepts from the 11th edition of *Essentials of Marketing*. When used in combination with the text, the CD will enhance each lesson and engage you in real-world marketing situations.

STUDENT RESOURCE CD-ROM

The Student Resource CD-ROM includes a variety of useful resources to help students learn and study. Learning with Ads shows print advertisements and demonstrates how real companies are applying concepts from each chapter. Students can reinforce learning and prepare for tests with the Flashcards, Glossary, and Self-Test Quizzes included on the CD. Other new and updated features on the Student CD are described below and on the following page.

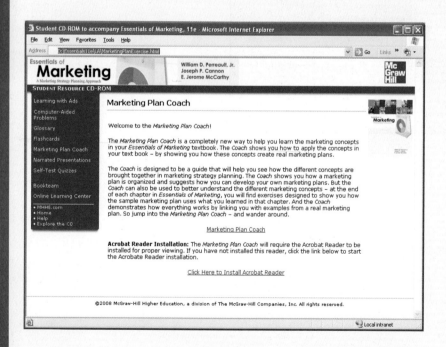

MARKETING PLAN COACH

A flexible new addition to our learning package, the *Marketing Plan Coach* demonstrates the marketing strategy planning process in action. The *Coach* links concepts from the book with a real marketing plan. We designed this tool so you can see how marketing concepts fit together and how they are applied by marketing managers. The tool can be used to reinforce learning, show links across concepts—and even to help you develop your own marketing plan. The *Coach* works like a website (but you don't need to be connected to the Internet)—with links between different concepts and a sample marketing plan.

NARRATED SLIDE SHOWS

Eight narrated slide shows provide an overview of key marketing concepts and reinforce how sections of the text fit together. They include full-motion video clips, photos, ads, and commentary that further illustrate ideas covered in lectures, class discussion, and independent reading.

COMPUTER-AIDED PROBLEMS

Award-winning spreadsheets, preprogrammed specifically for ease of use with the computer-aided problems at the end of each chapter, are fully integrated with the other applications on the Student CD. This software allows you to enter your answers to questions on screen and then print out both the spreadsheet and answer. These interesting problems give you practice in working with marketing concepts to see how they impact a firm's overall profitability and effectiveness in serving customers.

ONLINE SUPPORT.

Understanding that you have a variety of classes and responsibilities to worry about, *Essentials of Marketing* offers flexible online study and support tools that will fit into any busy schedule. If you have a few moments in the library or when you're checking e-mail, you have enough time to visit the website to enhance your marketing education experience.

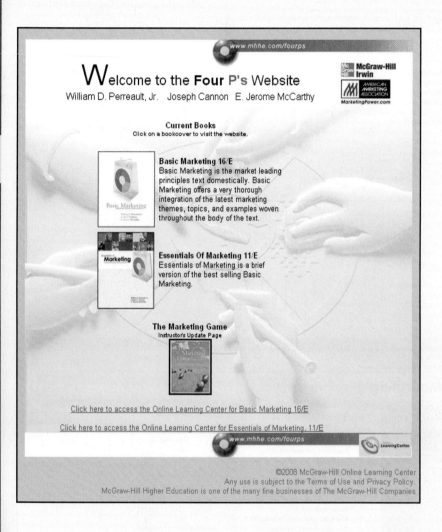

WEBSITE

Essentials of Marketing's website (www.mhhe.com/fourps) provides a cutting-edge, interactive resource on marketing education.

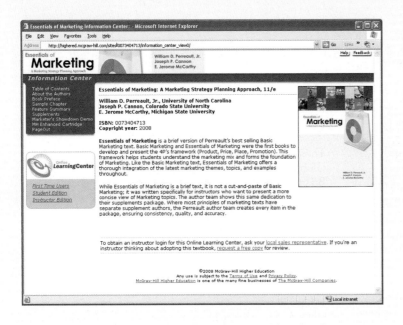

ONLINE LEARNING CENTER

The Online Learning Center is part of the text's website at www.mhhe.com/fourps. This website includes a variety of tools that will help you study and learn the concepts in *Essentials of Marketing*.

ONLINE APPLICATIONS IN ESSENTIALS OF MARKETING

In *Online Applications in Essentials of Marketing*, we have collected links to current articles, podcasts, videos, and websites. These resources are organized according to the topic areas in your *Essentials of Marketing* textbook. Whether your instructor assigns them or you simply want to learn more on your own, these resources will give you a deeper understanding of how some firms are successfully applying the marketing concepts in this textbook.

Acknowledgments

Essentials of Marketing has been influenced and improved by the inputs of more people than it is possible to list. We do, however, want to express our appreciation to those who have played the most significant roles, especially in this edition.

We are especially grateful to our many students who have criticized and made comments about materials in *Essentials of Marketing*. Indeed, in many ways, our students have been our best teachers.

We owe our greatest debt of gratitude to Lin Davis. The book probably wouldn't exist if it weren't for her—because without her help it would have been just too overwhelming and we'd have quit! Lin has been part of this team for over 20 years. During that time she has made contributions in every aspect of the text and package. For this edition she spent countless hours researching photos and case histories, and she critiqued thousands of manuscript pages through countless revisions of the text and all the accompanying materials. She has reviewed, edited, and critiqued every word we've written. Her hard work, positive attitude, and dedication to quality throughout the whole process is without match. We could not have asked for a better friend and colleague.

Many improvements in recent editions were stimulated by feedback from a number of colleagues around the country. Their feedback took many forms. In particular, we would like to recognize the helpful contributions of

Ainsworth Bailey, *University of Toledo*
Turina Bakker, *University of Wisconsin*
Jeff Bauer, *University of Cincinnati—Batavia*
Amy Beattie, *Nichols College of Champlain*
Cathleen Behan, *Northern VA Community College*
Suzeanne Benet, *Grand Valley State University*
David Blackmore, *University of Pittsburgh*
Jonathan Bohlman, *Purdue University*
Kit Brenan, *Northland Community College*
Richard Brien, *De Anza College*
Denny Bristow, *St. Cloud State University*
Derrell Bulls, *Texas Women's University*
Helen Burdenski, *Notre Dame College of Ohio*
Nancy Bush, *Wingate University*
Carmen Calabrese, *University of North Carolina—Pembroke*
James Carlson, *Manatee Community College*
Donald Caudill, *Bluefield State College*
Kenny Chan, *California State University—Chico*
E. Wayne Chandler, *Eastern Illinois University*
Paris Cleanthous, *New York University—Stern School*

Thomas Cline, *St. Vincent College*
Gloria Cockerell, *Collin County Community College*
Brian Connett, *California State University—Northridge*
Sherry Cook, *Southwest Missouri State*
Matt Critcher, *University of Arkansas Community College—Batesville*
Tammy Crutchfield, *Mercer University*
Charles Davies, *Hillsdale College*
J. Charlene Davis, *Trinity University*
Susan Higgins DeFago, *John Carroll University*
Les Dlabay, *Lake Forest College*
Glenna Dod, *Wesleyan College*
Gary Donnelly, *Casper College*
Paul Dowling, *University of Utah*
Michael Drafke, *College of DuPage*
John Drea, *Western Illinois University*
Steven Engel, *University of Colorado*
Peter Fader, *University of Pennsylvania*
Ken Fairweather, *LeTourneau University*
Lori S. Feldman, *Purdue University*
Richard Kent Fields, *Carthage College*
Michael Fitzmorris, *Park University*
Richard Fogg, *Kansas State University*
Kim Folkers, *Wartburg College*
Frank Franzak, *Virginia Commonwealth University*
John Gaffney, *Hiram College*
John Gaskins, *Longwood University*
Norman Govoni, *Babson College*
Gary Grandison, *Alabama State University*
Mitch Griffin, *Bradley University*
Mike Griffith, *Cascade College*
Alice Griswold, *Clarke College*
Khalil Hairston, *Indiana Institute of Technology*
Adam Hall, *Western Kentucky University*
Dorothy Harpool, *Wichita State University*
LeaAnna Harrah, *Marion Technical College*
Lewis Hershey, *University of North Carolina—Pembroke*
Wolfgang Hinck, *Louisiana State University—Shreveport*
Pamela Homer, *California State University—Long Beach*
Ronald Hoverstad, *University of the Pacific*
Janet Hunter, *Northland Pioneer College*
Annette Jaiko, *Triton College/College of DuPage*
Carol Johanek, *Washington University*
Fahri Karakaya, *University of Massachusetts*
Pat Karush, *Thomas College*
Eileen Kearney, *Montgomery County Community College*
Robin Kelly, *Cuyahoga Community College*
Rob Kleine, *Ohio Northern University*
Kathleen Krentler, *San Diego State University*
Dmitri Kuksov, *Washington University*
Linda Lamarca, *Tarleton State University*
Kevin Lambert, *Southeast Community College*

Richard LaRosa, *Indiana University of Pennsylvania*
Marilyn Lavin, *University of Wisconsin—Whitewater*
David Levy, *Bellevue University*
Doug Livermore, *Morningside College*
Lori Lohman, *Augsburg College*
Paul James Londrigan, *Mott Community College*
Terry Lowe, *Heartland Community College*
Richard Lutz, *University of Florida*
Michele McCarren, *Southern State Community College*
Kevin McEvoy, *University of Connecticut—Stamford*
Phyllis Mansfield, *Pennsylvania State University—Erie*
Rosalynn Martin, *Mid-South Community College*
Rajiv Mehta, *New Jersey Institute of Technology*
Sanjay Mehta, *Sam Houston State University*
Matt Meuter, *California State University—Chico*
Margaret Klayton Mi, *Mary Washington College*
Linda Mitchell, *Lindon State College*
Robert Montgomery, *University of Evansville*
Ed Mosher, *Laramie Community College*
Steve Mumsford, *Gwynedd-Mercy College*
Clara Munson, *Albertus Magnus*
Cynthia Newman, *Rider University*
David Oh, *California State University—Los Angeles*
Jeannie O'Laughlin, *Dakota Wesleyan University*
Louis Osuki, *Chicago State University*
Karen Palumbo, *University of St. Francis*
Terry Paridon, *Cameron University*
Stephen Peters, *Walla Walla Community College*
Brenda Ponsford, *Clarion University*
Tracy Proulx, *Park University*
Kathleen Radionoff, *Cardinal Stritch University*
Daniel Ricica, *Sinclair Community College*
Sandra Robertson, *Thomas Nelson Community College*
Kim Rocha, *Barton College*
Donald Roy, *Middle Tennessee State University*
Erika Schlomer-Fischer, *California Lutheran University*
Murphy Sewell, *University of Connecticut—Storrs*
Jeremy Sierra, *New Mexico State University*
Lisa Simon, *California Polytech—San Luis Obispo*
Aditya Singh, *Pennsylvania State University—McKeesport*
Mandeep Singh, *Western Illinois University*
Jill Slomski, *Mercyhurst College*
Robert Smoot, *Lees College*
Don Soucy, *University of North Carolina—Pembroke*
Roland Sparks, *Johnson C. Smith University*
Jim Stephens, *Emporia State University*
Tom Stevenson, *University of North Carolina*
Stephen Strange, *Henderson Community College*
Randy Stuart, *Kennesaw State University*
Rajneesh Suri, *Drexel University*
Uday Tate, *Marshall University*
A.J. Taylor, *Austin Peay State University*
Janice Taylor, *Miami University*
Jeff Thieme, *Syracuse University*
Dennis Tootelian, *California State University—Sacramento*
Gary Tschantz, *Walsh University*
Fran Ucci, *Triton College/College of DuPage*
David Urban, *Virginia Commonwealth University*
Peter Vantine, *Georgia Tech*
Steve Vitucci, *Tarleton State University*
Sharon Wagner, *Missouri Western State College*

Fred Whitman, *Mary Washington College*
Judy Wilkinson, *Youngstown State University*
Phillip Wilson, *Midwestern State University*
John Withey, *Indiana University—South Bend*
Jim Wong, *Shenandoah University*
Gary Young, *Worcester State College*

In addition, we appreciate people whose feedback on earlier editions had an ongoing influence on this revision. They are

Mary Albrecht, *Maryville University*
David Andrus, *Kansas State University at Manhattan*
Turina Bakker, *University of Wisconsin*
Jonathan Bohlman, *Purdue University*
John Brennan, *Florida State University*
Linda Jane Coleman, *Salem State College*
Brent Cunningham, *Jacksonville State University*
Scott Davis, *University of California at Davis*
Phillip Downs, *Florida State University*
Michael Drafke, *College of DuPage*
Sean Dwyer, *Louisiana Technical University*
Lou Firenze, *Northwood University*
Thomas Giese, *University of Richmond*
J. Lee Goen, *Oklahoma Baptist University*
David Good, *Central Missouri State University*
Susan Gupta, *University of Wisconsin at Milwaukee*
John Hadjmarcou, *University of Texas at El Paso*
Bobby Hall, *Wayland Baptist University*
Dorothy Harpool, *Wichita State University*
Pamela Homer, *California State University—Long Beach*
Deborah Baker Hulse, *University of Texas at Tyler*
Timothy Johnston, *University of Tennessee at Martin*
Eileen Kearney, *Montgomery County Community College*
James Kellaris, *University of Cincinnati*
Jean Laliberte, *Troy State University*
Debra Laverie, *Texas Tech University*
W. J. Mahony, *Southern Wesleyan University*
James McAloon, *Fitchburg State University*
Michael Mezja, *University of Las Vegas*
Robert Montgomery, *University of Evansville*
Todd Mooradian, *College of William and Mary*
Marlene Morris, *Georgetown University*
Brenda Moscool, *California State University—Bakersfield*
Reza Motameni, *California State University—Fresno*
Thomas Myers, *University of Richmond*
Philip S. Nitse, *Idaho State University at Pocatello*
J. R. Ogden, *Kutztown University*
Sam Okoroafo, *University of Toledo*
Esther S. Page-Wood, *Western Michigan University*
Daniel Rajaratnam, *Baylor University*
Catherine Rich-Duval, *Merrimack College*
Lee Richardson, *University of Baltimore*
Carlos Rodriguez, *Governors State University*
Robert Roe, *University of Wyoming*
Joel Saegert, *University of Texas at San Antonio*
Charles Schwepker, *Central Missouri State University*
Kenneth Shamley, *Sinclair College*
Doris Shaw, *Kent State University*
Donald Shifter, *Fontbonne College*
J.Taylor, *Austin Peay State University*

Janice Taylor, *Miami University*
Kimberly Taylor, *Florida International University*
Jeff Thieme, *Syracuse University*
Scott Thompson, *University of Wisconsin—Oshkosh*
David Urban, *Virginia Commonwealth University*
Jane Wayland, *Eastern Illinois University*
M.G.M. Wetzeis, *Universiteit Maastrict, The Netherlands*
Robert Witherspoon, *Triton College*
Joyce H. Wood, *N. Virginia Community College*
Newell Wright, *James Madison University*

W. Glynn Mangold
Robert Miller
J. R. Montgomery
Michael R. Mullen
Phillip Niffenegger
Deborah Owens
Thomas G. Ponzurick
George Prough
Peter Rainsford

Jane Reid
Roger Schoenfeldt
Thomas Shere
Jeanne M. Simmons
Rollie O. Tillman
Robert Welsh
Holt Wilson
Poh-Lin Yeou

We've always believed that the best way to build consistency and quality into the text and the other P.L.U.S. units is to do as much as possible ourselves. With the growth of multimedia technologies, it's darn hard to be an expert on them all. But we've had spectacular help in that regard.

We're indebted to Jay Carlson, Mandy Noelle Carlson, and Eric Karson for their creative work on the lecture-support PowerPoint presentation slides. David Urban, Milt Pressley, and Lewis Hershey participated in PowerPoint work on the previous editions and their influence is still felt. It's rare to find world-class marketing professors who also have their skill and experience with teaching technologies, so we are certainly fortunate that they've shared their brainwaves on this project.

Nick Childers at Shadows and Light Creative Services has been the guru behind the scenes in production work on the video package for many editions. He also worked with us in developing the first versions of our CDs. Nick Childers and Debra Childers continue to play an important role not only in the videos but in multimedia innovations.

For several editions Judy Wilkinson has played a big role as producer of the video series for the book. In that capacity she worked closely with us to come up with ideas, and she provided guidance to the talented group of marketing professors and managers who created or revised videos for this edition. Judy also is the author of several outstanding video segments. We express respect for and deep appreciation to Judy for her work on the video series.

Of course, like other aspects of *Essentials of Marketing*, the video series has evolved and improved over time, and its current strength is partly due to the insights of Phil Niffenegger, who served as producer for our early video efforts. The video series also continues to benefit from the contributions of colleagues who developed videos in earlier editions. They are

Gary R. Brockway
James Burley
David Burns
Debra Childers
Martha O. Cooper
Carolyn Costley
W. Davis Folsom

Douglas Hausknecht
Scott Johnson
Bart Kittle
Gene R. Lazniak
Bill Levy
Don McBane
Charles S. Madden

Faculty and students at our current and past academic institutions—Michigan State University, University of North Carolina, Colorado State University, Emory, Notre Dame, University of Georgia, Northwestern University, University of Oregon, University of Minnesota, and Stanford University—have significantly shaped the book. Professor Andrew A. Brogowicz of Western Michigan University contributed many fine ideas to early editions of the text and supplements. Neil Morgan, Charlotte Mason, Val Zeithaml, John Workman, Nicholas Didow, Barry Bayus, Ken Manning, and Ajay Menon have provided a constant flow of helpful suggestions.

We are also grateful to the colleagues with whom we collaborate to produce international adaptations of the text. In particular, Stan Shapiro, Ken Wong, and Pascale G. Quester have all had a significant impact on *Essentials of Marketing*.

The designers, artists, editors, and production people at McGraw-Hill/Irwin who worked with us on this edition warrant special recognition. All of them have shared our commitment to excellence and brought their own individual creativity to the project. First we should salute Christine Vaughan, who has done an excellent job as production manager for the project. Without her adaptive problem solving we could not have succeeded with a (very) rapid-response production schedule—which is exactly what it takes to be certain that teachers and students get the most current information possible. In the same vein, Lynn Bluhm is now our hardworking, "can-do" media producer for this edition. We appreciate her dedication to all of the details involved in bringing such a complex project to market.

Nancy Barbour has been the developmental editor on the project through many editions. Her consistent support and belief in our quality objectives have been an ongoing influence. Our projects create an enormous amount of work for her, and we appreciate what she does, especially now that her skills have been recognized with broader responsibilities for managing other development editors. Doug Hughes serves as executive editor (and commander-in-chief) for this edition and has handled those responsibilities with skill and energy.

Keith McPherson is a long-term, creative, and valuable contributor to the look and feel of *Essentials of Marketing*. He again took the creative lead in designing an attractive book; he also put his personal touch on every piece of art and all of the illustrations in the text. What a talent he is and what skill he exhibits in bringing it all together to create a book that not only discusses but really illustrates best practices in marketing! We also appreciate Mike Hruby, who again tracked down permissions for photos and ads we selected to use to illustrate important ideas.

Trent Whatcott is our marketing manager for the project. He has brought great ideas to the team. We also owe a debt of gratitude to Lynn Bluhm, Mark Christianson, and Charles Pelto, who have taken the internal lead at McGraw-Hill in producing all of the *Essentials of Marketing* technology initiatives.

In past editions, Rob Zwettler, Merrily Mazza, David Littlehale, John Biernat, and Jerry Saykes have all found time in their busy executive schedules to share their publishing insights—and they also gave us crucial top-management support. Steve Patterson is living proof that it is possible to survive and prosper after years as editor of this project, and his ongoing friendship and support is still much appreciated.

Our families have been patient and consistent supporters through all phases in developing *Essentials of Marketing*. The support has been direct and substantive. Pam Perreault and Chris Cannon have provided valuable assistance and more encouragement than you could imagine. Our kids—Suzanne, Will, Kelly, Ally, and Mallory—provide valuable suggestions and ideas as well as encouragement and support while their dads are too often consumed with a never-ending set of deadlines.

We are indebted to all the firms that allowed us to reproduce their proprietary materials here. Similarly, we are grateful to associates from our business experiences who have shared their perspectives and feedback and enhanced our sensitivity to the key challenges of marketing management. In that regard, we especially acknowledge Kevin Clancy, Peter Krieg, and their colleagues at Copernicus: The Marketing Investment Strategy Group. The combination of pragmatic experience and creative insight they bring to the table is very encouraging. If you want to see great marketing, watch them create it.

A textbook must capsulize existing knowledge while bringing new perspectives and organization to enhance it. Our thinking has been shaped by the writings of literally thousands of marketing scholars and practitioners. In some cases it is impossible to give unique credit for a particular idea or concept because so many people have played important roles in anticipating, suggesting, shaping, and developing it. We gratefully acknowledge these contributors—from the early thought-leaders to contemporary authors and researchers—who have shared their creative ideas. We respect their impact on the development of marketing and, more specifically, this book.

To all of these persons—and to the many publishers who graciously granted permission to use their materials—we are deeply grateful. Responsibility for any errors or omissions is certainly ours, but the book would not have been possible without the assistance of many others. Our sincere appreciation goes to all who contributed.

William D. Perreault, Jr.
Joseph P. Cannon
E. Jerome McCarthy

Brief Contents

ESSENTIALS OF MARKETING, 11e

Perreault / Cannon / McCarthy

www.mhhe.com/fourps

Contents

CHAPTER THREE

Focusing Marketing Strategy with Segmentation and Positioning 58

CHAPTER FOUR

Evaluating Opportunities in the Changing Marketing Environment 82

CHAPTER FIVE

Final Consumers and Their Buying Behavior 114

CHAPTER NINE

Product Management and New-Product Development 220

CHAPTER TEN

Place and Development of Channel Systems 250

CHAPTER ELEVEN

Distribution Customer Service and Logistics 274

CHAPTER TWELVE

Retailers, Wholesalers, and Their Strategy Planning 296

CHAPTER THIRTEEN

Promotion—Introduction to Integrated Marketing Communications 326

CHAPTER FOURTEEN

Personal Selling and Customer Service 354

CHAPTER FIFTEEN

Advertising and Sales Promotion 382

CHAPTER SIXTEEN

Pricing Objectives and Policies 410

CHAPTER SEVENTEEN

Price Setting in the Business World 438

CHAPTER EIGHTEEN

Ethical Marketing in a Consumer-Oriented World: Appraisal and Challenges 464

Video Cases 537

Cases 553

ESSENTIALS OF MARKETING

A Marketing Strategy Planning Approach

1

Marketing's Value to Consumers, Firms, and Society

When it's time to roll out of bed in the morning, does the alarm ringer on your Verizon cell phone wake you, or is it your Sony clock radio playing your favorite radio station? Is the station playing hip-hop, classical, or country music—or perhaps a Red Cross ad asking you to contribute blood? Will you slip into your Levi's jeans, your shirt from Abercrombie and Fitch, and your Nikes, or does the day call for your Brooks Brothers interviewing suit? Will breakfast be Lender's Bagels with cream cheese or will you finish off that box of Tiger Power, Kellogg's new cereal made with whole grain wheat from America's heartland? Will you have some calcium-fortified Minute Maid orange juice and brew a pot of Maxwell House coffee—or is this a day to meet a friend at the local Starbucks, where you'll pay someone else to fix you a Frappuccino while you use the wireless Internet connection to log on to MSN.com to check your e-mail? Or perhaps if you're running late you can grab a ride to class in your friend's new Toyota Prius and pop into the new Starbucks Drive Thru on the way. What? Your friend decided that the new hybrid was too pricey for someone with only a part-time job? Well then, maybe you'll just have to take the bus that the city bought from General Motors. At least as you ride along you can entertain yourself listening to tunes on your Apple iPod.

When you think about it, you can't get very far into a day without bumping into marketing—and what the whole marketing system does for you. It affects every aspect of our lives—often in ways we don't even consider.

In other parts of the world, people wake up each day to different kinds of experiences. A family in rural China may have little choice about what food they will eat or where their clothing will come from. A consumer in a large city like Tokyo may have many choices but not be familiar with names like Tony the Tiger, Lender's Bagels, or Brooks Brothers.

What's more, each element in the descriptions above could be viewed in more detail and through a different lens. Consider, for example, that visit to Starbucks. What exactly is it about Starbucks that makes so many customers so satisfied with the experience? Why do they come back time and time again when they could get a cup of coffee almost anywhere, at half the price? Do loyal customers use the Starbucks card because it lets them participate in sweepstakes and get e-mail notices of in-store promotions and new products? Or is it because the card makes it fast and easy to order and pay? Why does Starbucks sell music CDs and offer Internet wireless hot spots at some locations—and, by the way, who dreamed up the idea of calling that tasty icy thing a Frappuccino? Twenty years ago, Starbucks was just another tiny company in

of dollars to develop and promote it. It seemed like a good bet that this tasty and healthy new cereal could help Kellogg's take customers away from General Mills's Cheerios. But, alas, consumers didn't cooperate. Perhaps they were just too loyal to Cheerios, or maybe they were not all that loyal but instead just kept buying Cheerios out of habit. On the other hand, maybe they thought about trying Tiger Power but then didn't—because they incorrectly assumed that if Tony the Tiger was on the package the cereal would probably taste

Seattle; now it operates over 5,000 coffee bars, has expanded into distribution through supermarkets, and is one of the best-known brand names in the world (yes, even in Tokyo). If this is such a simple (and profitable) business idea, why didn't somebody else think of it earlier?[1]

And there's a flip side to the growth and success enjoyed by Starbucks. Many companies, even ones run by smart people, make business decisions that don't work out. Every day, all around you, consumers are disappointed in some purchase they've made, new products fail, stores close, and expensive ad campaigns are ignored. For example, do you remember the Tiger Power cereal mentioned earlier and shown in the picture? Maybe you don't. Kellogg's spent millions

like his famous Frosted Flakes. Or perhaps retailers didn't have the patience to continue to give up shelf space for a product that was slow to catch on. Whatever the reasons, even after spending a lot of money, Kellogg's hopeful plans for Tiger Power fizzled—and the firm pulled it from store shelves.

You can't help but wonder how a large, successful company like Kellogg's could invest so much talent and money in an idea and then have it fail. And if Kellogg's managers are going to try again with another new idea, what should it be? Indeed, if you were going to try to build your own marketing success, what would it be and how would you do it?[2]

LEARNING OBJECTIVES

In this text, we'll answer questions like those raised earlier. In this chapter, you'll see what marketing is all about and why it's important to you as a consumer. We'll also explore why it is so crucial to the success of individual firms and nonprofit organizations and the impact that it has on the quality of life in different societies.

When you finish this chapter, you should:

1. know what marketing is and why you should learn about it.

2. understand the difference between marketing and macro-marketing.

3. know the marketing functions and why marketing specialists—including middlemen intermediaries and marketing collaborators—develop to perform them.

4. understand what a market-driven economy is and how it adjusts the macro-marketing system.

5. know what the marketing concept is—and how it should guide a firm or nonprofit organization.

6. understand what customer value is and why it is important to customer satisfaction.

7. know how social responsibility and marketing ethics relate to the marketing concept.

8. understand the important new terms (shown in red).

MARKETING—WHAT'S IT ALL ABOUT?

Marketing is more than selling or advertising

Many people think that marketing means "selling" or "advertising." It's true that these are parts of marketing. But *marketing is much more than selling and advertising.*

How did all those bicycles get here?

To illustrate some of the other important things that are included in marketing, think about all the bicycles being peddled with varying degrees of energy by bike riders around the world. Most of us don't make our own bicycles. Instead, they are made by firms like Trek, Performance, Huffy, and Murray.

Most bikes do the same thing—get the rider from one place to another. But a bike rider can choose from a wide assortment of models. They are designed in different sizes and with or without gears. Off-road bikes have large knobby tires. Kids and older people may want more wheels—to make balancing easier. Some bikes need baskets or even trailers for cargo. You can buy a basic bike for less than $50. Or you can spend more than $2,500 for a custom frame.

This variety of styles and features complicates the production and sale of bicycles. The following list shows some of the things a firm should do before and after it decides to produce and sell a bike.

1. Analyze the needs of people who might buy a bike and decide if they want more or different models.
2. Predict what types of bikes—handlebar styles, type of wheels, brakes, and materials—different customers will want and decide which of these people the firm will try to satisfy.
3. Estimate how many of these people will want to buy bicycles, and when.
4. Determine where in the world these bike riders are and how to get the firm's bikes to them.

Selling and advertising are important parts of marketing, but modern marketing involves more. For example, to better satisfy its customers' needs and make traveling more enjoyable, this French railroad's customer service includes door-to-door delivery of the passenger's luggage. The ad says, "Your luggage is big enough to travel by itself. It's up to us to ensure you'd rather go by train."

5. Estimate what price they are willing to pay for their bikes and if the firm can make a profit selling at that price.
6. Decide which kinds of promotion should be used to tell potential customers about the firm's bikes.
7. Estimate how many competing companies will be making bikes, what kind, and at what prices.
8. Figure out how to provide warranty service if a customer has a problem after buying a bike.

The above activities are not part of **production**—actually making goods or performing services. Rather, they are part of a larger process—called *marketing*—that provides needed direction for production and helps make sure that the right goods and services are produced and find their way to consumers.

You'll learn much more about marketing activities in the next chapter. For now, it's enough to see that marketing plays an essential role in providing consumers with need-satisfying goods and services and, more generally, in creating customer satisfaction. Simply put, **customer satisfaction** is the extent to which a firm fulfills a customer's needs, desires, and expectations.

MARKETING IS IMPORTANT TO YOU

Marketing is important to every consumer

Marketing affects almost every aspect of your daily life. The choices you have among the goods and services you buy, the stores where you shop, and the radio and TV programs you tune in to are all possible because of marketing. In the process of providing all these choices, marketing drives organizations to focus on what it takes to satisfy you, the customer. Most of the things you want or need are available conveniently *when* and *where* you want or need them.

Some courses are interesting when you take them but never relevant again once they're over. That's not so with marketing—you'll be a consumer dealing with marketing for the rest of your life regardless of what career you pursue. Moreover, as a consumer, you pay for the cost of marketing activities. In advanced economies, marketing costs about 50 cents of every consumer dollar. For some goods and services, the percentage is much higher. It makes sense to be an educated consumer and to understand what you get and don't get from all that spending.

Marketing will be important to your job

Another reason for studying marketing is that it offers many exciting and rewarding career opportunities. Throughout this book you will find information about opportunities in different areas of marketing.

If you're aiming for a nonmarketing job, knowing something about marketing will help you do your own job better. Throughout the book, we'll discuss ways that marketing relates to other functional areas. Further, marketing is important to the success of every organization. The same basic principles used to sell soap are also used to "sell" ideas, politicians, mass transportation, health care services, conservation, museums, and even colleges. Even your job résumé is part of a marketing campaign to sell yourself to some employer![3]

Marketing affects innovation and standard of living

An even more basic reason for studying marketing is that marketing plays a big part in economic growth and development. One key reason is that marketing encourages research and **innovation**—the development and spread of new ideas, goods, and services. As firms offer new and better ways of satisfying consumer needs, customers have more choices among products and this fosters competition for consumers' money. This competition drives down prices. Moreover, when firms develop products that really satisfy customers, fuller employment and higher incomes can result. The combination of these forces means that marketing has a big impact on consumers' standard of living—and that makes it important to the future of all nations.[4]

HOW SHOULD WE DEFINE MARKETING?

There are micro and macro views of marketing

In our bicycle example, we saw that a producer of bicycles has to perform many customer-related activities besides just making bikes. The same is true for an insurance company or an art museum. This supports the idea of marketing as a set of activities done by an individual organization to satisfy its customers.

On the other hand, people can't survive on bicycles and art museums alone! In advanced economies, it takes goods and services from thousands of organizations to satisfy the many needs of society. Further, a society needs some sort of marketing system to organize the efforts of all the producers and middlemen needed to satisfy the varied needs of all its citizens. So marketing is also an important social process.

We can view marketing in two ways: *from a micro view, as a set of activities performed by organizations, and also from a macro view, as a social process.* Yet, in everyday use when people talk about marketing they have the micro view in mind. So that is the way we will define marketing here. However, the broader macro view that looks at the whole production-distribution system is also important, so later we will provide a separate definition and discussion of macro-marketing.

Marketing defined

Marketing is the performance of activities that seek to accomplish an organization's objectives by anticipating customer or client needs and directing a flow of need-satisfying goods and services from producer to customer or client.

Let's look at this definition.[5]

Applies to profit and nonprofit organizations

Marketing applies to both profit and nonprofit organizations. Profit is the objective for most business firms. But other types of organizations may seek more members—or acceptance of an idea. Customers or clients may be individual consumers, business firms, nonprofit organizations, government agencies, or even foreign nations. While most customers and clients pay for the goods and services they receive, others may receive them free of charge or at a reduced cost through private or government support.

More than just persuading customers

Marketing isn't just selling and advertising. Unfortunately, some executives still think of it that way. They feel that the job of marketing is to "get rid of" whatever the company happens to produce. In fact, the aim of marketing is to identify customers' needs and meet those needs so well that the product almost "sells itself." This is true whether the product is a physical good, a service, or even an idea. If the whole marketing job has been done well, customers don't need much persuading. They should be ready to buy. And after they buy, they'll be satisfied and ready to buy the same way the next time.

Begins with customer needs

Marketing should begin with potential customer needs—not with the production process. Marketing should try to anticipate needs. And then marketing, rather than production, should determine what goods and services are to be developed—including decisions about product design and packaging; prices or fees; credit and collection policies; use of middlemen; transporting and storing policies; advertising and sales policies; and, after the sale, installation, customer service, warranty, and perhaps even disposal policies.

Does not do it alone

This does not mean that marketing should try to take over production, accounting, and financial activities. Rather, it means that marketing—by interpreting customers' needs—should provide direction for these activities and try to coordinate them.

Marketing involves exchanges

The idea that marketing involves a flow of need-satisfying offerings from a producer to a customer implies that there is an exchange of the need-satisfying offering for something else, such as the customer's money. Marketing focuses on facilitating exchanges. In fact, *marketing doesn't occur unless two or more parties are willing to exchange something for something else*. For example, in a **pure subsistence economy**—in which each family unit produces everything it consumes—there is no need to exchange goods and services and no marketing is involved. (Although each producer-consumer unit is totally self-sufficient in such a situation, the standard of living is typically relatively low.)

Builds a relationship with the customer

Keep in mind that a marketing exchange is often part of an ongoing relationship, not just a single transaction. When marketing helps everyone in a firm really meet the needs of a customer before and after a purchase, the firm doesn't just get a single sale. Rather, it has a sale and an ongoing *relationship* with the customer. Then, in the future, when the customer has the same need again—or some other need that the firm can meet—other sales will follow. Often, the marketing *flow* of need-satisfying goods and services is not just for a single transaction but rather is part of building a long-lasting relationship that benefits both the firm and the customer.

The focus of this text— management-oriented micro-marketing

Since you are probably preparing for a career in management, the main focus of this text will be on managerial marketing. We will see marketing through the eyes of the marketing manager.

The marketing ideas we will be discussing throughout this text apply to a wide variety of situations. They are important for new ventures started by one person as well as big corporations, in domestic and international markets, and regardless of whether the focus is on marketing physical goods, services, or an idea or cause. They are equally critical whether the relevant customers or clients are individual consumers, businesses, or some other type of organization. For editorial convenience, we will sometimes use the term *firm* as a shorthand way of referring to any type of organization, whether it is a political party, a religious organization, a government agency, or the like. However, to reinforce the point that the ideas apply to all types of organizations, throughout the book we will illustrate marketing concepts in a wide variety of situations.

Although marketing within individual firms is the primary focus of this text, marketing managers must remember that their organizations are just small parts of a larger macro-marketing system. Therefore, next we will briefly look at a macro view of marketing. Then, we will develop this idea more fully in later chapters.

MACRO-MARKETING

Macro-marketing is a social process that directs an economy's flow of goods and services from producers to consumers in a way that effectively matches supply and demand and accomplishes the objectives of society.[6]

Emphasis is on whole system

With macro-marketing we are still concerned with the flow of need-satisfying goods and services from producer to consumer. However, the emphasis with macro-marketing is not on the activities of individual organizations. Instead, the emphasis is on *how the whole marketing system works*. This includes looking at how marketing affects society and vice versa.

Every society needs a macro-marketing system to help match supply and demand. Different producers in a society have different objectives, resources, and skills. Likewise, not all consumers share the same needs, preferences, and wealth. In other words, within every society there are both heterogeneous (highly varied) supply capabilities and heterogeneous demands for goods and services. The role of a macro-marketing system is to effectively match this heterogeneous supply and demand *and* at the same time accomplish society's objectives.

An effective macro-marketing system delivers the goods and services that consumers want and need. It gets products to them at the right time, in the right place, and at a price they're willing to pay. It keeps consumers satisfied after the sale and brings them back to purchase again when they are ready. That's not an easy job—especially if you think about the variety of goods and services a highly developed economy can produce and the many kinds of goods and services consumers want.

Separation between producers and consumers

Effective marketing in an advanced economy is difficult because producers and consumers are often separated in several ways. As Exhibit 1–1 shows, exchange between producers and consumers is hampered by spatial separation, separation in time, separation of information and values, and separation of ownership. You may love your MP3 player, but you probably don't know when or where it was produced or how it got to you. The people in the factory that produced it don't know about you or how you live.

Peruvian coffee farmers and their families provide coffee to Starbucks. But to overcome the spatial separation between growers and consumers, someone must first perform a variety of marketing functions, like standardizing and grading the coffee beans, transporting and storing them, and buying and selling them. When Starbucks sells consumers its branded coffee at one of its new "drive-thru" locations, it is providing the final activity of a process that began a continent away.

Exhibit 1–1   Marketing Facilitates Production and Consumption

Production Sector
Specialization and division of labor result in heterogeneous supply capabilities

Discrepancies of Quantity. Producers prefer to produce and sell in large quantities. Consumers prefer to buy and consume in small quantities.

Discrepancies of Assortment. Producers specialize in producing a narrow assortment of goods and services. Consumers need a broad assortment.

Marketing needed to overcome discrepancies and separations

Spatial Separation. Producers tend to locate where it is economical to produce, while consumers are located in many scattered places.

Separation in Time. Consumers may not want to consume goods and services at the time producers would prefer to produce them, and time may be required to transport goods from producer to consumer.

Separation of Information. Producers do not know who needs what, where, when, and at what price. Consumers do not know what is available from whom, where, when, and at what price.

Separation in Values. Producers value goods and services in terms of costs and competitive prices. Consumers value them in terms of economic utility and ability to pay.

Separation of Ownership. Producers hold title to goods and services that they themselves do not want to consume. Consumers want goods and services that they do not own.

Consumption Sector
Heterogeneous demand for different goods and services and when and where they need to be to satisfy needs and wants

In addition, most firms specialize in producing and selling large amounts of a narrow assortment of goods and services. This allows them to take advantage of mass production with its **economies of scale**—which means that as a company produces larger numbers of a particular product, the cost of each of these products goes down. Yet most consumers only want to buy a small quantity; they also want a wide assortment of different goods and services. These "discrepancies of quantity" and "discrepancies of assortment" further complicate exchange between producers and consumers (Exhibit 1–1). That is, each producer specializes in producing and selling large amounts of a narrow assortment of goods and services, but each consumer wants only small quantities of a wide assortment of goods and services.[7]

Marketing functions help narrow the gap

The purpose of a macro-marketing system is to overcome these separations and discrepancies. The "universal functions of marketing" help do this.

The **universal functions of marketing** are buying, selling, transporting, storing, standardization and grading, financing, risk taking, and market information. They must be performed in all macro-marketing systems. *How* these functions are performed—and *by whom*—may differ among nations and economic systems. But they are needed in any macro-marketing system. Let's take a closer look at them now.

Any kind of exchange usually involves buying and selling. The **buying function** means looking for and evaluating goods and services. The **selling function** involves promoting the product. It includes the use of personal selling, advertising, and other direct and mass selling methods. This is probably the most visible function of marketing.

The **transporting function** refers to the movement of goods from one place to another. The **storing function** involves holding goods until customers need them.

Standardization and grading involve sorting products according to size and quality. This makes buying and selling easier because it reduces the need for inspection and sampling. **Financing** provides the necessary cash and credit to produce, transport, store, promote, sell, and buy products. **Risk taking** involves bearing the uncertainties that are part of the marketing process. A firm can never be sure that customers will want to buy its products. Products can also be damaged, stolen, or outdated. The **market information function** involves the collection, analysis, and distribution of all the information needed to plan, carry out, and control marketing activities, whether in the firm's own neighborhood or in a market overseas.

Producers, consumers, and marketing specialists perform functions

Producers and consumers sometimes handle some of the marketing functions themselves. However, exchanges are often easier or less expensive when a marketing specialist performs some of the marketing functions. For example, both producers and consumers may benefit when an **intermediary** (or a **middleman**)—someone who specializes in trade rather than production—plays a role in the exchange process. In Chapters 11–12 we'll cover the variety of marketing functions performed by the two basic types of intermediaries: retailers and wholesalers. Imagine what it would be like to shop at many different factories and farms for the wide variety of brands of packaged foods that you like rather than at a well-stocked local grocery store. While intermediaries must charge for services they provide, this charge is usually offset by the savings of time, effort, and expense that would be involved without a middleman. So these intermediaries can help to make the whole macro-marketing system more efficient and effective.

A wide variety of other marketing specialists may also help smooth exchanges between producers, consumers, or intermediaries. These specialists are marketing **collaborators**—firms that facilitate or provide one or more of the marketing functions other than buying or selling. These collaborators include advertising agencies, marketing research firms, independent product-testing laboratories, Internet service providers, public warehouses, transporting firms, communications companies, and financial institutions (including banks).

Internet EXERCISE Go to the Wal-Mart home page (**www.walmart.com**) and click on a tab for one of the product categories. How many different manufacturers' products are shown? Would consumers be better off if each manufacturer just sold directly from its own website?

Some marketing specialists perform all the functions. Others specialize in only one or two. Marketing research firms, for example, specialize only in the market information function. Further, technology may make a certain function easier to perform. For example, the buying process may require that a customer first identify relevant sellers and where they are. Even though that might be accomplished quickly and easily with an online search of the Internet, the function hasn't been cut out.

New specialists develop to fill market needs

As the Internet example suggests, new types of marketing specialists develop when someone spots a way to make exchanges between producers and consumers more efficient or effective. Such changes can come quickly, as illustrated by the speed with which firms have adopted e-commerce. **E-commerce** refers to exchanges between individuals or organizations—and activities that facilitate these exchanges—based on applications of information technology. New Internet-based intermediaries—like Amazon.com and eBay.com—are helping to cut the costs of many marketing functions. Similarly, Internet service providers like MSN.com and Google.com that also operate websites are a new type of collaborator. They make it easier for many firms to satisfy their customers with Web-based information searches or transactions. Collectively, these developments have had a significant impact on the efficiency of our macro-marketing system. At the same time, an individual firm can take advantage of these innovations to improve profitability and customer satisfaction.[8]

Middlemen intermediaries and marketing collaborators develop and offer specialized services that facilitate exchanges between producers and customers.

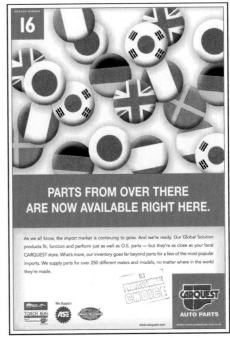

Through innovation, specialization, or economies of scale, marketing intermediaries and collaborators are often able to perform the marketing functions better—and at a lower cost—than producers or consumers can. This allows producers and consumers to spend more time on production, consumption, or other activities—including leisure.

Functions can be shifted and shared

From a macro-marketing viewpoint, all of the marketing functions must be performed by someone—an individual producer or consumer, an intermediary, a marketing collaborator, or, in some cases, even a nation's government. No function can be completely eliminated. *However, from a micro viewpoint, not every firm must perform all of the functions. Rather, responsibility for performing the marketing functions can be shifted and shared in a variety of ways. Further, not all goods and services require all the functions at every level of their production.* "Pure services"—like a plane ride—don't need storing, for example. But storing is required in the production of the plane and while the plane is not in service.

Regardless of who performs the marketing functions, in general they must be performed effectively and efficiently or the performance of the whole macro-marketing system will suffer. With many different possible ways for marketing functions to be performed in a macro-marketing system, how can a society hope to arrive at a combination that best serves the needs of its citizens? To answer this question, we can look at the role of marketing in different types of economic systems.

THE ROLE OF MARKETING IN ECONOMIC SYSTEMS

All societies must provide for the needs of their members. Therefore, every society needs some sort of **economic system**—the way an economy organizes to use scarce resources to produce goods and services and distribute them for consumption by various people and groups in the society.

How an economic system operates depends on a society's objectives and the nature of its political institutions.[9] But regardless of what form these take, all economic systems must develop some method—along with appropriate economic institutions—to decide what and how much is to be produced and distributed by whom, when, to whom, and why.

There are two basic kinds of economic systems: command economies and market-directed economies. Actually, no economy is entirely command-oriented or market-directed. Most are a mixture of the two extremes.

Government officials may make the decisions

In a **command economy,** government officials decide what and how much is to be produced and distributed by whom, when, to whom, and why. These decisions are usually part of an overall government plan, so command economies are also called "planned" economies. It sounds good for a government to have a plan, but as a practical matter attempts by a government to dictate an economic plan often don't work out as intended.

Producers in a command economy generally have little choice about what goods and services to produce. Their main task is to meet the production quotas assigned in the plan. Prices are also set by government planners and tend to be very rigid—not changing according to supply and demand. Consumers usually have some freedom of choice—it's impossible to control every single detail! But the assortment of goods and services may be quite limited. Activities such as market research, branding, and advertising usually are neglected. Sometimes they aren't done at all.

Government planning in a command economy may work fairly well as long as an economy is simple and the variety of goods and services is small. It may even be necessary under certain conditions—during wartime, drought, or political instability, for example. However, as economies become more complex, government planning becomes more difficult and tends to break down. Countries such as North Korea, Cuba, and China still rely on command-oriented economic systems. Even so, around the world there is a broad move toward market-directed economic systems—because they are more effective in meeting consumer needs.

A market-directed economy adjusts itself

In a **market-directed economy,** the individual decisions of the many producers and consumers make the macro-level decisions for the whole economy. In a pure market-directed economy, consumers make a society's production decisions when they make their choices in the marketplace. They decide what is to be produced and by whom—through their dollar "votes."

Price is a measure of value

Prices in the marketplace are a rough measure of how society values particular goods and services. If consumers are willing to pay the market prices, then apparently they feel they are getting at least their money's worth. Similarly, the cost of labor and materials is a rough measure of the value of the resources used in the production of goods and services to meet these needs. New consumer needs that can be served profitably—not just the needs of the majority—will probably be met by some profit-minded businesses.

Greatest freedom of choice

Consumers in a market-directed economy enjoy great freedom of choice. They are not forced to buy any goods or services, except those that must be provided for the good of society—things such as national defense, schools, police and fire protection, highway systems, and public-health services. These are provided by the community—and the citizens are taxed to pay for them.

Similarly, producers are free to do whatever they wish—provided that they stay within the rules of the game set by government *and* receive enough dollar "votes" from consumers. If they do their job well, they earn a profit and stay in business. But profit, survival, and growth are not guaranteed.

The role of government

The American economy and most other Western economies are mainly market-directed—but not completely. Society assigns supervision of the system to the

Marketing Helps India's Rural Poor

In recent decades India has experienced rapid economic growth. Many of its citizens now have more income and enjoy a higher quality of life. That helps to explain why Unilever's Indian subsidiary, Hindustani Lever Limited (HLL), has worked hard to build a 40 percent share of the Indian market with its product lines, which include soaps, toothpaste, and packaged foods.

So far, HLL has focused primarily on India's urban areas. Yet, two-thirds of India's 1 *billion*–plus people still live in rural areas. Only half of these rural villagers have access to electricity—and less than half have basic sanitation. Many of them have an income less than $2 a day. Conventional wisdom suggests that these poor rural villagers have too little money to be an attractive market. Further, villages are far flung, so it's expensive to distribute products to them.

But now that is changing. HLL's marketing managers have decided that Indian villagers represent an opportunity for growth—and that villagers might benefit if they could purchase the soaps, toothpaste, and packaged food products that HLL is successfully selling in urban areas of India.

HLL has tailored a new marketing strategy to this target market. First, many products have been repackaged in "sachets"—small bags that contain a one- or two-day supply. HLL prices the small sachets so that villagers can afford them—and that in turn gives customers a chance to try quality products that were previously unavailable.

HLL has created a "Shakti Ammas" (women entrepreneurs) program to communicate the benefits of its products and distribute them in remote rural areas. The program sets rural women up as home-based distributors and sales agents. These women stock HLL products at their homes and go door-to-door to sell them. They also organize meetings in local schools and at village fairs to educate their fellow villagers on health and hygiene issues.

HLL soon will have more than 100,000 Shakti Ammas operating in 500,000 villages. These women have a new source of income and are learning about business. Another positive social impact is that they are teaching rural villagers about the benefits of improved hygiene. And, of course, HLL hopes to clean up with a new source of growth.[10]

government. For example, besides setting and enforcing the "rules of the game," government agencies control interest rates and the supply of money. They also set import and export rules that affect international competition, regulate radio and TV broadcasting, sometimes control wages and prices, and so on. Government also tries to be sure that property is protected, contracts are enforced, individuals are not exploited, no group unfairly monopolizes markets, and producers deliver the kinds and quality of goods and services they claim to be offering.[11]

Is a macro-marketing system effective and fair?

The effectiveness and fairness of a particular macro-marketing system must be evaluated in terms of that society's objectives. Obviously, all nations don't share the same objectives. For example, Swedish citizens receive many "free" services—like health care and retirement benefits. Goods and services are fairly evenly distributed among the Swedish population. By contrast, North Korea places little emphasis on producing goods and services for individual consumers—and more on military spending. In India the distribution of goods and services is very uneven—with a big gap between the have-nots and the elite haves. Whether each of these systems is judged "fair" or "effective" depends on the objectives of the society.

So far, we have described how a market-directed macro-marketing system adjusts to become more effective and efficient by responding to customer needs. See Exhibit 1–2. As you read this book, you'll learn more about how marketing affects society and vice versa. You'll also learn more about specific marketing activities and be better informed when drawing conclusions about how fair and effective the macro-marketing

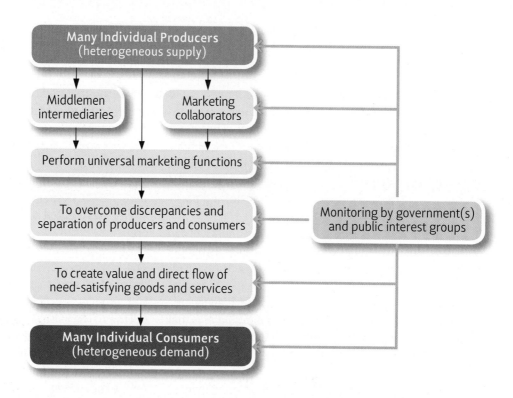

Exhibit 1–2
Model of a Market-Directed Macro-Marketing System

Many Individual Producers
(heterogeneous supply)

Middlemen intermediaries

Marketing collaborators

Perform universal marketing functions

To overcome discrepancies and separation of producers and consumers

Monitoring by government(s) and public interest groups

To create value and direct flow of need-satisfying goods and services

Many Individual Consumers
(heterogeneous demand)

system is. For now, however, we'll return to our general emphasis on a managerial view of the role of marketing in individual organizations.

MARKETING'S ROLE HAS CHANGED A LOT OVER THE YEARS

It's clear that marketing decisions are very important to a firm's success. But marketing hasn't always been so complicated. In fact, understanding how marketing thinking has evolved makes the modern view clearer. So we will discuss five stages in marketing evolution: (1) the simple trade era, (2) the production era, (3) the sales era, (4) the marketing department era, and (5) the marketing company era. We'll talk about these eras as if they applied generally to all firms—but keep in mind that *some managers still have not made it to the final stages*. They are stuck in the past with old ways of thinking.

Specialization permitted trade—and middlemen met the need

When societies first moved toward some specialization of production and away from a subsistence economy where each family raised and consumed everything it produced, traders played an important role. Early "producers for the market" made products that were needed by themselves and their neighbors. As bartering became more difficult, societies moved into the **simple trade era**—a time when families traded or sold their "surplus" output to local middlemen. These specialists resold the goods to other consumers or distant middlemen. This was the early role of marketing—and it is still the focus of marketing in many of the less-developed areas of the world. In fact, even in the United States, the United Kingdom, and other more advanced economies, marketing didn't change much until the Industrial Revolution brought larger factories a little over a hundred years ago.

From the production to the sales era

From the Industrial Revolution until the 1920s, most companies were in the production era. The **production era** is a time when a company focuses on production of a few specific products—perhaps because few of these products are available in the market. "If we can make it, it will sell" is management thinking characteristic of the production era. Because of product shortages, many nations—including China and many of the post-communist republics of Eastern Europe—continue to operate with production era approaches.

By about 1930, most companies in the industrialized Western nations had more production capability than ever before. Now the problem wasn't just to produce—but to beat the competition and win customers. This led many firms to enter the sales era. The **sales era** is a time when a company emphasizes selling because of increased competition.

To the marketing department era

For most firms in advanced economies, the sales era continued until at least 1950. By then, sales were growing rapidly in most areas of the economy. The problem was deciding where to put the company's effort. Someone was needed to tie together the efforts of research, purchasing, production, shipping, and sales. As this situation became more common, the sales era was replaced by the marketing department era. The **marketing department era** is a time when all marketing activities are brought under the control of one department to improve short-run policy planning and to try to integrate the firm's activities.

To the marketing company era

Since 1960, most firms have developed at least some managers with a marketing management outlook. Many of these firms have even graduated from the marketing department era into the marketing company era. The **marketing company era** is a time when, in addition to short-run marketing planning, marketing people develop long-range plans—sometimes five or more years ahead—and the whole company effort is guided by the marketing concept.

WHAT DOES THE MARKETING CONCEPT MEAN?

The **marketing concept** means that an organization aims *all* its efforts at satisfying its *customers*—at a *profit*. The marketing concept is a simple but very important idea. See Exhibit 1–3.

The marketing concept is not a new idea—it's been around for a long time. But some managers show little interest in customers' needs. These managers still have

Exhibit 1–3
Organizations with a Marketing Orientation Carry Out the Marketing Concept

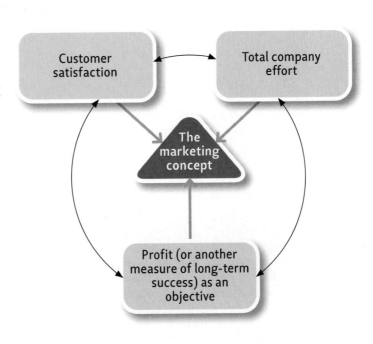

a **production orientation**—making whatever products are easy to produce and *then* trying to sell them. They think of customers existing to buy the firm's output rather than of firms existing to serve customers and—more broadly—the needs of society.

Well-managed firms have replaced this production orientation with a marketing orientation. A **marketing orientation** means trying to carry out the marketing concept. Instead of just trying to get customers to buy what the firm has produced, a marketing-oriented firm tries to offer customers what they need.

Three basic ideas are included in the definition of the marketing concept: (1) customer satisfaction, (2) a total company effort, and (3) profit—not just sales—as an objective. These ideas deserve more discussion.

Customer satisfaction guides the whole system

"Give the customers what they need" seems so obvious that it may be hard for you to see why the marketing concept requires special attention. However, people don't always do the logical—especially when it means changing what they've done in the past. In a typical company 40 years ago, production managers thought mainly about getting out the product. Accountants were interested only in balancing the books. Financial people looked after the company's cash position. And salespeople were mainly concerned with getting orders for whatever product was in the warehouse. Each department thought of its own activity as the center of the business. Unfortunately, this is still true in many companies today.

Work together to do a better job

Ideally, all managers should work together as a team. Every department may directly or indirectly impact customer satisfaction. But some managers tend to build "fences" around their own departments. There may be meetings to try to get them to work together—but they come and go from the meetings worried only about protecting their own turf.

We use the term *production orientation* as a shorthand way to refer to this kind of narrow thinking—and lack of a central focus—in a business firm. But keep in mind that this problem may be seen in sales-oriented sales representatives, advertising-oriented agency people, finance-oriented finance people, directors of nonprofit

In a firm, like SAP, that has adopted the marketing concept, everyone focuses their effort on satisfying customers at a profit. This isn't just a "feel good" philosophy. The investment made to satisfy customers creates long-run returns. As the Accion ad illustrates, marketing is now also widely accepted by many local, national, and international nonprofit organizations.

organizations, and so on. It is not a criticism of people who manage production. They aren't necessarily any more guilty of narrow thinking than anyone else.

The fences come down in an organization that has accepted the marketing concept. There may still be departments because specialization often makes sense. But the total system's effort is guided by what customers want—instead of what each department would like to do. The marketing concept provides a guiding focus that *all* departments adopt. It should be a philosophy of the whole organization, not just an idea that applies to the marketing department.

Survival and success require a profit

Firms must satisfy customers. But keep in mind that it may cost more to satisfy some needs than any customers are willing to pay. Or it may be much more costly to try to attract new customers than it is to build a strong relationship with—and repeat purchases from—existing customers. So profit—the difference between a firm's revenue and its total costs—is the bottom-line measure of the firm's success and ability to survive. It is the balancing point that helps the firm determine what needs it will try to satisfy with its total (sometimes costly!) effort.

ADOPTION OF THE MARKETING CONCEPT HAS NOT BEEN EASY OR UNIVERSAL

The marketing concept was first accepted by consumer products companies such as General Electric and Procter & Gamble. Competition was intense in their markets—and trying to satisfy customers' needs more fully was a way to win in this competition. Widespread publicity about the success of the marketing concept at these companies helped spread the message to other firms.[12]

Producers of industrial commodities—steel, coal, paper, glass, and chemicals—have accepted the marketing concept slowly if at all. Similarly, many traditional retailers have been slow to accept the marketing concept.

Service industries are catching up

Service industries—including airlines, power and telephone companies, banks, investment firms, lawyers, physicians, accountants, and insurance companies—were slow to adopt the marketing concept, too. But this has changed dramatically. This is partly due to changes in government regulations that forced many of these businesses to be more competitive.

Banks used to be open for limited hours that were convenient for bankers—not customers. Many closed during lunch hour! But now banks stay open longer and also offer more services for their customers—automated teller machines, banking over the Internet, or a "personal banker" to give financial advice.[13]

It's easy to slip into a production orientation

The marketing concept may seem obvious, but it's very easy to slip into a production-oriented way of thinking. For example, a company might rush a new product to market—rather than first finding out if it will fill an unsatisfied need. Many firms in high-technology businesses fall into this trap. Consider the thousands of new dot-com firms that have failed. They may have had a vision of what the technology could do, but they didn't stop to figure out all that it would take to satisfy customers or make a profit. Imagine how parents felt when eToys.com failed to deliver online purchases of Christmas toys on time. If you had that experience, would you ever shop there again? What would you tell others?

Take a look at Exhibit 1–4. It shows some differences in outlook between adopters of the marketing concept and typical production-oriented managers. As the exhibit suggests, the marketing concept forces the company to think through what it is doing—and why. And it motivates the company to develop plans for accomplishing its objectives.

Exhibit 1-4 Some Differences in Outlook between Adopters of the Marketing Concept and Typical Production-Oriented Managers

Topic	Marketing Orientation	Production Orientation
Attitudes toward customers	Customer needs determine company plans.	They should be glad we exist, trying to cut costs and bringing out better products.
An Internet website	A new way to serve customers.	If we have a website customers will flock to us.
Product offering	Company makes what it can sell.	Company sells what it can make.
Role of marketing research	To determine customer needs and how well company is satisfying them.	To determine customer reaction, if used at all.
Interest in innovation	Focus is on locating new opportunities.	Focus is on technology and cost cutting.
Importance of profit	A critical objective.	A residual, what's left after all costs are covered.
Customer service	Satisfy customer after the sale and he'll come back again.	An activity required to reduce consumer complaints.
Inventory levels	Set with customer requirements and costs in mind.	Set to make production more convenient.
Focus of advertising	Need-satisfying benefits of goods and services.	Product features and how products are made.
Role of sales force	Help the customer to buy if the product fits customer's needs, while coordinating with rest of firm.	Sell the customer, don't worry about coordination with other promotion efforts or rest of firm.
Relationship with customer	Customer satisfaction before and after sale leads to a profitable long-run relationship.	Relationship ends when a sale is made.
Costs	Eliminate costs that do not give value to customer.	Keep costs as low as possible.

THE MARKETING CONCEPT AND CUSTOMER VALUE

Take the customer's point of view

A manager who adopts the marketing concept sees customer satisfaction as the path to profits. And to better understand what it takes to satisfy a customer, it's useful to take the customer's point of view.

A customer may look at a market offering from two views. One deals with the potential benefits of that offering; the other concerns what the customer has to give up to get those benefits. Consider a student who has just finished an exam and is thinking about getting a cup of mocha latte from Starbucks. Our coffee lover might see this as a great-tasting snack, a personal reward, a quick pick-me-up, and even as a way to get to know an attractive classmate. Clearly, different needs are associated with these different benefits. The cost of getting these benefits would include the price of the coffee and any tip, but there might be other nondollar costs. For example, how difficult it will be to park is a convenience cost. Slow service would be an aggravation. And you might worry about another kind of cost if the professor whose exam you have the next day sees you "wasting time" at Starbucks.

Customer value reflects benefits and costs

As this example suggests, both benefits and costs can take many different forms, perhaps ranging from economic to emotional. They also may vary depending on the situation. However, it is the customer's view of the various benefits and costs that is important. This leads us to the concept of **customer value**—the difference between the benefits a customer sees from a market offering and the costs of obtaining those benefits. A consumer is likely to be more satisfied when the customer value is higher—when benefits exceed costs by a larger margin. On the other hand, a consumer who sees the costs as greater than the benefits isn't likely to become a customer.

Some people think that low price and high customer value are the same thing. But that may not be the case at all. A good or service that doesn't meet a consumer's needs results in low customer value, even if the price is very low. Yet a high price may be more than acceptable when it obtains the desired benefits. Think again about our Starbucks example. You can get a cup of coffee for a much lower price, but Starbucks offers more than *just* a cup of coffee.

Customer may not think about it very much

It's useful for a manager to evaluate ways to improve the benefits, or reduce the costs, of what the firm offers customers. However, this doesn't mean that customers stop and compute some sort of customer value score before making each purchase. If they did, there wouldn't be much time in life for anything else. So a manager's objective and thorough analysis may not accurately reflect the customer's impressions. Yet it is the customer's view that matters—even when the customer has not thought about it.

Where does competition fit?

You can't afford to ignore competition. Consumers usually have choices about how they will meet their needs. So a firm that offers superior customer value is likely to win and keep customers. See Exhibit 1–5.

Often the best way to improve customer value, and beat the competition, is to be first to satisfy a need that others have not even considered.

The competition between Pepsi and Coke illustrates this. Coke and Pepsi were spending millions of dollars on promotion—fighting head-to-head for the same cola customers. They put so much emphasis on the cola competition that they missed other opportunities. That gave firms like Snapple the chance to enter the market and steal away customers. For these customers, the desired benefits—and the greatest customer value—came from the variety of a fruit-flavored drink, not from one more cola.

Build relationships with customer value

Firms that embrace the marketing concept seek ways to build a profitable long-term relationship with each customer. Even the most innovative firm faces competition sooner or later. And trying to get new customers by taking them away from a competitor is usually more costly than retaining current customers by really satisfying their needs. Satisfied customers buy again and again. This makes their buying job easier, and it also increases the selling firm's profits.

Exhibit 1–5
Customer Value and Competition

Exhibit 1–6
Satisfying Customers with Superior Customer Value to Build Profitable Relationships

- Offer superior customer value
- Attract customers
- Satisfy customers
- Retain customers
- Build profitable relationships with customers
- Total company effort to satisfy customers

Building relationships with customers requires that everyone in a firm work together to provide customer value before *and after* each purchase. If there is a problem with a customer's bill, the accounting people can't just leave it to the salesperson to straighten it out or, even worse, act like it's "the customer's problem." The long-term relationship with the customer—and the lifetime value of the customer's future purchases—is threatened unless everyone works together to make things right for the customer. Similarly, the firm's advertising people can't just develop ads that try to convince a customer to buy once. If the firm doesn't deliver on the benefits promised in its ads, the customer is likely to go elsewhere the next time the need arises. And the same ideas apply whether the issue is meeting promised delivery dates, resolving warranty problems, giving a customer help on how to use a product, or even making it easy for the customer to return a purchase made in error.

In other words, any time the customer value is reduced—because the benefits to the customer decrease or the costs increase—the relationship is weakened.[14]

Exhibit 1–6 summarizes these ideas. In a firm that has adopted the marketing concept, everyone focuses on customer satisfaction. They offer superior customer value. That helps attract customers in the first place—and keeps them satisfied after they buy. Because customers are satisfied, they want to purchase from the firm again. The relationship with customers is profitable, so the firm is encouraged to find better ways to offer superior customer value. In other words, when a firm adopts the marketing concept, it wins and so do its customers.

THE MARKETING CONCEPT APPLIES IN NONPROFIT ORGANIZATIONS

Newcomers to marketing thinking

The marketing concept is as important for nonprofit organizations as it is for business firms. In fact, marketing applies to all sorts of public and private nonprofit organizations—ranging from government agencies, health care organizations,

L.L. Bean has always focused on customer satisfaction and customer value as a way to build long-term relationships with customers.

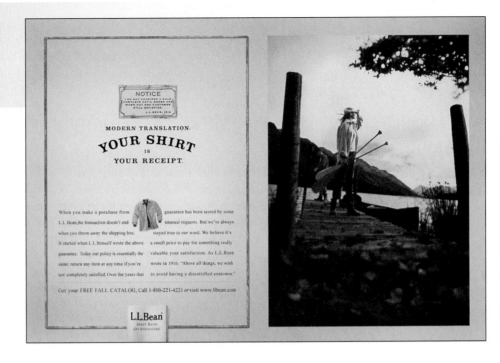

educational institutions, and religious groups to charities, political parties, and fine arts organizations.

Support may not come from satisfied "customers"

As with any business firm, a nonprofit organization needs resources and support to survive and achieve its objectives. Yet support often does not come directly from those who receive the benefits the organization produces. For example, the World Wildlife Fund protects animals. If supporters of the World Wildlife Fund are not satisfied with its efforts—that is, if they don't think the benefits are worth what it costs to provide them—they will, and should, put their time and money elsewhere.

Just as most firms face competition for customers, most nonprofits face competition for the resources and support they need. The Air Force faces a big problem if it can't attract new recruits. A shelter for the homeless may fail if supporters decide to focus on some other cause, such as AIDS education.

What is the "bottom line"?

As with a business, a nonprofit must take in at least as much money as it spends or it won't survive for long. However, a nonprofit organization does not measure "profit" in the same way as a firm. And its key measures of long-term success are also different. The YMCA, colleges, symphony orchestras, and the United Way, for example, all seek to achieve different objectives and need different measures of success. When everyone in an organization agrees to *some* measure(s) of long-run success, it helps the organization focus its efforts.[15]

Nonprofits achieve objectives by satisfying needs

A simple example shows how marketing thinking helped a small town reduce robberies. Initially the chief of police asked the town manager for a larger budget—for more officers and patrol cars. Instead of a bigger budget, the town manager suggested a different approach. She put two officers in charge of a community watch program. They helped neighbors to organize and notify the police of any suspicious situations. They also set up a program to engrave ID numbers on belongings. And new signs warned thieves that a community watch was in effect. Break-ins all but stopped—without increasing the police budget. What the town *really* needed was more effective crime prevention—not just more police officers.

Throughout this book, we'll be discussing the marketing concept and related ideas as they apply in many different settings. Often we'll simply say "in a firm" or "in a business"—but remember that most of the ideas can be applied in *any* type of organization.

THE MARKETING CONCEPT, SOCIAL RESPONSIBILITY, AND MARKETING ETHICS

Society's needs must be considered

The marketing concept is so logical that it's hard to argue with it. Yet when a firm focuses its efforts on satisfying some consumers—to achieve its objectives—there may be negative effects on society. For example, producers and consumers making free choices can cause conflicts and difficulties. This is called the **micro-macro dilemma**. What is "good" for some firms and consumers may not be good for society as a whole.

For example, many Americans want the convenience of disposable products and products in easy-to-use, small-serving packages. But these same "convenient" products and packages often lead to pollution of the environment and inefficient use of natural resources. Should future generations be left to pay the consequences of pollution that is the result of free choice by today's consumers?

Questions like these are not easy to answer. The basic reason is that many different people may have a stake in the outcomes—and social consequences—of the choices made by individual managers *and* consumers in a market-directed system. This means that marketing managers should be concerned with **social responsibility**—a firm's obligation to improve its positive effects on society and reduce its negative effects. As you read this book and learn more about marketing, you will also learn more about social responsibility in marketing—and why it must be taken seriously. You'll also see that being socially responsible sometimes requires difficult trade-offs.

Socially responsible marketing managers are concerned about the environmental impact of their decisions, and some firms are finding innovative ways to both help the environment and improve customer satisfaction at the same time.

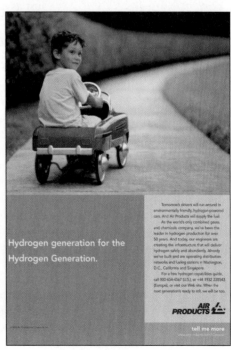

Hydrogen generation for the Hydrogen Generation.

Consider, for example, the environmental problems created by CFCs, chemicals that were used in hundreds of critical products, including fire extinguishers, cooling systems, and electronic circuit boards. When it was learned that CFCs deplete the earth's ozone layer, it was not possible to immediately stop producing and using all CFCs. For many products critical to society, there was no feasible short-term substitute. Du Pont and other producers of CFCs worked hard to balance these conflicting demands until substitute products could be found. Yet you can see that there are no easy answers for how such conflicts should be resolved.[16]

The issue of social responsibility in marketing also raises other important questions—for which there are no easy answers.

Should all consumer needs be satisfied?

Some consumers want products that may not be safe or good for them in the long run. Some critics argue that businesses should not offer high-heeled shoes, alcoholic beverages, or sugar-coated cereals because they aren't "good" for consumers in the long run.

Similarly, bicycles and roller blades are among the most dangerous products identified by the Consumer Product Safety Commission. Who should decide if these products will be offered to consumers?

What if it cuts into profits?

Being more socially conscious often seems to lead to positive customer response. For example, many consumers praise Wal-Mart as a "safe haven" for kids to shop because it does not carry CDs that are not suitable for children, lewd videos, plastic guns that look authentic, and video games judged to be too violent. Toyota and Honda have had a very good response to their offerings of hybrid cars that produce less pollution (even though the price is higher). And some consumers buy only from firms that certify that their overseas factories pay a "fair wage" and don't rely on child labor.[17]

Yet as the examples above show, there are times when being socially responsible conflicts with a firm's profit objective. Concerns about such conflicts have prompted critics to raise the basic question: Is the marketing concept really desirable?

Many socially conscious marketing managers are trying to resolve this problem. Their definition of customer satisfaction includes long-range effects—as well as immediate customer satisfaction. They try to balance consumer, company, *and* social interests.

The marketing concept guides marketing ethics

Certainly some concerns about social responsibility and marketing arise because some individual firm or manager has been intentionally unethical and cheated the market. Of course, a manager cannot be truly consumer-oriented and at the same time intentionally unethical. However, at times, problems and criticism may arise because a manager did not fully consider the ethical implications of a decision. In either case, there is no excuse for sloppiness when it comes to **marketing ethics**—the moral standards that guide marketing decisions and actions. Each individual develops moral standards based on his or her own values. That helps explain why opinions about what is right or wrong often vary from one person to another, from one society to another, and among different groups within a society. It is sometimes difficult to say whose opinions are "correct." Even so, such opinions may have a very real influence on whether an individual's (or a firm's) marketing decisions and actions are accepted or rejected. So marketing ethics are not only a philosophical issue, they are also a pragmatic concern.

Problems may arise when some individual manager does not share the same marketing ethics as others in the organization. One person operating alone can damage a firm's reputation and even survival.

To be certain that standards for marketing ethics are as clear as possible, many organizations have developed their own written codes of ethics. These codes usually state—at least at a general level—the ethical standards that everyone in the firm should follow in dealing with customers and other people. Many professional societies also have such codes. For example, the American Marketing Association's code of ethics—see Exhibit 1–7—sets specific ethical standards for many aspects of marketing.[18]

Exhibit 1–7   Code of Ethics, American Marketing Association

CODE OF ETHICS

Members of the American Marketing Association (AMA) are committed to ethical professional conduct. They have joined together in subscribing to this Code of Ethics embracing the following topics:

Responsibilities of the marketer

Marketers must accept responsibility for the consequences of their activities and make every effort to ensure that their decisions, recommendations, and actions function to identify, serve, and satisfy all relevant publics: customers, organizations, and society.

Marketers' professional conduct must be guided by:

1. The basic rule of professional ethics: not knowingly to do harm;
2. The adherence to all applicable laws and regulations;
3. The accurate representation of their education, training, and experience; and
4. The active support, practice, and promotion of this Code of Ethics.

Honesty and fairness

Marketers shall uphold and advance the integrity, honor, and dignity of the marketing profession by:

1. Being honest in serving consumers, clients, employees, suppliers, distributors, and the public;
2. Not knowingly participating in conflict of interest without prior notice to all parties involved; and
3. Establishing equitable fee schedules, including the payment or receipt of usual, customary, and/or legal compensation for marketing exchanges.

Rights and duties of parties in the marketing exchange process

Participants in the marketing exchange process should be able to expect that:

1. Products and services offered are safe and fit for their intended uses;
2. Communications about offered products and services are not deceptive;
3. All parties intend to discharge their obligations, financial and otherwise, in good faith; and
4. Appropriate internal methods exist for equitable adjustment and/or redress of grievances concerning purchases.

It is understood that the above would include, but is not limited to, the following responsibilities of the marketer:

In the area of product development and management,

- disclosure of all substantial risks associated with product or service usage;
- identification of any product component substitution that might materially change the product or impact on the buyer's purchase decision;
- identification of extra-cost added features.

In the area of promotions,

- avoidance of false and misleading advertising;
- rejection of high pressure manipulations or misleading sales tactics;
- avoidance of sales promotions that use deception or manipulation.

In the area of distribution,

- not manipulating the availability of a product for purpose of exploitation;
- not using coercion in the marketing channel;
- not exerting undue influence over the reseller's choice to handle a product.

In the area of pricing,

- not engaging in price fixing;
- not practicing predatory pricing;
- disclosing the full price associated with any purchase.

In the area of marketing research,

- prohibiting selling or fund raising under the guise of conducting research;
- maintaining research integrity by avoiding misrepresentation and omission of pertinent research data;
- treating outside clients and suppliers fairly.

Organizational relationships

Marketers should be aware of how their behavior may influence or impact on the behavior of others in organizational relationships. They should not demand, encourage, or apply coercion to obtain unethical behavior in their relationships with others, such as employees, suppliers, or customers.

1. Apply confidentiality and anonymity in professional relationships with regard to privileged information;
2. Meet their obligations and responsibilities in contracts and mutual agreements in a timely manner;
3. Avoid taking the work of others, in whole, or in part, and represent this work as their own or directly benefit from it without compensation or consent of the originator or owner;
4. Avoid manipulation to take advantage of situations to maximize personal welfare in a way that unfairly deprives or damages the organization or others.

Any AMA member found to be in violation of any provision of this Code of Ethics may have his or her Association membership suspended or revoked.

When a web surfer uses the search engine at Yahoo, one or more pop-up ads may appear. The advertising revenue pays for the service that Yahoo provides free to users, and some consumers click on interesting ads to get more information. However, most people think that pop-ups are too obtrusive.

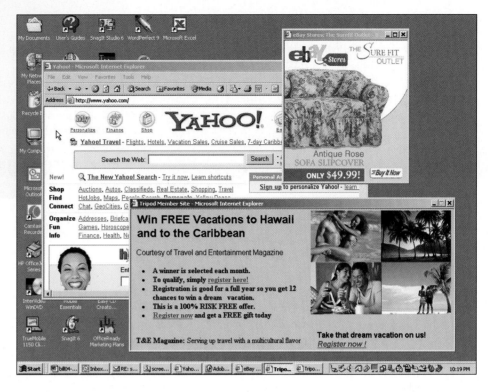

Throughout the text, we will be discussing the types of ethical issues individual marketing managers face. But we won't be moralizing and trying to tell you how you should think on any given issue. Rather, by the end of the course we hope that *you* will have some firm personal opinions about what is and is not ethical in micro-marketing activities.[19]

Fortunately, the prevailing practice of most businesspeople is to be fair and honest. However, not all criticisms of marketing focus on ethical issues.

Marketing has its critics

We must admit that marketing—as it exists in the United States and other developed societies—has many critics. Marketing activity is especially open to criticism because it is the part of business most visible to the public.

A number of typical complaints about marketing are summarized in Exhibit 1–8. Think about these criticisms and whether you agree with them or not. What complaints do you have that are not covered by one of the categories in Exhibit 1–8?

Such complaints should not be taken lightly. They show that many people are unhappy with some parts of the marketing system. Certainly, the strong public support for consumer protection laws proves that not all consumers feel they are being treated like royalty.

Exhibit 1–8   Sample Criticisms of Marketing

- Advertising is everywhere, and it's often annoying, misleading, or wasteful.
- The quality of products is poor and often they are not even safe.
- There are too many unnecessary products.
- Packaging and labeling are often confusing and deceptive.
- Middlemen add too much to the cost of distribution and just raise prices without providing anything in return.
- Marketing serves the rich and exploits the poor.

- Service stinks, and when a consumer has a problem nobody cares.
- Marketing creates interest in products that pollute the environment.
- Private information about consumers is collected and used to sell them things they don't want.
- Marketing makes people too materialistic and motivates them toward "things" instead of social needs.
- Easy consumer credit makes people buy things they don't need and can't afford.

As you consider the various criticisms of marketing, keep in mind that not all of them deal with the marketing practices of specific firms. Some of the complaints about marketing really focus on the basic idea of a market-directed macro-marketing system—and these criticisms often occur because people don't understand what marketing is—or how it works.[20] As you go through this book, we'll discuss some of these criticisms. Then in our final chapter, we will return to a more complete appraisal of marketing in our consumer-oriented society.

CONCLUSION

The basic purpose of this chapter is to introduce you to marketing and highlight its value for consumers, firms, and society. In the next chapter, we introduce a marketing strategy planning process that is the framework for ideas developed throughout the rest of the text—and that will guide your marketing thinking in the future. This chapter sets the stage for that by introducing basic principles that guide marketing thinking.

You've learned about two views of marketing, both of which are important. One takes a micro view and focuses on marketing activities by an individual business (or other type of organization). This is what most people (including most business managers) have in mind when they talk about marketing. But it's also important to understand that marketing also plays a more macro role. Macro-marketing is concerned with the way the whole marketing system works in a society or economy. It operates to make exchanges and relationships between producers and their customers more effective. We discussed the functions of marketing and who performs them. This includes not only producers and their customers but also marketing specialists who serve as intermediaries between producers and consumers and other specialists (like product-testing labs and advertising agencies) who are collaborators and facilitate marketing functions.

We explained how a market-directed economy works, through the macro-marketing system, to provide consumers with choices. We introduced macro-marketing in this chapter, and we'll consider macro-marketing issues throughout the text. But the major focus of this book is on marketing by individual organizations. Someone in an organization must plan and manage its activities to make certain that customer needs are satisfied.

That's why understanding the marketing concept is another objective. The marketing concept is the basic philosophy that provides direction to a marketing-oriented firm. It stresses that the company's efforts should focus on satisfying some target customers—at a profit. Production-oriented firms tend to forget this. The various departments within a production-oriented firm let their natural conflicts of interest get in the way of customer satisfaction.

We also introduced the customer value concept. It is marketing's responsibility to make certain that what the firm offers customers really provides them with value that is greater than they can obtain somewhere else. In today's competitive markets, a firm must offer superior customer value if it wants to attract customers, satisfy them, and build beneficial long-term relationships with them.

A final objective was for you to see how social responsibility and marketing ethics relate to the marketing concept. The chapter ends by considering criticisms of marketing—both of the way individual firms work and of the whole macro system. When you have finished reading this book, you will be better able to evaluate these criticisms.

By learning more about marketing-oriented decision making, you will be able to make more efficient and socially responsible decisions. This will help improve the performance of individual firms and organizations (your employers). And eventually it will help our macro-marketing system work better.

KEY TERMS

production, 5
customer satisfaction, 5
innovation, 6
marketing, 6
pure subsistence economy, 7
macro-marketing, 8
economies of scale, 9
universal functions of marketing, 9
buying function, 9
selling function, 9
transporting function, 10
storing function, 10

standardization and grading, 10
financing, 10
risk taking, 10
market information function, 10
intermediary (or middleman), 10
collaborators, 10
e-commerce, 10
economic system, 11
command economy, 12
market-directed economy, 12
simple trade era, 14
production era, 14

sales era, 15
marketing department era, 15
marketing company era, 15
marketing concept, 15
production orientation, 16
marketing orientation, 16
customer value, 18
micro-macro dilemma, 22
social responsibility, 22
marketing ethics, 23

QUESTIONS AND PROBLEMS

1. List your activities for the first two hours after you woke up this morning. Briefly indicate how marketing affected your activities.

2. If a producer creates a really revolutionary new product and consumers can learn about it and purchase it at a website on the Internet, is any additional marketing effort really necessary? Explain your thinking.

3. Distinguish between the micro and macro views of marketing. Then explain how they are interrelated, if they are.

4. Refer to Exhibit 1–1, and give an example of a purchase you made recently that involved separation of information and separation in time between you and the producer. Briefly explain how these separations were overcome.

5. Describe a recent purchase you made. Indicate why that particular product was available at a store and, in particular, at the store where you bought it.

6. Define the functions of marketing in your own words. Using an example, explain how they can be shifted and shared.

7. Online computer shopping at websites on the Internet makes it possible for individual consumers to get direct information from hundreds of companies they would not otherwise know about. Consumers can place an order for a purchase that is then shipped to them directly. Will growth of these services ultimately eliminate the need for retailers and wholesalers? Explain your thinking, giving specific attention to what marketing functions are involved in these "electronic purchases" and who performs them.

8. Explain why a small producer might want a marketing research firm to take over some of its information gathering activities.

9. Distinguish between how economic decisions are made in a command economy and how they are made in a market-directed economy.

10. Would the functions that must be provided and the development of wholesaling and retailing systems be any different in a command economy from those in a market-directed economy?

11. Explain why a market-directed macro-marketing system encourages innovation. Give an example.

12. Define the marketing concept in your own words, and then explain why the notion of profit is usually included in this definition.

13. Define the marketing concept in your own words, and then suggest how acceptance of this concept might affect the organization and operation of your college.

14. Distinguish between production orientation and marketing orientation, illustrating with local examples.

15. Explain why a firm should view its internal activities as part of a total system. Illustrate your answer for (*a*) a large grocery products producer, (*b*) a plumbing wholesaler, (*c*) a department store chain, and (*d*) a cell phone service.

16. Give examples of some of the benefits and costs that might contribute to the customer value of each of the following products: (*a*) a wristwatch, (*b*) a weight-loss diet supplement, (*c*) a cruise on a luxury liner, and (*d*) a checking account from a bank.

17. Give an example of a recent purchase you made where the purchase wasn't just a single transaction but rather part of an ongoing relationship with the seller. Discuss what the seller has done (or could do better) to strengthen the relationship and increase the odds of you being a loyal customer in the future.

18. Discuss how the micro-macro dilemma relates to each of the following products: high-powered engines in cars, nuclear power, bank credit cards, and pesticides that improve farm production.

19. A committee of the American Marketing Association recently updated the association's definition of marketing. It defines marketing as "an organizational function and a set of processes for creating, communicating, and delivering value to customers and for managing customer relationships in ways that benefit the organization and its stakeholders." The association's previous definition defined marketing as "the process of planning and executing the conception, pricing, promotion, and distribution of ideas, goods, and services to create exchanges that satisfy individual and organizational objectives." In your own words, explain what you think are the basic differences and similarities in the two definitions.

SUGGESTED CASES

1. McDonald's "Seniors" Restaurant   **2. Sunshine Foods, Inc.**   **18. Harrisburg Volunteer Fire Department**

COMPUTER-AIDED PROBLEM

1. REVENUE, COST, AND PROFIT RELATIONSHIPS

This problem introduces you to the computer-aided problem (CAP) software—which is on the CD that accompanies this text—and gets you started with the use of spreadsheet analysis for marketing decision making. This problem is simple. In fact, you could work it without the software. But by starting with a simple problem, you will learn how to use the program more quickly and see how it will help you with more complicated problems. Instructions for the software are available at the end of this text.

Sue Cline, the business manager at Magna University Student Bookstore, is developing plans for the next academic year. The bookstore is one of the university's nonprofit activities, but any "surplus" (profit) it earns is used to support the student activities center.

Two popular products at the bookstore are the student academic calendar and notebooks with the school name. Sue Cline thinks that she can sell calendars to 90 percent of Magna's 3,000 students, so she has had 2,700 printed. The total cost, including artwork and printing, is $11,500. Last year the calendar sold for $5.00, but Sue is considering changing the price this year.

Sue thinks that the bookstore will be able to sell 6,000 notebooks if they are priced right. But she knows that many students will buy similar notebooks (without the school name) from stores in town if the bookstore price is too high.

Sue has entered the information about selling price, quantity, and costs for calendars and notebooks in the spreadsheet program so that it is easy to evaluate the effect of different decisions. The spreadsheet is also set up to calculate revenue and profit, based on

$$\text{Revenue} = (\text{Selling price}) \times (\text{Quantity sold})$$

$$\text{Profit} = (\text{Revenue}) - (\text{Total cost})$$

Use the program to answer the questions that follow. Record your answers on a separate sheet of paper.

a. From the spreadsheet screen, how much revenue does Sue expect from calendars? How much revenue from notebooks? How much profit will the store earn from calendars? From notebooks?

b. If Sue increases the price of her calendars to $6.00 and still sells the same quantity, what is the expected revenue? The expected profit? (Note: Change the price from $5.00 to $6.00 on the spreadsheet and the program will recompute revenue and profit.) On your sheet of paper, show the calculations that confirm that the program has given you the correct values.

c. Sue is interested in getting an overview of how a change in the price of notebooks would affect revenue and profit, assuming that she sells all 6,000 notebooks she is thinking of ordering. Prepare a table—on your sheet of paper—with column headings for three variables: selling price, revenue, and profit. Show the value for revenue and profit for different possible selling prices for a notebook—starting at a minimum price of $1.60 and adding 8 cents to the price until you reach a maximum of $2.40. At what price will selling 6,000 notebooks contribute $5,400.00 to profit? At what price would notebook sales contribute only $1,080.00? (Hint: Use the "What If" analysis feature to compute the new values. Start by selecting "selling price" for notebooks as the value to change, with a minimum value of $1.60 and a maximum value of $2.40. Select the revenue and profit for notebooks as the values to display.)

For additional questions related to this problem, see Exercise 1-5 in the *Learning Aid for Use with Essentials of Marketing*, 11th edition.

CHAPTER TWO

Marketing Strategy Planning

There was a time when it didn't seem to be an exaggeration for Barnum & Bailey's ads to tout the circus as "the greatest show on earth." For a hundred years, circuses had brought excitement and family entertainment to towns all over the country. Parents hardly noticed the hard benches that they sat on as they watched their kids cheer for the acrobats, clowns, and animal acts. But by the 1980s the popularity of traditional circuses was in decline; many simply went out of business.

You can imagine why this sad state of affairs would be a concern for Guy Laliberté—a stilt walker, accordion player, and fire eater—and others in his band of performers. But instead of bemoaning the demise of the circus, they saw an opportunity for a new kind of entertainment—and their idea gave birth to "Cirque du Soleil."

Their new style of circus still traveled to the audience and set up a "big top" tent, but costly and controversial animal acts were eliminated. Instead, the entertainment focused on an innovative combination of acrobatics, music, and theater. This more sophisticated offering appealed to adults. Importantly, adults were willing to pay more for tickets when the show was targeted at them and not just kids—especially when the traditional circus benches were replaced with more comfortable seats.

Cirque du Soleil quickly struck a cord with audiences and soon the producers were developing new shows and also expanding tours to reach new markets. For example, seven different Cirque du Soleil shows now travel across Europe, Asia, and North America. Each show performs in a host city for anywhere from two weeks to three months. In addition, six other Cirque du Soleil shows now have permanent homes and target tourists. Five are in Las Vegas and one is in Orlando, Florida. Each show is different and has a unique theme. For example, the theme of *KÀ* highlights the martial arts, *O* emphasizes fire and water while incorporating Polynesian folklore, and *LOVE* celebrates the music of The Beatles.

As all of this suggests, Cirque du Soleil's marketing managers constantly evaluate new opportunities. A few years ago the company even considered a plan to diversify into hotels and spas based on the circus theme. This idea was screened out—at least for now—and instead the focus has been on developing new products for current and new markets. Each idea for a new show is judged on its creativity, uniqueness, and likelihood of becoming a real blockbuster. New product development is very ambitious. New shows can take more than five years and $100 million to develop. But these development costs can be recouped over each show's anticipated 10-year run. For example, a program now in development will feature the music of Elvis Presley and other new Cirque du Soleil shows will have permanent facilities in the Chinese resort city of Macao and Japan's capital, Tokyo.

Cirque du Soleil also now offers television specials and DVDs. This is another way for Cirque to reach new customers. These small screen shows not only generate additional revenue but they also give customers a taste of Cirque du Soleil and whet their appetite for a live show.

Once customers see a live Cirque du Soleil show, they want to see more. So Cirque's ad efforts focus on motivating customers to see that first show. For example, ads in airline magazines target travelers who are headed to cities with permanent shows and traveling shows are heavily advertised in local media. But publicity and word of mouth are also important. Local newspapers and TV shows are often interested in doing stories about touring productions that are coming to town. Cirque du Soleil's website helps reporters in this effort by providing photos, videos, and interviews for easy download. To encourage word of mouth, they also rely on exclusive "premiers" where influential people in the community are invited to a gala opening night. The troupe also offers free tickets and volunteers time to help build close relationships with local art and charitable organizations. After experiencing the troupe's magic, people often tell their friends and look forward to the next opportunity to see Cirque du Soleil in action.

These new fans are likely to visit Cirque du Soleil's website (www.cirquedusoleil.com), which gives information about all the shows. The site also encourages customers to join the hundreds of thousands who have already signed up for the free "Cirque Club." Members sign up for the specific news they want sent to their e-mail address. So those wanting information about the permanent shows in Orlando and traveling shows coming to Georgia get messages letting them know of advance ticket sales to the Atlanta show and changes at the Orlando show.

Cirque du Soleil has been very successful but it must continue to focus on ways to improve its customers' experiences. Imitators, like Slava's Snowshow, the Canadian Cirque Éloize, and Le Rêve in

Las Vegas now try to offer similar entertainment fare. The reputation of the powerful Cirque du Soleil brand name has given the troupe a competitive advantage when it introduces new shows. It also allows Cirque to charge a premium price for tickets, which range from $40 to over $200 for the exclusive *Tapis Rouge* (red carpet) tickets. Cirque du Soleil's carefully crafted marketing mix is now resulting in sales of more than half a billion dollars in tickets each year![1]

LEARNING OBJECTIVES

Marketing managers at Cirque du Soleil make many decisions as they develop marketing strategies. Making good marketing strategy decisions is never easy, yet knowing what basic decision areas to consider helps you to plan a more successful strategy. This chapter will get you started by giving you a framework for thinking about marketing strategy planning—which is what the rest of this book is all about.

When you finish this chapter, you should:

1. understand what a marketing manager does.

2. know what marketing strategy planning is—and why it is the focus of this book.

3. understand target marketing.

4. be familiar with the four Ps in a marketing mix.

5. know the difference between a marketing strategy, a marketing plan, and a marketing program.

6. understand what customer equity is and why marketing strategy planners seek to increase it.

7. be familiar with the text's framework for marketing strategy planning—and why it involves a process of narrowing down from broad opportunities to the most attractive marketing strategy.

8. know four broad types of marketing opportunities that help in identifying new strategies.

9. understand why strategies for opportunities in international markets should be considered.

10. understand the important new terms (shown in red).

THE MANAGEMENT JOB IN MARKETING

In Chapter 1 you learned about the marketing concept—a philosophy to guide the whole firm toward satisfying customers at a profit. From the Cirque du Soleil case, it's clear that marketing decisions are very important to a firm's success. So let's look more closely at how a marketing manager helps a firm to achieve its objectives. Because the marketing manager is a manager, let's look at the marketing management process.

The **marketing management process** is the process of (1) *planning* marketing activities, (2) directing the *implementation* of the plans, and (3) *controlling* these plans. Planning, implementation, and control are basic jobs of all managers—but here we will emphasize what they mean to marketing managers.

Exhibit 2–1 shows the relationships among the three jobs in the marketing management process. The jobs are all connected to show that the marketing management process is continuous. In the planning job, managers set guidelines for the implementing job and specify expected results. They use these expected results in the control job to determine if everything has worked out as planned. The link from the control job to the planning job is especially important. This feedback often leads to changes in the plans or to new plans.

Marketing managers should seek new opportunities

Marketing managers cannot be satisfied just planning present activities. Markets are dynamic. Consumers' needs, competitors, and the environment keep changing. Consider Parker Brothers, a company that seemed to have a "Monopoly" in family

Exhibit 2–1
The Marketing
Management Process

games. While it continued selling board games, firms like Sega, Sony, and Nintendo zoomed in with video game competition. Of course, not every opportunity is good for every company. Really attractive opportunities are those that fit with what the whole company wants to do and is able to do well.

Strategic management planning concerns the whole firm

The job of planning strategies to guide a whole company is called **strategic (management) planning**—the managerial process of developing and maintaining a match between an organization's resources and its market opportunities. This is a top-management job. It includes planning not only for marketing but also for production, finance, human resources, and other areas.

Although marketing strategies are not whole-company plans, company plans should be market-oriented. And the marketing plan often sets the tone and direction for the whole company. So we will use *strategy planning* and *marketing strategy planning* to mean the same thing.[2]

WHAT IS A MARKETING STRATEGY?

Marketing strategy planning means finding attractive opportunities and developing profitable marketing strategies. But what is a "marketing strategy"? We have used these words rather casually so far. Now let's see what they really mean.

Exhibit 2–2
A Marketing Strategy

A **marketing strategy** specifies a target market and a related marketing mix. It is a big picture of what a firm will do in some market. Two interrelated parts are needed:

1. A **target market**—a fairly homogeneous (similar) group of customers to whom a company wishes to appeal.
2. A **marketing mix**—the controllable variables the company puts together to satisfy this target group.

The importance of target customers in this process can be seen in Exhibit 2–2, where the target customer—the "C"—is at the center of the diagram. The customer is surrounded by the controllable variables that we call the "marketing mix." A typical marketing mix includes some product, offered at a price, with some promotion to tell potential customers about the product, and a way to reach the customer's place.

For example, the marketing strategy for The Learning Company's software aims at a specific group of target customers: young parents who have a computer at home and want their kids to learn while playing. The strategy calls for a variety of educational software products—like *Reader Rabbit* and *Where in the World Is Carmen Sandiego?* The firm's software is designed with entertaining graphics and sound, and it's tested on kids to be certain that it is easy to use. To make it convenient for target customers to buy the software, it can be ordered from the firm's own website (www.learningcompany.com) or from other retailers like Toys "R" Us. Promotion has helped build customer interest in the software. For instance, when marketing managers released *Where in Time Is Carmen Sandiego?* they not only placed ads in family-oriented computer magazines but also sent direct-mail flyers or e-mail to registered customers of the firm's other products. Some firms sell less-expensive games for kids, but parents are loyal to The Learning Company brand because it caters to their needs and offers first-class customer service—including a 90-day, no-questions-asked guarantee that assures the buyer of good customer value.[3]

SELECTING A MARKET-ORIENTED STRATEGY IS TARGET MARKETING

Target marketing is not mass marketing

Note that a marketing strategy specifies some *particular* target customers. This approach is called "target marketing" to distinguish it from "mass marketing." **Target marketing** says that a marketing mix is tailored to fit some specific target customers. In contrast, **mass marketing**—the typical production-oriented approach—vaguely aims at "everyone" with the same marketing mix. Mass marketing assumes that everyone is the same—and it considers everyone to be a potential customer. See Exhibit 2–3.

Mass marketers may do target marketing

Commonly used terms can be confusing here. The terms *mass marketing* and *mass marketers* do not mean the same thing. Far from it! *Mass marketing* means trying to sell to "everyone," as we explained above. *Mass marketers* like Kraft Foods and Wal-Mart are aiming at clearly defined target markets. The confusion with mass marketing occurs because their target markets usually are large and spread out.

Target marketing can mean big markets and profits

Target marketing is not limited to small market segments—only to fairly homogeneous ones. A very large market—even what is sometimes called the "mass market"—may be fairly homogeneous, and a target marketer will deliberately aim at it. For example, a very large group of parents of young children are homogeneous on many

Exhibit 2–3
Production-Oriented and Marketing-Oriented Managers Have Different Views of the Market

The production-oriented manager sees everyone as basically similar and practices "mass marketing"

The marketing-oriented manager sees everyone as different and practices "target marketing" dimensions, including their attitudes about changing baby diapers. In the United States alone, this group spends about $4 billion a year on disposable diapers—so it should be no surprise that it is a major target market for companies like Kimberly-Clark (Huggies) and Procter & Gamble (Pampers). On the other hand, babies and their parents are not the only ones who need disposable diapers. Many elderly people, especially those who are in nursing homes and have mobility problems, use diapers. Needless to say, the marketing mix that's right for babies isn't right for elder care. It's not just the sizes that are different, but also the forms. The elderly don't like the idea of needing "diapers"—so instead they wear disposable "pull ups."

The basic reason to focus on some specific target customers is so that you can develop a marketing mix that satisfies those customers' *specific* needs better than they are satisfied by some other firm. For example, E*trade uses an Internet site (www. etrade.com) to target knowledgeable investors who want a convenient, low-cost way to buy and sell stocks online without a lot of advice (or pressure) from a salesperson.

When a firm carefully targets its marketing mix, it is less likely to face direct competitors. So superior customer value is achieved with the benefits provided by the whole marketing mix rather than just by relying on a lower price. Whole Foods Market (WFM) is a good example. Most grocery stores sell the same brands—so they compete on price and profits tend to be weak. In contrast, WFM makes attractive profits with a differentiated marketing mix that delights its target customers. WFM sees itself as a buying agent for its customers and not the selling agent for manufacturers—so it evaluates the ingredients, freshness, safety, taste, nutritive value, and appearance of all the products it carries. It hires people who love food. WFM doesn't just sell food—but rather helps its customers appreciate the difference natural and organic products can make in the quality of their lives. Service is attentive, friendly, and offered with some flair, which helps make the store fun and inviting. Customers often socialize while they shop. Not everyone wants the marketing mix that WFM offers; but its target customers love shopping there—and they spread the word to others.[4]

DEVELOPING MARKETING MIXES FOR TARGET MARKETS

There are many marketing mix decisions

There are many possible ways to satisfy the needs of target customers. A product might have many different features. Customer service levels before or after the sale can be adjusted. The package, brand name, and warranty can be changed. Various advertising media—newspapers, magazines, cable, the Internet—may be used. A company's own sales force or other sales specialists can be used. The price can be changed, discounts can be given, and so on. With so many possible variables, is there any way to help organize all these decisions and simplify the selection of marketing mixes? The answer is yes.

The four "Ps" make up a marketing mix

It is useful to reduce all the variables in the marketing mix to four basic ones:

Product
Place
Promotion
Price

Exhibit 2-4
A Marketing Strategy—Showing the Four Ps of a Marketing Mix

It helps to think of the four major parts of a marketing mix as the "four Ps." Exhibit 2–4 emphasizes their relationship and their common focus on the target customer—"C."

Customer is not part of the marketing mix

The customer is shown surrounded by the four Ps in Exhibit 2–4. Some students assume that the customer is part of the marketing mix—but this is not so. The customer should be the *target* of all marketing efforts. The customer is placed in the center of the diagram to show this. The C stands for some specific customers—the target market.

Exhibit 2–5
Strategy Decision Areas
Organized by the Four Ps

Product	Place	Promotion	Price

• Physical good
• Service
• Features
• Benefits
• Quality level
• Accessories
• Installation
• Instructions
• Warranty
• Product lines
• Packaging
• Branding
	• Objectives
	• Channel type
	• Market exposure
	• Kinds of middlemen
	• Kinds and locations of stores
	• How to handle transporting and storing
	• Service levels
	• Recruiting middlemen
	• Managing channels
		• Objectives
		• Promotion blend
		• Salespeople
		  Kind
		  Number
		  Selection
		  Training
		  Motivation
		• Advertising
		  Targets
		  Kinds of ads
		  Media type
		  Copy thrust
		  Prepared by whom
		• Sales promotion
		• Publicity
			• Objectives
			• Flexibility
			• Level over product life cycle
			• Geographic terms
			• Discounts
			• Allowances

Exhibit 2–5 shows some of the strategy decision variables organized by the four Ps. These will be discussed in later chapters. For now, let's just describe each P briefly.

Product—the good or service for the target's needs

The Product area is concerned with developing the right "product" for the target market. This offering may involve a physical good, a service, or a blend of both. Keep in mind that Product is not limited to physical goods. For example, the Product of H&R Block is a completed tax form. The Product of a political party is the set of

A firm's product may involve a physical good or a service or a combination of both.

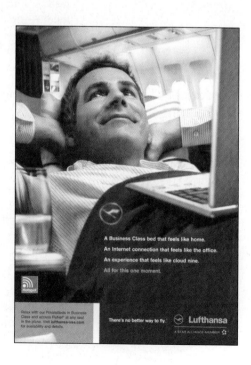

causes it will work to achieve. The important thing to remember is that your good or service should satisfy some customers' needs.

Along with other Product-area decisions like branding, packaging, and warranties, we will talk about developing and managing new products and whole product lines.

Place—reaching the target

Place is concerned with all the decisions involved in getting the "right" product to the target market's Place. A product isn't much good to a customer if it isn't available when and where it's wanted.

A product reaches customers through a channel of distribution. A **channel of distribution** is any series of firms (or individuals) that participate in the flow of products from producer to final user or consumer. Sometimes a channel of distribution is quite short—the financial services company Charles Schwab operates directly with most of its customers. See Exhibit 2–6. On the other hand, Nestlé's food products are handled by wholesalers and retailers before reaching consumers. Marketing managers must decide on the channel system that best meets target customers' needs.

We will also see how physical distribution service levels and decisions concerning logistics (transporting, storing, and handling products) relate to the other Place decisions and the rest of the marketing mix.

Promotion—telling and selling the customer

The third P—Promotion—is concerned with telling the target market or others in the channel of distribution about the "right" product. Sometimes promotion is focused on acquiring new customers, and sometimes it's focused on retaining current customers. Promotion includes personal selling, mass selling, and sales promotion. It is the marketing manager's job to blend these methods of communication.

Personal selling involves direct spoken communication between sellers and potential customers. Personal selling may happen face-to-face, over the telephone, or even via a videoconference over the Internet. Sometimes personal attention is required *after the sale*. **Customer service**—a personal communication between a seller and a customer who wants the seller to resolve a problem with a purchase—is often the key to building repeat business.

Exhibit 2–6
Four Examples of Basic Channels of Distribution for Consumer Products

Mass selling is communicating with large numbers of customers at the same time. The main form of mass selling is **advertising**—any *paid* form of nonpersonal presentation of ideas, goods, or services by an identified sponsor. **Publicity**—any *unpaid* form of nonpersonal presentation of ideas, goods, or services—is another important form of mass selling. Mass selling may involve a wide variety of media, ranging from newspapers and billboards to the Internet.

Sales promotion refers to those promotion activities—other than advertising, publicity, and personal selling—that stimulate interest, trial, or purchase by final customers or others in the channel. This can involve use of coupons, point-of-purchase materials, samples, signs, contests, events, catalogs, novelties, and circulars.

Price—making it right

In addition to developing the right Product, Place, and Promotion, marketing managers must also decide the right Price. Price setting must consider the kind of competition in the target market and the cost of the whole marketing mix. A manager must also try to estimate customer reaction to possible prices. Besides this, the manager must know current practices as to markups, discounts, and other terms of sale. And if customers won't accept the Price, all of the planning effort is wasted.

Each of the four Ps contributes to the whole

All four Ps are needed in a marketing mix. In fact, they should all be tied together. But is any one more important than the others? Generally speaking, the answer is no—all contribute to one whole. When a marketing mix is being developed, all (final) decisions about the Ps should be made at the same time. That's why the four Ps are arranged around the customer (C) in a circle—to show that they all are equally important.

Let's sum up our discussion of marketing mix planning thus far. We develop a *Product* to satisfy the target customers. We find a way to reach our target customers' *Place*. We use *Promotion* to tell the target customers (and others in the channel) about the product that has been designed for them. And we set a *Price* after estimating expected customer reaction to the total offering and the costs of getting it to them.

Toddler University's marketing strategy was successful because it developed a distinctive marketing mix that was precisely relevant to the needs of its target market.

Lifetime Value of Customers Can Be Very High—or Very Low

Investors lost millions when stock market values of dot-com firms collapsed after an initial, frenzied run-up. But why did values get so high in the first place, especially when most dot-coms were not yet profitable? The stock went up because many investors expected that the firms would earn profits in the future as more consumers went online and the early dot-coms accumulated customers. These hopes were fueled by dot-coms that made optimistic predictions about the lifetime value of the customers they were acquiring. The lifetime value of the customer concept is not new. For decades General Motors has known that a consumer who buys a GM car and is satisfied is likely to buy another one the next time. If that happens again and again, over a lifetime the happy customer could spend $250,000 on GM cars. Of course, this only works if the firm's marketing mix attracts the target customers and the relationship keeps them satisfied before, during, and after every purchase. If you don't satisfy and retain customers they don't have high lifetime value and don't generate sales. Of course, sales revenue alone does not guarantee profits. For example, a firm can't give away products—or spend so much on promotion to acquire new customers (or keep the ones it has)—that the revenue will never be able to offset the costs. Unfortunately, that is what happened with many of the dot-coms. They saw how the financial arithmetic might work—*assuming* that new customers kept buying and costs came under control. But without a sensible marketing strategy, that assumption was not realistic.[5]

Strategy jobs must be done together

It is important to stress—it cannot be overemphasized—that selecting a target market *and* developing a marketing mix are interrelated. Both parts of a marketing strategy must be decided together. It is *strategies* that must be evaluated against the company's objectives—not alternative target markets or alternative marketing mixes.

Understanding target markets leads to good strategies

The needs of a target market often virtually determine the nature of an appropriate marketing mix. So marketers must analyze their potential target markets with great care. This book will explore ways of identifying attractive market opportunities and developing appropriate strategies.

These ideas can be seen more clearly with an example in the children's fashion market.

Market-oriented strategy planning at Toddler University

The case of Jeff Silverman and Toddler University (TU), Inc., a shoe company he started, illustrates the strategy planning process. During high school and college, Silverman worked as a salesperson at local shoe stores. He also gained valuable experience during a year working for Nike. From these jobs he learned a lot about customers' needs and interests. He also realized that some parents were not satisfied when it came to finding shoes for their preschool children.

Silverman thought that there was a large, but hard to describe, mass market for general-purpose baby shoes—perhaps 60 or 70 percent of the potential for all kinds of baby shoes. Silverman did not focus on this market because it didn't make sense for his small company to compete head on with many other firms where he had no particular advantage. However, he identified four other markets that were quite different. In the following description of these markets, note that useful marketing mixes come to mind immediately.

The *Traditionalists* seemed to be satisfied with a well-manufactured shoe that was available from "quality" stores where they could seek help in selecting the right size and fit. They didn't mind if the design was old-fashioned and didn't change. They wanted a well-known brand that had a reputation for quality, even if it was a bit more expensive.

Many of the *Economy Oriented* parents were in the lower income group. They wanted a basic shoe at a low price. They saw baby shoes as all pretty much the same—so a "name" brand didn't have much appeal. They were willing to shop around to see what was on sale at local discount, department, or shoe stores.

The *Fashion Conscious* were interested in dressing up baby in shoes that looked like smaller versions of the latest styles that they bought for themselves. Fit was important, but beyond that a colorful design is what got their attention. They were more likely to look for baby-size shoes at the shop where they bought their own athletic shoes.

The *Attentive Parents* wanted shoes that met a variety of needs. They wanted shoes to be fun and fashionable and functional. They didn't want just a good fit but also design and materials that were really right for baby play and learning to walk. These well-informed, upscale shoppers were likely to buy from a store that specialized in baby items. They were willing to pay a premium price if they found the right product.

Silverman thought that Stride Rite and Buster Brown were meeting the needs of the Traditionalists quite well. The Economy Oriented and Fashion Conscious customers were satisfied with shoes from a variety of other companies, including Nike. But Silverman saw a way to get a toe up on the competition by targeting the Attentive Parents with a marketing mix that combined, in his words, "fit and function with fun and fashion." He developed a detailed marketing plan that attracted financial backers, and at age 24 his company came to life.

TU didn't have its own production facilities, so Silverman contracted with a producer in Taiwan to make shoes with his brand name and to his specs. And his specs were different—they improved the product for his target market. Unlike most rigid high-topped infant shoes, he designed softer shoes with more comfortable rubber soles. The shoes lasted longer because they were stitched rather than glued. An extra-wide opening made fitting easier on squirming feet. He also patented a special insert so parents could adjust the width. This change also helped win support from retailers. Since there are 11 sizes of children's shoes—and five widths—retailers usually need to stock 55 pairs of each model. TU's adjustable width reduced this stocking problem and made it more profitable for retailers to sell the line. It also made it possible for TU to resupply sold-out inventory faster than competitors. Silverman's Product and Place decisions worked together well to provide customer value and also to give him a competitive advantage.

For promotion, Silverman developed print ads with close-up photos of babies wearing his shoes and informative details about their special benefits. Creative packaging also helped promote the shoe and attract customers in the store. For example, he put one athletic-style shoe in a box that looked like a gray gym locker. Silverman also provided the stores with "shoe rides"—electric-powered rocking replicas of its shoes. The rides not only attracted kids to the shoe department, but since they were coin-operated, they paid for themselves in a year.

TU priced most of its shoes at $35 to $40 a pair. This is a premium price, but with today's smaller families, the Attentive Parents are willing to spend more on each child.

Internet EXERCISE

Jeffrey Silverman, the founder of Toddler University, recently started Preschoolians, which specializes in shoes for preschool kids. Go to the Preschoolians website (*www.preschoolians.com*) and review the site to learn about the company. Concisely describe its strategy.

In just four years, TU's sales jumped from $100,000 to over $40 million. To keep growth going, Silverman expanded distribution to reach new markets in Europe. To take advantage of TU's relationship with its satisfied target customers, he also added shoes for older kids to the Toddler University product assortment. Then Silverman made his biggest sale of all: He sold his company to Genesco, one of the biggest firms in the footwear business.[6]

THE MARKETING PLAN IS A GUIDE
TO IMPLEMENTATION AND CONTROL

Marketing plan fills out marketing strategy

As the Toddler University case illustrates, a marketing strategy sets a target market and a marketing mix. It is a big picture of what a firm will do in some market. A marketing plan goes farther. A **marketing plan** is a written statement of a marketing strategy *and* the time-related details for carrying out the strategy. It should spell out the following in detail: (1) what marketing mix will be offered, to whom (that is, the target market), and for how long; (2) what company resources (shown as costs) will be needed at what rate (month by month perhaps); and (3) what results are expected (sales and profits perhaps monthly or quarterly, customer satisfaction levels, and the like). The plan should also include some control procedures—so that whoever is to carry out the plan will know if things are going wrong. This might be something as simple as comparing actual sales against expected sales—with a warning flag to be raised whenever total sales fall below a certain level.

The multimedia CD that accompanies this text includes a feature called "Marketing Plan Coach." At the end of each chapter, there is a Marketing Plan Coach exercise that introduces you to aspects of a marketing plan that are related to the topics in that chapter. This gives you a step-by-step way to develop your plan-building skills as you progress through the text. In Chapter 18, we will review all of the elements in a marketing plan. At that point, you will have learned about all of the major strategy decision areas (Exhibit 2–5) and how to blend them into an innovative strategy.

Implementation puts plans into operation

After a marketing plan is developed, a marketing manager knows *what* needs to be done. Then the manager is concerned with **implementation**—putting marketing plans into operation. Strategies work out as planned only when they are effectively implemented. Many **operational decisions**—short-run decisions to help implement strategies—may be needed.

Managers should make operational decisions within the guidelines set down during strategy planning. They develop product policies, place policies, and so on as part of strategy planning. Then operational decisions within these policies probably will be necessary—while carrying out the basic strategy. Note, however, that as long as these

Campbell's has developed different soups (and related marketing mixes) that are targeted to the specific needs of different target markets. The marketing plan for each type of soup fits into Campbell's overall marketing program.

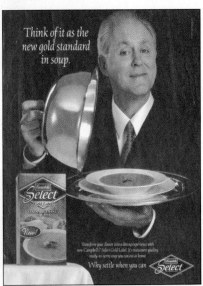

Exhibit 2-7 Relation of Strategy Policies to Operational Decisions for Baby Shoe Company

Marketing Mix Decision Area	Strategy Policies	Likely Operational Decisions
■ Product	Carry as limited a line of colors, styles, and sizes as will satisfy the target market.	Add, change, or drop colors, styles, and/or sizes as customer tastes dictate.
■ Place	Distribute through selected "baby-products" retailers that will carry the full line and provide good in-store sales support and promotion.	In market areas where sales potential is not achieved, add new retail outlets and/or drop retailers whose performance is poor.
■ Promotion	Promote the benefits and value of the special design and how it meets customer needs.	When a retailer hires a new salesperson, send current training package with details on product line; increase use of local newspaper print ads during peak demand periods (before holidays, etc.).
■ Price	Maintain a "premium" price, but encourage retailers to make large-volume orders by offering discounts on quantity purchases.	Offer short-term introductory price "deals" to retailers when a new style is first introduced.

operational decisions stay within the policy guidelines, managers are making no change in the basic strategy. If the controls show that operational decisions are not producing the desired results, however, the managers may have to reevaluate the whole strategy—rather than just working harder at implementing it.

It's easier to see the difference between strategy decisions and operational decisions if we illustrate these ideas using our Toddler University example. Possible four Ps or basic strategy policies are shown in the left-hand column in Exhibit 2–7, and examples of operational decisions are shown in the right-hand column.

Our focus in this text is on developing marketing strategies. But eventually marketing managers must control the marketing plans that they develop and implement. Thus, as we talk about each of the marketing decision areas, we will discuss some of the control problems. This will help you understand how control keeps the firm on course—or shows the need to plan a new course.[7]

Several plans make a whole marketing program

Most companies implement more than one marketing strategy—and related marketing plan—at the same time. They may have several products—some of them quite different—that are aimed at different target markets. The other elements of the marketing mix may vary too. Gillette's M3Power razor blades, its Duracell batteries, and its Right Guard deodorant all have different marketing mixes. Yet the strategies for each must be implemented at the same time.

Exhibit 2-8 Elements of a Firm's Marketing Program

Target market + Marketing mix } = Marketing strategy + Time-related details and control procedures } = Marketing plan + Other marketing plans } = A firm's marketing program

A **marketing program** blends all of the firm's marketing plans into one "big" plan. See Exhibit 2–8. This program, then, is the responsibility of the whole company. Typically, the whole *marketing program* is an integrated part of the whole-company strategic plan we discussed earlier.

THE MARKETING PROGRAM SHOULD BUILD CUSTOMER EQUITY

Expected profits depend on customer equity

We've highlighted the benefit for target customers when the firm does effective strategy planning and offers them superior customer value. Now it's time to expand this thinking and consider how the marketing program should also benefit the firm—by increasing customer equity. **Customer equity** is the expected earnings stream (profitability) of a firm's current and prospective customers over some period of time. Top management expects marketing strategy planners to help identify *opportunities that will lead to an increase in the firm's customer equity*. Let's consider the logic for and implications of this important idea.

Owners expect financial returns

A firm may be owned by management or by stockholders and other types of investors. The owners are better off the greater the earnings (profit) from the money they invest in the firm. So, the financial value of a firm—for example, the value of its stock or what the firm would be worth if it were sold—is based mainly on the earnings (profit) that can be expected from its current and future operations. Top executives are ultimately responsible to the owners for *increasing* the financial value of a firm. In turn, top executives expect marketing strategy planners to contribute to this effort.

Profit growth comes from customers

Profit is the difference between the firm's revenues (total dollar sales) and the total costs it runs up to make those sales. Customers are key; they are the source of the revenue. The revenue comes from the prices they are willing to pay for the quantity of purchases they make. There are also costs associated with attracting and serving customers. If those costs are too great, even high levels of revenue won't be profitable.

Obviously, a marketing manager doesn't control all of a firm's costs; for example, General Motors faces huge pension costs for retired workers regardless of its current marketing strategies. Even so, the marketing manager selects opportunities and creates marketing strategies—and should make choices where the revenues from target customers are greater than the costs of acquiring those customers, retaining their business, and (hopefully) increasing it. In other words, the best way to increase customer equity is to find cost-effective ways to increase earnings from current customers while bringing profitable new customers into the fold.

Each marketing strategy contributes to customer equity

Exhibit 2–9 illustrates what happens to customer equity over time for a new local bank that has just gone into business. The bank's initial strategy focuses on *acquiring* new customers. The bank's strategy here is to attract checking account customers with personal attention, friendly service, and free checks—none of which are available from the branches of big banks. The bank runs an advertising campaign to tell potential customers about these benefits. The amount of money earned from the bank's initial strategy (and the first target customers it attracts) is shown by the size of the green circle on the left of the exhibit. Note that at the start the firm gets only a small part of the earnings possible from these target customers. However, over time, the size of the green earnings circle should become larger as more of these target customers sign on.

If the bank satisfies the customers it serves, it will probably be able to retain those customers. In fact, the bank may be able to take advantage of its relationship with these customers to get more of their financial services business—and increase earnings. For example, the bank might be able to increase earnings by offering helpful financial planning services to customers who have large checking account balances.

Exhibit 2-9
Customer Equity
Increases as Firm
Attracts Customers,
Retains Them, and
Increases Earnings from
Business with Them

Growth in earnings from
retained customers

Earnings from initial
target customers

Customer equity
from whole
marketing program
grows over time

firm

Earnings from new
target customers

Business
enters market

time

Thus, each of several different strategies aimed at the bank's initial target customers might contribute to growth in the green earnings circle.

Customer equity might grow even faster if the firm simultaneously develops a different strategy—one that attracts a new target market. For example, some prospects are simply not interested in switching a checking account that is already established at another bank. The potential earnings from this group of people is shown by the small yellow circle in Exhibit 2–9. This target group is essentially outside of the firm's reach. However, a different strategy might attract these customers and produce earnings. For example, these consumers may be willing to pay a small fee to use the ATMs the bank has put in convenient locations. Over time, the bank might find other profitable ways to serve these new customers. For example, the color LCD display on an ATM provides a targeted way for the bank to reach these customers with short promotional videos that help "cross sell" other profitable products, such as home equity loans. Thus, over time earnings from these customers may also increase, as shown by the growth in the yellow earnings circle in Exhibit 2–9.

At the right side of Exhibit 2–9, you can see that the earnings from both groups of customers (and several different basic strategies) contribute to the customer equity created by the firm's overall marketing program.

The parts of the marketing program must work as a whole

In Chapter 1 we introduced the idea that firms acquire new customers and retain the ones that they have by offering superior customer value. The customer equity idea shows how this translates to increased earnings over time—and why it determines the value of the firm and the return on investment it produces for the owners. So, when seeking new opportunities, a marketing manager needs to carefully consider what strategies will work well together to produce an overall marketing program that increases customer equity.[8]

Planning for each strategy requires care

You can see that the success of the whole marketing program depends on the care that goes into planning individual strategies and how they will work together. Thus, in this text we will emphasize planning one marketing strategy at a time, rather than planning—or implementing—a whole marketing program. This is practical because it is important to plan each strategy carefully. Too many marketing managers fall into sloppy thinking. They try to develop too many strategies all at once— and don't develop any very carefully. However, when new strategies are evaluated, it makes sense to see how well they fit with the existing marketing program. So, throughout the book we'll discuss issues related to this fit as we cover the specific strategy decision areas.

THE IMPORTANCE OF MARKETING STRATEGY PLANNING

We emphasize the planning part of the marketing manager's job for a good reason. The "one-time" strategy decisions—the decisions that decide what business the company is in and the strategies it will follow—usually determine success or failure. An extremely good plan might be carried out badly and still be profitable, while a poor but well-implemented plan can lose money. The case history that follows shows the importance of planning and why we emphasize marketing strategy planning throughout this text.

Time for new strategies in the watch industry

The conventional watchmakers—both domestic and foreign—had always aimed at customers who thought of watches as high-priced, high-quality symbols to mark special events, like graduations or retirement. Advertising was concentrated around Christmas and graduation time and stressed a watch's symbolic appeal. Expensive jewelry stores were the main retail outlets.

This commonly accepted strategy of the major watch companies ignored people in the target market that just wanted to tell the time and were interested in a reliable, low-priced watch. So the U.S. Time Company developed a successful strategy around its Timex watches and became the world's largest watch company. Timex completely upset the watch industry—both foreign and domestic—not only by offering a good product (with a one-year repair or replace guarantee) at a lower price, but also by using new, lower-cost channels of distribution. Its watches were widely available in drugstores, discount houses, and nearly any other retail stores that would carry them.

Marketing managers at Timex soon faced a new challenge. Texas Instruments, a new competitor in the watch market, took the industry by storm with its low-cost but very accurate electronic watches—using the same channels Timex had originally developed. But other firms quickly developed a watch that used a more stylish liquid crystal display for the digital readout. Texas Instruments could not change quickly enough to keep up, and the other companies took away its customers. The competition became so intense that Texas Instruments stopped marketing watches altogether.

While Timex and others were focusing on lower-priced watches, Japan's Seiko captured a commanding share of the high-priced gift market for its stylish and accurate quartz watches by obtaining strong distribution. All of this forced many traditional watchmakers—like some of the once-famous Swiss brands—to close their factories.

Then Switzerland's Swatch launched its colorful, affordable plastic watches and changed what consumers see when they look at their watches. Swatch promoted its watches as fashion accessories and set them apart from those of other firms, whose ads squabbled about whose watches were most accurate and dependable. Swatch was also able to attract new retailers by focusing its distribution on upscale fashion and department stores. The total size of the watch market increased because many consumers bought several watches to match different fashions.

The economic downturn in the early 1990s brought more changes. Consumers were more cost conscious and less interested in expensive watches like those made by Rolex that were the "in" status symbol a few years earlier. The reemergence of value-seeking customers prompted Timex to return to its famous advertising

DON'T GET LOST.

TIMEX EXPEDITION WITH ELECTRONIC COMPASS TO KEEP YOU HEADED IN THE RIGHT DIRECTION.

TIMEX

tagline of the 1960s: "It takes a licking and keeps on ticking." Its position as the inexpensive-but-durable choice has helped it strengthen its distribution and has given it a leg up in getting shelf space for new products, such as its Indiglo line of watches.

By the turn of the century, the total market for watches was growing at only about 5 percent a year. To spark higher sales of its lines, Timex pushed to introduce more watches that combine time-telling and other needs. For example, Timex watches include heart-rate monitors, GPS systems to compute a runner's distance and speed, personal digital assistant functions (including data links to a computer), and Internet messenger capabilities so a watch can receive short text messages, like an alert from the wearer's stockbroker that it's time to sell. Of course, all the new features can make a watch more complicated to use, so Timex has promoted its I-control technology, which makes its watches "ridiculously easy to use." However, the competition is on the move as well. For example, Fossil, Inc., and Citizen Watch Company were the first watch companies to incorporate Microsoft's new operating system for SPOT (Small Personal Objective Technology). These watches connect to a wireless network to provide a variety of information services, including traffic and weather reports. With such changes always under way, marketing strategies at Timex must be constantly updated and revised.[9]

CREATIVE STRATEGY PLANNING NEEDED FOR SURVIVAL

Dramatic shifts in strategy—like those described earlier—may surprise conventional, production-oriented managers. But such changes should be expected. Managers who embrace the marketing concept realize that they cannot just define their line of business in terms of the products they currently produce or sell. Rather, they have to think about the basic consumer needs they serve, how those needs may change in the future, and how they can improve the value they offer to customers. If they are too nearsighted, they may fail to see what's coming until it is too late.

MARKETING PERFORMANCE:	TOTAL FAILURE	POOR	FAIR	GOOD	EXCEPTIONAL
	(Well below average) 2%	(Below average) 14%	68% (Average marketing program)	(Above average) 14%	(Well above average) 2%
Marketing Share	Dramatic decline	Significant decline	Modest decline	Increase	Dramatic increase
New Product Success	0%	5%	10%	25%	40%+
Advertising ROI	Negative	0%	1–4%	5–10%	20%
Sales Promotion	Disaster	Unprofitable	Marginally unprofitable	Profitable	Very profitable
Customer Satisfaction	0–59%	60–69%	70–79%	80–89%	90–95%
Customer Acquisition Efforts	Disturbing losses	Significant losses	Marginal losses	Break even	Profitable
Customer Retention/Loyalty	0–44%	45–59%	60–74%	75–89%	90–94%

Death-wish marketing ← → Best-practices marketing

Focus on "best practices" for improved results

The case studies and concepts in this chapter highlight effective marketing thinking. Throughout the text, we will continue with this thrust—focusing on marketing frameworks and concepts that produce good results. Some of these are new and innovative, and others are well established. What they have in common is that they all work well.

Sometimes we will warn you about marketing errors—so you can avoid them. But we won't just give you laundry lists of different approaches and then leave it to you to guess what might work. Rather, our focus will be on "best-practices" marketing.

There is an important reason for this approach. In too many firms, managers do a poor job planning and implementing marketing strategies and programs. And, as shown in Exhibit 2–10, this type of "death-wish" marketing is both costly and ineffective. In fact, you can see that even the average marketing program isn't producing great results—and that accounts for the majority of firms!

Exhibit 2–10 was developed by experts at Copernicus, one of the premier marketing research and consulting firms in the world. As these experts indicate in the chart, some managers are creating marketing programs that produce exceptional results for their companies. This book will help you do exactly that.

WHAT ARE ATTRACTIVE OPPORTUNITIES?

Effective marketing strategy planning matches opportunities to the firm's resources (what it can do) and its objectives (what top management wants to do). Successful strategies get their start when a creative manager spots an attractive market opportunity. Yet an opportunity that is attractive for one firm may not be attractive for

Attractive opportunities are often fairly close to markets the firm already knows. For example, Nike is a leader in tailoring products to the unique tastes of individual customers. At Nike's www.nikeid.com website, customers can select a style of shoe (or other Nike product) and then personalize the design with their own color preferences.

another. Attractive opportunities for a particular firm are those that the firm has some chance of doing something about—given its resources and objectives.

Breakthrough opportunities are best

Throughout this book, we will emphasize finding **breakthrough opportunities**—opportunities that help innovators develop hard-to-copy marketing strategies that will be very profitable for a long time. That's important because there are always imitators who want to "share" the innovator's profits—if they can. It's hard to continuously provide *superior* value to target customers if competitors can easily copy your marketing mix.

Competitive advantage is needed—at least

Even if a manager can't find a breakthrough opportunity, the firm should try to obtain a competitive advantage to increase its chances for profit or survival. **Competitive advantage** means that a firm has a marketing mix that the target market sees as better than a competitor's mix. A competitive advantage may result from efforts in different areas of the firm—cost cutting in production, innovative R&D, more effective purchasing of needed components, or financing for a new distribution facility. Similarly, a strong sales force, a well-known brand name, or good dealers may give it a competitive advantage in pursuing an opportunity. Whatever the source, an advantage only succeeds if it allows the firm to provide superior value and satisfy customers better than some competitor.[10]

Avoid hit-or-miss marketing with a logical process

You can see why a manager *should* seek attractive opportunities. But that doesn't mean that everyone does—or that everyone can turn an opportunity into a successful strategy. As Exhibit 2–10 shows, too many firms settle for the sort of death-wish marketing that doesn't satisfy customers or make a profit—to say nothing about achieving a breakthrough or providing superior value. It's all too easy for a well-intentioned manager to react in a piecemeal way to what appears to be an opportunity. Then by the time the problems are obvious, it's too late.

Developing a successful marketing strategy doesn't need to be a hit-or-miss proposition. And it won't be if you learn the marketing strategy planning process developed in this text. Exhibit 2–11 summarizes the marketing strategy planning process we'll be developing throughout the rest of the chapters.

Exhibit 2–11
Overview of Marketing
Strategy Planning
Process

Note: Marketing manager narrows down from screening broad market opportunities to develop a focused marketing strategy.

MARKETING STRATEGY PLANNING PROCESS HIGHLIGHTS OPPORTUNITIES

We've emphasized that a marketing strategy requires decisions about the specific customers the firm will target and the marketing mix the firm will develop to appeal to that target market. However, the idea isn't just to come up with *some* strategy. After all, there are hundreds or even thousands of combinations of marketing mix decisions and target markets (i.e., strategies) that a firm might try. Rather, the challenge is to zero in on the *best* strategy.

Process narrows down from broad opportunities to specific strategy

As Exhibit 2–11 suggests, it is useful to think of the marketing strategy planning process as a narrowing-down process. Later in this chapter and in the next two chapters we will go into more detail about strategy decisions relevant to each of the terms in this figure. Then, throughout the rest of the book, we will present a variety of concepts and "how to" frameworks that will help you improve the way you make these strategy decisions. As a preview of what's coming, let's briefly summarize the general logic of the process depicted in Exhibit 2–11.

The process starts with a broad look at a market—paying special attention to customer needs, the firm's objectives and resources, and competitors. This helps to identify new and unique opportunities that might be overlooked if the focus is narrowed too quickly.

Segmentation helps pinpoint the target

In the early stages of a search for opportunities we're looking for customers with needs that are not being satisfied as well as they might be. Of course, potential customers are not all alike. They don't all have the same needs—nor do they always want to meet needs in the same way. Part of the reason is that there are different possible types of customers with many different characteristics. In spite of the many possible differences, there often are subgroups (segments) of consumers who are similar and could be satisfied with the same marketing mix. Thus, we try to identify and understand these different subgroups—with market segmentation. We will explain approaches for segmenting markets later in Chapter 3. Then, in Chapters 5 and 6, we delve into the

Other firms offer hearing-aid batteries, but Duracell's EasyTab makes it easier for hearing-aid users to handle the small batteries. Many firms sell work clothes, but Workrite offers garments that are not only comfortable but also flame-resistant, which is critical for people who work in hazardous jobs.

many interesting aspects of customer behavior. For now, however, you should know that really understanding customers is at the heart of using market segmentation to narrow down to a specific target market. In other words, segmentation helps a manager decide to serve some segment(s)—subgroup(s) of customers—and not others.

Narrow down to a superior marketing mix

A marketing mix won't result in a competitive advantage if it *just* meets needs in the same way as some other firm. So in evaluating possible strategies, the marketing manager should think about whether there is a way to differentiate the marketing mix. **Differentiation** means that the marketing mix is distinct from and better than what is available from a competitor. Sometimes the difference is based mainly on one important element of the marketing mix—say, an improved product or faster delivery. However, differentiation often requires that the firm fine-tune all of the elements of its marketing mix to the specific needs of a distinctive target market. Differentiation is also more obvious to target customers when there is a consistent theme integrated across the four Ps decision areas. That emphasizes the difference so target customers will think of the firm as being in a unique position to meet their needs. For example, in Norway many auto buyers are particularly concerned about safety in the snow. So Audi offers a permanent four-wheel-drive system, called quattro, that helps the car to hold the road. Audi ads emphasize this differentiation. Rather than show the car, however, the ads feature things that are very sticky (like bubblegum!) and the only text is the headline "sticks like quattro" and the Audi brand name. Of course, handling is not Audi's only strength, but it is an important one in helping to position Audi as better than competing brands with this target market.

In Chapter 3, we'll introduce concepts relevant to this sort of positioning. Then, in Chapters 8 to 17, we'll cover the many ways in which the four Ps of the marketing mix can be differentiated. For now you can see that the thrust is to narrow down from all possible marketing mixes to one that is differentiated to meet target customers' needs particularly well. Of course, finding the best differentiation requires that we understand competitors as well as customers.

Screening criteria make it clear why you select a strategy

There are usually more different opportunities—and strategy possibilities—than a firm can pursue. Each one has its own advantages and disadvantages. Trends in the external market environment may make a potential opportunity more or less attractive. These complications can make it difficult to zero in on the best target market and marketing mix. However, developing a set of specific qualitative and quantitative screening criteria can help a manager define the business and markets in which the firm wants to compete. We will cover screening criteria in more detail in Chapter 4.

For now, you should realize that the criteria you select in a specific situation grow out of an analysis of the company's objectives and resources.

S.W.O.T. analysis highlights advantages and disadvantages

A useful aid for identifying relevant screening criteria and for zeroing in on a feasible strategy is **S.W.O.T. analysis**—which identifies and lists the firm's strengths and weaknesses and its opportunities and threats. The name S.W.O.T. is simply an abbreviation for the first letters of the words strengths, weaknesses, opportunities, and threats. A good S.W.O.T. analysis helps the manager focus on a strategy that takes advantage of the firm's opportunities and strengths while avoiding its weaknesses and threats to its success.

The marketing strategy developed by Amilya Antonetti illustrates the basic ideas behind a S.W.O.T. analysis. Her son was allergic to the chemicals in standard detergents—and her research showed that many other children had the same problem. So she started Soapworks and developed a line of hypoallergenic cleaning products to pursue this opportunity. Unlike the big firms, she didn't have relations with grocery chains or money for national TV ads. To get around these weaknesses, she used inexpensive radio ads in local markets and touted Soapworks as a company created for moms by a mom who cared about kids. She had a credible claim that the big corporations couldn't make. Her ads also helped her get shelf space because they urged other mothers to ask for Soapworks products and to tell friends about stores that carried them. This wasn't the fastest possible way to introduce a new product line, but her cash-strapped strategy played to her unique strengths with her specific target market.[11]

Exhibit 2–11 focuses on planning each strategy carefully. Of course, this same approach works well when several strategies are to be planned. Then, having an organized evaluation process is even more important. It forces everyone involved to think through how the various strategies fit together as part of an overall marketing program that increases customer equity.[12]

TYPES OF OPPORTUNITIES TO PURSUE

Many opportunities seem "obvious" only after someone else identifies them. So, early in the marketing strategy planning process it's useful for marketers to have a framework for thinking about the broad kinds of opportunities they may find. Exhibit 2–12 shows four broad possibilities: market penetration, market development, product development, and diversification.

Market penetration

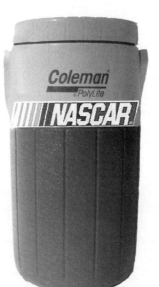

Market penetration means trying to increase sales of a firm's present products in its present markets—probably through a more aggressive marketing mix. The firm may try to strengthen its relationship with customers to increase their rate of use or repeat purchases, or it may try to attract competitors' customers or current nonusers. Coleman got a 50 percent increase in sales of its outdoor equipment, like camping lanterns and coolers, by reaching its target market with special promotional displays at outdoor events like concerts, fishing tournaments, and NASCAR races. For example, about 250,000 auto racing fans camp on-site at NASCAR races each year—so a display at the campground is an effective way to reach customers when they have leisure time to browse through product displays and demos.[13]

New promotion appeals alone may not be effective. A firm may need to make it easier for customers to place repeat orders on the Internet. Or it may need to add more stores in present areas for greater convenience. Short-term price cuts or coupon offers may help.

Many firms try to increase market penetration by developing closer relationships with customers so that they

Exhibit 2–12
Four Basic Types of
Opportunities

	Present products	New products
Present markets	Market penetration	Product development
New markets	Market development	Diversification

will be loyal. Frequent buyer clubs use this approach. Similarly, firms often analyze customer databases to identify "cross-selling" opportunities. For example, when a customer goes online to register Adobe's Photoshop, the web page promotes other related products, including its popular Acrobat Reader.

Market development

Market development means trying to increase sales by selling present products in new markets. This may involve searching for new uses for a product. E-Z-Go, a producer of golf carts, has done this. Its carts are now a quiet way for workers to get around malls, airports, and big factories. The large units are popular as utility vehicles on farms, at outdoor sports events, and at resorts. E-Z-Go even fits carts with ice compartments and cash drawers so they can be used for mobile food services.

Firms may also try advertising in different media to reach new target customers. Or they may add channels of distribution or new stores in new areas, including overseas.

For example, to reach new customers, McDonald's has opened outlets in airports, zoos, casinos, and military bases. And it has rapidly expanded into international markets with outlets in places like Russia, Brazil, and China.[14]

Product development

Product development means offering new or improved products for present markets. By knowing the present market's needs, a firm may see new ways to satisfy customers. For example, kids are the big consumers of ketchup. So Heinz figured out how ketchup could be more fun. Producing ketchup in gross green and funky purple colors—in an EZ Squirt dispenser molded to fit little hands—increased sales so much that the factory had to run 24/7. Ski resorts have developed trails for hiking and biking to bring their winter ski customers back in the summer. Nike moved beyond shoes and sportswear to offer its athletic target market a running watch, digital audio player, and even a portable heart-rate monitor. And of course Intel boosts sales by developing newer and faster chips.[15]

Diversification

Diversification means moving into totally different lines of business—perhaps entirely unfamiliar products, markets, or even levels in the production-marketing system. Products and customers that are very different from a firm's current base may look attractive to the optimists—but these opportunities are usually hard to evaluate. That's why diversification usually involves the biggest risk. McDonald's, for example, opened two hotels in Switzerland. The plan was to serve families on the weekend, but business travelers were the target during the week. Business travelers are not the group that McDonald's usually serves, and an upscale hotel is also very different from a fast-food restaurant. This helps to explain why operation of the Golden Arch hotels was taken over by a hospitality management company after two years. On the other hand, diversification can be successful—especially when the new strategy fits well with the firm's resources and marketing program.[16]

Which opportunities come first?

Most firms think first of greater market penetration. They want to increase profits where they already have experience and strengths. On the other hand, many firms are proving that market development—including the move into new international markets—is another profitable way to take advantage of current strengths.

Zippo is pursuing product development opportunities with its Multi-Purpose Lighter that is designed to light candles, fireplaces, grills, and more. Sara Lee is well known for its cheesecake and other baked goods. But Sara Lee's Bakery Breads are a product development opportunity that it hopes will increase customer equity.

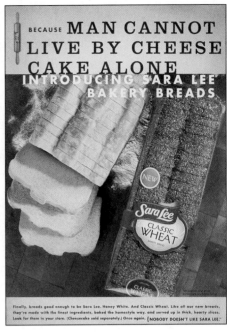

INTERNATIONAL OPPORTUNITIES SHOULD BE CONSIDERED

It's easy for a marketing manager to fall into the trap of ignoring international markets, especially when the firm's domestic market is prosperous. Yet there are good reasons to go to the trouble of looking elsewhere for opportunities.

The world is getting smaller

International trade is increasing all around the world, and trade barriers are coming down. In addition, advances in e-commerce, transportation, and communications are making it easier and cheaper to reach international customers. With an Internet website and e-mail, even the smallest firm can provide international customers with a great deal of information—and easy ways to order—at very little expense.

Develop a competitive advantage at home and abroad

If customers in other countries are interested in the products a firm offers—or could offer—serving them may improve economies of scale. Lower costs (and prices) may give a firm a competitive advantage both in its home markets *and* abroad. Black & Decker, for example, uses electric motors in many of its tools and appliances. By selling overseas as well as in the United States, it gets economies of scale and the cost per motor is very low.

Lipton is pursuing new customers and growth in more than 100 countries. For example, its multilingual website in Belgium explains how to make exotic cocktails from Ice Tea, and in Asia it encourages consumer trial with free samples.

Marketing managers who are only interested in the "convenient" customers in their own backyards may be rudely surprised to find that an aggressive, low-cost foreign producer is willing to pursue those customers. The owner of Purafil, a small firm in Atlanta that makes air purification equipment, puts it this way: "If I'm not [selling to an oil refinery] in Saudi Arabia, somebody else is going to solve their problem, then come attack me on my home turf."[17]

Get an early start in a new market

Different countries are at different stages of economic and technological development, and their consumers have different needs at different times.

A company facing tough competition, thin profit margins, and slow sales growth at home may get a fresh start in another country where demand for its product is just beginning to grow. A marketing manager may be able to transfer marketing know-how—or some other competitive advantage—the firm has already developed. Consider JLG, a Pennsylvania-based producer of equipment used to lift workers and tools at construction sites. Faced with tough competition, JLG's profits all but evaporated. By cutting costs, the company improved its domestic sales. But it got an even bigger boost from expanding overseas. In five years its international sales were greater than what its total sales had been before. Now that JLG has added distribution in China, international sales account for about half of its business.[18]

Find better trends in variables

Unfavorable trends in the marketing environment at home—or favorable trends in other countries—may make international marketing particularly attractive. For example, population growth in the United States has slowed and income is leveling off. In other places in the world, population and income are increasing rapidly.[19]

Screening must consider risks as well as benefits

International opportunities should be considered in the strategy planning process, but they don't always survive as the most attractive ones that are turned into strategies. As with local opportunities, managers should consider international opportunities relative to the firm's objectives and resources—as well as its strengths and weaknesses.

Screening criteria for international market development may include a variety of factors ranging from expected rate of population growth or cultural challenges to political instability or other economic risks. Risks are often higher with international opportunities. For example, while the 9/11 attack on the World Trade Center shows that horrible terrorist acts are not limited to overseas markets, most managers find it more difficult to protect a firm's employees—and its financial interests—in a remote market if the political structure, laws, resources, and culture are very different.

CONCLUSION

At a broad level, the purpose of this chapter is to introduce you to the basic decision areas involved in marketing strategy planning. The individual learning objectives for the chapter relate to this purpose and in combination explain the logic for the marketing strategy planning process summarized in Exhibit 2–11. In the remainder of this book we'll rely on this exhibit as a way to highlight the organization of the topics we are discussing.

In this chapter, you learned that the marketing manager must constantly study the market environment—seeking attractive opportunities and planning new strategies. A marketing strategy specifies a target market and the marketing mix the firm will offer to provide that target market with superior customer value. A marketing mix has four major decision areas: the four Ps—Product, Place, Promotion, and Price.

There are usually more potential opportunities than a firm can pursue, so possible target markets must be matched with marketing mixes the firm can offer. This is a narrowing-down process. The most attractive strategies—really, marketing plans and whole marketing programs—are chosen for implementation.

A marketing program that is implemented well should increase the firm's customer equity. Customer equity refers to the expected earnings from a firm's current or prospective customers. This is a forward-looking idea and reinforces the need not only to acquire customers but to satisfy them with superior customer value so that, in the future, earnings from them will grow because of repeat business.

Controls are needed to be sure that the plans are carried out successfully. If anything goes wrong along the way, continual feedback should cause the process to be started over again—with the marketing manager planning more attractive marketing strategies. Thus, the job of marketing management is one of continuous planning, implementing, and control. Strategies are not permanent; changes should be expected as market conditions change.

Firms need effective strategy planning to survive in our increasingly competitive markets. The challenge isn't just to come up with some strategy, but to zero in on the strategy that is best for the firm given its objectives and resources—and taking into consideration its strengths and weaknesses and the opportunities and threats that it faces. To improve your ability in this area,

this chapter introduces a framework for marketing strategy planning. The rest of this text is organized to deepen your understanding of this framework and how to use it to develop profitable marketing mixes for clearly defined target markets. After several chapters on analyzing target markets, we will discuss each of the four Ps in greater detail.

While market-oriented strategy planning is helpful to marketers, it is also needed by financial managers, accountants, production and personnel people, and all other specialists. A market-oriented plan lets everybody in the firm know what ballpark they are playing in and what they are trying to accomplish.

We will use the term *marketing manager* for editorial convenience, but really, when we talk about marketing strategy planning, we are talking about the planning that a market-oriented manager should do when developing a firm's strategic plans. This kind of thinking should be done—or at least understood—by everyone in the organization. And this includes even the entry-level salesperson, production supervisor, retail buyer, or personnel counselor.

KEY TERMS

QUESTIONS AND PROBLEMS

1. Distinguish clearly between a marketing strategy and a marketing mix. Use an example.

2. Distinguish clearly between mass marketing and target marketing. Use an example.

3. Why is the target customer placed in the center of the four Ps in the text diagram of a marketing strategy (Exhibit 2–4)? Explain, using a specific example from your own experience.

4. If a company sells its products only from a website, which is accessible over the Internet to customers from all over the world, does it still need to worry about having a specific target market? Explain your thinking.

5. Explain, in your own words, what each of the four Ps involves.

6. Evaluate the text's statement, "A marketing strategy sets the details of implementation."

7. Distinguish between strategy decisions and operational decisions, illustrating for a local retailer.

8. In your own words, explain what customer equity means and why it is important.

9. Distinguish between a strategy, a marketing plan, and a marketing program, illustrating for a local retailer.

10. Outline a marketing strategy for each of the following new products: (*a*) a toothbrush with a radically new design, (*b*) a new fishing reel, (*c*) a new wonder drug, and (*d*) a new industrial stapling machine.

11. Provide a specific illustration of why marketing strategy planning is important for all businesspeople, not just for those in the marketing department.

12. Exhibit 2–10 shows that only about three out of every four customers are, on average, satisfied by a firm's marketing programs. Give an example of a purchase you made where you were not satisfied and what the firm could have changed to satisfy you. If customer satisfaction is so important to firms, why don't they score better in this area?

13. Distinguish between an attractive opportunity and a breakthrough opportunity. Give an example.

14. Explain how new opportunities may be seen by defining a firm's markets more precisely. Describe a situation where you feel there is an opportunity—namely, an unsatisfied market segment—even if it is not very large.

15. In your own words, explain why the book suggests that you should think of marketing strategy planning as a narrowing-down process.

16. Explain the major differences among the four basic types of growth opportunities discussed in the text and cite examples for two of these types of opportunities.

17. Explain why a firm may want to pursue a market penetration opportunity before pursuing one involving product development or diversification.

18. In your own words, explain several reasons why a marketing manager should consider international markets when evaluating possible opportunities.

19. Give an example of a foreign-made product (other than an automobile) that you personally have purchased. Give some reasons why you purchased that product. Do you think that there was a good opportunity for a domestic firm to get your business? Explain why or why not.

CREATING MARKETING PLANS

The Marketing Plan Coach software on the Student CD includes a sample marketing plan for Hillside Veterinary Clinic. Skim through the different sections of the marketing plan. Look more closely at the "Marketing Strategy" section.

a. What is the target market for this marketing plan?

b. What is the strategy Hillside Veterinary Clinic intends to use?

c. What are your initial reactions to this strategy? Do you think it will be successful? Why or why not?

SUGGESTED CASES

3. NOCO Soccer Academy
4. Alvarez Technology Services
5. Applied Polymer Scienc

12. DrMarcus.com
29. Laser Castings, Inc.

COMPUTER-AIDED PROBLEM

2. TARGET MARKETING

Marko, Inc.'s managers are comparing the profitability of a target marketing strategy with a mass marketing "strategy." The spreadsheet gives information about both approaches.

The mass marketing strategy is aiming at a much bigger market. But a smaller percent of the consumers in the market will actually buy this product—because not everyone needs or can afford it. Moreover, because this marketing mix is not tailored to specific needs, Marko will get a smaller share of the business from those who do buy than it would with a more targeted marketing mix.

Just trying to reach the mass market will take more promotion and require more retail outlets in more locations—so promotion costs and distribution costs are higher than with the target marketing strategy. On the other hand, the cost of producing each unit is higher with the target marketing strategy—to build in a more satisfying set of features. But because the more targeted marketing mix is trying to satisfy the needs of a specific target market, those customers will be willing to pay a higher price.

In the spreadsheet, "quantity sold" (by the firm) is equal to the number of people in the market who will actually buy one each of the product—multiplied by the share of those purchases won by the firm's marketing mix. Thus, a change in the size of the market, the percent of people who purchase, or the share captured by the firm will affect quantity sold. And a change in quantity sold will affect total revenue, total cost, and profit.

a. On a piece of paper, show the calculations that prove that the spreadsheet "total profit" value for the target marketing strategy is correct. (Hint: Remember to multiply unit production cost and unit distribution cost by the quantity sold.) Which approach seems better—target marketing or mass marketing? Why?

b. If the target marketer could find a way to reduce distribution cost per unit by $.25, how much would profit increase?

c. If Marko, Inc., decided to use the target marketing strategy and better marketing mix decisions increased its share of purchases from 50 to 60 percent—without increasing costs—what would happen to total profit? What does this analysis suggest about the importance of marketing managers knowing enough about their target markets to be effective target marketers?

For additional questions related to this problem, see Exercise 2-4 in the *Learning Aid for Use with Essentials of Marketing*, 11th edition.

3

Focusing Marketing Strategy with Segmentation and Positioning

If you were a busy mom who took hundreds of snapshots of your kids, how would you get prints? Yes, a lot might depend on whether you use a trusty Kodak camera that shoots Kodak Gold 35mm film or, alternatively, a digital model—perhaps a new Hewlett-Packard (HP) Photosmart R817 that can store hundreds of 5 megapixel pictures.

If you use the HP Photosmart, you might select your best shots and print them yourself on the HP GoGo Photo printer that came with your camera. Or if you needed a lot of prints, you might upload the jpeg picture files to Snapfish.com, HP's online photo service. HP includes a coupon for 50 Snapfish prints with the camera, so trying the service is free. On the other hand, if you were the mom using that 35mm model, you'd probably be happy to leave your film at the local drugstore to be sent to Kodak for processing. That certainly would be the easiest approach if you are like many others who snap photos but don't know anything about megapixels, what a jpeg file is, or how to upload to some website.

Of course, there are other ways to get prints—but many of them involve HP. For example, HP recently made a push into retail photofinishing. Its self-service kiosks make instant prints from consumers' digital cameras, CDs, and other media. Many of these kiosks are next to full-service HP photo centers. In these centers, retailers create prints, posters, bound books, and other photo-specialty items. Customers can also upload pictures to Snapfish.com and have them printed in the HP center at a local store.

HP and Kodak serve similar customer needs, but the marketing mixes with which they compete are very different. And in a number of markets HP is well ahead of Kodak even though Kodak has been a worldwide leader in the photography business since 1888. To understand the success of HP's marketing program, let's take a longer-term look at how its strategies have evolved and become more focused with market segmentation.

When PCs were introduced in the early 1980s, most businesses wanted printer output that was faster and looked better than what was produced by the early dot-matrix models from firms like Epson. HP responded to this need with its initial Laser-Jet printer. It could handle big jobs quickly and its graphics and typefaces looked really good. It even handled jobs that previously required typesetting by a printing service. However, the LaserJet was difficult to set up and use—so HP sold it through a select group of computer dealers who could provide technical support. That basic LaserJet cost $3,000, but the market expanded rapidly as customers realized its value for desktop publishing.

Other firms introduced laser printers, but HP stayed a few steps ahead of them. HP improved the speed and quality of its basic printer but also fine-tuned strategies for different customer groups. For example, it developed high-capacity models that could be shared on corporate networks. At the same time, it came out with low-cost models to attract home-office users and expanded distribution into outlets such as Office Depot to reach them.

When Microsoft Windows became popular, HP saw the need for low-cost color printing and quickly introduced a limited line of inkjet printers. They were not as fast as lasers for text, but they offered color graphics at a reasonable cost. As it had previously done with the laser printers, HP quickly developed different marketing mixes for the inkjets' different target markets. For example, wide-format DeskJet printers were available through office supply stores. They were pricey but were popular with managers for printing presentations or big spreadsheets on oversized paper. The price was much lower and features were simpler

on basic models targeted at individual consumers. However, sales of replacement color print cartridges were very profitable—and demand grew as consumers used their printers for more purposes, ranging from photos and homemade greeting cards to holiday letters. So HP worked to expand distribution to make replacement cartridges easy to buy—placing them even in grocery stores and drugstores. HP also gave away software that made it even easier for consumers to use the printers in different ways.

The demand for low-cost color printing grew even faster as the Internet and digital photography became popular. However, competitors like Epson, Lexmark, and Canon offered models similar to those from HP, and that put downward pressure on prices—especially in the consumer market. To keep its lead, HP did more segmenting. Because most final consumers are price-sensitive, HP started by redesigning its printers to cut features that were costly but that consumers didn't value. For example, older models were more sturdy than most consumers needed. New models were lighter so they were less costly to ship to stores. But HP didn't just produce inexpensive models to appeal to budget-oriented consumers. Rather, the new-product designers used their knowledge of the needs of different segments to create more than 50 consumer products—inkjet printers, printers for digital cameras, "all-in-one" printer/fax/copier/scanners, portable printers for notebooks, and more. PhotoSmart Go Go printers, for example, go anywhere and print pictures from a digital camera without using a computer.

It's costly to produce so many different models for different segments. However, each segment is large enough that it is profitable to develop a specialized strategy that earns a larger share of purchases. Further, by innovating to meet the needs of new segments, HP is expanding the market and not just taking market share away from other brands of printers. For example, many consumers are turning to HP's new photo centers to create personalized gift items—like calendars illustrated with their own photos. It's possible to do this on a home computer, but the photo centers make it fast and easy for folks who aren't computer geeks.

HP will continue to invent. And its competitors will keep coming up with innovations of their own. For example, Kodak has introduced a new line of printers that produce color prints at about half the cost. However, it's the targeted strategy planning that HP has done so far that helps to explain why the majority of printers in use today carry the HP brand.[1]

LEARNING OBJECTIVES

As the HP case illustrates, a manager who develops an understanding of the needs and characteristics of specific groups of target customers within the broader market may see new, breakthrough opportunities. But it's not always obvious how to identify the real needs of a target market—or the marketing mix that those customers will see as different from, and better than, what is available from a competitor. This chapter covers concepts and approaches that will help you to succeed in the search for those opportunities.

When you finish this chapter, you should:

1. know how to define generic markets and product-markets.

2. know what market segmentation is and how to segment product-markets into submarkets.

3. know three approaches to market-oriented strategy planning.

4. know dimensions that may be useful for segmenting markets.

5. know what positioning is and why it is useful.

6. understand the important new terms (shown in red).

SEARCH FOR OPPORTUNITIES CAN BEGIN BY UNDERSTANDING MARKETS

Strategy planning is a narrowing-down process

In Chapter 2 we provided a framework for a logical marketing strategy planning process. It involves careful evaluation of the market opportunities available before narrowing down to focus on the most attractive target market and marketing mix. In this chapter we will discuss frameworks and concepts that can help guide that narrowing-down process. See Exhibit 3–1 for an overview.

Since this chapter is about bringing focus to the search for market opportunities, a good place to start is by discussing what we really mean when we use the term *market*.

What is a company's market?

Identifying a company's market is an important but sticky issue. In general, a **market** is a group of potential customers with similar needs who are willing to exchange something of value with sellers offering various goods or services—that is, ways of satisfying those needs. However, within a general market, marketing-oriented

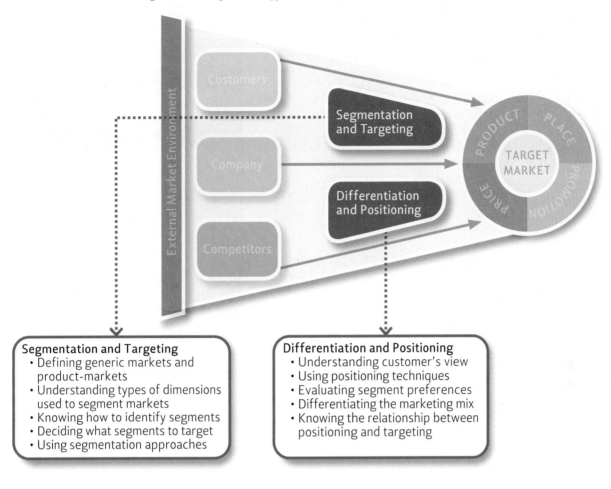

Segmentation and Targeting
- Defining generic markets and product-markets
- Understanding types of dimensions used to segment markets
- Knowing how to identify segments
- Deciding what segments to target
- Using segmentation approaches

Differentiation and Positioning
- Understanding customer's view
- Using positioning techniques
- Evaluating segment preferences
- Differentiating the marketing mix
- Knowing the relationship between positioning and targeting

managers develop marketing mixes for *specific* target markets. Getting the firm to focus on specific target markets is vital.

Don't just focus on the product

Some production-oriented managers don't understand this narrowing-down process. They get into trouble because they ignore the tough part of defining markets. To make the narrowing-down process easier, they just describe their markets in terms of *products* they sell. For example, producers and retailers of greeting cards might define their market as the "greeting card" market. But this production-oriented approach ignores customers—and customers make a market! This also leads to missed opportunities. Hallmark isn't missing these opportunities. Instead, Hallmark aims at the "personal expression" market. Hallmark stores offer all kinds of products that can be sent as "memory makers"—to express one person's feelings toward another. And as opportunities related to these needs change, Hallmark changes too. For example, at the Hallmark website (www.hallmark.com) it is easy to get shopping suggestions from an online "gift assistant," to order flowers, or to personalize an electronic greeting card to send over the Internet.[2]

From generic markets to product-markets

To understand the narrowing-down process, it's useful to think of two basic types of markets. A **generic market** is a market with *broadly* similar needs—and sellers offering various, *often diverse,* ways of satisfying those needs. In contrast, a **product-market** is a market with *very* similar needs and sellers offering various *close substitute* ways of satisfying those needs.[3]

Flam is an eat-on-the-go French snack "in a wrap" that contains pieces of pork and onions in a thick sauce made with soft white cheese. It is not a sandwich, but if it were available in this country it might compete in the same generic market with Blimpie's Panini. The products are different but they both serve the need for a convenient and tasty luncheon treat.

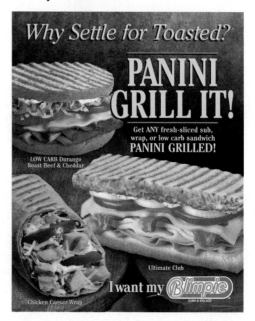

A generic market description looks at markets broadly and from a customer's viewpoint. Entertainment-seekers, for example, have several very different ways to satisfy their needs. An entertainment-seeker might buy a TiVo digital video recorder and plasma screen TV, sign up for a cruise on the Carnival Line, or reserve season tickets for the symphony. Any one of these *very different* products may satisfy this entertainment need. Sellers in this generic entertainment-seeker market have to focus on the need(s) the customers want satisfied—not on how one seller's product (digital TV system, vacation, or live music) is better than that of another producer.

It is sometimes hard to understand and define generic markets because *quite different product types may compete with each other.* For example, a person on a business trip to Italy might want a convenient way to record memories of the trip. Minolta's digital camera, Sony's video camcorder, Kodak's PalmPix digital accessory for a Palm, and even postcards from local shops may all compete to serve our traveler's needs. If customers see all these products as substitutes—as competitors in the same generic market—then marketers must deal with this complication.

Suppose, however, that our traveler decides to satisfy this need with a digital camera. Then—in this product-market—Minolta, Kodak, HP, Nikon, and many other brands may compete with each other for the customer's dollars. In this *product*-market concerned with digital cameras *and* needs to conveniently record memories, consumers compare similar products to satisfy their image needs.

Broaden market definitions to find opportunities

Broader market definitions—including both generic market definitions and product-market definitions—can help firms find opportunities. But deciding *how* broad to go isn't easy. Too narrow a definition limits a firm's opportunities—but too broad a definition makes the company's efforts and resources seem insignificant. Consider, for example, the mighty Coca-Cola Company. It has great success and a huge market share in the U.S. cola-drinkers' market. On the other hand, its share of all beverage drinking worldwide is very small.

Here we try to match opportunities to a firm's resources and objectives. So the *relevant market for finding opportunities* should be bigger than the firm's present product-market—but not so big that the firm couldn't expand and be an important competitor. A small manufacturer of screwdrivers in Mexico, for example, shouldn't define its market as broadly as "the worldwide tool users market" or as narrowly as "our present screwdriver customers." But it may have the production or marketing potential, or both, to consider "the handyman's hand-tool market in North America." Carefully naming your product-market can help you see possible opportunities.

NAMING PRODUCT-MARKETS AND GENERIC MARKETS

Some managers think about markets just in terms of the product they already produce and sell. But this approach can lead to missed opportunities. For example, think about how photographic film is being replaced with digital pictures, just as digital video recorders (DVRs) are replacing VCRs, and MP3 players are replacing portable CD players.

As this suggests, when evaluating opportunities, product-related terms do not—by themselves—adequately describe a market. A complete product-market definition includes a four-part description.

What:	1. Product type (type of good and type of service)
To meet what:	2. Customer (user) needs
For whom:	3. Customer types
Where:	4. Geographic area

We refer to these four-part descriptions as product-market "names" because most managers label their markets when they think, write, or talk about them. Such a four-part definition can be clumsy, however, so we often use a nickname. And the nickname should refer to people—not products—because, as we emphasize, people make markets!

Product type should meet customer needs

Product type describes the goods and/or services that customers want. Sometimes the product type is strictly a physical good or strictly a service. But marketing managers who ignore the possibility that *both* are important can miss opportunities.

Customer (user) needs refer to the needs the product type satisfies for the customer. At a very basic level, product types usually provide functional benefits such as nourishing, protecting, warming, cooling, transporting, cleaning, holding, saving time, and so forth. Although we need to identify such "basic" needs first, in advanced economies, we usually go on to emotional needs—such as needs for fun, excitement, pleasing appearance, or status. Correctly defining the need(s) relevant to a market is crucial and requires a good understanding of customers. We discuss these topics more fully in Chapters 5 and 6.

Customer type refers to the final consumer or user of a product type. Here we want to choose a name that describes all present (possible) types of customers. To define customer type, marketers should identify the final consumer or user of the product type, rather than the buyer—if they are different. For instance, producers should avoid treating middlemen as a customer type—unless middlemen actually use the product in their own business.

The *geographic area* is where a firm competes, or plans to compete, for customers. Naming the geographic area may seem trivial, but understanding the geographic boundaries of a market can suggest new opportunities. A firm aiming only at the domestic market, for example, may want to expand into world markets.

Product-market boundaries provide focus

This idea of making a decision about the boundaries of a market applies not just to geographic areas served but also to decisions about customer needs and product and customer types. Thus, naming the market is not simply an exercise in assigning labels.

Nestlé targets customers in many different geographic markets around the world, but often the product-markets in one country are different than in another. For example, Nestlé created banana flavored milk ice on a stick to fit the local tastes and preferences of Chinese consumers. The same product would probably not have a following in other places.

Rather, the manager's market definition sets the limits of the market(s) in which the firm will compete. For example, both final consumers and business customers have a variety of "fastening" needs that might be met with products ranging from screws and glues to tapes and welding. However, if a marketing manager decides that the firm should focus on business customers and not on individual consumers, then that should be explicit in the market definition. That decision limits the scope of the market and, at the same time, sharpens the focus.

No product type in generic market names

A generic market description *doesn't include any product-type terms*. It consists of only three parts of the product-market definition—without the product type. This emphasizes that any product type that satisfies the customer's needs can compete in a generic market. Exhibit 3–2 shows the relationship between generic market and product-market definitions.

Later we'll study the many possible dimensions for segmenting markets. But for now you should see that defining markets only in terms of current products is not the best way to find new opportunities. Instead, the most effective way to find opportunities is to use market segmentation.

Exhibit 3–2
Relationship between Generic and Product-Market Definitions

MARKET SEGMENTATION DEFINES POSSIBLE TARGET MARKETS

Market segmentation is a two-step process

Market segmentation is a two-step process of (1) *naming* broad product-markets and (2) *segmenting* these broad product-markets in order to select target markets and develop suitable marketing mixes.

This two-step process isn't well understood. First-time market segmentation efforts often fail because beginners start with the whole mass market and try to find one or two demographic characteristics to divide up (segment) this market. Customer behavior is usually too complex to be explained in terms of just one or two demographic characteristics. For example, not all elderly men buy the same products or brands. Other dimensions usually must be considered—starting with customer needs.

Naming broad product-markets is disaggregating

The first step in effective market segmentation involves naming a broad product-market of interest to the firm. Marketers must break apart—disaggregate—all possible needs into some generic markets and broad product-markets in which the firm may be able to operate profitably. See Exhibit 3–3. No one firm can satisfy everyone's needs. So the naming—disaggregating—step involves brainstorming about very different solutions to various generic needs and selecting some broad areas—broad product-markets—where the firm has some resources and experience. This means that a car manufacturer would probably ignore all the possible opportunities in food and clothing markets and focus on the generic market, "transporting people in the world," and probably on the broad product-market, "cars, trucks, and utility vehicles for transporting people in the world."

Market grid is a visual aid to market segmentation

Assuming that any broad product-market (or generic market) may consist of sub-markets, picture a market as a rectangle with boxes that represent the smaller, more homogeneous product-markets.

Exhibit 3–4, for example, represents the broad product-market of bicycle riders. The boxes show different submarkets. One submarket might focus on people who want basic transportation, another on people who want exercise, and so on. Alternatively, in the generic "transporting market" discussed earlier, we might see different product-markets of customers for bicycles, motorcycles, cars, airplanes, ships, buses, and "others."

Exhibit 3–3
Narrowing Down to Target Markets

Exhibit 3–4
A Market Grid Diagram
with Submarkets

Broad product-market (or generic market) name goes here
(The bicycle riders product-market)

| Submarket 1 (Exercisers) | Submarket 3 (Transportation riders) | Submarket 4 (Socializers) |

Submarket 2 (Off-road adventurers)

Submarket 5 (Environmentalists)

Segmenting is an aggregating process

Marketing-oriented managers think of **segmenting** as an aggregating process—clustering people with similar needs into a "market segment." A **market segment** is a (relatively) homogeneous group of customers who will respond to a marketing mix in a similar way.

This part of the market segmentation process (see Exhibit 3–3) takes a different approach from the naming part. Here we look for similarities rather than basic differences in needs. Segmenters start with the idea that each person is one of a kind but that it may be possible to aggregate some similar people into a product-market.

Segmenters see each of these one-of-a-kind people as having a unique set of dimensions. Consider a product-market in which customers' needs differ on two important segmenting dimensions: need for status and need for dependability. In Exhibit 3–5A, each dot shows a person's position on the two dimensions. While each person's position is unique, many of these people are similar in terms of how much status and dependability they want. So a segmenter may aggregate them into three (an arbitrary number) relatively homogeneous submarkets—A, B, and C. Group A might be called "status-oriented" and Group C "dependability-oriented." Members of Group B want both and might be called the "demanders."

How far should the aggregating go?

The segmenter wants to aggregate individual customers into some workable number of relatively homogeneous target markets and then treat each target market differently.

Look again at Exhibit 3–5A. Remember we talked about three segments. But this was an arbitrary number. As Exhibit 3–5B shows, there may really be six segments. What do you think—does this broad product-market consist of three segments or six?

Another difficulty with segmenting is that some potential customers just don't fit neatly into market segments. For example, not everyone in Exhibit 3–5B was put into one of the groups. Forcing them into one of the groups would have made these segments more heterogeneous and harder to please. Further, forming additional segments for them probably wouldn't be profitable. They are too few and not very similar in terms of the

Exhibit 3–5
Every Individual Has
His or Her Own Unique
Position in a Market—
Those with Similar
Positions Can Be
Aggregated into
Potential Target
Markets

A. Product-market showing three segments

B. Product-market showing six segments

Chef Magazine is an effective advertising medium for firms that want to promote specialized products for chefs. For example, VF Imagewear advertises its chef uniforms and Chefshoes.com wants chefs to know that it's on the Web and understands the problems of a chef who stands on a hard floor all day.

two dimensions. These people are simply too unique to be catered to and may have to be ignored—unless they are willing to pay a high price for special treatment.

The number of segments that should be formed depends more on judgment than on some scientific rule. But the following guidelines can help.

Criteria for segmenting a broad product-market

Ideally, "good" market segments meet the following criteria:

1. *Homogeneous (similar) within*—the customers in a market segment should be as similar as possible with respect to their likely responses to marketing mix variables *and* their segmenting dimensions.
2. *Heterogeneous (different) between*—the customers in different segments should be as different as possible with respect to their likely responses to marketing mix variables *and* their segmenting dimensions.
3. *Substantial*—the segment should be big enough to be profitable.
4. *Operational*—the segmenting dimensions should be useful for identifying customers and deciding on marketing mix variables.

It is especially important that segments be *operational*. This leads marketers to include demographic dimensions such as age, sex, income, location, and family size. In fact, it is difficult to make some Place and Promotion decisions without such information.

Target marketers aim at specific targets

Once you accept the idea that broad product-markets may have submarkets, you can see that target marketers usually have a choice among many possible target markets.

There are three basic ways to develop market-oriented strategies in a broad product-market.

1. The **single target market approach**—segmenting the market and picking one of the homogeneous segments as the firm's target market.
2. The **multiple target market approach**—segmenting the market and choosing two or more segments, then treating each as a separate target market needing a different marketing mix.
3. The **combined target market approach**—combining two or more submarkets into one larger target market as a basis for one strategy.

Note that all three approaches involve target marketing. They all aim at specific, clearly defined target markets. See Exhibit 3–6. For convenience, we call people who

Exhibit 3–6
Target Marketers Have
Specific Aims

follow the first two approaches the "segmenters" and people who use the third approach the "combiners."

Combiners try to satisfy "pretty well"

Combiners try to increase the size of their target markets by combining two or more segments. Combiners look at various submarkets for similarities rather than differences. Then they try to extend or modify their basic offering to appeal to these "combined" customers with just one marketing mix. See Exhibit 3–6.

A combined target market approach may help achieve some economies of scale. It may also require less investment than developing different marketing mixes for different segments—making it especially attractive for firms with limited resources.

Too much combining is risky

It is tempting to aim at larger combined markets instead of using different marketing mixes for smaller segmented markets. However, this makes it harder to develop marketing mixes that can satisfy potential customers. So a combiner faces the continual risk of innovative segmenters chipping away at the various segments of the combined target market—by offering more attractive marketing mixes to more homogeneous submarkets. ATI Technologies, a firm that is a leader in making graphics chips for PCs, saw this happen. It produced high-quality products with features desired by a very wide variety of computer users. But then ATI lost business to more specialized competitors like Nvidia Corp. Nvidia focused on the needs of video-game lovers who don't want to compromise when it comes to realistic special effects. Nvidia developed chips that did fewer things, but by doing those specialized things really well it captured much of the video-game lovers' business—until ATI did more segmenting.

Segmenters try to satisfy "very well"

Segmenters aim at one or more homogeneous segments and try to develop a different marketing mix for each segment. Segmenters usually fine-tune their marketing mixes for each target market—perhaps making basic changes in the product itself.

Instead of assuming that the whole market consists of a fairly similar set of customers (like the mass marketer does) or merging various submarkets together (like the combiner), segmenters believe that aiming at one, or some, of these smaller markets makes it possible to provide superior value and satisfy them better. This then provides greater profit potential for the firm.

Segmenting may produce bigger sales

Note that segmenters are not settling for a smaller sales potential or lower profits. Instead, they hope to increase sales by getting a much larger share of the business in the market(s) they target. A segmenter that really satisfies the target market can often build such a close relationship with customers that it faces no real competition. A segmenter that offers a marketing mix precisely matched to the needs of the target market can often charge a higher price that produces higher profits. Customers are willing to pay a higher price because the whole marketing mix provides better customer value.

Consider the success of the Aeron desk chair developed by Herman Miller (HM), an 80-year-old company that makes office furniture. Most firms that sell office furniture offer similar lines of executive desk chairs that are padded for comfort and convey the look of success. Marketing managers at HM realized that some customers felt that these traditional chairs were boring. Further, in an e-commerce world, even top executives sit at computers and want a chair that provides both good support and good looks. So to satisfy this upscale segment, HM designed a new type of chair from scratch. There's no fabric or padding, but everything about it adjusts to your body. It's so comfortable that HM positions it as "the chair you can wear." With a price tag close to $1,000, the Aeron chair became a status symbol for high-tech managers and has been as profitable as it is popular.[4]

Should you segment or combine?

Which approach should a firm use? This depends on the firm's resources, the nature of competition, and—most important—the similarity of customer needs, attitudes, and buying behavior.

In general, it's usually safer to be a segmenter—that is, to try to satisfy some customers *very* well instead of many just *fairly* well. That's why many firms use the single or multiple target market approach instead of the combined target market approach. Procter & Gamble, for example, offers many products that seem to compete directly with each other (e.g., Tide versus Cheer or Crest versus Gleem). However, P&G offers tailor-made marketing mixes to each submarket large and profitable enough to deserve a separate marketing mix. Though extremely effective, this approach may not be possible for a smaller firm with more limited resources. A smaller firm may have to use the single target market approach—focusing all its efforts at the one submarket niche where it sees the best opportunity.[5]

Kaepa, Inc., is a good example. Sales of its all-purpose sneakers plummeted as larger firms like Nike and Reebok stole customers with a multiple target market approach. They developed innovative products and aimed their promotion at specific needs—like jogging, aerobics, cross-training, and walking. Kaepa turned things around by catering to the needs of cheerleaders. Cheerleading squads can order Kaepa shoes with custom team logos and colors. The soles of the shoes feature finger grooves that make it easier for cheerleaders to build human pyramids. The Kaepa website (www.kaepa.com) attracts the cheerleader target market with links to a host of other cheering sites. Kaepa also carefully targets its market research and promotion. Kaepa salespeople attend the cheerleading camps that each summer draw 40,000 enthusiasts.[6]

Profit is the balancing point

In practice, cost considerations probably encourage more aggregating—to obtain economies of scale—while demand considerations suggest less aggregating—to satisfy needs more exactly.

Profit is the balancing point. It determines how unique a marketing mix the firm can afford to offer to a particular group.

Potential Target Market Dimensions	Effects on Strategy Decision Areas
1. Behavioral needs, attitudes, and how present and potential goods and services fit into customers' consumption patterns.	Affects *Product* (features, packaging, product line assortment, branding) and *Promotion* (what potential customers need and want to know about the firm's offering, and what appeals should be used).
2. Urgency to get need satisfied and desire and willingness to seek information, compare, and shop.	Affects *Place* (how directly products are distributed from producer to customer, how extensively they are made available, and the level of service needed) and *Price* (how much potential customers are willing to pay).
3. Geographic location and other demographic characteristics of potential customers.	Affects size of *Target Markets* (economic potential), *Place* (where products should be made available), and *Promotion* (where and to whom to target advertising and personal selling).

WHAT DIMENSIONS ARE USED TO SEGMENT MARKETS?

Segmenting dimensions guide marketing mix planning

Market segmentation forces a marketing manager to decide which product-market dimensions might be useful for planning marketing strategies. The dimensions should help guide marketing mix planning. Exhibit 3–7 shows the basic kinds of dimensions we'll be talking about in Chapter 5—and their probable effect on the four Ps. Ideally, we want to describe any potential product-market in terms of all three types of customer-related dimensions—plus a product type description—because these dimensions help us develop better marketing mixes.

Many segmenting dimensions may be considered

Customers can be described by many specific dimensions. Exhibit 3–8 shows some dimensions useful for segmenting consumer markets. A few are behavioral dimensions, others are geographic and demographic. We discuss these final consumer segmenting dimensions in Chapter 5. Exhibit 3–9 shows some additional dimensions for segmenting markets when the customers are businesses, government agencies, or other types of organizations. These dimensions for segmenting organizational customers are covered in Chapter 6. Regardless of whether customers are final consumers or organizations, segmenting a broad product-market *usually* requires using several different dimensions at the same time.[7]

Any hiking boot should repel water, and a product that doesn't meet that "qualifying need" probably wouldn't appeal to many hikers. Sorel wants its target customers to know that its boots go further in keeping feet dry because that difference may be important in determining which brand of boot they buy.

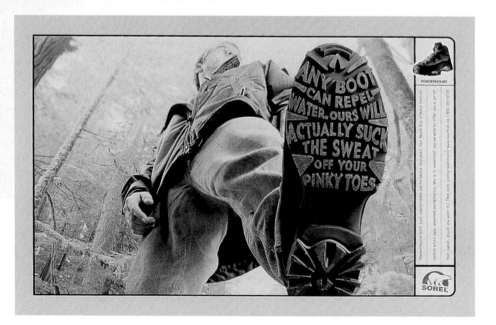

What are the qualifying and determining dimensions?

To select the important segmenting dimensions, think about two different types of dimensions. **Qualifying dimensions** are those relevant to including a customer type in a product-market. **Determining dimensions** are those that actually affect the customer's purchase of a specific product or brand in a product-market.

A prospective car buyer, for example, has to have enough money—or credit—to buy a car and insure it. Our buyer also needs a driver's license. This still doesn't guarantee a purchase. He or she must have a real need—like a job that requires "wheels" or kids who have to be carpooled. This need may motivate the purchase of *some* car. But these qualifying dimensions don't determine what specific brand or model car the person might buy. That depends on more specific interests—such as the kind of safety, performance, or appearance the customer wants. Determining dimensions related to these needs will affect the specific car the customer purchases. If safety is a determining dimension for a customer, a Volvo wagon that offers side impact protection, air bags, and all-wheel drive might be the customer's first choice.

Exhibit 3-8 Possible Segmenting Dimensions and Typical Breakdowns for Consumer Markets

Behavioral	
Needs	Economic, functional, physiological, psychological, social, and more detailed needs.
Benefits sought	Situation specific, but to satisfy specific or general needs.
Thoughts	Favorable or unfavorable attitudes, interests, opinions, beliefs.
Rate of use	Heavy, medium, light, nonusers.
Purchase relationship	Positive and ongoing, intermittent, no relationship, bad relationship.
Brand familiarity	Insistence, preference, recognition, nonrecognition, rejection.
Kind of shopping	Convenience, comparison shopping, specialty, none (unsought product).
Type of problem-solving	Routinized response, limited, extensive.
Information required	Low, medium, high.
Geographic	
Region of world, country	North America (United States, Canada), Europe (France, Italy, Germany), and so on.
Region in country	(Examples in United States): Pacific, Mountain, West North Central, West South Central, East North Central, East South Central, South Atlantic, Middle Atlantic, New England.
Size of city	No city; population under 5,000; 5,000–19,999; 20,000–49,999; 50,000–99,999; 100,000–249,999; 250,000–499,999; 500,000–999,999; 1,000,000–3,999,999; 4,000,000 and over.
Demographic	
Income	Under $5,000; $5,000–9,999; $10,000–14,999; $15,000–19,999; $20,000–29,999; $30,000–39,999; $40,000–59,999; $60,000 and over.
Sex	Male, female.
Age	Infant; under 6; 6–11; 12–17; 18–24; 25–34; 35–49; 50–64; 65 and over.
Family size	1, 2, 3–4, 5 or more.
Family life cycle	Young, single; young, married, no children; young, married, youngest child under 6; young, married, youngest child over 6; older, married, with children; older, married, no children under 18; older, single; other variations for single parents, divorced, etc.
Occupation	Professional and technical; managers, officials, and proprietors; clerical sales; craftspeople; foremen; operatives; farmers; retired; students; housewives; unemployed.
Education	Grade school or less; some high school; high school graduate; some college; college graduate.
Ethnicity	Asian, Black, Hispanic, Native American, White, multiracial.
Social class	Lower-lower, upper-lower, lower-middle, upper-middle, lower-upper, upper-upper.

Note: Terms used in this table are explained in detail later in the text.

Kind of relationship	Weak loyalty → strong loyalty to vendor Single source → multiple vendors "Arm's length" dealings → close partnership No cooperation → complete cooperation
Type of customer	Manufacturer, service producer, government agency, military, nonprofit, wholesaler or retailer (when end user), and so on
Demographics	Geographic location (region of world, country, region within country, urban → rural); Size (number of employees, sales volume); Primary business or industry (North American Industry Classification System); Number of facilities
How customer will use product	Installations, components, accessories, raw materials, supplies, professional services
Type of buying situation	Decentralized → centralized Buyer → multiple buying influence Straight rebuy → modified rebuy → new-task buying
Purchasing methods	Vendor analysis, purchasing specifications, Internet bids, negotiated contracts, long-term contracts, e-commerce websites

Note: Terms used in this table are explained in detail later in the text.

Determining dimensions may be very specific

How specific the determining dimensions are depends on whether you are concerned with a general product type or a specific brand. See Exhibit 3–10. The more specific you want to be, the more particular the determining dimensions may be. In a particular case, the determining dimensions may seem minor. But they are important because they *are* the determining dimensions.

Marketers at General Mills know this. Lots of people try to check e-mail or drive a car while eating breakfast or lunch. General Mills has figured out that for many of these target customers the real determining dimension in picking a snack is whether it can be eaten "one-handed."[8]

Exhibit 3–10 Finding the Relevant Segmenting Dimensions

Segmenting dimensions become more specific to reasons why the target segment chooses to buy a particular brand of the product

All potential dimensions	Qualifying dimensions	Determining dimensions (product type)	Determining dimensions (brand specific)
Dimensions generally relevant to purchasing behavior	Dimensions relevant to including a customer type in the product-market	Dimensions that affect the customer's purchase of a specific type of product	Dimensions that affect the customer's choice of a specific brand

Qualifying dimensions are important too

The qualifying dimensions help identify the "core benefits" that must be offered to everyone in a product-market. For example, people won't choose General Mills's one-handed snacks unless they qualify as being tasty. Qualifying and determining dimensions work together in marketing strategy planning.

Different dimensions needed for different submarkets

Note that each different submarket within a broad product-market may be motivated by a different set of dimensions. In the snack food market, for example, health food enthusiasts are interested in nutrition, dieters worry about calories, and economical shoppers with lots of kids may want volume to "fill them up."

Ethical issues in selecting segmenting dimensions

Marketing managers sometimes face ethical decisions when selecting segmenting dimensions. Problems may arise if a firm targets customers who are somehow at a disadvantage in dealing with the firm or who are unlikely to see the negative effects of their own choices. For example, some people criticize shoe companies for targeting poor, inner-city kids who see expensive athletic shoes as an important status symbol. Many firms, including producers of infant formula, have been criticized for targeting consumers in less-developed nations. Some nutritionists criticize firms that market soft drinks, candy, and snack foods to children.

Ethics QUESTION

A consumer group has criticized an encyclopedia publisher for targeting low-income parents. They respond well to sales appeals that focus on the low cost-per-day of encyclopedias that help kids enjoy learning. The critics say that the parents can't afford the books and don't understand the publisher's credit plan. In reply, the publisher cites a teacher group that touts the books as an excellent value. What do you think about this issue? If you were the marketing manager for the encyclopedia company, would you change its strategy?

Sometimes a marketing manager must decide whether a firm should serve customers it really doesn't want to serve. For example, banks sometimes offer marketing mixes that are attractive to wealthy customers but that basically drive off low-income consumers.

People often disagree about what segmenting dimensions are ethical in a given situation. A marketing manager needs to consider not only his or her own view but also the views of other groups in society. Even when there is no clear "right" answer, negative publicity may be very damaging. This is what Amazon.com encountered when it was revealed that it was charging some regular customers higher prices than new customers at its site.[9]

International marketing requires even more segmenting

Success in international marketing requires even more attention to segmenting. There are over 228 nations with their own unique cultures! And they differ greatly in language, customs (including business ethics), beliefs, religions, race, and income distribution patterns. (We'll discuss some of these differences in Chapters 4 and 5.) These additional differences can complicate the segmenting process. Even worse, critical data is often less available—and less dependable—as firms move into international markets. This is one reason why some firms insist that local operations and decisions be handled by natives. They, at least, have a feel for their markets.

There are more dimensions—but there is a way

Segmenting international markets may require more dimensions. But one practical method adds just one step to the approach discussed earlier. First, marketers segment by country or region—looking at demographic, cultural, and other characteristics, including stage of economic development. This may help them find regional or national submarkets that are fairly similar. Then—depending on whether the firm is aiming at final consumers or business markets—they apply the same basic approaches presented before.

Marketing researchers and managers often turn to computer-aided methods for help with the segmenting job. A detailed review of the possibilities is beyond the scope of this book. But a brief discussion will give you a flavor of how computer-aided methods work. In addition, the computer-aided problem for this chapter (3. Segmenting Customers) on the Student CD that accompanies the text gives you a hands-on feel for how managers use these techniques.

Clustering usually requires a computer

Clustering techniques try to find similar patterns within sets of data. Clustering groups customers who are similar on their segmenting dimensions into homogeneous segments. Clustering approaches use computers to do what previously was done with much intuition and judgment.

The data to be clustered might include such dimensions as demographic characteristics, the importance of different needs, attitudes toward the product, and past buying behavior. The computer searches all the data for homogeneous groups of people. When it finds them, marketers study the dimensions of the people in the groups to see why the computer clustered them together. The results sometimes suggest new, or at least better, marketing strategies.[10]

A cluster analysis of the toothpaste market, for example, might show that some people buy toothpaste because it tastes good (the sensory segment), while others are concerned with the effect of clean teeth and fresh breath on their social image (the sociables). Still others worry about decay or tartar (the worriers), and some are just interested in the best value for their money (the value seekers). Each of these market segments calls for a different marketing mix—although some of the four Ps may be similar.

Customer database can focus the effort

A variation of the clustering approach is based on customer relationship management methods. With **customer relationship management (CRM)**, the seller fine-tunes the marketing effort with information from a detailed customer database. This usually includes data on a customer's past purchases as well as other segmenting information.

Amazon.com sends e-mails to customers with recommendations based on their past purchases, which are analyzed in Amazon's customer relationship management system. Many customers find these messages useful, informing them of new books, music, or movies that actually match their interests.

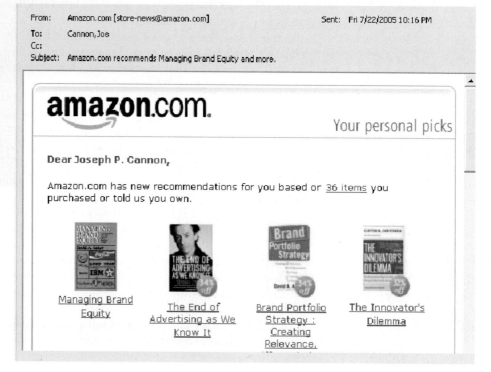

CDW Targets the Small Business Segment with Uncommon Service

Sellers in business markets often rely on customer size as a key segmentation dimension. When potential profit from serving a big customer is high, the selling firm may even treat that customer as a "segment of one"—and develop a unique marketing mix targeted to win and keep its business. Even if a unique marketing mix isn't justified, big customers in these segments often get volume discounts, extra services, and personalized attention. By contrast, smaller customers are often left to get information and handle orders themselves—at a seller's website. This can be efficient, reduce costs for both the seller and customer, and serve the need. But that is not always the case.

CDW is a wholesaler that sells all sorts of computer gear produced by many manufacturers. Most of its 360,000 business customers are too small to command much attention from equipment manufacturers. Yet they also have smaller IT departments and know less about buying IT equipment. CDW has enjoyed rapid growth because it offers a marketing mix that is atypical for these customers. Even the smallest customer gets a dedicated account manager (AM).

These salespeople don't just take orders; they go through months of CDW training so that they really understand a customer's needs and can help the buyer make the right purchases. The AM is a single point-of-contact with the account over time and is encouraged to act almost as an extension of the client's IT department. This relationship helps the AM anticipate client needs; the AM is also supported with customer relationship management databases that help predict when an upgrade is needed—rather than wait for the customer to ask. This is especially helpful to small customers who don't have backup systems in place to tide them over if something goes wrong. This is also why CDW fills orders fast—usually on the same day they are received. To provide that level of service with 17,000 orders a day, CDW operates a 450,000-square-foot distribution center and keeps about $130 million in inventory on hand. CDW's "high-touch" strategy is costly, but high volume keeps its prices competitive. And CDW's sales volume is high because CDW delivers superior customer value that wins a large share of its target customers' business.[11]

For example, an auto-repair garage that keeps a database of customer oil changes can send a reminder postcard when it's time for the next oil change. Similarly, a florist that keeps a database of customers who have ordered flowers for Mother's Day or Valentine's Day can call them in advance with a special offer. Firms that operate over the Internet may have a special advantage with these database-focused approaches. They are able to communicate with customers via a website or e-mail, which means that the whole effort is not only targeted but also very inexpensive. Further, it's fast and easy for a customer to reply.[12]

Internet EXERCISE

Visit the website for onContact Software (**www.oncontact.com**), and from the demo link at the top of the page select "screenshot tour" (*note:* the interactive tour requires that you register). Select the links to review the different examples of the firm's customer relationship management software. Give several examples of how this software could help a salesperson be more effective in working with customers.

DIFFERENTIATION AND POSITIONING TAKE THE CUSTOMER POINT OF VIEW

Differentiate the marketing mix—to serve customers better

As we've emphasized throughout, the reason for focusing on a specific target market—by using marketing segmentation approaches or tools such as cluster analysis or CRM—is so that you can fine-tune the whole marketing mix to provide some

Firms often use promotion to help "position" how a marketing mix meets target customers' specific needs. This Norwegian ad for the Audi Quattro simply says, "Sticks like quattro." Although it doesn't show the car at all, it helps to differentiate the Audi and its four-wheel-drive system that holds the road especially well, even in the snow.

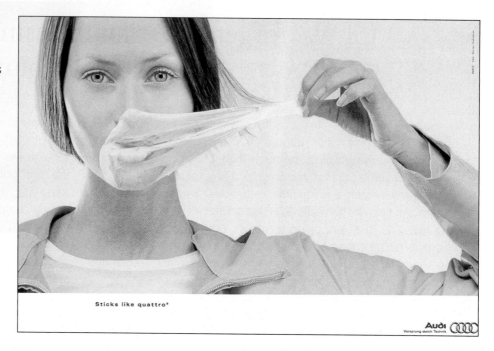

Sticks like quattro®

group of potential customers with superior value. By *differentiating* the marketing mix to do a better job meeting customers' needs, the firm builds a competitive advantage. When this happens, target customers view the firm's position in the market as uniquely suited to their preferences and needs. Further, because everyone in the firm is clear about what position it wants to achieve with customers, the Product, Promotion, and other marketing mix decisions can be blended better to achieve the desired objectives.

Although the marketing manager may want customers to see the firm's offering as unique, that is not always possible. Me-too imitators may come along and copy the firm's strategy. Further, even if a firm's marketing mix is different, consumers may not know or care. They're busy and, simply put, the firm's product may not be that important in their lives. Even so, in looking for opportunities it's important for the marketing manager to know how customers *do* view the firm's offering. It's also important for the marketing manager to have a clear idea about how he or she would like for customers to view the firm's offering. This is where another important concept, *positioning,* comes in.

Positioning is based on customers' views

Positioning refers to how customers think about proposed or present brands in a market. A marketing manager needs a realistic view of how customers think about offerings in the market. Without that, it's hard to differentiate. At the same time, the manager should know how he or she *wants* target customers to think about the firm's marketing mix.

Exhibit 3–11
"Product Space" Representing Consumers' Perceptions for Different Brands of Bar Soap

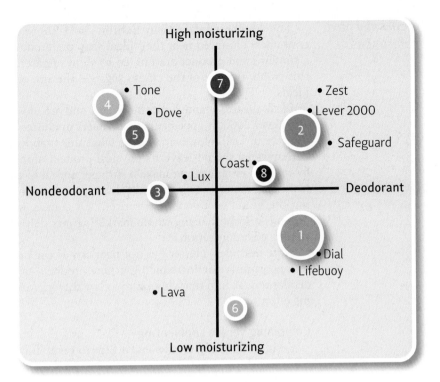

Positioning issues are especially important when competitors in a market appear to be very similar. For example, many people think that there isn't much difference between one provider of home owner's insurance and another. But State Farm Insurance uses advertising to emphasize the value of the service and personal attention from its agents, who live right in the customer's neighborhood. Low-price insurers who sell from websites or toll-free numbers can't make that claim.

Once you know what customers think, then you can decide whether to leave the product (and marketing mix) alone or reposition it. This may mean *physical changes in the product* or simply *image changes based on promotion*. For example, most cola drinkers can't pick out their favorite brand in a blind test—so physical changes might not be necessary (and might not even work) to reposition a cola.

Figuring out what customers really think about competing products isn't easy, but there are approaches that help. Most of them require some formal marketing research. The results are usually plotted on graphs to help show how consumers view the competing products. Usually, the products' positions are related to two or three product features that are important to the target customers.

Managers construct the graphs for positioning decisions by asking consumers to make judgments about different brands—including their "ideal" brand—and then using computer programs to summarize the ratings and plot the results. The details of positioning techniques—sometimes called *perceptual mapping*—are beyond the scope of this text. But Exhibit 3–11 shows the possibilities.[13]

Exhibit 3–11 shows the "product space" for different brands of bar soap using two dimensions—the extent to which consumers think the soaps moisturize and deodorize their skin. For example, consumers see Dove as quite high on moisturizing but low on deodorizing. Dove and Tone are close together—implying that consumers think of them as similar on these characteristics. Dial is viewed as different and is further away on the graph. Remember that positioning maps are based on *customers' perceptions*—the actual characteristics of the products (as determined by a chemical test) might be different!

The numbered circles in Exhibit 3–11 show different sets (submarkets) of consumers clustered near their ideal soap preferences. Groups of respondents with a similar ideal product are circled to show apparent customer concentrations. In this graph, the size of the circles suggests the size of the segments for the different ideals.

Ideal clusters 1 and 2 are the largest and are close to two popular brands—Dial and Lever 2000. It appears that customers in cluster 2 want more moisturizing than they see in Dial. However, exactly what this brand should do about this isn't clear. Perhaps Dial should leave its physical product alone—but emphasize moisturizing more in its promotion to make a stronger appeal to those who want moisturizers. A marketing manager talking about this approach might simply refer to it as "positioning the brand as a good moisturizer." Of course, whether the effort is successful depends on whether the whole marketing mix delivers on the promise of the positioning communication.

Note that ideal cluster 7 is not near any of the present brands. This may suggest an opportunity for introducing a new product—a strong moisturizer with some deodorizers. A firm that chooses to follow this approach would be making a segmenting effort.

Combining versus segmenting

Positioning analysis may lead a firm to combining—rather than segmenting—if managers think they can make several general appeals to different parts of a "combined" market. For example, by varying its promotion, Coast might try to appeal to segments 8, 1, and 2 with one product. These segments are all quite similar (close together) in what they want in an ideal brand. On the other hand, there may be clearly defined submarkets—and some parts of the market may be "owned" by one product or brand. In this case, segmenting efforts may be practical—moving the firm's own product into another segment of the general market area where competition is weaker.

A positioning analysis helps managers understand how customers see their market. It is a visual aid to understanding a product-market. The first time such an analysis is done, managers may be shocked to see how much customers' perceptions of a market differ from their own. For this reason alone, positioning analysis may be crucial. But a positioning analysis usually focuses on specific product features and brands that are close competitors in the product-market. Thus, it is a product-oriented approach. Important *customer*-related dimensions—including needs and attitudes—may be overlooked.

Premature emphasis on product features is dangerous in other ways as well. As our bar soap example shows, starting with a product-oriented definition of a market and how bar soaps compete against other bar soaps can make a firm miss more basic shifts in markets. For example, bars have lost popularity to liquid soaps. Other products, like bath oils or body shampoos for use in the shower, are now part of the relevant competition also. Managers wouldn't see these shifts if they looked only at alternative bar soap brands—the focus is just too narrow.

It's also important to realize that the way consumers look at a product isn't just a matter of chance. Let's return to our bar soap example. While many consumers do think about soap in terms of moisturizing and deodorizing, other needs shouldn't be overlooked. For example, some consumers are especially concerned about wiping out germs. Marketers for Dial soap recognized this need and developed ads that positioned Dial as "the choice" for these target customers. This helped Dial win new customers, including those who switched from Lifebuoy—which was otherwise similar to Dial (see Exhibit 3–11). In fact, what happened to Lifebuoy highlights what happens if managers don't update their marketing strategy as customer needs and competition change. Lifebuoy was the first deodorant soap on the market; it was a leading brand for over 100 years. But it gradually lost sales to competitors with stronger marketing mixes (clearer differentiation, better positioning, and superior customer value) until 2002, when Lever stopped selling it.

As we emphasize throughout the text, you must understand potential needs and attitudes when planning marketing strategies. If customers treat different products as substitutes, then a firm has to position itself against those products too. Customers won't always be conscious of all of the detailed ways that a firm's marketing mix might be different, but careful positioning can help highlight a unifying theme or benefits that relate to the determining dimensions of the target market. Thus, it's useful to think of positioning as part of the broader strategy planning process—because the purpose is to ensure that the whole marketing mix is positioned for competitive advantage.

CONCLUSION

In Chapter 2 we explained why firms need creative strategy planning to survive in our increasingly competitive markets. We also introduced a framework for strategy planning that starts with analysis of the broad market and then narrows down to a specific target market and marketing mix. The basic purpose of this chapter is to show how marketing managers use market segmentation and positioning to guide that narrowing-down process.

Now that you've read this chapter you should understand how to carefully define generic markets and product-markets and how that can help in identifying and evaluating opportunities. We stressed the shortcomings of a too narrow, product-oriented view of markets and explained why it's better to take a broader view that also includes consideration of customer needs, the product type, the customer type, and the geographic area.

We also discussed approaches for market segmentation—the process of naming and then segmenting broad product-markets to find potentially attractive target markets. Some people try to segment markets by starting with the mass market and then dividing it into smaller submarkets based on a few demographic characteristics. But this can lead to poor results. Instead, market segmentation should first focus on a broad product-market and then group similar customers into homogeneous submarkets. The more similar the potential customers are, the larger the

submarkets can be. Four criteria for evaluating possible product-market segments were presented.

Once a broad product-market is segmented, marketing managers can use one of three approaches to market-oriented strategy planning: (1) the single target market approach, (2) the multiple target market approach, or (3) the combined target market approach. In general, we encourage marketers to be segmenters rather than combiners.

We also covered computer-aided approaches such as clustering techniques, CRM, and positioning. We emphasized the role of positioning in providing a focus or theme to the various elements of a differentiated marketing mix that fits the preferences of target customers.

In summary, good marketers should be experts on markets and likely segmenting dimensions. By creatively segmenting markets, they may spot opportunities—even breakthrough opportunities—and help their firms succeed against aggressive competitors offering similar products. Segmenting is basic to target marketing. And the more you practice segmenting, the more meaningful market segments you will see. In Chapters 5 and 6 you'll learn more about the buying behavior of final consumers and organizational customers. As you enrich your understanding of customers and how they behave, you will develop command of a broader set of dimensions that are important for segmentation and positioning.

KEY TERMS

market, 60

generic market, 61

product-market, 61

market segmentation, 65

segmenting, 66

market segment, 66

single target market approach, 67

multiple target market approach, 67

combined target market approach, 67

combiners, 68

segmenters, 68

qualifying dimensions, 71

determining dimensions, 71

clustering techniques, 74

customer relationship management (CRM), 74

positioning, 76

QUESTIONS AND PROBLEMS

1. Distinguish between a generic market and a product-market. Illustrate your answer.

2. Explain what market segmentation is.

3. List the types of potential segmenting dimensions, and explain which you would try to apply first, second, and third in a particular situation. If the nature of the situation would affect your answer, explain how.

4. Explain why segmentation efforts based on attempts to divide the mass market using a few demographic dimensions may be very disappointing.

5. Illustrate the concept that segmenting is an aggregating process by referring to the admissions policies of your own college and a nearby college or university.

6. Review the types of segmenting dimensions listed in Exhibits 3–8 and 3–9, and select the ones you think should be combined to fully explain the market segment you personally would be in if you were planning to buy a new watch today. List several dimensions and try to develop a shorthand name, like "fashion-oriented," to describe your own personal market segment. Then try to estimate what proportion of the total watch market would be accounted for by your market segment. Next, explain if there are any offerings that come close to meeting the needs of your market. If not, what sort of a marketing mix is needed? Would it be economically attractive for anyone to try to satisfy your market segment? Why or why not?

7. Identify the determining dimension or dimensions that explain why you bought the specific brand you did in your most recent purchase of (a) a soft drink, (b) shampoo, (c) a shirt or blouse, and (d) a larger, more expensive item, such as a bicycle, camera, or boat. Try to express the determining dimension(s) in terms of your own personal characteristics rather than the product's characteristics. Estimate what share of the market would probably be motivated by the same determining dimension(s).

8. Consider the market for off-campus apartments in your city. Identify some submarkets that have different needs and determining dimensions. Then evaluate how well the needs in these market segments are being met in your geographic area. Is there an obvious breakthrough opportunity waiting for someone?

9. Explain how positioning analysis can help a marketing manager identify target market opportunities.

CREATING MARKETING PLANS

The Marketing Plan Coach software on the Student CD includes a sample marketing plan for Hillside Veterinary Clinic. Look through the "Customers" section.

a. How does the marketing plan segment the market?

b. Can you think of other segmentation dimensions that could be used?

c. What do you think of the approach Hillside used to determine target markets? Is it using a single target market, multiple target market, or combined target market approach?

d. How does Hillside plan to differentiate and position its offering?

SUGGESTED CASES

3. NOCO Soccer Academy

7. Kerikeri Lodge

10. Fulton's Ice Land

30. Saralyn Mills, Ltd.

COMPUTER-AIDED PROBLEM

3. SEGMENTING CUSTOMERS

The marketing manager for Audiotronics Software Company is seeking new market opportunities. He is focusing on the voice recognition market and has narrowed down to three segments: the Fearful Typists, the Power Users, and the Professional Specialists. The Fearful Typists don't know much about computers—they just want a fast way to create e-mail messages, letters, and simple reports without errors. They don't need a lot of special features. They want simple instructions and a program that's easy to learn. The Power Users know a lot about computers, use them often, and want a voice recognition program with many special features. All computer programs seem easy to them—so they aren't worried about learning to use the various features. The Professional Specialists have jobs that require a lot of writing. They don't know much about computers but are willing to learn. They want special features needed for their work—but only if they aren't too hard to learn and use.

The marketing manager prepared a table summarizing the importance of each of three key needs in the three segments (see table that follows).

Market Segment	Importance of Need (1 = not important; 10 = very important)		
	Features	Easy to Use	Easy to Learn
Fearful Typists	3	8	9
Power Users	9	2	2
Professional Specialists	7	5	6

Audiotronics's sales staff conducted interviews with seven potential customers who were asked to rate how important each of these three needs were in their work. The manager prepared a spreadsheet to help him cluster (aggregate) each person into one of the segments—along with other similar people. Each person's ratings are entered in the spreadsheet, and the clustering procedure computes a similarity score that indicates how similar (a low score) or dissimilar (a high score) the person is to the typical person in each of the segments. The manager can then "aggregate" potential customers into the segment that is most similar (that is, the one with the *lowest* similarity score).

a. The ratings for a potential customer appear on the first spreadsheet. Into which segment would you aggregate this person?

b. The responses for the seven potential customers who were interviewed are listed in the table below. Enter the ratings for a customer in the spreadsheet and then write down the similarity score for each segment. Repeat the process for each customer. Based on your analysis, indicate the segment into which you would aggregate each customer. Indicate the size (number of customers) of each segment.

c. In the interview, each potential customer was also asked what type of computer he or she would be using. The responses are shown in the table along with the ratings. Group the responses based on the customer's segment. If you were targeting the Fearful Typists segment, what type of computer would you focus on when developing your software?

d. Based on your analysis, which customer would you say is least like any of the segments? Briefly explain the reason for your choice.

For additional questions related to this problem, see Exercise 3-4 in the *Learning Aid for Use with Essentials of Marketing*, 11th edition.

Potential Customer	Importance of Need (1 = not important; 10 = very important)			
	Features	Easy to Use	Easy to Learn	Type of Computer
A.	8	1	2	Dell laptop
B.	6	6	5	HP desktop
C.	4	9	8	Apple
D.	2	6	7	Apple
E.	5	6	5	HP desktop
F.	8	3	1	Dell laptop
G.	4	6	8	Apple

CHAPTER FOUR

Evaluating Opportunities in the Changing Marketing Environment

Bank of America (BofA) is one of the best known brands in banking, so it's no surprise that when NationsBank acquired BofA it adopted that name. What is more surprising is how a small southern bank—North Carolina National Bank before it was renamed NationsBank—grew so quickly that it was ultimately able to acquire BofA, Fleet Bank, and other giant competitors. In fact, the innovative marketing strategy planning that originally fueled growth at NationsBank continues to make the new Bank of America unique.

BofA has offices in 31 countries and serves clients from 150 countries. It provides banking services for corporations, manages trusts for the wealthy, and offers investment services. But what differentiates BofA is that it has grown primarily by becoming a "local bank" that serves large numbers of final consumers and small businesses in communities across the land. Its banking centers are in 5,800 locations, and it has the largest network of ATMs—16,800 of them. It was also a pioneer in e-commerce and now, serving 14 million customers online, is the world's largest online banker.

The bank's customers benefit from this strategy. For the first time, consumers can count on easy access to their hometown bank virtually anywhere they live, work, play, and travel. BofA is right there—in person, online, or via telephone or ATM. Along with that convenience, BofA has raised the stakes for service quality in banking.

How did managers at NationsBank know which opportunities to pursue and turn into strategies? Part of the explanation is that they evaluated not only customer needs and competitive rivals, but also trends in the external market environment. Even though the marketing environment is constantly changing, they spotted new trends and took advantage of them. An obvious example of this is the way the bank responded to shifts in the technological environment. The bank quickly built capabilities in information technology because that helped its growing number of branches. Then that competitive strength catapulted the bank ahead when the Internet opened the door to online services. Moreover, using online banking to expand the retail customer base fit with the marketing program the bank had been pursuing for years.

Consider, for example, how changes in the competitive and legal environments have shaped the bank's strategies for acquiring new customers. Regulations once governed how banks could operate, interstate banking was restricted, and many states limited the number and location of branch offices. As regulations began to ease, banking became more competitive and more marketing-oriented. For example, in college towns the bank targeted students with special accounts to build relationships that would last when they moved to new locations after graduation.

By the time interstate banking was allowed, the firm already had experience managing many branches—and the financial resources to acquire other banks and their customers. Initially they screened opportunities to focus on banks in Sun Belt states where population and income growth was rapid, regulations were more favorable, and consumers were less satisfied with available banks. NationsBank's customer base grew quickly—and it held on to new customers by improving the value they received from their banking relationship.

Although NationsBank was very profitable and growing rapidly, it did not have the international reputation of banks like Citicorp that were based in big financial centers. That was a weakness during a period when economies were becoming more global. However, the merger with BofA helped to offset that weakness.

Because the bank operated in many regions across the United States, managers were less provincial than managers of many other banks. They quickly saw and responded to cultural shifts that were taking place. For example, BofA's banking centers in Texas and Florida served many Hispanic customers and the Atlanta bank had a large proportion of African American customers. As society became more multicultural, the bank recruited associates (employees) from diverse ethnic backgrounds and made BofA a welcoming place for them to work and bank. Now BofA is one of the best companies in America for minority workers. Similarly, it offers flexible hours and other progressive benefits to help ease the pressure on dual-career families. Having a loyal group of associates has helped build a team culture where everyone tries to win in the market by providing excellent and efficient service. Catherine Bessant, a global marketing executive, put it this way, "Our strong brand is a significant competitive advantage, and in building it everything matters. The substance of our people, culture, process, and presence uniquely sets us apart."[1]

LEARNING OBJECTIVES

The Bank of America case shows that a marketing manager must analyze customer needs and choose marketing strategy variables within the framework of the marketing environment and how it is changing.

When you finish this chapter, you should:

1. know the variables that shape the environment of marketing strategy planning.
2. understand why company objectives are important in guiding marketing strategy planning.
3. see how the resources of a firm affect the search for opportunities.
4. know how the different kinds of competitive situations affect strategy planning.
5. understand how the economic and technological environment can affect strategy planning.
6. know why you might be sent to prison if you ignore the political and legal environment.
7. understand the cultural and social environment and how key population trends affect strategy planning.
8. understand how to screen and evaluate marketing strategy opportunities.
9. understand the important new terms (shown in red).

THE MARKETING ENVIRONMENT

The marketing strategy planning process requires narrowing down to the best opportunities and developing a strategy that gives the firm a competitive advantage and provides target customers superior customer value. This narrowing-down process should consider the important elements of the marketing environment and how they are shifting.

A large number of forces shapes the marketing environment. The direct market environment includes customers, the company, and competitors. The external market environment is broader and includes four major areas:

1. Economic environment
2. Technological environment
3. Political and legal environment
4. Cultural and social environment

The marketing manager can't control the variables of the marketing environment. That's why it's useful to think of them as uncontrollable variables. On the other hand, the marketing manager should analyze the environment when making decisions that can be controlled. For example, a manager can select a strategy that leads the firm into a product-market where competition is not yet strong.

In this chapter, we'll look at the key marketing environment variables shown in Exhibit 4–1 in more detail. We'll see how they shape opportunities—limiting some possibilities but making others more attractive.

OBJECTIVES SHOULD SET FIRM'S COURSE

A company must decide where it's going, or it may fall into the trap expressed so well by the quotation: "Having lost sight of our objective, we redoubled our efforts." Company objectives should shape the direction and operation of the whole business.

It is difficult to set objectives that really guide the present and future development of a company. The marketing manager should be heard when the company is setting objectives. But setting whole-company objectives—within resource limits—is ultimately the responsibility of top management. Top management must look at the whole business, relate its present objectives and resources to the external environment, and then decide what the firm wants to accomplish in the future.

Three basic objectives provide guidelines

The following three objectives provide a useful starting point for setting a firm's objectives. They should be sought *together* because in the long run a failure in even one of the three areas can lead to total failure of the business. A business should

1. Engage in specific activities that will perform a socially and economically useful function.
2. Develop an organization to carry on the business and implement its strategies.
3. Earn enough profit to survive.[2]

A mission statement helps set the course

Our three general objectives provide guidelines, but a firm should develop its own objectives. This is important, but top executives often don't state their objectives clearly. If objectives aren't clear from the start, different managers may hold unspoken and conflicting objectives.

Many firms try to avoid this problem by developing a **mission statement,** which sets out the organization's basic purpose for being. For example, the mission of the Fort Smith Public Library (www.fspl.lib.ar.us) is "to serve the minds of the citizens in our community by providing easy access to resources that meet their informational and recreational needs." A good mission statement should focus on a few key goals rather than embracing everything. It should also supply guidelines when managers face difficult decisions. For example, if an employee of the library is trying to decide whether or not to write a proposal for the funding of a Spanish language story time or

Liquid Paper sales grew quickly when it was introduced as a correction fluid to cover up typewriter errors. However, sales disappeared as word-processing replaced typewriters.

new computers that provide Internet access, it should be clear that these services are within the scope of the library's stated mission. A mission statement may need to be revised as new market needs arise or as the marketing environment changes. But this would be a fundamental change and not one that is made casually.[3]

The whole firm must work toward the same objectives

A mission statement is important, but it is not a substitute for more specific objectives that provide guidance in screening possible opportunities. For example, top management might set objectives such as "earn 25 percent annual return on investment" and "introduce at least three innovative and successful products in the next two years."

Of course, when there are a number of specific objectives stated by top management, it is critical that they be compatible. For example, the objective of introducing new products is reasonable. However, if the costs of developing and introducing the new products cannot be recouped within one year, the return on investment objective is impossible.[4]

Company objectives should lead to marketing objectives

To avoid such problems, the marketing manager should at least be involved in setting company objectives. Company objectives guide managers as they search for and evaluate opportunities—and later plan marketing strategies. Particular *marketing* objectives should be set within the framework of larger company objectives. As shown in Exhibit 4–2, firms need a hierarchy of objectives—moving from company objectives to marketing department objectives. For each marketing strategy, firms also need objectives for each of the four Ps—as well as more detailed objectives. For example, in the Promotion area, we need objectives for personal selling, mass selling, *and* sales promotion.

Toyota provides an example. One of its company objectives is to achieve high customer satisfaction. So the R&D people design vehicles to meet specific reliability objectives. Similarly, the production people work to cut manufacturing defects. The marketing department, in turn, sets specific customer satisfaction objectives for every product. That leads to specific promotion objectives to ensure that the sales and advertising people don't promise more than the company can deliver. Dealers and customer service people, in turn, work to quickly fix a problem the first time it's reported.

Exhibit 4–2
A Hierarchy of
Objectives

Both company objectives and marketing objectives should be realistic and achievable. Overly ambitious objectives are useless if the firm lacks the resources to achieve them.

COMPANY RESOURCES MAY LIMIT SEARCH FOR OPPORTUNITIES

Every firm has some resources—hopefully some unique ones—that set it apart. Breakthrough opportunities—or at least some competitive advantage—come from making use of these strengths while avoiding direct competition with firms having similar strengths.

To find its strengths, a firm must evaluate its functional areas (production, research and engineering, marketing, general management, and finance) as well as its present products and markets. The knowledge of people at the firm can also be a unique resource. By analyzing successes or failures in relation to the firm's resources, management can discover why the firm was successful—or why it failed—in the past.

Harley-Davidson's motorcycle business was on the ropes, and it was losing customers to Japanese competitors. Studying the Japanese firms helped Harley identify ways to produce higher-quality motorcycles at lower cost. With these resource-use problems resolved, Harley was again on the road to achieving its objectives. As its sales and reputation grew, its close relationship with Harley owners became a resource that helped Harley introduce a profitable line of accessories. The Harley case highlights both manufacturing quality and relationships with existing customers as resources. Other resources that should be considered as part of an evaluation of strengths and weaknesses are discussed in the following sections.[5]

Financial strength

Some opportunities require large amounts of capital just to get started. Money may be required for R&D, production facilities, marketing research, or advertising before a firm makes its first sale. And even a really good opportunity may not be profitable for years. So lack of financial strength is often a barrier to entry into an otherwise attractive market.

Producing capability and flexibility

In many businesses, the cost of producing and selling each unit decreases as the quantity increases. Therefore, smaller firms can be at a great cost disadvantage if they try to win business from larger competitors.

Campbell Soup Company has strengths that make it a very tough competitor in the consumer market. Knorr doesn't have as large a consumer advertising budget or as much shelf space in supermarkets. However, in the restaurant market, chefs often want ingredients that are different from what consumers have at home—and that's a strength for Knorr.

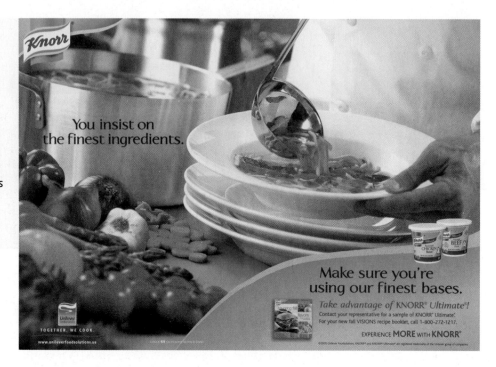

On the other hand, new—or smaller—firms sometimes have the advantage of flexibility. They are not handicapped with large, special-purpose facilities that are obsolete or poorly located.

Some firms are finding that they have the greatest flexibility by not having any "in-house" manufacturing at all. Sara Lee, the company that markets brands like Hanes and L'Eggs, is a good example. Sara Lee sold its manufacturing facilities for many of these textile-related markets. Sara Lee says it doesn't have a competitive advantage in manufacturing. Further, as its needs change in various markets around the world it will buy products from whatever suppliers are best able to meet its specifications.

Marketing strengths

Our marketing strategy planning framework (Exhibit 2–11) helps in analyzing current marketing resources. In the product area, for example, a familiar brand can be a big strength. Starbucks is famous for its coffee beverages. When Starbucks introduced its Coffee Ice Cream, many people quickly tried it because they knew what Starbucks flavor meant.[6]

A new idea or process may be protected by a *patent*. A patent owner has a 20-year monopoly to develop and use its new product, process, or material. If one firm has a strong patent, competitors may be limited to second-rate offerings—and their efforts may be doomed to failure.[7]

Good relations with established middlemen—or control of good locations—can be important resources. When marketing managers at Microsoft decided to introduce the Xbox game console, Microsoft software and computer accessories had already proved profitable for retailers like Best Buy that could reach the target market. So these retailers were willing to give the Xbox shelf space even if they were already carrying competing products from Nintendo or Sony.[8]

Promotion and price resources must be considered too. Fidelity Investments already has a skilled sales force. Marketing managers know these sales reps can handle new products and customers. And expertise to create an Internet website for online orders may enable a firm to expand.

Finally, thorough understanding of a target market can give a company an edge. Many companies fail in new product-markets because they don't really understand the needs of the new customers or the new competitive environment.

ANALYZING COMPETITORS AND THE COMPETITIVE ENVIRONMENT

Choose opportunities that avoid head-on competition

The **competitive environment** affects the number and types of competitors the marketing manager must face and how they may behave. Although marketing managers usually can't control these factors, they can choose strategies that avoid head-on competition. And where competition is inevitable, they can plan for it.

Economists describe four basic kinds of market (competitive) situations: pure competition, oligopoly, monopolistic competition, and monopoly. Understanding the differences among these market situations is helpful in analyzing the competitive environment, and our discussion assumes some familiarity with these concepts. (For a review, see Exhibit A–11 and the related discussion in Appendix A, which follows Chapter 18.)

Most product-markets head toward pure competition—or oligopoly—over the long run. In these situations, competitors offer very similar products. Because customers see the different available products (marketing mixes) as close substitutes, managers just compete with lower and lower prices, and profit margins shrink. Sometimes managers cut prices much too quickly, without really thinking through the question of how to add more customer value.

Avoiding pure competition is sensible and certainly fits with our emphasis on the need to find a competitive advantage. Marketing managers can't just adopt the same "good" marketing strategy being used by other firms. That just leads to head-on competition and a downward spiral in prices and profits.

Competitor-free environments are rare

Monopoly situations, in which one firm completely controls a broad product-market, are rare in market-directed economies. Further, governments commonly regulate monopolies. For example, in many parts of the world prices set by utility companies must be approved by a government agency. Although most marketing managers can't expect to operate with complete control in an unregulated monopoly, they can move away from head-on competition.

Monopolistic competition is typical—and a challenge

In monopolistic competition, a number of different firms offer marketing mixes that at least some customers see as different. Each competitor tries to get control (a monopoly) in its "own" target market. But competition still exists because some customers see the various alternatives as substitutes. Most marketing managers in developed economies face monopolistic competition.

Most consumers don't know the technical differences between various products for finishing wood, so Minwax ads emphasize that Minwax Polyshades saves them time by combining a stain and final finish in one product. Dirt Devil wants to convince customers that its Scorpion Hand Vac has more power than competitors so its ad gives the specific amp and watt rating. However, a consumer who does not know the ratings for other brands may not know that this is an advantage.

In monopolistic competition, marketing managers sometimes try to differentiate very similar products by relying on other elements of the marketing mix. For example, Clorox Bleach uses the same basic chemicals as other bleaches. But marketing managers for Clorox may help to set it apart from other bleaches by offering an improved pouring spout, by producing ads that demonstrate its stain-killing power, or by getting it better shelf positions in supermarkets. Yet such approaches may not work, especially if competitors can easily imitate each new idea.

Analyze competitors to find a competitive advantage

The best way for a marketing manager to avoid head-on competition is to find new or better ways to satisfy customers' needs and provide value. The search for a breakthrough opportunity—or some sort of competitive advantage—requires an understanding not only of customers but also of competitors. That's why marketing managers turn to **competitor analysis**—an organized approach for evaluating the strengths and weaknesses of current or potential competitors' marketing strategies.

The basic approach to competitor analysis is simple. You compare the strengths and weaknesses of your current (or planned) target market and marketing mix with what competitors are currently doing or are likely to do in response to your strategy.

The initial step in competitor analysis is to identify potential competitors. It's useful to start broadly and from the viewpoint of target customers. Companies may offer quite different products to meet the same needs, but they are competitors if customers see them as offering close substitutes. For example, disposable diapers, cloth diapers, and diaper rental services all compete in the same generic market concerned with baby care. Identifying a broad set of potential competitors helps marketing managers understand the different ways customers are currently meeting needs and sometimes points to new opportunities. For example, even parents who usually prefer the economy of cloth diapers may be interested in the convenience of disposables when they travel.

Usually, however, marketing managers quickly narrow the focus of their analysis to the set of **competitive rivals**—firms that will be the closest competitors. Rivals offering similar products are usually easy to identify. However, with a really new and different product concept, the closest competitor may be a firm that is currently serving similar needs with a different type of product. Although such firms may not appear to be close competitors, they are likely to fight back—perhaps with a directly competitive product—if another firm starts to take away customers.

Anticipate competition that will come

A successful strategy attracts copycats who jump in for a share of the profit. Sometimes a creative imitator figures out a way to provide customers with superior value. Then sales may disappear before the pioneer even knows what's happened.

Finding a sustainable competitive advantage requires special attention to competitor strengths and weaknesses. For example, it is very difficult to dislodge a firm that is already a market leader simply by attacking with a similar strategy. The leader can usually defend its position by quickly copying the best parts of what a new competitor is trying to do. On the other hand, an established competitor may not be able to defend quickly if it is attacked where it is weak. For example, Sony Walkman CD players had a large market share. When RCA added a new feature to its CD players that enabled them to also handle MP3 files, Sony was slow to respond. Sony executives were worried that more widespread use of MP3 files would hurt profits from the firm's music recording business.[9]

Watch for competitive barriers

In a competitor analysis, you also consider **competitive barriers**—the conditions that may make it difficult, or even impossible, for a firm to compete in a market. Such barriers may limit your own plans or, alternatively, block competitors' responses to an innovative strategy.

For example, Exhibit 4–3 summarizes a competitor analysis in the Japanese market for disposable diapers. P&G was about to replace its original Pampers, which were selling poorly, with a new version that offered improved fit and absorbency. Kao and Unicharm, the two leading Japanese producers, both had better distribution networks. Kao also had a better computer system to handle reorders. Because most Japanese

	P&G's Current and Planned Strategy	Kao's Strengths (+) and Weaknesses (−)	Unicharm's Strengths (+) and Weaknesses (−)
Target Market(s)	Upscale, modern parents who can afford disposable diapers	Same as for P&G	Same as for P&G, but also budget-conscious segment that includes cloth diaper users (+)
Product	Improved fit and absorbency (+); brand-name imagery weak in Japan (−)	Brand familiarity (+), but no longer the best performance (−)	Two brands—for different market segments—and more convenient package with handles (+)
Place	Distribution through independent wholesalers to both food stores and drugstores (+), but handled by fewer retailers (−)	Close relations with and control over wholesalers who carry only Kao products (+); computerized inventory reorder system (+)	Distribution through 80% of food stores in best locations (+); shelf space for two brands (+)
Promotion	Heaviest spending on daytime TV, heavy sales promotion, including free samples (+); small sales force (−)	Large efficient sales force (+); lowest advertising spending (−) and out-of-date ad claims (−)	Advertising spending high (+); effective ads that appeal to Japanese mothers (+)
Price	High retail price (−), but lower unit price for larger quantities (+)	Highest retail price (−), but also best margins for wholesalers and retailers (+)	Lowest available retail price (+); price of premium brand comparable to P&G (−)
(Potential) Competitive Barriers	Patent protection (+), limits in access to retail shelf space (−)	Inferior product (−), excellent logistics support system (+)	Economies of scale and lower costs (+); loyal customers (+)
Likely Response(s)	Improve wholesaler and retailer margins; faster deliveries in channel; change package to require less shelf space	Press retailers to increase in-store promotion; change advertising and/or improve product	Increase short-term sales promotions; but if P&G takes customers, cut price on premium brand

grocery stores and drugstores are very small, frequent restocking by wholesalers is critical. So getting cooperation in the channel was a potential competitive barrier for P&G. To overcome this problem, P&G changed its packaging to take up less space and offered wholesalers and retailers better markups.[10]

Seek information about competitors

A marketing manager should actively seek information about current or potential competitors. Although most firms try to keep the specifics of their plans secret, much public information may be available. Sources of competitor information include trade publications, alert sales reps, middlemen, and other industry experts. In business markets, customers may be quick to explain what competing suppliers are offering.

The Internet is a powerful way to get information about competitors. A firm that puts all of its marketing information on a public website for customers also makes it readily available to competitors. Similarly, it's easy to search through thousands of online publications and databases for any mention of a competitor. It's also increasingly common to specify what you want and instruct a software "robot" to send you a copy as soon as it's available.

Ethical issues may arise

The search for information about competitors sometimes raises ethical issues. For example, people who change jobs and move to competing firms may have a great deal of information, but is it ethical for them to use it? Similarly, some firms have been criticized for going too far—like waiting at a landfill for competitors' trash to find copies of confidential company reports. And the high-tech version of that occurs when computer "hackers" use the Internet to break into a competitor's computer network.

Beyond the moral issues, spying on competitors to obtain trade secrets is illegal. Damage awards can be huge. The courts ordered competing firms to pay Procter & Gamble about $125 million in damages for stealing secrets about its Duncan Hines soft cookies.[11]

You are a salesperson for a company that manufactures industrial lighting used in factories. During a recent sales call, an engineer at your customer firm complains about a new lighting product that his company is testing for a competing supplier. Your company was not aware of the competitor's new product—which you think may make one of your product lines obsolete. Should you pass along this competitive intelligence to your sales manager? Should you question the engineer or others at the customer firm to learn more? If you gather more information, should you share that with your company?

Competition may vary from country to country

A firm that faces very stiff competition may find that the competitive environment and the opportunities are much better in another country. For instance, eight years of slow growth and deregulation made the Japanese market extremely competitive. So Iris Ohyama Inc., a maker of plastic storage containers, started exporting to North America. Within three years, its sales to U.S. retailers like Staples were $60 million.[12]

THE ECONOMIC ENVIRONMENT

The **economic and technological environment** affects the way firms—and the whole economy—use resources. We will treat the economic and technological environments separately to emphasize that the technological environment provides a *base* for the economic environment. Technical skills and equipment affect the way companies convert an economy's resources into output. The economic environment, on the other hand, is affected by the way all of the parts of a macro-economic system interact. This then affects such things as national income, economic growth, and inflation. The economic environment may vary from one country to another, but economies around the world are linked.

Economic conditions change rapidly

The economic environment can, and does, change quite rapidly. The effects can be far-reaching and require changes in marketing strategy.

Even a well-planned marketing strategy may fail if a country or region goes through a rapid business decline. As consumers' incomes drop, they must shift their spending patterns. They may simply have to do without some products. When this happens, many businesses collapse. You can see how quickly this happens by considering what happened in Thailand in the late 1990s. In a few months, the buying power of Thai money (the baht) was cut by half. Imagine how *your* life would change if you suddenly had half as much money.

Economic changes are not always this dramatic. Consider the recent cooling off of the U.S. economy. The growth of the economy leading up to 2000 created a strong job market and increased incomes. Purchases of pricey items and luxuries trended up because of this "wealth effect." This trend changed when the economy turned, but for most products demand declined more gradually.

Interest rates and inflation affect buying

Changes in the economy are often accompanied by changes in the interest rate—the charge for borrowing money. Interest rates directly affect the total price borrowers must pay for products. So the interest rate affects when, and if, they will buy. This is an especially important factor in some business markets. But it also affects consumer purchases of homes, cars, and other items usually bought on credit.

Interest rates usually increase during periods of inflation, and inflation is a fact of life in many economies. In some Latin American countries, inflation has exceeded 400 percent a year in recent years. In contrast, recent U.S. levels—3 to 20 percent—

seem low. Still, inflation must be considered in strategy planning. When costs are rising rapidly and there are no more cost-cutting measures to take, a marketing manager may have to increase prices.

The global economy is connected

The economies of the world are connected—and changes in one economy quickly affect others. One reason for this is that the amount of international trade is increasing—and it is affected by changes in and between economies. For example, International Harvester (IH) was very successful selling its earth-moving equipment in Asia when construction was booming. However, when an economic downturn spread across Asia, many customers could no longer make payments and IH faced big losses.

Changes in the *exchange rate*—how much one country's money is worth in terms of another country's money—have an important effect on international trade. When the dollar is strong, it's worth more in foreign countries. This sounds good—but it makes U.S. products more expensive overseas and foreign products cheaper in the United States. New domestic competition arises as foreign products gain a competitive edge with lower prices.

Marketing managers must watch the economic environment carefully. In contrast to the cultural and social environment, economic conditions can move rapidly and require immediate strategy changes.[13]

THE TECHNOLOGICAL ENVIRONMENT

Technology affects opportunities

Technology is the application of science to convert an economy's resources to output. Technology affects marketing in two basic ways: with new products and with new processes (ways of doing things). For example, advances in information technology make it possible for people in different parts of the world to communicate with satellite videoconferencing and to send complex design drawings over the Internet. Websites enable sophisticated e-commerce exchanges between remote firms. These process changes are accompanied by an exciting explosion of high-tech products— from genome-based medicines to cars that contact the police if they are stolen.

Technology transfer is rapid

New technologies have created important industries that didn't even exist a few years ago. Fifteen years ago eBay didn't exist. Now it's one of the best known firms in the world. With such big opportunities at stake, you can also see why there is such rapid transfer of technology from one part of the world to another. But technology transfer is not automatic. Someone—perhaps you—has to see the opportunity.

Internet technologies are reshaping marketing

Many of the big advances in business have come from early recognition of new ways to do things. There is perhaps no better example of this than the World Wide Web and the Internet. The **Internet** is a system for linking computers around the world. The idea of linking computers in a network is not new. Even so, the Internet expands the network concept to include any computer anywhere and the World Wide Web makes the exchange of information easy. As a result, this technology is radically changing just about every aspect of marketing.

Consider the arena of promotion. The invention of TV changed marketing because it suddenly made it possible for a sponsor to broadcast a vivid message to millions of people at the same time. Now, the Internet makes it possible for that sponsor to select any of millions of messages and to simultaneously narrowcast any of them to millions of different individuals. It is just as easy for customers to request the information in the first place, or to respond electronically once they have it. Thus, the Internet's capability radically changes our ideas about how firms communicate with customers, and vice versa. Similarly, the Internet is creating totally different approaches to pricing. Airlines run online auctions of seats that might otherwise go unsold. To check out an online auction, go to www.ebay.com.

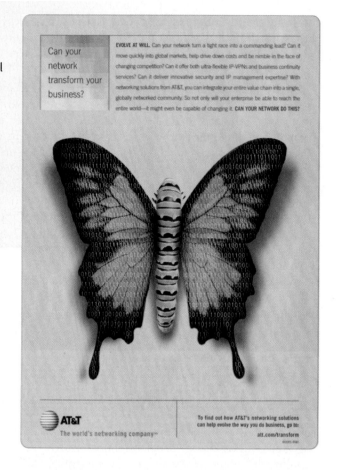

In hindsight, new approaches such as these seem obvious—given that the technology is available. But they are not obvious up front—unless you're really looking for them.[14]

Technology and ethical issues

Marketers often must help their firms decide what technological developments are ethically acceptable. For example, many firms track information about who "hits" the company web page and what website they have come from. The firm can then sell this information to whoever wants to use it to send promotional e-mail. Yet uninvited e-mail is just another form of invasion of privacy.

Some attractive technological developments may be rejected because of their long-run effects on the environment. Aseptic drink boxes, for example, are convenient but difficult to recycle. In a case like this, what's good for the firm and some customers may not be good for the cultural and social environment or acceptable in the political and legal environment. Being close to the market should give marketers a better feel for current trends and help firms avoid serious mistakes.[15]

THE POLITICAL ENVIRONMENT

The attitudes and reactions of people, social critics, and governments all affect the political environment. Consumers in the same country usually share a common political environment, but the political environment can also affect opportunities at a local or international level.

Nationalism can be limiting in international markets

Strong sentiments of **nationalism**—an emphasis on a country's interests before everything else—affect how macro-marketing systems work. They can affect how marketing managers work as well. Nationalistic feelings can reduce sales—or even block all marketing activity—in some international markets. For many years, China has made it difficult for outside firms to do business there—in spite of the fact that

Adero wants marketers to keep in mind that a website that can attract prospects from all over the world won't be successful in turning them into customers if it ignores nationalism and cultural differences.

Chinese producers have enjoyed rapid growth by establishing profitable markets in the United States, Europe, and other parts of the world.

The "Buy American" policy in many government contracts and business purchases reflects this same attitude in the United States. There is broad support for protecting U.S. producers—and jobs—from foreign competition.[16]

Regional groupings are becoming more important

Important dimensions of the political environment are likely to be similar among nations that have banded together to have common regional economic boundaries. The move toward the unification of Europe and free trade among the nations of North America are examples of this sort of regional grouping.

The unification of European markets

In the past, each country in Europe had its own unique trade rules and regulations. These differences made it difficult and expensive to move products from one country to the others. Now, the countries of the European Union (EU) are reducing conflicting laws, taxes, and other obstacles to trade within Europe. This is lowering costs and the prices European consumers pay.

Although Europe is becoming a large unified market, marketers will still encounter differences among European countries. What happened to Lands' End, the U.S.–based Internet and mail-order retailer, illustrates the issues. To better reach European consumers, Lands' End set up shop in England and Germany. As in the United States, its website touted the unconditional lifetime guarantee that is a key part of its strategy. However, German consumer protection rules prohibited promotion of the guarantee; the Germans argued that the promotion was misleading (on the logic that the cost of the guarantee was "hidden" in higher prices that consumers would pay). German officials wanted this ban to apply even if the German consumer purchased the product from a Lands' End website in England. If quirky local rules like this are allowed to prevail, they could erode the benefits that should come from more European unification.[17]

NAFTA is building trade cooperation

The international competition fostered by the moves to unify Europe provided impetus for other cooperative trade agreements, including the **North American Free Trade Agreement (NAFTA)**, which lays out a plan to reshape the rules of trade among the U.S., Canada, and Mexico. NAFTA basically enlarges the free-trade pact that had already knocked down most barriers to U.S.–Canada trade, and over a 15-year period it will eliminate most such barriers with Mexico. It also establishes a forum for resolving future trade disputes.

The changes that result from NAFTA may ultimately be as significant as those in Europe. Talks are under way to explore the concept of expanding NAFTA to create a free-trade zone for 34 countries across North, South, and Central America.

Of course, removal of some economic and political barriers—whether across all of the Americas or Europe—will not eliminate the need to adjust strategies to reach submarkets of consumers. Centuries of cultural differences will not disappear over-night. Some may never disappear.[18]

Some dramatic changes in the political environment—like the fall of communism in Eastern Europe—happen fast and are hard to predict. Yet many important political changes—both within and across nations—evolve more gradually. The development of consumerism is a good example.

Consumerism is here—and basic

Consumerism is a social movement that seeks to increase the rights and powers of consumers. In the last 45 years, consumerism has spread to many different countries, but it was born in America.

The basic goals of modern consumerism haven't changed much since 1962, when President Kennedy's "Consumer Bill of Rights" affirmed consumers' rights to safety, to be informed, to choose, and to be heard.

U.S. consumerism was much more visible in the early days. Consumers staged fre-quent boycotts and protest marches and attracted much media attention. Today, con-sumer groups provide information and work on special projects like product safety standards. Publications like *Consumer Reports* provide product comparisons and infor-mation on other consumer concerns.

Clearly, top management—and marketing managers—must continue to pay atten-tion to consumer concerns. The old, production-oriented ways of doing things are no longer acceptable.[19]

THE LEGAL ENVIRONMENT

Changes in the political environment often lead to changes in the legal environ-ment and in the way existing laws are enforced. The legal environment sets the basic rules for how a business can operate in society. To illustrate the effects of the legal environment, we will discuss how it has evolved in the United States. However, laws often vary from one country to another.

Trying to encourage competition

American economic and legislative thinking is based on the idea that competition among many small firms helps the economy. Therefore, attempts by business to limit competition are considered contrary to the public interest.

Starting in 1890, Congress passed a series of antimonopoly laws. Exhibit 4–4 shows the names and dates of these laws. Although the specific focus of each law is different, in general they are all intended to encourage competition.

Antimonopoly law and marketing mix planning

In later chapters, we will specifically apply antimonopoly law to the four Ps. For now you should note in Exhibit 4–4 what kind of proof the government must have to get a conviction under each of the major laws. You should also note which of the four Ps are most affected by each law.

Prosecution is serious—you can go to jail

Businesses and *individual managers* are subject to both criminal and civil laws. Pen-alties for breaking civil laws are limited to blocking or forcing certain actions—along with fines. Where criminal law applies, jail sentences can be imposed. For example, several managers at Beech-Nut Nutrition Corporation were fined $100,000 each and sent to jail. In spite of ads claiming that Beech-Nut's apple juice was 100 percent natural, they tried to bolster profits by secretly using low-cost artificial ingredients.[20]

Consumer protection laws are not new

Although antimonopoly laws focus on protecting competition, the wording of the laws in Exhibit 4–4 has, over time, moved toward protecting consumers. Some

Exhibit 4-4 Focus (mostly prohibitions) of Federal Antimonopoly Laws on the Four Ps

Law	Product	Place	Promotion	Price
Sherman Act (1890) Monopoly or conspiracy in restraint of trade	Monopoly or conspiracy to control a product	Monopoly or conspiracy to control distribution channels		Monopoly or conspiracy to fix or control prices
Clayton Act (1914) Substantially lessens competition	Forcing sale of some products with others— tying contracts	Exclusive dealing contracts (limiting buyers' sources of supply)		Price discrimination by manufacurers
Federal Trade Commission Act (1914) Unfair methods of competition		Unfair policies	Deceptive ads or selling practices	Deceptive pricing
Robinson-Patman Act (1936) Tends to injure competition		Prohibits paying allowances to "direct" buyers in lieu of middlemen costs (brokerage charges)	Prohibits "fake" advertising allowances or discrimination in help offered	Prohibits price discrimination on goods of "like grade and quality" without cost justification, and limits quanitity discounts
Wheeler-Lea Amendment (1938) Unfair or deceptive practices	Deceptive packaging or branding		Deceptive ads or selling claims	Deceptive pricing
Antimerger Act (1950) Lessens competition	Buying competitors	Buying producers or distributors		
Magnuson-Moss Act (1975) Unreasonable practices	Product warranties			

consumer protections are also built into the English and U.S. common law systems. A seller has to tell the truth (if asked a direct question), meet contracts, and stand behind the firm's product (to some reasonable extent). Beyond this, it is expected that vigorous competition in the marketplace will protect consumers—*so long as they are careful*.

Yet focusing only on competition didn't protect consumers very well in some areas. So the government found it necessary to pass other laws. For example, various laws regulate packaging and labels, telemarketing, credit practices, and environmental issues. Usually, however, the laws focus on specific types of products.

Foods and drugs are controlled

Consumer protection laws in the United States go back to 1906 when Congress passed the Pure Food and Drug Act. Unsanitary meat-packing practices in the Chicago stockyards stirred consumer support for this act. Before the law, it was assumed that common law and the old warning "let the buyer beware" would take care of consumers.

Later acts corrected some loopholes in the law. The law now bans the shipment of unsanitary and poisonous products and requires much testing of drugs. The Food and Drug Administration (FDA) attempts to control manufacturers of these products. It can seize products that violate its rules—including regulations on branding and labeling.

Product safety is controlled

The Consumer Product Safety Act (of 1972), another important consumer protection law, set up the Consumer Product Safety Commission. This group has broad power to set safety standards and can impose penalties for failure to meet those standards. There is some question as to how much safety consumers really want—the commission found the bicycle the most hazardous product under its control!

But given that the commission has the power to *force* a product off the market—or require expensive recalls to correct problems—it is obvious that safety must be considered in product design. And safety must be treated seriously by marketing managers. There is no more tragic example of this than the recalls of Firestone tires used as original equipment on Ford's Explorer SUV. Hundreds of consumers were killed or seriously injured in accidents.[21]

State and local laws vary

Besides federal legislation—which affects interstate commerce—marketers must be aware of state and local laws. There are state and city laws regulating minimum prices and the setting of prices, regulations for starting up a business (licenses, examinations, and even tax payments), and in some communities, regulations prohibiting certain activities—such as telephone selling or selling on Sundays or during evenings.

Internet EXERCISE

The Consumer Product Safety Commission's (CPSC) mission is to protect the public from hazardous products. The government agency also provides safety information for consumers. Go to the website (**www.cpsc.gov**) and click on "CPSC Publications." Look through one of the safety publications that interests you. Did you find it useful? Would it make you change your behavior?

Consumerists and the law say "let the seller beware"

The old rule about buyer–seller relations—let the buyer beware—has changed to *let the seller beware*. The shift to pro-consumer laws and court decisions suggests that lawmakers are more interested in protecting consumers. This may upset production-oriented managers. But times have changed—and managers must adapt to this new political and legal environment.[22]

THE CULTURAL AND SOCIAL ENVIRONMENT

The **cultural and social environment** affects how and why people live and behave as they do—which affects customer buying behavior and eventually the economic, political, and legal environment. Many variables make up the cultural and social environment. Some examples are the languages people speak, the type of education they have, their religious beliefs, what type of food they eat, the style of clothing and housing they have, and how they view work, marriage, and family.

Demographic data and trends tell us a lot about a society and its culture. Understanding the demographic dimensions is also important to marketing strategy planning, so it's useful to look at some key demographic patterns.

Where people are around the world

Exhibit 4–5 summarizes data for representative countries from different regions around the world. Even with a current population of over 309 million, the United States makes up less than 5 percent of the total world population, which is now over 6 billion.

Although the size of a market is important, the population trend is also important. The world's population is growing fast, but that population growth varies dramatically from country to country. In general, less-developed countries experience the fastest

Hybrid Cars Power toward Market Growth

For 100 years, gasoline-powered vehicles have been the king of the road. And unlike some cultures, people in the United States drive everywhere they go. Yet this has created problems. The high cost of gasoline, its environmental impact, and reliance on oil from the politically volatile Middle East long ago led to federal laws that required automakers to improve gas mileage. In response, automakers redesigned vehicles. Even so, progress has been slow. Many consumers prefer big gas-guzzler SUVs that are a better match for their suburban lifestyles.

In the 1990s, to help curb smog in cities like Los Angeles, desperate California lawmakers told automakers that by 2003, 10 percent of the autos and trucks they sell must produce *zero* emissions. To nudge toward that target, a few manufacturers offered electric vehicles. Yet battery-powered cars, like GM's EV1, were very costly, had a drive-range less than 100 miles, and were generally underpowered. A few wealthy celebrities drove them for publicity or to make an environmental "statement." But for most consumers, electric cars were too expensive and the need to plug them into an electric outlet was a real obstacle.

Toyota and Honda were the first to respond to this problem with hybrid vehicles, which combine power from gasoline and electric motors. Initial sales were good, especially given that many consumers are hesitant to adopt a new technology before it is proven to be reliable. Initial sales might have been even higher if it were not for a problem that was revealed by Toyota's marketing research. Even after there were thousands of hybrids on the road, about half of all consumers thought that hybrid models needed to be plugged in (or just didn't know). In light of this, Toyota worked with its ad agency to develop promotions to repeatedly remind consumers that "you never have to plug it in."

Now the market for hybrids is growing rapidly. Toyota and Honda have even had trouble keeping up with the demand for their Prius and Civic hybrids. Shortages existed even when all of the U.S. automakers promoted "employee discounts for everyone" as a way to slash prices on their standard models. Now, however, competition is encouraging innovations in hybrid technology. Costs are lower, mileage is higher, and power is better. Yet, consumers still must pay a premium to own a hybrid. An analysis in *Consumer Reports*, for example, showed that the higher initial cost of hybrids isn't offset by what consumers save on gasoline while they own the car. So, many consumers are still not motivated to pay extra to buy a "green" vehicle. This may explain why Ford's promotion focuses on the increased power of its hybrid SUVs and trucks rather than on an environmental appeal. In the future, we may see other innovations, perhaps hydrogen-powered cars where water is the only thing that comes out of the exhaust. But unless the U.S. culture changes, drivers will expect those vehicles to be big and to offer a lot of power.[23]

rates. Haiti, Madagascar, Nigeria, Somalia, and Uganda, for example, are projected to increase their populations by more than 50 percent between 2010 and 2030. The U.S. population, on the other hand, will grow about 18 percent. During the same time frame, the growth of China's large population is expected to be less than 9 percent while Japan, Russia, and many European countries are projecting population declines. You can see why so many marketers who face slow growth in their domestic markets have turned to international markets where population and sales revenues continue to grow.[24]

The shift to urban and suburban areas

The extent to which a country's population is clustered around urban areas varies a lot. In the United Kingdom, Argentina, Australia, Israel, and Singapore, for example, more than 85 percent of people live in urban areas. (See Exhibit 4–5.) By contrast, in Ethiopia, Nepal, and Uganda less than 16 percent of the people live in major urban areas.

Migration from rural to urban areas has been continuous in the United States since 1800. In 1920, about half the population lived in rural areas. By 1950, the number living on farms dropped to 15 percent—and now it is less than 2 percent. We have become an urban and suburban society.[25]

Exhibit 4-5 Demographic Dimensions for Representative Countries

Country	2010 Projected Population (000s)	2030 Projected Population (000s)	2010–2030 Projected Population Change (%)	2005 Population Density (per square mile)	2005 Percent of Population in Urban Areas	2004 GNI per Capita	2004 GDP (millions of $U.S.)	Estimated Illiteracy Percent
Algeria	34,555	41,600	20.4	36	49	2,280	84,649	32
Argentina	41,405	46,787	13.0	36	89	3,720	151,501	3
Australia	20,925	23,497	12.3	7	91	26,900	631,256	0
Bangladesh	159,765	219,636	37.5	2,594	23	440	56,844	59
Brazil	195,580	222,838	13.9	56	81	3,090	604,855	13
Canada	34,253	39,128	14.2	8	79	28,390	979,764	0
China	1,347,563	1,461,528	8.5	353	37	1,290	1,649,329	14
Egypt	84,348	109,044	29.3	191	43	1,310	75,148	44
Ethiopia	81,754	115,985	41.9	182	15	110	8,077	60
Finland	5,255	5,201	−1.0	40	62	32,790	186,597	0
France	61,638	63,185	2.5	285	76	30,090	2,002,582	0
Germany	82,283	79,572	−3.3	598	88	30,120	2,714,418	0
Greece	10,750	10,583	−1.6	218	60	16,610	203,401	3
Haiti	9,129	13,801	51.2	774	36	390	3,535	49
India	1,155,011	1,420,770	23.0	869	28	620	691,876	42
Israel	6,645	7,873	18.5	874	92	17,380	117,548	5
Italy	58,091	55,360	−4.7	505	90	26,120	1,672,302	2
Japan	127,195	116,338	−8.5	876	79	37,180	4,623,398	0
Kuwait	2,788	4,604	65.1	376	96	17,970	41,748	18
Madagascar	20,993	38,140	81.7	76	26	300	4,364	33
Mexico	112,469	135,172	20.2	142	75	6,770	676,497	9
Morocco	35,301	44,664	26.5	178	57	1,520	50,055	50
Mozambique	20,673	24,323	17.7	63	32	250	5,548	55
Nepal	30,758	42,839	39.3	446	14	260	6,707	57
Nigeria	145,032	231,000	59.3	369	44	390	72,106	35
Pakistan	179,592	244,093	35.9	528	34	600	96,115	56
Romania	22,181	20,827	−6.1	235	53	2,920	73,167	2
Russia	140,771	126,471	−10.2	22	73	3,410	582,395	0
Saudi Arabia	29,222	38,142	30.5	30	86	10,430	250,557	23
Singapore	4,701	5,130	9.1	17,946	100	24,220	106,818	7
Somalia	9,922	16,863	70.0	35	33	—	—	—
Spain	40,549	38,961	−3.9	223	76	21,210	991,442	2
Switzerland	7,623	7,756	1.7	467	68	48,230	359,465	0
Thailand	66,303	71,143	7.3	328	31	2,540	163,491	4
Uganda	32,500	67,604	108.0	289	12	270	6,833	32
U.K.	61,285	64,304	4.9	635	89	33,940	2,140,898	0
U.S.	309,163	363,811	17.7	80	79	41,400	11,667,515	0
Venezuela	27,134	33,429	23.2	76	87	4,020	109,322	7

For many firms, the concentration of people in major cities simplifies Place and Promotion decisions, especially for major cities in the wealthiest nations. Affluent, big-city consumers often have similar lifestyles and needs. Thus, many of the products successful in Toronto, New York, or Paris are likely to be successful in Caracas and Tokyo. The spread of the Internet, satellite TV, and other communication technologies will accelerate this trend.

However, keep in mind that many of the world's consumers—whether crowded in cities or widely spread in rural areas—live in deplorable conditions. These people have little hope of escaping the crush of poverty. They certainly have needs—but they don't have the income to do anything about their needs.

There's no market when there's no income

Profitable markets require income—as well as people. The amount of money people can spend affects the products they are likely to buy. When considering international markets, income is often one of the most important demographic dimensions.

There are a variety of different measures of national income. One widely used measure is **gross domestic product (GDP)**—the total market value of all goods and services provided in a country's economy in a year by both residents and non-residents of that country. *Gross national income (GNI)* is a measure that is similar to GDP, but GNI does not include income earned by foreigners who own resources in that nation. By contrast, GDP does include foreign income. (Note: Until recently, GNI was called gross national product or GNP, so many government documents still include that label.)

When you compare countries with different patterns of international investment, the income measure you use can make a difference. For example, Ford has a factory in Thailand. The GDP measure for Thailand would include the profits from that factory because they were earned in that country. However, Ford is not a Thai firm and most of its profit will ultimately flow out of Thailand. Thus, the Thai GNI would not include those profits. You should see that using GDP income measures can give the impression that people in less-developed countries have more income than they really do. In addition, in a country with a large population the

For firms interested in pursuing international markets, the growing concentration of population and income in major cities often simplifies Place and Promotion decisions.

income of the whole nation must be spread over more people. So GNI *per capita* (per person) is a useful figure because it gives some idea of the income level of people in the country.

Developed economies have most of the income

Exhibit 4–5 gives an estimate of GNI per capita and GDP for each country listed. You can see that the more developed industrial nations—including the United States, Japan, and Germany—account for the biggest share of the world's GDP. In these countries the GNI per capita is also quite high. This explains why so much trade takes place between these countries—and why many firms see them as the more important markets. In general, markets like these offer the best potential for products that are targeted at consumers with higher income levels. As a point of comparison, the GNI per capita in the United States is $41,400.[26]

Many managers, however, see great potential—and less competition—where GNI per capita is low. For example, Mars is making a big push to promote its candy in the countries of Eastern Europe. As with many other firms, it hopes to establish a relationship with consumers now, and then turn strong brand loyalty into profitable growth as consumer incomes increase.

Reading, writing, and marketing problems

The ability of a country's people to read and write has a direct influence on the development of its economy—and on marketing strategy planning. The degree of literacy affects the way information is delivered, which in marketing means promotion. The World Bank estimates that 18 percent of adults (age 15 or older) cannot read. You may be surprised by the high illiteracy rates for some of the countries in Exhibit 4–5.[27]

Much segmenting may be required

Exhibit 4–5 shows that marketers can learn a great deal about possible opportunities in different countries by studying available demographic data and trends. Much useful data is available. For example, *The World Factbook* is prepared by the Central Intelligence Agency (CIA) for the use of U.S. government officials, but it is available to everyone and can be accessed at the CIA's website (www.odci.gov/cia/publications/factbook). The World Bank publishes *The World Development Indicators*, another excellent source for statistics on individual countries. It is available at the World Bank's website (www.worldbank.org/data/wdi). The International Programs Center of the U.S. Census Bureau also publishes an analysis on world population and related topics called *World Population Profile*. You can also access useful statistics for individual countries at the Census Bureau's website (www.census.gov/ipc/idbsum.html).

After finding some countries or regions of possible interest (and eliminating unattractive ones), much more segmenting may be required. To illustrate how useful demographic dimensions can be in this effort, we will consider specific characteristics of the U.S. market in some detail. For additional data on the U.S. market, you can go to the Census Bureau's website (www.census.gov). Similar ideas apply to other markets around the world.

Internet EXERCISE

Michigan State University's Center for International Business Education and Research (CIBER) created globalEDGE—a website with information and tools for learning about global markets. At the home page for the globalEDGE website (*http://globaledge.msu.edu*) select "Resource Desk>Country Insights>View All Countries." Scroll down and select "Italy>Statistics." Examine the statistics listed under the headings "Economy" and "People." Now check the same statistics for Brazil. How are these countries similar? How are they different? What marketing opportunities might be available in each country?

POPULATION TRENDS IN THE U.S. CONSUMER MARKET

The U.S. population is shifting

We've said that the U.S. population is not growing as quickly as in some other countries, but Exhibit 4–6 shows that population growth varies a lot in different regions of the country. The states shaded blue and green in Exhibit 4–6 are growing at the fastest rate. Note that the greatest growth is in western states like Nevada, Arizona, Idaho, and Utah. Growth will continue in the Sun Belt states as well. With growth over 20 percent, Florida leads the way. But Texas, Georgia, North Carolina, and Virginia are also growing rapidly.

These different rates of growth are especially important to marketers. Sudden growth in one area may create a demand for many new shopping centers—while retailers in declining areas face tougher competition for a smaller number of customers.[28]

The mobile ones are an attractive market

As these shifts in population suggest, people move, stay awhile, and then move again. In fact, about 13 percent of Americans move each year. Although over 6 out of 10 moves are within the same county, both the local and long-distance mobiles are important market segments. Many marketing-oriented decisions have to be made fairly quickly after a move. Alert marketers try to locate these potential customers early—to inform them of offerings before they make their purchase decisions. Retail chains, "national" brands, and franchised services available in different areas have a competitive advantage with mobiles. The customer who moves to a new town may find a familiar Walgreens or Blockbuster sign down the street and never even try their local competitors.[29]

Local political boundaries don't define market areas

Marketers are more interested in the size of homogeneous *marketing* areas than in the number of people within political boundaries of a city or county. To meet this need, the U.S. Census Bureau also reports data by **Metropolitan Statistical Area (MSA)**, which is an integrated economic and social unit with a large population nucleus.

Exhibit 4-6 2004 Population (in thousands) and Percent Change in Population by State, 2000–2010

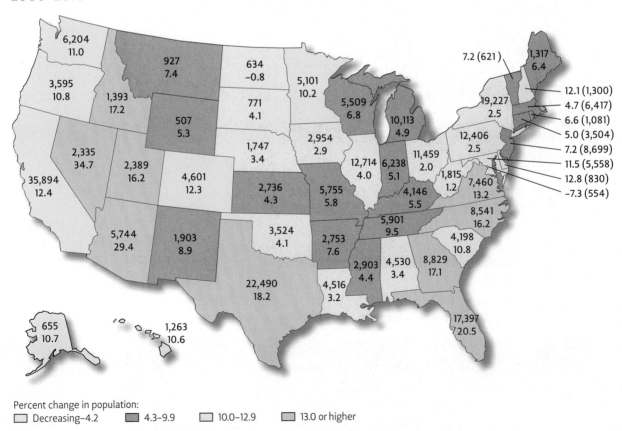

Percent change in population:
☐ Decreasing–4.2 ■ 4.3–9.9 ☐ 10.0–12.9 ■ 13.0 or higher

103

Evaluating Opportunities in the Changing Marketing Environment

Generally, an MSA centers on one city or urbanized area of 50,000 or more inhabitants and includes bordering urban areas.

The largest MSAs—basically those with a population of more than a million—are called Consolidated Metropolitan Statistical Areas. Almost 80 percent of all Americans live in MSAs, and about 40 percent live in the 20 largest CMSAs. More detailed data is available for areas within these sprawling, giant urban areas.

Big targets are attractive—but very competitive

Some national marketers sell only in these metro areas because having so many customers packed into a small area can simplify the marketing effort. They can use fewer middlemen and still offer products conveniently. One or two local advertising media—a city newspaper or TV station—can reach most residents. If a sales force is needed, it will incur less travel time and expense because people are closer together.

Metro areas are also attractive markets because they offer greater sales potential than their large population alone suggests. Consumers in these areas have more money to spend because wages tend to be higher. In addition, professionals—with higher salaries—are concentrated there. But remember that competition for consumer dollars is usually stiff in an MSA.[30]

The graying of America

Another important dimension of U.S. society is the age distribution. In 1980, the median age of the U.S. population was 30—but by 2010 the median age will be about 36. The median age is growing because the percentage of population in older age groups has increased.

Exhibit 4-7 Population Distribution (and percent growth rate) by Age Groups for Different 10-Year Periods

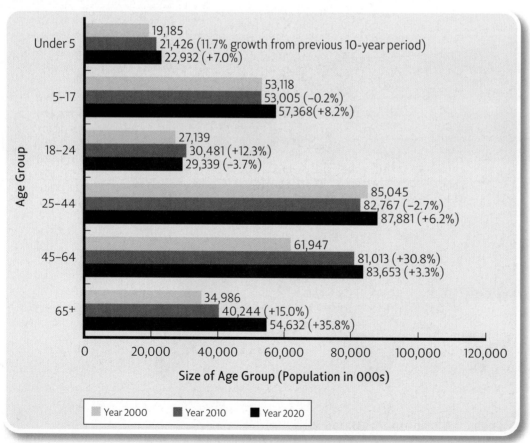

Highly targeted advertising media are proving especially effective at targeting messages to specific demographic groups. For example, AZN Television targets Asian Americans and Nickelodeon targets kids.

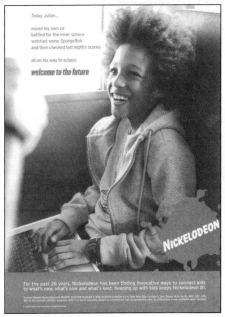

Stated another way, the percentage of the population in different age groups is changing. Exhibit 4–7 shows the number of people in different age groups in 2000—and the expected sizes for 2010 and 2020. Note the big increases under way in the 45 to 64 and 65 and older groups. From 2000 to 2010, the 45 to 64 group grows by 30.8 percent, but then growth in that age group slows to a 3.3 percent increase in the next decade. The over-65 age group is also increasing during this decade by 15.0 percent. However, from 2010 to 2020, a whopping increase of 35.8 percent is expected!

The major reason for the changing distribution is that the post–World War II baby boom produced over one-fourth of the U.S. population. Some of the effects of this big market are very apparent. For example, recording industry sales exploded—to the beat of rock-and-roll music and The Beatles—as the baby boom group moved into their record-buying teens. Soon after, colleges added facilities and faculty to handle the surge, but then had to cope with excess capacity and loss of revenue when the student-age population dwindled. To relieve financial strain, many colleges now add special-interest courses to attract the aging baby boomers, some of whom are beginning to retire. This ongoing growth creates new opportunities for such industries as tourism, health care, and financial services—all of which are important to the middle-aged and retired.

Modern medicine, improved sanitary conditions, and better nutrition help people live longer and are also adding to the proportion of the population in the **senior citizen group**—people over 65.[31]

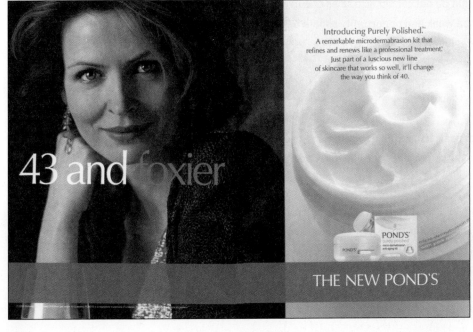

Changes come slowly   The demographic data we've been reviewing shows that changes in basic cultural values and social attitudes come slowly. As a result, an individual firm can't hope to encourage big changes in the short run. Instead, it should identify current attitudes and work within these constraints—as it seeks new and better opportunities.[32]

USING SCREENING CRITERIA TO NARROW DOWN TO STRATEGIES

Developing and applying screening criteria   After you analyze the firm's resources (for strengths and weaknesses), the environmental trends the firm faces, and the objectives of top management, you merge them all into a set of product-market screening criteria. These criteria should include both quantitative and qualitative components. The quantitative components summarize the firm's objectives: sales, profit, and return on investment (ROI) targets. (Note: ROI analysis is discussed briefly in Appendix B, which comes after Chapter 18.) The qualitative components summarize what kinds of businesses the firm wants to be in, what businesses it wants to exclude, what weaknesses it should avoid, and what resources (strengths) and trends it should build on.[33]

Exhibit 4–8   An Example of Product-Market Screening Criteria for a Small Retail and Wholesale Distributor ($10 million annual sales)

1. **Quantitative criteria**

   a. Increase sales by $1,500,000 per year for the next five years.

   b. Earn ROI of at least 25 percent before taxes on new ventures.

   c. Break even within one year on new ventures.

   d. Opportunity must be large enough to justify interest (to help meet objectives) but small enough so company can handle it with the resources available.

   e. Several opportunities should be pursued to reach the objectives—to spread the risks.

2. **Qualitative criteria**

   a. Nature of business preferred.

      (1) Should take advantage of our Internet order system and website promotion.

      (2) New goods and services for present customers to strengthen relationships and customer equity.

      (3) "Quality" products that do not cannibalize sales of current products.

      (4) Competition should be weak and opportunity should be hard to copy for several years.

      (5) There should be strongly felt (even unsatisfied) needs—to reduce promotion costs and permit "high" prices.

   b. Constraints.

      (1) Nature of businesses to exclude.

         (a) Manufacturing.

         (b) Any requiring large fixed capital investments.

         (c) Any requiring many support people who must be "good" all the time and would require much supervision.

      (2) Geographic.

         (a) United States, Mexico, and Canada only.

      (3) General.

         (a) Make use of current strengths.

         (b) Attractiveness of market should be reinforced by more than one of the following basic trends: technological, demographic, social, economic, political.

         (c) Market should not be bucking any basic trends.

Exhibit 4–9
Expected Sales and Cost Curves of Two Strategies over Five-Year Planning Periods

Developing screening criteria is difficult but worth the effort. They summarize in one place what the firm wants to accomplish. When a manager can explain the specific criteria that are relevant to selecting (or screening out) an opportunity, others can understand the manager's logic. Thus, marketing decisions are not just made or accepted based on intuition and gut feel.

The criteria should be realistic—that is, they should be achievable. Opportunities that pass the screen should be able to be turned into strategies that the firm can implement with the resources it has. For example, Exhibit 4–8 illustrates some product-market screening criteria for a small retail and wholesale distributor.

Whole plans should be evaluated

You need to forecast the probable results of implementing a marketing strategy to apply the quantitative part of the screening criteria because only implemented plans generate sales, profits, and return on investment. For a rough screening, you only need to estimate the likely results of implementing each opportunity over a logical planning period. If a product's life is likely to be three years, for example, a good strategy may not produce profitable results for 6 to 12 months. But evaluated over the projected three-year life, the product may look like a winner. When evaluating the potential of possible opportunities (product-market strategies), it is important to evaluate similar things—that is, *whole* plans.

Total profit approach can help evaluate possible plans

Note that managers can often evaluate different marketing plans at the same time. Exhibit 4–9 compares a much improved product and product concept (Product A) with a "me-too" product (Product B) for the same target market. In the short run, the me-too product will make a profit sooner and might look like the better choice—if managers consider only one year's results. The improved product, on the other hand, will take a good deal of pioneering—but over its five-year life it will be much more profitable.

PLANNING GRIDS HELP EVALUATE A PORTFOLIO OF OPPORTUNITIES

When a firm has many possibilities to evaluate, it usually has to compare quite different ones. This problem is easier to handle with graphical approaches—such as the nine-box strategic planning grid developed by General Electric and used by many other companies. Such grids can help evaluate a firm's whole portfolio of strategic plans or businesses.

General Electric looks for green positions

General Electric's (GE) strategic planning grid—see Exhibit 4–10—forces company managers to make three-part judgments (high, medium, and low) about the business strengths and industry attractiveness of all proposed or existing product-market plans. As you can see from Exhibit 4–10, this approach helps a manager organize information about the company's marketing environments (discussed earlier in this chapter) along with information about its strategy and translate it into relevant screening criteria.

Exhibit 4–10
General Electric's
Strategic Planning Grid

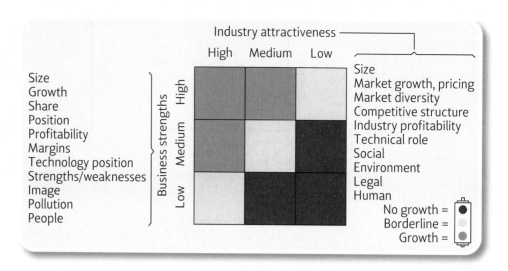

Size
Growth
Share
Position
Profitability
Margins
Technology position
Strengths/weaknesses
Image
Pollution
People

Size
Market growth, pricing
Market diversity
Competitive structure
Industry profitability
Technical role
Social
Environment
Legal
Human

No growth =
Borderline =
Growth =

The industry attractiveness dimension helps managers answer the question: Does this product-market plan look like a good idea? To answer that question, managers have to judge such factors (screening criteria) as the size of the market and its growth rate, the nature of competition, the plan's potential environmental or social impact, and how laws might affect it. Note that an opportunity may be attractive for *some* company—but not well suited to the strengths (and weaknesses) of a particular firm. That is why the GE grid also considers the business strengths dimension.

The business strengths dimension focuses on the ability of the company to pursue a product-market plan effectively. To make judgments along this dimension, a manager evaluates whether the firm has people with the right talents and skills to implement the plan, whether the plan is consistent with the firm's image and profit objectives, and whether the firm could establish a profitable market share given its technical capability, costs, and size. Here again, these factors suggest screening criteria specific to this firm and market situation.

GE feels opportunities that fall into the green boxes in the upper left-hand corner of the grid are its best growth opportunities. Managers give these opportunities high marks on both industry attractiveness and business strengths. The red boxes in the lower right-hand corner of the grid, on the other hand, suggest a no-growth policy. Existing red businesses may continue to generate earnings, but they no longer deserve much investment. Yellow businesses are borderline cases—they can go either way. GE may continue to support an existing yellow business but will probably reject a proposal for a new one. It simply wouldn't look good enough on the relevant screening criteria.

GE's "stoplight" evaluation method is a subjective, multiple-factor approach. It avoids the traps and possible errors of trying to use oversimplified, single-number criteria—like ROI or market share. Instead, top managers review detailed written summaries of many different screening criteria that help them make summary judgments. This approach helps everyone understand why the company supports some new opportunities and not others.[34]

General Electric considers factors that reflect its objectives. Another firm might modify the evaluation to emphasize other screening criteria—depending on its objectives and the type of product-market plans it is considering.

MULTIPRODUCT FIRMS HAVE A DIFFICULT STRATEGY PLANNING JOB

Multiproduct firms, like General Electric, obviously have a more difficult strategic planning job than firms with only a few products or product lines aimed at the same target markets. Multiproduct firms have to develop strategic plans for very different businesses. And they have to balance plans and resources so the whole company reaches its objectives. This means they must approve plans that make sense for the whole company—even if it means getting needed resources by milking some businesses and eliminating others.

Details on how to manage a complicated multiproduct firm are beyond the scope of this book. But you should be aware that the principles in this text are applicable—they just have to be extended. For example, some multiproduct firms form strategic business units (SBUs).

Strategic business units may help

A **strategic business unit (SBU)** is an organizational unit (within a larger company) that focuses on some product-markets and is treated as a separate profit center. By forming SBUs, a company formally acknowledges its very different activities. One SBU of Sara Lee, for example, produces baked goods for consumers and restaurants; another produces and markets Hanes brand T-shirts and underwear.

Some SBUs grow rapidly and require a great deal of attention and resources. Others produce only average profits and should be *milked*—that is, allowed to generate cash for the businesses with more potential. Product lines with poor market position, low profits, and poor growth prospects should be dropped or sold.

EVALUATING OPPORTUNITIES IN INTERNATIONAL MARKETS

Evaluate the risks

The approaches we've discussed apply to international markets just as they do to domestic ones. But in international markets it is often harder to fully understand the marketing environment variables. This may make it more difficult to see the risks involved in particular opportunities. Some countries are politically unstable; their governments and constitutions come and go. An investment safe under one government might become a takeover target under another.

To reduce the risk of missing some basic variable that may help screen out a risky opportunity, marketing managers sometimes need a detailed analysis of the market environment they are considering entering. Such an analysis can reveal facts about an

Lamb Weston is successful in international markets because potatoes—in many different forms—are common in the diet of most cultures. Other products are much more sensitive to cultural differences.

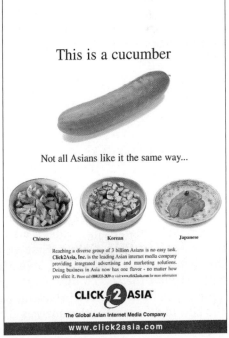

Exhibit 4–11
Continuum of
Environmental
Sensitivity

Insensitive		Sensitive
Industrial products	Basic commodity-type consumer products	Consumer products that are linked to cultural variables

unfamiliar market that a manager in a distant country might otherwise overlook. Further, a local citizen who knows the marketing environment may be able to identify an "obvious" problem ignored even in a careful analysis. Thus, it is very useful for the analysis to include input from locals—perhaps cooperative middlemen.[35]

Risks vary with environmental sensitivity

The farther you go from familiar territory, the greater the risk of making big mistakes. But not all products, or marketing mixes, involve the same risk. Think of the risks as running along a "continuum of environmental sensitivity." See Exhibit 4–11.

Some products are relatively insensitive to the economic and cultural environment they're placed in. These products may be accepted as is—or they may require just a little adaptation to make them suitable for local use. Most industrial products are near the insensitive end of this continuum.

At the other end of the continuum, we find highly sensitive products that may be difficult or impossible to adapt to all international situations. Consumer products closely linked to other social or cultural variables are at this end. For example, some cultures view dieting as unhealthy; that explains why products like Diet Pepsi that are popular in the United States have done poorly there.

This continuum helps explain why many of the early successes in international marketing were basic commodities such as gasoline, soap, transportation vehicles, mining equipment, and agricultural machinery. It also helps explain why some consumer products firms have been successful with basically the same promotion and products in different parts of the globe.

Yet some managers don't understand the reason for these successes. They think they can develop a global marketing mix for just about *any* product. They fail to see that firms producing and/or selling products near the sensitive end of the continuum should carefully analyze how their products will be seen and used in new environments—and plan their strategies accordingly.[36]

What if risks are still hard to judge?

If the risks of an international opportunity are still hard to judge, it may be wise to look first for opportunities that involve exporting. This gives managers a chance to build experience, know-how, and confidence over time. Then the firm will be in a better position to judge the prospects and risks of taking further steps.

CONCLUSION

Businesses need innovative strategy planning to survive in our increasingly competitive markets. In this chapter, we discussed the variables that shape the environment of marketing strategy planning and how they may affect opportunities. First we looked at how the firm's own resources and objectives may help guide or limit the search for opportunities. Then we went on to look at the need to understand competition and how to do a competitive analysis. Then we shifted our focus to the external market environments. They are important because changes in these environments present new opportunities, as well as problems, that a marketing manager must deal with in marketing strategy planning.

The economic environment—including chances of recession or inflation—also affects the choice of strategies. And the marketer must try to anticipate, understand, and deal with these changes—as well as changes in the technology underlying the economic environment.

The marketing manager must also be aware of legal restrictions and be sensitive to changing political climates. The acceptance of consumerism has already forced many changes.

The cultural and social environment affects how people behave and what marketing strategies will be successful.

Developing good marketing strategies within all these environments isn't easy. You can see that marketing management is a challenging job that requires the integration of information from many disciplines.

Eventually, managers need procedures for screening and evaluating opportunities. We explained an approach for developing qualitative and quantitative screening criteria—from an analysis of the strengths and weaknesses of the company's resources, the environmental trends it faces, and top management's objectives. We also discussed ways for evaluating and managing quite different opportunities—using the GE strategic planning grid and SBUs.

Now we can go on in the rest of the book to discuss how to turn opportunities into profitable marketing plans and programs.

KEY TERMS

mission statement, 85

competitive environment, 89

competitor analysis, 90

competitive rivals, 90

competitive barriers, 90

economic and technological
    environment, 92

technology, 93

Internet, 93

nationalism, 94

North American Free Trade Agreement
    (NAFTA), 95

consumerism, 96

cultural and social environment, 98

gross domestic product (GDP), 101

Metropolitan Statistical Area
    (MSA), 103

senior citizen group, 105

strategic business unit (SBU), 109

QUESTIONS AND PROBLEMS

1. Do you think it makes sense for a firm to base its mission statement on the type of product it produces? For example, would it be good for a division that produces electric motors to have as its mission: "We want to make the best (from our customers' point of view) electric motors available anywhere in the world"?

2. Explain how a firm's objectives may affect its search for opportunities.

3. Specifically, how would various company objectives affect the development of a marketing mix for a new type of Internet browser software? If this company were just being formed by a former programmer with limited financial resources, list the objectives the programmer might have. Then discuss how they would affect the development of the programmer's marketing strategy.

4. Explain how a firm's resources may limit its search for opportunities. Cite a specific example for a specific resource.

5. In your own words, explain how a marketing manager might use a competitor analysis to avoid situations that involve head-on competition.

6. The owner of a small hardware store—the only one in a medium-sized town in the mountains—has just learned that a large home improvement chain plans to open a new store nearby. How difficult will it be for the owner to plan for this new competitive threat? Explain your answer.

7. Discuss the probable impact on your hometown if a major breakthrough in air transportation allowed foreign producers to ship their products into any U.S. market for about the same transportation cost that domestic producers incur.

8. Will the elimination of trade barriers between countries in Europe eliminate the need to consider submarkets of European consumers? Why or why not?

9. What and who is the U.S. government attempting to protect in its effort to preserve and regulate competition?

10. For each of the *major* laws discussed in the text, indicate whether in the long run the law will promote or restrict competition (see Exhibit 4–4). As a consumer without any financial interest in business, what is your reaction to each of these laws?

11. Drawing on data in Exhibit 4–5, do you think that Romania would be an attractive market for a firm that produces home appliances? What about Finland? Discuss your reasons.

12. Discuss how the worldwide trend toward urbanization is affecting opportunities for international marketing.

13. Discuss how slower population growth will affect businesses in your local community.

14. Discuss the impact of changes in the size of the 18–24 age group on marketing strategy planning in the U.S.

15. Name three specific examples of firms that have developed a marketing mix to appeal to senior citizens. Name three examples of firms that have developed a marketing mix to appeal to teenagers.

16. Explain the components of product-market screening criteria that can be used to evaluate opportunities.

CREATING MARKETING PLANS

The Marketing Plan Coach software on the Student CD includes a sample marketing plan for Hillside Veterinary Clinic. The situation analysis section of the marketing plan includes sections labeled "Competitors" and "External Market Environment." Review those sections and answer the following questions.

a. In the Competitors section, what dimensions were used to analyze competitors? What other dimensions might have been examined?

b. How was competitor information gathered? How else could Hillside have gathered information about its competitors?

c. What aspects of the External Market Environment are included in the marketing plan? What do you think is the most important information in this section?

SUGGESTED CASES

2. Sunshine Foods, Inc.

6. International Steel Company

22. Bright Light Innovations

33. Collins & Sullivan

COMPUTER-AIDED PROBLEM

4. COMPETITOR ANALYSIS

Mediquip, Inc., produces medical equipment and uses its own sales force to sell the equipment to hospitals. Recently, several hospitals have asked Mediquip to develop a laser-beam "scalpel" for eye surgery. Mediquip has the needed resources, and 200 hospitals will probably buy the equipment. But Mediquip managers have heard that Laser Technologies—another quality producer—is thinking of competing for the same business. Mediquip has other good opportunities it could pursue—so it wants to see if it would have a competitive advantage over Laser Tech.

Mediquip and Laser Tech are similar in many ways, but there are important differences. Laser Technologies already produces key parts that are needed for the new laser product—so its production costs would be lower. It would cost Mediquip more to design the product—and getting parts from outside suppliers would result in higher production costs.

On the other hand, Mediquip has marketing strengths. It already has a good reputation with hospitals—and its sales force calls on only hospitals. Mediquip thinks that each of its current sales reps could spend some time selling the new product and that it could adjust sales territories so only four more sales reps would be needed for good coverage in the market. In contrast, Laser Tech's sales reps call on only industrial customers, so it would have to add 14 reps to cover the hospitals.

Hospitals have budget pressures—so the supplier with the lowest price is likely to get a larger share of the business. But Mediquip knows that either supplier's price will be set high enough to cover the added costs of designing, producing, and selling the new product—and leave something for profit.

Mediquip gathers information about its own likely costs and can estimate Laser Tech's costs from industry studies and Laser Tech's annual report. Mediquip has set up a spreadsheet to evaluate the proposed new product.

a. The initial spreadsheet results are based on the assumption that Mediquip and Laser Tech will split the business 50/50. If Mediquip can win at least 50 percent of the market, does Mediquip have a competitive advantage over Laser Tech? Explain.

b. Because of economies of scale, both suppliers' average cost per machine will vary depending on the quantity sold. If Mediquip had only 45 percent of the market and Laser Tech 55 percent, how would their costs (average total cost per machine) compare? What if Mediquip had 55 percent of the market and Laser Tech only 45 percent? What conclusion do you draw from these analyses?

c. It is possible that Laser Tech may not enter the market. If Mediquip has 100 percent of the market, and quantity purchases from its suppliers will reduce the cost of producing one unit to $6,500, what price would cover all its costs and contribute $1,125 to profit for every machine sold? What does this suggest about the desirability of finding your own unsatisfied target markets? Explain.

For additional questions related to this problem, see Exercise 4-4 in the *Learning Aid for Use with Essentials of Marketing*, 11th edition.

Final Consumers and Their Buying Behavior

When Sony introduced its Walkman in the late 1970s, it quickly became a popular way for on-the-go music lovers to play tapes of their favorite music—anywhere they went. Competing players quickly emerged, but Sony kept its lead by improving its Walkman and then offering models for CDs and digital audiotapes when those media came on the market.

In the late 1990s, the new MP3 format offered quality music from a small digital file that played on a computer or portable player. Diamond Multimedia's Rio was the first MP3 player. The Rio was innovative, but users had to download music from virus-ridden websites like Napster—or use special software to "rip" CDs to MP3 format. Many music buffs liked the idea of having songs at their fingertips but believed that getting the digital files was just too complicated. Further, lawsuits by music companies charged that sharing downloaded MP3 music files was illegal. All of this slowed down the initial adoption of MP3 players.

Attitudes quickly changed when Apple offered an innovative marketing mix that addressed the needs of these target customers. Its online iTunes.com store offered legal downloads of songs at a reasonable price and without the risk of viruses. Apple's free iTunes software made it easy to organize digital music on a computer and transfer it to Apple's iPod. The iPod was designed to be stylish and very easy to use in spite of its ability to play a huge number of songs. And Apple's ads made consumers aware of its new concept and motivated them with the promise of "a thousand songs in your pocket." Even skeptics who ignored the ads couldn't help but notice the distinctive white iPod cords dangling from the ears of a friend who was "in" on this cool new product. That prompted a lot of product conversations and persuasive on-the-spot iPod demos. Testimonials on blogs, website postings, and e-mails also helped spread the word.

Although most iPod owners were satisfied with their purchases, competitors like Dell, Sony, and Creative Labs raised expectations in the market by promoting benefits like longer battery life, capacity for more songs, and lower prices. For some consumers, all of this choice required a more careful purchase decision. For example, some would search for information and reviews on the Internet or talk with salespeople in stores to figure out which model was best. Of course, some iPod fanatics didn't bother with that extra effort; they just upgraded to whatever improved models Apple brought to market.

Apple also built on its relationship with loyal iPod users by offering profitable accessories, like a kit to allow an iPod to play through a car's radio.

In just a few years, annual iPod sales jumped to more than 22 million. They were becoming so common that some trendsetters thought they were no longer cool. But Apple rose to that challenge with a campaign of billboard, magazine, and TV ads showing silhouettes of people dancing. The ads were everywhere. At the same time, Apple actively encouraged other companies to develop iPod accessories—like new cases and portable speakers—so consumers could individualize their players.

Next, Apple began promoting iPod versions to appeal to different market segments. For example, a Harry Potter iPod, complete with Hogwarts' crest, appealed to kids, and a black U2 model targeted their parents. For customers who thought the iPod was too pricey, Apple developed the Shuffle. And by partnering with companies like Audible.com, which distributes downloadable books, Apple offered value for customers who wanted more than music.

By innovating, Apple provided consumers with fresh new styles, increased capacities, smaller sizes, and added features—like the ability to play videos. All of this also appealed to retailers. They liked the iPod's high profit margins and the large number of customers who returned to buy accessories.

Many consumers say they want a combination cell phone–MP3 player. This type of player is already popular in Japan, where the high-speed wireless network makes music downloads much faster than in the U.S. So, Apple partnered with Motorola to offer the ROKR, a cell phone and MP3 player that works with Apple iTunes. The ROKR's capacity is just 100 songs and it doesn't have iPod's stylish flair or brand name. However, perhaps Apple didn't want the ROKR to take customer attention away from the more profitable iPod. Even so, consumer desires can shift quickly. Apple will have to continue to adapt to changes in consumer behavior if it is to continue its success.[1]

LEARNING OBJECTIVES

Many variables influence consumer buying behavior. As the iPod case highlights, successful marketing strategy planning requires a clear understanding of how target consumers buy—and what factors affect their decisions. The learning objectives for this chapter will help you develop that understanding.

When you finish this chapter, you should:

1. be able to describe how economic needs and income influence the buyer decision process.

2. understand how psychological variables affect an individual's buying behavior.

3. understand how social influences affect an individual's buying behavior.

4. be able to explain how characteristics of the purchase situation influence consumer behavior.

5. be able to explain the process by which consumers make buying decisions.

6. understand important new terms (shown in red).

CONSUMER BEHAVIOR—WHY DO THEY BUY WHAT THEY BUY?

The iPod case shows that effective marketing strategy planning requires a real understanding of customers and why they buy as they do. Without that knowledge, it is difficult to zero in on the right target market or to develop a marketing mix that will provide the best value for those customers.

Understanding consumer behavior can be a challenge. Specific behaviors vary a great deal for different people, products, and purchase situations. In today's global markets, the variations on buying behavior are countless. That makes it impractical to catalog all the possibilities. But there are general behavioral principles—frameworks—that marketing managers can apply to better understand their specific target markets. In this chapter our approach focuses on developing your skill in working with these frameworks by exploring thinking from economics, psychology, sociology, and other behavioral disciplines. We'll take a look at the topics overviewed in Exhibit 5–1, which includes a simplified model of consumer behavior. Then we'll expand the model and cover the consumer decision process in more detail.

ECONOMIC NEEDS AFFECT MOST BUYING DECISIONS

Economic buyers seek the best uses of their money

Most economists assume that consumers are **economic buyers**—people who know all the facts and logically compare choices to get the greatest satisfaction from spending their time and money. The economic buyer theory says that consumers decide what to buy based on **economic needs**, which are concerned with making the best use of a consumer's time and money—as the consumer judges it. Some consumers look for the lowest price. Others will pay extra for convenience. And others may weigh price and quality for the best value. Some economic needs are

1. Economy of purchase or use.
2. Convenience.
3. Efficiency in operation or use.
4. Dependability in use.
5. Improvement of earnings.

Clearly, marketing managers must be alert to new ways of appealing to economic needs. Most consumers appreciate firms that offer them improved economic value for the money they spend. But improved value does not just mean offering lower and lower prices. For example, products can be designed to work better, require less service, or last longer. Promotion can inform consumers about product benefits in terms

Exhibit 5–1 Consumer Behavior for Marketing Strategy Planning

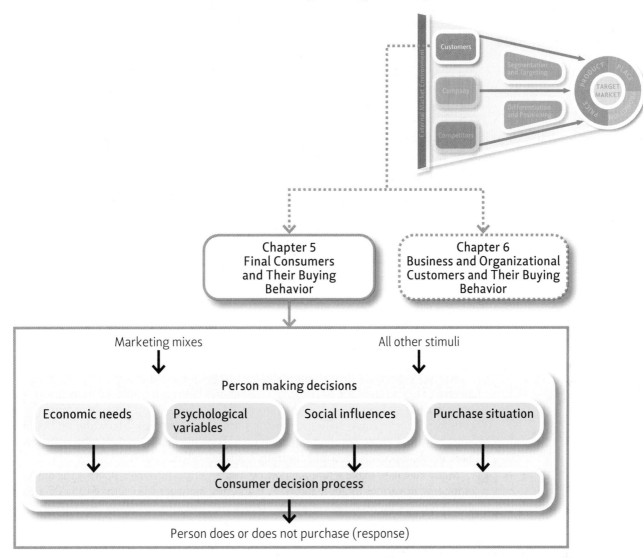

of measurable factors like operating costs, the length of the guarantee, or the time a product will save. Carefully planned Place decisions can make purchasing easier and faster for customers who face a poverty of time.

Discretionary income is elusive

In most households, people don't have enough income to buy everything that they want. For many products, these people can't be customers even if they want to be. For example, most families spend a good portion of their income on such necessities as food, rent or house payments, car and home furnishings, and insurance. A family's purchase of "luxuries" comes from **discretionary income**—what is left of income after paying taxes and paying for necessities.

Discretionary income is an elusive concept because the definition of necessities varies from family to family and over time. It depends on what they think is necessary for their lifestyle. A cable TV service purchased out of discretionary income by a lower-income family may be considered a necessity by a higher-income family.

The higher-income consumers receive a big share

It's useful to put these income effects on buying in perspective. Exhibit 5–2 divides all U.S. families into five equal-sized groups—from lowest to highest income—and shows the total income for each group. Exhibit 5–2 shows that higher-income

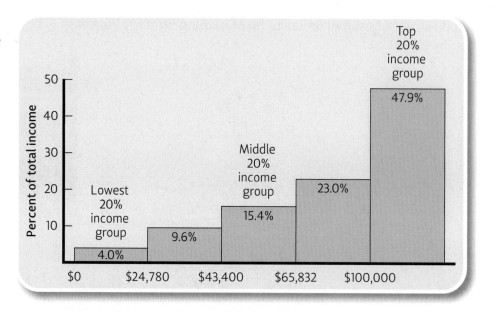

consumers receive a very large share of total income. The top 20 percent of the families—those with incomes over $100,000—receive almost 48 percent of the total income. This gives them extra buying power, especially for luxury items like memberships in country clubs and yachts. Well-to-do families with incomes over $173,640—the top 5 percent nationally—receive 21 percent of the total income.

At the lower end of the income scale, over 15 million families have less than $24,780 income. They account for 20 percent of all families but receive only 4.0 percent of total income. Half of them live below the poverty level of $19,307 for a family of four. These consumers may receive assistance in the form of food stamps, Medicare, and public housing, which increases their buying power. They may have enough money for some basic needs, especially food and clothing, but that's often about it.

How much income is "enough"?

Many managers make serious marketing strategy errors by overestimating the amount of income in various target markets. A marketing manager who earns $135,000 a year may have no clue what life is like for a family that lives on $25,000 a year.

Marketers are very aware that spending varies with income and other demographic dimensions.

Exhibit 5–3 A Model of Influences on Consumer Behavior

Person does or does not purchase (response)

The 2004 U.S. median family income of about $54,061 is a useful reference point because some college graduates start near that level. This may seem like a lot of money at first—but America's middle-income consumers have been hit hard by the spiraling costs of health care, housing, energy, cars, taxes, and tuition bills. More than ever, these consumers need to pinch their pennies and search for products that are a good value. This reality explains much of the buying behavior of lower and middle-income markets in the U.S.[2]

There's no doubt that income and economic needs are important factors in many purchase decisions. But most marketing managers think that buyer behavior is not as simple as the economic-buyer model suggests. Even when two people have the same income level, a product that one person sees as a good value—and is eager to buy—may be of no interest to someone else. So we can't expect to understand buying behavior without taking a broader view that includes the other behavioral dimensions that influence consumers. Exhibit 5–3 shows that a number of psychological variables, social influences, and the purchase situation itself combine with economic needs to affect buying behavior. We'll discuss these topics in the next few pages. Then we'll expand the model to include the consumer problem-solving process.

PSYCHOLOGICAL INFLUENCES WITHIN AN INDIVIDUAL

Needs motivate consumers

Everybody is motivated by needs and wants. **Needs** are the basic forces that motivate a person to do something. Some needs involve a person's physical well-being, others the individual's self-view and relationship with others. Needs are more basic than wants. **Wants** are "needs" that are learned during a person's life. For example, everyone needs water or some kind of liquid, but some people also have learned to want Clearly Canadian's raspberry-flavored sparkling water on the rocks.

When a need is not satisfied, it may lead to a drive. The need for liquid, for example, leads to a thirst drive. A **drive** is a strong stimulus that encourages action to reduce a need. Drives are internal—they are the reasons behind certain behavior patterns. In marketing, a product purchase results from a drive to satisfy some need.

Some critics imply that marketers can somehow manipulate consumers to buy products against their will. But trying to get consumers to act against their will is a waste of time. Instead, a good marketing manager studies what consumer drives, needs, and wants already exist and how they can be satisfied better.

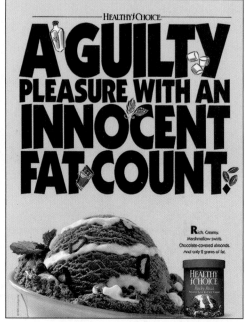

Consumers seek benefits to meet needs

We're all a bundle of needs and wants. Exhibit 5–4 lists some important needs that might motivate a person to some action. This list, of course, is not complete. But thinking about such needs can help you see what *benefits* consumers might seek from a marketing mix.

When a marketing manager defines a product-market, the needs may be quite specific. For example, the food need might be as specific as wanting a Domino's thick-crust pepperoni pizza—delivered to your door hot and ready to eat.

Several needs at the same time

Consumer psychologists often argue that a person may have several reasons for buying—at the same time. Maslow is well known for his five-level hierarchy of needs.

Exhibit 5–4 Possible Needs Motivating a Person to Some Action

Types of Needs	Specific Examples			
Physiological needs	Hunger Sex Rest	Thirst Body elimination	Activity Self-preservation	Sleep Warmth/coolness
Psychological needs	Aggression Family preservation Nurturing Playing-relaxing Self-identification	Curiosity Imitation Order Power Tenderness	Being responsible Independence Personal fulfillment Pride	Dominance Love Playing-competition Self-expression
Desire for . . .	Acceptance Affiliation Comfort Esteem Knowledge Respect Status	Achievement Appreciation Leisure Fame Prestige Retaliation Sympathy	Acquisition Beauty Distance—"space" Happiness Pleasure Self-satisfaction Variety	Affection Companionship Distinctiveness Identification Recognition Sociability Fun
Freedom from . . .	Fear Pain Harm	Depression Stress Ridicule	Discomfort Loss Sadness	Anxiety Illness Pressure

We will discuss a similar four-level hierarchy that is easier to apply to consumer behavior. Exhibit 5–5 illustrates the four levels along with an advertising slogan showing how a company has tried to appeal to each need. The lowest-level needs are physiological. Then come safety, social, and personal needs.[3]

Physiological needs are concerned with biological needs—food, drink, rest, and sex. **Safety needs** are concerned with protection and physical well-being (perhaps involving health, food, medicine, and exercise). **Social needs** are concerned with love, friendship, status, and esteem—things that involve a person's interaction with others. **Personal needs,** on the other hand, are concerned with an individual's need for personal satisfaction—unrelated to what others think or do. Examples include self-esteem, accomplishment, fun, freedom, and relaxation.

Motivation theory suggests that we never reach a state of complete satisfaction. As soon as we get our lower-level needs reasonably satisfied, those at higher levels become more dominant. This explains why marketing efforts targeted at affluent consumers in advanced economies often focus on higher-level needs. It also explains why these approaches may be useless in parts of the world where consumers' basic needs are not being met.

A particular product may satisfy more than one need at the same time. In fact, most consumers try to fill a *set* of needs rather than just one need or another in sequence. Determining which needs to satisfy may require careful analysis. Consider, for example, the lowly vegetable peeler. Marketing managers for OXO International realized that many people, especially young children and senior citizens, have trouble gripping the handle of a typical peeler. OXO redesigned the peeler with a bigger handle that addressed this physical need. OXO also coated the handle with dishwasher-safe rubber. This makes cleanup more convenient—and the sharp peeler is safer to use when the grip is wet. The attractively designed grip also appeals to consumers who get

Exhibit 5–5   The PSSP Hierarchy of Needs (physiological, safety, social, personal)

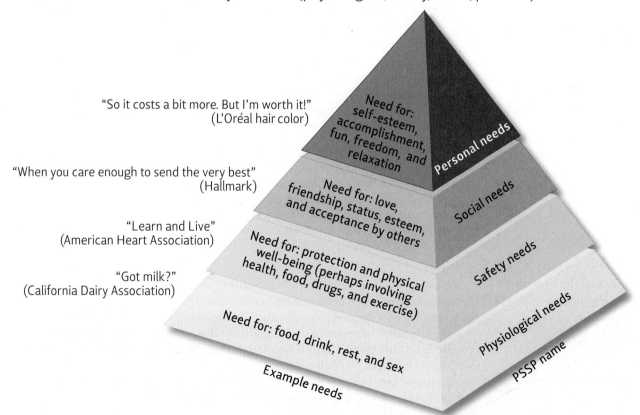

"So it costs a bit more. But I'm worth it!"
(L'Oréal hair color)

"When you care enough to send the very best"
(Hallmark)

"Learn and Live"
(American Heart Association)

"Got milk?"
(California Dairy Association)

Need for: self-esteem, accomplishment, fun, freedom, and relaxation — **Personal needs**

Need for: love, friendship, status, esteem, and acceptance by others — **Social needs**

Need for: protection and physical well-being (perhaps involving health, food, drugs, and exercise) — **Safety needs**

Need for: food, drink, rest, and sex — **Physiological needs**

Example needs

PSSP name

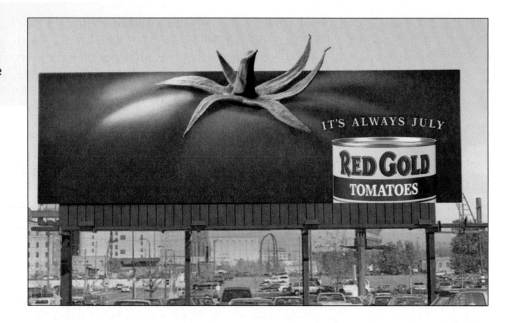

personal satisfaction from cooking. The premium-priced peeler has sold very well because it appeals to people with a variety of needs. Since that initial success, OXO has redesigned many everyday utensils, including its new scoop colander. The colander's long handle makes it safe and easy to scoop and drain cooked pasta—without handling a hot pan or boiling water.[4]

Perception determines what consumers see and feel

Consumers sometimes select varying ways to meet their needs because of differences in **perception**—how we gather and interpret information from the world around us.

We are constantly bombarded by stimuli—ads, products, stores—yet we may not hear or see anything. This is because we apply the following selective processes:

1. **Selective exposure**—our eyes and minds seek out and notice only information that interests us. How often have you closed a pop-up ad at a website without even noticing what it was for?
2. **Selective perception**—we screen out or modify ideas, messages, and information that conflict with previously learned attitudes and beliefs.
3. **Selective retention**—we remember only what we want to remember.

These selective processes help explain why some people are not affected by some advertising—even offensive advertising. They just don't see or remember it! Even if they do, they may dismiss it immediately.

Our needs affect these selective processes. And current needs receive more attention. For example, Goodyear tire retailers advertise some sale in the newspaper almost weekly. Most of the time we don't even notice these ads. Only when we need new tires do we tune in to Goodyear's ads.

Learning determines what response is likely

Learning is a change in a person's thought processes caused by prior experience. Learning is often based on direct experience: A little girl tastes her first cone of Ben & Jerry's Cherry Garcia flavor ice cream, and learning occurs! Learning may also be based on indirect experience or associations. If you watch an ad that shows other people enjoying Ben & Jerry's Chocolate Fudge Brownie low-fat frozen yogurt, you might conclude that you'd like it too.

Consumer learning may result from things that marketers do, or it may result from stimuli that have nothing to do with marketing. Either way, almost all consumer behavior is learned.[5]

Most people love homemade cake, but some think that baking and frosting a cake is a time-consuming hassle. Betty Crocker's new pourable frosting is fast and easy, but promotion such as this ad gives consumers a way to learn that it's available.

Introducing the world's first pourable frosting.
(Yes, it's that easy.)

Experts describe a number of steps in the learning process. We've already discussed the idea of a drive as a strong stimulus that encourages action. Depending on the **cues**—products, signs, ads, and other stimuli in the environment—an individual chooses some specific response. A **response** is an effort to satisfy a drive. The specific response chosen depends on the cues and the person's past experience.

Reinforcement of the learning process occurs when the response is followed by satisfaction—that is, reduction in the drive. Reinforcement strengthens the relationship between the cue and the response. And it may lead to a similar response the next time the drive occurs. Repeated reinforcement leads to development of a habit—making the individual's decision process routine. Exhibit 5–6 shows the relationships of the important variables in the learning process.

The learning process can be illustrated by a thirsty person. The thirst *drive* could be satisfied in a variety of ways. But if the person happened to walk past a vending machine and saw a Mountain Dew sign—a *cue*—then he might satisfy the drive with a *response*— buying a Mountain Dew. If the experience is satisfactory, positive *reinforcement* occurs, and our friend may be quicker to satisfy this drive in the same way in the future. This emphasizes the importance of developing good products that live up to the promises of the firm's advertising. People can learn to like or dislike Mountain Dew—reinforcement and learning work both ways. Unless marketers satisfy their customers, they must constantly try to attract new ones to replace the dissatisfied ones who don't come back.

Exhibit 5–6
The Learning Process

Drive → Cues → Response

Reinforcement

Positive cues help a marketing mix

Sometimes marketers try to identify cues or images that have positive associations from some other situation and relate them to their marketing mix. Many people associate the smell of lemons with a fresh, natural cleanliness. So companies often add lemon scent to household cleaning products—Clorox bleach and Pledge furniture polish, for example—because it has these associations. Similarly, firms like Calvin Klein use ads suggesting that people who use their products have more appeal to the opposite sex. Simple cues may even be important for a big purchase. Luxury-car makers try for a "new-car smell" with an aroma of leather and wood, even though the car really smells more like metal and adhesives as it comes off the production line in a factory.[6]

Many needs are culturally learned

Many needs are culturally (or socially) learned. The need for food, for instance, may lead to many specific food wants. Many Japanese enjoy sushi (raw fish), and their children learn to like it. Fewer Americans, however, have learned to enjoy it.

Some critics argue that marketing efforts encourage people to spend money on learned wants totally unrelated to any basic need. For example, Germans are less concerned about perspiration, and many don't buy or use antiperspirants. Yet Americans spend millions of dollars on such products. Advertising says that using Ban deodorant "takes the worry out of being close." But is marketing activity the cause of the difference in the two cultures? Most research says that advertising can't convince buyers of something contrary to their basic attitudes.

Attitudes relate to buying

An **attitude** is a person's point of view toward something. The "something" may be a product, an advertisement, a salesperson, a firm, or an idea. Attitudes are important because they affect selective processes, learning, and buying decisions.

Because attitudes are usually thought of as involving liking or disliking, they have some action implications. Beliefs are not so action-oriented. A **belief** is a person's opinion about something. Beliefs may help shape a consumer's attitudes but don't necessarily involve any liking or disliking. It is possible to have a belief—say, that Listerine PocketPak strips have a medicinal taste—without really caring what they taste like. On the other hand, beliefs about a product may have a positive or negative effect in shaping consumers' attitudes. For example, promotion for Splenda, a new no-cal sweetener in a yellow packet, informs consumers that it's "made from sugar so it tastes like sugar." A dieter who believes that Splenda will taste better because it is made from sugar might try it instead of just routinely rebuying another brand, like Equal. On the other hand, a person with diabetes might believe that he should avoid Splenda—like he avoids other products made from sugar—even though Splenda is actually suitable for people with diabetes.[7]

In an attempt to relate attitude more closely to purchase behavior, some marketers stretch the attitude concept to include consumer "preferences" or "intention to buy." Managers who must forecast how much of their brand customers will buy are particularly interested in the intention to buy. Forecasts would be easier if attitudes were good predictors of intentions to buy. Unfortunately, the relationships usually are not that simple. A person may have positive attitudes toward GPS navigation systems for cars, but no intention of buying one.

Try to understand attitudes and beliefs

Research on consumer attitudes and beliefs can sometimes help a marketing manager get a better picture of markets. For example, research showed that some consumers thought that Purina Dog Chow was a great dog food, but they didn't buy it all of the time. They believed that their dogs would get bored with it. But vets have found dogs benefit from a good, consistent diet. So Purina developed an ad campaign to convince these dog owners that what they believed was not true. Each ad gave a dog's-eye-view reaction to being fed a different dog food. In one ad, after taking a few bites, the dog looks into the camera with a pained expression and walks away. He returns with a packet of antacid, which he drops in his water bowl. Such ads helped convince consumers that switching foods was not good, and Dog Chow sales increased. Consumer beliefs—right or wrong—can have a significant impact on whether a strategy succeeds.[8]

Most marketers work with existing attitudes

Purina's efforts were successful in changing beliefs. But marketers generally try to understand the attitudes of their potential customers and work with them. Because attitudes tend to be enduring, it's usually more economical to work with consumer attitudes than to try to change them. Changing negative attitudes is probably the most difficult job marketers face.[9]

Ethical issues may arise

Part of the marketing job is to inform and persuade consumers about a firm's offering. An ethical issue sometimes arises, however, if consumers have *inaccurate* beliefs. For example, promotion of a "children's cold formula" may play off parents' fears that adult medicines are too strong—even though the basic ingredients in the children's formula are the same and only the dosage is different.

Salud! For Better Health, Spaniards Drink Bacteria for Breakfast

During the 1990s, many European consumers began to change their relaxed approach to meals. A bustling economy led to busier lifestyles, which prompted more interest in eat-on-the-go foods. This was even true of breakfast, which for many Europeans traditionally had meant a leisurely cup of coffee and a croissant. And, with more consumers entering the older age groups, there was also an increased interest in healthy eating.

Marketing managers for France's Danone spotted these trends and thought the firm's Actimel yogurt might address some of these needs. Indeed, scientists had already shown that consumers who regularly drink Actimel were healthier. Yet, there were challenges. Actimel is healthy because each serving contains over 10 billion live bacteria, like the "friendly" ones in the human body, that aid digestion. Yet, most consumers didn't understand that—and drinking bacteria doesn't sound like an appealing idea. To make things worse, marketing research revealed that consumers thought that yogurts were either tasty *or* healthy—but not both! They believed that healthy yogurts had an undesirable medicinal taste.

To help change this perception, Danone developed new Actimel flavors that would delight consumers once they tried the product. Even so, some consumers lost interest when they learned that the cost of Actimel was double that of regular yogurts. On the other hand, Actimel's higher price helped to pay for heavy introductory advertising to inform more consumers about its valuable health benefits. Actimel's attention-getting ads used appeals such as "Fight the cold. Practice self-defense." Still, many doubters remained unconvinced that Actimel could either improve their health or taste good. Danone was finally able to gain more trial and change attitudes with the "Actimel Challenge." With this challenge Danone promised to give consumers their money back if they didn't like Actimel and feel better after drinking it for two weeks.

Selling Actimel at health food stores might have reinforced its premium health positioning and provided more initial sales support. But Danone wanted customers to be able to find and buy Actimel easily. So distribution focused on placing four-packs in regular supermarkets and single-serve packages in convenience stores.

Over time, favorable consumer experience with this marketing mix has grown Actimel into a brand that many Europeans routinely purchase. In Spain it even outsells Coca-Cola. It has also sold well in other parts of the world, including Asia. Even so, Actimel never became popular among U.S. consumers. But Danone is still trying. It recently reintroduced the yogurt in the U.S. as Activia. Apparently, Activia's marketers hope that the American culture is now ready to accept the idea of drinking "bugs" as a tasty way to be healthy.[10]

Marketers also must be careful about promotion that might encourage false beliefs, even if the advertising is not explicitly misleading. For example, ads for Ultra Slim-Fast low-fat beverages don't claim that anyone who buys the product will lose weight and look like the slim models in the ads—but some critics argue that the advertising gives that impression.[11]

Meeting expectations is important

Attitudes and beliefs sometimes combine to form an **expectation**—an outcome or event that a person anticipates or looks forward to. Consumer expectations often focus on the benefits or value that the consumer expects from a firm's marketing mix. This is an important issue for marketers because a consumer is likely to be dissatisfied if his or her expectations are not met. Promotion that overpromises can create this problem. Finding the right balance, however, can be difficult. A few years ago Van Heusen came up with a new way to treat its wash-and-wear shirts so that they look better when they come out of the wash. Van Heusen promoted these shirts as "wrinkle-free." The new shirt is an improvement, but consumers who expected it to look as if it had been ironed were disappointed.[12]

Personality affects how people see things

Many researchers study how personality affects people's behavior, but the results have generally been disappointing to marketers. A trait like neatness can be associated with users of certain types of products—like cleaning materials. But marketing managers have not found a way to use personality in marketing strategy planning.[13] As a result, they've stopped focusing on personality measures borrowed from psychologists and instead developed lifestyle analysis.

Psychographics focus on activities, interests, and opinions

Psychographics or **lifestyle analysis** is the analysis of a person's day-to-day pattern of living as expressed in that person's Activities, Interests, and Opinions—sometimes referred to as AIOs. Exhibit 5–7 shows a number of variables for each of the AIO dimensions—along with some demographics used to add detail to the lifestyle profile of a target market.

Understanding the lifestyle of target customers has been especially helpful in providing ideas for advertising themes. Let's see how it adds to a typical demographic description. It may not help Toyota marketing managers much to know that an average member of the target market for a Highlander SUV is 34.8 years old, married, lives in a three-bedroom home, and has 2.3 children. Lifestyles help marketers paint a more human portrait of the target market. For example, lifestyle analysis might show that the 34.8-year-old is also a community-oriented consumer with traditional values who especially enjoys spectator sports and spends much time in other family activities.

Exhibit 5–7
Lifestyle Dimensions (and some related demographic dimensions)

Dimension	Examples		
Activities	Work Hobbies Social events	Vacation Entertainment Club membership	Surfing Web Shopping Sports
Interests	Family Home Job	Community Recreation Fashion	Food Media Achievements
Opinions	Themselves Social issues Politics	Business Economics Education	Products Future Culture
Demographics	Income Age Family life cycle	Geographic area Ethnicity Dwelling	Occupation Family size Education

The Harley-Davidson marketing mix often emphasizes the lifestyle and psychographics of its target customers, not just the features of its popular motorcycles.

"YOU, IN THE MINIVAN, HOW LONG YOU IN FOR?"

IT'S TIME TO RIDE. HARLEY-DAVIDSON MOTOR CYCLES

An ad might show the Highlander being used by a happy family at a ball game so the target market could really identify with the ad. And the ad might be placed on an ESPN show whose viewers match the target lifestyle profile.[14]

Marketing managers for consumer products firms who are interested in learning more about the lifestyle of a target market sometimes turn to outside specialists for help. For example, SRI Consulting Business Intelligence (SRIC-BI), a research firm, offers a service called geoVALS (VALS is an abbreviation for values, attitudes, and lifestyles). GeoVALS uses psychographics to show where customers live and why they behave as they do; it is especially useful for targeting direct-mail ad campaigns.[15]

Internet EXERCISE

Go to the SRIC-BI Internet site (*www.sric-bi.com*), click on VALS survey, and then click on "Take the Survey" to review the VALS questionnaire. If you wish, complete the short questionnaire online.

SOCIAL INFLUENCES AFFECT CONSUMER BEHAVIOR

We've been discussing some of the ways needs, attitudes, and other psychological variables influence the buying process. Now we'll look at how the individual interacts with family, social class, and other groups who may have influence.

Family life cycle influences needs

Relationships with other family members influence many aspects of consumer behavior. Family members may also share many attitudes and values, consider each other's opinions, and divide various buying tasks. Marital status, age, and the age of any children in the family have an especially important effect on how people spend their income. Put together, these dimensions tell us about the life-cycle stage of a family. Exhibit 5–8 shows a summary of stages in the family life cycle.[16]

Young people and families accept new ideas

Singles and young couples seem to be more willing to try new products and brands—and they are careful, price-conscious shoppers. Although many young people are waiting longer to marry, most do tie the knot eventually. These younger families—especially those with no children—are still accumulating durable goods, such as automobiles and home furnishings. Only as children arrive and grow does family spending shift to soft goods and services, such as education, medical, and personal care. This usually happens when the family head reaches the 35–49 age group. To meet expenses, people in this age group often make more purchases on credit, and they save less of their income.

Divorce—increasingly a fact of American life—disrupts the traditional family life-cycle pattern. The mother usually has custody of the children, and the father may pay child support. The mother and children typically have much less income than two-parent families. Such families spend a larger percent of their income on housing, child care, and other necessities—with little left for discretionary purchases. If a single parent remarries, the family life cycle may start over again.[17]

Exhibit 5–8   Stages in Modern Family Life Cycle

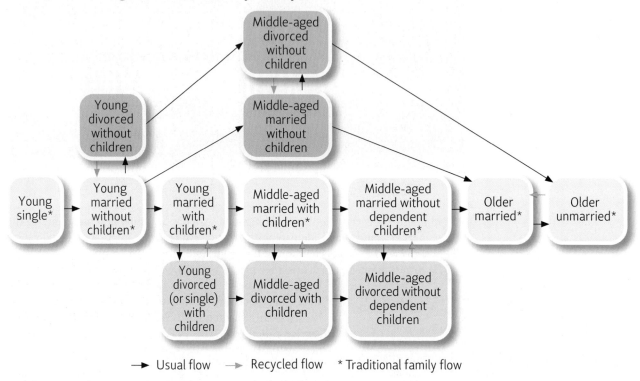

→ Usual flow   → Recycled flow   * Traditional family flow

Reallocation for teenagers

Once children become teenagers, further shifts in spending occur. Teenagers eat more, want to wear expensive clothes, and develop recreation and education needs that are hard on the family budget. America's teens currently spend over $170 billion a year. They are a target for many firms. MasterCard is targeting teens with its credit card promotions and Bausch & Lomb's contact-lens sales hit record levels when the firm refocused its marketing efforts on teens.[18]

Selling to the empty nesters

Another important category is the **empty nesters**—people whose children are grown and who are now able to spend their money in other ways. Usually these people are in the 50–64 age group. This tends to be a high-income period, especially for white-collar workers.

Empty nesters are an attractive market for many items. Often they spend more on travel and other things they couldn't afford before. Much depends on their income, of course.[19]

Who is the real decision maker in family purchases?

In years past, most marketers in the United States targeted the wife as the family

purchasing agent. Now, with sex-role stereotypes changed and with night and weekend shopping more popular, men and older children take more responsibility for shopping and decision making. Family roles vary from one culture to another.

Buying responsibility and influence vary greatly depending on the product and the family. Although only one family member may go to the store and make a specific purchase, other family members may have influenced the decision or really decided what to buy. Still others may use the product. That's why a lot of kids just have to have a Burger King hamburger because the Burger King crown giveaway is what they really want.[20]

Social class affects attitudes, values, and buying

Up to now, we've been concerned with individuals and their family relationships. Now let's consider how society looks at an individual and perhaps the family—in terms of social class. A **social class** is a group of people who have approximately equal social position as viewed by others in the society.

Almost every society has some social class structure. In most countries, social class is closely related to a person's occupation, but it may also be influenced by education, community participation, where a person lives, income, possessions, social skills, and other factors—including what family a person is born into.

In most countries—including the United States—there is *some* general relationship between income level and social class. But people with the same income level may be in different social classes. So income by itself is usually not a good measure of social class. And people in different social classes may spend, save, and borrow money in very different ways.

The U.S. class system is far less rigid than those in most countries. Children start out in the same social class as their parents—but they can move to a different social class depending on their educations and jobs. By contrast, India's social structure is more rigid, and individuals can't easily move up in the class system.

Marketers want to know what buyers in various social classes are like. In the United States, simple approaches for measuring social class groupings are based on a person's *occupation, education,* and *type and location of housing.* By using marketing research surveys or available census data, marketers can get a feel for the social class of a target market.

Many people think of America as a middle-class society. But in many marketing situations the social class groups are more distinct and they have different attitudes.

Reference groups are relevant too

A **reference group** refers to the people to whom an individual looks when forming attitudes about a particular topic. People normally have several reference groups for different topics. Some they meet face-to-face. Others they just wish to imitate. In either case, they may take values from these reference groups and make buying decisions based on what the group might accept.

Reference group influence is stronger for products that others "see" and which relate to status in the group. For one group, owning an expensive fur coat may be a sign of "having arrived." A group of animal lovers might view it as a sign of bad judgment.[21]

Reference group influence is usually more important when others will be able to see which product a consumer is using, but Jockey wants young people to view its underwear as in fashion and encourages them to "Let 'em know you're Jockey."

Reaching the opinion leaders who are buyers

An **opinion leader** is a person who influences others. Opinion leaders aren't necessarily wealthier or better educated. And opinion leaders on one subject aren't necessarily opinion leaders on another. For example, you may have a friend who is ahead of the curve in knowing about plasma TVs, but you might not want that friend's opinion about new clothing styles and cosmetics. On the other hand, sometimes a leader in one area earns respect in another.

Some marketing mixes aim especially at opinion leaders since their opinions affect others and they have many product-related discussions with "followers." Favorable word-of-mouth publicity from opinion leaders can really help a marketing mix. But the opposite is also true. If opinion leaders aren't satisfied, they're likely to spread the word. The Internet gives some opinion leaders influence over large numbers of consumers. Audible.com, for instance, encourages customer reviews of the audiobooks available for download at its website.[22]

Culture surrounds the other influences

Culture is the whole set of beliefs, attitudes, and ways of doing things of a reasonably homogeneous set of people. In this chapter, as well as Chapter 4, we looked at the broad impact of culture.

We can think of the American culture, the French culture, or the Latin American culture. People within these cultural groupings tend to be more similar in outlook and behavior. But often it is useful to think of subcultures within such groupings. For example, within the American culture, there are various religious, ethnic, and regional subcultures.

Failure to consider cultural differences, even subtle ones, can result in problems. To promote their product and get people to try it, marketers for Pepto-Bismol often provide free samples at festivals and street fairs. Their idea is that people tend to overindulge at such events. However, when they distributed sample packets at a festival in San Francisco's Chinatown, they insulted many of the people they wanted to influence. Booths with Chinese delicacies lined the streets, and many of the participants interpreted the sample packets (which featured the word "Nauseous" in large letters) as suggesting that Chinese delicacies were nauseating. The possibility of this misinterpretation may seem obvious in hindsight, but if it had been that obvious in advance the whole promotion would have been handled differently.[23]

Do ethnic groups buy differently?

America may be called the melting pot, but ethnic groups deserve special attention when analyzing markets. One basic reason is that people from different ethnic groups may be influenced by very different cultural variables. They may have quite varied needs and their own ways of thinking. Moreover, Americans are beginning to recognize the value of diversity. The United States is becoming a multicultural market. As a result, rather than disappearing in a melting pot, some important cultural and ethnic dimensions are being preserved and highlighted. This creates both opportunities and challenges for marketers.

Some important ethnic differences are obvious. For example, about 1 out of 5 families in the U.S. speaks a language other than English at home. Some areas have a much higher rate. In Miami and San Antonio, for example, about 1 out of 3 families speaks Spanish. This obviously affects promotion planning.

Stereotypes are common—and misleading

A marketer needs to study ethnic dimensions very carefully because they can be subtle and fast-changing. This is also an area where stereotyped thinking is the most common—and misleading. Many firms make the mistake of treating all consumers in a particular ethnic group as homogeneous. For example, some marketing managers treat all 40 million African American consumers as "the black market," ignoring the great variability among African American households on other segmenting dimensions.

Ethnic markets are becoming more important

More marketers pay attention to ethnic groups now because the number of ethnic consumers is growing at a much faster rate than the overall society. Much of this growth results from immigration. In addition, however, the median age of Asian Americans, African Americans, and Hispanics is much lower than that of whites—and the birthrate is higher. In combination, these factors have a dramatic effect.

Within the American culture, there are various religious, ethnic, and regional subcultures. For example, Univision's network appeals to the fast-growing Hispanic subculture, so Univision wants advertisers to know about the buying power of the Hispanic market.

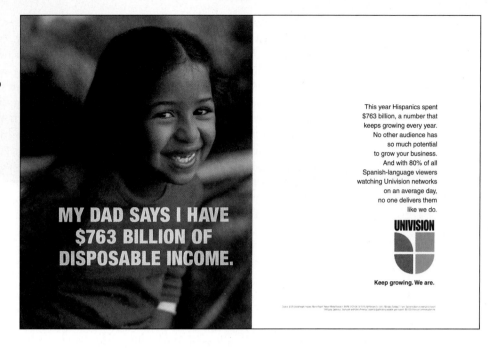

MY DAD SAYS I HAVE $763 BILLION OF DISPOSABLE INCOME.

This year Hispanics spent $763 billion, a number that keeps growing every year. No other audience has so much potential to grow your business. And with 80% of all Spanish-language viewers watching Univision networks on an average day, no one delivers them like we do.

UNIVISION

Keep growing. We are.

Hispanic market is growing

Let's take a closer look at Hispanic Americans—now the largest and fastest-growing ethnic group in the United States. Recently, their numbers have increased at the rate of about 1 million per year. By 2010, the Hispanic population will grow to about 48 million and make up 15.5 percent of the total population. To put this in perspective, the Hispanic population in the U.S. will be almost 20 percent greater than the population of Spain and almost 40 percent greater than the population of Canada. Hispanics also provide marketing opportunities for the future because they tend to be younger than the U.S. population as a whole.

Many companies are responding to this trend. For example, many Wells Fargo branches in the Southwest have added Latin-style decor, bicultural tellers, and Spanish-language promotion, including free coloring books for Hispanic kids. Efforts such as these have significantly increased Wells Fargo's business.

Asian American market is growing fast too

While there are fewer Asian Americans (about 14.2 million by 2010) the number has more than tripled since 1980. Asian Americans have the highest median family income ($65,132) of the major ethnic groups. Because of this growth and income, companies as varied as Kraft, Wal-Mart, and Allstate are targeting these consumers, especially in local markets where the Asian American population is concentrated.

Income and population create ethnic market buying power

The buying power of ethnic submarkets is also increasing rapidly. It's also important to marketers that much of this buying power is often concentrated in certain cities and states, which makes targeted promotion and distribution more efficient. For example, over 20 percent of San Francisco residents are Asians.

These ethnic shifts are changing the face of the American market. Already more than 36 percent of American children are African American, Hispanic, or Asian. Longer term, whites are expected to become a minority by 2050.[24]

Culture varies in international markets

Planning strategies that consider cultural differences in international markets can be even harder—and such cultures usually vary more. Each foreign market may need to be treated as a separate market with its own submarkets. Ignoring cultural differences—or assuming that they are not important—almost guarantees failure in international markets.

For example, only about 7 percent of Japanese households have a dishwasher. Appliance manufacturers who have tried to export their standard models to Japan have failed.

Japanese kitchens are too small for units that are standard in the U.S. Another problem is that many Japanese foods tend to be very sticky. A standard dishwasher won't clean the dishes well. To address these cultural differences, manufacturers have developed small countertop machines with powerful jets to do the cleaning. But another obstacle remains. Many traditional Japanese feel that it is the woman's duty to wash the dishes. For many housewives, the guilt of having dishes done by a machine is worse than the aggravation of doing the job. Foreign firms have missed that, but Matsushita, a Japanese firm, got big increases in sales by focusing its promotion on conserving hot water and hygiene—rather than convenience—as the important reasons to buy a dishwasher.[25]

From a target marketing point of view, a marketing manager probably wants to aim at people within one culture or subculture. A firm developing strategies for two cultures often needs two different marketing plans.[26]

INDIVIDUALS ARE AFFECTED BY THE PURCHASE SITUATION

Purchase reason can vary

Why a consumer makes a purchase can affect buying behavior. For example, a student buying a pen to take notes might pick up an inexpensive Bic. But the same student might choose a Cross pen as a gift for a friend. And a gadget-lover with some free time on his hands might buy a digital pen that transfers handwritten notes to a tablet computer—just for the fun of trying it.

Time affects what happens

Time influences a purchase situation. *When* consumers make a purchase—and the time they have available for shopping—will influence their behavior. Socializing with friends at a Starbucks induces different behavior than grabbing a quick cup of 7-Eleven coffee on the way to work.

The urgency of the need is another time-related factor. A sports buff who needs a digital video recorder with an "instant replay" feature in time for the Super Bowl—that evening—might spend an hour driving across town in heavy traffic to get the right unit. In a different circumstance, the same person might order a unit online from a website and figure that the extra time for it to be shipped is well worth the money saved.

On the other hand, how long something takes may be relative. Our online shopper might be frustrated by a web page that takes two minutes to load and abandon his virtual shopping cart after the digital video recorder is already selected. This happens all of the time online. On the other hand, you don't often see a consumer walk away from a shopping cart because of a two-minute wait in a checkout line at a store.

Surroundings affect buying too

Surroundings can affect buying behavior. The excitement of an on-site auction may stimulate impulse buying. Checking out an auction online might lead to a different response.

Surroundings may discourage buying too. For example, some people don't like to stand in a checkout line where others can see what they're buying—even if the other shoppers are complete strangers.[27]

Needs, benefits sought, attitudes, motivation, and even how a consumer selects certain products all vary depending on the purchase situation. So different purchase situations may require different marketing mixes—even when the same target market is involved.

THE CONSUMER DECISION PROCESS

The model in Exhibit 5–3 organizes the many different influences on consumer behavior. It helps explain *why* consumers make the decisions they make. Now, we'll expand that model with a closer look at the steps in the consumer decision process and a focus on *how* consumers make decisions.[28] See Exhibit 5–9.

Exhibit 5–9   An Expanded Model of Consumer Behavior

Recognizing a need creates a problem for the consumer

The consumer decision process begins when a consumer becomes aware of an unmet need. The consumer's problem-solving process then focuses on how best to meet that need. Problem recognition often happens quickly. A student on the way to class, for example, may realize that she's thirsty and wants something to drink. Or problem recognition may take shape over time. For example, a recent grad with a new apartment might want a comfortable place to sit. These situations present problems that may be solved with a purchase. But what purchase should it be?

How a consumer will solve the problem depends on the situation. Exhibit 5–10 highlights the basic problem-solving steps a consumer may go through to satisfy a need. A consumer may search for information, identify alternatives and what factors (criteria) are important, and then evaluate one or more alternative products that might meet the need. How long this process will take or how much conscious thought a consumer gives to each step varies from product to product. It is helpful, therefore, to recognize three levels of problem solving that consumers may use for any kind of product. See Exhibit 5–11.

Consumers use **extensive problem solving** when they put much effort into deciding how to satisfy a need—as is likely for a completely new purchase or to satisfy an important need. For example, an avid computer "gamer" may put in much effort before buying a new gaming computer. Our gamer might gather friends' opinions about the graphics speed and audio quality for different models before going online to compare options and prices and read technical reviews. Then, our gamer might visit a local store for a hands-on demo of a favorite game on a few computers. This is certainly not an impulse purchase!

Limited problem solving is used by consumers when *some* effort is required in deciding the best way to satisfy a need. This is typical when the consumer has some previous experience with a product but isn't quite sure which choice to make at the moment. A seasoned computer gamer, for instance, may already know that he likes sports games and what store has the newest releases. At the store he might get the

Exhibit 5–10
Consumer Problem Solving

Exhibit 5-11 Problem-Solving Continuum

Low involvement
Frequently purchased
Inexpensive
Little risk
Little information needed

Routinized response behavior | Limited problem solving | Extensive problem solving

High involvement
Infrequently purchased
Expensive
High risk
Much information desired

salesperson's advice and check out the video quality on a few games before deciding which to buy. This is a deliberate purchase, but only a limited amount of effort is expended before making the decision.

A consumer uses **routinized response behavior** when he or she regularly selects a particular way of satisfying a need when it occurs. Routinized response is typical when a consumer has considerable experience in how to meet a specific need and requires no new information. For example, our gamer might automatically buy the latest version of "Madden NFL" as soon as EA Sports makes it available.

Routine response behavior is also typical for **low-involvement purchases**—purchases that have little importance or relevance for the customer. Let's face it, buying a box of salt is probably not one of the burning issues in your life.[29]

Buying isn't always rational

The idea of a decision process does *not* imply that consumers always apply *rational* processes in their buying decisions. To the contrary, consumers don't always seek accurate information or make smart choices that provide the best economic value. This is often because of the influences on consumer behavior that we discussed earlier in the chapter.

Consumers can have second thoughts after a purchase

After making a purchase, buyers often have second thoughts and wonder if they made the right choice. The resulting tension is called **dissonance**—a feeling of uncertainty about whether the correct decision was made. This may lead a customer to seek additional information to confirm the wisdom of the purchase.

Post-purchase regret is a bigger problem

Sometimes uncertainty isn't the issue. Rather the consumer is certain about being unhappy with a purchase. The disappointment of a new pair of shoes that don't fit quite right can be experienced for a long time. A consumer may regret making a purchase for a variety of reasons. But, whatever the reason, regret is not likely to lead to the same decision in the future. In addition, research shows that consumers are more likely to share stories about being dissatisfied with a product than about being satisfied.[30]

New concepts require an adoption process

When consumers face a really new concept, their previous experience may not be relevant. These situations involve the **adoption process**—the steps individuals go through on the way to accepting or rejecting a new idea. Although the adoption process is similar to the decision-making process, learning plays a clearer role and promotion's contribution to a marketing mix is more visible.

In the adoption process, an individual moves through some fairly definite steps:

1. *Awareness*—the potential customer comes to know about the product but lacks details. The consumer may not even know how it works or what it will do.
2. *Interest*—if the consumer becomes interested, he or she will gather general information and facts about the product.
3. *Evaluation*—a consumer begins to give the product a mental trial, applying it to his or her personal situation.
4. *Trial*—the consumer may buy the product to experiment with it in use. A product that is either too expensive to try or isn't available for trial may never be adopted.

Some consumers think that different brands of sportswear are all the same. Columbia Sportswear ads use vivid humor to encourage consumers to evaluate Columbia not only on its style, but also on how comfortable it is in frigid weather.

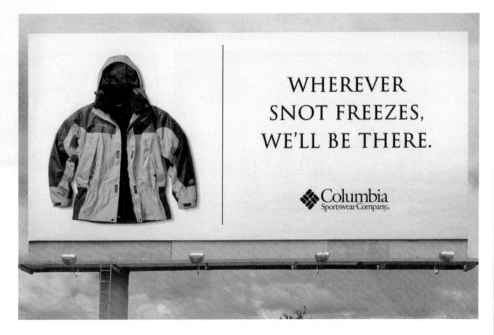

WHEREVER SNOT FREEZES, WE'LL BE THERE.

Columbia Sportswear Company.

5. *Decision*—the consumer decides on either adoption or rejection. A satisfactory evaluation and trial may lead to adoption of the product and regular use. According to psychological learning theory, reinforcement leads to adoption.

Internet EXERCISE To make it easier for consumers to visualize how certain fashions will look, the Lands' End website (**www.landsend.com**) has an interactive "virtual model" feature. Go to the Lands' End website, click on "My Model," and check out this feature. Do you think that it makes it easier to evaluate a potential purchase?

6. *Confirmation*—the adopter continues to rethink the decision and searches for support for the decision—that is, further reinforcement.[31]

PepsiCo had to work with the adoption process when it introduced Pepsi One, a low-calorie cola. Many consumers are interested in staying trim, but diet sodas have an image of bad taste. In light of that, Pepsi's initial ads didn't directly say that Pepsi One was a diet drink. Rather, they used the slogan "True Cola Taste. One Calorie." But that confused a lot of consumers who couldn't tell what made it different from Diet Pepsi. Because awareness and interest were low among consumers, retailers didn't devote much shelf space to Pepsi One, so it often wasn't even there for a consumer to consider. Even after a year on the market, trial was low. To help more consumers through the adoption process, Pepsi made changes. New ads explained that Pepsi One used a new sweetener that tasted better than the ones used in other diet drinks. The ads showed consumers drinking Pepsi One and not being able to taste the difference from a regular cola; they used the tagline "Too good to be one calorie, but it is." To generate more trial, Pepsi provided free samples on campuses, in office cafeterias, and at movie theaters.[32]

CONSUMER BEHAVIOR IN INTERNATIONAL MARKETS

All the influences interact—often in subtle ways

You're a consumer, so you probably have very good intuition about the many influences on consumer behavior that we've been discussing. That's good, but it's also a potential trap—especially when developing marketing mixes for consumers in inter-

In Saudi Arabia, McDonald's modifies its marketing mix to adapt to the local culture. For example, the McDonald's in Riyadh is segregated by sex with a separate section for women and children.

national markets. The less a marketing manager knows about the *specific* social and intrapersonal variables that shape the behavior of target customers, the more likely it is that relying on intuition or personal experience will be misleading. Many specific influences do not generalize from one culture to another.

Cadbury's effort to develop a Japanese market for its Dairy Milk Chocolate candy bar illustrates the point. In marketing research, Japanese consumers said that they didn't like the high milk-fat content of Cadbury's bar. But Cadbury's managers reasoned that this was because they were not accustomed to the candy. After all, in most other countries it's the rich taste of the candy that turns consumers into "chocoholics." When Cadbury introduced the bar in Japan, it was a real flop. Taste preferences in other countries simply didn't generalize to Japan.[33]

Sometimes an understanding of local cultural influences points to new ways to blend the four Ps. For example, Nestlé knew that free samples would be a good way to kick-start the adoption process when it wanted to introduce a new line of food flavorings in Brazil. In the United States, it's common to distribute samples at stores. But local Nestlé managers knew a more effective approach. In Brazil, cooks rely on stoves that run on gas rather than electricity, so local deliverymen regularly bring canisters of gas into consumers' kitchens. Nestlé paid the deliverymen to offer their customers samples of the flavorings and explain how to use them. Consumers showed more interest in the samples when the conversation took place right by the stove where the flavorings would be used.[34]

Watch out for stereotypes, and change

Consumers in a foreign culture may be bound by some similar cultural forces, but that doesn't mean that they are all the same. So it's important to watch out for oversimplifying stereotypes. Further, changes in the underlying social forces may make outdated views irrelevant.

Developing a marketing mix that really satisfies the needs of a target market takes a real understanding of consumer behavior and the varied forces that shape it. So when planning strategies for international markets, it's best to involve locals who have a better chance of understanding the experience, attitudes, and interests of your customers.

CONCLUSION

In this chapter, we analyzed the individual consumer as a problem solver who is influenced by economic needs, psychological variables, social influences, and the purchase situation. We showed how these variables influence the consumer decision process, what the steps in that process are, and why it is important to consider these steps when planning a marketing strategy. For example, we discussed three levels of problem solving that you can use to evaluate how consumers approach different types of purchase decisions. We also discussed how the consumer's experience after the purchase impacts what that consumer will do in the future.

From a broader perspective, this chapter makes it clear that each consumer and purchase decision is somewhat unique. So, it isn't possible to catalog all of the individual possibilities. Rather, the overall focus of this chapter is to provide you with general frameworks that you can use to analyze consumers regardless of what the particular product or decision may be. This also helps you to identify the dimensions of consumer behavior that are most important for segmenting the market and developing a targeted marketing mix.

By now it should be clear that expensive marketing errors can be made when you assume that other consumers will behave in the same manner as you or your family and friends. That's why we rely on the social and behavior sciences for insight about consumer behavior in general and why marketing research is so important to marketing managers when they are developing a marketing strategy for a particular target market. When managers understand how and why consumers behave the way they do, they are better able to develop effective marketing mixes that really meet the needs of their target market.

KEY TERMS

economic buyers, 116
economic needs, 116
discretionary income, 117
needs, 119
wants, 119
drive, 119
physiological needs, 121
safety needs, 121
social needs, 121
personal needs, 121
perception, 122
selective exposure, 122

selective perception, 122
selective retention, 122
learning, 122
cues, 123
response, 123
reinforcement, 123
attitude, 124
belief, 124
expectation, 125
psychographics, 126
lifestyle analysis, 126

empty nesters, 128
social class, 129
reference group, 129
opinion leader, 130
culture, 130
extensive problem solving, 133
limited problem solving, 133
routinized response behavior, 134
low-involvement purchases, 134
dissonance, 134
adoption process, 134

QUESTIONS AND PROBLEMS

1. In your own words, explain economic needs and how they relate to the economic-buyer model of consumer behavior. Give an example of a purchase you recently made that is consistent with the economic-buyer model. Give another that is not explained by the economic-buyer model. Explain your thinking.

2. Explain what is meant by a hierarchy of needs and provide examples of one or more products that enable you to satisfy each of the four levels of need.

3. Cut out or photocopy two recent advertisements: one full-page color ad from a magazine and one large display from a newspaper. In each case, indicate which needs the ads are appealing to.

4. Explain how an understanding of consumers' learning processes might affect marketing strategy planning. Give an example.

5. Briefly describe your own *beliefs* about the potential value of wearing automobile seat belts, your *attitude* toward seat belts, and your *intention* about using a seat belt the next time you're in a car.

6. Give an example of a recent purchase experience in which you were dissatisfied because a firm's marketing mix did not meet your expectations. Indicate how the purchase fell short of your expectations—and also explain whether your expectations were formed based on the firm's promotion or on something else.

7. Explain psychographics and lifestyle analysis. Explain how they might be useful for planning marketing strategies to reach college students, as opposed to average consumers.

8. A supermarket chain is planning to open a number of new stores to appeal to Hispanics in southern California. Give some examples that indicate how the four Ps might be adjusted to appeal to the Hispanic subculture.

9. How should social class influences affect the planning of a new restaurant in a large city? How might the four Ps be adjusted?

10. Illustrate how the reference group concept may apply in practice by explaining how you personally are influenced by some reference group for some product. What are the implications of such behavior for marketing managers?

11. Give two examples of recent purchases where the specific purchase situation influenced your purchase decision. Briefly explain how your decision was affected.

12. Give an example of a recent purchase in which you used extensive problem solving. What sources of information did you use in making the decision?

13. On the basis of the data and analysis presented in Chapters 4 and 5, what kind of buying behavior would you expect to find for the following products: (*a*) a haircut, (*b*) a shampoo, (*c*) a digital camera, (*d*) a tennis racket, (*e*) a dress belt, (*f*) a cell phone, (*g*) life insurance, (*h*) an ice cream cone, and (*i*) a new checking account? Set up a chart for your answers with products along the left-hand margin as the row headings and the following factors as headings for the columns: (*a*) how consumers would shop for these products, (*b*) how far they would travel to buy the products, (*c*) whether they would buy by brand, (*d*) whether they would compare with other products, and (*e*) any other factors they should consider. Insert short answers—words or phrases are satisfactory—in the various boxes. Be prepared to discuss how the answers you put in the chart would affect each product's marketing mix.

14. Review the model in Exhibit 5–9 and then reread the iPod case at the beginning of this chapter. List and briefly describe specific points in the case that illustrate the model.

15. Interview a friend or family member about two recent purchase decisions. One decision should be an important purchase, perhaps the choice of an automobile, a place to live, or a college. The second purchase should be more routine, such as a meal from a fast-food restaurant or a regularly purchased grocery item. For each purchase, ask your friend questions that will help you understand how the decision was made. Use the model in Exhibit 5–9 to guide your questions. Describe the similarities and differences between the two purchase decisions.

CREATING MARKETING PLANS

The Marketing Plan Coach software on the Student CD includes a sample marketing plan for Hillside Veterinary Clinic. Look through the "Customers" section and consider the following questions.

a. Based on the marketing plan, what do we know about the consumer behavior of the target market?

b. What additional information do you think would be helpful before developing a marketing strategy for Hillside?

SUGGESTED CASES

3. NOCO Soccer Academy
10. Fulton's Ice Land

8. Soprano's Ristorante
11. Runners Supply

9. Sleepy Inn Motel
30. Saralyn Mills, Ltd.

COMPUTER-AIDED PROBLEM

5. SELECTIVE PROCESSES

Submag, Inc., uses direct-mail promotion to sell magazine subscriptions. Magazine publishers pay Submag $3.12 for each new subscription. Submag's costs include the expenses of printing, addressing, and mailing each direct-mail advertisement plus the cost of using a mailing list. There are many suppliers of mailing lists, and the cost and quality of different lists vary.

Submag's marketing manager, Shandra Debose, is trying to choose between two possible mailing lists. One list has been generated from phone directories. It is less expensive than the other list, but the supplier acknowledges that about 10 percent of the names are out-of-date (addresses where people have moved away.) A competing supplier offers a list of active members of professional associations. This list costs 4 cents per name more than the phone list, but only 8 percent of the addresses are out-of-date.

In addition to concerns about out-of-date names, not every consumer who receives a mailing buys a subscription. For example, *selective exposure* is a problem. Some target customers never see the offer—they just toss out junk mail without even opening the envelope. Industry studies show that this wastes about 10 percent of each mailing—although the precise percentage varies from one mailing list to another.

Selective perception influences some consumers who do open the mailing. Some are simply not interested. Others don't want to deal with a subscription service. Although the price is good,
these consumers worry that they'll never get the magazines. Submag's previous experience is that selective perception causes more than half of those who read the offer to reject it.

Of those who perceive the message as intended, many are interested. But *selective retention* can be a problem. Some people set the information aside and then forget to send in the subscription order.

Submag can mail about 25,000 pieces per week. Shandra Debose has set up a spreadsheet to help her study the effects of the various relationships discussed earlier and to choose between the two mailing lists.

a. If you were Debose, which of the two lists would you buy based on the initial spreadsheet? Why?

b. For the most profitable list, what is the minimum number of items that Submag will have to mail to earn a profit of at least $3,500?

c. For an additional cost of $.01 per mailing, Submag can include a reply card that will reduce the percent of consumers who forget to send in an order (Percent Lost—Selective Retention) to 45 percent. If Submag mails 25,000 items, is it worth the additional cost to include the reply card? Explain your logic.

For additional questions related to this problem, see Exercise 5-5 in the *Learning Aid for Use with Essentials of Marketing*, 11th edition.

6

Business and Organizational Customers and Their Buying Behavior

MetoKote Corporation specializes in protective coating applications, like powder-coat and liquid paint, that other manufacturers need for the parts and equipment they make. For example, when you see John Deere agricultural, construction, or lawn and grounds-care equipment, many of the components have likely been coated (painted) in a MetoKote facility. In fact, Deere & Company and MetoKote have a close buyer–seller relationship. While Deere uses a variety of methods to identify suppliers and get competitive bids for many items it needs, it's different with MetoKote. Deere isn't going to switch to some other supplier just because other options provide cheaper coatings. MetoKote not only provides protective coatings for many John Deere products, it has built facilities right next to some Deere plants. When it's time for a component to be coated, a conveyer belt moves the part out of the John Deere plant and into the MetoKote facility. A short time later it's back—and it's green or yellow.

Deere favors this type of arrangement. It lets MetoKote's experts keep up with all of the environmental regulations and new technologies for coatings.

For a manufacturer, this type of relationship allows its facilities to be smaller and less costly to build and maintain, as the space isn't required for large spray booths. With MetoKote's facilities located nearby, newly coated parts for Deere do not have to be shipped, resulting in fewer scratches and dents—which results in higher-quality parts with less rework required.

Many people were involved in the decision to purchase coating services in this way. The responsibility for choosing vendors didn't just rest with the purchasing department but involved input from people in finance, quality control, and in some cases even the production employees.

John Deere needs high-quality protective finishes because its customers want durable, long-lasting equipment. Like John Deere, they want good value. Upholding Deere & Company's long-standing reputation for quality service is equally as important as the company's reputation for a quality product.

For example, if a huge commercial farm in Brazil needs a repair part, workers can contact the local John Deere dealer, or at any hour visit the company's website (www.johndeere.com) to access JDParts.com (www.jdparts.com), the online service that allows customers to learn which dealers have a needed part in inventory, check the price, and place an order for fast delivery. But helping John Deere customers and dealers earn better profits doesn't stop there.

For example, some John Deere farm equipment now includes a global positioning device that tracks exactly where the equipment goes when it is plowing, seeding, or cutting. The company's GreenStar™ system, which can easily be moved from machine to machine, uses advanced technology to measure average farm and field yields and facilitate documentation of tillage practices, planting, spraying, weather, and more. These Deere innovations can help a farmer make better management decisions and increase productivity.

John Deere recognizes that different customers have different needs. For example, golf courses buy Deere equipment to maintain their fairways, roughs, greens, and sand traps. Golf course managers value the reliability and durability of Deere equipment. However, they also need a variety of operating supplies—ranging from grass

seed and irrigation equipment to ball washers and chemicals. Golf course managers have many responsibilities besides purchasing, and it's time-consuming for them to have to work with many different suppliers. So, John Deere introduced its One Source service, which provides golf course managers with a "one-stop shop" for the things they need—all backed by the trusted Deere name. One Source strengthens Deere's relationships with both its dealers and their golf course customers. Of course, it creates new challenges for John Deere's purchasing department. It must identify, evaluate, monitor, and recommend the suppliers for the products that golf courses need. Deere's dealers and golf course customers rely on Deere's purchasing specialists to make the right decisions, and that's part of the customer value that Deere provides. Innovative approaches to delivering customer value, such as One Source for golf courses, make Deere the supplier of choice for many business customers.[1]

LEARNING OBJECTIVES

As the John Deere case illustrates, the buying behavior of organizational customers can be very different from the buying behavior of final consumers. Marketing strategy planning requires a solid understanding of who these organizational customers are and how they buy.

When you finish this chapter, you should:

1. know who the business and organizational buyers are.

2. see why business and organizational purchase decisions often involve multiple influences.

3. understand the problem-solving behavior of organizational buyers.

4. understand the different types of buyer–seller relationships and their benefits and limitations.

5. know the basic e-commerce methods used in organizational buying.

6. know about the number and distribution of manufacturers and why they are an important customer group.

7. know how buying by service firms, retailers, wholesalers, and governments is similar to—and different from—buying by manufacturers.

8. understand important new terms (shown in red).

BUSINESS AND ORGANIZATIONAL CUSTOMERS—A BIG OPPORTUNITY

Most people think about an individual final consumer when they hear the term *customer*. But many marketing managers aim at customers who are not final consumers. In fact, more purchases are made by businesses and other organizations than by final consumers.

Business and organizational customers are any buyers who buy for resale or to produce other goods and services. There are many different types of organizational customers, including

- *Producers of goods and services*—including manufacturers, farmers, real estate developers, hotel operators, bankers, and even doctors and lawyers.
- *Middlemen*—wholesalers and retailers.
- *Government units*—federal agencies in the United States and other countries as well as state and local governments.
- *Nonprofit organizations*—national organizations like the Red Cross and Girl Scouts as well as local organizations like museums and churches.

As this suggests, not all organizational customers are business firms. Even so, they are sometimes loosely referred to as *business buyers, intermediate buyers,* or *industrial buyers*—and marketing managers often refer to organizational customers collectively as the "business-to-business" market, or simply, the *B2B market*.

In this chapter, we'll focus on organizational customers and their buying behavior. See Exhibit 6–1. In Chapter 5 we focused on buying by final consumers, so here we'll start by covering important ways that organizational buying tends to be different from buying by final consumers. Then, later in the chapter, we'll focus on some key differences among the specific types of organizational customers.

So, keep in mind that, for many firms, marketing strategy planning is about meeting the needs of organizational customers, not final consumers. A firm can target both final consumers and organizations, but different marketing mixes may be needed. As you learn about the buying behavior of organizations, think about how a firm's marketing mix may need to be different and how it may be adjusted.

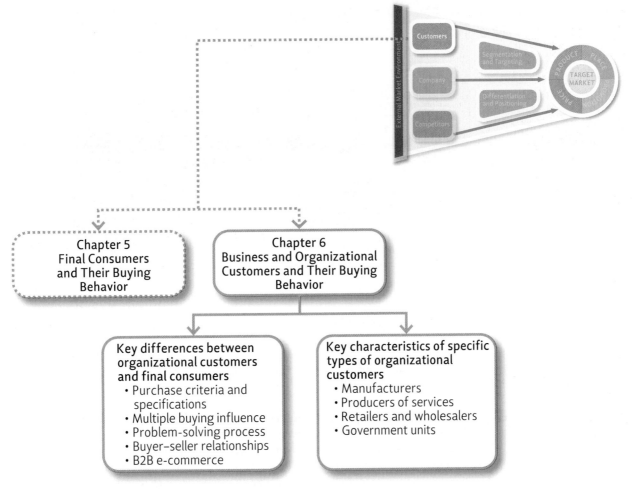

ORGANIZATIONAL CUSTOMERS ARE DIFFERENT

Organizations buy for a basic purpose

Like final consumers, organizations make purchases to satisfy needs. But it's often easier to understand an organization's needs because most organizations make purchases for the same basic reason. They buy goods and services that will help them meet the demand for the goods and services that they in turn supply to their markets. In other words, their basic need is to satisfy their own customers and clients. A producer buys because it wants to earn a profit by making and selling goods or services. A wholesaler or retailer buys products it can profitably resell to its customers. A town government wants to meet its legal and social obligations to its citizens.

Basic purchasing needs are economic

Organizations typically focus on economic factors when they make purchase decisions and are usually less emotional in their buying than final consumers.

Buyers try to consider the total cost of selecting a supplier and its particular marketing mix, not just the initial price of the product. For example, a hospital that needs a new type of digital X-ray equipment might look at both the original cost and ongoing costs, how it would affect doctor productivity, and, of course, the quality of the images it produces. The hospital might also consider the seller's reliability and its ability to provide speedy maintenance and repair.

The matter of dependability deserves further emphasis. An organization may not be able to function if purchases don't arrive when they're expected. For example, there's nothing worse to a manufacturer than shutting down a production line because

Promotion to organizational buyers often focuses on economic factors. Arlington's ad, from a trade magazine for electrical contractors, focuses on the time that contractors save by using its electric box extension rings with built-in nail-down clips and stabilizers. Sharp's ad, targeted at information technology managers, promises to double a customer's productivity by allowing a user to scan two-sided documents in a single pass.

sellers haven't delivered the goods. Dependable product quality is important too. For example, a bug in e-commerce software purchased by a firm might cause the firm's online order system to shut down. The costs of finding and correcting the problem—to say nothing about the cost of the lost business—could be much greater than the original cost of the software.

Even small differences are important

Understanding how the buying behavior of a particular organization differs from others can be very important. Even seemingly trivial differences in buying behavior may be important because success often hinges on fine-tuning the marketing mix.

Sellers often approach each organizational customer directly, usually through a sales representative. This gives the seller an opportunity to adjust the marketing mix for each individual customer. A seller may even develop a unique strategy for each individual customer. This approach carries target marketing to its extreme. But sellers often need unique strategies to compete for large-volume purchases.

Serving customers in international markets

Many marketers find good opportunities to serve business customers in different countries around the world. The basic approaches marketers use to deal with business customers in different parts of the world are much less varied than those required to reach individual consumers. This is probably why the shift to a global economy has been so rapid for many firms. Their business customers in different countries tend to buy in similar ways and can usually be reached with similar marketing mixes. Moreover, business customers are often willing to work with distant suppliers who have developed superior marketing mixes.

Specifications describe the need

Organizational buyers often buy on the basis of a set of **purchasing specifications**—a written (or electronic) description of what the firm wants to buy. When quality is highly standardized, as is often the case with manufactured items, the specification may simply consist of a brand name or part number. Often, however, the purchase requirements are more complicated; then the specifications may set out detailed information about the performance standards the product must meet. Purchase specifications for services tend to be detailed because services are less standardized and usually are not performed until after they're purchased.

Customers may expect quality certification

Organizational customers considering a new supplier or one from overseas may be concerned about product quality. However, this is becoming less of an obstacle because

144

of ISO 9000. **ISO 9000** is a way for a supplier to document its quality procedures according to internationally recognized standards.

ISO 9000 assures a customer that the supplier has effective quality checks in place, without the customer having to conduct its own costly and time-consuming audit. Some customers won't buy from any supplier who doesn't have it. To receive ISO 9000 certification, a company basically must prove to outside auditors that it documents in detail how the company operates and who is responsible for quality every step of the way.[2]

MANY DIFFERENT PEOPLE MAY INFLUENCE A DECISION

Purchasing managers are specialists

Many organizations rely on specialists to ensure that purchases are handled sensibly. These specialists have different titles in different firms (such as procurement officer, supply manager, purchasing agent, or buyer), but basically they are all **purchasing managers**—buying specialists for their employers. In large organizations, they usually specialize by product area and are real experts.

Some people think purchasing is handled by clerks who sit in cubicles and just do the paperwork to place orders. That view is out-of-date. Today, most firms look to their procurement departments to help cut costs and provide competitive advantage. In this environment, purchasing people have a lot of clout. And there are good job opportunities in purchasing for capable business graduates.

Salespeople often have to see a purchasing manager first—before they contact any other employee. These buyers hold important positions and take a dim view of sales reps who try to go around them. Rather than being "sold," these buyers want salespeople to provide accurate information that will help them buy wisely. They like information on new goods and services and tips on potential price changes, supply shortages, and other changes in market conditions. Sometimes all it takes for a sales rep to keep a buyer up-to-date is to send an occasional e-mail. But a buyer can tell when a sales rep has the customer firm's interest at heart.

Although purchasing managers usually coordinate relationships with suppliers, other people may also play important roles in influencing the purchase decision.[3]

Multiple buying influence in a buying center

Multiple buying influence means that several people—perhaps even top management—share in making a purchase decision. Possible buying influences include

1. *Users*—perhaps production line workers or their supervisors.
2. *Influencers*—perhaps engineering or R&D people who help write specifications or supply information for evaluating alternatives.
3. *Buyers*—the purchasing managers who have the responsibility for working with suppliers and arranging the terms of the sale.
4. *Deciders*—the people in the organization who have the power to select or approve the supplier—often a purchasing manager but perhaps top management for larger purchases.
5. *Gatekeepers*—people who control the flow of information within the organization—perhaps a purchasing manager who shields users or other deciders. Gatekeepers can also include receptionists, secretaries, research assistants, and others who influence the flow of information about potential purchases.

An example shows how the different buying influences work. Suppose Electrolux, the Swedish firm that produces vacuum cleaners, wants to buy a machine to stamp out the various metal parts it needs. An assistant to the purchasing manager does an Internet search to identify possible vendors. However, the list that the assistant (a gatekeeper) prepares for the manager excludes a few vendors on the basis of an initial evaluation of information from their websites. The manager e-mails a description of the problem to vendors on the list. It turns out that each of them is eager to get the business and submits a proposal. Several people (influencers) at Electrolux help to

A person who works on a utility firm's high-power wires needs safe, durable climbing gear. A number of different people may influence the decision about which gear the firm should buy.

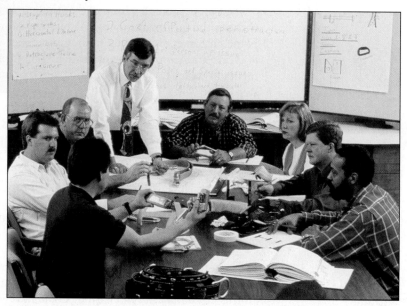

evaluate the vendors' proposals. A finance manager worries about the high cost and suggests leasing the machine. The quality control people want a machine that will do a more accurate job—although it's more expensive. The production manager is interested in speed of operation.

The company president (the decider) asks the purchasing department to assemble all the information but retains the power to select the supplier. The purchasing manager's assistant schedules visits for salespeople. After all these buying influences are considered, one of the purchasing agents for the firm (the buyer) will be responsible for making recommendations and arranging the terms of the sale.

It is helpful to think of a **buying center** as all the people who participate in or influence a purchase. Because different people may make up a buying center from one decision to the next, the salesperson must study each case carefully. Just learning who to talk with may be hard, but thinking about the various roles in the buying center can help. See Exhibit 6–2.

The salesperson may have to talk to every member of the buying center—stressing different topics for each. This not only complicates the promotion job but also lengthens it. Approval of a routine order may take anywhere from a day to several months. On very important purchases—a new computer system, a new building, or major equipment—the selling period may take a year or more.[4]

Exhibit 6–2
Multiple Influence and Roles in the Buying Center

Vendor analysis considers all of the influences

Considering all of the factors relevant to a purchase decision can be very complex. A supplier or product that is best in one way may not be best in others. To try to deal with these situations, many firms use **vendor analysis**—a formal rating of suppliers on all relevant areas of performance. The purpose isn't just to get a low price from the supplier on a given part or service. Rather, the goal is to lower the *total costs* associated with purchases. Analysis might show that the best vendor is the one that helps the customer reduce costs of excess inventory, retooling of equipment, or defective parts.[5]

Behavioral needs are relevant too

Vendor analysis tries to focus on economic factors, but purchasing in organizations may also involve many of the same behavioral dimensions we discussed in Chapter 5. Purchasing managers and others involved in buying decisions are human, and they want friendly relationships with suppliers.

The purchasing people in some firms are eager to imitate progressive competitors or even be the first to try new products. Such "innovators" deserve special attention when new products are being introduced.

The different people involved in purchase decisions are also human with respect to protecting their own interests and their own position in the company. That's one reason people from different departments may have different priorities in trying to influence what is purchased. Similarly, purchasing managers may want to avoid taking risks that might reflect badly on their decisions. If a new source delivers late or quality is poor, you can guess who will be blamed. Marketers who can help the buyer avoid risk have a definite appeal. In fact, this may make the difference between a successful and unsuccessful marketing mix.

A seller's marketing mix should satisfy *both* the needs of the customer company as well as the needs of individuals who influence the purchase. Therefore, sellers need to find an overlapping area where both can be satisfied.

Ethical conflicts may arise

Although organizational buyers are influenced by their own needs, most are serious professionals who are careful to avoid a conflict between their own self-interest and company outcomes. Marketers must be careful here. A salesperson who offers one of his company pens to a prospect may view the giveaway as part of the promotion effort—but the customer firm may have a policy against any employee accepting *any* gift from a supplier. For example, General Motors developed an ethics policy that forbids employees from accepting anything of value from a vendor. It specifically includes entertainment—like a golf outing, a steak dinner, or tickets to a sporting event.

A seller's marketing mix may need to consider both the needs of the customer company as well as the needs of the individuals who influence the purchase decision.

Most organizational buyers do their work ethically and expect marketers to do the same. Yet there have been highly publicized abuses. For example, the telephone company that serves New York found out that some of its buyers were giving contracts to suppliers who offered them vacation trips and other personal favors. Abuses of this sort have prompted many organizations to set up policies that prohibit a buyer or other employees from accepting anything from a potential supplier.

Marketers need to take concerns about conflict of interest very seriously. Part of the promotion job is to persuade different individuals who may influence an organization's purchase. Yet the whole marketing effort may be tainted if it even *appears* that a marketer has encouraged a person who influences a decision to put personal gain ahead of company interest.[6]

Purchasing may be centralized

If a large organization has facilities at many locations, much of the purchasing work may be done at a central location. With centralized buying, a sales rep may be able to sell to facilities all over a country—or even across several countries—without leaving a base city. Wal-Mart handles most of the purchase decisions for stores in its retail chain from its headquarters in Arkansas. Many purchasing decisions for agencies of the U.S. government are handled in Washington, D.C.

Many firms also have centralized control over who can make purchases. A person who needs to purchase something usually completes a **requisition**—a request to buy something. This is frequently handled online to cut time and paper shuffling. Even so, there may be delays before a supervisor authorizes the requisition and a purchasing manager can select the "best" seller and turn the authorization into a purchase order. The process may take a few hours for a simple purchase—but it may turn into months for a complex purchase.

Spend management systems control purchasing

Some firms use "spend management" systems to track every single purchase. In large firms this helps the purchasing department analyze the details of who is buying what and how. Sometimes this leads to cost-cutting opportunities or better purchasing policies. Computer purchases by a college illustrate the idea. Colleges buy hundreds of computers each year, but often they're purchased one at a time by different departments. If the college documents the total spending, it can contract for better terms from preferred vendors. The college might also change its policies so that any department can quickly order a standard computer from these vendors without approval from a purchasing manager.

The buying firm's values affect purchasing practices

A firm's own strategy and values often influence how suppliers are evaluated and who is selected. For example, Ben & Jerry's corporate values include helping the environment and reducing the effects of poverty. Its buyers spend more than half their purchasing budget with suppliers who share those priorities.[7]

ORGANIZATIONAL BUYERS ARE PROBLEM SOLVERS

Three kinds of buying processes are useful

In Chapter 5, we discussed problem solving by consumers and how it might vary from extensive problem solving to routine buying. In organizational markets, we can adapt these concepts slightly and work with three similar buying processes: a new-task buying process, a modified rebuy process, or a straight rebuy.[8] See Exhibit 6–3.

New-task buying occurs when an organization has a new need and the customer wants a great deal of information. New-task buying can involve setting product specifications, evaluating sources of supply, and establishing an order routine that can be followed in the future if results are satisfactory. Multiple buying influence is typical in new-task buying.

A **straight rebuy** is a routine repurchase that may have been made many times before. Buyers probably don't bother looking for new information or new sources of supply. Most of a company's small or recurring purchases are of this type—but they take only a small part of an organized buyer's time. Important purchases may be made this way too—but only after the firm has decided what procedure will be "routine."

The **modified rebuy** is the in-between process where some review of the buying situation is done—though not as much as in new-task buying. Sometimes a competitor will get lazy enjoying a straight rebuy situation. An alert marketer can turn these situations into opportunities by providing more information or a better marketing mix.

New-task buying requires information

Customers in a new-task buying situation are likely to seek information from a variety of sources. See Exhibit 6–4. Many of the impersonal sources in Exhibit 6–4 are readily available in online digital formats. How much information a customer collects depends on the importance of the purchase and the level of uncertainty about what choice might be best. The time and expense of searching for information may not be justified for a minor purchase. But a major purchase often involves real detective work by the buyer.

Of course, the flip side of the new-task buying situation is that a seller's promotion has much more chance to have an impact. At the very least, the marketer needs to be certain that his or her firm will turn up in the buyer's search. Later we will talk more about the role of e-commerce at this stage, but for now you should see that even a simple website is likely to turn up in a buyer's Internet search.[9]

Internet EXERCISE

Go to the BuyerZone website (**www.buyerzone.com**). What types of products could be purchased by requesting a free quote on this site? From the home page click "Furniture> Chairs> Chair Buyer's Guide," then look through this Buyer's Guide. Look at the Buyer's Guides for other products as well. What can be learned about buying different products from BuyerZone.com? For a marketing manager targeting smaller businesses, how could this site be helpful?

Exhibit 6–3
Organizational Buying Processes

Characteristics	Type of Process		
	New-Task Buying	Modified Rebuy	Straight Rebuy
Time required	Much	Medium	Little
Multiple influence	Much	Some	Little
Review of suppliers	Much	Some	None
Information needed	Much	Some	Little

Exhibit 6–4
Major Sources of
Information Used by
Organizational Buyers

	Marketing sources	Nonmarketing sources
Personal sources	• Salespeople • Others from supplier firms • Trade shows	• Buying center members • Outside business associates • Consultants and outside experts
Impersonal sources	• Advertising in trade publications • Sales literature • Sales catalogs • Web page	• Rating services • Trade associations • News publications • Product directories • Internet

What buying procedure becomes routine is critical

Once a buying firm gets beyond the early stages of a new-task buying decision, it needs to make important decisions about how it is going to deal with one or more suppliers to meet its needs. At one extreme, a buyer might want to rely on competition among all available vendors to get the best price on each and every order it places. At the other extreme, it might just routinely buy from one vendor with whom it already has a good relationship. In practice, there are many variations between these extremes. To better understand the variations, let's take a closer look at the benefits and limitations of different types of buyer–seller relationships.

BUYER–SELLER RELATIONSHIPS IN BUSINESS MARKETS

Close relationships may produce mutual benefits

There are often significant benefits of a close working relationship between a supplier and a customer firm. And such relationships are becoming common. Many firms are reducing the number of suppliers with whom they work—expecting more in return from the suppliers that remain. The best relationships involve real partnerships where there's mutual trust and a long-term outlook. Closely tied firms often share tasks at lower total cost than would be possible working at arm's length.

The partnership between AlliedSignal and Betz Laboratories, for example, shows the benefits of a good relationship. A while back, Betz was just one of several suppliers that sold Allied chemicals to keep the water in its plants from gunking up pipes and

In today's business markets, suppliers of both goods and services are working to build closer relationships with their business customers—to meet needs better and create a competitive advantage. Similarly, some customers are rewarding their best vendors by making them the "single source" of supply.

rusting machinery. But Betz didn't stop at selling commodity powders. Teams of Betz experts and Allied engineers studied each plant to find places where water was being wasted. In less than a year, a team in one plant found $2.5 million in potential cost reductions. For example, by adding a few valves to recycle the water in a cooling tower, Betz was able to save 300 gallons of water a minute, which resulted in savings of over $100,000 a year and reduced environmental impact. Because of ideas like this, Allied's use of water treatment chemicals decreased. However, Betz sales to Allied doubled because it became Allied's sole supplier.[10]

Relationships may not make sense

Although close relationships can produce benefits, they are not always best. A long-term commitment to a partner may reduce flexibility. When competition drives down prices and spurs innovation, the customer may be better off letting suppliers compete for the business. It may not be worth the customer's investment to build a relationship for purchases that are not particularly important or made that frequently.

It may at first appear that a seller would *always* prefer to have a closer relationship with a customer, but that is not so. Some customers may place orders that are too small or require so much special attention that the relationship would never be profitable for the seller. Also, in situations where a customer doesn't want a relationship, trying to build one may cost more than it's worth. Further, many small suppliers have made the mistake of relying too heavily on relationships with too few customers. One failed relationship may bankrupt the business.[11]

Relationships have many dimensions

Relationships are not "all or nothing" arrangements. Many firms may have a close relationship in some ways and not in others. It's useful to think about five key dimensions that help characterize most buyer–seller relationships: cooperation, information sharing, operational linkages, legal bonds, and relationship-specific adaptations. Purchasing managers for the buying firm and salespeople for the supplier usually coordinate the different dimensions of a relationship. However, as shown in Exhibit 6–5, close relationships often involve direct contacts between a number of people from other areas in both firms.[12]

Cooperation treats problems as joint responsibilities

In cooperative relationships, the buyer and seller work together to achieve both mutual and individual objectives. The two firms treat problems that arise as a joint responsibility. National Semiconductor (NS) and Siltec, a supplier of silicon wafers, found clever ways to cooperate and cut costs. Workers at the NS plant used to throw

Exhibit 6–5
Key Dimensions of Relationships in Business Markets

away the expensive plastic cassettes that Siltec uses to ship the silicon wafers. Now Siltec and NS cooperate to recycle the cassettes. This helps the environment and also saves more than $300,000 a year. Siltec passes along most of that to NS in the form of lower prices.[13]

Shared information is useful but may be risky

Some relationships involve open sharing of information. This might include the exchange of proprietary cost data, discussion of demand forecasts, and joint work on new product designs. Information might be shared through information systems or over the Internet. This is often a key facet of relationships that involve e-commerce.

Many firms provide relationship partners with access to password-protected websites. One big advantage of this approach is that it is fast and easy to update the information. It also saves time. A customer can check detailed product specs or the status of a job on the production line without having to wait for someone to respond.[14]

Information sharing can lead to better decisions, reduced uncertainty about the future, and better planning. However, firms don't want to share information if there's a risk that a partner might misuse it. For example, some suppliers claim that General Motors's former purchasing chief showed blueprints of its secret technology to competing suppliers. Violations of trust in a relationship are an ethical matter and should be taken seriously.

Operational linkages share functions between firms

Operational linkages are direct ties between the internal operations of the buyer and seller firms. These linkages usually involve ongoing coordination of activities between the firms. Shared activities are especially important when neither firm, working on its own, can perform a function as well as the two firms can working together.

Business customers often require operational linkages to reduce total inventory costs, maintain adequate inventory levels, and keep production lines moving. On the other hand, keeping too much inventory is expensive. Providing a customer with inventory when it's needed may require that a supplier be able to provide **just-in-time delivery**—reliably getting products there *just* before the customer needs them. We'll discuss just-in-time systems in more detail in Chapter 11. For now, it's enough to know that closer relationships between buyers and sellers involve operational linkages that lower costs and increase efficiency. Vertex Fasteners, for example, makes corrosion-resistant fasteners that are used by manufacturers in many different industries. Vertex creates value for its cost-conscious customers by working closely with a network of expert distributors. Distributors know each customer's specific needs so they can carefully label and pack orders for Vertex products in a way that saves the customer time and money when a truck is unloaded and shelves are stocked at the customer's factory.[15]

Operational linkages also may involve the routine activities of individuals who almost become part of the customer's operations. Design engineers, salespeople, and service representatives may participate in developing solutions to ongoing problems, conduct regular maintenance checks on equipment, or monitor inventory and coordinate orders. Consider the relationship between Johnson Controls, the supplier that makes instrument panels for Jeep's Liberty SUV, and its customer. When the Liberty was still in the planning stages, teams of people from both firms worked together to develop a special system of racks to move the instrument panels from JC's plant to the Jeep production line. Similar equipment was installed at the instrument panel plant and at the receiving dock for Jeep's assembly line. When the instrument panels get to the end of their own assembly line, the equipment automatically rolls them onto the racks in a waiting truck. The truck hauls the panels to the Jeep plant, and they are automatically unloaded, in sequence to match the next Liberty on the production line.[16]

Contracts spell out obligations

Many purchases in business markets are simple transactions. The seller's responsibility is to transfer title to goods or perform services, and the buyer's responsibility is to pay the agreed-upon price. However, more complex relationships may be spelled out in detailed legal contracts. An agreement may apply only for a short period, but long-term contracts are also common.

For example, a customer might ask a supplier to guarantee a 6 percent price reduction for a particular part for each of the next three years and pledge to virtually eliminate defects. In return, the customer might offer to double its orders and help the supplier boost productivity.

Sometimes the buyer and seller know roughly what is needed but can't fix all the details in advance. For example, specifications or total requirements may change over time. Then the relationship may involve **negotiated contract buying**, which means agreeing to contracts that allow for changes in the purchase arrangements. In such cases, the general project and basic price are described but include a provision for changes and price adjustments up or down.

Some managers figure that even a detailed contract isn't a good substitute for regular, good-faith reviews to make sure that neither party gets hurt by changing business conditions. Harley-Davidson used this approach when it moved toward closer relationships with a smaller number of suppliers. Purchasing executives tossed out detailed contracts and replaced them with a short statement of principles to guide relationships between Harley and its suppliers. This "handshake" approach is typical of relationships with Japanese firms.

Specific adaptations invest in the relationship

Relationship-specific adaptations involve changes in a firm's product or procedures that are unique to the needs or capabilities of a relationship partner. Industrial suppliers often custom design a new product for just one customer; this may require investments in R&D or new manufacturing technologies. MetoKote, in its relationship with John Deere described at the beginning of this chapter, made a specific adaptation by building its coating plant right next door to Deere's factory.

Buying firms may also adapt to a particular supplier; a computer maker may design around Intel's Pentium chip. However, buyers are often hesitant about making big investments that increase dependence on a specific supplier. Typically, they do it only when there isn't a good alternative—perhaps because only one or a few suppliers are available to meet a need—or if the benefits of the investment are clear before it's made.

Specific adaptations are usually made when the buying organization chooses to **outsource**—contract with an outside firm to produce goods or services rather than produce them internally. Many firms have turned to outsourcing to cut costs—and that's why much outsourcing is handled by suppliers in countries where labor costs are lower. For example, many American companies are outsourcing production to firms in China. Similarly, Dell Computer outsources handling of some of its telephone technical support and customer service inquiries to a firm in India that operates a call center.[17]

Powerful customer may control the relationship

Although a marketing manager may want to work in a cooperative partnership, that may be impossible with large customers who have the power to dictate how the relationship will work. For example, Duall/Wind, a plastics producer, was a supplier of small parts for Polaroid. But when Duall/Wind wanted to raise its prices to cover increasing costs, Polaroid balked. Polaroid's purchasing manager demanded that Duall/Wind show a breakdown of all its costs, from materials to labor to profit. As Duall/Wind's president said, "I had a tough time getting through my head that Polaroid wanted to come right in here and have us divulge all that." But Polaroid is a big account—and it got the information it wanted. Polaroid buyers agreed to a price increase only after they were confident that Duall/Wind was doing everything possible to control costs.[18]

Buyers still may use several sources to spread their risk

Even if a marketing manager develops the best marketing mix possible and cultivates a close relationship with the customer, the customer may not give *all* of its business to one supplier. Buyers often look for several dependable sources of supply to protect themselves from unpredictable events such as strikes, fires, or floods in one of their suppliers' plants. However, a good marketing mix is still likely to win a larger share of the total business—which can prove to be very important. From a buyer's point of view, it may not seem like a big deal to give a particular supplier a 30 percent share of the orders rather than a 20 percent share. But for the seller that's a 50 percent increase in sales![19]

TECHNOLOGY IS RESHAPING MANY BUSINESS MARKETS

The Internet and B2B e-commerce have changed the way many purchasing decisions are made. The cost of searching for market information is lower. Communication back and forth between buyers and sellers is more efficient. Transaction costs often decrease, too. For example, online ordering systems eliminate the old paper-shuffling bottlenecks, speed delivery, and reduce inventory costs.

Organizational buyers rely on a variety of important tools for e-commerce. To clarify the role that each plays in purchasing, we'll review them separately. However, often one website (or set of linked sites) combines them.

Buyers rely heavily on search engines

Purchasing managers rely heavily on Internet search engines to quickly identify new suppliers, better ways of meeting needs, and information to improve decisions. In a survey of business buyers, over 90 percent said their *first step* to satisfy new or unfamiliar needs is to turn to a search engine. Buyers often rely on specialized search engines that meet specific needs—like an engine that can find all types of steel that meet certain technical specifications and then compare delivered prices. But buyers also use general-purpose search engines like Google. A search across the whole Web can often locate off-the-shelf products that eliminate the need to buy expensive, custom-made items. For example, a firm in Saudi Arabia ordered $1,000 worth of tiny rubber grommets from Allstates Rubber & Tool, a small firm in the suburbs of Chicago. If the buyer's search hadn't located Allstates's website, the only alternative would have been to pay much more for custom-made grommets—and Allstates wouldn't have picked up a new customer.[20]

Marketing managers in B2B markets know that it is critical to have a website that gives buyers the information they need about the firm's whole marketing mix. To

In business-to-business markets, the Internet is making it faster, easier, and less expensive for firms to search for and identify suppliers who can meet their needs.

ensure that buyers find the website, many firms pay search engine services for special placement in the list of search results. Usually this takes the form of a sponsored link (ad) to the seller's website and appears on the first page of the list of search results.

Online marketplaces connect buyers and sellers in particular industries

Online marketplaces offer information of interest to firms that operate in specific markets or industries. These sites help customers find suppliers and vice versa, but many also offer newsletters, bookstores, market research reports, and job search tools. At VertMarkets (www.vertmarkets.com), there are links to 68 distinct online marketplaces that cover businesses ranging from semiconductor manufacturing to food service. Online marketplaces provide some organizational buyers with "one-stop shopping"; they can keep up with industry news, identify suppliers, gather information relevant to a purchase, and place an order. For sellers, marketplaces are a good way to generate new sales leads.

Catalog sites automate search and delivery

Catalog sites typically make it easy to search for and order products that are produced by many different suppliers. For example, for 75 years W.W. Grainger, a wholesaler, has sold a vast array of supplies for maintenance, repairs, and operations that are used in a wide range of industries. Now, its site (www.grainger.com) makes it fast and easy for customers to search its 3,700+ page electronic catalog.

Most catalog websites indicate if a product is available in inventory and allow customers to track delivery status. Many sites are also improving the quality of the information available. For instance, rather than provide just a basic description of an electric motor, a B2B catalog website might provide a download file with detailed engineering drawings and electrical details.

Procurement sites operate for the benefit of buyers

Procurement sites direct suppliers to companies (or divisions of a company) that need to make purchases. These sites make it easy for a large number of suppliers to find out about the purchase needs of the organizations that sponsor the sites. As a result, the number of sellers competing for the buyer's business is likely to increase, and this drives down prices or provides benefits to the buyer with respect to other terms of the sale. For example, when California's Department of Transportation was planning $4 billion in new construction projects, it established a procurement site so that potential suppliers knew what was required to be considered or selected as a vendor.

Reverse auction sites foster competition among sellers

Many websites that are designed to help buyers in B2B markets offer interactive systems for generating **competitive bids**—the terms of sale offered by different suppliers in response to the purchase specifications posted by the buyer.

In an e-marketplace, a buyer posts a specific purchase need to a website—and sellers bid for the business. For example, BuyerZone targets small business customers. A customer can go to its site (www.buyerzone.com), post a request related to any of about 100 product categories, and quickly get a response from interested suppliers. For instance, the owner of a 30-person mortgage firm in Bronx, New York, was looking for a service to handle his payroll. Within a few days of listing his request online at BuyerZone.com he had six bids. He saved 20 percent with the one he accepted. BuyerZone helps buyers generate competition for their purchases, but it also gives suppliers of all sizes—even multinational corporations like Toyota and Mitsubishi—a low-cost way to connect with customers when they are ready to purchase.[21]

Competitive bidding has been around for a long time. However, before the Internet, going through multiple rounds of bids was slow and inconvenient. Now it's fast and easy. A buyer who is ready to make a purchase can run a reverse auction. Vendors are invited to place a bid for specific goods or services. Usually the bidding focuses on price, but sometimes other terms of sale (like warranty or delivery time) are considered as well. Typically, auctions take place over a period of several hours—making it fast, cost-effective, and convenient for buyers looking for the lowest price. Some companies use reverse auctions to drive down the prices offered by their regular suppliers, but the downside of this is that it may harm the buyer–supplier relationship. Reverse auctions work best for undifferentiated products, including products such as plastic resin, personal computers, or transportation services that customers view as commodities. Reverse auctions are less effective when the value provided to the customer comes from a complete marketing mix, not just a low price.

Auction sites focus on unique items

At auction sites, the sellers describe what they have for sale, and potential buyers bid what they're willing to pay. A variety of formats are used, but in general the highest bidder prior to a deadline wins the auction. Auction sites tend to be seller-driven and are especially popular for surplus inventory, used items, and perishable products—such as unsold advertising space or produce. Auction sites help sellers because they attract buyers from far and wide. For example, Alibaba.com operates an auction site that connects sellers in China with global buyers and importers.[22]

Collaboration hubs support cooperation

Collaboration hubs go beyond matching buyers and sellers for one-time transactions. Many are designed to help people in different firms work together. The collaborative effort might involve design, manufacturing, and distribution. Many of these sites focus on the needs of smaller firms in a specific industry. For example, at CTSpace (www.ctspace.com) construction contractors and architects can collaborate on projects by sharing blueprints, working through building permit requirements, and purchasing building materials.

The Italian site, 1city.biz, created its Procurement Executive Circle as a collaboration hub for purchasing and supply chain executives to share common business interests and concerns. One hundred CEOs and purchasing managers from the largest

Online marketplace sites offer information of interest to firms that operate in specific markets.

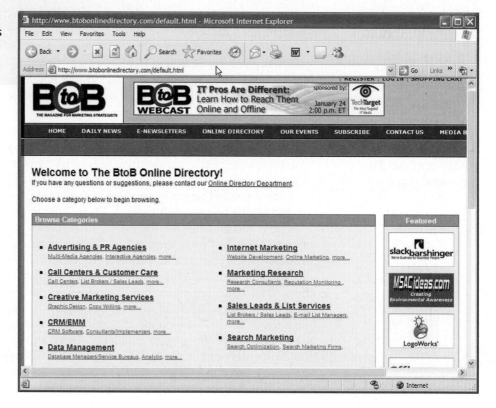

GXS Trades on Success with B2B E-commerce

GXS is a large corporation that provides business-to-business e-commerce services to firms from many industries, but it didn't start out that way. It got its start as the Global eXchange Services division at General Electric (GE). GE was a pioneer in B2B e-commerce, but its early efforts to solicit bids from vendors over the Internet ran into problems. Bidders with the lowest price got the business, but in the process GE got a lot of lowball quotes from untested vendors who couldn't fill the orders. By 1995, GE was on a smarter track with an Internet-based system called the Trading Process Network (TPN). It eliminated the delays of traditional purchasing approaches that used paper documents and snail mail.

With TPN, a buyer for GE's lighting division could search the Internet for possible suppliers of the custom-made machine tools he or she needed. To eliminate the paper shuffle, electronic blueprints and a bid request were sent via e-mail. As one GE purchasing manager put it, "You could simply point and click and a bid package would be sent to suppliers around the world." Vendors could respond quickly, too. A bid process that previously took a month was reduced to days, and sometimes even hours.

When GE executives saw how e-commerce improved their purchasing process, they decided to offer the TPN service to outside companies. A small firm could try the TPN Web for a fee of only $65 per month;

however, a large company paid $70,000 per month. That pricing hints at the kind of savings a large company could reap—and why GE's Global eXchange Services (GXS) division pushed to develop a full-service B2B Internet portal. Soon GSX was linking 100,000 trading partners involved in 1 billion exchanges a year worth $1 trillion in goods and services. In 2002, GE sold GXS for a whopping $800 million and today it operates as an independent company.

As e-commerce continues to evolve, a larger number of companies are exchanging different types of information. They range from payment instructions and computer-design files for new products to data on inventory levels and delivery status. Yet, different firms rely on incompatible digital formats and information management systems. So, GXS has introduced services to help buyers and sellers translate information so it is compatible across their separate systems.

For example, its Trading Grid helps buyers and suppliers from many different industries. They save money because they don't need to change their internal systems to match those of their trading partners. Firms that now benefit by using Trading Grid are as varied as retailer JCPenney, chemical manufacturer Rohm and Haas, and computer maker Ingram Micro, Inc. Even so, in the fast-changing world of e-commerce, GXS will have to continue to find new ways to meet firms' e-commerce needs if it is to stay ahead.[23]

Italian companies, as well as academics and consultants, share their knowledge about major issues that affect their businesses.[24]

More progress is needed

When everything else about a supplier's marketing mix is the same, a buyer would obviously prefer low prices. But "everything else" is not always the same. We considered examples of this earlier when we reviewed why a buyer might prefer closer relationships with fewer sellers. So Internet tools that focus primarily on lowering the purchase price do not necessarily lower total purchasing costs or provide a benefit in all types of purchases.

E-commerce order systems are common

E-commerce computer systems now *automatically* handle a large portion of routine order-placing. Buyers program decision rules that tell the computer how to order and leave the details of following through to the computer. For example, when an order comes in that requires certain materials or parts, the computer system automatically orders them from the appropriate suppliers, the delivery date is set, and production is scheduled.

If economic conditions change, buyers modify the computer instructions. When nothing unusual happens, however, the computer system continues to routinely rebuy as needs develop—electronically sending purchase orders to the regular supplier.

Obviously, it's a big sale to be selected as the major supplier that routinely receives all of a customer's electronic orders for the products you sell. Often this type of customer will be more impressed by an attractive marketing mix for a whole *line* of products than just a lower price for a particular order. Further, it may be too expensive and too much trouble to change the whole buying system just because somebody is offering a low price on a particular day.

It pays to have an ongoing relationship

In a routine order situation, it's very important to be one of the regular sources of supply. For straight rebuys, the buyer (or computer) may place an order without even considering other potential sources. However, if a buyer believes that there are several suppliers who could meet the specs, the buyer may request competitive bids. If different suppliers' quality, dependability, and delivery schedules all meet the specs, the buyer will select the low-price bid. But a creative marketer needs to look carefully at the purchaser's specs—and the need—to see if other elements of the marketing mix could provide a competitive advantage.

Sellers' sales reps (and perhaps whole teams of people) regularly call on these customers, but *not* to sell a particular item. Rather, they want to maintain relations, become a preferred source, or point out new developments that might cause the buyer to reevaluate the present straight rebuy procedure and give more business to the sales rep's company.

Variations in buying by customer type

We've been discussing aspects of relationships and e-commerce that generally apply with different types of customer organizations—in both the U.S. and internationally. However, it's also useful to have more detail about specific types of customers.

MANUFACTURERS ARE IMPORTANT CUSTOMERS

There are not many big ones

One of the most striking facts about manufacturers is how few there are compared to final consumers. This is true in every country. In the United States, for example, there are about 351,000 factories. Exhibit 6–6 shows that the majority of these are quite small—over half have less than 10 workers. But output from these small firms accounts for less than 3 percent of manufacturing value. In small plants, the owners often do the buying. And they buy less formally than buyers in the relatively few large manufacturing plants—which employ most of the workers and produce a large share of the value added by manufacturing. For example, only about 3 percent of all plants have 250 or more employees, yet they employ nearly half of the production workers and produce about 60 percent of the value added by manufacturers.

In other countries, the size distribution of manufacturers varies. But across different countries, the same general conclusion holds: Marketers often segment industrial markets on the basis of customer size because large firms do so much of the buying.

Customers cluster in geographic areas

In addition to concentration by company size, industrial markets are concentrated in certain geographic areas. Internationally, industrial customers are concentrated in countries that are at the more advanced stages of economic development. From all the talk in the news about the United States shifting from an industrial economy to a service and information economy, you might conclude that the U.S. is an exception—that the industrial market in this country is shrinking. But that's a myth. U.S. manufacturing output is higher than at any other time in the nation's history. The rate of growth, however, is fastest in countries where labor is cheap.

Within a country, there is often further concentration in specific areas. In the U.S., many factories are concentrated in big metropolitan areas—especially in New York, Pennsylvania, Ohio, Illinois, Texas, and California.[25] There is also concentration by industry. In Germany, for example, the steel industry is concentrated in the Ruhr Valley. Similarly, U.S. manufacturers of high-tech electronics are

Exhibit 6-6 Size Distribution of Manufacturing Establishments

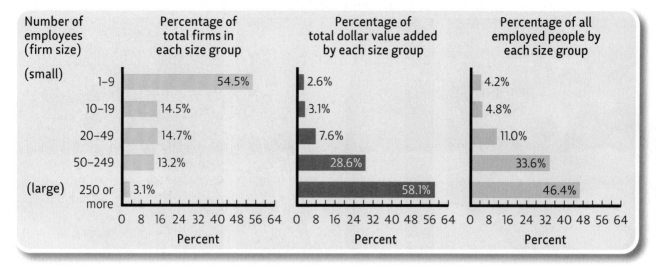

concentrated in California's famous Silicon Valley near San Francisco and also along Boston's Route 128.

Business data often classifies industries

The products an industrial customer needs to buy depend on the business it is in. Because of this, sales of a product are often concentrated among customers in similar businesses. For example, apparel manufacturers are the main customers for zippers. Marketing managers must focus their marketing mixes on prospective customers who exhibit characteristics similar to their current customers.

Detailed information is often available to help a marketing manager learn more about customers in different lines of business. The U.S. government collects and publishes data by the **North American Industry Classification System (NAICS) codes**—groups of firms in similar lines of business. (NAICS is pronounced "nakes.") The number of establishments, sales volumes, and number of employees—broken down by geographic areas—are given for each NAICS code. A number of other countries collect similar data, and some of them try to coordinate their efforts with an international variation of the NAICS system. However, in many countries data on business customers is incomplete or inaccurate.

The U.S. adopted NAICS as a standard in 1997 and is phasing it in over time. The phase-in makes it easier to use the system because in the past data was reported using Standard Industrial Classification (SIC) codes. Many of the codes are similar; check the website at www.naics.com for details. The move to the NAICS system helps business marketers. It is suited to identifying new or fast-changing industries—and for marketers that spells opportunity. NAICS is also more detailed than SIC and works better for services such as financial institutions, health care providers, and firms in the entertainment business. The general logic of NAICS and SIC is similar. So let's take a closer look at how the NAICS codes work.

The NAICS code breakdowns start with broad industry categories such as construction (23), manufacturing (31), wholesale trade (42), finance and insurance (52), and so on. Within each two-digit industry breakdown, much more detailed data may be available for three-digit industries (that is, subindustries of the two-digit industries). For example, within the two-digit manufacturing industry (code 31) there are manufacturers of food (311), beverages and tobacco (312), and others, including apparel manufacturers (315). Then each three-digit group of firms is further subdivided into more detailed four-, five-, and six-digit classifications. For instance, within the three-digit

A firm like Alcoa Aluminum is likely to find that the majority of its customers are concentrated within a few industries that it can identify by North American Industry Classification System code number.

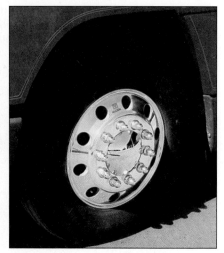

(315) apparel manufacturers there are four-digit subgroups for knitting mills (3151), cut and sew firms (3152), and producers of apparel accessories (3159). Exhibit 6–7 illustrates that breakdowns are more detailed as you move to codes with more digits. However, detailed data (say, broken down at the four-digit level) isn't available for all industries in every geographic area. The government does not provide detail when only one or two plants are located in an area.

Exhibit 6–7 Illustrative NAICS Code Breakdown for Apparel Manufacturers

- Construction (23)
- Manufacturing (31)
- others...

- Food (311)
- Apparel (315)
- others...

- Knitting mills (3151)
- Cut and sew apparel (3152)
- Apparel accessories (3159)
- others...

- Women's & girls' (31523)
- Men's & boys' (31522)
- Other cut & sew apparel (31529)
- others...

- Underwear & nightwear (315221)
- Suits and coats (315222)
- Shirts (315223)
- others...

Many firms find their *current* customers' NAICS codes and then look at NAICS-coded lists for similar companies that may need the same goods and services. Other companies look at which NAICS categories are growing or declining to discover new opportunities.[26]

PRODUCERS OF SERVICES—SMALLER AND MORE SPREAD OUT

The service side of the U.S. economy is large and has been growing fast. Service operations are also growing in some other countries. There are many good opportunities to provide these service companies with the products they need to support their operations. But there are also challenges.

The United States has about 4 million service firms—over 11 times as many as it has manufacturers. Some of these are big companies with international operations. Examples include AT&T, Hilton Hotels, Prudential Insurance, CitiGroup, and EDS (Electronic Data Systems). These firms have purchasing departments that are like those in large manufacturing organizations. But as you might guess given the large number of service firms, most of them are small. They're also more spread out around the country than manufacturing concerns. Factories often locate where transportation facilities are good, raw materials are available, and it is less costly to produce goods in quantity. Service operations, in contrast, often have to be close to their customers.

Buying may not be as formal

Purchases by small service firms are often handled by whoever is in charge. This may be a doctor, lawyer, owner of a local insurance agency, or manager of a hotel. Suppliers who usually deal with purchasing specialists in large organizations may have trouble adjusting to this market. Personal selling is still an important part of promotion, but reaching these customers in the first place often requires more advertising. And small service firms may need much more help in buying than a large corporation.

Canon, the familiar name in office copiers, was very successful serving the needs of smaller service firms like law offices. Canon developed promotion materials to help first-time buyers understand differences between copiers and emphasized that its machines were much easier to use and maintain. Canon also used retail channels to make its copiers available in less populated areas where there wasn't enough business to justify the expense of a dedicated sales rep.[27]

Small service customers like Internet buying

Small service companies that don't attract much personal attention from salespeople often rely on e-commerce for many of their purchases. Purchases by small customers can add up—so for many suppliers these customers are an important target market. Increasingly, suppliers cater to the needs of these customers with specially designed websites. A well-designed website can be efficient for both customers and suppliers. Customers can get information, place orders, or follow up with a call or e-mail for personal attention from a salesperson or customer service rep when it's needed.

RETAILERS AND WHOLESALERS BUY FOR THEIR CUSTOMERS

Most retail and wholesale buyers see themselves as purchasing agents for their target customers—remembering the old saying that "Goods well bought are half sold." Typically, retailers do *not* see themselves as sales agents for particular manufacturers. They buy what they think they can profitably sell. For example, the buying specialist at Walgreens Drugstores who handles products targeted at ethnic consumers is a real expert. He knows what ethnic customers want and won't be persuaded by a sales rep for a manufacturer who can't provide it. Of course, there is a place for collaboration, as when the Walgreens buyer works with people at Soft Sheen Products to develop a new product for the African American target market. That's profitable for both firms.

Committee buying is impersonal

Space in retail stores is limited, and buyers for retail chains simply are not interested in carrying every product that some salesperson wants them to sell. In an average week, 150 to 250 new items are offered to the buying offices of a large chain like Safeway. If the chain accepted all of them, it would add 10,000 new items during a single year! Obviously, these firms need a way to deal with this overload.[28]

The entrepreneurs who started PenAgain, for example, had to have more than a unique product to get shelf space at Wal-Mart. Their presentation to Wal-Mart had to include hard data that showed their marketing mix was already working well in other retail stores and evidence of their ability to supply the large quantities a retailer the size of Wal-Mart would need.[29]

Decisions to add or drop lines or change buying policies may be handled by a *buying committee*. The seller still calls on and gives a pitch to a buyer—but the buyer does not have final responsibility. Instead, the buyer prepares forms summarizing proposals for new products and passes them on to the committee for evaluation. The seller may not get to present her story to the buying committee in person. This rational, almost cold-blooded approach certainly reduces the impact of a persuasive salesperson. On the other hand, it may favor a firm that has hard data on how its whole marketing mix will help the retailer attract and keep customers.

Buyers watch computer output closely

Most larger firms now use sophisticated computerized inventory replenishment systems. Scanners at retail checkout counters keep track of what goes out the door—and computers use this data to update the records. Even small retailers and wholesalers use automated control systems that create daily reports showing sales of every product.

Buyers with this kind of information know, in detail, the profitability of the different competing products. If a product isn't moving, the retailer isn't likely to be impressed by a salesperson's request for more in-store attention or added shelf space.

Reorders are straight rebuys

Retailers and wholesalers usually carry a large number of products. A drug wholesaler, for example, may carry up to 125,000 products. Because they deal with so many products, most intermediaries buy their products on a routine, automatic reorder basis—straight rebuys—once they make the initial decision to stock specific items. Automatic computer ordering is a natural outgrowth of computerized checkout systems. Sellers to these markets must understand the size of the buyer's job and have something useful to say and do when they call.

Some are not "open to buy"

Retail buyers are sometimes controlled by a miniature profit and loss statement for each department or merchandise line. In an effort to make a profit, the buyer tries to forecast sales, merchandise costs, and expenses. The figure for "cost of merchandise" is the amount buyers have budgeted to spend over the budget period. If the money has not yet been spent, buyers are **open to buy**—that is, the buyers have budgeted funds that can be spent during the current period. However, if the budget has been spent, they are no longer in the market and no amount of special promotion or price-cutting is likely to induce them to buy.[30]

Resident buyers may help a firm's buyers

Resident buyers are independent buying agents who work in central markets (New York City, Paris, Rome, Hong Kong, Chicago, Los Angeles) for several retailer or wholesaler customers based in outlying areas or other countries. They buy new styles and fashions and fill-in items as their customers run out of stock during the year.

Resident buying organizations fill a need. They help small channel members (producers and middlemen) reach each other inexpensively. Resident buyers usually are paid an annual fee based on their purchases.

THE GOVERNMENT MARKET

Size and diversity

Some marketers ignore the government market because they think that government red tape is more trouble than it's worth. They probably don't realize how big the government market really is. Government is the largest customer group in many

Government agencies are important customers for a wide variety of products.

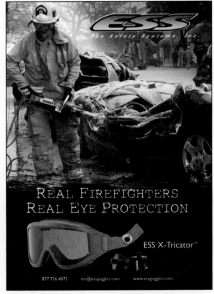

countries—including the United States. About 30 percent of the U.S. gross domestic product is spent by various government units; the figure is much higher in some economies. Different government units in the United States spend about $3,558,600,000,000 (think about it!) a year to buy almost every kind of product. They run not only schools, police departments, and military organizations, but also supermarkets, public utilities, research laboratories, offices, hospitals, and even liquor stores. These huge government expenditures cannot be ignored by an aggressive marketing manager.

Competitive bids may be required

Government buyers in the United States are expected to spend money wisely—in the public interest—so their purchases are usually subject to much public review. To avoid charges of favoritism, most government customers buy by specification using a mandatory bidding procedure. Often the government buyer must accept the lowest bid that meets the specifications. You can see how important it is for the buyer to write precise and complete specifications. Otherwise, sellers may submit a bid that fits the specs but doesn't really match what is needed. By law, a government unit might have to accept the lowest bid—even for an unwanted product.

Writing specifications is not easy—and buyers usually appreciate the help of well-informed salespeople. Salespeople *want* to have input on the specifications so their product can be considered or even have an advantage. A contract can be landed without the lowest bid when lower bids don't meet minimum or requested specifications.

Rigged specs are an ethical concern

At the extreme, a government customer who wants a specific brand or supplier may try to write the description so that no other supplier can meet all the specs. The buyer may have good reasons for such preferences—a more reliable product, prompt delivery, or better service after the sale. This kind of loyalty sounds great, but marketers must be sensitive to the ethical issues involved. Laws that require government customers to get bids are intended to increase competition among suppliers, not reduce it. Specs that are written primarily to defeat the purpose of these laws may be viewed as illegal bid rigging.

The approved supplier list

Specification and bidding difficulties aren't problems in all government orders. Items that are bought frequently—or for which there are widely accepted standards—are purchased routinely. The government unit simply places an order at a previously approved price. To share in this business, a supplier must be on the list of approved suppliers and agree on a price that will stay the same for a specific period—perhaps a year.

Negotiated contracts are common too

Negotiation is often necessary when there are many intangible factors. Unfortunately, this is exactly where favoritism and influence can slip in. And such influence is not unknown—especially in city and state government. Nevertheless, negotiation is an important buying method in government sales—so a marketing mix should emphasize more than just low price.[31]

Learning what government wants

In the United States, there are more than 87,575 local government units (school districts, cities, counties, and states) as well as many federal agencies that make purchases. Keeping on top of all of them is nearly impossible. Potential suppliers should focus on the government units they want to cater to and learn the bidding methods of those units. Then it's easier to stay informed since most government contracts are advertised. Target marketing can make a big contribution here—making sure the marketing mixes are well matched with the different bid procedures.

A marketer can learn a lot about potential government target markets from various government publications and by using the Internet. For example, the General Services Administration handles vendor contracts for off-the-shelf goods and services; information for vendors is available at www.gsa.gov. There is an online resource center for government contracting at www.govcon.com. The Small Business Administration (www.sba.gov) offers many resources, including the *U.S. Purchasing, Specifications, and Sales Directory*. It explains government procedures to encourage competition for such business. Various state and local governments also offer guidance, as do government units in many other countries.

Dealing with foreign governments

Selling to government units in foreign countries can be a real challenge. In many cases, a firm must get permission from the government in its own country to sell to a foreign government. Moreover, most government contracts favor domestic suppliers if they are available. Even if such favoritism is not explicit, public sentiment may make it very difficult for a foreign competitor to get a contract. Or the government bureaucracy may simply bury a foreign supplier in so much red tape that there's no way to win.

Is it unethical to "buy help"?

In some countries, government officials expect small payments (grease money) just to speed up processing of routine paperwork, inspections, or decisions from the local bureaucracy. Outright influence peddling—where government officials or their friends request bribe money to sway a purchase decision—is common in some markets. In the past, marketers from some countries have looked at such bribes as a cost of doing business. However, the **Foreign Corrupt Practices Act**, passed by the U.S. Congress in 1977, prohibits U.S. firms from paying bribes to foreign officials. A person who pays bribes, or authorizes an agent to pay them, can face stiff penalties. However, the law was amended in 1988 to allow small grease money payments if they are customary in a local culture. Further, a manager isn't held responsible if an agent in the foreign country secretly pays bribes.[32]

CONCLUSION

In this chapter, we examined organizational buying and how it differs from final consumer buying. We saw that organizational buyers rely heavily on economic factors and cost–benefit analysis to make purchase decisions. The chapter showed how multiple influences are important in buying decisions—and how marketing managers must recognize and attend to the needs of all members of the buying center.

Buying behavior—and marketing opportunities—may change when there's a close relationship between a supplier and a customer. However, close relationships are not all or nothing. There are different ways that a supplier can build close relationships with its customers. We identified key dimensions of relationships and their benefits and limitations.

This chapter also showed how buying differs with the buying situation. The problem-solving modes used by final consumers and discussed in Chapter 5 also apply here—with some modification.

Advances in technology and e-commerce play a key role in changes in organizational buying and B2B marketing. We introduced some of the different ways that these technologies are being employed.

We saw that organizational buyers buy for resale or to produce other goods and services—and include manufacturers, farms, distributors, retailers, government agencies, and nonprofit organizations. There are many similarities in how these organizations buy—but also differences. The chapter concludes by providing insights about buying practices particular to manufacturers, service firms, and governments.

Understanding how organizations buy can help marketing managers identify logical dimensions for segmenting markets and developing marketing mixes. But the nature of products being offered may require further adjustments in the mix. Different product classes are discussed in Chapter 8. Variations by product may provide additional segmenting dimensions to help a marketing manager fine-tune a marketing strategy.

KEY TERMS

QUESTIONS AND PROBLEMS

1. In your own words, explain how the buying behavior of business customers in different countries may have been a factor in speeding the spread of international marketing.

2. Compare and contrast the buying behavior of final consumers and organizational buyers. In what ways are they most similar and in what ways are they most different?

3. Briefly discuss why a marketing manager should think about who is likely to be involved in the buying center for a particular purchase. Is the buying center idea useful in consumer buying? Explain your answer.

4. If a nonprofit hospital were planning to buy expensive MRI scanning equipment (to detect tumors), who might be involved in the buying center? Explain your answer and describe the types of influence that different people might have.

5. Describe the situations that would lead to the use of the three different buying processes for a particular product—lightweight bumpers for a pickup truck.

6. Why would an organizational buyer want to get competitive bids? What are some of the situations when competitive bidding can't be used?

7. How likely would it be for each of the following to use competitive bids? (a) a small town that needed a road resurfaced, (b) a scouting organization that needed a printer to print its scouting handbook, (c) a hardware retailer that wants to add a new lawn mower line, (d) a grocery store chain that wants to install new checkout scanners, and (e) a sorority that wants to buy a computer to keep track of member dues. Explain your answers.

8. Discuss the advantages and disadvantages of just-in-time supply relationships from an organizational buyer's point of view. Are the advantages and disadvantages merely reversed from the seller's point of view?

9. Explain why a customer might be willing to work more cooperatively with a small number of suppliers rather than pitting suppliers in a competition against each other. Give an example that illustrates your points.

10. Would a tool manufacturer need different marketing strategies for (a) a big retail chain like Home Depot and (b) a single hardware store run by its owner? Discuss your answer.

11. How do you think a furniture manufacturer's buying habits and practices would be affected by the specific type of product to be purchased? Consider fabric for upholstered furniture, a lathe for the production line, cardboard for shipping cartons, and lubricants for production machinery.

12. Discuss the importance of target marketing when analyzing organizational markets. How easy is it to isolate homogeneous market segments in these markets?

13. Explain how NAICS codes might be helpful in evaluating and understanding business markets. Give an example.

14. Considering the nature of retail buying, outline the basic ingredients of promotion to retail buyers. Does it make any difference what kinds of products are involved? Are any other factors relevant?

15. The government market is obviously an extremely large one, yet it is often slighted or even ignored by many firms. Red tape is certainly one reason, but there are others. Discuss the situation and be sure to include the possibility of segmenting in your analysis.

16. Some critics argue that the Foreign Corrupt Practices Act puts U.S. businesses at a disadvantage when competing in foreign markets with suppliers from other countries that do not have similar laws. Do you think that this is a reasonable criticism? Explain your answer.

CREATING MARKETING PLANS

The Marketing Plan Coach software on the Student CD includes a sample marketing plan for Hillside Veterinary Clinic. Hillside decided to focus on final consumers and their pets rather than include organizational customers that might need veterinary care for animals. Such customers might range from dog breeders and farmers to animal protection shelters and law enforcement agencies that work with dogs. Would it be easy or hard for Hillside to expand its focus to serve customers who are not final consumers? Explain your thinking.

SUGGESTED CASES

5. Applied Polymer Sciences   6. International Steel Company

COMPUTER-AIDED PROBLEM

6. VENDOR ANALYSIS

CompuTech, Inc., makes circuit boards for microcomputers. It is evaluating two possible suppliers of electronic memory chips.

The chips do the same job. Although manufacturing quality has been improving, some chips are always defective. Both suppliers will replace defective chips. But the only practical way to test for a defective chip is to assemble a circuit board and "burn it in"—run it and see if it works. When one chip on a board is defective at that point, it costs $2.00 for the extra labor time to replace it. Supplier 1 guarantees a chip failure rate of not more than 1 per 100 (that is, a defect rate of 1 percent). The second supplier's 2 percent defective rate is higher, but its price is lower.

Supplier 1 has been able to improve its quality because it uses a heavier plastic case to hold the chip. The only disadvantage of the heavier case is that it requires CompuTech to use a connector that is somewhat more expensive.

Transportation costs are added to the price quoted by either supplier, but Supplier 2 is farther away so transportation costs are higher. And because of the distance, delays in supplies reaching CompuTech are sometimes a problem. To ensure that a sufficient supply is on hand to keep production going, CompuTech must maintain a backup inventory—and this increases inventory costs. CompuTech figures inventory costs— the expenses of finance and storage—as a percentage of the total order cost.

To make its vendor analysis easier, CompuTech's purchasing agent has entered data about the two suppliers on a spreadsheet. He based his estimates on the quantity he thinks he will need over a full year.

a. Based on the results shown in the initial spreadsheet, which supplier do you think CompuTech should select? Why?

b. CompuTech estimates it will need 100,000 chips a year if sales go as expected. But if sales are slow, fewer chips will be needed. This isn't an issue with Supplier 2; its price is the same at any quantity. However, Supplier 1's price per chip will be $1.95 if CompuTech buys less than 90,000 during the year. If CompuTech only needs 84,500 chips, which supplier would be more economical? Why?

c. If the actual purchase quantity will be 84,500 and Supplier 1's price is $1.95, what is the highest price at which Supplier 2 will still be the lower-cost vendor for CompuTech? (Hint: You can enter various prices for Supplier 2 in the spreadsheet—or use the analysis feature to vary Supplier 2's price and display the total costs for both vendors.)

For additional questions related to this problem, see Exercise 6-3 in the *Learning Aid for Use with Essentials of Marketing*, 11th edition.

7

Improving Decisions with Marketing Information

When you see the array of products on drugstore shelves—strips, gels, swabs, and more—to make your smile whiter and brighter, it's easy to forget that just a few years ago this category of products—for a combination of oral care and beauty needs—didn't exist. Movie stars would pay Hollywood dentists thousands of dollars for special whitening treatments, but the rest of us would just envy their pearly smiles.

That changed after research convinced marketing managers for Crest oral care products that this unmet need was a big opportunity. A variety of marketing research firms, including National Opinion Research and Semaphore, helped with the research. For example, focus group interviews suggested that consumers would be excited about a do-it-yourself whitening treatment that was effective, simple to use, and affordable. Responses by representative samples of consumers to survey questionnaires confirmed that this was a large market. Online product concept tests revealed that there would be demand even at a price around $50, which would cover development and introductory promotion costs. On the other hand, research also revealed that dentists, who are influential in recommending oral care products, were concerned that the product might eat into their business.

When the R&D people came up with the idea of using a clear, tape-like strip that works by sticking to the teeth, product effectiveness tests confirmed that consumers could see a difference in whiteness. Research also showed that 30 minutes was the consumer limit for wearing the strips. Research even helped in selecting a brand name, Crest Whitestrips, and in focusing the positioning with advertising copy on "easy to use" and "superior whitening versus toothpaste" benefits.

Rather than work with traditional test markets in retail stores, marketing managers used infomercials and ads in consumer magazines to explain the product and direct consumers to a website (www.whitestrips.com) where they could buy Whitestrips. That approach not only produced sales quickly but also showed retailers that there was strong demand, even at a $44 retail price. Moreover, by doing studies on the Internet, researchers were able to deliver consumer test market input to marketing managers within days. For example, when researchers found that 80 percent of customers were female rather than the 50/50 split of men and women that was expected, the ad agency refined the focus of the advertising media.

When Whitestrips went into national distribution, the new product launch was one of the most successful in 20 years. Within a year, sales of Whitestrips surpassed $200 million and the product became the category leader. A professional version of Whitestrips for dentists to sell contributed to this success. Some dentists reported that the strips even helped increase interest in other types of cosmetic dentistry.

Crest soon faced competition from entries such as Mentadent's Tooth Whitening System and Colgate's Simply White, which was half the price of Whitestrips. Although more consumers were buying whiteners, data from Information Resources, Inc., showed that Whitestrips's market share was slipping. Consumer research also showed that customers wanted more convenience, so Crest fought back with new products. One was a premium version of Whitestrips that works in half the time. Another was Crest Night

Effects—a lower-price product that is dabbed on the teeth and worn while sleeping. Many retailers took shelf space away from Mentadent to stock all three of Crest's whitening products. They could see in their routine sales analysis reports that Mentadent was losing sales to both Colgate and Crest.

Crest also switched its promotion to attract new customers. Although early adopters had wanted scientific evidence of the effectiveness of whiteners, research revealed that consumers adopting the product later were more focused on what other people thought. So Crest developed advertising that urged consumers to try Whitestrips for special social occasions, like a wedding or college reunion.

In spite of adjustments in strategy, growth in the U.S. market has slowed. However, Crest has introduced Whitestrips into the fast-growing Chinese marketplace, where it already has a 25 percent share of toothpaste sales.[1]

LEARNING OBJECTIVES

The Whitestrips case shows that successful marketing strategies require information about potential target markets and their likely responses to marketing mixes—as well as information about competition and other marketing environment variables. Managers also need information for implementation and control. Without good information, managers are left to guess—and in today's fast-changing markets, that invites failure. In this chapter, we discuss how marketing managers get the information that they need.

When you finish this chapter, you should:

1. know about marketing information systems.

2. understand the scientific approach to marketing research.

3. know about methods for collecting secondary and primary data.

4. understand the role of observing, questioning, and using experimental methods in marketing research.

5. understand important new terms (shown in red).

EFFECTIVE MARKETING REQUIRES GOOD INFORMATION

Information is a bridge to the market

To make good marketing decisions, managers need accurate information about what is happening in the market. They usually can't get all of the information that they'd like, but part of their job is to find cost-effective ways to get the information that they really must have.

In this chapter, we'll focus on the two key sources that marketing managers turn to for information to make better decisions. One source is **marketing research**—procedures that develop and analyze new information about a market. Marketing research may involve the use of questionnaires, interviews with customers, experiments, and many other approaches. But most marketing managers have some information needs that would take too long, or cost too much, to address with one-at-a-time marketing research projects. So, in many companies, marketing managers also routinely get help from a **marketing information system (MIS)**—which is an organized way of continually gathering, accessing, and analyzing information that marketing managers need to make ongoing decisions.

Marketing managers may need marketing research, an MIS, or a combination of both to get the information they need to make decisions during any step in the marketing strategy planning process—or to improve implementation and control. See Exhibit 7–1. In this chapter, we'll discuss ways to make marketing research and an MIS more useful and the key issues that marketing managers face in using them.

Success requires cooperation with specialists

Most large companies have a separate marketing research department to plan and manage research projects. People in these departments often rely on outside specialists—like interviewing and tabulating services—to carry out the work on particular projects. Further, they may call in specialized marketing consultants and marketing research organizations to take charge of a whole project.

Smaller companies usually don't have separate marketing research departments. They often depend on their salespeople or managers to conduct what research they do.

Some nonprofit organizations have begun to use marketing research—usually with the help of outside specialists. For example, there are research firms that specialize in conducting marketing research for colleges, museums, and politicians.

Most companies also have a separate department with information technology specialists to help set up and maintain an MIS. Even small firms may have a person who handles all of the technical work on computer systems. Increasingly, both small and large firms are turning to outside consultants and service providers for help with information systems. As we will discuss, collaboration between the marketing manager and these internal and external technical specialists is sometimes a challenge.

CHANGES ARE UNDER WAY IN MARKETING INFORMATION SYSTEMS

Marketing managers for some companies make decisions based almost totally on their own judgment—with very little hard data. The manager may not even know that he or she is about to make the same mistake that the previous person in that job already made! When it's time to make a decision, they may wish they had more information. But by then it's too late, so they do without.

MIS makes information available and accessible

Many firms realize that it doesn't pay to wait until you have important questions you can't answer. They anticipate the information they will need. They work to develop a *continual flow of information* that is available and quickly accessible from an MIS when it's needed.

We won't cover all of the technical details of planning for an MIS. But you should understand what an MIS is and know some of the possibilities. So we'll be discussing the elements of a complete MIS as shown in Exhibit 7–2. As part of that review, we'll highlight how technology is changing MIS use.

Exhibit 7-2   Elements of a Complete Marketing Information System

| Information sources | Questions and answers | Decision maker | Results |

Market research studies

New information

Marketing models

Internal data sources

Inputs   Questions   Answers

External data sources

Databases ("data warehouse")

Decision support system (DSS)

Marketing manager decisions

Outcomes (sales, profit, customer reactions, etc.)

Information technology specialists

Feedback

Get more information—faster and easier

Advances in information technology have ushered in *radical* improvements in marketing information systems. Now it's easy to set up and use an MIS and exchange data among remote computers. Managers have access to much more information. It's instantly available, and often just a mouse click away.

The *type* of information available is also changing dramatically. Until recently, marketing managers relied on computers mainly for number crunching. The multimedia revolution in computing lifted that limitation. Now it doesn't matter whether marketing information takes the form of a report, spreadsheet, database,

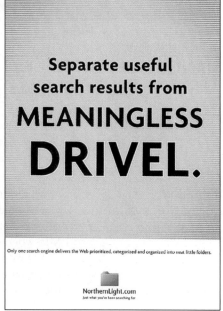

presentation, photo, graphic, video, or table of statistics. It is all being created on computer. So it can be easily stored and accessed by computer. When we talk about a "database" of marketing information, it may include all types of information, not just numbers.

An intranet is easy to update

Many firms, even very small ones, have their own **intranet**—a system for linking computers within a company. An intranet works like the Internet. However, to maintain security, access to websites or data on an intranet is usually limited to employees. Even so, information is available on demand. Further, it's a simple matter to "publish" new information to a website as it becomes available.

You seldom have all the information you need. Both customers and competitors can be unpredictable. Getting the precise information you want may cost too much or take too long. For example, data on international markets is often incomplete, outdated, or difficult to obtain. So a manager often must decide what information is really critical and how to get it.

Marketing managers must help develop an MIS

In some companies, an MIS is set up by a person or group that provides *all* departments in the firm with information technology support. Or it may be set up by marketing specialists.

These specialists are important, but the marketing manager should play an important role, too. Marketing managers know what data they've routinely used or needed in the past. They can also foresee what decisions they must make and what types of data might be useful. They should communicate these needs to the specialists so the information will be there when they want it and in the form they want it.

Decision support systems put managers online

An MIS system organizes incoming information into a **data warehouse**—a place where databases are stored so that they are available when needed. You can think of a data warehouse as a sort of electronic library, where all of the information is indexed extremely well. Firms with an MIS often have information technology specialists who help managers get specialized reports and output from the warehouse. However, to get better decisions, most MIS systems now provide marketing managers with a decision support system. A **decision support system (DSS)** is a computer program that makes it easy for a marketing manager to get and use information *as he or she is making decisions*.

A decision support system usually involves some sort of **search engine**—a computer program that helps a marketing manager find information that is needed. For example, a manager who wants sales data for the previous week might search for any database or computer file that references the term *unit sales* as well as the relevant dates. The search engine would identify any files where that term appeared. If there were many, the manager could narrow the search further (say by specifying the product of interest).

When the search is focused on numerical data, simply finding the information may not go far enough. Thus, a DSS typically helps change raw data—like product sales for the previous day—into more *useful information*. For example, it may draw graphs to show relationships in data—perhaps comparing yesterday's sales to the sales on the same day in the last four weeks.

Information for planning, implementation, and control

At Verizon Communications, marketing managers' computers display a "marketing dashboard." Like the speedometer and fuel gauge on a car, a marketing dashboard displays up-to-the-minute marketing data in an easy-to-read format. A marketing dashboard is usually customized to a manager's areas of responsibility. A Verizon dashboard might show the percentage of customer calls dropped by cell towers or the number and location of repair trucks in the field. With early warning about potential problems, the manager can quickly make corrections. For example, a manager might call in extra customer service help if too many customers are "on hold."

Some decision support systems go even further. They allow a manager to see how answers to questions might change in various situations. For example, a manager at Home Depot may need to decide whether to use radio advertising or newspaper inserts to stimulate paint sales in a particular store or market area. The Home Depot MIS has data on sales by product and store over time, as well as data on spending for different types of promotion by market. Drawing on data about how a promotion has worked in the past (in this market and in other markets), the DSS will make sales estimates using a marketing model. A **marketing model** is a statement of relationships among marketing variables. The manager can look at the sales (and costs) expected with different types of promotion and select the marketing mix that is best for that target market.[2]

In short, the decision support system puts managers online so they can study available data and make better marketing decisions—faster.[3]

Sales and performance analyses show what's happening

Marketers are always interested in what sort of results they are achieving, but it is usually not enough to simply know totals or summary information. Detailed sales data helps them understand what is happening in the market. A manager can use an MIS to conduct a **sales analysis**—a detailed breakdown of a company's sales records. For example, a sales manager might compare sales data for different salespeople, products, types of customers, or channels of distribution. Of course, a manager may be interested in aspects of performance other than sales. Other marketing "metrics"—including costs, profitability, market share, and like—can also be developed.

Managers for Staples, the big office supplies chain, used these types of analyses to help make better decisions on everything from where to locate new stores to how to organize display space. One analysis, which considered sales and costs in detail, led to the conclusion that the chain's basic emphasis on furniture lines (like desks and file cabinets) was a mistake. While these high-ticket furniture lines provided better gross margins than everyday office supplies (like Bic pens and Scotch tape), they took up much more floor space and required more time from salespeople. So Staples shrunk or eliminated the furniture department in most of its stores—and sales and profits improved.[4]

Many firms are not there yet

Of course, not every firm has a complete MIS system. And in some firms that do, managers don't know how to use what's there. A major problem is that many managers are used to doing it the old way—and they don't think through what information they need.

One sales manager thought he was progressive when he asked his assistant for a report listing each sales rep's sales for the previous month and the current month. The assistant quickly found the relevant information on the firm's intranet, put it into an Excel spreadsheet, and printed out the report. Later, however, she was surprised to see the sales manager working on the list with a calculator. He was figuring the percentage change in sales for the month and ranking the reps from largest increase in sales to smallest. The spreadsheet software could have done all of that—instantly—but the sales manager got what he *asked for,* not what he really needed. An MIS can provide information—but only the marketing manager knows what problem needs solving. It's the job of the manager—not the computer or the MIS specialist—to ask for the right information in the right form.[5]

THE SCIENTIFIC METHOD AND MARKETING RESEARCH

The scientific method—combined with the strategy planning framework we discussed in Chapter 2—can help marketing managers make better decisions.

The **scientific method** is a decision-making approach that focuses on being objective and orderly in *testing* ideas before accepting them. With the scientific method, managers don't just *assume* that their intuition is correct. Instead, they use their intuition and observations to develop **hypotheses**—educated guesses about the relationships between things or about what will happen in the future. Then they test their hypotheses before making final decisions.

A manager who relies only on intuition might introduce a new product without testing consumer response. But a manager who uses the scientific method might say, "I think (hypothesize) that consumers currently using the most popular brand will prefer our new product. Let's run some consumer tests. If at least 60 percent of the consumers prefer our product, we can introduce it in a regional test market. If it doesn't pass the consumer test there, we can make some changes and try again." With this approach, decisions are based on evidence, not just hunches.

The scientific method forces an orderly research process. Some managers don't carefully specify what information they need. They blindly move ahead—hoping that research will provide "the answer." Other managers may have a clearly defined problem or question but lose their way after that. These hit-or-miss approaches waste both time and money.

FIVE-STEP APPROACH TO MARKETING RESEARCH

The **marketing research process** is a five-step application of the scientific method that includes:

1. Defining the problem.
2. Analyzing the situation.
3. Getting problem-specific data.
4. Interpreting the data.
5. Solving the problem.

Exhibit 7–3 shows the five steps in the process. Note that the process may lead to a solution before all of the steps are completed. Or as the feedback arrows show, researchers may return to an earlier step if needed. For example, the interpreting step may point to a new question—or reveal the need for additional information—before a final decision can be made.

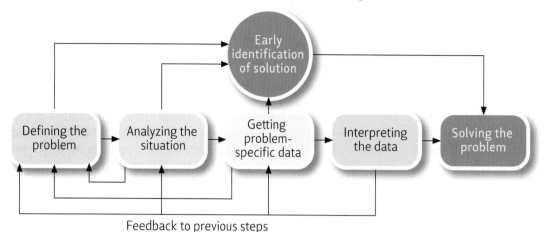

Feedback to previous steps

Effective research usually requires cooperation

Good marketing research requires cooperation between researchers and marketing managers. Researchers must be sure their research focuses on real problems.

Marketing managers must be able to explain what their problems are and what kinds of information they need. They should be able to communicate with specialists in the specialists' language. Marketing managers may only be "consumers" of research. But they should be informed consumers—able to explain exactly what they want from the research. They should also know about some of the basic decisions made during the research process so they know the limitations of the findings.

For this reason, our discussion of marketing research won't emphasize mechanics but rather how to plan and evaluate the work of marketing researchers.[6]

DEFINING THE PROBLEM—STEP 1

Defining the problem is often the most difficult step in the marketing research process. But it's important for the objectives of the research to be clearly defined. The best research job on the wrong problem is wasted effort.

Finding the right problem level almost solves the problem

Our strategy planning framework is useful for guiding the problem definition step. It can help the researcher identify the real problem area and what information is needed. Do we really know enough about our target markets to work out all of the four Ps? Before deciding how to position our product, do we understand our competitors' strengths and weaknesses? Do we know enough to decide what celebrity to use in an ad or how to handle the price war in New York City or Tokyo? If not, we may want to do research rather than rely on intuition.

Don't confuse problems with symptoms

The problem definition step sounds simple—and that's the danger. It's easy to confuse symptoms with the problem. When this happens, the research objectives are not clear, and researchers may ignore relevant questions—while analyzing unimportant questions in expensive detail.

Setting research objectives may require more understanding

Sometimes the research objectives are very clear. A manager wants to know if the targeted households have tried a new product and what percent of them bought it a second time. But research objectives aren't always so simple. The manager might also want to know *why* some didn't buy or whether they had even heard of the product. Companies rarely have enough time and money to study everything. A manager must narrow the research objectives. One good way is to develop a list of research questions that includes all the possible problem areas. Then the manager can consider the items on the list more completely—in the situation analysis step—before narrowing down to final research objectives.

ANALYZING THE SITUATION—STEP 2

What information do we already have?

When the marketing manager thinks the real problem has begun to surface, a situation analysis is useful. A **situation analysis** is an informal study of what information is already available in the problem area. It can help define the problem and specify what additional information, if any, is needed.

Pick the brains around you

The situation analysis usually involves informal talks with informed people. Informed people can be others in the firm, a few good middlemen who have close contact with customers, or others knowledgeable about the industry. In industrial markets—where relationships with customers are close—researchers may even call the customers themselves.

Situation analysis helps educate a researcher

The situation analysis is especially important if the researcher is a research specialist who doesn't know much about the management decisions to be made or if the marketing manager is dealing with unfamiliar areas. They both must be sure they understand the problem area—including the nature of the target market, the marketing mix, competition, and other external factors. Otherwise, the researcher may rush ahead and make costly mistakes or simply discover facts that management already knows. The following case illustrates this danger.

A marketing manager at the home office of a large retail chain hired a research firm to do in-store interviews to learn what customers liked most, and least, about some of its stores in other cities. Interviewers diligently filled out their questionnaires. When the results came in, it was apparent that neither the marketing manager nor the researcher had done their homework. No one had even talked with the local store managers! Several of the stores were in the middle of some messy remodeling—so all the customers' responses concerned the noise and dust from the construction. The research was a waste of money.

> **Internet EXERCISE**
>
> Assume that your boss has asked you to do a customer satisfaction survey. As part of a situation analysis, you want to get ideas about what others have done in this area. Go to the website for the Google search engine (*www.google.com*). In the dialogue box type 'customer satisfaction survey' (include the single quote marks) and click on Google search. Look at some of the websites identified. How helpful is this? How could it be improved?

Secondary data may provide the answers—or some background

The situation analysis should also find relevant **secondary data**—information that has been collected or published already. Later, in Step 3, we will cover **primary data**—information specifically collected to solve a current problem. Too often researchers rush to gather primary data when much relevant secondary information is already available—at little or no cost! See Exhibit 7–4.

Much secondary data is available

Ideally, much secondary data is already available from the firm's MIS. Data that has not been organized in an MIS may be available from the company's files and reports. Secondary data also is available from libraries, trade associations, government agencies, and private research organizations; increasingly, these organizations are putting their information online. So one of the first places a researcher should look for secondary data is the Internet.

Exhibit 7–4   Sources of Secondary and Primary Data

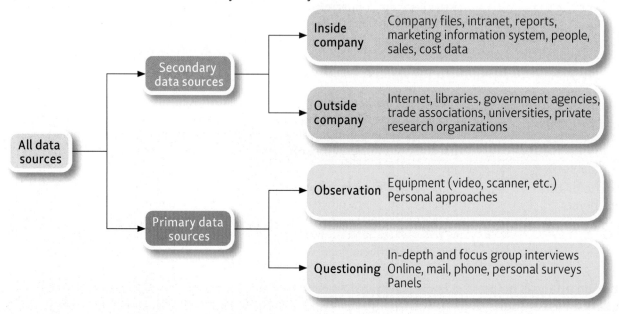

Search the Internet for information

Marketing managers can find a treasure trove of useful information on the Internet. It's all readily accessible from a computer (or a wireless PDA or perhaps even a cell phone). But available is not the same as reliable. Anyone can post anything on the Internet. So, as with any other research source, you should carefully evaluate the accuracy of Internet sources.

The key to the Internet is finding what's needed. Internet subject directories that categorize websites by topic are a good place to start. Yahoo.com has a popular directory, but libraries and other organizations have created many more. Two good directory resources are the Librarians' Index to the Internet (www.lii.org) and INFOMINE (http://infomine.ucr.edu). Powerful Internet search engines, like the ones at Google.com and Ask.com, provide lists of links to websites that include words or phrases specified by the researcher. A problem is that searches often identify too many irrelevant sources.

Search engines miss important databases

Many managers don't realize that much of the information stored on the Internet is in database formats that standard website search engines can't find. To search for information in those databases you must first locate the website with the relevant database and then use software at the site to search inside the database. Directories that describe database sites help with the first step. The directory at www.completeplanet.com, for example, provides an organized listing of more than 70,000 searchable databases.

Special interest groups on the Web

Many marketing managers join discussion groups or newsgroups that share information on topics of specific interest. Belonging to these groups is like subscribing to an electronic newsletter. Similarly, some websites provide automatic e-mail notifications when information is updated. This service can be valuable for information you need to come to you automatically—before you even know it's available. Indeed, it may be available at the website of a competing firm. A competitor's press releases or job listings sometimes provide important information about future plans. Microsoft, for example, was alerted to a competitor's plans by looking at its online job postings.

Some marketing managers take a more hands-on approach. They log in to blogs or online discussion groups to "eavesdrop" or ask questions as customers chat about

A firm's own data on customers' past purchases, if properly analyzed, can be an important source of information for evaluating new opportunities.

companies or brands of interest. Specialized search engines like Blogdex and Google Groups locate this type of site.[7]

Government data is inexpensive

Federal and state governments publish data on many subjects. Government data is often useful in estimating the size of markets. In Chapter 4 we gave a number of examples of the different types of data that are available and suggested some websites. Distribution of government data is not limited to the Internet, however. Almost all government data is available in inexpensive publications. Much of it is also available in computer form ready for further analysis.

Sometimes it's more practical to use summary publications for leads to more detailed reports. For the U.S. market, one of the most useful summary references is the *Statistical Abstract of the United States*. Like an almanac, it is issued in print form each year and gives 1,500 summary tables from more than 200 published sources. Detailed footnotes guide readers to more specific information on a topic. The abstract and much of the source material on which it is based are available online at www.census.gov. Similarly, the *United Nations Statistical Yearbook* is one of the finest summaries of worldwide data; like many other international statistical references, it is available on CD-ROM and online (www.un.org/depts/unsd).

Secondary data is very limited on some international markets. However, most countries with advanced economies have government agencies that help researchers get the data they need. For example, Statistics Canada (www.statcan.ca) compiles a great deal of information on the Canadian market. Eurostat (europa.eu.int/comm/eurostat), the statistical office for the European Union countries, and the Organization for Economic Cooperation (in Paris) offer many publications packed with data on Europe. In the United States, the Department of Commerce (www.doc.gov) distributes statistics compiled by all other federal departments. Some city and state governments have similar agencies for local data. The Yahoo! website (www.yahoo.com) provides an index to a large amount of information about different governments.

Private sources are useful, too

Many private research organizations—as well as advertising agencies, newspapers, and magazines—regularly compile and publish data. A good business library is valuable for sources such as *Sales & Marketing Management, Advertising Age, Journal of Global Marketing,* and the publications of the National Industrial Conference Board.

The *Encyclopedia of Associations* lists 75,000 U.S. and international trade and professional associations that can be a good source of information. For example, the American Marketing Association (www.ama.org) has an information center with many marketing publications.

Most trade associations compile data from and for their members. Some also publish magazines that focus on important topics in the industry. *Chain Store Age,* for example, has much information on retailing (www.chainstoreage.com).

Situation analysis yields a lot—for very little

The virtue of a good situation analysis is that it can be very informative but takes little time. And it's inexpensive compared with more formal research efforts—like a large-scale survey. Situation analysis can help focus further research or even eliminate the need for it entirely. The situation analyst is really trying to determine the exact nature of the situation and the problem.

Determine what else is needed

At the end of the situation analysis, you can see which research questions—from the list developed during the problem definition step—remain unanswered. Then you have to decide exactly what information you need to answer those questions and how to get it. This may require discussion between technical experts and the marketing manager. Often companies use a written **research proposal**—a plan that specifies what information will be obtained and how—to be sure no misunderstandings occur later. The research plan may include information about costs, what data will be collected, how it will be collected, who will analyze it and how, and how long the process will take.

GETTING PROBLEM-SPECIFIC DATA—STEP 3

Gathering primary data

The next step is to plan a formal research project to gather primary data. There are different methods for collecting primary data. Which approach to use depends on the nature of the problem and how much time and money are available.

In most primary data collection, the researcher tries to learn what customers think about some topic or how they behave under some conditions. There are two basic methods for obtaining information about customers: *questioning* and *observing.* Questioning can range from qualitative to quantitative research. And many kinds of observing are possible.

Qualitative questioning— open-ended with a hidden purpose

Qualitative research seeks in-depth, open-ended responses, not yes or no answers. The researcher tries to get people to share their thoughts on a topic—without giving them many directions or guidelines about what to say.

A researcher might ask different consumers, "What do you think about when you decide where to shop for food?" One person may talk about convenient location, another about service, and others about the quality of the fresh produce. The real advantage of this approach is *depth*. Each person can be asked follow-up questions so the researcher really understands what *that* respondent is thinking. The depth of the qualitative approach gets at the details—even if the researcher needs a lot of judgment to summarize it all.

Focus groups stimulate discussion

The most widely used form of qualitative questioning in marketing research is the **focus group interview**, which involves interviewing 6 to 10 people in an informal group setting. The focus group also uses open-ended questions, but here the interviewer wants to get group interaction—to stimulate thinking and get immediate reactions.

A skilled focus group leader can learn a lot from this approach. A typical session may last an hour, so participants can cover a lot of ground. Sessions are often videotaped (or broadcast over the Internet or by satellite) so different managers can form their own impressions of what happened. Some research firms create electronic focus groups in which participants log onto a specified website and with others participate in a chat session; each person types in comments that are shared on the computer screen of each of the other participants. What they type is the record of the session.[8]

MOD-PAC, a large printing company, faced a problem: Business from its traditional large customers was drying up. MOD-PAC managers wanted to know if there were niche markets willing to buy printing services over the Internet. So, they conducted *online* focus groups, each with prospects from a different target market. The focus groups helped MOD-PAC managers see that each group had different needs and used different terms to discuss its problems. Each focus group also indicated that there was interest in buying printing services online. In response, MOD-PAC developed its PrintLizard.com website; the home page uses tabs to route customers from different segments to the part of the site that caters to their specific needs.[9]

Online focus groups can offset some of the limitations of traditional focus groups. Participants who meet online feel freer to express their honest thoughts—and an aggressive individual is less likely to dominate the group. For example, AOL found that men were often embarrassed to admit to others in a traditional focus group that they had trouble controlling spam on their computers. In online groups, they revealed their real concerns. The online groups' input helped in AOL's revamp of its spam blocker system and in its ads explaining the benefits of using AOL.[10]

Regardless of how a focus group is conducted, conclusions reached from a session usually vary depending on who watches it. A typical problem—and serious limitation—with qualitative research is that it's hard to measure the results objectively. The results seem to depend largely on the viewpoint of the researcher. In addition, people willing to participate in a focus group—especially those who talk the most—may not be representative of the broader target market.

Focus groups can be conducted quickly and at relatively low cost—an average of about $3,500 each. This is part of their appeal. But focus groups are probably being overused. It's easy to fall into the trap of treating an idea arising from a focus group as a "fact" that applies to a broad target market.

To avoid this trap, some researchers use qualitative research to prepare for quantitative research. For example, the Jacksonville Symphony Orchestra wanted to broaden its base of support and increase ticket sales. It hired a marketing research firm to conduct focus group interviews. These interviews helped the marketing managers refine their ideas about what these target "customers" liked and did not like about the orchestra. The ideas were then tested with a larger, more representative sample. When the managers planned their promotion and the orchestra's program on the basis of research, ticket sales nearly doubled.[11]

Focus groups are popular, and well-run groups can provide a lot of useful information. As with any type of marketing research, a marketing manager should be aware of both the advantages and limitations of this approach when drawing conclusions and making decisions.

Qualitative research can provide good ideas—hypotheses. But we need other approaches—perhaps based on more representative samples and objective measures— to *test* the hypotheses.

Structured questioning gives more objective results

When researchers use identical questions and response alternatives, they can summarize the information quantitatively. Samples can be larger and more representative, and various statistics can be used to draw conclusions. For these reasons, most survey research is **quantitative research**—which seeks structured responses that can be summarized in numbers, like percentages, averages, or other statistics. For example, a marketing researcher might calculate what percentage of respondents have tried a new product and then figure an average score for how satisfied they were.

Fixed responses speed answering and analysis

Survey questionnaires usually provide fixed responses to questions to simplify analysis of the replies. This multiple-choice approach also makes it easier and faster for respondents to reply. Simple fill-in-a-number questions are also widely used in quantitative research. Fixed responses are also more convenient for computer analysis, which is how most surveys are analyzed.

Surveys come in many forms

Decisions about what specific questions to ask and how to ask them usually depend on how respondents will be contacted—by mail (or electronic mail), via a website, on the phone, or in person. What question and response approach is used may also affect the survey. There are many possibilities. For example, whether the survey is self-administered or handled by an interviewer, the questionnaire may be on paper or in an interactive computer format (perhaps distributed on a CD or disk or displayed on a website). The computer can be programmed to skip certain questions, depending on answers given. Computerized questionnaires also allow the researcher to show pictures or play audio/video clips (for example, to get reactions to an advertising jingle). In an automated telephone interview, questions may be prerecorded on an audio tape or computer and the subject may respond by pushing touch-tone buttons on the phone.

Mail and online surveys are common and convenient

A questionnaire distributed by mail, e-mail, or online is useful when extensive questioning is necessary. Respondents can complete the questions at their convenience.

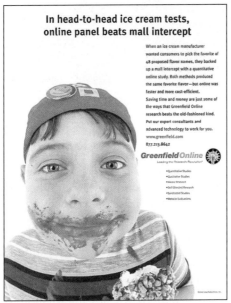

In head-to-head ice cream tests, online panel beats mall intercept

When an ice cream manufacturer wanted consumers to pick the favorite of 48 proposed flavor names, they backed up a mall intercept with a quantitative online study. Both methods produced the same favorite flavor—but online was faster and more cost-efficient. Saving time and money are just some of the ways that Greenfield Online research beats the old-fashioned kind. Put our expert consultants and advanced technology to work for you.

www.greenfield.com

877.213.8642

Greenfield Online
Leading the Research Revolution*

• Quantitative Studies
• Qualitative Studies
• Media Research
• Self-Directed Research
• Syndicated Studies
• Website Evaluations

They may be more willing to provide personal information—since a questionnaire can be completed anonymously. But the questions must be simple and easy to follow since no interviewer is there to help. If the respondent is likely to be a computer user, it may be possible to send the questionnaire on a disk (or put it on a website) and include a help feature with additional directions for people who need them.

A big problem with questionnaires is that many people don't complete them. The **response rate**—the percentage of people contacted who complete the questionnaire—is often low and respondents may not be representative. Mail, e-mail, and online surveys are economical if a large number of people respond. But they may be quite expensive if the response rate is low. Worse, the results may be misleading if the respondents are not representative. For example, people who complete online questionnaires tend to be younger, better educated, or different in other ways—all of which impacts how they answer.

Distributing questionnaires by e-mail, or at a website, is popular. It is quick, and the responses come back in computer form. Surveys sent by regular mail usually take a lot longer.

Regardless of how quickly a questionnaire is distributed, it often takes a month or more to get the data back. That is too slow for some decisions. Moreover, it is difficult to get respondents to expand on particular points. In markets where illiteracy is a problem, it may not be possible to get any response. In spite of these limitations, the convenience and economy of self-administered surveys makes them popular.

Telephone surveys—fast and effective

Telephone interviews are also popular. They are effective for getting quick answers to simple questions. Telephone interviews allow the interviewer to probe and really learn what the respondent is thinking. In addition, with computer-aided telephone interviewing, answers are immediately recorded on a computer, resulting in fast data analysis. On the other hand, many consumers find calls intrusive—and about a third refuse to answer any questions. Moreover, respondents can't be certain who is calling or how personal information might be used.

Personal interview surveys—can be in-depth

A personal interview survey is usually much more expensive per interview than e-mail, mail, or telephone surveys. But it's easier to get and keep the respondent's

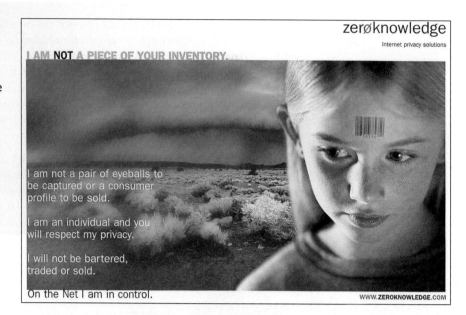

attention when the interviewer is right there. The interviewer can also help explain complicated directions and perhaps get better responses. For these reasons, personal interviews are commonly used for research on business customers. To reduce the cost of locating consumer respondents, interviews are sometimes done at a store or shopping mall. This is called a *mall intercept interview* because the interviewer stops a shopper and asks for responses to the survey.

Researchers have to be careful that having an interviewer involved doesn't affect the respondent's answers. Sometimes people won't give an answer they consider embarrassing. Or they may try to impress or please the interviewer. Further, in some cultures people don't want to give any information. For example, many people in Africa, Latin America, and Eastern Europe are reluctant to be interviewed.[12]

Sometimes questioning has limitations. In such cases, observing may be more accurate or economical.

Observing—what you see is what you get

Observing—as a method of collecting data—focuses on a well-defined problem. Here we are not talking about the casual observations that may stimulate ideas in the early steps of a research project. With the observation method, researchers try to see or record what the subject does naturally. They don't want the observing to *influence* the subject's behavior.

In some situations, consumers are recorded on video. This may be in a store, at home, or out with friends. Later, researchers can study the tape by running the film at very slow speed or actually analyzing each frame. Researchers use this technique to study the routes consumers follow through a store or how they select products. A dog food manufacturer put video cameras on the pet food aisle in supermarkets to learn more about how people choose dog food and treats. The videos showed that kids often picked the treats, but that the kids' parents chose the food. The videos also revealed that kids couldn't reach treats when they were on higher shelves. Sales immediately increased when the treats were moved to lower shelves.[13]

Many franchise companies use the observation method to check how well a franchisee is performing. Krispy Kreme hires people to go to its stores and act like normal customers. Then these "secret shoppers" report back to Krispy Kreme on the quality of the food, how they were treated, and the cleanliness of the store. The report may include digital pictures or videos that are instantly sent over the Internet from a laptop computer.

Marketers sometimes can find ways to improve products by observing customers as they use them. For example, product developers at Microsoft watch customers try new software products so that they can change features that are confusing or hard to learn.[14]

Observing is common in advertising research

Observation methods are common in advertising research. For example, Nielsen Media Research (www.nielsenmedia.com) uses a device called the "people meter" that adapts the observation method to television audience research. This device is attached to the TV set in the homes of selected families. It records when the set is on and what station is tuned in. Similarly, Arbitron developed its Portable People Meter (PPM) to automatically measure radio listening habits.

Checkout scanners see a lot

Computerized scanners at retail checkout counters help researchers collect very specific, and useful, information. Often this type of data feeds directly into a firm's MIS. Managers of a large chain of stores can see exactly what products have sold each day and how much money each department in each store has earned. But the scanner also has wider applications for marketing research.

Information Resources, Inc. (www.infores.com), and ACNielsen (acnielsen.com) use **consumer panels**—a group of consumers who provide information on a continuing basis. Whenever a panel member shops for groceries, he or she gives an ID card to the clerk, who scans the number. Then the scanner records every purchase— including brands, sizes, prices, and any coupons used. In a variation of this approach, consumers use a hand-held scanner to record purchases once they get home. Sometimes members of a panel answer questions and the answers are merged with the scanner data.

Analysis of panel data revealed that Ocean Spray was seeing sales slip to competitors. Households with kids are the heaviest purchasers of juice; yet they were purchas-

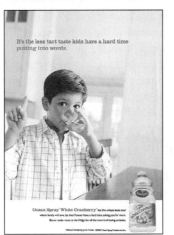

It's the less tart taste kids have a hard time putting into words.

Ocean Spray White Cranberry

ing Ocean Spray on a less frequent basis. Further research with these panel members revealed this was due to its "too tart" taste and tendency to stain. To combat this, the company focused its energies on developing White Cranberry Juice Drinks by harvesting the berries before they develop their traditional red color and pungent taste. An ad for the new product depicted a mom and her small son enjoying the taste of the new White Cranberry juice. When the boy accidentally spills it on the floor, it's also clear that it doesn't stain. Now that the "no stain" message has sunk in, Ocean Spray's ads put more emphasis on the idea that kids love the taste.[15]

Data captured by electronic scanners is equally important to e-commerce in business-to-business markets. Increasingly, firms mark their shipping cartons and packages with computer-readable bar codes that make it fast and easy to track inventory, shipments, orders, and the like. As information about product sales or shipments becomes available, it is instantly included in the MIS and accessible over the Internet.[16]

Experimental method controls conditions

A marketing manager can get a different kind of information—with either questioning or observing—using the experimental method. With the **experimental method**, researchers compare the responses of two (or more) groups that are similar except on the characteristic being tested. Researchers want to learn if the specific characteristic—which varies among groups—*causes* differences in some response among the groups. For example, a researcher might be interested in comparing the responses of consumers who have seen an ad for a new product with consumers who have not seen the ad. The "response" might be an observed behavior—like the

Exhibit 7–5   Illustration of Experimental Method in Comparing Effectiveness of Two Ads

purchase of a product—or the answer to a specific question—like "How interested are you in this new product?" See Exhibit 7–5.

Marketing managers for Mars—the company that makes Snickers candy bars—used the experimental method to help solve a problem. They wanted to know if making their candy bar bigger would increase sales enough to offset the higher cost. To decide, they conducted a marketing experiment in which the company carefully varied the size of candy bars sold in *different* markets. Otherwise, the marketing mix stayed the same. Then researchers tracked sales in each market area to see the effect of the different sizes. They saw a big difference immediately: The added sales more than offset the cost of a bigger candy bar.

Test-marketing of new products is another type of marketing experiment. In a typical approach, a company tries variations on its planned marketing mix in a few geographic market areas. The results of the tests help to identify problems or refine the marketing mix—before the decision is made to go to broader distribution. However, alert competitors may disrupt such tests—perhaps by increasing promotion or offering retailers extra discounts.[17]

Syndicated research shares data collection costs

Some private research firms specialize in collecting data and then sell it to managers in many different client firms. Often the marketing manager subscribes to the research service and gets regular updates. About 40 percent of marketing research spending is for syndicated research, and this helps explain why it can be an economical approach when marketing managers from many different firms need the same type of data. For example, many different auto producers use J.D. Power's (www.jdpa.com) surveys of customer satisfaction—often as the basis for advertising claims. Subscription data services are available for many different industries—ranging from food service to prescription drugs to micro electronic devices.[18]

Understand the costs and benefits of research

Whether collecting secondary data for a situation analysis or primary data from a focus group or survey, marketing research takes time and money. A good marketing manager knows that the value of additional information lies in the ability to design more effective marketing strategies. Similarly, different research methods provide different insights—and come at different costs. There are also benefits to getting information quickly—particularly in some markets. Small companies with limited budgets often must be creative in identifying low-cost ways to get the information they need.

When millions are at stake, Kraft Foods doesn't blink at spending $100,000 or more for a single market research project. Managers in small companies can only dream of having the research budgets to do that. But, ironically, not having good information may pose an even greater risk for small companies. While a big firm with deeper pockets can survive a marketing misstep or two, a mistake in an important marketing strategy decision can put a small firm out of business.

With a little creativity a good marketing manager can generate a lot of information using relatively little cash. For example, if you were thinking about starting a soccer training academy for kids, you might start by asking a lot of questions. Ask your friends for ideas about what to do and where to advertise. Go out to local soccer fields and question parents. Are they interested? When would they want the training to be available? How much are they willing to pay? Talk to kids, too. What could make soccer camp more fun?

If a firm's target market is accessible via the Internet, online surveys can be an economical way for running ideas and questions past a larger group. Greenfield Online (www.greenfieldonline.com), for instance, recruits people to respond to the online surveys it hosts for clients. For about $6,000, Greenfield can get responses to a 12-question survey from a representative sample of 150 people— and do it within a week. Look for other, do-it-yourself approaches. For example, Waterpik offers new customers a $5 coupon to encourage them to fill out its online survey.

Managers at small companies can learn a lot by studying competitors' promotion material, monitoring their websites, and shopping in their stores. Get on competitors' e-mail lists and study their advertising, products, and pricing on a regular basis. Firms that compete in business markets can also check each other out at trade shows. And trade magazines have articles, ads, and even letters to the editor that can alert you to new developments.

Make everyone in your company a researcher. Let them know you want them to be aware of important information that they see and to share useful ideas that they hear from a customer, a similar business in a different market, or the like. Above all, keep an eye on your current customers. Be sincere and regular about asking them, "Is there anything we can do better?" Be sure to listen when they answer. Set up internal monitoring systems that alert you to the loss of a customer—and then be conscientious about calling to find out what happened. What you learn might help you prevent another customer from defecting—and it might even get the old customer back.

Finally, don't be unnecessarily frugal. Marketing managers should remember the scientific method and be wary of shortcuts that can result in misleading information and bad decisions. For example, don't skip the step of pretesting a questionnaire; that may save some money or a few hours of work but waste the total amount spent on a real study with a "bad" questionnaire. Samples should still represent the target market, and that includes focus groups. A focus group with a group of employees may be convenient, but it isn't the same as using real customers.[19]

INTERPRETING THE DATA—STEP 4

What does it really mean?

After someone collects the data, it has to be analyzed to decide what it all means. In quantitative research, this step usually involves statistics. **Statistical packages**—easy-to-use computer programs that analyze data—have made this step easier. As we noted earlier, some firms provide *decision support systems* so managers can use a statistical package to interpret data themselves. More often, however, technical specialists are involved at the interpretation step.

Cross-tabulation is one of the most frequently used approaches for analyzing and interpreting marketing research data. It shows the relationship of answers to two different questions. Exhibit 7–6 is an example. The cross-tab analysis in this exhibit shows that customers who had moved in the last year were much more likely than nonmovers to have adopted "Caller ID" on their phones at home.

There are many other approaches for statistical analysis—the best one depends on the situation. The details of statistical analysis are beyond the scope of this book. But

Exhibit 7–6
Cross-Tabulation
Breakdown of
Responses to a Phone
Company Consumer
Survey

| | **Have You Moved in the Last Year?** | | |
| | | | |
Answers:	No	Yes	Total
Do you have "Caller ID" on your phone at home?			
Yes	10.2%	23.4%	15.5%
No	89.8	76.6	84.5
Total	100.0%	100.0%	100.0%

Interpretation: 15.5 percent of people in the survey said that they had "Caller ID" on their phone at home. However, the percentage was much higher (23.4%) among people who had moved in the last year, and lower (10.2%) among people who had not moved.

a good manager should know enough to understand what a research project can and can't do.[20]

Is your sample really representative?

It's usually impossible for marketing managers to collect all the information they want about everyone in a **population**—the total group they are interested in. Marketing researchers typically study only a **sample**, a part of the relevant population. How well a sample *represents* the total population affects the results. Results from a sample that is not representative may not give a true picture.

The manager of a retail store might want a phone survey to learn what consumers think about the store's hours. If interviewers make all of the calls during the day, consumers who work outside the home during the day won't be represented. Those interviewed might say the limited store hours are "satisfactory." Yet it would be a mistake to assume that *all* consumers are satisfied.

Research results are not exact

An estimate from a sample, even a representative one, usually varies somewhat from the true value for a total population. Managers sometimes forget this. They assume that survey results are exact. Instead, when interpreting sample estimates, managers should think of them as *suggesting* the approximate value.

Validity problems can destroy research

Even if the sampling is carefully planned, it is also important to evaluate the quality of the research data itself.

Managers and researchers should be sure that research data really measures what it is supposed to measure. Many of the variables marketing managers are interested in

As suggested by the copy for the Schick Quattro ad, sometimes the results of a survey are easy to analyze and interpret. However, research results developed from samples that are not really representative of the target market may be inaccurate and misleading.

are difficult to measure accurately. Questionnaires may let us assign numbers to consumer responses, but that still doesn't mean that the result is precise. An interviewer might ask, "How much did you spend on soft drinks last week?" A respondent may be perfectly willing to cooperate—and be part of the representative sample—but just not be able to remember.

Validity concerns the extent to which data measures what it is intended to measure. Validity problems are important in marketing research because many people will try to answer even when they don't know what they're talking about. Further, a poorly worded question can mean different things to different people and invalidate the results. Often, pretests of a research project are required to evaluate the quality of the questions and measures and to ensure that potential problems have been identified.

Poor interpretation can destroy research

Besides sampling and validity problems, a marketing manager must consider whether the analysis of the data supports the *conclusions* drawn in the interpretation step. Sometimes technical specialists pick the right statistical procedure—their calculations are exact—but they misinterpret the data because they don't understand the management problem. In one survey, car buyers were asked to rank five cars in order from "most preferred" to "least preferred." One car was ranked first by slightly more respondents than any other car so the researcher reported it as the "most liked car." That interpretation, however, ignored the fact that 70 percent of the respondents ranked the car *last*!

Interpretation problems like this can be subtle but crucial. Some people draw misleading conclusions on purpose to get the results they want. Marketing managers must decide whether *all* of the results support the interpretation and are relevant to their problem.

Marketing manager and researcher should work together

Marketing research involves many technical details. But the marketing researcher and the marketing manager must work together to be sure that they really do solve the problem facing the firm. If the whole research process has been a joint effort, then the interpretation step can move quickly toward solving the problem.

Ethics involved in interpreting and presenting results

Marketing managers want information they can trust when they make marketing decisions. But research often involves many hidden details. A person who wants to misuse research to pursue a personal agenda can often do so.

Perhaps the most common ethical issues concern decisions to withhold certain information about the research. For example, a manager might selectively share only those results that support his or her viewpoint. Others involved in a decision might never know that they are getting only partial truths.[21]

You're the new marketing manager for a small firm that offers computer repair services. The company's owner approves your proposal for a telephone survey to learn more about the needs of firms that are not current customers. You identify local firms for the sample and hire a researcher to call them. The interviewer tells respondents that their answers will be anonymous and used only for research purposes. About halfway through the data collection, the interviewer tells you that respondents are confused by one of the questions and that their answers to that question are probably useless. The question concerns the issue that is most important to your new boss. Do you admit the problem to others in your company? If the sales manager asks for the completed questionnaires, including all the names and responses, what would you say?

SOLVING THE PROBLEM—STEP 5

The last step is solving the problem

In the problem solution step, managers use the research results to make marketing decisions.

Some researchers, and some managers, are fascinated by the interesting tidbits of information that come from the research process. They are excited if the research reveals

There are a large number of international marketing research firms that offer specialized services to marketing managers.

something they didn't know before. But if research doesn't have action implications, it has little value and suggests poor planning by the researcher and the manager.

When the research process is finished, the marketing manager should be able to apply the findings in marketing strategy planning—the choice of a target market or the mix of the four Ps. If the research doesn't provide information to help guide these decisions, the company has wasted research time and money.

We emphasize this step because it is the reason for and logical conclusion to the whole research process. This final step must be anticipated at each of the earlier steps.

INTERNATIONAL MARKETING RESEARCH

Research contributes to international success

Marketing research on overseas markets is often a major contributor toward international marketing success. Conversely, export failures are often due to a lack of home office expertise concerning customer interests, needs, and other segmenting dimensions, as well as environmental factors such as competitors' prices and products. Effective marketing research can help to overcome these problems.

Avoid mistakes with local researchers

Whether a firm is small and entering overseas markets for the first time or already large and well established internationally, there are often advantages to working with local marketing research firms. They know the local situation and are less likely to make mistakes based on misunderstanding the customs, language, or circumstances of the customers they study.

Many large research firms have a network of local offices around the world to help with such efforts. Similarly, multinational or local advertising agencies and middlemen can often provide leads on identifying the best research suppliers.

Some coordination and standardization make sense

When a firm is doing similar research projects in different markets around the world, it makes sense for the marketing manager to coordinate the efforts. If the manager doesn't establish some basic guidelines at the outset, the different research projects may vary so much that the results can't be compared from one market area to another. Such comparisons give a home office manager a better chance of understanding how the markets are similar and how they differ.

Companies with operations in various countries often attempt to centralize some market research functions. One reason is to reduce costs or achieve research economies of scale. The centralized approach also improves the firm's ability to transfer experience and know-how from one market area or project to another. For example, one of Eastman Kodak's International Divisions appointed a market research specialist in each subsidiary company throughout the Asian region. The specialists report to local marketing managers but also receive research direction from expert research managers in the head office in the U.S.

There is even greater opportunity and need to standardize and coordinate elements of a marketing information system in an international marketing operation. Computer databases and information systems are most useful when they are designed to include the same variables organized consistently over time. Without this, it is impossible for the manager to go into much depth in comparing and contrasting data from different markets.[22]

CONCLUSION

Marketing managers face difficult decisions in selecting target markets and managing marketing mixes, but they rarely have all the information they would like to have before making those decisions. Even less information may be available in international markets. This doesn't mean that managers have to rely solely on intuition; they can usually obtain some good information that will improve the quality of their decisions. Both large and small firms can take advantage of Internet and intranet capabilities to develop marketing information systems (MIS) that help to assure routinely needed data is available and quickly accessible.

Some questions can be answered only with marketing research. Marketing research should be guided by the scientific method. This approach to solving marketing problems involves five steps: (1) defining the problem, (2) analyzing the situation, (3) obtaining data, (4) interpreting data, and (5) developing and implementing a solution. This objective and organized approach helps to keep problem solving on task. It reduces the risk of doing costly and unnecessary research that doesn't achieve the desired end—solving the marketing problem.

Our strategy planning framework can be very helpful in evaluating marketing research. By finding and focusing on real problems, researchers and marketing managers may be able to move more quickly to a useful solution during the situation analysis stage—without the costs and risks of gathering primary data. With imagination, they may even be able to find answers in their MIS or in readily available secondary data. However, primary data from questioning, observing, or conducting experiments may be needed. Qualitative data often provides initial insights or hypotheses—which might be tested with more representative samples and quantitative approaches.

KEY TERMS

marketing research, 170

marketing information system (MIS), 170

intranet, 173

data warehouse, 173

decision support system (DSS), 173

search engine, 173

marketing model, 174

sales analysis, 174

scientific method, 175

hypotheses, 175

marketing research process, 175

situation analysis, 177

secondary data, 177

primary data, 177

research proposal, 180

qualitative research, 180

focus group interview, 181

quantitative research, 182

response rate, 183

consumer panels, 185

experimental method, 185

statistical packages, 187

population, 188

sample, 188

validity, 189

QUESTIONS AND PROBLEMS

1. Discuss the concept of a marketing information system and why it is important for marketing managers to be involved in planning the system.

2. In your own words, explain why a decision support system (DSS) can add to the value of a marketing information system. Give an example of how a decision support system might help.

3. If a firm's intranet and marketing decision support system do not include a search engine, would they still be useful to a marketing manager? Why?

4. Discuss how output from a marketing information system (MIS) might differ from the output of a typical marketing research department.

5. Discuss some of the likely problems facing the marketing manager in a small firm who plans to search the Internet for information on competitors' marketing plans.

6. Explain the key characteristics of the scientific method and show why these are important to managers concerned with research.

7. How is the situation analysis different from the data collection step? Can both of these steps be done at the same time to obtain answers sooner? Is this wise?

8. Distinguish between primary data and secondary data and illustrate your answer.

9. With so much secondary information now available free or at low cost over the Internet, why would a firm ever want to spend the money to do primary research?

10. If a firm were interested in estimating the distribution of income in the state of California, how could it proceed? Be specific.

11. If a firm were interested in estimating sand and clay production in Georgia, how could it proceed? Be specific.

12. Go to the library (or get on the Internet) and find (in some government publication or website) three marketing-oriented "facts" on international markets that you did not know existed or were available. Record on one page and show sources.

13. Explain why a company might want to do focus group interviews rather than individual interviews with the same people.

14. Distinguish between qualitative and quantitative approaches to research—and give some of the key advantages and limitations of each approach.

15. Define response rate and discuss why a marketing manager might be concerned about the response rate achieved in a particular survey. Give an example.

16. Prepare a table that summarizes some of the key advantages and limitations of mail, e-mail, telephone, and personal interview approaches for administering questionnaires.

17. Would a firm want to subscribe to a shared cost data service if the same data was going to be available to competitors? Discuss your reasoning.

18. Explain how you might use different types of research (focus groups, observation, survey, and experiment) to forecast market reaction to a new kind of disposable baby diaper, which is to receive no promotion other than what the retailer will give it. Further, assume that the new diaper's name will not be associated with other known products. The product will be offered at competitive prices.

19. Marketing research involves expense—sometimes considerable expense. Why does the text recommend the use of marketing research even though a highly experienced marketing executive is available?

20. A marketing manager is considering opportunities to export her firm's current consumer products to several different countries. She is interested in getting secondary data that will help her narrow down choices to countries that offer the best potential. The manager then plans to do more detailed primary research with consumers in those markets. What suggestions would you give her about how to proceed?

21. Discuss the concept that some information may be too expensive to obtain in relation to its value. Illustrate.

CREATING MARKETING PLANS

The Marketing Plan Coach software on the Student CD includes a sample marketing plan for Hillside Veterinary Clinic. Look through the "Customers" and "Competitors" sections in the Situation Analysis and consider the following questions.

a. What different types of marketing research were conducted to fill out these sections of the marketing plan?

b. What are the strengths of the research conducted? What are the weaknesses?

c. Keeping in mind probable cost and time to complete, what additional research would you recommend?

COMPUTER-AIDED PROBLEM

7. MARKETING RESEARCH

Texmac, Inc., has an idea for a new type of weaving machine that could replace the machines now used by many textile manufacturers. Texmac has done a telephone survey to estimate how many of the old-style machines are now in use. Respondents using the present machines were also asked if they would buy the improved machine at a price of $10,000.

Texmac researchers identified a population of about 5,000 textile factories as potential customers. A sample of these were surveyed, and Texmac received 500 responses. Researchers think the total potential market is about 10 times larger than the sample of respondents. Two hundred twenty of the respondents indicated that their firms used old machines like the one the new machine was intended to replace. Forty percent of those firms said that they would be interested in buying the new Texmac machine.

Texmac thinks the sample respondents are representative of the total population, but the marketing manager realizes that estimates based on a sample may not be exact when applied to the whole population. He wants to see how sampling error would affect profit estimates. Data for this problem appears in the spreadsheet. Quantity estimates for the whole market are computed from the sample estimates. These quantity estimates are used in computing likely sales, costs, and profit contribution.

a. An article in a trade magazine reports that there are about 5,200 textile factories that use the old-style machine. If the total market is really 5,200 customers—not 5,000 as Texmac originally thought—how does that affect the total quantity estimate and profit contribution?

b. Some of the people who responded to the survey didn't know much about different types of machines. If the actual number of old machines in the market is really 200 per 500 firms—not 220 as estimated from survey responses—how much would this affect the expected profit contribution (for 5,200 factories)?

c. The marketing manager knows that the percentage of textile factories that would actually buy the new machine might be different from the 40 percent who said they would in the survey. He estimates that the proportion that will replace the old machine might be as low as 36 and as high as 44 percent—depending on business conditions. Use the analysis feature to prepare a table that shows how expected quantity and profit contribution change when the sample percent varies between a minimum of 36 and a maximum of 44 percent. What does this analysis suggest about the use of estimates from marketing research samples? (Note: Use 5,200 for the number of potential customers and use 220 as the estimate of the number of old machines in the sample.)

For additional questions related to this problem, see Exercise 7–4 in the *Learning Aid for Use with Essentials of Marketing*, 11th edition.

Elements of Product Planning for Goods and Services

The Segway™ Personal Transporter (PT) isn't just a new product, it's a new product concept. A design engineer is likely to be excited by the Segway PT's unique features. Under the power of its rechargeable batteries, its onboard computers and five gyroscopes automatically balance the two-wheel super-scooter as its rider glides down the sidewalk at up to 12 mph. Even the two-tone plastic fenders that sit above the wheels are unique. They are coated with Sollx, a high-quality chemical film developed by General Electric; Sollx gleams like colorful paint, but it resists scratches.

Of course, most customers don't dwell on technical features like Sollx, gyroscopes, or central processors; instead, they think about the benefits and satisfaction that might come from using the product. The benefits that the Segway PT offers depend to some extent on whether it is sold as a consumer product or a business product. For example, a firm might buy a unit because it provides a fast, safe, and nonpolluting way for workers to get around inside a sprawling distribution center. Similarly, the Post Office has evaluated it as a way to cut costs as mail carriers go from house to house. Alternatively, upscale consumers who live in congested urban areas might see it as a fun, quiet, and flexible way to get around without worrying about traffic, parking, or fill-ups at a gas station. They might also appreciate that it costs only about 10 cents a day to charge the battery.

Before the Segway PT was introduced, the new-product development process was wrapped in secrecy. Rumors even spread on the Internet that it might be some sort of hovercraft. This created some unrealistic expectations, but it also stimulated media coverage, publicity, and initial sales at Amazon.com. Thousands of units sold that way. Now Segway's website (www.segway.com) lists the names and locations of Segway dealers. This is still a selective distribution effort. Distribution through dealers makes sense for this sort of product. A customer who visits a local dealer can inspect the different models in the Segway product line and a salesperson can answer questions. In addition, before spending $4,500 on a Segway PT, a customer is likely to ask "where do I get warranty service if I have a problem?" In fact, some customers were reminded of such after-the-sale service issues when Segway announced a voluntary product recall. The Consumer Product Safety Commission encouraged the recall to head off tipping-over problems that could occur if a rider ignored warning messages or the unit lacked power for a maneuver.

While Segway has had its share of publicity, the Segway Transporter remains little sought after in the marketplace. Consumers, not knowing quite what to make of a *personal transporter*, haven't exactly beat down the showroom doors—sales have not met expectations. To stimulate interest, Segway adapted its marketing mix, developing new models to address specific transportation needs: the Segway x2 Golf for the links, for instance, and the Segway x2 Adventure for the off-road enthusiast. The latest models have an improved steering system. Looking to address other potential needs, the company is considering multiperson versions of the PT and has already built a prototype.

In addition, special accessory packages aimed at specific markets are now included in the mix—for example, a commuter package contains a handlebar bag, headlamp, and cable lock. Teaming with Garmin International, Segway also offers free global positioning systems to new customers and, working with City Segway Tours, encourages people to try the product on guided tours in several major cities, including Washington, D.C., and Paris.

While these efforts have increased sales for Segway, the niche markets did not meet the company's original sales objectives. The company wants the PT to have broader appeal—but the jury is still out on the PT's long-term prospects. Dean Kamen, Segway's inventor, likes to compare the Segway PT to the Stanley Steamer and early automobiles. When the automobile was first available, it was a curiosity that only the rich could afford. At that time, a horse and carriage was cheaper and more reliable. No one was predicting that 25 years later there would be no more horses in cities. And who could have anticipated that those early automobiles would spark 100 years of sales growth and hundreds of competing brands—ranging from Hummers and Dodge Caravans to BMW Z8s and Toyota Priuses—meeting a variety of needs. So what do you think? Is a new product-market being pioneered, or is the Segway Transporter destined to become another interesting collector's item?[1]

LEARNING OBJECTIVES

Developing a marketing mix that provides superior customer value for target customers is ultimately the focus of the marketing strategy planning process. To develop a successful marketing mix, each of the four Ps must be carefully planned and work well with all the others. Many important strategy decisions are required. This chapter focuses on key ideas related to strategy planning for Product.

When you finish this chapter, you should:

1. understand what "Product" really means.

2. know the key differences between goods and services.

3. understand how product classes can help a marketing manager plan marketing strategies.

4. know the differences among various consumer and business product classes.

5. understand what branding is and how to use it in strategy planning.

6. understand the importance of packaging in strategy planning.

7. understand the role of warranties in strategy planning.

8. understand important new terms (shown in red).

THE PRODUCT AREA INVOLVES MANY STRATEGY DECISIONS

The Segway case highlights some of the important topics and strategy decision areas that we'll discuss in this chapter and the next. As shown in Exhibit 8–1, there are many strategy decisions in the Product area. They're the focus of Chapter 8. Then in Chapter 9, we'll take a "how to" look at developing new products and also explain how strategy usually changes as products move through their life in the market.

We'll start here by looking at Product through the eyes of the customer. This focuses attention on the total benefits provided by the Product—regardless of whether it is a physical good, a service, or both. Taking the customer's view also leads us to consider product classes. The product classes, which are based on how customers think about and shop for products, help show how strategy decisions for Product relate to decisions for Place, Promotion, and Price. Then we'll review strategy decisions for three important Product areas: branding, packaging, and warranties.

WHAT IS A PRODUCT?

Customers buy satisfaction, not parts

When Kodak sells an EasyShare digital camera, is it just selling a certain number of switches and buttons, a plastic case, a lens, and megapixels of memory?

When Air Jamaica sells a ticket for a flight to the Caribbean, is it just selling so much wear and tear on an airplane and so much pilot fatigue?

The answer to these questions is *no*. Instead, what these companies are really selling is the satisfaction, use, or benefit the customer wants.

Consumers care that their EasyShare camera makes it easy to take great pictures *and* share them. They care that with the EasyShare's software they can organize or e-mail their photos, or send them to the EasyShare website when they want prints. Retailers who sell cameras add their own needs. They would like for customers to come into the store asking for the camera by name—so that it's easy to sell. And they want an attractive package that calls attention to all of these benefits.

Exhibit 8-1   Product Decisions for Marketing Strategy Planning

Product idea	Product classes	Branding	Packaging	Warranty
• Physical good/ service • Experience • Features • Benefits • Quality level • Installation • Instructions • Product line	• Consumer product classes • Business product classes	• Individual or family • Manufacturer or dealer	• Protection • Promotion • Enhance product	• None • Limited • Full • Extended

Similarly, Air Jamaica's customers want a safe, comfortable flight—but they also want quick and accurate reservations, smooth check-in at the airport, and luggage that arrives undamaged and on time. In other words, marketing managers deliver the highest level of satisfaction when the customer's *entire experience* with the product meets the customer's needs.

Product refers to the need-satisfying offering of a firm. The idea of "Product" as potential customer satisfaction or benefits is very important. Many business managers get wrapped up in the technical details involved in producing a product. But most customers think about a product in terms of the total satisfaction it provides. That satisfaction may require a "total" product offering that is really a combination of excellent service, a physical good with the right features, useful instructions, a convenient package, a trustworthy warranty, and perhaps even a familiar name that has satisfied the consumer in the past.

Product quality and customer needs

Product quality should also be determined by how customers view the product. From a marketing perspective, **quality** refers to a product's ability to satisfy a customer's needs or requirements. This definition focuses on the customer—and how the customer thinks a product will fit some purpose. For example, the "best" satellite TV service may not be the one with the highest number of channels but the one that includes a local channel that a consumer wants to watch. Similarly, the best-quality clothing for casual wear on campus may be a pair of jeans, not a pair of dress slacks made of a higher-grade fabric.

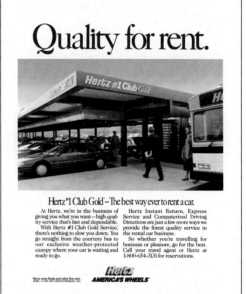

Among different types of jeans, the one with the most durable fabric might be thought of as having the highest grade or *relative quality* for its product type. Marketing managers often focus on relative quality when comparing their products to competitors' offerings. However, a product with better features is not a higher-quality product if the features aren't what the target market wants.

Quality and satisfaction depend on the total product offering. If potato chips get stale on the shelf because of poor packaging, the consumer will be dissatisfied. A broken button on a shirt will disappoint the customer—even if the laundry did a nice job cleaning and pressing the collar.[2]

Ethics QUESTION

Your construction firm was the low-price bidder on a plan to build three new runways at an airport. After winning the contract, you assured the airport commissioner that your work would far exceed the minimum quality specs in the contract. However, a test of the batch of concrete for the second runway shows that it's not as strong as the concrete you've been using. It does exceed the specs in the contract, but barely. Throwing the concrete away would eat up most of the profit expected from the job and also delay the airport in using the runway. There are various options. You could proceed with the project and be quiet about it, or perhaps call the commissioner and ask for quick approval. Alternatively, you could proceed but later admit what happened. With or without approval, you could offer a special warranty. Explain what you would do. What, if anything, would you say to your employees about your decision?[3]

Goods and/or services are the product

You already know that a product may be a physical *good* or a *service* or a *blend* of both. Exhibit 8–2 shows that a product can range from a 100 percent emphasis on physical good—for a commodity like steel pipe—to a 100 percent emphasis on service, like cell-phone service from Sprint PCS. Regardless of the emphasis involved, the marketing manager must consider most of the same elements in planning products and marketing mixes. Given this, we usually won't make a distinction between goods and services but will call all of them *Products*. Sometimes, however, understanding the differences in goods and services can help fine-tune marketing strategy planning. So let's look at some of these differences next.

Exhibit 8–2
Examples of Possible
Blends of Physical
Goods and Services in
a Product

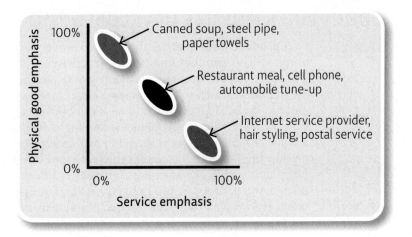

DIFFERENCES IN GOODS AND SERVICES

How tangible is the product?

Because a good is a physical thing, it can be seen and touched. You can try on a pair of Timberland shoes, thumb through the latest issue of *Rolling Stone* magazine, or smell Colombian coffee as it brews. A good is a *tangible* item. When you buy it, you own it. And it's usually pretty easy to see exactly what you'll get.

On the other hand, a **service** is a deed performed by one party for another. When you provide a customer with a service, the customer can't keep it. Rather, a service is experienced, used, or consumed. You go see a DreamWorks Pictures movie, but afterward all you have is a memory. You ride on a ski lift in the Alps, but you don't own the equipment. Services are not physical—they are *intangible*. You can't "hold" a service. And it may be hard to know exactly what you'll get when you buy it.

Most products are a combination of tangible and intangible elements. A Domino's pizza is tangible, but the fast home delivery is not.

Is the product produced before it's sold?

Goods are usually produced in a factory and then sold. A Sony flat-screen TV may be stored in a warehouse or store waiting for a buyer. By contrast, services are often sold first, then produced. And they're produced and consumed in the same time frame. Thus, goods producers may be far away from the customer, but service providers often work in the customer's presence.

A worker in a Sony TV factory can be in a bad mood—and customers will never know. But a rude bank teller can drive customers away.

Services can't be stored or transported

Services are perishable—they can't be stored. This makes it harder to balance supply and demand. An example explains the problem.

AT&T sells long-distance telephone services. Even on Mother's Day when demand is high, customers expect the service to be available. They don't want to hear "Sorry, all lines are busy." So AT&T must have enough equipment and employees to deal with peak demand times. But when customers aren't making many calls, AT&T's facilities are idle and the unused capacity (equipment and people) can't be saved and sold later.

It's often difficult to have economies of scale when the product emphasis is on service. *Services often have to be produced in the presence of the customer.* So service suppliers often need duplicate equipment and staff at places where the service is actually provided. Merrill Lynch sells investment advice along with financial products worldwide. That advice could, perhaps, be produced more economically in a single building in New York City and made available only on its website. But Merrill Lynch has offices all over the world because many customers want a personal touch from their stockbroker.[4]

WHOLE PRODUCT LINES MUST BE DEVELOPED TOO

A **product assortment** is the set of all product lines and individual products that a firm sells. A **product line** is a set of individual products that are closely related. The seller may see the products in a line as related because they're produced or operate in a similar way, sold to the same target market, sold through the same types of outlets, or priced at about the same level. Sara Lee, for example, has many product lines in its product assortment—including coffee, tea, luncheon meats, desserts, snacks, hosiery, sportswear, lingerie, and shoe polish. But Enterprise has only one product line—different types of vehicles to rent. An **individual product** is a particular product within a product line. It usually is differentiated by brand, level of service offered, price, or some other characteristic. For example, each size and scent of a brand of soap is an individual product. Intermediaries usually think of each separate product as a stockkeeping unit (SKU) and assign it a unique SKU number.

Each individual product and target market may require a separate strategy. For example, Sara Lee's strategy for selling its Café Pilão coffee in Brazil is different from its strategy for selling Hanes men's underwear in the United States. We'll focus mainly on developing one marketing strategy at a time. But remember that a marketing manager may have to plan *several* strategies to develop an effective marketing program for a whole company.

PRODUCT CLASSES HELP PLAN MARKETING STRATEGIES

You don't have to treat *every* product as unique when planning strategies. Some product classes require similar marketing mixes. These product classes are a useful starting point for developing marketing mixes for new products and evaluating present mixes.

Product classes start with type of customer

All products fit into one of two broad groups—based on the type of customer that will use them. **Consumer products** are products meant for the final consumer.

Allen Edmonds focuses its marketing effort on the high-quality leather shoes that make up its major product line. Within this line, it offers depth of assortment with a variety of sizes, styles, and colors. Other companies, like 3M, deal with a wider assortment of product lines, perhaps with less depth in each line.

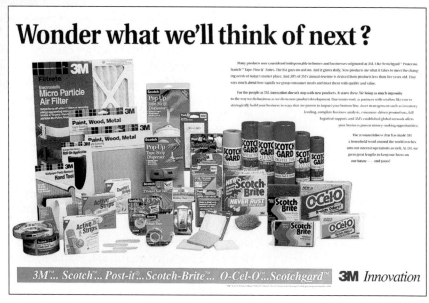

Business products are products meant for use in producing other products. Thus, the big difference between the consumer products market and the business products market is **derived demand**—the demand for business products derives from the demand for final consumer products. For example, car manufacturers buy about one-fifth of all steel products. But if demand for cars drops, they'll buy less steel. Then even the steel supplier with the best marketing mix is likely to lose sales.[5]

The same product—like Bertolli Olive Oil—*might* be both a consumer product and a business product. Consumers buy it to use in their own kitchens, but food processing companies and restaurants buy it in large quantities as an ingredient in the products they sell. Selling the same product to both final consumers and business customers requires (at least) two different strategies.

There are product classes within each group. Consumer product classes are based on *how consumers think about and shop for products.* Business product classes are based on *how buyers think about products and how they'll be used.*

CONSUMER PRODUCT CLASSES

Consumer product classes can be divided into four groups: (1) convenience, (2) shopping, (3) specialty, and (4) unsought. *Each class is based on the way people buy products.* See Exhibit 8–3 for a summary of how these product classes relate to marketing mixes.[6]

Convenience products—purchased quickly with little effort

Convenience products are products a consumer needs but isn't willing to spend much time or effort shopping for. These products are bought often, require little service or selling, don't cost much, and may even be bought by habit. A convenience product may be a staple, impulse product, or emergency product.

Staples are products that are bought often, routinely, and without much thought—like breakfast cereal, canned soup, and most other packaged foods used almost every day in almost every household.

Impulse products are products that are bought quickly—as *unplanned* purchases—because of a strongly felt need. True impulse products are items that the customer hadn't planned to buy, decides to buy on sight, may have bought the same way many times before, and wants right now. If the buyer doesn't see an impulse product at the right time, the sale may be lost.[7]

Emergency products are products that are purchased immediately when the need is great. The customer doesn't have time to shop around when a traffic accident occurs, a thunderstorm begins, or an impromptu party starts. The price of the ambulance service, raincoat, or ice cubes won't be important.

Shopping products— are compared

Shopping products are products that a consumer feels are worth the time and effort to compare with competing products. Shopping products can be divided into two types, depending on what customers are comparing: (1) homogeneous or (2) heterogeneous.

Homogeneous shopping products are shopping products the consumer sees as basically the same and wants at the lowest price. Some consumers feel that certain sizes and types of computers, television sets, washing machines, and even cars are very similar. So they shop for the best price. For some products, the Internet has become a way to do that quickly.

Firms may try to emphasize and promote their product differences to avoid head-to-head price competition. For example, Rustoleum says that its spray paint goes on smoother and does a better job of preventing rust. But if consumers don't think the differences are real or important in terms of the value they seek, they'll just look at price.

Heterogeneous shopping products are shopping products the consumer sees as different and wants to inspect for quality and suitability. Furniture, clothing, and

Exhibit 8–3   Consumer Product Classes and Marketing Mix Planning

Consumer Product Class	Marketing Mix Considerations	Consumer Behavior
Convenience products		
Staples	Maximum exposure required, with widespread, low-cost distribution; mass selling by producer; usually low price; branding is important.	Routinized (habitual), low effort, frequent purchases; low involvement.
Impulse	Widespread distribution required, with display at point of purchase.	Unplanned purchases bought quickly.
Emergency	Need widespread distribution near probable point of need; price sensitivity low.	Purchase made with time pressure when a need is great.
Shopping products		
Homogeneous	Need enough exposure to facilitate price comparison; price sensitivity high.	Customers see little difference among alternatives, seek lowest price.
Heterogeneous	Need distribution near similar products; promotion (including personal selling) to highlight product advantages; less price sensitivity.	Extensive problem solving; consumer may need help in making a decision (salesperson, website, etc.).
Specialty products	Price sensitivity is likely to be low; limited distribution may be acceptable, but should be treated as a convenience or shopping product (in whichever category product would typically be included) to reach persons not yet sold on its specialty product status.	Willing to expend effort to get specific product, even if not necessary; strong preferences make it an important purchase; Internet becoming important information source.
Unsought products		
New unsought	Must be available in places where similar (or related) products are sought; needs attention-getting promotion.	Need for product not strongly felt; unaware of benefits or not yet gone through adoption process.
Regularly unsought	Requires very aggressive promotion, usually personal selling.	Aware of product but not interested; attitude toward product may even be negative.

membership in a spa are good examples. Often the consumer expects help from a knowledgeable salesperson. Quality and style matter more than price. In fact, once the customer finds the right product, price may not matter as long as it's reasonable. For example, you may have asked a friend to recommend a good dentist without even asking what the dentist charges.

Branding may be less important for heterogeneous shopping products. The more carefully consumers compare price and quality, the less they rely on brand names or labels. Some retailers carry competing brands so consumers won't go to a competitor to compare items.

Specialty products— no substitutes please!

Specialty products are consumer products that the customer really wants and makes a special effort to find. Shopping for a specialty product doesn't mean comparing—the buyer wants that special product and is willing to search for it. It's the customer's *willingness to search*—not the extent of searching—that makes it a specialty product.

Any branded product that consumers insist on by name is a specialty product. Marketing managers want customers to see their products as specialty products and ask for

For many young people, life insurance is a regularly unsought product; however, they may change their opinion if promotion can show its value. In contrast, most people hate to wash dishes and know the benefits of having a dishwasher. Still, many consumers see dishwashers as homogeneous products and shop by price. But Bosch wants its target customers to see its distinctively quiet dishwashers as heterogeneous shopping products, or perhaps even specialty items.

them over and over again. Building that kind of relationship isn't easy. It means satisfying the customer every time. However, that's easier and a lot less costly than trying to win back dissatisfied customers or attract new customers who are not seeking the product at all.

Unsought products— need promotion

Unsought products are products that potential customers don't yet want or know they can buy. So they don't search for them at all. In fact, consumers probably won't buy these products if they see them—unless promotion can show their value.

There are two types of unsought products. **New unsought products** are products offering really new ideas that potential customers don't know about yet. Informative promotion can help convince customers to accept the product, ending its unsought status. Dannon's yogurt, Litton's microwave ovens, and Netscape's browser are all popular items now, but initially they were new unsought products.

Regularly unsought products are products—like gravestones, life insurance, and encyclopedias—that stay unsought but not unbought forever. There may be a need, but potential customers aren't motivated to satisfy it. For this kind of product, personal selling is *very* important.

Many nonprofit organizations try to "sell" their unsought products. For example, the Red Cross regularly holds blood drives to remind prospective donors of how important it is to give blood.

One product may be seen several ways

The same product might be seen in different ways by different target markets at the same time. For example, a product viewed as a staple by most consumers in the United States might be seen as a heterogeneous shopping product by consumers in another country. Similarly, a convenient place to shop often means very different things in different countries. In Japan, for example, retail stores tend to be smaller and carry smaller selections of products.

BUSINESS PRODUCT CLASSES—HOW THEY ARE DEFINED

Business product classes are based on how buyers think about products and how the products will be used. The classes of business products are (1) installations, (2) accessories,

Many items in Bush's Best line of food products sell as both consumer and business products, and different marketing mixes are required to reach the different target markets.

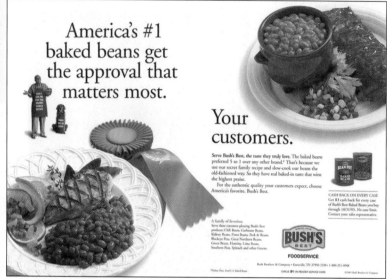

(3) raw materials, (4) components, (5) supplies, and (6) professional services. Exhibit 8-4 relates these product classes to marketing mix planning.

Installations—a boom-or-bust business

Installations—such as buildings, land rights, and major equipment—are important capital items. A **capital item** is a long-lasting product that can be used and depreciated for many years. Often it's very expensive. One-of-a-kind installations—like office buildings and custom-made machines—generally require special negotiations for each sale. Negotiations often involve top management and can stretch over months or even years. Standardized major equipment is treated more routinely.

Installations are a boom-or-bust business. During growth periods, firms may buy installations to increase capacity. But during a downswing, sales fall off sharply.[8]

Specialized services are needed as part of the product

Suppliers sometimes include special services with an installation at no extra cost. A firm that sells (or leases) equipment to dentists, for example, may install it and help the dentist learn to use it.

Accessories— important but short-lived capital items

Accessories are short-lived capital items—tools and equipment used in production or office activities—like Canon's small copy machines, Rockwell's portable drills, and Steelcase's filing cabinets. Accessories are more standardized than installations and they're usually needed by more customers.

Since these products cost less and last a shorter time than installations, multiple buying influence is less important. Operating people and purchasing agents, rather than top managers, may make the purchase decision. As with installations, some customers may wish to lease or rent—to expense the cost.

Raw materials become part of a physical good

Raw materials are unprocessed goods—such as logs, iron ore, and wheat—that are moved to the next production process with little handling. Unlike installations and accessories, *raw materials become part of a physical good and are expense items*. An **expense item** is a product whose total cost is treated as a business expense in the year it's purchased.

There are two types of raw materials: (1) farm products and (2) natural products. **Farm products** are grown by farmers—examples are oranges, sugar cane, and cattle.

Exhibit 8–4   Business Product Classes and Marketing Mix Planning

Business Product Classes	Marketing Mix Considerations	Buying Behavior
Installations	Usually require skillful personal selling by producer, including technical contacts, or understanding of applications; leasing and specialized support services may be required.	Multiple buying influence (including top management) and new-task buying are common; infrequent purchase, long decision period, and boom-or-bust demand are typical.
Accessory equipment	Need fairly widespread distribution and numerous contacts by experienced and sometimes technically trained personnel; price competition is often intense, but quality is important.	Purchasing and operating personnel typically make decisions; shorter decision period than for installations; Internet sourcing.
Raw materials	Grading is important, and transportation and storing can be crucial because of seasonal production and/or perishable products; markets tend to be very competitive.	Long-term contract may be required to ensure supply; online auctions.
Component parts and materials	Product quality and delivery reliability are usually extremely important; negotiation and technical selling typical on less-standardized items; replacement after market may require different strategies.	Multiple buying influence is common; online competitive bids used to encourage competitive pricing.
Maintenance, repair, and operating (MRO) supplies	Typically require widespread distribution or fast delivery (repair items); arrangements with appropriate middlemen may be crucial.	Often handled as straight rebuys, except important operating supplies may be treated much more seriously and involve multiple buying influence.
Professional services	Services customized to buyer's need; personal selling is very important; inelastic demand often supports high prices.	Customer may compare outside service with what internal people could provide; needs may be very specialized.

Natural products are products that occur in nature—such as timber, iron ore, oil, and coal.

The need for grading is one of the important differences between raw materials and other business products. Nature produces what it will—and someone must sort and grade raw materials to satisfy various market segments.

Most buyers of raw materials want ample supplies in the right grades for specific uses—fresh vegetables for Green Giant's production lines or logs for Weyerhaeuser's paper mills. To ensure steady quantities, raw materials customers often sign long-term contracts, sometimes at guaranteed prices.

Component parts and materials must meet specifications

Components are processed expense items that become part of a finished product. Component *parts* are finished (or nearly finished) items that are ready for assembly into the final product. ATI's graphics cards included in personal computers and TRW's air bags in cars are examples. Component *materials* are items such as wire, plastic, or textiles. They have already been processed but must be processed further before becoming part of the final product. Quality is important with components because they become part of the firm's own product.

Some components are custom-made. Then teamwork between the buyer and seller may be needed to arrive at the right specifications. So a buyer may develop a close partnership with a dependable supplier. In contrast, standardized component materials are more likely to be purchased online using a competitive bidding system.

Since component parts go into finished products, a replacement market often develops. Car tires are components originally sold in the *original equipment market* (OEM) that become consumer products in the *after market.*[9]

Supplies for maintenance, repair, and operations

Supplies are expense items that do not become part of a finished product. Supplies can be divided into three types: (1) maintenance, (2) repair, and (3) operating supplies—giving them their common name: MRO supplies.

Maintenance and small operating supplies are like convenience products. The item will be ordered because it is needed—but buyers won't spend much time on it. For such "nuisance" purchases branding is important, and so are breadth of assortment and the seller's dependability. Intermediaries usually handle the many supply items. They are often purchased via online catalog sites.[10]

Important operating supplies, like coal and fuel oil, receive special treatment. Usually there are several sources for such commodity products—and large volumes may be purchased at global exchanges on the Internet.

Professional services— pay to get it done

Professional services are specialized services that support a firm's operations. They are usually expense items. Management consulting services can improve the company's efficiency. Information technology services can maintain a company's networks and websites. Advertising agencies can help promote the firm's products. And food services can improve morale.

Managers compare the cost of buying professional services outside the firm (*outsourcing*) to the cost of having company people perform them. Work that was previously done by an employee is now often purchased from an independent specialist. Clearly, the number of service specialists is growing in our complex economy.

BRANDING NEEDS A STRATEGY DECISION TOO

There are so many brands—and we're so used to seeing them—that we take them for granted. But branding is an important strategy decision area, so we will treat it in some detail.

What is branding?

Branding means the use of a name, term, symbol, or design—or a combination of these—to identify a product. It includes the use of brand names, trademarks, and practically all other means of product identification.

Brand name has a narrower meaning. A **brand name** is a word, letter, or a group of words or letters. Examples include America Online (AOL), WD-40, 3M Post-its, and PT Cruiser.

Trademark is a legal term. A **trademark** includes only those words, symbols, or marks that are legally registered for use by a single company. A **service mark** is the same as a trademark except that it refers to a service offering.

The word *FedEx* can be used to explain these differences. The FedEx overnight delivery service is branded under the brand name FedEx (whether it's spoken or printed in any manner). When "FedEx" is printed in a certain kind of script, however, it becomes a trademark. A trademark need not be attached to the product. It need not even be a word—it can be a symbol. Exhibit 8–5 shows some common trademarks.

These differences may seem technical. But they are very important to business firms that spend a lot of money to protect and promote their brands. Sometimes a firm's brand name is the only element in its marketing mix that a competitor can't copy.

Exhibit 8–5 Recognized Trademarks and Symbols Help in Promotion

Brands meet needs

Well-recognized brands make shopping easier. Think of trying to buy groceries, for example, if you had to evaluate each of 25,000 items every time you went to a supermarket. Many customers are willing to buy new things—but having gambled and won, they like to buy a sure thing the next time. Brand names connect a product with the benefits a customer can expect. The connection may be learned from past consumer experience, from the firm's promotion, or in other ways. *Certified Angus Beef* stands for "tender, high-quality meat," and *Jiffy Lube* means "fast and convenient oil change." Consumers know what they will get when they buy these branded products.

Brand promotion has advantages for branders as well as customers. A good brand reduces the marketer's selling time and effort. Good brands can also improve the company's image—speeding acceptance of new products marketed under the same name. For example, many consumers quickly tried Listerine PocketPaks breath fresheners when they appeared because they already knew they trusted Listerine mouthwash.[11]

CONDITIONS FAVORABLE TO BRANDING

Can you recall a brand name for file folders, bed frames, electric extension cords, or nails? As these examples suggest, it's not always easy to establish a respected brand.

The following conditions are favorable to successful branding:

1. The product is easy to label and identify by brand or trademark.
2. The product quality is easy to maintain and provides the best value for the price.
3. Dependable and widespread availability is possible. (When customers start using a brand, they want to be able to continue using it.)
4. Demand is strong enough that the market price can be high enough to make the branding effort profitable.
5. There are economies of scale. (If the branding is really successful, costs should drop and profits should increase.)
6. Favorable shelf locations or display space in stores are available. This is something retailers can control when they brand their own products.

In general, these conditions are less common in less-developed economies, and that may explain why efforts to build brands in less-developed nations often fail.

ACHIEVING BRAND FAMILIARITY IS NOT EASY

Today, familiar brands exist for most product categories, ranging from crayons (Crayola) to real estate services (Century 21). However, what brand is familiar often varies from one country to another.

Brand acceptance must be earned with a good product and regular promotion. **Brand familiarity** means how well customers recognize and accept a company's brand. The degree of brand familiarity affects the planning for the rest of the marketing mix—especially where the product should be offered and what promotion is needed.

Five levels of brand familiarity

Five levels of brand familiarity are useful for strategy planning: (1) rejection, (2) nonrecognition, (3) recognition, (4) preference, and (5) insistence.

Some brands have been tried and found wanting. **Brand rejection** means that potential customers won't buy a brand unless its image is changed. Rejection may suggest a change in the product or perhaps only a shift to target customers who have a better image of the brand. Overcoming a negative image is difficult and can be very expensive.

Brand rejection is a big concern for service-oriented businesses because it's hard to control the quality of service. A business traveler who gets a dirty room in a Hilton Hotel in Caracas, Venezuela, might not return to a Hilton anywhere. Yet it's difficult for Hilton to ensure that every maid does a good job every time.

Some products are seen as basically the same. **Brand nonrecognition** means final consumers don't recognize a brand at all—even though intermediaries may use the brand name for identification and inventory control. Examples include school supplies, inexpensive dinnerware, many of the items that you'd find in a hardware store, and thousands of dot-coms on the Internet.

Brand recognition means that customers remember the brand. This may not seem like much, but it can be a big advantage if there are many "nothing" brands on the market. Even if consumers can't recall the brand without help, they may be reminded when they see it in a store among other less familiar brands.

Most branders would like to win **brand preference**—which means that target customers usually choose a particular brand over other brands, perhaps because of habit or favorable past experience.

It takes time and money to build brand awareness, so sometimes brands can be extended to new product offerings and different product categories. Dove has introduced moisturizing shampoos and conditioners and Johnson & Johnson has added Moisture Care Baby Wash. Both new products benefit from their well-recognized brand names.

Differentiation by Design

Today, many companies are finding that they can gain a competitive advantage by having designers involved in basic decisions about product features and functions—rather than just having them there to finalize the look. Designers now help with decisions about what benefits a product will offer, including the right look and feel to achieve ease of use.

Roomba, iRobot's innovative robotic vacuum cleaner, has a design that seems perfect for its target market—the large group of people who hate to vacuum. Roomba looks like a 13-inch disk and is less than 4 inches tall—not the odd-shaped clunker that our grandparents owned. It's a robot, but it requires no programming. You simply place it on the floor, press a button to turn it on, and Roomba automatically wanders around the room vacuuming. A next-generation Scooba robot that washes hardwood and tile floors appeals to the same target market.

Kaiser Permanente, the health care giant, conducted research that revealed that its facilities were alienating many patients. Most patients already had health concerns when they arrived, so the stark waiting rooms made them anxious, the poor signage was confusing, and small exam rooms were lonely. Kaiser turned to designers for help. In response, they expanded the exam rooms, added privacy curtains, and invited patients to have a friend wait with them. After the redesign, Kaiser's patients said they were more satisfied with the health care they received. The health care was the same, but the facilities were improved.

In Europe, the circulation of newspapers steadily declined for years. Young adults with fast-paced lifestyles and little time simply weren't reading them. However, Metro attracted many new customers from this demographic group after changing the morning newspaper experience. It did so by switching to a tabloid design and short-article format.

A decade ago, discount retailer Target relied on TV and magazine ads to try to build a cool image. But the products it carried were mostly the same stuff sold by rival Wal-Mart. To differentiate itself, Target put more emphasis on products with affordable, attractive, and functional designs. Target recruited designers like Michael Graves to create new lines of housewares, office supplies, furniture, toys, and games—all of which helped to reposition Target's image. Today, Target's design-centered differentiation helps it reduce direct price competition.

Trends in design change frequently because they depend on what look is in fashion as well as what functions well. So, it may be costly to follow design trends if they require frequent product updates. In recent years, Apple has been able to balance design, costs, and premium prices. By comparison, other companies, including Sony, have had a harder time keeping their design edge.[12]

Brand insistence means customers insist on a firm's branded product and are willing to search for it. This is an objective of many target marketers.

The right brand name can help

A good brand name can help build brand familiarity. It can help tell something important about the company or its product. Exhibit 8–6 lists some characteristics of a good brand name.

Exhibit 8–6
Characteristics of a Good Brand Name

• Short and simple	• Suggestive of product benefits
• Easy to spell and read	• Adaptable to packaging/labeling needs
• Easy to recognize and remember	• No undesirable imagery
• Easy to pronounce	• Always timely (does not go out-of-date)
• Can be pronounced in only one way	• Adaptable to any advertising medium
• Can be pronounced in all languages (for international markets)	• Legally available for use (not in use by another firm)

Companies that compete in international markets face a special problem in selecting brand names. A name that conveys a positive image in one language may be meaningless in another. Or, worse, it may have unintended meanings. GM's Nova car is a classic example. GM stuck with the Nova name when it introduced the car in South America. It seemed like a sensible decision because *nova* is the Spanish word for star. However, Nova also sounds the same as the Spanish words for "no go." Consumers weren't interested in a no-go car, and sales didn't pick up until GM changed the name.[13]

A respected name builds brand equity

Because it's costly to build brand recognition, some firms prefer to acquire established brands rather than try to build their own. The value of a brand to its current owner or to a firm that wants to buy it is sometimes called **brand equity**—the value of a brand's overall strength in the market. For example, brand equity is likely to be higher if many satisfied customers insist on buying the brand and if retailers are eager to stock it. That almost guarantees ongoing profits.

The financial value of the Yahoo! brand name illustrates the brand equity idea. In 1994, Yahoo! was just a tiny start-up trying to make it with a directory site on the Internet. Most people had never heard the name, and few even knew what the Internet was or why you'd need a directory site. As interest in the Internet grew, Yahoo! promoted its brand name with quirky TV and magazine ads. At a time when many people were just getting to know the Web, Yahoo! came across as an approachable and fun place to go on the Internet. Within a few years, Yahoo! attracted more than 100 million unique customer visits. Yahoo! wants its brand to be just as well known in places like Taiwan, China, and France—so it continues to use funny ads to make the brand and website feel comfortable to web surfers. Because Yahoo! charges fees to advertisers eager to reach these users, the familiarity of its brand translates directly into ad revenues.[14]

PROTECTING BRAND NAMES AND TRADEMARKS

U.S. common law and civil law protect the rights of trademark and brand-name owners. The **Lanham Act** (of 1946) spells out what kinds of marks (including brand names) can be protected and the exact method of protecting them. The law applies to goods shipped in interstate or foreign commerce.

The Lanham Act does not force registration. But registering under the Lanham Act is often a first step toward protecting a trademark to be used in international markets. That's because some nations require that a trademark be registered in its home country before they will register or protect it.

You must protect your own

A brand can be a real asset to a company. Each firm should try to see that its brand doesn't become a common descriptive term for its kind of product. When this happens, the brand name or trademark becomes public property—and the owner loses all rights to it. This happened with the names cellophane, aspirin, shredded wheat, and kerosene.[15]

Counterfeiting is accepted in some cultures

Even when products are properly registered, counterfeiters may make unauthorized copies. Many well-known brands—ranging from Levi's jeans to Rolex watches to Zantac acid reflux medicine—face this problem. Of course, pirated digital copies of songs, movies, and books are also routinely shared over the Internet. Counterfeiting is especially common in developing nations. In China, for example, many DVDs, CDs, and software programs are bootleg copies. Counterfeiting can be big business, so efforts to stop it may meet with limited success. There are also differences in cultural values. In South Korea, for example, many people don't see counterfeiting as unethical.[16]

WHAT KIND OF BRAND TO USE?

Keep it in the family

Branders of more than one product must decide whether they are going to use a **family brand**—the same brand name for several products—or individual brands for each product. Examples of family brands are Keebler snack food products and Sears's Kenmore appliances.

The use of the same brand for many products makes sense if all are similar in type and quality. The main benefit is that the goodwill attached to one or two products may help the others. Money spent to promote the brand name benefits more than one product, which cuts promotion costs for each product.

A special kind of family brand is a **licensed brand**—a well-known brand that sellers pay a fee to use. For example, the familiar Sunkist brand name has been licensed to many companies for use on more than 400 products in 30 countries.[17]

Individual brands for outside and inside competition

A company uses **individual brands**—separate brand names for each product—when it's important for each of the products to have a separate identity, as when products vary in quality or type.

If the products are really different, such as Elmer's glue and Borden's ice cream, individual brands can avoid confusion. Some firms use individual brands with similar products to make segmentation and positioning efforts easier. For example, when General Mills introduced a line of organic cereals, it used the Cascadian Farm name and the Big G logo was not on the box. The rationale was that consumers who try to avoid additives might not trust a big corporate brand.[18]

Internet EXERCISE

Go to the Procter & Gamble website (**www.pg.com**) and click on "Products," and then, under "Personal and Beauty," click on "Hair Care." Find out the brand names of the different shampoos that P&G makes. How are the different brands positioned, and what target markets do they appeal to?

Generic "brands"

Products that some consumers see as commodities may be difficult or expensive to brand. Some manufacturers and middlemen have responded to this problem with **generic products**—products that have no brand at all other than identification of their contents and the manufacturer or middleman. Generic products are usually offered in plain packages at lower prices. They are quite common in less-developed nations.[19]

General Mills uses the Cascadian Farm brand name to help reinforce the positioning of its organic line of cereals. However, both of its high-quality brands may have to compete for shelf space and consumer attention against similar store (dealer) brands of cereal, which often sell at lower prices.

WHO SHOULD DO THE BRANDING?

Manufacturer brands versus dealer brands

Manufacturer brands are brands created by producers. These are sometimes called *national brands* because the brand is promoted all across the country or in large regions. Note, however, that many manufacturer brands are distributed globally. Such brands include Nabisco, Campbell's, Whirlpool, Ford, and IBM. Many creators of service-oriented firms—like McDonald's, Orkin Pest Control, and Bank of America—promote their brands this way too.

Dealer brands, also called **private brands**, are brands created by middlemen. Examples of dealer brands include the brands of Kroger, Ace Hardware, Radio Shack, Wal-Mart, and Sears. Some of these are advertised and distributed more widely than many national brands. For example, national TV ads helped Original Arizona Jeans (by JCPenney) and Canyon River Blues (by Sears) compete with Levi's and Wrangler.

From the middleman's perspective, the major advantage of selling a popular manufacturer brand is that the product is already presold to some target customers. The major disadvantage is that manufacturers normally offer lower gross margins than the middleman might be able to earn with a dealer brand.

Who's winning the battle of the brands?

The **battle of the brands**, the competition between dealer brands and manufacturer brands, is just a question of whose brands will be more popular and who will be in control.

At one time, manufacturer brands were much more popular than dealer brands. Now sales of both kinds of brands are about equal—but sales of dealer brands are expected to

A consumer who needs a new showerhead is likely to pick the brand and style by comparing alternatives at a retail store. Waterpik's package makes it easy for the consumer to see and evaluate the product and the curved design helps to focus attention on the flexible hose. The package for Grillero beef looks different from the way most beef is packaged and also provides a way to tell French consumers that the product is organic.

continue growing. Middlemen have some advantages in this battle. With the number of large retail chains growing, they are better able to arrange reliable sources of supply at low cost. They can also give the dealer brand special shelf position or promotion.

Consumers benefit from the battle. Competition has already narrowed price differences between manufacturer brands and well-known dealer brands.[20]

THE STRATEGIC IMPORTANCE OF PACKAGING

Packaging involves promoting, protecting, and enhancing the product. Packaging can be important to both sellers and customers. See Exhibit 8–7. It can make a product more convenient to use or store. It can prevent spoiling or damage. Good packaging makes products easier to identify and promotes the brand at the point of purchase and even in use.

Packaging can enhance the product

A new package can make *the* important difference in a new marketing strategy—by meeting customers' needs better. Sometimes a new package makes the product easier or safer to use. For example, most drug and food products now have special seals to prevent product tampering. And clever packaging is an important part of a new effort by Campbell Soup Company to pump new life into an old product—soup. Campbell developed its Soup at Hand with a package that doesn't require a can opener or a stirring pot and instead is microwavable. Soup at Hand is just right for today's on-the-go consumers who want a portable meal solution, so it also helps Campbell get distribution in convenience stores and vending machines. Consumers value convenience, so the Soup at Hand price of $1.49 (versus $.79 for a traditional can of soup) also produces attractive profits.[21]

Packaging sends a message

Packaging can tie the product to the rest of the marketing strategy. Packaging for Energizer batteries features the pink bunny seen in attention-getting TV ads and reminds consumers that the batteries are durable. A good package sometimes gives a firm more promotional effect than it could get with advertising. Customers see the package in stores, when they're actually buying.

Exhibit 8–7 Some Ways Packaging Benefits Consumers and Marketers

Opportunity to Add Value	Some Decision Factors	Examples
Promotion	Link product to promotion	The bunny on the Energizer battery package is a reminder that it "keeps going and going."
	Branding at point of purchase or consumption	Coke's logo greets almost everyone each time the refrigerator is opened.
	Product information	Kraft's nutrition label helps consumers decide which cheese to buy, and a UPC code reduces checkout time and errors.
Protection	For shipping and storing	Sony's MP3 player is kept safe by Styrofoam inserts.
	From spoiling	Tylenol's safety seal prevents tampering.
	From shoplifting	Cardboard hang-tag on Gillette razor blades is too large to hide in hand.
Enhance product	The environment	Tide detergent bottle can be recycled.
	Convenience in use	Squeezable tube of Yoplait Go-Gurt is easy to eat on the go and in new situations.
	Added product functions	Plastic tub is useful for refrigerator leftovers after the Cool Whip is gone.

Packaging may lower distribution costs

Better protective packaging is very important to manufacturers and wholesalers. They sometimes have to pay the cost of goods damaged in shipment. Retailers need protective packaging too. It can reduce storing costs by cutting down on breakage, spoilage, and theft. Good packages also save space and are easier to handle and display.[22]

WHAT IS SOCIALLY RESPONSIBLE PACKAGING?

Laws reduce confusion and clutter

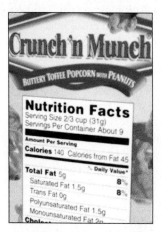

In the United States, consumer criticism finally led to the passage of the **Federal Fair Packaging and Labeling Act** (of 1966)—which requires that consumer goods be clearly labeled in easy-to-understand terms—to give consumers more information. The law also calls on industry to try to reduce the number of package sizes and make labels more useful. Since then there have been further guidelines. The most far-reaching are based on the Nutrition Labeling and Education Act of 1990. It requires food manufacturers to use a uniform format that allows consumers to compare the nutritional value of different products. Recently there have been more changes, including a requirement to clearly show the fat content of food.[23]

Current laws also offer more guidance on environmental issues. Some states require a consumer to pay a deposit on bottles and cans until they're returned. These laws mean well, but they can be a challenge. Channels of distribution are usually set up to distribute products, not return empty packages.[24]

Internet EXERCISE

How well do you understand food labels? The Food and Drug Administration's website has a quiz to test your food label knowledge. Go to the quiz at **www.foodsafety.gov/~dms/lab-gen.html** and then click the link "Quiz Yourself! Test Your Food Label Knowledge!" Try the five questions. What did you learn? What else do you think could be done to improve food labels? Should companies be required to label packages—or should it be their option? Why?

Ethical decisions remain

Although various laws provide guidance on many packaging issues, many areas still require marketing managers to make ethical choices. For example, some firms have been criticized for designing packages that conceal a downsized product, giving consumers less for their money. Similarly, some retailers design packages and labels for their private-label products that look just like, and are easily confused with, manufacturer brands. Are efforts such as these unethical, or are they simply an attempt to make packaging a more effective part of a marketing mix? Different people will answer differently.

Empty packages litter our streets, and some plastic packages will lie in a city dump for decades. But some consumers like the convenience that accompanies these problems. Is it unethical for a marketing manager to provide a choice for consumers with different preferences? Some critics argue that it is. Others praise firms that give consumers choices.

Many critics think that labeling information is too often incomplete or misleading. For example, what does it really mean if a label says a food product is "organic" or "low fat"? How far should a marketing manager go in putting potentially negative information on a package? For example, should Häagen-Dazs affix a label that says "this product will clog your arteries"? That sounds extreme, but what type of information *is* appropriate?[25]

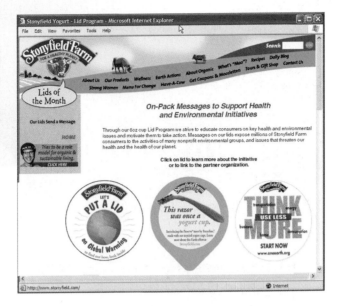

Stonyfield Farm wants its customers to know that it is sensitive to the environment. It communicates how it is trying to improve the environmental performance of its packaging with messages on the lids of its yogurt containers and at the company's website.

WARRANTY POLICIES ARE A PART OF STRATEGY PLANNING

Warranty puts promises in writing

A **warranty** explains what the seller promises about its product. A marketing manager should decide whether to offer a specific warranty and, if so, what the warranty will cover and how it will be communicated to target customers. This is an area where the legal environment—as well as customer needs and competitive offerings—must be considered.

U.S. common law says that producers must stand behind their products—even if they don't offer a specific warranty. A written warranty provided by the seller may promise more than the common law provides. However, it may actually *reduce* the responsibility a producer would have under common law.

The federal **Magnuson-Moss Act** (of 1975) says that producers must provide a clearly written warranty if they choose to offer any warranty. The warranty does not have to be strong. However, Federal Trade Commission (FTC) guidelines try to ensure that warranties are clear and definite and not deceptive or unfair. A warranty also must be available for inspection before the purchase.

A company has to make it clear whether it's offering a full or limited warranty—and the law defines what *full* means. Most firms offer a limited warranty if they offer one at all. In recent years, many firms have reduced the period of warranty coverage. Apple's popular iPod music player, for example, has only a 90-day warranty.

Warranty may improve the marketing mix

Some firms use warranties to improve the appeal of their marketing mix. They design more quality into their goods or services and offer refunds or replacement, not just repair, if there is a problem. A strong warranty sends consumers a signal about brand quality. A few years ago, Hyundai, the South Korean car maker, pushed to improve quality. Yet among consumers its old reputation lingered. That changed after Hyundai put a 10-year warranty on its cars and used TV ads to tout it as "America's best warranty."

Service guarantees

Customer service guarantees are becoming more common as a way to attract, and keep, customers. Pizza Hut guarantees a luncheon pizza in five minutes or it's free. General Motors set up a fast-oil-change guarantee to compete with fast-lube specialists who were taking customers away from dealers. If the dealer doesn't get the job done in 29 minutes or less, the next oil change is free.

There's more risk in offering a service guarantee than a warranty on a physical product. A lazy employee or a service breakdown can create a big expense. However,

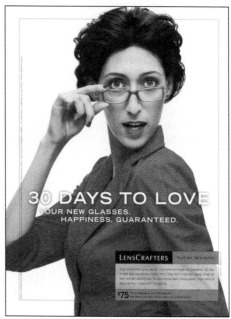

In a competitive market, a product's warranty or guarantee can be the critical difference in a firm's marketing mix.

without the guarantee, dissatisfied customers may just go away mad without ever complaining.

Warranty support can be costly

The cost of warranty support ultimately must be covered by the price that consumers pay. This has led some firms to offer warranty choices. The basic price for a product may include a warranty that covers a short time period or that covers parts but not labor. Consumers who want more or better protection pay extra for an extended warranty or a service contract.[26]

CONCLUSION

In this chapter, we looked at Product broadly—which is the right vantage point for marketing strategy planning. We saw that a product may be a good or a service, or some combination of both. And we saw that a firm's Product is what it offers to *satisfy the needs of its target market*—which may include the customer's experience both before and after the purchase.

We described some key marketing differences between goods and services. We also introduced both consumer product classes (based on *how consumers think about and shop for products*) and business product classes (based on *how buyers think about products and how they'll be used*). In addition, we showed how the product classes affect planning marketing mixes.

We reviewed the Product area strategy decisions required for branding and packaging—and saw how the right decisions can add value for customers and give a product a competitive edge. Customers view a

brand as a guarantee of quality, which leads to repeat purchases, lower promotion costs, higher sales figures, and greater customer equity. Packaging offers promotional opportunities and informs customers. Variations in packaging can also help a product appeal to different segments of the market. And packaging can help protect the product anywhere in the channel of distribution. Finally, we saw how warranties can play an important role in strategy planning—by reducing buying risk. Customers see warranties as a signal of quality.

The brand familiarity a product earns is a measure of the marketing manager's ability to carve out a separate market. Therefore, ultimately, brand familiarity affects place, price, and promotion decisions. Strategy planning for product and the rest of the marketing mix will vary across the product's life cycle—and this will be discussed in the next chapter.

KEY TERMS

QUESTIONS AND PROBLEMS

1. Define, in your own words, what a Product is.

2. Discuss several ways in which physical goods are different from pure services. Give an example of a good and a service to illustrate each of the differences.

3. What products are being offered by a shop that specializes in bicycles? By a travel agent? By a supermarket? By a new car dealer?

4. What kinds of consumer products are the following: (*a*) watches, (*b*) automobiles, and (*c*) toothpastes? Explain your reasoning.

5. Consumer services tend to be intangible, and goods tend to be tangible. Use an example to explain how the lack of a physical good in a pure service might affect efforts to promote the service.

6. How would the marketing mix for a staple convenience product differ from the mix for a homogeneous shopping product? How would the mix for a specialty product differ from the mix for a heterogeneous shopping product? Use examples.

7. Give an example of a product that is a *new* unsought product for most people. Briefly explain why it is an unsought product.

8. In what types of stores would you expect to find (*a*) convenience products, (*b*) shopping products, (*c*) specialty products, and (*d*) unsought products?

9. Cite two examples of business products that require a substantial amount of service in order to be useful.

10. Explain why a new law office might want to lease furniture rather than buy it.

11. Would you expect to find any wholesalers selling the various types of business products? Are retail stores required (or something like retail stores)?

12. What kinds of business products are the following: (*a*) lubricating oil, (*b*) electric motors, and (*c*) a firm that provides landscaping and grass mowing for an apartment complex? Explain your reasoning.

13. How do raw materials differ from other business products? Do the differences have any impact on their marketing mixes? If so, what specifically?

14. For the kinds of business products described in this chapter, complete the following table (use one or a few well-chosen words).

   1. *Kind of distribution facility(ies) needed and functions they will provide.*
   2. *Caliber of salespeople required.*
   3. *Kind of advertising required.*

Products	1	2	3
Installations			
Buildings and land rights			
Major equipment			
Standard			
Custom-made			
Accessories			
Raw materials			
Farm products			
Natural products			
Components			
Supplies			
Maintenance and small operating supplies			
Important operating supplies			
Professional services			

15. Is there any difference between a brand name and a trademark? If so, why is this difference important?

16. Is a well-known brand valuable only to the owner of the brand?

17. Suggest an example of a product and a competitive situation where it would *not* be profitable for a firm to spend large sums of money to establish a brand.

18. List five brand names and indicate what product is associated with the brand name. Evaluate the strengths and weaknesses of the brand name.

19. Explain family brands. Should Best Buy carry its own dealer brands to compete with some of the popular manufacturer brands it carries? Explain your reasons.

20. In the past, Sears emphasized its own dealer brands. Now it is carrying more well-known manufacturer brands. What are the benefits to Sears of carrying more manufacturer brands?

21. What does the degree of brand familiarity imply about previous and future promotion efforts? How does the degree of brand familiarity affect the Place and Price variables?

22. You operate a small hardware store with an emphasis on manufacturer brands and have barely been breaking even. Evaluate the proposal of a large wholesaler who offers a full line of dealer-branded hardware items at substantially lower prices. Specify any assumptions necessary to obtain a definite answer.

23. Give an example in which packaging costs probably (*a*) lower total distribution costs and (*b*) raise total distribution costs.

24. Is it more difficult to support a warranty for a service than for a physical good? Explain your reasons.

25. Explain some of the different aspects of the customer experience that could be managed to improve customer satisfaction if you were the marketing manager for: (*a*) an airport branch of a rental car agency, (*b*) a fast-food restaurant, (*c*) an online firm selling software directly to consumers from a website, and (*d*) a hardware store selling lawn mowers.

CREATING MARKETING PLANS

The Marketing Plan Coach software on the Student CD includes a sample marketing plan for Hillside Veterinary Clinic. Look through the "Marketing Strategy" section.

a. What goods does Hillside Veterinary Clinic sell?

b. What services does Hillside Veterinary Clinic sell?

c. What consumer product classes are offered by Hillside Veterinary Clinic?

d. The discussion of product classes in this chapter indicates what marketing mix is typical for different classes of products. Does the marketing strategy recommended in the marketing plan fit with those considerations? Why or why not?

SUGGESTED CASES

1. McDonald's "Seniors" Restaurant

3. NOCO Soccer Academy

13. Office Distributors, Inc.

31. Home Health, Inc.

COMPUTER-AIDED PROBLEM

8. BRANDING DECISION

Wholesteen Dairy, Inc., produces and sells Wholesteen brand condensed milk to grocery retailers. The overall market for condensed milk is fairly flat, and there's sharp competition among dairies for retailers' business. Wholesteen's regular price to retailers is $8.88 a case (24 cans). FoodWorld—a fast-growing supermarket chain and Wholesteen's largest customer—buys 20,000 cases of Wholesteen's condensed milk a year. That's 20 percent of Wholesteen's total sales volume of 100,000 cases per year.

FoodWorld is proposing that Wholesteen produce private-label condensed milk to be sold with the FoodWorld brand name. FoodWorld proposes to buy the same total quantity as it does now, but it wants half (10,000 cases) with the Wholesteen brand and half with the FoodWorld brand. FoodWorld wants Wholesteen to reduce costs by using a lower-quality can for the FoodWorld brand. That change will cost Wholesteen $.01 less per can than it costs for the cans that Wholesteen uses for its own brand. FoodWorld will also provide preprinted labels with its brand name—which will save Wholesteen an additional $.02 a can.

Wholesteen spends $70,000 a year on promotion to increase familiarity with the Wholesteen brand. In addition, Wholesteen gives retailers an allowance of $.25 per case for their local advertising, which features the Wholesteen brand. FoodWorld has agreed to give up the advertising allowance for its own brand, but it is only willing to pay $7.40 a case for the milk that will be sold with the FoodWorld brand name. It will continue under the old terms for the rest of its purchases.

Sue Glick, Wholesteen's marketing manager, is considering the FoodWorld proposal. She has entered cost and revenue data on a spreadsheet—so she can see more clearly how the proposal might affect revenue and profits.

a. Based on the data in the initial spreadsheet, how will Wholesteen profits be affected if Glick accepts the FoodWorld proposal?

b. Glick is worried that FoodWorld will find another producer for the FoodWorld private-label milk if Wholesteen rejects the proposal. This would immediately reduce Wholesteen's annual sales by 10,000 cases. FoodWorld might even stop buying from Wholesteen altogether. What would happen to profits in these two situations?

c. FoodWorld is rapidly opening new stores and sells milk in every store. The FoodWorld buyer says that next year's purchases could be up to 25,000 cases of Wholesteen's condensed milk. But Sue Glick knows that FoodWorld may stop buying the Wholesteen brand and want all 25,000 cases to carry the FoodWorld private-label brand. How will this affect profit? (Hint: Enter the new quantities in the "proposal" column of the spreadsheet.)

d. What should Wholesteen do? Why?

For additional questions related to this problem, see Exercise 8-5 in the *Learning Aid for Use with Essentials of Marketing*, 11th edition.

CHAPTER NINE

Product Management and New-Product Development

Kevin Plank was a business major and football player at the University of Maryland when he spotted an opportunity. He and his teammates wore cotton T-shirts under their football pads, but the T-shirts quickly became sweat-soaked, heavy, and uncomfortable during practices and games. When Plank began looking for a product that would perform better than a T-shirt, he learned about new types of fabrics and performance clothing for bicyclists and hikers. But he realized a shirt that would meet the needs of football players was a really new idea, not just a minor variation on existing clothing.

In New York City's garment district, Plank learned about a polyester-Lycra blend fabric that didn't trap moisture. He worked with a tailor to develop several prototype shirts and then asked friends who were players in the National Football League, like Vernon Davis of the San Francisco 49ers, to try them. The players really liked the skintight, compression shirts. They fit comfortably under football gear and wicked away sweat—keeping the players cooler, drier, and lighter. When Plank's friends clamored for more shirts, he knew he had a good start. However, he couldn't afford a big ad campaign to tout the benefits of his product, and he didn't have relationships with retailers who could help build demand with final consumers. So Plank moved to commercialization with a focus on a target market he knew: college football teams.

Plank went back to New York and ordered 500 shirts, the first products with the Under Armour brand name and the start of what became the Heat-Gear warm weather product line. Then he loaded his shirts in his SUV and traveled to colleges across the Southeast. He tried to persuade coaches, players, and equipment managers about the benefits of his unique shirts. Many were not initially convinced of the value—especially since the price was 3 to 5 times the price of a T-shirt. But its advantage was clear after a player would try one for a football practice—and praise for the product spread quickly.

Success with college and professional athletes helped the company build credibility. It also led to relationships with specialty-sports retailers who could reach the larger and more profitable consumer market. Sports retailers provided attractive displays and promoted the brand because they liked having a profitable new offering that was not available at lower prices in local discount or department stores.

As the market for sports-performance clothes grew, Nike, Adidas, and other firms came out with competing products. To fight back, Under Armour

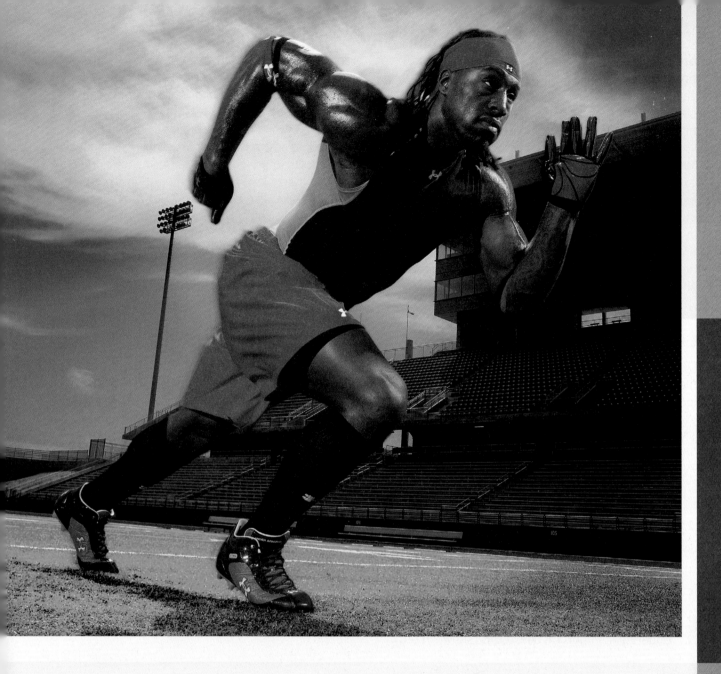

put more emphasis on creative promotion to build customer preference for the Under Armour brand. For example, Under Armour got a prominent product placement in the football movie *Any Given Sunday*. Similarly, Under Armour ran TV and print ads featuring professional athletes, like Dallas Cowboys football player (and former Plank teammate) Eric Ogbogu. When the muscular Ogbogu barked the firm's tag line, "Protect This House," it instantly became a part of popular sports culture. It was the rallying cry of players, fans, and banners in football stadiums across the country.

Of course, the firm continued to look for growth through new product ideas. One successful idea came from a coach who wanted a cold weather version of the shirt that would keep players warm as well as dry. Under Armour responded with the first products in its ColdGear line. New products for a variety of other athletic markets have followed, including leggings that are popular with skiers and polo shirts that are a hit with golfers.

It's tough to quickly steal away a large share of the customers in a mature product-market, but that is just what Under Armour accomplished with its new design for football cleats. The new-product development team researched playing surfaces, player movements, and body types to design cleats that were more durable, lighter, and more breathable. Player feedback led to even more refinements. Of course, it also took an innovative ad campaign and point-of-purchase promotion for the cleats to capture a 20 percent share of sales in this highly competitive market.

Even the best firms sometimes experience problems with new products, and Under Armour is no exception. Its initial line for women failed to meet expectations because of concerns about fit and quality. To fix the problems, Under Armour brought in more female designers and developed a clearer understanding of the needs of female athletes. The new line was expanded and included redesigned shorts, sleeveless tops, sports bras, and socks. The

brand manager supported the improved line with ads featuring soccer star Heather Mitts. Now the women's line accounts for more than one-fifth of the company's sales.

In just 10 years, Under Armour has grown from a start-up into a firm with over $430 million in annual sales. Of course, growth in the performance clothing market is now slowing and competition from big-name firms like Nike is increasing. But Kevin Plank is used to taking on bigger competitors. Once during his college football days, the 5-foot 11-inch, 229-pound Plank was assigned to block his 6-foot 4-inch, 269-pound buddy Ogbogu, and the bigger man ended up on his back with a concussion. Watch out Nike![1]

LEARNING OBJECTIVES

Developing new products and managing them for profitable growth are keys to success for most firms. Yet, many new products fail. Even products that succeed face new challenges as competition becomes more intense. So, the marketing strategy that supported the product's initial success usually needs to change as the market evolves. This chapter will help you understand this evolution and how it relates to effective new-product development and creative strategy changes for existing products—both of which are crucial to attracting and retaining target customers.

When you finish this chapter, you should:

1. understand how product life cycles affect strategy planning.

2. know what is involved in designing new products and what "new products" really are.

3. understand the new-product development process.

4. see why product liability must be considered in screening new products.

5. understand the need for product or brand managers.

6. understand how total quality management can improve goods and services.

7. understand important new terms (shown in red).

INNOVATION AND MARKET CHANGES CREATE OPPORTUNITIES

Successful new products, like those in the Under Armour case, are critical in driving profitable growth for both new and established companies. Under Armour pioneered a fast-growing new product-market—and "performance clothing" is meeting customer needs in new ways. Similarly, in Chapter 5, we looked at how the iPod and other innovations in digital media are changing personal entertainment. In fact, all around us there is a constant life-and-death struggle where old products are replaced by new products. Digital video recorders are quickly making videotapes obsolete, just as cell phones have replaced shortwave radios and phone booths and made it possible for people to communicate from places where it was previously impossible. Really new product ideas disrupt the old ways of doing things—not only for marketers, but also for consumers.

These innovations show that products, customer behavior, and competition change over time. These changes create opportunities for marketing managers and pose

Exhibit 9–1 The Role of Product Management and New-Product Development in Marketing Strategy

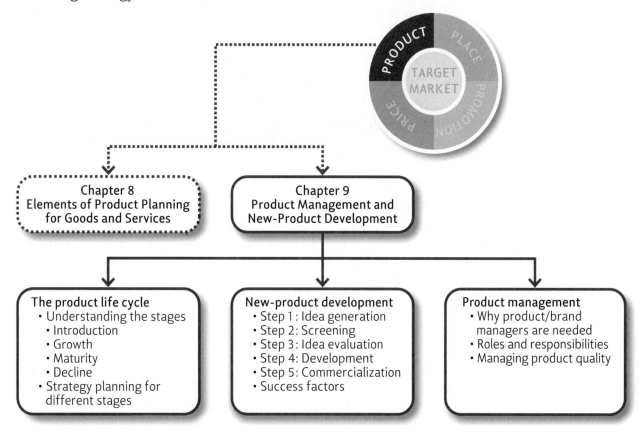

challenges as well. Developing new products and managing existing products to meet changing conditions is important to the success of every firm. In Chapter 8 we looked at important strategy decisions that need to be planned for new products or updated for existing products. In this chapter, we'll look at how successful new products are developed in the first place—and what marketing managers need to know and do to manage their growth. We'll start by explaining the cycle of growth and decline that new product innovations go through. When you understand the stages in this cycle, you can see *why* it is so critical for a firm to have an effective new-product development process—and why the challenges of managing a product change as it matures. See Exhibit 9–1.

MANAGING PRODUCTS OVER THEIR LIFE CYCLES

Revolutionary products create new product-markets. But competitors are always developing and copying new ideas and products—making existing products out-of-date more quickly than ever. Products, like consumers, go through life cycles.

Product life cycle has four major stages

The **product life cycle** describes the stages a really new product idea goes through from beginning to end. The product life cycle is divided into four major stages: (1) market introduction, (2) market growth, (3) market maturity, and (4) sales decline. The product life cycle is concerned with new types (or categories) of products in the market, not just what happens to an individual brand.

A particular firm's marketing mix usually must change during the product life cycle. There are several reasons why customers' attitudes and needs may change over the

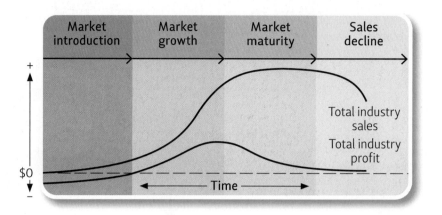

Exhibit 9-2
Typical Life Cycle of a
New Product Concept

product life cycle. The product may be aimed at entirely different target markets at different stages. And the nature of competition moves toward pure competition or oligopoly.

Further, total sales of the product—by all competitors in the industry—vary in each of its four stages. They move from very low in the market introduction stage to high at market maturity and then back to low in the sales decline stage. More important, the profit picture changes too. These general relationships can be seen in Exhibit 9–2. Note that sales and profits do not move together over time. *Industry profits decline while industry sales are still rising.*[2]

Market introduction—investing in the future

In the **market introduction** stage, sales are low as a new idea is first introduced to a market. Customers aren't looking for the product. Even if the product offers superior value, customers don't even know about it. Informative promotion is needed to tell potential customers about the advantages and uses of the new-product concept.

Even though a firm promotes its new product, it takes time for customers to learn that the product is available. Most companies experience losses during the introduction stage because they spend so much money for Product, Place, and Promotion development. Of course, they invest the money in the hope of future profits.

Market growth—profits go up and down

In the **market growth** stage, industry sales grow fast—but industry profits rise and then start falling. The innovator begins to make big profits as more and more customers buy. But competitors see the opportunity and enter the market. Some just copy the most successful product or try to improve it to compete better. Others try to refine their offerings to do a better job of appealing to some target markets. The new entries result in much product variety. So monopolistic competition—with down-sloping demand curves—is typical of the market growth stage.

This is the time of biggest profits *for the industry*. It is also a time of rapid sales and earnings growth for companies with effective strategies. *But it is toward the end of this stage when industry profits begin to decline* as competition and consumer price sensitivity increase. See Exhibit 9–2.

Some firms make big strategy planning mistakes at this stage by not understanding the product life cycle. They see the big sales and profit opportunities of the early market growth stage but ignore the competition that will soon follow. When they realize their mistake, it may be too late. This happened with many dot-coms during the late 1990s. Marketing managers who understand the cycle and pay attention to competitor analysis are less likely to encounter this problem.

Market maturity—sales level off, profits continue down

The **market maturity** stage occurs when industry sales level off and competition gets tougher. Many aggressive competitors have entered the race for profits—except in oligopoly situations. Industry profits go down throughout the market maturity stage because promotion costs rise and some competitors cut prices to attract business. Less

Whereas Garmin's automotive navigation systems have sold well in the growth stage of the product life cycle, many business customers think of steel as a commodity in market maturity. To change that perception, AK Steel differentiated its product by adding a coating that suppresses the growth of bacteria. The new coating adds value to the product, especially for companies that make ventilating systems, equipment for processing food or medicine, and kitchen appliances.

efficient firms can't compete with this pressure—and they drop out of the market. There is a long-run downward pressure on prices.

New firms may still enter the market at this stage—increasing competition even more. Note that late entries skip the early life-cycle stages, including the profitable market growth stage. And they must try to take a share of the saturated market from established firms, which is difficult and expensive. The market leaders have a lot at stake, so they fight hard to defend their share. Customers who are happy with their current relationship won't switch to a new brand. So late entrants usually have a tough battle.

Persuasive promotion becomes even more important during the market maturity stage. Products may differ only slightly. Most competitors have discovered effective appeals or just copied the leaders. As the various products become almost the same in the minds of potential consumers, price sensitivity is a real factor.[3]

The video game market vividly illustrates these competitive forces. By the time Microsoft introduced its Xbox game console, Nintendo's GameCube and Sony's Play-Station were already established leaders in the maturing market. Microsoft hoped to grab market share with a superior product designed to sell at a competitive price. To tout the advantages of the Xbox, it spent heavily on promotion. The others fought back with costly promotions of their own. Then Sony took advantage of its economies of scale and slashed the PlayStation II price by a third soon after Xbox hit the market. Nintendo followed with its own cuts. Experts estimate that, after matching the lower prices, Microsoft *lost* about $100 on each unit it sold. All the low prices did prompt renewed growth in unit sales. As the market leader, the added volume helped Sony make up for revenue lost from its price cut. However, for Microsoft, the expanded volume resulted in even greater total costs of coming into the market late. Time will tell if Microsoft's strengths will help it recoup profits by capturing market share in video game software—a market that is still growing.[4]

In the United States, the markets for most cars, boats, and many household appliances are in market maturity. This stage may continue for many years—until a basically new-product idea comes along—even though individual brands or models come and go. For example, high-definition digital TV (HDTV) is coming on now, and over time it will make obsolete not only the old-style TVs but also the broadcast systems on which they rely.

Sales decline—a time of replacement

During the **sales decline** stage, new products replace the old. Price competition from dying products becomes more vigorous—but firms with strong brands may make profits until the end because they have successfully differentiated their products.

As the new products go through their introduction stage, the old ones may keep some sales by appealing to their most loyal customers or those who are slow to try new ideas. These conservative buyers might switch later—smoothing the sales decline.

PRODUCT LIFE CYCLES SHOULD BE RELATED TO SPECIFIC MARKETS

Remember that product life cycles describe industry sales and profits for a *product idea* within a particular product-market. The sales and profits of an individual brand may not, and often do not, follow the life-cycle pattern. They may vary up and down throughout the life cycle—sometimes moving in the opposite direction of industry sales and profits. Further, a product idea may be in a different life-cycle stage in different markets.

Individual brands may not follow the pattern

A given firm may introduce or drop a specific product during *any* stage of the product life cycle. A "me-too" brand introduced during the market growth stage, for example, may never get sales at all and suffer a quick death. For instance, Wal-Mart tried to rent DVDs by mail—but the innovator, Netflix, was already established as the market leader. When customers did not see Wal-Mart's marketing mix as better, it failed to attract enough customers and closed operations.

Strategy planners who naively expect sales of an individual product to follow the general product life-cycle pattern are likely to be rudely surprised. In fact, it might be more sensible to think in terms of "product-market life cycles" rather than product life cycles—but we will use the term *product life cycle* because it is commonly accepted and widely used.

Each market should be carefully defined

How we see product life cycles depends on how broadly we define a product-market. For example, milk is a mature product in the United States. U.S. consumers drink about 18 times more milk than consumers in Asia. Milk is a good source of calcium in diets, so higher milk consumption there could help reduce Asia's high level of osteoporosis, a bone disease related to low calcium levels. To get sales growth in Asia, milk producers promote this benefit—but they've also added ginger and honey flavors to appeal to Asian palates.[5] As this example suggests, a firm with a mature product can sometimes find new growth in international markets.

How broadly we define the needs of customers in a product-market also affects how we view product life cycles—and who the competitors are. Consider the needs related

Nestlé's Hot Pockets have been available and popular in the U.S. for years, but the rollout of distribution to other countries has been gradual. They were just introduced in France by Nestlé under its Maggi brand, but if they become popular there, other firms are likely to introduce competing products.

to storing and preparing foods. Wax paper sales in the United States started to decline when Dow introduced Saran Wrap. Then sales of Saran Wrap (and other similar products) fell sharply when small plastic storage bags became popular. However, sales picked up again later when microwave cooking became popular. Then resealable bags like those from Ziploc took over because they can be used in both the freezer and the microwave.

If a market is defined broadly, there may be many competitors—and the market may appear to be in market maturity. On the other hand, if we focus on a narrow submarket—and a particular way of satisfying specific needs—then we may see much shorter product life cycles as improved product ideas come along to replace the old.

PRODUCT LIFE CYCLES VARY IN LENGTH

How long a whole product life cycle takes—and the length of each stage—varies a lot across products. The cycle may vary from 90 days—in the case of toys like the *Incredibles* movie line—to possibly 100 years for gas-powered cars.

Some products move fast

A new-product idea will move through the early stages of the life cycle more quickly when it has certain characteristics. For example, the greater the *comparative advantage* of a new product over those already on the market, the more rapidly its sales will grow. Sales growth is also faster when the product is *easy to use* and if its advantages are *easy to communicate*. If the product *can be tried* on a limited basis—without a lot of risk to the customer—it can usually be introduced more quickly. Finally, if the product is *compatible* with the values and experiences of target customers, they are likely to buy it more quickly.

The fast adoption of DVD players is a good example. The idea of renting or buying movies to view at home was already compatible with consumer lifestyles, but many consumers hesitated before buying a DVD player. They wanted to see if DVD movies would be readily available. As movies appeared, DVD player sales took off because they had advantages over VHS tape players. Consumers could tell that the picture and audio quality were better from a store demo—without buying anything. Further, ads highlighted DVD extras such as deleted scenes and interviews with

New products that do a better job of meeting the needs of specific target customers are more likely to move quickly and successfully through the introductory stage of the product life cycle.

directors. DVD players also worked with music CDs. Now that the price of DVD recorders and digital video recorders like TiVo have fallen, they are driving VHS recorders into the market decline stage of the product life cycle. Note, however, that DVD player adoption has not been as fast in less-developed countries where TV penetration is still low, movies are not available, and the costs are higher relative to consumer income.[6]

Product life cycles are getting shorter

Although the life of different products varies, in general product life cycles are getting shorter. This is partly due to rapidly changing technology. One new invention may make possible many new products that replace old ones. Tiny electronic microchips led to thousands of new products—from Texas Instruments calculators in the early days to microchip-controlled heart valves now.

Patents for a new product may not be much protection in slowing down competitors. Competitors can often find ways to copy the product idea without violating a specific patent.

Although life cycles keep moving in the developed economies, many advances bypass most consumers in less-developed economies. These consumers struggle at the subsistence level, without an effective macro-marketing system to stimulate innovation. However, some of the innovations and economies of scale made possible in the advanced societies do trickle down to benefit these consumers. Inexpensive antibiotics and drought-resistant plants, for example, are making a life-or-death difference.

The early bird usually makes the profits

The product life cycle means that firms must be developing new products all the time. Further, they must try to use marketing mixes that will make the most of the market growth stage—when profits are highest.

During the growth stage, competitors are likely to rapidly introduce product improvements. Fast changes in marketing strategy may be required here because profits don't necessarily go to the innovator. Sometimes fast copiers of the basic idea win in the market growth stage. General Motors's electric car, the EV1, was the first zero-emission vehicle on the market when it was first sold in California. However, Toyota and Honda leapfrogged past GM when they introduced hybrid vehicles powered by a combination of gas engine and electric motor. Their hybrids did not eliminate all emissions, but they met other needs better. They have more power and are less expensive. The market for low-emission hybrids is growing rapidly, yet GM is still playing catch-up. Marketers need to be innovative, but at the same time they must be flexible in adapting to the needs and attitudes of their target markets.[7]

The short happy life of fashions

The sales of some products are influenced by **fashion**—the currently accepted or popular style. Fashion-related products tend to have short life cycles. What is currently popular can shift rapidly. A certain color or style of clothing—baggy jeans, miniskirts, or four-inch-wide ties—may be in fashion one season and outdated the next. Marketing managers who work with fashions often have to make really fast product changes.[8]

How fast is fast enough? Zara, a women's fashion

retailer based in Spain, takes only about two weeks to go from a new fashion concept to having items on the racks of its stores. Zara's market-watching designers get a constant flow of new fashion ideas from music videos, fashion shows, and magazines. Zara quickly produces just enough of a design to test the waters and then sends it out for overnight delivery to some of its stores around the world. Stores track consumer preferences every day through point-of-sale computers and designers get online summaries of what's selling and where. If an item is hot, more is produced and shipped. Otherwise it's dropped. With this system items are rarely on the shelves of Zara stores for more than a few weeks.[9] Zara puts its catalog on its website so it can be updated quickly.

PLANNING FOR DIFFERENT STAGES OF THE PRODUCT LIFE CYCLE

Length of cycle affects strategy planning

Where a product is in its life cycle—and how fast it's moving to the next stage—should affect marketing strategy planning. Marketing managers must make realistic plans for the later stages. Exhibit 9–3 shows the relationship of the product life cycle to the marketing mix variables. The technical terms in this figure are discussed later in the book.

Introducing new products

Exhibit 9–3 shows that a marketing manager has to do a lot of strategy planning to introduce a really new product. Money must be spent developing the new product. Even if the product is unique, this doesn't mean that everyone will immediately come running to the producer's door. The firm will have to build channels of distribution—perhaps offering special incentives to win cooperation. Promotion is needed to build demand *for the whole idea*—not just to sell a specific brand. Because all this is expensive, it may lead the marketing manager to try to "skim" the market—charging a relatively high price to help pay for the introductory costs.

The correct strategy, however, depends on how quickly the new idea will be accepted by customers—and how quickly competitors will follow with their own versions of the product. When the early stages of the cycle will be fast, a low initial (penetration) price may make sense to help develop loyal customers early and keep competitors out.

Pioneer may need help from competitors

Sometimes it's not in the best interest of the market pioneer for competitors to stay out of the market. Building customer interest in a really new product idea—and obtaining distribution to make the product available—can be too big a job for a single company. Two or more companies investing in promotion to build demand may help to stimulate the growth of the whole product-market. Similarly, a new product may languish if it is not compatible with other products that customers rely on. This is what happened with Digital Video Express (Divx) video disks. When Divx came out, many consumer-electronics firms were launching DVD format products. Divx had advantages over DVD, but it was not compatible with many of the ordinary DVD players that were already on the market. Video stores didn't want to stock movies in both formats so Divx fizzled.[10]

New-product sales may not take off

Not all new-product ideas catch on. Customers or middlemen may not be satisfied with the marketing mix, or other new products may meet the same need better. But the success that eludes a firm with its initial strategy can sometimes be achieved by modifying the strategy. David Mintz invented a soy-based frozen dessert and started Tofutti Brands, Inc., to sell it. Tofutti was especially appealing to people who could not eat dairy products. Mintz's strategy was to offer a limited number of flavors and partner with a big company that already had national distribution in supermarkets. Häagen-Dazs agreed to the plan but wanted exclusive distribution rights. Sales grew quickly at first but then plummeted when conflicts between Mintz and Häagen-Dazs ended the relationship. To keep consumers interested in Tofutti while he slowly rebuilt distribution through a dozen specialized wholesalers, Mintz had to constantly offer new flavors.[11]

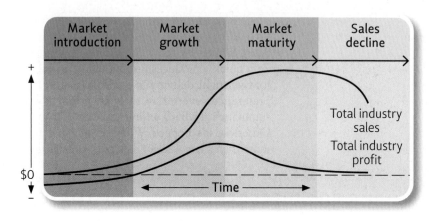

	Market introduction	Market growth	Market maturity	Sales decline
Product	One or few	Variety—try to find best product Build brand familiarity	All "same" Battle of brands	Some drop out
Place	Build channels Maybe selective distribution		Move toward more intensive distribution →	
Promotion	Build primary demand Pioneering-informing	Build selective demand ────────────→ Informing/Persuading ──→ Persuading/Reminding (frantically competitive)		
Price	Skimming or penetration	Meet competition (especially in oligopoly) ──→ or Price dealing and price cutting ──────────→		
Competitive situation	Monopoly or monopolistic competition	Monopolistic competition or oligopoly	Monopolistic competition or oligopoly heading toward pure competition	→

Managing maturing products

It's important for a firm to have some competitive advantage as it moves into market maturity. Even a small advantage can make a big difference—and some firms do very well by carefully managing their maturing products. They are able to capitalize on a slightly better product or perhaps lower production or marketing costs. Or they are simply more successful at promotion—allowing them to differentiate their more or less homogeneous product from competitors. For example, graham crackers were competing in a mature market and sales were flat. Nabisco used the same ingredients to create bite-sized Teddy Grahams and then promoted them heavily. These changes captured new sales and profits for Nabisco.[12]

Industry profits are declining in market maturity. Top managers must see this, or they will expect the attractive profits that are no longer possible. If top managers don't understand the situation, they may place impossible burdens on the marketing department—causing marketing managers to think about deceptive advertising or some other desperate attempt to reach impossible objectives.

Product life cycles keep moving. But that doesn't mean a firm should just sit by as its sales decline. There are other choices. A firm can improve its product or develop an innovative new product for the same market. Or it can develop a strategy for its

Some companies continue to do well in market maturity by improving their products or by finding new uses and applications. As shown in this ad, DuPont International's Lycra has expanded from personal apparel to furniture upholstery.

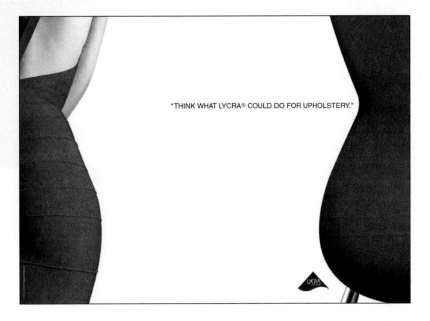

"THINK WHAT LYCRA® COULD DO FOR UPHOLSTERY."

product (perhaps with modifications) targeted at a new market. For example, it might find a market in a country where the life cycle is not so far along, or it might try to serve a new need. Or the firm can withdraw the product before it completes the cycle and refocus on better opportunities.

Improve the product or develop a new one

When a firm's product has won loyal customers, it can be successful for a long time—even in a mature or declining market. However, continued improvements may be needed as customers' needs shift. An outstanding example is Procter & Gamble's Tide. Introduced in 1947, Tide led to a whole new generation of powdered laundry products that cleaned better with fewer suds. But Tide continues to change because of new washing machines and fabrics. The Tide sold today has had at least 55 modifications.

Do product modifications—like those made with powdered Tide—create a wholly new product that should have its own product life cycle? Or are they technical adjustments of the original product idea? We will take the latter position—focusing on the product idea rather than changes in features. This means that some of these Tide changes were made in the market maturity stage. But this type of product improvement can help to extend the product life cycle.

On the other hand, a firm that develops an innovative new product may move to a new product life cycle. For example, by 1985 new liquid detergents like Wisk were moving into the growth stage, and sales of powdered detergents were declining. To share in the growth-stage profits for liquid detergents and to offset the loss of customers from powdered Tide, Procter & Gamble introduced Liquid Tide.

Even though regular powdered detergents are in the decline stage, traditional powdered Tide continues to sell well because it still does the job for some consumers. But sales growth is likely to come from liquid detergents and the new low-suds detergents.[13]

Develop new strategies for different markets

In a mature market, a firm may be fighting to keep or increase its market share. But if the firm finds a new use for the product, it may stimulate overall demand. DuPont's Teflon fluorocarbon resin is a good example. It was developed more than 50 years ago and has enjoyed sales growth as a nonstick coating for cookware and as a lining for chemically resistant equipment. But marketing managers for Teflon are not waiting to be stuck with declining profits in those mature markets. They are constantly developing strategies for new markets. For example, Teflon is now selling well as a special coating for the wires used in high-speed communications between computers and as an additive that improves bathroom cleaning products.[14]

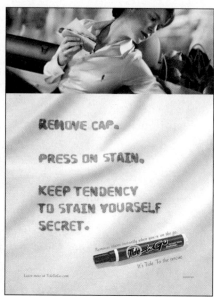

Tide detergent has been improved many times over the years and now comes in Rapid Action tablets so there's nothing to measure. Another innovation is its new portable instant stain remover called Tide to Go.

Phasing out dying products

Not all strategies have to be exciting growth strategies. If prospects are poor in a product-market, a phase-out strategy may be needed. The need for phasing out becomes more obvious as the sales decline stage arrives. But even in market maturity, it may be clear that a particular product is not going to be profitable enough to reach the company's objectives. In any case, it is wise to remember that marketing plans are implemented as ongoing strategies. Salespeople make calls, inventory moves in the channel, advertising is scheduled for several months into the future, and so on. So the firm usually experiences losses if managers end a plan too abruptly. Because of this, it's sometimes better to phase out the product gradually.

Phasing out a product may involve some difficult implementation problems. But phase-out is also a *strategy*—and it must be marketing-oriented to cut losses. In fact, it is possible to milk a dying product for some time if competitors move out more quickly and there is ongoing (though declining) demand. Some customers are willing to pay attractive prices to get their old favorite.

NEW-PRODUCT PLANNING

In most markets, progress marches on. So it is essential for a firm to develop new products or modify its current products to meet changing customer needs and competitors' actions. Not having an active new-product development process means that consciously, or subconsciously, the firm has decided to milk its current products and go out of business. New-product planning is not an optional matter. It has to be done just to survive in today's dynamic markets. Consider something as basic as a Bic lighter. It's always been a reliable product and a good value. For years, most of them were used to light cigarettes. But in response to changes in the cultural environment, Bic is coming out with new products for other needs. The Luminére lighter, for example, has a long stem that can move into several positions that make it ideal for lighting candles in hard-to-reach places.

What is a new product?

In discussing the introductory stage of product life cycles, we focused on the types of really new product innovations that tend to disrupt old ways of doing things. However, each year firms introduce many products that are basically refinements of existing products. So a **new product** is one that is new *in any way* for the company concerned.

A product can become "new" in many ways. A fresh idea can be turned into a new product and start a new product life cycle. For example, ALZA Corporation's time-release skin patches are replacing pills and injections for some medications.

Variations on an existing product idea can also make a product new. For example, Logitech has improved the lowly computer mouse by making it wireless and Gatorade has made its bottle easier to grip. Even small changes in an existing product can make it new.[15]

FTC says product is "new" only six months

A firm can call its product new for only a limited time. Six months is the limit according to the **Federal Trade Commission (FTC)**—the federal government agency that polices antimonopoly laws. To be called new, says the FTC, a product must be entirely new or changed in a "functionally significant or substantial respect."

Ethical issues in new-product planning

New-product decisions—and decisions to abandon old products—often involve ethical considerations. For example, some firms (including firms that develop drugs) have been criticized for holding back important new-product innovations until patents run out, or sales slow down, on their existing products.

At the same time, others have been criticized for "planned obsolescence"—releasing new products that the company plans to soon replace with improved new versions. Similarly, wholesalers and retailers complain that producers too often keep their new-product introduction plans a secret and leave intermediaries with dated inventory that they can sell only at a loss.

Companies also face ethical dilemmas when they decide to stop supplying a product or the service and replacement parts to keep it useful. An old model of a Cuisinart food processor, for example, might be in perfect shape except for a crack in the plastic mixing bowl. It's sensible for the company to improve the design if the crack is a frequent problem, but if consumers can't get a replacement part for the model they already own, they're left holding the bag.

Criticisms are also leveled at firms that constantly release minor variations of products that already saturate markets. Consider what happened with disposable diapers. Marketing managers thought that they were serving some customers' needs better when they offered diapers in boys' and girls' versions and in a variety of sizes, shapes, and colors. But many retailers felt that the new products were simply a ploy to get more shelf space. Further, some consumers complained that the bewildering array of choices made shopping difficult. Some people would level the same criticism at Huggies Little Swimmers Disposable Swimpants. But unlike other disposables, this product doesn't swell in the water. They have been a success because they seem to fill a different need.

Different marketing managers might have very different reactions to such criticisms. However, product management decisions often have a significant effect on customers and intermediaries. A too-casual decision may lead to a negative backlash that affects the firm's strategy or reputation.[16]

AN ORGANIZED NEW-PRODUCT DEVELOPMENT PROCESS IS CRITICAL

Identifying and developing new-product ideas—and effective strategies to go with them—is often the key to a firm's success and survival. But the costs of new-product development and the risks of failure are high. Experts estimate that consumer packaged-goods companies spend at least $20 million to introduce a new brand—and 70 to 80 percent of those new brands flop. In the service sector, the front-end cost of a failed effort may not be as high, but it can have a devastating long-term effect if dissatisfied consumers turn elsewhere for help.[17]

A new product may fail for many reasons. Most often, companies fail to offer a unique benefit or underestimate the competition. Sometimes the idea is good but the company has design problems—or the product costs much more to produce than was expected. Some companies rush to get a product on the market without developing a complete marketing plan.[18]

But moving too slowly can be a problem too. With the fast pace of change for many products, speedy entry into the market can be a key to competitive advantage. Marketing managers at Xerox learned this the hard way. Japanese competitors were taking market share with innovative new models of copiers. It turned out that the competitors were developing new models twice as fast as Xerox and at half the cost. For Xerox to compete, it had to slash its five-year product development cycle.[19]

The longer new-product development takes, the more likely it is that customer needs will be different when the product is actually introduced. Back in 2003, consumer interest in trucks and SUVs was high. General Motors expected that popularity to continue when planning new models. But by the time those vehicles were on the market in 2006, gasoline prices had skyrocketed—and consumer preferences were switching to smaller cars. In contrast, Honda's new-product planning had focused on more fuel efficiency, and its new 2006 models were in hot demand.

To move quickly and also avoid expensive new-product failures, companies should follow an organized new-product development process. The following pages describe such a process, which moves logically through five steps: (1) idea generation, (2) screening, (3) idea evaluation, (4) development (of product and marketing mix), and (5) commercialization.[20] See Exhibit 9–4.

The general process is similar for both consumer and business markets—and for both goods and services. There are some significant differences, but we will emphasize the similarities in the following discussion.

Process tries to kill new ideas—economically

An important element in the new-product development process is continued evaluation of a new idea's likely profitability and return on investment. The hypothesis tested is that the new idea will *not* be profitable. This puts the burden on the new

Generating innovative and profitable new products requires an understanding of customer needs—and an organized new-product development process.

Exhibit 9–4   New-Product Development Process

Idea generation	Screening	Idea evaluation	Development	Commercialization
Ideas from: Customers and users Marketing research Competitors Other markets Company people Middlemen, etc.	Strengths and weaknesses Fit with objectives Market trends Rough ROI estimate	Concept testing Reactions from customers Rough estimates of costs, sales, and profits	R&D Develop model or service prototype Test marketing mix Revise plans as needed ROI estimate	Finalize product and marketing plan Start production and marketing "Roll out" in select markets Final ROI estimate

idea—to prove itself or be rejected. Such a process may seem harsh, but experience shows that most new ideas have some flaw. Marketers try to discover those flaws early, and either find a remedy or reject the idea completely. Applying this process requires much analysis of the idea *before* the company spends money to develop and market a product. This is a major departure from the usual production-oriented approach—in which a company develops a product first and then asks sales to "get rid of it."

Step 1: Idea generation

Finding new-product ideas can't be left to chance. Instead, firms need a formal procedure to generate a continuous flow of ideas. New ideas can come from a company's own sales or production staff, middlemen, competitors, consumer surveys, or other sources such as trade associations, advertising agencies, or government agencies. By analyzing new and different views of the company's markets and studying present consumer behavior, a marketing manager can spot opportunities that have not yet occurred to competitors or even to potential customers. For example, ideas for new service concepts may come directly from analysis of consumer complaints.

No one firm can always be first with the best new ideas. So companies should pay attention to what competitors are doing. Some firms use what's called *reverse engineering*. For example, new-product specialists at Ford Motor Company buy other firms' cars as soon as they're available. Then they take the cars apart to look for new ideas or improvements. British Airways talks to travel agents to learn about new services offered by competitors.[21] Many firms now "shop" in international markets for new ideas. For instance, food companies in Europe are experimenting with an innovation recently introduced in Japan—a clear, odorless, natural film for wrapping food. Consumers don't have to unwrap it; when they put the product in boiling water or a microwave, the wrapper vanishes.[22]

Research shows that many new ideas in business markets come from customers who identify a need they have. Then they approach a supplier with the idea and perhaps even with a particular design or specification. These customers become the lead users of the product, but the supplier can also pursue the opportunity in other markets.[23]

Step 2: Screening

Screening involves evaluating the new ideas with the type of S.W.O.T analysis described in Chapter 2 and the product-market screening criteria described in Chapter 4. Recall that these criteria include the combined output of a resources (strengths and weaknesses) analysis, a long-run trends analysis, and a thorough understanding of the company's objectives. See Exhibit 2–11 and Exhibit 4–8. Further, a "good" new idea should eventually lead to a product (and marketing mix) that will give the firm a competitive advantage—hopefully, a lasting one.

The life-cycle stage at which a firm's new product enters the market has a direct bearing on its prospects for growth. So screening should consider how the strategy for a new product will hold up over the whole product life cycle.

Exhibit 9–5
Types of New-Product
Opportunities

		Immediate satisfaction	
		High	Low
Long-run consumer welfare	High	Desirable products	Salutary products
	Low	Pleasing products	Deficient products

Thinking about the strengths and weaknesses of a new-product idea from both a short-and long-term perspective can be a challenge. However, decisions about how the firm brings a new product to market often shape future market opportunities (and threats). A classic example is IBM's decision to license the operating system for the IBM PC when it was introduced. At that time, designing a PC to use an existing operating system (like the one then available from Microsoft) was a fast and low-cost way to get to market. However, the operating system ultimately produced more profit for Microsoft than the hardware did for IBM.

Some companies screen based on consumer welfare

Screening should also consider how a new product will affect consumers over time. Ideally, the product should increase consumer welfare, not just satisfy a whim. Exhibit 9–5 shows different kinds of new-product opportunities. Obviously, a socially responsible firm tries to find desirable opportunities rather than deficient ones. This may not be as easy as it sounds, however. Some consumers want pleasing products and give little thought to their own long-term welfare. And some competitors will offer consumers whatever they will buy.

Safety must be considered

Real acceptance of the marketing concept prompts managers to screen new products on the basis of how safe they are. Safety is not a casual matter. The U.S. **Consumer Product Safety Act** (of 1972) set up the Consumer Product Safety Commission to encourage safety in product design and better quality control. The commission has a great deal of power. It can set safety standards for products. It can order costly repairs or the return of unsafe products. And it can back up its orders with fines and jail sentences. The Food and Drug Administration has similar powers for foods and drugs.

Product safety complicates strategy planning because not all customers—even those who want better safety features—are willing to pay more for safer products. Some features cost a lot to add and increase prices considerably. These safety concerns must be considered at the screening step because a firm can later be held liable for unsafe products.

Products can turn to liabilities

Product liability refers to the legal obligation of sellers to pay damages to individuals who are injured by defective or unsafe products. Product liability is a serious matter. Liability settlements may exceed not only a company's insurance coverage but its total assets!

Relative to most other countries, U.S. courts enforce a very strict product liability standard. Sellers may be held responsible for injuries related to their products no matter how the items are used or how well they're designed. In one widely publicized judgment, McDonald's paid a huge settlement to a woman who was burned when her coffee spilled. The court concluded that there was not enough warning about how hot the coffee was.

Cases and settlements like this are common. Some critics argue that U.S. rules are so tough that they discourage innovation and economic growth. In contrast, Japan's

Independent product testing labs, like the Canadian Standards Association (CSA), give Canadian consumers added confidence that products are safe. Similar organizations operate in other countries. Honda is committed to developing new vehicles that provide "safety for everyone"—and that includes pedestrians who might be involved in an accident.

rules may be too slack. Japan's system discourages consumers from filing complaints because they are required to pay a percentage of any damages they seek as court costs—regardless of whether they win or lose.

Sometimes there is incentive for lawyers to push liability cases to take a share of the payments. Juries sometimes give huge settlements based on an emotional reaction to the case rather than scientific evidence. That seems to have happened in lawsuits over silicon breast implants.

Product liability is a serious ethical and legal matter. Many countries are attempting to change their laws so that they will be fair to both firms and consumers. But until product liability questions are resolved, marketing managers must be even more sensitive when screening new-product ideas.[24]

ROI is a crucial screening criterion

Getting by the initial screening criteria doesn't guarantee success for the new idea. But it does show that at least the new idea is in the right ballpark *for this firm*. If many ideas pass the screening criteria, a firm must set priorities to determine which ones go on to the next step in the process. This can be done by comparing the ROI (return on investment) for each idea—assuming the firm is ROI-oriented. The most attractive alternatives are pursued first.

Step 3: Idea evaluation

When an idea moves past the screening step, it is evaluated more carefully. Note that an actual product has not yet been developed—and this can handicap the firm in getting feedback from customers. For help in idea evaluation, firms use **concept testing**—getting reactions from customers about how well a new-product idea fits their needs. Concept testing uses marketing research—ranging from informal focus groups to formal surveys of potential customers.

Companies can often estimate likely costs, revenue, and profitability at this stage. And marketing research can help identify the size of potential markets. Even informal focus groups are useful—especially if they show that potential users are not excited about the new idea. If results are discouraging, it may be best to kill the idea at this stage. Remember, in this hypothesis-testing process, we're looking for any evidence that an idea is *not* a good opportunity for this firm and should be rejected.

Product planners must think about wholesaler and retailer customers as well as final consumers. Intermediaries may have special concerns about handling a proposed product. A Utah ice-cream maker was considering a new line of ice-cream novelty products—and he had visions of a hot market in California. But he had to drop his idea when he learned that grocery store chains wanted payments of $20,000 each just to stock his frozen novelties in their freezers.[25]

Idea evaluation is often more precise in business markets. Potential customers are more informed—and their needs focus on the economic reasons for buying rather than emotional factors. Further, given the derived nature of demand in business markets, most needs are already being satisfied in some way. So new products just substitute for existing ones. This means that product planners can compare the cost advantages and limitations of a new product with those currently being used. And by interviewing well-informed people, they can determine the range of product requirements and decide whether there is an opportunity.

Whatever research methods are used, the idea evaluation step should gather enough information to help decide whether there is an opportunity, whether it fits with the firm's resources, *and* whether there is a basis for developing a competitive advantage. With such information, the firm can estimate likely ROI in the various market segments and decide whether to continue the new-product development process.[26]

Step 4: Development

Product ideas that survive the screening and idea evaluation steps must now be analyzed further. Usually, this involves some research and development (R&D) and engineering to design and develop the physical part of the product. In the case of a new service offering, the firm will work out the details of what training, equipment, staff, and so on will be needed to deliver on the idea. Input from a firm's earlier efforts helps guide this technical work.

New computer-aided design (CAD) systems are sparking a revolution in design work. Designers can develop lifelike 3-D color drawings of packages and products. Changes can be made almost instantly. They can be sent by e-mail to managers all over the world for immediate review. They can even be put on a website for marketing research with remote customers. Then once the designs are finalized, they feed directly into computer-controlled manufacturing systems. Companies like Motorola and Timex have found that these systems cut their new-product development time in half—giving them a leg up on many competitors.

Even so, it is still useful to test models and early versions of the product in the market. This process may have several cycles. A manufacturer may build a model of a physical product or produce limited quantities; a service firm may try to train a small group of service providers. Product tests with customers may lead to revisions—*before* the firm commits to full-scale efforts.

With actual goods or services, potential customers can react to how well the product meets their needs. Focus groups, panels, and larger surveys can react to specific features and to the whole product idea. Sometimes that reaction kills the idea. For example, Coca-Cola Foods believed it had a great idea with Minute Maid Squeeze-Fresh, frozen orange juice concentrate in a squeeze bottle. In tests, however, Squeeze-Fresh bombed. Consumers loved the idea but hated the product. It was messy to use, and no one knew how much concentrate to squeeze in the glass.[27]

Microsoft Office Live Meeting makes it easy for managers to collaborate and share information without leaving their desks even if they are in different parts of the world. Capabilities such as this are helping to make new-product development efforts faster and more effective.

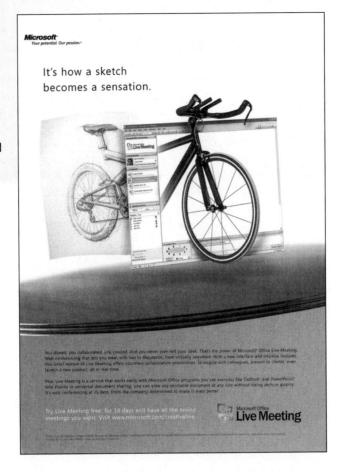

Firms often use full-scale market testing to get reactions in real-market conditions or to test variations in the marketing mix. For example, a firm may test alternative brands, prices, or advertising copy in different test cities. Note that the firm is testing the whole marketing mix, not just the product. For example, a hotel chain might test a new service offering at one location to see how it goes over.

Running market tests is costly, but *not* testing is risky too. Frito-Lay was so sure it understood consumers' snack preferences that it introduced a three-item cracker line without market testing. Even with network TV ad support, MaxSnax met with overwhelming consumer indifference. By the time Frito-Lay pulled the product from store shelves, it had lost $52 million.[28]

Step 5: Commercialization

A product idea that survives this far can finally be placed on the market. Putting a product on the market is expensive, and success usually requires cooperation of the whole company. Manufacturing or service facilities have to be set up. Goods have to be produced to fill the channels of distribution, or people must be hired and trained to provide services. Further, introductory promotion is costly—especially if the company is entering a very competitive market.

Because of the size of the job, some firms introduce their products city by city or region by region—in a gradual "rollout"—until they have complete market coverage. Sprint used this approach in introducing its broadband wireless service that included a rooftop transmission device. Detroit, Phoenix, and San Francisco were targeted first. Rollouts also permit more market testing, but the main purpose is to do a good job implementing the marketing plan. Marketing managers also need to pay close attention to control—to ensure that the implementation effort is working and that the strategy is on target.

NEW-PRODUCT DEVELOPMENT: A TOTAL COMPANY EFFORT

We've been discussing the steps in a logical, new-product development process. However, as shown in Exhibit 9–6, many factors can impact the success of the effort.

Top-level support is vital

Companies that are particularly successful at developing new goods and services seem to have one key trait in common: enthusiastic top-management support for new-product development. New products tend to upset old routines that managers of established products often try in subtle but effective ways to maintain. So someone with top-level support, and authority to get things done, needs to be responsible for new-product development.[29]

Put someone in charge

In addition, rather than leaving new-product development to someone in engineering, R&D, or sales who happens to be interested in taking the initiative, successful companies *put* someone in charge. It may be a person, department, or team. But it's not a casual thing. It's a major responsibility of the job.

A new-product development team with people from different departments helps ensure that new ideas are carefully evaluated and profitable ones are quickly brought

Exhibit 9–6 New-Product Development Success Factors

to market. It's important to choose the right people for the job. Overly conservative managers may kill too many, or even all, new ideas. Committees may create bureaucratic delays that make the difference between a product's success or failure.

Market needs guide R&D effort

From the idea generation stage to the commercialization stage, the R&D specialists, the operations people, and the marketing people must work together to evaluate the feasibility of new ideas. They may meet in person or communicate via e-mail or intranet sites, or perhaps teleconferencing or some other technology. There are many ways to share ideas. Obviously, it isn't sensible for a marketing manager to develop elaborate marketing plans for goods or services that the firm simply can't produce—or produce profitably. It also doesn't make sense for R&D people to develop a technology or product that does not have potential for the firm and its markets. Clearly, a balancing act is involved here. But the critical point is the basic one we've been emphasizing throughout the whole book: Marketing-oriented firms seek to satisfy customer needs at a profit with an integrated, whole company effort.

NEED FOR PRODUCT MANAGERS

Product variety leads to product managers

When a firm has only one or a few related products, everyone is interested in them. But when a firm has products in several different product categories, management may decide to put someone in charge of each category, or each brand, to be sure that attention to these products is not lost in the rush of everyday business. **Product managers** or **brand managers** manage specific products—often taking over the jobs formerly handled by an advertising manager. That gives a clue to what is often their major responsibility—Promotion—since the products have already been developed by the new-product people. However, some brand managers start at the new-product development stage and carry on from there.

Product managers are especially common in large companies that produce many kinds of products. Several product managers may serve under a marketing manager. Sometimes these product managers are responsible for the profitable operation of a particular product's whole marketing effort. Then they have to coordinate their efforts with others, including the sales manager, advertising agencies, production and research people, and even channel members. This is likely to lead to difficulties if product managers have no control over the marketing strategy for other related brands or authority over other functional areas whose efforts they are expected to direct and coordinate.

Consumer packaged-goods companies, like Nabisco, usually assign brand managers who are responsible for individual products. However, when there are a number of products in the same product category, there is often a higher-level manager who ensures that the marketing program for the whole category is effective.

To avoid these problems, in some companies the product manager serves mainly as a "product champion"—concerned with planning and getting the promotion effort implemented. A higher-level marketing manager with more authority coordinates the efforts and integrates the marketing strategies for different products into an overall plan.

The activities of product managers vary a lot depending on their experience and aggressiveness and the company's organizational philosophy. Today, companies are emphasizing marketing *experience*—because this important job takes more than academic training and enthusiasm. But it is clear that someone must be responsible for developing and implementing product-related plans, especially when a company has many products.[30]

MANAGING PRODUCT QUALITY

Total quality management meets customer requirements

In Chapter 8 we explained that product quality means the ability of a product to satisfy a customer's needs or requirements. Now we'll expand that idea and discuss some ways a manager can improve the quality of a firm's goods and services. We'll develop these ideas from the perspective of **total quality management (TQM)**, the philosophy that everyone in the organization is concerned about quality, throughout all of the firm's activities, to better serve customer needs.

The cost of poor quality is lost customers

Most of the early attention in quality management focused on reducing defects in goods produced in factories. At one time most firms assumed defects were an inevitable part of mass production. They saw the cost of replacing defective parts or goods as just a cost of doing business—an insignificant one compared to the advantages of mass production. However, many firms were forced to rethink this assumption when Japanese producers of cars, electronics, and cameras showed that defects weren't inevitable. Much to the surprise of some production-oriented managers, the Japanese experience showed that it is less expensive to do something right the first time than it is to pay to do it poorly and *then* pay again to fix problems. And their success in taking customers away from established competitors made it clear that the cost of defects wasn't just the cost of replacement!

From the customer's point of view, getting a defective product and having to complain about it is a big headache. The customer can't use the defective product and suffers the inconvenience of waiting for someone to fix the problem—if *someone* gets around to it. It certainly doesn't deliver superior value. Rather, it erodes goodwill and leaves customers dissatisfied. The big cost of poor quality is the cost of lost customers.

Firms that adopted TQM methods to reduce manufacturing defects soon used the same approaches to overcome many other problems. Their success brought attention to what is possible with TQM—whether the problem concerns poor customer service, flimsy packaging, or salespeople who can't answer customers' questions.

Getting a handle on doing things right the first time

The idea of identifying customer needs and doing things right the first time seems obvious, but it's easier said than done. Problems always come up, and it's not always clear what isn't being done as well as it could be. People tend to ignore problems that

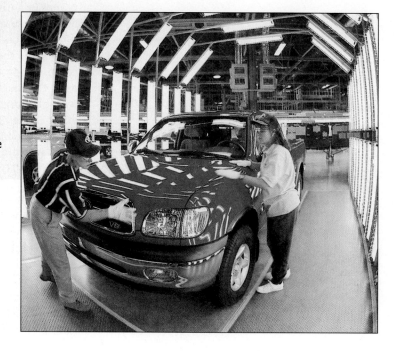

Customers want the paint on their new Toyota Tundra to be free from any scratches and that requires attention to implementation details. Factory workers take off their jewelry, wear shirts with rubber buttons, and use belts with special buckles that leave no metal exposed.

How to Be Innovative When You're a Hundred Years Old

3M is a 100-year-old company that has discovered its own "fountain of youth." Yet it's no secret what it does to constantly renew itself. 3M is fast and successful at spinning out new products that offer innovative and practical solutions to customers' problems. This doesn't happen by chance. It is an ongoing priority of top managers. For example, 3M's chief set an objective that 30 percent of sales should come from products that didn't exist four years earlier. You can see the emphasis on innovation in even the quickest visit to 3M's website (www.3m.com). One recent 3M innovation is wet-or-dry padding for casts—so the next time you break your arm, you can still go swimming or take a shower. Other innovations include special adhesives that allow metal-to-metal bonding, and a new type of hybrid power line that carries up to three times as much electricity as standard wires. Established 3M product lines are also continuously updated with new products—such as Scotch Stretchy Tape, Post-it Note Cards, and Scotch-Brite Tub & Tile Scrubber.

3M motivates innovation by staying close to customers, rewarding new-product champions, and sharing ideas among its many divisions. Teams from marketing, operations, and R&D screen new-product concepts for those with the highest profit potential. Then everyone works to bring the best ideas to market faster.

3M innovates not by giving customers what they *say* they want—but by probing deeper to find out what they really *need*. When laptop computer manufacturers asked for brighter monitors for laptop computers, 3M researchers asked why? They found that what their customers really needed was longer battery life because color displays use lots of power. So 3M invented a thin transparent film that channels more of the light directly to a user's eyes. The ultrathin plastic film brightens and clarifies the appearance of flat-screen displays—giving the effect of twice the brightness while not increasing battery usage. Now 3M's Vikuiti brand films not only improve the video screens on laptops, but cell phones and LCD TVs as well. As this suggests, 3M marketers are always looking for new needs that can be addressed with products it has already developed. Some of these ideas come from existing customers for other products. For example, Japanese automakers are working with 3M to evaluate Vikuiti film for the screens of their dashboard GPS navigation systems, where the distracting glare from windshields has been a problem.[31]

don't pose an immediate crisis. But firms that adopt TQM always look for ways to improve implementation with **continuous improvement**—a commitment to constantly make things better one step at a time. Once you accept the idea that there *may* be a better way to do something and you look for it, you may just find it! The place to start is to clearly define "defects" from the customer's point of view.

Things gone right and things gone wrong

Managers who use the TQM approach think of quality improvement as a sorting process—a sorting out of things gone right and things gone wrong. The sorting process calls for detailed measurements related to a problem. Then managers use a set of statistical tools to analyze the measurements and identify the problem areas that are the best candidates for fixing. The statistical details are beyond our focus here, but it's useful to get a feel for how managers use the tools.

Starting with customer needs

Let's consider the case of a restaurant that does well during the evening hours but wants to improve its lunch business. The restaurant develops a strategy that targets local businesspeople with an attractive luncheon buffet. The restaurant decides on a buffet because research shows that target customers want a choice of good healthy food and are willing to pay reasonable prices for it—as long as they can eat quickly and get back to work on time.

As the restaurant implements its new strategy, the manager wants a measure of how things are going. So she encourages customers to fill out comment cards that ask "How did we do today?" After several months of operation, things seem to be going reasonably well—although business is not as brisk as it was at first. The manager reads the comment cards and divides the ones with complaints into categories—to count up different reasons why customers weren't satisfied.

Slay the dragons first

Then the manager creates a graph (see Exhibit 9–7) showing a frequency distribution for the different types of complaints. Quality people call this a **Pareto chart**—a graph that shows the number of times a problem cause occurs, with problem causes ordered from most frequent to least frequent. The manager's Pareto chart reveals that customers complain most frequently that they have to wait for a seat. There were other common complaints—the buffet was not well organized, the table was not clean, and so on. However, the first complaint is much more common than the next most frequent one.

This is typical. The worst problems often occur over and over again. This focuses the manager's attention on which quality problem to fix first. A rule of quality management is to slay the dragons first—which simply means start with the biggest problem. After removing that problem, the battle moves on to the next most frequent problem. If you do this *continuously*, you solve a lot of problems—and you don't just satisfy customers, you delight them.

Figure out why things go wrong

So far, our manager has only identified the problem. To solve it, she creates a **fishbone diagram**—a visual aid that helps organize cause-and-effect relationships for "things gone wrong." See Exhibit 9–8. With this diagram, our restaurant manager discovers that customers wait to be seated because tables aren't cleared soon enough. In fact, the Pareto chart (Exhibit 9–7) shows that customers also complain frequently about tables not being clean. So the two implementation problems may be related.

The manager's fishbone diagram also summarizes other causes for tables not being cleaned quickly. There are different basic categories of causes—restaurant policy, procedures, people problems, and the physical environment. With this overview of different ways the service operation is going wrong, the manager can decide what to fix. She establishes different formal measures. For example, she counts how frequently different causes delay customers from being seated. She finds that the cashier's faulty credit card scanning machine holds up check processing. About half the time the cashier has to stop and enter the credit card information by hand. The fishbone diagram shows that restaurant policy is to clear the table after the entire party leaves. But

Exhibit 9–7
Pareto Chart Showing Frequency of Different Complaints

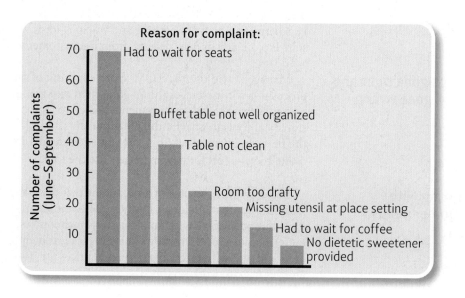

244

Exhibit 9-8 Fishbone Diagram Showing Cause and Effect for "Why Tables Are Not Cleared Quickly"

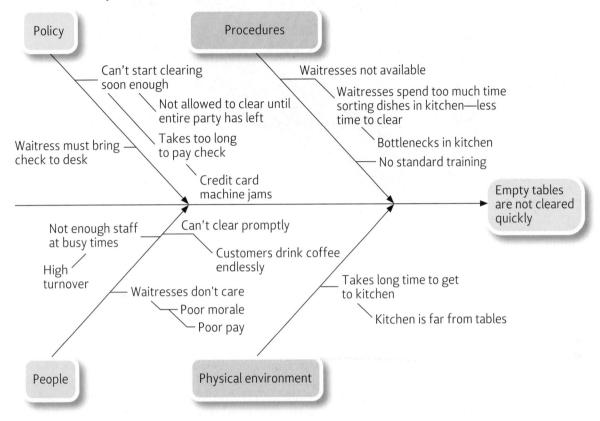

customers have to wait at their tables while the staff deals with the faulty credit card machine, and cleaning is delayed. With the credit card machine replaced, the staff can clear the tables sooner—and because they're not so hurried they do a better cleaning job. Two dragons are on the way to being slayed!

Our case shows that people in different areas of the restaurant affect customer satisfaction. The waitperson couldn't do what was needed to satisfy customers because the cashier had trouble with the credit card machine. The TQM approach helps everyone see and understand how their job affects what others do and the customer's satisfaction.[32]

Building quality into services

The restaurant case illustrates how a firm can improve product quality with TQM approaches. We used a service example because providing customer service is often a difficult area, regardless of whether a firm's product is primarily a service, primarily a physical good, or a blend of both. For example, a manufacturer of ball bearings isn't just providing wholesalers or producers with round pieces of steel. Customers need information about deliveries, they need orders filled properly, and they may have questions to ask the firm's accountant or engineers. Because almost every firm must manage the service it provides customers, let's focus on some of the special concerns of managing service quality.

Train people and empower them to serve

It's difficult to maintain consistent quality in services because the server is inseparable from the service. A person doing a specific service job may perform one specific task correctly but still annoy the customer in a host of other ways. So two keys to improving service quality are: (1) training and (2) empowerment.

All employees who have any contact with customers need training—many firms see 40 hours a year of training as a minimum. Good training usually includes role-playing on handling different types of customer requests and problems. A rental car attendant who is rude when a customer is trying to turn in a car may leave the customer dissatisfied—even if the rental car was perfect.

Companies can't afford an army of managers to inspect how each employee implements a strategy—and such a system usually doesn't work anyway. Quality cannot be "inspected in." It must come from the people who do the service jobs. So firms that commit to service quality empower employees to satisfy customers' needs. **Empowerment** means giving employees the authority to correct a problem without first checking with management. At a hotel, for instance, an empowered room-service employee knows it's OK to run across the street to buy the specific brand of bottled water a guest requests.

Managers lead the quality effort

Managers must show that they are committed to doing things right to satisfy customers and that quality is everyone's job. Without top-level support, some people won't get beyond their business-as-usual attitude—and TQM won't work.

Specify jobs and benchmark performance

Managers who develop successful quality programs clearly specify and write out exactly what tasks need to be done, how, and by whom. This may seem unnecessary. After all, most people know, in general, what they're supposed to do. However, if the tasks are clearly specified, it's easier to see what criteria should be used to measure performance.

Once criteria are established, there needs to be some basis on which to evaluate the job being done. In our restaurant example, one part of the job specification for the cashier is to process credit card payments. In that case, relevant criteria might include the amount of time that it takes and the number of people waiting in line to pay. If the restaurant manager had seen a record of how long it was taking to process credit cards, she would have known that for many customers it was taking too long. Without the measure, the precise nature of the problem was hidden.

That takes us to the issue of **benchmarking**—picking a basis of comparison for evaluating how well a job is being done. For example, consider a case in which an airline asks customers to rate their satisfaction with a flight. Then the company might benchmark each route against the others on average customer satisfaction. But if the service of all the airline's flights is poor, that isn't a sensible approach. The ones that stink the least would look good on a relative basis. Therefore, many firms try to benchmark against some external standard. For example, an airline might want to benchmark against a competitor. Or better, the manager might identify other travel firms that earn superlative customer satisfaction ratings and benchmark against them.

Getting a return on quality is important

While the cost of poor quality is lost customers, the type of quality efforts we've been discussing also result in costs. It's easy to fall into the trap of running up *unnecessary costs* trying to improve some facet of quality that really isn't that important to customer satisfaction or customer retention. When that happens, customers may still be satisfied, but the firm can't make a profit because of the extra costs. In other words, there isn't a financial return on the money spent to improve quality. A manager should focus on quality efforts that really provide the customer with superior value—quality that costs no more to provide than customers will ultimately be willing to pay.[33]

CONCLUSION

This chapter introduced the product life-cycle concept and showed how life cycles affect marketing strategy planning. The product life-cycle concept shows why new products are so important to growth in markets and also helps to explain why different strategies—including strategies for new improved products—need to be developed over time. Innovators—or fast copiers—that successfully bring new products to market are usually the ones who achieve the greatest growth in customer equity.

In today's highly competitive marketplace it is no longer profitable to simply sell "me-too" products. Markets, competition, and product life cycles are changing at a fast pace. New products help a company appeal to new target markets by appealing to unmet needs. New products can also encourage current customers to purchase more. In addition, they can help retain customers by adapting to changing customer needs.

Just because a product is new to a company doesn't mean that it is a really new innovation and starts a new-product life cycle. However, from a marketing manager's perspective, a product is new to the firm if it is new in any way or to any target market. Firms don't just develop and introduce new products; they do so within the context of the whole marketing strategy.

Many new products fail. But we presented an organized new-product development process that helps to prevent that fate. The process makes it clear that new-product success isn't just the responsibility of people from R&D or marketing but rather requires a total company effort.

We also described product and brand management. To help a product or brand grow, managers in these positions usually recommend ways to adjust all of the elements of the marketing mix, but the emphasis is often on Promotion.

Poor product quality results in dissatisfied customers. So alert marketers look for ways to design better quality into new products and to improve the quality of ones they already have. Approaches developed in the total quality management (TQM) movement can be a big help in this regard. Ultimately, the challenge is for the manager to focus on aspects of quality that really matter to the target customer. Otherwise, the cost of the quality offered may be higher than what target customers are willing to pay.

In combination, this chapter and Chapter 8 introduce strategy decision areas for Product and important frameworks that help you see how Product fits within an overall strategy. These chapters also start you down the path to a deeper understanding of the 4Ps. In Chapter 10, we expand on that base by focusing on the role of Place in the marketing mix.

KEY TERMS

product life cycle, 223
market introduction, 224
market growth, 224
market maturity, 224
sales decline, 225
fashion, 228
new product, 233

Federal Trade Commission (FTC), 233
Consumer Product Safety Act, 236
product liability, 236
concept testing, 238
product managers, 241
brand managers, 241
total quality management (TQM), 242

continuous improvement, 243
Pareto chart, 244
fishbone diagram, 244
empowerment, 246
benchmarking, 246

QUESTIONS AND PROBLEMS

1. Explain how industry sales and industry profits behave over the product life cycle.

2. Cite two examples of products that you think are currently in each of the product life-cycle stages. Consider services as well as physical goods.

3. Explain how you might reach different conclusions about the correct product life-cycle stage(s) in the worldwide automobile market.

4. Explain why individual brands may not follow the product life-cycle pattern. Give an example of a new brand that is not entering the life cycle at the market introduction stage.

5. Discuss the life cycle of a product in terms of its probable impact on a manufacturer's marketing mix. Illustrate using personal computers.

6. What characteristics of a new product will help it to move through the early stages of the product life cycle more quickly? Briefly discuss each characteristic—illustrating with a product of your choice. Indicate how each characteristic might be viewed in some other country.

7. What is a new product? Illustrate your answer.

8. Explain the importance of an organized new-product development process and illustrate how it might be used for (*a*) a new hair care product, (*b*) a new children's toy, and (*c*) a new subscribers-only cable television channel.

9. Discuss how you might use the new-product development process if you were thinking about offering some kind of summer service to residents in a beach resort town.

10. Explain the role of product or brand managers. When would it make sense for one of a company's current brand managers to be in charge of the new-product development process? Explain your thinking.

11. If a firm offers one of its brands in a number of different countries, would it make sense for one brand manager to be in charge, or would each country require its own brand manager? Explain your thinking.

12. Discuss the social value of new-product development activities that seem to encourage people to discard products that are not all worn out. Is this an economic waste? How worn out is all worn out? Must a shirt have holes in it? How big?

13. What are the major advantages of total quality management as an approach for improving the quality of goods and services? What limitations can you think of?

CREATING MARKETING PLANS

The Marketing Plan Coach software on the Student CD includes a sample marketing plan for Hillside Veterinary Clinic. Look through the "Marketing Strategy" section.

a. Hillside offers many different products. Identify several of these products and indicate where you think each of them is in its product life cycle.

b. Exhibit 9–3 summarizes some marketing mix characteristics based on where a product fits in the product life cycle. Is Hillside's marketing plan consistent with what this exhibit suggests? Why or why not?

SUGGESTED CASES

6. International Steel Company   20. Recreation Universe   22. Bright Light Innovations

COMPUTER-AIDED PROBLEM

9. GROWTH STAGE COMPETITION

AgriChem, Inc., has introduced an innovative new product—a combination fertilizer, weed killer, and insecticide that makes it much easier for soybean farmers to produce a profitable crop. The product introduction was quite successful, with 1 million units sold in the year of introduction. And AgriChem's profits are increasing. Total market demand is expected to grow at a rate of 200,000 units a year for the next five years. Even so, AgriChem's marketing managers are concerned about what will happen to sales and profits during this period.

Based on past experience with similar situations, they expect one new competitor to enter the market during each of the next five years. They think this competitive pressure will drive prices down about 6 percent a year. Further, although the total market is growing, they know that new competitors will chip away at AgriChem's market share—even with the 10 percent a year increase planned for the promotion budget. In spite of the competitive pressure, the marketing managers are sure that familiarity with AgriChem's brand will help it hold a large share of the total market and give AgriChem greater economies of scale than competitors. In fact, they expect that the ratio of profit to dollar sales for AgriChem should be about 10 percent higher than for competitors.

AgriChem's marketing managers have decided the best way to get a handle on the situation is to organize the data in a spreadsheet. They have set up the spreadsheet so they can change the "years in the future" value and see what is likely to happen to AgriChem and the rest of the industry. The starting spreadsheet shows the current situation with data from the first full year of production.

a. Compare AgriChem's market share and profit for this year with what is expected next year—given the marketing managers' current assumptions. What are they expecting? (Hint: Set number of years in the future to 1.)

b. Prepare a table showing AgriChem's expected profit, and the expected industry revenue and profit, for the current year and the next five years. Briefly explain what happens to industry sales and profits and why. (Hint: Do an analysis to vary the number of years in the future value in the spreadsheet from a minimum of 0—the current year—to a maximum of 5. Display the three values requested.)

c. If market demand grows faster than expected—say, at 280,000 units a year—what will happen to AgriChem's profits and the expected industry revenues and profits over the next five years? What are the implications of this analysis?

For additional questions related to this problem, see Exercise 9–4 in the *Learning Aid for Use with Essentials of Marketing*, 11th edition.

Place and Development of Channel Systems

Steve Kendal's firm creates video games. Growth seemed easy during his first five years in business. A few good wholesalers helped get his initial games into video game shops, gamers liked them, and they spread the word. But the market for video games was maturing. Competition was intense among game producers and also at the retail level. More retailers had started to sell video games at low prices. Many of the small shops were going out of business or joining chains. Kendal thought it was time to change his strategy, including his Place arrangements. He got the idea to shift his focus to *educational* video games from his wife, a teacher. She had told him about the surging popularity of products, like Disney's Baby Einstein videos, that targeted upscale parents who wanted ways to make their kids smarter. Kendal knew he could develop games that were fun, involving, and educational. Those benefits would make parents less price sensitive—and attract interest from retailers who wanted profitable new sales in the game category. Kendal was ready to act, but he knew that decisions he made about distribution channels would be critical to the success of his venture. And from his experience in the book business, he had an idea about how video game retailing was changing.

Kendal had been a manager for the Cozy Bookshop, a family-owned store that for decades had been *the* place to buy books in his college-town market. Kendal moved on to start his video game business before Cozy had its final inventory clearance sale. But its fate seemed clear because sales of books through independent bookshops dropped by over 25 percent in the 1990s. Like Cozy, many of these shops went out of business because of changes in the channels of distribution for books.

Competitors had emerged and slowly chipped away at Cozy's sales over the years. The mail-order book clubs, the religious book store that opened in town, and the used-textbook brokers all ate into business. But the coffin nail was driven by the growth of big national chains. They had buying clout with publishers and could demand lower prices for larger quantities. They also had aggressive marketing programs to woo consumers. Cozy had lost some customers to the frequent-buyer discount at Walden Books. Others went to Barnes & Noble for the selection—and the coffee bar. The local Costco store carried only a few best-sellers, but its low prices turned shoppers into impulse buyers. And many were buying from Amazon.com or from other online sellers who were able to sell at even lower prices than Amazon by linking their order systems to big wholesalers like Ingram Book Company that efficiently handled all of the inventory and shipping.

Kendal saw the same pattern unfolding in channel systems for video games. GameStop Corp. had recently acquired a big competitor, Electronics Boutique (EB). This combined their strengths: GameStop had great locations in growing suburban areas and EB added international strength. Stores were supplemented with the best features of the two websites, which had even larger selections, including used games.

With more than 4,500 stores and 2 million subscribers to its *Game Informer* magazine, GameStop now had more clout with game publishers like EA and Rockstar as well as with game system producers like Nintendo, Microsoft, and Sony. For example, GameStop holds special midnight sales events whenever there's an exciting new game or system because avid gamers are eager to buy the hottest releases. Because GameStop is a big player in the channel, suppliers make sure it has enough inventory for these events. Mass-merchandisers like Best Buy or Wal-Mart compete with low prices, but many gamers buy at GameStop before products get to competitors' shelves.

Kendal knew that it might be difficult for his small firm to get support from a powerful retailer like GameStop. Educational games are usually not big sellers, and there are other better-known brands. So, Kendal considered developing a line of educational games that GameStop could sell exclusively, perhaps even packaged as a GameStop dealer brand. This would mean the end of his good relationships with the small shops that had helped him get started. Yet, he felt that many of those shops would not survive for long anyway. Still, Kendal was worried about being too dependent on GameStop, so he decided to propose a line of games exclusive to GameStop and develop other games to sell directly from his own website.[1]

LEARNING OBJECTIVES

This case shows that offering customers a good product at a reasonable price is not the whole story. Marketing managers must make decisions about how they will make goods and services available to a target customer's Place when the customer wants them. This chapter's learning objectives will help you understand the role of Place in marketing strategy.

When you finish this chapter, you should:

1. understand what product classes suggest about Place objectives.

2. understand why some firms use direct channel systems while others work with intermediaries and indirect systems.

3. understand how and why marketing specialists develop to make channel systems more effective.

4. understand how to develop cooperative relationships and avoid conflict in channel systems.

5. know how channel members in vertical marketing systems shift and share functions to meet customer needs.

6. understand the differences between intensive, selective, and exclusive distribution.

7. understand important new terms (shown in red).

MARKETING STRATEGY PLANNING DECISIONS FOR PLACE

Managers must think about **Place**—making goods and services available in the right quantities and locations, when customers want them. And when different target markets have different needs, a number of Place variations may be required. Our opening case makes it clear that new Place arrangements can dramatically change the competition in a product-market. This is especially important in business today because information technology, including websites and e-commerce, makes it easier for firms to work together more efficiently and also to reach customers directly.

In this chapter and the two that follow, we'll deal with the many important marketing strategy decisions that a marketing manager must make concerning Place. Exhibit 10–1 gives an overview. We'll start here with a discussion of Place objectives and how they relate to product classes and the product life cycle—ideas introduced in the Product chapters (8 and 9). We'll then discuss the type of channel that's needed to meet customers' needs. We'll show why specialists are often involved and how they come together to form a **channel of distribution**—any series of firms or individuals who participate in the flow of products from producer to final user or consumer. We'll also consider how to manage relations among channel members to reduce conflict and improve cooperation. This chapter concludes by considering the desired level of market exposure and how many channel outlets are needed.

In Chapter 11, we'll expand the Place discussion to decisions that a marketing manager makes about physical distribution, including customer service level, transporting, and storing. Then, in Chapter 12, we'll take a closer look at the many different types of retailing and wholesaling firms. We'll consider their role in channels as well as the strategy decisions they make to satisfy their own customers.

PLACE DECISIONS ARE GUIDED BY "IDEAL" PLACE OBJECTIVES

All marketing managers want to be sure that their goods and services are available in the right quantities and locations—when customers want them. But customers may have different needs in these areas as they make different purchases.

Exhibit 10–1   Marketing Strategy Planning Decisions for Place

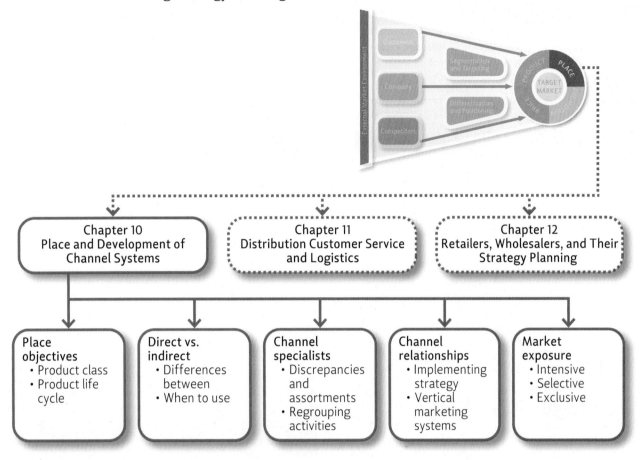

Product classes suggest Place objectives

In Chapter 8 we introduced the product classes, which summarize consumers' urgency to have needs satisfied and their willingness to seek information, shop, and compare. Now you should be able to use the product classes to handle Place decisions.

Exhibit 8–3 showed the relationship between consumer product classes and ideal Place objectives. Similarly, Exhibit 8–4 showed the business product classes and how they relate to customer needs. Study these exhibits carefully. They set the framework for making Place decisions. In particular, the product classes help us decide how much market exposure we'll need in each geographic area.

Place system is not automatic

Several different product classes may be involved if different market segments view a product in different ways. Thus, marketing managers may need to develop several strategies, each with its own Place arrangements. There may not be one Place arrangement that is best.

Place decisions have long-run effects

The marketing manager must also consider Place objectives in relation to the product life cycle; see Exhibit 9–3. Place decisions often have long-run effects. They're usually harder to change than Product, Promotion, and Price decisions. Many firms that thought they could quickly establish effective websites for direct online sales, for example, found that it took several years and millions of dollars to work out the kinks. It can take even longer and cost more to develop effective working relationships with others in the channel. Legal contracts with channel partners may limit changes. And it's hard to move retail stores and wholesale facilities once they are set up. Yet as products mature, they typically need broader distribution to reach different target customers.

When the market for premium pet foods grew, Procter & Gamble acquired the Iams brand and worked to increase sales by moving toward more intensive distribution in a variety of outlets, including pet superstores, mass-merchandisers, and online vendors. In contrast, the Science Diet brand uses selective distribution for its premium pet foods and reaches consumers in the U.S., Japan, France, and Italy mainly through veterinary offices and pet stores. Because Science Diet has developed cooperative relationships with members of its channel, they often give Science Diet products special promotion support at the point of purchase.

The distribution of premium pet foods followed this pattern. A decade ago, supermarkets wouldn't carry specialized pet foods because there wasn't much demand. So marketing managers for Science Diet products concentrated on getting distribution through pet shops and veterinary offices. Science Diet's sales in this channel grew rapidly. What's more, profit margins on the specialty foods were much higher than on traditional fare. Seeing this growth, Purina, Kal Kan, and other producers developed new products and worked with their supermarket channels to set up special "nutrition centers" on the pet food aisle. As market growth continued, Procter & Gamble bought Iams and pushed for distribution in pet superstores, at mass-merchandisers, and online.[2]

CHANNEL SYSTEM MAY BE DIRECT OR INDIRECT

One of the most basic Place decisions producers must make is whether to handle the whole distribution themselves—perhaps by relying on direct-to-customer e-commerce selling—or use wholesalers, retailers, and other specialists (see Exhibit 10–1). Intermediaries, in turn, must select the producers they'll work with.

Oakley wants its sunglasses to be conveniently available when customers want them, so it works with retailers who will carry a good selection. The Oakley website also has a dealer locator that lists retailers in the consumer's area and provides maps so the stores are easy to find.

Why a firm might want to use direct distribution

Many firms prefer to distribute directly to the final customer or consumer because they want to control the whole marketing job. They may think that they can serve target customers at a lower cost or do the work more effectively than intermediaries. Since middlemen often carry products of several competing producers, they might not give any one item the special emphasis its producer wants.

The Internet makes direct distribution easier

Website-based e-commerce systems give many firms direct access to customers whom it would have been impossible to reach in the past. Even small, specialized firms may be able to establish a web page and draw customers from all over the world.

Direct contact with customers

If a firm is in direct contact with its customers, it is more aware of changes in customer attitudes. It is in a better position to adjust its marketing mix quickly because there is no need to convince other channel members to help.

Suitable middlemen are not available

A firm may have to go direct if suitable middlemen are not available or will not cooperate. For example, Apple is again opening its own stores in hopes of getting more in-store promotional emphasis on what's different about its iMac computers. When Glacéau began selling its now popular Vitaminwater, distributors had little interest in carrying the brand. So the owner of the company started delivering the bottled water directly to small retailers in New York City. Once he proved his product would sell, distributor interest grew. When Glacéau entered the California market, it made an agreement with one distributor—an exclusive arrangement that enticed the middleman. The two companies then worked closely together to grow the market. Glacéau became a success, but many new products die because the producer can't find willing middlemen and doesn't have the financial resources to handle direct distribution.[3]

In the United States, the Census Bureau publishes detailed data concerning wholesalers and retailers, including breakdowns by kind of business, product line, and geographic territory. Similar information is available for many other countries. It can be very valuable in strategy planning—especially to learn whether potential channel members are already serving a target market. You can also learn what sales volume current intermediaries are achieving.

Common with business customers and services

Many business products are sold direct-to-customer. Alcan sells aluminum to General Motors direct. And Honda sells its motors direct to lawn mower producers. This is understandable since in business markets there are fewer transactions,

As a small company trying to obtain distribution and shelf space, Glacéau put freestanding, branded coolers for its Vitaminwater in stores, like Bed Bath & Beyond, which traditionally did not carry beverages. Thus, Glacéau didn't just compete for the same shelf space but rather expanded the available distribution outlets. Now its Vitaminwater coolers are in 50,000 locations.

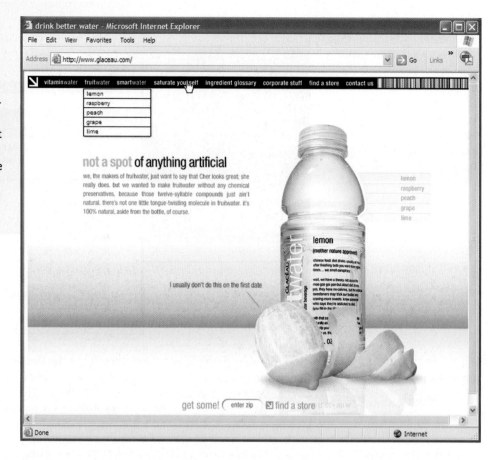

Internet EXERCISE

Gateway is a computer company that uses direct distribution to its customers in the U.S. Go to the Gateway website (*www.gateway.com*) and think about how it is organized. Is the website organized well to help Gateway reach different segments of customers (both consumer and business) in the U.S.?

orders are larger, and customers may be concentrated in one geographic area. Further, once relationships are established, e-commerce systems can efficiently handle orders.

Service firms often use direct channels. If the service must be produced in the presence of customers, there may be little need for middlemen. An accounting firm like PricewaterhouseCoopers, for example, must deal directly with its customers.

Many firms that produce physical goods turn to middlemen specialists to help provide the services customers expect. GE may hope that its authorized appliance dealers don't get many repair calls, but the service is available when customers need it. Here the intermediary produces the service.[4]

Some consumer products are sold direct

Many companies that produce consumer products have websites where a consumer can place a direct order. But for most consumer products this is still a small part of total sales. Most consumer products are sold through intermediaries.

Don't be confused by the term *direct marketing*

Even though most consumer products are sold through middlemen, an increasing number of firms rely on **direct marketing**—direct communication between a seller and an individual customer using a promotion method other than face-to-face personal selling. Sometimes direct marketing promotion is coupled with direct distribution from a producer to consumers. Park Seed Company, for example, sells the seeds it grows directly to consumers with a mail catalog and website. However, many firms that use direct marketing promotion distribute their products through middlemen. So the term *direct marketing* is primarily concerned with the Promotion area, not Place decisions. We'll talk about direct marketing promotion in more detail in Chapter 13.[5]

In the U.S. and many other developed nations, Unilever relies primarily on indirect distribution through a variety of wholesalers and retailers. However, in Spain it delivers frozen foods directly to consumer homes, and in Vietnam a mobile store brings products to local consumers. And now some products are sold direct to consumers from an Internet website.

When indirect channels are best

Even if a producer wants to handle the whole distribution job, sometimes it's simply not possible. Customers often have established buying patterns. For example, Square D, a producer of electrical supplies, might want to sell directly to electrical contractors. It can certainly set up a website for online orders or even open sales offices in key markets. But if contractors like to make all of their purchases in one convenient stop—at a local electrical wholesaler—the only practical way to reach them is through a wholesaler.

Similarly, consumers are spread throughout many geographic areas and often prefer to shop for certain products at specific places. Some consumers, for instance, see Sears as *the* place to shop for tires, so they'll only buy the brands that Sears carries. This is one reason most firms that produce consumer products rely so heavily on indirect channels (see Exhibit 2–6).[6]

Direct distribution usually requires a significant investment in facilities, people, and information technology. A company that has limited financial resources or that wants to retain flexibility may want to avoid that investment by working with established intermediaries.

Middlemen may further reduce a producer's need for working capital by buying the producer's output and carrying it in inventory until it's sold. If customers want a good "right now," there must be inventory available to make the sale. And if customers are spread over a large area, it will probably be necessary to have widespread distribution.

Until recently, Levi Strauss jeans were not distributed by Wal-Mart. However, many shoppers prefer to buy their jeans at Wal-Mart and other mass-merchandisers. To reach this segment, Levi Strauss created the Signature line. It features lighter-weight denim and less detailing and is now available at Wal-Mart, Target, and Kmart.

Some middlemen play a critical role by providing credit to customers at the end of the channel. A middleman who knows local customers can help reduce credit risks. As sales via the Internet grow, sellers are looking for faster and better ways to check the credit ratings of distant customers. It's an unhappy day when the marketing manager learns that a customer who was shipped goods based on an online order can't pay the invoice.

The most important reason for using an indirect channel of distribution is that an intermediary can often help producers serve customer needs better and at lower cost. Remember that we discussed this briefly in Chapter 1. Now we'll go into more detail.

The assortment and quantity of products customers want may be different from the assortment and quantity of products companies produce. Producers are often located far from their customers and may not know how best to reach them. Customers in turn may not know about their choices. Specialists develop to adjust these discrepancies and separations.[7]

Middlemen may supply needed information

Specialists often help provide information to bring buyers and sellers together. For example, most consumers don't know much about the wide variety of home and auto insurance policies available. A local independent insurance agent may help them decide which policy, and which insurance company, best fits their needs.

Middlemen who are close to their customers are often able to anticipate customer needs and forecast demand more accurately. This information can help reduce inventory costs in the whole channel—and it may help the producer smooth out production.

Producers often seek help from specialists when they first enter international markets. Specialists can provide crucial information about customer needs and insights into differences in the marketing environment.

Discrepancies of quantity and assortment

Discrepancy of quantity refers to the difference between the quantity of products it is economical for a producer to make and the quantity final consumers or users normally want. For example, most manufacturers of golf balls produce large quantities—perhaps 200,000 to 500,000 in a given time period. The average golfer, however, wants only a few balls at a time. Adjusting for this discrepancy usually requires middlemen—wholesalers and retailers.

Producers typically specialize by product—and therefore another discrepancy develops. **Discrepancy of assortment** refers to the difference between the lines a typical producer makes and the assortment final consumers or users want. Most golfers, for example, need more than golf balls. They want golf shoes, gloves, clubs, a bag, and, of course, a golf course to play on. And they usually don't want to shop for each item separately. So, again, there is a need for wholesalers and retailers to adjust these discrepancies.

Amazon, the large online retailer, doesn't charge customers for shipping on most orders over $25. That expands the market it serves but it also allows Amazon to compete effectively against many local booksellers because it offers such a huge assortment. It can do so because it economically accumulates products from many producers at its shipping and receiving facility and then breaks bulk to fill individual orders.

Channel specialists adjust discrepancies with regrouping activities

Regrouping activities adjust the quantities or assortments of products handled at each level in a channel of distribution.

There are four regrouping activities: accumulating, bulk-breaking, sorting, and assorting. When one or more of these activities is needed, a marketing specialist may develop to fill this need.

Adjusting quantity discrepancies by accumulating and bulk-breaking

Accumulating involves collecting products from many small producers. Much of the coffee that comes from Colombia is grown on small farms in the mountains. Accumulating the small crops into larger quantities is a way of getting the lowest transporting rate and making it more convenient for distant food processing companies to buy and handle it. Accumulating is especially important in less-developed countries and in other situations, like agricultural markets, where there are many small producers.

Accumulating is also important with professional services because they often involve the combined work of a number of individuals, each of whom is a specialized producer. A hospital makes it easier for patients by accumulating the services of a number of health care specialists, many of whom may not actually work for the hospital.

Many middlemen who operate from Internet websites focus on accumulating. Specialized sites for everything from Chinese art to Dutch flower bulbs bring together the output of many producers.

Bulk-breaking involves dividing larger quantities into smaller quantities as products get closer to the final market. The bulk-breaking may involve several levels of middlemen. Wholesalers may sell smaller quantities to other wholesalers or directly to retailers. Retailers continue breaking bulk as they sell individual items to their customers.

Adjusting assortment discrepancies by sorting and assorting

Different types of specialists adjust assortment discrepancies. They perform two types of regrouping activities: sorting and assorting.

Sorting means separating products into grades and qualities desired by different target markets. For example, an investment firm might offer its customers shares in a mutual fund made up only of stocks for companies that pay regular dividends. Similarly, a wholesaler that specializes in serving convenience stores may focus on smaller packages of frequently used products.

Assorting means putting together a variety of products to give a target market what it wants. This usually is done by those closest to the final consumer or user—retailers or wholesalers who try to supply a wide assortment of products for the convenience of their customers. Thus, a wholesaler selling Yazoo tractors and mowers to golf courses might also carry Pennington grass seed and Scotts fertilizer.

It's difficult for toy companies to grow in a mature market, but some toy companies are having success selling through outlets that do not traditionally handle toys. For example, John Deere's toy tractors at Home Depot are a hit with kids.

Watch for changes

Specialists should develop to adjust discrepancies *if they must be adjusted*. But there is no point in having middlemen just because that's the way it's been done in the past. Sometimes a breakthrough opportunity can come from finding a better way to reduce discrepancies. Some manufacturers of business products that previously relied on independent manufacturers' reps to sell their products on commission (leaving distribution to the firm) are finding that they can now reach more customers in distant markets with an Internet website. The website cost advantage can translate to lower prices and a marketing mix that is a better value for some target segments.[8]

CHANNEL RELATIONSHIP MUST BE MANAGED

Marketing manager must choose type of channel relationship

Middlemen specialists can help make a channel more efficient. But there may be problems getting the different firms in a channel to work together well. How well they work together depends on the type of relationship they have. This should be carefully considered since marketing managers usually have choices about what type of channel system to join or develop.

The whole channel should have a product-market commitment

Ideally, all of the members of a channel system should have a shared *product-market commitment*—with all members focusing on the same target market at the end of the channel and sharing the various marketing functions in appropriate ways. When members of a channel do this, they are better able to compete effectively for the customer's business. Unfortunately, many marketing managers overlook this idea because it's not the way their firms have traditionally handled channel relationships.

A channel captain can improve the performance of the whole channel—by developing strategies that help everyone in the channel do a better job of meeting the needs of target customers at the end of the channel.

Traditional channel systems involve weak relationships

In **traditional channel systems**, the various channel members make little or no effort to cooperate with each other. They buy and sell from each other—and that's the extent of their relationship. Each channel member does only what it considers to be in its own best interest. It doesn't worry about other members of the channel. This is shortsighted, but it's easy to see how it can happen. The objectives of the various channel members may be different. For example, General Electric wants a wholesaler of electrical building supplies to sell GE products. But a wholesaler who works with different producers may not care whose products get sold. The wholesaler just wants happy customers and a good profit margin.[9]

Conflict gets in the way

Specialization can make a channel more efficient—but not if the specialists are so independent that the channel doesn't work smoothly. Because members of traditional channel systems often have different objectives—and different ideas about how things should be done—conflict is common.

There are two basic types of conflict in channels of distribution. Vertical conflicts occur between firms at different levels in the channel of distribution. A vertical conflict may occur if a producer and a retailer disagree about how much shelf space or promotion effort the retailer should give the producer's product. For example, when Wherehouse Entertainment (a large retail music chain) started to sell used CDs—at about half the price of new ones—recording companies were concerned that the used CDs would hurt their sales.[10]

Horizontal conflicts occur between firms at the same level in the channel of distribution. For example, a furniture store that keeps a complete line of furniture on display isn't happy to find out that a discount chain store down the street is offering customers lower prices on special orders of the same items. The discounter is getting a free ride from the competing store's investment in inventory. And nothing gets an independent retailer more charged up than finding out that a chain store is selling some product for less than the wholesale price the independent pays.

Adding new channels creates conflict

Conflict often results when a manufacturer opens a new distribution channel that may compete with existing middlemen. In these situations, jilted channel members may fight back. For example, when Estée Lauder set up a website to sell its Bobbi Brown and Clinique brands direct to consumers, Dayton Hudson department stores cut back the space devoted to the Lauder brands. Lauder is certainly not the only firm that has made retailers unhappy by setting up a website.[11]

Managing conflict in channels

Some level of conflict may be inevitable—or even useful if that is what it takes for customers at the end of the channel to receive better value. However, most marketing managers try to avoid conflicts that harm relationships with channel partners. For example, a new channel is less likely to prompt conflict if it focuses on segments not already served by a current channel. Convenience stores, for example, do not directly compete with Costco for customers who want to make a quick purchase. So having the same product at both stores probably does not create competition between the two, especially if the package sizes are different.

Some firms try to minimize conflict by offering

Internet EXERCISE

Avon Products, Inc., has created a separate "mark" line of cosmetics and other beauty products that is targeted at young women. Avon sells mark at a website and through independent sales reps (agents), including college students who sell to their friends. Review the mark website (www.meetmark.com). Do you think that mark reps view the website as competing for their customers' purchases and as a source of conflict, or do you think that it helps them promote mark and identify new prospects? Explain your thinking.

different products through each channel. Gibson stopped selling guitars on its website after getting complaints from its traditional retailers and distributors. On the other hand, Gibson continued to sell accessories on its website. Dealers didn't want to carry inventory for all the variations of accessories, especially given that selling a few accessories wasn't very profitable.

Treating channel partners fairly—even when one partner is more powerful—tends to build trust and reduce conflict. When channel members trust each other they can work together in a cooperative relationship focused on a basic objective—satisfying target customers at the end of the channel. This leads us away from traditional channels to cooperative channel relationships and the channel captain concept.[12]

Channel captain can guide channel relationships

Ideally, each channel system should act as a unit, where each member of the channel collaborates to serve customers at the end of the channel. In this view, cooperation is everyone's responsibility. However, some firms are in a better position to take the lead in the relationship and coordinate the whole channel effort. This situation calls for a **channel captain**—a manager who helps direct the activities of a whole channel and tries to avoid or resolve channel conflicts.

For example, when Harley-Davidson wanted to expand sales of fashion accessories, it was difficult for motorcycle dealers to devote enough space to all of the different styles. Harley considered selling the items directly from its own website, but that would take sales away from dealers who were working hard to help Harley sell both cycles and fashions. So Harley's president asked a group of dealers and Harley managers to work together to come up with a plan they all liked. The result was a website that sells Harley products through the dealer that is closest to the customer.[13]

The concept of a single channel captain is logical. But most traditional channels don't have a recognized captain. The various firms don't act as a coordinated system. Yet firms are interrelated, even if poorly, by their policies. So it makes sense to try to avoid channel conflicts by planning for channel relations. The channel captain arranges for the necessary functions to be performed in the most effective way.[14]

Some producers lead their channels

In the U.S., producers frequently take the lead in channel relations. Middlemen often wait to see what the producer intends to do and wants them to do. Then they decide whether their roles will be profitable and whether they want to join in the channel effort.

Exhibit 10-2   How Channel Functions May Be Shifted and Shared in Different Channel Systems

A. How strategy decisions are handled
   in a producer-led channel

Producer's part of the job

Product
Price
Customers
Place
Promotion

Middleman's part of the job

B. How strategy decisions are handled
   in a retailer-led channel

Producer's part of the job

Product
Price
Customers

Middleman's part of the job

Place
Promotion

Exhibit 10–2A shows this type of producer-led channel system. Here the producer has selected the target market and developed the Product, set the Price structure, done some consumer and channel Promotion, and developed the Place setup. Middlemen are then expected to finish the Promotion job in their respective places. Of course, in a retailer-dominated channel system, the marketing jobs would be handled in a different way.

Some middlemen are channel captains

Sometimes wholesalers or retailers do take the lead. They are closer to the final user or consumer and are in an ideal position to assume the channel captain role. These middlemen analyze their customers' needs and then seek out producers who can provide these products at reasonable prices. With the growth of powerful chains like Wal-Mart and Best Buy, retailers now dominate the channel systems for many products in the United States. In Japan, very large wholesalers (trading companies) are often the channel captains.

Retailers like Sears and wholesalers like Ace Hardware who develop their own dealer brands in effect act like producers. They specify the whole marketing mix for a product and merely delegate production to a factory. Exhibit 10–2B shows how marketing strategy might be handled in this sort of retailer-led channel system.[15]

VERTICAL MARKETING SYSTEMS FOCUS ON FINAL CUSTOMERS

Many marketing managers accept the view that a coordinated channel system can help everyone in the channel. These managers are moving their firms away from traditional channel systems and instead developing or joining vertical market systems. **Vertical marketing systems** are channel systems in which the whole channel focuses on the same target market at the end of the channel. Such systems make sense, and are growing, because if the final customer doesn't buy the product, the whole channel suffers. There are three types of vertical marketing systems—corporate, administered, and contractual. Exhibit 10–3 summarizes some characteristics of these systems and compares them with traditional systems.

Corporate channel systems shorten channels

Some corporations develop their own vertical marketing systems by internal expansion or by buying other firms, or both. With **corporate channel systems**— corporate ownership all along the channel—we might say the firm is going "direct." But actually the firm may be handling manufacturing, wholesaling, *and* retailing—so it's more accurate to think of the firm as a vertical marketing system.

Exhibit 10–3   Characteristics of Traditional and Vertical Marketing Systems

Characteristics	Traditional	Vertical Marketing Systems		
		Administered	Contractual	Corporate
Amount of cooperation	Little or none	Some to good	Fairly good to good	Complete
Control maintained by	None	Economic power and leadership	Contracts	Ownership by one company
Examples	Typical channel of "independents"	General Electric, Miller Brewing Company, Scotts Lawn Products	McDonald's, Holiday Inn, Ace Hardware, Super Valu, Coca-Cola, Chevrolet	Florsheim Shoes, Sherwin-Williams, Mothers Work

Mothers Work is a good example of a corporate channel system started by a retailer. It began as a mail-order catalog specializing in maternity clothes. Now it sells more than a third of all maternity clothes in the U.S. Vertical integration has been a key factor in its ability to give its customers what they want. It has more than 700 company-run stores, its own designers, fabric-cutting operations, warehouses, and information systems to tie them all together.

Corporate channel systems may develop by **vertical integration**—acquiring firms at different levels of channel activity. For example, in England, most of the quaint local pubs are now actually owned and operated by the large beer breweries.

Vertical integration has potential advantages—stable sources of supplies, better control of distribution and quality, greater buying power, and lower executive overhead. Provided that the discrepancies of quantity and assortment are not too great at each level in a channel, vertical integration can be profitable. However, many managers have found that it's hard to be really good at running manufacturing, wholesaling, and retailing businesses that are very different from each other. Instead, they try to be more efficient at what they do best and focus on ways to get cooperation in the channel for the other activities. [16]

Administered and contractual systems may work well

Firms can often gain the advantages of vertical integration without building a costly corporate channel. A manager can develop administered or contractual channel systems instead. In **administered channel systems**, the channel members informally agree to cooperate with each other. They can agree to routinize ordering, share inventory and sales information over computer networks, standardize accounting, and coordinate promotion efforts. In **contractual channel systems,** the channel members agree by contract to cooperate with each other. With both of these systems, the members retain some of the flexibility of a traditional channel system.

The opportunities to reduce costs and provide customers with superior value are growing in these systems because of help from information technology. For example, Costco has a system that it calls "vendor managed inventory" in which key suppliers take over responsibility for managing a set of products, often a whole product category. Costco uses this approach with Kimberly-Clark (KC), the firm that makes Huggies. Every day, an analyst at KC's headquarters reviews Costco's online data that details Huggies' sales and inventory at every Costco store. If inventory is getting low, a new order is placed and shipping is scheduled. This system reduces buying and selling costs, inventory management, lost sales from inventory stock-outs, and consumer frustration. Because KC does this job well, it makes more money and so does Costco. [17]

Can I Download Some Popcorn with That Movie?

The market for entertainment is changing rapidly—and Hollywood has responded with new channels of distribution. For a long time, movie studios carefully managed how their films proceeded through tightly controlled channels. Movies took years to trickle down from theaters to premium cable TV channels like HBO and eventually to network television. This approach maximized the studios' revenue from each channel—and kept channel conflict at a minimum. But those days are gone and movie studios are scrambling to get revenue faster from more channels of distribution.

Each new outlet for movies has provided more convenience or a different consumer experience. In the late 1970s, the first video stores started renting movies for $10 a day. Studios also began selling movies. Disney's animated classics were especially popular at first because kids would watch the same movie many times. However, sales did not really take off until prices dropped below $25. As sales grew, distribution became more intense and retailers like Wal-Mart and Kmart were added to the mix. Blockbuster and other big rental chains also took off.

Now, if you don't feel like driving to pick up a flick, your cable channel or satellite television provider probably offers pay-per-view. Or, if you prefer, Netflix mails DVDs to your home and you can return them whenever you want. Blockbuster now takes that approach further—you can exchange a DVD that comes by mail for a new one at your local store.

Illegal channels have developed, too. Pirates often post movies on the Internet before they're even available in theaters, and some consumers copy DVDs on home computers and pass them around. However, new movie download services that are legal are also coming online, and smaller digital file formats make movies portable with a video cell phone or iPod. You may not care about portability if you've got your own comfy home theater setup. And bricks-and-mortar theaters, the traditional channel, are fighting to get customers back with stadium seating, bar and table service, and giant IMAX screens.

Concerns about movie piracy eroding sales have prompted movie studios to speed up the timing of movie distribution across channels. This has increased competition and conflict across channels. Some studios are releasing movies to theaters and on DVD at the same time—or skipping the theater channel altogether.

So where will you watch your next movie? Whether at an IMAX theater, in your home theater, or on your cell phone in a seat on a train—you can decide. These changes give you the power to choose—and movie studios hope all these channels get more people watching more movies.[18]

Vertical marketing systems—dominant force in the marketplace

Vertical systems in the consumer products area have a healthy majority of retail sales and should continue to increase their share in the future. Vertical marketing systems are becoming the major competitive units in the U.S. distribution system—and they are growing rapidly in other parts of the world as well.[19]

Short-term alliances are also popular

Firms that cooperate to build vertical marketing systems typically share a longer-term commitment. Sometimes, however, what a firm wants is a short-term collaboration to accomplish a specific objective. This may lead to an *alliance*, a partnership (usually informal) in which firms agree to work together to achieve an objective. An alliance may involve two firms, or a whole network of firms. The firms may be at the same level in the channel or at different levels. For example, a number of hardware, software, and service firms in the computer business have formed alliances to build a market for the Linux operating system. Some of these firms are even competitors (at least in some of their product-markets). Nevertheless, without the alliance it would be difficult for any of them to compete with Microsoft.[20]

THE BEST CHANNEL SYSTEM SHOULD ACHIEVE IDEAL MARKET EXPOSURE

You may think that all marketing managers want their products to have maximum exposure to potential customers. This isn't true. Some product classes require much less market exposure than others. **Ideal market exposure** makes a product available widely enough to satisfy target customers' needs but not exceed them. Too much exposure only increases the total cost of marketing.

Ideal exposure may be intensive, selective, or exclusive

Intensive distribution is selling a product through all responsible and suitable wholesalers or retailers who will stock or sell the product. **Selective distribution** is selling through only those middlemen who will give the product special attention. **Exclusive distribution** is selling through only one middleman in a particular geographic area. As we move from intensive to exclusive distribution, we give up exposure in return for some other advantage—including, but not limited to, lower cost.

Intensive distribution—sell it where they buy it

Intensive distribution is commonly needed for convenience products and business supplies—such as laser printer cartridges, ring binders, and copier paper—used by all offices. Customers want such products nearby. For example, Rayovac batteries were not selling well even though their performance was very similar to other batteries. Part of that was due to heavier advertising for Duracell and Energizer. But consumers usually don't go shopping for batteries. They're purchased on impulse 83 percent of the time. To get a larger share of purchases, Rayovac had to be in more stores. It offered retailers a marketing mix with less advertising and a lower price. In three

STIHL sells its high-quality chain saws through 8,000 independent STIHL dealers nationwide who give product demonstrations, good advice, and expert on-site service. These dealers know that the STIHL brand is not also distributed by retailers, like the big home-improvement warehouses, that put more emphasis on price competition and less on service.

years, the brand moved from being available in 36,000 stores to 82,000 stores—and that increase gave sales a big charge.[21]

Selective distribution—sell it where it sells best

Selective distribution covers the broad area of market exposure between intensive and exclusive distribution. It may be suitable for all categories of products. Only the better middlemen are used here. Companies commonly use selective distribution to gain some of the advantages of exclusive distribution—while still achieving fairly widespread market coverage.

Reduce costs and get better partners

A selective policy might be used to avoid selling to wholesalers or retailers that (1) place orders that are too small to justify making calls, (2) make too many returns or request too much service, (3) have a poor credit rating, or (4) are not in a position to do a satisfactory job.

Selective distribution is becoming more popular than intensive distribution as firms see that they don't need 100 percent coverage of a market to support national advertising. Often the majority of sales come from relatively few customers—and the others buy too little compared to the cost of working with them. This is called the 80/20 rule—80 percent of a company's sales often come from only 20 percent of its customers *until it becomes more selective in choosing customers*.

Esprit—a producer of women's clothing—was selling through about 4,000 department stores and specialty shops in the United States. But Esprit's sales analysis showed that sales in Esprit's own stores were about four times better than sales in other outlets. Profits increased when Esprit cut back to about half as many outlets and opened more of its own stores and a website. When competition from retailers like The Gap and Abercrombie & Fitch increased in the United States, Esprit focused on building profitability in its shops in Europe and Asia.[22]

Get special effort from channel members

Selective distribution can produce greater profits not only for the producer but for all channel members. Wholesalers and retailers are more willing to promote products aggressively if they know they're going to obtain the majority of sales through their own efforts. They may carry wider lines, increase promotion, and provide more service—all of which lead to more sales.

Selective often moves to intensive as market grows

In the early part of the life cycle of a new unsought good, a producer may have to use selective distribution. Well-known middlemen may have the power to get such products introduced, but sometimes on their own terms. That often means limiting the number of competing wholesalers and retailers. The producer may be happy with such an arrangement at first but dislike it later when more retailers want to carry the product.

Exclusive distribution sometimes makes sense

Exclusive distribution is just an extreme case of selective distribution—the firm selects only one middleman in each geographic area. Besides the various advantages of selective distribution, producers may want to use exclusive distribution to help control prices and the service offered in a channel.

Is limiting market exposure legal?

Exclusive distribution is a vague area under U.S. antimonopoly laws. Courts currently focus on whether an exclusive distribution arrangement hurts competition.

Horizontal arrangements among competitors are illegal

Horizontal arrangements—among *competing* retailers, wholesalers, or producers—to limit sales by customer or territory have consistently been ruled illegal by the U.S. Supreme Court. Courts consider such arrangements obvious collusion that reduces competition and harms customers.

Vertical arrangements may or may not be legal

The legality of vertical arrangements—between producers and middlemen—is not as clear-cut. A 1977 Supreme Court decision (involving Sylvania and the distribution of

TV sets) reversed an earlier ruling that it was always illegal to set up vertical relationships limiting territories or customers. Now courts can weigh the possible good effects against the possible restrictions on competition. They look at competition between whole channels rather than just focusing on competition at one level of distribution.

The Sylvania decision does not mean that all vertical arrangements are legal. Rather, it says that a firm has to be able to legally justify any exclusive arrangements.

Thus, firms should be extremely cautious about entering into *any* exclusive distribution arrangement. The courts can force a change in relationships that were expensive to develop. And even worse, the courts can award triple damages if they rule that competition has been hurt.

The same cautions apply to selective distribution. Here, however, less formal arrangements are typical—and the possible impact on competition is more remote. It is now more acceptable to carefully select channel members when building a channel system. Refusing to sell to some middlemen, however, should be part of a logical plan with long-term benefits to consumers.[23]

CHANNEL SYSTEMS CAN BE COMPLEX

Trying to achieve the desired degree of market exposure can lead to complex channels of distribution. Firms may need different channels to reach different segments of a broad product-market or to be sure they reach each segment. Sometimes this results in competition between different channels.

Consider the different channels used by a company that publishes computer books. See Exhibit 10–4. This publisher sells through a general book wholesaler who in turn sells to Internet book retailers and independent book retailers. The publisher may have some direct sales of its best-selling books to a large chain or even to consumers who order directly from its website. However, it might also sell through a computer supplies wholesaler that serves electronics superstores like Best Buy. This can cause problems because different wholesalers and retailers want different markups. It also increases

Exhibit 10–4   An Example of Multichannel Distribution by a Publisher of Computer Books

Note: Channel members may target different market segments; however, in some cases they may compete for the same customers. And, the channels shown here may also compete with channels for similar books by another publisher.

competition, including price competition. And the competition among different intermediaries may lead to conflicts between the intermediaries and the publisher.

Multichannel distribution systems may be needed

Multichannel distribution (sometimes called **dual distribution**) occurs when a producer uses several competing channels to reach the same target market—perhaps using several middlemen in addition to selling directly. Multichannel distribution is becoming more common. For instance, big retail chains want large quantities and low prices. A producer may sell directly to retail chains and rely on wholesalers to sell to smaller accounts. Some established middlemen resent this because they don't appreciate *any* competition—especially price competition set up by their own suppliers.

Other times, producers are forced to use multichannel distribution because their present channels are doing a poor job or aren't reaching some potential customers. For example, Reebok International had been relying on local sporting goods stores to sell its shoes to high school and college athletic teams. But Reebok wasn't getting much of the business. When it set up its own team-sales department to sell directly to the schools, it got a 30,000-unit increase in sales.[24]

Ethical decisions may be required

If competition changes or customers' Place requirements shift, the current channel system may not be effective. The changes required to serve customer needs may hurt one or more members of the channel. Ethical dilemmas in the channels area arise in situations like this—because not everyone in the channel can win.

For example, wholesalers and the independent retailers that they serve in a channel of distribution may trust a producer–channel captain to develop marketing strategies that will work for the whole channel. However, the producer may decide that consumers, and its own business, are best served by a change (say, dropping current middlemen and selling directly to big retail chains). A move of this sort, if implemented immediately, may not give current middlemen-partners a chance to make adjustments of their own. The more dependent they are on the producer, the more severe the impact is likely to be. It's not easy to determine the best or most ethical solution in these situations. However, marketing managers must think carefully about the consequences of Place strategy changes for other channel members. In channels, as in any business dealing, relationships of trust must be treated with care.[25]

Reverse channels should be planned

Most firms focus on getting products to their customers. But some marketing managers must also plan for **reverse channels**—channels used to retrieve products that customers no longer want. The need for reverse channels may arise in a variety of different situations. Toy companies, automobile firms, drug companies, pet food companies, and others sometimes have to recall products because of safety problems. A firm that makes an error in completing an order may have to take returns. If a ViewSonic computer monitor breaks while it's still under warranty, someone needs to get it to the repair center. Soft-drink companies may need to recycle empty bottles. Similarly, used inkjet and laser toner cartridges are often recycled and reused. And, of course, consumers sometimes buy something in error and want to return it. This is common with online purchases where consumers can't see, touch, or try the product before purchasing it.[26]

Another problem arises from products that are damaged in shipping or discontinued. Most manufacturers take them back. A grocery products trade group says that the cost of such unsalable products, in total, may be as much as $4 billion a year. To reduce such costs, P&G has adopted a no-returns policy and instead gives retailers a payment for damaged items. Some retailers don't like P&G's policy, but it is important to see that it is a specific plan and part of an overall strategy.

When marketing managers don't plan for reverse channels, the firm's customers may be left to solve "their" problem. That usually doesn't make sense. So a complete plan for Place may need to consider an efficient way to return products—with policies that different channel members agree on. It may also require specialists who were not involved in getting the product to the consumer. But if that's what it takes to satisfy customers, it should be part of marketing strategy planning.[27]

CONCLUSION

In this chapter we discussed the role of Place in marketing strategy. Place decisions are especially important because they may be difficult and expensive to change. So marketing managers must make Place decisions very carefully.

We discussed how product classes and the product life cycle are related to Place objectives. This helps us determine how much a firm should rely on indirect channel systems with intermediaries or direct systems.

Marketing specialists and channel systems develop to adjust discrepancies of quantity and assortment. Their regrouping activities are basic in any economic system. And adjusting discrepancies provides opportunities for creative marketers.

Channels of distribution tend to work best when there is cooperation among the members of a channel—and conflict is avoided. So we discussed the importance of planning channel systems and the role of a channel captain. We stressed that channel systems compete with each other and that vertical marketing systems seem to be winning.

Channel planning also requires firms to decide on the degree of market exposure they want. The ideal level of exposure may be intensive, selective, or exclusive. Finally, we discussed the legal issues marketing managers must consider in developing channel systems.

KEY TERMS

Place, 252
channel of distribution, 252
direct marketing, 256
discrepancy of quantity, 258
discrepancy of assortment, 258
regrouping activities, 259
accumulating, 259
bulk-breaking, 259

sorting, 259
assorting, 259
traditional channel systems, 261
channel captain, 262
vertical marketing systems, 263
corporate channel systems, 263
vertical integration, 264
administered channel systems, 264

contractual channel systems, 264
ideal market exposure, 266
intensive distribution, 266
selective distribution, 266
exclusive distribution, 266
multichannel distribution, 269
dual distribution, 269
reverse channels, 269

QUESTIONS AND PROBLEMS

1. Review the case at the beginning of the chapter and discuss the competitive advantages that Barnes & Noble would have over a small bookshop like Cozy Bookshop. What advantages does a small bookshop have?

2. Give two examples of service firms that work with other channel specialists to sell their products to final consumers. What marketing functions is the specialist providing in each case?

3. Discuss some reasons why a firm that produces installations might use direct distribution in its domestic market but use intermediaries to reach overseas customers.

4. Explain discrepancies of quantity and assortment using the clothing business as an example. How does the application of these concepts change when selling steel to the automobile industry? What impact does this have on the number and kinds of marketing specialists required?

5. Explain the four regrouping activities with an example from the building supply industry (nails, paint, flooring, plumbing fixtures, etc.). Do you think that many specialists develop in this industry, or do producers handle the job themselves? What kinds of marketing channels would you expect to find in this industry, and what functions would various channel members provide?

6. Insurance agents are middlemen who help other members of the channel by providing information and handling the selling function. Does it make sense for an insurance agent to specialize and work exclusively with one insurance provider? Why or why not?

7. Discuss the Place objectives and distribution arrangements that are appropriate for the following products (indicate any special assumptions you have to make to obtain an answer):

   a. A postal scale for products weighing up to 2 pounds.
   b. Children's toys: (1) radio-controlled model airplanes costing $80 or more, (2) small rubber balls.
   c. Heavy-duty, rechargeable, battery-powered nut tighteners for factory production lines.
   d. Fiberglass fabric used in making roofing shingles.

8. Give an example of a producer that uses two or more different channels of distribution. Briefly discuss what problems this might cause.

9. Explain how a channel captain can help traditional independent firms compete with a corporate (integrated) channel system.

10. Find an example of vertical integration within your city. Are there any particular advantages to this vertical integration? If so, what are they? If there are no such advantages, how do you explain the integration?

11. What would happen if retailer-organized channels (either formally integrated or administered) dominated consumer product marketing?

12. How does the nature of the product relate to the degree of market exposure desired?

13. Why would middlemen want to be exclusive distributors for a product? Why would producers want exclusive distribution? Would middlemen be equally anxious to get exclusive distribution for any type of product? Why or why not? Explain with reference to the following products: candy bars, batteries, golf clubs, golf balls, steak knives, televisions, and industrial woodworking machinery.

14. Explain the present legal status of exclusive distribution. Describe a situation where exclusive distribution is almost sure to be legal. Describe the nature and size of competitors and the industry, as well as the nature of the exclusive arrangement. Would this exclusive arrangement be of any value to the producer or intermediary?

15. Discuss the promotion a new grocery products producer would need in order to develop appropriate channels and move products through those channels. Would the nature of this job change for a new producer of dresses? For a new, small producer of installations?

CREATING MARKETING PLANS

The Marketing Plan Coach software on the Student CD includes a sample marketing plan for Hillside Veterinary Clinic. Look through the "Marketing Strategy" section.

a. Why does Hillside sell its product directly instead of indirectly?

b. Hillside has a small selection of pet supplies that it sells to people who bring in their pets. What products does it resell at retail? What channel functions does it provide, and what channel functions are performed by its suppliers?

SUGGESTED CASES

COMPUTER-AIDED PROBLEM

10. INTENSIVE VERSUS SELECTIVE DISTRIBUTION

Hydropump, Inc., produces and sells high-quality pumps to business customers. Its marketing research shows a growing market for a similar type of pump aimed at final consumers—for use with Jacuzzi-style tubs in home remodeling jobs. Hydropump will have to develop new channels of distribution to reach this target market because most consumers rely on a retailer for advice about the combination of tub, pump, heater, and related plumbing fixtures they need. Hydropump's marketing manager, Robert Black, is trying to decide between intensive and selective distribution. With intensive distribution, he would try to sell through all the plumbing supply, bathroom fixture, and hot-tub retailers who will carry the pump. He estimates that about 5,600 suitable retailers would be willing to carry a new pump. With selective distribution, he would focus on about 280 of the best hot-tub dealers (2 or 3 in the 100 largest metropolitan areas).

Intensive distribution would require Hydropump to do more mass selling—primarily advertising in home renovation magazines—to help stimulate consumer familiarity with the brand and convince retailers that Hydropump equipment will sell. The price to the retailer might have to be lower too (to permit a bigger markup) so they will be motivated to sell Hydropump rather than some other brand offering a smaller markup.

With intensive distribution, each Hydropump sales rep could probably handle about 300 retailers effectively. With selective distribution, each sales rep could handle only about 70 retailers because more merchandising help would be necessary.

Managing the smaller sales force and fewer retailers, with the selective approach, would require less manager overhead cost.

Going to all suitable and available retailers would make the pump available through about 20 times as many retailers and have the potential of reaching more customers. However, many customers shop at more than one retailer before making a final choice—so selective distribution would reach almost as many potential customers. Further, if Hydropump is using selective distribution, it would get more in-store sales attention for its pump and a larger share of pump purchases at each retailer.

Black has decided to use a spreadsheet to analyze the benefits and costs of intensive versus selective distribution.

a. Based on the initial spreadsheet, which approach seems to be the most sensible for Hydropump? Why?

b. A consultant points out that even selective distribution needs national promotion. If Black has to increase advertising and spend a total of $100,000 on mass selling to be able to recruit the retailers he wants for selective distribution, would selective or intensive distribution be more profitable?

c. With intensive distribution, how large a share (percent) of the retailers' total unit sales would Hydropump have to capture to sell enough pumps to earn $200,000 profit?

For additional questions related to this problem, see Exercise 10-3 in the *Learning Aid for Use with Essentials of Marketing*, 11th edition.

11

Distribution Customer Service and Logistics

If you want a Coca-Cola, there's usually one close by—no matter where you might be in the world. And that's no accident. An executive for the best-known brand name in the world stated the objective simply: "Make Coca-Cola available within an arm's reach of desire." To achieve that objective, Coke works with many different channels of distribution. But that's just the start. Think about what it takes for a bottle, can, or cup of Coke to be there whenever you're thirsty. In warehouses and distribution centers, on trucks, in gyms and sports arenas, and in thousands of other retail outlets, Coke handles, stores, and transports more than 400 billion servings of the soft drink a year. Getting all of that product to consumers could be a logistical nightmare, but Coke does it effectively and at a low cost. Think about it: A can of Coke at the store costs about the same as what it costs you to have the Post Office deliver a letter.

Fast information about what the market needs helps keep Coke's distribution on target. Coke uses an Internet-based data system that links about one million retailers and other sellers to Coke and its bottlers. The system lets Coke bottlers and retailers exchange orders, invoices, and pricing information online. Orders are processed instantly—so sales to consumers at the end of the channel aren't lost because of stock-outs. Similarly, computer systems show Coke managers exactly what's selling in each market; they can even estimate the effects of promotions as they plan inventories and deliveries. And Coke products move efficiently through the channel. In Cincinnati, for example, Coke built the beverage industry's first fully automated distribution center. And when Coke's truck drivers get to the retail store, they knowingly stock the shelves with the correct mix of products.

Coke's strategies in international markets rely on many of the same ideas. But the stage of market development varies in different countries, so Coke's emphasis varies as well. To increase sales in France, for example, Coke installed thousands of soft-drink coolers in French supermarkets. In Great Britain, Coke emphasizes multipacks because it wants to have more inventory at the point of consumption—in consumers' homes. In Japan, by contrast, Coke has relied heavily on an army of truck drivers to constantly restock 1 million Coke vending machines, more per capita than anywhere else in the world. And in Australia, some Coke vending machines have built-in cell phone systems; a press of a button makes a call so customers can charge the Coke to their cell phone accounts.

In less-developed areas, the Place system can make Coke products hard to find or costly. Until recently, retail stores in Afghanistan received Coke products shipped in from neighboring Pakistan—and a can of Coke sold for 40 cents. This priced many potential customers out of the market. After Coke built a local bottling plant and set up recycling systems, the price fell to about 13 cents—giving Coke a boost.

Coke is also working to increase fountain-drink sales in domestic and international markets. As part of that effort, Coke equips restaurants and food outlets with Coke dispensers. Once a Coke dispenser is installed, the retailer usually doesn't have room for a competitor's dispenser. The number of fountain outlets has grown so rapidly that one Coke account rep serves as many as 1,000 retail customers in a geographic area. That means that the little guys could get lost in the shuffle. However, to give them the service they need at a reasonable cost, Coke launched Coke.net, a password-protected Web portal where fountain customers can access account managers online, track syrup orders, request equipment repairs, or download marketing support materials.

Coke's successes and profitability have certainly been bolstered by its strengths in getting its colas to consumers—wherever they may be and whenever they want them. But no single element of the marketing mix makes a strategy a success. In fact, consumer demand for colas has slipped rapidly. Even Coca-Cola Classic has declining sales. More consumers now prefer other types of beverages—energy drinks, bottled waters, juices, premium coffees and teas, beverages with health appeals, and a variety of other new offerings. It seems that sales are growing for just about every beverage that does not have carbonation. That explains why Coke's marketers talk about their "sparkling" sodas rather than about carbonation. But changes in words won't fix the problem. In the past, Coke was too slow in developing new types of products to meet new needs—in large part because it was so focused on building its share in the cola competition with Pepsi. To remedy this, Coke is now introducing many noncola products in markets around the world. Clearly, a proliferation in the number of products to be distributed will make logistics even more of a challenge. However, if consumers want more choices, that is a challenge Coke will need to face.[1]

LEARNING OBJECTIVES

Choosing the right distribution channels is crucial in getting products to the target market's Place. But, as the Coca-Cola case shows, that alone doesn't ensure that products are placed "within an arm's reach of desire"—when, where, in the quantities that customers want them, and at a price they're willing to pay. In this chapter we discuss how marketing managers ensure that they also have physical distribution systems that meet their customers' needs—at both an acceptable service level and an affordable cost.

When you finish this chapter, you should:

1. understand why logistics (physical distribution) is such an important part of Place and marketing strategy planning.

2. understand why the physical distribution customer service level is a key marketing strategy variable.

3. understand the physical distribution concept and why the coordination of storing, transporting, and related activities is so important.

4. see how firms can cooperate and share logistics activities that will provide added value to their customers.

5. know about the advantages and disadvantages of various transport methods.

6. know how inventory and storage decisions affect marketing strategy.

7. understand the distribution center concept.

8. understand important new terms (shown in red).

PHYSICAL DISTRIBUTION GETS IT TO CUSTOMERS

Whenever Product includes a physical good, Place requires logistics decisions. **Logistics** is the transporting, storing, and handling of goods in ways that match target customers' needs with a firm's marketing mix—both within individual firms and along a channel of distribution. **Physical distribution (PD)** is another common name for logistics.

There are many different combinations of logistics decisions. Each combination can result in a different level of distribution service and different costs. So, firms must determine the best way to provide the level of distribution service that customers want and are willing to pay for. We start this chapter by considering these critical logistics decisions. See Exhibit 11–1. Next, we describe the choice among different modes of transportation: Each has its own costs and benefits. We conclude with decisions about inventory and the use of distribution centers.

Logistics costs are very important to both firms and consumers. These costs vary from firm to firm and, from a macro-marketing perspective, from country to country. For some products, a firm may spend half or more of its total marketing dollars on physical distribution activities. The amounts involved are often so large that even small improvements in this area can have a big effect on a whole macro-marketing system and consumers' quality of life. For example, in the 1990s many supermarket chains collaborated with their suppliers and producers to create a system called Efficient Consumer Response (ECR). The basic idea of ECR involves computer links between grocers and their suppliers, which leads to continuous restocking of what actually sells each day and lower inventory costs. ECR cut grocers' costs, and prices that consumers pay, by about 11 percent. That translated to savings of almost $30 billion a year for U.S. consumers! Although it started in the United States and Canada, it's no surprise that the ECR movement spread quickly across Europe and other global regions.[2]

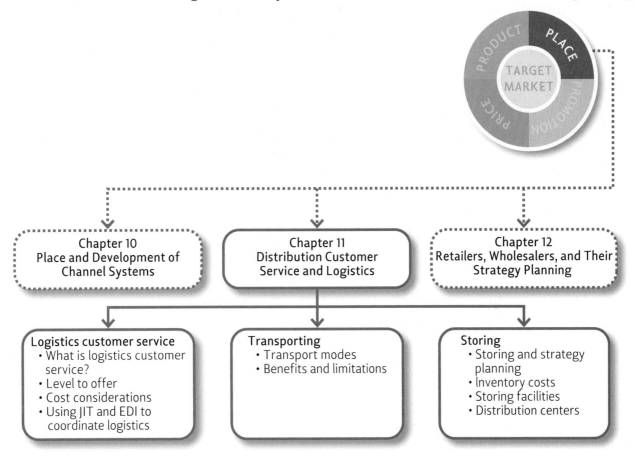

PHYSICAL DISTRIBUTION CUSTOMER SERVICE

From the beginning, we've emphasized that marketing strategy planning is based on meeting customers' needs. Planning for logistics and Place is no exception. So let's start by looking at logistics through a customer's eyes.

Customers want products, not excuses

Customers don't care how a product was moved or stored or what some channel member had to do to provide it. Rather, customers think in terms of the physical distribution **customer service level**—how rapidly and dependably a firm can deliver what they, the customers, want.

What does this really mean? It means that Toyota wants to have enough windshields delivered to make cars *that* day—not late so production stops *or* early so there are a lot of extras to move around or store. It means that business executives who rent cars from Hertz want them to be ready when they get off their planes. It means that when you order a blue shirt at the Lands' End website you receive blue, not pink. It means you want your Tostitos to be whole when you buy a bag at the snack bar—not crushed into crumbs from rough handling in a warehouse.

Physical distribution is invisible to most consumers

Physical distribution is, and should be, a part of marketing that is "invisible" to most consumers. It only gets their attention when something goes wrong. At that point, it may be too late to do anything that will keep them happy.

In countries where physical distribution systems are inefficient, consumers face shortages of the products they need. By contrast, most consumers in the United States and Canada don't think much about physical distribution. This probably means that these market-directed macro-marketing systems work pretty well—that a lot of individual marketing managers have made good decisions in this area. But it doesn't mean that the decisions are always clear-cut or simple. In fact, many trade-offs may be required.

Trade-offs of costs, service, and sales

Most customers would prefer very good service at a very low price. But that combination is hard to provide because it usually costs more to provide higher levels of service. So most physical distribution decisions involve trade-offs between costs, the customer service level, and sales.

If you want a new HP computer and the Staples store where you would like to buy it doesn't have it on hand, you're likely to buy it elsewhere; or if that model HP is hard to get you might just switch to some other brand. Perhaps the Staples store could keep your business by guaranteeing two-day delivery of your computer—by using airfreight from HP's factory. In this case, the store manager is trading the cost of storing inventory at the store for the extra cost of speedy delivery—assuming that the computer is available in inventory *somewhere* in the channel. In this example, missing one sale may not seem that important, but it all adds up. A few years ago a computer company lost over $500 million in sales because its computers weren't available when and where customers were ready to buy them.

Exhibit 11–2 illustrates trade-off relationships like those highlighted in the HP example. For instance, using faster but more expensive transportation may reduce the need for a costly inventory of computers. If the service level is too low, customers will buy elsewhere and sales will be lost. Alternatively, the supplier may hope that a higher service level will attract more customers. But if the service level is higher than customers want or are willing to pay for, sales will be lost to competitors.

The trade-offs that must be made in the PD area can be complicated. The lowest-cost approach may not be best—if customers aren't satisfied. If different target markets want different customer service levels, several different strategies may be needed.[3]

Many firms are trying to address these complications with e-commerce. Information technology can improve service levels and cut costs at the same time. Better information flows make it easier to coordinate logistics activities, improve efficiency, and add value for the customer.

Exhibit 11–2
Trade-Offs among Physical Distribution Costs, Customer Service Level, and Sales

*Note: Sales may be lost because of poor customer service or because of the high price charged to pay for too high a customer service level.

The physical distribution customer service level—including fast and reliable delivery of whatever assortment is needed—is critical to many business customers.

PHYSICAL DISTRIBUTION CONCEPT FOCUSES ON THE WHOLE DISTRIBUTION SYSTEM

The physical distribution concept

The **physical distribution (PD) concept** says that all transporting, storing, and product-handling activities of a business and a whole channel system should be coordinated as one system that seeks to minimize the cost of distribution for a given customer service level. This seems like common sense, but until recently most companies treated physical distribution functions as separate and unrelated activities.

Within a firm, responsibility for different distribution activities was spread among various departments—production, shipping, sales, warehousing, and others. No one person was responsible for coordinating storing and shipping decisions or customer service levels. It was even rarer for different firms in the channel to collaborate. Each just did its own thing. Unfortunately, in too many firms old-fashioned ways persist—with a focus on individual functional activities rather than the whole physical distribution system.[4]

Decide what service level to offer

With broader adoption of the physical distribution concept, this is changing. Firms work together to decide what aspects of service are most important to customers at the end of the channel. Then they focus on finding the least expensive way to achieve the target level of service.

Exhibit 11–3 shows a variety of factors that may influence the customer service level (at each level in the channel). The most important aspects of customer service depend on target market needs. Xerox might focus on how long it takes to deliver copy machine repair parts once it receives an order. When a copier breaks down, customers want the repair "yesterday." The service level might be stated as "we will deliver 90 percent of all emergency repair parts within 24 hours." This might require

Exhibit 11–3
Examples of Factors
That Affect PD Service
Levels

- Advance information on product availability
- Time to enter and process orders
- Backorder procedures
- Where inventory is stored
- Accuracy in filling orders
- Damage in shipping, storing, and handling
- Online status information

- Advance information on delays
- Time needed to deliver an order
- Reliability in meeting delivery date
- Complying with customer's instructions
- Defect-free deliveries
- How needed adjustments are handled
- Procedures for handling returns

that commonly needed parts be available on the service truck, that order processing be very fast, and that parts not available locally be sent by airfreight. Obviously, supplying this service level will affect the total cost of the PD system. But it may also beat competitors.

Fast PD service can be critical for retailers that appeal to consumers who are eager to get a new product that is in hot demand—the latest CD or DVD release, a best-selling book, or a popular toy or video game.

Increasing service levels may also be very profitable in highly competitive situations where the firm has little else to differentiate its marketing mix. Marketing managers at Clorox, for example, must do everything they can to develop and keep strong partnerships with middlemen. Many other firms sell products with precisely the same ingredients and are constantly trying to steal customers. Yet Clorox's high standards for customer service help it obtain a competitive advantage. For example, when the bleach buyer for a major retail chain went on vacation, the chain's central distribution center almost ran out of Clorox liquid bleach. But Clorox people identified the problem themselves—because of a computer system that allowed Clorox to access the chain's inventory records and sales data for Clorox products. Clorox rearranged production to get a shipment out fast enough

Both Sauder and Best Software try to help customer firms do a better job of tracking the status of orders and making certain that products are where they are needed at the right time.

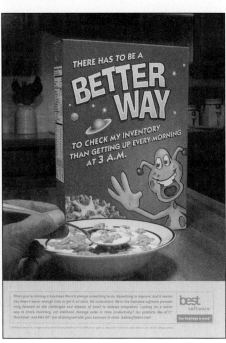

to prevent the chain, and Clorox, from losing sales. In the future when another bleach supplier tells buyers for the chain that "bleach is bleach," they'll remember the distribution service Clorox provides.[5]

Find the lowest total cost for the right service level

In selecting a PD system, the **total cost approach** involves evaluating each possible PD system and identifying *all* of the costs of each alternative. This approach uses the tools of cost accounting and economics. Costs that otherwise might be ignored—like inventory carrying costs—are considered. The possible costs of lost sales due to a lower customer service level may also be considered. The following example clarifies why the total cost approach is important.

A cost comparison of alternative systems

The Good Earth Vegetable Company was shipping produce to distant markets by train. The cost of shipping a ton of vegetables by train averaged less than half the cost of airfreight so the company assumed that rail was the best method. But then Good Earth managers did a more complete analysis. To their surprise, they found the airfreight system was faster and cheaper.

Exhibit 11–4 compares the costs for the two distribution systems—airplane and railroad. Because shipping by train was slow, Good Earth had to keep a large inventory in a warehouse to fill orders on time. And the company was also surprised at the extra cost of carrying the inventory in transit. Good Earth's managers also found that the cost of spoiled vegetables during shipment and storage in the warehouse was much higher when they used rail shipping.

In this case, total cost analyses showed that airfreight, while more costly by itself, provided better service than the conventional means—and at a lower total distribution cost. The case also illustrates why it is important to get beyond a focus on individual functional elements of PD and instead consider the costs and service level of a whole system. This broader focus should consider how the whole channel operates, not just individual firms.

Many firms are now applying this type of thinking to improve customer value and profits. For example, applying the total cost approach, National Semiconductor cut its standard delivery time in half, reduced distribution costs 2.5 percent, and increased sales by 34 percent. In the process, it shut down six warehouses around the globe and started to airfreight microchips to its worldwide customers from a new 125,000-square-foot distribution center in Singapore. In advance of these changes, no one would have said that this was an obvious thing to do. But it proved to be the smart thing.[6]

Exhibit 11–4
Comparative Costs of Airplane versus Rail and Warehouse

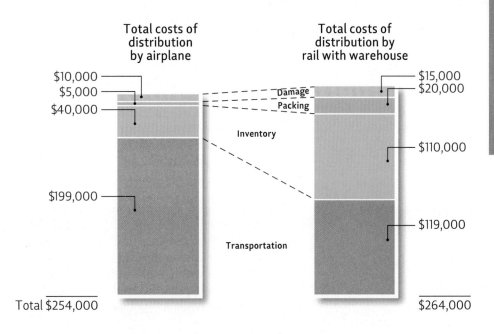

Total costs of distribution by airplane

Total costs of distribution by rail with warehouse

$10,000
$5,000
$40,000

$15,000
$20,000

Damage
Packing
Inventory

$110,000

$199,000

$119,000

Transportation

Total $254,000

$264,000

COORDINATING LOGISTICS ACTIVITIES AMONG FIRMS

Functions can be shifted and shared in the channel

As a marketing manager develops the Place part of a strategy, it is important to decide how physical distribution functions can and should be divided within the channel. Who will store, handle, and transport the goods—and who will pay for these services? Who will coordinate all of the PD activities?

There is no right sharing arrangement. Physical distribution can be varied endlessly in a marketing mix and in a channel system. And competitors may share these functions in different ways—with different costs and results.

How PD is shared affects the rest of a strategy

How the PD functions are shared affects the other three Ps—especially Price. The sharing arrangement can also make (or break) a strategy. Consider Channel Master, a firm that wanted to take advantage of the growing market for the dishlike antennas used to receive TV signals from satellites. The product looked like it could be a big success, but the small company didn't have the money to invest in a large inventory. So Channel Master decided to work only with wholesalers who were willing to buy (and pay for) several units—to be used for demonstrations and to ensure that buyers got immediate delivery.

In the first few months Channel Master earned $2 million in revenues—just by providing inventory for the channel. And the wholesalers paid the interest cost of carrying inventory—over $300,000 the first year. Here the wholesalers helped share the risk of the new venture, but it was a good decision for them, too. They won many sales from a competing channel whose customers had to wait several months for delivery. And by getting off to a strong start, Channel Master became a market leader.

A coordinated effort reduces conflict

If firms in the channel do not plan and coordinate how they will share PD activities, PD is likely to be a source of conflict rather than a basis for competitive advantage. Let's consider this point by taking a closer look at just-in-time (JIT) delivery systems (which we introduced in Chapter 6).

JIT requires a close, cooperative relationship

A key advantage of JIT for business customers is that it reduces their PD costs—especially storing and handling costs. However, if the customer doesn't have any backup inventory, there's no security blanket if a supplier's delivery truck gets stuck in traffic, there's an error in what's shipped, or there are any quality problems. Thus, a JIT system requires that a supplier have extremely high quality control in every PD activity.

A JIT system usually requires that a supplier respond to very short order lead times and the customer's production schedule. Thus, e-commerce order systems and information sharing over computer networks are often required. JIT suppliers often locate their facilities close to important customers. Trucks may make smaller and more frequent deliveries—perhaps even several times a day.

A JIT system shifts greater responsibility for PD activities backward in the channel. If the supplier can be more efficient than the customer could be in controlling PD costs—and still provide the customer with the service level required—this approach can work well for everyone in the channel. However, JIT is not always the best approach. It may be better for a supplier to produce and ship in larger, more economical quantities—if the savings offset the distribution system's total inventory and handling costs.[7]

Supply chain may involve even more firms

The relationships among firms in the distribution channel are sometimes part of a broader network of relationships in the **supply chain**—the complete set of firms and facilities and logistics activities that are involved in procuring materials, transforming them into intermediate or finished products, and distributing them to customers. For example, Honda not only works with dealers and customers but also with the supplier firms from which it buys parts. Those firms, in turn, coordinate with their own suppliers. What happens at each link can impact the whole chain. If the firm that produces seats

Disaster Relief Is No Logistics Picnic

Hurricanes, tsunamis, and earthquakes create immediate needs for emergency relief supplies. And the logistics involved in delivering them include many of the same activities found in the physical delivery of other goods. However, in a disaster situation, life and death often hinge upon the speed with which food, water, and medical supplies can be delivered. Yet, when bridges, roads, and airports are destroyed, local transportation can be complicated, if not impossible. And, even worse, there is no advance warning when or where aid will be needed. Imagine what it would be like for one business to be instantly ready to distribute millions of products to a target market that usually doesn't exist, moves around the world, and then without notice pops up somewhere with insatiable needs.

People in advanced societies have high expectations that help will be immediate when disaster strikes. Yet, it's nearly impossible for relief agencies to meet those expectations. Still, improved performance is on the way from both disaster relief agencies and private businesses, which have learned from recent efforts. For example, instead of stockpiling drugs, tents, and blankets, agencies are learning to rely on outsourcing. Agencies arrange open orders with suppliers who must be prepared to instantly ship supplies whenever and wherever they are needed.

Organizations with logistics expertise also lend a helping hand. As soon as Wal-Mart's emergency operation center learned that Hurricane Katrina was coming, it prestocked stores in the Gulf region with extra water, flashlights, and batteries as well as canned soups and meats. Residents survived with these crucial supplies before government aid arrived. Immediately following disasters in all parts of the world, transportation giants like FedEx, DHL, and China Southern Airlines have responded quickly with planes and trucks that facilitate delivery of needed supplies. Similarly, the Fritz Institute analyzes past relief efforts and consults with agencies to help them better prepare for future responses.

When chaos hits, coordination of relief efforts is possible only if there is good information. Agencies need to know what supplies are available, where they're located, what needs are greatest, and where and how quickly deliveries can be made. Having one central communication hub—to collect and share this type of information—and IT systems specifically dedicated to the task are key. A new system called Suma allows relief workers to manage incoming donations, put them in the right storage places, and establish shipping priorities.

Other physical distribution solutions are decidedly low-tech, but equally important. For example, boxes need to be color coded so it's obvious which ones contain critical medical supplies and perishable food. And donated goods must be packed in cartons light enough to be carried manually in locations that have no power or equipment.[8]

for Honda doesn't get the fabric from its supplier on time, the seats will be delayed in route to Honda and the car will be slow getting to the dealer and consumer.

Ideally, all of the firms in the supply chain should work together to meet the needs of the customer at the very end of the chain. That way, at each link along the chain the shifting and sharing of logistics functions and costs are handled to result in the most value for the final customer. This also helps all of the firms do a better job of competing against competitors who are involved in other supply chains.

It's still difficult for a manager in any one company to know what kind of logistics sharing arrangement will work best, or even be possible, in a whole series of other companies. Because of that, many firms turn to outside experts for help. For example, specialists may design the e-commerce computer systems that link all of the firms in a supply chain or figure out the best way to shift logistics functions among firms. Firms sometimes outsource the whole job of planning *and* implementing their logistics systems.[9]

Internet EXERCISE

Managers who are members of the Council of Supply Chain Management Professionals usually have responsibilities in purchasing, logistics, or materials management. The website of this organization (**www.cscmp.org**) provides many useful resources to members and nonmembers. Under "Resources" check the Supply Chain Innovation Award. Choose one of the nominees of this award and read how the nominee addressed a logistics challenge. Explain how other companies might learn from this firm's experience.

China is developing rapidly and becoming an economic powerhouse. However, this scene of a man peddling a tricycle loaded with monitors is a reminder of the legacy of China's command economy. In a modern market-directed economy, new marketing specialists, including logistics firms, will develop to efficiently meet the needs of fast-growing markets.

Better information helps coordinate PD

Coordinating all of the elements of PD has always been a challenge—even in a single firm. Trying to coordinate orders, inventory, and transportation throughout the whole supply chain is even tougher. But information shared over the Internet has been important in finding solutions to these challenges. Physical distribution decisions will continue to improve as more firms are able to have their computers "talk to each other" directly and as websites help managers get access to up-to-date information whenever they need it.

Electronic data interchange sets a standard

Until recently, differences in computer systems from one firm to another hampered the flow of information. Many firms attacked this problem by adopting **electronic data interchange (EDI)**—an approach that puts information in a standardized format easily shared between different computer systems. In many firms, purchase orders, shipping reports, and other paper documents were replaced with computerized EDI. With EDI, a customer transmits its order information directly to the supplier's computer. The supplier's computer immediately processes the order and schedules production, order assembly, and transportation. Inventory information is automatically updated, and status reports are available instantly. The supplier might then use EDI to send the updated information to the transportation provider's computer. In fact, most international transportation firms rely on EDI links with their customers.[10]

Improved information flow and better coordination of PD activities is a key reason for the success of Pepperidge Farm's line of premium cookies. Most of the company's delivery truck drivers use hand-held computers to record the inventory at each stop along their routes. They use a wireless Internet connection to instantly transmit the information into a computer at the bakeries, and cookies in short supply are produced. The right assortment of fresh cookies is quickly shipped to local markets, and delivery trucks are loaded with what retailers need that day. Pepperidge Farm moves cookies from its bakeries to store shelves in about three days; most cookie producers take about 10 days. That means fresher cookies for consumers, which helps to support Pepperidge Farm's high-quality positioning and premium price.[11]

Ethical issues may arise

Some ethical issues that arise in the PD area concern communications about product availability. For example, some critics say that Internet sellers too often take orders for products that are not available or which they cannot deliver as quickly as customers expect. Yet a marketing manager can't always know precisely how long it will take before a product will be available. It doesn't make sense for the marketer to lose a customer if it appears that he or she can satisfy the customer's needs. But the customer may be inconvenienced or face added cost if the marketer's best guess isn't accurate. Similarly, some critics say that stores too often run out of products that they promote to attract consumers to the store. Yet it may not be possible for the marketer to predict demand, or to know when placing an ad that deliveries won't arrive. Different people have different views about how a firm should handle such situations. Some retailers just offer rain checks.

Now that you see why the coordination of physical distribution activities is so important, let's take a closer look at some of the PD decision areas.

THE TRANSPORTING FUNCTION ADDS VALUE TO A MARKETING STRATEGY

Transporting aids economic development and exchange

Transporting is the marketing function of moving goods. Transportation makes products available when and where they need to be—at a cost. But the cost is less than the value added to products by moving them or there is little reason to ship in the first place.

Transporting can help achieve economies of scale in production. If production costs can be reduced by producing larger quantities in one location, these savings may more than offset the added cost of transporting the finished products to customers. Without low-cost transportation, both within countries and internationally, there would be no mass distribution as we know it today.

The cost of transportation adds little to the total cost of products—like pharmaceuticals—that are already valuable relative to their size and weight. But transporting costs can be a large part of the total cost for heavy products that are low in value, like sheet aluminum.

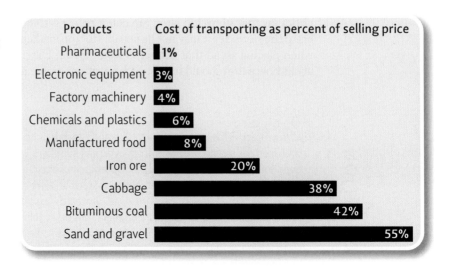

Exhibit 11–5
Transporting Costs as a
Percent of Selling Price
for Different Products

Products	Cost of transporting as percent of selling price
Pharmaceuticals	1%
Electronic equipment	3%
Factory machinery	4%
Chemicals and plastics	6%
Manufactured food	8%
Iron ore	20%
Cabbage	38%
Bituminous coal	42%
Sand and gravel	55%

Transporting can be costly

Transporting costs limit the target markets a marketing manager can serve. Shipping costs increase delivered cost—and that's what really interests customers. Transporting costs add little to the cost of products that are already valuable relative to their size and weight. A case of medicine, for example, might be shipped to a drugstore at low cost. But transporting costs can be a large part of the total cost for heavy products of low value—like many minerals and raw materials. You can imagine that shipping a massive roll of aluminum to a producer of soft-drink cans is an expensive proposition. Exhibit 11–5 shows transporting costs as a percent of the selling price for several products.[13]

Governments may influence transportation

Government often plays an important role in the development of a country's transportation system, including its roads, harbors, railroads, and airports. And different countries regulate transportation differently, although regulation has in general been decreasing.

For example, as part of their move toward unification, most European countries are reducing their transporting regulations. The construction of the tunnel under the English Channel is a dramatic example of the changes taking place. The "chunnel" allows trains to speed between England and the rest of Europe.

As regulations have decreased in the U.S., competition in the transportation industry has increased. As a result, a marketing manager generally has many carriers in one or more modes competing for the firm's transporting business. Or a firm can do its own transporting. So knowing about the different modes is important.[14]

WHICH TRANSPORTING ALTERNATIVE IS BEST?

Transporting function must fit the whole strategy

The transporting function should fit into the whole marketing strategy. But picking the best transporting alternative depends on the product, other physical distribution decisions, and what service level the company wants to offer. The best alternative should provide the level of service (for example, speed and dependability) required at as low a cost as possible. Exhibit 11–6 shows that different modes of transport have different strengths and weaknesses. You can find more detail at the website of the Bureau of Transportation Statistics (www.bts.gov). Low transporting cost is *not* the only criterion for selecting the best mode.[15]

Railroads—large loads moved at low cost

Railroads are still the workhorse of the U.S. transportation system. They carry more freight over more miles than any other mode. However, they account for less than 10 percent of transport revenues. They carry heavy and bulky goods—such as

Exhibit 11-6 Benefits and Limitations of Different Transport Modes

			Transporting Features			
Mode	Cost	Delivery Speed	Number of Locations Served	Ability to Handle a Variety of Goods	Frequency of Scheduled Shipments	Dependability in Meeting Schedules
Truck	High	Fast	Very extensive	High	High	High
Rail	Medium	Average	Extensive	High	Low	Medium
Water	Very low	Very slow	Limited	Very high	Very low	Medium
Air	Very high	Very fast	Extensive	Limited	High	High
Pipeline	Low	Slow	Very limited	Very limited	Medium	High

coal, steel, and chemicals—over long distances at relatively low cost. For example, in the United States the average cost to ship by rail runs about 2 to 3 cents a ton-mile. Because railroad freight usually moves more slowly than truck shipments, it is not as well suited for perishable items or those in urgent demand. Railroads are most efficient at handling full carloads of goods. Less-than-carload (LCL) shipments take a lot of handling, which means they usually move more slowly and at a higher price per pound than carload shipments.[16]

Trucks are more expensive, but flexible and essential

The flexibility and speed of trucks make them better at moving small quantities of goods for shorter distances. They can travel on almost any road. They go where the rails can't. They are also reliable in meeting delivery schedules, which is an essential requirement for logistics systems that provide rapid replenishment of inventory after a sale. In combination, these factors explain why at least 75 percent of U.S. consumer products travel at least part of the way from producer to consumer by truck. And in countries with good highway systems, trucks can give extremely fast service. Trucks compete for high-value items.[17]

Ship it overseas, but slowly

Water transportation is the slowest shipping mode, but it is usually the lowest-cost way of shipping heavy freight. Water transportation is very important for international shipments and often the only practical approach. This explains why port cities

Airfreight is helping to open up international markets for many products, including perishable items that need fast transportation to prevent spoiling.

like Boston, New York City, Rotterdam, Osaka, and Singapore are important centers for international trade.

Inland waterways are important too

Inland waterways (such as the Mississippi River and Great Lakes in the United States and the Rhine and Danube in Europe) are also important, especially for bulky, nonperishable products such as iron ore, grain, and gravel. However, when winter ice closes freshwater harbors, alternate transportation must be used.

Pipelines move oil and gas

Pipelines are used primarily to move oil and natural gas. So pipelines are important in both oil-producing and oil-consuming countries. Only a few major cities in the United States, Canada, Mexico, and Latin America are more than 200 miles from a major pipeline system. However, the majority of the pipelines in the United States are located in the Southwest, connecting oil fields and refineries.

Airfreight is expensive, but fast and growing

The most expensive cargo transport mode is airplane—but it is fast! Airfreight rates are on average three times higher than trucking rates—but the greater speed may offset the added cost.

High-value, low-weight goods—like high-fashion clothing and parts for the electronics industry—are often shipped by air. Perishable products that previously could not be shipped are now being flown across continents and oceans. Flowers and bulbs from Holland, for example, now are jet-flown to points all over the world. And airfreight has become very important for small emergency deliveries, like repair parts, special orders, and business documents that must be somewhere the next day.

But airplanes may cut the total cost of distribution

Using planes may reduce the cost of packing, unpacking, and preparing goods for sale and may help a firm reduce inventory costs by eliminating outlying warehouses. Valuable benefits of airfreight's speed are less spoilage, theft, and damage. Although the *transporting* cost of air shipments may be higher, the *total* cost of distribution may be lower. As more firms realize this, airfreight firms—like DHL Worldwide Express, FedEx, and Emery Air Freight—have enjoyed rapid growth. These firms are playing an especially important role in the growth of international business.[18]

Put it in a container— and move between modes easily

Products often move by several different modes and carriers during their journey. This is especially common for international shipments. Japanese firms, like Sony, ship stereos to the United States, Canada, and Europe by boat. When they arrive at the dock, they are loaded on trains and sent across the country. Then the units are delivered to a wholesaler by truck or rail.

Decisions in the logistics area often provide an opportunity to reduce both costs and environmental impacts. For example, packaging a detergent as a concentrate (with less water to ship, store, and handle) in a smaller package reduces logistics costs and at the same time offers improved benefits for the final consumer. Similarly, the U.S. Environmental Protection Agency's voluntary SmartWay Transport Partnership can help firms reduce fuel costs as well as air pollution.

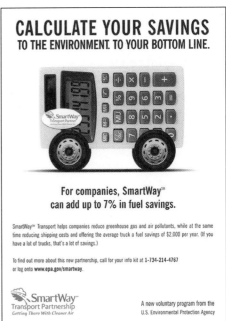

To better coordinate the flow of products between modes, transportation companies like CSX offer customers a complete choice of different transport modes. Then CSX, not the customer, figures out the best and lowest-cost way to shift and share transporting functions between the modes.[19]

Loading and unloading goods several times used to be a real problem. Parts of a shipment would become separated, damaged, or even stolen. And handling the goods, perhaps many times, raised costs and slowed delivery. Many of these problems are reduced with **containerization**—grouping individual items into an economical shipping quantity and sealing them in protective containers for transit to the final destination. This protects the products and simplifies handling during shipping. Some containers are as large as truck bodies.

Piggyback—a ride on two or more modes

Piggyback service means loading truck trailers—or flatbed trailers carrying containers—on railcars to provide both speed and flexibility. Railroads now pick up truck trailers at the producer's location, load them onto specially designed rail flatcars, and haul them as close to the customer as rail lines run. The trailers are then hooked up to a truck tractor and delivered to the buyer's door. Similar services are offered on oceangoing ships—allowing door-to-door service between cities around the world.

Transportation choices affect environmental costs too

Marketing managers must be sensitive to the environmental effects of transportation decisions. Some say trucks cause air pollution in already crowded cities. People who live near airports suffer from noise pollution. A damaged pipeline can spew thousands of gallons of oil before it can be repaired. The Exxon *Valdez* oil spill in Alaska is a dramatic example of the kind of environmental disaster that can happen when a transportation accident occurs.

Many firms are taking steps to reduce these problems. For example, Conoco is building ships with double hulls to reduce the risk of leaks. FedEx and UPS are revamping their fleets to reduce emissions. Some trucking and railroad firms have elaborate safety procedures for dealing with toxic cargo. Today, the public *expects* companies to manufacture, transport, sell, and dispose of products in an environmentally sound manner. Companies are even more sensitive to these issues in an era of terrorism. However, all these efforts increase the cost of distribution.[20]

THE STORING FUNCTION AND MARKETING STRATEGY

Store it and smooth out sales, increase profits and consumer satisfaction

Storing is the marketing function of holding goods so they're available when they're needed. **Inventory** is the amount of goods being stored.

Maintaining the right inventory level is difficult when it's hard to foresee likely demand. Consider what happened when Frito-Lay introduced Tostitos Gold, a thicker version of Tostitos tortilla snack chips that was developed to work well with dips and salsa. Marketing managers did not know if consumers would be willing to pay a premium price, normally reserved for low-fat or organic chips, for Tostitos Gold. To fuel demand, they ran a pair of celebrity ads on the Tostitos Fiesta Bowl national championship football game. In the ads, Jay Leno and Little Richard liven up parties with Tostitos Gold. The ads show how serving the chip "that's extra thick for hearty dips" can inject life into otherwise boring situations. The ads did a better job than expected in stirring interest, and chip lovers were so enthusiastic about Tostitos Gold that the chips were quickly out-of-stock at most supermarkets. The stock-outs resulted in lost sales of about $500,000 a week.[21]

A firm that stocks out when customers are ready to buy may not only lose the sale but also damage the relationship and the possibility of future sales. This problem contributed to Kmart's bankruptcy. Many consumers decided it was no longer a convenient place to shop when stores repeatedly ran out of basic staples that consumers expected to find.

Storing is necessary when production of goods doesn't match consumption. This is common with mass production. Nippon Steel, for example, might produce thousands of steel bars of one size before changing the machines to produce another size. It's often cheaper to produce large quantities of one size, and store the unsold quantity, than to have shorter production runs. Thus, storing goods allows the producer to achieve economies of scale in production.

Storing varies the channel system

Storing allows producers and middlemen to keep stocks at convenient locations, ready to meet customers' needs. In fact, storing is one of the major activities of some wholesalers.

Logistics activities are often invisible to consumers, but a breakdown in distribution customer service can result in dissatisfied consumers and lost business.

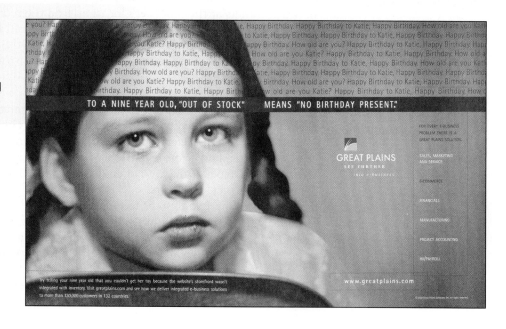

TO A NINE YEAR OLD, "OUT OF STOCK" MEANS "NO BIRTHDAY PRESENT."

290

Exhibit 11–7   Many Expenses Contribute to Total Inventory Cost

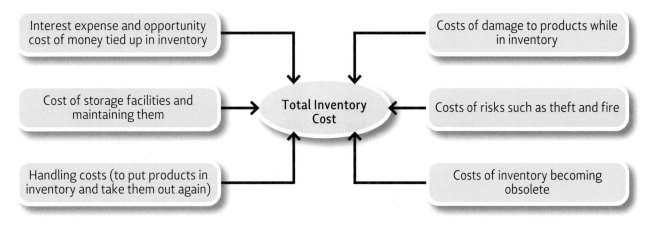

Most channel members provide the storing function for some length of time. Even final consumers store some things for their future needs. Which channel members store the product, and for how long, affects the behavior of all channel members. For example, the producer of Snapper lawn mowers tries to get wholesalers to inventory a wide selection of its machines. That way, retailers can carry smaller inventories since they can be sure of dependable local supplies from wholesalers. And the retailers might decide to sell Snapper—rather than Toro or some other brand that they would have to store at their own expense.

If final customers "store" the product, more of it may be used or consumed. Coke wants customers to buy six-packs and 2-liter bottles. Then consumers have an "inventory" in the refrigerator when thirst hits. Of course, consumers aren't always willing to hold the inventory. In China, for example, Coke had little success until it gave up pushing 2-liter bottles and switched to single-serving 75 ml bottles. Only 1 out of 10 Chinese families has a refrigerator—so they didn't have a good way to store a bottle once it was open.

Goods are stored at a cost

Storing can increase the value of goods, but *storing always involves costs* too. Different kinds of costs are involved. See Exhibit 11–7. Car dealers, for example, must store cars on their lots—waiting for the right customer. The interest expense of money tied up in the inventory is a major cost. In addition, if a new car on the lot is dented or scratched, there is a repair cost. If a car isn't sold before the new models come out, its value drops. There is also a risk of fire or theft—so the retailer must carry insurance. And, of course, dealers incur the cost of leasing or owning the display lot where they store the cars.

In today's competitive markets, most firms watch their inventories closely. They try to cut unnecessary inventory because it can make the difference between a strategy that is profitable and one that is not. On the other hand, a marketing manager must be very careful in making the distinction between unnecessary inventory and inventory needed to provide the distribution service level customers expect.[22]

Rapid response cuts inventory costs

Many firms are finding that they can cut inventory costs and still provide the desired customer service level—if they can reduce the time it takes to replace items that are sold. This is one important reason that JIT and ECR approaches have been widely adopted. The firms involved use EDI, the Internet, and similar computerized approaches to share information and speed up the order cycle and delivery process.

SPECIALIZED STORING FACILITIES MAY BE REQUIRED

New cars can be stored outside on the dealer's lot. Fuel oil can be stored in a specially designed tank. Coal and other raw materials can be stored in open pits. But most products must be stored inside protective buildings. Often, firms can choose among different types of specialized storing facilities. The right choice may reduce costs and serve customers better.

Private warehouses are common

Private warehouses are storing facilities owned or leased by companies for their own use. Most manufacturers, wholesalers, and retailers have some storing facilities either in their main buildings or in a separate location. A sales manager often is responsible for managing a manufacturer's finished-goods warehouse, especially if regional sales branches aren't near the factory.

Firms use private warehouses when a large volume of goods must be stored regularly. Yet private warehouses can be expensive. If the need changes, the extra space may be hard, or impossible, to rent to others.

Public warehouses fill special needs

Public warehouses are independent storing facilities. They can provide all the services that a company's own warehouse can provide. A company might choose a public warehouse if it doesn't have a regular need for space. For example, Tonka Toys uses public warehouses because its business is seasonal. Tonka pays for the space only when it is used. Public warehouses are also useful for manufacturers that must maintain stocks in many locations, including foreign countries. See Exhibit 11–8 for a comparison of private and public warehouses.[23]

Warehousing facilities cut handling costs too

The cost of physical handling is a major storing cost. Goods must be handled once when put into storage and again when removed to be sold. To reduce these costs, modern one-story buildings away from downtown traffic have replaced most old multistory warehouses. They eliminate the need for elevators and permit the use of power-operated lift trucks, battery-operated motor scooters, roller-skating order pickers, electric hoists for heavy items, and hydraulic ramps to speed loading and unloading. Bar codes, universal product code (UPC) numbers, and electronic radio frequency identification (RFID) tags make it easy for computers to monitor inventory, order needed stock, and track storing and shipping costs. For example, a warehouse worker may wear a tiny scanner ring when removing cartons from a shelf so that information in the bar codes can be instantly read and transmitted via a Bluetooth wireless network to the firm's information system. Similarly, RFID tags

Exhibit 11–8
A Comparison of Private and Public Warehouses

Characteristics	Type of Warehouse	
	Private	Public
Fixed investment	Very high	No fixed investment
Unit cost	High if volume is low; very low if volume is very high	Low: Charges are made only for space needed
Control	High	Low managerial control
Adequacy for product line	Highly adequate	May not be convenient
Flexibility	Low: Fixed costs have already been committed	High: Easy to end arrangement

Radio frequency identification (RFID) is an innovative technology that has great potential to improve the tracking of items during shipping and in inventory. It can also provide much more useful data—for information systems and for printed labels.

may transmit detailed information about the contents of a carton as it moves along a conveyor system. Some warehouses also have computer-controlled order-picking systems or conveyor belts that speed the process of locating and assembling the assortment required to fill an order.[24]

THE DISTRIBUTION CENTER—A DIFFERENT KIND OF WAREHOUSE

Is storing really needed?

Discrepancies of assortment or quantity between one channel level and another are often adjusted at the place where goods are stored. It reduces handling costs to regroup and store at the same place—*if both functions are required*. But sometimes regrouping is required when storing isn't.

Don't store it, distribute it

A **distribution center** is a special kind of warehouse designed to speed the flow of goods and avoid unnecessary storing costs. Anchor Hocking moves over a million pounds of its housewares products through its distribution center each day. Faster inventory turnover and easier bulk-breaking reduce the cost of carrying inventory.

Today, the distribution center concept is widely used by firms at all channel levels. Many products buzz through a distribution center without ever tarrying on a shelf; workers and equipment immediately sort the products as they come in and then move them to an outgoing loading dock and the vehicle that will take them to their next stop.

Managers must be innovative to provide customers with superior value

More competitive markets, improved technology, coordination among firms, and efficient new distribution centers are bringing big improvements to the PD area. Yet the biggest challenges may be more basic. As we've emphasized here, physical distribution activities transcend departmental, corporate, and even national boundaries. So taking advantage of ways to improve often requires cooperation all along the channel system. Too often, such cooperation doesn't exist—and changing ingrained ways of doing things is hard. But marketing managers who push for innovations in these areas are likely to win customers away from firms and whole channel systems that are stuck doing things in the old way.[25]

CONCLUSION

This chapter explained the major logistics activities and how they contribute to the value of products by getting them to the place that customers want or need them. *If the distribution customer service level meets their needs and can be provided at a reasonable cost, customers may not even think about the logistics activities that occur behind the scenes. But if products are not available when and where they need to be, a strategy will fail. So decisions in these areas are an important part of Place and marketing strategy planning.

We emphasized the relation between customer service level, transporting, and storing. The physical distribution concept focuses on coordinating all the storing, transporting, and product-handling activities into a smoothly working system—to deliver the desired service level and customer value at the lowest cost.

Marketing managers often want to improve service and may select a higher-cost alternative to improve their marketing mix. The total cost approach might reveal that it is possible to both reduce costs and improve customer service—perhaps by working closely with other members of the supply chain.

We discussed various modes of transporting and their advantages and disadvantages. We also discussed ways to reduce inventory costs. For example, distribution centers are an important way to cut storing and handling costs, and computerized information links—within firms and among firms in the channel—are increasingly important in blending all of the logistics activities into a smooth-running system.

Effective marketing managers make important strategy decisions about physical distribution. Creative strategy decisions may result in lower PD costs while maintaining or improving the customer service level. And production-oriented competitors may not even understand what is happening.

KEY TERMS

logistics, 276

physical distribution (PD), 276

customer service level, 277

physical distribution (PD) concept, 279

total cost approach, 281

supply chain, 282

electronic data interchange (EDI), 284

transporting, 285

containerization, 289

piggyback service, 289

storing, 290

inventory, 290

private warehouses, 292

public warehouses, 292

distribution center, 293

QUESTIONS AND PROBLEMS

1. Explain how adjusting the customer service level could improve a marketing mix. Illustrate.

2. Briefly explain which aspects of customer service you think would be most important for a producer that sells fabric to a firm that manufactures furniture.

3. Briefly describe a purchase you made where the customer service level had an effect on the product you selected or where you purchased it.

4. Discuss the types of trade-offs involved in PD costs, service levels, and sales.

5. Give an example of why it is important for different firms in the supply chain to coordinate logistics activities.

6. Discuss some of the ways computers are being used to improve PD decisions.

7. Explain why a just-in-time delivery system would require a supplier to pay attention to quality control. Give an example to illustrate your points.

8. Discuss the problems a supplier might encounter in using a just-in-time delivery system with a customer in a foreign country.

9. Review the list of factors that affect PD service level in Exhibit 11–3. Indicate which ones are most likely to be improved by EDI links between a supplier and its customers.

10. Explain the total cost approach and why it may cause conflicts in some firms. Give examples of how conflicts might occur between different departments.

11. Discuss the relative advantages and disadvantages of railroads, trucks, and airlines as transport methods.

12. Discuss why economies of scale in transportation might encourage a producer to include a regional merchant wholesaler in the channel of distribution for its consumer product.

13. Discuss some of the ways that air transportation can change other aspects of a Place system.

14. Explain which transport mode would probably be most suitable for shipping the following goods to a large Los Angeles department store:
    a. 300 pounds of Maine lobster.
    b. 15 pounds of screwdrivers from Ohio.
    c. Three dining room tables from High Point, North Carolina.
    d. 500 high-fashion dresses from the fashion district in Paris.
    e. A 10,000-pound shipment of exercise equipment from Germany.
    f. 600,000 pounds of various appliances from Evansville, Indiana.

15. Indicate the nearest location where you would expect to find large storage facilities. What kinds of products would be stored there? Why are they stored there instead of some other place?

16. When would a producer or middleman find it desirable to use a public warehouse rather than a private warehouse? Illustrate, using a specific product or situation.

17. Discuss the distribution center concept. Is this likely to eliminate the storing function of conventional wholesalers? Is it applicable to all products? If not, cite several examples.

18. Clearly differentiate between a warehouse and a distribution center. Explain how a specific product would be handled differently by each.

19. If a retailer operates only from a website and ships all orders by UPS, is it freed from the logistics issues that face traditional retailers? Explain your thinking.

CREATING MARKETING PLANS

The Marketing Plan Coach software on the Student CD includes a sample marketing plan for Hillside Veterinary Clinic. Look through the "Marketing Strategy" section. To provide veterinary care to pets, Hillside needs to have a variety of medical supplies on hand. To handle that, it relies on deliveries from suppliers and its own inventory decisions. It also sells some retail pet products to customers, and that requires a separate set of decisions about how it will handle inventory.

a. What logistics issues related to medical supplies should Hillside consider? Can you think of ways in which delivery from its suppliers or its own inventory decisions will be important in its ability to help its patients?

b. What level of customer service should customers expect with respect to the retail pet products that Hillside sells?

c. What issues are involved in the storage of pet supplies?

SUGGESTED CASES

16. Specialty Timber Company   26. National Packers, Inc.

COMPUTER-AIDED PROBLEM

11. TOTAL DISTRIBUTION COST

Proto Company has been producing various items made of plastic. It recently added a line of plain plastic cards that other firms (such as banks and retail stores) will imprint to produce credit cards. Proto offers its customers the plastic cards in different colors, but they all sell for $40 per box of 1,000. Tom Phillips, Proto's product manager for this line, is considering two possible physical distribution systems. He estimates that if Proto uses airfreight, transportation costs will be $7.50 a box, and its cost of carrying inventory will be 5 percent of total annual sales dollars. Alternatively, Proto could ship by rail for $2 a box. But rail transport will require renting space at four regional warehouses—at $26,000 a year each. Inventory carrying cost with this system will be 10 percent of total annual sales dollars. Phillips prepared a spreadsheet to compare the cost of the two alternative physical distribution systems.

a. If Proto Company expects to sell 20,000 boxes a year, what are the total physical distribution costs for each of the systems?

b. If Phillips can negotiate cheaper warehouse space for the rail option so that each warehouse costs only $20,000 per year, which physical distribution system has the lowest overall cost?

c. Proto's finance manager predicts that interest rates are likely to be lower during the next marketing plan year and suggests that Tom Phillips use inventory carrying costs of 4 percent for airfreight and 7.5 percent for railroads (with warehouse cost at $20,000 each). If interest rates are in fact lower, which alternative would you suggest? Why?

For additional questions related to this problem, see Exercise 11–3 in the *Learning Aid for Use with Essentials of Marketing*, 11th edition.

CHAPTER TWELVE

Retailers, Wholesalers, and Their Strategy Planning

When it comes to buying consumer electronics, are you a demon or an angel? If you don't know the answer, Best Buy probably does. Best Buy is evaluating its portfolio of customers to do a better job of segmenting the angels—customers who buy high-margin items like HDTVs at full price and then add accessories, an extended service contract, and perhaps Geek Squad installation help. Best Buy is cutting free from its demons, the 20 percent of its customers who are unprofitable. Some demons are just aggressive bargain hunters. They clip competitors' ads and demand price matches or "cherry pick" and buy only deeply discounted sale products. But an unscrupulous demon might go further and buy a videocam, use it on a vacation, send in for its rebate, and then return it for a refund. Best Buy is using its customer relationship management (CRM) system to identify demons and take them off its mail promotion list. It's also charging a 15 percent restocking fee on returns, phasing out rebates, and selling returned products on the Internet (which thwarts demons from rebuying their own returns at the lower, open-box price).

On a more positive (and profitable) note, Best Buy is targeting five key segments among its angel customers: upscale suburban moms, affluent professional males, teenage entertainment/gaming enthusiasts, budget-conscious families who are practical technology adopters, and small businesses. Best Buy is analyzing each store's sales data and demographics to identify which segments are most significant. Then it is converting stores, or creating a store-within-a-store, to better focus on those segments. For example, Best Buy's research showed that female shoppers buy 55 percent of electronic items but that they didn't like the Best Buy shopping experience. Now Best Buy is focusing on the most lucrative subset of women shoppers—busy moms in suburban areas. The retailer has a nickname for a woman in this segment. She's "Jill." In the past, sales staff either didn't explain things enough or talked down to and insulted Jill. So now a store that appeals to Jill offers "personal shopping assistants." They help Jill find what she wants in less time. Rather than ask, "How many megapixels do you need?" retrained salespeople ask Jill, "What do you want to photograph?"—and then they suggest what will best suit her needs. And, rather than organize cameras by brand on the shelf, models with similar features are displayed together so that Jill can compare them more easily. Stores that target Jill have learned that she is a great candidate for small appliances when they carry a broader assortment and place them in the regular aisles on easy-to-reach shelves—not off in a corner with the stoves.

Segmented stores differ depending on the target market. Stores that target the affluent male professional ("Barry"), for instance, have a private in-store home theater demo room, complete with comfy leather viewing chairs and popcorn. Barry likes the newest DVDs. So, on days when hot DVDs are released, home theater specialists roam the aisles, look for Barry, and steer him to preview DVDs in the demo room. You know you're an angel—and probably a Barry—if a $12,000 home theater setup is an impulse buy after a visit to the demo room.

Best Buy first tested the targeted stores concept in California. The test stores showed significant increases in sales, profits, and the percentage of customers who made a purchase. The reasons for these successes were measured and analyzed and then rolled out to other similar stores.

Best Buy's marketing strategy planning has not always been so sophisticated. Rather, it started in 1966 as Sound of Music, which was a conventional, limited-line retail store that sold a few select brands of hi-fi equipment. Since then, Best Buy's strategies for growth mirror some of the important trends that have emerged in retailing. Perhaps most basic, it was one of the first stores to adopt the mass-merchandising approach in selling consumer electronics; it focused on lower prices and faster turnover—rather than high markups—to draw customers and increase revenues and profits. Like other retailers who grew by creating multistore chains, it has achieved economies of scale in areas such as buying, promotion, and management. Over time it has scrambled its product line toward innovative and profitable new products—not just stereo equipment but also categories such as digital cameras and camcorders, video systems including HDTV, and now its full line of Geek Squad in-home technical services. Similarly, Best Buy was an innovator among bricks-and-mortar retailers when it quickly took advantage of Internet retailing with a website that complements its stores' offerings. It also has developed state-of-the-art distribution centers and logistics systems, which have reduced its reliance on traditional merchant wholesalers and helped to cut costs. On the other hand, some progressive wholesalers have benefited from these changes. For example, Best Buy uses Internet-based brokers to find construction firms that can help it cut costs when it builds new stores.

Forbes magazine has named Best Buy a "company of the year" and Fortune has ranked it #4 on its list of most admired companies. So you know that it has been doing a lot of things right. But, it is also facing tough competition on several fronts. Further, Best Buy will soon be at a saturation level, with about 1,000 stores in North America. So it is unlikely to continue its growth by opening new outlets in the same broad product-market. It has to generate more profit from the stores that it has—with better targeting and profitable services like Geek Squad. At the same time, it is evaluating new retailing formats, like its Best Buy Mobile concept stores, which sell mobile phones and service, and its EQ-Life concept stores, which may become for health-and-wellness retailing what its current stores are for electronics.[1]

LEARNING OBJECTIVES

Retail and wholesale organizations exist as members of marketing channel systems. But they also do their own strategy planning as they compete for target customers. As the Best Buy case shows, these firms make decisions about Product, Place, Promotion, and Price. This chapter overviews the strategy planning decisions of different types of retailers and wholesalers. The chapter shows how retailing and wholesaling are evolving—to give you a sense of how things may change in the future.

When you finish this chapter, you should:

1. understand how retailers plan their marketing strategies.

2. know about the many kinds of retailers that work with producers and wholesalers as members of channel systems.

3. understand the differences among the conventional and nonconventional retailers—including Internet merchants and others who accept the mass-merchandising concept.

4. understand scrambled merchandising and the "wheel of retailing."

5. see why size or belonging to a chain can be important to a retailer.

6. know what progressive wholesalers are doing to modernize their operations and marketing strategies.

7. know the various kinds of merchant wholesalers and agent middlemen and the strategies they use.

8. understand why retailing and wholesaling have developed in different ways in different countries.

9. see why the Internet is impacting both retailing and wholesaling.

10. understand important new terms (shown in red).

RETAILERS AND WHOLESALERS PLAN THEIR OWN STRATEGIES

In Chapter 10, we discussed the vital role that retailers and wholesalers perform in channel systems. Now we'll look at the decisions that retailers and wholesalers make in developing their own strategies. See Exhibit 12–1. The chapter begins with a discussion of strategy planning for retailers. Retailers must create a marketing mix that provides value for a target market. We also discuss how retailing has evolved and where it stands today, including some important international differences. The chapter concludes by considering strategy planning by different types of wholesalers.

Exhibit 12-1 Marketing Strategy Planning for Retailers and Wholesalers

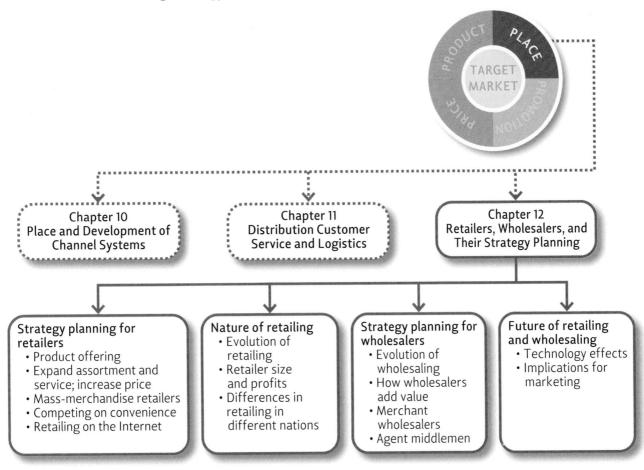

Understand how
retailing and
wholesaling are
evolving

Understanding the how and why of past changes in retailing and wholesaling will help you know what to expect in the future. It will also make it clear that it is the whole strategy, not just one aspect of it, that ultimately is a success or failure. This may seem obvious, but it's a point that many people have ignored—at great cost.

Consider the dramatic changes prompted by the Internet. A few years ago many people were proclaiming that it had changed everything we thought about successful retailing. Yet, many creative ideas for online retailing bombed precisely because managers of dot-coms failed to understand why retailing has evolved as it has. For many consumers and many types of purchases, it won't matter that an online retailer posts low prices for an incredible assortment if there's no way to get customer service, products are not actually available, or it's a hassle to return a green shirt that looked blue on the website. *You* want to avoid the trap of this sort of incomplete thinking!

So in this chapter we'll focus on decisions that apply to all retailers and wholesalers, while highlighting how their strategies are changing.

THE NATURE OF RETAILING

Retailing covers all of the activities involved in the sale of products to final consumers. Retailers range from large chains of specialized stores, like Toys "R" Us, to individual merchants like the woman who sells baskets from an open stall in the central market in Ibadan, Nigeria. Some retailers operate from stores and others operate without a store—by selling online, on TV, with a printed catalog, from vending machines, or even in consumers' homes. Most retailers sell physical goods produced by someone else. But in the case of service retailing—like dry cleaning, fast food, tourist attractions, online bank accounts, or one-hour photo processing—the retailer is also the producer. Because they serve individual consumers, even the largest retailers face the challenge of handling small transactions. And the total number of transactions with consumers is much greater than at other channel levels.

Retailing is crucial to consumers in every macro-marketing system. For example, consumers spend $4.1 *trillion* (that's $4,100,000,000,000!) a year buying goods and services from U.S. retailers.

The nature of retailing and its rate of change are generally related to the stage and speed of a country's economic development. In the U.S., retailing is more varied and dynamic than in most other countries. By studying the U.S. system, you will better understand where retailing is headed in other parts of the world.

PLANNING A RETAILER'S STRATEGY

Retailers interact directly with final consumers—so strategy planning is critical to their survival. If a retailer loses a customer to a competitor, the retailer is the one who suffers. Producers and wholesalers still make *their* sale regardless of which retailer sells the product.

Consumers have reasons for buying from particular retailers

Different consumers prefer different kinds of retailers. But many retailers either don't know or don't care why. All too often, beginning retailers just rent a store and assume customers will show up. As a result, in the U.S. about three-fourths of new retailing ventures fail during the first year. Even an established retailer will quickly lose if its customers find a better way to meet their needs. To avoid this fate, a retailer should carefully identify possible target markets and try to understand why these people buy where they do. That helps the retailer fine-tune its marketing mix to the needs of specific target markets.[2]

Retailer's whole offering is its Product

Most retailers in developed nations sell more than one kind of product. So the brands and product assortment they carry can be critical to success. Yet it's best to take a broader view in thinking about the Product strategy decisions for a retailer's marketing mix. The retailer's *whole* offering—assortment of goods and services, advice from salesclerks, convenience, and the like—is its "Product."

Different consumers have different needs—and needs vary from one purchase situation to another. Which retailer's Product offers the best customer value depends on the needs that a customer wants to satisfy. Whatever the effect of other consumer needs, economic needs are usually very important in shaping the choice of a retailer. Social and individual needs may also come into play. Our discussion of consumer behavior in Chapter 5 applies here.

Features of offering relate to needs

Features of a retailer's offering that relate to economic needs include

- *Convenience* (available hours, finding needed products, fast checkout, location, parking).
- *Product selection* (width and depth of assortment, quality).
- *Special services* (special orders, home delivery, gift wrap, entertainment).
- *Fairness in dealings* (honesty, correcting problems, return privileges, purchase risks).
- *Helpful information* (courteous sales help, displays, demonstrations, product information).
- *Prices* (value, credit, special discounts, taxes or extra charges).

Some features that relate to social and emotional needs include

- *Social image* (status, prestige, "fitting in" with other shoppers).
- *Shopping atmosphere* (comfort, safety, excitement, relaxation, sounds, smells).

In later chapters we'll go into much more detail on the promotion and price decisions that all firms, including retailers and wholesalers, make.

Strategy requires carefully set policies

In developing a strategy a retailer should consciously make decisions that set policies on *all* of the issues above. Each of them can impact a customer's view of the costs and benefits of choosing that retailer. And in combination they differentiate one retailer's offering and strategy from another. If the combination doesn't provide superior value to some target market, the retailer will fail.

Consumer needs relate to segmentation and positioning

Segmentation and positioning decisions are important to retailers. And ignoring either economic or social and emotional needs in those decisions can lead to serious errors in a retailer's strategy planning.

Consider, for example, how the shopping atmosphere may have an emotional effect on a consumer's view of a retailer. How merchandise is displayed, what decorations, colors, and finishes are used, and even the temperature, sounds, and smell of a store all contribute to its "atmospherics" and store image. Tiffany's, for example, offers luxury surroundings and inventive displays to attract upscale consumers—or ones who get an ego boost from Tiffany's prestige image. Of course, interesting surroundings are usually costly, and the prices that consumers pay must cover that expense. An online jewelry retailer offers a completely different shopping experience and deals with a different set of needs. So a retailer's atmosphere and image may be a plus or a minus, depending on the target market. And there's no single right answer about which target market is best. Like Tiffany's, Dollar General has been very profitable. But it has a "budget" image and atmosphere that appeals to working-class customers, many of whom just prefer to shop where they don't feel out of place.[3]

It's best to think of a retailer's Product as its whole offering—including its assortment of goods and services, advice from salespeople, the convenience of shopping, and hours it is available.

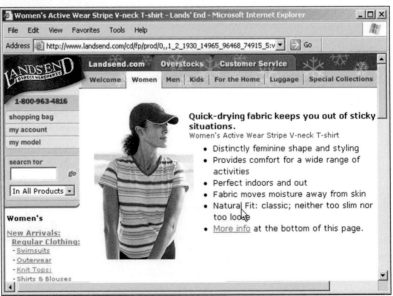

| Different types of retailers emphasize different strategies | Retailers have an almost unlimited number of ways in which to alter their offerings—their marketing mixes—to appeal to a target market. Because of all the variations, it's oversimplifying to classify retailers and their strategies on the basis of a single characteristic—such as merchandise, services, sales volume, or even whether they operate in cyberspace. But a good place to start is by considering basic types of retailers and some differences in their strategies. |

CONVENTIONAL RETAILERS—TRY TO AVOID PRICE COMPETITION

| Single-line, limited-line retailers specialize by product | A hundred and fifty years ago, **general stores**—which carried anything they could sell in reasonable volume—were the main retailers in the United States. But with the growing number of consumer products after the Civil War, general stores couldn't offer enough variety in all their traditional lines. So some stores began specializing in dry goods, apparel, furniture, or groceries. |

Now most *conventional* retailers are **single-line** or **limited-line stores**—stores that specialize in certain lines of related products rather than a wide assortment. Many specialize not only in a single line, such as clothing, but also in a *limited line* within the broader line. Within the clothing line, a retailer might carry *only* shoes, formal wear, or even neckties but offer depth in that limited line.

| Single-line, limited-line stores are being squeezed | The main advantage of limited-line retailers is that they can satisfy some target markets better. Perhaps some are just more conveniently located. But most adjust to suit specific customers. They build a relationship with their customers and earn a position as *the* place to shop for a certain type of product. But these retailers face the costly problem of having to stock some slow-moving items in order to satisfy their target markets. Many of these stores are small—with high expenses relative to sales. So they try to keep their prices up by avoiding competition on identical products. |

Conventional retailers like this have been around for a long time and are still found in every community. They are a durable lot and clearly satisfy some people's needs. In fact, in most countries conventional retailers still handle the vast majority of all retailing sales. However, this situation is changing fast. Nowhere is the change clearer than in the United States. Conventional retailers are being squeezed by retailers who modify their mixes in the various ways suggested in Exhibit 12–2. Let's look closer at some of these other types of retailers.

EXPAND ASSORTMENT AND SERVICE—TO COMPETE AT A HIGH PRICE

| Specialty shops usually sell shopping products | A **specialty shop**—a type of conventional limited-line store—is usually small and has a distinct "personality." Specialty shops sell special types of shopping products, such as high-quality sporting goods, exclusive clothing, cameras, or even antiques. They aim at a carefully defined target market by offering a unique product assortment, knowledgeable salesclerks, and better service. |

Catering to certain types of customers whom the management and salespeople know well simplifies buying, speeds turnover, and cuts costs due to obsolescence and style changes. Specialty shops probably will continue to be a part of the retailing scene as long as customers have varied tastes and the money to satisfy them.[4]

| Department stores combine many limited-line stores and specialty shops | **Department stores** are larger stores that are organized into many separate departments and offer many product lines. Each department is like a separate limited-line store and handles a wide variety of a shopping product, such as men's wear or housewares. They are usually strong in customer services, including credit, merchandise return, delivery, and sales help. |

Department stores are still a major force in big cities. But in the U.S., the number of department stores, the average sales per store, and their share of retail business has declined continuously since the 1970s. Well-run limited-line stores compete with good service and often carry the same brands. In the U.S. and many other countries, mass-merchandising retailers have posed an even bigger threat.[5]

EVOLUTION OF MASS-MERCHANDISING RETAILERS

Mass-merchandising is different from conventional retailing

Conventional retailers think that demand in their area is fixed—and they have a "buy low and sell high" philosophy. Many modern retailers reject this idea. They accept the **mass-merchandising concept**—which says that retailers should offer low prices to get faster turnover and greater sales volumes—by appealing to larger markets. The mass-merchandising concept applies to many types of retailers, including both those that operate stores and those that sell online. But to understand mass-merchandising better, let's look at its evolution from the development of supermarkets and discounters to modern mass-merchandisers like Wal-Mart in the U.S., Tesco in the U.K., and Amazon.com on the Internet.

Supermarkets started the move to mass-merchandising

From a world view, most food stores are relatively small limited-line operations. Shopping for food is inconvenient and expensive. Many Italians, for example, still go to one shop for pasta, another for meat, and yet another for milk. This may seem outdated, but many of the world's consumers don't have access to **supermarkets**—large stores specializing in groceries with self-service and wide assortments.

The basic idea for supermarkets developed in the U.S. during the 1930s Depression. Some innovators introduced self-service to cut costs but provided a broad assortment in large bare-bones stores. Profits came from large-volume sales, not from high traditional markups.[6]

Modern supermarkets carry 40,000 product items and stores average around 45,000 square feet. To be called a supermarket, a store must have annual sales of at least $2 million, but the average supermarket sells about $17 million a year. In the

Although U.S. supermarkets were the first mass-merchandisers, the mass-merchandising concept has now been introduced by many retailers. Single-line mass-merchandisers like Office Depot offer selections and prices that make it difficult for traditional retailers to compete.

U.S., there are about 32,000 supermarkets, and in most areas they are at the saturation level and competition is intense. In many other countries, however, they are just becoming a force.[7]

Supermarkets are planned for maximum efficiency. Scanners at checkout make it possible to carefully analyze the sales of each item and allocate more shelf space to faster-moving and higher-profit items. *Survival* depends on efficiency. Net profits in supermarkets usually run a thin 1 percent of sales *or less!*

Some supermarket operators have opened "super warehouse" stores. These 50,000- to 100,000-square-foot stores carry more items than supermarkets, but they usually put less emphasis on perishable items like produce or meat. These efficiently run, warehouse-like facilities can sell groceries at up to 25 percent less than the typical supermarket price.[8]

Discount houses upset some conventional retailers

After World War II, some retailers started to focus on discount prices. These **discount houses** offered "hard goods" (cameras, TVs, and appliances) at substantial price cuts to customers who would go to the discounter's low-rent store, pay cash, and take care of any service or repair problems themselves. These retailers sold at 20 to 30 percent off the list price being charged by conventional retailers.

In the early 1950s, with war shortages finally over, manufacturer brands became more available. The discount houses were able to get any brands they wanted and to offer wider assortments. At this stage, many discounters turned respectable—moving to better locations and offering more services and guarantees. It was from these origins that today's mass-merchandisers developed.

Mass-merchandisers are more than discounters

Mass-merchandisers are large, self-service stores with many departments that emphasize "soft goods" (housewares, clothing, and fabrics) and staples (like health and beauty aids) but still follow the discount house's emphasis on lower margins to get faster turnover. Mass-merchandisers, like Wal-Mart and Target, have checkout counters in the front of the store and little sales help on the floor. Today, the average mass-merchandiser has nearly 60,000 square feet of floor space, but many new stores are 100,000 square feet or more. Mass-merchandisers have grown rapidly—and they've become the primary place to shop for many frequently purchased consumer products.

By itself, Wal-Mart handles 30 percent or more of the total national sales for whole categories of products. Even if you don't shop at Wal-Mart, Sam Walton (who started the company) has had a big impact on your life. He pioneered the use of high-tech systems to take inefficiencies out of retailing logistics. That brought down costs *and* prices and attracted more customers, which gave Wal-Mart even more clout in pressuring manufacturers to lower prices. Other retailers are still scrambling to catch up. It was competition from Wal-Mart on staples such as health and beauty aids and household cleaning products that prompted firms in the supermarket supply chain to start the Efficient Consumer Response movement we discussed in Chapter 11.

Although these mass-merchandisers are the driving force in much of retailing in the U.S. today, their growth rate in the U.S. has slowed substantially. For future growth, they're expanding internationally.[9]

Supercenters meet all routine needs

Some supermarkets and mass-merchandisers have moved toward becoming **supercenters (hypermarkets)**—very large stores that try to carry not only food and drug items but all goods and services that the consumer purchases *routinely*. These superstores look a lot like a combination of the supermarkets, drugstores, and mass-merchandisers from which they have evolved, but the concept is different. A supercenter is trying to meet *all* the customer's routine needs at a low price. Supercenter operators include Meijer, Fred Meyer, Super Target, and Wal-Mart. In fact, Wal-Mart's supercenters have turned it into the largest food retailer in the U.S.

Supercenters average more than 150,000 square feet and carry about 50,000 items. Their assortment in one place is convenient, but many time-pressured consumers think that the crowds, lines, and "wandering around" time in the store are not.[10]

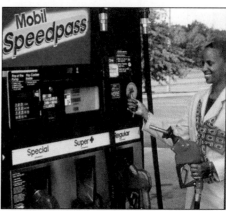

Retailers are hoping that more consumers will become comfortable with self-service checkout and payment—and that it will save shoppers time and help cut operating costs. Self-checkout grocery-store scanners are slowly beginning to catch on, but Mobil's Speedpass system already shows that self-service can be more convenient. A miniature electronic device identifies the driver and signals Speedpass to turn on the pump. The customer doesn't even need a credit card.

New mass-merchandising formats keep coming

The warehouse club is another retailing format that quickly gained popularity. Sam's Club and Costco are two of the largest. Consumers usually pay an annual membership fee to shop in these large, no-frills facilities. Among the 3,500 items per store, they carry food, appliances, yard tools, tires, and other items that many consumers see as homogeneous shopping items and want at the lowest possible price. The growth of these clubs has also been fueled by sales to small-business customers. That's why some people refer to these outlets as wholesale clubs. However, when half or more of a firm's sales are to final consumers, it is classified as a retailer, not a wholesaler.[11]

Single-line mass-merchandisers are coming on strong

Since 1980, many retailers focusing on single product lines have adopted the mass-merchandisers' approach. IKEA (furniture), Home Depot (home improvements), Circuit City (electronics), PetSmart (pet supplies), and Office Depot (office supplies) attract large numbers of customers with their large assortment and low prices in a specific product category. These stores are called *category killers* because it's so hard for less specialized retailers to compete.[12]

It's reasonable to think about the move to 24-hours-a-day online selling—by the established retailers, new firms that never relied on stores, or both—as a next step in the evolution of mass-merchandising. But we'll have a more complete basis for evaluating the strengths and limitations of selling and shopping on the Web if we first look at some retailers who have targeted consumers who want more convenience, even if the price is higher.

SOME RETAILERS FOCUS ON ADDED CONVENIENCE

Convenience (food) stores must have the right assortment

Convenience (food) stores are a convenience-oriented variation of the conventional limited-line food stores. Instead of expanding their assortment, however, convenience stores limit their stock to pickup or fill-in items like bread, milk, beer, and eat-on-the-go snacks. Many also sell gas. Stores such as 7-Eleven and Stop-N-Go aim to fill consumers' needs between trips to a supermarket, and many of them are competing with fast-food outlets. They offer convenience, not assortment, and often charge prices 10 to 20 percent higher than nearby supermarkets. However, as many other retailers have expanded their hours, intense competition is driving down convenience store prices and profits.[13]

| Vending machines are convenient | **Automatic vending** is selling and delivering products through vending machines. Vending machine sales account for only about 1.5 percent of total U.S. retail sales. Yet for some target markets this retailing method can't be ignored.

While vending machines can be costly to operate, consumers like their convenience. Traditionally, soft drinks, candy bars, and snack foods have been sold by vending machines. Now some higher-margin products are beginning to use this channel. Redbox rents DVD movies from vending machines at some McDonald's restaurants. In Japan, it's common to find digital cameras in vending machines, and now Zoom Systems is selling cameras and iPods that way in the U.S.[14]

| Shop at home, in a variety of ways | In-home shopping in the U.S. started in the pioneer days with **door-to-door selling**—a salesperson going directly to the consumer's home. Variations on this approach are still important for firms like Amway and Mary Kay. It meets some consumers' need for convenient personal attention. It is also growing in popularity in some international markets, like China, where it provides salespeople with a good income. In the U.S., it now accounts for less than 1 percent of retail sales. It's getting harder to find someone at home during the day.

On the other hand, time-pressured, dual-career families are a prime target market for **telephone and direct-mail retailing** that allow consumers to shop at home—usually placing orders by mail or via a toll-free long-distance telephone call and charging the purchase to a credit card. Typically, catalogs and ads on TV let customers see the offerings, and purchases are delivered by UPS. Some consumers really like this convenience, especially for products not available in local stores.

This approach reduces costs by using computer mailing lists to target specific customers and by using warehouse-type buildings and limited sales help. And shoplifting—a big expense for most retailers—isn't a problem. In recent years, many of these firms have faced increased competition, slower sales growth, and lower profits. As we will discuss, however, the Internet is opening up new growth opportunities for many of them.[15]

| Put the catalog on cable TV or computer | QVC, Home Shopping Network, and others are succeeding by devoting cable TV channels to home shopping. The explosion in the number of available cable channels and new interactive cable services have helped sales from this approach grow even faster. In addition, QVC has opened a major website on the Internet. However, selling on the Internet is much more than just a variation of selling on TV or from a catalog.[16]

RETAILING ON THE INTERNET

| It's still in its infancy | Internet retailing is still in the growth stages. On the one hand, Internet usage continues to rise and consumer e-commerce purchases have grown at a fast rate. In 1997, consumers spent about $2.7 billion on the Internet. To put that in perspective, it took about 3 percent of Wal-Mart's stores to rack up the same sales. By 2005 that number leaped to over $80 billion, and that does not include spending for travel or financial services, which more than double the amount. But don't confuse the effect that the Internet may have on retailing with the reality of its immediate economic impact. So far, it accounts for only 4 percent of retailing sales dollars. So, in absolute dollars, retailing on the Internet is in its infancy. Thus, it's useful to consider what's different about it today and how it is likely to evolve. See Exhibit 12–3.

Exhibit 12–3 Some Illustrative Differences between Online and In-Store Shopping

Characteristics	Online Shopping	In-Store Shopping
Customer characteristics	Younger, better educated, more upscale	Cross section; depends on store
Day-of-week emphasis	Higher percent of purchases during weekdays	Higher percent of purchases on the weekend
Customer service	Weak but improving	Varies, but usually better than online
Products purchased	More emphasis on one-time purchases	More emphasis on routine purchases
Availability of product	Not available for inspection or immediate use	Usually available for inspection and immediate use
Comparative information about products	Much more extensive, but sometimes poorly organized	Often weak (for example, limited to what is on packages)
Entertainment value	A media experience	Often a social experience
Charges	Product prices often lower, but shipping and handling costly	Product prices and taxes higher, but usually no delivery expense
Shopping hours and preparation	Completely flexible if online access is available	Depends on store and available transportation to store

Moving information versus moving goods

The Internet produces the biggest gains in businesses where faster, lower-cost information flows result in more efficiency. That's what happens in much online B2B e-commerce. On the other hand, sellers in consumer markets have the challenge of getting many small purchases to the *consumer's* place. To date, much of the investment in Internet retailing systems has been directed toward moving information (like orders), not physical goods. It takes, for example, about $25 million to build a world-class website for consumer e-commerce. But it costs about $150 million to build a distribution center and systems to support a large-scale consumer web operation. Therefore, much of the attention so far has been on the "front door" of the Internet "store" and not on the back end of retailing operations, where more of the big costs accumulate. The failure to understand "back door" costs has led to the downfall of many online retailers.

The investments and innovations will come into balance over time, just as they have with other retailing shifts. But demand is what will shape investments in new supply capabilities. So far, the basic patterns of consumer demand have changed slowly.

Convenience takes on new meanings

Traditional thinking about retail stores looked at shopping convenience from the perspective of product assortments and location. On the Internet, by contrast, a consumer can get to a very wide assortment, perhaps from different sellers, by clicking from one website to another. The assortment moves toward being unlimited.

But the Internet makes shopping inconvenient in other ways. You have to plan ahead. You can't touch a product. When you buy something, you've actually just ordered it and you don't have it to use. Someone else has to deliver it, and that involves delays and costs.

More and less information at the same time

On the Internet a consumer can't really inspect a product. Many consumers see that as a disadvantage. On the other hand, in a retail store it's often hard to get good information. At a website detailed product information is just a mouse-click away.

Some consumers look on the Internet for low prices on products that they need, but buying sight-unseen is sometimes a problem. For example, some U.S. consumers order low-price drugs over the Internet from Canada, but as this GlaxoSmithKline ad suggests, the customer doesn't really know where the drugs come from when they're ordered this way. On the other hand, many people have confidence in the brand-name medicines that they buy for their pets at discount prices from www.1800PetMeds.com.

Better information available on the Internet makes many consumers better shoppers, even if they buy in a store rather than online. That's what many web surfers do now. That reduces the risk of buying the wrong thing and the hassles of returning it if there's a problem.

More powerful computers are also opening up many more possibilities for multimedia information—pictures, product-demo videos, and audio explanations. The Internet is also a good medium for messaging and videoconferencing, so consumers can often get help from a real person while at a website. Many failed dot-com retailers figured out too late that cutting costs by dropping human customer service support was a big mistake. They ignored the lessons learned by mass-merchandisers when they tried to do the same thing in their early days.

Lost in the "aisles" of the Internet

If you know what you want, you can usually find it fast on the Internet. You can look for "Revo sunglasses" and get a list of sellers and see pictures of every style made. However, you may get too much information or the wrong information when you do a search. So there is a need for better "virtual malls"—databases with lots of information that can be viewed lots of ways—to make it easier to get information you want and avoid irrelevant clutter. Retailers like Amazon have improved their websites to make progress on this front.

Internet EXERCISE

Go to the websites for Amazon (**www. amazon. com**), Abebooks (**www.abebooks. com**), and Audible (**www.audible.com**). Choose a popular book title and search for it at each site. Is it available at each site? In what formats? New and used? How do prices compare? Are there shipping charges? What additional information is provided at each site? How are the sites similar and how are they different?

The costs are sometimes misleading

The Internet makes it easy to compare products and prices from different sellers. That has put price pressure on Internet sellers who have not figured out how else to differentiate what they offer. For more expensive items, a discount price may offset delivery costs. That often isn't the case with less-expensive items. Low-cost ways of handling post-purchase deliveries need to be developed for the Internet to

Many retail chains, like Best Buy, are combining "clicks and mortar" to meet consumers' needs better than would be possible with only an online website. However, specialty retailers, like Home Theater Direct, compete primarily for online customers by offering a focused product line and useful product information that is not conveniently available at stores in customers' local markets.

be really practical for everyday purchases. However, some firms are making this work. For example, Tesco in England sells groceries from a website and delivers them within 24 hours.

Retailers are refining their online efforts

At least four distinct approaches are used by different online retailers. Retailers who have bricks-and-mortar stores at many locations often use a website to *supplement* their stores and the other types of promotion they use. For example, Target and Home Depot are large chains that use their websites mainly to drive traffic into their stores. Retailers who use this approach often offer a more limited product assortment at the website than in stores. The website promotes select items that have the highest profit margins. For example, Target's site emphasizes products such as bedding and apparel rather than household supplies.

In contrast, some retailers take a strong multichannel approach and use their websites to *complement* their stores or catalogs. This is more common among retailers who have higher profit margins on the lines they sell. For example, Williams-Sonoma sells upscale housewares. It closely coordinates its online, catalog, and store outlets so that they focus on different benefits. For example, at its stores customers are free to handle items and see how they look next to each other, while the website provides more detailed product information and convenient ordering.

Among online-only retailers, some try to differentiate their offering primarily by being *more efficient* than competitors. They focus on offering consumers low prices on products that are in very competitive product-markets—like books, computers, and shoes—that have lower profit margins. These online sellers, including Amazon, Dell, and Zappos, need high sales volume to offset the large investments they must make in their e-commerce and logistics systems.

The essence of the fourth online approach is to differentiate by being very *focused* on the specific needs of target customers, many of whom don't have similar offerings available in their local markets. Good examples include outdoor-gear seller L.L. Bean and jeweler Ross-Simons. Retailers in this category typically use the Web to supplement a catalog operation or a limited number of stores. Smaller companies who can't afford expensive brand-building advertising campaigns often use this approach also. They rely on targeted direct-mail (or e-mail) promotions to acquire new customers and provide exceptional customer service to retain customers they already have.[17]

And the Winning Bidder Is eBay

There have been lots of innovations in retailing, but most people wouldn't put flea markets or estate auctions in among them. But, if you take those two ideas and then throw in a state-of-the-art website and more than 70 million active buyers and sellers, you get eBay, an innovative online shopping mall. Today, eBay operates in over 30 countries and helps customers complete more than $40 billion in exchanges a year. It sells a car every two minutes, a CD every 7 seconds, and takes its cut of every transaction. eBay is a retailing innovation that has proved very profitable.

At the eBay "shopping mall," sellers offer products ranging from once-worn wedding gowns to collectible trading cards as well as practical items like computer parts, cookware, and cars. eBay's basic success comes from identifying and meeting a need that previously wasn't being met; it helps individual buyers and sellers connect. And it does it well because it uses the latest technology to continually improve its service. The popular auction site allows consumers to find and bid on items they need. The highest bidder pays the seller—often using eBay's secure online PayPal system. The seller then ships the product. At the end, buyers and sellers leave positive or negative "feedback" for each other—building either good or bad reputations on both sides. Sellers with high positive marks earn greater trust and generate higher bids.

While many eBay sales are true auctions, eBay also has a "buy it now" feature that allows a buyer to skip the bidding by agreeing to pay a higher set price. eBay's virtual mall provides links to more than 180,000 stores.

Despite eBay's successes, in the fast-moving world of Internet retailing, it would be dangerous for eBay to rest on its laurels. Amazon, Google, and Yahoo! are formidable competitors in the online auction world, and others are strong outside the United States. In fact, opportunities for future growth are likely to be greatest in international markets. Yahoo! grabbed an early lead in China by partnering with the auction pioneer Alibaba Taobao. eBay is doing some partnering of its own. It acquired Skype, the online telephone service company, hoping to make it easier for buyers and sellers to talk. Skype's strength has been in international markets, and eBay's greatest strength has been in the U.S., where Skype had little penetration. So the combined companies should be even stronger in going after future growth.[18]

WHY RETAILERS EVOLVE AND CHANGE

The wheel of retailing keeps rolling

The **wheel of retailing theory** says that new types of retailers enter the market as low-status, low-margin, low-price operators and then, if successful, evolve into more conventional retailers offering more services with higher operating costs and higher prices. Then they're threatened by new low-status, low-margin, low-price retailers—and the wheel turns again. Department stores, supermarkets, and mass-merchandisers went through this cycle. Some Internet sellers are on this path.

The wheel of retailing theory, however, doesn't explain all major retailing developments. Vending machines entered as high-cost, high-margin operations. Convenience food stores are high-priced. Suburban shopping centers don't emphasize low price.

Scrambled merchandising— mixing product lines for higher profits

Conventional retailers tend to specialize by product line. But most modern retailers are moving toward **scrambled merchandising**—carrying any product lines they think they can sell profitably. Supermarkets and drugstores sell anything they can move in volume—panty hose, phone cards, one-hour photo processing, motor oil, potted plants, and computer software. Mass-merchandisers don't just sell everyday items but also cell phones, plasma TVs, and jewelry.[19]

Exhibit 12-4 Retailer Life Cycles—Timing and Years to Market Maturity

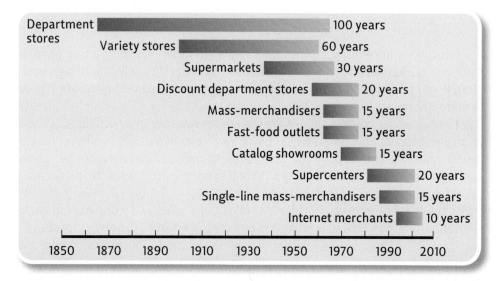

Department stores — 100 years
Variety stores — 60 years
Supermarkets — 30 years
Discount department stores — 20 years
Mass-merchandisers — 15 years
Fast-food outlets — 15 years
Catalog showrooms — 15 years
Supercenters — 20 years
Single-line mass-merchandisers — 15 years
Internet merchants — 10 years

1850 1870 1890 1910 1930 1950 1970 1990 2010

Product life-cycle concept applies to retailer types too

A retailer with a new idea may have big profits—for a while. But if it's a really good idea, the retailer can count on speedy imitation and a squeeze on profits. Other retailers will copy the new format or scramble their product mix to sell products that offer them higher margins or faster turnover. That puts pressure on the original firm to change or lose its market.

Some conventional retailers are in decline as these life and death cycles continue. Recent innovators, like the Internet merchants, are still in the market growth stage. See Exhibit 12–4. Some retailing formats that are mature in the United States are only now beginning to grow in other countries.

Ethical issues may arise

Most retailers face intense competitive pressure. The desperation that comes with such pressure has pushed some retailers toward questionable marketing practices.

Critics argue, for example, that retailers too often advertise special sale items to bring price-sensitive shoppers into the store or to a website but then don't stock enough to meet demand. Other retailers are criticized for pushing consumers to trade up to more expensive items. What is ethical and unethical in situations like these, however, is subject to debate. Retailers can't always anticipate demand perfectly, and deliveries may not arrive on time. Similarly, trading up may be a sensible part of a strategy—if it's done honestly.

The marketing concept should guide firms away from unethical treatment of customers. However, a retailer on the edge of going out of business may lose perspective on the need to satisfy customers in both the short and the long term.[20]

Ethics QUESTION

Farmers in poor countries get very little money for crops—such as coffee, cocoa, and bananas—that they grow for export. Some consumers in prosperous nations are willing to pay retailers higher prices for "fair trade" goods so that the farmers receive greater compensation. But critics question whether fair trade works as it should. For example, Sainsbury's is a popular British food retailer. It was charging $2.74 per pound for "fair trade" bananas versus only $.69 per pound for regular bananas. Farmers, however, only got $.16 extra from that $2.05 price premium. Critics charge that Sainsbury's makes more from the "fair trade" promotion than the farmers it is supposed to help. Many retailers have similar programs. Do you think that Sainsbury's is acting ethically? What do you think Sainbury's and other similar retailers should do? Why?[21]

RETAILER SIZE AND PROFITS

A few big retailers do most of the business

The large number of retailers (1,115,906) might suggest that retailing is a field of small businesses. To some extent this is true. When the last census of retailers was published, over 56 percent of all the retail stores in the United States had annual sales of less than $1 million. But that's only part of the story. Those same retailers accounted for less than 8 cents of every $1 in retail sales!

The larger retail stores—those selling more than $5 million annually—do most of the business. Only about 11 percent of the retail stores are this big, yet they account for almost 70 percent of all retail sales. Many small retailers are being squeezed out of business.[22]

Big chains are building market clout

The main way for a retailer to achieve economies of scale is with a corporate chain. A **corporate chain** is a firm that owns and manages more than one store—and often it's many. Chains have grown rapidly and now account for about half of all retail sales. You can expect chains to continue to grow and take business from independent stores.

Large chains use central buying for different stores. They take advantage of quantity discounts and develop their own efficient distribution centers. They can use computer networks to control inventory costs and stock-outs. They may also spread promotion, information technology, and management costs to many stores. Retail chains also have their own dealer brands. Many of these chains are becoming powerful members, or channel captains, in their channel systems. In fact, the most successful of these big chains, like Home Depot and Wal-Mart, control access to so many consumers that they have the clout to dictate almost every detail of relationships with their suppliers.[23]

Independents form chains too

Competitive pressure from corporate chains encouraged the development of both cooperative chains and voluntary chains. **Cooperative chains** are retailer-sponsored groups—formed by independent retailers—that run their own buying organizations and conduct joint promotion efforts. Cooperative chains face a tough battle. Some, like True Value Hardware, are still adapting as they identify the weakness of corporate chains. For example, ads remind consumers that they don't need to waste a half-hour lost in a big store to pick up some simple item.

Many independent retail stores are finding it difficult to compete with the large retail chains that now account for the majority of all retail sales in the U.S. Lowe's home-improvement warehouses, for example, offer huge product assortments at good prices and are open long hours. However, some independents are working together to compete more effectively. For example, Ace Hardware is a wholesaler-sponsored voluntary chain that provides store owners with some of the advantages of a corporate chain operation—without giving up their independence.

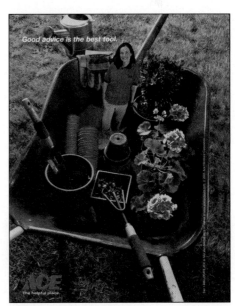

Voluntary chains are wholesaler-sponsored groups that work with "independent" retailers. Some are linked by contracts stating common operating procedures and requiring the use of common storefront designs, store names, and joint promotion efforts. Examples include SuperValu in groceries and Ace in hardware.

Franchisors form chains too

In a **franchise operation**, the franchisor develops a good marketing strategy, and the retail franchise holders carry out the strategy in their own units. Each franchise holder benefits from its relationship with the larger company and its experience, buying power, promotion, and image. In return, the franchise holder usually signs a contract to pay fees and commissions and to strictly follow franchise rules designed to continue the successful strategy.

Franchise holders' sales account for about half of all retail sales. One reason is that franchising is especially popular with service retailers, a fast-growing sector of the economy.[24]

DIFFERENCES IN RETAILING IN DIFFERENT NATIONS

New ideas spread across countries

New retailing approaches that succeed in one part of the world are often quickly adapted to other countries. Self-service approaches that started with supermarkets in the United States are now found in retail operations worldwide. The supercenter concept, on the other hand, initially developed in Europe.

Mass-merchandising requires mass markets

The low prices, selections, and efficient operations offered by mass-merchandisers might be attractive to consumers everywhere. But consumers in less-developed nations often don't have the income to support mass distribution. The small shops that survive in these economies sell in very small quantities, often to a small number of consumers.

Some countries block change

The political and legal environment severely limits the evolution of retailing in some nations. Japan is a prime example. For years its Large Store Law—aimed at protecting the country's politically powerful small shopkeepers—has been a real barrier to retail change. The law restricts development of large stores by requiring special permits, which are routinely denied.

Japan is taking steps to change the Large Store Law. One such change allowed Toys "R" Us to move into the Japanese market. Even so, most experts believe that it will be years before Japan moves away from its system of small, limited-line shops. Many countries in other parts of Asia and South America impose similar restrictions. On the other hand, the European Union is prompting member countries to drop such rules.[25]

WHAT IS A WHOLESALER?

It's hard to define what a wholesaler is because there are so many different wholesalers doing different jobs. Some of their activities may even seem like manufacturing. As a result, some wholesalers describe themselves as "manufacturer and dealer." Some like to identify themselves with such general terms as *merchant, agent, dealer,* or *distributor.* And others just take the name commonly used in their trade—without really thinking about what it means.

To avoid a long technical discussion on the nature of wholesaling, we'll use the U.S. Bureau of the Census definition:

Wholesaling is concerned with the *activities* of those persons or establishments that sell to retailers and other merchants, or to industrial, institutional, and commercial users, but that do not sell in large amounts to final consumers.

So **wholesalers** are firms whose main function is providing wholesaling activities. Wholesalers sell to all of the different types of organizational customers described in Chapter 6.

Wholesaling activities are just variations of the basic marketing functions—gathering and providing information, buying and selling, grading, storing, transporting, financing, and risk taking—we discussed in Chapter 1. You can understand wholesalers' strategies better if you look at them as members of channels. They add value by doing jobs for their customers and for their suppliers.

WHOLESALING IS CHANGING WITH THE TIMES

A hundred years ago wholesalers dominated distribution channels in the United States and most other countries. The many small producers and small retailers needed their services. This situation still exists in less-developed economies. However, in the developed nations, as producers became larger many bypassed the wholesalers. Similarly, large retail chains often take control of jobs that were previously handled by wholesalers. Now e-commerce is making it easier for producers and customers to "connect" without having a wholesaler in the middle of the exchange.

In light of these changes, many people have predicted a gloomy future for wholesalers. In the 1980s that seemed to be the pattern. Now, however, many wholesalers are adapting rapidly and finding new ways to add value in the channel. For example, some of the biggest B2B e-commerce sites on the Internet are wholesaler operations, and many wholesalers are enjoying significant growth.

Producing value and profits, not chasing orders

Progressive wholesalers are becoming more concerned with their customers and with their place in channel systems. Many are using technology to offer better service. Others work more closely to understand customers' needs and design a marketing mix that adds real value in the channel.

Frieda's, Inc., is a good example; it is a wholesaler that each year supplies supermarkets and food-service distributors with $30 million worth of exotic fruits and vegetables. It was started by Frieda Caplan in 1962; now, her daughters Karen and Jackie run the company. It is a sign of the marketing savvy of these women that artichokes, Chinese donut peaches, alfalfa sprouts, and spaghetti squash no longer seem very exotic. All of these crops were once viewed as unusual. Few farmers grew them, supermarkets didn't handle them, and consumers didn't know about them. Caplan helped to change all of that. She realized that some supermarkets wanted to attract less price-sensitive consumers who preferred more interesting choices in the hard-to-manage produce department. So she looked for products that would help her retailer-customers meet this need. For example, the funny looking kiwi fruit with its fuzzy brown skin was popular in New Zealand but virtually unknown to U.S. consumers. Caplan worked with small farmer-producers to ensure that she could provide her retailer-customers with a steady supply. She packaged kiwi with interesting recipes and promoted it to consumers. Because of her efforts, demand has grown and most supermarkets now carry kiwi. That has attracted competition from larger wholesalers. But that doesn't bother the Caplans. When one of their specialty items becomes a commodity with low profit margins, another novel item replaces it. In a typical year, Frieda's introduces about 40 new products—like Asian pears, kiwano melons, sun-dried yellow tomatoes, and hot Asian chiles.

Frieda's also has an advantage because of the special services it provides. It was the first wholesaler to routinely use airfreight for orders and send produce managers a weekly "hot sheet" about the best sellers. The Caplans also use seminars and press releases to inform produce buyers about how to improve sales. For example, one attention-getting story about Frieda's "El Mercado de Frieda" line helped retailers do a better job serving Hispanic customers. Similarly, Frieda's website attracts final consumers with helpful tips and recipes. And now that more consumers are eating out, Frieda's has established a separate division to serve the special needs of food-service distributors.[26]

Perhaps good-bye to some

Not all wholesalers are progressive, and less efficient ones will fail. Some wholesalers will disappear as the functions they provided in the past are shifted and shared in different ways in the channel. Cost-conscious buyers for Wal-Mart, Lowe's, and other chains are refusing to deal with some of the middlemen who represent small producers. They want to negotiate directly with the producer. Similarly, many manufacturers see advantages in having closer direct relationships with fewer suppliers—and they're paring out weaker vendors. Efficient delivery services like DHL, UPS, and FedEx are also making it easy for many producers to ship directly to their customers, even ones in foreign markets. The Internet is putting pressure on wholesalers whose primary role is providing information to bring more buyers and sellers together.[27]

Is it an ethical issue?

All of this is squeezing some wholesalers out of business. Some critics, including many of the wounded wholesalers, argue that it's unethical for powerful suppliers or customers to simply cut out wholesalers who have spent money and time, perhaps decades, developing markets. Contracts between channel members and laws sometimes define what is or is not legal. But the ethical issues are often more ambiguous.

For example, Amana notified Cooper Distributing Co. that it intended to cancel their distribution agreement in 10 days. Cooper had handled Amana appliances for 30 years, and Amana products represented 85 percent of Cooper's sales. Amana's explanation to Cooper? "We just think we can do it better."

Situations like this arise often. They may be cold-hearted, but are they unethical? We argue that it isn't fair to cut off the relationship with such short notice. But most wholesalers realize that their business is *always* at risk—if they don't perform channel functions better or cheaper than their suppliers or customers can do themselves.[28]

Survivors will need effective strategies

The wholesalers who do survive will need to be efficient, but that doesn't mean they'll all have low costs. Some wholesalers' higher operating expenses result from the strategies they select, including the special services they offer to *some* customers.

WHOLESALERS ADD VALUE IN DIFFERENT WAYS

Exhibit 12–5 compares the number, sales volume, and operating expenses of some major types of wholesalers. The differences in operating expenses suggest that each of these types performs, or does not perform, certain wholesaling functions. But which

Exhibit 12–5
U.S. Wholesale Trade by
Type of Wholesale
Operation

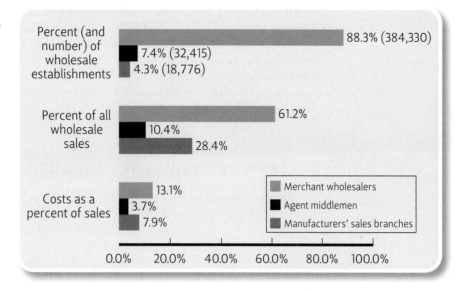

ones and why? And why do manufacturers use merchant wholesalers—costing 13.1 percent of sales—when agent middlemen cost only 3.7 percent?

To answer these questions, we must understand what these wholesalers do and don't do. Exhibit 12–6 gives a big-picture view of the major types of wholesalers we'll discuss. There are lots more specialized types, but our discussion will give you a sense of the diversity. Note that a major difference between merchant and agent wholesalers is whether they *own* the products they sell. Before discussing these wholesalers, we'll briefly consider producers who handle their own wholesaling activities.

Manufacturers' sales branches are considered wholesalers

Manufacturers who just take over some wholesaling activities are not considered wholesalers. However, when they have **manufacturers' sales branches**—warehouses that producers set up at separate locations away from their factories—they're classified as wholesalers by the U.S. Census Bureau and by government agencies in many other countries.

Exhibit 12–6   Types of Wholesalers

In the United States, these manufacturer-owned branch operations account for about 4.3 percent of wholesale facilities—but they handle 28.4 percent of total wholesale sales. One reason sales per branch are so high is that the branches are usually placed in the best market areas. This also helps explain why their operating costs, as a percent of sales, are often lower. It's also easier for a manufacturer to coordinate information and logistics functions with its own branch operations than with independent wholesalers.[29]

MERCHANT WHOLESALERS ARE THE MOST NUMEROUS

Merchant wholesalers own (take title to) the products they sell. They often specialize by certain types of products or customers. For example, Fastenal is a wholesaler that specializes in distributing threaded fasteners used by a variety of manufacturers. It owns (takes title to) the fasteners for some period before selling to its customers. If you think all merchant wholesalers are fading away, Fastenal is proof that they can serve a needed role. In the last decade Fastenal's profits have grown at about the same pace as Microsoft's.[30]

Exhibit 12–5 shows that almost 90 percent of the wholesaling establishments in the United States are merchant wholesalers—and they handle over 61 percent of wholesale sales. Merchant wholesalers are even more common in other countries. Japan is an extreme example. Products are often bought and sold by a series of merchant wholesalers on their way to the business user or retailer.[31]

Service wholesalers provide all the functions

Service wholesalers are merchant wholesalers that provide all the wholesaling functions. Within this basic group are three types: (1) general merchandise, (2) single-line, and (3) specialty.

General merchandise wholesalers are service wholesalers that carry a wide variety of nonperishable items such as hardware, electrical supplies, furniture, drugs, cosmetics, and automobile equipment. With their broad line of convenience and shopping products, they serve hardware stores, drugstores, and small department stores. *Mill supply houses* operate in a similar way, but they carry a broad variety of accessories and supplies to serve the needs of manufacturers.

Single-line (or general-line) wholesalers are service wholesalers that carry a narrower line of merchandise than general merchandise wholesalers. For example, they might carry only food, apparel, or certain types of industrial tools or supplies. In consumer products, they serve the single- and limited-line stores. In business products, they cover a wider geographic area and offer more specialized service.

Specialty wholesalers are service wholesalers that carry a very narrow range of products and offer more information and service than other service wholesalers. For example, a firm that produces specialized lights for vehicles might rely on specialty wholesalers to help reach auto makers in different countries. A consumer products specialty wholesaler might carry only health foods instead of a full line of groceries. Some limited-line and specialty wholesalers are growing by helping independent retailer-customers compete with mass-merchandisers. But in general, many consumer-products wholesalers have been hit hard by

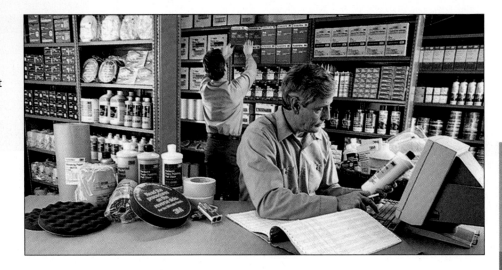

3M produces 1,600 products that are used by auto body repair shops in the U.S., Europe, Japan, and other countries. To reach this target market, 3M works with hundreds of specialty wholesalers.

the growth of retail chains that set up their own distribution centers and deal directly with producers.

A specialty wholesaler of business products might limit itself to fields requiring special technical knowledge or service. Richardson Electronics is an interesting example. It specializes in distributing replacement parts, such as electron tubes, for old equipment that many manufacturers still use on the factory floor. Richardson describes itself as "on the trailing edge of technology," but many of its customers operate in countries where new technologies are not yet common. Richardson gives them easy access to information from its website (www.rell.com) and makes its products available quickly by stocking them in locations around the world.[32]

Limited-function wholesalers provide some functions

Limited-function wholesalers provide only *some* wholesaling functions. In the following paragraphs, we briefly discuss the main features of these wholesalers. Although less numerous in some countries, these wholesalers are very important for some products.

Cash-and-carry wholesalers want cash

Cash-and-carry wholesalers operate like service wholesalers—except that the customer must pay cash. In the U.S., big warehouse clubs have taken much of this business. But cash-and-carry operators are common in less-developed nations where very small retailers handle the bulk of retail transactions. Full-service wholesalers often refuse to grant credit to small businesses that may have trouble paying their bills.

Drop-shippers do not handle the products

Drop-shippers own (take title to) the products they sell—but they do *not* actually handle, stock, or deliver them. These wholesalers are mainly involved in selling. They get orders and pass them on to producers. Then the producer ships the order directly to the customer. Drop-shippers commonly sell bulky products (like lumber) for which additional handling would be expensive and possibly damaging. Drop-shippers in the U.S. are already feeling the squeeze from buyers and sellers connecting directly via the Internet. But the progressive ones are fighting back by setting up their own websites and getting fees for referrals.

Truck wholesalers deliver—at a cost

Truck wholesalers specialize in delivering products that they stock in their own trucks. Their big advantage is that they promptly deliver perishable products that regular wholesalers prefer not to carry. A 7-Eleven store that runs out of potato chips on a busy Friday night doesn't want to be out of stock all weekend!

The Internet has helped many wholesalers expand their market opportunities. For example, databases at Orchard Network help producers identify a wholesaler that might be a good channel partner and help business customers find the right wholesaler-supplier.

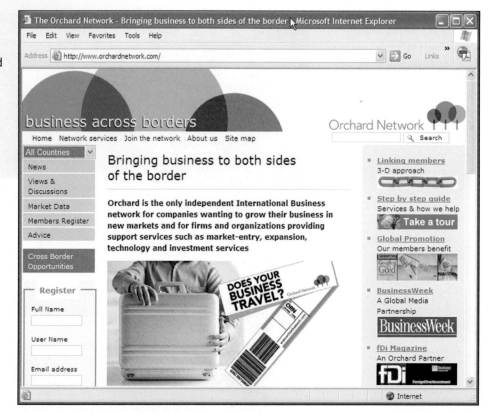

Truck wholesalers help retailers keep a tight rein on inventory, and they seem to meet a need.

Rack jobbers sell hard-to-handle assortments

Rack jobbers specialize in hard-to-handle assortments of products that a retailer doesn't want to manage—and rack jobbers usually display the products on their own wire racks. For example, a grocery store or mass-merchandiser might rely on a rack jobber to decide which paperback books or magazines it sells. The wholesaler knows which titles sell in the local area and applies that knowledge in many stores.

Catalog wholesalers reach outlying areas

Catalog wholesalers sell out of catalogs that may be distributed widely to smaller industrial customers or retailers that might not be called on by other middlemen. Customers place orders at a website or by mail, e-mail, fax, or telephone. These wholesalers sell lines such as hardware, jewelry, sporting goods, and computers. For example, Inmac uses a catalog that is printed in six languages and a website (www.inmac.com) to sell a complete line of computer accessories. Many of its customers don't have a local wholesaler, but they can place orders from anywhere in the world. Most catalog wholesalers quickly adapted to the Internet. It fits what they were already doing and makes it easier. But they're facing more competition too; the Internet allows customers to compare prices from more sources of supply.[33]

AGENT MIDDLEMEN ARE STRONG ON SELLING

They don't own the products

Agent middlemen are wholesalers who do *not* own the products they sell. Their main purpose is to help in buying and selling. Agent middlemen normally specialize by customer type and by product or product line. But they usually provide even fewer functions than the limited-function wholesalers. They operate at relatively low cost—sometimes 2 to 6 percent of their selling price—or less in the case of website-based agents who simply bring buyers and sellers together. Worldwide, the role of agent

A few years ago, auctions were used for only a few specialized product categories. But now online services like eBay are making auctions a convenient and popular approach for buying and selling many different types of new and used products.

middlemen is rapidly being transformed by the Internet. Those who didn't get on board this fast-moving train have been left behind.

They are important in international trade

Agent middlemen are common in international trade. Many markets have only a few well-financed merchant wholesalers. The best many producers can do is get local representation through agents and then arrange financing through banks that specialize in international trade.

Agent middlemen are usually experts on local business customs and regulations in their own countries. Sometimes a marketing manager can't work through a foreign government's red tape without the help of a local agent.

Manufacturers' agents—freewheeling sales reps

Manufacturers' agents sell similar products for several noncompeting producers—for a commission on what is actually sold. Such agents work almost as members of each company's sales force, but they're really independent middlemen. More than half of all agent middlemen are manufacturers' agents.

Their big plus is that they already call on some customers and can add another product line at relatively low cost—and at no cost to the producer until something sells!

Agents can be especially useful for introducing new products. For this service, they may earn 10 to 15 percent commission. (In contrast, their commission on large-volume established products may be quite low—perhaps only 2 percent.) A 10 to 15 percent commission rate may seem small for a new product with low sales. Once a product sells well, however, a producer may think the rate is high and begin using its own sales reps.

Export or **import agents** are basically manufacturers' agents who specialize in international trade. These agent middlemen operate in every country and help international firms adjust to unfamiliar market conditions in foreign markets.

Manufacturers' reps will continue to play an important role in businesses that need an agent to perform order-getting tasks. But manufacturers' reps everywhere are feeling pressure when it comes to routine business contacts. More producers are turning to telephone selling, websites, e-mail, teleconferencing, and faxes to contact customers directly.[34]

Brokers provide information

Brokers bring buyers and sellers together. Brokers usually have a *temporary* relationship with the buyer and seller while a particular deal is negotiated. They are especially useful when buyers and sellers don't come into the market very often. The broker's product is information about what buyers need and what supplies are available. If the transaction is completed, they earn a commission from whichever party hired them. **Export** and **import brokers** operate like other brokers, but they specialize in bringing together buyers and sellers from different countries. Smart brokers quickly saw new opportunities to expand their reach by using the Internet. As the Internet causes consolidation, it will also provide more value. A smaller number of cyberbrokers will cut costs and dominate the business with larger databases of buyers and sellers.

Selling agents—almost marketing managers

Selling agents take over the whole marketing job of producers—not just the selling function. A selling agent may handle the entire output of one or more producers, even competing producers, with almost complete control of pricing, selling, and advertising. In effect, the agent becomes each producer's marketing manager.

Financial trouble is one of the main reasons a producer calls in a selling agent. The selling agent may provide working capital but may also take over the affairs of the business. But selling agents also work internationally. A **combination export manager** is a blend of manufacturers' agent and selling agent—handling the entire export function for several producers of similar but noncompeting lines.

Auction companies speed up the sale

Auction companies provide a place where buyers and sellers can come together and bid to complete a transaction. Traditionally they were important in certain lines—such as livestock, fur, tobacco, and used cars—where demand and supply conditions change rapidly.

Auto Auction Network Limited (Aucsat), based in New Zealand, is a good example of a progressive auction company that put the bid process on the Internet. Its very successful used-car auction runs from a website (www.aucsat.co.nz). It provides bidders with a thorough online rating of the quality of each car. In the past, most auction companies said, "What you see is what you get." Because the ratings add value and are credible, Aucsat attracts more dealers. The Internet has spurred growth of all sorts of auction companies in lines of business where auctions have previously not been common.[35]

WHAT WILL HAPPEN TO RETAILERS AND WHOLESALERS IN THE FUTURE?

A common theme in this chapter—and the two before it—is that channels of distribution are in the midst of dynamic changes. There have been dramatic improvements in logistics, the Internet, and e-commerce. But before all of this, the evolution of retailing and wholesaling was ongoing. Middlemen that find new and better ways to add value prosper.

In time, more revolutionary change may come. Imagine, for example, what it would take for you—and everyone you know—to do most of your routine shopping on the Internet. What new marketing functions would be needed, and who would provide them?[36]

Let's admit it. You can only speculate about what changes may come. But perhaps it's good to speculate a little. The way markets work in the future will depend on creative innovations that people like you imagine, analyze, and ultimately turn into profitable marketing strategies.[36]

CONCLUSION

Modern retailing is scrambled—and we'll probably see more changes in the future. In such a dynamic environment, a producer's marketing manager must choose very carefully among the available kinds of retailers. And retailers must plan their marketing mixes with their target customers' needs in mind—while at the same time becoming part of an effective channel system.

In this chapter we described many different types of retailers, each offering different marketing mixes that appeal to different target customers. Lower margins and faster turnover are the modern philosophy for mass-merchandisers, but this is no guarantee of success as retailers' life cycles move on.

Retailing tends to evolve in predictable patterns—and we discussed the wheel of retailing theory to help understand this. But the growth of chains and scrambled merchandising will continue as retailing evolves to meet changing consumer demands. Important breakthroughs are possible—perhaps with the Internet—and consumers probably will continue to move away from conventional retailers.

Wholesalers can provide functions for those both above and below them in a channel of distribution.

These services are closely related to the basic marketing functions. There are many types of wholesalers. Some provide all the wholesaling functions—while others specialize in only a few. Eliminating wholesalers does not eliminate the need for the functions they now provide, but technology is helping firms to perform these functions in more efficient ways.

Merchant wholesalers are the most numerous and account for the majority of wholesale sales. Their distinguishing characteristic is that they take title to (own) products. Agent middlemen, on the other hand, act more like sales representatives for sellers or buyers—and they do not take title.

Despite dire predictions, wholesalers continue to exist. The more progressive ones are adapting to a changing environment. But some less-progressive wholesalers will fail. The Internet is already taking its toll. On the other hand, new types of intermediaries are evolving. Some are creating new ways of helping producers and their customers achieve their objectives by finding new ways to add value.

KEY TERMS

QUESTIONS AND PROBLEMS

1. What sort of a "product" are specialty shops offering? What are the prospects for organizing a chain of specialty shops?

2. Distinguish among discount houses, price-cutting by conventional retailers, and mass-merchandising. Forecast the future of low-price selling in food, clothing, and appliances. How will the Internet affect that future?

3. Discuss a few changes in the marketing environment that you think help to explain why telephone, mail-order, and Internet retailing have been growing so rapidly.

4. What are some advantages and disadvantages to using the Internet for shopping?

5. Apply the wheel of retailing theory to your local community. What changes seem likely? Will established retailers see the need for change, or will entirely new firms have to develop?

6. What advantages does a retail chain have over a retailer who operates with a single store? Does a small retailer have any advantages in competing against a chain? Explain your answer.

7. Many producers are now seeking new opportunities in international markets. Are the opportunities for international expansion equally good for retailers? Explain your answer.

8. Discuss how computer systems affect wholesalers' and retailers' operations.

9. Consider the evolution of wholesaling in relation to the evolution of retailing. List several changes that are similar, and several that are fundamentally different.

10. Do wholesalers and retailers need to worry about new-product planning just as a producer needs to have an organized new-product development process? Explain your answer.

11. How do you think a retailer of Maytag washing machines would react if Maytag set up a website, sold direct to consumers, and shipped direct from its distribution center? Explain your thinking.

12. What risks do merchant wholesalers assume by taking title to goods? Is the size of this risk about constant for all merchant wholesalers?

13. Why would a manufacturer set up its own sales branches if established wholesalers were already available?

14. What is an agent middleman's marketing mix?

15. Why do you think that many merchant wholesalers handle competing products from different producers, while manufacturers' agents usually handle only noncompeting products from different producers?

16. What alternatives does a producer have if it is trying to expand distribution in a foreign market and finds that the best existing merchant wholesalers won't handle imported products?

17. Discuss the future growth and nature of wholesaling if chains, scrambled merchandising, and the Internet continue to become more important. How will wholesalers have to adjust their mixes? Will wholesalers be eliminated? If not, what wholesaling functions will be most important? Are there any particular lines of trade where wholesalers may have increasing difficulty?

CREATING MARKETING PLANS

The Marketing Plan Coach software on the Student CD includes a sample marketing plan for Hillside Veterinary Clinic. Look through the "Marketing Strategy" section.

a. What kind of retail operation is the vet clinic? Does it fit any of the types described in this chapter?

b. How could Hillside make use of a website?

c. The marketing plan notes future plans to offer kennel (boarding) services and pet supplies. How will this change Hillside's current strategy? Does the marketing plan provide a good sense of what needs to be done? Do you have other recommendations for Hillside?

SUGGESTED CASES

11. Runners Supply
12. DrMarcus.com
14. Digital Depot

15. Sanchez & Associates
16. Specialty Timber Company

COMPUTER-AIDED PROBLEM

12. SELECTING CHANNEL INTERMEDIARIES

Art Glass Productions, a producer of decorative glass gift items, wants to expand into a new territory. Managers at Art Glass know that unit sales in the new territory will be affected by consumer response to the products. But sales will also be affected by which combination of wholesalers and retailers Art Glass selects. There is a choice between two wholesalers. One wholesaler, Giftware Distributing, is a merchant wholesaler that specializes in gift items; it sells to gift shops, department stores, and some mass-merchandisers. The other wholesaler, Margaret Degan & Associates, is a manufacturers' agent that calls on many of the gift shops in the territory.

Art Glass makes a variety of glass items, but the cost of making an item is usually about the same—$5.20 a unit. The items would sell to Giftware Distributing at $12.00 each—and in turn the merchant wholesaler's price to retailers would be $14.00—leaving Giftware with a $2.00 markup to cover costs and profit. Giftware Distributing is the only reputable merchant wholesaler in the territory, and it has agreed to carry the line only if Art Glass is willing to advertise in a trade magazine aimed at retail buyers for gift items. These ads will cost $8,000 a year.

As a manufacturers' agent, Margaret Degan would cover all of her own expenses and would earn 8 percent of the $14.00 price per unit charged the gift shops. Individual orders would be shipped directly to the retail gift shops by Art Glass, using United Parcel Service (UPS). Art Glass would pay the UPS charges at an average cost of $2.00 per item. In contrast, Giftware Distributing would anticipate demand and place larger orders in advance. This would reduce the shipping costs, which Art Glass would pay, to about $.60 a unit.

Art Glass's marketing manager thinks that Degan would only be able to sell about 75 percent as many items as Giftware Distributing—since she doesn't have time to call on all of the smaller shops and doesn't call on any department stores. On the other hand, the merchant wholesaler's demand for $8,000 worth of supporting advertising requires a significant outlay.

The marketing manager at Art Glass has decided to use a spreadsheet to determine how large sales would have to be to make it more profitable to work with Giftware and to see how the different channel arrangements would contribute to profits at different sales levels.

a. Given the estimated unit sales and other values shown on the initial spreadsheet, which type of wholesaler would contribute the most profit to Art Glass Productions?

b. If sales in the new territory are slower than expected, so that the merchant wholesaler was able to sell only 3,000 units—or the agent 2,250 units—which wholesaler would contribute the most to Art Glass's profits? (Note: Assume that the merchant wholesaler only buys what it can sell; that is, it doesn't carry extra inventory beyond what is needed to meet demand.)

c. Prepare a table showing how the two wholesalers' contributions to profit compare as the quantity sold varies from 3,500 units to 4,500 units for the merchant wholesaler and 75 percent of these numbers for the manufacturers' agent. Discuss these results. (Note: Use the analysis feature to vary the quantity sold by the merchant wholesaler, and the program will compute 75 percent of that quantity as the estimate of what the agent will sell.)

For additional questions related to this problem, see Exercise 12–4 in the *Learning Aid for Use with Essentials of Marketing*, 11th edition.

13

Promotion— Introduction to Integrated Marketing Communications

The classic MINI Cooper was a pop icon in England in the 1960s. John Lennon and Paul McCartney were MINI owners when they wrote "Baby, You Can Drive My Car." But the quirky MINI never made a splash in the U.S. (only 10,000 classic MINIs were sold from 1960–67). Now, however, all of that has changed— with the help of effective promotion.

After the BMW Group took ownership of the MINI brand, a new-product development team designed a new model. They gave it updated styling and high-tech features (including six standard airbags, Corner Brake Control, Dynamic Stability Control, ABS, heated seats, and a six-speaker CD stereo). Tiny compacts were already popular in Europe. Yet, in the U.S. where SUVs rule the road, the new MINI was the smallest car on the American road. The BMW Group hoped that the U.S. launch of the MINI would attract a segment of adventurous, fun-loving innovators who would boost sales. Kerri Martin, the Marketing Communications Manager for MINI U.S.A., planned the promotion to make that happen. Her team faced several challenges. The MINI brand had to be launched independently of any BMW brand as-sociation, so promotion had to simultaneously launch a new brand, two models, and a new small car segment. Further, Martin's team didn't have the big promotion budget typical for high-volume cars because first-year production was limited to 20,000 units.

Martin needed distinctive promotion to appeal to prospects who saw the unique MINI as a form of self-expression, not just as a way to get to work. She selected the Crispin Porter + Bogusky (CPB) ad agency to help. They were creative—and not scared off by her warning to avoid costly TV campaigns and traditional ads.

Before the MINI's introduction, CPB staged a series of sales promotion events to give the MINI a personality—and draw traffic to the newly cre-ated website. For example, they mounted a MINI on top of a jumbo SUV and drove it to auto shows and around major metropolitan cities like New York and San Francisco. A sign on the SUV said, "What are you doing for fun this weekend?" The big idea was that your fun stuff always goes on top, whether it be your skis, mountain bikes, or your MINI Cooper. Next CPB tore out seats at the Superdome in New Orleans and put a MINI right in with the fans for a game. The publicity stunts drew national TV coverage, including coverage on Monday Night Football. To get as much attention from TV ads would have cost

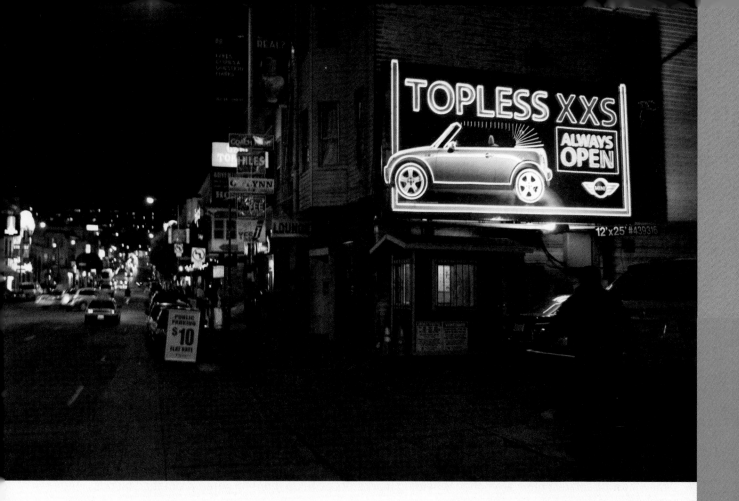

millions of dollars. Before the rollout to dealers, CPB added cheeky billboards like one that simply said, "The SUV backlash officially starts now," followed by the "LET'S MOTOR" tagline and the MINI web address www.MINIUSA.com.

Those efforts received attention that helped draw 125,000 consumers to the website—before cars even hit the showroom. Thousands played interactive video games and mailed electronic MINI greeting cards to friends, which helped spread the buzz. "MINI Insiders" signed up to receive e-mail newsletters, while others used the dealer locator to go see a MINI in person and take a test drive. The dealers' MINI motoring advisors (MINI didn't call them salespeople) added personal selling to the promotion blend. They explained MINI's options, negotiated prices, completed orders, and arranged deliveries. After the sale, MINI owners could turn to the dealer for follow-up information or help.

A couple of years later, when MINI brought out a convertible model, Martin faced a different product-market. Awareness of MINI at that point was 71 percent, compared to 7 percent during its initial launch. MINI also had a larger budget and

higher sales targets. While this allowed for some television advertising, MINI wanted to maintain its counterculture image and continued to use a variety of media. MINI sought to differentiate its convertible from others—so its promotion associated the new model with other open-air vehicles like motorcycles. The "Always Open" campaign encouraged drivers to keep the top down regardless of the weather. One element in that campaign was a magazine ad that included a "contract" that "required" new owners to keep their cars' tops down most of the time. An outdoor ad with moving neon lighting gave the illusion of the MINI's top going down.

More than half of MINIs are custom ordered—and buyers often wait two to three months for delivery. So the company maintains contact with customers through its "Make Waiting Fun" program. The "Where's my baby?" website allows customers to check the progress of their MINIs as they make their way through manufacturing and shipping. They can also request welcome kits, which include retro 1950s games like Interstate Highway Bingo and a stencil that allows them to spray paint "MINI Parking Only" on their garage floor. After the sale, follow-up communications from MINI keep customer satisfaction high and maintain the brand's personality. MINI sends regular e-mails to owners notifying them of new features on the website, and everyone receives an e-card celebrating their car's first birthday. All 150,000 U.S. owners received a MINI "Spy Kit" by mail. The kit included a decoder that helped them interpret jumbled text in magazine ads and directed them to a website with special offers. These types of messages make owners feel like members of a club rather than targets of mass selling. MINI hopes that its happy customers will encourage others to buy and that a few years down the road they replace their current MINI with a new one.[1]

LEARNING OBJECTIVES

As the MINI Cooper example shows, there are many decisions that a marketing manager must make concerning Promotion, and it is an important part of marketing strategy planning. Marketing managers usually blend a variety of different promotion methods to achieve promotion objectives because each method has its own strengths and limitations. In this chapter we introduce the major promotion options and how to integrate them into an effective whole.

When you finish this chapter, you should:

1. know the advantages and disadvantages of the promotion methods a marketing manager can use in strategy planning.

2. understand the integrated marketing communications concept and why firms use a blend of different promotion methods.

3. understand the importance of promotion objectives.

4. know how the communication process affects promotion planning.

5. know how direct-response promotion is helping marketers develop more targeted promotion blends.

6. understand how customer-initiated interactive communication is different.

7. know how typical promotion plans are blended to get an extra push from middlemen and help from customers in pulling products through the channel.

8. understand how promotion blends typically vary over the adoption curve and product life cycle.

9. understand how to determine how much to spend on promotion efforts.

10. understand important new terms (shown in red).

PROMOTION COMMUNICATES TO TARGET MARKETS

Promotion is communicating information between the seller and potential buyer or others in the channel to influence attitudes and behavior. The promotion part of the marketing mix involves telling target customers that the right Product is available at the right Place at the right Price. Just as Promotion must be fine-tuned for a specific target market, it must fit with the other variables of the marketing mix and reinforce the strategy's differentiation and positioning. See Exhibit 13–1.

This is the first of three chapters that discuss issues important for Promotion. We begin with an overview of the major promotion methods. Marketing managers can choose from several basic types of promotion: personal selling, mass selling, and sales promotion (see Exhibit 13–1). Because these different methods have different strengths and limitations, a marketing manager usually uses them in combination to achieve specific objectives. We also discuss the specialists who are involved in managing different types of promotion and why it is important for them to work together as a team. This chapter also provides models that will help you understand how

Exhibit 13-1   Promotion and Marketing Strategy Planning

communication works. Finally, we look at some concepts that help marketing managers develop the best promotion blend.

In Chapter 14, we take a closer look at the important promotion strategy decisions that marketing and sales managers make in personal selling and customer service. Chapter 15 provides a closer look at mass selling. It discusses the role of publicity and the strategy planning decisions for advertising. It shows how sales promotion complements these methods and fits with the overall promotion blend.

While we'll go into some detail about the different promotion methods, a key challenge for marketing managers is how best to blend them. So, it's helpful to begin with a brief overview of the promotion methods available.

SEVERAL PROMOTION METHODS ARE AVAILABLE

Personal selling—flexibility is its strength

Personal selling involves direct spoken communication between sellers and potential customers. Salespeople get immediate feedback, which helps them to adapt. Although some personal selling is included in most marketing mixes, it can be very expensive. So it's often desirable to combine personal selling with mass selling and sales promotion.

Mass selling involves advertising and publicity

Mass selling is communicating with large numbers of potential customers at the same time. It's less flexible than personal selling, but when the target market is large and scattered, mass selling can be less expensive.

Some critics argue that people are bombarded with too much advertising. The Cow Placard Company in Switzerland, for example, paints logos and slogans on cows—and then releases them to graze in pastures along Swiss highways. Swiss apparel company Alprausch used this approach and it attracted a lot of attention. Some people thought it was interesting—but there was also negative publicity by animal rights groups.

Advertising is the main form of mass selling. **Advertising** is any *paid* form of non-personal presentation of ideas, goods, or services by an identified sponsor. It includes the use of traditional media like magazines, newspapers, radio and TV, signs, and direct mail as well as new media such as the Internet. While advertising must be paid for, another form of mass selling—publicity—is "free."

Publicity avoids media costs

Publicity is any *unpaid* form of nonpersonal presentation of ideas, goods, or services. Of course, publicity people are paid. But they try to attract attention to the firm and its offerings *without having to pay media costs*. For example, movie studios try to get celebrities on TV talk shows because this generates a lot of interest and sells tickets to new movies without the studio paying for TV time.

Many companies write press releases hoping to generate publicity in newspapers, magazines, or on television. Southwest Airlines, for example, wanted its press releases to help promote special fares and new routes. So its public relations staff used a targeted approach to get attention from news reporters. Many reporters research story ideas on specialized search engines like Yahoo! News. So the PR staff at Southwest wanted its press releases to appear at the top of the reporters' search lists. Southwest's PR staff researched what keywords reporters used most frequently on these search engines—and then put those words in press releases. For example, PR used the phrase "cheap airfare" because it was in four times as many search requests as "cheap airline tickets." Southwest also put a hot link to its special promotion fare web page at the very start of each press release. The link allowed Southwest PR staff to track which press release worked best, and then it used that information to fine-tune other messages. These extra efforts paid off. Southwest generated $1.5 million in online ticket sales with just four press releases.[2]

If a firm has a really new message, publicity may be more effective than advertising. Trade magazines, for example, may carry articles featuring the newsworthy products of regular advertisers—in part because they *are* regular advertisers. The firm's publicity people write the basic copy and then try to convince magazine editors to print it. A consumer might carefully read a long magazine story but ignore an ad with the same information.

Some companies prepare videotapes designed to get free publicity for their products on TV news shows. For example, after learning that Seattle Mariner Jay Buhner loves Cheerios, a General Mills marketing manager had 162 boxes of the cereal stuffed into his spring-training locker and videotaped Buhner's surprise on opening his locker. TV news programs in 12 major markets showed the video. It would have cost hundreds of thousands of dollars to get as much attention with advertising.[3]

One problem with publicity is that the media don't always say or show what the firm intends. When Segway got an order from the vice president of the United States, it seemed like a perfect opportunity for publicity. It looked even better at the White House when President Bush got on to take a ride—until he fell off the Segway with photographers snapping pictures.[4]

You are the marketing manager at a small company that creates software for kids. The software helps young kids produce e-books with their own stories, photos, and recordings. Then it uploads the books to a website so friends can see them. The editor of *Fun 4 Kids* magazine calls and says that he has been invited to talk about holiday gift ideas on a national TV program. He says he is thinking about mentioning your product, but would like $5,000 to help cover the costs of his "research." The publicity would certainly generate sales to more than cover that cost. What else, if anything, would you want to know before making a decision? Would you agree to his request? If you knew that the TV show would mention that the editor receives endorsement fees, would your decision be any different?[5]

Sales promotion tries to spark immediate interest

Sales promotion refers to promotion activities—other than advertising, publicity, and personal selling—that stimulate interest, trial, or purchase by final customers or others in the channel. Sales promotion may be aimed at consumers, at middlemen, or at a firm's own employees. Examples are listed in Exhibit 13–2. Relative to other promotion methods, sales promotion can usually be implemented quickly and get results sooner. In fact, most sales promotion efforts are designed to produce immediate results.

Less is spent on advertising than on personal selling or sales promotion

Many people incorrectly think that promotion money gets spent primarily on advertising—because advertising is all around them. But all the special sales promotions—coupons, sweepstakes, trade shows, and the like—add up to even more money. Similarly, much personal selling goes on in the channels and in other business markets. In total, firms spend less money on advertising than on personal selling or sales promotion.

SOMEONE MUST PLAN, INTEGRATE, AND MANAGE THE PROMOTION BLEND

Each promotion method has its own strengths and weaknesses. In combination, they complement each other. Each method also involves its own distinct activities and requires different types of expertise. As a result, it's usually the responsibility of

Exhibit 13–2
Example of Sales Promotion Activities

Aimed at final consumers or users	Aimed at middlemen	Aimed at company's own sales force
Contests	Price deals	Contests
Coupons	Promotion allowances	Bonuses
Aisle displays	Sales contests	Meetings
Samples	Calendars	Portfolios
Trade shows	Gifts	Displays
Point-of-purchase materials	Trade shows	Sales aids
Banners and streamers	Meetings	Training materials
Frequent-buyer programs	Catalogs	
Sponsored events	Merchandising aids	
	Videos	

specialists—such as sales managers, advertising managers, and promotion managers—to develop and implement the detailed plans for the various parts of the overall promotion blend.

Sales managers manage salespeople

Sales managers are concerned with managing personal selling. Often the sales manager is responsible for building good distribution channels and implementing Place policies. In smaller companies, the sales manager may also act as the marketing manager and be responsible for advertising and sales promotion.

Advertising managers work with ads and agencies

Advertising managers manage their company's mass-selling effort—in television, newspapers, magazines, and other media. Their job is choosing the right media and developing the ads. Advertising departments within their own firms may help in these efforts—or they may use outside advertising agencies. The advertising manager may handle publicity too. Or it may be handled by an outside agency or by whoever handles **public relations**—communication with noncustomers, including labor, public interest groups, stockholders, and the government.

Sales promotion managers need many talents

Sales promotion managers manage their company's sales promotion effort. In some companies, a sales promotion manager has independent status and reports directly to the marketing manager. If a firm's sales promotion spending is substantial, it probably *should* have a specific sales promotion manager. Sometimes, however, the sales or advertising departments handle sales promotion efforts—or sales promotion is left as a responsibility of individual brand managers. Regardless of who the manager is, sales promotion activities vary so much that many firms use both inside and outside specialists.

Marketing manager talks to all, blends all

Although many specialists may be involved in planning for and implementing specific promotion methods, determining the blend of promotion methods is a strategy decision—and it is the responsibility of the marketing manager.

The various promotion specialists tend to focus on what they know best and their own areas of responsibility. A creative web page designer or advertising copywriter in New York may have no idea what a salesperson does during a call on a wholesaler. In addition, because of differences in outlook and experience, the advertising, sales, and sales promotion managers often have trouble working with each other as partners. Too often they just view other promotion methods as using up budget money they want.

The marketing manager must weigh the pros and cons of the various promotion methods, then devise an effective promotion blend—fitting in the various departments and personalities and coordinating their efforts. Then the advertising, sales, and sales promotion managers should develop the details consistent with what the marketing manager wants to accomplish.

Send a consistent and complete message with integrated marketing communications

Effective blending of all of the firm's promotion efforts should produce **integrated marketing communications**—the intentional coordination of every communication from a firm to a target customer to convey a consistent and complete message.

An example of integrated marketing communications is Nortel Networks's Mobility Solutions group, which sells wireless communication tools to many different business customers. While personal selling plays an important role in its promotion efforts, Nortel's marketing managers also use trade shows, ads in trade magazines, weekly web seminars, and online case studies. In addition, Nortel developed an online, virtual trade show. It helped Nortel and its partners demonstrate the complete package of solution-oriented products they provide. While Nortel relies on a variety of communication approaches to address the technical needs of its customers, it works to make the different messages consistent so they will be more effective.[6]

It seems obvious that a firm's different communications to a target market should be consistent. However, when a number of different people are working on different promotion elements, they are likely to see the same big picture only if a marketing manager ensures that it happens. Getting consistency is harder when different firms handle different aspects of the promotion effort. For example, different firms in the channel may have conflicting objectives.

To get effective coordination, everyone involved with the promotion effort must clearly understand the plan for the overall marketing strategy. They all need to realize how each promotion method will contribute to achieve specific promotion objectives.[7]

Stanley depends on a blend of integrated marketing communications, including sales presentations and product demonstration tours, trade ads focused on retailers, ads targeted at end users, and a website that provides information on the whole line.

WHICH METHODS TO USE DEPENDS ON PROMOTION OBJECTIVES

Overall objective is to affect behavior

The different promotion methods are all different forms of communication. They should encourage customers to choose a *specific* product. Therefore, promotion must (1) reinforce present attitudes or relationships that might lead to favorable behavior or (2) actually change the attitudes and behavior of the firm's target market.

Informing, persuading, and reminding are basic promotion objectives

Promotion objectives must be clearly defined—because the right promotion blend depends on what the firm wants to accomplish. It's helpful to think of three basic promotion objectives: *informing*, *persuading*, and *reminding* target customers about the company and its marketing mix. All try to affect buyer behavior by providing more information.

It's also useful to set more specific promotion objectives that state *exactly who* you want to inform, persuade, or remind, and *why*. This is unique to each company's strategy—and specific objectives vary by promotion method. We'll talk about more specific promotion objectives in the next two chapters. Here we'll focus on the three basic promotion objectives and how you can reach them.

Informing is educating

Potential customers must know something about a product if they are to buy at all. A firm with a really new product may not have to do anything but inform consumers about it and show that it meets consumer needs better than other products. Sometimes consumers try to become better educated before buying. A consumer who wants a digital camera, for example, can go to Best Buy's website to learn about digital cameras, find technical specifications, and read reviews by other customers.

Persuading usually becomes necessary

When competitors offer similar products, the firm must not only *inform* customers that its product is available but also persuade them to buy it. A *persuading* objective means the firm will try to develop a favorable set of attitudes so customers will buy, and keep buying, its product. A persuading objective often tries to demonstrate how one brand is better than others. To convince consumers to buy Brawny paper towels, ads show Brawny as the towel that's best for tough cleanup jobs. Spray 'n Wash convinces customers firsthand with in-store demonstrations that show how the product removes stains caused by spaghetti sauce or red wine.[8]

Reminding may be enough, sometimes

If target customers already have positive attitudes about a firm's marketing mix—or a good relationship with a firm—a *reminding* objective might be suitable. Customers who have been attracted and sold once are still targets for competitors' appeals. Reminding them of their past satisfaction may keep them from shifting to a competitor. Campbell realizes that most people know about its soup—so much of its advertising is intended to remind.

Promotion objectives relate to adoption process

In Chapter 5, we looked at consumer buying as a problem-solving process in which buyers go through steps on the way to adopting (or rejecting) an idea or product. The three basic promotion objectives relate to these steps. See Exhibit 13–3. *Informing* and *persuading* may be needed to affect the potential customer's knowledge and attitudes about a product and then bring about its adoption. Later promotion can simply *remind* the customer about that favorable experience and confirm the adoption decision.

The AIDA model is a practical approach

The basic promotion objectives and adoption process fit very neatly with another action-oriented model—called AIDA—that we will use in this and the next two chapters to guide some of our discussion.

The **AIDA model** consists of four promotion jobs: (1) to get *Attention*, (2) to hold *Interest*, (3) to arouse *Desire*, and (4) to obtain *Action*. (As a memory aid, note that the first letters of the four key words spell AIDA, the well-known opera.)

Exhibit 13–3
Relation of Promotion Objectives, Adoption Process, and AIDA Model

Promotion Objectives	Adoption Process	AIDA Model
Informing	Awareness	Attention
	Interest	Interest
Persuading	Evaluation	Desire
	Trial	
Reminding	Decision	Action
	Confirmation	

Exhibit 13–3 shows the relationship of the adoption process to the AIDA jobs. Getting attention is necessary to make consumers aware of the company's offering. Holding interest gives the communication a chance to build the consumer's interest in the product. Arousing desire affects the evaluation process, perhaps building preference. And obtaining action includes gaining trial, which may lead to a purchase decision. Continuing promotion is needed to confirm the decision and encourage an ongoing relationship and additional purchases.

British marketers for Pampers diapers generated interest and awareness with TV ads that showed the world from a baby's perspective. To encourage desire and action, they used creative in-store and point-of-purchase advertising. For example, on the doors of restrooms with baby-changing facilities, fake door knobs were placed unreachably high, with the message: "Babies have to stretch for things. That's why they like the extra stretchiness of Pampers Active fit." They also put huge footprints on the floor in the diaper aisle. And on store shelves, in a play on babies' disobedient nature, pull-out Pampers information cards were marked "Do Not Pull."[9]

PROMOTION REQUIRES EFFECTIVE COMMUNICATION

Communication can break down

Promotion is wasted when it doesn't communicate effectively. There are many reasons why a promotion message can be misunderstood or not heard at all. To understand this, it's useful to think about the whole **communication process**—which means a source trying to reach a receiver with a message. Exhibit 13–4 shows the elements of the communication process. Here we see that a **source**—the sender of a message—is trying to deliver a message to a **receiver**—a potential customer.

Exhibit 13–4   The Traditional Communication Process

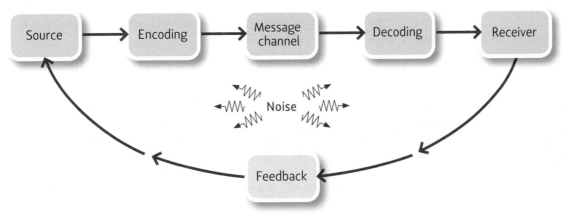

Customers evaluate both the message and the source of the message in terms of trustworthiness and credibility. For example, American Dental Association (ADA) studies show that Listerine mouthwash helps reduce plaque buildup on teeth. Listerine mentions the ADA endorsement in its promotion to help make the promotion message credible.

A major advantage of personal selling is that the source—the seller—can get immediate feedback from the receiver. It's easier to judge how the message is being received and to change it if necessary. Mass sellers usually must depend on marketing research or total sales figures for feedback—and that can take too long. Many marketers include toll-free telephone numbers and website addresses as ways of building direct-response feedback from consumers into their mass-selling efforts.

The **noise**—shown in Exhibit 13–4—is any distraction that reduces the effectiveness of the communication process. Conversations and snack-getting during TV ads are noise. The clutter of competing ads on the Internet is noise. Advertisers who plan messages must recognize that many possible distractions—noise—can interfere with communications.

Encoding and decoding depend on a common frame of reference

The basic difficulty in the communication process occurs during encoding and decoding. **Encoding** is the source deciding what it wants to say and translating it into words or symbols that will have the same meaning to the receiver. **Decoding** is the receiver translating the message. This process can be very tricky. The meanings of various words and symbols may differ depending on the attitudes and experiences of the two groups. People need a common frame of reference to communicate effectively. See Exhibit 13–5. Maidenform encountered this problem with its promotion aimed at working women. The company ran a series of ads depicting women stockbrokers and doctors wearing Maidenform lingerie. The men in the ads were fully dressed. Maidenform was trying to show women in positions of authority, but some women felt the ads presented them as sex objects. In this case, the promotion people who encoded the message didn't understand the attitudes of the target market and how they would decode the message.[10]

Different audiences may interpret a message differently. Such differences are common in international marketing when cultural differences or translation are problems. In Taiwan, the translation of the Pepsi slogan "Come alive with the Pepsi Generation" came out as "Pepsi will bring your ancestors back from the dead." Worse, a campaign for Schweppes Tonic Water in Italy translated the name into Schweppes Toilet Water. Many firms run into problems like this.[11]

Exhibit 13–5
This Same Message May Be Interpreted Differently

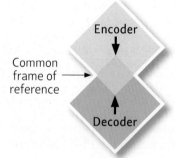

Encoder

Common frame of reference

Decoder

Message channel is important too

The communication process is complicated even more because the message is coming from a source through some **message channel**—the carrier of the message. A source can use many message channels to deliver a message. The salesperson does it in person with voice and action. Advertising must do it with media such as magazines, TV, e-mail, or Internet websites. A particular message channel may enhance or detract from a message. A TV ad, for example, can *show* that Dawn dishwashing detergent "takes the grease away"; the same claim might not be convincing if it arrives in a consumer's e-mail.

Ethical issues in marketing communications

Promotion is one of the most often criticized areas of marketing. Many criticisms focus on whether communications are honest and fair. Marketers must sometimes make ethical judgments in considering these charges and in planning their promotion.

For example, when a TV news program broadcasts a video publicity release, consumers don't know it was prepared to achieve marketing objectives. They think the news staff is the source. That may make the message more credible, but is it fair? Many say yes—as long as the publicity information is truthful. But gray areas still remain.

Davis Wright Tremaine LLP is a law firm that wants potential clients to know that it will be deadly serious about representing their interests. People could decode that sort of message differently, but the use of humor in the firm's magazine ad conveys the message in a vivid way that will help make it stick.

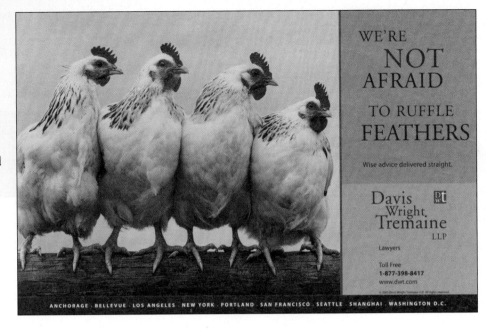

Critics raise similar concerns about the use of celebrities in advertisements. A person who plays the role of an honest and trustworthy person on a popular TV series may be a credible message source in an ad, but is using such a person misleading to consumers? Some critics believe it is. Others argue that consumers recognize advertising when they see it and know celebrities are paid for their endorsements.

The most common criticisms of promotion relate to exaggerated claims. If an ad or a salesperson claims that a product is the "best available," is that just a personal opinion or should every statement be backed up by proof? What type of proof should be required? Some promotions do misrepresent the benefits of a product. However, most marketing managers want relationships with, and repeat purchases from, their customers. They realize that customers won't come back if the marketing mix doesn't deliver what the promotion promises. Further, many consumers are skeptical about all the claims they hear and see. As a result, most marketing managers work to make promotion claims specific and believable.[12]

INTEGRATED DIRECT-RESPONSE PROMOTION IS VERY TARGETED

The challenge of developing promotions that reach *specific* target customers has prompted many firms to turn to direct marketing—direct communication between a seller and an individual customer using a promotion method other than face-to-face personal selling. Most direct marketing communications are designed to prompt immediate feedback—a direct response—by customers. That's why this type of communication is often called *direct-response promotion.*

Early efforts in the direct-response area focused on direct-mail advertising. A carefully selected mailing list—perhaps from the firm's customer relationship management (CRM) database—allowed advertisers to reach customers with specific interests. And direct-mail advertising proved to be very effective when the objective was to get a direct response from the customer.

Now it's more than direct-mail advertising

Achieving a measurable, direct response from specific target customers is still the heart of direct promotion. But direct-response media now include telephone, print, e-mail, a website, broadcast, and even interactive video. The customer's response may be a purchase (or donation), a question, or a request for more information. At a

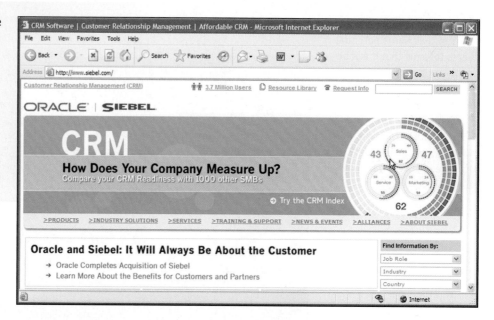

Siebel has long been one of the leading names in customer relationship management (CRM) software. Now that Oracle, the world's leading database firm, has acquired Siebel, the combined offering will give marketers even stronger and more flexible tools for managing marketing information and analysis.

website, the response may be a simple mouse-click to link to more information, a click to put an item in a virtual shopping cart, or a click to purchase.

Often the customer responds by calling a toll-free telephone number or, in the case of business markets, by sending a fax or an e-mail. Then a salesperson calls and follows up. That might involve filling an order or scheduling a personal visit with a prospect. There are many variations on this approach, and direct-response promotion is often an important component of integrated marketing communications programs. What distinguishes this general approach is that the marketer targets more of its promotion effort at specific individuals who respond directly.[13]

Target customer directly with a CRM database

Direct-response promotion usually relies on a customer relationship management (CRM) database to target specific prospects. The database includes customers' names and their home and e-mail addresses—as well as past purchases and other segmenting characteristics. Marketing managers like to be in regular contact with customers to stimulate customer interest or a call for action. Greenpeace and the Cousteau Society mail newsletters to people interested in environmental issues—keeping them informed of the cause or asking for donations. To customers who request it, Circuit City sends out weekly specials via an e-mail newsletter.

CRM databases are also useful for business customers. HP sends customized e-newsletters to its business customers to announce new products and to give advice on frequently asked service questions. These newsletters have increased sales of HP's new products and reduced calls to its service center. Effective e-mail programs give customers targeted information they find timely and useful.[14]

However, marketing managers should be careful they don't create ill will by bombarding customers with "spam"—e-mail messages they don't want. Growing concerns about spam have led many businesses and individuals to use filters that screen it out. But spam filters often delete useful messages—including requested e-newsletters. So marketing managers can't rely too heavily on e-mail because they can't be sure their target customers are even getting the message.[15]

Direct-response methods raise ethical concerns

Direct-response promotion and CRM database targeting have become an important part of many marketing mixes. But critics argue that thousands of acres of trees are consumed each week just to make the paper for direct-response "junk mail" that consumers don't want. In addition, many consumers don't like getting direct-promotion telephone solicitations at any time, but especially during evening meal times when these calls are particularly frequent. Similarly, most e-mail users resent that they need to spend time dealing with the constant flow of spam that floods their e-mail boxes; there's so much spam that it slows down the whole Internet. There are many other privacy issues related to how a direct-response database might be used, especially if it includes details of a consumer's purchases.

Most firms that use direct-response promotion are very sensitive to these concerns and take steps to address them. However, many people feel that solutions to these problems require other steps. As a result, laws in these areas are changing. For example, most states have passed laws prohibiting automatic calling systems that use prerecorded messages rather than a live salesperson. Many states have their own "do not call" laws and federal laws are under review. A host of new regulations concerning consumer privacy are also being considered by lawmakers. So marketers who do not heed warnings about consumer concerns in this area may find themselves in trouble—not only with customers but in the courts.[16]

THE CUSTOMER MAY INITIATE THE COMMUNICATION PROCESS

Traditional thinking about promotion—and for that matter, the communication process itself—has usually been based on the idea that it's the seller ("source") who initiates the communication. Of course, for decades consumers have been looking in the Yellow Pages for information or asking retail salespeople for help. Similarly, it's not news that organizational buyers contact potential vendors to ask questions or request bids.

In the past, a marketer usually viewed the buyer as a passive message receiver—at least until the marketer has done something to stimulate attention, interest, and desire. That's one reason that targeting is so important—so that the promotion expense isn't wasted on someone who isn't interested. Moreover, most mass-selling messages are based on the idea that you can get a customer's attention and interest for

Internet search engines have reduced the time it takes for customers to search for information about products and stores. Some marketing managers have tried to understand how search engines work so that their sites show up early in the list of results. Another approach is to pay a search engine firm for a sponsored link (ad) on the first page of results. See the sponsored links on the Google results screen produced by a search for "yo yo."

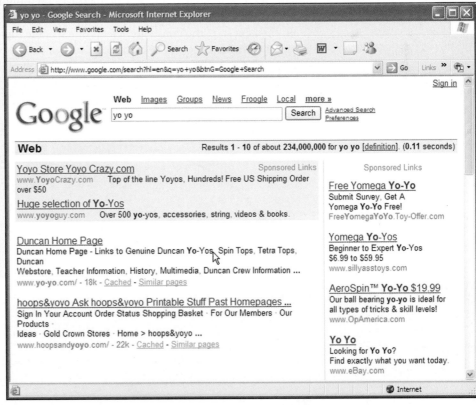

only a minute or two. Even with direct-response promotion, the marketer typically has taken the first step.

New electronic media enable interactive communication

However, this is changing. Buyers can now access a great deal of information (including pictures, video, and audio, as well as text) and place an order without the seller having been directly involved at all. The interactive technologies enabling this change take many different forms. Some of the most important are websites, e-mail list-servers, caller-controlled fax-on-demand, computerized telephone voice-messaging systems, video kiosks in malls, CD and DVD disks on personal computers, and MSN TV.

Internet EXERCISE

Visit the Campbell Soup Company website (*www.campbellsoup.com*). Does the website make it easy for you to get information? Does it make you want to spend more time and get more information? Explain your answer.

Work is underway on interactive cable systems in which icons will appear on-screen as consumers watch a program or movie. For example, an icon might appear on a jacket worn by a talk show guest. A consumer who is interested in the product will be able to press a button on a remote control to pause the show and get more information about the product and where to buy it—or even to place an order. The same concept is already implemented on DVDs for some movies. When this type of system is available via cable (or with streaming video over the Internet), it will reshape the way many marketing communications are handled.

Consider the simple model of customer- ("receiver-") initiated interactive communication shown in Exhibit 13–6. At first it doesn't seem very different from the traditional communication model we considered earlier (Exhibit 13–4). However, the differences are significant.

Consumer initiates communication with a search process

In the model in Exhibit 13–6, a customer initiates the communication process with a decision to search for information in a particular message channel. The most far-reaching message channel to search is the Internet. The message channel is still the carrier of the message, as was the case before, but "searchable" message channels usually feature an archive of existing messages on a number of topics. There may be many available topics—even millions.

In the next step, the consumer selects one specific topic on which to receive a message. Selecting a topic might be done in one of a variety of ways, depending on the message channel. The most typical approaches involve using a mouse, remote control

Exhibit 13–6
A Model of Customer-Initiated Interactive Communication

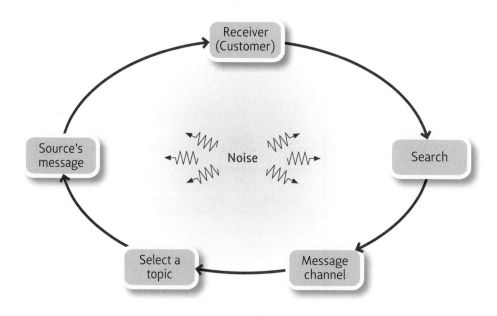

device, or keypad to highlight a selection from an initial list (like a table of contents or index). Of course, other approaches are common. Many dial-up telephone systems use voice-recognition.

Many consumers initiate communication when they enter search keywords into a search engine like Google or Yahoo! What does this mean for a marketer? An online retailer that sells golf gear wants to appear near the top of the search results when someone searches for "Big Bertha golf," Callaway's popular line of golf clubs. In this case, the retailer might pay a search engine company to put a sponsored (advertising) link near the top of the list. Or, there are other technical approaches that make it more likely that a seller's website will appear near the top of the search results. Either way, the marketer wants to be sure that when customers "look" that its business is "seen"—or the firm's message won't be communicated.

Consumer decides how much information to get

Once a specific topic has been selected, the message for that topic is displayed. Typically, the message is brief. But it may include a simple way to get more detailed information, select another related topic, return to the original selection process, or quit the search. Thus, after each message the consumer can decide whether to search further (say, to get more detail). This interactive approach makes it easy for the consumer to get as much information as desired. However, noise may still be a problem. For example, a consumer may waste time and still not find what is needed—because it is not available or is too hard to find. Of course, an online seller doesn't want to lose a customer who has made it to the website but then encountered some problem. So, many online sellers have a live person who is ready to help if a customer needs it. At the Lands' End site, a customer can click a button to have a salesperson call on the phone and give help or, alternatively, give online help in an instant-messaging chat session.

Action, including purchase, may be immediate

The action required to make a purchase by interactive media is usually fast and easy. At many Internet sites, for example, a consumer can click on an item to place it in a virtual shopping cart, charge it to a credit card, and arrange for shipping.

Custom communications will be more personalized

The traditional principles of communication discussed earlier in the chapter are still important in customer-initiated interactive communication. At the same time, the interactive approach allows the marketer to customize communication to the needs and responses of the consumer. As new approaches develop in this arena, we are seeing more promotion targeted at single-person "segments." For example, many websites place "cookies" on a customer's computer so that when the customer revisits their sites the system can "remember" the customer and automatically recall past purchase activity. When a customer returns to Amazon.com, the site recommends books based on that customer's purchase history.[17]

HOW TYPICAL PROMOTION PLANS ARE BLENDED AND INTEGRATED

Get a push in the channel with promotion to middlemen

When a channel of distribution involves middlemen, their cooperation can be crucial to the success of the overall marketing strategy. **Pushing** (a product through a channel) means using normal promotion effort—personal selling, advertising, and sales promotion—to help sell the whole marketing mix to possible channel members. This approach emphasizes the importance of securing the wholehearted cooperation of channel members to promote the product in the channel and to the final user.

Producers usually take on much of the responsibility for the pushing effort in the channel. However, wholesalers often handle at least some of the promotion to retailers. Similarly, retailers often handle promotion in their local markets. The overall effort is most likely to be effective when all of the individual messages are carefully integrated.

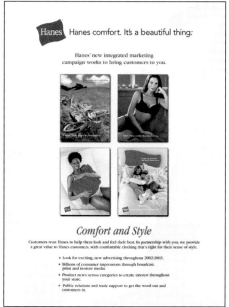

The Hanes ad (on the left) is targeted at parents and kids and designed to stimulate demand and help pull Hanes's popular products through the channel of distribution. The Hanes trade ad (on the right) is targeted at retailers and designed to inform them about the consumer promotion and encourage them to carry Hanes brand products.

Promotion to middlemen emphasizes personal selling

Salespeople handle most of the important communication with middlemen. Middlemen don't want empty promises. They want to know what they can expect in return for their cooperation and help. A salesperson can answer questions about what promotion will be directed toward the final consumer, each channel member's part in marketing the product, and important details on pricing, markups, promotion assistance, and allowances. A salesperson can also help the firm determine when it should adjust its marketing mix from one middleman to another.

When suppliers offer similar products and compete for attention and shelf space, middlemen usually pay attention to the one with the best profit potential. So sales promotions targeted at middlemen usually focus on short-term arrangements that will improve the middleman's profits. For example, a soft-drink bottler might offer a convenience store a free case of drinks with each two cases it buys. The free case improves the store's profit margin on the whole purchase.

Firms run ads in trade magazines to recruit new middlemen or to inform channel members about a new offering. Trade ads usually encourage middlemen to contact the supplier for more information, and then a salesperson takes over.

Push within a firm— with promotion to employees

Some firms emphasize promotion to their own employees—especially salespeople or others in contact with customers. This type of *internal marketing* effort is basically a variation on the pushing approach. One objective of an annual sales meeting is to inform reps about important elements of the marketing strategy—so they'll work together as a team to implement it. Some firms use promotion to motivate employees to provide better customer service or achieve higher sales. This is typical in services where the quality of the employees' efforts is a big part of the product. Some ads, for example, use the theme "we like to see you smile." The ads communicate to customers, but also remind employees that the service they provide is crucial to customer satisfaction.

Pulling policy— customer demand pulls the product through the channel

Most producers focus a significant amount of promotion on customers at the end of the channel. This helps to stimulate demand and pull the product through the channel of distribution. **Pulling** means getting customers to ask middlemen for the product.

Pulling and pushing are usually used in combination. See Exhibit 13–7. However, if middlemen won't work with a producer—perhaps because they're already carrying a competing brand—a producer may try to use a pulling approach by itself. This involves highly aggressive promotion to final consumers or users—perhaps using coupons or samples—temporarily bypassing middlemen. If the promotion works, the middlemen are forced to carry the product to satisfy customer requests. However, this approach is risky. Customers may lose interest before reluctant middlemen make the product available. At minimum, middlemen should be told about the planned pulling effort—so they can be ready if the promotion succeeds.

Who handles promotion to final customers at the end of the channel varies in different channel systems, depending on the mix of pushing and pulling. Further, the promotion blend typically varies depending on whether customers are final consumers or business users.[18]

Promotion to final consumers

The large number of consumers almost forces producers of consumer products and retailers to emphasize advertising and sales promotion. Sales promotion—such as coupons, contests, or free samples—builds consumer interest and short-term sales of a product. Effective mass selling may build enough brand familiarity so that little personal selling is needed, as in self-service and discount operations.[19]

Personal selling can be effective too. But aggressive personal selling to final consumers usually is found in expensive channel systems, such as those for financial services, furniture, consumer electronics, designer clothing, and automobiles.

Promotion to business customers

Producers and wholesalers that target business customers often emphasize personal selling. This is practical because there are fewer of these customers and their purchases are typically larger. Sales reps can be more flexible in adjusting their companies' appeals to suit each customer—and personal contact is usually required to close a sale. A salesperson is also able to call back later to follow up, resolve any problems, and nurture the relationship with the customer.

While personal selling dominates in business markets, mass selling is necessary too. A typical sales call on a business customer costs about $200.[20] That's because salespeople spend less than half their time actually selling. The rest is consumed by such

LivePerson is the leading provider of hosted solutions for managing online customer interactions. LivePerson helps firms identify the best prospects who visit the firm's website so that a salesperson can then immediately reach out and move these prospects through the sales process or provide customer support. LivePerson recently released Timpani, which combines live chat, e-mail management, and self-service/knowledge base.

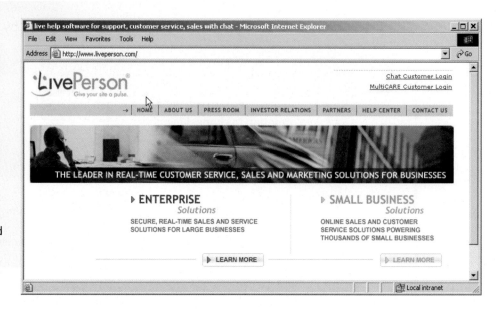

tasks as traveling, paperwork, sales meetings, and strictly service calls. So it's seldom practical for salespeople to carry the whole promotion load.

Ads in trade magazines or at a B2B e-commerce website, for instance, can inform potential customers that a product is available. Most trade ads give a toll-free telephone number, fax number, or website address to stimulate direct inquiries. Domestic and international trade shows also help identify prospects. Even so, most sellers who target business customers spend only a small percentage of their promotion budget on mass selling and sales promotion.

Each market segment may need a unique blend

Knowing what type of promotion is typically emphasized with different targets is useful in planning the promotion blend. But each unique market segment may need a separate marketing mix and a different promotion blend. You should be careful not to slip into a shotgun approach when what you really need is a rifle approach—with a more careful aim.

ADOPTION PROCESSES CAN GUIDE PROMOTION PLANNING

The AIDA and adoption processes look at individuals. This emphasis on individuals helps us understand how promotion affects the way that people behave. But it's also useful to look at markets as a whole. Different segments of customers within a market may behave differently—with some taking the lead in trying new products and, in turn, influencing others.

Promotion must vary for different adopter groups

Research on how markets accept new ideas has led to the adoption curve model. The **adoption curve** shows when different groups accept ideas. It emphasizes the relations among groups and shows that individuals in some groups act as leaders in accepting a new idea. Promotion efforts usually need to change over time to adjust to differences among the adopter groups.

Exhibit 13–8 shows the adoption curve for a typical successful product. Some of the important characteristics of each of these customer groups are discussed next. Which one are you?

Innovators don't mind taking some risks

The **innovators** are the first to adopt. They are eager to try a new idea and willing to take risks. Innovators tend to be young and well educated. They are likely to be

Exhibit 13-8   The Adoption Curve

mobile and have many contacts outside their local social group and community. Business firms in the innovator group are often specialized and willing to take the risk of doing something new.

Innovators tend to rely on impersonal and scientific information sources, or other innovators, rather than salespeople. They often search for information on the Internet, read articles in technical publications, or look for informative ads in special-interest magazines.

Early adopters are often opinion leaders

Early adopters are well respected by their peers and often are opinion leaders. They tend to be younger, more mobile, and more creative than later adopters. But unlike innovators, they have fewer contacts outside their own social group or community. Business firms in this category also tend to be specialized.

Of all the groups, this one tends to have the greatest contact with salespeople. Mass media are important information sources too. Marketers should be very concerned with attracting and selling the early adopter group. Its acceptance is crucial. The next group, the early majority, looks to the early adopters for guidance. The early adopters can help the promotion effort by spreading *word-of-mouth* information and advice among other consumers.

Opinion leaders help spread the word

Marketers know the importance of personal recommendations by opinion leaders. For example, some movie fans like to be the first to see new flicks. If they like a movie, they quickly tell their friends and word-of-mouth publicity does the real selling job. When online grocer FreshDirect opened in New York City, positive word of mouth keyed its fast growth. However, consumers are even more likely to talk about a negative experience than a positive one. So, if early groups reject the product, it may never get off the ground. In a study of consumers, 64 percent said they would not shop at a store after being told about someone else's negative experience there.[21]

While word of mouth has always had a powerful influence on consumer choice, the popularity of blogs, online review sites, and similar web media give "word of mouse" an even more far-reaching impact. When Hot Hot Hot, a retailer that specializes in hot sauces for food, established its website, it urged customers to click a link and e-mail its web address to their friends. Very quickly, largely because of these referrals, 1,500 people were visiting the website each day.

When consumers are not motivated to spread the word, a company called BzzAgent helps marketing managers get conversations started. BzzAgent works with about 125,000 "agents." Agents who sign up to help with a particular campaign receive product samples and information. If they like the product, they are urged to pass the word. But BzzAgent encourages them to be ethical and disclose their status as "buzz agents." Kraft Foods, General Mills, and Dockers have run campaigns like this.[22]

While publicity stunts and word of mouth can create awareness, they aren't a substitute for a complete marketing mix that addresses a target market's needs. Consider Pontiac's giveaway of 276 of its new G6 cars to the audience of Oprah Winfrey's TV show. The giveaway generated a lot of publicity and initial word-of-mouth "buzz" was very favorable, but in the end the G6 didn't score well with consumers.[23]

Early majority group is deliberate

The **early majority** group avoids risk and waits to consider a new idea after many early adopters have tried it—and liked it. Average-sized business firms that are less specialized often fit in this category. If successful companies in their industry adopt the new idea, they will too.

The early majority has a great deal of contact with mass media, salespeople, and early adopter opinion leaders. Members usually aren't opinion leaders themselves.

Late majority is cautious

The **late majority** group is cautious about new ideas. Often members of this group are older and more set in their ways, so they are less likely to follow early adopters. In fact, strong social pressure from their own peer group may be needed before they adopt a new product. Business firms in this group tend to be conservative, smaller-sized firms with little specialization.

The late majority makes little use of marketing sources of information—mass media and salespeople. It tends to be oriented more toward other late adopters rather than outside sources it doesn't trust.

Laggards or nonadopters hang on to tradition

Laggards or **nonadopters** prefer to do things the way they've been done in the past and are very suspicious of new ideas. They tend to be older and less well educated. The smallest businesses with the least specialization often fit this category. They cling to the status quo and think it's the safe way.

The main source of information for laggards is other laggards. This certainly is bad news for marketers. In fact, it may not pay to bother with this group.[24]

Marketers Are Wading into the Blogosphere

Many marketers are adding a new dimension to their promotion blend by using blogs. A *blog*, short for *web log*, is a website that provides a running stream of messages, links, and comments. Blogs are usually created by an individual to express personal opinions about some topic. But many marketers like the first-person, conversational style that is typical of blogs. As with other types of personal communication, including personal selling, blogs can help make a connection with customers and enhance the relationship with them, but at a low cost.

Lego uses a blog (www.bricksonthebrain.com) to build a sense of community for its small but influential adult hobbyist segment. These Lego fanatics account for only 5 percent of sales, but their huge Lego displays often get media coverage and help to generate buzz. Lego's blog provides a way for these hobbyists to share ideas, photos, and suggestions. Similarly, yogurt maker Stonyfield Farm uses blogs to reinforce the healthy and wholesome positioning of its foods. Its "Baby Babble" blog targets new parents and "The Bovine Bugle" tells about daily activities at a farm that supplies Stonyfield with milk.

Most blogs rely on and reflect the passions of their creators. Ed Brill is a global sales executive for IBM's Lotus Notes software. Each day about 13,000 Lotus users check what he's thinking at his blog (www.edbrill.com).

One reason is that Brill provides important news fast. For example, when the general manager of Lotus was replaced, Brill posted the news within hours and explained what it would mean for customers. But Brill's site isn't strictly business. It includes photos of Brill and his friends and comments on personal matters, like the fancy watch he received as a Valentine's gift. IBM is a big company and Lotus is a huge brand, but Brill's personal blog helps to humanize them and build relationships with customers.

Marketers for GourmetStation, a Web-based retailer of high-end food, wanted to generate a little buzz. They thought a blog "written" by the website's fictional connoisseur of fine food and wine, T. Alexander, would be just the ticket. Soon Alexander was blogging away, recommending foods and wines. However, some bloggers are very protective of "their" media—and don't like the idea of any blog that appears too commercial. Some of these critics quickly blogged their criticism of GourmetStation's blog for not being authentic—and one gave it a "Beyond Lame Award." In this case, the criticisms didn't seem to matter to customers—and instead all the attention generated more hits for the website. However, marketers need to be aware that creative promotion on the Web can draw critics. Still, firms that keep their focus on the target market are likely to win in the long run.[25]

PROMOTION BLENDS VARY OVER THE LIFE CYCLE

Stage of product in its life cycle

The adoption curve helps explain why a new product goes through the product life-cycle stages described in Chapter 9. Promotion blends usually have to change to achieve different promotion objectives at different life-cycle stages.

Market introduction stage—"this new idea is good"

During market introduction, the basic promotion objective is informing. If the product is a really new idea, the promotion must build **primary demand**—demand for the general product idea—not just demand for the company's own brand. Video phone service and "smart" appliances (that connect to the Internet) are good examples of product concepts where primary demand is just beginning to grow. There may be few potential innovators during the introduction stage, and personal selling can help find them. Firms also need salespeople to find good channel members and persuade them to carry the new product. Sales promotion may be targeted at salespeople or channel members to get them interested in selling the new product. And sales promotion may also encourage customers to try it.

Market growth stage— "our brand is best"

In the market growth stage, more competitors enter the market, and promotion emphasis shifts from building primary demand to stimulating **selective demand**—

Stays on the job all day, just like you.

Only BAND-AID® Brand TOUGH-STRIPS™ have a rugged fabric exterior and Super-Stick adhesive for heavy duty protection that keeps out dirt and germs all day.

For more information, go to www.band-aid.com.

BAND-AID
BRAND ADHESIVE BANDAGES

FINGER-CARE
TOUGH-STRIPS™

Johnson-Johnson

Pourquoi ne se sent-on jamais coupable après avoir goûté au plaisir d'une pomme ?

Bref, mangez des pommes.

Johnson & Johnson's ad for Tough Strips for finger care seeks to build selective demand for the Band-Aid brand. By contrast, apple producers (in France) created an ad to increase primary demand for apples—rather than one particular brand of apple.

demand for a company's own brand. The main job is to persuade customers to buy, and keep buying, the company's product.

Now that there are more potential customers, mass selling becomes more economical. But salespeople and personal selling must still work in the channels, expanding the number of outlets and cementing relationships with channel members.

ConAgra's Banquet Homestyle Bakes product illustrates this stage. When ConAgra Foods introduced Homestyle Bakes, it was the first shelf-stable meal kit with the meat already in the package. ConAgra, also the producer of Armour processed meats, had the expertise to create a tasty product that a consumer could prepare in a few minutes and then just stick in the oven. When Homestyle Bakes came out there was no direct competition. The sales force used marketing research data to convince retailers to give the product shelf space, and ads used humor to highlight that the package was so heavy because it already included meat. However, over time promotion shifted to emphasize that Homestyle Bakes was adding a variety of new flavors and 10 percent more meat. Similarly, the sales force shifted its efforts to get retailers to participate in Homestyle Bakes's "Super Meals/Super Moms" contests, which offered harried moms prizes, such as a visit to a spa, to keep them interested in the Homestyle brand.[26]

Market maturity stage—"our brand is better, really"

In the market maturity stage, mass selling and sales promotion may dominate the promotion blends of consumer products firms. Business products may require more aggressive personal selling—perhaps supplemented by more advertising. The total dollars allocated to promotion may rise as competition increases.

If a firm already has high sales—relative to competitors—it may have a real advantage in promotion at this stage. For example, sales of Tylenol tablets are about four times the sales of Motrin competing tablets. If both Tylenol and Motrin spend the same percentage of sales (say 35 percent) on promotion, Tylenol will spend four times as much as its smaller competitor and will probably communicate to more people.

Firms that have differentiated their marketing mixes may favor mass selling because they have something to talk about. For instance, a firm with a strong brand may use reminder-type advertising or target frequent-buyer promotions at current customers to strengthen the relationship and keep customers loyal. This may be more effective than costly efforts to win customers away from competitors.

However, as a market drifts toward pure competition, some companies resort to price-cutting. This may temporarily increase the number of units sold, but it is also likely to reduce total revenue and the money available for promotion. The temporary sales gains disappear and prices are dragged down even lower when competitors retaliate with their own short-term sales promotions, like price-off coupons. As cash flowing into the business declines, spending may have to be cut back.[27]

Sales decline stage—"let's tell those who still want our product"

During the sales decline stage, the total amount spent on promotion usually decreases as firms try to cut costs to remain profitable. Since some people may still want the product, firms need more targeted promotion to reach these customers.

On the other hand, some firms may increase promotion to try to slow the cycle, at least temporarily. Crayola had almost all of the market for children's crayons, but sales were slowly declining as new kinds of markers came along. Crayola increased ad spending to urge parents to buy their kids a "fresh box."

SETTING THE PROMOTION BUDGET

Size of budget affects promotion efficiency and blend

There are some economies of scale in promotion. An ad on national TV might cost less *per person* reached than an ad on local TV. Similarly, citywide radio, TV, and newspapers may be cheaper than neighborhood newspapers or direct personal contact. But the *total cost* for some mass media may force small firms, or those with small promotion budgets, to use promotion alternatives that are more expensive per contact. For example, a small retailer might want to use local television but find that there is only enough money for a web page, an ad in the Yellow Pages, and an occasional newspaper ad.

The most common method of budgeting for promotion expenditures is to compute a percentage of either past sales or sales expected in the future. The virtue of this method is its simplicity. However, just because this mechanical approach is common doesn't mean that it's smart. It leads to expanding marketing expenditures when business is good and cutting back when business is poor. When business is poor, this approach may just make the problem worse—especially if weak promotion is the reason for declining sales.

Find the task and budget for it

In the light of our continuing focus on planning marketing strategies to reach objectives, the most sensible approach to budgeting promotion expenditures is the

Many marketing managers view promotion on the Internet and in the Yellow Pages as "must buys" in a promotion budget.

task method—basing the budget on the job to be done. This method helps the marketing manager set priorities so that the money spent produces specific results. In fact, this approach makes sense for *any* marketing expenditure, but here we'll focus on promotion.

A practical approach is to determine which promotion objectives are most important and which promotion methods are most economical and effective for the communication tasks relevant to each objective. The costs of these tasks are then totaled—to determine how much should be budgeted for promotion (just as money is allocated for other marketing activities required by the strategy). In other words, the firm can assemble its total promotion budget directly from detailed plans rather than by simply relying on historical patterns or ratios.

This method also helps to eliminate budget fights between managers responsible for different promotion methods who see themselves as pitted against each other for limited budget dollars. The specialists may still make their own suggestions about how to perform tasks. But then the budget allocations are based on the most effective ways of getting things done, not on what the firm did last year, what some competitor does, or even on internal politics. With this approach, different promotion specialists are also more likely to recognize that they must all work together to achieve truly integrated marketing communications.[28]

CONCLUSION

Promotion is an important part of any marketing mix. Most consumers and intermediate customers can choose from among many products. To be successful, a producer must not only offer a good product at a reasonable price but also inform potential customers about the product and where they can buy it. Further, producers must tell wholesalers and retailers in the channel about their product and marketing mix. These intermediaries, in turn, must use promotion to reach their customers. And the promotion blend must fit with the rest of the marketing mix and the target market.

In this chapter, we introduced different promotion methods and we discussed the advantages and disadvantages of each method. We also discussed the integrated marketing communications concept and explained why most firms use a blend of different promotion methods. While the overall promotion objective is to affect buying behavior, the basic promotion objectives are informing, persuading, and reminding.

These objectives help guide the marketing manager's decisions about the promotion blend.

Models from the behavioral sciences help us understand the communication process and how it can break down. These models recognize different ways to communicate. We discussed direct-response promotion for developing more targeted promotion blends. And we described an approach where customers initiate and interact with the marketer's communications. It provides new and different challenges for marketing managers.

This chapter also recognized other factors that influence decisions about promotion blends. Marketing managers must make decisions about how to split promotion that is directed at final consumers or business customers—and channel members. Promotion blends are also influenced by the adoption curve and the product life-cycle stages. Finally, we described how promotion budgets are set and how they influence promotion decisions.

KEY TERMS

QUESTIONS AND PROBLEMS

1. Briefly explain the nature of the three basic promotion methods available to a marketing manager. What are the main strengths and limitations of each?

2. In your own words, discuss the integrated marketing communications concept. Explain what its emphasis on "consistent" and "complete" messages implies with respect to promotion blends.

3. Relate the three basic promotion objectives to the four jobs (AIDA) of promotion using a specific example.

4. Discuss the communication process in relation to a producer's promotion of an accessory product—say, a new electronic security system businesses use to limit access to areas where they store confidential records.

5. If a company wants its promotion to appeal to a new group of target customers in a foreign country, how can it protect against its communications being misinterpreted?

6. Promotion has been the target of considerable criticism. What specific types of promotion are probably the object of this criticism? Give a particular example that illustrates your thinking.

7. With direct-response promotion, customers provide feedback to marketing communications. How can a marketing manager use this feedback to improve the effectiveness of the overall promotion blend?

8. How can a promotion manager target a message to a certain target market with electronic media (like the Internet) when the customer initiates the communication? Give an example.

9. What promotion blend would be most appropriate for producers of the following established products? Assume average- to large-sized firms in each case and support your answer.
   a. Chocolate candy bar.
   b. Car batteries.
   c. Panty hose.
   d. Castings for truck engines.
   e. A special computer used by manufacturers for control of production equipment.
   f. Inexpensive plastic rainhats.
   g. A digital tape recorder that has achieved specialty-product status.

10. A small company has developed an innovative new spray-on glass cleaner that prevents the buildup of electrostatic dust on computer screens and TVs. Give examples of some low-cost ways the firm might effectively promote its product. Be certain to consider both push and pull approaches.

11. Would promotion be successful in expanding the general demand for: (*a*) almonds, (*b*) air travel, (*c*) golf clubs, (*d*) walking shoes, (*e*) high-octane unleaded gasoline, (*f*) single-serving, frozen gourmet dinners, and (*g*) bricks? Explain why or why not in each case.

12. Explain how an understanding of the adoption process would help you develop a promotion blend for digital tape recorders, a new consumer electronics product that

produces high-quality recordings. Explain why you might change the promotion blend during the course of the adoption process.

13. Explain how opinion leaders affect a firm's promotion planning.

14. Discuss how the adoption curve should be used to plan the promotion blend(s) for a new automobile accessory—an electronic radar system that alerts a driver if he or she is about to change lanes into the path of a car that is passing through a blind spot in the driver's mirrors.

15. If a marketing manager uses the task method to budget for marketing promotions, are competitors' promotion spending levels ignored? Explain your thinking and give an example that supports your point of view.

16. Discuss the potential conflict among the various promotion managers. How could this be reduced?

CREATING MARKETING PLANS

The Marketing Plan Coach software on the Student CD includes a sample marketing plan for Hillside Veterinary Clinic. Look through the "Marketing Strategy" section.

a. What are Hillside's promotion objectives? How do they differ for the various goods and services the company offers?

b. Do the promotion activities recommended in the plan fit with the promotion objectives? Create a table to compare them. Label the columns: good/service, promotion objective, and promotion activities.

c. Based on the situation analysis, target market, and intended positioning, recommend other (low-cost) promotion activities for Hillside.

SUGGESTED CASES

18. Harrisburg Volunteer Fire Department   19. ourWedding.com

COMPUTER-AIDED PROBLEM

13. SELECTING A COMMUNICATIONS CHANNEL

Helen Troy, owner of three Sound Haus stereo equipment stores, is deciding what message channel (advertising medium) to use to promote her newest store. Her current promotion blend includes direct-mail ads that are effective for reaching her current customers. She also has knowledgeable salespeople who work well with consumers once they're in the store. However, a key objective in opening a new store is to attract new customers. Her best prospects are professionals in the 25–44 age range with incomes over $38,000 a year. But only some of the people in this group are audiophiles who want the top-of-the-line brands she carries. Troy has decided to use local advertising to reach new customers.

Troy narrowed her choice to two advertising media: an FM radio station and a biweekly magazine that focuses on entertainment in her city. Many of the magazine's readers are out-of-town visitors interested in concerts, plays, and restaurants. They usually buy stereo equipment at home. But the magazine's audience research shows that many local professionals do subscribe to the magazine. Troy doesn't think that the ob-

jective can be achieved with a single ad. However, she believes that ads in six issues will generate good local awareness with her target market. In addition, the magazine's color format will let her present the prestige image she wants to convey in an ad. She thinks that will help convert aware prospects to buyers. Specialists at a local advertising agency will prepare a high-impact ad for $2,000, and then Troy will pay for the magazine space.

The FM radio station targets an audience similar to Troy's own target market. She knows repeated ads will be needed to be sure that most of her target audience is exposed to her ads. Troy thinks it will take daily ads for several months to create adequate awareness among her target market. The FM station will provide an announcer and prepare a tape of Troy's ad for a one-time fee of $200. All she has to do is tell the station what the message content for the ad should say.

Both the radio station and the magazine gave Troy reports summarizing recent audience research. She decides that comparing the two media in a spreadsheet will help her make a better decision.

a. Based on the data displayed on the initial spreadsheet, which message channel (advertising medium) would you recommend to Troy? Why?

b. The agency that offered to prepare Troy's magazine ad will prepare a fully produced radio ad—including a musical jingle—for $2,500. The agency claims that its musical ad will have much more impact than the ad the radio station will create. The agency says its ad should produce the same results as the station ad with 20 percent fewer insertions. If the agency claim is correct, would it be wise for Troy to pay the agency to produce the ad?

c. The agency will not guarantee that its custom-produced radio ad will reach Troy's objective—making 80 percent of the prospects aware of the new store. Troy wants to see how lower levels of awareness—between 50 percent and 70 percent—would affect the advertising cost per buyer and the cost per aware prospect. Use the analysis feature to vary the percent of prospects who become aware. Prepare a table showing the effect on the two kinds of costs. What are the implications of your analysis?

For additional questions related to this problem, see Exercise 13–3 in the *Learning Aid for Use with Essentials of Marketing*, 11th edition.

Personal Selling and Customer Service

As a student in the College of Business at the University of Illinois, Pooja Gupta wanted a job that would offer interesting challenges, provide opportunities for professional growth, and value her enthusiasm. She found what she wanted with Ferguson. Ferguson was actively recruiting on college campuses to find the brightest and best candidates for its sales jobs—so, in a way, the job found her.

Gupta knew that motivated young people with ability often find the best opportunities for advancement in fast-growing companies. She didn't expect, however, that her fast-growing company would be a wholesaler of plumbing supplies, pipes, valves, and fittings. To the contrary, she'd heard that many wholesalers were declining. But that didn't apply to Ferguson. For decades it has doubled in size about every five years—and now it's the largest distributor of plumbing products in the United States. And in a business that serves such a wide variety of customer types—large industrial firms, city water works, commercial builders and subcontractors, kitchen and bath dealers, and final consumers—you don't get that kind of growth without strong marketing strategy planning—and a very effective sales force.

It's Ferguson's sales force that gets the initial orders with new customers, builds the relationships that instill customer loyalty, and provides the exceptional customer service support that Ferguson emphasizes in its marketing strategy. What's more, salespeople at Ferguson are real experts. They understand their customers' business problems and how Ferguson's products, e-commerce, and state-of-the-art logistics systems can help solve them. An effective sales force like the one at Ferguson doesn't just happen. Someone needs to figure out the promotion jobs that require personal selling and then get the right people on the job. As the president of the company put it, "In a time when computer interfaces often replace face-to-face contact and a handshake, and quality is sacrificed for convenience, Ferguson remains committed to our long-standing philosophy. We never settle for less than the best in products, in customer service provided, and in the associates who are the Ferguson team." Ferguson's sales, which were over $7 billion in 2005, are a tribute to that philosophy.

The strength of Ferguson's parent company, Wolseley PLC, also contributes to the overall success of Ferguson's sales force. Wolseley is an international business that operates in 14 countries, has 64,000 employees, and recently had annual sales over $20 billion. Wolseley focuses on distribution of construction products, so approaches that prove successful in one of its businesses are transferred to others.

Ferguson carries over a million products, provides service centers at nearly 1,100 locations, and has divisions that specialize by different customer segments. It would be futile for sales reps to try to be expert in everything. Instead, sales managers carefully match each salesperson to particular territories, customers, and product lines. Gupta, for example, helps contractors in the Virginia market figure out how to satisfy the needs of final consumers for whom they are building homes. She knows the current fashions in bathroom sinks for million-dollar homes, how to reduce "behind-the-wall" installation costs in big subdivisions, and the advantages and limitations of hundreds of brands from companies like Kohler, Elkay, Moen, and Jacuzzi. Other Ferguson salespeople work with cities and huge waterworks contractors on projects such as updating water purification facilities. And salespeople for Ferguson's Integrated Systems Division (ISD) are really selling a big business idea rather than "pipe." They show top executives at customer firms why they should invest millions of dollars in a full-service supply relationship where Ferguson does all of the purchasing and warehousing for entire manufacturing facilities. In stark contrast, the main sales job in one of Ferguson's new self-service Xpress outlets is to ring up sales when hurried plumbers need repair parts for a current job.

To be certain that these varied jobs are done well, Ferguson's sales managers recruit talented people using a wide variety of methods. For example, the careers section of Ferguson's website collects job applicant profiles on an ongoing basis. When a position opens up, qualified candidates are notified. And Ferguson actively recruits on college campuses, hiring over 1,000 graduates every year. After a pre-interview on campus, candidates go to a regional office and meet a number of managers from that area. After the best people are selected, Ferguson provides the sales training to make them even better. Of course, the training is different for different people. For example, most new college recruits work for a short time in a Ferguson warehouse, which helps them understand the company's logistics system, its products, and its industry, as well as the company's "can-do" culture. Other training methods range from self-study computer modules to role playing to working in the field with experienced managers who help them build professional problem-solving skills as well as technical knowledge. Even experienced sales reps need ongoing training on new strategies or policies (for example, ways in which the Ferguson service experience should be similar for customers regardless of what branch or division is handling the business).

To be sure that each salesperson is highly motivated, Ferguson's sales managers must make certain that sales compensation arrangements and benefits reward salespeople for producing needed results. All of that growth isn't possible unless everyone is doing their best work and being rewarded for it. For example, the evaluation considers how well individuals work with others on a team—because part of the customer-service culture at Ferguson is based on everyone being adaptable in embracing new challenges.[1]

LEARNING OBJECTIVES

Promotion is communicating with potential customers and others in the channel. As the Ferguson case suggests, personal selling is often the best way to do it. While face to face with prospects, salespeople can adjust what they say or do to the prospect's interests, needs, questions, and feedback. If, and when, the prospect is ready to buy, the salesperson is there to ask for the order. And afterward, the salesperson works to be certain that the customer is satisfied and will buy again in the future. In this chapter, you'll learn about the key strategy decisions related to personal selling that marketing managers and the sales managers who work with them make.

When you finish this chapter, you should:

1. understand the importance and nature of personal selling.

2. know the three basic sales tasks—order-getting, order-taking, and supporting—and what the various kinds of salespeople can be expected to do.

3. understand why customer service presents different challenges than other personal selling tasks.

4. know the different ways sales managers can organize salespeople so that personal selling jobs are handled effectively.

5. know how sales technology affects the way sales tasks are performed.

6. know what the sales manager must do, including selecting, training, and organizing salespeople to carry out the personal selling job.

7. understand how the right compensation plan can help motivate and control salespeople.

8. understand when and where to use the three types of sales presentations.

9. understand important new terms (shown in red).

THE IMPORTANCE AND ROLE OF PERSONAL SELLING

Personal selling requires strategy decisions

In this chapter, we'll discuss the importance and nature of personal selling and customer service so you'll understand the strategy decisions in this area. See Exhibit 14–1.

We'll also discuss a number of frameworks and how-to approaches that guide these strategy decisions. Because these approaches apply equally to domestic and international markets, we won't emphasize that distinction in this chapter. This does not mean, however, that personal selling techniques don't vary from one country to another. To the contrary, in dealing with *any* customer, the salesperson must adjust for cultural influences and other factors that might affect communication. For example, a Japanese customer and an Arab customer might respond differently to subtle aspects of a salesperson's behavior. The Arab customer might expect to be very close to a salesperson, perhaps only two feet away, while they talk. The Japanese customer might consider that distance rude. Similarly, what topics of discussion are considered sensitive, how messages are interpreted, and which negotiating styles are used vary from one country to another. A salesperson must know how to communicate effectively with each customer—wherever and whoever that customer is.[2]

Personal selling is important

Personal selling is absolutely essential in the promotion blends of some firms. Consider how you would feel if you regularly had to meet payrolls and somehow, almost miraculously, your salespeople kept coming in with orders just in time to keep the business profitable.

Personal selling is often a company's largest single operating expense. This is another reason why it is important to understand sales management decisions. Bad ones are costly in terms of both lost sales and actual out-of-pocket expenses.

Exhibit 14–1   Strategy Planning and Personal Selling

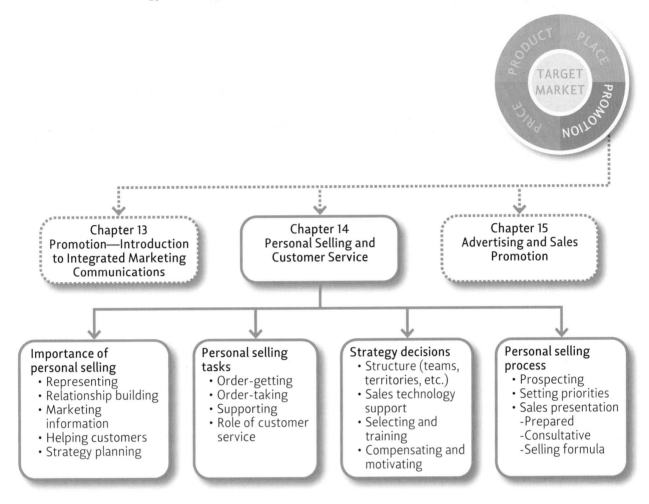

Every economy needs and uses many salespeople. In the United States, one person out of every ten in the total labor force is involved in sales work.

Helping to buy is good selling

Good salespeople don't just try to *sell* the customer. Rather, they try to *help the customer buy*—by understanding the customer's needs and presenting the advantages and disadvantages of their products. Such helpfulness results in satisfied customers and long-term relationships. And strong relationships often form the basis for a competitive advantage, especially in business markets.

You may think in terms of an old-time stereotype of a salesperson: a bag of wind with no more to offer than a funny story, a big expense account, and an engaging grin. But that isn't true any more. Old-time salespeople are being replaced by real professionals—problem solvers—who have something definite to contribute to their employers *and* their customers.

Salespeople represent the whole company— and customers too

The salesperson is often a representative of the whole company—responsible for explaining its total effort to customers rather than just pushing products. The salesperson may provide information about products, explain company policies, and even negotiate prices or diagnose technical problems.

The sales rep is often the only link between the firm and its customers, especially if customers are far away. When a number of people from the firm work with the customer organization—which is common when suppliers and customers form close

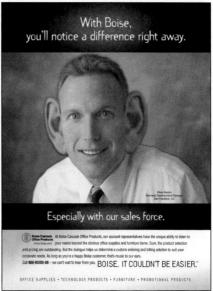

relationships—it is usually the sales rep who coordinates the relationship for his or her firm. See Exhibit 6–5.

The salesperson also represents the *customer* back inside the selling firm. Recall that feedback is an essential part of both the communication process *and* the basic management process of planning, implementing, and control. For example, it's likely to be the sales rep who explains to the production manager why a customer is unhappy with product quality or to the e-commerce specialist how better order status information available on the website could cut the customer's costs.

As evidence of these changing responsibilities, some companies give their salespeople such titles as account representative, field manager, sales consultant, market specialist, or sales engineer.

Sales force aids in marketing information function as well

The sales force can aid in the marketing information function too. The sales rep may be the first to hear about a new competitor or a competitor's new strategy. And sales reps who are well attuned to customers' needs can be a key source of ideas for new products or new uses for existing products.

Material Sciences Corporation developed a product called Quiet Steel, two thin layers of steel bonded together to absorb vibration so that it doesn't rattle. A sales rep who worked with the Ford team developing the new F-150 truck probed to understand where Ford was trying to reduce noise and recommended how Quiet Steel could help. Feedback to the company about the most promising applications helps Quiet Steel reps who call on other car makers pursue similar applications. And the R&D department for Quiet Steel benefits from hearing from the sales reps about applications where the current product isn't quite right, but where there might be an opportunity for a new product.[3]

Salespeople can be strategy planners too

Some salespeople are expected to be marketing managers in their own territories. And some become marketing managers by default because top management hasn't provided detailed strategy guidelines. Either way, the salesperson may have choices about (1) what target customers to aim at, (2) which particular products to emphasize, (3) which middlemen to rely on or help, (4) how to use promotion money, and (5) how to adjust prices. A salesperson who can put together profitable strategies and implement them well can rise very rapidly. The opportunity is there for those prepared and willing to work.[4]

WHAT KINDS OF PERSONAL SELLING ARE NEEDED?

If a firm has too few salespeople, or the wrong kind, some important personal selling tasks may not be completed. And having too many salespeople wastes money. In addition, the balance that is right may change over time with other changes in strategy or the marketing environment. That's why many firms have to restructure their sales forces.

One of the difficulties of determining the right number and kind of salespeople is that every sales job is different. While an engineer or accountant can look forward to fairly specific duties, the salesperson's job changes constantly. However, there are three basic types of sales tasks. This gives us a starting point for understanding what sales tasks need to be done and how many people are needed to do them.

Personal selling is divided into three tasks

The three **basic sales tasks** are order-getting, order-taking, and supporting. For convenience, we'll describe salespeople by these terms—referring to their primary task—*although one person may do all three tasks in some situations*.

ORDER GETTERS DEVELOP NEW BUSINESS RELATIONSHIPS

Order getters are concerned with establishing relationships with new customers and developing new business. **Order-getting** means seeking possible buyers with a well-organized sales presentation designed to sell a good, service, or idea.

Order getters must know what they're talking about, not just be personal contacts. Order-getting salespeople normally are well paid—many earn more than $80,000 a year.

Producers' order getters—find new opportunities

Producers of all kinds of products, especially business products, have a great need for order getters. They use order getters to locate new prospects, open new accounts, see new opportunities, and help establish and build channel relationships.

Top-level customers are more interested in ways to save or make more money than in technical details. Good order getters cater to this interest. They help the customer

Customers who are making an important purchase want relationships with salespeople whose advice they can trust.

Producers sometimes aid in the personal selling effort by providing innovative displays that communicate not only the features but also the benefits of their products. To help salespeople explain the benefits of its Profile washer and dryer, GE places this interactive display in dealers' stores.

identify ways to solve problems; then they sell concepts and ideas, not just physical products. The goods and services they supply are merely the means of achieving the customer's end.

To be effective at this sort of "solutions selling," an order getter often needs to understand a customer's whole business as well as technical details about the product and its applications. For example, a salesperson for automated manufacturing equipment must understand a prospect's production process as well as the technical details of converting to computer-controlled equipment.

Order getters for professional services—and other products where service is a crucial element of the marketing mix—face a special challenge. The customer usually can't inspect a service before deciding to buy. The order getter's communication and relationship with the customer may be the only basis on which to evaluate the quality of the supplier.

Wholesalers' order getters—almost hand it to the customer

Agent middlemen often are order getters—particularly the more aggressive manufacturers' agents and brokers. They face the same tasks as producers' order getters. But, unfortunately for them, once the order-getting is done and the customers become established and loyal, producers may try to eliminate the agents and save money with their own order takers.

Retail order getters influence consumer behavior

Convincing consumers about the value of products they haven't seriously considered takes a high level of personal selling ability. Order getters for unsought consumer products must help customers see how a new product can satisfy needs now being filled by something else. Without order getters, many common products—ranging from mutual funds to air conditioners—might have died in the market introduction stage. The order getter helps bring products out of the introduction stage into the market growth stage.

Order getters are also helpful for selling *heterogeneous* shopping products. Consumers shop for many of these items on the basis of suitability and value. They welcome useful information.

ORDER TAKERS NURTURE RELATIONSHIPS TO KEEP THE BUSINESS COMING

Order takers sell to the regular or established customers, complete most sales transactions, and maintain relationships with their customers. After a customer becomes interested in a firm's products through an order getter or supporting salesperson or through advertising or sales promotion, an order taker usually answers any final questions and completes the sale. **Order-taking** is the routine completion of sales made regularly to target customers. It usually requires ongoing follow-up to make certain that the customer is totally satisfied.

Producers' order takers—train, explain, and collaborate

Order takers work on improving the whole relationship with their accounts, not just on completing a single sale. Even in e-commerce, where customers place routine orders with computerized order systems and EDI, order takers do a variety of important jobs that are essential to the business relationship. Someone has to explain details, make adjustments, handle complaints, explain new prices or terms, place sales promotion materials, and keep customers informed of new developments. An order taker who fails to meet a customer's expectations on any of these activities might jeopardize the relationship and future sales.

Firms sometimes use order-taking jobs to train potential order getters and managers. Such jobs give them an opportunity to meet customers and better understand their needs. And frequently, they run into some order-getting opportunities.

Order takers who are alert to order-getting possibilities can make the big difference in generating new sales. Some firms lose sales just because no one ever asks for the order. Banks try to avoid this problem. For example, when a customer walks into a Bank of America branch to make a deposit, the teller's computer screen shows information about the customer's accounts. If the balance in a checking account is high but the customer does not use any of the bank's other investment services, the teller is trained to ask if the customer would be interested in learning about the bank's certificates of deposit. Some banks use more sophisticated customer relationship management (CRM) database systems that figure out which specific financial service would be best for the teller to recommend.[5]

Wholesalers' order takers—not getting orders but keeping them

While producers' order takers usually handle relatively few items, wholesalers' order takers often sell thousands of items. Sales reps who handle that many items may single out a few of the newer or more profitable items for special attention, but it's not possible to give aggressive sales effort to many. So the main job of wholesalers' order takers is to maintain close contact with customers, place orders, and check to be sure the company fills orders promptly. Order takers also handle any adjustments or complaints and generally act as liaisons between the company and its customers.

Retail order takers—often they are poor salesclerks

Order-taking may be almost mechanical at the retail level—for example, at the supermarket checkout counter. Some retail clerks perform poorly because they aren't paid much—often only the minimum wage. Even so, retail order takers play a vital role in a retailer's marketing mix. Customers expect prompt and friendly service. They will find a new place to shop, or to do their banking or have their car serviced, rather than deal with a salesclerk who is rude or acts annoyed by having to complete a sale.

SUPPORTING SALES FORCE INFORMS AND PROMOTES IN THE CHANNEL

Supporting salespeople help the order-oriented salespeople, but they don't try to get orders themselves. Their activities are aimed at enhancing the relationship with the customer and getting sales in the long run. For the short run, however, they are ambassadors of goodwill who may provide specialized services and information. There are three types of supporting salespeople: missionary salespeople, technical specialists, and customer service reps.

Missionary salespeople can increase sales

Missionary salespeople are supporting salespeople who work for producers—calling on their middlemen and their customers. They try to develop goodwill and stimulate demand, help intermediaries train their salespeople, and often take orders for delivery by intermediaries. Missionary salespeople are sometimes called *merchandisers* or *detailers*.

Producers who rely on merchant wholesalers or e-commerce to obtain widespread distribution often use missionary salespeople. The sales rep can give a promotion boost to a product that otherwise wouldn't get much attention because it's just one of many. A missionary salesperson for Vicks cold remedy products, for example, might visit pharmacists during the cold season and encourage them to use a special end-of-aisle display for Vicks cough syrup—and then help set it up. The wholesaler that supplies the drugstore would benefit from any increased sales but might not take the time to urge use of the special display.

An imaginative missionary salesperson can double or triple sales for a company. Naturally, this doesn't go unnoticed. Missionary sales jobs are often a route to order-oriented jobs.

Technical specialists are experts who know product applications

Technical specialists are supporting salespeople who provide technical assistance to order-oriented salespeople. Technical specialists are often science or engineering graduates with the know-how to understand the customer's applications and explain the advantages of the company's product. They are usually more skilled in showing the technical details of their product than in trying to persuade customers to buy it. Before the specialist's visit, an order getter probably has stimulated interest. The technical specialist provides the details.

Customer service reps solve problems after a purchase

Customer service reps work with customers to resolve problems that arise with a purchase, usually after the purchase has been made. *Every* marketing-oriented company needs good people to handle customer service. Customer service is important to

When a customer firm, like a supermarket chain, buys Hobart equipment, technical support people provide training for the firm's employees.

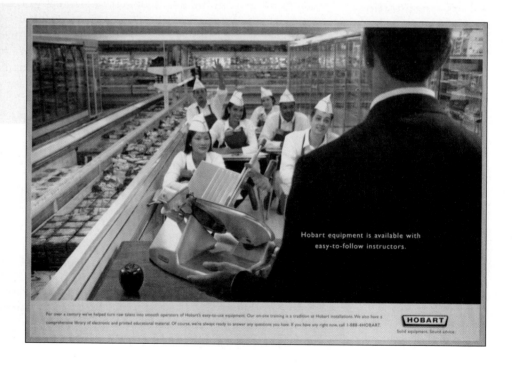

Hobart equipment is available with easy-to-follow instructors.

For over a century we've helped turn raw talent into smooth operators of Hobart's easy-to-use equipment. Our on-site training is a tradition at Hobart installations. We also have a comprehensive library of electronic and printed educational material. Of course, we're always ready to answer any questions you have. If you have any right now, call 1-888-4HOBART.

HOBART
Solid equipment. Sound advice.

both business customers and final consumers. There are times when a customer's problem simply can't be resolved without a personal touch.

In general, all types of personal selling help to win customers, but effective customer service is especially critical in keeping them. It is often the key to building repeat business. It's useful to think of customer service reps as *the salespeople who promote a customer's next purchase—by being sure that the customer is satisfied with a previous purchase.* In this chapter, you'll see that the strategy decisions for customer service reps are the same as for others involved in personal selling. In spite of this, some firms don't view customer service as a personal selling activity—or as part of the firm's integrated marketing communications. They manage it as a production operation and think of the output as responses to questions or complaints from "problem customers." That approach is one reason that customer service is often a challenging area for firms. So, it's useful to take a closer look at why customer service activities are so important and why firms should manage them as part of the personal selling effort.

CUSTOMER SERVICE PROMOTES THE NEXT PURCHASE

Customer service is not the product

People sometimes use the term *customer service* as a catch-all expression for anything that helps customers. Our focus here is on the service that is required *to solve a problem that a customer encounters with a purchase.* In that regard, it is useful to think about the difference between customer service and the service (or support) that is part of the product that a customer buys.

In Chapter 8, we discussed the idea that a firm's product is its need-satisfying offering, and that it may be a physical good, a service, or a combination of the two. See Exhibit 8–2. Citibank offers consumers credit card services for a fee. Wolf Camera makes prints from customers' digital images. In these situations, customers see service as an important aspect of what they are purchasing.

However, from a customer's perspective, that kind of service is different from the customer service that is required to fix a problem when something doesn't work as the customer hopes or expects. For example, our customer doesn't expect the Citibank ATM to eat her credit card when she's on a trip and doesn't want Wolf to charge more than the advertised price for her pictures or for them to be smudged. These problems are breakdowns in the firms' marketing mixes. What the customer expected from the seller is not what the customer got.

When a customer service rep works to solve a customer's problem, it often involves taking steps to remedy what went wrong. But repairing a negative experience is fundamentally different from providing a positive experience in the first place. No matter how effective the customer service solution, the problem is an inconvenience or involves other types of costs to the customer. Thus, the customer value from the firm's marketing mix is lower than what the customer bargained for.

Why customer service is part of promotion

We mentioned before that customers weigh negative experiences more heavily than positive experiences when they decide whether to buy the same product (or buy from the same company) again. They are also more likely to tell other people about bad experiences with a company than about good ones. The practical matter is that customer service interactions arise because the customer is unhappy. So, if the firm doesn't have an effective way to provide customer service it is, consciously or unconsciously, making a decision to kiss that customer good-bye. In today's highly competitive markets, that can be a big mistake, especially in situations where it's costly to acquire new customers or when the lifetime value of a customer is significant. Poor customer service reduces the firm's customer equity.

This is why firms should view customer service reps as a key part of personal selling. They are not just fixing the customer's problem, but rather fixing the *company's* problem, which is the risk of losing customers.

Customer service reps are customer advocates

A breakdown in any element of the marketing mix can result in a requirement for customer service. Ideally, a firm should deliver what it promises, but marketing is a human process and mistakes do happen. Consider, for example, a customer who decides to use Verizon cell phone service because its ad—or the salesperson at the Radio Shack who sold the phone—said that the first month of service would be free. If Verizon bills the customer for the first month, is it a pricing problem, a promotion problem, or a lack of coordination in the channel? From the customer's perspective, it really doesn't matter. What does matter is that expectations have been dashed. The customer doesn't need explanations or excuses but instead needs an advocate to make things right.

Sometimes the marketing mix is fine, but the customer makes a purchase that is a mistake. Or customers may simply change their minds. Either way, customers usually expect sellers to help fix purchasing errors. Firms need policies about how customer service reps should deal with customer errors. But, most firms simply can't afford to alienate customers, even ones who have made an error, if they expect them to come back in the future. Sometimes the toughest sales job is figuring out how to keep a customer who is unhappy.

Regardless of whether the firm or customer causes the problem, customer service reps need to be effective communicators, have good judgment, and realize that they are advocates not only for their firm but also for its customers. As that implies, the rest of the company needs to be organized to provide the support reps need to fix problems.

THE RIGHT STRUCTURE HELPS ASSIGN RESPONSIBILITY

We have described three sales tasks—order-getting, order-taking, and supporting. A sales manager must organize the sales force so that all the necessary tasks are done well. In many situations, a particular salesperson might be given two, or all three, of these tasks. For example, 10 percent of a particular job may be order-getting, 80 percent order-taking, and the additional 10 percent customer service. On the other hand, organizations are often structured to have different salespeople specializing by different sales tasks and by the target markets they serve.

Sales tasks may be handled by a team

If different people handle different sales tasks, firms often rely on **team selling**—when different people work together on a specific account. Sometimes members of a sales team are not from the sales department at all. If improving the relationship with

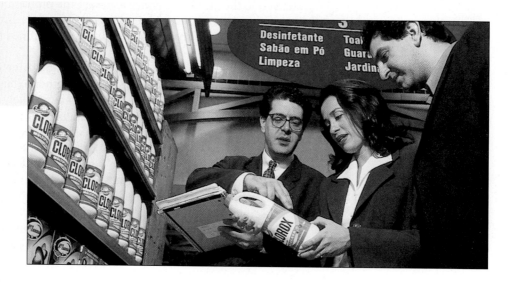

The Clorox sales team responsible for the launch of liquid beach in the Brazilian market drew on people from R&D, marketing, and sales.

the customer calls for input from the quality control manager, then that person becomes a part of the team, at least temporarily. Producers of high-ticket items often use team selling. IBM uses team selling to sell information technology solutions for a whole business. Different specialists handle different parts of the job—but the whole team coordinates its efforts to achieve the desired result.

Different target markets need different sales tasks

Sales managers often divide sales force responsibilities based on the type of customer involved. For example, Bigelow—a company that makes quality carpet for homes and office buildings—divided its sales force into groups of specialists. Some Bigelow salespeople call only on architects to help them choose the best type of carpet for new office buildings. These reps know all the technical details, such as how well a certain carpet fiber will wear or its effectiveness in reducing noise from office equipment. Often no sale is involved because the architect only suggests specifications and doesn't actually buy the carpet. Other Bigelow salespeople call on retail carpet stores. These reps encourage the store manager to keep a variety of Bigelow carpets in stock. They also introduce new products, help train the store's salespeople, and try to solve any problems that occur. Bigelow also has a group of customer service reps who are available via a toll-free number. They help final consumers who have purchased carpet but have a problem that the carpet store can't resolve.

Big accounts get special treatment

Very large customers often require special sales effort—and relationships with them are treated differently. Moen, a maker of plumbing fixtures, has a regular sales force to call on building material wholesalers and an elite **major accounts sales force** that sells directly to large accounts—like Lowe's or other major retail chains that carry plumbing fixtures.

You can see why this sort of special attention is justified when you consider Procter & Gamble's relationship with Wal-Mart. Wal-Mart accounts for one-fourth or more of the total national sales in many of the product categories in which P&G competes. For instance, Wal-Mart sells about one-third of the toothpaste in the United States. If P&G wants to grow its share of the toothpaste market, it has to make certain that it stimulates an effective sales effort with Wal-Mart.

Some salespeople specialize in telephone selling

Some firms have a group of salespeople who specialize in **telemarketing**—using the telephone to "call" on customers or prospects. In Chapter 13, we highlighted the consumer backlash to the use of cold call telemarketing for prospecting. However, the reception to telephone selling in business markets is often quite different.

In business markets, an "inside" sales force can often build profitable relationships with small or hard-to-reach customers the firm might otherwise have to ignore. Telephone selling is also used to extend personal selling efforts to new target markets or increase the frequency of contact with current customers. The big advantage of telephone selling by an inside sales group in these situations is that it saves time and money for the seller, and it gives customers a fast and easy way to solve a purchasing problem. For example, many firms use toll-free telephone lines to make it convenient for customers to call the inside sales force for assistance or to place an order. Firms also rely heavily on telephone selling to provide support a customer may need in an e-commerce situation.

Companies that produce goods and services for final consumers also rely heavily on toll-free telephone lines to give final consumers easy access to customer service reps. In most cases, there is no other practical way for the producer to be sure that retailers are taking care of customers or their problems. A customer service call center provides a way for the producer to get direct feedback from customers—and perhaps find solutions to potential problems.[6]

Sales tasks are done in sales territories

Often companies organize selling tasks on the basis of a **sales territory**—a geographic area that is the responsibility of one salesperson or several working together. A territory might be a region of a country, a state, or part of a city, depending on the market potential. An airplane manufacturer like Boeing might consider a whole country as *part* of a sales territory for one salesperson.

Carefully set territories can reduce travel time and the cost of sales calls. Assigning territories can also help reduce confusion about who has responsibility for a set of sales tasks.

Sometimes simple geographic division isn't easy. A company may have different products that require very different knowledge or selling skills—even if products sell in the same territory or to the same customer. For example, Du Pont makes special films for hospital X-ray departments as well as chemicals used in laboratory blood tests.

Size of sales force depends on workload

Once the important sales tasks have been specified and the responsibilities divided, the sales manager must decide how many salespeople are needed. The first step is estimating how much work can be done by one person in some time period. Then the sales manager can make an educated guess about how many people are required in total, as the following example shows.

For many years, the Parker Jewelry Company was very successful selling its silver jewelry to department and jewelry stores in the southwestern region of the United States. But top managers wanted to expand into the big urban markets in the northeastern states. They realized that most of the work for the first few years would require order getters. They felt that a salesperson would need to call on each account at least once a month to get a share of this competitive business. They estimated that a salesperson could make only five calls a day on prospective buyers and still allow time for travel, waiting, and follow-up on orders that came in. This meant that a sales rep who made calls 20 days a month could handle about 100 stores (5 a day × 20 days)

The managers used a CD-ROM database that included all of the telephone Yellow Pages listings for the country. Then they simply divided the total number of stores by 100 to estimate the number of salespeople needed. This also helped them set up territories—by defining areas that included about 100 stores for each salesperson. Obviously, managers might want to fine-tune this estimate for differences in territories—such as travel time. But the basic approach can be adapted to many different situations.[7]

Some managers forget that over time the right number of salespeople may change as sales tasks change. Then when a problem becomes obvious, they try to change everything in a hurry—a big mistake. Consideration of what type of salespeople and how many should be ongoing. If the sales force needs to be reduced, it doesn't make sense to let a lot of people go all at once, especially when that could be avoided with some planning.

Sometimes technology can substitute for personal selling

Some sales tasks that have traditionally been handled by a person can now be handled effectively and at lower cost by an e-commerce system or other technology. The situation that the firm faces may influence which approach makes the most sense and how many salespeople are really needed. See Exhibit 14–2.

A salesperson is required in important selling situations where there is a need to create and build relationships. Here the salesperson (or customer service rep) focuses on tasks like creative problem solving, persuading, coordinating among people who do different jobs, and finding ways to support the customer. On the other hand, information technology is cost effective for handling needs related to the recurring exchange of standardized information (such as inventory, orders, and delivery status). Similarly, details of product specifications and prices can be organized at a website. Of course, there should be some way to provide good customer service when needs arise. In a complex relationship, using technology for standard information frees the sales rep to spend time on value-added communication.

Digital self-service is not a cure-all

When relationship building by a sales rep is not required and there is not a recurring need for routine information, a firm may be able to meet customer needs best by providing digital self-service. This is basically the role of ATMs for banks—to service

Exhibit 14-2
Examples of Possible
Personal Selling
Emphasis in Some
Different Business-
Market Selling
Situations

	Low	**High**
High Standardized information exchanged on a recurring basis (orders, invoices, delivery status, product information, prices)	Emphasis on standardized e-commerce (with customer service)	Emphasis on both personal selling and customized e-commerce
Low	Emphasis on digital self-service	Emphasis on personal selling

Relationship building required
(problem solving, coordination, support, cooperation)

customers who don't want to wait until a teller is available. Similarly, Amazon's virtual shopping carts play this role. But digital self-service can be more sophisticated.

Some firms provide an "intelligent agent" at their websites. An intelligent agent is a computer program that helps customers solve their own problems. At the CompUSA website, a customer who wants to buy a notebook computer can respond to a series of structured questions about how the computer will be used, and the intelligent agent recommends which features are most important and what brands have those features.

While digital self-service works well in many situations, it has risks when it's used for customer service problems. A customer service rep can be a customer's advocate, but technology can't. The more serious the customer's problem, the less likely it is

The website for the Hass Avocado Board provides self-service information for firms that buy avocados from Hass growers. The buyers are already experts, so many of their routine information needs can be served well with an up-to-date website, without the expense of personal contact from a salesperson.

that digital self-service can resolve it; and a problem can easily escalate when the customer can't get help. For example, it may appear cost-efficient to rely on a telephone menu system that offers customers a series of choices, but if the process wastes time or doesn't work, customers will be even more frustrated. Worse, the company won't know there's a problem to fix. Personal communication is expensive, but so is the cost of losing customers because they can't get help.

We've focused on technology that substitutes for personal contact by a salesperson. But marketing managers also need to make decisions about providing sales technology support to help salespeople communicate more effectively.

INFORMATION TECHNOLOGY PROVIDES TOOLS TO DO THE JOB

Changes in how sales tasks are handled

How sales tasks and responsibilities are planned and handled is changing in many companies because of the new sales technology tools that are available. It is usually the sales manager's job—perhaps with help from specialists in technology—to decide what types of tools are needed and how they will be used.

To get a sense of what is involved, consider a day in the life of a sales rep for a large consumer packaged goods firm. Over a hasty breakfast, she plans the day's sales calls on her laptop's organizer, logs onto the company network, and sorts through a dozen e-mail messages she finds there. One is from a buyer for a supermarket chain. Sales in the chain's paper towel category are off 10 percent, and he wants to know if the rep can help. The rep downloads sales trend data for the chain and its competitors from her firm's intranet. A spreadsheet analysis of the data reveals that the sales decline is due to new competition from warehouse clubs. After a videoconference with a brand manager and a company sales promotion specialist to seek advice, she prepares a PowerPoint presentation, complete with a proposed shelf-space plan, that recommends that the buyer promote larger size packages of both her company's and competitors' brands. Before leaving home, the rep e-mails an advance copy of the report to the buyer and her manager. In her car, she calls the buyer to schedule an appointment.

Information technology is making the modern sales force more efficient and giving salespeople new ways to meet the needs of their customers while achieving the objectives of their jobs. Salesforce.com is an online solution to sales force automation.

Salespeople Work Smarter— with Their Fingertips

Tablet PCs, PDAs, and laptops are helping more salespeople work smarter, not just harder. Salespeople are using computers in many different ways.

Without a laptop, it was impossible for a wholesaler's salespeople to master Cincinnati Milacron's product line. Now a computer asks a series of questions and then helps the salesperson figure out which of 65,000 grinding wheels and hundreds of cutting fluids to sell to each metal shop. After adding this system, Milacron doubled its market share—without adding any new salespeople.

Sales reps for Crown Beer Distributors found that laptops were too bulky to take with them when they called on accounts along their routes. However, a hand-held tablet PC was just right for the task. The sales reps enter inventory data and orders right into the tablet. The screen is small, but they can instantly pull up whatever information a customer may want to see. With everything at their fingertips, some salespeople save an hour each day—and in the process handle required administrative reporting without it becoming tedious. As the president of the firm noted, "When you start to multiply that out for distributors with 20 or 30 salespeople, that's a significant amount of savings."

Salespeople for Metropolitan Life Insurance Company use laptops to help customers analyze the financial implications of different investments. For example, when the manager of a pension fund wanted to see what would happen if she switched money from one investment to another, the salesperson used spreadsheet software on the laptop to do the analysis—on the spot. The customer was convinced, and the sales rep closed a $633,000 sale.

Herman Miller, the office equipment company, provides dealers who sell its furniture with software that allows their sales reps to do a better job in a variety of tasks ranging from competitor analysis to preparation of realistic three-dimensional graphics that show an arrangement of furniture in a customer's office space. The competitor database provides very useful information about the limitations of office furniture available from many other firms. For instance, a sales rep learned that a prospect was leaning toward buying a competitor's office cubicles. She got back on track when the database revealed that the cubicles had no electrical outlets.

Results like these explain why the number of companies equipping salespeople with technology is growing so rapidly. Multimedia computers that handle massive amounts of information, including full-motion video for demonstrations and presentations, wireless Internet access, and e-commerce applications are standard equipment. Further, Web-enabled PDAs and cell phones now offer capabilities once reserved only for computers, providing a link to company databases and all the resources of the Internet.[8]

New software and hardware provide a competitive advantage

The sales rep in this example relies on support from an array of software and hardware that wasn't available a decade ago. Software for CRM, spreadsheet sales analysis, digital presentations, time management, sales forecasting, customer contact, and shelf-space management are at the salesperson's fingertips. Commonplace hardware includes everything from PDAs with wireless Internet access to personal videoconferencing systems. In many situations, these technologies give sales reps new ways to meet customers' needs while achieving the objectives of their jobs.

These tools change how well the job is done. Yet this is not simply a matter that is best left to individual sales reps. Use of these tools may be necessary just to compete effectively. For example, if a customer expects a sales rep to access data on past sales and provide an updated sales forecast, a sales organization that does not have this capability will be at a real disadvantage in keeping that customer's business.

On the other hand, these tools have costs. There is an obvious expense of buying the technology. But there is also the training cost of keeping everyone up-to-date. Often that is not an easy matter. Some salespeople who have done the sales job well

Videoconferencing technology allows a salesperson to make a sales presentation to a customer anywhere in the world.

for a long time "the old-fashioned way" resent being told that they have to change what they are doing, even if it's what customers expect. So if a firm expects salespeople to be able to use these technologies, that requirement needs to be included in selecting and training people for the job.[9]

SOUND SELECTION AND TRAINING TO BUILD A SALES FORCE

Selecting good salespeople takes judgment, plus

It is important to hire *well-qualified* salespeople who will do a good job. But selection in many companies is done without serious thought about exactly what kind of person the firm needs. Managers may hire friends and relations, or whoever is available, because they feel that the only qualifications for sales jobs are a friendly personality. This approach leads to poor sales, lost customers, and costly sales force turnover.

Progressive companies are more careful. They constantly update a list of possible job candidates. They invite applications at the company's website. They schedule candidates for multiple interviews with various executives and do thorough background checks. Unfortunately, such techniques don't guarantee success. But a systematic approach based on several different inputs results in a better sales force.

One problem in selecting salespeople is that two different sales jobs with identical titles may involve very different selling or supporting tasks and require different skills. A carefully prepared job description helps avoid this problem.

Job descriptions should be in writing and specific

A **job description** is a written statement of what a salesperson is expected to do. It might list 10 to 20 specific tasks—as well as routine prospecting and sales report writing. Each company must write its own job specifications. And it should provide clear guidelines about what selling tasks the job involves. This is critical to determine the kind of salespeople who should be selected—and later it provides a basis for seeing how they should be trained, how well they are performing, and how they should be paid.

Good salespeople are trained, not born

The idea that good salespeople are born that way may have some truth—but it isn't the whole story. A salesperson needs to be taught about the company and its products, about giving effective sales presentations, and about building relationships with customers. But this isn't always done. Many salespeople do a poor job because they haven't had good training. Firms often hire new salespeople and immediately send them out on the road, or the retail selling floor, with no grounding in the basic selling steps and no information about the product or the customer. They just get a price list and a pat on the back. This isn't enough!

Many firms turn to outside specialists, like Caliper, who can help sales managers improve the selection, training, and motivation of their sales reps.

All salespeople need some training

It's up to sales and marketing management to be sure that salespeople know what they're supposed to do and how to do it. Hewlett-Packard Development Co. recently faced this problem. For years the company was organized into divisions based on different product lines—printers, networks servers, and the like. However, sales reps who specialized in the products of one division often couldn't compete well against firms that could offer customers total solutions to computing problems. When a new top executive came in and reorganized the company, all sales reps needed training in their new responsibilities, how they would be organized, and what they should say to their customers about the benefits of the reorganization.

Sales training should be modified based on the experience and skills of the group involved. But the company's sales training program should cover at least the following areas: (1) company policies and practices, (2) product information, (3) building relationships with customer firms, and (4) professional selling skills.

Selling skills can be learned

Many companies spend the bulk of their training time on product information and company policy. They neglect training in selling techniques because they think selling is something anyone can do. But training in selling skills can pay off. Estée Lauder, for example, has selling skills for the "beauty advisors" who sell its cosmetics down to a fine art—and its training manual and seminars cover every detail. Its advisors who take the training seriously immediately double their sales.[10] Training can also help salespeople learn how to be more effective in cold calls on new prospects, in listening carefully to identify a customer's real objections, in closing the sale, and in working with customers in difficult customer service situations.

Training often starts in the classroom with lectures, case studies, and videotaped trial presentations and demonstrations. But a complete training program adds

Customers who rent heavy construction equipment want to deal with a knowledgeable salesperson. So Caterpillar selects salespeople who have experience with the applications for which the equipment will be used and gives them training on Cat products and new developments in the market.

on-the-job observation of effective salespeople and coaching from sales supervisors. Many companies also use Web-based training, weekly sales meetings or work sessions, annual conventions, and regular e-mail messages and newsletters, as well as ongoing training sessions, to keep salespeople up-to-date.[11]

Internet EXERCISE

The Motivating Tape Company rents and sells various sales training videos. Go to the firm's website (**www.achievement.com**) and then scroll down and select "Sales Training Videos." Review the list of sales training videos offered. If a sales manager were going to rely on some of these tapes for training people just moving into a sales career, what key areas of sales training would he have to cover by some other approach?

COMPENSATING AND MOTIVATING SALESPEOPLE

To recruit, motivate, and keep good salespeople, a firm has to develop an effective compensation plan. Ideally, sales reps should be paid in such a way that what they want to do—for personal interest and gain—is in the company's interest too. Most companies focus on financial motivation—but public recognition, sales contests, and simple personal recognition for a job well done can be highly effective in encouraging greater sales effort.[12] Our main emphasis here, however, will be on financial motivation.[13]

Two basic decisions must be made in developing a compensation plan: (1) the level of compensation and (2) the method of payment.

Compensation varies with job and needed skills

To build a competitive sales force, a company must pay at least the going market wage for different kinds of salespeople. To be sure it can afford a specific type of salesperson, the company should estimate—when the job description is written—how valuable such a salesperson will be. A good order getter may be worth $100,000 to one company but only $15,000 to $25,000 to another—just because the second firm doesn't have enough to sell! In such a case, the second company should rethink its job specifications, or completely change its promotion plans, because the going rate for order getters is much higher than $15,000 a year.

If a job requires extensive travel, aggressive pioneering, or customer service contacts with troublesome customers, the pay may have to be higher. But the salesperson's compensation level should compare, at least roughly, with the pay scale of the rest of the firm. Normally, salespeople earn more than the office or production force but less than top management.

Payment methods vary

Given some competitive level of compensation, there are three basic methods of payment: (1) straight salary, (2) straight commission (incentive), or (3) a combination plan. A straight salary offers the most security for the salesperson. Commission pay, in contrast, offers the most incentive and is tied to results actually achieved. A commission is often based on a percentage of dollar sales, but it may be a financial incentive based on other outcomes—such as the number of new accounts, customer satisfaction ratings, or customer service problems resolved in some time period. Most salespeople want some security, and most companies want salespeople to have some incentive to do better work, so the most popular method is a combination plan that includes some salary and some commission. Bonuses, profit sharing, pensions, stock plans, insurance, and other fringe benefits may be included, too.

Salary gives control— if there is close supervision

A salesperson on straight salary earns the same amount regardless of how he or she spends time. So the salaried salesperson is expected to do what the sales manager asks—whether it is order-taking, supporting sales activities, solving customer service problems, or completing sales call reports. However, the sales manager maintains control *only* by close supervision. As a result, straight salary or a large salary element in the compensation plan increases the amount of sales supervision needed.

Commissions can both motivate and direct

If personal supervision would be difficult, a firm may get better control with a compensation plan that includes some commission, or even a straight commission plan, with built-in direction. One trucking company, for example, has a sales incentive plan that pays higher commissions on business needed to balance freight shipments—depending on how heavily traffic has been moving in one direction or another. Another company that wants to motivate its salespeople to devote more time to developing new accounts could pay higher commissions on shipments to a new customer. However, a salesperson on a straight commission tends to be his or her own boss. The sales manager is less likely to get help on sales activities that won't increase the salesperson's earnings.

An incentive compensation plan can help motivate salespeople, but incentives must be carefully aligned with the firm's objectives. For example, IBM at one time had a sales commission plan that resulted in IBM salespeople pushing customers to buy expensive computers that were more powerful than they needed. The sales reps got sales and increased their income, but later many customers were dissatisfied and switched to other suppliers. Now most IBM sales reps receive incentive pay that is in part based on satisfaction ratings they earn from their customers. Many firms use variations of this approach—because incentives that just focus on short-term sales objectives may not motivate sales reps to develop long-term, need-satisfying relationships with their customers.

Incentives should link efforts to results

The incentive portion of a sales rep's compensation should be large only if there is a direct relationship between the salesperson's effort and results. Otherwise, a salesperson in a growing territory might have rapidly increasing earnings, while the sales rep in a poor area will have little to show for the same amount of work. Such a situation isn't fair, and it can lead to high turnover and much dissatisfaction. A sales manager can take such differences into consideration when setting a salesperson's **sales quota**—the specific sales or profit objective a salesperson is expected to achieve.

Exhibit 14–3
Relation between Personal Selling Expenses and Sales Volume—for Three Basic Personal Selling Compensation Alternatives

Commissions reduce need for working capital

Small companies that have limited working capital or uncertain markets often prefer straight commission, or combination plans with a large commission element. When sales drop off, costs do too. Such flexibility is similar to using manufacturers' agents who get paid only if they deliver sales. This advantage often dominates in selecting a sales compensation method. Exhibit 14–3 shows the general relation between personal selling expenses and sales volume for each of the basic compensation alternatives.

Compensation plans should be clear

Salespeople are likely to be dissatisfied if they can't see the relationship between the results they produce and their pay. A compensation plan that includes different commissions for different products or types of customers can become quite complicated. Simplicity is best achieved with straight salary. But in practice, it's usually better to sacrifice some simplicity to gain some incentive, flexibility, and control. The best combination of these factors depends on the job description and the company's objectives.

To make it easier for a sales rep to see the relationship between effort and compensation, some firms provide the rep with that information online. For example, Oracle, a company that sells database systems, developed a system that allows sales reps, at any point, to check a website and see how they are doing. As new sales results come in, the report at the website is updated. Sales managers can also make changes quickly—for example, by putting a higher commission on a product or more weight on customer satisfaction scores. Other firms use the same idea but just give their sales reps a spreadsheet so that they can keep their own information up-to-date.[14]

Sales managers must plan, implement, and control

Managers must regularly evaluate each salesperson's performance and be certain that all the needed tasks are being done well. The compensation plan may have to be changed if the pay and work are out of line. And by evaluating performance, firms can also identify areas that need more attention—by the salesperson or management.[15]

PERSONAL SELLING TECHNIQUES—PROSPECTING AND PRESENTING

We've stressed the importance of training in selling techniques. Now let's discuss these ideas in more detail so you understand the basic steps each salesperson should follow—including prospecting and selecting target customers, planning sales presentations, making sales presentations, and following up after the sale. Exhibit 14–4 shows the steps we'll consider. You can see that the salesperson is just carrying out a planned communication process, as we discussed in Chapter 13.[16]

Exhibit 14–4
Key Steps in the
Personal Selling Process

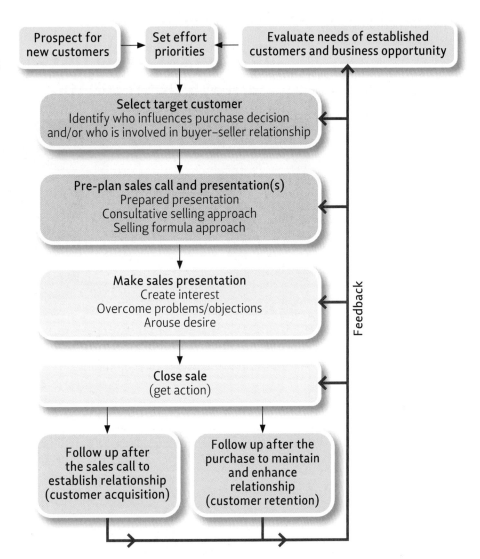

**Prospecting—
narrowing down to
the right target**

Narrowing the personal selling effort down to the right target requires constant, detailed analysis of markets and much prospecting. Basically, **prospecting** involves following all the leads in the target market to identify potential customers.

Finding live prospects who will help make the buying decision isn't as easy as it sounds. In business markets, for example, the salesperson may need to do some hard detective work to find the real purchase decision makers.

Some companies provide prospect lists or a customer relationship management (CRM) database to make this part of the selling job easier. Inquiries that come in at the firm's website, for example, can be passed along to a sales rep for follow-up. In other cases, a more indirect approach may be required. For example, one insurance company checks the local newspaper for marriage announcements—then a salesperson calls to see if the new couple is interested in finding out more about life insurance.

**All customers are
not equal**

While prospecting focuses on identifying new customers, established customers require attention

Internet EXERCISE

Sage Software sells various software products, including ACT! personal management software that is used by many salespeople to organize information about their customers, sales calls, and tasks they need to do. Visit the ACT! website (**www.act. com**) for information about this product. Give a few specific examples of ways that a salesperson could use ACT! to build better relationships with customers.

too. It's often time-consuming and expensive to establish a relationship with a customer, so once established it makes sense to keep the relationship healthy. That requires the rep to routinely review active accounts, rethink customers' needs, and reevaluate each customer's long-term business potential. Some small accounts may have the potential to become big accounts, and some accounts that previously required a lot of costly attention may no longer warrant it. So a sales rep may need to set priorities both for new prospects and existing customers.

How long to spend with whom?

Once a set of prospects and customers who need attention have been identified, the salesperson must decide how much time to spend with each one. A sales rep must qualify customers—to see if they deserve more effort. The salesperson usually makes these decisions by weighing the potential sales volume as well as the likelihood of a sale. This requires judgment. But well-organized salespeople usually develop some system because they have too many demands on their time.[17]

Many firms provide their reps with customer relationship management (CRM) systems to help with this process. Most of them use some grading scheme. A sales rep might estimate how much each prospect is likely to purchase and the probability of getting and keeping the business given the competition. The computer then combines this information and grades each prospect. Attractive accounts may be labeled A—and the salesperson may plan to call on them weekly until the sale is made, the relationship is in good shape, or the customer is moved into a lower category. B customers might offer somewhat lower potential and be called on monthly. C accounts might be called on only once a year—unless they happen to contact the salesperson. And D accounts might be transferred to a telemarketing group.[18]

Three kinds of sales presentations may be useful

Once the salesperson selects a target customer, it's necessary to make a **sales presentation**—a salesperson's effort to make a sale or address a customer's problem. But someone has to plan what kind of sales presentation to make. This is a strategy decision. The kind of presentation should be set before the sales rep goes calling. And in situations where the customer comes to the salesperson—in a retail store, for instance—planners have to make sure that prospects are brought together with salespeople.

A marketing manager can choose two basically different approaches to making sales presentations: the prepared approach or the consultative selling approach. Another approach, the selling formula approach, is a combination of the two. Each of these has its place.

The prepared sales presentation

The **prepared sales presentation** approach uses a memorized presentation that is not adapted to each individual customer. This approach says that a customer faced with a particular stimulus will give the desired response—in this case, a yes answer to the salesperson's prepared statement, which includes a **close**, the salesperson's request for an order.

If one trial close doesn't work, the sales rep tries another prepared presentation and attempts another closing. This can go on for some time—until the salesperson runs out of material or the customer either buys or decides to leave. Exhibit 14–5 shows the relative participation of the salesperson and customer in the prepared approach. Note that the salesperson does most of the talking.

Firms may rely on this canned approach when only a short presentation is practical. It's also sensible when salespeople aren't very skilled. The company can control what they say and in what order. For example, Novartis uses missionary salespeople to tell doctors about new drugs when they're introduced. Doctors are busy, so they only give the rep a minute or two. That's just enough time to give a short, prepared pitch and leave some samples. To get the most out of the presentation, Novartis refines it based on feedback from doctors whom it pays to participate in focus groups.[19]

But a canned approach has a weakness. It treats all potential customers alike. It may work for some and not for others. A prepared approach may be suitable for simple order-taking—but it is no longer considered good selling for complicated situations.

Consultative selling—builds on the marketing concept

The **consultative selling approach** involves developing a good understanding of the individual customer's needs before trying to close the sale. This name is used because the salesperson is almost acting as a consultant to help identify and solve the customer's problem. With this approach, the sales rep makes some general benefit statements to get the customer's attention and interest. Then the salesperson asks questions and *listens carefully* to understand the customer's needs. Once they agree on needs, the seller tries to show the customer how the product fills those needs and to close the sale. This is a problem-solving approach—in which the customer and salesperson work together to satisfy the customer's needs. That's why it's sometimes called the need-satisfaction approach. Exhibit 14–6 shows the participation of the customer and the salesperson during such a sales presentation.

The consultative selling approach takes skill and time. The salesperson must be able to analyze what motivates a particular customer and show how the company's offering would help the customer satisfy those needs. The sales rep may even conclude that the customer's problem is really better solved with someone else's product. That might result in one lost sale, but it also is likely to build real trust and more sales opportunities over the life of the relationship with the customer. That's why this kind of selling is typical in business markets when a salesperson already has established a close relationship with a customer.

Exhibit 14–5
Prepared Approach to
Sales Presentation

Exhibit 14–6
Consultative Selling
Approach to Sales
Presentation

Exhibit 14–7
Selling Formula
Approach to Sales
Presentation

**Selling formula
approach—some
of both**

The **selling formula approach** starts with a prepared presentation outline—much like the prepared approach—and leads the customer through some logical steps to a final close. The prepared steps are logical because we assume that we know something about the target customer's needs and attitudes.

Exhibit 14–7 shows the selling formula approach. The salesperson does most of the talking at the beginning of the presentation—to communicate key points early. This part of the presentation may even have been prepared as part of the marketing strategy. As the sales presentation moves along, however, the salesperson brings the customer into the discussion to help clarify just what needs this customer has. The salesperson's job is to discover the needs of a particular customer to know how to proceed. Once it is clear what kind of customer this is, the salesperson comes back to show how the product satisfies this specific customer's needs and to close the sale.

**AIDA helps plan
sales presentations**

Recall the AIDA model from Chapter 13 —Attention, Interest, Desire, and Action. Most sales presentations follow this AIDA sequence. The time a sales rep spends on each of the steps varies depending on the situation and the selling approach being used. But it is still necessary to begin a presentation by getting the prospect's *attention* and, hopefully, to move the customer to *action*.[20]

**Ethical issues
may arise**

As in every other area of marketing communications, ethical issues arise in the personal selling area. The most basic issue, plain and simple, is whether a salesperson's presentation is honest and truthful. But addressing that issue is a no-brainer. No company is served well by a salesperson who lies or manipulates customers to get their business.

Ethics QUESTION

Assume that you are a sales rep and sell costly electronic systems used in automated factories. You made a sales presentation to a customer, but he didn't place an order—and then wouldn't take your calls when you tried to inform him that your company was coming out with a more reliable model at the same price. Months later, he faxes a purchase order for immediate delivery on the model you originally discussed. You have the old model in stock, and it will be difficult to sell once the new model arrives in two weeks. Do you try to contact the customer again to tell him about the new model, or do you do what he has requested and immediately fill the order with the old model? Either way, if you make the sale, the commission will pay for your upcoming vacation to the Caribbean. Explain what you would do and why.

Keebler salespeople use an interactive tool called Instant Data Evaluation Access ("IDEA") Wizard on their laptop computers. It provides research data related to the marketing of cookies and crackers on topics such as shelf-space management and consumer purchase patterns. The sales rep can use the Wizard to support a consultative selling approach in working to develop closer relationships with retailers.

On the other hand, most sales reps sooner or later face a sales situation in which they must make more difficult ethical decisions about how to balance company interests, customer interests, and personal interests. Conflicts are less likely to arise if the firm's marketing mix really meets the needs of its target market. Similarly, they are less likely to occur when the firm sees the value of developing a longer-term relationship with the customer. Then the salesperson is arranging a happy marriage. By contrast, ethical conflicts are more likely when the sales rep's personal outcomes (such as commission income) or the selling firm's profits hinge on making sales to customers whose needs are only partially met by the firm's offering. A number of financial services firms, for example, have garnered bad publicity—and even legal problems—from situations like this.

Ideally, companies can avoid the whole problem by supporting their salespeople with a marketing mix that really offers target customers unique benefits. Moreover, top executives, marketing managers, and sales managers set the tone for the ethical climate in which a salesperson operates. If they set impossible goals or project a "do-what-you-need-to-do" attitude, a desperate salesperson may yield to the pressure of the moment. When a firm clearly advocates ethical selling behavior and makes it clear that manipulative selling techniques are not acceptable, the salesperson is not left trying to swim "against the flow."[21]

CONCLUSION

In this chapter, we discussed the importance and nature of personal selling. Selling is much more than just getting rid of the product. In fact, a salesperson who is not given strategy guidelines may have to become the strategy planner for the market he or she serves. Ideally, however, the sales manager and marketing manager work together to set some strategy guidelines: the kind and number of

salespeople needed, what sales technology support will be provided, the kind of sales presentation desired, and selection, training, and motivation approaches.

We discussed the three basic sales tasks: (1) order-getting, (2) order-taking, and (3) supporting. Most sales jobs combine at least two of these three tasks. Once a firm specifies the important tasks, it can decide on the structure of its sales organization and the number of salespeople it needs. The nature of the job and the level and method of compensation also depend on the blend of these tasks. Firms should develop a job description for each sales job. This, in turn, provides guidelines for selecting, training, and compensating salespeople.

Once the marketing manager agrees to the basic plan and sets the budget, the sales manager must implement the plan, including directing and controlling the sales force. This includes assigning sales territories and controlling performance. You can see that the sales manager has more to do than jet around the country sipping martinis and entertaining customers. A sales manager is deeply involved with the basic management tasks of planning and control—

as well as ongoing implementation of the personal selling effort.

We also reviewed some basic selling techniques and identified three kinds of sales presentations. Each has its place—but the consultative selling approach seems best for higher-level sales jobs. In these kinds of jobs, personal selling is achieving a new, professional status because of the competence and level of personal responsibility required of the salesperson. The day of the old-time glad-hander is passing in favor of the specialist who is creative, industrious, persuasive, knowledgeable, highly trained, and therefore able to help the buyer. This type of salesperson always has been, and probably always will be, in short supply. And the demand for high-level salespeople is growing.

KEY TERMS

basic sales tasks, 359
order getters, 359
order-getting, 359
order takers, 361
order-taking, 361
supporting salespeople, 361
missionary salespeople, 362

technical specialists, 362
customer service reps, 362
team selling, 364
major accounts sales force, 365
telemarketing, 365
sales territory, 365
job description, 370

sales quota, 373
prospecting, 375
sales presentation, 377
prepared sales presentation, 377
close, 377
consultative selling approach, 377
selling formula approach, 378

QUESTIONS AND PROBLEMS

1. What strategy decisions are needed in the personal selling area? Why should the marketing manager make these strategy decisions?

2. What kind of salesperson (or what blend of the basic sales tasks) is required to sell the following products? If there are several selling jobs in the channel for each product, indicate the kinds of salespeople required. Specify any assumptions necessary to give definite answers.
   a. Laundry detergent.
   b. Costume jewelry.
   c. Office furniture.
   d. Men's underwear.
   e. Mattresses.
   f. Corn.
   g. Life insurance.

3. Distinguish among the jobs of producers', wholesalers', and retailers' order-getting salespeople. If one order getter is needed, must all the salespeople in a channel be order getters? Illustrate.

4. Discuss the role of manufacturers' agents in a marketing manager's promotion plans. What kind of salesperson is a manufacturers' agent? What type of compensation plan is used for a manufacturers' agent?

5. Discuss the future of the specialty shop if producers place greater emphasis on mass selling because of the inadequacy of retail order-taking.

6. Compare and contrast missionary salespeople and technical specialists.

7. Explain how a compensation plan could be developed to provide incentives for experienced salespeople and yet make some provision for trainees who have not yet learned the job.

8. Cite an actual local example of each of the three kinds of sales presentations discussed in the chapter. Explain for each situation whether a different type of presentation would have been better.

9. Are the benefits and limitations of a canned presentation any different if it is supported with a slide show

or videotape than if it is just a person talking? Why or why not?

10. Describe a consultative selling sales presentation that you experienced recently. How could it have been improved by fuller use of the AIDA framework?

11. How would our economy operate if personal salespeople were outlawed? Could the economy work? If so, how? If not, what is the minimum personal selling effort necessary? Could this minimum personal selling effort be controlled by law?

CREATING MARKETING PLANS

The Marketing Plan Coach software on the Student CD includes a sample marketing plan for Hillside Veterinary Clinic. Look through the "Marketing Strategy" section.

a. What personal selling tasks are performed at Hillside Veterinary Clinic and who does them?

b. Suppose Hillside wants to put more emphasis on "order-getting" to promote growth. What ideas do you have for how to do it?

c. Based on the situation analysis, target market, and intended positioning, recommend some ways that Hillside could actively work to improve its reputation for customer service.

SUGGESTED CASES

12. DrMarcus.com   21. Global Materials, Inc.   23. Valley Furniture   28. ACT, Inc.

COMPUTER-AIDED PROBLEM

14. SALES COMPENSATION

Franco Welles, sales manager for Nanek, Inc., is trying to decide whether to pay a sales rep for a new territory with straight commission or a combination plan. He wants to evaluate possible plans—to compare the compensation costs and profitability of each. Welles knows that sales reps in similar jobs at other firms make about $36,000 a year.

The sales rep will sell two products. Welles is planning a higher commission for Product B—because he wants it to get extra effort. From experience with similar products, he has some rough estimates of expected sales volume under the different plans and various ideas about commission rates. The details are found in the spreadsheet. The program computes compensation and how much the sales rep will contribute to profit. "Profit contribution" is equal to the total revenue generated by the sales rep minus sales compensation costs and the costs of producing the units.

a. For the initial values shown in the spreadsheet, which plan—commission or combination—would give the rep the highest compensation, and which plan would give the greatest profit contribution to Nanek, Inc.?

b. Welles thinks a sales rep might be motivated to work harder and sell 1,100 units of Product B if the commission rate (under the commission plan) were increased to 10 percent. If Welles is right (and everything else stays the same), would the higher commission rate be a good deal for Nanek? Explain your thinking.

c. A sales rep interested in the job is worried about making payments on her new car. She asks if Welles would consider paying her with a combination plan but with more guaranteed income (an $18,000 base salary) in return for taking a 3 percent commission on Products B and A. If this arrangement results in the same unit sales as Welles originally estimated for the combination plan, would Nanek, Inc., be better off or worse off under this arrangement?

d. Do you think the rep's proposal will meet Welles's goals for Product B? Explain your thinking.

For additional questions related to this problem, see Exercise 14-3 in the *Learning Aid for Use with Essentials of Marketing*, 11th edition.

CHAPTER FIFTEEN

Advertising and Sales Promotion

In the summer of 1965, 17-year-old Fred DeLuca was trying to figure out how to pay for college. A family friend suggested that Fred open a sandwich shop—and then the friend invested $1,000 to help get it started. Within a month, they opened their first sandwich shop. From that humble start grew the Subway franchise chain with over 25,500 outlets in 84 countries.

Targeted advertising and sales promotion have been important to Subway's growth. Some memorable Subway ads featured Jared Fogle, a college student who was overweight but lost 245 pounds by eating only Subway's low-fat sandwiches, like the "Veggie Delite." Jared says it was a fluke that he ended up in Subway's ads. After all, he was recruited to do the ads because of good publicity that Subway got after national media picked up a story that Jared's friend wrote about him in a college newspaper. On the other hand, Subway's strategy at that time focused on its line of seven different sandwiches with under 6 grams of fat. The objective was to set Subway apart from other fast food in a way that would appeal to health-conscious eaters and spark new sales growth. Jared walked past a nearby Subway every day, but what pulled him in the first time was Subway's point-of-purchase promotion for the "7 under 6" menu. So maybe it wasn't as random as it seems to Jared.

As soon as Jared's ads began to run, word of his inspiring story spread and consumer awareness of Subway and its healthy fare increased. It's always hard to isolate the exact impact of ads on sales, but sales grew more than 18 percent that year. Another benefit was that the ads attracted attention from potential franchisees. Many of them followed up by requesting the franchise brochure, which explains how Subway's strategy works and why it is profitable for franchisees. For instance, it describes how franchisees elect a group to help manage advertising and media buying decisions— so that Subway outlets get the most return from their advertising dollars. Subway headquarters also supports franchisees by providing materials and guidance for the local advertising and sales promotion they do to reach their own target customers.

Recently, Subway has been squeezed at the high end by rival sandwich shops like Quiznos Sub and Panera Bread. So Subway has to balance both its menu and promotion to appeal to two different segments— those customers most interested in taste *and* those most interested in low fat. Subway balances the menu with a line of "Subway Selects" sandwiches made with zesty sauces and special breads. It turned to a new ad-agency, Fallon Worldwide, to create new ads that would balance the copy thrust. Fallon, in turn, called on specialized agencies, like one in Miami that focused on advertising to Hispanics, to help with specific parts of Subway's campaign. But the relationship with Fallon did not last long—and Subway went back to an agency that had experience with Jared. Subway also gets cooperative promotional support from Coca-Cola now that it has taken over as the exclusive supplier for all Subway outlets.

Subway includes many other elements in its promotion blend. For example, Subway made Jared available to help people keep New Year's resolutions to lose weight. Dieters who signed up at Subway's website received recorded phone calls from Jared that encouraged them to eat healthy and stay active. The website also provides tips on dieting and exercise as well as nutritional details about Subway sandwiches. These details help consumers who want all the

health-related facts. The available information also makes sense given the scrutiny the Federal Trade Commission is giving to firms that make promotional claims related to weight loss and health.

Subway also leveraged its healthy fast-food positioning and stepped up efforts to combat childhood obesity and increase sales to kids and teens.

Subway's F.R.E.S.H. Steps promotion encouraged kids and their parents to "Feel Responsible, Energized, Satisfied, and Happy." A television advertising campaign let parents and kids know how to make healthy eating choices and live a more active life-style. As a national sponsor of Little League Base-ball and Soft-ball, Subway advertises in *Little League* magazine and targets little leaguers and their parents via direct mail and with point of sale materials. Subway also teamed up with Discovery Kids cable TV where it told kids 6 to 12 years old to "play hard and fresh." This promotion included tie-ins with the network's *Endurance* show, where kids compete in outdoor activities. Subway developed an online Endurance game, a sweepstakes to win extreme sports vacation trips, and a Kids' Pak meal that includes toys promoting outdoor activities.

Subway is in a very competitive, dynamic market. More change is sure to come. But so far, Subway has achieved profitable growth with a targeted strategy that includes effective use of promotion.[1]

LEARNING OBJECTIVES

The Subway case shows that advertising and sales promotion are often critical elements in the success or failure of a strategy. But many firms do a poor job with advertising and promotion—so just copying how other firms handle these important strategy decisions is not "good enough." There is no sense in imitating bad practices. This chapter helps you understand important decisions that help to make effective use of advertising and sales promotion.

When you finish this chapter, you should:

1. understand why a marketing manager sets specific objectives to guide the advertising effort.

2. understand when the various kinds of advertising are needed.

3. understand how to choose the "best" medium.

4. understand the main ways that advertising on the Internet differs from advertising in other media.

5. understand how to plan the "best" message—that is, the copy thrust.

6. understand what advertising agencies do and how they are paid.

7. understand how to advertise legally.

8. understand the importance and nature of sales promotion.

9. know the advantages and limitations of different types of sales promotion.

10. understand important new terms (shown in red).

ADVERTISING, SALES PROMOTION, AND MARKETING STRATEGY PLANNING

Advertising and sales promotion can play a central role in the promotion blend. On a per-contact basis, these promotion methods provide a relatively low-cost way to inform, persuade, and activate customers. Advertising and sales promotion can position a firm's marketing mix as the one that meets customer needs. They can help motivate channel members or a firm's own employees, as well as final customers.

Unfortunately the results that marketers *actually achieve* with advertising and sales promotion are very uneven. It's often said that half of the money spent on these activities is wasted—but that most managers don't know which half. Mass selling can be exciting and involving, or it can be downright obnoxious. Sometimes it's based on careful research, yet much of it is based on someone's pet idea. A creative idea may produce great results or be a colossal waste of money. Ads may stir emotions or go unnoticed.

This chapter explains approaches to help you understand how successful advertising and sales promotion works. See Exhibit 15–1. After a brief overview of the cost of advertising, we look at the different decisions marketing managers—and the advertising agencies they may work with—have to make: (1) advertising objectives and what they want to achieve, (2) who the target audience is, (3) what kind of advertising to use, (4) which media to use to reach target customers, (5) what to say (the copy thrust), and (6) who will do the work—the firm's own marketing or advertising people or outside agencies. We also discuss legal issues in advertising.

There are challenges in managing sales promotion, but it offers advantages over advertising for some objectives. So, this chapter also presents decisions that must be made with respect to different types of sales promotion for different targets.

Exhibit 15–1   Marketing Strategy Planning, Advertising, and Sales Promotion

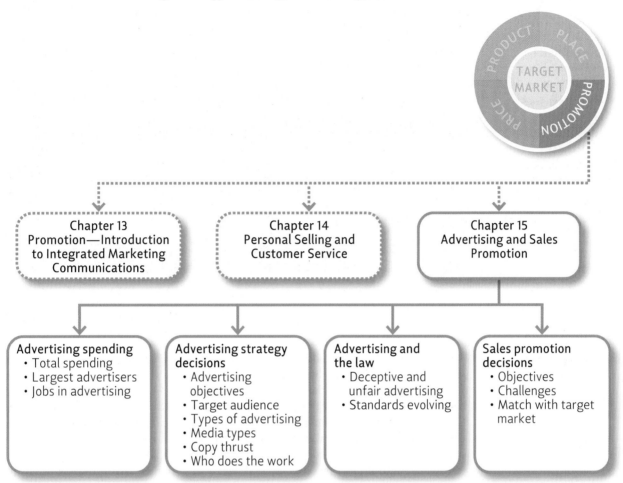

International dimensions are important

The basic strategy planning decisions for advertising and sales promotion are the same regardless of where in the world the target market is located. However, the look and feel of advertising and sales promotion vary a lot in different countries. The choices available to a marketing manager within each of the decision areas may also vary dramatically from one country to another.

Commercial television may not be available. If it is, government rules may limit the type of advertising permitted or when ads can be shown. Radio broadcasts in a market area may not be in the target market's language. The target audience may not be able to read. Access to interactive media like the Internet may be nonexistent. Cultural influences may limit ad messages. Ad agencies that already know a nation's unique advertising environment may not be available.

International dimensions also impact sales promotion. Trade promotion may be difficult, or even impossible, to manage. A typical Japanese grocery retailer with only 250 square feet of space, for example, doesn't have room for *any* special end-of-aisle displays. Consumer promotions may be affected, too. In some developing nations, samples can't be distributed through the mail, because they're routinely stolen before they get to target customers. And some countries ban consumer sweepstakes because they see it as a form of gambling.

In this chapter we'll consider a number of these international issues, but we'll focus on the array of choices available in the United States and other advanced economies.[2]

Traditional media choices are more limited in some international markets, so marketers like Procter & Gamble (P&G) must be creative to communicate their messages. In Thailand, P&G used a large green comb installed near the top of a utility pole to promote its Rejoice conditioners. The tagline on the comb says, "Tangles? Switch to Rejoice conditioners." In China, P&G used a 12-stories-tall white shirt mounted on a building to promote its Ariel detergent.

ADVERTISING IS BIG BUSINESS

Total spending is big—and growing internationally

As an economy grows, advertising becomes more important—because more consumers have income and advertising can get results. But good advertising results cost money. And spending on advertising is significant. In 1946, U.S. advertising spending was slightly more than $3 billion. By 2005, it was about $276 billion.

During the last decade, the rate of advertising spending has increased even more rapidly in other countries. However, advertising in the U.S. accounts for roughly half of worldwide ad spending. Europe and Asia account for about 33 percent and about 14 percent, respectively, though spending in Asia is growing rapidly, especially in China. For most countries in other regions, advertising spending has traditionally been quite low.[3]

Most advertisers aren't really spending that much

While total spending on advertising seems high, U.S. corporations spend an average of only about 2.5 percent of their sales dollars on advertising. Worldwide, the percentage is even smaller. Exhibit 15–2 shows, however, that advertising spending as a percent of sales dollars varies significantly across product categories. Producers of consumer products generally spend a larger percent than firms that produce business products. For example, U.S. companies that make soap and detergent spend about 10 percent. However, companies that sell plastics to manufacturers spend only about 1.2 percent on advertising. Some business products companies—those that depend on e-commerce or personal selling—may spend less than $1/10$ of 1 percent.

Of course, percentages don't tell the whole story. Nissan, which spends less than 1 percent of sales on advertising, is among the top 12 advertisers worldwide. The really big spenders are very important to the advertising industry because they account for a large share of total advertising spending. Worldwide, the top 100 global advertisers spend about $100 billion a year. That's about 17 percent of total worldwide advertising.[4]

Advertising doesn't employ that many people

While total advertising expenditures are large, the advertising industry itself employs relatively few people. The major expense is for media time and space. In the United States, the largest share of this—26 percent—goes for television (including cable). Direct mail takes about 20 percent of the total and newspapers about 18 percent. The shares for radio (7 percent), the Yellow Pages (5 percent), magazines (5 percent), the Internet (3 percent), and outdoor (2 percent) are much smaller.[5]

Exhibit 15–2   Advertising Spending as Percent of Sales for Illustrative Product Categories

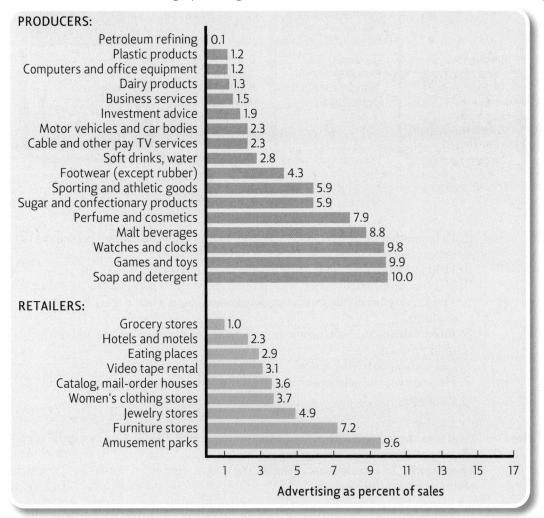

Many students hope for a glamorous job in advertising, but there are fewer jobs in advertising than you might think. In the United States, only about 500,000 people work directly in the advertising industry. Advertising agencies employ only about half of all these people.[6]

ADVERTISING OBJECTIVES ARE A STRATEGY DECISION

Advertising objectives must be specific

Every ad and every advertising campaign should have clearly defined objectives. These should grow out of the firm's overall marketing strategy and the promotion jobs assigned to advertising. It isn't enough for the marketing manager to say "Promote the product." The marketing manager must decide exactly what advertising should do.

Advertising objectives should be more specific than personal selling objectives. One of the advantages of personal selling is that a salesperson can shift the presentation for a specific customer. Each ad, however, must be effective not just for one customer but for thousands, or millions, of them.

The marketing manager sets the overall direction

The marketing manager might give the advertising manager one or more of the following specific objectives, along with the budget to accomplish them:

Exhibit 15-3 Examples of Different Types of Advertising over Adoption Process Stages

Awareness	Interest	Evaluation and trial	Decision	Confirmation
Teaser campaigns Pioneering ads Jingles/slogans Viral advertising Announcements	Informative or descriptive ads Image/celebrity ads Flash ads Demonstration of benefits	Competitive ads Persuasive copy Comparative ads Testimonials	Direct-action retail ads Point-of-purchase ads Price deal offers	Reminder ads Informative "why" ads

1. Help position the firm's brand or marketing mix by informing and persuading target customers or intermediaries about its benefits.
2. Help introduce new products to specific target markets.
3. Help obtain desirable outlets and tell customers where they can buy a product.
4. Provide ongoing contact with target customers, even when a salesperson isn't available.
5. Prepare the way for salespeople by presenting the company's name and the merits of its products.
6. Get immediate buying action.
7. Help to maintain relationships with satisfied customers and encourage more purchases.

If you want half the market, say so!

If a marketing manager really wants specific results, they should be clearly stated. A general objective is "To help expand market share." This could be rephrased more specifically: "To increase shelf space in our cooperating retail outlets by 25 percent during the next three months."

Objectives guide implementation too

The specific objectives obviously affect what type of advertising is best. Exhibit 15–3 shows that the type of advertising that achieves objectives for one stage of the adoption process may be off target for another. For example, Peerflix.com is an online club where members trade DVD movies. Peerflix created an online game with a movie theme and a viral advertising campaign to build awareness when it was getting started. Teaser ads were posted on gaming and entertainment-related blogs. The game site generated over 2 million visits in its first three months. On the other hand, Taco Bell used informative television ads and in-store point-of-purchase materials to encourage consumers to buy its Chicken Caesar Grilled Stuft Burrito.[7]

OBJECTIVES DETERMINE THE KINDS OF ADVERTISING NEEDED

The advertising objectives largely determine which of two basic types of advertising to use—product or institutional. See Exhibit 15–4. **Product advertising** tries to sell a product. We will discuss three categories of product advertising—pioneering, competitive, and reminder—which focus on getting consumers to know, like, and remember something. Then we will discuss **institutional advertising**, which promotes an organization's image, reputation, or ideas rather than a specific product.

Pioneering advertising builds primary demand

Pioneering advertising tries to develop primary demand for a product category rather than demand for a specific brand. Pioneering advertising is usually done in

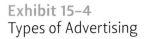

Exhibit 15–4
Types of Advertising

the early stages of the product life cycle; it informs potential customers about the new product and helps turn them into adopters. When digital cameras first came out, consumers didn't know their benefits or why they might want one—and at the same time they worried about how they could get printed pictures. So advertising for the early products in the market had to explain these basics and build primary demand. Now that there are a hundred brands of digital cameras, each brand's ads try to highlight its own advantages—like the number of megapixels, amount of memory, or ease of use.

Competitive advertising emphasizes selective demand

Competitive advertising tries to develop selective demand for a specific brand. A firm is forced into competitive advertising as the product life cycle moves along—to hold its own against competitors.

Competitive advertising may be either direct or indirect. The **direct type** aims for immediate buying action. The **indirect type** points out product advantages to affect future buying decisions.

Most of Delta Airlines's advertising is of the competitive variety. Much of it tries for immediate sales—so the ads are the direct type with prices, timetables, and phone numbers to call for reservations. Some of its ads are the indirect type. They focus on the quality of service and suggest you check Delta's website the next time you travel.

Comparative advertising is even rougher. **Comparative advertising** means making specific brand comparisons—using actual product names. A recent comparative ad for Clorox Disinfecting Wipes, for example, claimed that a competing wipe from Windex didn't disinfect as well.

Many countries forbid comparative advertising, but that situation is changing. In the United States, the Federal Trade Commission decided to encourage comparative ads because it thought they would increase competition and provide consumers with more useful information. Superiority claims are supposed to be supported by research evidence—but the guidelines aren't clear. When P&G's Dryel did not fare well in independent test comparisons with stain removal by professional dry cleaners, P&G changed its ad claims. However, some firms just keep running tests until they get the results they want. Others talk about minor differences that don't reflect a product's overall benefits. Comparative ads can also backfire by calling attention to competing products that consumers had not previously considered.[8]

Reminder advertising reinforces a favorable relationship

Reminder advertising tries to keep the product's name before the public. It may be useful when the product has achieved brand preference or insistence, perhaps in the market maturity or sales decline stages. It is used primarily to reinforce previous promotion. Here the advertiser may use soft-sell ads that just mention or show the name—as a reminder. Hallmark, for example, often relies on reminder ads because most consumers already know the brand name and, after years of promotion, associate it with high-quality cards and gifts.

When General Mills introduced its Milk 'n Cereal bars, it used a comparative ad that made direct comparisons with other brands to highlight the advantages of its bars (50 percent larger, twice the calcium, and three times the iron of Kellogg's bars). By contrast, Philips uses effective institutional ads that promote the company's name and image rather than trying to sell one of its many product lines.

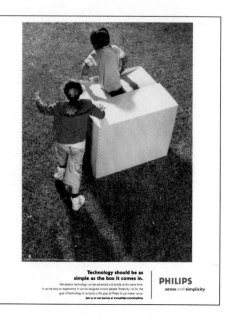

Institutional advertising— remember our name

Institutional advertising usually focuses on the name and prestige of an organization or industry. It may seek to inform, persuade, or remind. Its basic objective is to develop goodwill or improve an organization's relations with various groups—not only customers but also current and prospective channel members, suppliers, shareholders, employees, and the general public. The British government, for instance, uses institutional advertising to promote England as a place to do business. Many Japanese firms, like Hitachi, emphasize institutional advertising, in part because they often use the company name as a brand name.

Some organizations use institutional advertising to advocate a specific cause or idea. Insurance companies and organizations like Mothers Against Drunk Driving, for example, use these advocacy ads to encourage people not to drink and drive.[9]

COORDINATING ADVERTISING EFFORTS WITH COOPERATIVE RELATIONSHIPS

Vertical cooperation— advertising allowances, cooperative advertising

Sometimes a producer knows that an advertising job can be done more effectively or more economically by someone further along in the channel. Alternatively, a retail chain like Best Buy may approach a manufacturer like Panasonic with an ad program and tell them how much it will cost to participate. In either case, the producer may offer **advertising allowances**—price reductions to firms further along in the channel to encourage them to advertise or otherwise promote the firm's products locally.

Cooperative advertising involves middlemen and producers sharing in the cost of ads. This helps wholesalers and retailers compete in their local markets. It also helps the producer get more promotion for the advertising dollar because media usually give local advertisers lower rates than national or international firms. In addition, a retailer or wholesaler who is paying a share of the cost is more likely to follow through.

Integrated communications from cooperative relationships

Coordination and integration of ad messages in the channel is another reason for cooperative advertising. One big, well-planned, integrated advertising effort is often better than many different, perhaps inconsistent, local efforts.

To get this coordination, producers often provide a master of an ad on a DVD, CD, website, or printed sheets. The middlemen add their identification before turning the ad over to local media.

However, allowances and support materials alone don't ensure cooperation. When channel members don't agree with the advertising strategy, it can be a serious source of conflict. For example, Wendy's strategy includes an objective to be the late-night, quick-serve restaurant of choice for its target market. This requires staying open late at night and advertising the longer hours. However, some Wendy's restaurants are franchise operations rather than company-owned. A franchise operator who does not think that late-night hours will be profitable in his or her local market may not want to stay open for the longer hours or pay franchise fees to support the national ad campaign.[10]

Ethical concerns may arise

Ethical issues sometimes arise concerning advertising allowance programs. For example, a retailer may run one producer's ad to draw customers to the store but then sell them another brand. Is this unethical? Some producers think it is. A different view is that retailers are obligated to the producer to run the ad but obligated to consumers to sell them what they want, no matter whose brand it may be. A producer can often avoid the problem by setting the allowance amount as a percent of the retailer's *actual purchases*. Smart producers also insist on proof that the advertising was really done. That way, a retailer who doesn't produce sales—or even run the ads—doesn't get the allowance.[11]

CHOOSING THE "BEST" MEDIUM—HOW TO DELIVER THE MESSAGE

What is the best advertising medium? There is no simple answer to this question. Effectiveness depends on how well the medium fits with the rest of a marketing strategy—that is, it depends on (1) your promotion objectives, (2) what target markets you want to reach, (3) the funds available for advertising, and (4) the nature of the media, including who they *reach*, with what *frequency*, with what *impact*, and at what *cost*.

Exhibit 15–5 shows ad spending, percent growth, and some pros and cons of major kinds of media. However, some of the advantages noted in this table may not apply in all markets. For example, direct mail may not be a flexible choice in a country with a weak postal system. Internet ads might be worthless if few target customers have access to the Internet. Similarly, TV audiences are often less selective and targeted, but a special-interest cable TV show may reach a very specific audience.[12]

Highly targeted advertising media are proving especially effective at targeting messages to specific demographic, social, and cultural groups.

Exhibit 15-5 Ad Spending, Percent Growth, and Advantages and Disadvantages of Major Media

Kinds of Media	Ad Spending 2004 ($ in billions)	Two-Year Percent Growth	Advantages	Disadvantages
Television and cable	$67.8	25.3%	Demonstrations, good attention, wide reach	Expensive in total, "clutter," less-selective audience
Direct mail	52.2	16.8	Selected audience, flexible, can personalize	Relatively expensive per contact, "junk mail," hard to retain attention
Newspaper	46.6	5.9	Flexible, timely, local market	May be expensive, short life, no "pass along"
Radio	19.6	9.5	Wide reach, segmented audience, inexpensive	Weak attention, many different rates, short exposure
Yellow Pages	14.0	1.4	Reaches local customers seeking purchase information	Many other competitors listed in same place, hard to differentiate
Magazine	12.3	11.8	Very targeted, good detail, good "pass along"	Inflexible, long lead times
Internet	6.9	40.8	Ads link to more detailed website, some "pay for results," easier to track results	Hard to compare costs with other media
Outdoor	5.8	11.5	Flexible, repeat exposure, inexpensive	"Mass market," very short exposure

Specific promotion objectives

The medium should support the promotion objectives. If the objective requires demonstrating product benefits, TV may be the best alternative. If the objective is to inform, telling a detailed story and using precise pictures, then Internet advertising might be right. Alternatively, with a broad target market, print media like magazines and newspapers may be better. For example, Jockey switched its advertising to magazines from television when it decided to show the variety of styles of its men's briefs. Jockey worried that there were problems with modeling men's underwear on television. However, Jockey might have stayed with TV if it had been targeting consumers in France or Brazil, where nudity in TV ads is common.[13]

Match your market with the media

To guarantee good media selection, the advertiser first must *clearly* specify its target market. Then the advertiser can choose media that reach those target customers.

The media available in a country may limit the choices. In less-developed nations, for example, radio is often the only way to reach a broad-based market of poor consumers who may not be able to read or afford television.

Advertisers pay for the whole audience

Another problem is that the audience for media that *do* reach your target market may also include people who are *not* in the target group. But *you pay for the whole audience the media delivers*, including those who aren't potential customers. For example, Delta Faucet, a faucet manufacturer that wanted its ads to reach plumbers, placed ads on ESPN's Saturday college football telecasts. Research showed that many plumbers watched the ESPN games. Yet plumbers are only a very small portion of the total college football audience—and the size of the total audience determined the cost of the advertising time.[14]

Because it's hard to pick the best media, media analysts often focus on cost per thousand of audience size or circulation. This may seem an objective approach, but

Advertising space on a race car reaches racing fans and often benefits from extended TV coverage. But the cost for primary sponsors can be millions of dollars.

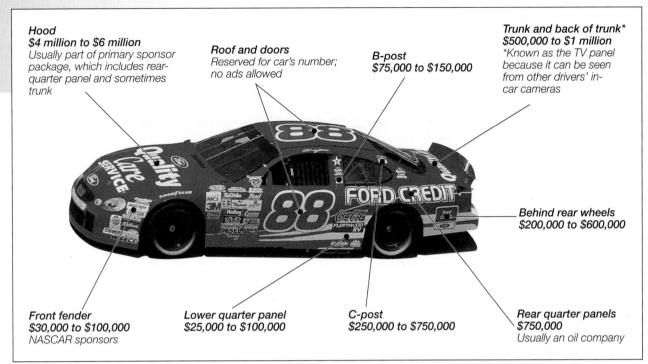

Hood
$4 million to $6 million
Usually part of primary sponsor package, which includes rear-quarter panel and sometimes trunk

Roof and doors
Reserved for car's number; no ads allowed

B-post
$75,000 to $150,000

Trunk and back of trunk*
$500,000 to $1 million
*Known as the TV panel because it can be seen from other drivers' in-car cameras

Behind rear wheels
$200,000 to $600,000

Front fender
$30,000 to $100,000
NASCAR sponsors

Lower quarter panel
$25,000 to $100,000

C-post
$250,000 to $750,000

Rear quarter panels
$750,000
Usually an oil company

advertisers preoccupied with keeping these costs down may ignore the relevant segmenting dimensions and slip into mass marketing.

Some media help zero in on specific target markets

Today, the major media direct more attention to reaching smaller, more defined target markets. The most obvious evidence of this is in the growth of spending on direct-mail advertising to consumers in databases. For example, Germany's Otto Versand (since renamed Otto Group), the world's largest mail-order company, maintains CRM databases that track each customer's past purchases and responses to previous mailings. These data help the firm to accurately predict whether a customer will respond to a particular mailing. Such data also help mail-order firms segment customers, develop better messages, and increase the efficiency of their direct-mail campaigns.[15] However, other media, even traditional ones, are becoming more targeted as well.

TV is a good example. Cable TV channels—like CNN, Nickelodeon, ESPN, and MTV—are taking advertisers away from the networks because they target specific audiences. ESPN, for example, has an audience heavily weighted toward affluent, male viewers. Moreover, being specialized doesn't necessarily mean that the target market is small. MTV appeals most strongly to young viewers, but its programming is seen in nearly 400 million homes worldwide—more than any other programmer.

Radio has also become a more specialized medium. Some stations cater to particular ethnic and racial groups, such as Hispanics, African Americans, or French Canadians. Others aim at specific target markets with rock, country, or classical music. Now that radio stations can get their programming to a larger number of consumers over the Internet and via satellite broadcast systems, expect even more targeting.

Many magazines serve only special-interest groups, such as fishermen, new parents, and personal computer users. In fact, the most profitable magazines seem to be the ones aimed at clearly defined markets. Many specialty magazines also have international editions that help marketers reach consumers with similar interests in different parts of the world. *PC Magazine*, for example, offers European, Japanese, and other editions.

There are also trade magazines in many fields, such as chemical engineering, furniture retailing, electrical wholesaling, farming, and the aerospace market. *Standard Rate and Data* provides a guide to the thousands of magazines now available in the United States. Similar guides exist in most other countries.

Specialized media are small, but gaining

The advertising media listed in Exhibit 15–5 are attracting the vast majority of advertising media budgets. But advertising specialists always look for cost-effective new media that will help advertisers reach their target markets. For example, one company successfully sells space for signs on bike racks that it places in front of 7-Eleven stores. A new generation of ATMs show video ads while customers wait to get their money.[16] Purina has created podcasts—downloadable files that can be listened to on an MP3 player or computer—that offer pet owners advice on issues ranging from helping pets lose weight to pet health insurance. In the United Kingdom, the leading cellular carrier, Orange, launched a program called Orange Wednesdays. Customers can sign up to receive special offers—like two-for-one movie tickets—via a text message voucher.[17] And, of course, the Internet is a medium that can be highly targeted.

"Must buys" may use up available funds

Selecting which media to use is still pretty much an art. The media buyer starts with a budgeted amount and tries to buy the best blend to reach the target audience.

Some media are obvious "must buys," like the local newspaper for a retailer in a small town. Most firms serving local markets view a Yellow Pages listing as a must buy. Website advertising is increasingly seen as a must buy. It may be the only medium for firms trying to reach business buyers in overseas markets. Must-buy ads may even use up the available funds.

For many firms, even national advertisers, the high cost of television may eliminate it from the media blend. The average cost just to produce a national TV ad is now about $250,000—and a big impact ad can easily cost twice that. In the United States, it costs an average of $150,000 to run a 30-second commercial during the prime evening time, but on hit shows like *American Idol* the cost can be more than $700,000 per 30-second spot. Prices can soar even higher for "big event" shows; 30 seconds of advertising on the 2006 Super Bowl cost sponsors about $2.5 million.[18]

ADVERTISING ON THE INTERNET—NEW OPPORTUNITIES AND NEW CHALLENGES

Internet advertising accounts for a small proportion of total ad spending, but it is growing fast as more consumers head to the Web for news, information, and entertainment. In addition, the interactive technology of the Internet creates both opportunities and challenges for advertisers who want to target specific customers or segments.

Most Internet ads seek a direct response

Advertising on the Internet takes a variety of forms, but the purpose is usually to attract the interest of people in the advertiser's target market so they'll click through to the firm's website. Many people try to ignore any advertising—and on the Internet they may even use software that eliminates some types of ads. However, to get the attention of web surfers, Internet advertisers have created many different types of ads.

Banner ads are small rectangular boxes that usually include text, graphics, and sometimes video to create interest. Because banner ads can be easy to ignore, advertisers turned to *pop-up ads* that open in a new browser window (and block what the web user is trying to view—until they're closed). A variation is the *pop-under ad*, which opens under the web page being viewed, so it usually isn't noticed until after the web browser is closed. Most people find these ads very annoying and many use software to block them. Yet some advertisers still use them because they do get responses. Some firms that *sell*

Does Advertising That's Everywhere Get Us Anywhere?

There's no holiday from advertising. You get to the beach, look down, and huge versions of the Skippy peanut butter logo are embossed in the sand. You roll your eyes in dismay and catch a view of a plane pulling a 100-foot-long banner ad with Catherine Zeta-Jones urging you to "Sign up for T-Mobile's free Friday minutes." You walk down the street and try to ignore the billboards and bus stop shelter ads. But it's hard not to notice trucks whose trailers are billboards—and there are even ads on the trucks' mud flaps. A bus drives by wrapped in an ad for McDonald's—and you see a cab with hubcaps advertising Taco Bell. You *are* getting hungry, but you packed a lunch and seek refuge in a nearby park. Not quite an escape from ads—the bench you sit on is an ad for a check-cashing service—and just for good measure the banana you pull out of your lunch bag has a sticker advertising Florida oranges. A couple of girls walk by wearing T-shirts emblazoned with "Abercrombie & Fitch" and "Old Navy." Then you hear a deep voice—but it's just a cell phone—the ring tone of the guy sitting next to you is promoting Stephen King's new movie with the author's voice. Then your cell phone displays a text message that offers you a discounted admission at a nearby club—how do they know where you are?

You need to get away from this commercial overload, so you head back to your condo to kick back, watch a movie, play computer games, and maybe read e-mail. But this is no escape! An ad and discount for the local Hard Rock Café are printed on the key to your rented condo. The "ad-free" pay-per-view movie—*Minority Report*—has product placements from Coca-Cola, Nokia, Gap, and Lexus. You pull out your laptop and load up Tony Hawk's American Wasteland video game—but you can't miss all the Jeep Wranglers, Cherokees, and Liberties driving around in the game—not a coincidence. So you close the game and check your e-mail. Getting onto a wireless Internet connection, your pop-up blocker stops many ads, but some still worm through. You sort through your e-mails—half of which are uninvited spam messages. Ugh. Is there no place to hide?

There are certainly many cases where promotion benefits both the consumer and the firm and, after all, it is revenues from advertising that cover the cost of lots of great stuff consumers get for free. Yet sometimes you can't help but wish that you—and your wallet—were not the targets that so many companies are aiming at![19]

Internet advertising will probably continue to look for ways around ad blocking software in an effort to try to force consumers to view an ad. But that approach probably doesn't make much sense for a marketing-oriented firm. Rather, it is better to try to reach target customers who are actually interested in what the firm has to communicate.

Sites often target specific customers

Target marketers try to place ads on websites that are designed to appeal to the firm's target market. For example, Morningstar's website attracts many investors who want current financial information about the stock market, so E*Trade posts its online brokerage ads there. And Electric Cyclery, a retailer of electric bikes and scooters, runs ads at the TreeHugger blog because it attracts environmentalists.

Advertisers who seek exposure to a broader target market can place an ad at a popular web portal like Yahoo! or MSN. These sites get 20 to 25 million visits a day. But they are expensive—up to $500,000 per day for a banner ad on the main page.

Internet EXERCISE

Go to the Google website (*www.google.com*) and click on the "Advertising Programs" link. Read about the benefits of the different options. What are some advantages of advertising on Google as compared to *Time* magazine or a local radio station? What are some disadvantages?

Search ads know what customers are looking for

Google and other search engine sites know customers' interests based on the keywords they use in a search. Many consumers conduct searches to get information for buying decisions. So Circuit City might pay a search engine firm for a sponsored search ad that appears with the search results when specific search terms, like *camcorder*, are entered.

Some ads know where customers have been on the Web

Behavioral targeting delivers ads to consumers based on previous websites the customer has visited. Some websites place a small file called a cookie on the computer of people who visit the site. These cookies give an advertiser some information about the consumer. For example, cookies could indicate whether a web surfer has been to the company's website before, made a purchase on the last visit, or perhaps abandoned a partially full shopping cart. Or, based on what other sites a customer has visited, it is sometimes possible to determine likely interest in an offering. For example, a California theme park wanted to increase vacation package sales at its website. Special ads were delivered to web surfers whose computers had cookies to indicate that they lived in specific western states and had also visited a travel site in the previous two weeks. This proved to be a cost-effective way to target ads and boost online sales.

Some advertisers pay only if ads deliver

Many websites charge advertisers a fee based on how frequently or how long an ad is shown. However, competition for advertisers has prompted *pay-per-click* advertising, where advertisers only pay when a customer clicks on the ad and links to the advertiser's website. For example, Omaha Steaks, which sells frozen meat by mail order, uses Google search ads. Its ads appear when any of about 1,600 search terms, including *Omaha steaks* or *filet mignon*, are entered at Google. Omaha Steaks pays about 70 cents for each click-through.

This is a big shift from traditional media where firms have to pay for their ads whether they work or not. A lot more firms will put ads on websites if there is a direct relationship between costs and results. Moreover, this arrangement gives a website more incentive to attract an audience that some specific advertiser wants to reach.

Websites need to maintain interest and create desire

After a customer clicks on an ad and links to a company's website, that site has to provide something of interest or the customer will immediately click away. Some ads simply link customers to the firm's home page. However, a customized "landing page" helps keep customers at the site by increasing their interest and desire. For instance,

Autobytel uses search ads to target car buyers at MSN. The landing page at the Autobytel website depends on the search term the customer enters. For example, a customer who searches on the phrase *used Ford Focus* would land on a page with information about the Ford Focus and a photo.

Once customers get to a company's website, the site can provide much more interactivity than traditional advertising. For example, sites often provide a link so that visitors can see a different language. MSN uses this approach. Increasingly, content moves beyond the text and pictures typical of print ads and instead includes videos, sound, a product database, customer reviews or forums, and order-entry shopping carts. The website can also offer a great deal more information than advertising and allow customers to self-direct to pages that are of the greatest interest. In addition, a website can provide links to outside sources of information. Or a web page can invite the viewer to sign up for more information via e-mail or even start a chat session with a salesperson.[20]

PLANNING THE "BEST" MESSAGE—WHAT TO COMMUNICATE

Specifying the copy thrust

Once you decide *how* the messages will reach the target audience, you have to decide on the **copy thrust**—what the words and illustrations should communicate.

Carrying out the copy thrust is the job of advertising specialists. But the advertising manager and the marketing manager need to understand the process to be sure that the job is done well.

Let AIDA help guide message planning

Basically, the overall marketing strategy should determine *what* the message should say. Then management judgment, perhaps aided by marketing research, can help decide how to encode this content so it will be decoded as intended.

As a guide to message planning, we can use the AIDA concept: getting Attention, holding Interest, arousing Desire, and obtaining Action.

Getting attention

Getting attention is an ad's first job. Many readers leaf through magazines without paying attention to any of the ads, and viewers get snacks during TV commercials. When watching a program on TiVo, they may zip past the commercial with a flick of a button. On the Internet, they may use a pop-up blocker or click on the next website before the ad message finishes loading onto the screen.

Many attention-getting devices are available. A large headline, computer animation, shocking statements, attractive models, animals, special effects—anything different or eye-catching—may do the trick. However, the attention-getting device can't detract from, and hopefully should lead to, the next step, holding interest.

The right copy thrust helps an ad clearly communicate to its target market.

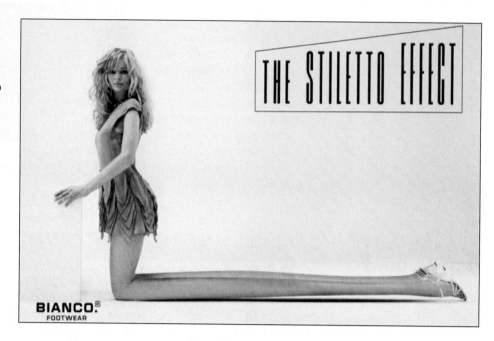

Holding interest

Holding interest is more difficult. A humorous ad, an unusual video effect, or a clever photo may get your attention—but once you've seen it, then what? If there is no relation between what got your attention and the marketing mix, you'll move on. To hold interest, the tone and language of the ad must fit with the experiences and attitudes of the target customers and their reference groups. As a result, many advertisers develop ads that relate to specific emotions. They hope that the good feeling about the ad will stick, even if its details are forgotten.

To hold interest, informative ads need to speak the target customer's language. Persuasive ads must provide evidence that convinces the customer. For example, TV ads often demonstrate a product's benefits.

Layouts for print ads should be arranged to encourage the eye to move smoothly through the ad—perhaps from a headline that starts in the upper left-hand corner to the illustration or body copy in the middle and finally to the lower right-hand corner where the ad's "signature" usually gives the company or brand name, toll-free number, and website address. If all of the elements of the ad work together as a whole, they will help to hold interest and build recall.[22]

Arousing desire

Arousing desire to buy a particular product is one of an ad's most difficult jobs. The ad must convince customers that the product can meet their needs. Testimonials may persuade a consumer that other people with similar needs like the product. Product comparisons may highlight the advantages of a particular brand.

Although products may satisfy certain emotional needs, many consumers find it necessary to justify their purchases on some logical basis. Snickers candy bar ads help ease the guilt of calorie-conscious snackers by assuring them that "Snickers satisfies you when you need an afternoon energy break."

An ad should usually focus on a *unique selling proposition* that aims at an important unsatisfied need. This can help differentiate the firm's marketing mix and position its brand as offering superior value to the target market. For example, Altoids has used humor in its ads to highlight the "curiously strong" flavor of its mints. Too many advertisers ignore the idea of a unique selling proposition. Rather than using an integrated blend of communications to tell the whole story, they cram too much into each ad—and then none of it has any impact.

Obtaining action

Getting action is the final requirement—and not an easy one. From communication research, we now know that prospective customers must be led beyond considering how the product *might* fit into their lives to actually trying it.

Direct-response ads can sometimes help promote action by encouraging interested consumers to do *something* even if they are not ready to make a purchase. For example, Fidelity Investments has run TV ads featuring colorful graphs and a sign with "Wow!"—followed by the company's phone number and website address. And just in case viewers don't "get it," Blondie's song "Call Me" plays in the background. Fidelity wants to encourage interested consumers to make the first step in building a relationship.

Careful research on attitudes in the target market may help uncover strongly felt *unsatisfied* needs. Appealing to important needs can get more action and also provide the kind of information buyers need to confirm the correctness of their decisions. Some customers seem to read more advertising *after* a purchase than before.

Can global messages work?

Many international consumer products firms try to use one global advertising message all around the world. Of course, they translate the message or make other minor adjustments—but the focus is one global copy thrust. Some do it to cut the cost of developing different ads for each country. Others feel their customers' basic needs are the same, even in different countries. Some just do it because it's fashionable to "go global."

This approach works for some firms. Coca-Cola and IBM, for example, believe that the needs their products serve are very similar for customers around the world. They focus on the similarities among customers who make up their target market rather than the differences. However, most firms who use this approach experience terrible results. They may save money by developing fewer ads, but they lose sales because they don't develop advertising messages, and whole marketing mixes, aimed at specific target markets. They just try to appeal to a global "mass market."[23]

ADVERTISING AGENCIES OFTEN DO THE WORK

An advertising manager manages a company's advertising effort. Many advertising managers, especially those working for large retailers, have their own advertising departments that plan specific advertising campaigns and carry out the details. Others turn over much of the advertising work to specialists—the advertising agencies.

Ad agencies are specialists

Advertising agencies are specialists in planning and handling mass-selling details for advertisers. Agencies play a useful role. They are independent of the advertiser and have an outside viewpoint. They bring experience to an individual client's problems because they work for many other clients. They can often do the job more economically than a company's own department. And if an agency isn't doing a good job, the client can select another. However, ending a relationship with an agency is a serious decision. Too many marketing managers just use their advertising agency as a scapegoat. Whenever anything goes wrong, they blame the agency.

Some full-service agencies handle any activities related to advertising, publicity, or sales promotion. They may even handle overall marketing strategy planning as well as marketing research, product and package development, and sales promotion. Other agencies are more specialized. For example, in recent years there has been rapid growth of firms that specialize in developing websites and Internet ads.

The biggest agencies handle much of the advertising

The vast majority of advertising agencies are small, with 10 or fewer employees. But the largest agencies account for most of the billings. Over the past two decades many of the big agencies have merged, creating mega-agencies with offices worldwide. For example, the top six mega-agencies have combined annual billings of over $30 billion.

The move toward international marketing is a key reason behind the mergers. The mega-agency can offer varied services, wherever in the world a marketing manager needs them. This may be especially important for managers in large corporations—like Toyota, Renault, Unilever, NEC, and PepsiCo—that advertise worldwide.[24]

The really big agencies are less interested in smaller accounts. Smaller agencies will continue to appeal to customers who want more personal attention and a close relationship that is more attuned to their marketing needs.

Are they paid too much?

Traditionally, U.S. advertising agencies have been paid a commission of about 15 percent on media and production costs. This arrangement evolved because media usually have two prices: one for national advertisers and a lower rate for local advertisers, such as local retailers. The advertising agency gets a 15 percent commission on national rates but not on local rates. This makes it worthwhile for producers and national middlemen to use agencies. National advertisers have to pay the full media rate anyway, so it makes sense to let the agency experts do the work and earn their commission. Local retailers—allowed the lower media rate—seldom use agencies.

Firms that spend huge amounts for help from advertising agencies are increasingly involving their purchasing departments in the process of negotiating agency compensation and other terms of the agency-client relationship. Procurement specialists may also set up procedures to audit agency charges for "billable hours" or other expenses. Auditing may become even more common in the future because of a few highly publicized cases in which agency executives have been accused of padding their time sheets.

Some firms pay the agency based on results

A number of advertisers now grade the work done by their agencies—and the agencies' pay depends on the grade. General Foods was the first to do this. It lowered its basic commission to about 13 percent. However, it paid the agency a bonus of about 3 percent on campaigns that earned an A rating. If the agency only earned a B, it lost the bonus. If it earned a C, it had to improve fast or GF removed the account. Variations on this approach are becoming common. For example, Carnation directly links its agency's compensation with how well its ads score in market research tests. This approach forces the advertiser and agency to agree on very specific objectives for their ads and what they expect to achieve. It also reduces the likelihood of the creative people in an agency focusing on ads that will win artistic approval in their industry rather than ads that do what the firm needs done.[25]

Ethical conflicts may arise

Ad agencies usually work closely with their clients, and they often have access to confidential information. This can create ethical conflicts if an agency is working with two or more competing clients. Most agencies are sensitive to the potential problems and keep people and information from competing accounts separated. Even so, that doesn't always happen. For example, PepsiCo got a restraining order to stop an ad agency from assigning four people who had worked on advertising for its Aquafina

Different specialty agencies help firms with specific advertising and sales promotion needs. For example, WonderGroup is a leading agency that focuses on the youth market. FLOORgraphics helps firms with point-of-sale ads on the floors of retail stores.

bottled water to the account for Coca-Cola's competing brand, Dasani. Coca-Cola, in turn, yanked the account away from the agency. Because of situations like this, many advertisers refuse to work with any agency that handles any competing accounts, even if they are handled in different offices.[26]

MEASURING ADVERTISING EFFECTIVENESS IS NOT EASY

Success depends on the total marketing mix

It would be convenient if we could measure the results of advertising by looking at sales. Some breakthrough ads do have a very direct effect on a company's sales—and the advertising literature is filled with success stories that "prove" advertising increases sales. Similarly, marketing research firms like Information Resources can sometimes compare sales levels before and after the period of an ad campaign. Yet we usually can't measure advertising success just by looking at sales. The total marketing mix—not just advertising—is responsible for the sales result. Sales results are also affected by what competitors do and by other changes in the external marketing environment. Only with direct-response advertising can a company make a direct link between advertising and sales results.

Research and testing can improve the odds

Ideally, advertisers should pretest advertising before it runs rather than relying solely on their own guesses about how good an ad will be. The judgment of creative people or advertising experts may not help much. They often judge only on the basis of originality or cleverness of the copy and illustrations.

Many progressive advertisers now demand laboratory or market tests to evaluate an ad's effectiveness. For example, split runs on cable TV systems in test markets are an important approach for testing ads in a normal viewing environment. Scanner sales data from retailers in those test markets can provide an estimate of how an ad is likely to affect sales. This approach will become even more powerful in the future as more cable systems allow viewers to provide immediate feedback to an ad as it appears on TV or on the Internet.

Hindsight may lead to foresight

After ads run, researchers may try to measure how much consumers recall about specific products or ads. The response to radio or television commercials or magazine

Mercedes used the ad (below) to help introduce its new model and attract younger customers in Latin America. A bad economy dampened sales, but the ad did pull the target market into showrooms. This increased names in the dealers' customer database, used to target other promotions, by 50 percent. Firms like QuickTake.com do research to help advertisers determine if a creative ad is also effective.

The new Mercedes-Benz A-Class. A dream come true.

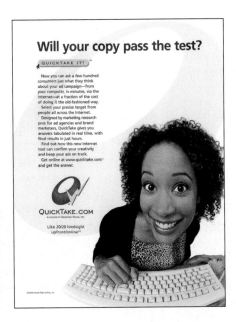

Will your copy pass the test?

readership can be estimated using various survey methods to check the size and composition of audiences (the Nielsen and Starch reports are examples). Similarly, most Internet advertisers keep track of how many "hits" on the firm's website come from ads placed at other websites.[27]

HOW TO AVOID UNFAIR ADVERTISING

Government agencies may say what is fair

In most countries, the government takes an active role in deciding what kinds of advertising are allowable, fair, and appropriate. For example, France and Japan limit the use of cartoon characters in advertising to children, and Canada bans *any* advertising targeted directly at children. In Switzerland, an advertiser cannot use an actor to represent a consumer. New Zealand limits political ads on TV. In the United States, print ads must be identified so they aren't confused with editorial matter; in other countries ads and editorial copy can be intermixed. Most countries limit the number and length of commercials on broadcast media.

What is seen as positioning in one country may be viewed as unfair or deceptive in another. For example, when Pepsi was advertising its cola as "the choice of the new generation" in most countries, Japan's Fair Trade Committee didn't allow it—because in Japan Pepsi was not "the choice."[28]

Differences in rules mean that a marketing manager may face very specific limits in different countries, and local experts may be required to ensure that a firm doesn't waste money developing ads that will never be shown or which consumers will think are deceptive.

FTC controls unfair practices in the United States

In the United States, the Federal Trade Commission (FTC) has the power to control unfair or deceptive business practices, including deceptive advertising. The FTC has been policing deceptive advertising for many years. And it may be getting results now that advertising agencies as well as advertisers must share equal responsibility for false, misleading, or unfair ads.

This is a serious matter. If the FTC decides that a particular practice is unfair or deceptive, it has the power to require affirmative disclosures—such as the health warnings on cigarettes—or **corrective advertising**—ads to correct deceptive advertising. Years ago the FTC forced Listerine to spend millions of dollars on advertising to "correct" earlier ads that claimed the mouthwash helped prevent colds. Advertisers still remember that lesson. The possibility of large financial penalties or the need to pay for corrective ads have caused more agencies and advertisers to stay well within the law.

However, sometimes ad claims seem to get out of hand anyway. For example, there have been many ads and infomercials that tout various gadgets and dietary supplements as effective for weight loss. For most of these products there is no evidence that they work (unless used while training to compete in a marathon). Given the heightened concerns about obesity, the FTC has started to crack down on claims related to weight loss and health. For example, KFC quickly stopped running several of its TV ads after the FTC objected to the ads and opened an investigation. KFC's ads positioned fried chicken as a healthy choice in fast food, but they also included lots of small print at the bottom of the screen to qualify the claims.[29]

What is unfair or deceptive is changing

What constitutes unfair and deceptive advertising is a difficult question. The law provides some guidelines, but the marketing manager must make personal judgments as well. The social and political environment is changing worldwide. Practices considered acceptable some years ago are now questioned or considered deceptive. Saying or even implying that your product is best may be viewed as deceptive. And a 1988 revision of the Lanham Act protects firms whose brand names are unfairly tarnished in comparative ads.

| Supporting ad claims is a fuzzy area | It's really not hard to figure out how to avoid criticisms of being unfair and deceptive. A little puffing is acceptable, and probably always will be. But marketing managers need to put a stop to the typical production-oriented approach of trying to use advertising to differentiate me-too products that are not different and don't offer customers better value.[30] |

SALES PROMOTION—DO SOMETHING DIFFERENT TO STIMULATE CHANGE

The nature of sales promotion

Sales promotion refers to those promotion activities—other than advertising, publicity, and personal selling—that stimulate interest, trial, or purchase by final customers or others in the channel. Exhibit 13–2 shows examples of typical sales promotions targeted at final customers, channel members, or a firm's own employees.

Sales promotion is generally used to complement the other promotion methods. While advertising campaigns and sales force strategy decisions tend to have longer-term effects, a particular sales promotion activity usually lasts for only a limited time period. But sales promotion can often be implemented quickly and get sales results sooner than advertising. Further, sales promotion objectives usually focus on prompting some short-term action. For a middleman, such an action might be a decision to stock a product, provide a special display space, or give the product extra sales emphasis. For a consumer, the desired action might be to try a new product, switch from another brand, or buy more of a product. The desired action by an employee might be a special effort to satisfy customers.

Sales promotion objectives and situation should influence decision

There are many different types of sales promotion, but what type is appropriate depends on the situation and objectives. For example, Exhibit 15–6 shows some possible ways that a short-term promotion might affect sales. The sales pattern in the graph on the left might occur if Hellmann's issues coupons to help clear its excess mayonnaise inventory. Some consumers might buy earlier to take advantage of the coupon, but unless they use extra mayonnaise their next purchase will be delayed. In the center graph, kids might convince parents to eat more Big Macs while McDonald's has a *Lord of the Rings* promotion, but when it ends things go back to normal. The graph on the right shows a Burger King marketer's dream come true: Free samples of a new style of french fries quickly pull in new customers who like what they try and keep coming back after the promotion ends. This is also the kind of long-term result that is the aim of effective advertising. From these examples, you can see that the situation and the objective of the promotion should determine what specific type is best.

Exhibit 15–6 Some Possible Effects of a Sales Promotion on Sales

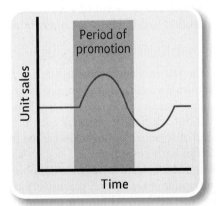

Sales temporarily increase, then decrease, then return to regular level

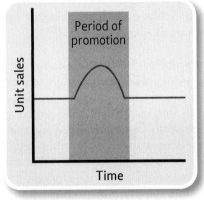

Sales temporarily increase and then return to regular level

Sales increase and then remain at higher level

| Sales promotion
spending has grown
in mature markets | Sales promotion involves so many different types of activities that it is difficult to estimate accurately how much is spent in total. There is general consensus, however, that the total spending on sales promotion exceeds spending on advertising.[31]

One reason for increased use of sales promotion by many consumer products firms is that they are generally competing in mature markets. There's only so much soap that consumers want to buy, regardless of how many brands there are vying for their dollars. There's also only so much shelf space that retailers will allocate to a particular product category.

The competitive situation is intensified by the growth of large, powerful retail chains. They have put more emphasis on their own dealer brands and also demanded more sales promotion support for the manufacturer brands they do carry.

Perhaps in part because of this competition, many consumers have become more price sensitive. Many sales promotions, like coupons, have the effect of lowering the prices consumers pay. So sales promotion has been used as a tool to overcome consumer price resistance.

The growth of sales promotion has also been fostered by the availability of more ad agencies and specialists who plan and implement sales promotion programs. Of course, the most basic reason for the growth of spending on sales promotion is that it can be very effective if it is done properly. But there are problems in the sales promotion area. |
|---|---|

PROBLEMS IN MANAGING SALES PROMOTION

| Does sales promotion
erode brand loyalty? | Some experts think that marketing managers—especially those who deal with consumer packaged goods—put too much emphasis on sales promotion. They argue that the effect of most sales promotion is temporary and that money spent on advertising and personal selling helps the firm more over the long term. When the market is not growing, sales promotion may just encourage "deal-prone" customers (and middlemen) to switch back and forth among brands. Here, all the expense of the sales promotion simply contributes to lower profits. It also increases the prices that consumers pay because it increases selling costs.

However, once a marketing manager is in this situation there may be little choice other than to continue. In mature markets, frequent sales promotions may be needed just to offset the effects of competitors' promotions. One escape from this competitive rat race is for the marketing manager to seek new opportunities—with a strategy that doesn't rely solely on short-term sales promotions for competitive advantage. |
|---|---|
| There are alternatives | Procter & Gamble is a company that changed its strategy, and promotion blend, to decrease its reliance on sales promotion targeted at middlemen. It is offering middlemen lower prices on many of its products and supporting those products with more advertising and promotion to final consumers. P&G believes that this approach builds its brand equity, serves consumers better, and leads to smoother-running relationships in its channels. Not all retailers are happy with P&G's changes. However, many other producers are following P&G's lead.[32] |
| Sales promotion is
hard to manage | Another problem in the sales promotion area is that it is easy to make big, costly mistakes. Because sales promotion includes such a wide variety of activities, it's difficult for the typical company to develop skill in managing all of them. Even large firms and agencies that specialize in sales promotion run into difficulties because each promotion is typically custom-designed and then used only once. Yet mistakes caused by lack of experience can be costly or hurt relationships with customers.

In a promotion for Pampers diapers that was designed to reward loyal buyers and steal customers away from competing Huggies, marketing managers offered parents Fisher-Price toys if they collected points printed on Pampers' packages. At first the promotion seemed to be a big success because so many parents were collecting points. But that turned into a problem when Fisher-Price couldn't produce enough toys to redeem all the |

Some successful sales promotion ideas at first seem pretty wild. Marketers for Charmin toilet tissue outfitted trucks with fancy bathrooms and sent the portable potties to big events, like the Super Bowl, where public restrooms would be in short supply. Two million curious consumers tried out these facilities. The payoff? Research shows a 14 percent increase in Charmin sales among those people.

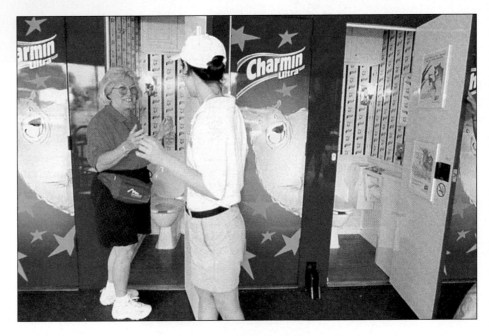

points. Pampers had to add 50 toll-free phone lines to handle all the complaints, and a lot of angry parents stopped buying Pampers for good. Problems like this are common.[33]

Not a sideline for amateurs

Sales promotion mistakes are likely to be worse when a company has no sales promotion manager. If the personal selling or advertising managers are responsible for sales promotion, they often treat it as a "stepchild." They allocate money to sales promotion if there is any "left over" or if a crisis develops.

Making sales promotion work is a learned skill, not a sideline for amateurs. That's why specialists in sales promotion have developed, both inside larger firms and as outside consultants. Some of these people are real experts. But it's the marketing manager's responsibility to set sales promotion objectives and policies that will fit in with the rest of each marketing strategy.[34]

DIFFERENT TYPES OF SALES PROMOTION FOR DIFFERENT TARGETS

Sales promotion for final consumers or users

Much of the sales promotion aimed at final consumers or users tries to increase demand, perhaps temporarily, or speed up the time of purchase. Such promotion might involve developing materials to be displayed in retailers' stores, including banners, sample packages, calendars, and various point-of-purchase materials. It might include sweepstakes contests as well as coupons designed to get customers to buy a product by a certain date. Coupon distribution has dropped off some in recent years but still averages about 3,000 coupons per household in America! However, only about 1 percent of all coupons are redeemed.[35]

All of these sales promotion efforts are aimed at specific objectives. For example, if customers already have a favorite brand, it may be hard to get them to try anything new. A free trial-sized bottle of mouthwash might be just what it takes to get cautious consumers to try the new product. Samples might be distributed house to house, by mail, at stores, or attached to other products sold by the firm. In this type of situation, sales of the product might start to pick up as soon as customers try the product and find out that they like it. And sales will continue at the higher level after the promotion is over if satisfied customers make repeat purchases. Thus, the cost of the sales promotion in this situation might be viewed as a long-term investment.

Internet EXERCISE

Catalina Marketing Corporation is a supplier of in-store, at-home, and online consumer promotions. Go to the Catalina website (*www.catmktg.com*) and select "Retail Services," then click on "Products & Services" under that category. Review the information about its Retail Services. Go back and check out "Manufacturer Services" in the same way. Briefly describe, in your own words, how the "Checkout Prizes" program works, and describe a situation in which both a retailer and a manufacturer might find it useful.

Once a product is established, consumer sales promotion usually focuses on short-term sales increases. For example, after a price-off coupon for a soft drink is distributed, sales might temporarily pick up as customers take advantage of buying at a lower price. When the objective of the promotion is focused primarily on producing a short-term increase in sales, it's sensible for the marketing manager to evaluate the cost of the promotion relative to the extra sales expected. If the increase in sales won't at least cover the cost of the promotion, it probably doesn't make sense to do it. Otherwise, the firm is "buying sales" at the cost of reduced profit.

Sales promotion directed at industrial customers might use the same kinds of ideas. In addition, the sales promotion people might set up and staff trade show exhibits. Here, attractive models are often used to encourage buyers to look at a firm's product, especially when it is displayed near other similar products in a circuslike atmosphere. Trade shows are a cost-effective way to reach target customers and generate a list of "live" prospects for sales rep follow-up. However, many firms handle these leads badly. One study indicates that 85 percent of leads are not followed up by anyone.

Some sellers give away promotion items—pen sets, watches, or clothing (perhaps with the firm's brand name on them)—to remind business customers of their products. This is common, but it can be a problem. Some companies do not allow buyers to accept any gifts.[36]

Sales promotion for middlemen

Sales promotion aimed at middlemen—sometimes called *trade promotion*—emphasizes price-related matters. The objective may be to encourage middlemen to stock new items, buy in larger quantity, buy early, or stress a product in their own promotion efforts.

The tools used here include merchandise allowances, promotion allowances, and perhaps sales contests to encourage retailers or wholesalers to sell specific items or the company's whole line. Offering to send contest winners to Hawaii, for example, may increase sales.

About half of the sales promotion spending targeted at middlemen has the effect of reducing the price that they pay for merchandise. So we'll go into more detail on different types of trade discounts and allowances in the next chapter.

Sales promotion for company's own employees

Sales promotion aimed at the company's own sales force might try to encourage providing better service, getting new customers, selling a new product, or selling the company's whole line. Depending on the objectives, the tools might be contests, bonuses on sales or number of new accounts, and holding sales meetings at fancy resorts to raise everyone's spirits.

Ongoing sales promotion work might also be aimed at the sales force—to help sales management. Sales promotion might be responsible for preparing sales portfolios, digital videos, PowerPoint presentations, displays, and other sales aids, as well as sales training material.

Service-oriented firms such as hotels and restaurants use sales promotions targeted at their employees. Some, for example, give a monthly cash prize for the employee who provides the "best service." And the employee's picture is displayed to give recognition.[37]

CONCLUSION

It may seem simple to develop an advertising campaign. Just pick the medium and develop a message. But it's not that easy.

This chapter discussed why marketing managers should set specific objectives to guide the entire advertising effort. Knowing what they want to achieve, marketing managers can determine what kind of advertising—product or institutional—to use. We also discussed three basic types of product advertising: pioneering, competitive (direct and indirect), and reminder.

Marketing managers must also choose from various media—so we discussed their advantages and disadvantages. Because the Internet offers new advertising opportunities and challenges we discussed how it is similar to and different from other media. And, of course, marketing managers must determine the message—or copy thrust—that will appear in ads.

Many technical details are involved in mass selling. Advertising agencies often handle these jobs. But specific objectives must be set for agencies, or their advertising may have little direction and be almost impossible to evaluate. This chapter also discussed how to make sure that advertising is done legally.

Sales promotion spending is big and growing. This approach is especially important in prompting action—by customers, intermediaries, or salespeople. There are many different types of sales promotion, and it is a problem area in many firms because it is difficult for a firm to develop expertise given all of the possibilities.

Advertising and sales promotion are often important parts of a promotion blend, but in most blends personal selling also plays an important role. Further, promotion is only a part of the total marketing mix a marketing manager must develop to satisfy target customers. So to broaden your understanding of the four Ps and how they fit together, in the next two chapters we'll go into more detail on the role of Price in strategy decisions.

KEY TERMS

product advertising, 388

institutional advertising, 388

pioneering advertising, 388

competitive advertising, 389

direct type advertising, 389

indirect type advertising, 389

comparative advertising, 389

reminder advertising, 389

advertising allowances, 390

cooperative advertising, 390

copy thrust, 397

advertising agencies, 399

corrective advertising, 402

QUESTIONS AND PROBLEMS

1. Identify the strategy decisions a marketing manager must make in the advertising area.

2. Discuss the relation of advertising objectives to marketing strategy planning and the kinds of advertising actually needed. Illustrate.

3. List several media that might be effective for reaching consumers in a developing nation with low per capita income and a high level of illiteracy. Briefly discuss the limitations and advantages of each medium you suggest.

4. Give three examples where advertising to intermediaries might be necessary. What is the objective(s) of such advertising?

5. What does it mean to say that "money is invested in advertising"? Is all advertising an investment? Illustrate.

6. Find advertisements to final consumers that illustrate the following types of advertising: (*a*) institutional, (*b*) pioneering, (*c*) competitive, and (*d*) reminder. What objective(s) does each of these ads have? List the needs each ad appeals to.

7. Describe the type of media that might be most suitable for promoting: (*a*) tomato soup, (*b*) greeting cards, (*c*) a business component material, and (*d*) playground equipment. Specify any assumptions necessary to obtain a definite answer.

8. Briefly discuss some of the pros and cons an advertising manager for a producer of sports equipment might want to think about in deciding whether to advertise on the Internet.

9. Discuss the use of testimonials in advertising. Which of the four AIDA steps might testimonials accomplish? Are they suitable for all types of products? If not, for which types are they most suitable?

10. Find a magazine ad that you think does a particularly good job of communicating to the target audience. Would the ad communicate well to an audience in another country? Explain your thinking.

11. Johnson & Johnson sells its baby shampoo in many different countries. Do you think baby shampoo would be a good product for Johnson & Johnson to advertise with a single global message? Explain your thinking.

12. Discuss the future of smaller advertising agencies now that many of the largest are merging to form mega-agencies.

13. Does advertising cost too much? How can this be measured?

14. How would your local newspaper be affected if local supermarkets switched their weekly advertising and instead used a service that delivered weekly, freestanding ads directly to each home?

15. Is it unfair to criticize a competitor's product in an ad? Explain your thinking.

16. Explain why P&G and other consumer packaged goods firms are trying to cut back on some types of sales promotion like coupons for consumers and short-term trade promotions such as "buy a case and get a case free."

17. Discuss some ways that a firm can link its sales promotion activities to its advertising and personal selling efforts— so that all of its promotion efforts result in an integrated effort.

18. Indicate the type of sales promotion that a producer might use in each of the following situations and briefly explain your reasons:

    a. A firm has developed an improved razor blade and obtained distribution, but customers are not motivated to buy it.

    b. A competitor is about to do a test market for a new brand and wants to track sales in test market areas to fine-tune its marketing mix.

    c. A big grocery chain won't stock a firm's new popcorn-based snack product because it doesn't think there will be much consumer demand.

19. Why wouldn't a producer of toothpaste just lower the price of its product rather than offer consumers a price-off coupon?

20. If sales promotion spending continues to grow—often at the expense of media advertising—how do you think this might affect the rates charged by mass media for advertising time or space? How do you think it might affect advertising agencies?

CREATING MARKETING PLANS

The Marketing Plan Coach software on the Student CD includes a sample marketing plan for Hillside Veterinary Clinic. Look through the "Marketing Strategy" section.

a. What are Hillside's advertising objectives?

b. What types of advertising and media are being proposed? Why are these types used and not others?

c. What type of copy thrust is recommended? Why?

d. What sales promotion activities are being planned? What are the goals of sales promotion?

SUGGESTED CASES

18. Harrisburg Volunteer Fire Department   20. Recreation Universe

COMPUTER-AIDED PROBLEM

15. SALES PROMOTION

As a community service, disc jockeys from radio station WMKT formed a basketball team to help raise money for local nonprofit organizations. The host organization finds or fields a competing team and charges $5 admission to the game. Money from ticket sales goes to the nonprofit organization.

Ticket sales were disappointing at recent games, averaging only about 300 people per game. When WMKT's marketing manager, Bruce Miller, heard about the problem, he suggested using sales promotion to improve ticket sales. The PTA for the local high school—the sponsor for the next game—is interested in the idea but is concerned that its budget doesn't include any promotion money. Miller tries to help them by reviewing his idea in more detail.

Specifically, he proposes that the PTA give a free T-shirt (printed with the school name and date of the game) to the first 500 ticket buyers. He thinks the T-shirt giveaway will create a lot of interest. In fact, he says he is almost certain the promotion would help the PTA sell 600 tickets, double the usual number. He speculates that the PTA might even have a sellout of all 900 seats in the school gym. Further, he notes that the T-shirts will more than pay for themselves if the PTA sells 600 tickets.

A local firm that specializes in sales promotion items agrees to supply the shirts and do the printing for $2.40 a shirt if the PTA places an order for at least 400 shirts. The PTA thinks the idea is interesting but wants to look at it more closely to see what will happen if the promotion doesn't increase ticket sales. To help the PTA evaluate the alternatives, Miller sets up a spreadsheet with the relevant information.

a. Based on the data from the initial spreadsheet, does the T-shirt promotion look like a good idea? Explain your thinking.

b. The PTA treasurer worries about the up-front cost of printing the T-shirts and wants to know where they would stand if they ordered the T-shirts and still sold only 300 tickets. He suggests it might be safer to order the minimum number of T-shirts (400). Evaluate his suggestion.

c. The president of the PTA thinks the T-shirt promotion will increase sales but wonders if it wouldn't be better just to lower the price. She suggests $2.60 a ticket, which she arrives at by subtracting the $2.40 T-shirt cost from the usual $5.00 ticket price. How many tickets would the PTA have to sell at the lower price to match the money it would make if it used the T-shirt promotion and actually sold 600 tickets? (Hint: Change the selling price in the spreadsheet and then vary the quantity using the analysis feature.)

For additional questions related to this problem, see Exercise 15–3 in the *Learning Aid for Use with Essentials of Marketing*, 11th edition.

16

Pricing Objectives and Policies

In the early 1960s, the electric toothbrush was a new idea. A number of brands were on the market, and the American Dental Association declared that electric brushes were better at cleaning teeth. Yet when Consumers Union found that the available models created an electric shock hazard, demand fizzled. In the 1990s, SonicCare introduced a safe, rechargeable unit at a premium price. Braun and other competitors followed its lead. But demand was limited. Few consumers saw an electric brush priced at more than $50 as a good value.

In 1998, John Osher and his three business partners had an idea for a battery-powered toothbrush that has changed the market. Even before 1998, Osher had been successful developing new-product ideas and then selling them to big companies. One hit was the Spin Pop, a spinning lollipop attached to a battery-powered plastic handle. After selling Spin Pop to Hasbro, Osher and his partners searched for their next big idea. While looking at the toothbrush display at a Wal-Mart store, they realized that they could adapt the Spin Pop idea to create an electric toothbrush. They reasoned that many consumers would trade up to their product if it was more effective than the premium manual brushes—and not much more expensive. So they spent the next year and a half researching, designing, and sourcing a high-quality brush that could sell for $5, including the batteries.

Their next challenge was to prove that the brush would sell. Large firms typically support new-product introductions with a hefty advertising budget and by giving retailers introductory deals or allowances. Then, to cover all the costs, they charge a premium price—at least until competition heats up. But Osher's small firm wanted to penetrate the market at a low initial price, where demand would be the greatest. And at a low price it couldn't afford all of the promotion. Instead, they decided to build interest at the point of purchase with packaging that said "Try me" and that left the button exposed so consumers could see the brush work. With the help of a salesperson who had experience working with big discount chains, they set up a test market. In the test, their new SpinBrush outsold the leading manual brush nearly 3 to 1. Using that sales data as evidence of the profit a retailer could make selling SpinBrush, they persuaded Walgreens Drugstores and then other retailers to carry it. Within a year, by the end of 2000, their new SpinBrush had expanded sales in the electric toothbrush market by 300 percent.

With that track record, Osher approached Procter & Gamble about buying SpinBrush. The timing was good. Price competition was making it tough for P&G's Crest oral care line to meet its profit objectives. Worse, Colgate had just launched its $19.95 ActiBrush electric toothbrush and it was off to a fast start. So P&G quickly struck a deal and soon was selling the SpinBrush with the Crest brand name. P&G kept the suggested retail price of the Spin-Brush at $5.99, and relied on its sales reps to expand distribution. Even without TV ads, sales took off like a rocket.

ActiBrush suffered in comparison, so by 2002 Colgate cut its price to $12 and also introduced a brush like the SpinBrush at the same $5.99 price. However, by then marketing managers for Spin-Brush had introduced new models, including new colors and designs to appeal to kids.

The Dora the Explorer SpinBrush appeals to preschoolers who enjoy the popular television show of the same name. P&G pays Nickelodeon a license fee to use the Dora character, but that extra cost is more than covered by the $7.99 price P&G charges for that model. The higher price also allows retailers to get a higher markup, so they have extra incen-tive to give SpinBrush more shelf space. Even at a higher price consumers see SpinBrush as a good value; that was confirmed when *Consumers Digest* declared it a best buy.

Marketing managers at Gillette didn't want to sit by while P&G's SpinBrush took customers from their Oral-B brand manual brushes and high-end electrics, so they added the CrossAction battery brush in the middle of the Oral-B product line. To help fend off the increased competition, P&G came out with testimonial ads for SpinBrush that also included a $1-off coupon. The coupons didn't leave much profit margin, but they attracted new customers who will be profitable when they buy replacement brushes packaged two for $5.95.

By 2005, SpinBrush's annual sales were $110 million—with 80 percent of its sales in the United States. But when P&G wanted to acquire Gillette, European antitrust regulators were concerned that P&G would control too much of the toothbrush market. To win their approval, P&G sold SpinBrush to a competing firm that markets oral care brands Mentadent and Aim. That firm paid a hefty $100 million for the SpinBrush business.[1]

LEARNING OBJECTIVES

The SpinBrush case demonstrates the importance of Price and how it interacts with the other marketing mix variables to influence customer behavior. This chapter will help you better understand pricing objectives and policies that influence how firms make pricing decisions.

When you finish this chapter, you should:

1. understand how pricing objectives should guide strategy planning for pricing decisions.
2. understand choices marketing managers must make about price flexibility.
3. know what a marketing manager should consider when setting the price level for a product in the early stages of the product life cycle.
4. understand the many possible variations of a price structure, including discounts, allowances, and who pays transportation costs.
5. understand the value pricing concept and its role in obtaining a competitive advantage and offering target customers superior value.
6. understand the legality of price level and price flexibility policies.
7. understand important new terms (shown in red).

PRICE HAS MANY STRATEGY DIMENSIONS

Price is one of the four major strategy decision variables that a marketing manager controls. Pricing decisions affect both the number of sales a firm makes and how much money it earns. Price is what a customer must give up to get the benefits offered by the rest of a firm's marketing mix, so it plays a direct role in shaping customer value.

Guided by the company's objectives, marketing managers develop specific pricing objectives. See Exhibit 16–1. These objectives drive decisions about key pricing policies: (1) how flexible prices will be, (2) the level of prices over the product life cycle, (3) to whom and when discounts and allowances will be given, and (4) how transportation costs will be handled. After we've looked at these specific areas, we will discuss how they combine to impact customer value as well as laws that are relevant. In Chapter 17, we will discuss how prices are set.

Ragged Mountain wants its customers to know that its price is a good value compared to what they get at other ski resorts.

Our weekday lift tickets are just $19.
Ironically, the same price
for Tic-Tacs at other mountains.

RAGGED MT.
Danbury, New Hampshire 603-768-3475 www.ragged-mt.com

Exhibit 16–1 Strategy Planning and Pricing Objectives and Policies

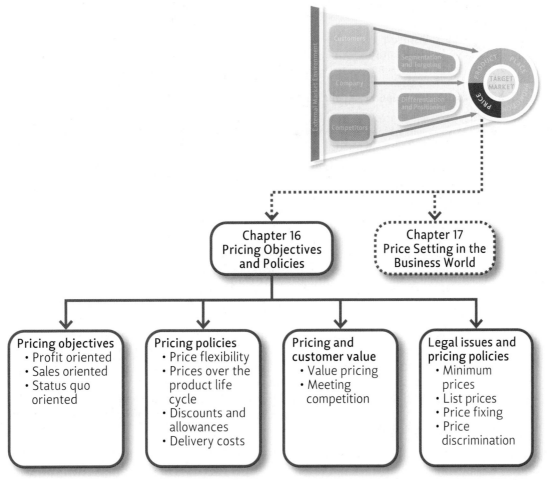

It's not easy to define price in real-life situations because price reflects many dimensions. People who don't realize this can make big mistakes.

Suppose you've been saving to buy a new car and you see in an ad that, after a $1,000 rebate, the base price for the new-year model is $16,494—5 percent lower than the previous year. At first this might seem like a real bargain. However, your view of this deal might change if you found out you also had to pay a $400 transportation charge and an extra $480 for an extended service warranty. The price might look even less attractive if you discovered that the fancy stereo, side air bags, and moonroof that were standard the previous year are now options that cost $1,400. The cost of the higher interest rate on the car loan and the sales tax on all of this might come as an unpleasant surprise too. Further, how would you feel if you bought the car anyway and then learned that a friend who just bought the exact same model got a much lower price from the dealer by using a broker he found on the Internet?[2]

The price equation: Price equals something of value

This example emphasizes that when a seller quotes a price, it is related to *some* assortment of goods and services. So **Price** is the amount of money that is charged for "something" of value. Of course, price may be called different things in different settings. Colleges charge tuition. Landlords collect rent. Motels post a room rate. Country clubs get dues. Banks ask for interest when they loan money. Airlines have fares. Doctors set fees. Employees want a wage. People may call it different things, but *almost every business transaction in our modern economy involves an exchange of money—the Price—for something.*

Exhibit 16–2
Price as Seen by
Consumers or Users

Price	Equals	Something of Value

List Price
 	
Less: *Discounts*
    Quantity
    Seasonal
    Cash
    Temporary sales
Less: *Allowances*
    Trade-ins
    Damaged goods
Less: *Rebate and coupon value*
Plus: *Transportation and taxes*
	equals	*Product*
		    Physical good
		    Service
		    Assurance of quality
		    Repair facilities
		    Packaging
		    Credit
		    Warranty
		Place of delivery or when available

The something can be a physical product in various stages of completion, with or without supporting services, with or without quality guarantees, and so on. Or it could be a pure service—dry cleaning, a lawyer's advice, or insurance on your car.

The nature and extent of this something determines the amount of money exchanged. Some customers pay list price. Others obtain large discounts or allowances because something is *not* provided. Exhibit 16–2 summarizes some possible variations for consumers or users, and Exhibit 16–3 does the same for channel members. These variations are discussed more fully below, and then we'll consider the customer value concept more fully—in terms of competitive advantage. But here it should be clear that Price has many dimensions. How each of these dimensions is handled affects customer value. If a customer sees greater value in spending money in some other way, no exchange will occur.

OBJECTIVES SHOULD GUIDE STRATEGY PLANNING FOR PRICE

Pricing objectives should flow from, and fit in with, company-level and marketing objectives. Pricing objectives should be *explicitly stated* because they have a direct effect on pricing policies as well as the methods used to set prices. Exhibit 16–4 shows the various types of pricing objectives we'll discuss.

Exhibit 16–3
Price as Seen by
Channel Members

Price	Equals	Something of Value

List Price
 	
Less: *Discounts*
    Quantity
    Seasonal
    Cash
    Trade or functional
    Temporary "deals"
Less: *Allowances*
    Damaged goods
    Advertising
    Push money
    Stocking
Plus: *Transportation, taxes,
    and tariffs*
	equals	*Product*
		    Branded—well known
		    Guaranteed
		    Warranted
		    Service—repair facilities
		    Convenient packaging for handling
		Place
		    Availability—when and where
		Promotion
		    Promotion aimed at customers
		Price
		    Price-level guarantee
		    Sufficient margin to allow chance
		    for profit

Exhibit 16–4
Possible Pricing
Objectives

PROFIT-ORIENTED OBJECTIVES

**Target returns provide
specific guidelines**

A **target return objective** sets a specific level of profit as an objective. Often this amount is stated as a percentage of sales or of capital investment. A large manufacturer like Motorola might aim for a 15 percent return on investment. The target for Safeway and other supermarket chains might be a 1 percent return on sales.

A target return objective has administrative advantages in a large company. Performance can be compared against the target. Some companies eliminate divisions, or drop products, that aren't yielding the target rate of return. For example, General Electric sold its small appliance division to Black & Decker because it felt it could earn higher returns in other product-markets.

**Some just want
satisfactory profits**

Some managers aim for only satisfactory returns. They just want returns that ensure the firm's survival and convince stockholders they're doing a good job. Similarly, some small family-run businesses aim for a profit that will provide a comfortable lifestyle.[3]

Many private and public nonprofit organizations set a price level that will just recover costs. In other words, their target return figure is zero. For example, a government agency may charge motorists a toll for using a bridge but then drop the toll when the cost of the bridge is paid.

Similarly, firms that provide critical public services—including many utility and insurance companies, transportation firms, and defense contractors—sometimes pursue only satisfactory long-run targets. They are well aware that the public expects them to set prices that are in the public interest. They may also have to face public or government agencies that review and approve prices.[4]

**Profit maximization
can be socially
responsible**

A **profit maximization objective** seeks to get as much profit as possible. It might be stated as a desire to earn a rapid return on investment—or, more bluntly, to charge all the traffic will bear.

Pricing to achieve profit maximization doesn't always lead to high prices. Low prices may expand the size of the market and result in greater sales and profits. For example, when prices of cell phones were very high, only businesses and wealthy people bought them. When producers lowered prices, nearly everyone bought one.

If a firm is earning a very large profit, other firms will try to copy or improve on what the company offers. Frequently, this leads to lower prices.[5]

Some consumers and lawmakers think prices for some drugs are too high. Merck wants consumers and lawmakers to know that higher drug prices provide pharmaceutical companies with an incentive to invest in research needed for innovative medicines.

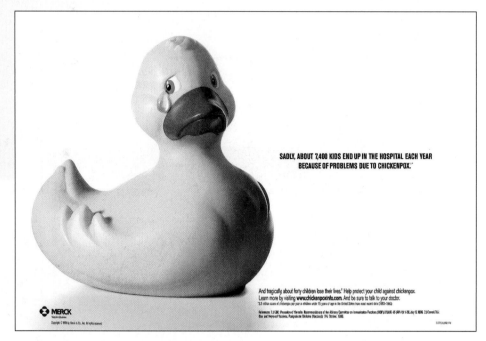

SADLY, ABOUT 7,400 KIDS END UP IN THE HOSPITAL EACH YEAR BECAUSE OF PROBLEMS DUE TO CHICKENPOX.

And tragically, about forty children lose their lives. Help protect your child against chickenpox. Learn more by visiting **www.chickenpoxinfo.com**. And be sure to talk to your doctor.

SALES-ORIENTED OBJECTIVES

A **sales-oriented objective** seeks some level of unit sales, dollar sales, or share of market—*without referring to profit.*

Sales growth doesn't necessarily mean big profits

Some managers are more concerned about sales growth than profits. They think sales growth always leads to more profits. This kind of thinking causes problems when a firm's costs are growing faster than sales. Some major corporations have had declining profits in spite of growth in sales. At the extreme, many dot-coms kept lowering prices to increase market share but never earned any profits. Pets.com had growing sales until it burned through investors' money and went bankrupt. Generally, however, business managers now pay more attention to profits, not just sales.[6]

Some nonprofit organizations set prices to increase market share—precisely because they are *not* trying to earn a profit. For example, many cities set low fares to fill up their buses. Buses cost the same to run empty or full, and there's more benefit when they're full even if the total revenue is no greater.

Market share objectives are popular

Many firms seek to gain a specified share (percent) of a market. If a company has a large market share, it may have better economies of scale than its competitors. In addition, it's usually easier to measure a firm's market share than to determine if profits are being maximized.

A company with a longer-run view may aim for increased market share when the market is growing. The hope is that future volume will justify sacrificing some profit in the short run. Companies as diverse as 3M and Coca-Cola look at opportunities in Eastern Europe and Southeast Asia this way.

Of course, market share objectives have the same limitations as straight sales growth objectives. A larger market share, if gained at too low a price, may lead to profitless "success." This is a too-common symptom of death-wish marketing.[7]

Giving your product away helps you charge more

Some firms use low prices or giveaways to help sell another product or sell to other customers. For example, Google doesn't charge for its search services and CNN.com offers free news and information. These companies are not simply being generous.

416

Google and CNN can sell advertising to business customers at a higher price if more of those businesses target customers who use the Google and CNN sites.

STATUS QUO PRICING OBJECTIVES

Don't-rock-the-boat objectives

Managers satisfied with their current market share and profits sometimes adopt **status quo objectives**—don't-rock-the-*pricing*-boat objectives. Managers may say that they want to stabilize prices, or meet competition, or even avoid competition. This don't-rock-the-boat thinking is most common when the total market is not growing.

Or stress nonprice competition instead

A status quo pricing objective may be part of an aggressive overall marketing strategy focusing on **nonprice competition**—aggressive action on one or more of the Ps other than Price. Some Internet firms originally thought that they'd compete with low prices and still earn high profits from volume. However, when they didn't get the sales volume they hoped for, they realized that there were also some nonprice ways to compete. For example, Zappos.com offers free shipping and guarantees that it will meet local shoe store prices. But it wins customers with its enormous selection of shoes, a website that makes it easy for customers to find what they want, and excellent customer service before and after the sale.[8]

MOST FIRMS SET SPECIFIC PRICING POLICIES—TO REACH OBJECTIVES

Administered prices help achieve objectives

Price policies usually lead to **administered prices**—consciously set prices. In other words, instead of letting daily market forces (or auctions) decide their prices, most firms set their own prices. They may hold prices steady for long periods of time or change them more frequently if that's what's required to meet objectives.

If a firm doesn't sell directly to final customers, it usually wants to administer both the price it receives from middlemen and the price final customers pay. After all, the price final customers pay will ultimately affect the quantity it sells.

Yet it is often difficult to administer prices throughout the channel. Other channel members may also wish to administer prices to achieve their own objectives. This is what happened to Alcoa, one of the largest aluminum producers. To reduce its excess inventory, Alcoa offered its wholesalers a 30 percent discount off its normal price. Alcoa expected the wholesalers to pass most of the discount along to their customers to stimulate sales throughout the channel. Instead, wholesalers bought *their* aluminum at the lower price but passed on only a small discount to customers. As a result, the quantity Alcoa sold didn't increase much, and it still had excess inventory, while the wholesalers made much more profit on the aluminum they did sell.[9]

Some firms don't even try to administer prices. They just meet competition—or worse, mark up their costs with little thought to demand. They act as if they have no choice in selecting a price policy.

Remember that Price has many dimensions. Managers usually *do* have many choices. They *should* administer their prices. And they should do it carefully because, ultimately, customers must be willing to pay these prices before a whole marketing mix succeeds. In the rest of this chapter, we'll talk about policies a marketing manager must set to do an effective job of administering Price.[10]

PRICE FLEXIBILITY POLICIES

One-price policy— the same price for everyone

One of the first decisions a marketing manager has to make is whether to use a one-price or a flexible-price policy. A **one-price policy** means offering the same price to all customers who purchase products under essentially the same conditions and in the same quantities. The majority of U.S. firms use a one-price policy—mainly for administrative convenience and to maintain goodwill among customers.

A one-price policy makes pricing easier. But a marketing manager must be careful to avoid a rigid one-price policy. This can amount to broadcasting a price that competitors can undercut, especially if the price is somewhat high. One reason for the growth of mass-merchandisers is that conventional retailers rigidly applied traditional margins and stuck to them.

Flexible-price policy—different prices for different customers

A **flexible-price policy** means offering the same product and quantities to different customers at different prices. When computers are used to implement flexible pricing, the decisions focus more on what type of customer will get a price break.

Pricing databases make flexible pricing easier

Various forms of flexible pricing are more common now that most prices are maintained in a central computer database. Frequent changes are easier. You see this when supermarket chains give frequent-shopper club members reduced prices on weekly specials. The checkout scanner reads the code on the package, then the computer looks up the club price or the regular price depending on whether a club card has been scanned.

Some marketing managers have set up relationships with Internet companies whose ads invite customers to "set your own price." For example, Priceline operates a website at www.priceline.com. Visitors to the website specify the desired schedule for an airline flight and what price they're willing to pay. Priceline electronically forwards the information to airlines and if one accepts the offer the consumer is notified.

It may appear that these marketing managers have given up on administering prices. Just the opposite is true. They are carefully administering a flexible price. Most airlines, for example, set a very high list price. Not many people pay it. Travelers who plan ahead or who accept nonpeak flights get a discount. Business travelers who want high-demand flights on short notice pay the higher prices. However, it doesn't make sense to stick to a high price and fly the plane half empty. So the airline continuously adjusts the price on the basis of how many seats are left to fill. If seats are still empty at the last minute, the website offers a rock-bottom fare. Other firms, especially service businesses, use this approach when they have excess capacity.[11]

Marketing managers for Trico Winter Wiper Blades consciously set prices so that consumers receive a good value at a price that will yield attractive profits for both the producer and the retailer. Carnival's managers use flexible pricing—including discounts for retired people.

The only thing they clear better than snow is profits.

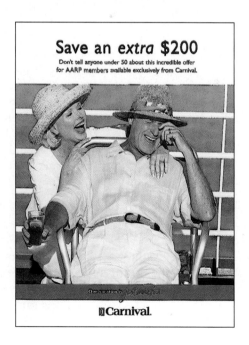

Save an *extra* $200

Don't tell anyone under 50 about this incredible offer for AARP members available exclusively from Carnival.

Carnival.

Salespeople can adjust prices to the situation	Flexible pricing is most common in the channels, in direct sales of business products, and at retail for expensive shopping products. Retail shopkeepers in less-developed economies typically use flexible pricing. These situations usually involve personal selling, not mass selling. The advantage of flexible pricing is that the salesperson can adjust price—considering prices charged by competitors, the relationship with the customer, and the customer's bargaining ability. Flexible-price policies often specify a *range* in which the actual price charged must fall.[12]
Too much price-cutting erodes profits	Some sales reps let price-cutting become a habit. This can lead to a lower price level and lower profit. A small price cut may not seem like much; but keep in mind that all of the revenue that is lost would go to profit. If salespeople for a producer that usually earns profits equal to 15 percent of its sales cut prices by an average of about 5 percent, profits would drop by a third!
Disadvantages of flexible pricing	Flexible pricing does have disadvantages. A customer who finds that others paid lower prices for the same marketing mix will be unhappy. This can cause real conflict in channels. For example, the Winn-Dixie supermarket chain stopped carrying products of some suppliers who refused to give Winn-Dixie the same prices available to chains in other regions of the country. Similarly, companies that post different prices for different segments on a website that all can see often get complaints.

If buyers learn that negotiating is in their interest, the time needed for bargaining will increase. This can increase selling costs and reduce profits. It can also frustrate customers. For example, most auto dealers use flexible pricing and bargain for what they can get. Inexperienced consumers, reluctant to bargain, often pay hundreds of dollars more than the dealer is willing to accept. By contrast, CarMax has earned high customer-satisfaction ratings by offering haggle-weary consumers a one-price policy.[13] |

PRICE-LEVEL POLICIES—OVER THE PRODUCT LIFE CYCLE

Marketing managers who administer prices must consciously set a price-level policy. As they enter the market, they have to set introductory prices that may have long-run effects. They must consider where the product life cycle is and how fast it's moving. And they must decide if their prices should be above, below, or somewhere in between relative to the market.

Skimming pricing— feeling out demand at a high price	A **skimming price policy** tries to sell the top (skim the cream) of a market—the top of the demand curve—at a high price before aiming at more price-sensitive customers. Skimming may maximize profits in the market introduction stage for an innovation, especially if there are few substitutes or if some customers are not price sensitive. Skimming is also useful when you don't know very much about the shape of the demand curve. It's sometimes safer to start with a high price that customers can refuse and then reduce it if necessary.
Skimming has critics	Some critics argue that firms should not try to maximize profits by using a skimming policy on new products that have important social consequences—a patent-protected, life-saving drug or a technique that increases crop yields, for example. Many of those who need the product may not have the money to buy it. This is a serious concern. However, it's also a serious problem if firms don't have any incentive to take risks and develop new products.[14]
Price moves down the demand curve	A skimming policy usually involves a slow reduction in price over time. See Exhibit 16–5A. Note that as price is reduced, new target markets are probably being sought. So as the price level steps down the demand curve, new Place, Product, and Promotion policies may be needed too.

Exhibit 16–5   Alternative Introductory Pricing Policies

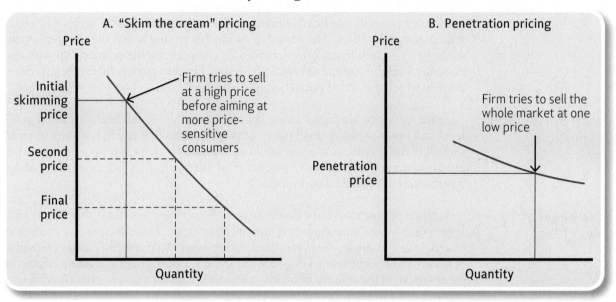

This is happening with hang-on-the-wall, flat-panel TVs. In 2000, the average selling price for a plasma TV was $12,000. Most of these units were sold by dealers who sell commercial lines to business customers who are less price sensitive. For instance, a firm that wanted a plasma TV to display product demo videos at a trade show was more likely to focus on picture quality, saving space, and the "wow factor." Yet by 2001, about 16,000 of these pricey plasma TVs had been sold to early-adopter consumers. When Sony, Panasonic, and other firms saw that trend, they came out with consumer models and distributed them through electronics superstores, like Best Buy. These retailers used a lower markup (about 30 percent) than the commercial dealers. Their lower prices stimulated consumer demand, so producers built more factories. Then, with more production capacity than demand, price competition increased—and producers came out with new models to appeal to different market segments. As the demand for flat-panel TVs surged, manufacturers of computer LCD displays added TV tuners and improved the picture quality on their large screens. By 2006, general-merchandise retailers like Sears and Wal-Mart were selling flat-panel TVs, and firms like Dell and HP had added them to their lines. At that point, prices were only about 25 percent of where they had started—and they continue to fall as demand grows and more firms switch from producing traditional TVs to flat-panel ones.[15]

Penetration pricing—get volume at a low price

A **penetration pricing policy** tries to sell the whole market at one low price. This approach might be wise when the elite market—those willing to pay a high price—is small. This is the case when the whole demand curve is fairly elastic. See Exhibit 16–5B. A penetration policy is even more attractive if selling larger quantities results in lower costs because of economies of scale. Penetration pricing may be wise if the firm expects strong competition very soon after introduction.

When the first version of the PalmPilot was introduced, competitors were close behind. In addition, Apple had failed when it tried to introduce the Newton personal information manager at a skimming price of $1,000. So the focus for Palm was on a combination of features and price that would be a good value and help penetrate the market quickly. The initial price of about $250 resulted in sales of a million units in 24 months. A $250 retail price may not seem that low now that the PDA market is maturing and the Palm Zire, for example, is priced at about $70 to appeal to first-time PDA buyers. However, Palm's initial price was low enough to discourage some competitors from quickly entering the market.

DuPont Corian, a solid countertop material, was costly to develop. When Corian was introduced, there was little direct competition and a premium price helped to recover development costs. Now that there is more competition, discounted prices are sometimes available. Marketing managers for PalmPilot used a different approach. With penetration pricing they sold a million units of the innovative PalmPilot within 24 months of its introduction. Then Palm introduced an even lower-priced Zire model targeted at parents.

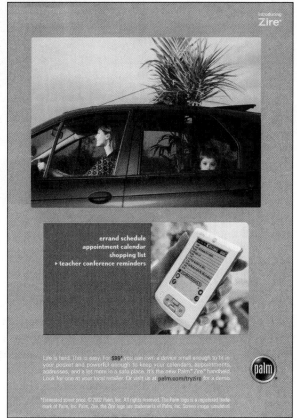

Even a very low penetration price usually won't keep competitors out of a growth market permanently—and product life cycles do march on. For instance, competition is now intense among firms that sell PDAs, and different models appeal to different segments. Higher-priced PDAs that combine a cell phone, digital camera, and Internet access as well as MP3 and video players compete with single-use products in other product categories.[16]

Introductory price dealing—temporary price cuts

Low prices do attract customers. Therefore, marketers often use **introductory price dealing**—temporary price cuts—to speed new products into a market and get customers to try them. However, don't confuse these *temporary* price cuts with low penetration prices. The plan here is to raise prices as soon as the introductory offer is over. By then, hopefully, target customers will have decided it is worth buying again at the regular price.

Established competitors often choose not to meet introductory price dealing—as long as the introductory period is not too long or too successful. However, some competitors match introductory price deals with their own short-term sale prices to discourage customers from shopping around.

Different price-level policies through the channel

The price of a product sold to channel members should be set so that channel members can cover their costs and make a profit. For example, a producer of a slightly better product might set a price level that is low relative to competitors when selling to retailers but suggest an above-the-market retail price. This encourages retailers to emphasize the product because it yields higher profits.

The price of money may affect the price level

We've been talking about the price level of a firm's product. But a nation's money also has a price level—what it is worth in some other currency. For example, on March 1, 2007, one U.S. dollar was worth 0.51 British pounds. In other words, the exchange rate for the British pound against the U.S. dollar was 0.51. Exhibit 16–6 lists exchange rates for money from several countries over a number of years. From this exhibit you can see that exchange rates change over time—and sometimes the changes are significant. For example, on April 16, 2001, a U.S. dollar was worth 1.13 euros; in April 2005 it was worth only 0.77 euros.

Exchange rate changes can have a significant effect on international trade. From a manager's viewpoint, they also affect whether or not a price level has the expected result. As the following example shows, this can be an important factor even for a small firm that sells only in its own local market.

In 2001, the marketing manager for EControl, Inc.—a small firm that produces electronic controllers for producers of satellite TV receiving dishes—set a meeting-competition wholesale price of about $100 for a carton of the controllers. The profit margin on the controllers at that price was about $10 per carton. The wholesalers who distribute the controllers also carried a product by a British firm. Its wholesale price was also $100, which means that the British firm got about 70 British pounds ($100 × 0.70 pounds per dollar) per carton. Prices were stable for some time. However, when the exchange rate for the pound against the dollar fell from 0.70 to 0.64, the British producer got 6 fewer pounds for each $100 carton of controllers (70 pounds − 64 pounds = 6 pounds).

Because EControl's marketing manager was only selling controllers in the domestic market, she didn't pay any attention to the drop in the exchange rate at first. However, she did pay attention when the British producer decided to raise its wholesale price to $110 a carton. At the $110 price, the British firm got about 70.4 pounds per carton ($110 × 0.64 pounds per dollar)—about the same as it was getting before the exchange rate change. EControl's market share and sales increased substantially—at the British competitor's expense—because EControl's price was $10 lower than its British competitor. EControl's

Exhibit 16–6
Exchange Rates for Various Currencies against the U.S. Dollar over Time

Base Currency	Number of Units of Base Currency per U.S. Dollar*			
	1999	2001	2003	2005
British pound	0.62	0.70	0.64	0.53
Thai baht	37.40	45.65	42.89	39.62
Japanese yen	117.86	124.58	120.04	107.65
Australian dollar	1.55	1.96	1.64	1.30
Canadian dollar	1.49	1.56	1.46	1.24
Euro	1.07	1.13	0.92	0.77

*Units shown are for April 16th in each year.

marketing manager concluded that it would probably take a while for the British firm to lower its price, even if the exchange rate went up again. So she decided that she could safely raise her price level by 5 percent—up to $105—and still have a solid price advantage over the British supplier. At a price of $105 per carton, EControl's profit per carton jumped from $10 to $15, a 50 percent increase in profit.

Things turned out well for EControl even though the manager initially ignored exchange rates. Note, however, that during the 1999–2001 period the exchange rate for the British pound against the U.S. dollar *increased*. So in the 1999–2001 period EControl's situation might have been reversed![17]

MOST PRICE STRUCTURES ARE BUILT AROUND LIST PRICES

Prices start with a list price

Most price structures are built around a base price schedule or list price. **Basic list prices** are the prices final customers or users are normally asked to pay for products. In this book, unless noted otherwise, list price refers to basic list price.

In the next chapter, we discuss how firms set these list prices. For now, however, we'll consider variations from list price and why they are made.

DISCOUNT POLICIES—REDUCTIONS FROM LIST PRICES

Discounts are reductions from list price given by a seller to buyers who either give up some marketing function or provide the function themselves. Discounts can be useful in marketing strategy planning. In the following discussion, think about what function the buyers are giving up, or providing, when they get each of these discounts.

Quantity discounts encourage volume buying

Quantity discounts are discounts offered to encourage customers to buy in larger amounts. This lets a seller get more of a buyer's business, or shifts some of the storing function to the buyer, or reduces shipping and selling costs—or all of these. There are two kinds of quantity discounts: cumulative and noncumulative.

Cumulative quantity discounts apply to purchases over a given period—such as a year—and the discount usually increases as the amount purchased increases. Cumulative discounts encourage *repeat* buying by reducing the customer's cost for additional purchases. This is a way to develop loyalty and ongoing relationships with customers. For example, a Lowe's lumberyard might give a cumulative quantity discount to a building contractor who is not able to buy all of the needed materials at once. Lowe's wants to reward the contractor's patronage and discourage shopping around.

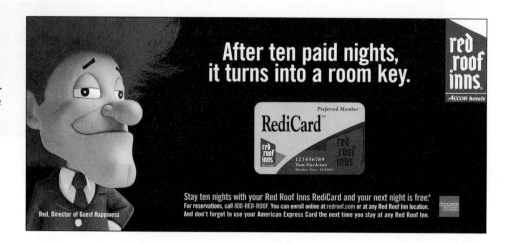

A cumulative quantity discount is often attractive to business customers who don't want to run up their inventory costs. They are rewarded for their loyalty—buying large quantities, even though individual orders may be smaller.

Noncumulative quantity discounts apply only to individual orders. Such discounts encourage larger orders but do not tie a buyer to the seller after that one purchase. Lowe's lumberyard may resell insulation products made by several competing producers. Owens-Corning might try to encourage Lowe's to stock larger quantities of its pink insulation by offering a noncumulative quantity discount.

Seasonal discounts—buy sooner

Seasonal discounts are discounts offered to encourage buyers to buy earlier than present demand requires. If used by a manufacturer, this discount tends to shift the storing function further along in the channel. It also tends to even out sales over the year. For example, Kyota offers wholesalers a lower price on its garden tillers if they buy in the fall, when sales are slow.

Service firms that face irregular demand or excess capacity often use seasonal discounts. For example, some tourist attractions, like ski resorts, offer lower weekday rates when attendance would otherwise be down.

Payment terms and cash discounts set payment dates

Most sales to businesses are made on credit. The seller sends a bill (invoice) by mail or electronically, and the buyer's accounting department processes it for payment. Some firms depend on their suppliers for temporary working capital (credit). Therefore, it is very important for both sides to clearly state the terms of payment—including the availability of cash discounts—and to understand the commonly used payment terms.

Net means that payment for the face value of the invoice is due immediately. These terms are sometimes changed to net 10 or net 30, which means payment is due within 10 or 30 days of the date on the invoice.

Cash discounts are reductions in price to encourage buyers to pay their bills quickly. The terms for a cash discount usually modify the net terms.

2/10, net 30 means the buyer can take a 2 percent discount off the face value of the invoice if the invoice is paid within 10 days. Otherwise, the full face value is due within 30 days. And it usually is stated or understood that an interest charge will be added after the 30-day free-credit period.

Why cash discounts are given and should be evaluated

Smart buyers carefully evaluate cash discounts. A discount of 2/10, net 30 may not look like much at first. But the buyer earns a 2 percent discount for paying the invoice just 20 days sooner than it should be paid anyway. By not taking the discount, the company in effect is borrowing at an annual rate of 36 percent. That is, assuming a 360-day year and dividing by 20 days, there are 18 periods during which the company could earn 2 percent—and 18 times 2 equals 36 percent a year.

PayPal is an online financial service that makes it easier and less risky for firms or individuals who sell over the Internet to receive payment from a distant buyer.

Consumers say "charge it"

Credit sales are also important to retailers. Most retailers use credit card services, such as Visa or MasterCard, and pay a percent of the revenue from each credit sale for this service. For this reason, some retailers offer discounts to consumers who pay cash.

Many consumers like the convenience of credit card buying. But some critics argue that the cards make it too easy for consumers to buy things they really can't afford. Credit card interest rates can increase the total costs to consumers.

Trade discounts often are set by tradition

A **trade (functional) discount** is a list price reduction given to channel members for the job they are going to do. A manufacturer, for example, might allow retailers a 30 percent trade discount from the suggested retail list price to cover the cost of the retailing function and their profit. Similarly, the manufacturer might allow wholesalers a *chain* discount of 30 percent and 10 percent off the suggested retail price. In this case, the wholesalers would be expected to pass the 30 percent discount on to retailers.[18]

Special sales reduce list prices— temporarily

A **sale price** is a temporary discount from the list price. Sale price discounts encourage immediate buying. In other words, to get the sale price, customers give up the convenience of buying when they want to buy and instead buy when the seller wants to sell.

Special sales provide a marketing manager with a quick way to respond to changing market conditions without changing the basic marketing strategy. For example, a retailer might use a sale to help clear extra inventory or to meet a competing store's price.

In recent years, sale prices and deals have become much more common. Some retailers have sales so often that consumers just wait to purchase when there's a sale. Others check out a website like www.fatwallet.com to figure out where the product they want is already on sale. But prices that change constantly erode brand loyalty.

To avoid these problems, some firms that sell consumer convenience products offer **everyday low pricing**—setting a low list price rather than relying on frequent sales, discounts, or allowances. Many supermarkets use this approach.

Sale prices should be used carefully, consistent with well-thought-out pricing objectives and policies. A marketing manager who constantly uses temporary sales to adjust the price level probably has not done a good job setting the normal price.[19]

ALLOWANCE POLICIES—OFF LIST PRICES

Allowances, like discounts, are given to final consumers, customers, or channel members for doing something or accepting less of something.

Advertising allowances—something for something

Advertising allowances are price reductions given to firms in the channel to encourage them to advertise or otherwise promote the supplier's products locally. For example, Sony might give an allowance (3 percent of sales) to its retailers. They, in turn, are expected to spend the allowance on local advertising.

Stocking allowances—get attention and shelf space

Stocking allowances—sometimes called *slotting allowances*—are given to a middleman to get shelf space for a product. For example, a producer might offer a retailer cash or free merchandise to stock a new item. Stocking allowances are used mainly to get supermarket chains to handle new products. Supermarkets are more willing to give space to a new product if the supplier will offset their handling costs and risks. With a big stocking allowance, the intermediary makes extra profit—even if a new product fails and the producer loses money.

Are stocking allowances ethical?

Critics say that retailer demands for big stocking allowances slow new-product introductions and make it hard for small producers to compete. Some producers feel that retailers' demands are unethical—just a different form of extortion. Retailers, on the other hand, point out that the fees protect them from producers that simply want to push more and more me-too products onto their shelves. Perhaps the best way for a producer to cope with the problem is to develop new products that really do offer consumers superior value. Then it benefits everyone in the channel, including retailers, to get the products to the target market.[20]

PMs—push for cash

Push money (or prize money) allowances—sometimes called *PMs* or *spiffs*—are given to retailers by manufacturers or wholesalers to pass on to the retailers' salesclerks for aggressively selling certain items. PM allowances are used for new items, slower-moving items, or higher-margin items. They are often used for pushing furniture, clothing, consumer electronics, and cosmetics. A salesclerk, for example, might earn an additional $5 for each new model Panasonic DVD player sold.

Bring in the old, ring up the new—with trade-ins

A **trade-in allowance** is a price reduction given for used products when similar new products are bought. Trade-ins give the marketing manager an easy way to lower the effective price without reducing list price. Proper handling of trade-ins is important when selling durable products.

Coupons for consumer products are popular and prompt customers to action.

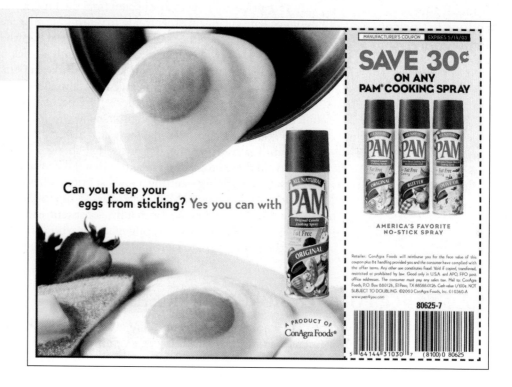

Rebates—Rip-off or Reward?

Over the last decade the use of rebates has become much more common. In total, firms offer about 400 million rebates each year. Rebate amounts range from 50 cents to thousands of dollars. But is this use of rebates a good thing?

Firms use rebates because, like other price cuts, they boost sales. But why do producers offer rebates rather than just take the rebate amount off the price charged intermediaries? When producers first started to offer rebates it was to ensure that final consumers actually got the lower price the producer planned. Otherwise, middlemen might not pass the savings along to consumers—especially if they thought that they'd make more profit by selling the usual amount at the usual price but with a higher profit margin. So rebates got their start as a way for producers to administer prices at the end of the channel.

However, what really explains the big increase in the use of rebates in recent years is that many consumers buy a product because of the rebate—but then don't request the refund. TiVo offered a holiday-season $100 rebate on its digital video recorders (DVRs) and got a huge surge in sales, but then about half of the buyers never claimed the refund. So TiVo never had to shell out that $5 million in refunds. Now, many managers *count* on a rebate offer giving them a bump in demand without having to pay for all the rebates. In fact, this also explains why some retailers use mail-in rebates of their own—and why they can afford to promote items that are "free after rebate." Customers buy the "free" items at inflated prices, many never request refunds, and some buy other products once they're in the store.

Critics say that many firms set complex rebate requirements because they never intend for customers to get the refund; firms say it's to protect against consumer fraud. There's no debate that the requirements are often complicated. CompUSA offered a $300 "bundle" of accessories for free (after the rebates) with a laptop purchase. Unsuspecting buyers had to mail in 20 separate rebate requests; worse, the rules for some rebates in the bundle conflicted with others. So many consumers complained that CompUSA told them to just send in one request with a copy of the receipt. But many firms deny rebate refunds if consumers don't precisely follow every rule. And some firms send rebate checks in envelopes that look like junk mail—and consumers throw them away unopened. Rebate checks that are never cashed also save the seller money. A number of firms have even faced fraud charges because they made no attempt to send refunds.

When you add all of this up, processing rebates involves a lot of hassle and expense for both sellers and buyers. Because of the growing consumer backlash against rebates and the threat of government regulation, firms like Best Buy say they will drop rebates altogether. Others, like Staples, are making it easier for consumers by providing an easy online rebate request form. The basic lesson here is that marketers are likely to have problems when they do things that don't create value for the customer.[21]

SOME CUSTOMERS GET SOMETHING EXTRA

Clipping coupons—more for less

Many producers and retailers offer discounts (or free items) through coupons distributed in packages, mailings, print ads, or at the store. By presenting a coupon to a retailer, the consumer is given a discount off list price. This is especially common in the consumer packaged goods business—but the use of price-off coupons is also growing in other lines of business.

Internet EXERCISE

FatWallet (*www.fatwallet.com*) is one of many websites that can help consumers find good deals. To see how it works, assume that you are interested in buying a new printer for your personal computer. Start by selecting a specific model that you like at the HP website (*www.hpshopping.com*). Then, search at www.fatwallet.com to see what you can learn about buying that printer. For example, check for advice in the consumer forums and see if there are any coupons. Identify different retailers that sell the printer, and read the ratings of those retailers. Where would you buy the printer, and why did you choose that retailer?

Retailers are willing to redeem producers' coupons because it increases their sales—and they usually are paid for the trouble of handling the coupons. For example, a retailer that redeems a 50-cents-off coupon might be repaid 75 cents.[22]

Cash rebates when you buy

Some firms offer **rebates**—refunds paid to consumers after a purchase. Sometimes the rebate is very large. Some automakers offer rebates of $500 to $6,000 to promote sales of slow-moving models. Rebates are also used on lower-priced items, ranging from Duracell batteries and Memorex CD-Rs to Logitech webcams and Paul Masson wines. Rebates give a producer a way to be certain that final consumers actually get the price reduction. If the rebate amount were just taken off the price charged intermediaries, they might not pass the savings along to consumers.

A pricing consultant has suggested that your firm set a premium price for the paper-shredding machines it sells through office equipment stores—but that there be a $20 mail-in rebate with each unit. The consultant says his research shows that, when an office shredder wears out, it's usually the administrative assistant who is sent to buy a replacement. The consultant says that many of these buyers will pick your firm's shredder, in spite of the higher price, so that they can pocket the rebate. At the end of his report he says, "This is an accepted way to motivate the decision maker. Think about all those executives who rack up frequent-flier miles on business trips and then use the free tickets they get for family vacations." Your boss has left the decision up to you. Would you follow the consultant's advice? Why or why not?

LIST PRICE MAY DEPEND ON GEOGRAPHIC PRICING POLICIES

Retail list prices sometimes include free delivery. Or free delivery may be offered to some customers as an aid to closing the sale. But deciding who pays the freight charge is more important on sales to business customers than to final consumers because more money is involved. Purchase orders usually specify place, time, method of delivery, freight costs, insurance, handling, and other charges. There are many possible variations for an imaginative marketing manager, and some specialized terms have developed.

F.O.B. pricing is easy

A commonly used transportation term is **F.O.B.**—which means free on board some vehicle at some place. Typically, F.O.B. pricing names the place—often the location of the seller's factory or warehouse—as in F.O.B. Taiwan or F.O.B. mill. This means that the seller pays the cost of loading the products onto some vehicle, then title to the products passes to the buyer. The buyer pays the freight and takes responsibility for damage in transit.

If a firm wants to pay the freight for the convenience of customers, it can use F.O.B. delivered or F.O.B. buyer's factory. In this case, title does not pass until the products are delivered. If the seller wants title to pass immediately but is willing to prepay freight (and then include it in the invoice), F.O.B. seller's factory-freight prepaid can be used.

F.O.B. shipping point pricing simplifies the seller's pricing—but it may narrow the market. Since the delivered cost varies depending on the buyer's location, a customer located farther from the seller must pay more and might buy from closer suppliers.

Zone pricing smooths delivered prices

Zone pricing means making an average freight charge applicable to all buyers within specific geographic areas. The seller pays the actual freight charges and bills each customer for an average charge. For example, a company in Canada might divide the United States into seven zones, then bill all customers in the same zone the same amount for freight even though actual shipping costs might vary.

Zone pricing reduces the wide variation in delivered prices that results from an F.O.B. shipping point pricing policy. It also simplifies transportation charges.

Uniform delivered pricing—one price to all

Uniform delivered pricing means making an average freight charge applicable to all buyers. It is a kind of zone pricing—an entire country may be considered as one zone—that includes the average cost of delivery in the price. Uniform delivered pricing is most often used when (1) transportation costs are relatively low and (2) the seller wishes to sell in all geographic areas at one price, perhaps a nationally advertised price.

Freight-absorption pricing—competing on equal grounds in another territory

When all firms in an industry use F.O.B. shipping point pricing, a firm usually competes well near its shipping point but not farther away. As sales reps look for business farther away, delivered prices rise and the firm finds itself priced out of the market.

This problem can be reduced with **freight-absorption pricing**—which means absorbing freight cost so that a firm's delivered price meets that of the nearest competitor. This amounts to cutting list price to appeal to new market segments. Some firms look at international markets this way; they just figure that any profit from export sales is a bonus.

PRICING POLICIES COMBINE TO IMPACT CUSTOMER VALUE

Look at Price from the customer's viewpoint

We've discussed pricing policies separately so far, but from the customer's view they all combine to impact customer value. So when we talk about Price we are really talking about the whole set of price policies that define the real price level. On the other hand, superior value isn't just based on having a lower price than some competitor but rather on the whole marketing mix.

Value pricing leads to superior customer value

Smart marketers look for the combination of Price decisions that result in value pricing. **Value pricing** means setting a fair price level for a marketing mix that really gives the target market superior customer value.

Value pricing doesn't necessarily mean cheap if cheap means bare-bones or low-grade. It doesn't mean high prestige either if the prestige is not accompanied by the right quality goods and services. Rather, the focus is on the customer's requirements and how the whole marketing mix meets those needs.

Different pricing policies combine to impact customer value. For example, Transamerican Wholesale increases its customer value (and expands the market it serves) by offering free delivery to most metropolitan areas. Dawn detergent emphasizes that it offers superior value because it "does 20 percent more greasy dishes while suds last."

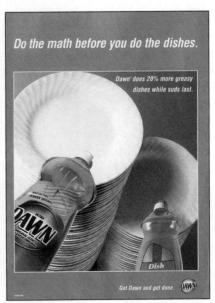

Toyota is a firm that has been effective with value pricing. It has different marketing mixes for different target markets. But from the $10,000 Echo to the $55,000 Land Cruiser, the Japanese automaker consistently offers better quality and lower prices than its competitors. Among fast-food restaurants, Wendy's has a good reputation for value pricing.

Companies that use value pricing deliver on their promises. They try to give the consumer pleasant surprises—like an unexpected service—because it increases value and builds customer loyalty. They return the price if the customer isn't completely satisfied. They avoid unrealistic price levels—prices that are high only because consumers already know the brand name. They build relationships so customers will come back time and again.

There are Price choices in most markets

Some marketing managers miss the advantages of value pricing. They've heard economists say that in perfect competition it's foolish to offer products above or below the market price. But most firms *don't* operate in perfect competition where what firms offer is exactly the same.

Most operate in monopolistic competition, where products and whole marketing mixes are *not* exactly the same. This means that there are pricing options. At one extreme, some firms are clearly above the market—they may even brag about it. Tiffany's is well known as one of the most expensive jewelry stores in the world. Other firms emphasize below-the-market prices in their marketing mixes. Prices offered by discounters and mass-merchandisers, such as Wal-Mart and Tesco, illustrate this approach. They may even promote their pricing policy with catchy slogans like "guaranteed lowest prices."

Value pricers define the target market and the competition

In making price decisions and using value pricing, it is important to clearly define the *relevant target market* and *competitors* when making price comparisons.

Consider Wal-Mart prices again from this view. Wal-Mart may have lower camera prices than conventional camera retailers, but it offers less help in the store, less selection, and it won't take old cameras in trade. Wal-Mart may be appealing to budget-oriented shoppers who compare prices *and* value among different mass-merchandisers. But a specialty camera store may be trying to appeal to different customers and not even be a direct competitor!

Epeda sells high-quality mattresses. It wants customers to know that its higher price is worth it. This ad says, "Lots of mattresses are cheap to buy. The reason is to make you forget how much sleeping on them is going to cost you."

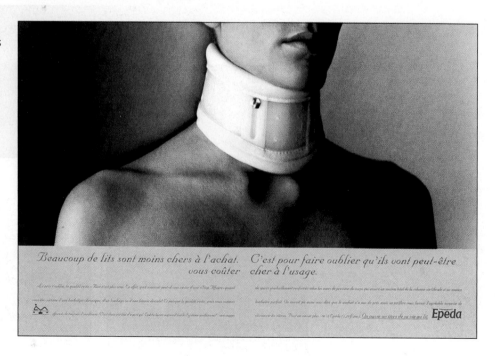

A camera producer with this point of view might offer the specialty store models that are not available to Wal-Mart—to ensure that customers don't view price as the only difference between the two stores.

Further, the specialty store needs to communicate clearly to its target market *how* it offers superior value. Wal-Mart is certainly going to communicate that it offers low prices. If that's all customers hear, it's no wonder that they just focus on price. The specialty retailer has to be certain that consumers understand that price is not the only thing of value that is different. This same logic applies to comparisons between Internet sellers and bricks-and-mortar competitors. Each may have advantages or disadvantages that relate to value.

Meeting competitors' prices may be necessary

In a mature market there is downward pressure on both prices and profit margins. Moreover, differentiating the value a firm offers may not be easy when competitors can quickly copy new ideas. Extending our camera example, if our speciality store is in a city with a number of similar stores with the same products, there may be no real pricing choice other than to "meet the competition." Thin profit margins would quickly disappear—or turn into losses—at a lower price. And a higher price would simply prompt competitors to promote their price advantage.[23]

Similarly, a B2B supplier may have a better marketing mix than competitors; but if buyers have decided to use a procurement hub and reverse auction as the only way to buy, the supplier may not have any choice but to decide what the lowest price is that it will bid to get the business. Winning the bid at a profit-losing price doesn't help.

Even though competition can be intense, too many marketers give up too easily. They often can find a way to differentiate, even if it's something that competitors

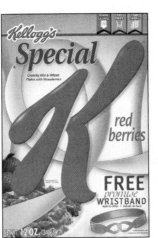

dismiss as less important. For example, Kellogg Company was facing soggy sales and tough competition in the dry cereal category. Dealer brands made price competition even tougher. However, when Kellogg added freeze-dried fruit to create Special K Red Berries cereal, it attracted many customers away from competing brands. The berries did increase costs, but Kellogg's profits still improved. In Europe, where price sensitivity was greatest, Kellogg kept the price the same but reduced the size of the Red Berries box. In the U.S., the size of the box is standard but the price was increased enough to provide profit margins. Even though General Mills later copied the idea, Kellogg had a head start and quickly came out with other fruit-added cereals. And both producers benefited by having a way to differentiate from the low-price store brands in their category.[24]

There may be little choice about Price in oligopoly situations. Pricing at the market—that is, meeting competition—may be the only sensible policy. To raise prices might lead to a large loss in sales, unless competitors adopt the higher price too. And cutting prices might lead to similar reductions by competitors—downward along an inelastic industry demand curve. This can only lead to a decrease in total revenue for the industry and probably for each firm. The major airlines faced these problems recently.

To avoid these problems, each oligopolist may choose a status quo pricing objective and set its price at the competitive level. Some critics call this pricing behavior conscious parallel action, implying it is unethical and the same as intentional conspiracy among firms. As a practical matter, however, that criticism seems overly harsh. It obviously isn't sensible for firms to ignore their competitors.

Consumers often use websites like mySimon.com that search for the best prices on particular items. When it's easy for customers to compare prices, marketers must clearly communicate to the customer how the rest of the marketing mix is better and why it justifies a higher price.

Value pricing fits with market-oriented strategy planning

There are times when the marketing manager's hands are tied and there is little that can be done to differentiate the marketing mix. However, most marketing managers do have choices—many choices. They can vary strategy decisions with respect to all of the marketing mix variables, not just Price, to offer target customers superior value. And when a marketer's hands are really tied, it's time to look for new opportunities that offer more promise.

LEGALITY OF PRICING POLICIES

This chapter discusses the many pricing decisions that must be made. However, some pricing decisions are limited by government legislation. The first step to understanding pricing legislation is to know the thinking of legislators and the courts. To get a better idea of the "why" of legislation, we'll focus on U.S. legislation here, but many other countries have similar pricing laws.[25]

Minimum prices are sometimes controlled

Unfair trade practice acts put a lower limit on prices, especially at the wholesale and retail levels. They have been passed in more than half the states in the United States. Selling below cost in these states is illegal. Wholesalers and retailers are usually required to take a certain minimum percentage markup over their merchandise-plus-transportation costs. The practical effect of these laws is to protect certain limited-line food retailers—such as dairy stores—from the kind of "ruinous" competition supermarkets might offer if they sold milk as a leader, offering it below cost for a long time.

The United States and most other countries control the minimum price of imported products with antidumping laws. **Dumping** is pricing a product sold in a foreign market below the cost of producing it or at a price lower than in its domestic market. These laws are usually designed to protect the country's domestic producers and jobs. But there is debate about how well they work.

Consider what happened in 2002 when U.S. steel producers pushed for tariffs because overseas steel mills, many of which are subsidized by their own governments, were selling at a lower price in the U.S. than at home. Most U.S. steel producers suffered losses and were forced to cut jobs. After the tariffs went into place, U.S. steel producers increased their profits by raising prices. But, as a result, other U.S. firms that needed to buy steel faced higher costs. Yet these firms couldn't raise *their* prices because they still had global competitors in their own product-markets. Some critics argued that U.S. steel companies were inefficient and that the tariffs protected them by sacrificing their customers. Late in 2003, the U.S. dropped the steel tariffs. However,

Many stores guarantee that they have the lowest price and promise a refund if a customer finds an item priced lower somewhere else. Some stores woo customers with automatic refunds. They hire an outside firm to do daily price checks. When a customer is due a refund, it is sent automatically.

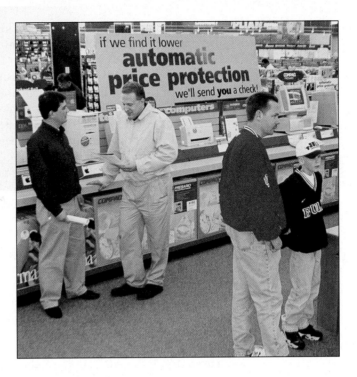

by then other countries seized the excuse to impose tariffs of their own, which made it harder for U.S. companies to get export business. Dumping can have big macro-marketing effects, but it is a difficult problem to fix.[26]

Even very high prices may be OK

Generally speaking, firms can charge high prices—even outrageously high prices—as long as they don't conspire with their competitors to fix prices, discriminate against some of their customers, or lie.

Of course, there are exceptions. Firms in regulated businesses may need to seek approval for their prices. For example, in the United States, most states regulate automobile insurance rates. Some countries impose more general price controls—to reduce inflation or try to control markets. However, most countries have followed the move toward a market-directed economy. That doesn't mean, however, that there aren't important regulations in the pricing area.

You can't lie about prices

Phony list prices are prices customers are shown to suggest that the price has been discounted from list. Some customers seem more interested in the supposed discount than in the actual price. Most businesses, trade associations, and government agencies consider the use of phony list prices unethical. In the United States, the FTC tries to stop such pricing—using the **Wheeler Lea Amendment**, which bans "unfair or deceptive acts in commerce."[27]

A few years ago, some electronics retailers, like Best Buy, were criticized on these grounds. For example, they might advertise a $300 discount on a computer when the customer signed up for an Internet service provider, but not make it clear to the consumer that a three-year commitment—costing over $700—would be required.

Price fixing is illegal— you can go to jail

Difficulties with pricing—and violations of pricing legislation—usually occur when competing marketing mixes are quite similar. When the success of an entire marketing strategy depends on price, there is pressure (and temptation) to make agreements with competitors (conspire). And **price fixing**—competitors getting together to raise, lower, or stabilize prices—is common and relatively easy. *But it is also completely illegal in the United States.* It is considered "conspiracy" under the Sherman Act and the Federal Trade Commission Act. To discourage price fixing, both companies and individual managers are held responsible. In a recent case, an executive at Archer Daniels Midland (ADM) Company was sentenced to three years in jail and the company was fined $100 million.

Federal price-fixing laws in the United States focus on protecting customers who purchase directly from a supplier. For example, a wholesaler could bring action against a producer-supplier for fixing prices. However, retailers or consumers who bought the producer's products from the wholesaler could not bring action. In contrast, many state laws now allow "indirect customers" in the channel to sue the price fixer.[28]

Different countries have different rules concerning price fixing, and this has created problems in international trade. Japan, for example, allows price fixing, especially if it strengthens the position of Japanese producers in world markets.

U.S. antimonopoly laws ban price discrimination unless...

Price level and price flexibility policies can lead to price discrimination. The **Robinson-Patman Act** (of 1936) makes illegal any **price discrimination**—selling the same products to different buyers at different prices—*if it injures competition.* The law does permit some price differences—but they must be based on (1) cost differences or (2) the need to meet competition. Both buyers and sellers are considered guilty if they know they're entering into discriminatory agreements.

What does "like grade and quality" mean?

Firms in businesses as varied as transportation services, book publishing, and auto parts have been charged with violations of the Robinson-Patman Act in recent, nationally publicized cases. Competitors who have been injured by a violation of the law have incentive to go to court because they can receive a settlement that is three times larger than the damage suffered.

The Robinson-Patman Act allows a marketing manager to charge different prices for similar products if they are *not* of "like grade and quality." But the FTC

says that if the physical characteristics of a product are similar, then they are of like grade and quality. A landmark U.S. Supreme Court ruling against the Borden Company upheld the FTC's view that a well-known label *alone* does not make a product different from one with an unknown label. The company agreed that the canned milk it sold at different prices under different labels was basically the same.

But the FTC's victory in the Borden case was not complete. The U.S. Court of Appeals found no evidence of injury to competition and further noted that there could be no injury unless Borden's price differential exceeded the "recognized consumer appeal of the Borden label." How to measure "consumer appeal" was not spelled out, so producers who want to sell several brands—or dealer brands at lower prices than their main brand—probably should offer physical differences, and differences that are really useful.[29]

Can cost analysis justify price differences?

The Robinson-Patman Act allows price differences if there are cost differences—say, for larger quantity shipments or because middlemen take over some of the physical distribution functions. But justifying cost differences is a difficult job. And the justification must be developed *before* different prices are set. The seller can't wait until a competitor, disgruntled customer, or the FTC brings a charge. At that point, it's too late.[30]

Can you legally meet price cuts?

Under the Robinson-Patman Act, meeting a competitor's price is permitted as a defense in price discrimination cases. A major objective of antimonopoly laws is to protect competition, not competitors. And "meeting competition in good faith" still seems to be legal.

Special promotion allowances might not be allowed

Some firms violate the Robinson-Patman Act by providing push money, advertising allowances, and other promotion aids to some customers and not others. The act prohibits such special allowances, *unless they are made available to all customers on "proportionately equal" terms.*[31]

How to avoid discriminating

Because price discrimination laws are complicated and penalties for violations heavy, many business managers follow the safest course by offering few or no quantity discounts and the same cost-based prices to *all* customers. This is *too* conservative a reaction. But when firms consider price differences, they may need a lawyer involved in the discussion!

CONCLUSION

The Price variable offers an alert marketing manager many possibilities for varying marketing mixes. This chapter began by discussing how a firm's pricing objectives may be oriented toward profit, sales, or maintaining the status quo. Clear pricing objectives help in making decisions about the firm's important pricing policies.

This chapter discussed the pros and cons of flexible pricing and some of the approaches that firms use to implement it. It also considered the initial price level decision—skim the cream or penetration—that the marketing manager must make with new products at the introductory stage of their life cycle. We also discussed a variety of ways that marketing managers adjust the basic list price under different circumstances—by using different types of discounts, allowances, and transportation costs. These policies need to be clearly defined by the marketing manager.

The chapter described how the different components of price are traded off against the other marketing mix variables to create something of value for the customer. We also discuss value pricing and how to create a competitive advantage by offering customers superior value—which isn't the same as just offering lower and lower prices.

Pricing comes under greater scrutiny from the law than some other marketing mix variables. So it is important to understand key legal constraints that influence pricing decisions.

This chapter provided a foundation for understanding the objectives and policies that guide pricing decisions. This information provides input into the price-setting process, which we describe in greater detail in the following chapter when we look at both cost and demand-oriented approaches to pricing.

KEY TERMS

Price, 413

target return objective, 415

profit maximization objective, 415

sales-oriented objective, 416

status quo objectives, 417

nonprice competition, 417

administered prices, 417

one-price policy, 417

flexible-price policy, 418

skimming price policy, 419

penetration pricing policy, 420

introductory price dealing, 421

basic list prices, 423

discounts, 423

quantity discounts, 423

cumulative quantity discounts, 423

noncumulative quantity discounts, 424

seasonal discounts, 424

net, 424

cash discounts, 424

2/10, net 30, 424

trade (functional) discount, 425

sale price, 425

everyday low pricing, 425

allowances, 425

advertising allowances, 426

stocking allowances, 426

push money (or prize money) allowances, 426

trade-in allowance, 426

rebates, 428

F.O.B, 428

zone pricing, 428

uniform delivered pricing, 429

freight-absorption pricing, 429

value pricing, 429

unfair trade practice acts, 432

dumping, 432

phony list prices, 433

Wheeler Lea Amendment, 433

price fixing, 433

Robinson-Patman Act, 434

price discrimination, 434

QUESTIONS AND PROBLEMS

1. Identify the strategy decisions a marketing manager must make in the Price area. Illustrate your answer for a local retailer.

2. How should the acceptance of a profit-oriented, a sales-oriented, or a status quo–oriented pricing objective affect the development of a company's marketing strategy? Illustrate for each.

3. Distinguish between one-price and flexible-price policies. Which is most appropriate for a hardware store? Why?

4. What pricing objective(s) is a skimming pricing policy most likely implementing? Is the same true for a penetration pricing policy? Which policy is probably most appropriate for each of the following products: (a) a new type of home lawn-sprinkling system, (b) a skin patch drug to help smokers quit, (c) a DVD of a best-selling movie, and (d) a new children's toy?

5. How would differences in exchange rates between different countries affect a firm's decisions concerning the use of flexible-price policies in different foreign markets?

6. Are seasonal discounts appropriate in agricultural businesses (which are certainly seasonal)?

7. What are the effective annual interest rates for the following cash discount terms: (a) 1/10, net 20; (b) 1/5, net 10; and (c) net 25?

8. Do stocking allowances increase or reduce conflict in a channel of distribution? Explain your thinking.

9. Why would a manufacturer offer a rebate instead of lowering the suggested list price?

10. How can a marketing manager change a firm's F.O.B. terms to make an otherwise competitive marketing mix more attractive?

11. What type of geographic pricing policy is most appropriate for the following products (specify any assumptions necessary to obtain a definite answer): (a) a chemical by-product, (b) nationally advertised candy bars, (c) rebuilt auto parts, and (d) tricycles?

12. How would a ban on freight absorption (that is, requiring F.O.B. factory pricing) affect a producer with substantial economies of scale in production?

13. Give an example of a marketing mix that has a high price level but that you see as a good value. Briefly explain what makes it a good value.

14. Think about a business from which you regularly make purchases even though there are competing firms with similar prices. Explain what the firm offers that improves value and keeps you coming back.

15. Cite two examples of continuously selling above the market price. Describe the situations.

16. Explain the types of competitive situations that might lead to a meeting-competition pricing policy.

17. Would consumers be better off if all nations dropped their antidumping laws? Explain your thinking.

18. How would our marketing system change if manufacturers were required to set fixed prices on *all* products sold at retail and *all* retailers were required to use these prices? Would a manufacturer's marketing mix be easier to develop? What kind of an operation would retailing be in this situation? Would consumers receive more or less service?

19. Is price discrimination involved if a large oil company sells gasoline to taxicab associations for resale to individual taxicab operators for $2\frac{1}{2}$ cents a gallon less than the price charged to retail service stations? What happens if the cab associations resell gasoline not only to taxicab operators but to the general public as well?

CREATING MARKETING PLANS

The Marketing Plan Coach software on the Student CD includes a sample marketing plan for Hillside Veterinary Clinic. Look through the "Marketing Strategy" section.

a. A veterinary clinic located in another town gives its customers a 10 percent discount on their next vet bill if they refer a new pet owner to the clinic. Do you think that this would be a good idea for Hillside? Does it fit with Hillside's strategy?

b. The same clinic offered customers a sort of cumulative discount—an end-of-year refund if their total spending at the clinic exceeded a certain level. That clinic sees it as a way of being nice to people whose pets have had a lot of problems. Do you think that this is a good idea for Hillside? Why or why not?

SUGGESTED CASES

13. **Office Distributors, Inc.**   25. **PlastiTech Mfg., Inc.**

COMPUTER-AIDED PROBLEM

16. CASH DISCOUNTS

Joe Tulkin owns Tulkin Wholesale Co. He sells paper, tape, file folders, and other office supplies to about 120 retailers in nearby cities. His average retailer-customer spends about $900 a month. When Tulkin started business in 1991, competing wholesalers were giving retailers invoice terms of 3/10, net 30. Tulkin never gave the issue much thought—he just used the same invoice terms when he billed customers. At that time, about half of his customers took the discount. Recently, he noticed a change in the way his customers were paying their bills. Checking his records, he found that 90 percent of the retailers were taking the cash discount. With so many retailers taking the cash discount, it seems to have become a price reduction. In addition, Tulkin learned that other wholesalers were changing their invoice terms.

Tulkin decides he should rethink his invoice terms. He knows he could change the percent rate on the cash discount, the number of days the discount is offered, or the number of days before the face amount is due. Changing any of these, or any combination, will change the interest rate at which a buyer is, in effect, borrowing money if he does not take the discount. Tulkin decides that it will be easier to evaluate the effect of different invoice terms if he sets up a spreadsheet to let him change the terms and quickly see the effective interest rate for each change.

a. With 90 percent of Tulkin's customers now taking the discount, what is the total monthly cash discount amount?

b. If Tulkin changes his invoice terms to 1/5, net 20, what interest rate is each buyer paying by not taking the cash discount? With these terms, would fewer buyers be likely to take the discount? Why?

c. Tulkin thinks 10 customers will switch to other wholesalers if he changes his invoice terms to 2/10, net 30, while 60 percent of the remaining customers will take the discount. What interest rate does a buyer pay by not taking this cash discount? For this situation, what will the total gross sales (total invoice) amount be? The total cash discount? The total net sales receipts after the total cash discount? Compare Tulkin's current situation with what will happen if he changes his invoice terms to 2/10, net 30.

For additional questions related to this problem, see Exercise 16-3 in the *Learning Aid for Use with Essentials of Marketing*, 11th edition.

CHAPTER SEVENTEEN

Price Setting in the Business World

Wal-Mart is the largest retailer in the world. It sells more food than any supermarket chain and more toys than Toys "R" Us. Procter & Gamble and Kimberly-Clark are giants in consumer packaged goods, but more than 20 percent of their sales are at Wal-Mart; for many major producers, it's more than 20 percent of sales. In 2006, Wal-Mart's sales revenue was $345 billion, more than 12 times what it was in 1990. Back then, Wal-Mart and Kmart had equal sales. However, Wal-Mart made about twice as much profit for each dollar of revenue. Trying to compete with Wal-Mart over the decade of the 90s ultimately pushed Kmart into bankruptcy. Now, out of bankruptcy and trying to streamline operations, Kmart is back trying to compete with Wal-Mart again. That's a tough fight.

What explains the big difference in growth and profits when the two chains are in many ways similar? Part of the answer is that Wal-Mart has more sales volume in each store. Even after Kmart closed about 25 percent of its poorer stores, Wal-Mart's sales revenue per square foot is about twice that at Kmart. Wal-Mart's lower prices on similar products increases demand in its stores. But that also reduces its fixed operating costs as a percentage of sales. That means it can add a smaller markup, still cover its operating expenses, and make a larger profit. And as ongoing price rollbacks pull in more and more customers, its percentage of overhead costs to sales revenue continues to drop—from about 20.2 percent in 1980 to about 17 percent now.

Wal-Mart has become even more efficient in cutting unnecessary inventory. In one sweeping set of improvements a few years ago, Wal-Mart cut more than $2 billion in average inventory, thereby saving $150 million in carrying costs and reducing the need for markdowns. Now Wal-Mart gets close to 10 stockturns on its inventory each year, while most other mass-merchandisers average about 7. Wal-Mart also has lower costs for the goods it sells. Its buyers are tough in negotiating the best prices from suppliers—to be able to offer Wal-Mart customers the brands they want at low prices. But Wal-Mart also works closely with producers to reduce costs in the channel. For example, Wal-Mart was one of the first major retailers to insist that all orders be placed by computer and more recently has been one of the first to use radio frequency ID "smart tags" to precisely track the flow of goods from vendors through its distribution centers to stores. That reduces stock-outs on store shelves and lost sales at the checkout counter. Wal-Mart also works with vendors to create quality private-label brands, like Sam's Choice Cola.

Even with its lower costs, Wal-Mart isn't content to take the convenient route to price setting by just adding a standard percentage markup on different items. The company was one of the first retailers to give managers in every department in every store frequent, detailed information about what is selling and what isn't. Managers drop items that are collecting dust and roll back prices on the ones with the fastest turnover and highest margins. That not only increases stockturns but also puts the effort behind products with the most potential. For instance, Wal-Mart's analysis of checkout-scanner sales data revealed that parents often pick up more than one kid's video at a time. So now managers make certain that special displays feature several videos and that the rest of the selection is close by.

While Wal-Mart wants to attract customers with low prices, it doesn't want to miss opportunities for growth. For example, Wal-Mart's consumer research revealed that many of its higher-income customers left the store after buying just food and cleaning supplies. To get a larger "share of wallet"

from these consumers, Wal-Mart added upgrades to its clothing and home furnishings lines. Similarly, Wal-Mart increased the floor space for the consumer electronics category and aggressively promoted its electronics line, including some new higher-priced models from Sony and Philips. Even with these changes, Wal-Mart still offers low prices relative to competitors. For example, Wal-Mart sells extended warranties at about half the price of major competitors.

To return to where we started, Kmart is trying to fight back, but as yet it is not clear what its new strategy will be. What is clear is that Sears and Kmart have merged and are trying to figure out a new, differentiated strategy so they won't have to compete just on low prices. That will require creativity, but other Wal-Mart rivals have found ways to differentiate themselves from the retail giant. However, Wal-Mart will continue to leverage its sales volume, purchasing power, low logistics costs, and margins to make it difficult for rivals to win on price. So, unless Wal-Mart somehow stumbles because of its enormous size, its low prices will continue to attract many customers.[1]

LEARNING OBJECTIVES

Ultimately, the price that a firm charges must cover the costs of the whole marketing mix or the firm will not make a profit. So, it's important for marketing managers to understand costs and how they relate to pricing. On the other hand, it doesn't make sense to set prices based just on costs because customers won't buy a product if they don't think that it represents a good value for their money. So, setting prices is not an easy task and marketing managers must carefully balance costs, customer price sensitivity, and other factors. This chapter will help you better understand these issues and how to evaluate them in setting prices.

When you finish this chapter, you should:

1. understand how most wholesalers and retailers set their prices by using markups.

2. understand why turnover is so important in pricing.

3. understand the advantages and disadvantages of average-cost pricing.

4. know how to use break-even analysis to evaluate possible prices.

5. understand the advantages of marginal analysis and how to use it for price setting.

6. understand the various factors that influence customer price sensitivity.

7. know the many ways that price setters use demand estimates in their pricing.

8. understand how bid pricing and negotiated prices work.

9. understand important new terms (shown in red).

PRICE SETTING IS A KEY STRATEGY DECISION

In Chapter 16 we discussed the idea that pricing objectives and policies should guide pricing decisions. We described different dimensions of the pricing decision and how they combine to create value for customers. This chapter builds on those concepts—all of which influence price setting—and gives you additional frameworks that will help you understand how marketing managers set prices. See Exhibit 17–1.

There are many ways to set prices. But, for simplicity, they can be reduced to two basic approaches—*cost-oriented* and *demand-oriented* price setting. We will discuss cost-oriented approaches first because they are most common. Also, understanding the problems of relying on a cost-oriented approach shows why a marketing manager must consider customer demand and price sensitivity to make good Price decisions. We conclude the chapter with a discussion of some special price setting issues— pricing full lines of products, bid pricing, and negotiated pricing. Let's begin by looking at markups, which is how most retailers and wholesalers set cost-oriented prices.

SOME FIRMS JUST USE MARKUPS

Markups guide pricing by intermediaries

Some firms, including most retailers and wholesalers, set prices by using a **markup**—a dollar amount added to the cost of products to get the selling price. For example, suppose that a CVS drugstore buys a bottle of Pert Plus shampoo and conditioner for $2. To make a profit, the drugstore obviously must sell Pert Plus for more than $2. If it adds $1 to cover operating expenses and provide a profit, we say that the store is marking up the item $1.

Markups, however, usually are stated as percentages rather than dollar amounts. And this is where confusion sometimes arises. Is a markup of $1 on a cost of $2 a markup of 50 percent? Or should the markup be figured as a percentage of the selling price—$3.00—and therefore be 33 1/3 percent? A clear definition is necessary.

Exhibit 17-1   Price Setting and Strategy Planning

Markup percent is based on selling price—a convenient rule

Unless otherwise stated, **markup (percent)** means percentage of selling price that is added to the cost to get the selling price. So the $1 markup on the $3.00 selling price is a markup of 33⅓ percent. Markups are related to selling price for convenience.

There's nothing wrong with the idea of markup on cost. However, to avoid confusion, it's important to state clearly which markup percent you're using.[2]

A manager may want to change a markup on selling price to one based on cost, or vice versa. The calculations used to do this are simple. (See the section on markup conversion in Appendix B on marketing arithmetic. The appendixes follow Chapter 18.)

Many use a standard markup percent

Many intermediaries select a standard markup percent and then apply it to all their products. This makes pricing easier. When you think of the large number of items the average retailer and wholesaler carry—and the small sales volume of any one item—this approach may make sense. Spending the time to find the best price to charge on every item in stock (day to day or week to week) might not pay.

Moreover, different companies in the same line of business often use the same markup percent. There is a reason for this: Their operating expenses are usually similar. So they see a standard markup as acceptable as long as it's large enough to cover the firm's operating expenses and provide a reasonable profit.

Markups are related to gross margins

How does a manager decide on a standard markup in the first place? A standard markup is often set close to the firm's *gross margin*. Managers regularly see gross margins on their operating (profit and loss) statements. The gross margin is the amount left—after subtracting the cost of sales (cost of goods sold) from net sales—to cover the expenses of selling products and operating the business. (See Appendix B on marketing arithmetic if you are unfamiliar with these ideas.) Our CVS manager knows that there won't be any profit if the gross margin is not large enough. For this reason,

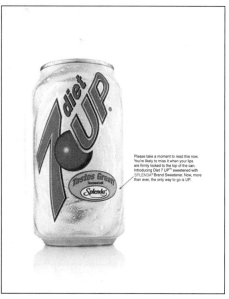

Kohler is an example of a firm with specialized products that relies on selective distribution and sells in smaller volumes, usually offering retailers higher markups to offset the retailer's higher carrying costs and marketing expenses. Splenda, the low-cal sweetener, faced tough competition from Equal and Sweet 'n Low when it came out. It built distribution as it became more popular with consumers, and then targeted food makers to use Splenda as an ingredient in their products because the large base of established Splenda fans would help with sales.

CVS might accept a markup percent on Pert Plus that is close to the store's usual gross margin percent.

Smart producers pay attention to the gross margins and standard markups of middlemen in their channel. They usually allow trade (functional) discounts similar to the standard markups these intermediaries expect.

Markup chain may be used in channel pricing

Different firms in a channel often use different markups. A **markup chain**—the sequence of markups firms use at different levels in a channel—determines the price structure in the whole channel. The markup is figured on the *selling price* at each level of the channel.

For example, Black & Decker's selling price for a cordless electric drill becomes the cost the Ace Hardware wholesaler pays. The wholesaler's selling price becomes the hardware retailer's cost. And this cost plus a retail markup becomes the retail selling price. Each markup should cover the costs of running the business and leave a profit.

Exhibit 17–2 illustrates the markup chain for a cordless electric drill at each level of the channel system. The production (factory) cost of the drill is $43.20. In this case, the producer takes a 10 percent markup and sells the product for $48. The markup is 10 percent of $48 or $4.80. The producer's selling price now becomes the wholesaler's cost—$48. If the wholesaler is used to taking a 20 percent markup on selling price, the markup is $12—and the wholesaler's selling price becomes $60. The $60 now becomes the cost for the hardware retailer. A retailer who is used to a 40 percent markup adds $40, and so the retail selling price becomes $100.

High markups don't always mean big profits

Some people, including many conventional retailers, think high markups mean big profits. Often this isn't true. A high markup may result in a price that's too high—a price at which few customers will buy. You can't earn much if you don't sell much, no matter how high your markup on a single item. So high markups may lead to low profits.

Exhibit 17–2 Example of a Markup Chain and Channel Pricing

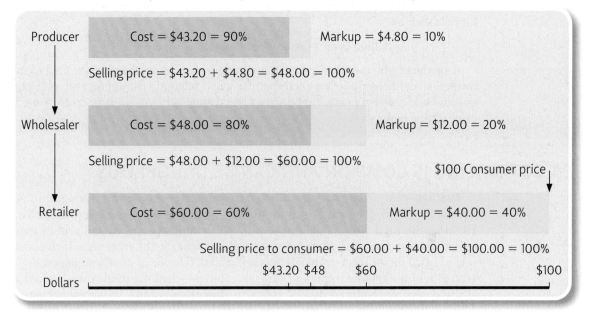

Producer   Cost = $43.20 = 90%   Markup = $4.80 = 10%

Selling price = $43.20 + $4.80 = $48.00 = 100%

Wholesaler   Cost = $48.00 = 80%   Markup = $12.00 = 20%

Selling price = $48.00 + $12.00 = $60.00 = 100%

$100 Consumer price

Retailer   Cost = $60.00 = 60%   Markup = $40.00 = 40%

Selling price to consumer = $60.00 + $40.00 = $100.00 = 100%

$43.20 $48 $60 $100

Dollars

Lower markups can speed turnover and the stockturn rate

Some retailers and wholesalers, however, try to speed turnover to increase profit—even if this means reducing their markups. They realize that a business runs up costs over time. If they can sell a much greater amount in the same time period, they may be able to take a lower markup and still earn higher profits at the end of the period.

An important idea here is the **stockturn rate**—the number of times the average inventory is sold in a year. Various methods of figuring stockturn rates can be used (see the section "Computing the Stockturn Rate" in Appendix B). A low stockturn rate may be bad for profits.

At the very least, a low stockturn increases inventory carrying cost and ties up working capital. If a firm with a stockturn of 1 (once per year) sells products that cost it $100,000, it has that much tied up in inventory all the time. But a stockturn of 5 requires only $20,000 worth of inventory ($100,000 cost ÷ 5 turnovers a year). If annual inventory carrying cost is about 20 percent of the inventory value, that reduces costs by $16,000 a year. That's a big difference on $100,000 in sales!

Whether a stockturn rate is high or low depends on the industry and the product involved. An electrical parts wholesaler may expect an annual rate of 2—while a supermarket might expect 8 stockturns on average but 20 stockturns for soaps and 70 stockturns for fresh fruits and vegetables.

Mass-merchandisers run in fast company

Although some middlemen use the same standard markup percent on all their products, this policy ignores the importance of fast turnover. Mass-merchandisers know this. They put low markups on fast-selling items and higher markups on items that sell less frequently. For example, Wal-Mart may put a small markup on fast-selling health and beauty aids (like toothpaste or shampoo) but higher markups on appliances and clothing.

Where does the markup chain start?

Some markups eventually become standard in a trade. Most channel members tend to follow a similar process—adding a certain percentage to the previous price. But who sets price in the first place? The firm that brands a product is usually the one that sets its basic list price. It may be a large retailer, a large wholesaler, or most often, the producer.

Some producers just start with a cost per unit figure and add a markup—perhaps a standard markup—to obtain their selling price. Or they may use some rule-of-thumb formula such as:

Selling price = Average production cost per unit × 3

A producer who uses this approach might develop rules and markups related to its own costs and objectives. Yet even the first step—selecting the appropriate cost per unit to build on—isn't easy. Let's discuss several approaches to see how cost-oriented price setting really works.

AVERAGE-COST PRICING IS COMMON AND CAN BE DANGEROUS

Average-cost pricing means adding a reasonable markup to the average cost of a product. A manager usually finds the average cost per unit by studying past records. Dividing the total cost for the last year by all the units produced and sold in that period gives an estimate of the average cost per unit for the next year. If the cost was $32,000 for all labor and materials and $30,000 for fixed overhead expenses—such as selling expenses, rent, and manager salaries—then the total cost is $62,000. If the company produced 40,000 items in that time period, the average cost is $62,000 divided by 40,000 units, or $1.55 per unit. To get the price, the producer decides how much profit per unit to add to the average cost per unit. If the company considers 45 cents a reasonable profit for each unit, it sets the new price at $2.00. Exhibit 17–3A shows that this approach produces the desired profit if the company sells 40,000 units.

It does not make allowances for cost variations as output changes

It's always a useful input to pricing decisions to understand how costs operate at different levels of output. Further, average-cost pricing is simple. But it can also be dangerous. It's easy to lose money with average-cost pricing. To see why, let's follow this example further.

Exhibit 17–3 Results of Average-Cost Pricing

A. Calculation of Planned Profit if 40,000 Items Are Sold		B. Calculation of Actual Profit if Only 20,000 Items Are Sold	
Calculation of Costs:		**Calculation of Costs:**	
Fixed overhead expenses	$30,000	Fixed overhead expenses	$30,000
Labor and materials ($.80 a unit)	32,000	Labor and materials ($.80 a unit)	16,000
Total costs	$62,000	Total costs	$46,000
"Planned" profit	18,000		
Total costs and planned profit	$80,000		
Calculation of Profit (or Loss):		**Calculation of Profit (or Loss):**	
Actual unit sales × Price ($2.00*)	$80,000	Actual unit sales × Price ($2.00*)	$40,000
Minus: total costs	62,000	Minus: total costs	46,000
Profit (loss)	$18,000	Profit (loss)	($6,000)
Result:		**Result:**	
Planned profit of $18,000 is earned if 40,000 items are sold at $2.00 each.		Planned profit of $18,000 is not earned. Instead, $6,000 loss results if 20,000 items are sold at $2.00 each.	

*Calculation of "reasonable" price: $\dfrac{\text{Expected total costs and planned profit}}{\text{Planned number of items to be sold}} = \dfrac{\$80,000}{40,000} = \$2.00$

First, remember that the average cost of $2.00 per unit was based on output of 40,000 units. But if the firm is only able to produce and sell 20,000 units in the next year, it may be in trouble. Twenty thousand units sold at $2.00 each ($1.55 cost plus 45 cents for expected profit) yield a total revenue of only $40,000. The overhead is still fixed at $30,000, and the variable material and labor cost drops by half to $16,000—for a total cost of $46,000. This means a loss of $6,000, or 30 cents a unit. The method that was supposed to allow a profit of 45 cents a unit actually causes a loss of 30 cents a unit! See Exhibit 17-3B.

The basic problem with the average-cost approach is that it doesn't consider cost variations at different levels of output. In a typical situation, costs are high with low output, and then economies of scale set in—the average cost per unit drops as the quantity produced increases. This is why mass production and mass distribution often make sense. It's also why it's important to develop a better understanding of the different types of costs a marketing manager should consider when setting a price.

MARKETING MANAGERS MUST CONSIDER VARIOUS KINDS OF COSTS

Average-cost pricing may lead to losses because there are a variety of costs—and each changes in a *different* way as output changes. Any pricing method that uses cost must consider these changes. To understand why, we need to define six types of cost.

There are three kinds of total cost

1. **Total fixed cost** is the sum of those costs that are fixed in total—no matter how much is produced. Among these fixed costs are rent, depreciation, managers' salaries, property taxes, and insurance. Such costs stay the same even if production stops temporarily.

2. **Total variable cost**, on the other hand, is the sum of those changing expenses that are closely related to output—expenses for parts, wages, packaging materials, outgoing freight, and sales commissions.

Businesses worry when the cost of ingredients goes up, or fluctuates often, because it can reduce the profitability of products they sell, increase pressure to raise prices on those products, or both.

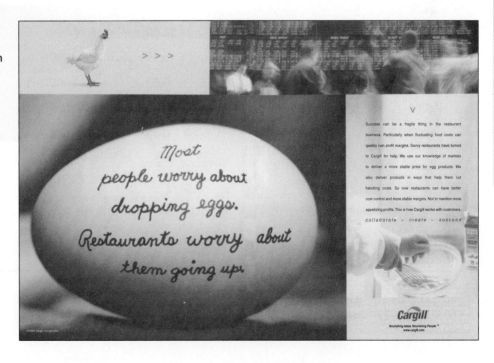

At zero output, total variable cost is zero. As output increases, so do variable costs. If Levi's doubles its output of jeans in a year, its total cost for denim cloth also (roughly) doubles.

3. **Total cost** is the sum of total fixed and total variable costs. Changes in total cost depend on variations in total variable cost, since total fixed cost stays the same.

There are three kinds of average cost

The pricing manager usually is more interested in cost per unit than total cost because prices are usually quoted per unit.

1. **Average cost (per unit)** is obtained by dividing total cost by the related quantity (that is, the total quantity that causes the total cost).
2. **Average fixed cost (per unit)** is obtained by dividing total fixed cost by the related quantity.
3. **Average variable cost (per unit)** is obtained by dividing total variable cost by the related quantity.

An example shows cost relations

A good way to get a feel for these different types of costs is to extend our average-cost pricing example (Exhibit 17–3A). Exhibit 17–4 shows the six types of cost and how they vary at different levels of output. The line for 40,000 units is highlighted because that was the expected level of sales in our average-cost pricing example. For simplicity, we assume that average variable cost is the same for each unit. Notice, however, that total variable cost increases when quantity increases.

Exhibit 17–4 Cost Structure of a Firm

Quantity (Q)	Total Fixed Costs (TFC)	Average Fixed Costs (AFC)	Average Variable Costs (AVC)	Total Variable Costs (TVC)	Total Cost (TC)	Average Cost (AC)
0	$30,000	——	——	——	$ 30,000	——
10,000	30,000	$3.00	$0.80	$ 8,000	38,000	$3.80
20,000	30,000	1.50	0.80	16,000	46,000	2.30
30,000	30,000	1.00	0.80	24,000	54,000	1.80
40,000	**30,000**	**0.75**	**0.80**	**32,000**	**62,000**	**1.55**
50,000	30,000	0.60	0.80	40,000	70,000	1.40
60,000	30,000	0.50	0.80	48,000	78,000	1.30
70,000	30,000	0.43	0.80	56,000	86,000	1.23
80,000	30,000	0.38	0.80	64,000	94,000	1.18
90,000	30,000	0.33	0.80	72,000	102,000	1.13
100,000	30,000	0.30	0.80	80,000	110,000	1.10

$$\begin{bmatrix} 110,000 \ (TC) \\ -80,000 \ (TVC) \\ \overline{30,000} \ (TFC) \end{bmatrix} \quad (Q) \ 100,000 \ \overline{\big)\,30,000 \ (TFC)}^{\ 0.30 \ (AFC)} \quad \begin{bmatrix} 100,000 \ (Q) \\ \times 0.80 \ (AVC) \\ \overline{80,000} \ (TVC) \end{bmatrix} \quad \begin{bmatrix} 30,000 \ (TFC) \\ +80,000 \ (TVC) \\ \overline{110,000} \ (TC) \end{bmatrix} \quad (Q) \ 100,000 \ \overline{\big)\,110,000 \ (TC)}^{\ 1.10 \ (AC)}$$

Customers Have a Soft Spot for Coach

Coach is best known for its fine leather handbags, but it has found a profitable place in the broader product-market for fashion accessories with a line that also includes brief cases, jewelry, belts, and silk scarves. Marketing managers at Coach have developed marketing strategies that help it achieve a 35 percent operating margin—the best ratio of profit to sales in its industry.

Coach is successful in targeting the "affordable luxury" segment. Coach positions its products between lower-priced mass-market brands and those from the priciest fashion designers. The Coach marketing mix combines a strong luxury brand name, a broad product line, and relatively affordable prices—from $38 key chains to $698 suede satchels. Coach handbags typically sell between $200 and $400, but that is about 50 percent less than European luxury brands from Louis Vuitton and Prada. Coach's lower-priced items help attract new customers, and once they become more familiar with the Coach line they often move up to more expensive items. Coach is luxury, but it's still affordable.

While Coach's product line is sold at many department stores, more than half of its sales are through company-owned stores or other outlets where Coach has greater control over product presentation and pricing. Coach's flagship stores are located in upscale shopping districts—like Rodeo Drive in Beverly Hills and New York's Madison Avenue. They help to showcase the brand and build its prestige. The salespeople at these stores know how to explain the value of Coach products—and encourage customers to handle them so they can feel the quality of the soft leathers and other materials. These stores have all of Coach's latest designs and they sell at Coach's full list price. Coach also has factory outlet stores which sell styles that are 6 to 12 months old at 25 to 35 percent discounts from list price. However, these outlets don't put price pressure on other Coach channels because they're carefully located at least 60 miles away. Coach also operates Internet and catalog outlets, which provide convenience to some customers, but Coach products have the most appeal when customers can see and touch them.

Different channels allow Coach to serve different target markets. Shoppers at full-price stores tend to be younger than outlet shoppers—but both target groups have proven to be very loyal. Coach's research shows that full-price customers spend an average of $1,170 per year on the brand and outlet customers $770. But Coach must be careful with pricing and distribution decisions. Calvin Klein, Tommy Hilfiger, and others lost their exclusive image and power to command luxury prices after selling in discount channels. But for now, it seems that Coach has found the sweet spot as it grows customer equity in two significant target markets.[3]

Exhibit 17–5 shows the three average cost curves from Exhibit 17–4. Notice that average fixed cost goes down steadily as the quantity increases. Although the average variable cost remains the same, average cost decreases continually too. This is because average fixed cost is decreasing. With these relations in mind, let's reconsider the problem with average-cost pricing.

Ignoring demand is the major weakness of average-cost pricing

Average-cost pricing works well if the firm actually sells the quantity it used to set the average-cost price. Losses may result, however, if actual sales are much lower than expected. On the other hand, if sales are much higher than expected, then profits may be very good. But this will only happen by luck—because the firm's demand is much larger than expected.

To use average-cost pricing, a marketing manager must make *some* estimate of the quantity to be sold in the coming period. Without a quantity estimate, it isn't possible to compute average cost. But unless this quantity is related to price—that is, unless the firm's demand curve is considered—the marketing manager may set a price that doesn't even cover a firm's total cost! You saw this happen in Exhibit 17–3B, when the firm's price of $2.00 resulted in demand for only 20,000 units and a loss of $6,000.

The demand curve is still important even if a manager doesn't take time to think about it. For example, Exhibit 17–6 shows the demand curve for the firm we're discussing. This demand curve shows *why* the firm lost money when it tried to use average-cost pricing. At the $2.00 price, quantity demanded is only 20,000. With this demand curve and the costs in Exhibit 17–4, the firm will incur a loss whether management sets the price at a high $3 or a low $1.20. At $3, the firm will sell only 10,000 units for a total revenue of $30,000. But total cost will be $38,000—for a loss of $8,000. At the $1.20 price, it will sell 60,000 units—at a loss of $6,000. However, the curve suggests that at a price of $1.65 consumers will demand about 40,000 units, producing a profit of about $4,000.

In short, average-cost pricing is simple in theory but often fails in practice. In stable situations, prices set by this method may yield profits but not necessarily *maximum* profits. And note that such cost-based prices may be higher than a price that would be more profitable for the firm, as shown in Exhibit 17–6. When demand conditions are changing, average-cost pricing is even more risky.

Exhibit 17–6
Evaluation of Various
Prices along a Firm's
Demand Curve

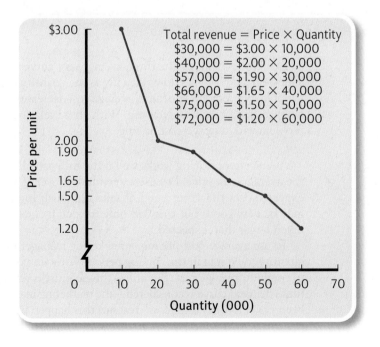

Exhibit 17–7
Summary of
Relationships among
Quantity, Cost, and Price
Using Cost-Oriented
Pricing

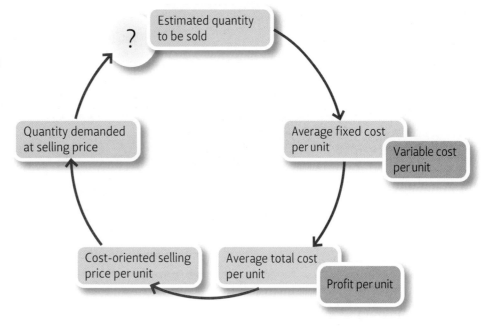

Exhibit 17–7 summarizes the relationships just discussed. Cost-oriented pricing requires an estimate of the total number of units to be sold. That estimate determines the *average* fixed cost per unit and thus the average total cost. Then the firm adds the desired profit per unit to the average total cost to get the cost-oriented selling price. How customers react to that price determines the actual quantity the firm will be able to sell. But that quantity may not be the quantity used to compute the average cost![4]

Don't ignore competitors' costs

Another danger of average-cost pricing is that it ignores competitors' costs and prices. Just as the price of a firm's own product influences demand, the price of available substitutes may impact demand. We saw this in our Wal-Mart case at the start of this chapter. By finding ways to cut costs, Wal-Mart was able to offer prices lower than competitors and still make an attractive profit.

BREAK-EVEN ANALYSIS CAN EVALUATE POSSIBLE PRICES

Some price setters use break-even analysis in their pricing. **Break-even analysis** evaluates whether the firm will be able to break even—that is, cover all its costs—with a particular price. This is important because a firm must cover all costs in the long run or there is not much point being in business. This method focuses on the **break-even point (BEP)**—the quantity where the firm's total cost will just equal its total revenue.

Break-even charts help find the BEP

To help understand how break-even analysis works, look at Exhibit 17–8, an example of the typical break-even chart. *The chart is based on a particular selling price*—in this case, $1.20 a unit. The chart has lines that show total costs (total variable plus total fixed costs) and total revenues at different levels of production. The break-even point on the chart is at 75,000 units, where the total cost and total revenue lines intersect. At that production level, total cost and total revenue are the same—$90,000.

Exhibit 17–8
Break-Even Chart for a
Particular Situation

The difference between the total revenue and total cost at a given quantity is the profit—or loss! The chart shows that below the break-even point, total cost is higher than total revenue and the firm incurs a loss. The firm makes a profit above the break-even point. However, the firm will only reach the break-even point, or get beyond it into the profit area, *if* it can sell at least 75,000 units at the $1.20 price.

Break-even analysis can be helpful if used properly, so let's look at this approach more closely.

How to compute a break-even point

A break-even chart is an easy-to-understand visual aid, but it's also useful to be able to compute the break-even point.

The BEP, in units, can be found by dividing total fixed costs (TFC) by the **fixed-cost (FC) contribution per unit**—the assumed selling price per unit minus the variable cost per unit. This can be stated as a simple formula:

$$\text{BEP (in units)} = \frac{\text{Total fixed cost}}{\text{Fixed cost contribution per unit}}$$

This formula makes sense when we think about it. To break even, we must cover total fixed costs. Therefore, we must figure the contribution each unit will make to covering the total fixed costs (after paying for the variable costs to produce the item). When we divide this per-unit contribution into the total fixed costs that must be covered, we have the BEP (in units).

To illustrate the formula, let's use the cost and price information in Exhibit 17–8. The price per unit is $1.20. The average variable cost per unit is 80 cents. So the FC contribution per unit is 40 cents ($1.20 − 80 cents). The total fixed cost is $30,000 (see Exhibit 17-8). Substituting in the formula:

$$\text{BEP} = \frac{\$30,000}{.40} = 75,000 \text{ units}$$

From this you can see that if this firm sells 75,000 units, it will exactly cover all its fixed and variable costs. If it sells even one more unit, it will begin to show a profit—in this case, 40 cents per unit. Note that once the fixed costs are covered, the part of revenue formerly going to cover fixed costs is now *all profit*.

Break-even analysis is helpful—but not a pricing solution

Break-even analysis is helpful for evaluating alternatives. It is also popular because it's easy to use. Yet break-even analysis is too often misunderstood. Beyond the BEP, profits seem to be growing continually. And the graph—with its straight-line total

The money that a firm spends on marketing and other expenses must be at least covered by a firm's price if it is to make a profit. That's why Gillette enjoys big economies of scale by selling the same razors in many markets around the world.

revenue curve—makes it seem that any quantity can be sold at the assumed price. But this usually isn't true. It is the same as assuming a perfectly horizontal demand curve at that price. In fact, most managers face down-sloping demand situations. And their total revenue curves do *not* keep going up.

Break-even analysis is a useful tool for analyzing costs and evaluating what might happen to profits in different market environments. But it is a cost-oriented approach. Like other cost-oriented approaches, it does not consider the effect of price on the quantity that consumers will want—that is, the demand curve.

So to really zero in on the most profitable price, marketers are better off estimating the demand curve itself and then using marginal analysis, which we'll discuss next.[5]

MARGINAL ANALYSIS CONSIDERS BOTH COSTS AND DEMAND

Marginal analysis helps find the right price

The best pricing tool marketers have for looking at costs and revenue (demand) at the same time is marginal analysis. **Marginal analysis** focuses on the changes in total revenue and total cost from selling one more unit to find the most profitable price and quantity. Marginal analysis shows how costs, revenue, and profit change at different prices. The price that maximizes profit is the one that results in the greatest difference between total revenue and total cost.[6]

Demand estimates involve "if-then" thinking

Since the price determines what quantity will be sold, a manager needs an estimate of the demand curve to compute total revenue. A practical approach here is for managers to think about a price that appears to be too high and one that is too low. Then, for a number of prices between these two extremes, the manager estimates what quantity it might be possible to sell. You can think of this as a summary of the answers to a series of what-if questions—*What* quantity will be sold *if* a particular price is selected?

Profit is the difference between total revenue and total cost

The first two columns in Exhibit 17–9 give quantity and price combinations (demand) for an example firm. Total revenue in column 3 of Exhibit 17–9 is equal to a price multiplied by its related quantity. Costs at the different quantities are also shown. The profit at each quantity and price is the difference between total revenue

Exhibit 17–9   Revenue, Cost, and Profit at Different Prices for a Firm

(1) Quantity (Q)	(2) Price (P)	(3) Total Revenue (TR)	(4) Total Variable Cost (TVC)	(5) Total Cost (TC)	(6) Profit (TR − TC)
0	$150	$ 0	$ 0	$200	$−200
1	140	140	96	296	− 156
2	130	260	116	316	− 56
3	117	351	131	331	+ 20
4	105	420	144	344	+ 76
5	92	460	155	355	+ 105
6	**79**	**474**	**168**	**368**	**+ 106**
7	66	462	183	383	+ 79
8	53	424	223	423	+ 1
9	42	378	307	507	− 129
10	31	310	510	710	− 400

and total cost. In this example, the best price is $79 (and a quantity of six units sold) because that combination results in the highest profit ($106).

Profit maximization with total revenue and total cost curves

Exhibit 17–10 graphs the total revenue, total cost, and total profit relationships for the numbers we've been working with in Exhibit 17–9. The highest point on the total profit curve is at a quantity of six units. This is also the quantity where we find the greatest vertical distance between the total revenue curve and the total cost curve. Exhibit 17–9 shows that it is the $79 price that results in selling six units, so $79 is the price that leads to the highest profit. A price lower than $79 would result in a higher sales volume. But you can see that the total profit curve declines beyond a quantity of six units. So a profit-maximizing marketing manager would not be interested in setting a lower price.

A profit range is reassuring

Marginal analysis focuses on the price that earns the *highest* profit. But a slight miss doesn't mean failure because demand estimates don't have to be exact. There is usually a range of profitable prices. You can see this in Exhibit 17–9 and in the section of Exhibit 17–10 shown in yellow. Although the price that would result in the highest profit is $79, the firm's strategy would be profitable all the way from a price of $53 to $117. So the effort of trying to estimate demand will probably lead to being some place in the profitable range. In contrast, mechanical use of average-cost pricing could lead to a price that is much too high—or much too low.

DEMAND-ORIENTED APPROACHES FOR SETTING PRICES

Evaluating the customer's price sensitivity

A manager who knows what influences target customers' price sensitivity can do a better job estimating the demand curve that the firm faces. Marketing researchers have identified a number of factors that influence price sensitivity across many different market situations.

The first is the most basic. When customers have *substitute ways* of meeting a need, they are likely to be more price sensitive. A cook who wants a cappuccino maker to

Exhibit 17–10
Graphic Determination of the Price Giving the Greatest Total Profit for a Firm

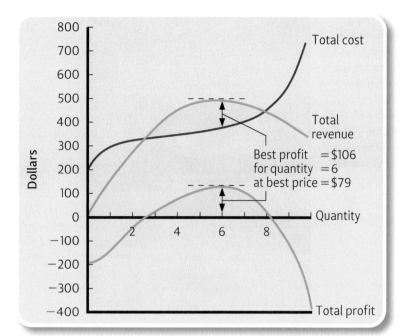

be able to serve something distinctive to guests at a dinner party may be willing to pay a high price. However, if different machines are available and our cook sees them as pretty similar, price sensitivity will be greater. It's important not to ignore dissimilar alternatives if the customer sees them as substitutes. If a machine for espresso were much less expensive than one for cappuccino, our cook might decide that an espresso machine would meet her needs just as well.

The impact of substitutes on price sensitivity is greatest when it is easy for customers to *compare prices*. For example, unit prices make it easier for our cook to compare the prices of espresso and cappuccino grinds on the grocery store shelf. Many people believe that the ease of comparing prices on the Internet increases price sensitivity and brings down prices. If nothing else, it may make sellers more aware of competing prices.

Internet
EXERCISE

Bizrate.com is a website that makes it easy to find different brands of products from different sellers and compare prices. Go to the website (*www.bizrate.com*) and search for "popcorn makers." Review the products and prices listed and check a few of the links to related information. How useful is this sort of service? Is there more variety in features and prices than you expected? Do you think that this sort of comparison makes people more price sensitive? Why or why not?

People tend to be less price sensitive when someone else pays the bill or *shares the cost*. Perhaps this is just human nature. Insurance companies think that consumers would reject high medical fees if they were paying all of their own bills. And executives might plan longer in advance to get better discounts on airline flights if their companies weren't footing the bills.

Customers tend to be more price sensitive the greater the *total expenditure*. Sometimes a big expenditure can be broken into smaller pieces. Mercedes knows this. When its ads focused on the cost of a monthly lease rather than the total price of the car, more consumers got interested in biting the bullet.

Customers are less price sensitive the greater the *significance of the end benefit* of the purchase. Computer makers will pay more to get Intel processors if they believe that having an "Intel inside" sells more machines. Positioning efforts often focus on emotional benefits of a purchase to increase the significance of a benefit. Ads for L'Oréal hair color, for example, show closeups of beautiful hair while popular celebrities like Heather Locklear tell women to buy it "because you're worth it." A consumer who cares about the price of a bottle of hair color might still have no question that she's worth the difference in price.

Customers are sometimes less price sensitive if there are *switching costs*—costs that a customer faces by buying a product that is different from what has been purchased or used

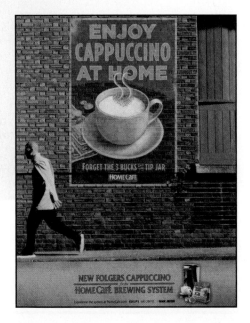

Consumers who really love cappuccino may be less price sensitive and willing to pay $3 a cup at a local coffee bar, but that doesn't mean that they wouldn't prefer a substitute way of meeting that need—like Folgers Home Café Brewing System—if they view it as offering better customer value.

in the past. Switching costs can be quite high for some business customers. For example, once a firm's employees know how to use Microsoft Excel, a company may not want to incur the financial cost and time it would take to train employees in a new software package. But switching costs can apply to final consumers as well. For example, if a hair salon raises its prices, many customers will not switch to a new salon. The hassles of looking for a new stylist—and the risk of ending up with a bad hair day—usually make it easier to simply pay the higher price.

These factors apply in many different purchase situations, so it makes sense for a marketing manager to consider each of them in refining estimates of how customers might respond at different prices.[7]

Value in use pricing—how much will the customer save?

Organizational buyers think about how a purchase will affect their total costs. Many marketers who aim at business markets keep this in mind when estimating demand and setting prices. They use **value in use pricing**—which means setting prices that will capture some of what customers will save by substituting the firm's product for the one currently being used.

For example, a producer of computer-controlled machines used to assemble cars knows that the machine doesn't just replace a standard machine. It also reduces labor costs, quality control costs, and—after the car is sold—costs of warranty repairs. The marketer can estimate what each auto producer will save by using the machine—and then set a price that makes it less expensive for the auto producer to buy the computerized machine

Porsche wants target customers to frame the price of its exciting sports car relative to the thrill of each mile driven, not some other car. "A dollar a mile for the first 42,600. Free after that."

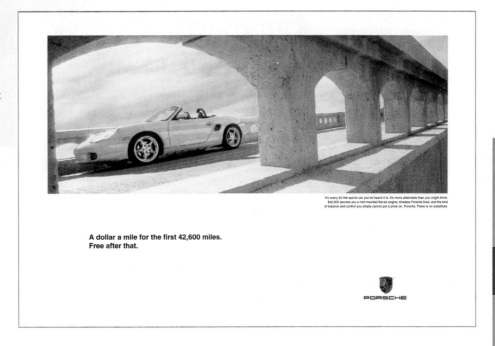

A dollar a mile for the first 42,600 miles.
Free after that.

than to stick with the old methods. The number of customers who have different levels of potential savings also provides some idea about the shape of the demand curve.

Creating a superior product that could save customers money doesn't guarantee that customers will be willing to pay a higher price. To capture the value created, the seller must convince buyers of the savings—and buyers are likely to be skeptical. A salesperson needs to be able to show proof of the claims.[8]

Auctions show what a customer will pay

Auctions have always been a way to determine exactly what some group of potential customers would pay, or not pay, for a product. However, the use of online auctions has dramatically broadened the use of this approach for both consumer and business products. About 5 million auctions are on eBay each day. And some firms are setting up their own auctions, especially for products in short supply. The U.S. government is using online auctions as well. It recently auctioned off airwave rights for cell phone services. Count on more growth in online auctions.[9]

Some sellers use sequential price reductions

Some sellers are taking the auction approach and adapting it by using sequential price reductions over time. The basic idea is that the seller starts with a relatively high price and sells as much of the product as possible at that price, but plans from the start on a series of step-by-step price reductions until the product is sold out. This approach is most commonly used with products that have a short life or are in short supply, but which would just run up inventory costs if they were not sold. Retailers like TJ Maxx use this approach with women's fashions, and grocery stores use it with perishable food like fruits and vegetables. Cruise lines sell space this way; they don't want the ship to sail with empty cabins. Some people may think of this as a "clearance" sale. But the difference here is that the plan from the outset is to work down the demand curve in steps—appealing to segments who are least price sensitive first—until all of a product is sold. However, sellers hope that if they offer the right products they'll never get to price reductions (which earn lower margins). Rather, they prefer to be bringing in the next round of products to start the process over again.

Customers may have reference prices

Some people don't devote much thought to what they pay for the products they buy, including some frequently purchased goods and services. But consumers often have a **reference price**—the price they expect to pay—for many of the products they purchase. And different customers may have different reference prices for the same basic type of purchase. For example, a person who really enjoys reading might have a higher reference price for a popular paperback book than another person who is only an occasional reader.[10]

If a firm's price is lower than a customer's reference price, customers may view the product as a better value and demand may increase. See Exhibit 17–11. Sometimes a firm will try to position the benefits of its product in such a way that consumers compare it with a product that has a higher reference price. Public Broadcasting System TV stations do this when they ask viewers to make donations that match what they pay for "just one month of cable service." Insurance companies frame the price of premiums for homeowners' coverage in terms of the price to repair flood damage—and advertising makes the damage very vivid. Some retailers just want consumers to use the manufacturer's list price as the reference price, even if no one anywhere actually pays that list price.

Leader pricing—make it low to attract customers

Leader pricing means setting some very low prices—real bargains—to get customers into retail stores. The idea is not only to sell large quantities of the leader items but also to get customers into the store to buy other products. Certain products are picked for their promotion value and priced low but above cost. In food stores, the leader prices are the "specials" that are advertised regularly to give an image of low prices. Leader pricing is normally used with products for which consumers do have a specific reference price.

Leader pricing can backfire if customers buy only the low-priced leaders. To avoid hurting profits, managers often select leader items that aren't directly competitive with major lines—as when bargain-priced blank CDs are a leader for an electronics store.[11]

Bait pricing—offer a steal, but sell under protest

Bait pricing is setting some very low prices to attract customers but trying to sell more expensive models or brands once the customer is in the store. For example, a furniture store may advertise a color TV for $199. But once bargain hunters come to

Exhibit 17–11 How a Customer's Reference Price Influences Perceived Value (for a marketing mix with a given set of benefits and costs)

the store, salespeople point out the disadvantages of the low-priced TV and try to convince them to trade up to a better, and more expensive, set. Bait pricing is something like leader pricing. But here the seller *doesn't* plan to sell many at the low price.

If bait pricing is successful, the demand for higher-quality products expands. This approach may be a sensible part of a strategy to trade up customers. And customers may be well served if—once in the store—they find a higher-priced product offers features better suited to their needs. But bait pricing is also criticized as unethical.

Is bait pricing ethical?

Extremely aggressive and sometimes dishonest bait-pricing advertising has given this method a bad reputation. Some stores make it very difficult to buy the bait item. The Federal Trade Commission considers this type of bait pricing a deceptive act and has banned its use in interstate commerce. Even well-known chains like Sears have been criticized for bait-and-switch pricing.

If the price of a product is lower than the target market's reference price, it is likely to be viewed as offering better customer value. eCampus's ad claims that it saves students up to 50 percent on textbooks that come with free shipping. Hallmark's ad prompts consumers to think of the reference price for a greeting card in terms of the value it creates for the person who receives the card.

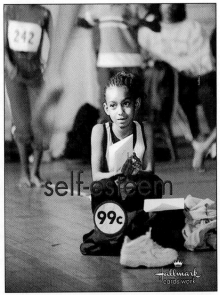

Psychological pricing—some prices just seem right

Price lining—a few prices cover the field

Psychological pricing means setting prices that have special appeal to target customers. Some people think there are whole ranges of prices that potential customers see as the same. So price cuts in these ranges do not increase the quantity sold. But just below this range, customers may buy more. Then, at even lower prices, the quantity demanded stays the same again—and so on. Exhibit 17–12 shows the kind of demand curve that leads to psychological pricing. Vertical drops mark the price ranges that customers see as the same. Pricing research shows that there *are* such demand curves.[12]

Odd-even pricing is setting prices that end in certain numbers. For example, products selling below $50 often end in the number 5 or the number 9—such as 49 cents or $24.95. Prices for higher-priced products are often $1 or $2 below the next even dollar figure—such as $99 rather than $100.

Some marketers use odd-even pricing because they think consumers react better to these prices—perhaps seeing them as "substantially" lower than the next highest even price. Marketers using these prices seem to assume that they have a rather jagged demand curve—that slightly higher prices will substantially reduce the quantity demanded. Long ago, some retailers used odd-even prices to force their clerks to make change. Then the clerks had to record the sale and could not pocket the money.[13]

Price lining is setting a few price levels for a product line and then marking all items at these prices. This approach assumes that customers have a certain reference price in mind that they expect to pay for a product. For example, many neckties are priced between $20 and $50. In price lining, there are only a few prices within this range. Ties will not be priced at $20, $21, $22, $23, and so on. They might be priced at four levels—$20, $30, $40, and $50.

Price lining has advantages other than just matching prices to what consumers expect to pay. The main advantage is simplicity—for both salespeople and customers. It is less confusing than having many prices. Some customers may consider items in only one price class. Their big decision, then, is which item(s) to choose at that price.

Demand-backward pricing starts with the retail price for a particular item and then works backward—subtracting the typical margins that channel members expect.

For retailers, price lining has several advantages. Sales may increase because (1) they can offer a bigger variety in each price class and (2) it's easier to get customers to make decisions within one price class. Stock planning is simpler because demand is larger at the relatively few prices. Price lining can also reduce costs because inventory needs are lower.

Demand-backward pricing and prestige pricing

Demand-backward pricing is setting an acceptable final consumer price and working backward to what a producer can charge. It is commonly used by producers of consumer products, especially shopping products such as women's clothing and appliances. It is also used with gift items for which customers will spend a specific amount—because they are seeking a $10 or a $15 gift. Here a reverse cost-plus pricing process is used. This method has been called market-minus pricing.

The producer starts with the retail (reference) price for a particular item and then works backward—subtracting the typical margins that channel members expect. This gives the approximate price the producer can charge. Then the average or planned marketing expenses can be subtracted from this price to find how much can be spent producing the item. Candy companies do this. They alter the size of the candy bar to keep the bar at the expected price.

Prestige pricing is setting a rather high price to suggest high quality or high status. Some target customers want the best, so they will buy at a high price. But if the price seems cheap, they worry about quality and don't buy. Prestige pricing is most common for luxury products such as furs, jewelry, and perfume.

Exhibit 17-13
Demand Curve Showing a Prestige Pricing Situation

It is also common in service industries, where the customer can't see the product in advance and relies on price to judge its quality. Target customers who respond to prestige pricing give the marketing manager an unusual demand curve. Instead of a normal down-sloping curve, the curve goes down for a while and then bends back to the left again.[14] See Exhibit 17–13.

PRICING A FULL LINE

Our emphasis has been, and will continue to be, on the problem of pricing an individual product mainly because this makes our discussion clearer. But most marketing managers are responsible for more than one product. In fact, their "product" may be the whole company line! So we'll discuss this matter briefly.

Full-line pricing—market- or firm-oriented

Full-line pricing is setting prices for a whole line of products. How to do this depends on which of two basic situations a firm is facing.

In one case, all products in the company's line are aimed at the same general target market, which makes it important for all prices and value to be logically related. This is a common approach with shopping products. A producer of TV sets might offer several models with different features at different prices to give its target customers some choice. The difference among the prices and benefits should appear reasonable when the target customers are evaluating them. Customer perceptions can be important here. A low-priced item, even one that is a good value at that price, may drag down the image of the higher end of the line. Alternatively, one item that consumers do not see as a good value may spill over to how they judge other products in the line.

In other cases, the different products in the line are aimed at entirely different target markets so there doesn't have to be any relation between the various prices. A chemical producer of a wide variety of products with several target markets, for example, probably should price each product separately.

Costs are complicated in full-line pricing

The marketing manager must try to recover all costs on the whole line—perhaps by pricing quite low on more competitive items and much higher on ones with unique benefits. However, estimating costs for each product is a challenge because there is no single right way to assign a company's fixed costs to each of the products. Regardless of how costs are allocated, any cost-oriented pricing method that doesn't consider demand can lead to very unrealistic prices. To avoid mistakes, the marketing manager should judge demand for the whole line as well as demand for each individual product in each target market.

Complementary product pricing

Complementary product pricing is setting prices on several products as a group. This may lead to one product being priced very low so that the profits from another product will increase, thus increasing the product group's total profits. When Gillette introduced the M3Power battery-powered wet-shaving system, the shaver, two blade cartridges, and a Duracell battery had a relatively low suggested retail price of $14.99. However, the blade refill cartridges, which must be replaced frequently, come in a package of four at a hefty price of $10.99.

Complementary product pricing differs from full-line pricing because different production facilities may be involved—so there's no cost allocation problem. Instead, the problem is really understanding the target market and the demand curves for each of the complementary products. Then various combinations of prices can be tried to see what set will be best for reaching the company's pricing objectives.

Product-bundle pricing—one price for several products

A firm that offers its target market several different products may use **product-bundle pricing**—setting one price for a set of products. Firms that use product-bundle pricing usually set the overall price so that it's cheaper for the customer to buy the products at the same time than separately. Drugstores sometimes bundle the cost of a roll of film and the cost of the processing. A bank may offer a product-bundle price for a safe-deposit box, traveler's checks, and a savings account. Sprint bundles wireless minutes and long distance. Bundling encourages customers to spend more and buy products that they might not otherwise buy—because the added cost of the extras is not as high as it would normally be, so the value is better.

Most firms that use product-bundle pricing also set individual prices for the unbundled products. This may increase demand by attracting customers who want one item in a product assortment but don't want the extras. Many firms treat services this way. A software company may have a product-bundle price for its software and access to a toll-free telephone assistance service. However, customers who don't need help can pay a lower price and get just the software.[15]

BID PRICING AND NEGOTIATED PRICING DEPEND HEAVILY ON COSTS

A new price for every job

We introduced the issue of competitive bidding and reverse auctions in Chapter 6. But now let's take a closer look at bid pricing. **Bid pricing** means offering a specific price for each possible job rather than setting a price that applies for all customers. In an e-commerce reverse auction for a standardized product, this may just require that the manager decide the firm's lowest acceptable selling price. But in many situations bid pricing is more complicated. For example, building contractors usually must bid on possible projects. And many companies selling services (like cleaning or data processing) must submit bids for jobs they would like to have.

A big problem in bid pricing on a complicated job is estimating all the costs that will apply. This may sound easy, but a complicated bid may involve thousands of cost components. Further, management must include an overhead charge and a charge for profit.

Because many firms use an e-mail distribution list or website to solicit bids, the process is fast and easy for the buyer. But a seller has to be geared up to set a price and respond quickly. However, this system does allow the seller to set a price based on the precise situation and what costs and revenue are involved.

Bids are usually based on purchase specifications provided by the customer. The specs may be sent as an attachment to an e-mail message or, increasingly, they are posted on a website. Sometimes the seller can win the business, even with a higher bid price, by suggesting changes in the specs that save the customer money.

At times it isn't possible to figure out specs or costs in advance. This may lead to a negotiated contract where the customer agrees to pay the supplier's total cost plus an agreed-on profit figure (say, 10 percent of costs or a dollar amount)—after the job is finished.

Ethical issues in cost-plus bid pricing

Some unethical sellers give bid prices based on cost-plus contracts a bad reputation by faking their records to make costs seem higher than they really are. In other cases, there may be honest debate about what costs should be allowed. We've already considered, for instance, the difficulties in allocating fixed costs.

Demand must be considered too

Competition must be considered when adding in overhead and profit for a bid price. Usually, the customer will get several bids and accept the lowest one. So unthinking addition of typical overhead and profit rates should be avoided. Some bidders use the same overhead and profit rates on all jobs, regardless of competition, and then are surprised when they don't get some jobs.[16]

Negotiated prices— what will a specific customer pay?

Sometimes the customer asks for bids and then singles out the company that submits the *most attractive* bid, not necessarily the lowest, for further bargaining. What a customer will buy—if the customer buys at all—depends on the **negotiated price**, a price set based on bargaining between the buyer and seller. As with simple bid pricing, negotiated pricing is most common in situations where the marketing mix is adjusted for each customer—so bargaining may involve the whole marketing mix, not just the price level. Through the bargaining process, the seller tries to determine what aspects of the marketing mix are most important—and worth the most—to the customer.

Sellers must know their costs to negotiate prices effectively. However, negotiated pricing is a demand-oriented approach. Here the seller analyzes very carefully a particular customer's position on a demand curve, or on different possible demand curves based on different offerings, rather than the overall demand curve for a group of customers.

The Internet is making it fast and easy for customers to communicate their needs to a larger number of suppliers to solicit competitively based bid prices.

CONCLUSION

In this chapter, we discussed various approaches to price setting. Generally, retailers and wholesalers use markups. Some just use the same markups for all their items because it is simpler, but this is usually not the best approach. It's more effective to consider customer demand, competition, and how markups relate to turnover and profit.

It's important for marketing managers to understand costs; if customers are not willing to pay a price that is at least high enough to cover all of the costs of the marketing mix the firm won't be profitable. So, we describe the different types of cost that a marketing manager needs to understand and how average-cost pricing is used to set prices. But, we note that this approach can fail because it ignores demand. We look at break-even analysis, which is a variation of the cost-oriented approach. It is useful for analyzing possible prices. However, managers must estimate demand to evaluate the chance of reaching these possible break-even points.

The major difficulty with demand-oriented pricing involves estimating the demand curve. But experienced managers, perhaps aided by marketing research, can estimate the nature of demand for their products. Even if estimates are not exact, they can help to get prices in the right ballpark—and there's usually a profitable range around the most profitable price. So marketers should consider demand when setting prices. We see this with value in use pricing, psychological pricing, odd-even pricing, full-line pricing, and even bid pricing. Understanding the factors that influence customer price sensitivity can make these approaches more effective.

While we do not recommend that cost-oriented approaches be used by themselves, they do help the marketing manager understand the firm's profitability. Pricing decisions should consider the cost of offering the whole marketing mix. But smart marketers do not accept cost as a given—target marketers always look for ways to be more efficient—to reduce costs while improving the value that they offer customers.

KEY TERMS

markup, 440

markup (percent), 441

markup chain, 442

stockturn rate, 443

average-cost pricing, 444

total fixed cost, 445

total variable cost, 445

total cost, 446

average cost (per unit), 446

average fixed cost (per unit), 446

average variable cost (per unit), 446

break-even analysis, 449

break-even point (BEP), 449

fixed-cost (FC) contribution per unit, 450

marginal analysis, 451

value in use pricing, 454

reference price, 455

leader pricing, 456

bait pricing, 456

psychological pricing, 458

odd-even pricing, 458

price lining, 458

demand-backward pricing, 459

prestige pricing, 459

full-line pricing, 459

complementary product pricing, 460

product-bundle pricing, 460

bid pricing, 460

negotiated price, 461

QUESTIONS AND PROBLEMS

1. Why do many department stores seek a markup of about 30 percent when some discount houses operate on a 20 percent markup?

2. A producer distributed its riding lawn mowers through wholesalers and retailers. The retail selling price was $800, and the manufacturing cost to the company was $312. The retail markup was 35 percent and the wholesale markup 20 percent. (*a*) What was the cost to the wholesaler? To the retailer? (*b*) What percentage markup did the producer take?

3. Relate the concept of stock turnover to the growth of mass-merchandising. Use a simple example in your answer.

4. If total fixed costs are $200,000 and total variable costs are $100,000 at the output of 20,000 units, what are the probable total fixed costs and total variable costs at an output of 10,000 units? What are the average fixed costs, average variable costs, and average costs at these two output levels? Explain what additional information you would want to determine what price should be charged.

5. Construct an example showing that mechanical use of a very large or a very small markup might still lead to unprofitable operation while some intermediate price would be profitable. Draw a graph and show the break-even point(s).

6. The Davis Company's fixed costs for the year are estimated at $200,000. Its product sells for $250. The variable cost per unit is $200. Sales for the coming year are expected to reach $1,250,000. What is the break-even point? Expected profit? If sales are forecast at only $875,000, should the Davis Company shut down operations? Why?

7. Discuss the idea of drawing separate demand curves for different market segments. It seems logical because each target market should have its own marketing mix. But won't this lead to many demand curves and possible prices? And what will this mean with respect to functional discounts and varying prices in the marketplace? Will it be legal? Will it be practical?

8. Distinguish between leader pricing and bait pricing. What do they have in common? How can their use affect a marketing mix?

9. Cite a local example of psychological pricing and evaluate whether it makes sense.

10. Cite a local example of odd-even pricing and evaluate whether it makes sense.

11. How does a prestige pricing policy fit into a marketing mix? Would exclusive distribution be necessary?

12. Is a full-line pricing policy available only to producers? Cite local examples of full-line pricing. Why is full-line pricing important?

CREATING MARKETING PLANS

The Marketing Plan Coach software on the Student CD includes a sample marketing plan for Hillside Veterinary Clinic. Look through the "Marketing Strategy" section.

a. A veterinary clinic must have some system for dealing with emergencies that occur on weekends and at night when the clinic is closed. Individual vets usually rotate so that someone is always on call to handle emergencies. The price for emergency care is usually 50 percent higher than the price for care during normal hours. Do you think that Hillside should charge higher prices for emergency care? Does it fit with Hillside's strategy?

b. Some customers have expensive pedigree dogs and cats and are less price sensitive than others about fees for veterinary care. Do you think that it would be possible for Hillside to charge higher prices in caring for expensive pets? Why or why not?

SUGGESTED CASES

17. Healthy Water, Inc.   24. Custom Wire, Inc.   27. Premier Molding, Inc.   35. Pepe's Pizza

COMPUTER-AIDED PROBLEM

17. BREAK-EVEN/PROFIT ANALYSIS

This problem lets you see the dynamics of break-even analysis. The starting values (costs, revenues, etc.) for this problem are from the break-even analysis example in this chapter (see Exhibit 17–8).

The first column computes a break-even point. You can change costs and prices to figure new break-even points (in units and dollars). The second column goes further. There you can specify target profit level, and the unit and dollar sales needed to achieve your target profit level will be computed. You can also estimate possible sales quantities, and the program will compute costs, sales, and profits. Use this spreadsheet to address the following issues.

a. Vary the selling price between $1.00 and $1.40. Prepare a table showing how the break-even point (in units and dollars) changes at the different price levels.

b. If you hope to earn a target profit of $15,000, how many units would you have to sell? What would total cost be? Total sales dollars? (*Note:* Use the right-hand ["profit analysis"] column in the spreadsheet.)

c. Using the "profit analysis" column (column 2), allow your estimate of the sales quantity to vary between 64,000 and 96,000. Prepare a table that shows, for each quantity level, what happens to average cost per unit and profit. Explain why average cost changes as it does over the different quantity values.

For additional questions related to this problem, see Exercise 17-4 in the *Learning Aid for Use with Essentials of Marketing*, 11th edition.

Ethical Marketing in a Consumer-Oriented World: Appraisal and Challenges

The worldwide drive toward market-directed economies is dramatic evidence that consumer-citizens want freedom and choices not only in politics but in markets. Command economies simply weren't able to meet needs. Even in China, government officials have been gradually softening their hard line on central planning and now allow Western firms to market products that will improve the life of Chinese consumers.

Although there's much talk about the world as a global village, we're not there yet. Someone in a real village on the plains of Kenya may be able to get a glimpse of the quality of life that consumers in the advanced Western economies enjoy, but for that person it doesn't seem real. What is real is the struggle to meet the basic physical needs of life—to survive starvation, malnutrition, and epidemic-carrying water. The plight of consumers doesn't seem quite as severe in the emerging democracies, like those in Eastern Europe. But the vast majority of citizen-consumers in those societies can still only wonder if they'll ever have choices among a wide variety of goods and services—and the income to buy them—that most consumers take for granted in the United States, Canada, England, most countries in Western Europe, Australia, and a few other advanced economies.

The challenges faced by consumers, and marketing managers, in the advanced economies seem minor by contrast. In England, for example, some consumers who live in villages that are off the beaten path may worry, instead, that they are not included in the 96 percent of the British population served by Tesco delivery vans. Tesco, the largest supermarket chain in England, created its online shopping service for groceries (and hundreds of other products) just a few years ago, but now its fleet of vans make over 100,000 deliveries a week.

If online shopping for groceries has had a slower start in the U.S., it just may be because many Americans are more interested in instant gratification. We expect the corner convenience store to have a nice selection of frozen gourmet dinners that we can prepare in minutes in a microwave oven. Or perhaps that's too much hassle. After all, Domino's will deliver a hot pizza in less than 30 minutes. And McDonald's has our McGriddles ready when we pull up at the drive-thru at 7 in the morning. In a relative sense, few of the world's consumers can expect so much, and get so much of what they expect.

But is it a good thing that firms give us what we want? For example, national attention is now directed toward problems of obesity, especially among children. In the U.S., 37 percent of children weigh too much. However, that surge of obesity among children is a global trend. Nutritionists say that in the U.S. and elsewhere, a key culprit is too much fat, starch, and sugar in diets. World Health Organization experts say that today's levels of childhood obesity will later lead to an explosion of illnesses (like heart disease, diabetes, and hypertension) that will drain economies, create enormous suffering, and cause premature deaths. Many nutritionists and public-health officials point the finger of blame at food processors and fast food. When a group of obese teenagers sued McDonald's, claiming that it made them fat, the widely publicized case was fodder for jokes on late-night TV shows. But fast-food companies are not laughing. The judge threw out the case but left open the door for future suits. Some legal experts say that this is just the beginning of legal actions—and they draw the parallel with suits against tobacco companies 30 years ago. Many fast-food companies are scrambling to add salads and other low-fat fare to their menus. But should consumers have

the right to choose high-fat foods if that is what they want?

When you think about the contrast between problems of starvation and too much fast food, it's not hard to decide which consumers are better off. But is that just a straw man comparison? Is the situation in the less-developed nations one extreme, with the system in the United States and similar societies just as extreme—only in a different way?

Would we be better off if we didn't put quite so much emphasis on marketing?

Do we need so many brands of products? Does all the money spent on advertising really help consumers? Should we expect to be able to get fast food any hour of the day—or order groceries over the Internet and have a van deliver them to the front door? Or, conversely, do all of these choices just increase the prices consumers pay without really adding anything of value? More generally, does marketing serve society well?

These questions are what this chapter is about. Now that you have a better understanding of what marketing is all about, and how the marketing manager contributes to the macro-marketing process, you should be able to decide whether marketing costs too much.[1]

LEARNING OBJECTIVES

Throughout the text we've discussed ways that marketing can help customers while also meeting a firm's objectives. We've also considered many related ethical and societal questions. In this chapter, we evaluate the overall costs and benefits of marketing to society. This leads into an explanation of how to prepare a marketing plan—because the marketing plan integrates all of the decisions in the marketing strategy planning process and thus guides the firm toward more effective marketing.

When you finish this chapter, you should:

1. understand why marketing must be evaluated differently at the micro and macro levels.

2. understand why the text argues that micro-marketing costs too much.

3. understand why the text argues that macro-marketing does not cost too much.

4. understand all of the elements of the marketing strategy planning process and strategy decisions for the four Ps.

5. know how to prepare a marketing plan and how it relates to the marketing strategy planning process.

6. know some of the challenges marketers face as they work to develop ethical marketing strategies that serve consumers' needs.

HOW SHOULD MARKETING BE EVALUATED?

We must evaluate at two levels

We've stressed the need for marketing to satisfy customers at a cost that customers consider a good value. So, in this final chapter we'll focus on both customer satisfaction and the costs of marketing as we evaluate marketing's impact on society (see Exhibit 18–1). As we discussed in Chapter 1, it's useful to distinguish between the two levels of marketing: managerial (micro) marketing (how an individual firm runs) and macro marketing (how the whole markeing system works). Some complaints against marketing are aimed at only one of these levels at a time. In other cases, the criticisms seem to be directed to one level but actually are aimed at the other. Some critics of specific ads, for example, probably would not be satisfied with any advertising. When evaluating marketing, we must treat each of these levels separately.

Some critics argue that the many choices in some product categories, like cell phone services, can be confusing to consumers. It is true that a market-directed economy produces many choices, but is that a bad thing? Would you rather make a choice that best fits your own preferences—or have things simpler with choices made for you by someone else, perhaps the critics?

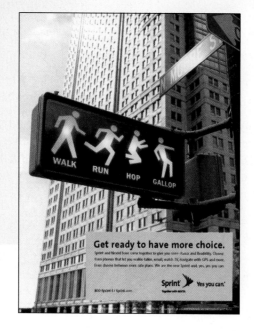

Exhibit 18–1   Ethical Marketing in a Consumer-Oriented World

Nation's objectives affect evaluation

Different nations have different social and economic objectives. Dictatorships, for example, may be mainly concerned with satisfying the needs of society as seen by the political elite. In a socialist state, the objective might be to satisfy society's needs as defined by government planners.

Consumer satisfaction is the objective in the United States

In the United States, *the basic objective of our market-directed economic system has been to satisfy consumer needs as they, the consumers, see them.* This objective implies that political freedom and economic freedom go hand in hand and that citizens in a free society have the right to live as they choose. The majority of American consumers would be unwilling to give up the freedom of choice they now enjoy. The same can be said for Canada, Great Britain, and most other countries in the European Union. However, for focus we will concentrate on marketing as it exists in American society.

Therefore, let's try to evaluate the operation of marketing in the American economy—where the present objective is to satisfy consumer needs *as consumers see them*. This is the essence of our system.

CAN CONSUMER SATISFACTION BE MEASURED?

Since consumer satisfaction is our objective, marketing's effectiveness must be measured by *how well* it satisfies consumers. There have been various efforts to measure overall consumer satisfaction not only in the United States but also in other countries. For example, a team of researchers at the University of Michigan has created the American Customer Satisfaction Index based on regular interviews with thousands of customers of about 200 companies in 39 industries. Similar studies are available for member countries of the European Union.

Satisfaction depends on individual aspirations

This sort of index makes it possible to track changes in consumer satisfaction measures over time and even allows comparison among countries. That's potentially useful. Yet there are limits to interpreting any measure of consumer satisfaction when we try to evaluate macro-marketing effectiveness in any absolute sense. One basic issue is that satisfaction depends on and is *relative to* your level of aspiration or expectation. Less prosperous consumers begin to expect more out of an economy as they see the higher living standards of others. Also, aspiration levels tend to rise with repeated successes and fall with failures. Products considered satisfactory one day may not be satisfactory the next day, or vice versa. Twenty-five years ago, most people were satisfied with a 21-inch color TV that pulled in three or four channels. But once you become accustomed to a large-screen HD model and enjoy all the options possible with a digital satellite receiver and a DVR, that old TV is never the same again. And when interactive "on demand" broadcast systems become more widespread, today's most satisfying units won't seem quite so acceptable.

In addition, consumer satisfaction is a highly personal concept—and looking at the "average" satisfaction of a whole society does not provide a complete picture for evaluating macro-marketing effectiveness. At a minimum, some consumers are more satisfied than others. So although efforts to measure satisfaction are useful, any evaluation of macro-marketing effectiveness has to be largely subjective.

Probably the supreme test is whether the macro-marketing system satisfies enough individual consumer-citizens so that they vote—in the ballot box—to keep it running. So far, we've done so in the United States.[2]

Planetfeedback.com is a website that makes it easy for consumers to give feedback to companies. Of course, some feedback is clear from customers' choices in the marketplace. For example, Country Inns & Suites by Carlson has gained positive feedback by providing customers with a satisfying experience at an affordable price. J.D. Power and Associates ranked it "Highest in Guest Satisfaction among Mid-Price Hotel Chains with Limited Service."

There are many measures of micro-marketing effectiveness

Measuring the marketing effectiveness of an individual firm is also difficult, but it can be done. Expectations may change just as other aspects of the marketing environment change—so firms have to do a good job of coping with the change. Individual business firms can and should try to measure how well their marketing mixes satisfy their customers (or why they fail). In fact, most large firms now have some type of ongoing effort to determine whether they're satisfying their target markets. For example, the J.D. Power and Associates marketing research firm is well known for its studies of consumer satisfaction with different makes of automobiles and computers. And the American Customer Satisfaction Index is also used to rate individual companies.

Many large and small firms measure customer satisfaction with attitude research studies. Other widely used methods include comment cards, e-mail response features on websites, unsolicited consumer responses (usually complaints), opinions of middlemen and salespeople, market test results, and profits. Of course, customers may be very satisfied about some aspects of what a firm is doing but dissatisfied about other dimensions of performance.[3]

> **Internet EXERCISE**
>
> Let's take a closer look at the American Customer Satisfaction Index (ACSI). Go to the organization's website (**www.theacsi.org**). Click on "ACSI Scores" and look at "Scores by Industry." In some industries, ACSI has been measuring customer satisfaction since 1994. What industries have shown the greatest improvement since that time? What industries have declined in customer satisfaction? Why do you think some industries have moved up, while others have moved down?

In our market-directed system, it's up to each customer to decide how effectively individual firms satisfy his or her needs. Usually, customers will buy more of the products that satisfy them—and they'll do it repeatedly. That's why firms that develop really satisfying marketing mixes are able to develop profitable long-term relationships with the customers that they serve. Because efficient marketing plans can increase profits, profits can be used as a rough measure of a firm's efficiency in satisfying customers. Nonprofit organizations have a different bottom line, but they too will fail if they don't satisfy supporters and get the resources they need to continue to operate.

Evaluating marketing effectiveness is difficult, but not impossible

It's easy to see why opinions differ concerning the effectiveness of micro- and macro-marketing. If the objective of the economy is clearly defined, however—and the argument is stripped of emotion—the big questions about marketing effectiveness probably *can* be answered.

In this chapter, we argue that micro-marketing (how individual firms and channels operate) frequently *does* cost too much but that macro-marketing (how the whole marketing system operates) *does not* cost too much, *given the present objective of the American economy—consumer satisfaction*. Don't accept this position as *the* answer but rather as a point of view. In the end, you'll have to make your own judgment.[4]

MICRO-MARKETING OFTEN DOES COST TOO MUCH

Throughout the text, we've explored what marketing managers could or should do to help their firms do a better job of satisfying customers—while achieving company objectives. Many firms implement highly successful marketing programs, but others are still too production-oriented and inefficient. For customers of these latter firms, micro-marketing often does cost too much.

Research shows that many consumers are not satisfied. But you know that already. All of us have had experiences when we weren't satisfied—when some firm didn't deliver on its promises. And the problem is much bigger than some marketers want to

Maxwell House ready-to-drink coffee came in a package that looked like a milk carton, but it had an inner foil liner that caused problems when consumers heated the carton in a microwave. There was no mention on the package that it might make good iced coffee. Fixing these problems might not have made the product a success, but *not* fixing them certainly contributed to its failure.

believe. Research suggests that the majority of consumer complaints are never reported. Worse, many complaints that are reported never get fully resolved.

The failure rate is high

Further evidence that too many firms are too production-oriented—and not nearly as efficient as they could be—is the fact that so many new products fail. New and old businesses—even ones that in the past were leaders in their markets—fail regularly too.

Generally speaking, marketing inefficiencies are due to one or more of three reasons:

1. Lack of interest in or understanding of the sometimes fickle customer.
2. Improper blending of the four Ps—caused in part by overemphasis on internal problems as contrasted with a customer orientation.
3. Lack of understanding of or adjustment to the marketing environment, especially what competitors do.

Any of these problems can easily be a fatal flaw—the sort of thing that leads to business failures. A firm can't create value if it doesn't have a clue what customers think or say. Even if a firm listens to the "voice of the customer," there's no incentive for the customer to buy if the benefits of the marketing mix don't exceed the costs. And if the firm succeeds in coming up with a marketing mix with benefits greater than costs, it still won't be a superior value unless it's better than what competitors offer.

The high cost of missed opportunities

Another sign of failure is the inability of firms to identify new target markets and new opportunities. A new marketing mix that isn't offered doesn't fail—but the lost opportunity can be significant for both a firm and society. Too many managers seize on whatever strategy seems easiest rather than seeking really new ways to satisfy customers. Too many companies stifle really innovative thinking. Layers of bureaucracy and a "that's not the way we do things" mentality just snuff it out.

On the other hand, not every new idea is a good idea for every company. For example, there is no doubt that e-commerce is having a dramatic effect in improving how many firms serve their customers. But many firms have lost millions of dollars with failed efforts to capitalize on the Internet or some "hot" technology. Just jumping on the "what's new" bandwagon—without stopping to figure out how it is going to really satisfy the customer and result in profit for the firm—is as much a ticket for failure as being too slow or bureaucratic.

Your firm has a new strategy that will make its established product obsolete. However, it will take a year before you are ready to implement the new strategy. If you announce your plan in advance, profits will disappear because many customers and intermediaries will delay purchases until the new product is released. If you don't announce the new plan, customers and middlemen will continue to buy the established product as their needs dictate, but some will be stuck owning the inferior product and won't do business with you again in the future. How would you decide what to do?

Micro-marketing does cost too much, but things are changing

For reasons like these, marketing does cost too much in many firms. Despite much publicity, the marketing concept is not applied in many places.

But not all firms and marketers deserve criticism. More of them *are* becoming customer-oriented. And many are paying more attention to market-oriented planning to carry out the marketing concept more effectively. Throughout the text, we've highlighted firms and strategies that are making a difference. The successes of innovative firms—like Wal-Mart, Bank of America, 3M, IKEA, Best Buy, Tesco, GE, and Starbucks—do not go unnoticed. Yes, they make some mistakes. That's human—and marketing is a human enterprise. But they have also shown the results that market-oriented strategy planning can produce.

Another encouraging sign is that more companies are recognizing that they need a diverse set of backgrounds and talents to meet the increasingly varied needs of their increasingly global customers. They're shedding "not-invented-here" biases and embracing new technologies, comparing what they do with the best practices of firms in totally different industries, and teaming up with outside specialists who can bring a fresh perspective.

Managers who adopt the marketing concept as a way of business life do a better job. They look for target market opportunities and carefully blend the elements of the marketing mix to meet their customers' needs. As more of these managers rise in business, we can look forward to much lower micro-marketing costs and strategies that do a better job of satisfying customer needs.

MACRO-MARKETING DOES NOT COST TOO MUCH

Some critics of marketing take aim at the macro-marketing system. They typically argue that the macro-marketing system causes a poor use of resources and leads to an unfair distribution of income. Most of these complaints imply that some marketing activities by individual firms should not be permitted—and because they are, our macro-marketing system does a less-than-satisfactory job. Let's look at some of these positions to help you form your own opinion.

Micro-efforts help the economy grow

Some critics feel that marketing helps create a monopoly or at least monopolistic competition. Further, they think this leads to higher prices, restricted output, and reduction in national income and employment.

It's true that firms in a market-directed economy try to carve out separate monopolistic markets for themselves with new products. But consumers do have a choice. They don't *have* to buy the new product unless they think it's a better value. The old products are still available. In fact, to meet the new competition, prices of the old products usually drop. And that makes them even more available.

Over several years, the innovator's profits may rise—but rising profits also encourage further innovation by competitors. This leads to new investments, which contribute to economic growth and higher levels of national income and employment. Around the world, many countries failed to achieve their potential for economic growth under command systems because this type of profit incentive didn't exist.

Even in mature product categories, marketing stimulates innovation and the development of new ways to meet customers' needs. For example, greater interest in healthy eating has prompted Sara Lee to develop a whole grain bread that tastes like regular white bread, and Marie's salad dressing achieves its straight-from-the-garden taste with no preservatives or trans fat.

Even now, many of the regulations that are imposed by the developed countries are left over from old ways of thinking and get in the way of progress.

Increased profits also attract competition. Profits and prices then begin to drop as new competitors enter the market and begin producing somewhat similar products. (Recall the rise and fall of industry profit during the product life cycle.)

Is advertising a waste of resources?

Advertising is the most criticized of all micro-marketing activities. Indeed, many ads *are* annoying, insulting, misleading, and downright ineffective. This is one reason why micro-marketing often does cost too much. However, advertising can also make both the micro- and macro-marketing processes work better.

Advertising is an economical way to inform large numbers of potential customers about a firm's products. Provided that a product satisfies customer needs, advertising can increase demand for the product—resulting in economies of scale in manufacturing, distribution, and sales. Because these economies may more than offset advertising costs, advertising can actually *lower* prices to the consumer.[5]

Consumers are not puppets

The idea that firms can manipulate consumers to buy anything the company chooses to produce simply isn't true. A consumer who buys a soft drink that tastes terrible won't buy another can of that brand, regardless of how much it's advertised. In fact, many new products fail the test of the market. Not even large corporations are assured of success every time they launch a new product. Consider, for example, the dismal fate of Pets.com and eToys.com, Ford's Edsel, Sony's beta format VCRs, Xerox's personal computers, and half of the TV programs put on the air in recent years by NBC. And if powerful corporations know some way to get people to buy products against their will, would companies like Lucent, General Motors, and Eastern Airlines ever have gone through long periods losing hundreds of millions of dollars?

Needs and wants change

Consumer needs and wants change constantly. Few of us would care to live the way our grandparents lived when they were our age. Marketing's job is not just to satisfy consumer wants as they exist at any particular point in time. Rather, marketing must keep looking for new *and* better ways to create value and serve consumers.[6]

Does marketing make people materialistic?

There is no doubt that marketing caters to materialistic values. However, people disagree as to whether marketing creates these values or simply appeals to values already there.

Even in the most primitive societies, people want to accumulate possessions. The tendency for ancient pharaohs to surround themselves with wealth and treasures can hardly be attributed to the persuasive powers of advertising agencies!

Products do improve the quality of life

Clearly, the quality of life can't be measured just in terms of quantities of material goods. But when we view products as the means to an end rather than the end itself, they *do* make it possible to satisfy higher-level needs. The Internet, for example, empowers people with information in ways that few of us could have even imagined a decade ago.

Marketing reflects our own values

Critics say that advertising elevates the wrong values—for example, by relying on sex appeal to get attention—and generally sending the signal that what really matters most is self-gratification. For example, GoDaddy.com sells Internet domain names and related services. Its stated objective for its 2005 Super Bowl ad was to create the most talked about ad ever, and it figured that a risqué ad was the way to

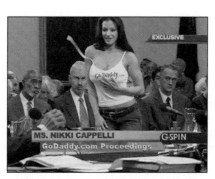

go. The ad that it ultimately aired (after trying another dozen or so ideas that were rejected as inappropriate for TV) was a spoof on Janet Jackson's "wardrobe malfunction" during the Super Bowl halftime show the previous year. The sexy woman dancing around in the commercial doesn't have anything to do with GoDaddy.com, but she did get a lot of attention and GoDaddy's awareness levels went up significantly. A survey showed that it was one of the four most liked commercials during the Super Bowl and the year, but also one of the four most disliked. There are thousands of other ads that rely on something related to sex to get attention. But, is it advertising that creates interest in sex or something else? Experts who study values seem to agree that, in the short run, marketing reflects social values, while in the long run it enhances and reinforces them. Further, many companies work hard to figure out their customers' beliefs and values. Then they refuse to use ads that would be offensive to their target customers.[7]

Not all needs are met

Some critics argue that our macro-marketing system is flawed because it does not provide solutions to important problems, such as questions about how to help the homeless, the uneducated, dependent children, minorities who have suffered discrimination, the elderly poor, and the sick. Many of these people do live in dire circumstances. But is that the result of a market-directed system?

There is no doubt that many firms focus their effort on people who can pay for what they have to offer. But as the forces of competition drive down prices, more people are able to afford more of what they need. And the matching of supply and demand stimulates economic growth, creates jobs, and spreads income among more people. In other words, a market-directed economy makes efficient use of resources. However, it can't guarantee that government aid programs are effective. It doesn't ensure that all voters and politicians agree on which problems should be solved first— or how taxes should be set and allocated. It can't eliminate the possibility of a child being ignored.

These are important societal issues. Citizen-consumers in a democratic society assign some responsibilities to business and some to government. Ultimately, consumer-citizens vote in the ballot box for how they want governments to deal with these concerns—just as they vote with their dollars for which firms to support. As more managers in the public sector understand and apply marketing concepts, we should be able to do a better job meeting the needs of all people.

MARKETING STRATEGY PLANNING PROCESS REQUIRES LOGIC AND CREATIVITY

We've said that our macro-marketing system *does not* cost too much, given that customer satisfaction is the present objective of our economy. But we admit that the performance of many business firms leaves a lot to be desired. This presents a challenge to serious-minded students and marketers—and raises the question: What needs to be done?

We hope that this book has convinced you that a large part of the answer to that question is that the effectiveness and *value of marketing efforts in individual firms is improved significantly when managers take the marketing concept seriously—and when they apply the marketing strategy planning process we've presented.* So, let's briefly review these ideas and show how they can be integrated into a marketing plan.

Marketing strategy planning process brings focus to efforts

Developing a good marketing strategy and turning the strategy into a marketing plan requires creative blending of the ideas we've discussed throughout this text. Exhibit 18–2 provides a broad overview of the major areas we've been talking about. You saw this exhibit before in Chapter 2—before you learned what's really involved in each idea. Now we must integrate ideas about these different areas to narrow down to logical marketing strategies and marketing plans.

As suggested in Exhibit 18–2, developing an effective marketing strategy involves a process of narrowing down to a specific target market and marketing mix that represents a real opportunity. This narrowing-down process requires a thorough understanding of the market. That understanding is enhanced by careful analysis of customers' needs, current or prospective competitors, and the firm's own objectives and resources. Similarly, trends in the external marketing environment may make a potential opportunity more or less attractive.

Swagelok is known in business markets for the quality of the engineering in its fluid system components. Promotion in this product-market typically focuses on technical issues. In contrast, this ad uses a creative image to highlight the extraordinary reliability that differentiates Swagelok's strategy.

www.swagelok.com

If only you could use Swagelok®
for everything.

Extraordinarily reliable industrial fluid system components.
From research and production to distribution and support, the Swagelok mission remains: every component, every connection, each as reliable as the next. For components you can count on, count on Swagelok. Brought to you by more than 200 independent sales and service centers around the globe. So reliable, you wouldn't use anything else, even if you could.

Swagelok

Unfailing reliability from people you rely on.

Exhibit 18-2
Overview of Marketing
Strategy Planning
Process

There are usually more different strategy possibilities than a firm can pursue. Each possible strategy usually has a number of different potential advantages and disadvantages. This can make it difficult to zero in on the best target market and marketing mix. However, as we discussed in Chapter 4, developing a set of specific qualitative

Treif's marketing mix, targeted at firms that process meat, includes this ad for its high-quality slicing equipment, which uses the brand name Zebra-CE. The brand name and the picture of zebras with thick and thin stripes are intended to highlight the thick and thin cutting technology of the equipment, but a potential customer might miss the point and instead be distracted with thoughts of sliced zebra meat. Gardenburger's ad takes a humorous approach, which might appeal to consumers who are cynical about advertisers' sales pitches. On the other hand, Hindu consumers (who would logically be potential customers for Gardenburger products) might find it offensive that the ad alludes to Hindu religious beliefs.

Exhibit 18-3
Strategy Decision
Areas Organized by
the Four Ps

Product	Place	Promotion	Price

• Physical good
• Service
• Features
• Benefits
• Quality level
• Accessories
• Installation
• Instructions
• Warranty
• Product lines
• Packaging
• Branding
	• Objectives
	• Channel type
	• Market exposure
	• Kinds of middlemen
	• Kinds and locations of stores
	• How to handle transporting and storing
	• Service levels
	• Recruiting middlemen
	• Managing channels
		• Objectives
		• Promotion blend
		• Salespeople
		  Kind
		  Number
		  Selection
		  Training
		  Motivation
		• Advertising
		  Targets
		  Kinds of ads
		  Media type
		  Copy thrust
		  Prepared by whom
		• Sales promotion
		• Publicity
			• Objectives
			• Flexibility
			• Level over product life cycle
			• Geographic terms
			• Discounts
			• Allowances

and quantitative screening criteria—to define what business and market(s) the firm wants to compete in—can help eliminate potential strategies that are not well suited to the firm.

Careful analysis helps the manager focus on a strategy that takes advantage of the firm's strengths and opportunities while avoiding its weaknesses and threats to its success. These strengths and weaknesses can be compared with the pros and cons of strategies that are considered. For example, if a firm is considering a strategy that focuses on a target market that is already satisfied by a competitor's offering, finding a competitive advantage might require an innovative new product, improved distribution, more effective promotion, or a better price. Just offering a marketing mix that is like what is available from competitors usually doesn't provide any real basis for the firm to position or differentiate its marketing mix as offering superior customer value.

Marketing manager must blend the four Ps

Exhibit 18–3 reviews the major marketing strategy decision areas organized by the four Ps. Each of these requires careful decision making. Yet marketing planning involves much more than just independent decisions and assembling the parts into a marketing mix. The four Ps must be creatively *blended*—so the firm develops the best mix for its target market. In other words, each decision must work well with all of the others to make a logical whole.

In our discussion, we've given the job of integrating the four Ps strategy decisions to the marketing manager. Now you should see the need for this integrating role. It is easy for specialists to focus on their own areas and expect the rest of the company to work for or around them. This is especially true in larger firms where the size of the whole marketing job is too big for one person. Yet the ideas of the product manager, the advertising manager, the sales manager, the logistics manager, and whoever makes pricing decisions may have to be adjusted to improve the whole mix. It's critical that each marketing mix decision work well with all of the others. A breakdown in any one decision area may doom the whole strategy to failure.

THE MARKETING PLAN BRINGS ALL THE DETAILS TOGETHER

Marketing plan provides a blueprint for implementation

Once the manager has selected the target market, decided on the (integrated) marketing mix to meet that target market's needs, and developed estimates of the costs and revenue for that strategy, it's time to put it all together in the marketing plan. As we explained in Chapter 2, a marketing plan includes the time-related details—including costs and revenues—for a marketing strategy. Thus, the plan basically serves as a blueprint for what the firm will do.

Exhibit 18-4 provides a summary outline of the different sections of a complete marketing plan. You can see that this outline is basically an abridged overview of the topics we've covered throughout the text. Thus, you can flesh out your thinking for any portion of a marketing plan by reviewing the section of the book where that topic is discussed in more detail. Further, the Hillside Veterinary Clinic case on your Student CD gives you a real example of the types of thinking and detail that are included.

Marketing plan spells out the timing of the strategy

Some time schedule is implicit in any strategy. A marketing plan simply spells out this time period and the time-related details. Usually, we think in terms of some reasonable length of time—such as six months, a year, or a few years. But it might be only a month or two in some cases, especially when rapid changes in fashion or technology are important. Or a strategy might be implemented over several years, perhaps the length of the early stages of the product's life.

Although the outline in Exhibit 18-4 does not explicitly show a place for the time frame for the plan or the specific costs for each decision area, these should be included in the plan—along with expected estimates of sales and profit—so that the plan can be compared with *actual performance* in the future. In other words, the plan not only makes it clear to everyone what is to be accomplished and how—it also provides a basis for the control process after the plan is implemented.[8]

A complete plan spells out the reasons for decisions

The plan outline shown in Exhibit 18-4 is quite complete. It doesn't just provide information about marketing mix decisions—it also includes information about customers (including segmenting dimensions), competitors' strategies, other aspects of the marketing environment, and the company's objectives and resources. This material provides important background information relevant to the "why" of the marketing mix and target market decisions.

Too often, managers do not include this information; their plans just lay out the details of the target market and the marketing mix strategy decisions. This shortcut approach is more common when the plan is really just an update of a strategy that has been in place for some time. However, that approach can be risky.

Managers too often make the mistake of casually updating plans in minor ways—perhaps just changing some costs or sales forecasts—but otherwise sticking with what was done in the past. A big problem with this approach is that it's easy to lose sight of why those strategy decisions were made in the first place. When the market situation changes, the original reasons may no longer apply. Yet if the logic for those strategy decisions is not retained, it's easy to miss changes taking place that should result in a plan being reconsidered. For example, a plan that was established in the growth stage of the product life cycle may have been very successful for a number of years. But a marketing manager can't be complacent and assume that success will continue forever. When market maturity hits, the firm may be in for big trouble—unless the basic strategy and plan are modified. If a plan spells out the details of the market analysis and logic for the marketing mix and target market selected, then it is a simple matter to routinely check and update it. Remember: The idea is for all of the analysis and strategy decisions to fit together as an integrated whole. Thus, as some of the elements of the plan or marketing environment change, the whole plan may need a fresh approach.

Exhibit 18–4   Summary Outline of Different Sections of Marketing Plan

<u>Situation Analysis</u>

Company Analysis
  Company objectives and overall marketing objectives
  Company resources (marketing, production, financial, human, etc.)
  Other marketing plans (marketing program)
  Previous marketing strategy
  Major screening criteria relevant to product-market opportunity selected
      Quantitative (ROI, profitability, risk level, etc.)
      Qualitative (nature of business preferred, social responsibility, etc.)
  Major constraints
  Marketing collaborators (current and potential)

Customer Analysis (organizational customers and/or final consumers)
  Product-market
  Possible segmenting dimensions (customer needs, other characteristics)
      Qualifying dimensions and determining dimensions
  Identify target market(s) (one or more specific segments)
      Operational characteristics (demographics, geographic locations, etc.)
  Potential size (number of people, dollar purchase potential, etc.) and likely growth
  Key economic, psychological, and social influences on buying
  Type of buying situation
  Nature of relationship with customers

Competitor Analysis
  Nature of current/likely competition
  Current and prospective competitors (or rivals)
      Current strategies and likely responses to plan
  Competitive barriers to overcome and sources of potential competitive advantage

Analysis of the Market Context—External Market Environment
  Economic environment
  Technological environment
  Political and legal environment
  Cultural and social environment

Key Factors from Situation Analysis
  S.W.O.T.: Strengths, weaknesses, opportunities, and threats from situation analysis

<u>Marketing Plan Objectives</u>
  Specific objectives to be achieved with the marketing strategy

<u>Differentiation and Positioning</u>
  How will marketing mix be differentiated from the competition?
  How will the market offering be positioned?

<u>Marketing Strategy</u>

Overview of the Marketing Strategy
  General direction for the marketing strategy
  Description of how the four Ps fit together

Target Market(s)
  Summary of characteristics of the target market(s) to be approached

Product
  Product class (type of consumer or business product)
  Current product life-cycle stage
  New-product development requirements (people, dollars, time, etc.)
  Product liability, safety, and social responsibility considerations
  Specification of core physical good or service
      Features, quality, etc.
  Supporting service(s) needed
  Warranty (what is covered, timing, who will support, etc.)
  Branding (manufacturer versus dealer, family versus individual, etc.)

Packaging
  Promotion and labeling needs
  Protection needs
Cultural sensitivity of product
Fit with product line

Place
Objectives
  Degree of market exposure required
  Distribution customer service level required
Type of channel (direct, indirect)
  Other channel members or collaborators required
  Type /number of wholesalers (agent, merchant, etc.)
  Type/number of retailers
  How discrepancies and separations will be handled
  How marketing functions will be shared
Coordination needed in company, channel, and supply chain
  Information requirements (EDI, the Internet, e-mail, etc.)
Transportation requirements
Inventory product-handling requirements
Facilities required (warehousing, distribution centers, etc.)
Reverse channels (for returns, recalls, etc.)

Promotion
Objectives
Major message theme(s) (for integrated marketing communications/positioning)
Promotion blend
  Advertising (type, media, copy thrust, etc.)
  Personal selling (type and number of salespeople, compensation, effort allocation, etc.)
  Sales promotion (for customers, channel members, employees)
  Publicity
  Interactive media
Mix of push and pull required
Who will do the work?

Price
Nature of demand (price sensitivity, price of substitutes)
Demand and cost analyses (marginal analysis)
Markup chain in channel
Price flexibility
Price level(s) (under what conditions) and impact on customer value
Adjustments to list price (geographic terms, discounts, allowances, etc.)

<u>Marketing Information Requirements</u>
Marketing research needs (with respect to customers, 4Ps, external environment, etc.)
Secondary and primary data needs
Marketing information system needs, models to be used, etc.

<u>Implementation and Control</u>
Special Implementation Problems to Overcome
People required
Manufacturing, financial, and other resources needed

Control
Marketing information systems and data needed
Criterion measures/comparison with objectives (customer satisfaction, sales, cost, performance analysis, etc.)

Budget, Sales Forecasts, and Estimates of Profit
Costs (all elements in plan, over time)
Sales (by market, over time, etc.)
Estimated operating statement (pro forma)

Timing
Specific sequence of activities and events, etc.
Likely changes over the product life cycle

Risk Factors and Contingency Plans

CHALLENGES FACING MARKETERS

Marketers face the challenge of preparing creative and innovative marketing plans, but that in itself will not improve the value of marketing to society. We need to face up to other basic challenges that require new ways of thinking.

Change is the only thing that's constant

We need better marketing performance at the firm level. Progressive firms pay attention to changes in the market—including trends in the marketing environment—and how marketing strategies need to be improved to consider these changes. Exhibit 18–5 lists some of the important trends and changes we've discussed throughout this text.

Most of the changes and trends summarized in Exhibit 18–5 are having a positive effect on how marketers serve society. And this ongoing improvement is self-directing. As consumers shift their support to firms that do meet their needs, laggard businesses are forced to either improve or get out of the way.

If it ain't broke, improve it

Marketing managers must constantly evaluate their strategies to be sure they're not being left in the dust by competitors who see new and better ways of doing things. It's crazy for a marketing manager to constantly change a strategy that's working well. But too many managers fail to see or plan for needed changes. They're afraid to do anything different and adhere to the idea that "if it ain't broke, don't fix it." But a firm can't always wait until a problem becomes completely obvious to do something about it. When customers move on and profits disappear, it may be too late to fix the problem. Marketing managers who take the lead in finding innovative new markets and approaches get a competitive advantage.

We need to welcome international competition

Marketers can't afford to bury their heads in the sand and hope that international competition will go away. Rather, they must realize that it is part of today's marketing environment. It creates even more pressure on marketing managers to figure out what it takes to gain a competitive advantage—both at home and in foreign markets. But with the challenge comes opportunities. The forces of competition in and among market-directed economies will help speed the diffusion of marketing advances to consumers everywhere. As macro-marketing systems improve worldwide, more consumers will have income to buy products—from wherever in the world those products come.

We need to use technology wisely

We live in a time of dramatic new technologies. Many marketers hate the idea that what they've learned from years of on-the-job experience may no longer apply when a technology like the Internet comes along. Or they feel that it's the job of the technical specialist to figure out how a new technology can help the firm serve its customers. But marketers can't just pawn that responsibility off on "somebody else." If that means learning about new technologies, then that is just part of the marketing job.

At a broader level, firms face the challenge of determining what technologies are acceptable and which are not. For example, gene research has opened the door to life-saving medicines, genetically altered crops that resist drought or disease, and even cloning of human beings. Yet in all of these arenas there is intense conflict among different groups about what is appropriate. How should these decisions be made? There is no simple answer to this question, but it's clear that old production-oriented views are *not* the answer. Perhaps we will move toward developing answers if some of the marketing ideas that have been applied to understanding individual needs can be extended to better understand the needs of society as a whole.

May need more social responsibility

Good business managers put themselves in the consumer's position. A useful rule to follow might be: Do unto others as you would have others do unto you. In practice, this means developing satisfying marketing mixes for specific target markets. It may mean building in more quality or more safety. The consumer's long-run satisfaction should be considered too. How will the product hold up in use? What about service guarantees? While trying to serve the needs of some target market, does the marketing

Communication Technologies
The Internet and intranets
Satellite communications
HTML e-mail and instant messaging
Videoconferencing and Internet phones
Cell phones

Role of Computerization
E-commerce, websites
Computers and PDAs
Spreadsheet analysis
Wireless networks
Scanners, bar codes, and RFID for tracking
Multimedia integration

Marketing Research
Search engines
Growth of marketing information systems
Decision support systems
XML data exchange
Single source data (and scanner panels)
Data warehouses and data mining
Multimedia data and questionnaires
Customer relationship management (CRM) systems

Demographic Patterns
"Wired" households
Explosion in senior and ethnic submarkets
Aging of the baby boomers
Population growth slowdown in U.S.
Geographic shifts in population
Slower real income growth in U.S.

Business and Organizational Customers
Closer relationships and single sourcing
Just-in-time inventory systems/EDI
Web portals and Internet sourcing
Interactive bidding and proposal requests
Shift to NAICS
ISO 9000
E-commerce and supply chain management

Product
More attention to "really new" products
Faster new-product development
Computer-aided design (CAD)
R&D teams with market-driven focus
More attention to quality
More attention to service technologies
More attention to design, including packages
Category management

Channels and Logistics
Internet selling (wholesale and retail)
More vertical marketing systems
Clicks and bricks (multichannel)
Larger, more powerful retail chains
More attention to distribution service
Real-time inventory replenishment
Rapid response, JIT, and ECR
Automated warehousing and handling
Cross-docking at distribution centers
Logistics outsourcing
Cross-channel logistics coordination
Growth of mass-merchandising

Sales Promotion
Database-directed promotion
Point-of-purchase promotion
Trade promotion becoming more sensible
Event sponsorships
Product placement
Better support from agencies
Customer loyalty programs
Customer acquisition cost analysis

Personal Selling
Post-sale customer service
Sales technology
Use of laptop computers
Major accounts specialization
More telemarketing and team selling
Use of e-mail, fax, and voice mail

Mass Selling
Interactive media (Internet ads, etc.)
Integrated marketing communications
More targeted media
   Blogs
   Specialty publications
   Specialty radio and TV (cable, satellite)
   Point-of-purchase
Growth of interactive agencies
Consolidation of global agencies
Consolidation of media companies
Changing agency compensation
Direct-response advertising
Shrinking media budgets

Pricing
Electronic bid pricing and auctions
Value pricing
Overuse of sales and deals
Bigger differences in functional discounts
More attention to exchange rate effects
Lower markups on higher stockturn items
Spreadsheets for marginal analysis

International Marketing
More international market development
Global competitors—at home and abroad
Global communication over Internet
New trade rules (NAFTA, WTO, EU, etc.)
More attention to exporting by small firms
International expansion by retailers
Impact of "pop" culture on traditional cultures
Tensions between "have" and "have-not" cultures
Growing role of airfreight

General
Explicit mission statements
S.W.O.T. analysis
Privacy issues
Benchmarking and total quality management
More attention to positioning and differentiation
Less regulation of business
Increased use of alliances
Shift away from diversification
More attention to profitability, not just sales
Greater attention to superior value
Addressing environmental concerns

strategy disregard the rights and needs of other consumers or create problems that will be left for future generations?[9]

The environment is everyone's need

Marketers need to work harder and smarter at finding ways to satisfy consumer needs without sacrificing the environment. All consumers need the environment, whether they realize it yet or not. We are only beginning to understand the consequences of the environmental damage that's already been done. Acid rain, depletion of the ozone layer, global warming, and toxic waste in water supplies—to mention but a few current environmental problems—have catastrophic effects.

In the past, most firms didn't pass the cost of environmental damage on to consumers in the prices that they paid. Pollution was a hidden and unmeasured cost for most companies. That is changing rapidly. Firms are already paying billions of dollars to correct problems, including problems created years ago. The government isn't accepting the excuse that "nobody knew it was a big problem."[10]

Consumer privacy needs to be protected

Marketers must also be sensitive to consumers' rights and privacy. Today, sophisticated marketing research methods, the Internet, and other technologies make it easier to abuse these rights. For example, credit card records—which reveal much about consumers' purchases and private lives—are routinely computerized and sold to anybody who pays for the list.

Most consumers don't realize how much data about their personal lives—some of it incorrect but treated as fact—is collected and available. A simple computer billing error may land consumers on a bad-credit list without their knowledge or poor security can result in identity theft. Marketing managers should use technology responsibly to improve the quality of life, not disrupt it. If you don't think privacy is a serious matter, enter your social security number in an Internet search engine and see what pops up. You may be surprised.[11]

May need to change laws and how they are enforced

One of the advantages of a market-directed economic system is that it operates automatically. But in our version of this system, consumer-citizens provide certain constraints (laws), which can be modified at any time. Managers who ignore consumer attitudes must realize that their actions may cause new restraints.

Before piling on too many new rules, however, some of the ones we have may need to be revised—and others may need to be enforced more carefully. Antitrust laws, for

Environmental problems pose a major challenge to society, but they're also an opportunity for innovative firms—because there will be rewards for firms that develop better ways of addressing them.

Promotion Managers Go Back to School

Schools are a targeted place for youth-oriented marketers to promote their products to the 51 million elementary and secondary students in the U.S. Coke and Pepsi are eager to contribute scoreboards (or is that billboards?) for high school sports fields. In school cafeterias, which serve over 34 million meals a day, Kellogg's cereal and Dannon's yogurt sponsor programs to motivate learning (and increase consumption). A school district in Colorado got national attention for selling advertising space on the sides of its school buses. Targeting students who are captive at school is not a new idea. The National Dairy Council has promoted dairy products in the schools since 1915.

Even so, the growth of the practice raises questions. The launch of the Channel One television network with ads and programming for schools brought new attention, and controversy, to the issue. Many critics saw it as a crass attempt to exploit classroom students. Some schools even hand out coupons tied in with the ads. Channel One notes that schools get benefits. Besides the excellent news programs, they get video equipment and chances to win support for Internet access. Even Internet access can be a mixed blessing. It's a great educational tool, but there are virtually no limits on Internet advertising banners, including ones that link to pornographic websites. To prevent that sort of problem, many schools use a Web-filtering program from N2H2, Inc. But critics are troubled that N2H2 sells information about student surfing habits collected by the program.

To find more targeted ways of reaching students, some consumer products firms turn to promotion specialists, like Sampling Corporation of America (SCA). About 70 percent of all schools participate in SCA programs. For example, every Halloween SCA provides schools with safety literature wrapped around product samples or coupons provided by sponsor companies. Other firms create teaching materials or sponsor programs for school assemblies. Dole Foods, for example, created a multimedia CD featuring 30 animated fruits and vegetables. It also sponsored a series of staged performances by the National Theatre for Children (NTC). The NTC performances highlighted nutrition issues (and brand recognition for Dole's line of fruits and salads). For a fee, NTC has developed programs for other companies.

There is no question that in-school promotion efforts do provide budget-strapped educators with added resources, including useful teaching materials. Yet promotions targeted at students also raise sensitive issues of educational standards, ethics, and taste. Because of that, Coke and Pepsi have new guidelines for their bottlers that limit cola sales in some schools or make juice and water available at the same price. Kraft has gone further and stopped all promotions in schools. But self-control doesn't go far enough for some state legislatures which have passed stricter regulations on what foods and drinks can be sold in schools. Marketers who are not responsive to concerns such as these may provoke a hostile public backlash, including a host of new regulations.[12]

example, are often applied to protect competitors from each other—but they were originally intended to encourage competition.

Specifically, U.S. antitrust laws were developed so that all firms in a market would compete on a level playing field. But in many markets, that level playing field no longer exists. In our global economy, individual U.S. firms now compete with foreign firms whose governments urge them to cooperate with each other. Such foreign firms don't see each other as competitors; rather they see U.S. firms, as a group, as the competitors.

Laws should affect top managers

Strict enforcement of present laws could have far-reaching results if more price fixers, fraudulent or deceptive advertisers, and others who violate existing laws—thus affecting the performance of the

Internet EXERCISE

Obvious Implementations Corp. is a small consulting and manufacturing firm. Go to its website (**www.obviously.com**) and then select "How to stop junk mail, e-mail, and phone calls." Read through the information and, if you wish, follow some of the links to other sites listed. Should it be easier to avoid mail, spam, and calls you don't want? Explain your thinking.

The Utah Transit Authority (UTA) thought that more university students would ride the bus long-term if they were motivated by personal benefit rather than environmental or social conscience. For most people, the pros and cons of riding the bus, like other product choices, are more a personal matter. So UTA decided it should offer an answer to the question, "What's in it for me?" The answer in this particular UTA ad is "social opportunities." Although public transit is not exactly a sexy product, the ad employs a "sex sells" approach. What do you think? Is this a good idea? Why?

Chemistry 101

You can learn a lot on the bus.

University of Utah students ride free with student I.D. **U T A**

macro-marketing system—were sent to jail or given heavy fines. A quick change in attitudes might occur if unethical top managers—those who plan strategy—were prosecuted, instead of the salespeople or advertisers expected to deliver on weak or undifferentiated strategies.

Laws merely define minimal ethical standards

Whether a marketer is operating in his or her own country or in a foreign nation, the legal environment sets the *minimal* standards of ethical behavior as defined by a society. In addition, the American Marketing Association's code of ethics (Exhibit 1–7) provides a checklist of basic guidelines that a marketing manager should observe. But marketing managers constantly face ethical issues where there are no clearly defined answers. Every marketing manager should make a personal commitment to carefully evaluate the ethical consequences of marketing strategy decisions.

On the other hand, innovative new marketing strategies *do* sometimes cause problems for those who have a vested interest in the old ways. Some people try to portray anything that disrupts their own personal interest as unethical. But that is not an appropriate ethical standard. The basic ethical charge to marketers is to find new *and* better ways to serve society's needs.

Need socially responsible consumers

We've stressed that marketers should act responsibly—but consumers have responsibilities too. Some consumers abuse policies about returning goods, change price tags in self-service stores, and are downright abusive to salespeople. Others think nothing of ripping off businesses because "they're rich." Shoplifting is a major problem for most traditional retailers, averaging almost 2 percent of sales nationally. In supermarkets, losses to shoplifters are on average greater than profits. Online retailers, in turn, must fight the use of stolen or fraudulent credit cards. Honest consumers pay for the cost of this theft in higher prices.[13]

Americans tend to perform their dual role of consumer-citizens with a split personality. We often behave one way as consumers and then take the opposite position in the ballot box. For example, we cover our beaches and parks with garbage and litter while urging our legislators to take stiff action to curb pollution. We protest sex and

Both consumers and businesses have social responsibilities.

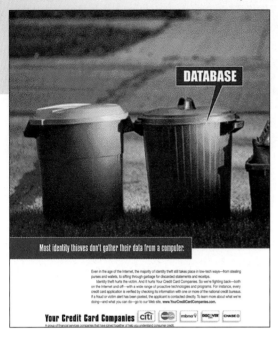

Most identity thieves don't gather their data from a computer.

Your Credit Card Companies

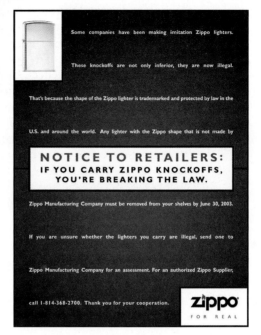

NOTICE TO RETAILERS:
IF YOU CARRY ZIPPO KNOCKOFFS,
YOU'RE BREAKING THE LAW.

violence in the media, but some of the most profitable websites on the Internet are purveyors of pornography. Parents complain about advertising aimed at children but use TV as a Saturday morning babysitter.

Unethical or illegal behavior is widespread. In a major survey of workers, managers, and executives from a wide range of industries, 48 percent admitted to taking unethical or illegal actions in the past year. Offenses included things like cheating on expense accounts, paying or accepting kickbacks, trading sex for sales, lying to customers, leaking company secrets, and looking the other way when environmental laws are violated. Think about it—we're talking about half of the workforce.[14]

As consumer-citizens, each of us shares the responsibility for preserving an effective macro-marketing system. And we should take this responsibility seriously. That even includes the responsibility to be smarter customers. Let's face it, a majority of consumers ignore most of the available information that could help them spend money (and guide the marketing process) more wisely. Consumerism has encouraged nutritional labeling, open dating, unit pricing, truth-in-lending, plain-language contracts and warranties, and so on. Many companies provide extensive information at their websites or in brochures. Government agencies publish many consumer buying guides on everything from tires to appliances, as do organizations such as Consumers Union. Most of this information is available from home, over the Internet. It makes sense to use it.

HOW FAR SHOULD THE MARKETING CONCEPT GO?

Should marketing managers limit consumers' freedom of choice?

Achieving a better macro-marketing system is certainly a desirable objective. But what part should a marketer play in deciding what products to offer?

This is extremely important, because some marketing managers, especially those in large corporations, can have an impact far larger than they do in their roles as consumer-citizens. For example, should they refuse to produce hazardous products, like skis or motorcycles, even though such products are in strong demand? Should they install safety devices that increase costs but that customers don't want?

These are difficult questions to answer. Some things marketing managers do clearly benefit both the firm and consumers because they lower costs or improve consumers' options. But other decisions may actually reduce consumer choice and conflict with a desire to improve the effectiveness of our macro-marketing system.

Consumer-citizens should vote on the changes

It seems fair to suggest, therefore, that marketing managers should be expected to improve and expand the range of goods and services they make available—always trying to add value and better satisfy consumers' needs and preferences. This is the job we've assigned to business.

If pursuing this objective makes excessive demands on scarce resources or has an unacceptable ecological effect, then consumer-citizens have the responsibility to vote for laws restricting individual firms that are trying to satisfy consumers' needs. This is the role that we, as consumers, have assigned to the government—to ensure that the macro-marketing system works effectively.

It is important to recognize that some *seemingly minor* modifications in our present system *might* result in very big, unintended problems. Allowing some government agency to prohibit the sale of products for seemingly good reasons could lead to major changes we never expected and could seriously reduce consumers' present rights to freedom of choice, including "bad" choices.

CONCLUSION

Macro-marketing does *not* cost too much. Consumers have assigned business the role of satisfying their needs. Customers find it satisfactory and even desirable to permit businesses to cater to them and even to stimulate wants. As long as consumers are satisfied, macro-marketing will not cost too much—and business firms will be permitted to continue as profit-making entities.

But business exists at the consumer's discretion. It's mainly by satisfying the consumer that a particular firm—and *our* economic system—can justify its existence and hope to keep operating.

In carrying out this role—granted by consumers—business firms are not always as effective as they could be. Many business managers don't understand the marketing concept or the role that marketing plays in our way of life. They seem to feel that business has a God-given right to operate as it chooses. And they proceed in their typical production-oriented ways. Further, many managers have had little or no training in business management and are not as competent as they should be. Others fail to adjust to the changes taking place around them. And a few dishonest or unethical managers can do a great deal of damage before consumer-citizens take steps to stop them. As a result, marketing by individual firms often *does* cost too much. But the situation is improving. More business training is now available, and more competent people are being attracted to mar-

keting and business generally. Clearly, *you* have a role to play in improving marketing activities in the future.

The marketing strategy planning process presented in this book provides a framework that will guide you to more effective marketing decisions—and marketing that really does deliver superior value to customers. It also benefits the firm, through profits and growth. It's truly a "win-win" situation. And in our competitive, market-driven economy, managers and firms that lead the way in creating these successes will not go unnoticed. As effective marketing management spreads to more companies, the whole macro-marketing system will be more efficient and effective.

To keep our system working effectively, individual firms should implement the marketing concept in a more efficient, ethical, and socially responsible way. At the same time, we—as consumers—should consume goods and services in an intelligent and socially responsible way. Further, we have the responsibility to vote and ensure that we get the kind of macro-marketing system we want. What kind do you want? What should you do to ensure that fellow consumer-citizens will vote for your system? Is your system likely to satisfy you as well as another macro-marketing system? You don't have to answer these questions right now—but your answers will affect the future you'll live in and how satisfied you'll be.

QUESTIONS AND PROBLEMS

1. Explain why marketing must be evaluated at two levels. What criteria should be used to evaluate each level of marketing? Defend your answer. Explain why your criteria are better than alternative criteria.

2. Discuss the merits of various economic system objectives. Is the objective of the American economic system sensible? Could it achieve more consumer satisfaction if sociologists or public officials determined how to satisfy the needs of lower-income or less-educated consumers? If so, what education or income level should be required before an individual is granted free choice?

3. Should the objective of our economy be maximum efficiency? If your answer is yes, efficiency in what? If not, what should the objective be?

4. Discuss the conflict of interests among production, finance, accounting, and marketing executives. How does this conflict affect the operation of an individual firm? The economic system? Why does this conflict exist?

5. Why does adoption of the marketing concept encourage a firm to operate more efficiently? Be specific about the impact of the marketing concept on the various departments of a firm.

6. In the short run, competition sometimes leads to inefficiency in the operation of our economic system. Many people argue for monopoly in order to eliminate this inefficiency. Discuss this solution.

7. How would officially granted monopolies affect the operation of our economic system? Consider the effect on allocation of resources, the level of income and employment, and the distribution of income. Is the effect any different if a firm obtains a monopoly by winning out in a competitive market?

8. Comment on the following statement: "Ultimately, the high cost of marketing is due only to consumers."

9. Distinguish clearly between a marketing strategy and a marketing plan. If a firm has a really good strategy, does it need to worry about developing a written plan?

10. How far should the marketing concept go? How should we decide this issue?

11. Should marketing managers, or business managers in general, refrain from producing profitable products that some target customers want but that may not be in their long-run best interest? Should firms be expected to produce "good" but less profitable products? What if such products break even? What if they are unprofitable but the company makes other profitable products—so on balance it still makes some profit? What criteria are you using for each of your answers?

12. Should a marketing manager or a business refuse to produce an "energy-gobbling" appliance that some consumers are demanding? Should a firm install an expensive safety device that will increase costs but that customers don't want? Are the same principles involved in both these questions? Explain.

13. Discuss how one or more of the trends or changes shown in Exhibit 18–5 are affecting marketing strategy planning for a specific firm that serves the market where you live.

14. Discuss how slower economic growth or no economic growth would affect your college community—in particular, its marketing institutions.

CREATING MARKETING PLANS

The Marketing Plan Coach software on the Student CD includes a sample marketing plan for Hillside Veterinary Clinic. Review the entire marketing plan.

a. How will do the pieces fit together?
b. Does the marketing strategy logically follow from the target market dimensions?
c. Does the marketing strategy logically follow from the differentiation and positioning?
d. Does the plan appear reasonable given the stated objectives?

SUGGESTED CASES

17. Healthy Water, Inc.   22. Bright Light Innovations   28. ACT, Inc.   30. Saralyn Mills, Ltd.   32. Lever, Ltd.

Economics Fundamentals

LEARNING OBJECTIVES

The economist's traditional analysis of supply and demand is a useful tool for analyzing markets. In particular, you should master the concepts of a demand curve and demand elasticity. A firm's demand curve shows how the target customers view the firm's Product—really, its whole marketing mix. And the interaction of demand and supply curves helps set the size of a market and the market price. The interaction of supply and demand also determines the nature of the competitive environment, which has an important effect on strategy planning. The following sections of this appendix discuss these ideas more fully.

When you finish this appendix, you should:

1. understand the "law of diminishing demand."

2. understand demand and supply curves and how they set the size of a market and its price level.

3. know about elasticity of demand and supply.

4. know why demand elasticity can be affected by availability of substitutes.

5. know the different kinds of competitive situations and understand why they are important to marketing managers.

6. understand important new terms (shown in red).

PRODUCTS AND MARKETS AS SEEN BY CUSTOMERS AND POTENTIAL CUSTOMERS

Economists see individual customers choosing among alternatives

A basic idea from economics is that most customers have a limited income and simply cannot buy everything they want. They must balance their needs and the prices of various products. Economists usually assume that customers have a fairly definite set of preferences and that they evaluate alternatives in terms of whether the alternatives will make them feel better or in some way improve their situation.

But what exactly is the nature of a customer's desire for a particular product?

Usually economists answer this question in terms of the extra utility the customer can obtain by buying more of a particular product—or how much utility would be lost if the customer had less of the product. It is easier to understand the idea of utility if we look at what happens when the price of one of the customer's usual purchases changes.

The law of diminishing demand

Suppose that consumers buy potatoes in 10-pound bags at the same time they buy other foods such as bread and rice. If the consumers are mainly interested in buying a certain amount of food and the price of the potatoes drops, it seems reasonable to expect that they will switch some of their food money to potatoes and away from some other foods. But if the price of potatoes rises, you expect our consumers to buy fewer potatoes and more of other foods.

The general relationship between price and quantity demanded illustrated by this food example is called the **law of diminishing demand**—which says that if the price of a product is raised, a smaller quantity will be demanded and if the price of a product is lowered, a greater quantity will be demanded. Experience supports this relationship between price and total demand in a market, especially for broad product categories or commodities such as potatoes.

The relationship between price and quantity demanded in a market is what economists call a "demand schedule." An example is shown in Exhibit A–1. For each row in the table, column 2 shows the quantity consumers will want (demand) if they have to pay the price given in column 1. The third column shows that the total revenue (sales) in the potato market is equal to the quantity demanded at a given price times that price. Note that as prices drop, the total *unit* quantity increases, yet the total *revenue* decreases. Fill in the blank lines in the third column and observe the behavior

Exhibit A–1
Demand Schedule for Potatoes (10-pound bags)

Point	(1) Price of Potatoes per Bag (P)	(2) Quantity Demanded (bags per month) (Q)	(3) Total Revenue per Month (P × Q = TR)
A	$1.60	8,000,000	$12,800,000
B	1.30	9,000,000	_____
C	1.00	11,000,000	11,000,000
D	0.70	14,000,000	_____
E	0.40	19,000,000	_____

of total revenue, an important number for the marketing manager. We will explain what you should have noticed, and why, a little later.

The demand curve—usually down-sloping

If your only interest is seeing at which price the company will earn the greatest total revenue, the demand schedule may be adequate. But a demand curve shows more. A **demand curve** is a graph of the relationship between price and quantity demanded in a market, assuming that all other things stay the same. Exhibit A–2 shows the demand curve for potatoes—really just a plotting of the demand schedule in Exhibit A–1. It shows how many potatoes potential customers will demand at various possible prices. This is a "down-sloping demand curve."

Most demand curves are down-sloping. This just means that if prices are decreased, the quantity customers demand will increase.

Demand curves always show the price on the vertical axis and the quantity demanded on the horizontal axis. In Exhibit A–2, we have shown the price in dollars. For consistency, we will use dollars in other examples. However, keep in mind that these same ideas hold regardless of what money unit (dollars, yen, euros, pounds, etc.) is used to represent price. Even at this early point, you should keep in mind that markets are not necessarily limited by national boundaries—or by one type of money.

Note that the demand curve only shows how customers will react to various possible prices. In a market, we see only one price at a time, not all of these prices. The curve, however, shows what quantities will be demanded, depending on what price is set.

Microwave oven demand curve looks different

To get a more complete picture of demand-curve analysis, let's consider another product that has a different demand schedule and curve. A demand schedule for standard 1-cubic-foot microwave ovens is shown in Exhibit A–3. Column (3) shows the total revenue that will be obtained at various possible prices and quantities. Again, as the price

Exhibit A–2
Demand Curve for Potatoes (10-pound bags)

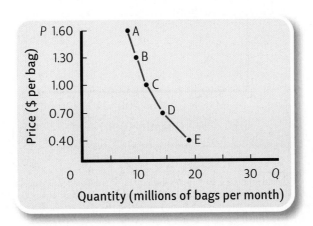

Point	(1) Price per Microwave Oven (P)	(2) Quantity Demanded per Year (Q)	(3) Total Revenue (TR) per Year (P × Q = TR)
A	$300	20,000	$6,000,000
B	250	70,000	15,500,000
C	200	130,000	26,000,000
D	150	210,000	31,500,000
E	100	310,000	31,000,000

goes down, the quantity demanded goes up. But here, unlike the potato example, total revenue increases as prices go down—at least until the price drops to $150.

Every market has a demand curve, for some time period

These general demand relationships are typical for all products. But each product has its own demand schedule and curve in each potential market, no matter how small the market. In other words, a particular demand curve has meaning only for a particular market. We can think of demand curves for individuals, groups of individuals who form a target market, regions, and even countries. And the time period covered really should be specified, although this is often neglected because we usually think of monthly or yearly periods.

The difference between elastic and inelastic

The demand curve for microwave ovens (see Exhibit A–4) is down-sloping—but note that it is flatter than the curve for potatoes. It is important to understand what this flatness means.

We will consider the flatness in terms of total revenue, since this is what interests business managers.*

When you filled in the total revenue column for potatoes, you should have noticed that total revenue drops continually if the price is reduced. This looks undesirable for sellers and illustrates inelastic demand. **Inelastic demand** means that although the quantity demanded increases if the price is decreased, the quantity demanded will not "stretch" enough—that is, it is not elastic enough—to avoid a decrease in total revenue.

---

*Strictly speaking, two curves should not be compared for flatness if the graph scales are different, but for our purposes now we will do so to illustrate the idea of "elasticity of demand." Actually, it would be more accurate to compare two curves for one product on the same graph. Then both the shape of the demand curve and its position on the graph would be important.

In contrast, **elastic demand** means that if prices are dropped, the quantity demanded will stretch (increase) enough to increase total revenue. The upper part of the microwave oven demand curve is an example of elastic demand.

But note that if the microwave oven price is dropped from $150 to $100, total revenue will decrease. We can say, therefore, that between $150 and $100, demand is inelastic—that is, total revenue will decrease if price is lowered from $150 to $100.

Thus, elasticity can be defined in terms of changes in total revenue. *If total revenue will increase if price is lowered, then demand is elastic. If total revenue will decrease if price is lowered, then demand is inelastic.* (Note: A special case known as "unitary elasticity of demand" occurs if total revenue stays the same when prices change.)

Total revenue may increase if price is raised

A point often missed in discussions of demand is what happens when prices are raised instead of lowered. With elastic demand, total revenue will *decrease* if the price is *raised*. With inelastic demand, however, total revenue will *increase* if the price is *raised*.

The possibility of raising price and increasing dollar sales (total revenue) at the same time is attractive to managers. This only occurs if the demand curve is inelastic. Here total revenue will increase if price is raised, but total costs probably will not increase—and may actually go down—with smaller quantities. Keep in mind that profit is equal to total revenue minus total costs. So when demand is inelastic, profit will increase as price is increased!

The ways total revenue changes as prices are raised are shown in Exhibit A–5. Here total revenue is the rectangular area formed by a price and its related quantity. The larger the rectangular area, the greater the total revenue.

P_1 is the original price here, and the total potential revenue with this original price is shown by the area with blue shading. The area with red shading shows the total revenue with the new price, P_2. There is some overlap in the total revenue areas, so the important areas are those with only one color. Note that in the left-hand figure—where demand is elastic—the revenue added (the red-only area) when the price is increased is less than the revenue lost (the blue-only area). Now let's contrast this to the right-hand figure, when demand is inelastic. Only a small blue revenue area is given up for a much larger (red) one when price is raised.

Exhibit A–5
Changes in Total Revenue as Prices Increase

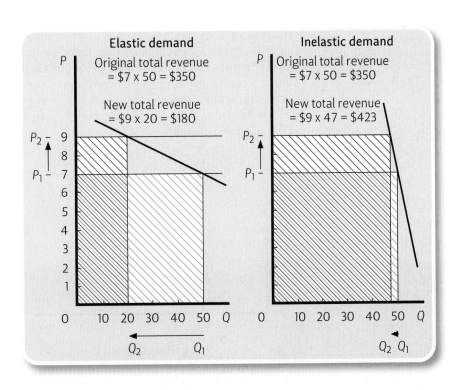

An entire curve is not elastic or inelastic

It is important to see that it is *wrong to refer to a whole demand curve as elastic or inelastic.* Rather, elasticity for a particular demand curve refers to the change in total revenue between two points on the curve, not along the whole curve. You saw the change from elastic to inelastic in the microwave oven example. Generally, however, nearby points are either elastic or inelastic—so it is common to refer to a whole curve by the degree of elasticity in the price range that normally is of interest—the *relevant range.*

Demand elasticities affected by availability of substitutes and urgency of need

At first, it may be difficult to see why one product has an elastic demand and another an inelastic demand. Many factors affect elasticity, such as the availability of substitutes, the importance of the item in the customer's budget, and the urgency of the customer's need and its relation to other needs. By looking more closely at one of these factors—the availability of substitutes—you will better understand why demand elasticities vary.

Substitutes are products that offer the buyer a choice. For example, many consumers see grapefruit as a substitute for oranges and hot dogs as a substitute for hamburgers. The greater the number of "good" substitutes available, the greater will be the elasticity of demand. From the consumer's perspective, products are "good" substitutes if they are very similar (homogeneous). If consumers see products as extremely different, or heterogeneous, then a particular need cannot be satisfied easily by substitutes. And the demand for the most satisfactory product may be quite inelastic.

As an example, if the price of hamburger is lowered (and other prices stay the same), the quantity demanded will increase a lot, as will total revenue. The reason is that not only will regular hamburger users buy more hamburger, but some consumers who formerly bought hot dogs or steaks probably will buy hamburger too. But if the price of hamburger is raised, the quantity demanded will decrease, perhaps sharply. Still, consumers will buy some hamburger, depending on how much the price has risen, their individual tastes, and what their guests expect (see Exhibit A–6).

In contrast to a product with many "substitutes"—such as hamburger—consider a product with few or no substitutes. Its demand curve will tend to be inelastic. Motor oil is a good example. Motor oil is needed to keep cars running. Yet no one person or family uses great quantities of motor oil. So it is not likely that the quantity of motor oil purchased will change much as long as price changes are *within a reasonable range.* Of course, if the price is raised to a staggering figure, many people will buy less oil (change their oil less frequently). If the price is dropped to an extremely low level, manufacturers may buy more—say, as a lower-cost substitute for other chemicals typically used in making plastic (Exhibit A–7). But these extremes are outside the relevant range.

Demand curves are introduced here because the degree of elasticity of demand shows how potential customers feel about a product—and especially whether they see substitutes for the product. But to get a better understanding of markets, we must extend this economic analysis.

Exhibit A–6
Demand Curve for Hamburger (a product with many substitutes)

Exhibit A–7
Demand Curve for
Motor Oil (a product
with few substitutes)

MARKETS AS SEEN BY SUPPLIERS

Customers may want some product—but if suppliers are not willing to supply it, then there is no market. So we'll study the economist's analysis of supply. And then we'll bring supply and demand together for a more complete understanding of markets.

Economists often use the kind of analysis we are discussing here to explain pricing in the marketplace. But that is not our intention. Here we are interested in how and why markets work and the interaction of customers and potential suppliers. Later in this appendix we will review how competition affects prices, but how individual firms set prices, or should set prices, is discussed fully in Chapters 16 and 17.

Supply curves reflect supplier thinking

Generally speaking, suppliers' costs affect the quantity of products they are willing to offer in a market during any period. In other words, their costs affect their supply schedules and supply curves. While a demand curve shows the quantity of products customers will be willing to buy at various prices, a **supply curve** shows the quantity of products that will be supplied at various possible prices. Eventually, only one quantity will be offered and purchased. So a supply curve is really a hypothetical (what-if) description of what will be offered at various prices. It is, however, a very important curve. Together with a demand curve, it summarizes the attitudes and probable behavior of buyers and sellers in regard to a particular product in a particular market—that is, in a product-market.

Some supply curves are vertical

We usually assume that supply curves tend to slope upward—that is, suppliers will be willing to offer greater quantities at higher prices. If a product's market price is very high, it seems only reasonable that producers will be anxious to produce more of the product and even put workers on overtime or perhaps hire more workers to increase the quantity they can offer. Going further, it seems likely that producers of other products will switch their resources (farms, factories, labor, or retail facilities) to the product that is in great demand.

On the other hand, if consumers are only willing to pay a very low price for a particular product, it's reasonable to expect that producers will switch to other products, thus reducing supply. A supply schedule (Exhibit A–8) and a supply curve (Exhibit A–9) for potatoes illustrate these ideas. This supply curve shows how many potatoes would be produced and offered for sale at each possible market price in a given month.

In the very short run (say, over a few hours, a day, or a week), a supplier may not be able to change the supply at all. In this situation, we would see a vertical supply curve. This situation is often relevant in the market for fresh produce. Fresh strawberries, for example, continue to ripen, and a supplier wants to sell them quickly—preferably at a higher price—but in any case, they must be sold.

If the product is a service, it may not be easy to expand the supply in the short run. Additional barbers or medical doctors are not quickly trained and licensed, and they

Point	Possible Market Price per 10-lb. Bag	Number of Bags Sellers Will Supply per Month at Each Possible Market Price
A	$1.60	17,000,000
B	1.30	14,000,000
C	1.00	11,000,000
D	0.70	8,000,000
E	0.40	3,000,000

Note: This supply curve is for a month to emphasize that farmers might have some control over when they deliver their potatoes. There would be a different curve for each month.

only have so much time to give each day. Further, the prospect of much higher prices in the near future cannot easily expand the supply of many services. For example, a hit play or an "in" restaurant or nightclub is limited in the amount of product it can offer at a particular time.

Elasticity of supply

The term *elasticity* also is used to describe supply curves. An extremely steep or almost vertical supply curve, often found in the short run, is called **inelastic supply** because the quantity supplied does not stretch much (if at all) if the price is raised. A flatter curve is called **elastic supply** because the quantity supplied does stretch more if the price is raised. A slightly up-sloping supply curve is typical in longer-run market situations. Given more time, suppliers have a chance to adjust their offerings, and competitors may enter or leave the market.

DEMAND AND SUPPLY INTERACT TO DETERMINE THE SIZE OF THE MARKET AND PRICE LEVEL

We have treated market demand and supply forces separately. Now we must bring them together to show their interaction. The *intersection* of these two forces determines the size of the market and the market price—at which point (price and quantity) the market is said to be in *equilibrium*.

The intersection of demand and supply is shown for the potato data discussed above. In Exhibit A–10, the demand curve for potatoes is now graphed against the supply curve in Exhibit A–9.

496

Exhibit A–10
Equilibrium of Supply and Demand for Potatoes (10-pound bags)

In this potato market, demand is inelastic—the total revenue of all the potato producers would be greater at higher prices. But the market price is at the **equilibrium point**—where the quantity and the price sellers are willing to offer are equal to the quantity and price that buyers are willing to accept. The $1.00 equilibrium price for potatoes yields a smaller *total revenue* to potato producers than a higher price would. This lower equilibrium price comes about because the many producers are willing to supply enough potatoes at the lower price. *Demand is not the only determiner of price level. Cost also must be considered—via the supply curve.*

Some consumers get a surplus

Presumably, a sale takes place only if both buyer and seller feel they will be better off after the sale. But sometimes the price a consumer pays in a sales transaction is less than what he or she would be willing to pay.

The reason for this is that demand curves are typically down-sloping, and some of the demand curve is above the equilibrium price. This is simply another way of showing that some customers would have been willing to pay more than the equilibrium price—if they had to. In effect, some of them are getting a bargain by being able to buy at the equilibrium price. Economists have traditionally called these bargains the **consumer surplus**—that is, the difference to consumers between the value of a purchase and the price they pay.

Some business critics assume that consumers do badly in any business transaction. In fact, sales take place only if consumers feel they are at least getting their money's worth. As we can see here, some are willing to pay much more than the market price.

DEMAND AND SUPPLY HELP US UNDERSTAND THE NATURE OF COMPETITION

The elasticity of demand and supply curves and their interaction help predict the nature of competition a marketing manager is likely to face. For example, an extremely inelastic demand curve means that the manager will have much choice in strategy planning, especially price setting. Apparently customers like the product and see few substitutes. They are willing to pay higher prices before cutting back much on their purchases.

The elasticity of a firm's demand curve is not the only factor that affects the nature of competition. Other factors are the number and size of competitors and the uniqueness of each firm's marketing mix. Understanding these market situations is important because the freedom of a marketing manager, especially control over price, is greatly reduced in some situations.

Important Dimensions	Types of Situations			
	Pure Competition	Oligopoly	Monopolistic Competition	Monopoly
Uniqueness of each firm's product	None	None	Some	Unique
Number of competitors	Many	Few	Few to many	None
Size of competitors (compared to size of market)	Small	Large	Large to small	None
Elasticity of demand facing firm	Completely elastic	Kinked demand curve (elastic and inelastic)	Either	Either
Elasticity of industry demand	Either	Inelastic	Either	Either
Control of price by firm	None	Some (with care)	Some	Complete

A marketing manager operates in one of four kinds of market situations. We'll discuss three kinds: pure competition, oligopoly, and monopolistic competition. The fourth kind, monopoly, isn't found very often and is like monopolistic competition. The important dimensions of these situations are shown in Exhibit A–11.

When competition is pure

Many competitors offer about the same thing

Pure competition is a market situation that develops when a market has

1. Homogeneous (similar) products.
2. Many buyers and sellers who have full knowledge of the market.
3. Ease of entry for buyers and sellers; that is, new firms have little difficulty starting in business—and new customers can easily come into the market.

More or less pure competition is found in many agricultural markets. In the potato market, for example, there are thousands of small producers—and they are in pure competition. Let's look more closely at these producers.

Although the potato market as a whole has a down-sloping demand curve, each of the many small producers in the industry is in pure competition, and each of them faces a flat demand curve at the equilibrium price. This is shown in Exhibit A–12.

As shown at the right of Exhibit A-12, an individual producer can sell as many bags of potatoes as he chooses at $1—the market equilibrium price. The equilibrium price is determined by the quantity that all producers choose to sell given the demand curve they face.

But a small producer has little effect on overall supply (or on the equilibrium price). If this individual farmer raises 1/10,000th of the quantity offered in the market, for example, you can see that there will be little effect if the farmer goes out of business—or doubles production.

The reason an individual producer's demand curve is flat is that the farmer probably couldn't sell any potatoes above the market price. And there is no point in selling below the market price! So in effect, the individual producer has no control over price.

Markets tend to become more competitive

Not many markets are *purely* competitive. But many are close enough so we can talk about "almost" pure competition situations—those in which the marketing manager has to accept the going price.

Exhibit A–12 Interaction of Demand and Supply in the Potato Industry and the Resulting Demand Curve Facing Individual Potato Producers

Such highly competitive situations aren't limited to agriculture. Wherever *many* competitors sell *homogeneous* products—such as textiles, lumber, coal, printing, and laundry services—the demand curve seen by *each producer* tends to be flat.

Markets tend to become more competitive, moving toward pure competition (except in oligopolies—see below). On the way to pure competition, prices and profits are pushed down until some competitors are forced out of business. Eventually, in long-run equilibrium, the price level is only high enough to keep the survivors in business. No one makes any profit—they just cover costs. It's tough to be a marketing manager in this situation!

When competition is oligopolistic

A few competitors offer similar things

Not all markets move toward pure competition. Some become oligopolies. **Oligopoly** situations are special market situations that develop when a market has

1. Essentially homogeneous products—such as basic industrial chemicals or gasoline.
2. Relatively few sellers—or a few large firms and many smaller ones who follow the lead of the larger ones.
3. Fairly inelastic industry demand curves.

The demand curve facing each firm is unusual in an oligopoly situation. Although the industry demand curve is inelastic throughout the relevant range, the demand curve facing each competitor looks "kinked." See Exhibit A–13. The current market price is at the kink.

There is a market price because the competing firms watch each other carefully—and they know it's wise to be at the kink. Each firm must expect that raising its own price above the market price will cause a big loss in sales. Few, if any, competitors will follow the price increase. So the firm's demand curve is relatively flat above the market price. If the firm lowers its price, it must expect competitors to follow. Given inelastic industry demand, the firm's own demand curve is inelastic at lower prices, assuming it keeps its share of this market at lower prices. Since lowering prices along such a curve will drop total revenue, the firm should leave its price at the kink—the market price.

Sometimes there are price fluctuations in oligopolistic markets. This can be caused by firms that don't understand the market situation and cut their prices to try to get business. In other cases, big increases in demand or supply change the basic nature of the situation and lead to price cutting. Price cuts can be drastic, such as Du Pont's price cut of 25 percent for Dacron. This happened when Du Pont decided that

Exhibit A–13 Oligopoly—Kinked Demand Curve—Situation

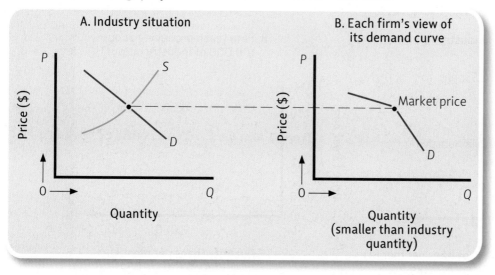

A. Industry situation

B. Each firm's view of its demand curve

industry production capacity already exceeded demand, and more plants were due to start production.

It's important to keep in mind that oligopoly situations don't just apply to whole industries and national markets. Competitors who are focusing on the same local target market often face oligopoly situations. A suburban community might have several gas stations, all of which provide essentially the same product. In this case, the "industry" consists of the gas stations competing with each other in the local product-market.

As in pure competition, oligopolists face a long-run trend toward an equilibrium level, with profits driven toward zero. This may not happen immediately—and a marketing manager may try to delay price competition by relying more on other elements in the marketing mix.

When competition is monopolistic

A price must be set

You can see why marketing managers want to avoid pure competition or oligopoly situations. They prefer a market in which they have more control. **Monopolistic competition** is a market situation that develops when a market has

1. Different (heterogeneous) products—in the eyes of some customers.
2. Sellers who feel they do have some competition in this market.

The word *monopolistic* means that each firm is trying to get control in its own little market. But the word *competition* means that there are still substitutes. The vigorous competition of a purely competitive market is reduced. Each firm has its own down-sloping demand curve. But the shape of the curve depends on the similarity of competitors' products and marketing mixes. Each monopolistic competitor has freedom—but not complete freedom—in its own market.

Judging elasticity will help set the price

Since a firm in monopolistic competition has its own down-sloping demand curve, it must make a decision about price level as part of its marketing strategy planning. Here, estimating the elasticity of the firm's own demand curve is helpful. If it is highly inelastic, the firm may decide to raise prices to increase total revenue. But if demand is highly elastic, this may mean there are many competitors with acceptable substitutes. Then the price may have to be set near that of the competition. And the marketing manager probably should try to develop a better marketing mix.

CONCLUSION

The economist's traditional demand and supply analysis provides a useful tool for analyzing the nature of demand and competition. It is especially important that you master the concepts of a demand curve and demand elasticity. How demand and supply interact helps determine the size of a market and its price level. The interaction of supply and demand also helps explain the nature of competition in different market situations. We discuss three competitive situations: pure competition, oligopoly, and monopolistic competition. The fourth kind, monopoly, isn't found very often and is like monopolistic competition.

The nature of supply and demand—and competition—is very important in marketing strategy planning. We discuss these topics more fully in Chapters 3 and 4 and then build on them throughout the text. This appendix provides a good foundation on these topics.

KEY TERMS

law of diminishing demand, 490

demand curve, 491

inelastic demand, 492

elastic demand, 493

substitutes, 494

supply curve, 495

inelastic supply, 496

elastic supply, 496

equilibrium point, 497

consumer surplus, 497

pure competition, 498

oligopoly, 499

monopolistic competition, 500

QUESTIONS AND PROBLEMS

1. Explain in your own words how economists look at markets and arrive at the "law of diminishing demand."

2. Explain what a demand curve is and why it is usually down-sloping. Then give an example of a product for which the demand curve might not be down-sloping over some possible price ranges. Explain the reason for your choice.

3. What is the length of life of the typical demand curve? Illustrate your answer.

4. If the general market demand for men's shoes is fairly elastic, how does the demand for men's dress shoes compare to it? How does the demand curve for women's shoes compare to the demand curve for men's shoes?

5. If the demand for perfume is inelastic above and below the present price, should the price be raised? Why or why not?

6. If the demand for shrimp is highly elastic below the present price, should the price be lowered?

7. Discuss what factors lead to inelastic demand and supply curves. Are they likely to be found together in the same situation?

8. Why would a marketing manager prefer to sell a product that has no close substitutes? Are high profits almost guaranteed?

9. If a manufacturer's well-known product is sold at the same price by many retailers in the same community, is this an example of pure competition? When a community has many small grocery stores, are they in pure competition? What characteristics are needed to have a purely competitive market?

10. List three products that are sold in purely competitive markets and three that are sold in monopolistically competitive markets. Do any of these products have anything in common? Can any generalizations be made about competitive situations and marketing mix planning?

11. Cite a local example of an oligopoly, explaining why it is an oligopoly.

B

Marketing Arithmetic

LEARNING OBJECTIVES

Marketing students must become familiar with the essentials of the language of business. Businesspeople commonly use accounting terms when talking about costs, prices, and profit. And using accounting data is a practical tool in analyzing marketing problems. The objectives of this appendix and the sections that follow will help you understand these concepts and how they are used by marketing managers.

When you finish this appendix, you should:

1. understand the components of an operating statement (profit and loss statement).
2. know how to compute the stockturn rate.
3. understand how operating ratios can help analyze a business.
4. understand how to calculate markups and markdowns.
5. understand how to calculate a return on investment (ROI) and return on assets (ROA).
6. understand the basic forecasting approaches and why they are used.
7. understand important new terms (shown in red).

THE OPERATING STATEMENT

An **operating statement** is a simple summary of the financial results of a company's operations over a specified period of time. Some beginning students may feel that the operating statement is complex, but as we'll soon see, this really isn't true. *The main purpose of the operating statement is determining the net profit figure and presenting data to support that figure.* This is why the operating statement is often referred to as the *profit and loss statement.*

Exhibit B–1 shows an operating statement for a wholesale or retail business. The statement is complete and detailed so you will see the framework throughout the discussion, but the amount of detail on an operating statement is *not* standardized. Many companies use financial statements with much less detail than this one. They emphasize clarity and readability rather than detail. To really understand an operating statement, however, you must know about its components.

Only three basic components

The basic components of an operating statement are *sales*—which come from the sale of goods and services; *costs*—which come from the producing and selling process; and the balance—called *profit or loss*—which is just the difference between sales and costs. So there are only three basic components in the statement: sales, costs, and profit (or loss). Other items on an operating statement are there only to provide supporting details.

Time period covered may vary

There is no one time period an operating statement covers. Rather, statements are prepared to satisfy the needs of a particular business. This may be at the end of each day or at the end of each week. Usually, however, an operating statement summarizes results for one month, three months, six months, or a full year. Since the time period does vary, this information is included in the heading of the statement as follows:

Perry Company
Operating Statement
For the (Period) Ended (Date)

Also see Exhibit B–1.

Perry Company
Operating Statement
For the Year Ended December 31, 200X

Gross sales			$540,000
Less: Returns and allowances			40,000
Net sales			$500,000
Cost of sales:			
Beginning inventory at cost		$ 80,000	
Purchases at billed cost.	$310,000		
Less: Purchase discounts	40,000		
Purchases at net cost	270,000		
Plus: freight-in	20,000		
Net cost of delivered purchases.		290,000	
Cost of goods available for sale		370,000	
Less: Ending inventory at cost		70,000	
Cost of sales.			300,000
Gross margin (gross profit)			200,000
Expenses:			
Selling expenses:			
Sales salaries	60,000		
Advertising expense.	20,000		
Website updates	10,000		
Delivery expense.	10,000		
Total selling expense		100,000	
Administrative expense:			
Office salaries	30,000		
Office supplies.	10,000		
Miscellaneous administrative expense	5,000		
Total administrative expense		45,000	
General expense:			
Rent expense.	10,000		
Miscellaneous general expenses.	5,000		
Total general expense.		15,000	
Total expenses.			160,000
Net profit from operation			$ 40,000

Management uses of operating statements

Before going on to a more detailed discussion of the components of our operating statement, let's think about some of the uses for such a statement. Exhibit B–1 shows that a lot of information is presented in a clear and concise manner. With this information, a manager can easily find the relation of net sales to the cost of sales, the gross margin, expenses, and net profit. Opening and closing inventory figures are available—as is the amount spent during the period for the purchase of goods for resale. Total expenses are listed to make it easier to compare them with previous statements and to help control these expenses.

All this information is important to a company's managers. Assume that a particular company prepares monthly operating statements. A series of these statements is a valuable tool for directing and controlling the business. By comparing results from one month to the next, managers can uncover unfavorable trends in the sales, costs, or profit areas of the business and take any needed action.

A skeleton statement gets down to essential details

Let's refer to Exhibit B–1 and begin to analyze this seemingly detailed statement to get first-hand knowledge of the components of the operating statement.

As a first step, suppose we take all the items that have dollar amounts extended to the third, or right-hand, column. Using these items only, the operating statement looks like this:

Gross sales	$540,000
Less: Returns and allowances	40,000
Net sales	500,000
Less: Cost of sales	300,000
Gross margin.	200,000
Less: Total expenses.	160,000
Net profit (loss)	$ 40,000

Is this a complete operating statement? The answer is *yes*. This skeleton statement differs from Exhibit B–1 only in supporting detail. All the basic components are included. In fact, the only items we must list to have a complete operating statement are

Net sales	$500,000
Less: Costs	460,000
Net profit (loss).	$ 40,000

These three items are the essentials of an operating statement. All other subdivisions or details are just useful additions.

Meaning of sales

Now let's define the meaning of the terms in the skeleton statement.

The first item is sales. What do we mean by sales? The term **gross sales** is the total amount charged to all customers during some time period. However, there is always some customer dissatisfaction or just plain errors in ordering and shipping goods. This results in returns and allowances, which reduce gross sales.

A **return** occurs when a customer sends back purchased products. The company either refunds the purchase price or allows the customer dollar credit on other purchases.

An **allowance** usually occurs when a customer is not satisfied with a purchase for some reason. The company gives a price reduction on the original invoice (bill), but the customer keeps the goods and services.

These refunds and price reductions must be considered when the firm computes its net sales figure for the period. Really, we're only interested in the revenue the company manages to keep. This is **net sales**—the actual sales dollars the company receives. Therefore, all reductions, refunds, cancellations, and so forth made because of returns and allowances are deducted from the original total (gross sales) to get net sales. This is shown below.

Gross sales	$540,000
Less: Returns and allowances	40,000
Net sales	$500,000

Meaning of cost of sales

The next item in the operating statement—**cost of sales**—is the total value (at cost) of the sales during the period. We'll discuss this computation later. Meanwhile, note that after we obtain the cost of sales figure, we subtract it from the net sales figure to get the gross margin.

Meaning of gross margin and expenses

Gross margin (gross profit) is the money left to cover the expenses of selling the products and operating the business. Firms hope that a profit will be left after subtracting these expenses.

Selling expense is commonly the major expense below the gross margin. Note that in Exhibit B–1, **expenses** are all the remaining costs subtracted from the gross margin to get the net profit. The expenses in this case are the selling, administrative, and general expenses. (Note that the cost of purchases and cost of sales are not included in this total expense figure—they were subtracted from net sales earlier to get the gross margin. Note, also, that some accountants refer to cost of sales as cost of goods sold.)

Net profit—at the bottom of the statement—is what the company earned from its operations during a particular period. It is the amount left after the cost of sales and the expenses are subtracted from net sales. *Net sales and net profit are not the same.* Many firms have large sales and no profits—they may even have losses! That's why understanding costs, and controlling them, is important.

DETAILED ANALYSIS OF SECTIONS OF THE OPERATING STATEMENT

Cost of sales for a wholesale or retail company

The cost of sales section includes details that are used to find the cost of sales ($300,000 in our example).

In Exhibit B–1, you can see that beginning and ending inventory, purchases, purchase discounts, and freight-in are all necessary to calculate cost of sales. If we pull the cost of sales section from the operating statement, it looks like this:

Cost of sales:		
Beginning inventory at cost		$ 80,000
Purchases at billed cost....................	$310,000	
Less: Purchase discounts	40,000	
Purchases at net cost......................	270,000	
Plus: Freight-in	20,000	
Net cost of delivered purchases		290,000
Cost of goods available for sale.............		370,000
Less: Ending inventory at cost............		70,000
Cost of sales..........................		$300,000

Cost of sales is the cost value of what is *sold,* not the cost of goods on hand at any given time.

Inventory figures merely show the cost of goods on hand at the beginning and end of the period the statement covers. These figures may be obtained by physically counting goods on hand on these dates or estimated from perpetual inventory records that show the inventory balance at any given time. The methods used to determine the inventory should be as accurate as possible because these figures affect the cost of sales during the period and net profit.

The net cost of delivered purchases must include freight charges and purchase discounts received since these items affect the money actually spent to buy goods and bring them to the place of business. A **purchase discount** is a reduction of the original invoice amount for some business reason. For example, a cash discount may be given for prompt payment of the amount due. We subtract the total of such discounts from the original invoice cost of purchases to get the *net* cost of purchases. To this figure we add the freight charges for bringing the goods to the place of business. This gives the net cost of *delivered* purchases. When we add the net cost of delivered purchases to the beginning inventory at cost, we have the total cost of goods available for sale during the period. If we now subtract the ending inventory at cost from the cost of the goods available for sale, we get the cost of sales.

One important point should be noted about cost of sales. The way the value of inventory is calculated varies from one company to another—and it can cause big differences in the cost of sales and the operating statement. (See any basic accounting textbook for how the various inventory valuation methods work.)

Exhibit B–1 shows the way the manager of a wholesale or retail business arrives at his cost of sales. Such a business *purchases* finished products and resells them. In a manufacturing company, the purchases section of this operating statement is replaced by a section called cost of production. This section includes purchases of raw materials and parts, direct and indirect labor costs, and factory overhead charges (such as heat, light, and power) that are necessary to produce finished products. The cost of production is added to the beginning finished products inventory to arrive at the cost of products available for sale. Often, a separate cost of production statement is prepared, and only the total cost of production is shown in the operating statement. See Exhibit B–2 for an illustration of the cost of sales section of an operating statement for a manufacturing company.

Expenses

Expenses go below the gross margin. They usually include the costs of selling and the costs of administering the business. They do not include the cost of sales, either purchased or produced.

There is no right method for classifying the expense accounts or arranging them on the operating statement. They can just as easily be arranged alphabetically or according to amount, with the largest placed at the top and so on down the line. In a business of

Exhibit B–2
Cost of Sales Section of an Operating Statement for a Manufacturing Firm

Cost of sales:			
Finished products inventory (beginning)		$ 20,000	
Cost of production (Schedule 1)		100,000	
Total cost of finished products available for sale		120,000	
Less: Finished products inventory (ending) ...		30,000	
Cost of sales...........................			$ 90,000
Schedule 1, Schedule of cost of production			
Beginning work in process inventory			15,000
Raw materials:			
Beginning raw materials inventory............		10,000	
Net cost of delivered purchases		80,000	
Total cost of materials available for use		90,000	
Less: Ending raw materials inventory		15,000	
Cost of materials placed in production		75,000	
Direct labor.....................................		20,000	
Manufacturing expenses:			
Indirect labor	$4,000		
Maintenance and repairs....................	3,000		
Factory supplies	1,000		
Heat, light, and power	2,000		
Total manufacturing expenses		10,000	
Total manufacturing costs			105,000
Total work in process during period			120,000
Less: Ending work in process inventory........			20,000
Cost of production			$100,000

any size, though, it is clearer to group the expenses in some way and use subtotals by groups for analysis and control purposes. This was done in Exhibit B–1.

Summary on operating statements

The statement presented in Exhibit B–1 contains all the major categories in an operating statement—together with a normal amount of supporting detail. Further detail can be added to the statement under any of the major categories without changing the nature of the statement. The amount of detail normally is determined by how the statement will be used. A stockholder may be given a sketchy operating statement—while the one prepared for internal company use may have a lot of detail.

COMPUTING THE STOCKTURN RATE

A detailed operating statement can provide the data needed to compute the **stockturn rate**—a measure of the number of times the average inventory is sold during a year. Note that the stockturn rate is related to the *turnover during a year*, not the length of time covered by a particular operating statement.

The stockturn rate is a very important measure because it shows how rapidly the firm's inventory is moving. Some businesses typically have slower turnover than others. But a drop in turnover in a particular business can be very alarming. It may mean that the firm's assortment of products is no longer as attractive as it was. Also, it may mean that the firm will need more working capital to handle the same volume of sales. Most businesses pay a lot of attention to the stockturn rate, trying to get faster turnover (and lower inventory costs).

Three methods, all basically similar, can be used to compute the stockturn rate. Which method is used depends on the data available. These three methods, which usually give approximately the same results, are shown below.[*]

(1) $$\frac{\text{Cost of sales}}{\text{Average inventory at cost}}$$

(2) $$\frac{\text{Net sales}}{\text{Average inventory at selling price}}$$

(3) $$\frac{\text{Sales in units}}{\text{Average inventory in units}}$$

Computing the stockturn rate will be illustrated only for Formula 1, since all are similar. The only difference is that the cost figures used in Formula 1 are changed to a selling price or numerical count basis in Formulas 2 and 3. (Note: Regardless of the method used, you must have both the numerator and denominator of the formula in the same terms.)

If the inventory level varies a lot during the year, you may need detailed information about the inventory level at different times to compute the average inventory. If it stays at about the same level during the year, however, it's easy to get an estimate. For example, using Formula 1, the average inventory at cost is computed by adding the beginning and ending inventories at cost and dividing by 2. This average inventory figure is then divided into the cost of sales (in cost terms) to get the stockturn rate.

For example, suppose that the cost of sales for one year was $1,000,000. Beginning inventory was $250,000 and ending inventory $150,000. Adding the two inventory figures and dividing by 2, we get an average inventory of $200,000. We next divide the cost of sales by the average inventory ($1,000,000 ÷ $200,000) and get a stockturn rate of 5. The stockturn rate is covered further in Chapter 17.

---

*Differences occur because of varied markups and nonhomogeneous product assortments. In an assortment of tires, for example, those with low markups might have sold much better than those with high markups. But with Formula 3, all tires would be treated equally.

OPERATING RATIOS HELP ANALYZE THE BUSINESS

Many businesspeople use the operating statement to calculate **operating ratios**—the ratio of items on the operating statement to net sales—and to compare these ratios from one time period to another. They can also compare their own operating ratios with those of competitors. Such competitive data is often available through trade associations. Each firm may report its results to a trade association, which then distributes summary results to its members. These ratios help managers control their operations. If some expense ratios are rising, for example, those particular costs are singled out for special attention.

Operating ratios are computed by dividing net sales into the various operating statement items that appear below the net sales level in the operating statement. The net sales is used as the denominator in the operating ratio because it shows the sales the firm actually won.

We can see the relation of operating ratios to the operating statement if we think of there being another column to the right of the dollar figures in an operating statement. This column contains percentage figures, using net sales as 100 percent. This approach can be seen below.

Gross sales.	$540,000	
Less: Returns and allowances	40,000	
Net sales	500,000	100%
Less: Cost of sales	300,000	60
Gross margin	200,000	40
Less: Total expenses	160,000	32
Net profit	$ 40,000	8%

The 40 percent ratio of gross margin to net sales in the above example shows that 40 percent of the net sales dollar is available to cover selling and administrative expenses and provide a profit. Note that the ratio of expenses to sales added to the ratio of profit to sales equals the 40 percent gross margin ratio. The net profit ratio of 8 percent shows that 8 percent of the net sales dollar is left for profit.

The value of percentage ratios should be obvious. The percentages are easily figured and much easier to compare than large dollar figures.

Note that because these operating statement categories are interrelated, only a few pieces of information are needed to figure the others. In this case, for example, knowing the gross margin percent and net profit percent makes it possible to figure the expenses and cost of sales percentages. Further, knowing just one dollar amount and the percentages lets you figure all the other dollar amounts.

MARKUPS

A **markup** is the dollar amount added to the cost of sales to get the selling price. The markup usually is similar to the firm's gross margin because the markup amount added onto the unit cost of a product by a retailer or wholesaler is expected to cover the selling and administrative expenses and to provide a profit.

The markup approach to pricing is discussed in Chapter 17, so it will not be discussed at length here. But a simple example illustrates the idea. If a retailer buys an article that costs $1 when delivered to his store, he must sell it for more than this cost if he hopes to make a profit. So he might add 50 cents onto the cost of the article to cover his selling and other costs and, hopefully, to provide a profit. The 50 cents is the markup.

The 50 cents is also the gross margin or gross profit from that item *if* it is sold. But note that it is *not* the net profit. Selling expenses may amount to 35 cents, 45 cents, or even 55 cents. In other words, there is no guarantee the markup will cover costs. Further, there is no guarantee customers will buy at the marked-up price. This may require markdowns, which are discussed later in this appendix.

Markup conversions

Often it is convenient to use markups as percentages rather than focusing on the actual dollar amounts. But markups can be figured as a percent of cost or selling price. To have some agreement, *markup (percent)* will mean percentage of selling price unless stated otherwise. So the 50-cent markup on the $1.50 selling price is a markup of 33⅓ percent. On the other hand, the 50-cent markup is a 50 percent markup on cost.

Some retailers and wholesalers use markup conversion tables or spreadsheets to easily convert from cost to selling price, depending on the markup on selling price they want. To see the interrelation, look at the two formulas below. They can be used to convert either type of markup to the other.

$$(4) \qquad \frac{\text{Percent markup}}{\text{on selling price}} = \frac{\text{Percent markup on cost}}{100\% + \text{Percent markup on cost}}$$

$$(5) \qquad \frac{\text{Percent markup}}{\text{on cost}} = \frac{\text{Percent markup on selling price}}{100\% - \text{Percent markup on selling price}}$$

In the previous example, we had a cost of $1, a markup of 50 cents, and a selling price of $1.50. We saw that the markup on selling price was 33⅓ percent—and on cost, it was 50 percent. Let's substitute these percentage figures—in Formulas 4 and 5—to see how to convert from one basis to the other. Assume first of all that we only know the markup on selling price and want to convert to markup on cost. Using Formula 5, we get

$$\text{Percent markup on cost} = \frac{33\tfrac{1}{3}\%}{100\% - 33\tfrac{1}{3}\%} = \frac{33\tfrac{1}{3}\%}{66\tfrac{2}{3}\%} = 50\%$$

On the other hand, if we know only the percent markup on cost, we can convert to markup on selling price as follows:

$$\text{Percent markup on selling price} = \frac{50\%}{100\% + 50\%} = \frac{50\%}{150\%} = 33\tfrac{1}{3}\%$$

These results can be proved and summarized as follows:

$$\text{Markup } \$0.50 = 50\% \text{ of cost, or } 33\tfrac{1}{3}\% \text{ of selling price}$$

$$\underline{+ \text{ Cost } \$1.00 = 100\% \text{ of cost, or } 66\tfrac{2}{3}\% \text{ of selling price}}$$

$$\text{Selling price } \$1.50 = 150\% \text{ of cost, or } 100\% \text{ of selling price}$$

Note that when the selling price ($1.50) is the base for a markup calculation, the markup percent (33 ⅓ percent = $.50/$1.50) must be less than 100 percent. As you can see, that's because the markup percent and the cost percent (66 ⅔ percent = $1.00/$1.50) sum to exactly 100 percent. So if you see a reference to a markup percent that is greater than 100 percent, it could not be based on the selling price and instead must be based on cost.

MARKDOWN RATIOS HELP CONTROL RETAIL OPERATIONS

The ratios we discussed above were concerned with figures on the operating statement. Another important ratio, the **markdown ratio**, is a tool many retailers use to measure the efficiency of various departments and their whole business. But note that it is *not directly related to the operating statement*. It requires special calculations.

A **markdown** is a retail price reduction required because customers won't buy some item at the originally marked-up price. This refusal to buy may be due to a variety of reasons—soiling, style changes, fading, damage caused by handling, or an original price that was too high. To get rid of these products, the retailer offers them at a lower price.

Markdowns are generally considered to be due to business errors, perhaps because of poor buying, original markups that are too high, and other reasons. (Note, however, that some retailers use markdowns as a way of doing business rather than a way to correct errors. For example, a store that buys out overstocked fashions from other retailers may start by marking each item with a high price and then reduce the price each week until it sells.) Regardless of the reason, however, markdowns are reductions in the original price—and they are important to managers who want to measure the effectiveness of their operations.

Markdowns are similar to allowances because price reductions are made. Thus, in computing a markdown ratio, markdowns and allowances are usually added together and then divided by net sales. The markdown ratio is computed as follows:

$$\text{Markdown \%} = \frac{\text{\$ Markdowns} + \text{\$ Allowances}}{\text{\$ Net sales}} \times 100$$

The 100 is multiplied by the fraction to get rid of decimal points.

Returns are *not* included when figuring the markdown ratio. Returns are treated as consumer errors, not business errors, and therefore are not included in this measure of business efficiency.

Retailers who use markdown ratios usually keep a record of the amount of markdowns and allowances in each department and then divide the total by the net sales in each department. Over a period of time, these ratios give management one measure of the efficiency of buyers and salespeople in various departments.

It should be stressed again that the markdown ratio is not calculated directly from data on the operating statement since the markdowns take place before the products are sold. In fact, some products may be marked down and still not sold. Even if the marked-down items are not sold, the markdowns—that is, the reevaluations of their value—are included in the calculations in the time period when they are taken.

The markdown ratio is calculated for a whole department (or profit center), *not* individual items. What we are seeking is a measure of the effectiveness of a whole department, not how well the department did on individual items.

RETURN ON INVESTMENT (ROI) REFLECTS ASSET USE

Another off-the-operating-statement ratio is **return on investment (ROI)**—the ratio of net profit (after taxes) to the investment used to make the net profit, multiplied by 100 to get rid of decimals. Investment is not shown on the operating statement. But it is shown on the **balance sheet** (statement of financial condition), which is another accounting statement that shows a company's assets, liabilities, and net worth. It may take some digging or special analysis, however, to find the right investment number.

Investment means the dollar resources the firm has invested in a project or business. For example, a new product may require $4 million in new money—for inventory, accounts receivable, promotion, and so on—and its attractiveness may be judged by its likely ROI. If the net profit (after taxes) for this new product is expected to be $1 million in the first year, then the ROI is 25 percent—that is, ($1 million ÷$4 million) × 100.

There are two ways to figure ROI. The *direct* way is

$$\text{ROI (in \%)} = \frac{\text{Net profit (after taxes)}}{\text{Investment}} \times 100$$

The *indirect* way is

$$\text{ROI (in \%)} = \frac{\text{Net profit (after taxes)}}{\text{Sales}} = \frac{\text{Sales}}{\text{Investment}} \times 100$$

This way is concerned with net profit margin and turnover—that is,

$$\text{ROI (in \%)} = \text{Net profit margin} \times \text{Turnover} \times 100$$

This indirect way makes it clearer how to *increase* ROI. There are three ways:

1. Increase profit margin (with lower costs or a higher price).
2. Increase sales.
3. Decrease investment.

Effective marketing strategy planning and implementation can increase profit margins or sales, or both. And careful asset management can decrease investment.

ROI is a revealing measure of how well managers are doing. Most companies have alternative uses for their funds. If the returns in a business aren't at least as high as outside uses, then the money probably should be shifted to the more profitable uses.

Some firms borrow more than others to make investments. In other words, they invest less of their own money to acquire assets—what we called *investments*. If ROI calculations use only the firm's own investment, this gives higher ROI figures to those who borrow a lot—which is called *leveraging*. To adjust for different borrowing proportions—to make comparisons among projects, departments, divisions, and companies easier—another ratio has come into use. **Return on assets (ROA)** is the ratio of net profit (after taxes) to the assets used to make the net profit—times 100. Both ROI and ROA measures are trying to get at the same thing—how effectively the company is using resources. These measures became increasingly popular as profit rates dropped and it became more obvious that increasing sales volume doesn't necessarily lead to higher profits—or ROI or ROA. Inflation and higher costs for borrowed funds also force more concern for ROI and ROA. Marketers must include these measures in their thinking or top managers are likely to ignore their plans and requests for financial resources.

FORECASTING TARGET MARKET POTENTIAL AND SALES

Effective strategy planning and developing a marketing plan require estimates of future sales, costs, and profits. Without such information, it's hard to know if a strategy is potentially profitable.

The marketing manager's estimates of sales, costs, and profits are usually based on a forecast (estimate) of target **market potential**—what a whole market segment might buy—and a **sales forecast**—an estimate of how much an industry or firm hopes to sell to a market segment. Usually we must first try to judge market potential before we can estimate what share a particular firm may be able to win with its particular marketing mix.

Three levels of forecasts are useful

We're interested in forecasting the potential in specific market segments. To do this, it helps to make three levels of forecasts.

Some economic conditions affect the entire global economy. Others may influence only one country or a particular industry. And some may affect only one company or one product's sales potential. For this reason, a common top-down approach to forecasting is to

1. Develop a *national income forecast* (for each country in which the firm operates) and use this to
2. Develop an *industry sales forecast*, which then is used to
3. Develop forecasts for a *specific company*, its *specific products*, and the *segments* it targets.

SunLite maintains a large domestic inventory of its casual outdoor furniture so it can quickly resupply its retailer-customers. A number of firms, like Third Wave Research Group, now offer marketers software or databases to help them more accurately forecast sales for specific market areas, products, or segments.

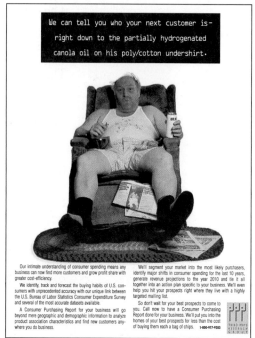

Generally, a marketing manager doesn't have to make forecasts for a national economy or the broad industry. This kind of forecasting—basically trend projecting—is a specialty in itself. Such forecasts are available in business and government publications, and large companies often have their own technical specialists. Managers can use just one source's forecast or combine several. Unfortunately, however, the more targeted the marketing manager's earlier segmenting efforts have been, the less likely that industry forecasts will match the firm's product-markets. So managers have to move directly to estimating potential for their own companies and for their specific products.

Two approaches to forecasting

Many methods are used to forecast market potential and sales, but they can all be grouped into two basic approaches: (1) extending past behavior and (2) predicting future behavior. The large number of methods may seem confusing at first, but this variety has an advantage. Forecasts are so important that managers often develop forecasts in two or three different ways and then compare the differences before preparing a final forecast.

Extending past behavior can miss important turning points

When we forecast for existing products, we usually have some past data to go on. The basic approach, called **trend extension**, extends past experience into the future. With existing products, for example, the past trend of actual sales may be extended into the future. See Exhibit B–3.

Ideally, when extending past sales behavior, we should decide why sales vary. This is the difficult and time-consuming part of sales forecasting. Usually we can gather a lot of data about the product or market or about changes in the marketing environment. But

Exhibit B–3
Straight-Line Trend Projection—Extends Past Sales into the Future

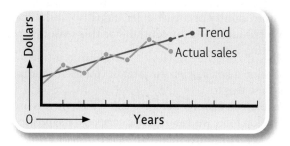

unless we know the *reason* for past sales variations, it's hard to predict in what direction, and by how much, sales will move. Graphing the data and statistical techniques—including correlation and regression analysis—can be useful here. (These techniques, which are beyond our scope, are discussed in beginning statistics courses.)

Once we know why sales vary, we can usually develop a specific forecast. Sales may be moving directly up as population grows in a specific market segment, for example. So we can just estimate how population is expected to grow and project the impact on sales.

The weakness of the trend extension method is that it assumes past conditions will continue unchanged into the future. In fact, the future isn't always like the past. An agent wholesaler's business may have been on a steady path, but the development of the Internet may have added a totally new factor. The past trend for the agent's sales has changed because now the agent can quickly reach a broader market.

As another example, for years the trend in sales of disposable diapers moved closely with the number of new births. However, as the number of women in the workforce increased and as more women returned to jobs after babies were born, use of disposable diapers increased, and the trend changed. As in these examples, trend extension estimates will be wrong whenever big changes occur. For this reason—although they may extend past behavior for one estimate—most managers look for another way to help them forecast sharp market changes.

Predicting future behavior takes judgment

When we try to predict what will happen in the future, instead of just extending the past, we have to use other methods and add more judgment. Some of these methods (to be discussed later) include juries of executive opinion, salespeople's estimates, surveys, panels, and market tests.

FORECASTING COMPANY AND PRODUCT SALES BY EXTENDING PAST BEHAVIOR

Past sales can be extended

At the very least, a marketing manager ought to know what the firm's present markets look like and what it has sold to them in the past. A detailed sales analysis for products and geographic areas helps to project future results.

Just extending past sales into the future may not seem like much of a forecasting method. But it's better than just assuming that next year's total sales will be the same as this year's.

Factor method includes more than time

A simple extension of past sales gives one forecast. But it's usually desirable to tie future sales to something more than the passage of time.

The factor method tries to do this. The **factor method** tries to forecast sales by finding a relation between the company's sales and some other factor (or factors). The basic formula is: Something (past sales, industry sales, etc.) *times* some factor *equals* sales forecast. A **factor** is a variable that shows the relation of some other variable to the item being forecast. For instance, in our example above, both the birthrate and the number of working mothers are factors related to sales of disposable diapers.

A bread producer example

The following example, about a bread producer, shows how firms can make forecasts for many geographic market segments using the factor method and available data. This general approach can be useful for any firm—producer, wholesaler, or retailer.

Analysis of past sales relationships showed that the bread manufacturer regularly sold one-tenth of 1 percent (0.001) of the total retail food sales in its various target markets. This is a single factor. By using this single factor, a manager could estimate the producer's sales in a new market for the coming period by multiplying a forecast of expected retail food sales by 0.001.

Sales & Marketing Management magazine makes retail food sales estimates each year. Exhibit B–4 shows the kind of geographically detailed data available.

Exhibit B–4 Sample Page from *Sales & Marketing Management's* Survey of Buying Power: Metro and County Totals

COLORADO

METRO AREA County City	Total Population (000s)	18-24	25-34	35-49	50+	House-holds (000s)	Total Retail Sales	Food & Beverage Stores	Food Service & Drinking Establishments	General Merchandise	Furniture & Home Furnish. & Electron. & Appliances	Motor Vehicle & Parts Dealers	Total EBI ($000)	Median Hsld. EBI	A $20,000-$34,999	B $35,000-$49,999	C $50,000 & Over	Buying Power Index
BOULDER-LONGMONT	303.7	13.6	15.5	25.6	22.4	119.6	5,081,227	1,001,555	556,377	448,453	247,484	1,220,087	7,716,546	51,714	17.8	17.1	51.6	0.1360
BOULDER	303.7	13.6	15.5	25.6	22.4	119.6	5,081,227	1,001,555	556,377	448,453	247,484	1,220,087	7,716,546	51,714	17.8	17.1	51.6	0.1360
•Boulder	97.1	26.4	18.8	20.0	20.1	40.7	2,147,663	439,133	267,970	121,357	117,520	447,464	2,480,204	43,427	21.5	15.8	43.1	0.0479
•Longmont	74.6	8.7	14.6	25.3	23.6	28.0	1,126,804	250,483	122,965	125,103	40,068	272,449	1,531,271	47,526	19.4	20.1	46.8	0.0290
COLORADO SPRINGS	537.3	10.7	14.4	24.7	22.6	200.1	7,883,675	819,826	647,101	984,753	465,488	2,031,112	10,259,019	42,082	24.7	21.0	38.7	0.1994
EL PASO	537.3	10.7	14.4	24.7	22.6	200.1	7,883,675	819,826	647,101	984,753	465,488	2,031,112	10,259,019	42,082	24.7	21.0	38.7	0.1994
•Colorado Springs	373.1	10.5	14.8	24.5	23.7	146.5	6,786,693	628,690	549,107	858,048	443,063	1,848,219	7,353,670	41,212	24.9	20.9	37.5	0.1515
DENVER	2,199.5	9.2	16.2	25.0	23.8	858.0	33,750,880	4,700,116	3,232,590	3,615,646	2,518,616	9,368,057	52,585,220	49,109	18.8	19.0	48.9	0.9282
ADAMS	382.9	10.5	16.7	23.3	21.1	134.3	4,558,882	670,017	371,810	416,956	385,657	1,466,781	6,459,840	42,802	22.5	22.4	38.7	0.1253
Thornton	87.3	9.7	17.5	24.9	18.0	30.6	707,386	152,812	68,679	122,478	40,099	150,769	1,594,293	48,053	19.4	22.4	46.8	0.0270
Westminster	105.4	9.9	17.1	26.0	20.3	40.1	1,052,771	153,993	114,177	292,678	100,304	88,416	2,368,971	51,512	17.0	21.6	51.9	0.0384
ARAPAHOE	505.4	8.8	15.1	25.7	23.9	197.5	9,846,119	1,160,676	872,314	963,885	595,477	4,049,257	13,314,002	52,887	18.2	18.6	53.1	0.2422
Aurora	286.8	10.4	17.2	24.0	21.0	109.0	3,889,713	531,245	378,269	566,166	225,882	1,236,463	5,874,943	47,398	20.7	21.5	46.0	0.1076
DENVER	568.5	11.1	19.9	22.1	25.1	243.7	9,287,630	1,235,129	1,270,413	730,810	755,362	1,701,220	13,899,851	42,540	21.6	18.4	41.0	0.2474
•Denver	568.5	11.1	19.9	22.1	25.1	243.7	9,275,551	1,224,988	1,269,426	730,810	755,362	1,700,815	13,899,851	42,540	21.6	18.4	41.0	0.2474
DOUGLAS	200.7	4.9	15.9	29.6	18.0	69.6	2,725,601	517,182	250,871	294,714	289,389	355,394	5,147,699	59,715	10.9	18.2	64.7	0.0851
JEFFERSON	542.0	8.3	13.2	26.8	26.5	212.9	7,332,648	1,117,112	467,182	1,209,281	492,731	1,795,405	13,763,828	54,470	16.4	18.6	55.1	0.2282
Arvada	104.0	8.0	11.9	25.9	28.1	40.0	1,007,245	224,707	79,597	133,524	60,181	74,965	2,332,241	51,557	18.1	19.3	51.8	0.0376
Lakewood	148.0	9.9	15.2	24.1	28.8	62.3	2,065,827	297,529	149,068	292,832	124,879	567,796	3,451,207	46,782	20.8	21.1	45.2	0.0599
DENVER-BOULDER-GREELEY CONSOLIDATED AREA	2,695.8	10.0	15.9	24.9	23.6	1,044.7	40,882,936	5,939,206	3,929,714	4,267,775	2,809,610	11,246,398	63,170,157	48,397	19.2	19.0	47.9	1.1216

Population — % Population by Age Group; Retail Sales by Store Group ($000); Effective Buying Income — % of Hslds by EBI Group

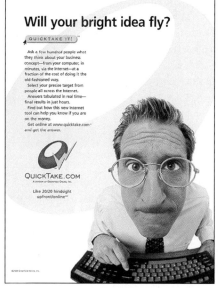

Let's carry this bread example further—using the data in Exhibit B–4 for the Denver, Colorado, metro area. Denver's food sales were $4,700,116,000 for the previous year. By simply accepting last year's food sales as an estimate of next year's sales and multiplying the food sales estimate for Denver by the 0.001 factor (the firm's usual share of food purchases in such markets), the manager would have an estimate of next year's bread sales in Denver. That is, last year's food sales estimate ($4,700,116,000) times 0.001 equals this year's bread sales estimate of $4,700,116.

Factor method can use several factors

The factor method is not limited to just one factor; several factors can be used together. For example, *Sales & Marketing Management* regularly gives a "buying power index" (BPI) as a measure of the potential in different geographic areas. See Exhibit B–4. This index considers (1) the population in a market, (2) the retail sales in that market, and (3) income in that market. The BPI for the Denver, Colorado, metro area, for example, is 0.9282— that is, Denver accounts for 0.9282 percent of the total U.S. buying power. This means that consumers who live in Denver have higher than average buying power. We know this because Denver accounts for about 0.7723 percent of the U.S. population.

Using several factors rather than only one uses more information. And in the case of the BPI, it gives a single measure of a market's potential. Rather than falling back on using population only, or income only, or trying to develop a special index, the BPI can be used in the same way that we used the 0.001 factor in the bread example.

PREDICTING FUTURE BEHAVIOR CALLS FOR MORE JUDGMENT AND SOME OPINIONS

These past-extending methods use quantitative data—projecting past experience into the future and assuming that the future will be like the past. But this is risky in competitive markets. Usually, it's desirable to add some judgment to other forecasts before making the final forecast yourself.

Jury of executive opinion adds judgment

One of the oldest and simplest methods of forecasting—the **jury of executive opinion**—combines the opinions of experienced executives, perhaps from marketing, production, finance, purchasing, and top management. Each executive estimates market potential and sales for the *coming years*. Then they try to work out a consensus.

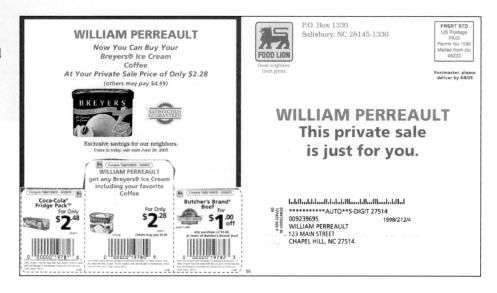

The main advantage of the jury approach is that it can be done quickly and easily. On the other hand, the results may not be very good. There may be too much extending of the past. Some of the executives may have little contact with outside market influences. But their estimates could point to major shifts in customer demand or competition.

Estimates from salespeople can help too

Using salespeople's estimates to forecast is like the jury approach. But salespeople are more likely than home office managers to be familiar with customer reactions and what competitors are doing. Their estimates are especially useful in some business markets where the few customers may be well known to the salespeople. But this approach can be useful in any type of market.

However, managers who use estimates from salespeople should be aware of the limitations. For example, new salespeople may not know much about their markets. Even experienced salespeople may not be aware of possible changes in the economic climate or the firm's other environments. And if salespeople think the manager is going to use the estimates to set sales quotas, the estimates may be low!

Surveys, panels, and market tests

Special surveys of final buyers, retailers, or wholesalers can show what's happening in different market segments. Some firms use panels of stores—or final consumers—to keep track of buying behavior and to decide when just extending past behavior isn't enough.

Surveys are sometimes combined with market tests when the company wants to estimate customers' reactions to possible changes in its marketing mix. A market test might show that a product increased its share of the market by 10 percent when its price was dropped 1 cent below competition. But this extra business might be quickly lost if the price were increased 1 cent above competition. Such market experiments help the marketing manager make good estimates of future sales when one or more of the four Ps is changed.

Accuracy depends on the marketing mix

Forecasting can help a marketing manager estimate the size of possible market opportunities. But the accuracy of any sales forecast depends on whether the firm selects and implements a marketing mix that turns these opportunities into sales and profits.

KEY TERMS

QUESTIONS AND PROBLEMS

1. Distinguish between the following pairs of items that appear on operating statements: (*a*) gross sales and net sales, and (*b*) purchases at billed cost and purchases at net cost.

2. How does gross margin differ from gross profit? From net profit?

3. Explain the similarity between markups and gross margin. What connection do markdowns have with the operating statement?

4. Compute the net profit for a company with the following data:

Beginning inventory (cost)	$ 150,000
Purchases at billed cost	330,000
Sales returns and allowances	250,000
Rent.....................................	60,000
Salaries.................................	400,000
Heat and light...........................	180,000
Ending inventory (cost)	250,000
Freight cost (inbound)	80,000
Gross sales..............................	1,300,000

5. Construct an operating statement from the following data:

Returns and allowances.................	$ 150,000
Expenses	20%
Closing inventory at cost	600,000
Markdowns..............................	2%
Inward transportation	30,000
Purchases	1,000,000
Net profit (5%).........................	300,000

6. Compute net sales and percent of markdowns for the data given below:

Markdowns	$ 40,000
Gross sales..........................	400,000
Returns..............................	32,000
Allowances	48,000

7. (*a*) What percentage markups on cost are equivalent to the following percentage markups on selling price: 20, $37\frac{1}{2}$, 50, and $66\frac{2}{3}$? (*b*) What percentage markups on selling price are equivalent to the following percentage markups on cost: $33\frac{1}{3}$, 20, 40, and 50?

8. What net sales volume is required to obtain a stockturn rate of 20 times a year on an average inventory at cost of $100,000 with a gross margin of 25 percent?

9. Explain how the general manager of a department store might use the markdown ratios computed for her various departments. Is this a fair measure? Of what?

10. Compare and contrast return on investment (ROI) and return on assets (ROA) measures. Which would be best for a retailer with no bank borrowing or other outside sources of funds (that is, the retailer has put up all the money that the business needs)?

11. Explain the difference between a forecast of market potential and a sales forecast.

12. Suggest a plausible explanation for sales fluctuations for (*a*) computers, (*b*) ice cream, (*c*) washing machines, (*d*) tennis rackets, (*e*) oats, (*f*) disposable diapers, and (*g*) latex for rubber-based paint.

13. Explain the factor method of forecasting. Illustrate your answer.

14. Based on data in Exhibit B–4, discuss the relative market potential of the city of Boulder, Colorado, and the city of Lakewood, Colorado, for (*a*) prepared cereals, (*b*) automobiles, and (*c*) furniture.

Career Planning
in Marketing

LEARNING OBJECTIVES

One of the hardest decisions facing most college students is the choice of a career. Of course you are the best judge of your own objectives, interests, and abilities. Only you can decide what career you should pursue. However, you owe it to yourself to at least consider the possibility of a career in marketing. This chapter's objectives will help organize your thinking about a career and the marketing plan you could develop to help you achieve your career goals.

When you finish this appendix, you should:

1. know there is a job or career for you in marketing.

2. know that marketing jobs can be rewarding, pay well, and offer opportunities for growth.

3. understand the difference between "people-oriented" and "thing-oriented" jobs.

4. know about the many marketing jobs you can choose from.

5. know some ways to use the Internet to help with career planning.

THERE'S A PLACE IN MARKETING FOR YOU

We're happy to tell you that many opportunities are available in marketing. There's a place in marketing for everyone, from a service provider in a fast-food restaurant to a vice president of marketing in a large company such as Microsoft or Procter & Gamble. The opportunities range widely, so it will help to be more specific. In the following pages, we'll discuss (1) the typical pay for different marketing jobs, (2) setting your own objectives and evaluating your interests and abilities, and (3) the kinds of jobs available in marketing. We'll also provide some ideas about using the Internet to get more information and perhaps apply for a job or post your own information; this material is in the box titled "Getting Wired for a Career in Marketing."

THERE ARE MANY MARKETING JOBS, AND THEY CAN PAY WELL

There are many interesting and challenging jobs for those with marketing training. You may not know it, but 60 percent of graduating college students take their initial job in a sales, marketing, or customer service position regardless of their stated major. So you'll have a head start because you've been studying marketing, and companies are always looking for people who already have skills in place. In terms of upward mobility, more CEOs have come from the sales and marketing side than all other fields combined. The sky is the limit for those who enter the sales and marketing profession prepared for the future!

Further, marketing jobs open to college-level students do pay well. At the time this went to press, marketing graduates were being offered starting salaries around $33,800, with a range from about $25,000 to $55,000 a year. Students with a master's in marketing averaged about $60,000; those with an MBA averaged about $75,000. Starting salaries can vary considerably, depending on your background, experience, and location.

Starting salaries in marketing compare favorably with many other fields. They are lower than those in such fields as computer science and electrical engineering, where college graduates are currently in demand. But there is even better opportunity for personal growth, variety, and income in many marketing positions. The *American Almanac of Jobs and Salaries* ranks the median income of marketers number 10 in a list of 125 professions. Marketing also supplies about 50 percent of the people who achieve senior management ranks.

How far and fast your career and income rise above the starting level, however, depends on many factors, including your willingness to work, how well you get along with people, and your individual abilities. But most of all, it depends on *getting results*—individually and through other people. And this is where many marketing jobs offer the newcomer great opportunities. It is possible to show initiative, ability, creativity, and judgment in marketing jobs. And some young people move up very rapidly in marketing. Some even end up at the top in large companies or as owners of their own businesses.

Marketing is often the route to the top

Marketing is where the action is! In the final analysis, a firm's success or failure depends on the effectiveness of its marketing program. This doesn't mean the other functional areas aren't important. It merely reflects the fact that a firm won't have much need for accountants, finance people, production managers, and so on if it can't successfully meet customers' needs and sell its products.

Because marketing is so vital to a firm's survival, many companies look for people with training and experience in marketing when filling key executive positions. In general, chief executive officers for the nation's largest corporations are more likely to have backgrounds in marketing and distribution than in other fields such as production, finance, and engineering.

DEVELOP YOUR OWN PERSONAL MARKETING STRATEGY

Now that you know there are many opportunities in marketing, your problem is matching the opportunities to your own personal objectives and strengths. Basically the problem is a marketing problem: developing a marketing strategy to sell a product—yourself—to potential employers. Just as in planning strategies for products, developing your own strategy takes careful thought. Exhibit C–1 shows how you can organize your own strategy planning. This exhibit shows that you should evaluate

Exhibit C–1
Organizing Your Own Personal Marketing Strategy Planning

yourself first—a personal analysis—and then analyze the environment for opportunities. This will help you sharpen your own long-and short-run objectives, which will lead to developing a strategy. Finally, you should start implementing your own personal marketing strategy. These ideas are explained more fully below.

CONDUCT YOUR OWN PERSONAL ANALYSIS

You are the product you are going to include in your own marketing plan. So first you have to decide what your long-run objectives are—what you want to do, how hard you want to work, and how quickly you want to reach your objectives. Be honest with yourself—or you will eventually face frustration. Evaluate your own personal strengths and weaknesses—and decide what factors may become the key to your success. Finally, as part of your personal analysis, set some preliminary timetables to guide your strategy planning and implementation efforts. Let's spell this out in detail.

Set broad long-run objectives

Your strategy planning may require some trial-and-error decision making. But at the very beginning, you should make some tentative decisions about your own objectives—what you want out of a job and out of life. At the very least, you should decide whether you are just looking for a job or whether you want to build a career. Beyond this, do you want the position to be personally satisfying—or is the financial return enough? And just how much financial return do you need? Some people work only to support themselves (and their families) and their leisure-time activities. These people try to find job opportunities that provide adequate financial returns but aren't too demanding of their time or effort.

Other people look first for satisfaction in their job—and they seek opportunities for career advancement. Financial rewards may be important too, but these are used mainly as measures of success. In the extreme, the career-oriented individual may be willing to sacrifice a lot, including leisure and social activities, to achieve success in a career.

Once you've tentatively decided these matters, then you can get more serious about whether you should seek a job or a career in marketing. If you decide to pursue a career, you should set your broad long-run objectives to achieve it. For example, one long-run objective might be to pursue a career in marketing management (or marketing research). This might require more academic training than you planned, as well as a different kind of training. If your objective is to get a job that pays well, on the other hand, then this calls for a different kind of training and different kinds of job experiences before completing your academic work.

Evaluate personal strengths and weaknesses

What kind of a Job is right for you?

Because of the great variety of marketing jobs, it's hard to generalize about what aptitudes you should have to pursue a career in marketing. Different jobs attract people with various interests and abilities. We'll give you some guidelines about what kinds of interests and abilities marketers should have. However, if you're completely lost about your own interests and abilities, see your campus career counselor and take some vocational aptitude and interest tests. These tests will help you to compare yourself with people who are now working in various career positions. They will *not* tell you what you should do, but they can help, especially in eliminating possibilities you are less interested in or less able to do well in.

Are you people-oriented or thing-oriented?

One useful approach is to decide whether you are basically "people-oriented" or "thing-oriented." This is a very important decision. A people-oriented person might be very unhappy in an inventory management job, for example, whereas a thing-oriented person might be miserable in a personal selling or retail management job that involves a lot of customer contact.

Getting Wired for a Career in Marketing

The Internet is a great resource at every stage of career planning and job hunting. It can help you learn: how to do a self-assessment, the outlook for different industries and jobs, what firms have jobs open, how to improve a résumé and post it online for free, and just about anything else you can imagine. Here we'll highlight just a few ideas and websites that can help you get started. However, if you start with some of these suggestions, each website you visit will provide links to other relevant sites that will give you new ideas.

One good place to start is at Yahoo! (www.yahoo.com). Select "employment and work" under the "business" heading, and then click "careers and jobs." Take a look at all of the information and services that are available when you select the Career Tools link. For example, you can browse résumé tools and salary information, look at job listings, and much more. You may also want to study the similar information at www.monster.com.

Another website to check is at www.marketingjobs.com. It has listings of marketing jobs, links to a number of companies with openings, a résumé center with ideas for preparing a résumé and posting it on the Internet, and lists of helpful periodicals. You might also go to www.careerjournal.com. There are job listings, job-hunting advice, career articles from *The Wall Street Journal*, and more. You can create and post a résumé there as well. Professional associations are another great resource. For example, the American Marketing Association website is at www.marketingpower.com, and the Sales and Marketing Executives International website is at www.smei.org. The Council of Supply Chain Management Professionals website is at www.cscmp.org.

Another potentially useful website address is www.collegegrad.com. It has links for posting a résumé, information on writing cover letters and getting references, and ideas about how to find a company with job openings. To get a sample of what's possible in tracking down jobs, visit the website at www.thejobresource.com and experiment with its search engine, which lets you look at what's available by state. For example, you might want to search through job listings that mention terms such as *entry level*, *marketing*, *advertising*, and *sales*.

This should get you started. Remember, however, that in Chapter 7 we gave addresses for a number of websites with search engines. You can use one of them to help find more detail on any topic that interests you. For example, you might go to www.google.com and search on terms such as *marketing jobs*, *salary surveys*, *post a résumé*, or *entry level position*.

Marketing has both people-oriented and thing-oriented jobs. People-oriented jobs are primarily in the promotion area—where company representatives must make contact with potential customers. This may be direct personal selling or customer service activities—for example, in technical service or installation and repair. Thing-oriented jobs focus more on creative activities and analyzing data—as in advertising and marketing research—or on organizing and scheduling work—as in operating warehouses, transportation agencies, or the back-end of retailers.

People-oriented jobs tend to pay more, in part because such jobs are more likely to affect sales, the lifeblood of any business. Thing-oriented jobs, on the other hand, are often seen as cost generators rather than sales generators. Taking a big view of the whole company's operations, the thing-oriented jobs are certainly necessary—but without sales, no one is needed to do them.

Thing-oriented jobs are usually done at a company's facilities. Further, especially in lower-level jobs, the amount of work to be done and even the nature of the work may be spelled out quite clearly. The time it takes to design questionnaires and tabulate results, for example, can be estimated with reasonable accuracy. Similarly, running a warehouse, analyzing inventory reports, scheduling outgoing shipments, and so on are more like production operations. It's fairly easy to measure an employee's effectiveness and productivity in a thing-oriented job. At the least, time spent can be used to measure an employee's contribution.

A sales rep, on the other hand, might spend all weekend thinking and planning how to make a half-hour sales presentation on Monday. For what should the sales rep be compensated—the half-hour presentation, all of the planning and thinking that went into it, or the results? Typically, sales reps are rewarded for results—and this helps account for the sometimes extremely high salaries paid to effective order getters. At the same time, some people-oriented jobs can be routinized and are lower paid. For example, salespeople in some retail stores are paid at or near the minimum wage.

Managers needed for both kinds of jobs

Here we have oversimplified deliberately to emphasize the differences among types of jobs. Actually, of course, there are many variations between the two extremes. Some sales reps must do a great deal of analytical work before they make a presentation. Similarly, some marketing researchers must be extremely people-sensitive to get potential customers to reveal their true feelings. But the division is still useful because it focuses on the primary emphasis in different kinds of jobs.

Managers are needed for the people in both kinds of jobs. Managing others requires a blend of both people and analytical skills—but people skills may be the more important of the two. Therefore, people-oriented individuals are often promoted into managerial positions more quickly.

What will differentiate your product?

After deciding whether you're generally people-oriented or thing-oriented, you're ready for the next step—trying to identify your specific strengths (to be built on) and weaknesses (to be avoided or remedied). It is important to be as specific as possible so you can develop a better marketing plan. For example, if you decide you are more people-oriented, are you more skilled in verbal or written communication? Or if you are more thing-oriented, what specific analytical or technical skills do you have? Are you good at working with numbers, using a computer, solving complex problems, or coming to the root of a problem? Other possible strengths include past experience (career-related or otherwise), academic performance, an outgoing personality, enthusiasm, drive, motivation, and so on.

It is important to see that your plan should build on your strengths. An employer will be hiring you to do something—so promote yourself as someone who is able to do something *well*. In other words, find your competitive advantage in your unique strengths—and then communicate these unique things about *you* and what you can do. Give an employer a reason to pick you over other candidates by showing that you'll add superior value to the company.

While trying to identify strengths, you also must realize that you may have some important weaknesses, depending on your objectives. If you are seeking a career that requires technical skills, for example, then you need to get those skills. Or if you are seeking a career that requires independence and self-confidence, then you should try to develop those characteristics in yourself—or change your objectives.

Set some timetables

At this point in your strategy planning process, set some timetables to organize your thinking and the rest of your planning. You need to make some decisions at this point to be sure you see where you're going. You might simply focus on getting your first job, or you might decide to work on two marketing plans: (1) a short-run plan to get your first job and (2) a longer-run plan—perhaps a five-year plan—to show how you're going to accomplish your long-run objectives. People who are basically job-oriented may get away with only a short-run plan, just drifting from one opportunity to another as their own objectives and opportunities change. But those interested in careers need a longer-run plan. Otherwise, they may find themselves pursuing attractive first-job opportunities that satisfy short-run objectives but quickly leave them frustrated when they realize that they can't achieve their long-run objectives without additional training or other experiences that require starting over again on a new career path.

Exhibit C–2   Some Career Paths and Salary Ranges

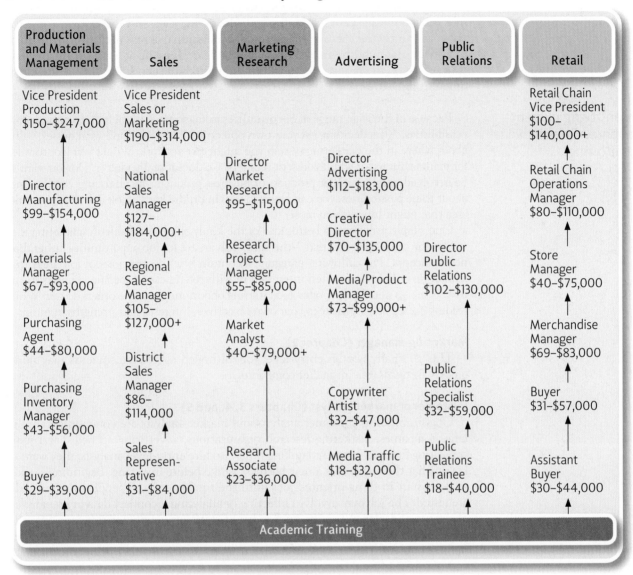

ENVIRONMENT ANALYSIS

Strategy planning is a matching process. For your own strategy planning, this means matching yourself to career opportunities. So let's look at opportunities available in the marketing environment. (The same approach applies, of course, in the whole business area.) Exhibit C–2 shows some of the possibilities and salary ranges.

Keep in mind that the salary ranges in Exhibit C–2 are rough estimates. Salaries for a particular job often vary depending on a variety of factors, including company size, industry, and geographic area. People in some firms also get big bonuses that are not counted in their salary. The salary figures in this exhibit were assembled from several sources, including the salary surveys conducted by the U.S. Bureau of Labor Statistics and the useful "salary wizard" at www.salary.com. (You can use it to update the information in the exhibit for your region and to explore salaries for other positions; when this data was assembled in the spring of 2006, the average starting salary for a college graduate with a marketing degree was about $33,800.) Note that the ranges in the table are not the very lowest and highest salaries for the positions, but rather the range includes the majority of people in that position. There are many other sources of salary information. For example, *Advertising Age* publishes an annual survey of salary levels for different marketing and advertising jobs, with breakdowns by company size and other factors. Many trade associations, across a variety of different industries, also publish surveys. If you use the search engine at www.google.com and do a search on *salary survey*, you will find hundreds of such surveys for a number of different industries.

Identifying current opportunities in marketing

Because of the wide range of opportunities in marketing, it's helpful to narrow your possibilities. After deciding on your own objectives, strengths, and weaknesses, think about where in the marketing system you might like to work. Would you like to work for manufacturers, or wholesalers, or retailers? Or does it really matter? Do you want to be involved with consumer products or business products? By analyzing your feelings about these possibilities, you can begin to zero in on the kind of job and the functional area that might interest you most.

One simple way to get a better idea of the kinds of jobs available in marketing is to review the chapters of this text—this time with an eye for job opportunities rather than new concepts. The following paragraphs contain brief descriptions of job areas that marketing graduates are often interested in with references to specific chapters in the text. Some, as noted below, offer good starting opportunities, while others do not. While reading these paragraphs, keep your own objectives, interests, and strengths in mind.

Marketing manager (Chapter 2)

This is usually not an entry-level job, although aggressive students may move quickly into this role in smaller companies.

Customer or market analyst (Chapters 3, 4, and 5)

Opportunities as consumer analysts and market analysts are commonly found in large companies, marketing research organizations, advertising agencies, and some consulting firms. Investment banking firms also hire entry-level analysts; they want to know what the market for a new business is like before investing. Beginning market analysts start in thing-oriented jobs until their judgment and people-oriented skills are tested. The job may involve collecting or analyzing secondary data or preparation of reports and plans. Because knowledge of statistics, computer software, Internet search techniques, or behavioral sciences is very important, marketing graduates often find themselves competing with majors from statistics, sociology, computer science, and economics. Graduates who have courses in marketing *and* one or more of these areas may have the best opportunities.

Purchasing agent/buyer (Chapter 6)

Entry-level opportunities are commonly found in large companies, and there are often good opportunities in the procurement area. Many companies are looking for bright newcomers who can help them find new and better ways to work with suppliers. To get off on the right track, beginners usually start as trainees or assistant buyers under the supervision of experienced buyers. That's good preparation for a promotion to more responsibility.

Marketing research opportunities (Chapter 7)

There are entry-level opportunities at all levels in the channel (but especially in large firms where more formal marketing research is done in-house), in advertising agencies, and in marketing research firms. Some general management consulting firms also have marketing research groups. Quantitative and behavioral science skills are extremely important in marketing research, so some firms are more interested in business graduates who have studied statistics or psychology as electives. But there still are many opportunities in marketing research for marketing graduates, especially if they have some experience in working with computers and statistical software. A recent graduate might begin in a training program—conducting interviews or summarizing open-ended answers from questionnaires and helping to prepare electronic slide presentations for clients—before being promoted to a position as an analyst, assistant project manager, account representative, and subsequent management positions.

Packaging specialists (Chapter 8)

Packaging manufacturers tend to hire and train interested people from various backgrounds—there is little formal academic training in packaging. There are many sales opportunities in this field—and with training, interested people can become specialists fairly quickly in this growing area.

Product/brand manager (Chapters 8 and 9)

Many multiproduct firms have brand or product managers handling individual products—in effect, managing each product as a separate business. Some firms hire marketing graduates as assistant brand or product managers, although larger firms typically recruit MBAs for these jobs. Many firms prefer that recent college graduates spend some time in the field doing sales work or working with an ad agency or sales promotion agency before moving into brand or product management positions.

Product planner (Chapter 9)

This is usually not an entry-level position. Instead, people with experience on the technical side of the business or in sales might be moved onto a new-product development team as they demonstrate judgment and analytical skills. However, new employees with winning ideas for new products don't go unnoticed—and they sometimes have the opportunity to grow fast with ideas they spearhead. Having a job that puts you in contact with customers is often a good way to spot new needs.

Distribution channel management (Chapter 10)

This work is typically handled or directed by sales managers and therefore is not an entry-level position. However, many firms form teams of specialists who work closely with their counterparts in other firms in the channel to strengthen coordination and relationships. Such a team often includes new people in sales or purchasing because it gives them exposure to a different part of the firm's activities. It's also not unusual for people to start working in a particular industry and then take a different job at a different level in the channel. For example, a graduate who has trained to be a store manager for a chain of sporting goods stores might go to work for a manufacturers' representative that handles a variety of sports equipment.

Logistics opportunities (Chapter 11)

There are many sales opportunities with physical distribution specialists—but there are also many thing-oriented jobs involving traffic management, warehousing, and materials handling. Here training in accounting, finance, and computer methods could be very useful. These kinds of jobs are available at all levels in channels of distribution.

Retailing opportunities (Chapter 12)

Not long ago, most entry-level marketing positions in retailing involved some kind of sales work. That has changed rapidly in recent years because the number of large retail chains is expanding and they often recruit graduates for their management training programs. Retailing positions tend to offer lower-than-average starting salaries—but they often provide opportunities for very rapid advancement. In a fast-growing chain, results-oriented people can move up very quickly. Most retailers require new employees to have some selling experience before managing others—or buying. A typical marketing graduate can expect to work as an assistant manager or do some sales work and manage one or several departments before advancing to a store management position—or to a staff position that might involve buying, advertising, location analysis, and so on.

Wholesaling opportunities (Chapter 12)

Entry-level jobs with merchant wholesalers typically fall into one of two categories. The first is in the logistics area—working with transportation management, inventory control, distribution customer service, and related activities. The other category usually involves personal selling and customer support. Agent wholesalers typically focus on selling, and entry-level jobs often start out with order-taking responsibilities that grow into order-getting responsibilities. Many wholesalers are moving much of their information to the Internet, so marketing students with skills and knowledge in this arena may find especially interesting opportunities.

Personal selling opportunities (Chapter 14)

Because there are so many different types of sales jobs and so many people are employed in sales, there are many good entry-level opportunities in personal selling. This might be order-getting, order-taking, customer service, or missionary selling. Many sales jobs now rely on sales technology, so some of the most challenging opportunities will go to students who know how to prepare spreadsheets and presentation materials using software programs like Microsoft Office. Many students are reluctant to get into personal selling—but this field offers benefits that are hard to match in any other field. These include the opportunity to earn high salaries and commissions quickly, a chance to develop your self-confidence and resourcefulness, an opportunity to work with minimal supervision—almost to the point of being your own boss—and a chance to acquire product and customer knowledge that many firms consider necessary for a successful career in product/brand management, sales management, and marketing management. On the other hand, many salespeople prefer to spend their entire careers in selling. They like the freedom and earning potential that go with a sales job over the headaches and sometimes lower salaries of sales management positions.

Customer service opportunities (Chapter 14)

As this book points out, marketing managers are recognizing the growing importance in providing customers with service after the sale. There are a number of different opportunities in customer service. Many firms need qualified customer service representatives who work with customers to fulfill their needs and help assure customer satisfaction. Customer service reps may interact with customers on the phone, by online chat, or via e-mail. But other service representatives help customers at their businesses with installations or equipment repair. While some of the entry-level positions that require only a high school education are being outsourced to other countries, positions requiring strong communication skills and a good education provide an opportunity for marketing majors. There are also management positions that develop customer service strategies, control costs, and focus on hiring, training, and retaining customer service reps and enhancing customer satisfaction.

Advertising opportunities (Chapters 13 and 15)

Job opportunities in this area are varied and highly competitive. And because the ability to communicate and a knowledge of the behavioral sciences are important, marketing and advertising graduates often find themselves competing with majors from fields such as English, communication, psychology, and sociology. There are thing-oriented jobs such as copywriting, media buying, art, computer graphics, and so on. Competition for these jobs is very strong—and they go to people with a track record. So the entry-level positions are as assistant to a copywriter, media buyer, or art director. There are also people-oriented positions involving work with clients, which are probably of more interest to marketing graduates. This is a glamorous but small and extremely competitive industry where young people can rise very rapidly—but they can also be as easily displaced by new bright young people. Entry-level salaries in advertising are typically low. There are sometimes good opportunities to get started in advertising with a retail chain that prepares its advertising internally. Another way to get more experience with advertising is to take a job with one of the media, perhaps in sales or as a customer consultant. Selling advertising space on a website or cable TV station or newspaper may not seem as glamorous as developing TV ads, but media salespeople help their customers solve promotion problems and get experience dealing with both the business and creative side of advertising.

Sales promotion opportunities (Chapters 13 and 15)

The number of entry-level positions in the sales promotion area is growing because the number of specialists in this area is growing. For example, specialists might help a company plan a special event for employees, figure out procedures to distribute free samples, or perhaps set up a database to send customers a newsletter. Because clients' needs are often different, creativity and judgment are required. It is usually difficult for an inexperienced person to show evidence of these skills right out of school, so entry-level people often work with a project manager until they learn the ropes. In companies that handle their own sales promotion work, a beginner usually starts by getting some experience in sales or advertising.

Pricing opportunities (Chapters 16 and 17)

Pricing decisions are usually handled by experienced executives. However, in some large companies and consulting firms there are opportunities as pricing analysts for marketing graduates who have quantitative skills. These people work as assistants to higher-level executives and collect and analyze information about competitors' prices and costs, as well as the firm's own costs. Thus, being able to work with accounting numbers and computer spreadsheets is often important in these jobs. However, sometimes the route to these jobs is through experience in marketing research or product management.

Credit management opportunities

Specialists in credit have a continuing need for employees who are interested in evaluating customers' credit ratings and ensuring that money gets collected. Both people skills and thing skills can be useful here. Entry-level positions normally involve a training program and then working under the supervision of others until your judgment and abilities are tested.

International marketing opportunities

Many marketing students are intrigued with the adventure and foreign travel promised by careers in international marketing. Some firms hire recent college graduates for positions in international marketing, but more often these positions go to MBA graduates. However, that is changing as more and more firms are pursuing international markets. It's an advantage in seeking an international marketing job to know a second language and to know about the culture of countries where you would like to work. Your college may have courses or international exchange programs that would help in these areas. Graduates aiming for a career in international marketing usually must spend time mastering the firm's domestic marketing operations before being sent abroad. So a good way to start is to focus on firms that are already involved in international marketing, or who are planning to move in that direction soon. On the other hand, there are many websites with listings of international jobs. For example, you might want to visit www.overseasjobs.com.

Customer relations/consumer affairs opportunities (Chapters 13 and 18)

Most firms are becoming more concerned about their relations with customers and the general public. Employees in this kind of work, however, usually have held various positions with the firm before doing customer relations.

Study trends that may affect your opportunities

A strategy planner should always be evaluating the future because it's easier to go along with trends than to buck them. This means you should watch for political, technical, or economic changes that might open, or close, career opportunities.

If you can spot a trend early, you may be able to prepare yourself to take advantage of it as part of your long-run strategy planning. Other trends might mean you should avoid certain career options. For example, technological changes in computers and communications, including the Internet, are leading to major changes in retailing and advertising, as well as in personal selling. Cable television, telephone selling, and direct-mail selling may reduce the need for routine order takers, while increasing the need for higher-level order getters. More targeted and imaginative sales presentations for delivery by mail, e-mail, phone, or Internet websites may be needed. The retailers that prosper will have a better understanding of their target markets. And they may need to be supported by wholesalers and manufacturers that can plan targeted promotions that make economic sense. This will require a better understanding of the production and physical distribution side of business, as well as the financial side. And this means better training in accounting, finance, inventory control, and so on. So plan your personal strategy with such trends in mind.

One good way to get more detailed analysis is to go to the U.S. Bureau of Labor Statistics website at http://stats.bls.gov and use the search procedure to look for the term *occupational outlook*. The Bureau provides detailed comments about the outlook for employment and growth in different types of jobs, industries, and regions.

Evaluate business practices

Finally, you need to know how businesses really operate and the kind of training required for various jobs. We've already seen that there are many opportunities in marketing—but not all jobs are open to everyone, and not all jobs are entry-level jobs. Positions such as marketing manager, brand manager, and sales manager are higher rungs on the marketing career ladder. They become available only when you have a few years of experience and have shown leadership and judgment. Some positions require more education than others. So take a hard look at your long-run objectives—and then see what degree you may need for the kinds of opportunities you might like.

DEVELOP OBJECTIVES

Once you've done a personal analysis and environment analysis—identifying your personal interests, your strengths and weaknesses, and the opportunities in the environment—define your short-run and long-run objectives more specifically.

Develop long-run objectives

Your long-run objectives should clearly state what you want to do and what you will do for potential employers. You might be as specific as indicating the exact career area you want to pursue over the next 5 to 10 years. For example, your long-run objective might be to apply a set of marketing research and marketing management tools to the food manufacturing industry, with the objective of becoming director of marketing research in a small food manufacturing company.

Your long-run objectives should be realistic and attainable. They should be objectives you have thought about and for which you think you have the necessary skills (or the capabilities to develop those skills) as well as the motivation to reach the objectives.

Develop short-run objectives

To achieve your long-run objective(s), you should develop one or more short-run objectives. These should spell out what is needed to reach your long-run objective(s). For example, you might need to develop a variety of marketing research skills *and* marketing management skills—because both are needed to reach the longer-run objective. Or you might need an entry-level position in marketing research for a large food manufacturer to gain experience and background. An even shorter-run objective might be to take the academic courses that are necessary to get that desired entry-level job. In this example, you would probably need a minimum of an undergraduate degree in marketing, with an emphasis on marketing research. (Note that, given the longer-run objective of managerial responsibility, a business degree would probably be better than a degree in statistics or psychology.)

DEVELOPING YOUR MARKETING PLAN

Now that you've developed your objectives, move on to developing your own personal marketing plan. This means zeroing in on likely opportunities and developing a specific marketing strategy for these opportunities. Let's talk about that now.

Identify likely opportunities

An important step in strategy planning is identifying potentially attractive opportunities. Depending on where you are in your academic training, this can vary all the way from preliminary exploration to making detailed lists of companies that offer the kinds of jobs that interest you. If you're just getting started, talk to your school's career counselors and placement officers about the kinds of jobs being offered to your school's graduates. Your marketing instructors can help you be realistic about ways you can match your training, abilities, and interests to job opportunities. Also, it helps to read business publications such as *BusinessWeek, Fortune, The Wall Street Journal,* and *Advertising Age.* If you are interested in opportunities in a particular industry, check at your library or on the Internet to see if there are trade publications or websites that can bring you up to speed on the marketing issues in that area. Your library or college may also have an online service to make it easier to search for articles about specific companies or industries. And many companies have their own websites that can be a very useful source of information.

Don't overlook the business sections of your local newspapers to keep in touch with marketing developments in your area. And take advantage of any opportunity to talk with marketers directly. Ask them what they're doing and what satisfactions they find in their jobs. Also, if your college has a marketing club, join it and participate actively in the club's programs. It will help you meet marketers and students with serious interest in the field. Some may have had interesting job experiences and can provide you with leads on part-time jobs or exciting career opportunities.

If you're far along in your present academic training, list companies that you know something about or are willing to investigate, trying to match your skills and interests with possible opportunities. Narrow your list to a few companies you might like to work for.

If you have trouble narrowing down to specific companies, make a list of your personal interest areas—sports, travel, reading, music, or whatever. Think about the companies that compete in markets related to these interests. Often your own knowledge about these areas and interest in them can give you a competitive advantage in getting a job. This helps you focus on companies that serve needs you think are important or interesting. A related approach is to do a search on the Internet for websites related to your areas of interest. Websites often display ads or links to firms that are involved in that specific interest area. Further, many companies post job openings on their own websites or at websites that specialize in promoting job searches by many companies.

Then do some research on these companies. Find out how they are organized, their product lines, and their overall strategies. Try to get clear job descriptions for the kinds of positions you're seeking. Match these job descriptions against your understanding of these jobs and your objectives. Jobs with similar titles may offer very different opportunities. By researching job positions and companies in depth, you should begin to have a feel for where you would be comfortable as an employee. This will help you narrow your target market of possible employers to perhaps five firms. For example, you may decide that your target market for an entry-level position consists of large corporations with (1) in-depth training programs, (2) a wide product line, and (3) a wide variety of marketing jobs that will enable you to get a range of experiences and responsibilities within the same company.

Planning your product

Just like any strategy planner, you must decide what product features are necessary to appeal to your target market. Identify which credentials are mandatory and which are optional. For example, is your present academic program enough, or will you need more training? Also, identify what technical skills are needed, such as computer programming or accounting. Further, are there any business experiences or extracurricular activities that might help make your product more attractive to employers? This might involve active participation in college organizations or work experience, either on the job or in internships.

Planning your promotion

Once you identify target companies and develop a product you hope will be attractive to them, you have to tell these potential customers about your product. You can write directly to prospective employers, sending a carefully developed résumé that reflects your strategy planning. Or you can visit them in person (with your résumé). Many colleges run well-organized interviewing services. Seek their advice early in your strategy planning effort.

IMPLEMENTING YOUR MARKETING PLAN

When you complete your personal marketing plan, you have to implement it, starting with working to accomplish your short-run objectives. If, as part of your plan, you decide that you need specific outside experience, then arrange to get it. This may mean taking a low-paying job or even volunteering to work in political organizations or volunteer organizations where you can get that kind of experience. If you decide that you need skills you can learn in academic courses, plan to take those courses. Similarly, if you don't have a good understanding of your opportunities, then learn as much as you can about possible jobs by talking to professors, taking advanced courses, and talking to businesspeople. Of course, trends and opportunities can change—so continue to read business publications, talk with professionals in your areas of interest, and be sure that the planning you've done still makes sense.

Strategy planning must adapt to the environment. If the environment changes or your personal objectives change, you have to develop a new plan. This is an ongoing process—and you may never be completely satisfied with your strategy planning. But even trying will make you look much more impressive when you begin your job interviews. Remember, while all employers would like to hire a Superman or a Wonder Woman, they are also impressed with candidates who know what they want to do and are looking for a place where they can fit in and make a contribution. So planning a personal strategy and implementing it almost guarantee you'll do a better job of career planning, and this will help ensure that you reach your own objectives, whatever they are.

Whether or not you decide to pursue a marketing career, the authors wish you the best of luck in your search for a challenging and rewarding career, wherever your interests and abilities may take you.

Video Cases

Essentials of Marketing includes two different types of marketing cases: the 8 special video cases in this section and the 35 traditional cases in the next section. All of the cases offer you the opportunity to evaluate marketing concepts at work in a variety of real-world situations. However, the video cases add a multimedia dimension because we have produced a special video to accompany each of the written cases. The videos are available to professors who adopt *Essentials of Marketing* for use in their course. (These case-based videos are in addition to the teaching videos we have custom produced and made available to instructors for possible use with other parts of the text.)

The videos bring to life many of the issues considered in each case. However, you can read and analyze the written case descriptions even if there is no time or opportunity to view the video. Either way, you'll find the case interesting and closely tied to the important concepts you've studied in the text.

The set of questions at the end of each case will get you started in thinking about the marketing issues in the case. Further, we provide instructors with a number of suggestions on using the video cases—both for group discussion in class or individual assignments. Thus, as is also true with the traditional cases in the next section, the video cases can be used in many different ways and sequences. You can analyze all of the cases, or only a subset. In fact, the same case can be analyzed several times for different purposes. As your understanding of marketing deepens throughout the course, you'll "see" many more of the marketing issues considered in each case.

1. Chick-fil-A: "Eat Mor Chikin" (Except on Sunday)*

There aren't many companies like Chick-fil-A. Most U.S. companies struggle to balance ambitious financial objectives with the desire to be ethical in business dealings and demonstrate a social conscience. Chick-fil-A easily surpasses industry norms for financial performance and eagerly embraces and protects a corporate culture rich with religious values and charity. The contrast is striking to most observers. Yet the Chick-fil-A phenomenon is easily understood when you study its entrepreneurial heritage.

S. Truett Cathy, founder, chairman, and CEO of Chick-fil-A started his restaurant career in 1946 when he and his brother Ben opened a restaurant in Atlanta called the Dwarf Grill (renamed the Dwarf House two years later). It was not until 1967 that Cathy opened the first Chick-fil-A restaurant in Atlanta's Greenbriar Shopping Center. He is credited with introducing the original boneless breast of chicken sandwich and pioneering the placement of fast-food restaurants in shopping malls. Today, Chick-fil-A is the second-largest quick-service chicken restaurant chain in the United States, based on sales ($1.975 billion in 2005). It operates more than 1,250 restaurants in 37 states and Washington, D.C.

Chick-fil-A's unique corporate culture derives from Cathy's Christian background and his desire to inspire and influence people. The company's official statement of corporate purpose is "to glorify God by being a faithful steward of all that is entrusted to us and to have a positive influence on all who come in contact with Chick-fil-A." This level of commitment to religious values is reflected in a number of ways. For example, all Chick-fil-A locations, in a mall or stand-alone, are closed on Sundays. Cathy has been quoted on numerous occasions as saying, "Our decision to close on Sunday (starting in 1946) was our way of honoring God and directing our attention to things more important than our business. If it took seven days to make a living with a restaurant, then we needed to be in some other line of work. Through the years, I have never wavered from that position."

Chick-fil-A also has an extensive corporate giving program. The company has helped thousands of restaurant employees, foster children, and other young people through the WinShape Foundation that Cathy established in 1984 to help "shape winners." The foundation sponsors WinShape Homes, which currently operates 14 homes in Georgia, Tennessee, Alabama, and Brazil. The WinShape College Program at Berry College in Rome, Georgia, is a co-op program offering joint four-year scholarship funding to incoming freshmen of up to $32,000. In addition to the WinShape scholarships, Chick-fil-A offers $1,000 college scholarships to its restaurant team members. Camp WinShape is a summer camp for boys and girls. WinShape Marriage provides development, education, and encouragement for married couples on the campus of WinShape Retreat, a multiuse conference and retreat facility located on the Mountain Campus of Berry College.

Chick-fil-A's unique corporate culture is matched by its equally unique marketing efforts, especially in the advertising and promotion areas. Its "Eat Mor Chikin" campaign is one of the longest-running advertising campaigns in the United States. Started in June 1995 when the first Chick-fil-A billboard was erected in Atlanta, the Eat Mor Chikin cows have become cult figures, convincing diners to stray from the herd of beef-burger eateries and to "eat mor chikin"—particularly in Chick-fil-A restaurants. In focus groups, respondents rate the cows as one of the three things they like best about the Chick-fil-A brand—the other two being the food and the company's policy of being closed on Sundays.

The Eat Mor Chikin theme, created by Dallas-based ad agency the Richards Group, was first introduced in 1995 as a three-dimensional billboard concept depicting a black-and-white cow sitting atop the back of another cow painting the words "Eat-Mor-Chikin" on the billboard. Since then, the theme has been used as the basis of an integrated marketing campaign, which encompasses billboards, in-store point-of-purchase materials, promotions, radio and TV advertising, clothing and merchandise (e.g., plush cows, bobble-head cows), and calendars. Introduced in 1998, Chick-fil-A's cow calendars have been a marketer's dream come true. The calendar is produced annually by the Richards Group. Sales have sharply increased—from 337,000 for the first printed calendar to 1.5 million for the 2006 renaissance-themed calendar entitled "Cows in Shining Armor," featuring "famous" medieval cows named Angus Kahn, Charbroilemagne, Boldhoof, Lady Guineveal, and Moolius Caesar. The calendars sell for $5 and contain Chick-fil-A food and beverage coupon offers.

Sponsorship of collegiate sports such as the Chick-fil-A Peach Bowl (renamed the Chick-fil-A Bowl in 2006) are another way in which Chick-fil-A builds its brand. A local promotion emphasis at the market and restaurant level completes Chick-fil-A's integrated marketing approach.

In 1998, the Eat Mor Chikin campaign won a national silver EFFIE award in the Fast Food/Restaurants category for creativity and effectiveness in advertising. The outdoor Advertising Association of America recognized Chick-fil-A and its renegade cows with the organization's OBIE Hall of Fame Award in 2006.

Chick-fil-A is growing rapidly through store openings and menu additions. Menu additions include Chick-fil-A Chick-n Strips in 1995, Chick-fil-A Cool Wraps in 2001, Chick-fil-A Southwest chargrilled salad in 2003, fruit cup in 2004, and a breakfast menu featuring Chick-fil-A Chick-n Minis, a chicken or sausage breakfast burrito, and a chicken, egg, and cheese bagel in 2004. The chain introduced the industry's first premium two-blend coffee line in 2005 with Café Blends and the complementary Cinnamon Cluster. Hand-Spun milkshakes were launched in 2006.

The company had sales of $1.975 billion in 2005 and forecasts sales of $3 billion by 2010. Also by 2010, the company looks to double its current size in terms of new locations, primarily through stand-alone restaurants and aggressive expansion into the western United States. Chick-fil-A also has licensed restaurants in nontraditional locations such as airports, corporate offices, hospitals, and college campuses.

Dan Cathy, the son of S. Truett Cathy and Chick-fil-A's current president and COO, takes restaurant openings seriously. The openings are not simple ribbon-cuttings. Cathy

---

*This case was prepared by Dr. J. B. Wilkinson, professor emeritus, Youngstown State University.

holds a dedication dinner during which he and other company leaders wait on newly hired employees. He also "camps out" the night before a store opening with Chick-fil-A raving fans and customers. Beginning in 2003, Chick-fil-A offered the first 100 customers in line at its new stores a free combo meal each week for a year. People lined up hours in advance, setting up tents and lawn chairs overnight in the parking lot to ensure a place in line. Observing this, Cathy decided to join them and since then, camping out with Chick-fil-A fans and customers at store openings has become a tradition for him.

Dan Cathy takes his role as a leader seriously and defines his role through his interaction with customers and employees. He frequently visits Chick-fil-A restaurants and often pitches in to help. Like his father, Dan Cathy is on a mission to meet customers, franchisees, and employees face to face and spread the Chick-fil-A business philosophy of "Second Mile" service, great food, and influencing others.

1. What types of marketing strategies is Chick-fil-A following?
2. How would you describe Chick-fil-A's positioning strategy?
3. Is closing on Sunday a competitive advantage for Chick-fil-A? Explain.
4. Should other retailers consider closing on Sunday? Why? Why not?

2. Suburban Regional Shopping Malls: Can the Magic Be Restored?*

The suburban regional shopping mall is regarded by many as the "crown jewel" of shopping experiences. In a single location, shoppers can visit over a hundred stores, go to a movie, eat, walk, and lounge for an entire day in a secure, pleasant atmosphere sheltered from undesirable weather and the demands of everyday life. Most Americans at one time or another have escaped for the day to such a mall and felt "uplifted" in spirit by the experience. So pervasive is the suburban regional shopping mall that William Kowinski in *The Malling of America* (1985) claims that in the United States alone there are more enclosed malls than cities, four-year colleges, or television stations! Indeed, few of us can remember a time when shopping was a trip to "downtown" or the central business district (CBD) of a large city.

Many suburban regional shopping malls are over one million square feet in size, contain over a hundred stores, and offer shoppers free parking, restaurants, play facilities, lounge facilities, restrooms, and movie theaters. Some centers even provide amusement rides and other entertainment opportunities. One of the dominant features of these large shopping complexes is the presence of multiple department stores that "anchor" the extreme points of the mall's layout and "pull" shoppers to the mall from surrounding suburban areas. Department stores also encourage shoppers to walk through the mall. In fact, department stores were the driving force behind the original development of suburban regional shopping malls and have played a critical role in their continuing success.

The movement of traditional department stores from CBD locations to the suburbs, complete with large "full-line" departments, contributed greatly to the explosive growth of suburban regional shopping malls during the post–World War II era. At its inception, the suburban regional shopping mall was designed to be a substitute, or even a replacement, for a city's CBD, but without the usual congestion or parking difficulties. This strategy was particularly attractive after the opening of Southdale Center in suburban Minneapolis in 1956 (www.southdale.com), which demonstrated the viability of a regional shopping mall with multiple anchors.

In 2002 there were a total of 46,336 shopping centers in the United States, of which about 1,200 could be considered regional or superregional malls (www.icsc.org). In addition to regional and superregional malls, numerous types of shopping centers have evolved since the 1950s. The International Council of Shopping Centers has defined eight principal shopping center types: neighborhood, community, regional, superregional, fashion/specialty, power, theme/festival, and outlet.

The suburban regional shopping malls and their department store anchors enjoyed great success for almost 50 years and seemed virtually invincible to threats until the final decade of the twentieth century. During that era, several chinks developed in the competitive armor of this type of retail institution, and the problems seem to be getting worse. Shopper activity is declining: the number of tenant vacancies is increasing; and the delinquency rate on mall mortgages is disturbing. Increasingly larger percentages of consumer discretionary income are being spent elsewhere. To make matters worse, many of the older malls need renovating to remain attractive to shoppers. Renovation of an older mall can cost tens of millions of dollars.

Changes in consumers and in their wants and needs appear to be the major factor that underlies the woes of suburban regional shopping malls. Since the first multi-anchor center opened in 1956, the lifestyles of American families have changed significantly. In 1950, for instance, only 24 percent of wives worked outside the home; today, that percentage exceeds 60 percent. Women between the ages of 18 and 45, the mainstay of mall shoppers, simply do not have the time to shop like they once had. As a result, shopping has become much more purpose-driven. Shopping statistics bear this out. Shoppers are visiting suburban regional shopping malls less frequently, visiting fewer stores when they do shop, and also spending less time at the mall when they do shop. Shoppers, however, are more likely to make a purchase when they do visit a mall. Yet the typical suburban regional shopping mall was designed for a "shop-all-day" or a "shop-'til-you-drop" philosophy.

Another consumer trend that spells trouble for suburban regional shopping malls is increased shopper price sensitivity. A wider selection of shopping alternatives from which to choose and the desire to make the family income go farther

---

*This case and the script for the accompanying video were prepared by Dr. J. B. Wilkinson, professor emeritus, Youngstown State University, and Dr. David J. Burns, Xavier University.

(which, in essence, is equal to a pay increase) have proven to be strong forces pushing shoppers to comparison shop between retail establishments—something that most malls are not designed to facilitate. Despite the large number of stores contained within a regional suburban shopping mall, comparison shopping between stores is not an easy task. Most malls are laid out to cater to a leisure-oriented shopper. Similar stores are located in different wings of the shopping mall to encourage shoppers to walk through the entire center. Shoppers may walk upwards to a quarter-mile in their quest to compare products! This is not consistent with the desire for shopping convenience and efficiency on the part of most consumers.

Competition also has played a role in the problems that plague suburban regional shopping malls. High levels of competition characterize most mature industries, and the shopping center industry is no exception. Regional malls have both direct and indirect competitors. Direct competitors are nearby shopping centers with either similar or dissimilar formats. Indirect competitors comprise other types of retail store sites like freestanding or clustered sites and nonstore retailing sites. Nonstore retailing includes online shopping, catalog shopping, home TV shopping, telemarketing, and other forms of direct marketing, all of which have made considerable inroads into retail store sales. Suburban regional shopping malls have been especially vulnerable to both forms of competition.

Many of the more successful retailers (e.g., Kohl's, Home Depot) are located on freestanding sites or in large open-air centers—locations that have greater appeal to time-pressed, purpose-driven shoppers than mall locations. Similarly, many outlet malls, which cater to price-sensitive shoppers, are typically open-air centers to facilitate store access. In addition, some of the newer small shopping centers cater to a focused lifestyle (teen or professional woman) or have an organizing theme (home decor, hobby) that satisfies the specific needs of a market niche by offering a more focused product assortment than what can be found in a suburban regional shopping mall.

Oversupply of retail space has posed considerable problems to all shopping centers. The United States has 20 square feet for every man, woman, and child, compared to 1.4 square feet per person in Great Britain. Sales per square foot of retail space is declining in the United States. In fact, revenue from retail sales is contracting. It grew an average of 2.5 percent in the 1970s; 1.3 percent in the 1980s; and only 0.8 percent in the 1990s, adjusted for inflation. The result has been retail consolidation, store closings, and bankruptcies, leaving shopping centers fighting for a shrinking base of retail tenants.

Finally, department stores, the primary traffic generators for suburban regional shopping malls, are experiencing serious competitive problems. Over the past two decades, department stores have lost half of their market share to discounters and specialty stores. They also have suffered a significant sales revenue decline, causing store closings and consolidation. Given the role department stores have played as traffic generators for shopping malls, the problems of department stores have added to the problems of suburban regional shopping malls. Quite simply, fewer department store shoppers have meant fewer shoppers in the mall. To make matters worse, an empty department store space in a mall gives shoppers less reason to visit that portion of the mall and often leads to the closure of nearby stores. Besides being unproductive, the resulting empty retail space is unsightly, projecting the same image that empty storefronts in the CBDs of cities do—decay and decline.

The predictable outcome of all these changes is that construction of new suburban regional shopping malls has virtually come to a halt. Furthermore, a significant number of existing centers are being "decommissioned"—converted into alternative uses such as office space, learning centers, and telemarketing call centers, or torn down to be replaced by other forms of retail centers. Over 300 malls have been decommissioned since the mid-1990s, a trend which is expected to continue.

The dim outlook for suburban regional shopping malls has stimulated much creative thought about turnaround strategies for those still in operation. One turnaround strategy that has been suggested deals with the way suburban regional shopping malls are traditionally configured and involves changing the way stores in the center are arranged with respect to one another. The traditional layout locates similar stores in different wings or corridors of the center to encourage shoppers to travel through the entire center in their quest to locate and compare products. This type of layout maximizes customer interchange between stores but does not address shopping efficiency. Zonal merchandising represents a different approach to a center's layout. Under zonal merchandising, similar tenants are located in close proximity to one another. This reduces shopping time for shoppers who come to the mall to purchase a specific product. It also creates opportunities for differentiating mall areas in terms of decor, music, amenities, and special events to suit the tastes of shoppers who are most likely to be visiting stores in those areas.

Zonal merchandising has been used most commonly for fast food. Called "food courts," these clusters of fast-food providers have been very successful. Food court tenants have experienced higher levels of sales than under traditional layouts. Food courts also have shown that they are able to draw shoppers from other locations in the mall, similar to the traffic-generating role of a traditional anchor store.

Based on the success of the food court, several attempts to implement zonal merchandising on a wider scale have been made. Beginning with Bridgewater Commons in New Jersey (www.bridgewatercommons.com), several new projects have incorporated zonal merchandising principles, including Rivertown Crossings in Grand Rapids, Michigan (www.rivertown crossings.com), which has grouped some categories of stores by product line carried, and Park Meadows in Denver, Colorado (www.parkmeadows.com), which has grouped stores by customer lifestyle. The results of these endeavors have been promising, and General Growth (www.generalgrowth.com), the developer of Rivertown Crossings, plans to implement some form of clustering at all of its future projects. Attempts to reconfigure existing centers around zonal merchandising ideas, such as the changes at Glendale Galleria in Glendale, California (www.glendalegalleria.com), seem to be successful as well.

An alternative strategy, which has been proposed for turning around traditional suburban regional shopping malls, is the incorporation of entertainment within the center. The idea behind this strategy is quite simple: add value to the shopper's visit to a mall and give shoppers additional reasons to shop in the mall rather than at home. Entertainment can run the gamut from simple play areas or a carousel for children to video arcades and virtual golf courses to a full-scale amusement park, such as the Mall of America (www.mallofamerica.com). However, adding entertainment offerings to suburban regional shopping malls does not guarantee success. The entertainment must be something that will attract shoppers and keep their interest for a lengthy period of time—not something which shoppers tire of easily. Also the effect of the entertainment activities on a center's retailing activities must be considered. Entertainment centers in suburban regional malls often attract people with social goals instead of shopping goals, which does not benefit a center's merchandise-based stores.

Some industry analysts suggest that the key to revitalizing the suburban regional shopping mall is to make the shopping experience itself more exciting. Even at Mall of America, the home of the largest mall-based entertainment facility in the United States, the primary attraction of the center is the entertainment and excitement provided by the shopping experience itself; shoppers find stores and products which they cannot find elsewhere in the region.

Most suburban regional shopping malls are unexciting. They offer shoppers a relatively nondescript homogeneous shopping experience. They look alike, possess the same stores, and sell the same products. What has been forgotten by mall managers is that entertainment, in a mall sense, is not necessarily what activities can be added to the center, but what entertainment is provided by the shopping experience. Shoppers are searching for shopping experiences that are fresh, different, and fun. To provide this experience, suburban regional shopping malls need to attract stores and sell products that are unique, interesting, and ever-changing. The recent addition of the Build-a-Bear Workshop to the offerings of several suburban regional shopping malls is one such example. The Build-a-Bear Workshop (www.buildabear.com) is a novel retail concept that provides a playful, creative environment. The challenge for mall managers is to find new and exciting retailing concepts like Build-a-Bear Workshop on a continual basis.

The Easton Town Center in Columbus, Ohio (www.eastontowncenter.com) is an example of a suburban regional shopping center that was explicitly designed to provide shoppers with a fun, exciting, entertaining place to shop. Easton Town Center was designed as an open-air center that mimics small-town America over 50 years ago. The center possesses an entertainment-oriented product mix with numerous restaurants, 30 movie theaters, spas, a comedy club, a cabaret, specialty stores, and Nordstrom and Lazarus as anchor department stores. The center has a "town square" and special event areas. It is considered to be one of the most successful retail centers in the region.

The challenge to mall developers and managers is clear. Since the opening of Southdale Center in 1956, changes in competition, retailing, and consumer shopping behavior have resulted in significant threats and opportunities. If suburban regional shopping malls are to enjoy continued success, they must creatively adapt to the new industry and shopping environment. Managers and owners of suburban regional shopping malls must determine the change strategy that is best for them. A number of considerations should guide their thinking—the competition, the needs of shoppers in their area, the opportunities available, and the center's resources. Just as one size does not fit all, the same turnaround strategy will not suit all suburban regional shopping malls.

1. Imagine yourself as the manager of a struggling local suburban regional shopping mall. What do you think the mall should do to improve its performance?
2. What shopping trends do you foresee over the next 10 years? How might these trends affect suburban regional shopping malls?
3. What new retail concepts can you identify? How might you learn about more? What strategies do you suggest for learning about new retail concepts?

3. Celestial Seasonings*

In the late 1960s, the era of Woodstock and Summer of Love music festivals, Mo and Peggy Siegel and two friends began picking herbs in the mountains around Aspen, Colorado. They decided to start a company that they named after one of their friends—Lucinda Ziesing, whose nickname was Celestial. The next year, 10,000 muslin bags of Mo's 36 Herb Tea were sewn, filled, and sold to a health-food store in Boulder, Colorado. A year later, Sleepytime Herb Tea was created, and the business was moved to a barn in Boulder. But that didn't last long. Mo and his friends were onto something hot! Soon they were purchasing herbs around the world and learning how to mass produce their product in a factory. Loose-pack tea was eventually replaced with single-serve tea bags, and additional flavors were created—all of which fueled sales. Today, Celestial Seasonings is recognized as a leader in herbal products, accounting for half the herbal tea market in the United States and expanding worldwide.

Celestial Seasonings' core business is herbal teas. Along with Mo's 36 Herb, Red Zinger, and their best-selling product, Sleepytime, the company has created over 60 different herbal teas.

The tea market comprises black teas, herbal and medicinal teas, diet teas, iced teas, and Chai, a sweet Indian spiced blend. The U.S. tea market has an annual growth rate of about 10 percent in recent years. Herbal and medicinal teas represent two-thirds of the total tea market and are growing at about 12 percent a year. Celestial Seasonings is the leading competitor in the herbal tea category, holding 50 percent market share. Other herbal tea competitors include Republic of Tea, Tazo (Starbucks), Yogi Tea, and Oregon Chai.

Herbal teas compete with traditional black teas, dominated by Lipton Tea Company. In the 70s, Celestial revolutionized the tea industry when it introduced the idea of herbal teas as flavorful, healthy beverages for everyday consumption. At that

*This case and the script for the accompanying video were prepared by Professor Davis Folsom of USC Beaufort.

time, herbal teas were perceived as foul-tasting medicinal brews. Few retail stores carried a complete line of herbal teas, so creating awareness, favorable image, and distribution posed a daunting challenge to the company. Initially, Celestial Seasonings promoted and distributed its products through health-food stores.

In 1984, food industry giant Kraft Foods bought Celestial Seasonings. With its marketing muscle and channel power, Kraft expanded distribution of Celestial Seasonings and added a line of gourmet black teas under the Celestial brand name. Shortly after the Kraft buyout, Mo Siegel retired from the company, and Barney Feinblum was named successor. However, the Kraft way of doing business sometimes conflicted with Celestial's culture, which from the beginning was influenced by "hippie-style" entrepreneurship, employee involvement, and earth-friendly community initiatives.

The values of the company are epitomized in its belief statement:

> We believe in marketing and selling healthful and naturally oriented products that nurture people's bodies and uplift their souls. Our products must be superior in quality, of good value, beautifully artistic, and philosophically inspiring.

In 1988, Celestial Seasonings management along with a venture capital firm bought the company back from Kraft. A new board of directors was created, and new headquarters were constructed outside of Boulder, Colorado. In 1991, Mo Siegel returned as CEO and chairman of the board and agreed to stay until 1997.

During Mo's second period of leadership, Celestial Seasonings went public and attempted a variety of product diversifications. A partnership with Perrier was formed to license and produce a line of ready-to-drink bottled teas under the Celestial Seasonings brand. A line of After Dinner Teas was launched, targeting more upscale consumers than Celestial's original back-to-the-earth customers and promoting tea as an after-dinner beverage. Iced Delight teas were created and marketed as "Brews in Your Fridge." A licensing agreement with Warner-Lambert produced Celestial Seasonings Soothers, herbal throat drops. In 1995, with HP Hood Company, Celestial created iced tea flavored frozen popsicles, but they were not a market success. That same year, Celestial developed its first medicinal herb tea—Herbal Comfort. In 1997, based on the success of Herbal Comfort, Celestial Seasonings expanded the line of medicinal teas to include Echinacea, Green Tea, GinkoSharp, Diet Partner, GingerEase, Detox A.M., LaxaTea, and Melatonin P.M. Celestial Seasonings now has 46 percent (up from 24 percent in June 1998) of the fast-growing medicinal tea category.

In 1998, Celestial acquired Mountain Chai, a Boulder-based manufacturer of concentrated Indian-style tea. Six varieties of Mountain Chai were reformulated and introduced under the Celestial logo. That same year, a line of six green teas was launched. Green teas have been used in Asian cultures for hundreds of years and are known for their curative qualities. Green teas were introduced to the American market in the 60s but were not widely successful due to their bland taste.

In 1997, Mo Siegel's commitment to manage the company ended, and Steve Hughes, known in the industry for growing the Healthy Choice line of food products, became Celestial's CEO. With Hughes at the helm, Celestial Seasonings entered a new phase. Saying that Celestial was "a $500 million brand trapped in a $100 million business," Hughes initiated a series of efforts to leverage the Celestial brand name, including the creation of herbal supplements. According to Hughes,

> For 25 years we've cared about one thing—creating healthy, natural products that make our customers feel good. Our herbal supplement line is a natural extension of that mission. We know the power of herbs and the simple solutions they provide for good health. We want to share that.

Launched in April 1998 in capsule form, the herbal supplements line included nine single-herb extracts and eight advanced-formula blend products. The timing seemed perfect. Herbal supplements were rapidly gaining consumer acceptance as alternatives and additions to traditional health and wellness products. A 1998 Market Facts survey showed the percentage of Americans who reported using herbal supplements had grown from just 3 percent in 1990 to 37 percent in 1998, and almost 80 percent of respondents felt herbal supplements were safe to take. Herbal supplements also have a number of logical synergies with Celestial's existing products. Many of the same ingredients are used, and herbal supplements can be sold through the same distribution channels.

Herbal supplements are promoted on the company's Natural Wellness website (www.celestialseasonings.com):

> We do our best to eat right, get enough rest, and exercise, and the benefits are undeniable. But our health can be affected by things we can't control. Environmental toxins, emotional and physical stress and simply getting older create concerns that show up in many ways—as wrinkles, low energy, a flagging mood, and more. We're not defenseless, though. Nature, as usual, provides what we need.

Clearly, Celestial Seasonings is appealing to specific target market segments, like aging baby boomers and health-conscious consumers of all ages. In fact, whenever a new Celestial product or service is proposed, the first question asked is "What will Tracy think?" Tracy Jones is the company's nickname for their primary target market: a 35- to 54-year-old, college-educated, socially involved woman with a focus on healthy lifestyle and household income greater than $50,000. Tracy also is not a major viewer of television. Herbal supplements are primarily targeted to Tracy and secondarily targeted to other health-conscious consumers. With labels that talk about "Tummy Mint" and "Tension Tamer," these new herbal supplements are designed to strike an emotional chord in Tracy.

Launched with a $4 million campaign and priced at a premium, the herbal supplements line brought in 21 percent of Celestial's revenues in 1998. But just as things looked as bright as a summer day in the Rockies, Celestial learned a classic marketing lesson. The market for herbal supplements peaked at the same time two major competitors, One a Day and Centrum, entered the market. Also, 1999 SPINS and ACNielsen market research data indicated a variety of changes in the herbal market. Green teas, medicinal blend teas, and Chai were gaining sales, but previously popular single-herb supplements, including St. John's Wort and Ginseng, showed sharp declines.

In response, Celestial restaged the herbal supplements line in 1999 by dropping six products, reducing the advertising budget, and doubling the number of capsules per bottle. Celestial's herbal supplements line still represents a major part of company sales, but initial enthusiasm has mellowed, and the marketing team has begun to look for new opportunities. Also, companies specializing in herbal supplements face several ethical and legal issues.

Almost 80 percent of American consumers believe that herbal supplements are *safe*. However, as one FDA director has stated, "Realize that the label term 'natural' doesn't guarantee that a product is safe. Think of poisonous mushrooms. They're natural." Herbal supplements companies must abide by FDA rules regarding claims of effectiveness of their products; they cannot represent their products as medicines. Mike Gross, Celestial's regulatory expert, explains, "What it all boils down to is that you cannot make any claim to cure, treat, prevent, mitigate, or diagnose any disease state—or even mention a disease! For example, you cannot say 'for the treatment of prostate enlargement' but you can say 'to keep your prostate healthy.'"

One new direction under consideration at most consumer goods companies is the Internet. The Internet initiative at Celestial started in the Information Technology division of the organization. Celestial started a modest web storefront designed to educate consumers and sell seasonal items and gifts from its mail-order catalog. Then the catalog manager got onboard and the marketing group joined in to build this alternative channel.

Part of the success of Celestial's catalog and Internet sales is attributable to the company kitchen! Started in 1973 as a free lunch program for employees, outsiders began to drift in, wanting to buy products. As more and more customers visited the factory, the idea of a factory tour gained favor. Between 1994 and 1999, over 350,000 people took Celestial's factory tour, creating a huge database for catalog and Internet marketing strategies.

1. What kinds of synergies do herbal supplements have with herbal teas?
2. What environmental trends seem to be fueling sales growth for herbal supplements? What environmental trends pose threats to the sales and profits of herbal supplements?
3. What kinds of new products should Celestial Seasonings develop? What criteria would you use to evaluate new product ideas for Celestial Seasonings? Why?

4. Toyota Prius: The Power of Excellence in Product Innovation and Marketing*

Prius (Latin for "to go before") was introduced to the Japanese market in 1997 amid much publicity and extravaganza. It was the world's first mass-produced car powered by a combination of gasoline and electricity. For the Toyota Motor Corporation, the Prius product launch represented a major strategic commitment and a long-term financial gamble.

The Prius story begins in the early 1990s when Toyota released its first Earth Charter, setting the goal of minimizing its overall environmental impact. In September 1993, the company began to plan for the development of a car for the next century. Called Globe 21st Century, or G21, the plan was to produce a car with better fuel economy and lower emissions than existing automobiles.

Alternative ideas were considered before deciding to press ahead with a gas-electric hybrid system; these included direct-injection diesel engines, electric motors, hydrogen-powered fuel cells, and solar-powered vehicles. Mass production of gasoline-electric hybrids was not possible until recently. Improved technology with respect to batteries and powerful control electronics to coordinate the two propulsion systems made the idea more attractive.

GM (as well as Ford, Honda, and Toyota) failed to successfully market electric cars in the 1990s. Although GM's EV1 was a technical triumph, consumers were scared off by its limited battery life. All three American carmakers developed diesel-electric hybrid cars in the 1990s, but none were deemed acceptable to the market. A diesel engine is more expensive than a gasoline engine, so a diesel hybrid required a higher price premium. Development of a hydrogen-powered fuel cell vehicle was simply not technically feasible within the time frame that Toyota had set for its goal.

The hybrid technology chosen to power the Prius combines a gasoline engine with an integrated electric-drive system. Like conventional cars and trucks, the hybrid system relies on a gasoline-fueled engine to generate power; the electric motor system provides a second power channel. These two complementary systems work together to create a more efficient powertrain.

At start-up, only the electric motor is used, and it powers the vehicle at low-to mid-range speeds. Under normal driving conditions, the gas engine is engaged and power is allocated between the two engines to maximize efficiency during operations such as acceleration, deceleration, coasting, and stopping. In the city, with its stop-and-go traffic, the Prius relies more on the electric engine, whereas for highway driving, the gas engine is the primary power producer. The benefits of this powertrain combination are greater fuel efficiency and low exhaust emissions. Compared to electric cars, the hybrid system offers a high level of convenience since the battery is recharged from surplus engine power.

The Prius development effort took four years. The biggest challenges Toyota engineers faced were handling the powerful voltage between the battery and the electric motor and determining how to fit the gas engine, the electric motor, and a jumbo battery into a compact car frame. Solving these problems involved adapting the heavy-duty transistors used in Japan's bullet trains and shrinking the parts through computer modeling. A prototype car was shown to the public in 1995 and in December 1997, the first production car rolled out of Toyota's Takaoka factory in Toyota City near Nagoya. For the next two years, Toyota sold Prius only in Japan. First year sales were around 12,000 units due to limited production capability. Toyota elected to defer capital investment in manufacturing facilities and to produce the Prius on existing assembly lines: a "hedging" strategy in case the hybrid "flopped." The initial price was just $16,929, which industry analysts say was below the estimated cost of building a

---

*This case was prepared by Dr. J. B. Wilkinson, professor emeritus, Youngstown State University.

Prius. However, even at that price, buyers paid a premium of several thousand dollars for a Prius compared to similar-size conventional cars. Industry analysts speculated that Toyota would have to sell around 250,000 Priuses a year to make a profit.

Prius was introduced to the U.S. market in 2000. The Honda Insight, a two-seater gas-electric hybrid, had been in the U.S. market for a year with first-year sales of about 3,500. Toyota limited U.S. sales of the Prius to 17,000 units during the introductory year. Base price for the Prius was $19,995 (roughly the same as for a Honda Insight). Both the Prius and the Insight were priced below cost but several thousand dollars higher than similar-sized conventional cars. However, the higher price was partially offset by better gasoline mileage (52 m.p.g. in city driving for the first-generation Prius).

The advertising campaign that launched the Prius into the U.S. market used "Prius Genius" as its tagline and courted leading-edge buyers of the technological generation. Celebrity buyers like Cameron Diaz heightened Toyota's publicity efforts, which included an "Engine of Change" tour—a 15-city circuit where the Prius was shown to leaders in government, media, and environmental groups. In addition, the Prius was seen by millions of Academy Award viewers as an "alternative limo" used by environmentally friendly Hollywood celebrities.

Toyota enjoyed a dramatic jump in Prius sales after its U.S. debut. Sales were so strong that demand outstripped production capability. It was not uncommon for buyers to wait up to six months to receive their new Prius. By 2004, global sales totaled 250,000, and Toyota was earning a modest profit per vehicle. The second-generation Prius (Prius II) hit U.S. showrooms in October 2003. As other car manufacturers (Ford, GM) entered the market with hybrid vehicles and Honda increased its number of hybrid models (Civic), Toyota changed its marketing strategy to emphasize its Hybrid Synergy Drive in Prius II as the powertrain of choice—a classic selective demand-building strategy, suitable for the growth stage in a product's life cycle. The objective of this strategy was to differentiate Toyota's hybrid technology from other hybrid systems emerging in the market. Unlike competitive systems on the market in 2004, the new high-voltage/high-power Hybrid Synergy Drive powertrain

was capable of operating in either gas or electric modes, as well as a mode in which both the gas engine and electric motor are in operation. Compared to the original Toyota Hybrid System (THS) in Prius I, the new Hybrid Synergy Drive system delivered significantly more power and performance, best-in-class fuel economy, and best-in-market emissions performance. Toyota also worked to reduce the cost of its hybrids. Because gasoline-electric hybrids employ two motors under the hood, hybrids are more expensive to produce than conventional gas-powered vehicles (about $3,000 more). Cost reductions would lead to price reductions, making Toyota's hybrid cars more affordable.

The 2004 second-generation Prius was designed to appeal to a broader market. It was larger, more powerful, with numerous technical improvements and aerodynamic styling (plus a four-door, lift-back configuration), and loaded with high-tech options like the Smart Entry/Smart Start, which allows the driver to open and start the vehicle without inserting a key. Other options included a hands-free cell phone system and a navigation system. Base price was held at $19,995, the same as the first Prius cost during its introductory year in the United States. This second-generation car won some of the industry's most prestigious awards and was named European Car of the Year 2005.

The success of the Prius has provided Toyota with numerous product opportunities, including hybrid technology extension and licensing strategies. Toyota recently introduced a hybrid Lexus RX400h (2004) and Highlander (2005). A hybrid Camry and Lexus GS sedan were planned for 2006. Toyota expects that a quarter of its unit sales in the United States will use gasoline-electric technology by 2010. To achieve that goal, virtually all Toyota vehicles, including trucks, will offer hybrid power systems.

1. In what stage of the product life cycle is the Toyota Prius? Explain.
2. Describe the marketing strategies being followed by Toyota for the Prius.
3. Do you think Toyota should convert all of its cars to hybrids? Why? Why not?

5. Potbelly Sandwich Works Grows through "Quirky" Marketing*

Want an inexpensive gourmet sandwich served in a fun and funky place by friendly young people? Lots of people do, including celebrities Will Ferrell, Sandra Bullock, and Keanu Reaves. In fact, Potbelly Sandwich Works was ranked as one of the top fastest-growing chains in the restaurant industry.[1]

Chances are you have never eaten at a Potbelly, but you probably will in the near future. Under the leadership of Bryant Keil, chairman and CEO, Chicago-based Potbelly Sandwich Works is expanding rapidly (see Table 1). Keil

bought the original Potbelly in 1996. Prior to that, it was a very successful neighborhood sandwich shop run by a couple who had originally started the business as an antique store in 1977. They added homemade sandwiches and desserts to bolster the business and soon the food became more popular than the antiques. As time went on, booths were added along with ovens for toasting the sandwiches and the antiques became "décor" rather than merchandise for sale. A prominently placed antique potbelly stove provided inspiration for the sandwich shop's name.

Although Potbelly has many sandwich shop rivals and competition in the fierce quick-serve segment of the restaurant industry, Potbelly has more than held its own. Billed as "a unique and quirky sandwich joint," it has a unique appeal.

*This case was prepared by Dr. J. B. Wilkinson, professor emeritus, Youngstown State University.

[1]"Way to Grow: A Tight Real Estate Market Doesn't Deter Top Chains' Expansion Plans," *Restaurants and Institutions*, July 2005, p. 121.

Table 1 Potbelly Store Openings by Year and City, 1997–2005

Market	1997	1998	1999	2000	2001	2002	2003	2004	2005	Total
Chicago	1	1	1	2	3	8	11	9	11	48*
Washington, D.C.						8	3	4	3	18
Michigan							4	2	1	7
Minnesota							1	3	2	6
Wisconsin							2		2	4
Indiana								1	1	2
Texas								3	8	11
Ohio									6	6
Total	1	1	1	2	3	16	21	22	34	102

*Includes the original Potbelly opened in 1977 and bought by Keil in 1996.

Potbelly's core strategy elements include *product, place, promotion,* and *price*.

Product

According to Keil, "Anyone can sell a sandwich. You need to sell an experience." Industry observers point to several aspects of the Potbelly experience that make it the first choice for young professionals on a quick lunch break. First is the menu, which features made-to-order toasted sandwiches, soups, homemade desserts, malts, shakes, and yogurt smoothies. Toasting is part of what makes Potbelly's sandwiches distinctive. Quality ingredients, including a freshly baked Italian sub roll and freshly sliced meats and cheese also contribute to superior value. Friendly service and an upbeat atmosphere, live music, antique fixtures, real books for customers to read or borrow, and vintage memorabilia create a homey environment for customers. The idea behind Potbelly is simple: superior value, fun-filled atmosphere, warm, comfy décor, and quick, friendly service.

Place

Potbelly stores average 2,200 square feet but can top 4,000 square feet. Most units have indoor seating for more than 50 and outdoor seating during warmer months. Geographic locations are selected carefully. Keil looks for cities that are not saturated with sandwich chains and have a urban/suburban density of core customers—young professionals less than 35 years old. Locations must be convenient for them since Potbelly stores rely on high repeat business. All units are corporate owned and operated.

Promotion

Historically, Potbelly Sandwich Works has not had an ad budget. Promotions are keyed to events like store openings and National Sandwich Day. For example, on National Sandwich Day, Potbelly hosts a "Belly Buster" sandwich-eating contest at Potbelly stores. Prizes are awarded to winners and runners-up. Diners randomly receive free meals. Other events promotions raise money for local charities such as food banks and community-based reading and music appreciation programs.

Price

Potbelly sandwiches sell for $3.79. Sheila's Dream Bar, made of oatmeal, caramel and chocolate, is $1.29, while homemade chocolate chip or sugar cookies go for only 99 cents. Checks average about $6.50. Pricing is an integral part of the value Potbelly offers customers and can be summed up as, "Just good food at good prices!"

Considered separately, any one of Potbelly's marketing strategy elements may not seem overly powerful as a competitive weapon, but combined and implemented with zeal, they are a significant competitive threat to national, regional, and local competitors. Brands like Subway, Quizno's, Cosi, Panera, Jimmy John's, and Schlotzsky's Deli are wary that Potbelly will become a major national competitor. The Potbelly experience appears to be difficult to duplicate. For example, Quizno's may have similar food quality but not similar atmosphere; Cosi may have the hangout ambience down but not the food! Subway is especially vulnerable since it has neither the food nor the warm and comfy fun store environment.

Yet Potbelly has a tough road ahead. It requires management to maintain the superior performance of current units while creating new Potbelly units in new markets. Each Potbelly is special in terms of location, décor, and staff. The unit must be tailored to its neighborhood and community. Attentive, enthusiastic workers must be found. Food quality and fun atmosphere must become an integral part of the store culture. Not an easy task!

1. Identify and describe Potbelly's strategy in terms of product (present or new) and market (present or new).
2. How would you describe Potbelly's positioning strategy?
3. What types of environmental opportunities and threats do you see in Potbelly's external environment? How might they affect Potbelly's current strategy?

6. Girl Scouts*

Girl Scouting is dedicated to and available to all girls age 5 to 17. Today there are approximately 3.6 million Girl Scouts in the U.S., including over 2.7 million girls and nearly 900,000 adult members, most of whom are volunteers. Membership categories for the girls are

Category	Age	Grade
Daisy	5–6	K, 1
Brownie	6, 7, 8	1, 2, 3
Junior Girl Scout	8, 9, 10, 11	3, 4, 5, 6
Cadette Girl Scout	11, 12, 13, 14	6, 7, 8, 9
Senior Girl Scout	14–17	9–12

Membership is at an all-time high. In 1999, as a result of specific target market initiatives, growth was especially strong among Hispanic (a 6.3 percent increase) and African American (a 5.9 percent increase) girls. And membership is not just limited to the United States. Through its membership in the World Association of Girl Guides and Girl Scouts, Girl Scouts of the U.S.A. (GSUSA) is part of a larger entity of over 10 million girls in 140 countries. Although some programs for overseas travel and adventure exist, the international link is still being developed and is not nearly as strong as the link between GSUSA and the local councils.

As is true for many nonprofit organizations, the Girl Scouts organization operates on two levels. At the corporate or head-quarters level is Girl Scouts of the U.S.A., located in New York. A board of directors, a national president, and a national executive director run GSUSA. From these offices, plans are made for the national parent and for the local councils. These local councils may be thought of as strategic business units (SBUs) for the Girl Scouts. Over 300 local councils serve to direct the activities of the more than 226,000 troops in the United States and overseas. A local board of directors and an executive director manages each of these local councils. To become a part of GSUSA, each of these local councils must go through a type of accreditation review by the national organization. Every four years each council is reviewed, and if it continues to meet the established criteria, it will be rechartered. This chartering process provides GSUSA with a strong weapon to maintain some level of consistency for the strategies and actions of the member Girl Scout councils.

Strategic marketing planning clearly is necessary to run such a large organization. GSUSA does extensive corporate-level planning and also provides the local councils with assistance for their own formulation and execution of plans. Strategic marketing planning at the corporate level is the responsibility of the president and the board, with input from board committees, board task groups, community leaders, and community groups.

Four steps are involved. The first step is a S.W.O.T. analysis, a review of internal strengths and external trends. This includes using the database maintained by GSUSA that details membership, program attendance, financial and development data, and similar benchmarks. The study of external trends results in the *Environmental Scanning Report,* which uses social, economic, political, and technological data from a variety of sources. This document is then made available to corporate- and council-level planners. One result of this S.W.O.T. analysis is the identification of a set of critical issues facing GSUSA. These issues are then used in the second step: to develop corporate goals covering a six-year period. These goals are reviewed at the midpoint of the planning period. In the third step, the group develops strategic guidelines, strategies, and long-range projects. Finally, the group develops long-range resource strategies that are needed to support the projects identified in the third step.

Staff and volunteers involved in implementing the strategic plans are responsible for the development of one-year plans (tactical planning). At this fourth step, priorities are established; specific operational goals are set; action plans are developed, including decisions about who, how, what, and when; and the operational budget is determined.

The completed corporate plan shapes all efforts and programs at the national level. However, local planners can exercise some discretion in planning for their markets. To accomplish local planning, some councils hold planning retreats with local board and community experts; some hold planning sessions for just staff; and some limit the efforts to a committee of the board. Whatever the process, the council board develops a set of five-year goals that it reviews annually. While these usually mirror national goals, each local council has the opportunity to change priorities or to add other goals peculiar to their local efforts. Using these goals, the staff develops proposals for specific objectives and action steps for board approval. These approved objectives and action steps form the basis for the local council's annual operating plan.

During the year, results are measured, compared to objectives, and subjected to corrective actions. Also during the year, the staff has the opportunity to reevaluate the goals that have been set by the board for the coming year and may provide suggestions to the board. The board then meets again early in the following year to plan for that year and to add goals for the fifth year in the current plan. Thus, the local council board always has a plan that looks five years ahead.

Marketing plans and efforts must be directed at three distinct groups. First, plans must be developed for recruiting and marketing efforts directed to the target market for Scouting: girls and their families. In addition, marketing plans also must target volunteers. Scouting could not function nearly as effectively without its giant network of volunteers, both at the local and national levels. There are over 880,000 adult members of Girl Scouting and most of them are volunteers. Many of these volunteers were involved in scouting when they were young. Others are parents of current scouts.

Finally, the community at large represents an important stakeholder group. This group includes donors, both corporate and individual, who provide financial and other resources; schools and school counselors; church organizations and the

---

*This case and accompanying video script were prepared by Dr. George Prough, the University of Akron, with assistance from Lori Arguelles, Communications Director, GSUSA, and Mary Kintz, Director of Member Services, Western Reserve Girl Scouts Council.

like. During the S.W.O.T. analysis, all three groups are studied, and this provides input for recruitment plans and for the ongoing marketing efforts.

Quite clearly, young girls in the target demographic are the first and most important marketing target. Marketing efforts aimed at this group include recruitment efforts as well as retention efforts (keeping existing Scouts delighted with their experiences).

Plans of both types must consider the competition faced by Girl Scouting. All organizations face competition of various sorts, but Girl Scouts planners face an unusual situation. Essentially, the competition for Scouting is other activities that compete for a girl's time. This includes school clubs and other school-related activities; sports; private lessons such as piano, ballet, and music; church; and other social activities, including dating boys. However, the thinking about competition at Girl Scouts is different. Girl Scouting does not attempt to defeat the competition. Instead, Scouting embraces many of these competing activities and offers them as part of their product mix. If it finds that a certain activity is becoming more important to young girls, then Scouting looks at the possibility of incorporating that activity into its product mix of activities.

As girls mature, this kind of competition grows more intense. Older girls have more choices, making retention in these categories more difficult. As a result, there has been a growing concern that the programs and offerings of Girl Scouting, especially in the older age categories, is not sufficiently contemporary. Retention of these older girls is a problem. For instance, analysis of the U.S. membership shows the following data regarding the number of girls served by the Girl Scouts in each membership category:

Category	Girls Served in the Category
Daisy	1 of every 8
Brownie	1 of every 4
Junior Girl Scout	1 of every 7
Cadette Girl Scout	1 of every 25
Senior Girl Scout	1 of every 73

To better understand customers and the competing demands on their lives, Girl Scouts USA is beginning to do extensive market and customer research among young girls. During the fall of 2000, GSUSA launched the Girl Scout Research Institute, a research and public policy information center focusing on the healthy development of girls. Through this Institute, the GSUSA hopes to develop a large database of information on girls, with the additional goal of positioning itself as an information resource and expert on girls.

Within this competitive market, the GSUSA uses a variety of plans and strategies in order to attract new girls. The national website offers an overview for interested girls; however, it is not very interactive and has limited recruiting value. Nationally prepared brochures and literature are also available. Often these can be useful as stuffers in store, mall, and other point-of-sale display units. But many councils choose to localize and personalize these efforts. For these councils, most of the recruitment and marketing

efforts are planned and developed at the local level. Local websites, school visits, locally prepared fliers, recruiting efforts at malls, churches, and other similar local activities lend a more personal touch to their recruiting.

Specific to certain types of competition, GSUSA has responded with a changing product mix. Each year, Girl Scouts adds to its diversity of activities and merit badges, all awarded for participation and mastery of particular tasks. With the increase in girls participating in sporting activities, Girl Scouts developed *GirlSports*, a program offering senior Girl Scouts from around the country a chance to spend a week during the summer developing certain sporting skills. During the 2000 version, 26 girls met in Oakland, California, with local athletes and trainers, learned 13 extreme sports, and studied with ESPN fitness experts and Olympic athletes. An expanded version of *GirlSports* is being developed to include over 100,000 girls competing in nearly 2,300 different sporting events in over 300 councils.

Another trend identified was the increasing interest of girls in the sciences. As a result, the *Girl at the Center* program was developed. This is a science and technology program in which local councils can take advantage of partnerships between the Girl Scouts and over 31 science museums, encouraging families and girls to explore and learn more about the sciences. *Girl at the Center* and the *GirlSports* program are examples of how the Girl Scouts organization is forming partnerships with others to make its programs relevant and successful.

Girl Scouting uses several methods to appeal to its second target, its volunteers—both to attract them and to keep them motivated and involved. To attract volunteers at the national level, the website offers valuable insight as do the nationally prepared brochures highlighting the benefits of volunteering and the many ways of doing so. But again, the local councils often develop their own marketing efforts. Parents are targeted by maintaining a parents' network and involving parents in meetings and events. When the local council has events at malls or churches, the council staff involved makes every attempt to sell volunteering to adults as much as they do scouting to young girls. Additionally, many local councils work with area organizations in an attempt to generate volunteers. Universities, schools, the local housing authority, and other volunteer-based organizations have proven to be excellent sources of interns or other types of volunteers.

To keep volunteers motivated and involved, GSUSA national offers a variety of adult development and training opportunities. These include programs at the corporate training center, a number of online training offerings, and certification programs that support and enable the volunteers to improve their abilities to perform their functions.

Girl Scouting's third target, its stakeholder group, consists of the community at large. Efforts to interact with this stakeholder group can be planned, and suggestions are made at the national level; however, many of these efforts involve personal contacts and one-on-one relationships with donors or other partnership targets. As a result, many of these efforts are developed and conducted by people at the local council level.

1. Compare strategic marketing planning by the Girl Scouts with planning by for-profit organizations. What are the similarities? What are the differences?
2. What changes would you suggest to improve the planning process in the Girl Scouts?

7. The GM HUMMER: Brand Equity, Positioning, and Development*

Few brands have the cachet, exotic heritage, and unique identity that GM's HUMMER exudes. It has a brand image and equity that sets it apart from most automobiles in the industry. Within General Motors Corp., it represents an important growth opportunity in a highly competitive and dynamic market.

The HUMMER can trace its roots to AM General (formerly Willys-Overland Motors, Inc.) and the year 1979 when the U.S. Army issued a draft specification for a new light tactical vehicle that could replace light civilian trucks and various other specially designed Army vehicles. The specifications indicated that the Army wanted a versatile, cross-country vehicle capable of performing both combat and combat-support roles. Other required attributes and characteristics included durability, mobility, and reliability; diesel-power and automatic transmission; and the capability of being modified to carry communications and weapons systems (missiles, automatic weapons). Thus, the concept for a High-Mobility Multipurpose Wheeled Vehicle (HMMWV), nicknamed HUMVEE, was conceived. AM General became one of three contenders awarded an Army contract for the design and construction of 11 prototype HMMWVs—six weapons carriers and five utility vehicles. These prototypes were tested in various off-road conditions in combat environments—rocky hills, sand, mud and water, desert heat, and Arctic cold. In March 1983, AM General was awarded a five-year contract for 55,000 HMMWVs in 15 different configurations. Most were to be used in the Army, but some were allocated to the Marine Corps, Air Force, and Navy. By mid-1991, more than 72,000 vehicles had been produced. The total as of 2006 is more than 190,000, including international sales.

Civilians learned about the HUMVEE during the 1991 Gulf War (Operation: Desert Storm). Photographs and video broadcasts from Kuwait spawned a great deal of interest in the HUMVEE from the American public. Arnold Schwarzenegger was so taken with the vehicle that he persuaded AM General to sell him one and to make them available to civilians under the brand name HUMMER. In 1992, AM General began selling the HUMMER H1. In 2002, AM General began producing the HUMMER H2, which was marketed and sold by General Motors.

HUMMER H1 was essentially a civilian version of the military HUMVEE—a large, heavy vehicle (over 8,500 lbs.) with a large diesel engine and complex driveline. It got about 10 mpg, but was excellent off-road—an icon of strength, durability, and rugged individualism. It originally cost about $50,000 ($140,000 in 2006) and attracted off-road enthusiasts, celebrities, and men who wanted to make a "tough-guy" statement. H1 buyers are 95 percent male, and sales have been about 700 a year. There are about 12,000 of these macho-mobiles on the road today. The last HUMMER H1 for commercial sale rolled off the assembly line in 2006. In a statement issued by HUMMER General Manager Martin Walsh, the reason for dropping the HUMMER H1 from the line was to focus

on models with broader appeal instead of the small niche market attracted to H1.

In 1999, AM General sold the marketing rights to the HUMMER brand name to General Motors. Under this agreement, AM General continued to produce the HUMMER H1. In 2002, AM General opened a new plant to produce the HUMMER H2 SUV and later in 2005 an SUT sport utility truck variant. However, GM has exclusive ownership of the HUMMER brand name and has been very active in licensing it for use on colognes, flashlights, bicycles, laptops, apparel, jewelry, CD players, and other items.

HUMMER H2 was positioned as a kinder, gentler vehicle, while maintaining the macho mystique of the brand. Many of the print ads for the H2 showed it sitting still in a vast outdoor setting, which made it look petite. One of the original commercials featured a well-dressed woman behind the wheel. However, one of the ads bragged, "In a world where SUVs have begun to look like their owners, with love handles and mushy seats, the H2 proves that there is still one out there that can drop and give you 20." In fact, the H2 was only slightly smaller and lighter than the H1 with tires as high as a kitchen table and side mirrors as big as manila folders. Yet, it performed more like a well-mannered SUV. It also came in bright colors (e.g., bright yellow and red) with cup-holders, heated seats, and other comforts. At a price of around $50,000, it competed with luxury SUVs like the Range Rover, Lincoln Navigator, and Cadillac Escalade. Buyers for the H2 were "successful achievers" and "rugged individualists." A large percentage of buyers for the H2 are women (about 25 percent). Celebrity owners of the H2 include Arnold Schwarzenegger, LeBron James, and Patti Labelle.

HUMMER H3 was introduced in spring 2005. Configured as a midsize SUV and priced around $30,000 to $40,000, the H3 looked a lot like the HUMMER H2 but was much smaller and got an EPA estimated 20 mpg highway. The lower price made the H3 affordable for a younger demographic. Standard features included full power equipment and door locks with lockout protection; electric rear-window defogger; exterior power-adjustable, manually folding rear-view mirrors; three 12-volt covered auxiliary power outlets; instrument cluster and center stack with a brushed finish in the interior; and other items. Options included a DVD-based navigation radio, a large power sunroof, and accessories to personalize the vehicle. However, the H3 had the same off-road prowess as the larger H2 and was infused with the same militaristic styling and take-the-hill attitude.

The commercials for HUMMER H3 were designed for mass-market appeal to connect with a wider cross section of consumers than the HUMMER brand had sought out in the past. In one commercial, a group of exasperated HUMMER executives stand around a boardroom table, trying to come up with the next hot product—something new. Ed the Courier, a very short guy, comes in and says, "Why not make a smaller one?" In another commercial, the camera focuses on an empty parking spot. As music from the Richard Strauss symphony "Also Sprach Zarathustra" plays, a HUMMER H3

*This case was prepared by Dr. J. B. Wilkinson, professor emeritus, Youngstown State University.

pulls up to the spot and parallel parks effortlessly. To prove the H3 still has the "right stuff," another commercial has the H3 plowing through mountain roads and scaling boulders, much like the H2 did in its commercials. More recently, a 2006 Super Bowl ad called "Monsters" showed a Godzilla clone squaring off against a giant robot. Instead of fighting, they fall in love. When the female monster gives birth, a red H3 is born.

GM is counting on the HUMMER H3 to increase the volume and accessibility of the brand to more customers through its 172 HUMMER dealers. As part of its brand recognition strategy, GM now sells HUMMERS through separate dealerships that all have a distinctive design—sort of a militaristic steel, glass, and concrete Quonset hut look.

Possible future plans for the brand include a diesel and a hybrid-electric engine for the H2. A prototype called the HUMMER H2H, powered by a hydrogen fuel cell, is on loan to Governor Arnold Schwarzenegger. Opportunities in international markets are strong. Beginning in 2006, GM will be assembling HUMMERS at a plant in Port Elizabeth, South Africa, for local South African consumption and for export to other markets.

1. How would you describe the brand image and positioning of the original HUMMER H1?
2. How has the brand image and positioning changed with the HUMMER H2 and HUMMER H3?
3. What is the major risk in GM's repositioning strategy for the HUMMER brand?

8. Segway Finds Niche Markets for Its Personal Transporter Technology*

Amid heavy media coverage and much speculation, "Ginger" made its debut on ABC's *Good Morning America* on December 3, 2001. It thrilled some and disappointed others, but the technology was breathtaking to all.

Now known as the Segway Personal Transporter (PT), Ginger was the brainchild of inventor and entrepreneur Dean Kamen, who is best known for his inventions in the medical field. While in college, Kamen invented the first wearable drug-infusion pump. In the following years, he invented the first portable insulin pump, the first portable dialysis machine, and an array of heart stents. This string of successes established Kamen's reputation and turned DEKA Research and Development Corp., the R&D lab he founded, into a premier company for medical-devise design.

The inspiration for Ginger occurred during the development of the IBOT wheelchair at DEKA. Developed for and funded by Johnson & Johnson, the IBOT wheelchair is a gyro-stabilized, microprocessor-controlled wheelchair that gives disabled people the same kind of mobility the rest of us take for granted. Officially called the Independence IBOT mobility system, this six-wheel machine can go up and down curbs, cruise effortlessly through sand or gravel, climb stairs, and rise up on its wheels to lift its occupant to eye level while maintaining balance and maneuverability with such stability that it can't be knocked over. The IBOT wheelchair has been likened to a sophisticated robot.

As Kamen and his team at DEKA were working on the IBOT, it dawned on them that they could build a device using similar technology for pedestrians—one that could go farther, move more quickly, and carry more. The IBOT was also the source of the "Ginger" code name for the Segway PT during its development stage. Watching the IBOT "dance up the stairs," Kamen's team likened it to Fred Astaire—hence the name Ginger for its smaller partner with only two wheels!

Segway's breakthrough technology is based on dynamic stabilization. A self-balancing, electric-powered transport device, the Segway PT contains gyroscopes and sensors that monitor a user's center of gravity and respond to subtle shifts in weight. Lean forward, go forward; lean back, go back; lean back a bit more and you go in reverse; turn by twisting your wrist; arch your back a tad and you slow to a halt. Exactly how the Segway achieves this is difficult to explain, but in every Segway, there are gyroscopes that act like your inner ear, a computer that acts like your brain, motors that act like your muscles, and wheels that act like your feet. You step aboard and it "oscillates" for a few seconds, getting the feel of you, and then it's fully cruise-able at 6 mph in "learning mode," and 12.5 miles per hour "flat-out." It has a range of about 17 to 25 miles per battery charge and can support weights of 80 pounds. It has no brakes, no engine, no throttle, no gearshift, no steering wheel, and gives off no emissions. It is much cleaner than a car and faster than a bike. It is more pedestrian-friendly than bikes or scooters and safer than a skateboard.

The commercial potential for Segway is enormous. For this reason, Kamen decided to move development and manufacturing of the Segway PT to a new company with the vision to develop highly efficient, zero-emission transportation solutions using dynamic stabilization technology. The new company, Segway LLC (changed to Segway Inc. in 2005) is headquartered in Bedford, New Hampshire, and construction of a manufacturing and assembly plant was completed in 2001.

Kamen has openly stated that the Segway "will be to the car what the car was to the horse and buggy!" He imagines them everywhere: in parks, on battlefields, on factory floors, zipping around distribution centers, and especially on downtown sidewalks. But market acceptance and penetration has been slow for this engineering marvel.

The Segway PT was initially marketed to major corporations and government agencies. Kamen personally demonstrated the Segway to the postmaster general who was keen to put letter carriers on Segways and to the head of the National Park Service who wanted to do the same with park rangers. Both were among Segway's first customers. The Pentagon's research agency, DARPA, bought Segways to give to robotics labs. The objective was to use Segway bases in the development

---
*This case was prepared by Dr. J. B. Wilkinson, professor emeritus, Youngstown State University.

of robots to do menial tasks (cleaning, picking crops), specialized jobs (nurses aids), and dangerous missions (bomb removal or rescue work in earthquake debris). Amazon.com, GE Plastics, and Delphi Automotive Systems purchased Segways for use in warehouses and manufacturing plants. Police departments, cities, and airports bought Segways for use by foot patrols, security personnel, and meter readers. Customer studies by these early buyers showed double-digit productivity gains and reduced reliance on motorized transport. For postal workers, the Segway has increased their carrying capacity and delivery speed. Test studies with police officers and security personnel have shown faster response times and better sightlines from being higher in the air than pedestrians.

In 2002, Segways went on sale to the public for the first time on Amazon.com at a price of around $5,000. In 2003, the retail store Brookstone became the first retailer to sell the Segway PT. By January 2004, it was estimated by industry observers that about 6,000 Segways had been sold. Given Kamen's stated ambition of replacing automobiles and other forms of personal transport alternatives, initial consumer sales were disappointing.

However, the Segway PT is still in the early stages of its product life cycle. According to product life-cycle theories and related empirical studies on diffusion of innovations, products move through their life cycles in different ways and the length of any particular stage varies according to many factors. In general, the speed with which a product moves through its introduction and growth stages varies according to product characteristics, market characteristics, competition, and environmental factors. The initial marketing strategy for a product will also affect market acceptance (adoption). A product will move quickly through the introduction and growth stages when it has high relative advantage—cost and benefits—compared to alternative products and is highly compatible with a buyer's current attitudes, lifestyle, and usage situation. The more complex a product is to understand and use, the slower will be its rate of adoption. In addition, if the product can be tried in small amounts, potential buyers perceive less risk associated with initial trial and this will speed adoption. Communication of the new product will affect market acceptance since buyers must first learn about a new product before the buying process can be initiated. Thus, a company's communication strategies and the degree to which favorable word-of-mouth opinion occurs will impact sales. Finally, new products will have higher rates of market acceptance if market conditions, competition, and environmental trends are favorable.

Industrial and government applications for the Segway PT continue to be positive. It's ideally suited for use in large-scale manufacturing plants and warehousing operations, for use by the police and security personnel in certain types of situations, for meter reading, for corporate and university campus transportation, and for package and mail delivery. And it has found a number of new niches in recent years. For example, tour groups are using Segways to move tourists between attractions in cities where tour buses and cars have operational difficulties. For example, Bill and Emily Neuenschwander's tours use Segways equipped with a radio on the handlebars that provide a running commentary to guide customers through tours of the Minneapolis, Minnesota, riverfront and surrounding historic landmarks. Visitors to theme parks, museums, and islands (e.g., Amelia Island Plantation Resort) use them.

Some lawyers use them between offices and courtrooms. Some medics use them to reach injured people faster.

However, in the consumer market, the Segway PT is still an unsought product for many people. Industry observers believe that the automobile is a preferred alternative for a number of reasons, including the infrastructure of cities, commuting distances, weather, and the American family lifestyle. Most people agree that the use of a Segway PT on highways and busy streets is dangerous. Also, many commuters live more than 5 miles from work. The need to recharge Segways raises the question of public sources of electricity. Issues related to public safety also have slowed consumer sales. Although the Segway PT is approved in most states for use on sidewalks, restrictions have been placed on speed, helmet use, minimum operating age, and use on streets and highways. At the local level, additional regulations apply. For example, San Francisco banned their use on city sidewalks, and they are outlawed in subways in Washington, D.C. Many see the mix of pedestrians, bicycles, skateboards, roller skates, ATVs, scooters, and Segways as a dangerous mix on sidewalks, hiking trails, and other public areas.

On the other hand, the Segway PT has obvious advantages to walking and other types of personal transport in some types of situations where people need to get from one place to another quickly and efficiently using a clean, quiet, and environmental-friendly transport device. The market potential for the product has barely been tapped. Early consumer buyers were mostly "techies" who like to own new, high-tech products, and they have played an important role in communicating the benefits and fun of owning a Segway PT. They have established local clubs across America and have started a number of websites devoted to Segway. In 2003, owners and enthusiasts held the first SegwayFest to celebrate all things Segway. The Fest has been held every year since.

In 2004, Segway launched a repositioning campaign to change the image of the Segway PT from "staid," "high-tech," and "serious" to "fun, smart transportation." The new and more traditional marketing campaign included new customer materials, dealer displays, and cable TV advertising with the tagline "Get Moving." Segway also has been increasing the number of dealerships and distributors worldwide. The new distribution strategy allows potential buyers to see the different models and to try them out before buying. The dealer network increases the visibility of the product and lowers buyers' perceived risk associated with servicing. Publicity, media appearances, and product placement on television shows such as *Frasier, Arrested Development,* and *The Simpsons* continue to provide important market exposure.

The new positioning strategy emphasizes the leisure aspect of the Segway PT. New models aimed at the recreation market have been introduced. For example, the Segway x2 Golf is geared toward golf enthusiasts and includes a golf bag carrier. The Segway x2 Adventure is the company's off-road vehicle, which can perform well in a variety of environments. The Centaur is a four-wheeled ATV-like vehicle that can pick up its wheels to climb over obstacles or simply glide on two wheels at 25 mph.

To further develop the market for the Segway technology, the company has started to market Segway Smart Motion Technology through licensing and partnering with third parties to codevelop new products. Under this program, any number of specialized products could emerge.

The future for Segway is ultimately unlimited. America's commitment to end its dependence on petroleum and reduce harmful emissions is not likely to change. Segway technology has part of the answer to how this can occur. The consumer market for Segway has developed slowly, but the future is assured. For this "new-to-the-world" product, the life cycle will be long and classically configured. Its impact on all sectors of the economy will be profound. How we work, play, and get around will radically change in the 21st century. From the company's perspective, this is just dandy! Its ultimate goal is to "be to the car what the car was to the horse and buggy!"

1. How might Segway, Inc., further develop the market for Segway technology? (Hint: What types of marketing strategies are associated with sales growth?)
2. What would be some advantages and disadvantages of using a Segway PT to get around on campus?
3. What types of applications and usage situations are there for Segway PTs in your area?
4. What kinds of problems would the use of Segway PTs create in your area? What are some possible solutions for these problems? Explain.

Cases

Guide to the use of these cases

Cases can be used in many ways. And the same case can be analyzed several times for different purposes.

"Suggested cases" are listed at the end of most chapters, but these cases can also be used later in the text. The main criterion for the order of these cases is the amount of technical vocabulary—or text principles—that is needed to read the case meaningfully. The first cases are "easiest" in this regard. This is why an early case can easily be used two or three times—with different emphasis. Some early cases might require some consideration of Product and Price, for example, and might be used twice, perhaps regarding product planning and later pricing. In contrast, later cases, which focus more on Price, might be treated more effectively *after* the Price chapters are covered.

In some of the cases, we have disguised certain information—such as names or proprietary financial data—at the request of the people or firms involved in the case. However, such changes do not alter the basic substantive problems you will be analyzing in a case.

1. McDonald's "Seniors" Restaurant

Bridgett Bowen is manager of a McDonald's restaurant in a city with many "seniors." She has noticed that some senior citizens have become not just regular patrons—but patrons who come for breakfast and stay on until about 3 PM. Many of these older customers were attracted initially by a monthly breakfast special for people aged 55 and older. The meal costs $1.99, and refills of coffee are free. Every fourth Monday, between 100 and 150 seniors jam Bridgett's McDonald's for the special offer. But now almost as many of them are coming every day—turning the fast-food restaurant into a meeting place. They sit for hours with a cup of coffee, chatting with friends. On most days, as many as 100 will stay from one to four hours.

Bridgett's employees have been very friendly to the seniors, calling them by their first names and visiting with them each day. In fact, Bridgett's McDonald's is a happy place—with her employees developing close relationships with the seniors. Some employees have even visited customers who have been hospitalized. "You know," Bridgett says, "I really get attached to the customers. They're like my family. I really care about these people." They are all "friends" and it is part of McDonald's corporate philosophy (as reflected in its website, www.mcdonalds.com) to be friendly with its customers and to give back to the communities it serves.

These older customers are an orderly group and very friendly to anyone who comes in. Further, they are neater than most customers and carefully clean up their tables before they leave. Nevertheless, Bridgett is beginning to wonder if anything should be done about her growing "non-fast-food" clientele. There's no crowding problem yet, during the time when the seniors like to come. But if the size of the senior citizen group continues to grow, crowding could become a problem. Further, Bridgett is concerned that her restaurant might come to be known as an "old people's" restaurant—which might discourage some younger customers. And if customers felt the restaurant was crowded, some might feel that they wouldn't get fast service. On the other hand, a place that seems busy might be seen as "a good place to go" and a "friendly place."

Bridgett also worries about the image she is projecting. McDonald's is a fast-food restaurant (there are over 30,000 of them in 119 countries), and normally customers are expected to eat and run. Will allowing people to stay and visit change the whole concept? In the extreme, Bridgett's McDonald's might become more like a European-style restaurant where the customers are never rushed and feel very comfortable about lingering over coffee for an hour or two! Bridgett knows that the amount her senior customers spend is similar to the average customer's purchase—but the seniors do use the facilities for a much longer time. However, most of the older customers leave McDonald's by 11:30, before the noon crowd comes in.

Bridgett is also concerned about another possibility. If catering to seniors is OK, then should she do even more with this age group? In particular, she is considering offering bingo games during the slow morning hours—9 AM to 11 AM. Bingo is popular with some seniors, and this could be a new revenue source—beyond the extra food and drink purchases that probably would result. She figures she could charge $5 per person for the two-hour period and run it with two underutilized employees. The prizes would be coupons for purchases at her store (to keep it legal) and would amount to about two-thirds of the bingo receipts (at retail prices). The party room area of her McDonald's would be perfect for this use and could hold up to 150 persons.

Evaluate Bridgett Bowen's current strategy regarding senior citizens. Does this strategy improve this McDonald's image? What should she do about the senior citizen market—that is, should she encourage, ignore, or discourage her seniors? What should she do about the bingo idea? Explain.

2. Sunshine Foods, Inc.

It is 2006, and Jon Moore, newly elected president of Sunshine Foods, Inc., faces a severe decline in profits. Sunshine Foods, Inc., is a 127-year-old California-based food processor. Its multiproduct lines are widely accepted under the Sunshine Foods brand. The company and its subsidiaries prepare, package, and sell canned and frozen foods, including fruits, vegetables, pickles, and condiments. Sunshine Foods, which operates more than 30 processing plants in the United States, is one of the larger U.S. food processors—with annual sales of about $650 million.

Until 2004, Sunshine Foods was a subsidiary of a major midwestern food processor, and many of the present managers came from the parent company. Sunshine Foods' last president recently said:

The influence of our old parent company is still with us. As long as new products look like they will increase the company's sales volume, they are introduced. Traditionally, there has been little, if any, attention paid to margins. We are well aware that profits will come through good products produced in large volume.

Alfredo Bose, a 25-year employee and now production manager, agrees with the multiproduct-line policy. As he puts it: "Volume comes from satisfying needs. We will can or freeze any vegetable or fruit we think consumers might want." Alfredo Bose also admits that much of the expansion in product lines was encouraged by economics. The typical plants in the industry are not fully used. By adding new products to use this excess capacity, costs are spread over greater volume. So the production department is always looking for new ways to make more effective use of its present facilities.

Sunshine Foods has a line-forcing policy, which requires that any store wanting to carry its brand name must be willing to carry most of the 65 items in the Sunshine Foods line. This policy, coupled with its wide expansion of product lines, has resulted in 88 percent of the firm's sales coming from major supermarket chain stores, such as Safeway, Kroger, and A&P.

Smaller stores are generally not willing to accept the Sunshine Foods policy. Alfredo Bose explains, "We know that only large stores can afford to stock all our products. But the large stores are the volume! We give consumers the choice of any Sunshine Foods product they want, and the result is maximum sales." Many small retailers have complained about Sunshine Foods' policy, but they have been ignored because they are considered too small in potential sales volume per store to be of any significance.

In late 2006, a stockholders' revolt over low profits (in 2006, they were only $500,000) resulted in Sunshine Foods' president and two of its five directors being removed. Jon Moore, an accountant from the company's outside auditing firm, was brought in as president. One of the first things he focused on was the variable and low levels of profits in the past several years. A comparison of Sunshine Foods' results with comparable operations of some large competitors supported his concern. In the past 13 years, Sunshine Foods' closest competitors had an average profit return on shareholders' investment of 5 to 9 percent, while Sunshine Foods averaged only 1.5 percent. Further, Sunshine Foods' sales volume has not increased much from the 1987 level (after adjusting for inflation)—while operating costs have soared upward. Profits for the firm were about $8 million in 1987. The closest Sunshine Foods has come since then is about $6 million—in 1995. The outgoing president blamed his failure on an inefficient sales department. He said, "Our sales department has deteriorated. I can't exactly put my finger on it, but the overall quality of salespeople has dropped, and morale is bad. The team just didn't perform." When Jon Moore e-mailed Peter Holmes, the vice president of sales, with this charge, his reply was,

It's not our fault. I think the company made a key mistake in the early 80s. It expanded horizontally—by increasing its number of product offerings—while major competitors were expanding vertically, growing their own raw materials and making all of their packing materials. They can control quality and make profits in manufacturing that can be used in promotion. I lost some of my best people from frustration. We just aren't competitive enough to reach the market the way we should with a comparable product and price.

In a lengthy e-mail from Peter Holmes, Jon Moore learned more about the nature of Sunshine Foods' market. Although all the firms in the food-processing industry advertise heavily, the size of the market for most processed foods hasn't grown much for many years. Further, most consumers are pressed for time and aren't very selective. If they can't find the brand of food they are looking for, they'll pick up another brand rather than go to some other store. No company in the industry has much effect on the price at which its products are sold. Chain store buyers are very knowledgeable about prices and special promotions available from all the competing suppliers, and they are quick to play one supplier against another to keep the price low. Basically, they have a price they are willing to pay—and they won't exceed it. However, the chains will charge any price they wish on a given brand sold at retail. (That is, a 48-can case of beans might be purchased from any supplier for $23.10, no matter whose product it is. Generally, the shelf price for each is no more than a few pennies different, but chain stores occasionally attract customers by placing a well-known brand on sale.)

Besides insisting that processors meet price points, like for the canned beans, some chains require price allowances if special locations or displays are desired. They also carry nonadvertised brands and/or their own brands at lower price—to offer better value to their customers. And most will willingly accept producers' cents-off coupons, which are offered by Sunshine Foods as well as most of the other major producers of full lines.

At this point, Jon Moore is trying to decide why Sunshine Foods, Inc., isn't as profitable as it once was. And he is puzzled about why some competitors are putting products on the market with low potential sales volume. (For example, one major competitor recently introduced a line of exotic foreign vegetables with gourmet sauces.) And others have been offering frozen dinners or entrees with vegetables for several years. Apparently, Sunshine Foods' managers considered trying such products several years ago but decided against it because of the small potential sales volumes and the likely high costs of new-product development and promotion.

Evaluate Sunshine Foods' present situation. What would you advise Jon Moore to do to improve Sunshine Foods' profits? Explain why.

3. NOCO Soccer Academy

Jermain Dyer came to the U.S. from the U.K. in 1996 on a soccer scholarship. Jermain grew up playing soccer on many competitive teams through high school and had a brief professional career in England. When St. Albans College recruited him to play soccer, he thought it would open his life to a grand adventure. That adventure changed his life.

While at St. Albans, Dyer met his future wife, Randy Simpson, who also played soccer there. She graduated a year ahead of him and went to Fort Collins, Colorado, where she played on the semiprofessional Fort Collins Force women's soccer team. When Dyer finished college he followed Simpson to northern Colorado. Simpson was captain of the Force and worked for the sports marketing company that owned the team.

Dyer got a job at a local meat packing plant, but soccer was his passion. He made the practice squad for the Colorado

Rapids Major League Soccer team, but injuries cut his professional career short. Another passion for Dyer became teaching kids soccer. He has a natural talent for coaching. Dyer is charismatic, kids enjoy his easygoing demeanor and British accent, and he really knows soccer and how to teach the game to youngsters.

In 2002, Dyer founded the NOCO (for NOrthern COlorado) Soccer Academy. At first he trained small groups of young players aged 7–14. He grouped them by age, gender, and skill and conducted training sessions for small groups of 5–7 at a local park. The first kids he attracted came by word of mouth as they quickly told friends and teammates about "this British guy who teaches soccer and makes it fun." His small after-school camps quickly grew to include more than 50 kids. Word continued to get around, and by the following summer Dyer conducted 10 different camps—and quit his job at the meat packing plant. He also trained 11 different NOCO 3v3 soccer teams that competed in tournaments across the state and nation during the summer. All of his players had bright blue jerseys with the NOCO name across the front, and the success of these teams made the jerseys a great promotion vehicle. In 2004, four of his teams competed in the national 3v3 soccer tournament, with one winning a national championship.

To keep up with the rapid growth, Dyer brought a few friends over from England to assist with training. Charlie King moved to the U.S. to become Dyer's assistant director of coaching. Dyer and King planned to work year-round as trainers and hire a couple of local coaches to help them conduct training sessions. During the summer he added a couple of local college soccer players and a few former teammates from England. The summer season works nice for his British mates, because that is the off-season for those still playing professionally. Dyer is confident he can hire and train more coaches if he needs them to handle future growth.

Youth soccer is big in Colorado and across much of the United States. It is the largest participation sport for kids. Fort Collins is a soccer hotbed, and this has helped Dyer's business grow. He now trains about 600 kids per year. But he has even greater ambitions. For example, he would like to build a training facility; the space he currently rents is not always well-suited to soccer. However, he figures he would need to double his business to justify the cost of the soccer complex he wants to build. So he is now wondering how to grow his business.

About 90 percent of his current customers live in Fort Collins, which has a population of about 110,000 people. Dyer believes awareness of his program is close to 100 percent among competitive soccer players ages 11–14—and is probably at about 40 percent among families with soccer-playing kids ages 6–10. Most of his customers are 10–13 and enroll in two to three NOCO programs per year. He has also run a few camps in Boulder and Northglenn, which are about 50 miles from Fort Collins. These have been successful but are currently limited.

There are several small cities within 25 miles of Fort Collins. Loveland, a city of about 60,000, borders Fort Collins on the south. Greeley and Longmont, each with about 80,000 people, are about 25 miles away by interstate highway. These areas have very limited soccer training programs except for their competitive teams, and awareness of NOCO is not very high. Those who have heard of his academy are often not familiar with its philosophy and programs. Dyer is not sure if parents in these communities would be willing to drive their kids to Fort Collins for training. If not, he would have to run his programs there.

Dyer knows that he wants to grow his business, but wonders how he can accomplish his goal. He currently sees a few options:

1. His current customer retention rate is pretty high: about 80 percent. However, when the kids reach 14 or 15 years old, other high school sports and activities make them less interested in extra soccer training. One option is to try to increase retention by developing programs targeted at kids over 14.

2. Another option is to develop a marketing strategy that would encourage his current customers to buy more. He wonders if they have other needs that he might be able to serve.

3. Dyer could try to grow the business by entering new markets and acquiring new customers. His market penetration with kids 6–9 years old is still quite modest. He might develop new programs to better meet this group's needs.

4. Another new market option would be to serve more kids from Loveland, Longmont, and Greeley.

Evaluate Dyer's different options for growing NOCO's customer equity. Develop a set of marketing strategy ideas for each of the options. What could Dyer do for marketing research to better assess his options?

4. Alvarez Technology Services

Katie Alvarez is getting desperate about her new business. She's not sure she can make a go of it—and she really wants to stay in her hometown of Petoskey, Michigan, a beautiful summer resort area along the eastern shore of Lake Michigan. The area's permanent population of 10,000 more than triples in the summer months and doubles at times during the winter skiing and snowmobiling season.

Katie spent four years in the Navy after college graduation, returning home in June 2005. When she couldn't find a good job in the Petoskey area, she decided to go into business for herself and set up Alvarez Technology Services. Katie's plan was to work by herself and basically serve as a "for hire" computer consultant and troubleshooter for her customers. She knew that many of the upscale summer residents relied on a home computer to keep in touch with business dealings and friends at home, and it seemed that someone was always asking her for computer advice. She was optimistic that she could keep busy with a variety of "on-site" services—setting up a

customer's new computer, repairing hardware problems, installing software or upgrades, creating a wireless network, correcting problems created by viruses, and the like.

Katie thought that her savings would allow her to start the business without borrowing any money. Her estimates of required expenditures were: $7,000 for a used SUV; $1,125 for tools, diagnostic equipment, and reference books; $1,700 for a laptop computer, software, and accessories; $350 for an initial supply of fittings and cables; and $500 for insurance and other incidental expenses. This total of $10,675 still left Katie with about $5,000 in savings to cover living expenses while getting started.

Katie chose the technology services business because of her previous work experience. She worked at a computer "help desk" in college and spent her last year in the Navy troubleshooting computer network problems. In addition, from the time Katie was 16 until she finished college, she had also worked during the summer for Joe Carson. Carson operates the only successful computer services company in Petoskey. (There was one other local computer store that also did some "on location" service work when the customer bought equipment at the store, but that store recently went out of business.)

Carson prides himself on quality work and has been able to build up a good business with repeat customers. Specializing in services to residential, small business, and professional offices, Carson has built a strong customer franchise. For 20 years, Carson's major source of new business has been satisfied customers who tell friends or coworkers about his quality service. He is highly regarded as a capable person who always treats clients fairly and honestly. For example, seasonal residents often give Carson the keys to their vacation homes so that he can do upgrades or maintenance while they are away for months at a time. Carson's customers are so loyal, in fact, that Fix-A-Bug—a national computer service franchise—found it impossible to compete with him. Even price-cutting was not an effective weapon against Carson.

From having worked with Carson, Katie Alvarez thought that she knew the computer service business as well as he did; in fact, she had sometimes been able to solve technical problems that left him stumped. Katie was anxious to reach her $60,000-per-year sales objective because she thought this would provide her with a comfortable living in Petoskey. While aware of opportunities to do computer consulting for larger businesses, Katie felt that the sales volume available there was limited because many firms had their own computer specialists or even IT departments. As Katie saw it, her only attractive opportunity was direct competition with Carson.

To get started, Katie spent $1,400 to advertise her business in the local newspaper and on an Internet website. With this money she bought two large announcement ads and 52 weeks of daily ads in the classified section, listed under Miscellaneous Residential and Business Services. The website simply listed businesses in the Petoskey area and gave a telephone number, e-mail address, and brief description. She put magnetic sign boards on her SUV and waited for business to take off.

Katie had a few customers, but much of the time she wasn't busy and she was able to gross only about $200 a week. Of course, she had expected much more. Many of the people who did call were regular Carson customers who had some sort of crisis when he was already busy. While these people agreed that Katie's work was of the same quality as Carson's, they preferred Carson's "quality-care" image and they liked the fact that they had an ongoing relationship with him.

Sometimes Katie did get more work than she could handle. This happened during April and May, when seasonal businesses were preparing for summer openings and owners of summer homes and condos were ready to "open the cottage." The same rush occurred in September and October, as many of these places were being closed for the winter; those customers often wanted help backing up computer files or packing up computer equipment so they could take it with them. During these months, Katie was able to gross about $150 to $200 a day.

Toward the end of her discouraging first year in business, Katie Alvarez is thinking about quitting. While she hates to think about leaving Petoskey, she can't see any way of making a living there with her independent technology services business. Carson seems to dominate the market, except in the rush seasons and for people who need emergency help. And the resort market is not growing very rapidly, so there is little hope of a big influx of new businesses and homeowners to spur demand.

Evaluate Katie Alvarez's strategy planning for her new business. Why isn't she able to reach her objective of $60,000? What should Katie do now? Explain.

5. Applied Polymer Sciences

Jan Jensen, a chemist in Applied Polymer Sciences' resins laboratory, is trying to decide how hard to fight for the new product she has developed. Jensen's job is to find new, more profitable applications for the company's present resin products—and her current efforts are running into unexpected problems.

During the last four years, Jensen has been under heavy pressure from her managers to come up with an idea that will open up new markets for the company's foamed polystyrene.

Two years ago, Jensen developed the "foamed-dome concept"—a method of using foamed polystyrene to make dome-shaped roofs and other structures. She described the procedure for making domes as follows: The construction of a foamed dome involves the use of a specially designed machine that bends, places, and bonds pieces of plastic foam together into a predetermined dome shape. In forming a dome, the machine head is mounted on a boom, which swings around a pivot like the hands of a clock, laying and bonding layer upon layer of foam board in a rising spherical form.

According to Jensen, polystyrene foamed boards have several advantages:

1. Foam board is stiff—but can be formed or bonded to itself by heat alone.
2. Foam board is extremely lightweight and easy to handle. It has good structural rigidity.
3. Foam board has excellent and permanent insulating characteristics. (In fact, the major use for foam board is as an insulator.)
4. Foam board provides an excellent base on which to apply a variety of surface finishes, such as a readily available concrete-based stucco that is durable and inexpensive.

Using her good selling abilities, Jensen easily convinced her managers that her idea had potential.

According to a preliminary study by the marketing research department, the following were areas of construction that could be served by the domes:

1. Bulk storage.
2. Cold storage.
3. Educational construction.
4. Covers for industrial tanks.

5. Light commercial construction.
6. Planetariums.
7. Recreational construction (such as golf-course starter houses).

The marketing research study focused on uses for existing dome structures. Most of the existing domes are made of cement-based materials. The study showed that large savings would result from using foam boards, due to the reduction of construction time.

Because of the new technology involved, the company decided to do its own contracting (at least for the first four to five years). Jensen thought this was necessary to make sure that no mistakes were made by inexperienced contractor crews. (For example, if not applied properly, the plastic may burn.)

After building a few domes in the United States to demonstrate the concept, Jensen contacted some leading U.S. architects. Reactions were as follows:

"It's very interesting, but we're not sure the fire marshal of Chicago would ever give his OK."

"Your tests show that foamed domes can be protected against fires, but there are no *good* tests for unconventional building materials as far as I am concerned."

"I like the idea, but foam board does not have the impact resistance of cement."

"We design a lot of recreational facilities, and kids will find a way to poke holes in the foam."

"Building codes in our area are written for wood and cement structures. Maybe we'd be interested if the codes change."

After this unexpected reaction, management didn't know what to do. Jensen still thinks they should go ahead with the project. She wants to build several more demonstration projects in the United States and at least three each in Europe and Japan to expose the concept in the global market. She thinks architects outside the United States may be more receptive to really new ideas. Further, she says, it takes time for potential users to "see" and accept new ideas. She is sure that more exposure to more people will speed acceptance. And she is convinced that a few reports of well-constructed domes in leading trade papers and magazines will go a long way toward selling the idea. She is working on getting such reports right now. But her managers aren't sure they want to OK spending more money on "her" project. Her immediate boss is supportive, but the rest of the review board is less sure about more demonstration projects or going ahead at all—just in the United States or in global markets.

Evaluate how Applied Polymer Sciences got into the present situation. What should Jan Jensen do? What should Jensen's managers do? Explain.

6. International Steel Company

International Steel Company is one of two major producers of wide-flange beams in the United States. The other producer is United Steel Corporation (now USX). A number of small firms also compete, but they tend to compete mainly on price in nearby markets where they can keep transport costs low. Typically, all interested competitors charge the same delivered price, which varies some depending on how far the customer is from either of the two major producers. In other words, local prices are higher in more remote geographic markets.

Wide-flange beams are one of the principal steel products used in construction. They are the modern version of what are commonly known as I-beams. USX rolls a full range of wide flanges from 6 to 36 inches. International entered the field about 30 years ago, when it converted an existing mill to produce this product. International's mill is limited to flanges up to 24 inches, however. At the time of the conversion, International felt that customer usage of sizes over 24 inches was likely to be small. In recent years, however, there has been a definite trend toward the larger and heavier sections.

The beams produced by the various competitors are almost identical—since customers buy according to standard dimensional and physical-property specifications. In the smaller size range, there are a number of competitors. But above 14 inches, only USX and International compete. Above 24 inches, USX has no competition.

All the steel companies sell these beams through their own sales forces. The customer for these beams is called a structural fabricator. This fabricator typically buys unshaped beams and other steel products from the mills and shapes them according to the specifications of each customer. The fabricator sells to the contractor or owner of the structure being built.

The structural fabricator usually must sell on a competitive-bid basis. The bidding is done on the plans and specifications prepared by an architectural or structural engineering firm and forwarded to the fabricator by the contractor who wants the bid. Although thousands of structural fabricators compete in the U.S., relatively few account for the majority of wide-flange tonnage in the various geographical regions. Since the price is the same from all producers, they typically buy beams on the basis of availability (i.e., availability to meet production schedules) and performance (i.e., reliability in meeting the promised delivery schedule).

Several years ago, International's production schedulers saw that they were going to have an excess of hot-rolled plate capacity in the near future. At the same time, development of a new production technology allowed International to weld three plates together into a section with the same dimensional and physical properties and almost the same cross section as a rolled wide-flange beam. This development appeared to offer two key advantages to International: (1) It would enable International to use some of the excess plate capacity, and (2) larger sizes of wide-flange beams could be offered. Cost analysts showed that by using a fully depreciated plate mill and the new welding process it would be possible to produce and sell larger wide-flange beams at competitive prices—that is, at the same price charged by USX.

International's managers were excited about the possibilities, because customers usually appreciate having a second source of supply. Also, the new approach would allow the production of up to a 60-inch flange. With a little imagination, these larger sizes might offer a significant breakthrough for the construction industry.

International decided to go ahead with the new project. As the production capacity was converted, the salespeople were kept well informed of the progress. They, in turn, promoted this new capability to their customers, emphasizing that soon they would be able to offer a full range of beam products. International sent several general information letters to a broad mailing list but did not advertise. The market development section of the sales department was very busy explaining the new possibilities of the process to fabricators at engineering trade associations and shows.

When the new production line was finally ready to go, the market reaction was disappointing. No orders came in and none were expected. In general, customers were wary of the new product. The structural fabricators felt they couldn't use it without the approval of their customers, because it would involve deviating from the specified rolled sections. And as long as they could still get the rolled section, why make the extra effort for something unfamiliar, especially with no price advantage? The salespeople were also bothered with a very common question: How can you take plate that you sell for about $460 per ton and make a product that you can sell for $470? This question came up frequently and tended to divert the whole discussion to the cost of production rather than to the way the new product might be used or its value in the construction process.

Evaluate International's situation. What should International do?

7. Kerikeri Lodge

Nestled in the high country of New Zealand's South Island is a getaway adventure playground aimed unashamedly at the world's very wealthy. Presidents, playboys, and other such globe-trotters are the prime targets of this fledgling tourism business developed by Kerikeri Lodge. The lodge offers this exclusive niche the opportunity of a secluded holiday in a little-known paradise. Guests, commonly under public scrutiny in their everyday lives, can escape such pressures at a hunting retreat designed specifically with their needs in mind.

A chance meeting between a New Zealand Department of Conservation investigator and the son of the former Indonesian president marked the beginning of this specialty tourist operation. Recognizing that "filthy rich" public figures are constantly surrounded by security and seldom have the luxury of going anywhere incognito, the New Zealander, Gerard Olde-Olthof, suggested that he and his new friend purchase a high-country station and hunting-guide company that was for sale. Olde-Olthof believed that the facilities, and their secluded and peaceful environment, would make an ideal holiday haven for this elite group. His Indonesian partner concurred.

Olde-Olthof, who was by now the company's managing director, developed a carefully tailored package of goods and services for the property. Architecturally designed accommodations, including a game trophy room and eight guest rooms, were constructed using high-quality South Island furniture and fittings, to create the ambience necessary to attract and satisfy the demands of their special clientele.

Although New Zealand had an international reputation for being sparsely populated and green, Olde-Olthof knew that rich travelers frequently complained that local accommodations were below overseas standards. Since the price (NZ$700 a night) was not a significant variable for this target market, sumptuous guest facilities were built. These were designed to be twice the normal size of most hotel rooms, with double-glazed windows that revealed breathtaking views. Ten fulltime staff and two seasonal guides were recruited to ensure that visitors received superior customized service, in fitting with the restrained opulence of the lodge.

The 28,000 hectares of original farmland that made up the retreat and backed onto the South Island's Mount Cook National Park were converted into a big-game reserve. All merino sheep on the land were sold, and deer, elk, chamois, and wapiti were brought in and released. This was a carefully considered plan. Olde-Olthof, the former conservationist, believed that financially and environmentally this was the correct decision. Not only do tourists, each staying for one week and taking part in safari shooting, inject as much cash into the business as the station's annual wool clip used to fetch, but the game does less harm to the environment than sheep. Cattle, however, once part of the original station, were left to graze on lower riverflat areas.

For those high-flying customers seeking less bloodthirsty leisure activities, Kerikeri developed photographic "safaris" and other product-line extensions. Horse-trekking, golfing on a nearby rural course (with no need for hordes of security forces), helicopter trips around nearby Lake Tekapo, nature walks, and other such activities formed part of the exclusive package.

While still in the early stages of operation, this retreat has already attracted a steady stream of visitors. To date, the manager has relied solely on positive word of mouth, publicity, and public relations to draw in new customers. Given the social and business circles in which his potential target market moves, Olde-Olthof considers these to be the most appropriate forms of marketing communication. The only real concern for Kerikeri Lodge has been the criticism of at least one New Zealand lobby group that the company is yet another example of local land passing into "foreign" hands, and that New Zealanders are prevented from using the retreat and excluded from its financial returns. However, this unwelcome attention has been fairly short-lived.

Identify the likely characteristics of the market segment being targeted by the company. Why are most target customers likely to be foreigners rather than New Zealanders? Suggest what expectations target customers are likely to have regarding the quality, reliability, and range of services. What are the implications for Kerikeri Lodge? How difficult is it for Kerikeri Lodge to undertake marketing research? Elaborate.

8. Soprano's Ristorante

Sophie Soprano, the owner and manager of Soprano's Ristorante, is reviewing the slow growth of her restaurant. She's also thinking about the future and wondering if she should change her strategy. In particular, she is wondering if she should join a fast-food or family restaurant franchise chain. Several are located near her, but there are many franchisors without local restaurants. After doing some research on the Internet, she has learned that with help from the franchisors, some of these places gross $500,000 to $1 million a year. Of course, she would have to follow someone else's strategy and thereby lose her independence, which she doesn't like to think about. But those sales figures do sound good, and she has also heard that the return to the owner-manager (including salary) can be over $150,000 per year. She has also considered putting a web page for Soprano's Ristorante on the Internet but is not sure how that will help.

Soprano's Ristorante is a fairly large restaurant—about 3,000 square feet—located in the center of a small shopping center completed early in 2005. Soprano's sells mainly full-course "home-cooked" Italian-style dinners (no bar) at moderate prices. In addition to Soprano's restaurant, other businesses in the shopping center include a supermarket, a hair salon, a liquor store, a video rental store, and a vacant space that used to be a hardware store. The hardware store failed when a Home Depot located nearby. Sophie has learned that a pizzeria is considering locating there soon. She wonders how that competition will affect her. Ample parking space is available at the shopping center, which is located in a residential section of a growing suburb in the East, along a heavily traveled major traffic route.

Sophie graduated from a local high school and a nearby university and has lived in this town with her husband and two children for many years. She has been self-employed in the restaurant business since her graduation from college in 1988. Her most recent venture before opening Soprano's was a large restaurant that she operated successfully with her brother from 1996 to 2002. In 2002, Sophie sold out her share because of illness. Following her recovery, she was anxious for something to do and opened the present restaurant in April 2005. Sophie feels her plans for the business and her opening were well thought out. When she was ready to start her new restaurant, she looked at several possible locations before finally deciding on the present one. Sophie explained: "I looked everywhere, but here I particularly noticed the heavy traffic when I first looked at it. This is the crossroads for three major interstate highways. So obviously the potential is here."

Having decided on the location, Sophie signed a 10-year lease with option to renew for 10 more years, and then eagerly attacked the problem of outfitting the almost empty store space in the newly constructed building. She tiled the floor, put in walls of surfwood, installed plumbing and electrical fixtures and an extra washroom, and purchased the necessary restaurant equipment. All this cost $120,000—which came from her own cash savings. She then spent an additional $1,500 for glassware, $2,000 for an initial food stock, and $2,125 to advertise Soprano's Ristorante's opening in the local newspaper. The paper serves the whole metro area, so the $2,125 bought only three quarter-page ads. These expenditures also came from her own personal savings. Next she hired five waitresses at $275 a week and one chef at $550 a week. Then, with $24,000 cash reserve for the business, she was ready to open. Reflecting her sound business sense, Sophie knew she would need a substantial cash reserve to fall back on until the business got on its feet. She expected this to take about one year. She had no expectations of getting rich overnight. (Her husband, a high school teacher, was willing to support the family until the restaurant caught on.)

The restaurant opened in April and by August had a weekly gross revenue of only $2,400. Sophie was a little discouraged with this, but she was still able to meet all her operating expenses without investing any new money in the business. By September business was still slow, and Sophie had to invest an additional $3,000 in the business just to survive.

Business had not improved in November, and Sophie stepped up her advertising—hoping this would help. In December, she spent $1,200 of her cash reserve for radio advertising—10 late-evening spots on a news program at a station that aims at middle-income America. Sophie also spent $1,600 more during the next several weeks for some metro newspaper ads.

By April 2006, the situation had begun to improve, and by June her weekly gross was up to between $3,100 and $3,300. By March 2007, the weekly gross had risen to about $4,200. Sophie increased the working hours of her staff six to seven hours a week and added another cook to handle the increasing number of customers. Sophie was more optimistic for the future because she was finally doing a little better than breaking even. Her full-time involvement seemed to be paying off. She had not put any new money into the business since summer 2006 and expected business to continue to rise. She had not yet taken any salary for herself, even though she had built up a small surplus of about $9,000. Instead, she planned to put in a bigger air-conditioning system at a cost of $5,000 and was also planning to use what salary she might have taken for herself to hire two new waitresses to handle the growing volume of business. And she saw that if business increased much more she would have to add another cook.

Evaluate Sophie's past and present marketing strategy. What should she do now? Should she seriously consider joining some franchise chain?

9. Sleepy Inn Motel

Eng Huang is trying to decide whether he should make some minor changes in the way he operates his Sleepy Inn Motel or if he should join either the Days Inn or Holiday Inn motel chains. Some decision must be made soon because his present operation is losing money. But joining either of the chains will require fairly substantial changes, including new capital investment if he goes with Holiday Inn.

Huang bought the recently completed 60-room motel two years ago after leaving a successful career as a production manager for a large producer of industrial machinery. He was looking for an interesting opportunity that would be less demanding than the production manager job. The Sleepy Inn is located at the edge of a very small town near a rapidly expanding resort area and about one-half mile off an interstate highway. It is 10 miles from the tourist area, with several nationally franchised full-service resort motels suitable for "destination" vacations. There is a Best Western, a Ramada Inn, and a Hilton Inn, as well as many mom and pop and limited-service, lower-priced motels—and some quaint bed and breakfast facilities—in the tourist area. The interstate highway near the Sleepy Inn carries a great deal of traffic, since the resort area is between several major metropolitan areas. No development has taken place around the turnoff from the interstate highway. The only promotion for the tourist area along the interstate highway is two large signs near the turnoffs. They show the popular name for the area and that the area is only 10 miles to the west. These signs are maintained by the tourist area's Tourist Bureau. In addition, the state transportation department maintains several small signs showing (by symbols) that near this turnoff one can find gas, food, and lodging. Huang does not have any signs advertising Sleepy Inn except the two on his property. He has been relying on people finding his motel as they go toward the resort area.

Initially, Huang was very pleased with his purchase. He had traveled a lot himself and stayed in many different hotels and motels—so he had some definite ideas about what travelers wanted. He felt that a relatively plain but modern room with a comfortable bed, standard bath facilities, and free cable TV would appeal to most customers. Further, Huang thought a swimming pool or any other nonrevenue-producing additions were not necessary. And he felt a restaurant would be a greater management problem than the benefits it would offer. However, after many customers commented about the lack of convenient breakfast facilities, Huang served a free continental breakfast of coffee, juice, and rolls in a room next to the registration desk.

Day-to-day operations went fairly smoothly in the first two years, in part because Huang and his wife handled registration and office duties as well as general management. During the first year of operation, occupancy began to stabilize around 55 percent of capacity. But according to industry figures, this was far below the average of 68 percent for his classification—motels without restaurants.

After two years of operation, Huang was concerned because his occupancy rates continued to be below average. He decided to look for ways to increase both occupancy rate and profitability and still maintain his independence.

Huang wanted to avoid direct competition with the full-service resort motels. He stressed a price appeal in his signs and brochures and was quite proud of the fact that he had been able to avoid all the "unnecessary expenses" of the full-service resort motels. As a result, Huang was able to offer lodging at a very modest price—about 40 percent below the full-service hotels and comparable to the lowest-priced resort area motels. The customers who stayed at Sleepy Inn said they found it quite acceptable. But he was troubled by what seemed to be a large number of people driving into his parking lot, looking around, and not coming in to register.

Huang was particularly interested in the results of a recent study by the regional tourist bureau. This study revealed the following information about area vacationers:

1. 68 percent of the visitors to the area are young couples and older couples without children.
2. 40 percent of the visitors plan their vacations and reserve rooms more than 60 days in advance.
3. 66 percent of the visitors stay more than three days in the area and at the same location.
4. 78 percent of the visitors indicated that recreational facilities were important in their choice of accommodations.
5. 13 percent of the visitors had family incomes of less than $27,000 per year.
6. 38 percent of the visitors indicated that it was their first visit to the area.

After much thought, Huang began to seriously consider affiliating with a national motel chain in hopes of attracting more customers and maybe protecting his motel from the increasing competition. There were constant rumors that more motels were being planned for the area. After some investigating, he focused on two national chain possibilities: Days Inn and Holiday Inn. Neither had affiliates in the area even though they each have about 2,000 units nationwide.

Days Inn of America, Inc., is an Atlanta-based chain of economy lodgings. It has been growing rapidly and is willing to take on new franchisees. A major advantage of Days Inn is that it would not require a major capital investment by Huang. The firm is targeting people interested in lower-priced motels, in particular, senior citizens, the military, school sports teams, educators, and business travelers. In contrast, Holiday Inn would probably require Huang to upgrade some of his facilities, including adding a swimming pool. The total new capital investment would be between $300,000 and $500,000, depending on how fancy he got. But then Huang would be able to charge higher prices, perhaps $75 per day on the average rather than the $45 per day per room he's charging now.

The major advantages of going with either of these national chains would be their central reservation systems and their national names. Both companies offer nationwide, toll-free reservation lines, which produce about 40 percent of all bookings in affiliated motels. Both companies also offer websites (www.daysinn.com and www.holiday-inn.com) that help find a specific hotel by destination, rate, amenities, quality rating, and availability.

A major difference between the two national chains is their method of promotion. Days Inn uses little TV advertising and less print advertising than Holiday Inn. Instead, Days Inn emphasizes sales promotions. In one campaign, for example, Blue Bonnet margarine users could exchange proof-of-purchase seals for a free night at a Days Inn. This tie-in led to the Days Inn system *selling* an additional 10,000 rooms. Further, Days Inn operates a September Days Club for travelers 50 and over who receive such benefits as discount rates and a quarterly travel magazine.

Days Inn also has other membership programs, including its InnCentives loyalty club for frequent business and leisure travelers. Other programs targeted to business travelers include two Corporate Rate programs and its new Days Business Place hotels. Not to be outdone, Holiday Inn has a membership program called Priority Club Worldwide.

Both firms charge 8 percent of gross room revenues for belonging to their chain—to cover the costs of the reservation service and national promotion. This amount is payable monthly. In addition, franchise members must agree to maintain their facilities and make repairs and improvements as required. Failure to maintain facilities can result in losing the franchise. Periodic inspections are conducted as part of supervising the whole chain and helping the members operate more effectively.

Evaluate Eng Huang's present strategy. What should he do? Explain.

10. Fulton's Ice Land

Steve Fulton, the manager of Fulton's Ice Land, is trying to decide what strategies to use to increase profits.

Fulton's Ice Land is an ice-skating rink with a conventional hockey rink surface (85 feet × 200 feet). It is the only indoor ice rink in a northern U.S. city of about 450,000. The city's recreation department operates some outdoor rinks in the winter, but they don't offer regular ice skating programs because of weather variability.

Steve runs a successful hockey program that is more than breaking even—but this is about all he can expect if he only offers hockey. To try to increase his profits, Steve is trying to expand and improve his public skating program. With such a program, he could have as many as 700 people in a public session at one time, instead of limiting the use of the ice to 12 to 24 hockey players per hour. While the receipts from hockey can be as high as $200 an hour (plus concession sales), the receipts from a two-hour public skating session—charging $5 per person—could yield up to $3,500 for a two-hour period (plus much higher concession sales). The potential revenue from such large public skating sessions could make Fulton's Ice Land a really profitable operation. But, unfortunately, just scheduling public sessions doesn't mean that a large number will come. In fact, only a few prime times seem likely: Friday and Saturday evenings and Saturday and Sunday afternoons.

Steve has included 14 public skating sessions in his ice schedule, but so far they haven't attracted as many people as he hoped. In total, they only generate a little more revenue than if the times were sold for hockey use. Offsetting this extra revenue are extra costs. More staff people are needed to handle a public skating session—guards, a ticket seller, skate rental, and more concession help. So the net revenue from either use is about the same. He could cancel some of the less attractive public sessions—like the noon-time daily sessions, which have very low attendance—and make the average attendance figures look a lot better. But he feels that if he is going to offer public skating he must have a reasonable selection of times. He does recognize, however, that the different public skating sessions do seem to attract different people and really different kinds of people.

The Saturday and Sunday afternoon public skating sessions have been the most successful, with an average of 200 people attending during the winter season. Typically, this is a "kid-sitting" session. More than half of the patrons are young children who have been dropped off by their parents for several hours, but there are also some family groups.

In general, the kids and the families have a good time—and a fairly loyal group comes every Saturday and/or Sunday during the winter season. In the spring and fall, however, attendance drops about in half, depending on how nice the weather is. (Steve schedules no public sessions in the summer, focusing instead on hockey clinics and figure skating.)

The Friday and Saturday evening public sessions are a big disappointment. The sessions run from 8 until 10, a time when he had hoped to attract teenagers and young adult couples. At $5 per person, plus $1.50 for skate rental, this would be an economical date. In fact, Steve has seen quite a few young couples—and some keep coming back. But he also sees a surprising number of 8- to 14-year-olds who have been dropped off by their parents. The younger kids tend to race around the rink playing tag. This affects the whole atmosphere, making it less appealing for dating couples and older patrons.

Steve has been hoping to develop a teenage and young-adult market for a "social activity," adapting the format used by roller-skating rinks. Their public skating sessions feature a variety of couples-only and group games as well as individual skating to dance music. Turning ice skating sessions into such social activities is not common, however, although industry newletters suggest that a few ice-rink operators have had success with the roller-skating format. Seemingly, the ice skating sessions are viewed as active recreation, offering exercise or a sports experience.

Steve installed some soft lights to try to change the evening atmosphere. The music was selected to encourage people to skate to the beat and couples to skate together. Some people complained about the "old" music; but it was "danceable," and some skaters really liked it. For a few sessions, Steve even tried to have some couples-only skates. The couples liked it, but this format was strongly resisted by the young boys who felt that they had paid their money and there was no reason why they should be kicked off the ice. Steve also tried to attract more young people and especially couples by bringing in a local rock radio station disk jockey to broadcast from Fulton's Ice Land—playing music and advertising the Friday and Saturday evening public sessions. But this had no effect on attendance, which varies from 50 to 100 per two-hour session during the winter.

Steve seriously considered the possibility of limiting the Friday and Saturday evening sessions to people age 14 and over—to try to change the environment. He knew it would take time to change people's attitudes. But when he counted the customers, he realized this would be risky. More than a quarter of his customers on an average weekend night appear to be 13 or under. This means that he would have to make a serious commitment to building the teen and young-adult market. And, so far, his efforts haven't been successful. He has already invested over $3,000 in lighting changes and over $9,000 promoting the sessions over the rock music radio station, with very disappointing results. Although the station's sales rep said they reached teenagers all over town, an on-air offer for a free skating session did not get a single response!

Some days, Steve feels it's hopeless. Maybe he should accept that most public ice skating sessions are a mixed bag. Or maybe he should just sell the time to hockey groups. Still he keeps hoping that something can be done to improve weekend evening public skating attendance, because the upside potential is so good. And the Saturday and Sunday afternoon sessions are pretty good money-makers.

Evaluate Fulton's Ice Land's situation. What should Steve Fulton do? Why?

11. Runners Supply

Julie Yellowrobe, owner of Runners Supply, is trying to decide what she should do with her retail business and how committed she should be to her current target market.

Julie is 42 years old, and she started her Runners Supply retail store in 1990 when she was only 24 years old. She was a nationally ranked runner herself and felt that the growing interest in jogging offered real potential for a store that provided serious runners with the shoes and advice they needed. The jogging boom quickly turned Runners Supply into a profitable business selling high-end running shoes—and Julie made a very good return on her investment for the first 10 years. From 1990 until 2000, Julie emphasized Nike shoes, which were well accepted and seen as top quality. Nike's aggressive promotion and quality shoes resulted in a positive image that made it possible to get a $5 to $7 per pair premium for Nike shoes. Good volume and good margins resulted in attractive profits for Julie Yellowrobe.

Committing so heavily to Nike seemed like a good idea when its marketing and engineering was the best available. In addition to running shoes, Nike had other athletic shoes Julie could sell. So even though they were not her primary focus, Julie did stock other Nike shoes including walking shoes, shoes for aerobic exercise, basketball shoes, tennis shoes, and cross-trainers. She also added more sportswear to her store and put more emphasis on fashion rather than just function.

Even with this broadened product line, Julie's sales flattened out—and she wasn't sure what to do to get her business back in growth mode. She realized that she was growing older and so were many of her longer-term customers. Many of them were finding that jogging isn't just hard work—it's hard on the body, especially the knees. So many of her previously loyal runner-customers were switching to other, less demanding exercise programs. However, when she tried to orient her store and product line more toward these people she wasn't as effective in serving the needs of serious runners—still an important source of sales for the store.

She was also facing more competition on all fronts. Many consumers who don't really do any serious exercise buy running shoes as their day-to-day casual shoes. As a result, many department stores, discount stores, and regular shoe stores have put more and more emphasis on athletic shoes in their product assortment. When Julie added other brands and put more emphasis on fashion she found that she was in direct competition with a number of other stores, which put more pressure on her to lower prices and cut her profit margins. For example, in Julie's area there are a number of local and online retail chains offering lower-cost and lower-quality versions of similar shoes as well as related fashion apparel. Wal-Mart also expanded its assortment of athletic shoes—and it offers rock-bottom prices. Other chains, like Foot Locker, have focused their promotion and product lines on specific target markets. Still, all of them (including Julie's Runners Supply, the local chains, Wal-Mart, and Foot Locker) are scrambling to catch up with rival category killers whose selections are immense.

In the spring of 2006 Julie tried an experiment. She took on a line of high-performance athletic shoes that were made to order. The distinctive feature of these shoes was that the sole was molded to precisely fit the customer's foot. A pair of these custom-made shoes cost about $170, so the market was not large. Further, Julie didn't put much promotional emphasis on this line. However, when a customer came in the store with a serious interest in high-performance shoes, Julie's sales clerks would tell them about the custom shoe alternative and show a sample. When a customer was interested, a mold of the customer's bare foot was made at the store, using an innovative material that hardened in just a few minutes without leaving a sticky mess. Julie sent the mold off to the manufacturer by UPS, and about two weeks later the finished shoes arrived. Customers who tried these shoes were delighted with the result. However, the company that offered them ran into financial trouble and went out of business.

Julie recently learned about another company that is offering a very similar custom shoe program. However, that company requires more promotion investment by retailers and in return provides exclusive sales territories. Another requirement is that the store establish a website promoting the shoes and providing more detail on how the order process works. All of a retailer's salesclerks are also required to go through a special two-day training program so that they know how to present the benefits of the shoe and do the best job creating the molds. The training program is free, but Julie would have to pay travel, hotel, and food expenses for her salespeople. So before even getting started, the new program would cost her several thousand dollars.

Julie is uncertain about what to do. Although sales have dropped, she is still making a reasonable profit and has a relatively good base of repeat customers, with the serious runners still more than half of her sales and profits. She thinks that the custom shoe alternative is a way to differentiate her store from the mass-merchandisers and to sharpen her focus on the target market of serious runners. On the other hand, that doesn't really solve the problem that the "runners" market seems to be shrinking. It also doesn't address the question of how best to keep a lot of the aging customers she already serves who seem to be shifting away from an emphasis on running. She also worries that she'll lose the loyalty of her repeat customers if she shifts the store further away from her running niche and more toward fashionable athletic shoes or fashionable casual wear. Yet athletic wear—women's, in particular—has come a long way in recent years. Designers like Donna Karan, Calvin

Klein, Georgio Armani, and Ralph Lauren are part of the fast-growing women's wear business.

So Julie is trying to decide if there is anything else she can do to better promote her current store and product line, or if she should think about changing her strategy in a more dramatic way. Any change from her current focus would involve retraining her current salespeople and perhaps hiring new salespeople. Adding and maintaining a website isn't an insurmountable challenge, but it is not an area where she has either previous experience or skill.

Clearly, a real shift in emphasis would require that Julie make some hard decisions about her target market and her whole marketing mix. She's got some flexibility—it's not like she's a manufacturer of shoes with a big investment in a factory that can't be changed. On the other hand, she's not certain she's ready for a big change, especially a change that would mean starting over again from scratch. She started Runners Supply because she was interested in running and felt she had something special to offer. Now she worries that she's just grasping at straws without a real focus or any obvious competitive advantage. She also knows that she is already much more successful than she ever dreamed when she started her business—and in her heart she wonders if she wasn't just spoiled by growth that came fast and easy at the start.

Evaluate Julie Yellowrobe's present strategy. Evaluate the alternative strategies she is considering. Is her primary problem her emphasis on running shoes, her emphasis on trying to hang on to her current customers, or is it something else? What should she do? Why?

12. DrMarcus.com—Custom Vitamins and Supplements

Dr. Marcus West has to decide how to handle a complaint letter from a customer. When he received the letter, he passed it along to Alberto Skinner, the firm's customer service manager, to get his recommendation. Now West has a reply from Skinner, and he must decide how to respond to the customer and determine if changes are needed in his company's customer service operations.

Dr. West has a reputation as a health and nutrition guru. His fame grew after he published two books—both of which were very popular and received a lot of attention in the press. Five years ago, Internet entrepreneur Trishia Bauder approached him with the idea of creating a website to sell custom vitamins under Dr. Marcus' name.

West and Bauder became partners, and the business enjoyed success in its first four years of operation. Bauder handles the website technology, inventory, production, and shipping. Dr. West is the health expert, creates content provided on the website, and is in charge of marketing and customer service.

The complaint letter and reply from Skinner follow:

Dear Dr. West,

I am a longtime fan of your books and like to visit your website for health tips. As a new grandmother, my health is even more important to me. I want to see my grandchildren graduate from high school, go to college, and have kids of their own.

You have made me a bit of a guru as well. I work out every day. People always ask me how I stay so fit and healthy. Having read both your books, I tell them they should exercise regularly and take vitamins and supplements for long-term health. I always recommend your DrMarcus.com website and especially the section on your custom vitamins. That is my favorite part of your website. I really like that you take information about me and my medical history—and then recommend custom vitamins and supplements. I also like how you send me packages that each contain a daily dose.

But after my recent experiences, my loyalty to you and your company are now in jeopardy. Here is my story.

Six months ago, I went to the website to reorder my vitamins and supplements. The home page announced a new and improved health survey and custom health program. So, I went through the survey and filled out all the details—it would have been nice if you had saved some of them from my previous survey. At the end of the survey the website offered me a 90-day supply of a custom set of vitamins and supplements selected for my specific needs. The $212 price was about $50 more than my previous 90-day supply, but I trusted your advice so I placed the order.

About two-and-a-half months later, I phoned DrMarcus.com to place a refill order. The person on the phone was very nice and asked if I wanted to set up automatic refills. I said no because I hate those automatic programs. They remind me of those book clubs that automatically send you books you don't want if you do not reply fast enough. About a week later my order arrived—then two days later another identical order arrived. I did not understand this, but I figured I would eventually use them up and I kept everything (and I was billed for both orders—$424 on my credit card). I should mention there was no e-mail explaining this mystery delivery. I was a little annoyed and sent an e-mail to customer service seeking an explanation. I received an automated response, "Thank you for your inquiry, someone will get back to you within 24 hours." No one ever replied, but I forgot about it.

Then two weeks ago I received an e-mail from DrMarcus.com telling me my refill order had been shipped and would arrive in a few days. But I did not place a refill order! I did not even need more vitamins because I was still working off the two 90-day supplies that I received three months ago. So I replied by e-mail that I did not want the order and to cancel it. A reply e-mail (from Clara) told me that I had signed up for automatic refill six months ago. I replied that I certainly had not and that I would not pay for the order that was being sent.

A few days later I received a call from Alberto Skinner, your director of customer service. He told me that I had originally signed up for automatic refill and that was why I received vitamins. I told him that was impossible, and he told me that unless I checked some box on my original order that this was done automatically, "for my convenience." He said there were also several warnings and that I must have missed those. *Basically, I think he told me this was my fault. I did not like that one bit!!!* Mr. Skinner told me the vitamins were on their way, but I could refuse delivery of them. He offered to let me have them for

20 percent off if I simply kept them. Unfortunately, the vitamins were on my doorstep when I arrived home that day. I had to take the vitamins to UPS to get them shipped back to you.

You guys are no longer very good at your business. You might have a great product, but I am now seeing other vitamin companies offering the same products. I have no doubt these other companies offer better customer service. If you want me back as a customer, I would expect a formal apology from Mr. Skinner and a free 90-day supply. Otherwise, I figure my business will be welcomed at one of your competitors— and I will be sure all my friends know about my experience at DrMarcus.com.

Sincerely,

Roseanne Hester

Below is the reply that Alberto Skinner sent to Dr. West concerning the letter.

Dear Marcus,

As per your request, I reviewed Mrs. Hester's order history. Yes, she is a very good customer who spent almost $800 with us last year. And she is a member of our referral program— and we can count at least seven new customers she has directed to us in the last 18 months.

But I want to clarify some of this particular situation.

- You might recall that our automatic refill program has been a big success. Since we instituted the program a year ago, our customer retention rate has jumped by 10 percent. There are occasional complaints, but given the large number of customers we serve, the complaints are really just a "drop in the bucket."
- When Mrs. Hester placed her order six months ago there were at least two different warnings about the automatic

refill program—customers have to check a box at the bottom of the screen to "opt out" of the program. We all agreed that it was better to make them part of the program automatically, but to give them two chances to remove themselves from automatic delivery.

- I do not know if we replied to her e-mail asking for customer service help.
- I did not tell Mrs. Hester that this was her fault, but I did tell her that when she signed up there were two chances for her to choose to not be part of the automatic refill program.
- Mrs. Hester did not get an e-mail notifying her of the first refill order because that system was not in place yet. But this has now been fixed, and the e-mail notifying her when we ship shows that this works.
- I offered her 20 percent off as is our standard policy when we make a mistake. Considering this was her mistake, I thought this was generous.
- If Mrs. Hester had called and asked, I could have had UPS come out and pick up the package for return to us.

I do not recommend giving her a free 90-day supply. This may simply encourage her to complain again in the future. Besides, this was not our mistake. We may be better off without certain customers—and I think Mrs. Hester falls into this category.

Feel free to call me if you have any more questions.

Regards, Alberto

Assess the customer service operations at DrMarcus.com. What should West do about Mrs. Hester? What changes, if any, should West make to customer service and ordering operations?

13. Office Distributors, Inc.*

Tiffany Lui, marketing manager for Office Distributors, Inc. (ODI) must decide whether she should permit her largest customer to buy some of ODI's commonly used file folders under the customer's brand rather than ODI's own FILEX brand. She is afraid that if she refuses, this customer—Business Center, Inc.—will go to another file folder producer and ODI will lose this business.

Business Center, Inc., is a major distributor of office supplies and has already managed to put its own brand on more than 45 high-sales-volume office supply products. It distributes these products—as well as the branded products of many manufacturers—through its nationwide distribution network, which includes 150 retail stores. Now Rick Mann, vice president of marketing for Business Center, is seeking a line of file folders similar in quality to ODI's FILEX brand, which now has over 60 percent of the market.

This is not the first time that Business Center has asked ODI to produce a file folder line for Business Center. On both previous occasions, Tiffany Lui turned down the requests and Business Center continued to buy. In fact, Business Center not

only continued to buy the file folders but also the rest of ODI's product lines. And total sales continued to grow as Business Center built new stores. Business Center accounts for about 30 percent of Tiffany Lui's business. And FILEX brand file folders account for about 35 percent of this volume.

In the past ODI consistently refused such dealer-branding requests as a matter of corporate policy. This policy was set some years ago because of a desire (1) to avoid excessive dependence on any one customer and (2) to sell its own brands so that its success is dependent on the quality of its products rather than just a low price. The policy developed from a concern that if it started making products under other customers' brands, those customers could shop around for a low price and the business would be very fickle. At the time the policy was set, Tiffany Lui realized that it might cost ODI some business. But it was felt wise nevertheless, to be better able to control the firm's future.

ODI has been in business 28 years and now has a sales volume of $40 million. Its primary products are file folders, file markers and labels, and a variety of indexing systems. ODI offers such a wide range of size, color, and type that no competition can match it in its part of the market. About 40 percent of ODI's file folder business is in specialized lines such as files

---

*Adapted from a case written by Professor Hardy, University of Western Ontario, Canada.

for oversized blueprint and engineer drawings; see-through files for medical markets; and greaseproof and waterproof files for marine, oil field, and other hazardous environmental markets. ODI's competitors are mostly small paper converters. But excess capacity in the industry is substantial, and these converters are always hungry for orders and willing to cut price. Further, the raw materials for the FILEX line of file folders are readily available.

ODI's distribution system consists of 10 regional stationery suppliers (40 percent of total sales), Business Center, Inc. (30 percent), and more than 40 local stationers who have wholesale and retail operations (30 percent). The 10 regional stationers each have about six branches, while the local stationers each have one wholesale and three or four retail locations. The regional suppliers sell directly to large corporations and to some retailers. In contrast, Business Center's main volume comes from sales to local businesses and walk-in customers at its 150 retail stores.

Tiffany Lui has a real concern about the future of the local stationers' business. Some are seriously discussing the formation of buying groups to obtain volume discounts from vendors and thus compete more effectively with Business Center's 150 retail stores, the large regionals, and the superstore chains, which are spreading rapidly. These chains—for example, Staples, Office World, Office Max, and Office Depot—operate stores of 16,000 to 20,000 square feet (i.e., large stores compared to the usual office supply stores) and let customers wheel through high-stacked shelves to supermarket-like checkout counters. These chains stress convenience, wide selection, and much lower prices than the typical office supply retailers. They buy directly from manufacturers, such as ODI, bypassing wholesalers like Business Center. It is likely that the growing pressure from these chains is causing Business Center to renew its proposal to buy a file line with its own name. For example, Staples offers its own dealer brand of files and many other types of products.

None of Tiffany's other accounts is nearly as effective in retailing as Business Center, which has developed a good reputation in every major city in the country. Business Center's profits have been the highest in the industry. Further, its brands are almost as well known as those of some key producers—and its expansion plans are aggressive. And now, these plans are being pressured by the fast-growing superstores, which are already knocking out many local stationers.

Tiffany is sure that ODI's brands are well entrenched in the market, despite the fact that most available money has been devoted to new-product development rather than promotion of existing brands. But Tiffany is concerned that if Business Center brands its own file folders it will sell them at a discount and may even bring the whole market price level down. Across all the lines of file folders, Tiffany is averaging a 35 percent gross margin, but the commonly used file folders sought by Business Center are averaging only a 20 percent gross margin. And cutting this margin further does not look very attractive to Tiffany.

Tiffany is not sure whether Business Center will continue to sell ODI's FILEX brand of folders along with Business Center's own file folders if Business Center is able to find a source of supply. Business Center's history has been to sell its own brand and a major brand side by side, especially if the major brand offers high quality and has strong brand recognition.

Tiffany is having a really hard time deciding what to do about the existing branding policy. ODI has excess capacity and could easily handle the Business Center business. And she fears that if she turns down this business, Business Center will just go elsewhere and its own brand will cut into ODI's existing sales at Business Center stores. Further, what makes Business Center's offer especially attractive is that ODI's variable manufacturing costs would be quite low in relation to any price charged to Business Center—that is, there are substantial economies of scale, so the extra business could be very profitable—if Tiffany doesn't consider the possible impact on the FILEX line. This Business Center business will be easy to get, but it will require a major change in policy, which Tiffany will have to sell to Dan Powell, ODI's president. This may not be easy. Dan is primarily interested in developing new and better products so the company can avoid the "commodity end of the business."

Evaluate ODI's current strategy. What should Tiffany Lui do about Business Center's offer? Explain.

14. Digital Depot

Mark Johannson, manager of Digital Depot, is looking for ways to increase profits. But he's turning cautious after the poor results of his last effort, during the previous Christmas season. Digital Depot (DD), is located along a busy crosstown street about two miles from the downtown of a metropolitan area of 1 million and near a large university. It sells a wide variety of products used for its different types of multimedia presentations. Its lines include high-quality video and digital cameras, color scanners for use with computers, teleprompters and projection equipment, including video-beam overhead projectors and electronic projectors that produce large-screen versions of computer output. Most of the sales of this specialized equipment are made to area school boards for classroom use, to industry for use in research and sales, and to the university for use in research and instruction.

Digital Depot also offers a good selection of production-quality video media, specialized supplies (such as the large-format acetates used with backlit signs), video and audio editing equipment, and a specialized video editing service. Instead of just duplicating videos on a mass production basis, Digital Depot gives each video editing job individual attention—to add an audio track or incorporate computer graphics as requested by a customer. This service is really appreciated by local firms that need help producing high-quality DVDs—for example, for training or sales applications.

To encourage the school and industrial trade, Digital Depot offers a graphics consultation service. If a customer wants to create a video or computerized presentation, professional advice is readily available. In support of this free service, Digital Depot carries a full line of computer software for multimedia presentations and graphics work.

Digital Depot has four full-time store clerks and two outside sales reps. The sales reps call on business firms, attend trade shows, make presentations for schools, and help both present and potential customers in their use and choice of multimedia materials. Most purchases are delivered by the sales reps or the store's delivery truck. Many repeat orders come in by phone or mail, but e-mail and electronic file exchange have become common.

The people who make most of the over-the-counter purchases are (1) serious amateurs and (2) some professionals who prepare videos or computerized presentation materials on a fee basis. Digital Depot gives price discounts of up to 25 percent off the suggested retail price to customers who buy more than $2,000 worth of goods per year. Most regular customers qualify for the discount.

In recent years, many amateur photo buffs have purchased digital cameras to capture family pictures. Frequently, the buyer is a computer user who wants to use the computer as a digital darkroom—and the cameras now available make this easy. Digital Depot has not previously offered the lower-priced and lower-quality digital models such buyers commonly want. But Mark Johannson knew that lots of such digital cameras were bought and felt that there ought to be a good opportunity to expand sales during the Christmas gift-giving season. Therefore, he planned a special pre-Christmas sale of two of the most popular brands of digital cameras and discounted the prices to competitive discount store levels—about $129 for one and $189 for the other. To promote the sale, he posted large signs in the store windows and ran ads in a Christmas gift-suggestion edition of the local newspaper. This edition appeared each Wednesday during the four weeks before Christmas. At these prices and with this promotion, Mark hoped to sell at least 100 cameras. However, when the Christmas returns were in, total sales were five cameras. Mark was extremely disappointed with these results—especially because trade experts suggested that sales of digital cameras in these price and quality ranges were up 300 percent over last year—during the Christmas selling season.

Evaluate what Digital Depot is doing and what happened with the special promotion. What should Mark Johannson do to increase sales and profits?

15. Sanchez & Associates

Melita Sanchez, owner of Sanchez & Associates, is deciding whether to take on a new line. She is very concerned, however, because although she wants more lines she feels that something is wrong with her latest possibility.

Melita Sanchez graduated from a large midwestern university in 2004 with a B.S. in business. She worked selling cell phones for a year. Then Melita decided to go into business for herself and formed Sanchez & Associates. Looking for opportunities, Melita placed several ads in her local newspaper in Columbus, Ohio, announcing that she was interested in becoming a sales representative in the area. She was quite pleased to receive a number of responses. Eventually, she became the sales representative in the Columbus area for three local computer software producers: Accto Company, which produces accounting-related software; Saleco, Inc., a producer of sales management software; and Invo, Inc., a producer of inventory control software. All of these companies were relatively small and were represented in other areas by other sales representatives like Melita Sanchez.

Melita's main job was to call on possible customers. Once she made a sale, she would fax the signed license agreement to the respective producer, who would then UPS the programs directly to the customer or provide a key code for a website download. The producer would bill the customer, and Sanchez would receive a commission varying from 5 to 10 percent of the dollar value of the sale. Sanchez was expected to pay her own expenses. And the producers would handle any user questions, either by using 800 numbers for out-of-town calls or by e-mail queries to a technical support group.

Sanchez called on anyone in the Columbus area who might use the products she sold. At first, her job was relatively easy, and sales came quickly because she had little competition. Many national companies offer similar products, but at that time they were not well represented in the Columbus area. Most small businesses needed someone to demonstrate what the software could do.

In 2006, Sanchez sold $250,000 worth of Accto software, earning a 10 percent commission; $100,000 worth of Saleco software, also earning a 10 percent commission; and $200,000 worth of Invo software, earning a 7 percent commission. She was encouraged with her progress and looked forward to expanding sales in the future. She was especially optimistic because she had achieved these sales volumes without overtaxing herself. In fact, she felt she was operating at about 60 percent of her capacity and could easily take on new lines. So she began looking for other products she could sell in the Columbus area. A local software company has recently approached Melita about selling its newly developed software, which is basically a network security product. It is designed to secretly track all of the keystrokes and mouse clicks of each employee as he or she uses the computer—so that an employer can identify inappropriate uses of its computers or confidential data. Melita isn't too enthusiastic about this offer because the commission is only 2 percent on potential annual sales of about $150,000—and she also doesn't like the idea of selling a product that might undermine the privacy of employees who are not doing anything wrong.

Now Melita Sanchez is faced with another decision. The owner of the MetalCoat Company, also in Columbus, has made what looks like an attractive offer. She called on MetalCoat to see if the firm might be interested in buying her accounting software. The owner didn't want the software, but he was very impressed with Melita. After two long discussions, he asked if she would like to help MetalCoat solve its current problem. MetalCoat is having trouble with marketing and the owner would like Melita Sanchez to take over the whole marketing effort.

MetalCoat produces solvents used to make coatings for metal products. It sells mainly to industrial customers in the mid-Ohio area and faces many competitors selling essentially the same products and charging the same low prices. MetalCoat is a small manufacturer. Last year's sales were $500,000. It could handle at least four times this sales volume with ease, and is willing to expand to increase sales—its main objective in the short run. MetalCoat's owner is offering Melita a 12 percent commission on all sales if she will take charge of their pricing, advertising, and sales efforts. Melita is flattered by the offer, but she is a little worried because it is a different type of product and she would have to learn a lot about it. The job also might require a great deal more traveling than she is doing now. For one thing, she would have to call on new potential customers in mid-Ohio, and she might have to travel up to 200 miles around Columbus to expand the solvent business. Further, she realizes that she is being asked to do more than just sell. But she did have marketing courses in college, and thinks the new opportunity might be challenging.

Evaluate Melita Sanchez's current strategy and how the proposed solvent line fits in with what she is doing now. What should she do? Why?

16. Specialty Timber Company

Jacque Patrice, owner of Specialty Timber Company, feels his business is threatened by a tough new competitor. And now Jacque must decide quickly about an offer that may save his business.

Jacque Patrice has been a sales rep for lumber mills for about 20 years. He started selling in a clothing store but gave it up after two years to work in a lumberyard because the future looked much better in the building materials industry. After drifting from one job to another, Jacque finally settled down and worked his way up to manager of a large wholesale building materials distribution warehouse in Buffalo, New York. In 1990, he formed Specialty Timber Company and went into business for himself, selling carload lots of lumber to lumberyards in western New York and Pennsylvania.

Jacque works with five large lumber mills on the West Coast. They notify him when a carload of lumber is available to be shipped, specifying the grade, condition, and number of each size board in the shipment. Jacque isn't the only person selling for these mills—but he is the only one in his area. He isn't required to take any particular number of carloads per month—but once he tells a mill he wants a particular shipment, title passes to him and he has to sell it to someone. Jacque's main function is to find a buyer, buy the lumber from the mill as it's being shipped, and have the railroad divert the car to the buyer.

Having been in this business for 20 years, Jacque knows all of the lumberyard buyers in his area very well and is on good working terms with them. He does most of his business over the telephone or by e-mail from his small office, but he tries to see each of the buyers about once a month. He has been marking up the lumber between 4 and 6 percent—the standard markup, depending on the grades and mix in each car—and has been able to make a good living for himself and his family. The going prices are widely publicized in trade publications and are listed on the Internet, so the buyers can easily check to be sure Jacque's prices are competitive.

In the last few years, a number of Jacque's lumberyard customers have gone out of business—and others have lost sales. The main problem is competition from several national home-improvement chains that have moved into Jacque's market area. These chains buy lumber in large quantities direct from a mill, and their low prices, available inventory, and one-stop shopping are taking some customers away from the traditional lumberyards. Some customers think the quality of the lumber is not quite as good at the big chains, and some contractors stick with the lumberyards out of loyalty or because they get better service, including rush deliveries when they're needed. However, if it weren't for low interest rates and a boom in the construction market—helping to make up for lost market share—Jacque's profits would have taken an even bigger hit.

Six months ago, things got worse. An aggressive young salesman set up in the same business, covering about the same area but representing different lumber mills. This new salesman charges about the same prices as Jacque but undersells him once or twice a week in order to get the sale. On several occasions he even set up what was basically an e-mail-based auction to quickly sell excess wood that was not moving fast enough. Many lumber buyers—feeling the price competition from the big chains and realizing that they are dealing with a homogeneous product—seem to be willing to buy from the lowest-cost source. This has hurt Jacque financially and personally—because even some of his old friends are willing to buy from the new competitor if the price is lower. The near-term outlook seems dark, since Jacque doubts that there is enough business to support two firms like his, especially if the markup gets shaved any closer. Now they seem to be splitting the shrinking business about equally, as the newcomer keeps shaving his markup.

A week ago, Jacque was called on by Ken Rivers of Horizon Mfg. Co., a large manufacturer of windows, raised-panel doors, and accessories. Horizon doesn't sell to the big chains and instead distributes its quality line only through independent lumberyards. Rivers knows that Jacque is well acquainted with the local lumberyards and wants him to become Horizon's exclusive distributor (sales rep) of residential windows and accessories in his area. Rivers gave Jacque several brochures on Horizon's product lines. He also explained Horizon's new support program, which will help train and support Jacque and interested lumberyards on how to sell the higher markup accessories. Later, in a lengthy e-mail, Rivers explained how this program will help Jacque and interested lumberyards differentiate themselves in this very competitive market.

Most residential windows of specified grades are basically "commodities" that are sold on the basis of price and availability, although some premium and very low end windows are sold also. The national home-improvement chains usually stock and sell only the standard sizes. Most independent lumberyards do not stock windows because there are so many possible sizes. Instead, the lumberyards custom order from the stock sizes each factory offers. Stock sizes are not set by industry standards; they vary from factory to factory, and some offer more sizes. Most factories can deliver these custom orders in two to six weeks, which is usually adequate to satisfy contractors who buy and install them according to architectural plans. This part of the residential window business is well established, and most lumberyards buy from several different window manufacturers—to ensure sources of supply in case of strikes, plant fires, and so on. How the business is split depends on price and the personality and persuasiveness of the sales reps. And given that prices are usually similar, the sales rep–customer relationship can be quite important.

Horizon Mfg. Co. gives more choice than just about any other supplier. It offers many variations in $1/8$-inch increments—to cater to remodelers who must adjust to many situations. Horizon has even set up a special system on an Internet website. The lumberyard can connect to the website, enter the specs for a window online, and within seconds get a price quote and estimated delivery time.

One reason Rivers has approached Jacque Patrice is because of Jacque's many years in the business. But the other reason is that Horizon is aggressively trying to expand—relying on its made-to-order windows, a full line of accessories, and a newly developed factory support system to help differentiate it from the many other window manufacturers.

To give Jacque a quick big picture of the opportunity he is offering, Rivers explained the window market as follows:

1. For commercial construction, the usual building code ventilation requirements are satisfied with mechanical ventilation. So the windows do not have to operate to permit natural ventilation. They are usually made with heavy-grade aluminum framing. Typically, a distributor furnishes and installs the windows. As part of its service, the distributor provides considerable technical support, including engineered drawings and diagrams to the owners, architects, and/or contractors.

2. For residential construction, on the other hand, windows must be operable to provide ventilation. Residential windows are usually made of wood, frequently with light-gauge aluminum or vinyl on the exterior. The national chains get some volume with standard size windows, but lumberyards are the most common source of supply for contractors in Jacque's area. These lumberyards do not provide any technical support or engineered drawings. A few residential window manufacturers do have their own sales centers in selected geographic areas, which provide a full range of support and engineering services, but none are anywhere near Jacque's area.

Horizon Mfg. Co. feels a big opportunity exists in the commercial building repair and rehabilitation market (sometimes called the retrofit market) for a crossover of residential windows to commercial applications—and it has designed some accessories and a factory support program to help lumberyards get this "commercial" business. For applications such as nursing homes and dormitories (which must meet commercial codes), the wood interior of a residential window is desired, but the owners and architects are accustomed to commercial grades and building systems. And in some older facilities, the windows may have to provide supplemental ventilation for a deficient mechanical system. So what is needed is a combination of the residential *operable* window with a heavy-gauge commercial exterior frame that is easy to specify and install. And this is what Horizon Mfg. Co. is offering with a combination of its basic windows and easily adjustable accessory frames. Two other residential window manufacturers offer a similar solution, but neither has pushed its products aggressively and neither offers technical support to lumberyards or trains sales reps like Jacque to do the necessary job. Rivers feels this could be a unique opportunity for Jacque.

The sales commission on residential windows would be about 5 percent of sales. Horizon Mfg. Co. would do the billing and collecting. By getting just 20 to 30 percent of his lumberyards' residential window business, Jacque could earn about half of his current income. But the real upside would come from increasing his residential window share. To do this, Jacque would have to help the lumberyards get a lot more (and more profitable) business by invading the commercial market with residential windows and the bigger markup accessories needed for this market. Jacque would also earn a 20 percent commission on the accessories, adding to his profit potential.

Jacque is somewhat excited about the opportunity because the retrofit market is growing. And owners and architects are seeking ways of reducing costs (which Horizon's approach does—over usual commercial approaches). But he is also concerned that a lot of sales effort will be needed to introduce this new idea. He is not afraid of work, but he is concerned about his financial survival.

Jacque thinks he has three choices:

1. Take Rivers' offer and sell both window and lumber products.
2. Take the offer and drop lumber sales.
3. Stay strictly with lumber and forget the offer.

Rivers is expecting an answer within one week, so Jacque has to decide soon.

Evaluate Jacque Patrice's current strategy and how the present offer fits in. What should he do now? Why?

17. Healthy Water, Inc.

Manish (Manny) Krishna established his company, Healthy Water, Inc. (HWI), to market a product designed to purify drinking water. The product, branded as the PURITY II Naturalizer Water Unit, is produced by Environmental Control, Inc., a corporation that focuses primarily on water purification and filtering products for industrial markets.

Healthy Water is a small but growing business. Manny started the business with initial capital of only $20,000, which came from his savings and loans from several relatives. Manny manages the company himself. He has a secretary and six full-time salespeople. In addition, he employs two college students part-time; they make telephone calls to prospect for customers and set up appointments for a salesperson to demonstrate the unit in the consumer's home. By holding spending to a minimum, Manny has kept the firm's monthly operating budget at only $4,500—and most of that goes for rent, his secretary's salary, and other necessities like computer supplies and telephone bills.

The PURITY II system uses a reverse osmosis purification process. Reverse osmosis is the most effective technology known for improving drinking water. The device is certified by the Environmental Protection Agency to reduce levels of most foreign substances, including mercury, rust, sediment, arsenic, lead, phosphate, bacteria, and most insecticides.

Each PURITY II unit consists of a high-quality 1-micron sediment removal cartridge, a carbon filter, a sediment filter, a housing, a faucet, and mounting hardware. The compact system fits under a kitchen sink or a wet bar sink. An HWI salesperson can typically install the PURITY II in about a half hour. Installation involves attaching the unit to the cold-water supply line, drilling a hole in the sink, and fastening the special faucet. It works equally well with water from a municipal system or well water and it can purify up to 15 gallons daily. HWI sells the PURITY II to consumers for $395, which includes installation.

The system has no movable parts or electrical connections and it has no internal metal parts that will corrode or rust. However, the system does use a set of filters that must be replaced after about two years. HWI sells the replacement filters for $80. Taking into consideration the cost of the filters, the system provides drinking water at a cost of approximately $.05 per gallon for the average family.

There are two major benefits from using the PURITY II system. First, water treated by this system tastes better. Blind taste tests confirm that most consumers can tell the difference between water treated with the PURITY II and ordinary tapwater. Consequently, the unit improves the taste of coffee, tea, frozen juices, ice cubes, mixed drinks, soup, and vegetables cooked in water. Perhaps more important, the PURITY II's ability to remove potentially harmful foreign matter makes the product of special interest to people who are concerned about health and the safety of the water they consume.

The number of people with those concerns is growing. In spite of increased efforts to protect the environment and water supplies, there are many problems. Hundreds of new chemical compounds—ranging from insecticides to industrial chemicals to commercial cleaning agents—are put into use each year. Some of the residue from chemicals and toxic waste eventually enters water supply sources. Further, floods and hurricanes have damaged or completely shut down water treatment facilities in some cities. Problems like these have led to rumors of possible epidemics of such dread diseases as cholera and typhoid—and more than one city has recently experienced near-panic buying of bottled water.

Given these problems and the need for pure water, Manny believes that the market potential for the PURITY II system is very large. Residences, both single-family and apartment, are one obvious target. The unit is also suitable for use in boats and recreational vehicles; in fact, the PURITY II is standard equipment on several upscale RVs. And it can be used in taverns and restaurants, in institutions such as schools and hospitals, and in commercial and industrial buildings.

There are several competing ways for customers to solve the problem of getting pure water. Some purchase bottled water. Companies such as Ozarka deliver water monthly for an average price of $.60 per gallon. The best type of bottled water is distilled water; it is absolutely pure because it is produced by the process of evaporation. However, it may be *too pure*. The distilling process removes needed elements such as calcium and phosphate—and there is some evidence that removing these trace elements contributes to heart disease. In fact, some health-action groups recommend that consumers not drink distilled water.

A second way to obtain pure water is to use some system to treat tapwater. PURITY II is one such system. Another system uses an ion exchange process that replaces ions of harmful substances like iron and mercury with ions that are not harmful. Ion exchange is somewhat less expensive than the PURITY II process, but it is not well suited for residential use because bacteria can build up before the water is used. In addition, there are a number of other filtering and softening systems. In general, these are less expensive and less reliable than the PURITY II. For example, water softeners remove minerals but do not remove bacteria or germs.

Manny's first year with his young company has gone quite well. Customers who have purchased the system like it, and there appear to be several ways to expand the business and increase profits. For example, so far he has had little time to make sales calls on potential commercial and institutional users or residential builders. He also sees other possibilities such as expanding his promotion effort or targeting consumers in a broader geographic area.

At present, HWI distributes the PURITY II in the 13-county gulf coast region of Texas. Because of the Robinson-Patman Act, the manufacturer cannot grant an exclusive distributorship. However, HWI is currently the only PURITY II distributor in this region. In addition, HWI has the right of first refusal to set up distributorships in other areas of Texas. The manufacturer has indicated that it might even give HWI distribution rights in a large section of northern Mexico.

The agreement with the manufacturer allows HWI to distribute the product to retailers, including hardware stores, plumbing supply dealers, and the like. Manny has not yet pursued this channel, but a PURITY II distributor in Florida reported some limited success selling the system to retailers at a wholesale price of $275. Retailers for this type of product typically expect a markup of about 33 percent of their selling price.

Environmental Control, Inc., ships the PURITY II units directly from its warehouse to the HWI office via UPS. The manufacturer's $200 per unit selling price includes the cost of shipping. HWI only needs to keep a few units on hand because the manufacturer accepts faxed orders and then ships immediately—so delivery never takes more than a few days. Further, the units are small enough to inventory in the back room of the HWI sales office. Several of the easy-to-handle units will fit in the trunk of a salesperson's car.

Manny is thinking about recruiting additional salespeople. Finding capable people has not been a problem so far. However, there has already been some turnover, and one of the current salespeople is complaining that the compensation is not high enough. Manny pays salespeople on a straight commission basis. A salesperson who develops his or her own prospects gets

$100 per sale; the commission is $80 per unit on sales leads generated by the company's telemarketing people. For most salespeople, the mix of sales is about half and half. HWI pays the students who make the telephone contacts $4 per appointment set up and $10 per unit sold from an appointment.

An average HWI salesperson easily sells 20 units per month. However, Manny believes that a really effective and well-prepared salesperson can sell much more, perhaps 40 units per month.

HWI and its salespeople get good promotion support from Environmental Control, Inc. For example, Environmental Control supplies sales training manuals and sales presentation flip charts. The materials are also well done, in part because Environment Control's promotion manager previously worked for Electrolux vacuum cleaners, which are sold in a similar way. The company also supplies print copy for magazine and newspaper advertising and tapes of commercials for radio and television. Thus, all HWI has to do is buy media space or time. In addition, Environmental Control furnishes each salesperson with a portable demonstration unit, and the company recently gave HWI three units to be placed in models of condominium apartments.

Manny has worked long hours to get his company going, but he realizes that he has to find time to think about how his strategy is working and to plan for the future.

Evaluate Manish Krishna's current marketing strategy for Healthy Water. How do you think he's doing so far, and what should he do next? Why?

18. Harrisburg Volunteer Fire Department

Jesse Delaney raced out the front door of the Target store where he worked as soon as his beeper sounded. In his pickup truck he heard the call on his special radio scanner, "Highway 18 Fire Department, there is a grass fire at the old Larson place. That's a mile down the old dirt road just past the Wilson house." The directions might appear cryptic to someone who had not grown up around Harrisburg, but it was all Jesse needed to know. Upon arriving at the fire, Jesse quickly pulled on his fire-retardant bunker pants and boots. He left his Nomex hood, helmet, and fire pants in the back of his truck— he would not need them for this fire.

Less than 10 minutes from the time the call was placed, Jesse and 20 other members of the Harrisburg Volunteer Fire Department (HVFD) arrived at the old Larson place. They were able to put out the fire in less than half an hour, but not before a football-field-size patch of grass was scorched. Their quick response saved the neighbor's barn and kept the fire from spreading to a nearby forest. A third straight year of drought has the crew on high alert.

Jesse threw his gear in the back of his truck and headed back to finish his shift at Target. He had worked there as a department manager for two years, ever since he graduated from the local state college with a marketing degree. As he drove, Jesse thought about what HVFD Chief Sherry Martin recently asked him to do. Over the last few years, the fire department had more to do but fewer people to do it with. So Chief Martin asked Jesse to draw up a marketing plan to recruit new volunteers.

Jesse had already started to gather information for the marketing plan. From an online search he found that HVFD was one of an estimated 30,000 volunteer fire departments in the U.S. and that these departments had almost a million volunteers. Jesse was surprised that more than 75 percent of all U.S. firefighters were volunteers. Harrisburg, a small city of just over 100,000 and hours from a big city, only had volunteer firefighters.

There are 48 firefighters currently in the HVFD—down from 55 five years ago. While there was a surge of interest in the year following the terrorist attacks in 2001, only a few of those volunteers remain. Over time, HVFD has found that about half of new recruits quit before their three-year anniversary. Those who remain usually stay with the department until they can't keep up with the job's physical demands. Sherry Martin has been chief for the last three years. She replaced long-time Chief Clyde Owen, who retired after being with HVFD for more than 40 years—the last 10 as chief.

The current volunteers include 44 men and four women; more than half of the force is over 40 years old and Jesse is one of only five members younger than 30. Almost all of them started volunteering while still in their 20s or early 30s. The crew represents all walks of life, and their ranks include a lawyer, a real estate salesperson, a college professor, a carpenter, a stay-at-home mom, and a few guys from the local factory. Many entered firefighting for the thrill of it or because they hoped the experience might help them land a paid firefighting job in a bigger city. But most of the crew stay with it because they feel good about giving back to their community, view it as a hobby, and enjoy the camaraderie with the other firefighters.

Being a volunteer firefighter is much different than Jesse thought it would be when he started. Last year he counted 238 hours volunteering for HVFD, but less than a third of that was actually responding to emergencies. And fewer than half of the emergencies were actual fires. He spent about a quarter of this time in required training and drills. He had to be trained for the many different possible calls, including car accidents, hazardous chemical spills, and terrorist attacks. Another 20 percent of his time was spent in meetings and a similar amount helping with fund-raising. Depending upon financial needs, HVFD holds at least four fund-raising events a year—some years six or eight. These include annual activities like a chili cook-off, pancake breakfast, and booth at the county fair—and as-needed events like pie auctions, turkey shoots, and basketball tournaments.

The biggest requirement to be a volunteer firefighter is the willingness to make the time commitment. Jesse's time commitment and allocation of hours is typical of all the firefighters at HVFD. Volunteers have to be able to attend at least 80 percent of the twice monthly drills—scheduled on the second and fourth Tuesdays of every month. Firefighters also have to live or work near the city of Harrisburg so they can quickly respond to an emergency. They also have to be at least 18 years old and have a valid driver's license. There is a physical ability test to make sure that firefighters can stand the rigors of the job. While one doesn't have to be a weightlifter, the job requires volunteers to be in good physical shape.

HVFD has never really had a marketing strategy or any formal promotion efforts. Most of Jesse's fellow volunteers heard about HVFD through word of mouth. People are always curious when a volunteer firefighter runs out the door from work or suddenly leaves a party. These occasions give volunteers a chance to tell others about what they do. Sometimes those questions bring someone out to see drills and to apply to become a volunteer. One of Jesse's high school friends was a volunteer and he encouraged Jesse to join up while Jesse was in his junior year of college. But still, awareness of volunteer firefighting in the Harrisburg area is still very low. When Jesse tells friends about his volunteer work, most are surprised and think the town has full-time paid staff fighting fires.

Jesse thinks his marketing strategy should focus mostly on promotion. From his studies he remembers the AIDA model and integrated marketing communications. But he also wonders if his plan should focus only on gaining new recruits or if current volunteers might also be the target of new promotion. Jesse also considers how and what he should communicate to his target market. He knows he will have limited funding for his efforts.

Evaluate the promotion objectives Jesse Delaney should include in his plan. What promotion methods should he use to achieve those objectives?

19. ourWedding.com

Jessica Stone is happy with her life but disappointed that the idea she had for starting her own business hasn't taken off as expected. Within a few weeks she either has to renew the contract for her Internet website or decide not to put any more time and money into her idea. She knows that it doesn't make sense to renew the contract if she can't come up with a plan to make her website-based business profitable—and she doesn't like to plan. She's a "doer," not a planner.

Jessica's business, ourWedding.com, started as an idea 18 months ago as she was planning her own wedding. She attended a bridal fair at the convention center in Raleigh, North Carolina, to get ideas for a wedding dress, check out catering companies and florists, and in general learn more about the various services available to newlyweds. While there she and her fiancé went from one retailer's booth to another to sign up for their wedding gift registries. Almost every major retailer in the city—ranging from the Home Depot warehouse to the Belk's department store to the specialty shops that handle imported crystal glassware—offered a gift registry. Some had computers set up to provide access to their online registries. Being listed in all of the registries improved the odds that her wedding gifts would be items she wanted and could use—and it saved time and hassle for gift-givers. On the way back from the fair, Jessica and her fiancé discussed the idea that it would be a lot easier to register gift preferences once on a central Internet site than to provide lots of different stores with bits and pieces of information. A list at a website would also make it easier for gift-givers, at least those who were computer users.

When Jessica got home, she did an Internet search and found several sites that focused on weddings. The biggest seemed to be www.weddingchannel.com. It had features for couples who were getting married, including a national gift registry. The site featured products from a number of companies, especially large national retail chains; however, there was a search feature to locate people who provide wedding-related services in a local ZIP code area. Jessica thought that the sites she found looked quite good, but that they were not as helpful as a site could be with a more local focus.

The more Jessica and her fiancé discussed the idea of a website offering local wedding-related services, the more it looked like an interesting opportunity. Except for the annual bridal fair, there was no other obvious local place for consumers to get information about planning a wedding and buying wedding-related services. And for local retailers, florists, catering companies, insurance agents, home builders, and many other types of firms, there was no other central place to target promotion at newlyweds. Further, the amount of money spent on weddings and wedding gifts is very substantial, and right before and after getting married many young couples make many important purchase decisions for everything from life insurance to pots and pans. Spending on the wedding itself can easily exceed the cost of a year of college.

Jessica was no stranger to the Internet. She worked as a website designer for a small firm whose one and only client was IBM. That IBM was the only client was intentional rather than accidental. A year earlier IBM had decided that it wanted to outsource certain aspects of its website development work and have it handled by an outside contractor. After negotiating a three-year contract to do IBM's work, several IBM employees quit their jobs and started the business. IBM was a good client, and all indications were that IBM could give the firm as much work as it could handle as it hired new people and prospected for additional accounts over the next few years. Jessica especially liked the creative aspects of designing the "look" of a website, and technical specialists handled a lot of the subtle details.

Before joining this new company, Jessica had several marketing-related jobs—but none had been the glamorous ad agency job she dreamed of in college as an advertising major. Her first job as a college graduate was with an ad agency, but she was in a backroom operation handling a lot of the arrangements for printing and mailing large-scale direct-mail promotions. In spite of promises that it was a path to other jobs at the agency, the pay was bad, the work was always pressured, and every aspect of what she had to do was boring. After six punishing months, she quit and went looking for something else.

When a number of job applications didn't turn up something quickly, she took a part-time job doing telemarketing calls for a mortgage refinance company. Jessica's boss told her that she was doing a great job reeling in prospects—but she hated disturbing people at night and just didn't like making sales pitches. Fortunately for her, that pain didn't last long. A neighbor in Jessica's apartment complex got Jessica an interview for a receptionist position at an ad agency. That, at least, got her foot in the door. Her job description wasn't very interesting, but in a small agency she had the opportunity to learn a lot about all aspects of the business—ranging from working on client proposals and media plans to creative sessions for new campaigns. In fact, it was from a technician at that agency that she learned to work with the graphics software used to create ad layouts and website pages. When the website design job came open at the new firm, her boss gave her a glowing recommendation, and in two days she was off on her new career.

Although Jessica's jobs had not been high-profile positions, they did give her some experience in sales promotion, personal selling, and advertising. Those skills were complemented by the technical computer skills of her fiancé (now husband), who made a living as a database programmer for a large software consulting firm. Taking everything as a whole, they thought that they could get a wedding-related website up and running and make it profitable.

There were several different facets to the original plan for ourWedding.com. One facet focused on recruiting local advertisers and "sponsors" who would pay to be listed at the website and be allocated a web page (which Jessica would design) describing their services, giving contact information, and links to their own websites. Another facet focused on services for people who were planning to be married. In addition to an online wedding gift registry, sections of the website provided information about typical wedding costs, planning checklists, details about how to get a required marriage license, and other helpful information (including a discussion forum with comments about the strengths and weaknesses of various local suppliers). Jessica had also started a blog that helped foster more feedback from customers. A man and woman could sign up for the service online and could pay the modest $20 "membership" fee for a year by credit card. Friends, family, and invited guests could visit the website at no charge and get information about wedding preferences, local hotels, discounts on local car rentals, and even printable maps to all of the churches and synagogues in the area.

When Jessica told friends about her plan they all thought it sounded like a great idea. In fact, each time she discussed it someone came up with another idea for a locally oriented feature to add to the website. Several friends said that they had tried national websites but that the information was often too general. But generating more new ideas was not the problem. The problem was generating revenue. Jessica had already contracted for space from an Internet service provider and created some of the initial content for the website, but she only had four paying sponsors, two of whom happened to be family friends.

Jessica started by creating a colorful flyer describing the website and sent it to most of the firms that had participated in the bridal fair. When no one sent back the reply coupon for more information, Jessica started to make calls (mainly during her lunch hour at her full-time job). Some stores seemed intrigued by the concept, but no one seemed ready to sign up. One reason was that they all seemed surprised at the cost to participate and get ad space at the website—$2,400 a year (about the same as a $1/16$-page display ad in the Raleigh Yellow Pages). Another problem was that no one wanted to be the first to sign up. As one florist shop owner put it, "If you pull this off and other florists sign up, then come back and I will too."

Getting couples to sign up went slowly too. Jessica paid for four display ads in local Sunday newspapers in the society section, sent information sheets about the website to clergy in the area, listed the website with about 25 Internet search engines, and sent carefully crafted press releases announcing the service to almost every publication in the area. One article that resulted from a press release got some attention, and for a few weeks there was a flurry of e-mail inquiries about her web page. But after that it slowed to a trickle again.

Jessica's diagnosis of the problem was simple. Most people thought it was a great idea, but few couples knew to look on the Internet for such a service. Similarly, potential advertisers—many of them small local businesses—were not accustomed to the idea of paying for Internet advertising. They didn't know if the cost was reasonable or if her site would be effective in generating business.

Jessica's life as a married person was going great and her job as a web page designer kept her very busy. Her free time outside of work was always in short supply because the young crowd at her office always had some scheme for how to keep entertained. So she wasn't about to quit her job to devote full time to her business idea. Further, she thought that once it got rolling she would only have to devote 10 hours a week to it to earn an extra $30,000 a year. She didn't have delusions of becoming a "dot-com millionaire." She just wanted a good locally oriented business.

However, it still wasn't clear how to get it rolling. After a year of trying on and off, she only had four paying ad sponsors, and one of them had already notified her that he didn't plan to sign up again because it wasn't clear that the website had generated any direct leads or sales. Further, it looked like anything she could do to attract more "members" would end up being expensive and inefficient.

Jessica thinks the idea has real potential, and she's willing to do the work. But she's not certain if she can make it pay off. She has to decide soon, however, because the bill for the Internet service provider is sitting on her desk.

What is Jessica's strategy? What should she do? If she were to move forward, what strategy would you recommend? Does her financial goal seem realistic? Why?

20. Recreation Universe

Mike Kidd, owner of Recreation Universe, is worried about his business' future. He has tried various strategies for two years now, and he's still barely breaking even.

Two years ago, Mike Kidd bought the inventory, supplies, equipment, and business of Recreation Universe, located on the edge of Minneapolis, Minnesota. The business is in an older building along a major highway leading out of town, several miles from any body of water. The previous owner had sales of about $500,000 a year but was just breaking even. For this reason—plus the desire to retire to Arizona—the owner sold to Mike for roughly the value of the inventory.

Recreation Universe had been selling two well-known brands of small pleasure boats, a leading outboard motor, two brands of snowmobiles and jet-skis, and a line of trailer and pickup-truck campers. The total inventory was valued at $250,000—and Mike used all of his own savings and borrowed some from two friends to buy the inventory and the business. At the same time, he took over the lease on the building—so he was able to begin operations immediately.

Mike had never operated a business of his own before, but he was sure that he would be able to do well. He had worked in a variety of jobs—as a used-car salesman, an auto repairman, and a jack-of-all-trades in the maintenance departments of several local businesses.

Soon after starting his business, Mike hired his friend, Henri, who had a similar background. Together, they handle all selling and setup work on new sales and do maintenance work as needed. Sometimes the two are extremely busy—at the peaks of each sport season. Then both sales and maintenance keep them going up to 16 hours a day. At these times it's difficult to have both new and repaired equipment available as soon as customers want it. At other times, however, Mike and Henri have almost nothing to do.

Mike usually charges the prices suggested by the various manufacturers, except at the end of a weather season when he is willing to make deals to clear the inventory. He is annoyed that some of his competitors sell mainly on a price basis—offering 10 to 30 percent off a manufacturer's suggested list prices—even at the beginning of a season! Mike doesn't want to get into that kind of business, however. He hopes to build a loyal following based on friendship and personal service. Further, he doesn't think he really has to cut price because all of his lines are exclusive for his store. No stores within a five-mile radius carry any of his brands, although nearby retailers offer many brands of similar products. Right now, the Internet does not provide much competition, but he fears future price competition from online boat shows.

To try to build a favorable image for his company, Mike occasionally places ads in local papers and buys some radio spots. The basic theme of this advertising is that Recreation Universe is a friendly, service-oriented place to buy the equipment needed for the current season. Sometimes he mentions the brand names he carries, but generally Mike tries to build an image for concerned, friendly service—both in new sales and repairs—stressing "We do it right the first time." He chose this approach because, although he has exclusives on the brands he carries, there generally are 10 to 15 different manufacturers' products being sold in the area in each product category—and most of the products are quite similar. Mike feels that this similarity among competing products almost forces him to try to differentiate himself on the basis of his own store's services.

The first year's operation wasn't profitable. In fact, after paying minimal salaries to Henri and himself, the business just about broke even. Mike made no return on his $250,000 investment.

In hopes of improving profitability, Mike jumped at a chance to add a line of lawn mowers, tractors, and trimmers as he was starting into his second year of business. This line was offered by a well-known equipment manufacturer who wanted to expand into the Minneapolis area. The equipment is similar to that offered by other lawn equipment manufacturers. The manufacturer's willingness to do some local advertising and to provide some point-of-purchase displays appealed to Mike. And he also liked the idea that customers probably would want this equipment sometime earlier than boats and other summer items. So he thought he could handle this business without interfering with his other peak selling seasons.

It's two years since Mike bought Recreation Universe—and he's still only breaking even. Sales have increased a little, but costs have gone up too because he had to hire some part-time help. The lawn equipment helped to expand sales—as he had expected—but unfortunately, it did not increase profits as he had hoped. Mike needed part-time helpers to handle this business—in part because the manufacturer's advertising had generated a lot of sales inquiries. Relatively few inquiries resulted in sales, however, because many people seemed to be shopping for deals. So Mike may have even lost money handling the new line. But he hesitates to give it up because he doesn't want to lose that sales volume, and the manufacturer's sales rep has been most encouraging, assuring Mike that things will get better and that his company will be glad to continue its promotion support during the coming year.

Mike is now considering the offer of a mountain bike producer that has not been represented in the area. The bikes have become very popular with students and serious bikers in the last several years. The manufacturer's sales rep says industry sales are still growing (but not as fast as in the past) and probably will grow for many more years. The sales rep has praised Mike's service orientation and says this could help him sell lots of bikes because many mountain bikers are serious about buying a quality bike and then keeping it serviced. He says Mike's business approach would be a natural fit with bike customers' needs and attitudes. As a special inducement to get Mike to take on the line, the sales rep says Mike will not have to pay for the initial inventory of bikes, accessories, and repair parts for 90 days. And, of course, the company will supply the usual promotion aids and a special advertising allowance of $10,000 to help introduce the line to Minneapolis. Mike kind of likes the idea of carrying mountain bikes because he has one himself and knows that they do require some service year-round. But he also knows that the proposed bikes are very similar in price and quality to the ones now being offered by the bike shops in town. These bike shops are service- rather than price-oriented, and Mike feels that they are doing a good job on service—so he is concerned with how he could be "different."

Evaluate Mike Kidd's overall strategy(ies) and the mountain bike proposal. What should he do now?

21. Global Materials, Inc.

Global Materials, Inc., is a multinational producer of various chemicals and plastics with plants in the United States, England, France, and Germany. It is run from its headquarters in New Jersey.

Greg Donaldson is marketing manager of Global Materials' plastics business. Greg is reconsidering his promotion approach. He is evaluating what kind of promotion—and how much—should be directed to car producers and to other major plastics customers worldwide. Currently, Greg has one salesperson who devotes most of his time to the car industry. This man is based in the Detroit area and focuses on GM, Ford, and DaimlerChrysler—as well as the various firms that mold plastics to produce parts to supply the car industry. This approach worked well when relatively little plastic was used in each car *and* the auto producers did all of the designing themselves and then sent out specifications for very price-oriented competitive bidding. But now the whole product planning and buying system is changing—and of course foreign producers with facilities in the U.S. are much more important.

How the present system works can be illustrated in terms of the approach DaimlerChrysler used on its project to design the Crossfire.

Instead of the old five-year process of creating a new automobile in sequential steps, the new system is a team approach. Under the old system, product planners would come up with a general concept and then expect the design team to give it artistic form. Next engineering would develop the specifications and pass them on to manufacturing and suppliers. There was little communication between the groups and no overall project responsibility.

Under the new approach, representatives from all the various functions—planning, design, engineering, purchasing, marketing, and manufacturing—work together. In fact, representatives from key suppliers are usually involved from the outset. The whole team takes final responsibility for a car. Because all of the departments are involved from the start, problems are resolved as the project moves on—before they cause a crisis. Manufacturing, for example, can suggest changes in design that will result in higher productivity or better quality.

In the Crossfire project, DaimlerChrysler engineers followed the Japanese lead and did some reverse engineering of their own. They dismantled several competitors' cars, piece by piece, looking for ideas they could copy or improve. This helped them learn how the parts were assembled and how they were designed. Eventually, DaimlerChrysler incorporated almost all of the best features into its design of the Crossfire. For example, the Crossfire platform is even more rigid than that of the Porsche 911.

In addition to reverse engineering, DaimlerChrysler researchers conducted a series of market studies. This led to the inclusion of additional features, such as 18-inch wheels, a six-speed transmission, and its finely tuned exhaust system that gives a sports car tone.

DaimlerChrysler also asked assembly-line workers for suggestions before the car was redesigned and then incorporated their ideas into the new car. Most bolts had the same-size head, for example, so workers didn't have to switch from one wrench to another.

Finally, DaimlerChrysler included its best suppliers as part of the planning effort. Instead of turning to a supplier after the car's design was completed, DaimlerChrysler invited them to participate in product planning.

Most other vehicles are now developed with an approach similar to this, and DaimlerChrysler is not alone in the effort. Ford, for example, used a very similar team approach to redesign its new Mustang. And major firms in most other industries are using similar approaches. A major outgrowth of this effort has been a trend by these producers to develop closer working relationships with a smaller number of suppliers.

For example, the suppliers selected for the Crossfire project were major suppliers who had already demonstrated a serious commitment to the car industry. They had not only the facilities, but also the technical and professional managerial staff who could understand—and become part of—the program management approach. DaimlerChrysler expected these major suppliers to join in its total quality management push and to be able to provide just-in-time delivery systems. DaimlerChrysler dropped suppliers whose primary sales technique was to entertain buyers and then submit bids on standard specifications.

Because many firms have moved to these team-oriented approaches and developed closer working relationships with a subset of their previous suppliers, Greg Donaldson is trying to determine if Global Materials' present effort is still appropriate. Greg's strategy has focused primarily on responding to inquiries and bringing in Global Materials' technical people as the situation seems to require. Potential customers with technical questions are sometimes referred to other noncompeting customers already using the materials or to a Global Materials plant—to be sure that all questions are answered. But basically, all producer-customers are treated more or less alike. The sales reps make calls and try to find good business wherever they can.

Each Global Materials sales rep usually has a geographic area. If an area like Detroit needs more than one rep, each may specialize in one or several similar industries. But Global Materials uses the same basic approach—call on present users of plastic products and try to find opportunities for getting a share (or bigger share) of existing purchases or new applications. The sales reps are supposed to be primarily order getters rather than technical specialists. Technical help can be brought in when the customer wants it or sometimes the sales rep simply sets up a conference call between Global Materials' technical experts, the buyer, and the users at the buyer's facility.

Greg sees that some of his major competitors—including General Electric and Dow Chemical—are becoming more aggressive. They are seeking to affect specifications and product design from the start rather than after a product design is completed. This takes a lot more effort and resources, but

Greg thinks it may get better results. A major problem he sees, however, is that he may have to drastically change the nature of Global Materials' promotion. Instead of focusing primarily on buyers and responding to questions, it may be necessary to try to contact *all* the multiple buying influences and not only answer their questions but help them understand what questions to raise—to find solutions. Such a process may even require more technically trained sales reps. In fact, it may require that people from Global Materials' other departments—engineering, manufacturing, R&D, and distribution—get actively involved in discussions with their counterparts in customer firms. Further, use of e-mail and an Internet website might make ongoing contacts faster and easier.

While Greg doesn't want to miss the boat if changes are needed, he also doesn't want to go off the deep end. After all, many of the firm's customers don't seem to want Global Materials to do anything very different from what it's been doing. In fact, some say that they're very satisfied with their current supply arrangements and really have no interest in investing in a close relationship with a single supplier.

Contrast the previous approach to designing and producing cars to Crossfire's program management approach, especially as it might affect suppliers' promotion efforts. Given that many other major producers have moved in the program management direction, what promotion effort should Greg Donaldson develop for Global Materials? Should every producer in every geographic area be treated alike, regardless of size? Explain.

22. Bright Light Innovations: The Starlight Stove*

The top management team of Bright Light Innovations is preparing to meet and review their market situation. The team is a combination of students and faculty from Colorado State University's (CSU) Colleges of Business and Engineering: Dr. Bryan Wilson, Paul Hudnut, Sachin Joshi, Dan Mastbergen, Katie Lucchesi, Chaun Sims, Ajay Jha, and Ryan Palmer. They are excited about the Starlight Stove product they have developed—and passionate about the opportunity that it provides to improve the quality of life for some of the world's poorest people. They know they have a great technology, but they need a marketing plan to bring this product to market.

Every day, over 2.4 billion people—one-third of the world's population—burn solid biomass fuel (wood, charcoal, dung, and coal) for cooking and heating. These fuels are usually burned indoors in open pits or traditional cook stoves. About two-thirds of the people using this fuel also have no electricity so the open fires often burn into the night to provide light. These fires create indoor air pollution that is a leading contributor to respiratory diseases in these countries. U.N. Secretary General Kofi Annan has called for greater energy efficiency and noted that "indoor air pollution has become one of the top 10 causes of mortality and premature death." It is estimated that this source of pollution contributes each year to the deaths of 1 million children under the age of five, and it is a leading cause of miscarriage and women's health problems.

Hoping to address these consumers' needs for safe cooking and electricity, CSU's Engines and Energy Conversion Laboratory developed the Starlight Stove. The Starlight Stove's improved technology requires 50 to 70 percent less biomass fuel than traditional stoves. It also has a thermo-electric generator that converts heat from the stove into electricity that can power a small light bulb or be stored in a rechargeable battery for later use. The technology has been refined and the team believes it is ready to go to market.

There are other competing enclosed cook stoves, but none produce electricity. Solar panels can provide electricity, but they are expensive—costing $360 each. Micro-hydro power allows households to convert the power from streams and rivers into electricity, but homes must be close to a river and water flow in many areas of the country is seasonal. These technologies—solar panels and hydro power—are understood by many consumers and are already in use in some areas. The Starlight Stove, on the other hand, offers a new technology, and that may slow its adoption.

The management team decided on Nepal as the initial target market for the Starlight Stove. Several factors made this market particularly attractive. The climate is relatively cold and only 11 percent of the households have access to electricity, so the heat and electricity production of the stove are particularly beneficial. Eighty-eight percent of the population uses firewood as their main source of energy. In addition, deforestation creates environmental problems in Nepal because it contributes to erosion and flooding. So the social benefits of the Starlight Stove will be particularly appealing to the Nepalese government and aid organizations.

There are approximately 9.2 million households in Nepal but the gross national income per capita is only about $260, with most adults making between $1 and $3 per day. Nepal is largely rural, with only 14 percent of the population living in urban areas. The country is divided into 75 districts. Each district is further divided into about 60 village development committees (a sort of local government) consisting of about 450 households. The similar characteristics of northern India— immediately south of Nepal—make it a logical follow-up market.

The Starlight Stove offers several benefits to this population. For example, the longer hours with light—thanks to the electricity—and less time required to collect wood or other fuel, could allow families to earn money by weaving, farming, or producing other crafts. Family productivity could increase 20 percent or more per day. Or the added hours with light might allow children to gain an education. If the product were manufactured locally, it could provide jobs for the population and help them learn the benefits of technology.

With obvious benefits for such a large number of people, the Bright Light team could look to donations to subsidize the Starlight Stove for the Nepalese people. But the team has concerns about this traditional form of aid. Financing in the form of grants, government relief, or donations is unreliable. If it is not renewed, projects wallow or die. Further, grants often fail to teach disadvantaged people skills and responsibility. So

---

*This case is based on a business plan written by Ajay Jha, Sachin Joshi, Katie Lucchesi, Dan Mastbergen, Ryan Palmer, and Chaun Sims.

the team wants to create a sustainable venture that provides benefits for all—and has set up Bright Light Innovations as a for-profit business.

The management team has to make a number of marketing decisions. For example, they have to decide how to price the Starlight Stove. They estimate that the stove will cost about $60 to manufacture after setting up a plant in Nepal. They expect that microfinancing organizations will provide loans for families. If units are sold for $80 the loan can be financed at 20 percent interest for three years with payments of $0.68 per week (microfinancing institutions typically collect on a weekly, or sometimes daily, basis). The team thinks that it will be easy to find a microfinancing institution to provide these loans. But the team is still unsure about whether this price will provide adequate margins for distributors.

The team also has to decide how to promote the stove to a population where less than half the adults can read. However, the team does have contacts with some business leaders, government officials, and nongovernmental organizations that may be able to provide advice and help.

What should be the Bright Light Innovation team's marketing strategy for the Starlight Stove? Why?

23. Valley Furniture

Dora Abila, owner of Valley Furniture, is discouraged with her salespeople and is even thinking about hiring some new blood. Abila has been running Valley Furniture for 10 years and has slowly built the sales to $3.5 million a year. Her store is located on the outskirts of a growing city of 275,000 population. This is basically a factory city, and she has deliberately selected blue-collar workers as her target market. She carries some higher-priced furniture lines but emphasizes budget combinations and easy credit terms.

Abila is concerned that she may have reached the limit of her sales growth—her sales have not been increasing during the last two years even though total furniture sales have been increasing in the city as new people move in. Her local cable TV spots and newspaper advertising seem to attract her target market, but many of these people come in, shop around, and leave. Some of them come back—but most do not. She thinks her product selections are very suitable for her target market and is concerned that her salespeople don't close more sales with potential customers. Several times, she has discussed this matter with her 10 salespeople. Her staff feels they should treat customers the way they personally want to be treated. They argue that their role is to answer questions and be helpful when asked—not to make suggestions or help customers make decisions. They think this would be too "hard sell."

Abila says their behavior is interpreted as indifference by the customers attracted to the store by her advertising. She has tried to convince her salespeople that customers must be treated on an individual basis and that some customers need more help in looking and deciding than others. Moreover, Abila is convinced that some customers would appreciate more help and suggestions than the salespeople themselves might want. To support her views, she showed her staff the data from a study of furniture store customers (see Table 1 below and Table 2 on the next page) that she found on the Internet website for a furniture trade association. She tried to explain the differences in demographic groups and pointed out that her store was definitely trying to aim at specific people. She argued that they (the salespeople) should cater to the needs and attitudes of their customers and think less about how they would like to be treated themselves. Further, Abila announced that she is considering changing the sales compensation plan or hiring new blood if the present employees can't do a better job. Currently, the sales reps are paid $26,000 per year plus a 5 percent commission on sales.

Contrast Dora Abila's strategy and thoughts about her salespeople with their apparent view of her strategy and especially their role in it. What should she do now? Explain.

Table 1

In Shopping for Furniture I Found (Find) That	Group A	Group B	Group C	Group D
I looked at furniture in many stores before I made a purchase.	78%	72%	52%	50%
I went (am going) to only one store and bought (buy) what I found (find) there.	2	5	10	11
To make my purchase I went (am going) back to one of the stores I shopped in previously.	63	59	27	20
I looked (am looking) at furniture in no more than three stores and made (will make) my purchase in one of these.	20	25	40	45
I like a lot of help in selecting the right furniture.	27	33	62	69
I like a very friendly salesperson.	23	28	69	67

The header for Group A, B, C, D falls under "Demographic Groups".

Table 2 The Sample Design

Demographic Status
Upper class (Group A); 13% of sample
This group consists of managers, proprietors, or executives of large businesses; professionals, including doctors, lawyers, engineers, college professors, and school administrators; and research personnel and sales personnel, including managers, executives, and upper-income salespeople above level of clerks. *Family income over $60,000*
Middle class (Group B); 37% of sample
Group B consists of white-collar workers, including clerical, secretarial, salesclerks, bookkeepers, etc. It also includes school teachers, social workers, semiprofessionals, proprietors or managers of small businesses, industrial foremen, and other supervisory personnel. *Family income between $35,000 and $70,000*
Lower middle class (Group C); 36% of sample
Skilled workers and semiskilled technicians are in this category, along with custodians, elevator operators, telephone linemen, factory operatives, construction workers, and some domestic and personal service employees. *Family income between $20,000 and $45,000. No one in this group has above a high school education.*
Lower class (Group D); 14% of sample
Nonskilled employees, day laborers. It also includes some factory operatives and domestic and service people. *Family income under $28,000. None have completed high school; some have only a grade school education.*

24. Custom Wire, Inc.

Meggie Stillwater, marketing manager of consumer products for Custom Wire, Inc., is trying to set a price for her most promising new product—a space-saving shoe rack suitable for small homes or apartments.

Custom Wire, Inc.—located in Ft. Worth, Texas—is a custom producer of industrial wire products. The company has a lot of experience bending wire into many shapes and also can chrome- or gold-plate finished products. The company was started 16 years ago and has slowly built its sales volume to $3.6 million a year. Just one year ago, Meggie Stillwater was appointed marketing manager of the consumer products division. It is her responsibility to develop this division as a producer and marketer of the company's own branded products—as distinguished from custom orders, which the industrial division produces for others.

Stillwater has been working on a number of different product ideas for almost a year now and has developed several designs for DVD holders, racks for soft-drink cans, plate holders, doll stands, collapsible book ends, and other such products. Her most promising product is a shoe rack for crowded homes and apartments. The wire rack attaches to the inside of a closet door and holds eight pairs of shoes.

The rack is very similar to one the industrial division produced for a number of years for another company. That company sold the shoe rack and hundreds of other related items out of its "products for organizing and storing" mail-order catalog. Managers at Custom Wire were surprised by the high sales volume the catalog company achieved with the rack. In fact, that is what interested Custom Wire in the consumer market and led to the development of the separate consumer products division.

Stillwater has sold hundreds of the shoe racks to various local hardware, grocery, and general merchandise stores, and wholesalers on a trial basis, but each time she has negotiated a price—and no firm policy has been set. Now she must determine what price to set on the shoe rack, which she plans to push aggressively wherever she can. Actually, she hasn't decided on exactly which channels of distribution to use. But trials in the local area have been encouraging, and as noted earlier, the experience in the industrial division suggests that there is a large market for this type of product. Further, she has noticed that a Wal-Mart store in her local area is selling a similar rack made of plastic. When she talked casually about her product with the store manager, he suggested that she contact the chain's housewares buyer in the home office in Arkansas.

The manufacturing cost of her rack—when made in reasonable quantities—is approximately $2.80 if it is painted black and $3.60 if it is chromed. Similar products have been selling at retail in the $9.95 to $19.95 range. The sales and administrative overhead to be charged to the division will amount to $95,000 a year. This will include Stillwater's salary and some travel and office expenses. She expects that a number of other products will be developed in the near future. But for the coming year, she hopes the shoe rack will account for about half the consumer products division's sales volume.

Evaluate Meggie Stillwater's strategy planning so far. What should she do now? What price should she set for the shoe rack?

25. PlastiTech Mfg., Inc.

Barry Summers, the marketing manager of PlastiTech Mfg., Inc., wants to increase sales by adding sales reps rather than "playing with price." That's how Barry describes what Bill Summers, his father and PlastiTech's president, is suggesting. Bill is not sure what to do either. But he does want to increase sales, so something new is needed.

PlastiTech Mfg., Inc.—of Long Beach, California—is a leading producer in the plastic forming machinery industry. It has patents covering over 200 variations, but PlastiTech's customers seldom buy more than 30 different types in a year. The machines are sold to plastic forming manufacturers to increase production capacity or replace old equipment.

Established in 1970, the company has enjoyed a steady growth to its present position with annual sales of $50 million.

Twelve U.S. firms compete in the U.S. plastic forming machinery market. Several Japanese, German, and Swedish firms compete in the global market, but the Summers have not seen much of them on the West Coast. Apparently the foreign firms rely on manufacturers' agents who have not provided an ongoing presence. They are not good about following up on inquiries, and their record for service on the few sales they have made on the East Coast is not satisfactory. So the Summers are not worried about them right now.

Each of the 12 U.S. competitors is about the same size and manufactures basically similar machinery. Each has tended to specialize in its own geographic region. Six of the competitors are located in the East, four in the Midwest, and two— including PlastiTech—on the West Coast. The other West Coast firm is in Tacoma, Washington. All of the competitors offer similar prices and sell F.O.B. their factories. Demand has been fairly strong in recent years. As a result, all of the competitors have been satisfied to sell in their geographic areas and avoid price-cutting. In fact, price-cutting is not a popular idea in this industry. About 15 years ago, one firm tried to win more business and found that others immediately met the price cut—but industry sales (in units) did not increase at all. Within a few years, prices returned to their earlier level, and since then competition has tended to focus on promotion and avoid price.

PlastiTech's promotion depends mainly on six company sales reps, who cover the West Coast. In total, these reps cost about $880,000 per year including salary, bonuses, supervision, travel, and entertaining. When the sales reps are close to making a sale, they are supported by two sales engineers—at a cost of about $130,000 per year per engineer. PlastiTech does some advertising in trade journals—less than $100,000—and occasionally uses direct mailings and trade show exhibits. It also has a simple website on the Internet. But the main promotion emphasis is on personal selling. Any personal contact outside the West Coast market is handled by manufacturers' agents who are paid 4 percent on sales—but sales are very infrequent.

Bill Summers is not satisfied with the present situation. Industry sales have leveled off and so have PlastiTech's sales—although the firm continues to hold its share of the market. Bill would like to find a way to compete more effectively in the other regions because he sees great potential outside the West Coast.

Competitors and buyers agree that PlastiTech is the top-quality producer in the industry. Its machines have generally been somewhat superior to others in terms of reliability, durability, and productive capacity. The difference, however, usually has not been great enough to justify a higher price—because the others are able to do the necessary job—unless a Plasti-Tech sales rep convinces the customer that the extra quality will improve the customer's product and lead to fewer production line breakdowns. The sales rep also tries to sell the advantages of PlastiTech's better sales engineers and technical service people—and sometimes is successful. But if a buyer is mainly interested in comparing delivered prices for basic machines—the usual case—PlastiTech's price must be competitive to get the business. In short, if such a buyer has a choice between PlastiTech's and another machine *at the same price*, PlastiTech will usually win the business in its part of the West Coast market. But it's clear that PlastiTech's price has to be at least competitive in such cases.

The average plastic forming machine sells for about $220,000, F.O.B. shipping point. Shipping costs within any of the three major regions average about $4,000—but another $3,000 must be added on shipments between the West Coast and the Midwest (either way) and another $3,000 between the Midwest and the East.

Bill Summers is thinking about expanding sales by absorbing the extra $3,000 to $6,000 in freight cost that occurs if a midwestern or eastern customer buys from his West Coast location. By doing this, he would not actually be cutting price in those markets but rather reducing his net return. He thinks that his competitors would not see this as price competition and therefore would not resort to cutting prices themselves.

Barry Summers, the marketing manager, disagrees. Barry thinks that the proposed freight absorption plan would stimulate price competition in the Midwest and East and perhaps on the West Coast. He proposes instead that PlastiTech hire some sales reps to work the Midwest and Eastern regions—selling quality—rather than relying on the manufacturers' agents. He argues that two additional sales reps in each of these regions would not increase costs too much and might greatly increase the sales from these markets over that brought in by the agents. With this plan, there would be no need to absorb the freight and risk disrupting the status quo. Adding more of PlastiTech's own sales reps is especially important, he argues, because competition in the Midwest and East is somewhat hotter than on the West Coast—due to the number of competitors (including foreign competitors) in those regions. A lot of expensive entertaining, for example, seems to be required just to be considered as a potential supplier. In contrast, the situation has been rather quiet in the West—because only two firms are sharing this market and each is working harder near its home base. The eastern and midwestern competitors don't send any sales reps to the West Coast—and if they have any manufacturers' agents, they haven't gotten any business in recent years.

Bill Summers agrees that his son has a point, but industry sales are leveling off and Bill wants to increase sales. Further, he thinks the competitive situation may change drastically in the near future anyway, as global competitors get more aggressive and some possible new production methods and machines become more competitive with existing ones. He would rather be a leader in anything that is likely to happen rather than a follower. But he is impressed with Barry's comments about the greater competitiveness in the other markets and therefore is unsure about what to do.

Evaluate PlastiTech's current strategies. Given Bill Summers' sales objective, what should PlastiTech Mfg. do? Explain.

26. National Packers, Inc.

Scott Wallace, president of National Packers, Inc., is not sure what he should propose to the board of directors. His recent strategy change isn't working. And Harry Mason, National's only sales rep (and a board member), is so frustrated that he refuses to continue his discouraging sales efforts. Mason wants Scott Wallace to hire a sales force or do *something.*

National Packers, Inc., is a long-time processor in the highly seasonal vegetable canning industry. National packs and sells canned beans, peas, carrots, corn, peas and carrots mixed, and kidney beans. It sells mainly through food brokers to merchant wholesalers, supermarket chains (such as Kroger, Safeway, A&P, and Jewel), cooperatives, and other outlets, mostly in the Midwest. Of less importance, by volume, are sales to local institutions, grocery stores, and supermarkets—and sales of dented canned goods at low prices to walk-in customers.

National is located in Wisconsin's Devil's River Valley. The company has more than $28 million in sales annually (exact sales data is not published by the closely held corporation). Plants are located in strategic places along the valley, with main offices in the valley also. The National brand is used only on canned goods sold in the local market. Most of the goods are sold and shipped under a retailer's label or a broker's/wholesaler's label.

National is well known for the consistent quality of its product offerings. And it's always willing to offer competitive prices. Strong channel relations were built by Ron Placar, National's former chairman of the board and chief executive officer. Placar—who still owns controlling interest in the firm—worked the Chicago area as the company's sales rep in its earlier years, before he took over from his father as president in 1972. Placar was an ambitious and hardworking top manager—the firm prospered under his direction. He became well known within the canned food processing industry for technical/product innovations.

During the off-canning season, Placar traveled widely. In the course of his travels, he arranged several important business deals. His 1986 and 1997 trips resulted in the following two events: (1) inexpensive pineapple was imported from Taiwan and sold by National, primarily to expand the product line, and (2) a technically advanced continuous process cooker (65 feet high) was imported from England and installed at one of National's plants. It was the first of its kind in the United States and cut processing time sharply while improving quality.

Placar retired in 2004 and named his son-in-law, 35-year-old Scott Wallace, as his successor. Wallace is intelligent and hardworking. He has been concerned primarily with the company's financial matters and only recently with marketing problems. During his seven years as financial director, the firm received its highest credit rating and was able to borrow working capital ($5 million to meet seasonal can and wage requirements) at the lowest rate ever.

The fact that the firm isn't unionized allows some competitive advantage. However, changes in minimum wage laws have increased costs. And these and other rising costs have squeezed profit margins. This led to the recent closing of two plants as they became less efficient to operate. National expanded capacity of the remaining two plants (especially warehouse facilities) so they could operate more profitably with maximum use of existing processing equipment.

Shortly after Placar's retirement, Scott Wallace reviewed the company's situation with his managers. He pointed to narrowing profit margins, debts contracted for new plants and equipment, and an increasingly competitive environment. Even considering the temporary labor-saving competitive advantage of the new cooker system, there seemed to be no way to improve the status quo unless the firm could sell direct—as they do in the local market—thereby eliminating the food brokers' 5 percent commission on sales. This was the plan decided on, and Harry Mason was given the new sales job. An inside salesperson was retained to handle incoming orders and do some telemarketing to smaller accounts.

Harry Mason, the only full-time outside sales rep for the firm, lives in Devil's River Valley. Other top managers do some selling but not much. Being a nephew of Placar, Harry Mason is also a member of the board of directors. He is well qualified in technical matters and has a college degree in food chemistry. Although Harry Mason formerly did call on some important customers with the brokers' sales reps, he is not well-known in the industry or even by National's usual customers.

It is now five months later. Harry Mason is not doing very well. He has made several selling trips, placed hundreds of telephone calls, and maintained constant e-mail contacts with prospective customers—all with discouraging results. He is unwilling to continue sales efforts on his own. There seems to be too many potential customers for one person to reach. And much negotiating, wining, and dining seems to be needed—certainly more than he can or wants to do.

Mason insists that National hire a sales force to continue the present way of operating. Sales are down in comparison both to expectations and to the previous year's results. Some regular supermarket chain customers have stopped buying—though basic consumer demand has not changed. Further, buyers for some supermarket chains that might be potential new customers have demanded quantity guarantees much larger than National Packers can supply. Expanding supply would be difficult in the short run—because the firm typically must contract with growers to ensure supplies of the type and quality they normally offer.

Placar, still the controlling stockholder, has asked for a special meeting of the board in two weeks to discuss the present situation.

Evaluate National's past and current strategy planning. What should Scott Wallace tell Ron Placar? What should National do now?

27. Premier Molding, Inc.

Deb Glendon is trying to decide whether to leave her present job to buy into another business and be part of top management.

Glendon is now a sales rep for a plastics components manufacturer. She calls mostly on large industrial accounts—such as refrigerator manufacturers—who might need large quantities of custom-made products like door liners. She is on a straight salary of $45,000 per year, plus expenses and a company car. She expects some salary increases but doesn't see much long-run opportunity with this company.

As a result, she is seriously considering changing jobs and investing $60,000 in Premier Molding, Inc., an established Chicago (Illinois) thermoplastic molder (manufacturer). Josiah Tooner, the present owner, is nearing retirement and has not trained anyone to take over the business. He has agreed to sell the business to Jerry Natchez, a lawyer, who has invited Deb Glendon to invest and become the sales manager. Jerry Natchez has agreed to match Glendon's current salary plus expenses, plus a bonus of 2 percent of profits. However, she must invest to become part of the new company. She will get a 5 percent interest in the business for the necessary $60,000 investment—all of her savings.

Premier Molding, Inc., is well established and last year had sales of $3.2 million but zero profits (after paying Tooner a salary of $80,000). In terms of sales, cost of materials was 46 percent; direct labor, 13 percent; indirect factory labor, 15 percent; factory overhead, 13 percent; and sales overhead and general expenses, 13 percent. The company has not been making any profit for several years—but it has been continually adding new computer-controlled machines to replace those made obsolete by technological developments. The machinery is well maintained and modern, but most of it is similar to that used by its many competitors. Most of the machines in the industry are standard. Special products are made by using specially made dies with these machines.

Sales have been split about two-thirds custom-molded products (that is, made to the specification of other producers or merchandising concerns) and the balance proprietary items (such as housewares and game items, like poker chips).

The housewares are copies of items developed by others and indicate neither originality nor style. Tooner is in charge of selling the proprietary items, which are distributed through any available wholesale channels. The custom-molded products are sold through two full-time sales reps—who receive a 10 percent commission on individual orders up to $30,000 and then 3 percent above that level—and also by three manufacturers' reps who get the same commissions.

The company seems to be in fairly good financial condition, at least as far as book value is concerned. The $60,000 investment will buy almost $88,000 in assets—and ongoing operations should pay off the seven-year note (see Table 1). Jerry Natchez thinks that with new management the company has a good chance to make big profits. He expects to make some economies in the production process—because he feels most production operations can be improved. He plans to keep custom-molding sales at approximately the present $2 million level. His new strategy will try to increase the proprietary sales volume from $1.2 million to $3 million a year. Deb Glendon is expected to be a big help here because of her sales experience. This will bring the firm up to about capacity level—but it will mean adding additional employees and costs. The major advantage of expanding sales will be spreading overhead.

Some of the products proposed by Jerry Natchez for expanding proprietary sales are listed below.

New products for consideration:

Safety helmets for cyclists.

Water bottles for cyclists and in-line skaters.

Waterproof cases for digital cameras.

Toolboxes.

Closet organizer/storage boxes for toys.

Short legs for furniture.

Step-on garbage cans without liners.

Outside house shutters and siding.

Importing and distributing foreign housewares.

Table 1 Premier Molding, Inc., Statement of Financial Conditions, December 31, 2006

Assets			Liabilities and Net Worth		
Cash		$ 19,500	Liabilities:		
Accounts receivable		82,500	Accounts payable		$ 105,000
Building	$ 337,500		Notes payable—7 years (machinery)		291,000
Less: depreciation	112,500				
		225,000			
Machinery	2,100,000		Net worth:		
Less: depreciation	675,000		Capital stock		1,350,000
		1,425,000	Retained earnings		6,000
Total assets		$1,752,000	Total liabilities and net worth		$1,752,000

Premier Molding faces heavy competition from many other similar companies, including firms that have outsourced production to China and Eastern Europe where labor costs are much lower. Further, most retailers expect a wide margin, sometimes 50 to 60 percent of the retail selling price. Even so, manufacturing costs are low enough so Premier Molding can spend some money for promotion while still keeping the price competitive. Apparently, many customers are willing to pay for novel new products—if they see them in stores. And Glendon isn't worried too much by tough competition. She sees plenty of that in her present job. And she does like the idea of being an "owner and sales manager."

Evaluate Premier Molding's situation and Jerry Natchez's strategy. What should Deb Glendon do? Why?

28. ACT, Inc.

Carroll Taylor, president and marketing manager of Accurate Cutting Tools, Inc., is deciding what strategy, or strategies, to pursue.

Accurate Cutting Tools (ACT) is a manufacturer of industrial cutting tools. These tools include such items as lathe blades, drill press bits, and various other cutting edges used in the operation of large metal cutting, boring, or stamping machines. Carroll Taylor takes great pride in the fact that his company—whose $5,700,000 sales in 2006 is small by industry standards—is recognized as a producer of a top-quality line of cutting tools.

Competition in the cutting-tool industry is intense. ACT competes not only with the original machine manufacturers, but also with many other larger domestic and foreign manufacturers offering cutting tools as one of their many different product lines. This has had the effect, over the years, of standardizing the price, specifications, and, in turn, the quality of the competing products of all manufacturers. It has also led to fairly low prices on standard items.

About a year ago, Carroll was tiring of the financial pressure of competing with larger companies enjoying economies of scale. At the same time, he noted that more and more potential cutting-tool customers were turning to small tool-and-die shops that used computer-controlled equipment to meet specialized needs that could not be met by the mass production firms. Carroll thought perhaps he should consider some basic strategy changes. Although he was unwilling to become strictly a custom producer, he thought that the recent trend toward buying customized cutting edges suggested new markets might be developing—markets too small for the large, multiproduct-line companies to serve profitably but large enough to earn a good profit for a flexible company of ACT's size.

Carroll hired a marketing research company, MResearch-Pro, to study the feasibility of serving these markets. The initial results were encouraging. It was estimated that ACT might increase sales by 65 percent and profits by 90 percent by serving the emerging markets. The research showed that there are many large users of standard cutting tools who buy directly from large cutting-tool manufacturers (domestic or foreign) or wholesalers who represent these manufacturers. This is the bulk of the cutting-tool business (in terms of units sold and sales dollars). But there are also many smaller users all over the United States who buy in small but regular quantities. And some of these needs are becoming more specialized. That is, a special cutting tool may make a machine and/or worker much more productive, perhaps eliminating several steps with time-consuming setups. This is the area that the research company sees as potentially attractive.

Next, Carroll had the sales manager hire two technically oriented market researchers (at a total cost of $85,000 each per year, including travel expenses) to maintain continuous contact with potential cutting-tool customers. The researchers were supposed to identify any present or future needs that might exist in enough cases to make it possible to profitably produce a specialized product. The researchers were not to take orders or sell ACT's products to the potential customers. Carroll felt that only through this policy could these researchers talk to the right people.

The initial feedback from the market researchers was most encouraging. Many firms (large and small) had special needs—although it often was necessary to talk to the shop foreman or individual machine operators to find these needs. Most operators were making do with the tools available. Either they didn't know customizing was possible or doubted that their supervisors would do anything about it if they suggested that a more specialized tool could increase productivity. But these operators were encouraging because they said that it would be easier to persuade supervisors to order specialized tools if the tools were already produced and in stock than if they had to be custom made. So Carroll decided to continually add high-quality products to meet the ever-changing, specialized needs of users of cutting tools and edges.

ACT's potential customers for specialized tools are located all over the United States. The average sale per customer is likely to be less than $500, but the sale will be repeated several times within a year. Because of the widespread market and the small order size, Carroll doesn't think that selling direct—as is done by small custom shops—is practical. At the present time, ACT sells 90 percent of its regular output through a large industrial wholesaler—Summit Mill Supply—which serves the area east of the Mississippi River and carries a very complete line of industrial supplies (to "meet every industrial need"). Summit Mill Supply carries over 10,000 items. Some sales come from customers who know exactly what they want and just place orders directly by fax or at the firm's Internet website. But most of the selling is by Summit's sales reps, who work from an electronic catalog on a laptop computer. Summit Mill Supply, although very large and well-known, is having trouble moving cutting tools. Summit is losing sales of cutting tools in some cities to newer wholesalers specializing in the cutting-tool industry. The new wholesalers are able to give more technical help to potential customers and therefore better service. Summit's president is convinced that the newer, less-experienced concerns will either realize that a substantial profit margin can't be maintained along with their aggressive strategies, or they will eventually go broke trying to overspecialize.

From Carroll's standpoint, the present wholesaler has a good reputation and has served ACT well in the past. Summit Mill Supply has been of great help in holding down Carroll's inventory costs—by increasing the inventory in Summit's 35 branch locations. Although Carroll has received several complaints about the lack of technical assistance given by Summit's sales reps—as well as their lack of knowledge about ACT's new special products—he feels that the present wholesaler is providing the best service it can. All its sales reps have been told about the new products at a special training session, and new pages have been added to the electronic catalog on their laptops. So regarding the complaints, Carroll says, "The usual things you hear when you're in business."

Carroll thinks there are more urgent problems than a few complaints. Profits are declining, and sales of the new cutting tools are not nearly as high as forecast—even though all research reports indicate that the company's new products meet the intended markets' needs perfectly. The high costs involved in producing small quantities of special products and in adding the market research team—together with lower-than-expected sales—have significantly reduced ACT's profits. Carroll is wondering whether it is wise to continue to try to cater to the needs of many specific target markets when the results are this discouraging. He also is considering increasing advertising expenditures in the hope that customers will pull the new products through the channel.

Evaluate ACT's situation and Carroll Taylor's present strategy. What should he do now?

29. Laser Castings, Inc.

Roger Lansing, marketing manager for Laser Castings, Inc., is trying to figure out how to explain to his boss why a proposed new product line doesn't make sense for them. Roger is sure it's wrong for Laser Castings, but isn't able to explain why.

Laser Castings, Inc., is a producer of malleable iron castings for automobile and aircraft manufacturers and a variety of other users of castings. Last year's sales of castings amounted to over $70 million.

Laser Castings also produces about 30 percent of all the original equipment bumper jacks installed in new U.S.-made automobiles each year. This is a very price-competitive business, but Laser Castings has been able to obtain its large market share with frequent personal contact between the company's executives and its customers—supported by very close cooperation between the company's engineering department and its customers' buyers. This has been extremely important because the wide variety of models and model changes frequently requires alterations in the specifications of the bumper jacks. All of Laser Castings' bumper jacks are sold directly to the automobile manufacturers. No attempt has been made to sell bumper jacks to final consumers through hardware and automotive channels—although they are available through the manufacturers' automobile dealers.

Karl Minelli, Laser Castings' production manager, now wants to begin producing hydraulic garage jacks for sale through automobile-parts wholesalers to retail auto parts stores. Minelli saw a variety of hydraulic garage jacks at a recent automotive show and knew immediately that his plant could produce these products. This especially interested him because of the possibility of using excess capacity. Further, he says "jacks are jacks," and the company would merely be broadening its product line by introducing hydraulic garage jacks. (Note: Hydraulic garage jacks are larger than bumper jacks and are intended for use in or around a garage. They are too big to carry in a car's trunk.)

As Karl Minelli became more enthusiastic about the idea, he found that Laser Castings' engineering department already had a patented design that appeared to be at least comparable to the products now offered on the market. Further, Minelli says that the company would be able to produce a product that is better made than the competitive products (i.e., smoother castings)—although he agrees that most customers probably wouldn't notice the difference. The production department estimates that the cost of producing a hydraulic garage jack comparable to those currently offered by competitors would be about $48 per unit.

Roger Lansing, the marketing manager, has just received an e-mail from Jaime Neilsen, the company president, explaining the production department's enthusiasm for broadening Laser Castings' present jack line into hydraulic jacks. Jaime Neilsen seems enthusiastic about the idea too, noting that it would be a way to make fuller use of the company's resources and increase its sales. Neilsen's e-mail asks for Roger's reaction, but Jaime Neilsen already seems sold on the idea.

Given Neilsen's enthusiasm, Roger Lansing isn't sure how to respond. He's trying to develop a good explanation of why he isn't excited about the proposal. The firm's six sales reps are already overworked with their current accounts. And Roger couldn't possibly promote this new line himself—he's already helping other reps make calls and serving as sales manager. So it would be necessary to hire someone to promote the line. And this sales manager would probably have to recruit manufacturers' agents (who probably will want 10 to 15 percent commission on sales) to sell to automotive wholesalers who would stock the jack and sell to the auto parts retailers. The wholesalers will probably expect trade discounts of about 20 percent, trade show exhibits, some national advertising, and sales promotion help (catalog sheets, mailers, and point-of-purchase displays). Further, Roger Lansing sees that Laser Castings' billing and collection system will have to be expanded because many more customers will be involved. It will also be necessary to keep track of agent commissions and accounts receivable.

Auto parts retailers are currently selling similar hydraulic garage jacks for about $99. Roger Lansing has learned that such retailers typically expect a trade discount of about 35 percent off of the suggested list price for their auto parts.

All things considered, Roger Lansing feels that the proposed hydraulic jack line is not very closely related to the company's present emphasis. He has already indicated his lack of enthusiasm to Karl Minelli, but this made little difference in Karl's thinking. Now it's clear that Roger will have to convince the president or he will soon be responsible for selling hydraulic jacks.

Contrast Laser Castings, Inc.'s current strategy and the proposed strategy. What should Roger Lansing say to Jaime Neilsen to persuade him to change his mind? Or should he just plan to sell hydraulic jacks? Explain.

---

30. Saralyn Mills, Ltd.*

Nicole Vichon, marketing manager of Saralyn Mills, Ltd.—a Canadian company—is being urged to approve the creation of a separate marketing plan for Quebec. This would be a major policy change because Saralyn Mills' international parent is trying to move toward a global strategy for the whole firm and Vichon has been supporting Canada-wide planning.

Nicole Vichon has been the marketing manager of Saralyn Mills, Ltd., for the last four years—since she arrived from international headquarters in Minneapolis. Saralyn Mills, Ltd., headquartered in Toronto, is a subsidiary of a large U.S.-based consumer packaged-food company with worldwide sales of more than $2.8 billion in 2005. Its Canadian sales are just over $450 million, with the Quebec and Ontario markets accounting for 69 percent of the company's Canadian sales.

The company's product line includes such items as cake mixes, puddings, pie fillings, pancakes, prepared foods, and frozen dinners. The company has successfully introduced at least six new products every year for the last five years. Products from Saralyn Mills are known for their high quality and enjoy much brand preference throughout Canada, including the Province of Quebec.

The company's sales have risen every year since Nicole Vichon took over as marketing manager. In fact, the company's market share has increased steadily in each of the product categories in which it competes. The Quebec market has closely followed the national trend except that, in the past two years, total sales growth in that market began to lag.

According to Vichon, a big advantage of Saralyn Mills over its competitors is the ability to coordinate all phases of the food business from Toronto. For this reason, Vichon meets at least once a month with her product managers—to discuss developments in local markets that might affect marketing plans. While each manager is free to make suggestions and even to suggest major changes, Nicole Vichon has the responsiblity of giving final approval for all plans.

One of the product managers, Marie LeMans, expressed great concern at the last monthly meeting about the poor performance of some of the company's products in the Quebec market. While a broad range of possible reasons—ranging from inflation and the threat of job losses to politics—were reviewed to try to explain the situation, LeMans insisted that it was due to a basic lack of understanding of that market. She felt not enough managerial time and money had been spent on the Quebec market— in part because of the current emphasis on developing all-Canada plans on the way to having one global strategy.

Marie LeMans felt the current marketing approach to the Quebec market should be reevaluated because an inappropriate marketing plan may be responsible for the sales slowdown. After all, she said, "80 percent of the market is French-speaking. It's in the best interest of the company to treat that market as being separate and distinct from the rest of Canada."

Marie LeMans supported her position by showing that Quebec's per capita consumption of many product categories (in which the firm competes) is above the national average (see Table 1). Research projects conducted by Saralyn Mills also support the "separate and distinct" argument. Over the years, the firm has found many French–English differences in brand attitudes, lifestyles, usage rates, and so on.

LeMans argued that the company should develop a unique Quebec marketing plan for some or all of its brands. She specifically suggested that the French-language advertising plan for a particular brand be developed independently of the plan for English Canada. Currently, the Toronto agency assigned to the brand just translates its English-language ads for the French market. Nicole Vichon pointed out that the present advertising approach assured Saralyn Mills of a uniform brand image across Canada. Marie LeMans said she knew what the agency is doing, and that straight translation into Canadian-French may not communicate the same brand image. The discussion that followed suggested that a different brand image might be needed in the French market if the company wanted to stop the brand's decline in sales.

Table 1   Per Capita Consumption Index, Province of Quebec (Canada = 100)*

Cake mixes	107	Soft drinks	126
Pancakes	87	Pie fillings	118
Puddings	114	Frozen dinners	79
Salad dressings	85	Prepared packaged foods	83
Molasses	132	Cookies	123

*An index shows the relative consumption as compared to a standard. In this table, the standard is all of Canada. The data shows that per capita consumption of cake mixes is 7% higher in Quebec and pancake consumption 13% lower compared to all of Canada.

---

*This case was adapted from one written by Professor Roberta Tamilia, University of Windsor, Canada.

The managers also discussed the food distribution system in Quebec. The major supermarket chains have their lowest market share in that province. Independents are strongest there—the "mom-and-pop" food stores fast disappearing outside Quebec remain alive and well in the province. Traditionally, these stores have stocked a higher proportion (than supermarkets) of their shelf space with national brands, an advantage for Saralyn Mills.

Finally, various issues related to discount policies, pricing structure, sales promotion, and cooperative advertising were discussed. All of these suggested that things were different in Quebec and that future marketing plans should reflect these differences to a greater extent than they do now.

After the meeting, Nicole Vichon stayed in her office to think about the situation. Although she agreed with the basic idea that the Quebec market was in many ways different, she wasn't sure how far the company should go in recognizing this fact. She knew that regional differences in food tastes and brand purchases existed not only in Quebec but in other parts of Canada as well. But people are people, after all, with far

more similarities than differences, so a Canadian and eventually a global strategy makes some sense too.

Nicole Vichon was afraid that giving special status to one region might conflict with top management's objective of achieving standardization whenever possible—one global strategy for Canada, on the way to one worldwide global strategy. She was also worried about the long-term effect of such a policy change on costs, organizational structure, and brand image. Still, enough product managers had expressed their concern over the years about the Quebec market to make her wonder if she shouldn't modify the current approach. Perhaps they could experiment with a few brands—and just in Quebec. She could cite the language difference as the reason for trying Quebec rather than any of the other provinces. But Vichon realizes that any change of policy could be seen as the beginning of more change, and what would Minneapolis think? Could she explain it successfully there?

Evaluate Saralyn Mills, Ltd.'s present strategy. What should Nicole Vichon do now? Explain.

31. Home Health, Inc.

Sharon Warren, executive director of Home Health, Inc., is trying to clarify her strategies. She's sure some changes are needed, but she's less sure about how *much* change is needed and/or whether it can be handled by her people.

Home Health, Inc. (HHI), is a nonprofit organization that has been operating—with varying degrees of success—for 25 years, offering nursing services in clients' homes. Some of its funding comes from the local United Way—to provide emergency nursing services for those who can't afford to pay. The balance of the revenues—about 90 percent of the $2.2 million annual budget—comes from charges made directly to the client or to third-party payers, including insurance companies, health maintenance organizations (HMOs), and the federal government, for Medicare or Medicaid services.

Sharon Warren has been executive director of HHI for two years. She has developed a well-functioning organization able to meet most requests for service that come from some local doctors and from the discharge officers at local hospitals. Some business also comes by self-referral—the client finds the HHI name in the Yellow Pages of the local phone directory.

The last two years have been a rebuilding time—because the previous director had personnel problems. This led to a weakening of the agency's image with the local referring agencies. Now the image is more positive. But Sharon is not completely satisfied with the situation. By definition, Home Health is a nonprofit organization. But it still must cover all its costs: payroll, rent payments, phone expenses, and so on, including Sharon's own salary. She can see that while HHI is growing slightly and is now breaking even, it doesn't have much of a cash cushion to fall back on if (1) the demand for HHI nursing services declines, (2) the government changes its rules about paying for HHI's kind of nursing services, either cutting back what it will pay for or reducing the amount it will pay for specific services, or (3) new competitors enter the market. In fact, the last possibility concerns Sharon greatly. Some

hospitals, squeezed for revenue, are expanding into home health care—especially nursing services as patients are being released earlier from hospitals because of payment limits set by government guidelines. For-profit organizations (e.g., Kelly Home Care Services) are expanding around the country to provide a complete line of home health care services, including nursing services of the kind offered by HHI. These for-profit organizations appear to be efficiently run, offering good service at competitive and sometimes even lower prices than some nonprofit organizations. And they seem to be doing this at a profit, which suggests that it would be possible for these for-profit companies to lower their prices if nonprofit organizations try to compete on price.

Sharon is considering whether she should ask her board of directors to let her offer a complete line of home health care services—that is, move beyond just nursing services into what she calls "care and comfort" services.

Currently, HHI is primarily concerned with providing professional nursing care in the home. But HHI nurses are much too expensive for routine home health care activities—helping fix meals, bathing and dressing patients, and other care and comfort activities. The full cost of a nurse to HHI, including benefits and overhead, is about $65 per hour. But a registered nurse is not needed for care and comfort services. All that is required is someone who is honest, can get along with all kinds of people, and is willing to do this kind of work. Generally, any mature person can be trained fairly quickly to do the job—following the instructions and under the general supervision of a physician, a nurse, or family members. The full cost of aides is $9 to $16 per hour for short visits and as low as $75 per 24 hours for a live-in aide who has room and board supplied by the client.

The demand for all kinds of home health care services seems to be growing. With more dual-career families and more single-parent households, there isn't anyone in the family to take over home health care when the need arises—due to emergencies or long-term disabilities. Further, hospitals send patients home earlier than in the past. And with people living longer, there are more single-survivor family situations where there is no one nearby to take care of the needs of these older people. But often some family members—or third-party payers such as the government or insurers—are willing to pay for some home health care services. Sharon now occasionally recommends other agencies or suggests one or another of three women who have been doing care and comfort work on their own, part-time. But with growing demand, Sharon wonders if HHI should get into this business, hiring aides as needed.

Sharon is concerned that a new, full-service home health care organization may come into her market and be a single source for both nursing services *and* less-skilled home care and comfort services. This has happened already in two nearby but somewhat larger cities. Sharon fears that this might be more appealing than HHI to the local hospitals and other referrers. In other words, she can see the possibility of losing nursing service business if HHI does not begin to offer a complete home health care service. This would cause real problems for HHI—because overhead costs are more or less fixed. A loss in revenue of as little as 10 percent would require some cutbacks—perhaps laying off some nurses or secretaries, giving up part of the office, and so on.

Another reason for expanding beyond nursing services— using paraprofessionals and relatively unskilled personnel—is to offer a better service to present customers *and* make more effective use of the computer systems and organization structure that she has developed over the last two years. Sharon estimates that the administrative and office capabilities could handle twice as many clients without straining the system. It would be necessary to add some clerical help—if the expansion were quite large. But this increase in overhead would be minor compared to the present proportion of total revenue that goes to covering overhead. In other words, additional clients or more work for some current clients could increase revenue and ensure the survival of HHI, provide a cushion to cover the normal fluctuations in demand, and ensure more job security for the administrative personnel.

Further, Sharon thinks that if HHI were successful in expanding its services—and therefore could generate some surplus—it could extend services to those who aren't now able to pay. Sharon says one of the worst parts of her job is refusing service to clients whose third-party benefits have run out or for whatever reason can no longer afford to pay. She is uncomfortable about having to cut off service, but she must schedule her nurses to provide revenue-producing services if she's going to meet the payroll every two weeks. By expanding to provide more services, she might be able to keep serving more of these nonpaying clients. This possibility excites Sharon because her nurse's training has instilled a deep desire to serve people in need, whether they can pay or not. This continual pressure to cut off service because people can't pay has been at the root of many disagreements and even arguments between the nurses serving the clients and Sharon, as executive director and representative of the board of directors.

Sharon knows that expanding into care and comfort services won't be easy. Some decisions would be needed about relative pay levels for nurses, paraprofessionals, and aides. HHI would also have to set prices for these different services and tell current customers and referral agencies about the expanded services.

These problems aren't bothering Sharon too much, however—she thinks she can handle them. She is sure that care and comfort services are in demand and could be supplied at competitive prices.

Her primary concern is whether this is the right thing for Home Health—basically a nursing organization—to do. HHI's whole history has been oriented to supplying *nurses' services.* Nurses are dedicated professionals who bring high standards to any job they undertake. The question is whether HHI should offer less-professional services. Inevitably, some of the aides will not be as dedicated as the nurses might like them to be. And this could reflect unfavorably on the nurse image. At a minimum, she would need to set up some sort of training program for the aides. As Sharon worries about the future of HHI, and her own future, it seems that there are no easy answers.

Evaluate HHI's present strategy. What should Sharon Warren do? Explain.

32. Lever, Ltd.*

Alan Cooke is product manager for Guard Deodorant Soap. He was just transferred to Lever, Ltd., a Canadian subsidiary of Lever Group, Inc., from world headquarters in New York. Alan is anxious to make a good impression because he is hoping to transfer to Lever's London office. He is working on developing and securing management approval of next year's marketing plan for Guard. His first job is submitting a draft marketing plan to Wendy Lee, his recently appointed group product manager, who is responsible for several such plans from product managers like Alan.

Alan's marketing plan is the single most important document he will produce on this assignment. This annual marketing plan does three main things:

1. It reviews the brand's performance in the past year, assesses the competitive situation, and highlights problems and opportunities for the brand.
2. It spells out marketing strategies and the plan for the coming year.
3. Finally, and most importantly, the marketing plan sets out the brand's sales objectives and advertising/promotion budget requirements.

In preparing this marketing plan, Alan gathered the information in Table 1.

---

*Adapted from a case prepared by Daniel Aronchick, who at the time of its preparation was marketing manager at Thomas J. Lipton, Limited.

Table 1 Past 12-Month Share of Bar Soap Market (percent)

	Maritimes	Quebec	Ontario	Manitoba/Saskatchewan	Alberta	British Columbia
Deodorant segment						
Zest	21.3%	14.2%	24.5%	31.2%	30.4%	25.5%
Dial	10.4	5.1	12.8	16.1	17.2	14.3
Lifebuoy	4.2	3.1	1.2	6.4	5.8	4.2
Guard	2.1	5.6	1.0	4.2	4.2	2.1
Beauty bar segment						
Camay	6.2	12.3	7.0	4.1	4.0	5.1
Lux	6.1	11.2	7.7	5.0	6.9	5.0
Dove	5.5	8.0	6.6	6.3	6.2	4.2
Lower-priced bars						
Ivory	11.2	6.5	12.4	5.3	5.2	9.0
Sunlight	6.1	3.2	8.2	4.2	4.1	8.0
All others (including stores' own brands)	26.9	30.8	18.6	17.2	16.0	22.6
Total bar soap market	100.0%	100.0%	100.0%	100.0%	100.0%	100.0%

Alan was somewhat surprised at the significant regional differences in the bar soap market:

1. The underdevelopment of the deodorant bar segment in Quebec, with a corresponding overdevelopment of the beauty bar segment. But some past research suggested that this is due to cultural factors—English-speaking people have been more interested than others in cleaning, deodorizing, and disinfecting. A similar pattern is seen in most European countries, where the adoption of deodorant soaps has been slower than in North America. For similar reasons, the perfumed soap share is highest in French-speaking Quebec.
2. The overdevelopment of synthetic bars (Zest, Dial) in the Prairies (Manitoba/Saskatchewan and Alberta). These bars, primarily in the deodorant segment, lather better in the hard water of the Prairies. Nonsynthetic bars lather very poorly in hard-water areas and leave a soap film.
3. The overdevelopment of the "all-other" segment in Quebec. This segment, consisting of smaller brands, fares better in Quebec, where 43 percent of the grocery trade is done by independent stores. Conversely, large chain grocery stores dominate in Ontario and the Prairies.

Alan's brand, Guard, is a highly perfumed deodorant bar. His business is relatively weak in the key Ontario market. To confirm this share data, Alan calculated consumption of Guard per thousand people in each region (see Table 2).

These differences are especially interesting since per capita sales of all bar soap products are roughly equal in all provinces.

A consumer attitude and usage research study was conducted approximately a year ago. This study revealed that consumer "top-of-mind" awareness of the Guard brand differed greatly across Canada. This was true despite the even—by population—expenditure of advertising funds in past years. Also, trial of Guard was low in the Maritimes, Ontario, and British Columbia (see Table 3 on the next page).

The attitude portion of the research revealed that consumers who had heard of Guard were aware that its deodorant protection came mainly from a high fragrance level. This was the main selling point in the copy, and it was well communicated by Guard's advertising. The other important finding was that consumers who had tried Guard were satisfied with the product. About 70 percent of those trying Guard had repurchased the product at least twice.

Table 2 Standard Cases of 3-Ounce Bars Consumed per 1,000 People in 12 Months

	Maritimes	Quebec	Ontario	Manitoba/Saskatchewan	Alberta	British Columbia
Guard	4.1	10.9	1.9	8.1	4.1	6.2
Sales index	66	175	31	131	131	100

Table 3 Usage Results (in percent)

	Maritimes	Quebec	Ontario	Manitoba/ Saskatchewan	Alberta	British Columbia
Respondents aware of Guard	20%	58%	28%	30%	32%	16%
Respondents ever trying Guard	3	18	2	8	6	4

Alan has also discovered that bar soap competition is especially intense in Ontario. It is Canada's largest market, and many competitors want a share of it. The chain stores are also quite aggressive in promotion and pricing—offering specials, in-store coupons, and so on. They want to move goods. And because of this, two key Ontario chains have put Guard on their pending delisting sheets. These chains, which control about half the grocery volume in Ontario, are dissatisfied with how slowly Guard is moving off the shelves.

Now Alan feels he is ready to set a key part of the brand's marketing plan for next year: how to allocate the advertising/sales promotion budget by region.

Guard's present advertising/sales promotion budget is 20 percent of sales. With forecast sales of $4 million, this would amount to an $800,000 expenditure. Traditionally such funds have been allocated in proportion to population (see Table 4).

Alan feels he should spend more heavily in Ontario where the grocery chain delisting problem exists. Last year, 36 percent of Guard's budget was allocated to Ontario, which accounted for only 12 percent of Guard's sales. Alan wants to increase Ontario spending to 48 percent of the total budget by taking funds evenly from all other areas. Alan expects this will increase business in the key Ontario market, which has over a third of Canada's population, because it is a big increase and will help Guard "outshout" the many other competitors who are promoting heavily.

Alan presented this idea to Wendy, his newly appointed group product manager. Wendy strongly disagrees. She has also been reviewing Guard's business and feels that promotion funds have historically been misallocated. It is her strong belief that, to use her words, "A brand should spend where its business is." Wendy believes that the first priority in allocating funds regionally is to support the areas of strength. She suggested to Alan that there may be more business to be had in the brand's strong areas, Quebec and the Prairies, than in chasing sales in Ontario. The needs and attitudes toward Guard, as well as competitive pressures, may vary a lot among the provinces. Therefore, Wendy suggested that spending for Guard in the coming year be proportional to the brand's sales by region rather than to regional population.

Alan is convinced this is wrong, particularly in light of the Ontario situation. He asked Wendy how the Ontario market should be handled. Wendy said that the conservative way to build business in Ontario is to invest incremental promotion funds. However, before these incremental funds are invested, a test of this Ontario investment proposition should be conducted. Wendy recommended that some of the Ontario money should be used to conduct an investment-spending market test in a small area or town in Ontario for 12 months. This will enable Alan to see if the incremental spending results in higher sales and profits—profits large enough to justify higher spending. In other words, an investment payout should be assured before spending any extra money in Ontario. Similarly, Wendy would do the same kind of test in Quebec—to see if more money should go there.

After several e-mails back and forth, Alan feels this approach would be a waste of time and unduly cautious, given the importance of the Ontario market and the likely delistings in two key chains.

Evaluate the present strategy for Guard and Alan's and Wendy's proposed strategies. How should the promotion money be allocated? Should investment-spending market tests be run first? Why? Explain.

Table 4 Allocation of Advertising/Sales Promotion Budget, by Population

	Maritimes	Quebec	Ontario	Manitoba/ Saskatchewan	Alberta	British Columbia	Canada
Percent of population	10%	27%	36%	8%	8%	11%	100%
Possible allocation of budget based on population (in 000s)	$80	$216	$288	$64	$64	$88	$800
Percent of Guard business at present	7%	51%	12%	11%	11%	8%	100%

33. Collins & Sullivan

The partners of Collins & Sullivan are having a serious discussion about what the firm should do in the near future.

Collins & Sullivan (CS) is a medium-size regional certified public accounting firm based in Grand Rapids, Michigan, with branch offices in Lansing and Detroit. Collins & Sullivan has nine partners and a professional staff of approximately 105 accountants. Gross service billings for the fiscal year ending June 30, 2006, were $6.9 million. Financial data for 2006, 2005, and 2004 are presented in Table 1.

CS' professional services include auditing, tax preparation, bookkeeping, and some general management consulting. Its client base includes municipal governments (cities, villages, and townships), manufacturing companies, professional organizations (attorneys, doctors, and dentists), and various other small businesses. A good share of revenue comes from the firm's municipal practice. Table 1 gives CS' gross revenue by service area and client industry for 2006, 2005, and 2004.

At the monthly partners' meeting held in July 2006, Alex Collins, the firm's managing partner (CEO), expressed concern about the future of the firm's municipal practice. Collins' presentation to his partners appears below:

> Although our firm is considered to be a leader in municipal auditing in our geographic area, I am concerned that as municipals attempt to cut their operating costs, they will solicit competitive bids from other public accounting firms to perform their annual audits. Three of the four largest accounting firms in the world have local offices in our area. Because they concentrate their practice in the manufacturing industry—which typically has December 31 fiscal year-ends—they have "available" staff during the summer months.

> Therefore, they can afford to low-ball competitive bids to keep their staffs busy and benefit from on-the-job training provided by municipal clientele. I am concerned that we may begin to lose clients in our most established and profitable practice area.*

Amy Sullivan, a senior partner in the firm and the partner in charge of the firm's municipal practice, was the first to respond to Alex Collins' concern.

> Alex, we all recognize the potential threat of being underbid for our municipal work by our large accounting competitors. However, CS is a leader in municipal auditing in Michigan, and we have much more local experience than our competitors. Furthermore, it is a fact that we offer a superior level of service to our clients—which goes beyond the services normally expected during an audit to include consulting on financial and other operating issues. Many of our less sophisticated clients depend on our nonaudit consulting assistance. Therefore, I believe, we have been successful in differentiating our services from our competitors. In many recent situations, CS was selected over a field of as many as 10 competitors even though our proposed prices were much higher than those of our competitors.

The partners at the meeting agreed with Amy Sullivan's comments. However, even though CS had many success stories regarding their ability to retain their municipal clients—despite being underbid—they had lost three large municipal clients during the past year. Amy Sullivan was asked to

---

*Organizations with December fiscal year-ends require audit work to be performed during the fall and in January and February. Those with June 30 fiscal year-ends require auditing during the summer months.

Table 1 Fiscal Year Ending June 30

	2006	2005	2004
Gross billings	$6,900,000	$6,400,000	$5,800,000
Gross billings by service area:			
Auditing	3,100,000	3,200,000	2,750,000
Tax preparation	1,990,000	1,830,000	1,780,000
Bookkeeping	1,090,000	745,000	660,000
Other	720,000	625,000	610,000
Gross billings by client industry:			
Municipal	3,214,000	3,300,000	2,908,000
Manufacturing	2,089,000	1,880,000	1,706,000
Professional	1,355,000	1,140,000	1,108,000
Other	242,000	80,000	78,000

comment on the loss of those clients. She explained that the lost clients are larger municipalities with a lot of in-house financial expertise and therefore less dependent on CS' consulting assistance. As a result, CS' service differentiation went largely unnoticed. Amy explained that the larger, more sophisticated municipals regard audits as a necessary evil and usually select the low-cost reputable bidder.

Alex Collins then requested ideas and discussion from the other partners at the meeting. One partner, Zack Denver, suggested that CS should protect itself by diversifying. Specifically, he felt a substantial practice development effort should be directed toward manufacturing. He reasoned that since manufacturing work would occur during CS' off-season, CS could afford to price very low to gain new manufacturing clients. This strategy would also help to counter (and possibly discourage) low-ball pricing for municipals by the three large accounting firms mentioned earlier.

Another partner, Bob LaMott, suggested that "if we have consulting skills, we ought to promote them more, instead of hoping that the clients will notice and come to appreciate us. Further, maybe we ought to be more aggressive in calling on smaller potential clients."

Another partner, Will Ruiz, agreed with LaMott, but wanted to go further. He suggested that they recognize that there are at least two types of municipal customers and that two (at least) different strategies be implemented, including lower prices for auditing only for larger municipal customers and/or higher prices for smaller customers who are buying consulting too. This caused a big uproar from some who said this would lead to price-cutting of professional services and CS didn't want to be price cutters: "One price for all is the professional way."

However, another partner, Megan Cullen, agreed with Will Ruiz and suggested they go even further—pricing consulting services separately. In fact, she suggested that the partners consider setting up a separate department for consulting—like the large accounting firms have done. This can be very profitable business. But it is a different kind of business and eventually may require different kinds of people and a different organization. For now, however, it may be desirable to appoint a manager for consulting services—with a budget—to be sure it gets proper attention. This suggestion too caused serious disagreement. Partners pointed out that having a separate consulting arm had led to major conflicts, especially in some larger accounting firms. The initial problems were internal. The consultants often brought in more profit than the auditors, but the auditors controlled the partnership and the successful consultants didn't always feel that they got their share of the rewards. But there had also been serious external problems and charges of unethical behavior based on the concern that big accounting firms had a conflict of interest when they did audits on publicly traded companies that they in turn relied on for consulting income. Because of problems in this area, the Securities Exchange Commission created new guidelines that have changed how the big four accounting firms handle consulting. On the other hand, several partners argued that this was really an opportunity for CS because their firm handled very few companies listed with the SEC, and the conflict of interest issues didn't even apply with municipal clients.

Alex Collins thanked everyone for their comments and encouraged them to debate these issues in smaller groups and to share ideas by e-mail before coming to a one-day retreat (in two weeks) to continue this discussion and come to some conclusions.

Evaluate CS' situation. What strategy(ies) should the partners select? Why?

34. Alumco Worldwide*

Matt Garrity, newly hired VP of marketing for Alumco Worldwide, is reviewing the firm's international distribution arrangements because they don't seem to be very well thought out. He is not sure if anything is wrong, but he feels that the company should follow a global strategy rather than continuing its current policies.

Alumco based in Atlanta, Georgia, produces finished aluminum products, such as aluminum ladders, umbrella-type clothes racks, scaffolding, and patio tables and chairs that fold flat. Sales in 2006 reached $25 million, primarily to U.S. customers.

In 2002, Alumco decided to try selling in select foreign markets. The sales manager, Amber Moss, believed the growing affluence of European workers would help the company's products gain market acceptance quickly.

Amber's first step in investigating foreign markets was to join a trade mission to Europe, a tour organized by the U.S. Department of Commerce. This trade mission visited Italy, Germany, Denmark, Holland, France, and England. During this trip,

*Adapted from a case written by Professor Hardy, University of Western Ontario, Canada.

Amber was officially introduced to leading buyers for department store chains, import houses, wholesalers, and buying groups. The two-week trip convinced Amber that there was ample buying power to make exporting a profitable opportunity.

On her return to Atlanta, Amber's next step was to obtain credit references for the firms she considered potential distributors. To those who were judged creditworthy, she sent letters expressing interest and samples, brochures, prices, and other relevant information.

The first orders were from a French wholesaler. Sales in this market totaled $70,000 in 2003. Similar success was achieved in Germany and England. Italy, on the other hand, did not produce any sales. Amber felt the semiluxury nature of the company's products and the lower incomes in Italy encouraged a "making do" attitude rather than purchase of goods and services that would make life easier.

In the United States, Alumco distributes through fairly aggressive and well-organized merchant hardware distributors and buying groups, such as cooperative and voluntary hardware chains, which have taken over much of the strategy planning for cooperating producers and retailers. In its foreign markets, however, there is no recognizable pattern. Channel systems vary from country to country. To avoid channel conflict, Alumco has only one account in each country. The chosen distributor is the exclusive distributor.

In France, Alumco distributes through a wholesaler based in Paris. This wholesaler has five salespeople covering the country. The firm specializes in small housewares and has contacts with leading buying groups, wholesalers, and department stores. Amber is impressed with the firm's aggressiveness and knowledge of merchandising techniques.

In Germany, Alumco sells to a Hamburg-based buying group for hardware wholesalers throughout the country. Amber felt this group would provide excellent coverage of the market because of its extensive distribution network.

In Denmark, Alumco's line is sold to a buying group representing a chain of hardware retailers. This group recently expanded to include retailers in Sweden, Finland, and Norway. Together this group purchases goods for about 500 hardware retailers. The buying power of Scandinavians is quite high, and it is expected that Alumco's products will prove very successful there.

In the United Kingdom, Alumco uses an importer-distributor, who both buys on his own account and acts as a sales agent. This firm sells to department stores and hardware wholesalers. This firm has not done very well overall, but it has done very well with Alumco's line of patio tables and chairs.

Australia is handled by an importer who operates a chain of discount houses. It heard about Alumco from a United Kingdom contact. After extensive e-mailing, this firm discovered it could land aluminum patio furniture in Melbourne at prices competitive with Chinese imports. So it started ordering because it wanted to cut prices in a high-priced garden furniture market.

The Argentina market is handled by an American who lives in Buenos Aires but came to the United States in search of new lines. Alumco attributes success in Argentina to the efforts of this aggressive and capable agent. He has built a sizable trade in aluminum ladders.

In Trinidad and Jamaica, Alumco's products are handled by traders who carry such diversified lines as insurance, apples, plums, and fish. They have been successful in selling aluminum ladders. This business grew out of inquiries sent to the U.S. Department of Commerce and in researching its website (www.commerce.gov), which Amber Moss followed up by phone.

Amber Moss's export policies for Alumco are as follows:

1. *Product:* No product modifications will be made in selling to foreign customers. This may be considered later after a substantial sales volume develops.

2. *Place:* New distributors will be contacted through foreign trade shows. Amber Moss considers large distributors desirable. She feels, however, that they are not as receptive as smaller distributors to a new, unestablished product line. Therefore, she prefers to appoint small distributors. Larger distributors may be appointed after the company has gained a strong consumer franchise in a country.

3. *Promotion:* The firm does no advertising in foreign markets. Brochures and sales literature already being used in the United States are supplied to foreign distributors, who are encouraged to adapt them or create new materials as required. Alumco will continue to promote its products by participating in overseas trade shows. These are handled by the sales manager. All inquiries are forwarded to the firm's distributor in that country.

4. *Price:* The company does not publish suggested list prices. Distributors add their own markup to their landed costs. Supply prices will be kept as low as possible. This is accomplished by (a) removing advertising expenses and other strictly domestic overhead charges from price calculations, (b) finding the most economical packages for shipping (smallest volume per unit), and (c) bargaining with carriers to obtain the lowest shipping rates possible.

5. *Financing:* Alumco sees no need to provide financial help to distributors. The company views its major contribution as providing good products at the lowest possible prices.

6. *Marketing and planning assistance:* Amber Moss feels that foreign distributors know their own markets best. Therefore, they are best equipped to plan for themselves.

7. *Selection of foreign markets:* The evaluation of foreign market opportunities for the company's products is based primarily on discretionary income and lifestyle patterns. For example, Amber fails to see any market in North Africa for Alumco's products, which she thinks are of a semiluxury nature. She thinks that cheaper products such as wood ladders (often homemade) are preferred to prefabricated aluminum ladders in regions such as North Africa and Southern Europe. Argentina, on the other hand, she thinks is a more highly industrialized market with luxury tastes. Thus, Amber sees Alumco's products as better suited for more highly industrialized and affluent societies.

Evaluate Alumco's present foreign markets strategies. Should it develop a global strategy? What strategy or strategies should Matt Garrity (the new VP of marketing) develop? Explain.

35. Pepe's Pizza

Angelina Cello, manager of the Pepe's Pizza store in Flint, Michigan, is trying to develop a plan for the "sick" store she just took over.

Pepe's Pizza is an owner-managed pizza take-out and delivery business with three stores located in Ann Arbor, Southfield, and Flint, Michigan. Pepe's business comes from telephone, fax, or walk-in orders. Each Pepe's store prepares its own pizzas. In addition to pizzas, Pepe's also sells and delivers a limited selection of soft drinks.

Pepe's Ann Arbor store has been very successful. Much of the store's success may be due to being close to the University of Michigan campus. Most of these students live within five miles of Pepe's Ann Arbor store.

The Southfield store has been moderately successful. It serves mostly residential customers in the Southfield area, a largely residential suburb of Detroit. Recently, the store advertised—using direct-mail flyers—to several office buildings within three miles of the store. The flyers described Pepe's willingness and ability to cater large orders for office parties, business luncheons, and so on. The promotion was quite successful. With this new program and Pepe's solid residential base of customers in Southfield, improved profitability at the Southfield location seems assured.

Pepe's Flint location has had mixed results during the last three years. The Flint store has been obtaining only about half of its orders from residential delivery requests. The Flint store's new manager, Angelina Cello, believes the problem with residential pizza delivery in Flint is due to the location of residential neighborhoods in the area. Flint has several large industrial plants (mostly auto industry related) located throughout the city. Small, mostly factory-worker neighborhoods are distributed in between the various plant sites. As a result, Pepe's store location can serve only two or three of these neighborhoods on one delivery run. Competition is also relevant. Pepe's has several aggressive competitors who advertise heavily, distribute cents-off coupons, and offer 2-for-1 deals. This aggressive competition is probably why Pepe's residential sales leveled off in the last year or so. And this competitive pressure seems likely to continue as some of this competition comes from aggressive national chains that are fighting for market share and squeezing little firms like Pepe's. For now, anyway, Angelina feels she knows how to meet this competition and hold on to the present residential sales level.

Most of the Flint store's upside potential seems to be in serving the large industrial plants. Many of these plants work two or three shifts, five days a week. During each work shift, workers are allowed one half-hour lunch break—which usually occurs at 11 AM, 8 PM, or 2:30 AM, depending on the shift.

Generally, a customer will phone or fax from a plant about 30 minutes before a scheduled lunch break and order several (5 to 10) pizzas for a work group. Pepe's may receive many orders of this size from the same plant (i.e., from different groups of workers). The plant business is very profitable for several reasons. First, a large number of pizzas can be delivered at the same time to the same location, saving transportation costs.

Second, plant orders usually involve many different toppings (double cheese, pepperoni, mushrooms, hamburger) on each pizza. This results in $11 to $14 revenue per pizza. The delivery drivers also like delivering plant orders because the tips are usually $1 to $2 per pizza.

Despite the profitability of the plant orders, several factors make it difficult to serve the plant market. Pepe's store is located 5 to 8 minutes from most of the plant sites, so Pepe's staff must prepare the orders within 20 to 25 minutes after it receives the telephone order. Often, inadequate staff and/or oven capacity means it is impossible to get all the orders heated at the same time.

Generally, plant workers will wait as long as 10 minutes past the start of their lunch break before ordering from various vending trucks that arrive at the plant sites during lunch breaks. (Currently, no other pizza delivery stores are in good positions to serve the plant locations and have chosen not to compete.) But there have been a few instances when workers refused to pay for pizzas that were only five minutes late! Worse yet, if the same work group gets a couple of late orders, they are lost as future customers. Angelina Cello believes that the inconsistent profitability of the Flint store is partly the result of such lost customers.

In an effort to rebuild the plant delivery business, Angelina is considering various methods to ensure prompt customer delivery. She thinks that potential demand during lunch breaks is significantly above Pepe's present capacity. Angelina also knows that if she tries to satisfy all phone or fax orders on some peak days, she won't be able to provide prompt service and may lose more plant customers.

Angelina has outlined three alternatives that may win back some of the plant business for the Flint store. She has developed these alternatives to discuss with Pepe's owner. Each alternative is briefly described below:

Alternative 1: Determine practical capacities during peak volume periods using existing equipment and personnel. Accept orders only up to that capacity and politely decline

Table 1 Practical Capacities and Sales Potential of Current Equipment and Personnel

	11 AM Break	8 PM Break	2:30 AM Break	Daily Totals
Current capacity (pizzas)	48	48	48	144
Average selling price per unit	$ 12.50	$ 12.50	$ 12.50	$ 12.50
Sales potential	$600	$600	$600	$1,800
Variable cost (approximately 40 percent of selling price)*	240	240	240	720
Contribution margin of pizzas	360	360	360	1,080
Beverage sales (2 medium-sized beverages per pizza ordered at 75¢ a piece)†	72	72	72	216
Cost of beverages (30% per beverage)	22	22	22	66
Contribution margin of beverages	50	50	50	150
Total contribution of pizza and beverages	$ 410	$ 410	$ 410	$ 1,230

*The variable cost estimate of 40% of sales includes variable costs of delivery to plant locations.
† Amounts shown are not physical capacities (there is almost unlimited physical capacity), but potential sales volume is constrained by number of pizzas that can be sold.

Table 2 Capacity and Demand for Plant Customer Market

	Estimated Daily Demand	Current Daily Capacity	Proposed Daily Capacity
Pizza units (1 pizza)	320	144	300

orders beyond. This approach will ensure prompt customer service and high product quality. It will also minimize losses resulting from customers' rejection of late deliveries. Financial analysis of this alternative—shown in Table 1—indicates that a potential daily contribution to profit of $1,230 could result if this alternative is implemented successfully. This would be profit before promotion costs, overhead, and net profit (or loss). Note: Any alternative will require several thousand dollars to reinform potential plant customers that Pepe's has improved its service and "wants your business."

Alternative 2: Buy additional equipment (one oven and one delivery car) and hire additional staff to handle peak loads. This approach would ensure timely customer delivery and high product quality as well as provide additional capacity to handle unmet demand. Table 2 is a conservative estimate of potential daily demand for plant orders compared to current capacity and proposed increased capacity. Table 3 gives the cost of acquiring the additional equipment and relevant information related to depreciation and fixed costs.

Using this alternative, the following additional pizza delivery and preparation personnel costs would be required:

	Hours Required	Cost per Hour	Total Additional Cost
Delivery personnel	6	6	$36.00
Preparation personnel	8	6	48.00
			$84.00

The addition of even more equipment and personnel to handle all unmet demand was not considered in this alternative because the current store is not large enough.

Alternative 3: Add additional equipment and personnel as described in alternative 2, but move to a new location that would reduce delivery lead times to two to five minutes. This move would probably allow Pepe's to handle all unmet demand—because the reduction in delivery time will provide for additional oven time. In fact, Pepe's might have excess capacity using this approach.

A suitable store is available near about the same number of residential customers (including many of the store's current residential customers). The available store is slightly larger than needed. And the rent is higher. Relevant cost information on the proposed store appears next:

Additional rental expense of proposed store over current store	$1,600 per year
Cost of moving to new store (one-time cost)	$16,000

Angelina Cello presented the three alternatives to Pepe's owner, Pepe Mandoso. Pepe was pleased that Angelina had done her homework. He decided that Angelina should make the final decision on what to do (in part because she had a profit-sharing agreement with Pepe) and offered the following comments and concerns:

1. Pepe agreed that the plant market was extremely sensitive to delivery timing. Product quality and pricing, although important, were of less importance.
2. He agreed that plant demand estimates were conservative. "In fact, they may be 10 to 30 percent low."
3. Pepe expressed concern that under alternative 2, and especially under alternative 3, much of the store's capacity would go unused over 80 percent of the time.
4. He was also concerned that Pepe's store had a bad reputation with plant customers because the prior store manager was not sensitive to timely plant delivery. So Pepe suggested that Angelina develop a promotion plan to improve Pepe's reputation in the plants and be sure that everyone knows that Pepe's has improved its delivery service.

Evaluate Angelina's possible strategies for the Flint store's plant market. What should Angelina do? Why? Suggest possible promotion plans for your preferred strategy.

Table 3 Cost of Required Additional Assets

	Cost	Estimated Useful Life	Salvage Value	Annual Depreciation*	Daily Depreciation[†]
Delivery car (equipped with pizza warmer)	$11,000	5 years	$1,000	$2,000	$5.71
Pizza oven	$20,000	8 years	$2,000	$2,250	$6.43

*Annual depreciation is calculated on a straight-line basis.
[†]Daily depreciation assumes a 350-day (plant production) year. All variable expenses related to each piece of equipment (e.g., utilities, gas, oil) are included in the variable cost of a pizza.

Computer-Aided Problems

Guide to the Use of Computer-Aided Problems

Computer-Aided Problem Solving

Marketing managers are problem solvers who must make many decisions. Solving problems and making good decisions usually involve analysis of marketing information. Such information is often expressed in numbers—like costs, revenues, prices, and number of customers or salespeople. Most marketing managers use a computer to keep track of the numbers and speed through calculations. The computer can also make it easier to look at a problem from many different angles—for example, to see how a change in the sales forecast might impact expected sales revenue, costs, and profit.

The computer can only take a manager so far. The manager is the one who puts it all together—and it still takes skill to decide what the information means. The computer-aided problems at the end of the chapters in this text were developed by the authors to help you develop this skill. To work on the problems, you use the computer-aided problem (CAP) software that is included on the *Student CD-ROM to Accompany Essentials of Marketing* shrinkwrapped with this text.

The problems are short descriptions of decisions faced by marketing managers. Each description includes information to help make the decision. With each problem there are several questions for you to answer. Further, the *Learning Aid for Use with Essentials of Marketing* includes additional questions related to each problem.

Although you will use the computer program to do an analysis, most problems ask you to indicate what decision you would make and why. Thus, in these problems—as in the marketing manager's job—the computer is just a tool to help you make better decisions.

Each problem focuses on one or more of the marketing decision areas discussed in the corresponding chapter. The earlier problems require less marketing knowledge and are simpler in terms of the analysis involved. The later problems build on the principles already covered in the text. The problems can be used in many ways. And the same problem can be analyzed several times for different purposes. Although it is not necessary to do all of the problems or to do them in a particular order, you will probably want to start with the first problem. This practice problem is simpler than the others. In fact, you could do the calculations quite easily without a computer. But this problem will help you see how the program works and how it can help you solve the more complicated problems that come later.

Spreadsheet Analysis of Marketing Problems

Marketing managers often use spreadsheet analysis to evaluate their alternatives—and the program for the computer-aided problems does computerized spreadsheet analysis. In spreadsheet analysis, costs, revenue, and other data related to a marketing problem are organized into a data table—a spreadsheet. The spreadsheet analysis allows you to change the value of one or more of the variables in the data table—to see how each change affects the value of other variables. This is possible because the relationships among the variables are already programmed into the computer. You do not need to do any programming. Let's look at an overly simple example.

You are a marketing manager interested in the total revenue that will result from a particular marketing strategy. You are considering selling your product at $10.00 per unit. You expect to sell 100 units. In our CAP analysis, this problem might be shown in a (very simple) spreadsheet that looks like this:

Variable	Value
Selling price	$10.00
Units sold	100
Total revenue	$1,000.00

There is only one basic relationship in this spreadsheet: Total revenue is equal to the selling price multiplied by the number of units sold. If that relationship has been programmed into the computer (as it is in these problems), you can change the selling price or the number of units you expect to sell, and the program will automatically compute the new value for total revenue.

But now you can ask questions like: What if I raise the price to $10.40 and still sell 100 units? What will happen to total revenue? To get the answer, all you have to do is enter the new price in the spreadsheet, and the program will compute the total revenue for you.

You may also want to do many "what-if" analyses—for example, to see how total revenue changes over a range of prices. Spreadsheet analysis allows you to do this quickly and easily. For instance, if you want to see what happens to total revenue as you vary the price between some minimum value (say, $8.00) and a maximum value (say, $12.00), the program will provide the results table for a what-if analysis showing total revenue for 11 different prices in the range from $8.00 to $12.00.

In a problem like this—with easy numbers and a simple relationship between the variables—the spreadsheet does not do that much work for you. You could do it in your head. But with more complicated problems, the spreadsheet makes it very convenient to more carefully analyze different alternatives or situations.

Using the Program

You don't have to know about computers or using a spreadsheet to use the computer-aided problems program. It was designed to be easy to learn and use. The Help button will give you more detailed information if you need it. But it's best to just try things out to see how it works. A mistake won't hurt anything.

You're likely to find that it's quicker and easier to just use the program than it is to read the instructions. So you may want to go ahead and install the CD-ROM on your own computer and try the practice problem now. Check the label on the CD-ROM for instructions about how to install the software. It takes just a few minutes and there's nothing to it.

The Spreadsheet Is Easy to Use

The spreadsheet software is very easy to use and specifically designed for the computer-aided problems. Like the other software on the Student CD-ROM, it follows conventions that are standard to browser programs (like Microsoft Internet Explorer or Netscape Navigator). If you have used a browser to surf the Internet, using this will be the same. Even if you have not used a browser before, using this program will make it easy for you to learn. However, if you want more general information about using Microsoft Windows software, you can review the Help file or tutorial that comes with the Windows operating system.

As with other browser-based programs, you typically use a mouse to move around in the program and select options. When you move the mouse, the cursor (which appears on your screen as an arrow) also moves. If you move the mouse so that the cursor is over one of the options on the screen and quickly press and release the left button on the mouse, the program will perform the action associated with that option. This process of using the mouse to position the cursor and then quickly pressing and releasing the left button is called "clicking" or "selecting." In these instructions, we'll refer to this often. For example, we'll say things like "click the Results button" or "select a problem from the list."

Let's use the first problem to illustrate how the program works.

Start by selecting a problem

When you start the *Essentials of Marketing* CD-ROM software, the first screen displayed is a home page with the title of the book and various options. Click on the label that says CAPs (short for computer-aided problems).

The computer-aided problem page will appear, and you will see a small window in the upper-left corner with the phrase "Choose a problem by clicking on the arrow." When you click the small arrow to the right of that label, a drop-down list of problems will appear. Select the problem you want to work (in this case, select the first one, "Revenue, Cost, and Profit Relationships").

Note: When you first select a problem, be patient while the program loads. It may take a minute or so. Once the program has loaded, calculations are immediate.

Once you select a problem, the problem description window appears. This is simply a convenient reminder of the problem description found in this text. (The assignment questions for each problem are in this book, so it's useful to have your book with you at the computer when you're working on a problem.)

Across the top of the box in which the problem description appears you will see buttons labeled Description, Spreadsheet, Results, Graph, and Calculator. After you've reviewed the problem description, click the Spreadsheet button.

Each spreadsheet consists of one or two columns of numbers. Each column and row is labeled. Look at the row and column labels carefully to see what variable is represented by the value (number) in the spreadsheet. Study the layout of the spreadsheet, and get a feel for how it organizes the information from the problem description. The spreadsheet displays the starting values for the problem. Keep in mind that sometimes the problem description does not provide as much detail about the starting values as is provided in the spreadsheet.

You will see that some of the values in the spreadsheet appear in a highlighted edit box. These are usually values related to the decision variables in the problem you are solving. You can change any value (number) that appears in one of these boxes. When you make a change, the rest of the values (numbers) in that column are recalculated to show how a change in the value of that one variable affects the others. Think about how the numbers relate to each other.

Making changes in values is easy. When the spreadsheet first appears your cursor appears as a free-floating arrow; however, when you pass the cursor over the box for the value that you want to change the cursor changes to the shape of an I-beam. When you click on the value in that box you can change it. Or to move the cursor to a value in a different box, just click on that box.

When you have selected the box with the value (number) you want to change, there are different ways to type in your new number. A good approach is to position the I-beam cursor before the first digit, and while depressing the mouse button drag the cursor across all of the digits in the number. This will highlight the entire number. Then simply type in the new number and the old one will be replaced. Alternatively, you can use other keys to edit the number. For example, you can use the backspace key to erase digits to the left of the I-beam cursor; similarly, you can use the Del key to erase digits to the right of the cursor. Or you can use the arrow keys to move the cursor to the point where you want to change part of a number. Then you just type in your change. You may want to experiment to see which of these editing approaches you like the best.

When you are finished typing the new number, press the Enter key and the other values in the spreadsheet will be recalculated to show the effect of your new value. Similarly, the other numbers will recalculate if you click on a different box after you have entered a number.

When you are typing numbers into the edit boxes, you'll probably find it most convenient to type the numbers and the decimal point with the keys on the main part of the keyboard (rather than those on the cursor control pad). For example, a price of one thousand dollars and 50 cents would be typed as 1000.50 or just 1000.5—using the number keys on the top row of the keyboard and the period key for the decimal point. *Do not type in the dollar sign or the commas to indicate thousands.* Be careful not to type the letters o or l (lowercase L) instead of the numbers 0 or 1.

Typing percent values is a possible point of confusion, since there are different ways to think about a percent. For example, "ten and a half" percent might be represented by 10.5 or .105. To avoid confusion, the program always expects you to enter percents using the first approach, which is the way percents are discussed in the problems. Thus, if you want to enter the value for ten and a half percent you would type 10.5.

To help prevent errors, each problem is programmed with a set of permitted values for each boxed field. After you click on a specific edit box, the range of permitted values is shown in the line at the bottom left corner of the spreadsheet window. It may be useful to explain what we mean by "permitted values." For example, if you accidentally type a letter when the computer program expects a number, the entry will turn red and what you typed will not be accepted. Further, the program won't allow you to enter a new value for a variable that is outside of a permitted range of values.

For example, if you try to type −10.00 as the price of a product, the entry will turn red. (It doesn't make sense to set the price as a negative number!) If you make an error, check what range of values is permitted—and then retype a new number that is in the permitted range, and press the Enter key to recompute the spreadsheet. When you have entered a permitted value, the value will no longer appear in red.

Remember that a value on the spreadsheet stays changed until you change it again. Some of the questions that accompany the problems ask you to evaluate results associated with different sets of values. It's good practice to check that you have entered all the correct values on a spreadsheet before interpreting the results.

In addition to changing values (numbers) on the spreadsheet itself, there are other options on the spreadsheet menu bar. Click the Description button to go back and review the problem description—or you can use the drop-down list again to select another problem. If you click the Results button, a new window will appear that shows the results table for a what-if analysis. We'll discuss what-if analysis after we cover printing.

Adding your comments and printing

After you have done an analysis, you may want to print a copy of your results (especially if you are expected to hand in your answers to the questions that accompany the computer-aided problem). In fact, the print feature gives you the opportunity to type your name and answers right on the sheet that is printed. To use this feature, just click the printer icon while the spreadsheet is displayed with the results you want to print. A new window will open with a printable version of your analysis. You will also see an edit box area where you can type in your comments. Each comment can be up to 500 characters, and that should be plenty of space for you to type your answers to a question. Sometimes you will want to print more than one spreadsheet (each with its own comments) to answer the different questions.

Once you are satisfied with any comments you have added, you are ready to print your results. Of course, to be able to print you will need to have a printer properly hooked up to your computer and configured for Windows. *Before you select the Print button, make sure that the printer is turned on and loaded with paper!*

Results of a what-if analysis

The Results button makes it easy for you to study in more detail the effect of changing the value of a particular variable. It systematically changes the value of one variable (which you select) and displays the effect that variable has on two other variables. You could do the same thing manually at the spreadsheet—by entering a value for a variable, checking the effect on other variables, and then repeating the process over and over again. But the manual approach is time-consuming and requires you to keep track of the results after each change. A what-if analysis does all this very quickly and presents the results table summary; you can also print or graph the results table if you wish.

Now let's take a step-by-step look at how you can get the exact what-if analysis that you want. The first step is to decide what variable (value) you want to vary and what result values you want to see in the results table.

You select the variables for your analysis by simply clicking the circle ("radio button") beside the number of interest. Click the radio button beside the value of the variable in an edit box that you want to vary. The radio button for the selected value is filled in. You can only select one variable to vary at a time. So if you want to vary some other variable, simply click on your new selection.

When you select a value to vary, the program computes a default "suggested" minimum value and maximum value for the range over which that variable may vary. The minimum value is usually 20 percent smaller than the value shown on the spreadsheet, and the maximum value is 20 percent larger. These default values are used as the minimum and maximum values to compute the results table for a what-if analysis (when you click the Results button).

You can also select the two variables that you want to display in the results table of the what-if analysis. Typically, you will want to display the results (computed values) for variables that will be affected by the variable you select to vary. Remember the example we used earlier. If you had specified that price was going to vary, you might want to display total revenue—to see how it changes at different price levels.

You select a variable to display in the same way that you select the variable you are going to vary. Simply click on the radio button beside a number on the spreadsheet that is not in an edit box. Then use this approach to select a second variable to be displayed in the results table. If you change your mind, you can click on the radio button for another variable. When you have completed this step, you will see a solid radio button next to the variable you chose to vary and solid radio buttons next to the two variables that you want to display.

Now you can let the computer take over. On the button bar at the top of the spreadsheet window, click the Results button and the results table for the what-if analysis will appear. Each row in the first column of the results table will show a different value for the variable you wanted to vary.

The minimum value will be in the first row. The maximum value will be in the bottom row. Evenly spaced values between the minimum and maximum will be in the middle rows. The other columns show the calculated results for the values you selected to display. Each column of values is labeled at the top to identify the column and row from the spreadsheet. The row portion of the label is a short version of the label from the spreadsheet. The results are based on the values that were in the spreadsheet when you selected the Results button, except for the value you selected to vary.

After the results table is displayed, you have the option of typing in your own minimum value and maximum value in the edit boxes below the results table. To do that, just use the same approach you used to enter new values in the spreadsheet. When you enter a new minimum or maximum, the results table will be updated based on the new range of values between the minimum and maximum you entered.

At this point you will want to study the results of your analysis. You can also print a copy of the results table by clicking the Print button. The button bar also shows other possibilities. For example, if you select the Spreadsheet button, the spreadsheet will reappear. The radio buttons will still show the values you selected in the previous analysis. From there you can make additional changes in the values in the spreadsheet, check the results table for a new what-if analysis, or select another problem to work. Or you can look at (and print) a graph of values in the results table for the what-if analysis.

Viewing a graph of your results

You can create a graph of values in the results table by clicking the Graph button. The horizontal axis for the graph will be the variable in the first column of the display. The vertical axis on the left side is based on the first variable you selected to display in the results table. The vertical axis on the right side of the graph is for the second variable. There will be a line on the graph that corresponds to each axis.

What to do next

The next section gives additional tips on the program. You will probably want to look through it after you have done some work with the practice problem. For now, however, you're probably tired of reading instructions. So work a problem or two. It's easier and faster to use the program than to read about it. Give it a try, and don't be afraid to experiment. If you have problems, remember that the Help button is available when you need it.

Some Tips on Using the CAP Program

Resetting the spreadsheet to the initial values

The initial spreadsheet for each problem gives the "starting values" for the problem. While working a problem, you will often change one or more of the starting values to a new number. A changed value stays in effect, unless you change it again. This is a handy feature. But after you make several changes, you may not be able to remember the starting values. There is a simple solution—you can click the button to return to the home page, then click the CAPs label again, and reselect the problem you want. The spreadsheet will appear with the original set of starting values.

Checking the computer's calculations

Some values appear in the spreadsheet as whole numbers, and others appear with one or more digits to the right of a decimal point. For example, dollar values usually have two digits to the right of the decimal point, indicating how many cents are involved. A value indicating, say, number of customers, however, will appear as a whole number.

When you are doing arithmetic by hand, or with a calculator, you sometimes have to make decisions about how much detail is necessary. For example, if you divide 13 by 3 the answer is 4.33, 4.333, 4.3333, or perhaps 4.33333, depending on how important it is to be precise. Usually we round off the number to keep things manageable. Similarly, computers usually display results after rounding off the numbers. This has the potential to create confusion and seeming inaccuracy when many calculations are involved. If the computer uses a lot of detail in its calculations and then displays intermediate results after rounding off, the numbers may appear to be inconsistent. To illustrate this, let's extend the example. If you multiply 4.33 times 2640, you get 11431.20. But if you multiply 4.333 by 2640, you get 11439.12. To make it easier for you to check relationships between the values on a spreadsheet, the CAP software does not use a lot of hidden detail in calculations. If it rounds off a number to display it in the spreadsheet, the rounded number is used in subsequent calculations.

It would be easy for the computer to keep track of all of the detail in its calculations—but that would make it harder for you to check the results yourself. If you check the results on a spreadsheet (perhaps with the calculator provided) and find that your numbers are close but do not match exactly, it is probably because you are making different decisions about rounding than were programmed into the spreadsheet.

The software was designed and tested to be easy to use and error free. In fact, it is programmed to help prevent the user from making typing errors. But it is impossible to anticipate every possible combination of numbers you might enter—and some combinations of numbers can cause problems. For example, a certain combination of numbers might result in an instruction for the computer to divide a number by zero, which is a mathematical impossibility. When a problem of this sort occurs, the word ERROR will appear in the spreadsheet (or in the results table for the what-if analysis) instead of a number. If this happens, you should recheck the numbers in the spreadsheet and redo the analysis—to make certain that the numbers you typed in were what you intended. That should straighten out the problem in almost every case. Yet with any computer program there can be a hidden bug that only surfaces in unusual situations or on certain computers. Thus, if you think you have found a bug, we would like to know so that we can track down the source of the difficulty.

Notes

CHAPTER 1

1. For more on Starbucks, see www.starbucks.com; "Starbucks, Yahoo! Make a Match," *Brandweek*, February 20, 2006, p. 23; "Starbucks Calls China Its Top Growth Focus," *Wall Street Journal*, February 14, 2006, p. B4; "A Tall Skinny Latte, a Nice, Comfy Chair and, Now, Kid Tunes," *Wall Street Journal*, February 14, 2006, p. B1ff.; "Starbucks, Kellogg Plot Cereal Killing," *Advertising Age*, February 6, 2006, p. 1ff.; "Starbucks Plans to Make Debut in Movie Business," *Wall Street Journal*, January 12, 2006, p. A1ff.; "Fill 'Er Up—with Latte," *Wall Street Journal*, January 6, 2006, p. A9ff.; "A Special Effort: Starbucks Is Reaching Out to People with Disabilities—Both as Employees and as Customers," *Wall Street Journal*, November 14, 2005, p. R8; "Lattes Lure Brits to Coffee," *Wall Street Journal*, October 20, 2005, p. B1ff.; "This Java Joint Is Jumping," *Brandweek*, October 10, 2005, p. M42ff.; "Starbucks to Offer Cold Drinks in Convenience Stores in Japan," *Wall Street Journal*, September 27, 2005, p. B4; "Brewing the Perfect Concept," *Investor's Business Daily*, September 12, 2005, p. A4; "At Starbucks, a Blend of Coffee and Music Creates a Potent Mix," *Wall Street Journal*, July 19, 2005, p. A1ff.; "Strong Lattes, Sour Notes," *Business Week*, June 20, 2005, pp. 58–60; "Coffee on the Double," *Wall Street Journal*, April 12, 2005, p. B1ff.; "New Bean Counters: Banks Share Space with Coffee Shops," *Wall Street Journal*, March 22, 2005, p. D3; "Starbucks Perking in Music Business as It Expands Its CD-Burning Outlets," *Investor's Business Daily*, February 17, 2005, p. A5; "Innovation Entrepreneurs: A Hot, Steaming Cup of Customer Awareness," *Fortune*, November 15, 2004, p. 192; "Maybe They'll Call It Starbooks," *Business Week*, October 25, 2004, p. 13; "Starbucks: Coffee Giant Aims to Win New Customers with Food, Music, Internet," *Investor's Business Daily*, August 9, 2004, p. A9; "How to Find a Hit as Big as Starbucks," *Business 2.0*, May 2004, pp. 66–68; "You Want It Your Way," *USA Today*, March 5, 2004, p. 1Aff.; "Hot Starbucks to Go," *Fortune*, January 26, 2004, pp. 60–74; "It's a Grande-Latte World," *Wall Street Journal*, December 15, 2003, p. B1ff.; "Starbucks Unwired," *Business Week*, November 10, 2003, pp. A20–A21; "Starbucks Brews Up New Prepaid Card," *USA Today*, October 13, 2003, p. 2B; "Starbucks' Road to China," *Wall Street Journal*, July 14, 2003, p. B1; "In Japan, Adding Beer, Wine to Latte List," *Wall Street Journal*, July 14, 2003, p. B1; "Another Overpriced Coffee Option," *Wall Street Journal*, June 17, 2003, p. D1; "Marketers of the Next Generation," *Brandweek*, April 7, 2003, p. 40; "Planet Starbucks," *Business Week*, September 9, 2002, p. 100; "Starbucks May Indeed Be a Robust Staple," *Wall Street Journal*, July 26, 2002, p. B4; "Starbucks Goes to Europe . . . with Humility and Respect," *Wall Street Journal*, April 9, 2002, p. B16; "The Best Global Brands," *Business Week*, August 6, 2001, p. 56; "Still Perking after All These Years," *Fortune*, May 24, 1999, p. 203; "Starbucks: Making Values Pay," *Fortune*, September 29, 1997, p. 261; "Restaurant Brands Fill Supermarkets," *USA Today*, August 26, 1997, p. 1B.

2. For more on Kellogg's Tiger Power cereal, see "Tony Spinoff Gets Declawed," *Advertising Age*, October 17, 2005, p. 4; "Cheerios Crushes Tony as Kellogg Launch Flops," *Advertising Age*, June 13, 2005; "Kellogg's Pounces on Toddlers: Tiger Power to Wrest Tot Monopoly Away from General Mills' $500M Cheerios Brand," *Advertising Age*, December 6, 2004.

3. Eric H. Shaw, "A Review of Empirical Studies of Aggregate Marketing Costs and Productivity in the United States," *Journal of the Academy of Marketing Science*, Fall, 1990, p. 285; Christopher H. Lovelock and Charles B. Weinberg, *Marketing for Public and Nonprofit Managers* (New York: John Wiley & Sons, 1984).

4. Gregory D. Upah and Richard E. Wokutch, "Assessing Social Impacts of New Products: An Attempt to Operationalize the Macromarketing Concept," *Journal of Public Policy and Marketing* 4 (1985), p. 166.

5. An American Marketing Association committee recently defined marketing as "an organizational function and a set of processes for creating, communicating, and delivering value to customers and for managing customer relationships in ways that benefit the organization and its stakeholders." For a discussion of the AMA's previous definition, see also Ernest F. Cooke, C. L. Abercrombie, and J. Michael Rayburn, "Problems with the AMA's New Definition of Marketing Offer Opportunity to Develop an Even Better Definition," *Marketing Educator*, Spring 1986, p. 1.

6. George Fisk, "Editor's Working Definition of Macromarketing," *Journal of Macromarketing* 2, no. 1 (1982), p. 3; Shelby D. Hunt and John J. Burnett, "The Macromarketing/Micromarketing Dichotomy: A Taxonomical Model," *Journal of Marketing*, Summer 1982, p. 11.

7. William McInnes, "A Conceptual Approach to Marketing," in *Theory in Marketing*, second series, ed. Reavis Cox, Wroe Alderson, and Stanley J. Shapiro (Homewood, IL: Richard D. Irwin, 1964), p. 51.

8. Thorsten Posselt and Eitan Gerstner, "Pre-Sale vs. Post-Sale E-Satisfaction: Impact on Repurchase Intention and Overall Satisfaction," *Journal of Interactive Marketing*, Autumn 2005, p. 35; Fang Wu, Vijay Mahajan, and Sridhar Balasubramanian, "An Analysis of E-Business Adoption and Its Impact on Business Performance," *Journal of the Academy of Marketing Science*, Fall 2003, p. 425; Peter R. Dickson, "Understanding the Trade Winds: The Global Evolution of Production, Consumption, and the Internet," *Journal of Consumer Research*, June 2000, p. 115; Hans H. Bauer, Mark Grether, and Mark Leach, "Building Customer Relations over the Internet," *Industrial Marketing Management*, February 2002, p. 155;

9. Marian Friestad and Peter Wright, "The Next Generation: Research for Twenty-First-Century Public Policy on Children and Advertising," *Journal of Public Policy & Marketing*, Fall 2005, p. 183; Kevin D. Bradford, Gregory T. Gundlach and William L. Wilkie, "Countermarketing in the Courts: The Case of Marketing Channels and Firearms Diversion," *Journal of Public Policy & Marketing*, Fall 2005, p. 284; Gary T. Ford and John E. Calfee, "Food Politics: How the Food Industry Influences Nutrition and Health/The Obesity Myth: Why America's Obsession with Weight Is Hazardous to Your Health/Fat Land: How Americans Became the Fattest People in the World," *Journal of Public Policy & Marketing*, Spring 2005, p. 174; Graham Hooley, Tony Cox, John Fahy, David Shipley et al. "Market Orientation in the Transition Economies of Central Europe: Tests of the Narver and Slater Market Orientation Scales," *Journal of Business Research*, December 2000, p. 273; Saeed Samiee, "Globalization, Privatization, and Free Market Economy," *Journal of the Academy of Marketing Science*, Summer 2001, p. 319; Robert A. Peterson and Ashutosh Prasad, "A General Theory of Competition: Resources, Competencies, Productivity, Economic Growth," *Journal of the Academy of Marketing Science*, Fall 2001, p. 422;

10. "Shakti—Changing Lives in Rural India," http://hll.com/citizen_lever/project_shakti.asp; P. Indu, Komal Chary, and Vivek Gupta, "Reviving Hindustan Lever Limited," ICFAI Center for Management Research, Case Study #306-410-1, 2006; V. Kasturi Rangan and Rhithari Rajan, "Unilever in India: Hindustan Lever's Project Shakti—Marketing FMCG to the Rural Consumer," Harvard Business School, Case #9-505-056, 2006; "Shakti: Growing the Market While Changing Lives in Rural India," Case Weatherhead School of Management Case #000362, 2005; C. K. Prahalad, *The Fortune at the*

Bottom of the Pyramid (Philadelphia: Wharton School Publishing, 2005); "Access to Electricity: White Paper on ABB's Initiative for Access to Electricity," April 2005, www.abb.com; "India—Water Supply and Sanitation: Bridging the Gap between Infrastructure and Service Executive Summary," The World Bank, siteresources.worldbank. org/INTINDIA/Resources/Bridging_the_Gap_Exec_Sum.pdf.

11. Victor V. Cordell, "Effects of Public Policy on Marketing," *Journal of Macromarketing*, Spring 1993, p. 20; James M. Carman and Robert G. Harris, "Public Regulation of Marketing Activity, Part III: A Typology of Regulatory Failures and Implications for Marketing and Public Policy," *Journal of Macromarketing*, Spring 1986, p. 51.

12. Ahmet H. Kirca, Satish Jayachandran and William O. Bearden, "Market Orientation: A Meta-Analytic Review and Assessment of Its Antecedents and Impact on Performance," *Journal of Marketing*, April 2005, p. 24; Ranjay Gulati and James B. Oldroyd, "The Quest for Customer Focus," *Harvard Business Review*, April 2005, p. 92; Dave Webb, Cynthia Webster, and Areti Krepapa, "An Exploration of the Meaning and Outcomes of a Customer-Defined Market Orientation," *Journal of Business Research*, May 2000, p. 101; Jagdish N. Sheth, Rajendra S. Sisodia, and Arun Sharma, "The Antecedents and Consequences of Customer-Centric Marketing," *Journal of the Academy of Marketing Science*, Winter 2000, p. 55; Karen Norman Kennedy, Jerry R. Goolsby, and Eric J. Arnould, "Implementing a Customer Orientation: Extension of Theory and Application," *Journal of Marketing*, October 2003, p. 67; see also Charles R. Weiser, "Championing the Customer," *Harvard Business Review*, November–December 1995, p. 113; Stanley F. Slater and John C. Narver, "Market Orientation and the Learning Organization," *Journal of Marketing*, July 1995, p. 63; R.W. Ruekert, "Developing a Market Orientation: An Organizational Strategy Perspective," *International Journal of Research in Marketing*, August 1992, p. 225; Bernard J. Jaworski and Ajay K. Kohli, "Market Orientation: Antecedents and Consequences," *Journal of Marketing*, July 1993, p. 53; Franklin S. Houston, "The Marketing Concept: What It Is and What It Is Not," *Journal of Marketing*, April 1986, p. 81.

13. For more on the marketing concept in the banking industry, see "The Wal-Mart of Banking," *Advertising Age*, October 3, 2005, p. 3; "Branded ATMs Become Billboards for Banks," *Advertising Age*, August 29, 2005, p. 9; "Now Open: The Bank of VW," *Wall Street Journal*, November 3, 2004, p. D1ff.; "Beyond the Toaster: Banks Step Up Freebies," *Wall Street Journal*, October 14, 2004, p. D1ff.; "Service Charge: As Banks Elbow for Consumers, Washington Mutual Thrives," *Wall Street Journal*, November 6, 2003, p. A1; "Is This Any Way to Run a Bank?" *Business Week*, October 13, 2003, p. 44; "Bank of the Americas," *Fortune*, April 14, 2003, p. 144; "A New Banking Model," *Fortune*, March 31, 2003, p. 102; "Do You Really Need a Bank?" *Wall Street Journal*, July 10, 2002, p. D1; "Why Banks Are Getting Nicer," *Wall Street Journal*, May 29, 2002, p. D1; "A Mini-Mall in Your ATM," *Time*, April 8, 2002, p. 61; "What a Bank Should Be: A Colorado Startup Reinvents Small-Business Lending with Fanatical Service," *Business Week Small Biz*, July 16, 2001, pp. 24–28; "Banks Cozy Up to Customers," *Wall Street Journal*, April 26, 2001, p. B1. For more on the marketing concept and churches, see "The Message: God Is Cool, Ice Cream, Frisbees, and Marketing Get the Word Out," *USA Today*, August 22, 2005, p. 4D; "If You Billed It around Faith, They Will Certainly Come," *USA Today*, July 22, 2005, p. 1Aff.; "Earthly Empires . . . Borrowing from the Business Playbook," *Business Week*, May 23, 2005, pp. 78–88; "What Churches Have in Store," *Wall Street Journal*, December 17, 2004, p. W1ff.; for more on the marketing concept and the academic community, see "Going to College Gets the Hard Sell," *USA Today*, August 31, 2005, p. 5D; "The New U: A Tough Market Is Reshaping Colleges," *Business Week*, December 22, 1997, p. 96; for more on the marketing concept and the dental and medical professions, see "House Calls," *Newsweek*, February 7, 2005, pp. 52–53; "Some Hospital ERs Begin Guaranteeing Quick Service, or Your Room May Be Free," *USA Today*, December 3, 2004, p. 1Aff.; "Drill Down to Customer Concerns," *Investor's Business Daily*, December 15, 2003, p. A9; "Hospital Chic: The ER Gets a Makeover," *Wall Street Journal*, July 8, 2003, p. D1ff.; "Some Hospitals Offer New Service: Helping Patients Complain," *Wall Street Journal*, June 19, 2003, p. D1ff.; "Massaging More than Your Gums," *Wall Street Journal*, September 11, 2002, p. D1; "Grocery List: Milk, Bread, QuickMedx," *USA Today*, January 23, 2001, p. 3B.

14. "Would You Recommend Us?" *Business Week*, January 30, 2006, pp. 94–95; "Pyromarketing: Up in Flames," *Point*, December 2005, pp. 14–18; "Progressive Businesses," *Brandweek*, November 28, 2005, pp. 16–26; "Get Creative! How to Build Innovative Companies," *Business Week*, August 1, 2005, pp. 60–79; "In Search of the Next iPod," *Brandweek*, June 20, 2005, pp. S8–S18; "Cult Brands," *Business Week*, August 2, 2004, pp. 64–67; "Inventing to Order," *Business Week*, July 5, 2004, pp. 84–85; "When the Factory Is a Theme Park," *Business Week*, May 3, 2004, p. 94; "Go for the Outrageous," *Investor's Business Daily*, January 3, 2004, p. A4; "Will Jeff Immelt's New Push Pay Off for GE? Helping Customers Beyond the Call of Duty," *Business Week*, October 13, 2003, pp. 94–96; "Remedies for an Economic Hangover," *Fortune*, June 25, 2001, p. 130; "The Best Little Grocery Store in America," *Inc.*, June 2001, p. 54; "Fanatics!" *Inc.*, April 2001, p. 36; "Why Some Customers Are More Equal than Others," *Fortune*, September 19, 1994, p. 215. See also Youn-Kyung Kim, "Consumer Value: An Application to Mall and Internet Shopping," *International Journal of Retail & Distribution Management*, no. 11 (2002), p. 595; Ronald L. Hess, Jr., Shankar Ganesan, and Noreen M. Klein, "Service Failure and Recovery: The Impact of Relationship Factors on Customer Satisfaction," *Journal of the Academy of Marketing Science*, Spring 2003, p. 127; Mihaly Csikszentmihalyi, "The Costs and Benefits of Consuming," *Journal of Consumer Research*, September 2000, p. 267; Jaishankar Ganesh, Mark J. Arnold, and Kristy E. Reynolds, "Understanding the Customer Base of Service Providers: An Examination of the Differences between Switchers and Stayers," *Journal of Marketing*, July 2000, p. 65; C. B. Bhattacharya and Sankar Sen, "Consumer-Company Identification: A Framework for Understanding Consumers' Relationships with Companies," *Journal of Marketing*, April 2003, p. 76; George S. Day, "Managing Market Relationships," *Journal of the Academy of Marketing Science*, Winter 2000, p. 24; Deepak Sirdeshmukh, Jagdip Singh and Barry Sabol, "Consumer Trust, Value, and Loyalty in Relational Exchanges," *Journal of Marketing*, January 2002, p. 15; Stanley F. Slater and John C. Narver, "Market Orientation, Customer Value, and Superior Performance," *Business Horizons*, March–April 1994, p. 22; Sharon E. Beatty, "Keeping Customers," *Journal of Marketing*, April 1994, p. 124; Thomas W. Gruen, "Relationship Marketing: The Route to Marketing Efficiency and Effectiveness," *Business Horizons*, November–December 1997, p. 32.

15. Wolfgang Ulaga and Andreas Eggert, "Value-Based Differentiation in Business Relationships: Gaining and Sustaining Key Supplier Status," *Journal of Marketing*, January 2006, p. 119; Christian Homburg, Nicole Koschate and Wayne D. Hoyer, "Do Satisfied Customers Really Pay More? A Study of the Relationship between Customer Satisfaction and Willingness to Pay," *Journal of Marketing*, April 2005, p. 84; Karen Norman Kennedy, Jerry R. Goolsby and Eric J. Arnould, "Implementing a Customer Orientation: Extension of Theory and Application," *Journal of Marketing*, October 2003, p. 67; Roger Baxter and Sheelagh Matear, James C. Anderson, James A. Narus, and Wouter van Rossum, "Customer Value Propositions in Business Markets," *Harvard Business Review*, March 2006, p. 90; "Helping Nonprofits Find Hidden Gold," *Business 2.0*, December 2005, p. 40; "Uncle Sam Wants You in the Worst Way," *Business Week*, August 11, 2005, p. 40; "Advertising . . . Nonprofit Organizations Are Going Commercial," *New York Times*, February 20, 2004, p. C4; "When Nonprofits Go after Profits," *Business Week*, June 26, 2000, p. 173; "Modern Marketing Helps Sell Life as a Nun," *Wall Street Journal*, May 11, 1999, p. B1; see also Glenn B. Voss and Zannie Giraud Voss, "Strategic Orientation and Firm Performance in an Artistic Environment," *Journal of Marketing*, January 2000, p. 67; Dennis B. Arnett, Steve D. German, and Shelby D. Hunt, "The

Identity Salience Model of Relationship Marketing Success: The Case of Nonprofit Marketing," *Journal of Marketing*, April 2003, p. 89; "Public Policy, Technology, and Ethics: Marketing Decisions for NASA's Space Shuttle," *Journal of Marketing*, Summer 1984, p. 56.

16. "Companies Try Keeping Ice Cream Frozen, Emissions Down," *Wall Street Journal*, May 4, 2005, p. B1ff.; "The Black Market Vs. the Ozone," *Business Week*, July 7, 1997, p. 128; "CFC-Span: Refrigerant's Reign Nears an End," *USA Today*, August 22, 1994, p. 5B; "Air-Conditioner Firms Put Chill on Plans to Phase Out Use of Chlorofluorocarbons," *Wall Street Journal*, May 10, 1993, p. B1. See also Alan R. Andreasen, "Social Marketing: Its Definition and Domain," *Journal of Public Policy & Marketing*, Spring 1994, p. 108.

17. "Wrestling with Your Conscience," *Time*, November 15, 1999, p. 72; "Wal-Mart Provides Many an Introduction to Sport Shooting," *Wall Street Journal*, April 15, 1999, p. A1; "GreenMountain.com Makes Pitch for Clean Energy," *Wall Street Journal*, May 1, 2000, p. A36; for more on overseas sweatshops, see "Sweatshops: Finally, Airing the Dirty Linen," *Business Week*, June 23, 2003, p. 100.

18. C. B. Bhattacharya and Sankar Sen, "Doing Better at Doing Good: When, Why and How Customers Respond to Corporate Social Initiatives," *California Management Review*, Fall 2004, p. 9; Grahame R. Dowling, "Corporate Reputations: Should You Compete on Yours?" *California Management Review*, Spring 2004, p. 19; Edward J. O'Boyle and Lyndon E. Dawson, Jr., "The American Marketing Association Code of Ethics: Instructions for Marketers," *Journal of Business Ethics*, December 1992, p. 921; Ellen J. Kennedy and Leigh Lawton, "Ethics and Services Marketing," *Journal of Business Ethics*, October 1993, p. 785.

19. Lawrence B. Chonko and Shelby D. Hunt, "Ethics and Marketing Management: A Retrospective and Prospective Commentary," *Journal of Business Research*, December 2000, p. 235; Barry J. Babin, James S. Boles, and Donald P. Robin, "Representing the Perceived Ethical Work Climate among Marketing Employees," *Journal of the Academy of Marketing Science*, Summer 2000, p. 345; Jeffrey G. Blodgett, Long-Chuan Lu, Gregory M. Rose, and Scott J. Vitell, "Ethical Sensitivity to Stakeholder Interests: A Cross-Cultural Comparison," *Journal of the Academy of Marketing Science*, Spring 2001, p. 190; George G. Brenkert, "Ethical Challenges of Social Marketing," *Journal of Public Policy & Marketing*, Spring 2002, p. 14;

20. "Too Much Corporate Power?" *Business Week*, September 11, 2000, p. 144; "Ad Nauseam," *Advertising Age*, July 10, 2000, p. 1; Stephen J. Arnold and Monika Narang Luthra, "Market Entry Effects of Large Format Retailers: A Stakeholder Analysis," *International Journal of Retail & Distribution Management*, (4) 2000, p. 139.

CHAPTER 2

1. See www.cirquedusoleil.com; "Super Pregame Show," MiamiHerald.com, January 10, 2007; "Cirque du Success," *U.S. News and World Report*, November 20, 2006, pp. 83–86; "The Onliness of Strong Brands," BusinessWeek.com, November 16, 2006; "Crazy for 'Delirium,'" *Billboard*, July 15, 2006, p. 22; "The Disney of the New Age," *Maclean's*, June 26, 2006, pp. 22–26; "Cirque du Balancing Act," *Fortune*, June 12, 2006, p. 54; "How Cirque du Soleil Uses Email to Sell Out Shows at Local Cities," MarketingSherpa.com, June 1, 2006; W. Chan Kim and Renée Mauborgne, *Blue Ocean Strategy* (Boston: Harvard Business School Press, 2005); "Join the Circus," *Fast Company*, July 1, 2005, p. 52; "Lord of the Rings," *Economist*, February 5, 2005, p. 61; "Best Launch: Zumanity," *Marketing Magazine*, November 11, 2004, p. 27; "Big Top Television," *Marketing Magazine*, August 9–16, 2004, p. 20; "Mario D'Amico—Cirque du Soleil," *Reveries*, July 2002.

2. Rebecca J. Slotegraaf and Peter R. Dickson, "The Paradox of a Marketing Planning Capability," *Journal of the Academy of Marketing Science*, Fall 2004, p. 371; Kwaku Atuahene-Gima and Janet Y. Murray, "Antecedents and Outcomes of Marketing Strategy Comprehensiveness," *Journal of Marketing*, October 2004, p. 33; Gail J. McGovern,

David Court, John A. Quelch and Blair Crawford, "Bringing Customers into the Boardroom," *Harvard Business Review*, November 2004, p. 70; Charles H. Noble, Rajiv K. Sinha, and Ajith Kumar, "Market Orientation and Alternative Strategic Orientations: A Longitudinal Assessment of Performance Implications," *Journal of Marketing*, October 2002, p. 25; Mary Anne Raymond and Hiram C. Barksdale, "Corporate Strategic Planning and Corporate Marketing: Toward an Interface," *Business Horizons*, September/October, 1989, p. 41; George S. Day, "Marketing's Contribution to the Strategy Dialogue," *Journal of the Academy of Marketing Science*, Fall 1992, p. 323; P. Rajan Varadarajan and Terry Clark, "Delineating the Scope of Corporate, Business, and Marketing Strategy," *Journal of Business Research*, October–November 1994, p. 93.

3. See www.learningco.com; "Broderbund: Identify a Need, Turn a Profit," *Fortune*, November 30, 1992, p. 78.

4. "Whole Foods Market on Growth Spurt," *Wall Street Journal*, December 14, 2005, p. B11A; "Pricier Gourmet Sodas Grab Attention," *Wall Street Journal*, December 8, 2005, p. B9A; "Eating Too Fast at Whole Foods," *Business Week*, October 24, 2005, pp. 82–84; "Marketers of the Year 2005: John Mackey; For Shoppers, It's Love," *Brandweek*, "Zigging while Wal-Mart Zags," *Investor's Business Daily*, June 20, 2005, p. A20; "Metropolitan Magnet," *Wall Street Journal*, May 11, 2005, p. B1ff.; "A Whole New Ballgame in Grocery Shopping," *USA Today*, March 9, 2005, p. 1Bff.; "Whole Foods Transcends Grocery Shopping Experience," *DSN Retailing Today*, June 7, 2004, p. 17; "No Preservatives, No Unions, Lots of Dough," *Fortune*, September 15, 2003, pp. 127–30; "Health-Food Chains Spar for Baby-Boomers," *Fortune*, April 3, 2000, pp. 56–57; "Peace, Love, and the Bottom Line," *Business Week*, December 7, 1998, pp. 79–87.

5. Rajkumar Venkatesan and V. Kumar, "A Customer Lifetime Value Framework for Customer Selection and Resource Allocation Strategy," *Journal of Marketing*, October 2004, p. 106; Edward C. Malthouse and Robert C. Blattberg, "Can We Predict Customer Lifetime Value?," *Journal of Interactive Marketing*, Winter 2004, p. 2; "The 5 Lessons of 2004," *Business 2.0*, December 2004, pp. 121–26; "What Customers Want," *Fortune*, July 7, 2003, p. 122; "The Unprofitable Customers," *Wall Street Journal Reports*, October 28, 2002, p. R7; "Will This Customer Sink Your Stock?" *Fortune*, September 30, 2002, p. 126; "Keep 'Em Coming Back," *Business Week E. Biz*, May 15, 2000, p. EB20; "Marketers Put a Price on Your Life," *USA Today*, July 7, 1999, p. 3B. See also Heinz K. Stahl, Kurt Matzler, and Hans H. Hinterhuber, "Linking Customer Lifetime Value with Shareholder Value," *Industrial Marketing Management*, May 2003, p. 267; Valarie A. Zeithaml, "Service Quality, Profitability, and the Economic Worth of Customers: What We Know and What We Need to Learn," *Journal of the Academy of Marketing Science*, Winter 2000, p. 67; Dipak Jain and Siddhartha S. Singh, "Customer Lifetime Value Research in Marketing: A Review and Future Directions," *Journal of Interactive Marketing*, Spring 2002, p. 34; Charlotte H. Mason, "Tuscan Lifestyles: Assessing Customer Lifetime Value," *Journal of Interactive Marketing*, Autumn 2003, p. 54; Vikas Mittal, "Driving Customer Equity: How Customer Lifetime Value Is Reshaping Corporate Strategy," *Journal of Marketing*, April 2001, p. 107;

6. For information on Silverman's new business, see www.preschoolians.com. For more on Toddler University see "Genesco Names New Executive of Children's Footwear Division," press release, Genesco, July 15, 1994; "Toddler University Ends Up in Westport," *Westport News*, March 8, 1991, p. A13; "Whiz Kid," *Connecticut*, August 1989, p. 56; "The Young and the Restless," *Children's Business*, May 1989, p. 29.

7. Orville C. Walker, Jr., and Robert W. Ruekert, "Marketing's Role in the Implementation of Business Strategies: A Critical Review and Conceptual Framework," *Journal of Marketing*, July 1987, p. 15; Thomas V. Bonoma, "A Model of Marketing Implementation," *1984 AMA Educators' Proceedings* (Chicago: American Marketing Association, 1984), p. 185; Kevin Romer and Doris C. Van Doren, "Implementing Marketing in a High-Tech Business," *Industrial Marketing Management*, August 1993, p. 177.

8. Roland T. Rust, Katherine N. Lemon, and Valarie A. Zeithaml, "Return on Marketing: Using Customer Equity to Focus Marketing Strategy," *Journal of Marketing*, January 2004, p. 109; Jacquelyn S. Thomas, Werner Reinartz, and V. Kumar, "Getting the Most Out of All Your Customers," *Harvard Business Review*, July 2004, p. 116; Michael D. Johnson, Andreas Herrmann, and Frank Huber, "The Evolution of Loyalty Intentions," *Journal of Marketing*, April 2006, p. 122; Peter C. Verhoef, "Understanding the Effect of Customer Relationship Management Efforts on Customer Retention and Customer Share Development," *Journal of Marketing*, October 2003, p. 30; Roland T. Rust, Valarie A. Zeithaml, and Katherine N. Lemon, "Customer-Centered Brand Management," *Harvard Business Review*, September 2004, p. 110.

9. "The Times They Are a-Changing," *Wall Street Journal*, January 18, 2006, p. D1ff.; "Watches Shift into Automatic," *Wall Street Journal*, November 12, 2005, p. P8; "The Clock Is Ticking for Aging Timex," *Advertising Age*, October 17, 2005, p. 6; "Timex Seeks New Faces to Capture 18-34 Range," *DM News*, September 19, 2005, pp. 12–13; "A Workout Pro Close at Hand," *Business Week*, August 15, 2005, pp. 89–90; Microsoft's Latest, Strapped to a Wrist," *New York Times*, January 8, 2004, p. E1ff.; "It's Comeback Time for Luxury Watches," *New York Times*, January 6, 2004, p. C1ff.; " "Now, Even Your Watch Can Help You Carry Your Computer Files," *Wall Street Journal*, September 25, 2003, p. B1; "Bill Has Designs on Your Wrist," *Business Week*, January 20, 2003, p. 68; "Timex Pursues Hip, Younger Set in Ads for Its New iControl Watch," *Wall Street Journal*, May 19, 2000, p. B2; "Swatch: Ready for Net Time," *Business Week*, February 14, 2000, p. 61; "Indiglo Watch Lights Up Better Times for Timex," *Brandweek*, April 25, 1994, p. 30.

10. George S. Day and Robin Wensley, "Assessing Advantage: A Framework for Diagnosing Competitive Superiority," *Journal of Marketing*, April 1988, p. 1; Michael E. Porter, *Competitive Advantage—Creating and Sustaining Superior Performance* (New York: Free Press, MacMillan, 1986); Mark B. Houston, "Competing for the Future: Breakthrough Strategies for Seizing Control of Your Industry and Creating the Markets of Tomorrow," *Journal of the Academy of Marketing Science*, Winter 1996, p. 77; Kevin P. Coyne, "Sustainable Competitive Advantage—What It Is, What It Isn't," *Business Horizons*, January/February 1986, p. 54.

11. See www.soapworks.com; "Taking On Procter & Gamble," *Inc.*, October 2000, p. 66.

12. Stephen J. Arnold, "Lessons Learned from the World's Best Retailers," *International Journal of Retail & Distribution Management*, no. 11 (2002), p. 562; Ashesh Mukherjee and Wayne D. Hoyer, "The Effect of Novel Attributes on Product Evaluation," *Journal of Consumer Research*, December 2001, p. 462; Douglas W. Vorhies and Neil A. Morgan, "A Configuration Theory Assessment of Marketing Organization Fit with Business Strategy and Its Relationship with Marketing Performance," *Journal of Marketing*, January 2003, p. 100; Jean L. Johnson, Ruby Pui-Wan Lee, Amit Saini, and Bianca Grohmann, "Market-Focused Strategic Flexibility: Conceptual Advances and an Integrative Model," *Journal of the Academy of Marketing Science*, Winter 2003, p. 74; Ian C. MacMillan and Rita G. McGrath, "Discovering New Points of Differentiation," *Harvard Business Review*, July–August 1997, p. 133.

13. For more on Coleman, see "The Grill of Their Dreams," *Business 2.0*, February 2002, p. 96; "Growing to Match Its Brand Name," *Fortune*, June 13, 1994, p. 114. See also Peter C. Verhoef, "Understanding the Effect of Customer Relationship Management Efforts on Customer Retention and Customer Share Development," *Journal of Marketing*, October 2003, p. 30; Youjae Yi and Hoseong Jeon, "Effects of Loyalty Programs on Value Perception, Program Loyalty, and Brand Loyalty," *Journal of the Academy of Marketing Science*, Summer 2003, p. 229.

14. For more on E-Z-Go, see "Off-Roading, Golf-Cart Style," *Wall Street Journal*, June 14, 2001, p. B1. For more on McDonald's, see www.mcdonalds.com; *2005 Annual Report*, McDonald's; "The Marketing Legacy of McDonald's," *Advertising Age*, July 25, 2005, pp. S1–S17; "Fast Fruit? At Wendy's and McDonald's, It's a Main Course," *Wall Street Journal*, February 9, 2005, p. B1ff.; "McDonald's: Fries with That Salad?" *Business Week*, July 5, 2004, pp. 82–84; "Phat Feeder Down with Diddy," *Advertising Age*, July 4, 2005, p. 1ff.; "100 Innovations: McD's Tests Wi-Fi, Self-Service and 'China,'" *Advertising Age*, August 11, 2003, p. 4; "McDonald's Salads Lure Women," *USA Today*, June 16, 2003, p. 7B; "It's Back to Basics for McDonald's," *USA Today*, May 21, 2003, p. 1B; "What's This? The French Love McDonald's?" *Business Week*, January 13, 2003, p. 50; "Why You Won't Find Any Egg McMuffins for Breakfast in Brazil," *Wall Street Journal*, October 23, 1997, p. A1; "Burger Wars Sizzle as McDonald's Clones the Whopper," *Wall Street Journal*, September 17, 1997, p. B1. See also Michael S. Garver, "Best Practices in Identifying Customer-Driven Improvement Opportunities," *Industrial Marketing Management*, August 2003, p. 455; John H. Roberts, "Developing New Rules for New Markets," *Journal of the Academy of Marketing Science*, Winter 2000, p. 31.

15. For more on Heinz' EZ Squirt, see *2005 Annual Report*, Heinz; "Wacky Colors, Unconventional Flavors Appeal to the Savvy Younger Set," *DSN Retailing Today*, May 19, 2003, p. 18; "Heinz Picks Purple as New EZ Squirt Color," *Brandweek*, June 25, 2001, p. 7; "Squeezing New from Old," *USA Today*, January 4, 2001, p. 1B. For more on ski resorts, see "Seeking Growth, Ski Areas Target Minorities," *Wall Street Journal*, December 22, 2004, p. B1ff.; "Bikers Give Ski Resorts Summer Time Lift," *Wall Street Journal*, July 7, 1994, p. B1. For more on Nike, see *2005 Annual Report*, Nike; "Nike Puts Its Swoosh on MP3 Players, Walkie-Talkies, Heart Monitors," *Wall Street Journal*, May 10, 2000, p. B1. See also Sarah J. Marsh and Gregory N. Stock, "Building Dynamic Capabilities in New Product Development Through Intertemporal Integration," *Journal of Product Innovation Management*, March 2003, p. 136; George C. Kingston and Beebe Nelson, "Leading Product Innovation: Accelerating Growth in a Product-Based Business," *Journal of Product Innovation Management*, November 2001, p. 414.

16. For more on McDonald's and its hotel diversification effort, see www.goldenarcheshotel.com; "Would You Like a Bed with Your Burger?" *Ad Age Global*, February 2001, p. 12; "The Golden Arches: Burgers, Fries and 4-Star Rooms," *Wall Street Journal*, November 17, 2000, p. B1.

17. For more on Purafil, see "Small Businesses Find International Success," *USA Today*, June 30, 2000, p. 1B.

18. For more on JLG, see "The Secret of U.S. Exports: Great Products," *Fortune*, January 10, 2000, pp. 154C–J.

19. For more on international marketing in China, see James McGregor, *One Billion Customers: Lessons from the Front Lines of Doing Business in China* (New York: Free Press, 2005); "Doing Business in China Is Complex," *USA Today*, November 21, 2005, p. 4B; "One Billion Opportunities?" *Wall Street Journal*, October 18, 2005, p. B1ff.; "Let a Thousand Brands Bloom," *Business Week*, October 17, 2005, pp. 58–60; "Relaxed Marketing Rules in China Open the Door for More Sales," *Investor's Business Daily*, October 7, 2005, p. A7; "Localizing the Brand," *Inc. Magazine*, October 2005, pp. 54–56; "Chinese Dragon, Hidden Treasure: The Peril and Promise of Selling in China," *Selling Power*, June 2005, pp. 54–61; "Nestlé Stumbles in China's Evolving Market," *Wall Street Journal*, December 8, 2004, p. A10; "Outsiders Get Smarter about China's Tastes," *Wall Street Journal*, August 5, 2004, p. B1ff.; "Getting a Foothold in China," *Wall Street Journal*, August 3, 2004, p. A9; "Cracking China's Market: Adapting to Chinese Customs, Cultural Changes . . .," *Wall Street Journal*, January 9, 2003, p. B1ff.; see also Naresh K. Malhotra, Francis M. Ulgado, and James Agarwal, "Internationalization and Entry Modes: A Multitheoretical Framework and Research Propositions," *Journal of International Marketing*, 2003, p. 1; Peter N. Golder, "Insights from Senior Executives about Innovation in International Markets," *Journal of Product Innovation Management*, September 2000, p. 326; Shaoming Zou and S. Tamer Cavusgil, "The GMS: A Broad Conceptualization of Global Marketing Strategy and Its Effect on Firm Performance," *Journal of Marketing*, October 2002, p. 40; Susan P. Douglas, "Exploring New Worlds: The Challenge of Global Marketing," *Journal of Marketing*, January 2001, p. 103.

CHAPTER 3

1. "Photo Marketers Hope to Inspire Seller Innovation," *USA Today*, February 27, 2006, p. 5B; "H-P Takes Another Shot at Making Digital Photos Click," *Wall Street Journal*, February 23, 2006, p. B1ff.; "The Downside of Photo-Storage Sites," *Wall Street Journal*, February 1, 2006, p. D1ff.; "Digital-Photo Prices Hit a New Low: Wal-Mart Sets Cost . . .," *Wall Street Journal*, September 27, 2005, p. D1ff.; "Digital Snaps in a Snap," *Wall Street Journal*, August 4, 2005, p. B1ff.; "New HP Printers Pop Out Photos in 14 Seconds Flat," *USA Today*, July 12, 2005, p. 3B; "Kodak Sharpens Digital Focus on Its Best Customers: Women," *Wall Street Journal*, July 6, 2005, p. A1ff.; "A Price War Hits Digital Photos," *Wall Street Journal*, March 17, 2005, p. D1ff.; "As Cameras Go Digital, a Race to Shape Habits of Consumers," *Wall Street Journal*, November 19, 2004, p. A1ff.; "As Kodak Eyes Digital Future, a Big Partner Starts to Fade," *Wall Street Journal*, January 23, 2004, p. A1ff.

2. See www.hallmark.com; *2005 Annual Report*, Hallmark; "Caring Enough about Loyalty," *Brandweek*, August 9, 2004, pp. 16–17; "Hallmark Cards' Joyce C. Hall," *Investor's Business Daily*, October 14, 2003, p. A3; "Hallmark Hits the Mark," *USA Today*, June 14, 2001, p. 1D.

3. Glen L. Urban and John R. Hauser, "Listening In to Find and Explore New Combinations of Customer Needs," *Journal of Marketing*, April 2004, p. 72; Terri C. Albert, "Need-Based Segmentation and Customized Communication Strategies in a Complex-Commodity Industry: A Supply Chain Study," *Industrial Marketing Management*, May 2003, p. 281; Stavros P. Kalafatis and Vicki Cheston, "Normative Models and Practical Applications of Segmentation in Business Markets," *Industrial Marketing Management*, November 1997, p. 519; Lisa R. Adam, "Nichecraft: Using Your Specialness to Focus Your Business, Corner Your Market, and Make Customers Seek You Out," *Journal of the Academy of Marketing Science*, Summer 1997, p. 259; Rajendra K. Srivastava, Mark I. Alpert, and Allan D. Shocker, "A Customer-Oriented Approach for Determining Market Structures," *Journal of Marketing*, Spring 1984, p. 32.

4. For more on Nvidia, see "Perseverance May Pay Off for Chipmaker," *USA Today*, June 27, 2005, p. 1Bff.; "Nvidia Packs New Chip with Speed," *Wall Street Journal*, June 22, 2005, p. D5; "Nvidia Swings into Hollywood," *Business 2.0*, July 2004, pp. 58–59; "ATI Is Enlisted to Design Chips for Xbox Console," *Wall Street Journal*, August 15, 2003, p. B5; "Little Niches that Grew," *Business Week*, June 18, 2001, p. 100. For more on Herman Miller, see www.hermanmillerred.com; *2005 Annual Report*, Herman Miller; "A Cult Chair Gets a Makeover," *Wall Street Journal*, September 17, 2002, p. D1; "The Net as a Lifeline," *Business Week E.Biz*, October 29, 2001, pp. EB16–EB23; "Reinventing Herman Miller," *Business Week E.Biz*, April 3, 2000, pp. EB89–EB96.

5. Sally Dibb and Lyndon Simkin, "Market Segmentation: Diagnosing and Treating the Barriers," *Industrial Marketing Management*, November 2001, p. 609; Terry Elrod and Russell S. Winer, "An Empirical Evaluation of Aggregation Approaches for Developing Market Segments," *Journal of Marketing*, Fall 1982, p. 32; Frederick W. Winter, "A Cost-Benefit Approach to Market Segmentation," *Journal of Marketing*, Fall 1979, p. 103.

6. See www.kaepa.com; "Tapping into Cheerleading," *Adweek's Marketing Week*, March 2, 1992, p. 17.

7. S. Tamer Cavusgil, Tunga Kiyak, and Sengun Yeniyurt, "Complementary Approaches to Preliminary Foreign Market Opportunity Assessment: Country Clustering and Country Ranking," *Industrial Marketing Management*, October 2004, p. 607; Malaika Brengman, Maggie Geuens, Bert Weijters, Scott M. Smith, and William R. Swinyard, "Segmenting Internet Shoppers Based on Their Web-Usage-Related Lifestyle: A Cross-Cultural Validation," *Journal of Business Research*, January 2005, p. 79; Amit Bhatnagar and Sanjoy

Ghose, "Segmenting Consumers Based on the Benefits and Risks of Internet Shopping," *Journal of Business Research*, December 2004, p. 1352; Richard J. Courtheoux, "Analysis of List Segmentation Efficacy and Campaign Optimization," *Journal of Interactive Marketing*, Winter 2004, p. 70; Clayton M. Christensen, Scott Cook, and Taddy Hall, "Marketing Malpractice," *Harvard Business Review*, December 2005, p. 74; Ruth N. Bolton and Matthew B. Myers, "Price-Based Global Market Segmentation for Services," *Journal of Marketing*, July 2003, p. 108; Philip A. Dover, "Segmentation and Positioning for Strategic Marketing Decisions," *Journal of the Academy of Marketing Science*, Summer 2000, p. 438; Alex Chernev, "The Effect of Common Features on Brand Choice: Moderating Role of Attribute Importance," *Journal of Consumer Research*, March 1997, p. 304; Robert L. Armacost and Jamshid C. Hosseini, "Identification of Determinant Attributes Using the Analytic Hierarchy Process," *Journal of the Academy of Marketing Science*, Fall 1994, p. 383; Joel S. Dubow, "Occasion-based vs. User-based Benefit Segmentation, A Case Study," *Journal of Advertising Research*, March/April 1992, p. 11; Peter R. Dickson and James L. Ginter, "Market Segmentation, Product Differentiation, and Marketing Strategy," *Journal of Marketing*, April 1987, p. 1; Russell I. Haley, "Benefit Segmentation—20 Years Later," *Journal of Consumer Marketing* 1, no. 2 (1984), p. 5.

8. For more on General Mills, see "General Mills Intends to Reshape Doughboy in Its Own Image," *Wall Street Journal*, July 18, 2000, p.A1. See also "Food Marketing," *Brandweek*, April 30, 2001, p. 20.

9. "Marketers Find 'Tweens' Too Hot to Ignore," *USA Today*, July 10, 2001, p. 13A; "Yamada Card Gives Credit to Struggling Brazilians," *Wall Street Journal*, March 27, 2001, p. B1; "Grown-Up Drinks for Tender Taste Buds," *Business Week*, March 5, 2001, p. 96; "Soda Pop That Packs a Punch," *Newsweek*, February 19, 2001, p. 45; Suzeanne Benet, Robert E. Pitts, and Michael LaTour, "The Appropriateness of Fear Appeal Use for Health Care Marketing to the Elderly: Is It OK to Scare Granny?" *Journal of Business Ethics*, January 1993, p.45; "New Converse Shoe Named Run 'N Gun Is Angering Critics," *Wall Street Journal*, February 8, 1993, p. B5; "Malt Liquor Makers Find Lucrative Market in the Urban Young," *Wall Street Journal*, March 9, 1992, p. A1; Richard W. Pollay, S.Siddarth, Michael Siegel, Anne Haddix et al., "The Last Straw? Cigarette Advertising and Realized Market Shares among Youths and Adults, 1979–1993," *Journal of Marketing*, April 1996, p. 1.

10. Girish Punj and David W. Stewart, "Cluster Analysis in Marketing Research: Review and Suggestions for Application," *Journal of Marketing Research*, May 1983, p. 134; Fernando Robles and Ravi Sarathy, "Segmenting the Computer Aircraft Market with Cluster Analysis," *Industrial Marketing Management*, February 1986, p. 1.

11. "CDW Taps Resellers as It Eyes Comeback in Business Spending," *Investor's Business Daily*, May 18, 2004, p. A6; "CDW Wins Gov't Contracts with Direct Sales," *BtoB*, May 3, 2004, p. 19; "Return of the Middleman," *Business 2.0*, March 2003, p. 52.

12. For more on Amazon, see "Amazon Moves to Front Line of Shaping Web Services," *USA Today*, September 30, 2003, p. 1B; "Amazon Plans a Search Service to Drive Sales," *Wall Street Journal*, September 25, 2003, p. B1; "New Chapter: A Web Giant Tries to Boost Profits by Taking on Tenants," *Wall Street Journal*, September 24, 2003, p. A1; "Mighty Amazon," *Fortune*, May 26, 2003, p. 60; "Secrets of the New Brand Builders," *Fortune*, June 22, 1998, p. 167. See also Katherine N. Lemon, Tiffany Barnett White, and Russell S. Winer, "Dynamic Customer Relationship Management: Incorporating Future Considerations into the Service Retention Decision," *Journal of Marketing*, January 2002, p. 1; Richard A. Feinberg, Rajesh Kadam, Leigh Hokama, and Iksuk Kim, "The State of Electronic Customer Relationship Management in Retailing," *International Journal of Retail & Distribution Management*, no. 10 (2002), p. 470; Jonghyeok Kim, Euiho Suh, and Hyunseok Hwang, "A Model for Evaluating the Effectiveness of CRM Using the Balanced Scorecard," *Journal of Interactive Marketing*, Spring 2003, p. 5. For more on privacy, see Chapter 13, footnote 16 and Chapter 18, footnote 11.

13. Girish Punj and Junyean Moon, "Positioning Options for Achieving Brand Association: a Psychological Categorization Framework," *Journal of Business Research*, April 2002, p. 275; Kalpesh Kaushik Desai and S. Ratneshwar, "Consumer Perceptions of Product Variants Positioned on Atypical Attributes," *Journal of the Academy of Marketing Science*, Winter 2003, p. 22; David A. Aaker and J. Gary Shansby, "Positioning Your Product," *Business Horizons*, May/June, 1982, p. 56; Al Ries and Jack Trout, *Positioning: The Battle for Your Mind* (New York: McGraw-Hill, 1981), p. 53. For some examples of positioning, see "Hulking Hummer Steers Nimbly around Critics," *Wall Street Journal*, November 15, 2005, p. D5; "Beauty's New Regimen: A Note from the Doctor," *Advertising Age*, July 25, 2005, p. 12; "Sparkler on the Other Hand," *Brandweek*, April 19, 2004, pp. 18–19; "Getting Corian Out of the Kitchen," *Wall Street Journal*, December 12, 2000, p. B1;

CHAPTER 4

1. See www.bofa.com; *2005 Annual Report*, Bank of America; "Bank of America Makes Deal for Credit-Card Issuer MBNA," *Wall Street Journal*, July 1, 2005, p. A1ff.; "BofA's $35 Bil Buy of Card Firm MBNA Will Create Biggest Credit Card Issuer," *Investor's Business Daily*, July 1, 2005, p. A1.

2. See Peter F. Drucker, *Management: Tasks, Responsibilities, Practices, and Plans* (New York: Harper and Row, 1973); Sev K. Keil, "The Impact of Business Objectives and the Time Horizon of Performance Evaluation on Pricing Behavior," *International Journal of Research in Marketing*, June 2001, p. 67; Kenneth E. Clow, "Marketing Strategy: The Challenge of the External Environment," *Journal of the Academy of Marketing Science*, Summer 2000, p. 437.

3. Lance Leuthesser and Chiranjeev Kohli, "Corporate Identity: The Role of Mission Statements," *Business Horizons*, May–June 1997, p. 59; Christopher K. Bart, "Sex, Lies, and Mission Statements," *Business Horizons*, November–December 1997, p. 9.

4. "Why Inflation Is Not Inevitable," *Fortune*, September 12, 1988, p.117.

5. See www.harley-davidson.com; *2005 Annual Report*, Harley-Davidson; "Motorcycle Sales Rev Up to Top 1 Million," *USA Today*, January 20, 2005, p. 1B; "Can Harley Ride the New Wave?" *Brandweek*, October 25, 2004, pp. 20–22; 2004, p. A9; "Why the Harley Brand's So Hot," *Advertising Age*, March 15, 2004, p. 26; "Hurdles on the Road to Hog Heaven," *Business Week*, November 10, 2003, p. 96; "Harley-Davidson Merchandising Goes Full Throttle," *USA Today*, August 25, 2003, p. 1B; "Where Hundreds Failed, Harley-Davidson Succeeded," *USA Today*, August 25, 2003, p. 3B; "How Harley Revved Online Sales," *Business 2.0*, December 2002, p. 44; "Gearing Up for the Cruiser Wars," *Fortune*, August 3, 1998, pp. 128B–L; "Killer Strategies That Make Shareholders Rich," *Fortune*, June 23, 1997, p. 70; "How Harley Beat Back the Japanese," *Fortune*, September 25, 1989, p. 155.

6. For more on Starbucks, see Chapter 1, endnote 1.

7. For more on the BlackBerry patent case, see "BlackBerry Case Could Spur Patent-Revision Efforts," *Wall Street Journal*, March 6, 2006, p. B4; "RIM to Pay NTP $612.5 Million to Settle BlackBerry Patent Suit," *Wall Street Journal*, March 4, 2006, p. A1ff.; "BlackBerry Gambles Patent Office Will Be on Its Side in Court," *Wall Street Journal*, January 17, 2006, p. B1ff.; "The BlackBerry Widow's Tale," *Business Week*, December 19, 2005, pp. 33–34; "Pay Up—or You're Done For," *Fortune*, December 12, 2005, pp. 29–30. For more on patents, see "The Patent Epidemic," *Business Week*, January 9, 2006, pp. 60–62; Patent Applications So Abundant that Examiners Can't Catch Up," *USA Today*, September 21, 2005, p. 3B; "Brothers of Invention: Design-Arounds Surge as More Companies Imitate Rivals Patented Products," *Wall Street Journal*, April 19, 2004, p. B1ff.; "Businesses Battle over Intellectual Property," *USA Today*, August 2, 2000, p. 1B; "New Teeth for Old Patents," *Business Week*, November 30, 1998, p. 92.

8. For more on the Xbox 360, see "EA's Net Drops 31% as Shortage of Xboxes Weakens Game Sales," *Wall Street Journal*, February 3, 2006, p. B4; "Microsoft Sales Miss as New Xbox Supply Lags Strong Demand," *Investor's Business Daily*, January 27, 2006, p. A5; "Xbox 360 Rollout from Microsoft Rattles Industry," *Wall Street Journal*, December 24, 2005, p. A1ff.; "For Every Xbox, a Big Fat Loss," *Business Week*, December 5, 2005, p. 13; "New Xbox Aim for Microsoft: Profitability," *Wall Street Journal*, May 24, 2005, p. C1ff.; "It's Xbox 360 vs. PlayStation 3, and War Is About to Begin," *Wall Street Journal*, May 9, 2005, p. B1ff.; "Microsoft Play Video Leapfrog," *Business Week*, May 10, 2004, p. 44. For more on the original Xbox, see "PlayStation 2 to Rivals: Game On!" *Brandweek*, November 17, 2003, p. 1; "Microsoft's Xbox to Use IBM Chips," *Wall Street Journal*, November 4, 2003, p. B4; "The Biggest Game in Town," *Fortune*, September 15, 2003, p. 132; "New Sony Videogame Camera Sells Well," *Wall Street Journal*, August 29, 2003, p.B6; "Is Nintendo Playing the Wrong Game?" *Business 2.0*, August 2003, p. 110; "Choosing Sides: Videogame Giant Links with Sony, Snubbing Microsoft," *Wall Street Journal*, May 12, 2003, p.A1; "Why Videogame Makers Are Taking Aim at You," *Wall Street Journal*, May 16, 2002, p. D1.

9. Peter J. Williamson, "Asia's New Competitive Game," *Harvard Business Review*, September–October 1997, p. 55; David J. Collis and Cynthia A. Montgomery, "Competing on Resources: Strategy in the 1990s," *Harvard Business Review*, July–August 1995, p. 118; "Firms Analyze Rivals to Help Fix Themselves," *Wall Street Journal*, May 3, 1994, p. B1; Thomas S. Gruca and D. Sudharshan, "A Framework for Entry Deterrence Strategy: The Competitive Environment, Choices, and Consequences," *Journal of Marketing*, July 1995, p. 44; Venkatram Ramaswamy, Hubert Gatignon, and David J. Reibstein, "Competitive Marketing Behavior in Industrial Markets," *Journal of Marketing*, April 1994, p. 45; Z. S. Deligonul and S. T. Cavusgil, "Does the Comparative Advantage Theory of Competition Really Replace the Neoclassical Theory of Perfect Competition?" *Journal of Marketing*, October 1997, p. 65; J. S. Armstrong, "Co-Opetition," *Journal of Marketing*, April 1997, p. 92.

10. Timothy B. Heath, Gangseog Ryu, Subimal Chatterjee, Michael S. McCarthy et al. "Asymmetric Competition in Choice and the Leveraging of Competitive Disadvantages," *Journal of Consumer Research*, December 2000, p. 291; *Kao* (Cambridge, MA: Harvard Business School Press, 1984); Bruce R. Klemz, "Managerial Assessment of Potential Entrants: Processes and Pitfalls," *International Journal of Research in Marketing*, June 2001, p. 37. For more on P&G's diaper competition in U.S., see "Value Positioning Becomes a Priority," *Advertising Age*, February 23, 2004; "Opportunity Knocks: In Lean Times, Big Companies Make a Grab for Market Share," *Wall Street Journal*, September 5, 2003, p. A1; "Rivals Take P&G to Court to Challenge Ads," *Wall Street Journal*, June 17, 2003, p. B1; "Dueling Diapers," *Fortune*, February 17, 2003, p. 115. For a different competitor analysis in the cosmetics market, see "Face-Off: An Unlikely Rival Challenges L'Oreal in Beauty Market," *Wall Street Journal*, January 9, 2003, p. A1; "L'Oreal's Global Makeover," *Fortune*, September 30, 2002, p. 141.

11. "P&G Wins Lawsuit, Loses Market," *Advertising Age*, September 18, 1989, p. 72. For more on corporate spying and competitive intelligence, see "Snooping on a Shoestring," *Business 2.0*, May 2003, p. 64; "More U.S. Trade Secrets Walk Out Door with Foreign Spies," *USA Today*, February 13, 2003, p. 1B; "The Case of the Corporate Spy," *Business Week*, November 26, 2001, p. 56; "Eyeing the Competition," *Time*, March 22, 1999, p. 58; "How Safe Are Your Secrets?" *Fortune*, September 8, 1997, p. 114. For more on the Oracle/Microsoft case, see "Oracle-Style Investigations Common, Experts Say," *USA Today*, June 29, 2000, p. 3B; "How Piles of Trash Became Latest Focus in Bitter Software Feud," *Wall Street Journal*, June 29, 2000, p. A1. See also Shaker A. Zahra, "Unethical Practices in Competitive Analysis: Patterns, Causes and Effects," *Journal of Business Ethics*, January 1994, p. 53.

12. "A Whole New Wave of Japanese Exports Is Headed Westward," *Wall Street Journal*, November 14, 1997, p. A1.

13. "Chinese Economic Engine Revs as Worldwide Low-Cost Leader," *Investor's Business Daily*, August 12, 2003, p. A1; "Follow the Leader: As U.S. Shows Signs of Strength, Global Economies Look Up, Too," *Wall Street Journal*, August 12, 2003, p. A1; Rajdeep Grewal, "Building Organizational Capabilities for Managing Economic Crisis: The Role of Market Orientation and Strategic Flexibility," *Journal of Marketing*, April 2001, p. 67; "Wary Consumers Watch as Inflation Nudges Prices Up," *USA Today*, April 30, 2001, p. 1B.

14. "High-Speed Internet over Power Lines Could Serve Millions," *Wall Street Journal*, December 19, 2005, p. B1ff.; "Computer, Heal Thyself," *Business Week*, December 5, 2005, pp. 74–75; "Internet to Ask, How May I Serve You?" *USA Today*, October 27, 2005, p. 1Bff.; "Technology," *Wall Street Journal Reports*, October 24, 2005, pp. R1–R13; "It's a Whole New Web," *Business Week*, September 26, 2005, pp. 76–90; "The Innovation Economy," *Business Week*, October 11, 2004, pp. 90–202; "Seven New Technologies that Change Everything," *Business 2.0*, September 2004, pp. 82–90; "Technology: Emerging Technologies," *USA Today (Bonus Section E)*, November 17, 2003; "Technology: There Goes the Status Quo," *Wall Street Journal Reports*, May 19, 2003; "The Internet Age," *Business Week*, October 4, 1999, p. 69. See also Gary S. Lynn, Sharon M. Lipp, Ali E. Akgun, and Alexander Cortex Jr., "Factors Impacting the Adoption and Effectiveness of the World Wide Web in Marketing," *Industrial Marketing Management*, January 2002, p. 35; P. Rajan Varadarajan and Manjit S Yadav, "Marketing Strategy and the Internet: An Organizing Framework," *Journal of the Academy of Marketing Science*, Fall 2002, p. 296; A. Parasuraman and George M. Zinkhan, "Marketing to and Serving Customers through the Internet: An Overview and Research Agenda," *Journal of The Academy of Marketing Science*, Fall 2002, p. 286; Guilherme D. Pires and Janet Aisbett, "The Relationship Between Technology Adoption and Strategy in Business-to-Business Markets: The Case of E-Commerce," *Industrial Marketing Management*, May 2003, p. 291; Paul Whysall, "Retailing and the Internet: A Review of Ethical Issues," *International Journal of Retail & Distribution Management*, no. 11 (2000), p. 481; Robert A. Peterson, Sridhar Balasubramanian, and Bart J. Bronnenberg, "Exploring the Implications of the Internet for Consumer Marketing," *Journal of the Academy of Marketing Science*, Fall 1997, p. 329; Karen A. Graziano, "The Innovator's Dilemma: When New Technologies Cause Great Firms to Fail," *Journal of Product Innovation Management*, January 1998, p. 95.

15. "Technology: A Tech To-Do List," *Wall Street Journal Reports*, November 17, 2003; "Advances in Car Technology Bring High-Class Headaches," *USA Today*, November 12, 2003, p. 1B; "Epidemic: Crippling Computer Viruses and Spam Attacks Threaten the Information Economy," *Business Week*, September 8, 2003, p. 28; "Technology: Just Make It Simpler," *Business Week*, September 8, 2003, p. 38; "Innovation on Hold," *Wall Street Journal*, May 29, 2003, p. B1; "Will Light Bulbs Go the Way of the Victrola?" *Business Week*, January 22, 2001, p. 94H; "High-Tech Applications Transform Old Economy," *USA Today*, September 7, 2000, p. 3B; "Noel Capon and Rashi Glazer, "Marketing and Technology: A Strategic Coalignment," *Journal of Marketing*, July 1987, p. 1. For more on privacy, see Chapter 13, footnote 16 and Chapter 18, footnote 11.

16. "Craftsman: Made in USA (Sort of)," *Business Week*, July 4, 2005, p. 12; "How China Will Change Your Business," *Inc. Magazine*, March 2005, pp. 70–84; "The China Price," *Business Week*, December 6, 2004, pp. 102–12; "Still Made in the U.S.A.," *Wall Street Journal*, July 8, 2004, p. B1ff.; "Lessons of a Crisis," *Business Week*, April 23, 2001, p. 56; "U.S. Backpedals on Law That Hung 'Made in China' Tag on European Goods," *Wall Street Journal*, August 8, 1997, p. A2. See also George Balabanis and Adamantios Diamantopoulos, "Domestic Country Bias, Country-of-Origin Effects, and Consumer Ethnocentrism: a Multidimensional Unfolding Approach," *Journal of the Academy of Marketing Science*, Winter 2004, p. 80; Zeynep Gurhan-Canli and Durairaj Maheswaran, "Determinants of Country-of-Origin Eval-

uations," *Journal of Consumer Research*, June 2000, p. 96; Kent L. Granzin and John J. Painter, "Motivational Influences on 'Buy Domestic' Purchasing: Marketing Management Implications from a Study of Two Nations," *Journal of International Marketing*, no. 2 (2001), p. 73; Gopalkrishnan R. Iyer, "Anticompetitive Practices in Japan: Their Impact on the Performance of Foreign Firms," *Journal of Marketing*, October 1997, p. 97.

17. For more on Lands' End example, see "German Shoppers May Get Sale Freedom," *Wall Street Journal*, January 23, 2002, p. B7A; "Border Crossings," *Wall Street Journal Reports*, November 22, 1999, p. R41. For another example, see "Corn Flakes Clash Shows the Glitches in European Union," *Wall Street Journal*, November 1, 2005, p. A1ff. For more on EU, see "Squeezed by the Euro," *Business Week*, June 6, 2005, pp. 52–54; "EU Expansion Brings USA Opportunities," *USA Today*, April 27, 2004, p. 1Bff.; "Expanded EU Will Be an Uneven One," *Wall Street Journal*, September 22, 2003, p.A16; "Mega Europe," *Business Week*, November 25, 2002, p. 62; "A Tale of Two Nations Shows Europe's Union Has Differing Sides," *Wall Street Journal*, July 28, 1997, p. A1; "Europe's Borders Fade and People and Goods Can Move More Freely," *Wall Street Journal*, May 18, 1993, p. A1. See also Andrew Paddison, "Retailing in the European Union: Structures, Competition and Performance," *International Journal of Retail & Distribution Management*, no. 6 (2003), p. 379.

18. For more on NAFTA, see www.nafta.org; "10 Years Ago, NAFTA Was Born," *USA Today*, December 31, 2003, p. 3B; "Was NAFTA Worth It? A Tale of What Free Trade Can and Cannot Do," *Business Week*, December 22, 2003, pp. 66–72; "Border Crossing? No Problema," *Business Week Small Biz*, July 16, 2001, p. 10; "NAFTA Scorecard: So Far, So Good," *Business Week*, July 9, 2001, p. 54; "In the Wake of NAFTA, a Family Firm Sees Business Go South," *Wall Street Journal*, February 23, 1999, p. A1; Kent Jones, "NAFTA Chapter 19: Is There Hope for Bilateral Dispute Resolution of Unfair Trade Law Decisions?" *Journal of Public Policy & Marketing*, Fall 1994, p. 300. See also "Central American Free Trade Agreement Faces Obstacles," *USA Today*, May 12, 2005, p. 1Bff.

19. Thomas L. Osterhus, "Pro-Social Consumer Influence Strategies: When and How Do They Work?" *Journal of Marketing*, October 1997, p. 16; Roger Swagler, "Evolution and Applications of the Term Consumerism: Theme and Variations," *Journal of Consumer Affairs*, Winter 1994, p. 347; Alan Morrison, "The Role of Litigation in Consumer Protection," *Journal of Consumer Affairs*, Winter, 1991, p. 209.

20. For more on Beech-Nut, see "What Led Beech-Nut Down the Road to Disgrace," *Business Week*, February 22, 1988, p. 124. See also Kersi D. Antia, Mark E. Bergen, Shantanu Dutta, and Robert J. Fisher, "How Does Enforcement Deter Gray Market Incidence?" *Journal of Marketing*, January 2006, p. 92; Debra M. Desrochers, Gregory T. Gundlach, and Albert A. Foer, "Analysis of Antitrust Challenges to Category Captain Arrangements," *Journal of Public Policy & Marketing*, Fall 2003, p. 201; "Stock Now, Pay Later," *Forbes*, October 27, 2003, p. 60; "EU Court Sends a Tough Antitrust Message," *Wall Street Journal*, October 24, 2003, p. A12; "Big Drug Wholesaler Fights Charges of Fakes, Price Fixing," *Wall Street Journal*, October 7, 2003, p. B1; "The EU vs. Microsoft: A Rugged Endgame," *Business Week*, August 25, 2003, p. 40; "Europe Decides to Fine Nintendo," *Wall Street Journal*, October 25, 2002, p. B5; "Sotheby's Taubman Is Sentenced to Jail Time, Fined $7.5 Million," *Wall Street Journal*, April 23, 2002, p. B4; "Hard Profits: A Cement Titan in Mexico Thrives by Selling to Poor," *Wall Street Journal*, April 22, 2002, p. A1; David A. Balto, "Emerging Antitrust Issues in Electronic Commerce," *Journal of Public Policy & Marketing*, Fall 2000, p. 277; "Europe: A Different Take on Antitrust," *Business Week*, June 25, 2001, p. 40; "In Archer-Daniels Saga, Now the Executives Face Trial," *Wall Street Journal*, July 9, 1998, p. B10. See also Mary W. Sullivan, "The Role of Marketing in Antitrust," *Journal of Public Policy & Marketing*, Fall 2002, p. 247; Jeff Langenderfer and Steven W. Kopp, "Which Way to the Revolution? The Consequences of Database Protection as a New Form of Intellectual Property," *Journal of Public Policy & Marketing*,

Spring 2003, p. 83; David E. M. Sappington and Donald K. Stockdale, Jr., "The Federal Communications Commission's Competition Policy and Marketing's Information Technology Revolution," *Journal of Public Policy & Marketing*, Spring 2003, p. 26; Ann C. Morales, "Corporate Officer Liability: FTC Expands Its Remedial Reach Over Deceptive Marketing Practices," *Journal of the Academy of Marketing Science*, Spring 1998, p. 163; Charles S. Gulas, "Marketing Strategies for Services: Globalization, Client-Orientation, Deregulation," *Journal of the Academy of Marketing Science*, Spring 1996, p. 178; Joan T. A. Gabel, "Lanham Act Not Limited to Advertisements Aimed at the Ultimate Consumer," *Journal of the Academy of Marketing Science*, Spring 1997, p. 178. See also Louis W. Stern and Thomas L. Eovaldi, *Legal Aspects of Marketing Strategy: Antitrust and Consumer Protection Issues* (Englewood Cliffs, NJ: Prentice Hall, 1984).

21. For more on auto safety, see "Surfing the Freeway: Cars Get PCs," *Wall Street Journal*, January 26, 2006, p. D1ff.; "Safety Features' Cost Turns Off Buyers," *Wall Street Journal*, December 6, 2005, p. D2; "Crash Test Smarties," *Business 2.0*, October 2005, p. 128; "How U.S. Shifted Gears to Find Small Cars Can Be Safe, Too," *Wall Street Journal*, September 26, 2005, p. A1ff.; "New Sticker Shock for Car Buyers," *Wall Street Journal*, May 18, 2005, p. D1ff.; "One in Twelve Cars Recalled Last Year," *Wall Street Journal*, March 4, 2004, p. D1ff.; "Savvy Safety Systems Are Developed for Cars," *Wall Street Journal*, March 2, 2004, p. B1ff.; "Ford Tests Ways to Keep Drivers from Dozing Off," *USA Today*, January 27, 2004, p. 1Bff; for more on food and drug safety, see "A Winded FDA Races to Keep Up with Drug Ads That Go Too Far," *USA Today*, May 31, 2005, p. 1Aff.; "Has Your Chicken Been Drugged?" *Wall Street Journal*, August 2, 2005, p. D1ff.; "Who Is Minding the USA's Food Store?" *USA Today*, January 27, 2004, p. 1Bff.; "The Big Gap at the FDA," *Fortune*, July 22, 2002, p. 113; see also "In a Bind over Stents," *Business Week*, August 8, 2005, pp. 48–50; "He Took on the Whole Power-Tool Industry," *Inc. Magazine*, July 2005, pp. 86–91; "Airline Turmoil Poses Safety Issues," *Wall Street Journal*, June 9, 2005, p. D1ff.; "Graco Fined $4M for Lack of Timely Reporting," *USA Today*, March 23, 2005, p. 3B; "A Stun-Gun Maker Struggles to Shake Off Safety Concerns," *Wall Street Journal*, March 21, 2005, p. A1ff.; "Worlds Apart on Product Safety," *Wall Street Journal*, September 15, 2004, p. A19.

22. "Marketing Law: A Marketer's Guide to Alphabet Soup," *Business Marketing*, January 1990, p. 56; Ray O. Werner, "Marketing and the Supreme Court in Transition, 1982–1984," *Journal of Marketing*, Summer 1985, p. 97; Ray O. Werner, "Marketing and the United States Supreme Court, 1975–1981," *Journal of Marketing*, Spring 1982, p. 73; Dorothy Cohen, "Trademark Strategy," *Journal of Marketing*, January 1986, p. 61.

23. "How Toyota Does It," *Fortune*, March 6, 2006, pp. 107–24; "Auto Insurer Gives Drivers of Hybrids a Break," *USA Today*, January 6, 2006, p. 4B; "Toyota's Little Green Machine," *Fortune*, December 12, 2005, p. S12; "Helping Employees into Hybrids," *Business 2.0*, November 2005, p. 38; "Honda's Experimental Hybrid May Help in Race with Toyota," *Wall Street Journal*, October 25, 2005, p. D6; "As Hybrid Cars Gain Traction, Industry Battles over Designs," *Wall Street Journal*, October 19, 2005, p. A1ff.; "Ford Teaches Hybrid Buyers How to Drive," *USA Today*, October 14, 2005, p. 5B; "Hybrid Nation? Nope," *Newsweek*, October 10, 2005, p. 46; "Cost Savings May Not Offset Higher Price for Hybrids," *USA Today*, June 1, 2005, p. 1B; "Are You Ready for a Hybrid?" *Business Week*, April 25, 2005, pp. 118–26; "Forget Rebates: The Hybrid-Car Markup," *Wall Street Journal*, June 10, 2004, p. D1ff.; "Hybrid Car Owners Want to Know: Where's the Mileage?" *USA Today*, February 4, 2004, p. 3B; "The Hybrid Car Moves beyond Curiosity Stage," *New York Times*, January 28, 2003, p. A1.

24. Based on U.S. Census International Data Base at www.census.gov/ipc/www/idbsum.html and other U.S. Census data, including, *Global Population Profile: 2002 (WP/02)* and *Global Population at a Glance: 2002 and Beyond, WP/02-1* and *An Aging World: 2001, P95/01-1* (Washington, DC: Government Printing Office). Also based on World Bank data at www.worldbank.org/data/dataquery.

html and other World Bank data, including, *World Development Report 2006: Equity and Development* and *World Development Indicators: 2005* (Washington, DC: International Bank for Reconstruction and Development/The World Bank). Also based on Population Reference Bureau data at www.prb.org/pubs/wpds2005 and other PRB data, including *2005 World Population Data Sheet* (Washington, DC: Population Reference Bureau). Also based on Central Intelligence Agency data at www.odci.gov/cia/publications/factbook. Also based on GlobalEDGE data from Michigan State University at http://globaledge.msu.edu. See also "Russia: Shoppers Gone Wild," Business Week, February 20, 2006, pp. 46–47; "India Rising," *Newsweek*, March 6, 2006, pp. 32–42; "The Battle for the Face of China," *Fortune*, December 12, 2005, pp. 156–78; "The Rise of Central Europe," *Business Week*, December 12, 2005, pp. 50–56; "India's Bumpy Ride," *Fortune*, October 31, 2005, pp. 135–47; "China & India," *Business Week* (special issue), August 22, 2005; "Global Aging: Now, the Geezer Glut," *Business Week*, January 31, 2005, pp. 44–47; "Techs Awaken to the Muslim Market," *Wall Street Journal*, July 29, 2004, p. B4; "To Put It in Perspective," *American Demographics*, June 2003, p. 9; "When Globalization Suffers, the Poor Take the Heat," *Business Week*, April 21, 2003, p. 28; "Global Baby Bust: Economic, Social Implications Are Profound as Birthrates Drop in Almost Every Nation," *Wall Street Journal*, January 24, 2003, p. B1; Tarun Khanna and Krishna Palepu, "Why Focused Strategies May Be Wrong for Emerging Markets," *Harvard Business Review*, July–August 1997, p. 41; Tamer S. Cavusgil, "Measuring the Potential of Emerging Markets: An Indexing Approach," *Business Horizons*, January–February 1997, p. 87.

25. Based on U.S. Census data and "Population of Rural America Is Swelling," *Wall Street Journal*, July 21, 1996, p. B1; "The Rural Rebound," *American Demographics*, May 1994, p. 24. See also Hugh M. Cannon and Attila Yaprak, "Will the Real-World Citizen Please Stand Up! The Many Faces of Cosmopolitan Consumer Behavior," *Journal of International Marketing*, no. 4 (2002), p. 30.

26. Based on World Bank GNI and GDP data and available online at http://devdata.worldbank.org.

27. Based on World Bank data at www.worldbank.org/data/dataquery.html and other World Bank data, including *World Development Report 2006: Equity and Development* and *World Development Indicators: 2005*; "The Lowdown on Literacy," *American Demographics*, June 1994, p. 6.; see also Madhubalan Viswanathan, Jose Antonio Rosa, and James Edwin Harris, "Decision Making and Coping of Functionally Illiterate Consumers and Some Implications for Marketing Management," *Journal of Marketing*, January 2005, p. 15; Natalie Ross Adkins, Julie L. Ozanne, Dawn Iacobucci, and Eric Arnould, "The Low Literate Consumer," *Journal of Consumer Research*, June 2005, p. 93.

28. Based on U. S. Census data, including U.S. Bureau of the Census, *Statistical Abstract of the United States 2006* (Washington, DC: U.S. Government Printing Office, 2005), pp. 21 and 23 and available at www.census.gov/statab; "Fastest Growth Found in Red States," *USA Today*, December 22, 2004, p. 3A; "Manifest Destiny 3.0," *American Demographics*, September 2004, pp. 29–34; "America's Gray Area Dilemma," *American Demographics*, July/August 2004, pp. 40–41; *Census 2000 Special Reports: Demographic Trends in the 20th Century CENSR-4* and "The Next 25 Years," *American Demographics* (Marketing Tools Sourcebook 2004), pp. D26–D29; "Moving West Is No Longer the Norm," *USA Today*, August 6, 2003, p. 1A; "Decade of Change for USA," *USA Today*, June 5, 2002, p. 3B; also based on data from Population Reference Bureau at www.prb.org.

29. Based on U.S. Census data, including U.S. Bureau of the Census, *Statistical Abstract of the United States 2006* pp. 36–37; "The Math of Moving," *American Demographics*, July/August 2004, pp. 8–9; "Movement at Warp Speed," *American Demographics*, August 2000, p. 61.

30. Based on U.S. Census data, including U.S. Bureau of the Census, *Statistical Abstract of the United States 2006*, pp. 29–35, and *Census 2000 Special Reports: Demographic Trends in the 20th Century CENSR-4*; "Population Boom Spawns Super Cities," *USA Today*, July 11, 2005, p. 6A; "The Cloning of Austin, TX," *American Demographics*,

July/August 2004, pp. 42–43; "Small-Town USA Goes Micropolitan," *USA Today*, June 28, 2004, p. 1Bff.; "Minorities Reshape Suburbs," *USA Today*, July 9, 2001, p. 1A; "Counting Change," *Advertising Age*, May 14, 2001, p. 16; "U.S. Cities Buck Trend with Boom Downtown," *USA Today*, May 7, 2001, p. 1A.

31. Based on U.S. Census data, including U.S. Bureau of the Census, *Statistical Abstract of the United States 2006*, pp. 14, 16, and 17, at www.census.gov/statab and *Census 2000 Special Reports: Demographic Trends in the 20th Century CENSR-4*; "Love Those Boomers," *Business Week*, October 24, 2005, pp. 94–102; "When We're All 64," *Wall Street Journal Reports*, September 26, 2005, p. R1ff.; "Half of Boomers Hit the 50 Mark, but Spending Not Likely to Slow Down," *Advertising Age*, July 4, 2005, p. 18; "The Next 25 Years," *American Demographics*, April 2003, p. 24; "The Boomer Attitude," *American Demographics*, October 2002, p. 42; "Chasing Youth," *American Demographics*, October 2002, p. 34; see also Linda L. Price, Eric J. Arnould, and Carolyn Folkman Curasi, "Older Consumers' Disposition of Special Possessions," *Journal of Consumer Research*, September 2000, p. 179; William R. Swinyard and Heikki J. Rinne, "The Six Shopping Worlds of Baby Boomers," *Business Horizons*, September–October 1994, p. 64.

32. For more on the changing nature of families, see Suraj Commuri and James W. Gentry, "Resource Allocation in Households with Women as Chief Wage Earners," *Journal of Consumer Research*, September 2005, p. 185. "How Corporate America Is Betraying Women," *Fortune*, January 10, 2005, pp. 64–74; "Power: Do Women Really Want It," *Fortune*, October 13, 2003, p. 80; "She Works, He Doesn't," *Newsweek*, May 12, 2003, p. 44; "Gen X Moms Have It Their Way," *USA Today*, May 7, 2003, p. 1D; "Mommy Is Really Home from Work," *Business Week*, November 25, 2002, p. 101; "How to Shrink the Pay Gap," *Business Week*, June 24, 2002, p. 151; "Career Matters," *American Demographics*, April 2002, p. 18; "Ads That Portray Women," *USA Today*, September 9, 1996, p. 4B. For more on changing food habits, see "The Fine Art of Finding the Fat," *Business Week*, October 13, 2003, p. 134; "Are They Safe? The Skinny on Fat and Sugar Substitutes," *Wall Street Journal*, August 12, 2003, p. D1; "The End of Nesting," *Wall Street Journal*, May 16, 2003, p. W1; "The New Kitchen—Your Car," *Wall Street Journal*, April 11, 2003, p. W10; "America Adds Salsa to Its Burgers and Fries," *Wall Street Journal*, January 2, 2003, p. A9; "Fleeing from Fast Food," *Wall Street Journal*, November 11, 2002, p. B1; for more on poverty of time, see "The Real Reasons You're Working So Hard . . .," *Business Week*, October 3, 2005, pp. 60–73; "America Untethered," *American Demographics*, March 2003, p. 34; "How Much Is Your Time Worth?" *Wall Street Journal*, February 26, 2003, p. D1; "The Price of Speed," *USA Today*, August 3, 2000, p. 10D; "The End of Leisure," *American Demographics*, July 2000, p. 50. See also Laura M. Milner and James M. Collins, "Sex-Role Portrayals and the Gender of Nations," *Journal of Advertising*, Spring 2000, p. 67; Eric Panitz, "Marketing in a Multicultural World: Ethnicity, Nationalism and Cultural Identity," *Journal of the Academy of Marketing Science*, Spring 1997, p. 169.

33. Frank R. Bacon, Jr., and Thomas W. Butler, Jr., *Planned Innovation*, rev. ed. (Ann Arbor: Institute of Science and Technology, University of Michigan, 1980).

34. Paul F. Anderson, "Marketing, Strategic Planning and the Theory of the Firm," *Journal of Marketing*, Spring 1982, p. 15; George S. Day, "Analytical Approaches to Strategic Market Planning," in *Review of Marketing 1981*, ed. Ben M. Enis and Kenneth J. Roering (Chicago: American Marketing Association, 1981), p. 89; Ronnie Silverblatt and Pradeep Korgaonkar, "Strategic Market Planning in a Turbulent Business Environment," *Journal of Business Research*, August 1987, p. 339.

35. Keith B. Murray and Edward T. Popper, "Competing under Regulatory Uncertainty: A U.S. Perspective on Advertising in the Emerging European Market," *Journal of Macromarketing*, Fall 1992, p. 38; "Inside Russia—Business Most Unusual," *UPS International Update*, Spring 1994, p. 1; "Freighted with Difficulties," *Wall Street Journal*, December 10, 1993, p. R4; "Russia Snickers after Mars Invades," *Wall Street Journal*, July 13, 1993, p. B1; Michael G. Harvey and James T. Rothe, "The Foreign Corrupt Practices Act: The Good, the Bad and the Future," in *1983 American Marketing Association Educators' Proceedings*, ed. P. E. Murphy et al. (Chicago: American Marketing Association, 1983), p. 374.

36. "Sensitive Export: Seeking New Markets for Tampons, P&G Faces Cultural Barriers," *Wall Street Journal*, December 8, 2000, p. A1; "Pizza Queen of Japan Turns Web Auctioneer," *Wall Street Journal*, March 6, 2000, p. B1; "What Makes Italy Easier?" *Going Global—Italy* (supplement to *Inc.*), 1994; "Jean Cloning," *Brandweek*, May 30, 1994, p. 15; "Double Entendre: The Life and the Life of Pepsi Max," *Brandweek*, April 18, 1994, p. 40; "Global Ad Campaigns, After Many Missteps, Finally Pay Dividends," *Wall Street Journal*, August 27, 1992, p. A1; Kamran Kashani, "Beware the Pitfalls of Global Marketing," *Harvard Business Review*, September–October 1989, p. 91.

CHAPTER 5

1. "Apple Rolls Out $69 iPods, New Showtime Downloads," *USA Today*, February 8, 2006, p. 1B; "More Music-Playing Phones Are Coming," *Wall Street Journal*, February 8, 2006, p. D11; "The Bug in Microsoft's Ear," *Business Week*, February 6, 2006, p. 38; "Preloaded iPods Prompt Legal Ponderings," *USA Today*, January 24, 2006, p. 1B; "What's That Ringing in iPod's Ears?" *Business Week*, January 16, 2006, pp. 70–71; "Album Sales Slump as Downloads Rise," *USA Today*, January 5, 2006, p. 1D; "The iPod: All Decked Out," *Business Week*, December 5, 2005, pp. 90–92; "Video iPod, I Love You," *Business Week*, November 7, 2005, p. 20; "The House That iPod Built," *Business Week*, November 7, 2005, pp. 82–85; "How Apple Does It," *Time*, October 24, 2005, pp. 65–70; "Will Viewing Habits Switch with Video iPod Programs?" *Brandweek*, October 17, 2005, p. 6; "Sony Introduces New Walkman in Next Bid to Outgun the iPod," *Wall Street Journal*, September 9, 2005, p. B3; "iPod's Latest Siblings," *Wall Street Journal*, September 8, 2005, p. B1ff.; "Cell Phones Challenging iPods, but Apple Device Still Has Edge," *Investor's Business Daily*, May 13, 2005, p. A4; "As Dell Fights Apple, It's All You Can Eat vs. Pay as You Go," *Investor's Business Daily*, February 25, 2005, p. A4; "Apple Tries a New Tack: Lower Prices," *Wall Street Journal*, January 12, 2005, p. D1ff.; "Apple Transcends Lifestyle Brand," *Advertising Age* (AdAge Marketer of the Year), December 15, 2003, pp. S1–S6; "Song in the Key of Steve," *Fortune*, May 12, 2003, pp. 52–62; "Music That You Don't Have to Steal," *Wall Street Journal*, April 30, 2003, p. D1ff.

2. Based on U.S. Census data, including U.S. Bureau of the Census, *Statistical Abstract of the United States 2006*, and "Table F-1. Income Limits for Each Fifth and Top 5 Percent of Families (All Races): 1947 to 2004," "Table F-2. Share of Aggregate Income Received by Each Fifth and Top 5 Percent of Families (All Races): 1947 to 2004," and "Table F-6. Regions—Families (All Races) by Median and Mean Income: 1953 to 2004" (all 3 tables at www.census.gov/hhes/income/hitinc). For more on income, see "A-Hunting We Will Go—After Time at the Spa," *USA Today*, December 1, 2005, p. 1Bff.; "McMansions on Wheels," *Business Week*, October 17, 2005, pp. 106–7; "As Consumers Find Other Ways to Splurge, Apparel Hits a Snag," *Wall Street Journal*, February 4, 2005, p. A1ff.; "New Luxury Goods Set Super-Wealthy Apart from Pack," *Wall Street Journal*, December 14, 2004, p. A1ff.; "Waking Up from the American Dream," *Business Week*, December 1, 2003, p. 54; "Middle Class Barely Treads Water," *USA Today*, September 15, 2003, p. 1B; "Economic Inequality Grew in 90's Boom, Fed Reports," *New York Times*, January 23, 2003, p. C1; see also Census data, including, *Income, Earnings, and Poverty from the 2004 American Community Survey*; *Money Income in the United States: 2002*; and *The Changing Shape of the Nation's Income Distribution*. For more on poverty, see www.census.gov/hhes/poverty; "Black Poverty's Human Face," *Business Week*, September 19, 2005, p. 148; "The Other America," *Newsweek*, September 19, 2005, pp. 42–48; "Working . . . and Poor," *Business Week*, May 31, 2004, pp. 58–68.

3. Kristina D. Frankenberger, "Consumer Psychology for Marketing," *Journal of the Academy of Marketing Science*, Summer 1996, p. 279; K. H. Chung, *Motivational Theories and Practices* (Columbus, OH: Grid, 1977), p. 40; A. H. Maslow, *Motivation and Personality* (New York: Harper & Row, 1970).

4. "Features Drive Kitchen Gadget Evolution," *DSN Retailing Today*, May 19, 2003, p. 20; "What Works for One Works for All," *Business Week*, April 20, 1992, p. 112.

5. See also Les Carlson, Russell N. Laczniak, and Ann Walsh, "Socializing Children about Television: An Intergenerational Study," *Journal of the Academy of Marketing Science*, Summer 2001, p. 276; Elizabeth Cowley and Andrew A. Mitchell, "The Moderating Effect of Product Knowledge on the Learning and Organization of Product Information," *Journal of Consumer Research*, December 2003, p. 443; Stacy L. Wood and John G. Lynch, Jr., "Prior Knowledge and Complacency in New Product Learning," *Journal of Consumer Research*, December 2002, p. 416; Naomi Mandel and Eric J. Johnson, "When Web Pages Influence Choice: Effects of Visual Primes on Experts and Novices," *Journal of Consumer Research*, September 2002, p. 235; Elizabeth S. Moore and Richard J. Lutz, "Children, Advertising, and Product Experiences: A Multimethod Inquiry," *Journal of Consumer Research*, June 2000, p. 31; Julie A. Ruth, Frederic F. Brunel, and Cele C. Otnes, "Linking Thoughts to Feelings: Investigating Cognitive Appraisals and Consumption Emotions in a Mixed-Emotions Context," *Journal of the Academy of Marketing Science*, Winter 2002, p. 44; Stijn M. J. Van Osselaer and Chris Janiszewski, "Two Ways of Learning Brand Associations," *Journal of Consumer Research*, September 2001, p. 202; William E. Baker, "When Can Affective Conditioning and Mere Exposure Directly Influence Brand Choice?" *Journal of Advertising*, Winter 1999, p. 31; Jennifer Gregan-Paxton and Deborah R. John, "Consumer Learning by Analogy: A Model of Internal Knowledge Transfer," *Journal of Consumer Research*, December 1997, p. 266; M. C. Macklin, "Preschoolers' Learning of Brand Names from Visual Cues," *Journal of Consumer Research*, December 1996, p. 251; Jaideep Sengupta, Ronald C. Goodstein, and David S. Boninger, "All Cues Are Not Created Equal: Obtaining Attitude Persistence Under Low-Involvement Conditions," *Journal of Consumer Research*, March 1997, p. 351; John Kim, Jeen-Su Lim, and Mukesh Bhargava, "The Role of Affect in Attitude Formation: A Classical Conditioning Approach," *Journal of the Academy of Marketing Science*, Spring 1998, p. 143; Hairong Li, Terry Daugherty, and Frank Biocca, "The Role of Virtual Experience in Consumer Learning," *Journal of Consumer Psychology*, 2003, p. 395; Thomas W. Gruen, Talai Osmonbekov, and Andrew J. Czaplewski, "eWOM: The Impact Of Customer-to-Customer Online Know-How Exchange on Customer Value and Loyalty," *Journal of Business Research*, April 2006, p. 449; James C. Ward and Amy L. Ostrom, "The Internet as Information Minefield: An Analysis of the Source and Content of Brand Information Yielded by Net Searches," *Journal of Business Research*, November 2003, p. 907.

6. "Secrets of That New-Car Smell," *Car and Driver*, November 2003, p. 141; "Battling the Inferior-Interior Complex," *Wall Street Journal*, December 3, 2001, p. B1. See also Anna S. Mattila and Jochen Wirtz, "Congruency of Scent and Music as a Driver of In-Store Evaluations and Behavior," *Journal of Retailing*, Summer 2001, p. 273.

7. "Sweet Success," *Brandweek*, May 12, 2003, p. 22.

8. "Purina Dog Chow: Grand Effie Winner, Pet Care/Gold Winner," *Brandweek* (Special Effies Winner Supplement), 1997. See also Edward Rosbergen, Rik Pieters, and Michel Wedel, "Visual Attention to Advertising: A Segment-Level Analysis," *Journal of Consumer Research*, December 1997, p. 305; Gavan J. Fitzsimons and Vicki G. Morwitz, "The Effect of Measuring Intent on Brand-Level Purchase Behavior," *Journal of Consumer Research*, June 1996, p. 1; Ellen C. Garbarino and Julie A. Edell, "Cognitive Effort, Affect, and Choice," *Journal of Consumer Research*, September 1997, p. 147.

9. "Will the British Warm Up to Iced Tea? Some Big Marketers Are Counting on It," *Wall Street Journal*, August 22, 1994, p. B1. See also "Starbucks Hits a Humorous Note in Pitching Iced Coffee to Brits," *Wall Street Journal*, September 1, 1999, p. B7. See also Rohini Ahluwalia, "Examination of Psychological Processes Underlying Resistance to Persuasion," *Journal of Consumer Research*, September 2000, p. 217; J. Joseph Cronin Jr., Michael K. Brady, and G. T. M. Hult, "Assessing the Effects of Quality, Value, and Customer Satisfaction on Consumer Behavioral Intentions in Service Environments," *Journal of Retailing*, Summer 2000, p. 193; Yih Hwai Lee, "Manipulating Ad Message Involvement through Information Expectancy: Effects on Attitude Evaluation and Confidence," *Journal of Advertising*, Summer 2000, p. 29; Vikas Mittal, William T. Ross, and Patrick M. Baldasare, "The Asymmetric Impact of Negative and Positive Attribute-Level Performance on Overall Satisfaction and Repurchase Intentions," *Journal of Marketing*, January 1998, p. 33; Mary F. Luce, "Choosing to Avoid: Coping with Negatively Emotion-Laden Consumer Decisions," *Journal of Consumer Research*, March 1998, p. 409.

10. "Yogurt Cultivating Unprecedented Popularity," *USA Today*, January 23, 2006; "Benefits of Probiotic Drinks: Healthy Bugs" *The Independent* (London), November 7, 2005, p. 12.; "Health: It's Just a Gut Feeling: Millions of Us Drink Yogurts with 'Friendly Bacteria'," *The Independent* (London), March 1, 2005, p. 11; ""Yogurt: The Culture Catches On," *The Boston Globe*, September 13, 2004; *Trading Up Trends, Brands, and Practices, 2004 Research Update*, Boston Consulting Group, May 2004; "Actimel Leads the Culture Club," *Brand Strategy*, November 11, 2003, p. 23; "RKCR/Y&R Unveil the Actimel Challenge," *Campaign*, January 10, 2003, p. 8.

11. "For Asian Women, Weight-Loss Rule 1 Is Skip the Gym," *Wall Street Journal*, October 9, 2003, p. A1; "Unilever Expands Slim-Fast to Create a Diet Megabrand," *Advertising Age*, June 23, 2003, p. 8; "Living Larger," *USA Today*, March 16, 1998, p. 4D.

12. For more on wrinkle-free clothing, see "Botox for Broadcloth," *Wall Street Journal*, October 7, 2002, p. A19; "'Wrinkle-Free' Shirts Don't Live Up to the Name," *Wall Street Journal*, May 11, 1994, p. B1. For more on stain-resistant clothing, see "A Tie You Can Wipe Your Mouth With," *Wall Street Journal*, October 14, 2003, p. D1; "Look, Ma, No Stains," *Time*, December 9, 2002, p. 64. For more on service quality, see Chapter 8, endnote 4. For more on service expectations, see "Can I Get a Smile with My Burger and Fries?" *Wall Street Journal*, September 23, 2003, p. D6; "Service—with a Side of Sales," *Wall Street Journal Reports*, October 29, 2001, p. R13; "Why Service Stinks," *Business Week*, October 23, 2000, p. 118. See also Alain Genestre and Paul Herbig, "Service Expectations and Perceptions Revisited: Adding Product Quality to SERVQUAL," *Journal of Marketing Theory & Practice*, Fall 1996, p. 72; Valarie A. Zeithaml, Leonard L. Berry, and A. Parasuraman, "The Nature and Determinants of Customer Expectations of Service," *Journal of the Academy of Marketing Science*, Winter 1993, p. 1; Rashmi Adaval, "How Good Gets Better and Bad Gets Worse: Understanding the Impact of Affect on Evaluations of Known Brands," *Journal of Consumer Research*, December 2003, p. 352; Alexander Chernev, David Glen Mick, and Michael D. Johnson, "When More Is Less and Less Is More: The Role of Ideal Point Availability and Assortment in Consumer Choice," *Journal of Consumer Research*, September 2003, p. 170.

13. Harold H. Kassarjian and Mary Jane Sheffet, "Personality and Consumer Behavior: An Update," in H. Kassarjian and T. Robertson, *Perspectives in Consumer Behavior* (Glenview, IL: Scott, Foresman, 1981), p. 160; Todd A. Mooradian and James M. Olver, "I Can't Get No Satisfaction: The Impact of Personality and Emotion on Postpurchase Processes," *Psychology & Marketing*, July 1997, p. 379.

14. "It's Mind Vending . . . in the World of Psychographics," *Time* (Inside Business Bonus Section), October 2003; "Lifestyles Help Shape Innovation," *DSN Retailing Today*, August 4, 2003, p. 20; "Generation Next," *Advertising Age*, January 15, 2001, p. 14; "Head Trips," *American Demographics*, October 2000, p. 38; "Join the Club," *Brandweek*, February 15, 1999, p. 26; "The Frontier of Psychographics," *American Demographics*, July 1996, p. 38; W. D. Wells, "Psychographics: A Critical Review," *Journal of Marketing Research*, May 1975, p. 196.

15. See www.sric-bi.com; "Markets with Attitude," *American Demographics*, July 1994, p. 22; "New VALS 2 Takes Psychological Route," *Advertising Age*, February 13, 1989, p. 24; Lynn R. Kahle, Sharon E. Beatty, and Pamela Homer, "Alternative Measurement Approaches to Consumer Values: The List of Values (LOV) and Values and Life Styles (VALS)," *Journal of Consumer Research*, December 1986, p. 405.

16. "Families Spend Less on Food as They Pursue House, Car Dreams," *Advertising Age*, February 7, 2005, p. 34; "Buying Young," *Wall Street Journal*, November 26, 2004, p. W8; "Targeting Young Adults," *Wall Street Journal*, October 4, 2004, p. B1ff.; "Farther along the X Axis," *American Demographics*, May 2004, pp. 21–24; "La-Z-Boy: Up from Naugahyde," *Business Week*, April 12, 2004, pp. 88–90; "Work & Family," *Wall Street Journal*, March 31, 1997, p. 1ff. See also Richard G. Netemeyer, Thomas Brashear-Alejandro, and James S. Boles, "A Cross-National Model of Job-Related Outcomes of Work Role and Family Role Variables: A Retail Sales Context," *Journal of the Academy of Marketing Science*, Winter 2004, p. 49; Patrick E. Murphy and William A. Staples, "A Modernized Family Life Cycle," *Journal of Consumer Research*, June 1979, p. 12.

17. Based on U.S. Census data and "The American Consumer 2006," *Advertising Age*, January 2, 2006; "The State of Our Unions," *USA Today*, February 26, 2004, p. 1Aff.; "Do Us Part," *American Demographics*, September 2002, p. 9; "The Ex-Files," *American Demographics*, February 2001, p. 60. See also James A. Roberts, Chris Manolis, and John F. Tanner, Jr., "Family Structure, Materialism, and Compulsive Buying: a Reinquiry and Extension," *Journal of the Academy of Marketing Science*, Summer 2003, p. 300.

18. Based on U.S. Census data and "Trying to Connect with Generation Y," *Wall Street Journal*, October 13, 2005, p. B3; "American Express Tries to Find Its Place with a Younger Crowd," *Wall Street Journal*, September 22, 2005, p. A1ff.; "Wireless Services Get Wakeup Call from Youth," *Advertising Age*, June 6, 2005, p. 16; "Teens Shift Gears," *Display and Design Ideas*, October 2004, pp. 32–34; "Firms Aim Prepaid Credit Cards at Young Consumers," *USA Today*, August 4, 2004, p. 4B; "Nextel Chases Teen Market," *Wall Street Journal*, April 13, 2004, p. B2; "Verizon Wireless Upsells Youth via Instant Texting," *Advertising Age*, March 1, 2004, p. 3; "Hooking Up with Gen Y," *Business 2.0*, October 2003, pp. 49–52; "More Parents Are Leaving School Shopping to the Kids," *USA Today*, August 11, 2003, p.1A; "Kids, Tweens & Teens," *Advertising Age*, February 17, 2003, pp. S1–S6; "Rushing to Cash In on the New Baby Boom," *Wall Street Journal*, August 9, 2000, p. B1; "My, You've Grown: The Teen Economy Is Like Totally Awesome," *Wall Street Journal*, June 28, 2000, p. S3; "The Six Value Segments of Global Youth," *Brandweek*, May 22, 2000, p. 38.

19. Based on U.S. Census data and "Why Grown Kids Come Home," *USA Today*, January 11, 2005, p. 1Aff.; "Mom and Dad, I'm Home—Again," *Business Week*, November 3, 2003, p. 110; "Free at Last!" *Newsweek*, October 13, 2003, p. 62; "Bringing Up Adultolescents," *Newsweek*, March 25, 2002, p. 38; "The Joy of Empty Nesting," *American Demographics*, May 2000, p. 48; "Take My Stuff, Please!" *Wall Street Journal*, March 31, 2000, p. W1; "Extreme Nesting," *Wall Street Journal*, January 7, 2000, p. W1; Patti Williams and Aimee Drolet, "Age-Related Differences in Responses to Emotional Advertisements," *Journal of Consumer Research*, December 2005, p. 343.

20. For more on kids' influence in purchase decisions, see L. A. Flurry and Alvin C. Burns, "Children's Influence in Purchase Decisions: A Social Power Theory Approach," *Journal of Business Research*, May 2005, p. 593; "Walkie-Talkie Phones Hit the Family Market," *Wall Street Journal*, February 23, 2006, p. D1ff.; "Cell Phones for the Sandlot," *Business Week*, August 15, 2005, p. 20; "Marketing to Kids: More than Child's Play," *Poultry*, June/July 2005, pp. 28–30; "Kids," *Advertising Age*, February 21, 2005, pp. S1–S10; "Advertising Huggies and Pampers Are Seeking to Extend Their Brands . . .," *New York Times*, January 18, 2005, p. C12; "K-C Pampers Tots with Toiletries,"

Advertising Age, December 13, 2004, p. 6; "Toymakers Launch Videogame Consoles Aimed at Preschoolers," *Wall Street Journal*, September 8, 2004, p. B1ff.; "Computer Gadgets Get Downsized for Children," *Wall Street Journal*, August 25, 2004, p. D4; "Marketing to Kids, Tweens, & Teens," *Advertising Age*, March 29, 2004, pp. S1–S8; "Into the Mouth of Babes," *Brandweek*, May 6, 2002, pp. 26–34; "Catering to Kids," *Wall Street Journal*, May 3, 2002, p. W1; "Peek-a-Boo, I See You—Clearly," *Wall Street Journal*, January 25, 2002, p. W1; "Hey Kid, Buy This!" *Business Week*, June 30, 1997, p. 62. See also Sharon E. Beatty and Salil Talpade, "Adolescent Influence in Family Decision Making: A Replication with Extension," *Journal of Consumer Research*, September 1994, p. 332; Ugur Yavas, Emin Babakus, and Nejdet Deleners, "Family Purchasing Roles in Saudi Arabia: Perspectives from Saudi Wives," *Journal of Business Research*, September 1994, p. 75; Ellen R. Foxman, Patriya S. Tansuhaj, and Karin M. Ekstrom, "Adolescents' Influence in Family Purchase Decisions: A Socialization Perspective," *Journal of Business Research*, March 1989, p. 159; C. Lackman and J.M. Lanasa, "Family Decision-Making Theory: An Overview and Assessment," *Psychology & Marketing*, March/April 1993, p. 81. For more on women's influence in purchase decisions, see U.S. Census data, including "Women in the United States: A Profile, March 2000," at www.census.gov/population/www/socdemo/women; "A Guide to Who Holds the Purse Strings," *Wall Street Journal*, June 22, 2000, p. A14; "How to Market to Women," *Advertising Age*, June 12, 2000, p. 24.

21. "Consumers Enjoy Lap of Luxury," *Investor's Business Daily*, October 27, 2003, p. A7; "Downsized Luxury," *Wall Street Journal*, October 14, 2003, p. B1; "The Japanese Paradox," *Wall Street Journal*, September 23, 2003, p. B1; "Luxury for the Masses," *Brandweek*, June 25, 2001, p. 16; "Luxury Marketing," *Advertising Age*, June 11, 2001, p. S1ff.; "Which Is Luxury?" *USA Today*, May 4, 2001, p. 1B; "Class in America," *Fortune*, February 7, 1994, p. 114. See also Cornelia Pechmann and Susan J. Knight, "An Experimental Investigation of the Joint Effects of Advertising and Peers on Adolescents' Beliefs and Intentions about Cigarette Consumption," *Journal of Consumer Research*, June 2002, p. 5; Albert M. Muniz, Jr. and Thomas C. O'Guinn, "Brand Community," *Journal of Consumer Research*, March 2001, p. 412; Gary Cross, "Valves of Desire: A Historian's Perspective on Parents, Children, and Marketing," *Journal of Consumer Research*, December 2002, p. 441; Terry L. Childers and Akshay R. Rao, "The Influence of Familial and Peer-based Reference Groups on Consumer Decisions," *Journal of Consumer Research*, September 1992, p. 198; David B. Wooten and Americus Reed Ii, "Playing It Safe: Susceptibility to Normative Influence and Protective Self-Presentation," *Journal of Consumer Research*, December 2004, p. 551.

22. For more on opinion leaders and word-of-mouth publicity, see Chapter 13, endnote 23. See also "In Search of True Marketplace Influencers," *Advertising Age*, December 5, 2005, p. 22; "In Era of Consumer Control, Marketers Crave the Potency of Word-of-Mouth," *Advertising Age*, November 28, 2005, p. 32; "Blogs Cause Word of Mouth Business to Spread Quickly," *Brandweek*, October 3, 2005, p. 9; "How to Calculate Word-of-Mouth," *Advertising Age*, July 26, 2004, p. 4ff.; "The Net of Influence," *Business 2.0*, March 2004, p. 70; "Word of Mouth in the Digital Age: Marketers Win when Friends Hit 'Send,'" *Brandweek*, October 2, 2000, p. 24. See also Michael A. Belch, Kathleen A. Krentler, and Laura A. Willis-Flurry, "Teen Internet Mavens: Influence in Family Decision Making," *Journal of Business Research*, May 2005, p. 569; Ellen Garbarino and Michal Strahilevitz, "Gender Differences in the Perceived Risk of Buying Online and the Effects of Receiving a Site Recommendation," *Journal of Business Research*, July 2004, p. 768; Fred Thorsten Hennig-Thurau, Kevin P. Gwinner, Gianfranco Walsh, and Dwayne D. Gremler, "Electronic Word-of-Mouth Via Consumer-Opinion Platforms: What Motivates Consumers to Articulate Themselves on the Internet?" *Journal of Interactive Marketing*, Winter 2004, p. 38; Ronald A. Clark and Ronald E. Goldsmith, "Market Mavens: Psychological Influences," *Psychology & Marketing*, April 2005, p. 289; Barbara Bickart and

Robert M. Schindler, "Internet Forums as Influential Sources of Consumer Information," *Journal of Interactive Marketing*, Summer 2001, p. 31.

23. "Art of Noise," *Brandweek*, November 1, 1999, p. 78.

24. Based on "The American Consumer 2006," *Advertising Age*, January 2, 2006; *The Multicultural Economy 2004, America's Minority Buying Power*, Selig Center for Economic Growth, University of Georgia, and U.S. Census data, including *Census 2000 Special Reports: Demographic Trends in the 20th Century CENSR-4*. For an overview of ethnic populations in the U.S., see *Racial and Ethnic Diversity* (Ithaca, NY: New Strategist, 2000); "Airlines See Potential in Travel by Immigrants," *USA Today*, December 27, 2005, p. 1Bff.; "Give Me Your Tired, Your Poor, Your Beloved Products," *Business 2.0*, October 2005, pp. 29–30; "Embracing Illegals," *Business Week*, July 18, 2005, pp. 56–64; "Sears Tries Multicultural Style," *USA Today*, November 16, 2004, p. 4B; "The Art of Cultural Correctness," *American Demographics*, November 2004, pp. 27–33; "Zooming In on Diversity," *American Demographics*, July/August 2004, pp. 27–31; "Census Projects Growing Diversity," *USA Today*, March 18, 2004, pp. 1A–2A; "The New Face of Beauty," *Brandweek*, January 19, 2004, pp. 24–28; "Ads for Ethnic Hair Care Show a New Face" *Wall Street Journal*, July 21, 2003, p. B1; "Multicultural Marketing," *Advertising Age*, July 7, 2003, p. S1; "Ethnic Marketing," *DSN Retailing Today*, March 24, 2003, p. 13; Geng Cui, "Marketing to Ethnic Minority Consumers: An Historical Journey (1932–1997)," *Journal of Macromarketing* 21, no. 1 (June 2001), p. 23; Marilyn Halter, *Shopping for Identity: The Marketing of Ethnicity* (Schocken Books, 2000); "Micro Melting Pots," *American Demographics*, June 2001, p. 20; "Color Them Beautiful—and Visible," *USA Today*, May 2, 2001, p. 1B. For more on the white population, see U.S. Census data, including *The White Population: August 2001*. For more on the African American market, see U.S. Census data, including *The Black Population in the United States: April 2003* at www.census.gov/population/www/socdemo/race; "Has This Group Been Left Behind?" *Brandweek*, March 14, 2005, pp. 33–36; "Offerings Hope to Extend the Oprah Effect," *Advertising Age*, March 7, 2005, p. S12ff.; "Revival," *American Demographics*, October 2003, p. 26; "Color Bind," *American Demographics*, September 2003, p. 22; "Card Crafter Uses Creativity to Carve Out Niche," *USA Today*, March 19, 2003, p. 7B; "The New Demographics of Black Americans," *Business Week*, December 4, 2000, p. 14; Carol M. Motley, "Aunt Jemima, Uncle Ben, and Rastus: Blacks in Advertising, Yesterday, Today, and Tomorrow," *Journal of Marketing*, April 1995, p. 111. For more on the Hispanic market, see U.S. Census data, including *The Hispanic Population in the United States: March 2002* at www.census.gov/population/www/socdemo/race; "How Nextel Quickly Expanded Its Hispanic Sales," AdAge.com, May 25, 2005; "IKEA, Circuit City Stores Go Bilingual," *Advertising Age*, January 3, 2005, p. 19; "Hispanic Fact Pack," *Advertising Age*, 2004 and 2005 editions; "Hispanic Nation," *Business Week*, March 15, 2004; "P&G's Hispanic Accent," *Business Week Online*, March 15, 2004; "How Wells Fargo Banks on Hispanics," *Business Week Online*, March 15, 2004; "Marketing to Hispanics," *Advertising Age*, September 15, 2003, p. S1; "39 Million Make Hispanics Largest Minority Group," *USA Today*, June 19, 2003, p. 1A; "Advertisers Point and Click to Find Hispanic Audiences," *Adweek*, April 7, 2003, p. 8; "Fresh from the Border," *Time* (Inside Business), April 2003; "Advertisers Tap into Hispanic Gold Mine," *USA Today*, February 21, 2003, p. 1B. For more on the Asian-American market, see U.S. Census data, including *The Asian and PI Population in the United States: March 2002* at www.census.gov/population/www/socdemo/race; "The Invisible Market," *Brandweek*, January 30, 2006, pp. 22–26; "Banks Market to Asian Communities," *USA Today*, September 22, 2004, p. 4B; "For Asians in U.S. Mini-Chinatowns Sprout in Suburbia," *Wall Street Journal*, April 28, 2004, p. A1ff.; "The Asian American Blind Spot," *American Demographics*, July 2001, p. 16; "U.S. Asian Population Grew and Diversified, Census Shows," *Wall Street Journal*, May 15, 2001, p. B4; Sonya A. Grier, Anne M. Brumbaugh, and Corliss G. Thornton, "Crossover Dreams: Consumer Responses to Ethnic-Oriented Products," *Journal of Marketing*, April 2006, p. 35; David Luna and Laura A. Peracchio, "Advertising to Bilingual Consumers: The Impact of Code-Switching on Persuasion," *Journal of Consumer Research*, March 2005, p. 760; Shi Zhang and Bernd H. Schmitt, "Activating Sound and Meaning: The Role of Language Proficiency in Bilingual Consumer Environments," *Journal of Consumer Research*, June 2004, p. 220; Ainsworth Anthony Bailey, "A Year in the Life of the African-American Male in Advertising: A Content Analysis," *Journal of Advertising*, Spring 2006, p. 83; D. Anthony Platha and Thomas H. Stevenson, "Financial Services Consumption Behavior across Hispanic American Consumers," *Journal of Business Research*, August 2005, p. 1089; see also Lucette B. Comer and J. A. F. Nicholls, "Communication Between Hispanic Salespeople and Their Customers: A First Look," *Journal of Personal Selling & Sales Management*, Summer 2000, p. 121; Geng Cui, "Marketing Strategies in a Multi-Ethnic Environment," *Journal of Marketing Theory & Practice*, Winter 1997, p. 122; Michael Laroche, Chung K. Kim, and Madeleine Clarke, "The Effects of Ethnicity Factors on Consumer Deal Interests: An Empirical Study of French- and English-Canadians," *Journal of Marketing Theory & Practice*, Winter 1997, p. 100.

25. "Overcoming the Stigma of Dishwashers in Japan," *Wall Street Journal*, May 19, 2000, p. B1. See also "MTV's Passage to India," Fortune, August 9, 2004, pp. 117–25; "The New Land of Opportunity," *Business 2.0*, July 2004, pp. 71–79; "Product Pitfall Proliferate in a Global Cultural Maze," *Wall Street Journal*, May 14, 2001, p. B11; Sydney Roslow, "International Consumer Behavior: Its Impact on Marketing Strategy Development," *Journal of the Academy of Marketing Science*, Summer 1996, p. 278; R. Mead, "Where Is the Culture of Thailand?" *International Journal of Research in Marketing*, September 1994, p. 401.

26. Eric J. Arnould and Craig J. Thompson, "Consumer Culture Theory (CCT): Twenty Years of Research," *Journal of Consumer Research*, March 2005, p. 868; "Does Class Count in Today's Land of Opportunity?" *New York Times*, January 18, 2003, p. A17; John L. Graham, "How Culture Works," *Journal of Marketing*, April 1996, p. 134; Gary D. Gregory and James M. Munch, "Cultural Values in International Advertising: An Examination of Familial Norms and Roles in Mexico," *Psychology & Marketing*, March 1997, p. 99; Grant McCracken, "Culture and Consumption: A Theoretical Account of the Structure and Movement of the Cultural Meaning of Consumer Goods," *Journal of Consumer Research*, June 1986, p. 71.

27. "No More Shoppus Interruptus," *American Demographics*, May 2001, p. 39; "No Buy? Then Bye-Bye," *Business Week E.Biz*, April 16, 2001, p. EB6; "E-Tailing," *Business Week E.Biz*, May 15, 2000, pp. EB103–EB118. See also Jennifer Chang Coupland, Dawn Iacobucci, and Eric Arnould, "Invisible Brands: An Ethnography of Households and the Brands in Their Kitchen Pantries," *Journal of Consumer Research*, June 2005, p. 106; S. Christian Wheeler, Richard E. Petty, and George Y. Bizer, "Self-Schema Matching and Attitude Change: Situational and Dispositional Determinants of Message Elaboration," *Journal of Consumer Research*, March 2005, p. 787; Steven Bellman, Eric J. Johnson, Gerald L. Lohse, and Naomi Mandel, "Designing Marketplaces of the Artificial with Consumers in Mind: Four Approaches to Understanding Consumer Behavior in Electronic Environments," *Journal of Interactive Marketing*, Winter 2006, p. 21; Pratibha A. Dabholkar and Richard P. Bagozzi, "An Attitudinal Model of Technology-Based Self-Service: Moderating Effects of Consumer Traits and Situational Factors," *Journal of the Academy of Marketing Science*, Summer 2002, p. 184; Darren W. Dahl, Rajesh V. Manchanda, and Jennifer J. Argo, "Embarrassment in Consumer Purchase: The Roles of Social Presence and Purchase Familiarity," *Journal of Consumer Research*, December 2001, p. 473; Charles S. Areni, Pamela Kiecker, and Kay M. Palan, "Is It Better to Give than to Receive? Exploring Gender Differences in the Meaning of Memorable Gifts," *Psychology & Marketing*, January 1998, p. 81; Russell W. Belk, "Situational Variables and Consumer Behavior," *Journal of Consumer*

Research 2 (1975), p. 157; John F. Sherry, Jr., "Gift Giving in Anthropological Perspective," *Journal of Consumer Research,* September 1983, p. 157.

28. Adapted and updated from James H. Myers and William H. Reynolds, *Consumer Behavior and Marketing Management* (Boston: Houghton Mifflin, 1967), p. 49. See also Mary Frances Luce, Jianmin Jia, and Gregory W. Fischer, "How Much Do You Like It? Within-Alternative Conflict and Subjective Confidence in Consumer Judgments," *Journal of Consumer Research,* December 2003, p. 464; Ann E. Schlosser, David Glen Mick, and John Deighton, "Experiencing Products in the Virtual World: The Role of Goal and Imagery in Influencing Attitudes versus Purchase Intentions," *Journal of Consumer Research,* September 2003, p. 184; Jennifer Edson Escalas, Marian Chapman Moore, and Julie Edell Britton, "Fishing for Feelings? Hooking Viewers Helps!" *Journal of Consumer Psychology,* no. 1 (2004), p. 105; Eric J. Karson and Robert J. Fisher, "Predicting Intentions to Return to the Web Site: Extending the Dual Mediation Hypothesis," *Journal of Interactive Marketing,* Summer 2005, p. 2; Dipayan Biswas and Abhijit Biswas, "The Diagnostic Role of Signals in the Context of Perceived Risks in Online Shopping: Do Signals Matter More on the Web?" *Journal of Interactive Marketing,* Summer 2004, p. 30; Gordon R. Foxall and Victoria K. James, "The Behavioral Ecology of Brand Choice: How and What Do Consumers Maximize?" *Psychology & Marketing,* September 2003, p. 811; Ronald E. Goldsmith, "A Theory of Shopping," *Journal of the Academy of Marketing Science,* Fall 2000, p. 541; Judith Lynne Zaichkowsky, "Consumer Behavior: Yesterday, Today, and Tomorrow," *Business Horizons,* May/June 1991, p. 51; Dawn Iacobucci, Phipps Arabie, and Anand Bodapati, "Recommendation Agents on the Internet," *Journal of Interactive Marketing,* Summer 2000, p. 2; Dan Ariely, "Controlling the Information Flow: Effects on Consumers' Decision Making and Preferences," *Journal of Consumer Research,* September 2000, p. 233; Amitav Chakravarti and Chris Janiszewski, "The Influence of Macro-Level Motives on Consideration Set Composition in Novel Purchase Situations," *Journal of Consumer Research,* September 2003, p. 244; Ravi Dhar and Steven J. Sherman, "The Effect of Common and Unique Features in Consumer Choice," *Journal of Consumer Research,* December 1996, p. 193; Victor V. Cordell, "Consumer Knowledge Measures as Predictors in Product Evaluation," *Psychology & Marketing,* May 1997, p. 241; John V. Petrof and Naoufel Daghfous, "Evoked Set: Myth or Reality?" *Business Horizons,* May/June 1996, p. 72; Wayne D. Hoyer, "An Examination of Consumer Decision Making for a Common Repeat Purchase Product," *Journal of Consumer Research,* December 1984, p. 822; James R. Bettman, *An Information Processing Theory of Consumer Choice* (Reading, MA.: Addison-Wesley Publishing, 1979); Richard W. Olshavsky and Donald H. Granbois, "Consumer Decision Making: Fact or Fiction?" *Journal of Consumer Research,* September 1979, p. 93.

29. Craig J. Thompson, "Consumer Risk Perceptions in a Community of Reflexive Doubt," *Journal of Consumer Research,* September 2005, p. 235; Alice M. Tybout, Brian Sternthal, Prashant Malaviya, Georgios A. Bakamitsos, Se-Bum Park, Dawn Iacobucci, and Frank Kardes, "Information Accessibility as a Moderator of Judgments: The Role of Content versus Retrieval Ease," *Journal of Consumer Research,* June 2005, p. 76; Nitika Garg, J. Jeffrey Inman, Vikas Mittal, Dawn Iacobucci, and Stephen Nowlis, "Incidental and Task-Related Affect: A Re-Inquiry and Extension of the Influence of Affect on Choice," *Journal of Consumer Research,* June 2005, p. 154; Susan Jung Grant, Prashant Malaviya, and Brian Sternthal, "The Influence of Negation on Product Evaluations," *Journal of Consumer Research,* December 2004, p. 583; Laura L. Pingol and Anthony D. Miyazaki, "Information Source Usage and Purchase Satisfaction: Implications for Product-Focused Print Media," *Journal of Advertising Research,* March 2005, p. 132; Stijn M. J. Van Osselaer, Joseph W. Alba, and Puneet Manchanda, "Irrelevant Information and Mediated Intertemporal Choice,"

Journal of Consumer Psychology, 2004, p. 257; Judi Strebel, Tülin Erdem, and Joffre Swait, "Consumer Search in High Technology Markets: Exploring the Use of Traditional Information Channels," *Journal of Consumer Psychology,* no. 1 (2004), p. 96; Ram D. Gopal, Bhavik Pathak, Arvind K. Tripathi, and Fang Yin, "From Fatwallet to eBay: An Investigation of Online Deal-Forums and Sales Promotions," *Journal of Retailing,* June 2006, p. 155; Fuan Li, Paul W. Miniard, and Michael J. Barone, "The Facilitating Influence of Consumer Knowledge on the Effectiveness of Daily Value Reference Information," *Journal of the Academy of Marketing Science,* Summer 2000, p. 424; Robin A. Coulter, Linda L. Price, and Lawrence Feick, "Rethinking the Origins of Involvement and Brand Commitment: Insights from Postsocialist Central Europe," *Journal of Consumer Research,* September 2003, p. 151; Gal Zauberman, "The Intertemporal Dynamics of Consumer Lock-In," *Journal of Consumer Research,* December 2003, p. 405; Brian T. Ratchford, "The Economics of Consumer Knowledge," *Journal of Consumer Research,* March 2001, p. 397; Cele Otnes, Tina M. Lowrey, and L J. Shrum, "Toward an Understanding of Consumer Ambivalence," *Journal of Consumer Research,* June 1997, p. 80; Ronald E. Goldsmith, "Consumer Involvement: Concepts and Research," *Journal of the Academy of Marketing Science,* Summer 1996, p. 281; Jeffrey B. Schmidt and Richard A. Spreng, "A Proposed Model of External Consumer Information Search," *Journal of the Academy of Marketing Science,* Summer 1996, p. 246; Raj Arora, "Consumer Involvement—What It Offers to Advertising Strategy," *International Journal of Advertising* 4, no. 2 (1985), p. 119; J. Brock Smith and Julia M. Bristor, "Uncertainty Orientation: Explaining Differences in Purchase Involvement and External Search," *Psychology & Marketing,* November/December 1994, p. 587.

30. J. Jeffrey Inman and Marcel Zeelenberg, "Regret in Repeat Purchase Versus Switching Decisions: The Attenuating Role of Decision Justifiability," *Journal of Consumer Research,* June 2002, p. 116; Michael Tsiros and Vikas Mittal, "Regret: A Model of Its Antecedents and Consequences in Consumer Decision Making," *Journal of Consumer Research,* March 2000, p. 401; Thomas A. Burnham, Judy K. Frels, and Vijay Mahajan, "Consumer Switching Costs: A Typology, Antecedents, and Consequences," *Journal of the Academy of Marketing Science,* Spring 2003, p. 109; Ziv Carmon, Klaus Wertenbroch, and Marcel Zeelenberg, "Option Attachment: When Deliberating Makes Choosing Feel Like Losing," *Journal of Consumer Research,* June 2003, p. 15; Alan D. J. Cooke, Tom Meyvis, and Alan Schwartz, "Avoiding Future Regret in Purchase-Timing Decisions," *Journal of Consumer Research,* March 2001, p. 447; Anna S. Mattila, "The Impact of Cognitive Intertia on Postconsumption Evaluation Processes," *Journal of the Academy of Marketing Science,* Summer 2003, p. 287; William Cunnings and Mark Venkatesan, "Cognitive Dissonance and Consumer Behavior: A Review of the Evidence," *Journal of Marketing Research,* August 1976, p. 303; Sarah Fisher Gardial et al., "Comparing Consumers' Recall of Prepurchase and Postpurchase Product Evaluation Experience," *Journal of Consumer Research,* March 1994, p. 548.

31. Adapted from E. M. Rogers, *Diffusion of Innovation* (New York: Free Press, 2003). For other sampling examples, see "McDonald's Gives Free Samples of Chicken Selects," *USA Today,* February 16, 2005, p. 6B; "Test Drives Get a New Spin," *Wall Street Journal,* February 3, 2005, p. B1ff.; "Unilever Pitch to Hispanics: Taste Ragu, Register to Vote," *Wall Street Journal,* March 25, 2004, p. B1ff.; "Mr., Mrs., Meet Mr. Clean," *Wall Street Journal,* January 30, 2003, p. B1; "J&J Supports Marathon Runners at Point of Pain," *Brandweek,* December 2, 2002, p. 32; "Taking the Free Out of Free Samples," *Wall Street Journal,* September 25, 2002, p. D1; "Marketers Revel with Spring Breakers," *USA Today,* March 12, 2002, p. 3B; "When Free Samples Become Saviors," *Wall Street Journal,* August 14, 2001, p. B1; "Small Wonder," *Wall Street Journal,* June 25, 2001, p. R1; "Use of Samples in Drug Industry Raises Concern," *Wall Street Journal,* July 19, 2000, p. B1; "Try It. You'll Like It," *Wall Street Journal,* September 27,

1999, p. 15. See also Michael A. Jones, David L. Mothersbaugh, and Sharon E. Beatty, "Switching Barriers and Repurchase Intentions in Services," *Journal of Retailing*, Summer 2000, p. 259; Kevin Mason, Thomas Jensen, Scot Burton, and Dave Roach, "The Accuracy of Brand and Attribute Judgments: The Role of Information Relevancy, Product Experience, and Attribute-Relationship Schemata," *Journal of the Academy of Marketing Science*, Summer 2001, p. 307; Jan-Benedict E. M. Steenkamp and Katrijn Gielens, "Consumer and Market Drivers of the Trial Probability of New Consumer Packaged Goods," *Journal of Consumer Research*, December 2003, p. 368; Stephen J. Hoch, "Product Experience Is Seductive," *Journal of Consumer Research*, December 2002, p. 448.

32. "PepsiCo Tries to Clarify Pepsi One's Image," *Wall Street Journal*, February 25, 2000, p. B7.

33. Robert M. March, *The Honourable Customer: Marketing and Selling to the Japanese in the 1990s* (Melbourne, Vic.: Longman Professional, 1990); Robert Gottliebsen, "Japan's Stark Choices," *Business Review Weekly*, October 16, 1992. See also Lawrence Feick, Robin A. Coulter, and Linda L. Price, "Rethinking the Origins of Involvement and Brand Commitment: Insights from Postsocialist Central Europe," *Journal of Consumer Research*, September 2003, p. 151; Annamma Joy, "Gift Giving in Hong Kong and the Continuum of Social Ties," *Journal of Consumer Research*, September 2001, p. 239.

34. "Fuel and Freebies," *Wall Street Journal*, June 10, 2002, p. B1.

CHAPTER 6

1. See www.johndeere.com, www.jdparts.com, and www.metokote.com. See also *2005 Annual Report*, Deere & Company; "John Deere Cultivates Its Image," *Advertising Age*, July 25, 2005, p. 6; "Metokote Develops Customized Systems for Applying High Tech Coatings; More than Just Painting a Part," *Diesel Progress*, April 2003; and "John Deere Golf & Turf One Source," www.deere.com/en_US/golfturf/one_source_partners; "Deere Uses E-Hubs to Build Relationships with Dealers," *BtoB*, September 9, 2002, p. 18; "Outsourcing Is More than Cost Cutting," *Fortune*, October 26, 1998, p. 238C.

2. "Detroit to Suppliers: Quality or Else," *Fortune*, September 30, 1996, p. 134C. See also Thomas H. Stevenson and Frank C. Barnes, "What Industrial Marketers Need to Know Now about ISO 9000 Certification: A Review, Update, and Integration with Marketing," *Industrial Marketing Management*, November 2002, p. 695; Roger Calantone and Gary Knight, "The Critical Role of Product Quality in the International Performance of Industrial Firms," *Industrial Marketing Management*, November 2000, p. 493; Sime Curkovic and Robert Handfield, "Use of ISO 9000 and Baldrige Award Criteria in Supplier Quality Evaluation," *International Journal of Purchasing & Materials Management*, Spring 1996, p. 2.

3. Masaaki Kotabe and Janet Y. Murray, "Global Sourcing Strategy and Sustainable Competitive Advantage," *Industrial Marketing Management*, January 2004, p. 7; R. Bruce Money, "Word-of-Mouth Promotion and Switching Behavior in Japanese and American Business-to-Business Service Clients," *Journal of Business Research*, March 2004, p. 297; "The Push to Streamline Supply Chains," *Fortune*, March 3, 1997, pp. 108C–R; P. F. Johnson, Michiel R. Leenders, and Harold E. Fearon, "Evolving Roles and Responsibilities of Purchasing Organizations," *International Journal of Purchasing & Materials Management*, Winter 1998, p. 2; Scott Elliott, "Collaborative Advantage: Winning through Extended Enterprise Supplier Networks," *Journal of Product Innovation Management*, September 2001, p. 352; Chris Howgego, "Maximizing Competitiveness through the Supply Chain," *International Journal of Retail & Distribution Management*, no. 11 (2002), p. 603; Robert J. Trent and Robert M. Monczka, "Understanding Integrated Global Sourcing," *International Journal of Physical Distribution & Logistics Management*, no. 7 (2003), p. 607.

4. Jeffrey E. Lewin and Naveen Donthu, "The Influence of Purchase Situation on Buying Center Structure and Involvement: A Select Meta-Analysis of Organizational Buying Behavior Research," *Journal of Business Research*, October 2005, p. 1381; Jae H. Pae, Namwoon Kim, Jim K. Han, and Leslie Yip, "Managing Intraorganizational Diffusion of Innovations: Impact of Buying Center Dynamics and Environments," *Industrial Marketing Management*, November 2002, p. 719; Larry C. Giunipero and Judith F. Vogt, "Empowering the Purchasing Function: Moving to Team Decisions," *International Journal of Purchasing & Materials Management*, Winter 1997, p. 8; Jerome M. Katrichis, "Exploring Departmental Level Interaction Patterns in Organizational Purchasing Decisions," *Industrial Marketing Management*, March 1998, p. 135; Robert D. McWilliams, Earl Naumann, and Stan Scott, "Determining Buying Center Size," *Industrial Marketing Management*, February 1992, p. 43; Melvin R. Mattson, "How to Determine the Composition and Influence of a Buying Center," *Industrial Marketing Management*, August 1988, p. 205; Barbara C. Perdue, "The Size and Composition of the Buying Firm's Negotiation Team in Rebuys of Component Parts," *Journal of the Academy of Marketing Science*, Spring 1989, p. 121; R. Venkatesh, Ajay K. Kohli, and Gerald Zaltman, "Influence Strategies in Buying Centers," *Journal of Marketing*, October 1995, p. 71.

5. Daniel J. Flint, Robert B. Woodruff, and Sarah Fisher Gardial, "Exploring the Phenomenon of Customers' Desired Value Change in a Business-to-Business Context," *Journal of Marketing*, October 2002, p. 102; E. Stephen Grant, "Buyer-Approved Selling: Sales Strategies from the Buyers Side of the Desk," *Journal of the Academy of Marketing Science*, Winter 2004, p. 99; Minette E. Drumwright, "Socially Responsible Organizational Buying: Environmental Concern as a Noneconomic Buying Criterion," *Journal of Marketing*, July 1994, p. 1; Lisa M. Ellram, "A Structured Method for Applying Purchasing Cost Management Tools," *International Journal of Purchasing & Materials Management*, Winter 1996, p. 11; Morgan P. Miles, Linda S. Munilla, and Gregory R. Russell, "Marketing and Environmental Registration/Certification: What Industrial Marketers Should Understand about ISO 14000," *Industrial Marketing Management*, July 1997, p. 363; M. Bixby Cooper, Cornelia Droge, and Patricia J. Daugherty, "How Buyers and Operations Personnel Evaluate Service," *Industrial Marketing Management* 20, no. 1 (1991), p. 81.

6. Richard F. Beltramini, "Exploring the Effectiveness of Business Gifts: Replication and Extension," *Journal of Advertising*, Summer 2000, p. 75; Jeanette J. Arbuthnot, "Identifying Ethical Problems Confronting Small Retail Buyers during the Merchandise Buying Process," *Journal of Business Ethics*, May 1997, p. 745; Gail K. McCracken and Thomas J. Callahan, "Is There Such a Thing as a Free Lunch?" *International Journal of Purchasing & Materials Management*, Winter 1996, p. 44; Robert W. Cooper, Garry L. Frank, and Robert A. Kemp, "The Ethical Environment Facing the Profession of Purchasing and Materials Management," *International Journal of Purchasing & Materials Management*, Spring 1997, p. 2; I. Fredrick Trawick, John E. Swan, Gail W. McGee, and David R. Rink, "Influence of Buyer Ethics and Salesperson Behavior on Intention to Choose a Supplier," *Journal of the Academy of Marketing Science*, Winter 1991, p. 17; J. A. Badenhorst, "Unethical Behaviour in Procurement: A Perspective on Causes and Solutions," *Journal of Business Ethics*, September 1994, p. 739.

7. "Social and Environmental Assessment 2004," Ben and Jerry's, Burlington, VT.

8. Neeraj Bharadwaj, "Investigating the Decision Criteria Used in Electronic Components Procurement," *Industrial Marketing Management*, May 2004, p. 317; Jacques Verville and Alannah Halingten, "A Six-Stage Model of the Buying Process for ERP Software," *Industrial Marketing Management*, October 2003, p. 585; Michael D. Smith, "The Impact of Shopbots on Electronic Markets," *Journal of the Academy of Marketing Science*, Fall 2002, p. 446; Carol C. Bienstock, "Understanding Buyer Information Acquisition for the Purchase of Logistics Services," *International Journal of Physical Distribution & Logistics Management*, no. 8 (2002), p. 636; David Tucker and Laurie Jones, "Leveraging the Power of the Internet for Optimal Supplier Sourcing," *International Journal of Physical Distribution & Logistics Management*, no. 3 (2000), p. 255; H. L. Brossard, "Information Sources Used by an Organization during a Complex Decision Process: An Exploratory Study," *Industrial Marketing Management*, January 1998, p. 41; Michele D. Bunn, "Taxonomy of Buying Decision Approaches," *Journal of Marketing*, January 1993, p. 38; Mark A. Farrell and Bill Schroder, "Influence Strategies in Organizational Buying Decisions," *Industrial Marketing Management*, July 1996, p. 293; Richard G. Newman, "Monitoring Price Increases with Economic Data: A Practical Approach," *International Journal of Purchasing & Materials Management*, Fall 1997, p. 35; Barbara Kline and Janet Wagner, "Information Sources and Retailer Buyer Decision-Making: The Effect of Product-Specific Buying Experience," *Journal of Retailing*, Spring 1994, p. 75; Ellen Day and Hiram C. Barksdale, Jr., "How Firms Select Professional Services," *Industrial Marketing Management*, May 1992, p. 85; Edward F. Fern and James R. Brown, "The Industrial/Consumer Marketing Dichotomy: A Case of Insufficient Justification," *Journal of Marketing*, Spring 1984, p. 68.

9. "With Promise of Big Savings, Net Bill Paying Could Soon Win Fans among U.S. Businesses," *Investor's Business Daily*, February 26, 2001, p. A7; "How Baxter, PNC, Pratt & Whitney Make the Internet Work for Them," *Investor's Business Daily*, February 12, 2001, p. A1; "Look, Ma, No Humans," *Business Week E.Biz*, November 20, 2000, p. EB132; "Hewlett-Packard's Slick Procurement System," *Ecompany*, November 2000, p. 236; "Setting Standards for Corporate Purchasing on the Internet," *Fortune*, September 8, 1997, p. 156. See also Werner Delfmann, Sascha Albers, and Martin Gehring, "The Impact of Electronic Commerce on Logistics Service Providers," *International Journal of Physical Distribution & Logistics Management*, no. 3 (2002), p. 203; Daniel Knudsen, "Aligning Corporate Strategy and E-procurement Tools," *International Journal of Physical Distribution & Logistics Management*, no. 8 (2003), p. 720.

10. "The New Golden Rule of Business," *Fortune*, February 21, 1994, p. 60; Janet L. Hartley and Thomas Y. Choi, "Supplier Development: Customers as a Catalyst of Process Change," *Business Horizons*, July/August 1996, p. 37; Theodore P. Stank, Margaret A. Emmelhainz, and Patricia J. Daugherty, "The Impact of Information on Supplier Performance," *Journal of Marketing Theory & Practice*, Fall 1996, p. 94.

11. "Ford Seeks Big Savings by Overhauling Supply System," *Wall Street Journal*, September 29, 2005, p. A1ff.; "Turning Vendors into Partners," *Inc. Magazine*, August 2005, pp. 94–100; "A 'China Price' for Toyota," *Business Week*, February 21, 2005, pp. 50–51; "Ford to Suppliers: Let's Get Cozier," *Business Week*, September 20, 2004, pp. IM8–IM10; "How Would You Like Your Ford?" *Business Week*, August 9, 2004, p. 34; "Wal-Mart's Low-Price Obsession Puts Suppliers through Wringer," *Investor's Business Daily*, January 30, 2004; "Push from Above," *Wall Street Journal*, May 23, 1996, p. R24; Jan B. Heide, "Plural Governance in Industrial Purchasing," *Journal of Marketing*, October 2003, p. 18; Shibin Sheng, James R. Brown, Carolyn Y. Nicholson, and Laura Poppo, "Do Exchange Hazards Always Foster Relational Governance? An Empirical Test of the Role of Communication," *International Journal of Research in Marketing*, March 2006, p. 63; Erin Anderson and Sandy D. Jap, "The Dark Side of Close Relationships," *MIT Sloan Management Review*, Spring 2005, p. 75.

12. Much of the discussion in this section is based on research reported in Joseph P. Cannon and William D. Perreault, Jr., "Buyer-Seller Relationships in Business Markets," *Journal of Marketing Research*, November 1999. See also Joseph P. Cannon, "Buyer-Supplier Relationships and Customer Firm Costs," *Journal of Marketing*, January 2001, p. 29; Kishore Gopalakrishna Pillai and Arun Sharma, "Mature Relationships: Why Does Relational Orientation Turn into Transaction Orientation?" *Industrial Marketing Management*, November 2003, p. 643; Kelly Hewett, R. Bruce Money, and Subhash Sharma, "An Exploration of the Moderating Role of Buyer Corporate Culture in Industrial Buyer-Seller Relationships," *Journal of the Acad-*

emy of Marketing Science, Summer 2002, p. 229; Christian Homburg, Harley Krohmer, Joseph P. Cannon, and Ingo Kiedaisch, "Customer Satisfaction in Transnational Buyer-Supplier Relationships," *Journal of International Marketing*, no. 4 (2002), p. 1; Christopher R. Moberg, Bob D. Cutler, Andrew Gross, and Thomas W. Speh, "Identifying Antecedents of Information Exchange Within Supply Chains," *International Journal of Physical Distribution & Logistics Management*, no. 9 (2002), p. 755; William W. Keep, Stanley C. Hollander, and Roger Dickinson, "Forces Impinging on Long-Term Business-to-Business Relationships in the United States: An Historical Perspective," *Journal of Marketing*, April 1998, p. 31; Das Narayandas and V. Kasturi Rangan, "Building and Sustaining Buyer-Seller Relationships in Mature Industrial Markets," *Journal of Marketing*, July 2004, p. 63; Thomas Tellefsen and Gloria Penn Gloria Thomas, "The Antecedents and Consequences of Organizational and Personal Commitment in Business Service Relationships," *Industrial Marketing Management*, January 2005, p. 23; Mary T. Holden and Thomas O'Toole, "A Quantitative Exploration of Communication's Role in Determining the Governance of Manufacturer-Retailer Relationships," *Industrial Marketing Management*, August 2004, p. 539; Gerrit H. Van Bruggen, Manish Kacker, and Chantal Nieuwlaat, "The Impact of Channel Function Performance on Buyer-Seller Relationships in Marketing Channels," *International Journal of Research in Marketing*, June 2005, p. 141.

13. "Purchasing's New Muscle," *Fortune*, February 20, 1995, p. 75; "Can Chrysler Get Blood from a Supplier?" *Business Week*, December 25, 2000, p. 56; "Chrysler's Checks to Suppliers, Shoppers to Shrink," *Wall Street Journal*, December 8, 2000, p. B4.

14. See "Web Masters," *Sales & Marketing Management*, 2000 and 2001; Jeffrey K. Liker and Thomas Y. Choi, "Building Deep Supplier Relationships," *Harvard Business Review*, December, 2004, p. 2.

15. "Buyers and Suppliers Team Up for Greater Savings," *Purchasing*, March 5, 2005.

16. "Jeep Builds a New Kind of Plant," *Fortune*, November 11, 2002, pp. T168B–L.

17. For more on outsourcing, see "Big Three's Outsourcing Plan: Make Parts Suppliers Do It," *Wall Street Journal*, June 10, 2004, p. A1ff.; "Why Some Sony Gear Is Made in Japan—by Another Company," *Wall Street Journal*, June 14, 2001, p. A1; "Inside Outsourcing," *Fortune/CNET Technology Review*, Summer 2001, p. 85; "Outsourcing as a Strategic Option: It's about More than Saving Money," *Investor's Business Daily*, May 7, 2001, p.A1. For more on supplier speeds and costs, see "Custom Fit: One Size Does Not Fit All," *Point*, September 2005, pp. 20–23; "When Cool Heads Prevail," *Business Week*, June 11, 2001, p.114; "Should Suppliers Be Partners?" *Business Week*, June 4, 2001, pp. 30B–D; "Machete Time," *Business Week*, April 9, 2001, p. 42. For more on JIT, see "Parts Shortages Hamper Electronics Makers," *Wall Street Journal*, July 7, 2000, p. B5; "The Web at Work: Clorox Co." *Wall Street Journal*, October 9, 2000, p. B21; "Kimberly-Clark Keeps Costco in Diapers, Absorbing Costs Itself," *Wall Street Journal*, September 7, 2000, p. A1; "At Ford, E-Commerce Is Job 1," *Business Week*, February 28, 2000, p. 74; "Where 'Build to Order' Works Best," *Fortune*, April 26, 1999, pp. 160C–V. See also Leonard V. Coote, Edward J. Forrest, and Terence W. Tam, "An Investigation into Commitment in Non-Western Industrial Marketing Relationships," *Industrial Marketing Management*, October 2003, p. 595; Teresa M. McCarthy and Susan L. Golicic, "Implementing Collaborative Forecasting to Improve Supply Chain Performance," *International Journal of Physical Distribution & Logistics Management*, no. 6 (2002), p. 431; James Hoyt and Faizul Huq, "From Arms-Length to Collaborative Relationships in the Supply Chain, an Evolutionary Process," *International Journal of Physical Distribution & Logistics Management*, no. 9 (2002), p. 750.

18. For other examples of big/small partnerships, see "A Fruitful Relationship," *Business Week E.Biz*, November 20, 2000, pp. EB94–EB96; "Automating an Automaker," *Inc. Tech 2000*, no. 4, p. 86. See also "Polaroid Corp. Is Selling Its Technique for Limiting Supplier

Price Increases," *Wall Street Journal*, February 13, 1985, p. 36; "Making Honda Parts, Ohio Company Finds, Can Be Road to Ruin," *Wall Street Journal*, October 5, 1990, p. A1.

19. "A Blaze in Albuquerque Sets Off Major Crisis for Cell-Phone Giants," *Wall Street Journal*, January 29, 2001, p. A1; "Toyota's Fast Rebound after Fire at Supplier Shows Why It Is Tough," *Wall Street Journal*, May 8, 1997, p. A1; Larry R. Smeltzer and Sue P. Siferd, "Proactive Supply Management: The Management of Risk," *International Journal of Purchasing & Materials Management*, Winter 1998, p. 38.

20. For more on Allstates, see "The Role of Search in Business to Business Buying Decisions," *Enquiro Search Solutions*, October 27, 2004; "Net Marketing 100 Best B-to-B Websites," *BtoB*, August 11, 2003, p. 1; "A Bazaar World Continues Online with Business Exchanges Thriving," *Investor's Business Daily*, December 18, 2002, p. A4; "Building a Market," *Wall Street Journal Reports*, April 15, 2002, p. R14; "Exchanges: Making It Work," *Wall Street Journal*, February 11, 2002, p. R16; "Collaboration Software: Bic Finds Right Stuff for Cutting Costs in E-Rooms," *Investor's Business Daily*, August 9, 2001, p. A6; "B2B Tomorrow: Beyond Exchanges," *AME Info*, March 24, 2001; "Industries, from Steel to Chemicals, Say One Internet Site May Not Meet Needs," *Wall Street Journal*, February 28, 2000, p. A16. See also Goutam Chakraborty, Prashant Srivastava, and David L. Warren, "Understanding Corporate B2B Web Sites' Effectiveness from North American and European Perspective," *Industrial Marketing Management*, July 2005, p. 420; Samir Gupta, Jack Cadeaux, and Arch Woodside, "Mapping Network Champion Behavior in B2B Electronic Venturing," *Industrial Marketing Management*, July 2005, p. 495; Cindy Claycomb, Karthik Iyer, and Richard Germain, "Predicting the Level of B2B E-Commerce in Industrial Organizations," *Industrial Marketing Management*, April 2005, p. 221; D. Eric Boyd and Robert E. Spekman, "Internet Usage within B2B Relationships and Its Impact on Value Creation: A Conceptual Model and Research Propositions," *Journal of Business-to-Business Marketing*, no. 1 (2004), p. 9; B. Mahadevan, "Making Sense of Emerging Market Structures in B2B E-Commerce," *California Management Review*, Fall 2003, p. 86; C. M. Sashi and Bay O'Leary, "The Role of Internet Auctions in the Expansion of B2B Markets," *Industrial Marketing Management*, February 2002, p. 103; Geoff Easton and Luis Araujo, "Evaluating the Impact of B2B E-commerce: A Contingent Approach," *Industrial Marketing Management*, July 2003, p. 431; Irvine Clarke III and Theresa B. Flaherty, "Web-Based B2B Portals," *Industrial Marketing Management*, January 2003, p. 15; Rajdeep Grewal, "An Investigation into the Antecedents of Organizational Participation in Business-to-Business Electronic Markets," *Journal of Marketing*, July 2001, p. 17; LiPheng Khoo, Shu B. Tor, and Stephen S. G. Lee, "The Potential of Intelligent Software Agents in the World Wide Web in Automating Part Procurement," *International Journal of Purchasing & Materials Management*, Winter 1998, p. 46.

21. "Always Compare before a Big Purchase," *USA Today*, April 25, 2005; "Buying Online Yields Net Value," *New York Business*, June, 2004, p. 11; see also M. L. Emiliani, "Regulating B2B Online Reverse Auctions through Voluntary Codes of Conduct," *Industrial Marketing Management*, July 2005, p. 526; Shawn P. Daly and Prithwiraj Nath, "Reverse Auctions for Relationship Marketers," *Industrial Marketing Management*, February 2005, p. 157; Richard W. Schrader, Julie Toner Schrader, and Eric P. Eller, "Strategic Implications of Reverse Auctions," *Journal of Business-to-Business Marketing*, no. 1 (2004), p. 61.

22. "Buying Online Yields Net Value," *New York Business*, June, 2004.

23. See www.gxs.com, www.getradeweb.com, and www.gegxs.com. See also "Supply Chain Ends Share Data," *eWeek*, June 6, 2005, p. 34; "Can New GXS Service Revive the Trading Hub Concept?" January 2005, *Manufacturing Business Technology*, p. 38; "GXS, Sterling, Expand beyond EDI for B2B," *eWeek*, November 15, 2004, p. 17; "Why EDI Won't Die," *Business 2.0*, August 2003, p. 68; "Sales Are Clicking on Manufacturing's Internet Mart," *Fortune*, July 7, 1997, pp.136C–T.

24. Andrea Ordanini, "The Effects of Participation on B2B Exchanges: A Resource-Based View," *California Management Review* 47, no. 2, p. 97.

25. "Making It in the USA," *Business 2.0*, December 2003, p. 33; "Will 'Made in USA' Fade Away?" *Fortune*, November 24, 2003, p. 98; "Heroes of U.S. Manufacturing," *Fortune*, March 19, 2001, pp. 178C–HH. See also U. S. Census data, including "Table 5: Industry Statistics for Subsectors by Employment Size: 2002" from *2002 Economic Census—Manufacturing, Subject Series, General Summary* (Washington, DC: U.S. Government Printing Office, 2005) at www.census.gov.

26. See www.naics.com. See also "Classified Information," *American Demographics*, July 1999, p. 16; "SIC: The System Explained," *Sales and Marketing Management*, April 22, 1985, p. 52; "Enhancement of SIC System Being Developed," *Marketing News Collegiate Edition*, May 1988, p. 4.

27. For more on targeting small business, see "Small Firms Enjoy Courtship of Big Suppliers," *Wall Street Journal*, June 24, 2003, p. B9. For more on Canon, see "Perfecting the Pitch," *Wall Street Journal*, May 23, 1996, p. R26; *1996 Annual Report*, Canon; "Can Anyone Duplicate Canon's Personal Copiers' Success?" *Marketing and Media Decisions*, Spring 1985, p. 97.

28. *2005 Annual Report*, Safeway; *2005 Annual Report*, Food Lion; *2005 Annual Report*, Winn-Dixie; *2005 Annual Report*, A&P; Daulatram B. Lund, "Retail Scanner Checkout System: How Buying Committees Functioned," *Industrial Marketing Management* 18, no. 3 (1989), p. 179; Janet Wagner, Richard Ettenson, and Jean Parrish, "Vendor Selection among Retail Buyers: An Analysis by Merchandise Division," *Journal of Retailing*, Spring 1989, p. 58.

29. "The Long Road to Wal-Mart," *Wall Street Journal*, September 19, 2005, p. R1.

30. "Create Open-to-Buy Plans the Easy Way," *Retail Control*, December 1984, p. 21.

31. Based on U.S. Census data and "Eyes Wide Open," *Fortune*, September 19, 2005, pp. 316B-D; "How Bikers' Water Backpack Became Soldiers' Essential," *Wall Street Journal*, July 19, 2005, p. B1ff.; "Targeting the DHS," *Inc.*, May 2005, pp. 44–46; "Heavy Load Now Lighter with Bleex," *Investor's Business Daily*, December 29, 2004, p. A4; "Pentagon Sales Give Powerful Jolt to Ultralife's Business," *Investor's Business Daily*, April 6, 2004, p. A7; "Uncle Sam Is a Tough Customer," *Investor's Business Daily*, October 20, 2003, p. A8; "Super Soldiers," *Business Week*, July 28, 2003, p. 62; "For G.I. Joe, Smart Uniforms via Nanotech," *Business Week*, June 9, 2003, p. 125; "The Humvee of Laptops," *Business Week*, April 21, 2003, p. 74; "Invented to Save Gas, Kevlar Now Saves Lives," *USA Today*, April 16, 2003, p. 1B; "Raytheon on Target," *Business 2.0*, February 2003, p. 79; "Mickey Mouse, Nike Give Advice on Air Security," *Wall Street Journal*, January 24, 2002, p. B1; "The Marines Learn New Tactics—from Wal-Mart," *Business Week*, December 24, 2001, p. 74; Robert Gulbro and Paul Herbig, "Negotiating Successfully in Cross-Cultural Situations," *Industrial Marketing Management*, May 1996, p. 235; William C. Perkins, James C. Hershauer, Abbas Foroughi, and Michael M. Delaney, "Can a Negotiation Support System Help a Purchasing Manager?" *International Journal of Purchasing & Materials Management*, Spring 1996, p. 37.

32. For a detailed discussion of business ethics in a number of countries, see *Journal of Business Ethics*, October 1997. See also John B. Ford, Michael S. LaTour, and Tony L. Henthorne, "Cognitive Moral Development and Japanese Procurement Executives: Implications for Industrial Marketers," *Industrial Marketing Management*, November 2000, p. 589; "How Can a U.S. Company Go International, Avoid the Economic Disaster of a Thai Baht . . . and Pay No Bribes?" *USA Today*, November 17, 1997, p. 5B; Larry R. Smeltzer and Marianne M. Jennings, "Why an International Code of Business Ethics Would Be Good for Business," *Journal of Business Ethics*, January 1998, p. 57.

616

CHAPTER 7

1. See www.whitestrips.com; "P&G Seeks Renewal in Teeth Whitening," *Brandweek*, January 16, 2006, p. 6; "Broadening the Brand," *Strategy and Innovation*, July–August 2004, pp. 3–6; "Procter & Gamble's Likely Foray into Oral Care in India, *Indiainfoline.com*, March 11, 2004; "Crest Biting Back with Whiter Strips," *Brandweek*, September 8, 2003, p. 6; "P&G: New and Improved," *Business Week*, July 7, 2003, p. 52; "P&G Seeks Rejuvenating Effect for New Crest Line," *Brandweek*, June 16, 2003, p. 7; "The Cranky Consumer Works on Its Smile," *Wall Street Journal*, January 14, 2003, p. D1; "How Do You Feel about a $44 Tooth-Bleaching Kit?" *Business 2.0*, October 2001, p. 126.

2. Amy Miller and Jennifer Cioffi, "Measuring Marketing Effectiveness and Value: The Unisys Marketing Dashboard," *Journal of Advertising Research*, September 2004, p. 237; "Making Marketing Measure Up," *Business Week*, December 13, 2004; "How Verizon Flies by Wire," *CIO Magazine*, November 1, 2004.

3. Gary L. Lilien, Arvind Rangaswamy, Gerrit H. van Bruggen, and Berend Wierenga, "Bridging the Marketing Theory-Practice Gap with Marketing Engineering," *Journal of Business Research*, February 2002, p. 111; "Virtual Management," *Business Week*, September 21, 1998, p. 80; John T. Mentzer and Nimish Gandhi, "Expert Systems in Marketing: Guidelines for Development," *Journal of the Academy of Marketing Science*, Winter, 1992, p. 73; William D. Perreault, Jr., "The Shifting Paradigm in Marketing Research," *Journal of the Academy of Marketing Science*, Fall 1992, p. 367; J.M. McCann, W.G. Lahti, and J. Hill, "The Brand Manager's Assistant: A Knowledge-Based System Approach to Brand Management," *International Journal of Research in Marketing*, April 1991, p. 51.

4. See www.staples.com; "Supermarkets Slot Space for Staples," *DSN Retailing Today*, March 28, 2005, p. 3ff.; "Staples Blows into Chicago," *DSN Retailing Today*, March 14, 2005, p. 3ff.; "Easy Does It: Staples Enjoys Success of Recent Strategies," *DSN Retailing Today*, September 20, 2004, p. 1ff.; "Office Supplies Chain Pencils in a New Plan," *Investor's Business Daily*, September 14, 2004, p. A8; "Three-Way Competition Is Here to Stay," *DSN Retailing Today*, November 10, 2003, p. 13; "Fire Awards: Staples Finest in Office Supplies," *DSN Retailing Today*, September 8, 2003, p. 41; "Staples: Office-Supplies Chain Beats Economic Blues," *Investor's Business Daily*, September 2, 2003, p. A9; "Staples: Thinking Outside the Big Box," *Business Week*, August 11, 2002, p. 62; "When Worlds Collide," *Wall Street Journal Reports*, April 28, 2003, p. R1; "Looking for Intelligence in Ice Cream," *Fortune*, March 17, 2003, p. 114; "Advertising: Staples Is Changing Its Slogan to Stress the Ease of Shopping for Office Supplies in Its Stores," *New York Times*, February 27, 2003, p. C6; "Web Delivers Big Results for Staples," *BtoB*, November 11, 2002, p. 14; "The Architect of Happy Customers," *Business 2.0*, August 2002, p. 85; "How to Lower Marketing Costs—and Eliminate Guesswork," *Investor's Business Daily*, November 21, 2001, p. A1.

5. Larry Selden and Ian C. MacMillan, "Manage Customer-Centric Innovation–Systematically," *Harvard Business Review*, April 2006, p. 108; Bruce H. Clark, "Business Intelligence Using Smart Techniques," *Journal of the Academy of Marketing Science*, Fall 2003, p. 488; Mark Peyrot, Nancy Childs, Doris Van Doren, and Kathleen Allen, "An Empirically Based Model of Competitor Intelligence Use," *Journal of Business Research*, September 2002, p. 747; Stanley F. Slater and John C. Narver, "Intelligence Generation and Superior Customer Value," *Journal of the Academy of Marketing Science*, Winter 2000, p. 120; Deborah Utter, "Information-Driven Marketing Decisions: Development of Strategic Information Systems," *Journal of the Academy of Marketing Science*, Spring 1998, p. 157; Philip B. Evans and Thomas S. Wurster, "Strategy and the New Economics of Information," *Harvard Business Review*, September–October 1997, p. 70; James C. Bondra and Tim R. V. Davis, "Marketing's Role in Cross-Functional Information Management," *Industrial Marketing Management*, May 1996, p. 187; Jack J. Honomichl, "Point of View: Why Marketing Information Should Have Top Executive Status," *Journal of Advertising Research*, November/December 1994, p. 61; James M. Sinkula, "Market Information Processing and Organizational Learning," *Journal of Marketing*, January 1994, p. 35; Jim Bessen, "Riding the Marketing Information Wave," *Harvard Business Review*, September–October 1993, p.150; Lawrence B. Chonko, John F. Tanner, Jr., and Ellen Reid Smith, "The Sales Force's Role in International Marketing Research and Marketing Information Systems," *Journal of Personal Selling and Sales Management*, Winter, 1991, p. 69.

6. William Boulding, Richard Staelin, Michael Ehret, and Wesley J. Johnston, "A Customer Relationship Management Roadmap: What Is Known, Potential Pitfalls, and Where to Go," *Journal of Marketing*, October 2005, p. 155; Satish Jayachandran, Subhash Sharma, Peter Kaufman, and Pushkala Raman, "The Role of Relational Information Processes and Technology Use in Customer Relationship Management," *Journal of Marketing*, October 2005, p. 177; Yong Cao and Thomas S. Gruca, "Reducing Adverse Selection through Customer Relationship Management," *Journal of Marketing*, October 2005, p. 219; Darrell K. Rigby and Dianne Ledingham, "CRM Done Right," *Harvard Business Review*, November 2004, p. 118; Peter M. Chisnall, "The Effective Use of Market Research: A Guide for Management to Grow the Business," *International Journal of Market Research*, Summer 2000, p. 359; Seymour Sudman and Edward Blair, *Marketing Research: A Problem Solving Approach* (Burr Ridge, IL: Irwin/McGraw-Hill, 1998). See also Christine Moorman, Rohit Deshpande, and Gerald Zaltman, "Factors Affecting Trust in Market Research Relationships," *Journal of Marketing*, January 1993, p. 81.

7. "Finding Information on the Internet: A Tutorial," UC Berkeley—Teaching Library Internet Workshops, www.lib.berkeley.edu/TeachingLib/Guides/Internet/FindInfo.html; "Internet Tutorials," University Libraries, University at Albany, http://library.albany.edu/internet.

8. For more on focus groups, see "The Perils of Packaging: Nestlé Aims for Easier Openings," *Wall Street Journal*, November 17, 2005, p. B1ff.; "Puppet's Got a Brand-New Bag," *Business 2.0*, October 2005, p. 58; "Focus Groups Should Be Abolished," *Advertising Age*, August 8, 2005, p. 14; "Where the Stars Design the Cars," *Business 2.0*, July 2005, p. 32; "Sticky Fingers? How Avery Found an Office Problem to Solve," *Wall Street Journal*, July 13, 2004, p. B1ff.; "This Volvo Is Not a Guy Thing," *Business Week*, March 15, 2004, pp. 84–86; "The New Science of Focus Groups," *American Demographics*, March 2003, p. 29; "Selling Cellphone with Mixed Messages," *Wall Street Journal*, February 27, 2003, p. B5; "Web Enhances Market Research," *Advertising Age*, June 18, 2001, p. T18. See also William J. McDonald, "Focus Group Research Dynamics and Reporting: An Examination of Research Objectives and Moderator Influences," *Journal of the Academy of Marketing Science*, Spring 1993, p. 161; Thomas Kiely, "Wired Focus Groups," *Harvard Business Review*, January–February 1998, p. 12; see also James R. Stengel, Andrea L. Dixon and Chris T. Allen, "Listening Begins at Home," *Harvard Business Review*, November 2003, p. 106.

9. "How to Run an Online Focus Group to Discover What Business Prospects Really Want (+ Tips on Launching an E-Commerce Website)," *MarketingSherpa.com*, September 28, 2005.

10. "Shoot the Focus Group," *Business Week Online*, November 14, 2005; "Take Your Market Research Online," *Fortune Small Business*, May 29, 2005.

11. "Selling Sibelius Isn't Easy," *American Demographics*, the 1994 Directory, p. 24; "Symphony Strikes a Note for Research as It Prepares to Launch a New Season," *Marketing News*, August 29, 1988, p. 12.

12. For more on surveys, see "Electrolux Cleans Up," *Business Week*, February 27, 2006, pp. 42–43; "Chrysler's Made-Up Customers Get Real Living Space at Agency," *Wall Street Journal*, January 4, 2006, p. B9; "VW's American Road Trip," *Wall Street Journal*, January 4, 2006, p. B1ff.; "The Only Question That Matters," *Business 2.0*, September 2005, pp. 50–52; "Flour Power," *Business 2.0*, June 2004,

p. 80; "A New Style: QB Net . . . Japanese Consumers," *Wall Street Journal Reports*, September 22, 2003, p. R3; "Marketers Re-Evaluate Research," *BtoB*, February 10, 2003, p. 1; "Today, Brawny Men Help with the Kids and the Housework," *Wall Street Journal*, October 4, 2002, p. B2; "A Matter of Opinion," *Wall Street Journal Reports*, October 23, 2000, p. R46; "Online Testing Rated," *Advertising Age*, May 8, 2000, p. 64; "Market Research for the Internet Has Its Drawbacks," *Wall Street Journal*, March 2, 2000, p. B4. See also Pierre Chandon, Vicki G. Morwitz, and Werner J. Reinartz, "Do Intentions Really Predict Behavior? Self-Generated Validity Effects in Survey Research," *Journal of Marketing*, April 2005, p. 1; Stanley E. Griffis, Thomas J. Goldsby, and Martha Cooper, "Web-Based and Mail Surveys: A Comparison of Response, Data, and Cost," *Journal of Business Logistics*, no. 2 (2003), p. 237; Terry L. Childers and Steven J. Skinner, "Toward a Conceptualization of Mail Survey Response Behavior," *Psychology & Marketing*, March 1996, p. 185.

13. Paco, Underhill, *Why We Buy* (New York: Simon and Shuster, 1999); Stephen R. Rosenthal and Mark Capper, "Ethnographies in the Front End: Designing for Enhanced Customer Experiences," *Journal of Product Innovation Management*, May 2006, p. 215.

14. Pierre Berthon, James Mac Hulbert, and Leyland Pitt, "Consuming Technology: Why Marketers Sometimes Get It Wrong," *California Management Review*, Fall 2005, p. 110. See also "Why Are Tech Gizmos So Hard to Figure Out?" *USA Today*, November 2, 2005, p. 1Bff.; "Poll: Many Like Tech Gizmos but Are Frustrated," *USA Today*, October 31, 2005, p. 4B; "The Fine Art of Usability Testing," *Dev Source*, March, 2005; "Living on Internet Time: Product Development at Netscape, Yahoo!, NetDynamics, and Microsoft," *Harvard Business School*, April 21, 1997. See also "IBM.com Looks for Big Improvements from Some Subtle Design Tweaks," *Business Week Online*, April 5, 2001.

15. "Red, White, and Blue," *Beverage Industry*, February 2002, p. 20.

16. For more on types of observation, see "K-C Tries Seeing Things from Consumer's POV," *Brandweek*, September 5, 2005, p. 6; "Studying Messy Habits to Sweep Up a Market," *Wall Street Journal*, July 14, 2005, p. B1ff.; "P&G Chief's Turnaround Recipe: Find Out What Women Want," *Wall Street Journal*, June 1, 2005, p. A1ff.; "The World on a String," *Point*, February 2005, pp. 13–18; "Spying on the Sales Floor," *Wall Street Journal*, December 21, 2004, p. B1ff.; "Sharpening the Focus," *Brandweek*, November 3, 2003, p. 28; "Rear Window," *Business 2.0*, August 2003, p. 72; "Shop, You're on Candid Camera," *USA Today*, November 6, 2002, p. 1B; "Ethnographic Research: Watch Me Now," *American Demographics*, October 2002, pp. S1–S8; "McDonald's Asks Mystery Shoppers What Ails Sales," *Wall Street Journal*, December 17, 2001, p. B1; "P&G Checks Out Real Life," *Wall Street Journal*, May 17, 2001, p. B1; "The New Market Research," *Inc.*, July 1998, p. 87. See also Stephen J. Grove and Raymond P. Fisk, "Observational Data Collection Methods for Services Marketing: An Overview," *Journal of the Academy of Marketing Science*, Summer 1992, p. 217; Magid M. Abraham and Leonard M. Lodish, "An Implemented System for Improving Promotion Productivity Using Store Scanner Data," *Marketing Science*, Summer 1993, p. 248.

17. "Will Your Web Business Work? Take It for a Test Drive," *Ecompany*, May 2001, p. 101; "Ads Awaken to Fathers' New Role in Family Life," *Advertising Age*, January 10, 1994, p. S8; "AT&T's Secret MultiMedia Trials Offer Clues to Capturing Interactive Audiences," *Wall Street Journal*, July 28, 1993, p. B1; "Experimenting in the U.K.: Phone, Cable Deals Let U.S. Test Future," *USA Today*, June 28, 1993, p. 1B. See also Raymond R. Burke, "Virtual Shopping: Breakthrough in Marketing Research," *Harvard Business Review*, March–April 1996, p. 120; Glen L. Urban, Bruce D. Weinberg, and John R. Hauser, "Premarket Forecasting of Really-New Products," *Journal of Marketing*, January 1996, p. 47.

18. For more on Nielsen's people meters, see "Where's the Ratings, Dude?" *Wall Street Journal*, March 7, 2005, p. B1ff.; "Nielsen's Search for Hispanics Is a Delicate Job," *Wall Street Journal*, October 11, 2004, p. B1ff.; "How Nielsen Stood Up to Murdoch," *Business Week*, September 20, 2004, pp. 88–90; "For Nielsen, Fixing Old Ratings System Causes New Static," *Wall Street Journal*, September 16, 2004, p. A1ff.; "Outdoor Ads, Here's Looking at You," *Wall Street Journal*, July 12, 2004, p. B3; "Nielsen's Feud with TV Networks Shows Scarcity of Marketing Data," *Wall Street Journal*, October 29, 2003, p. A1; "Nielsen Adapts Its Methods as TV Evolves," *Wall Street Journal*, September 29, 2003, p. B1; "Confessions of a Nielsen Household," *American Demographics*, May 2001. See also "The Metrics System," *Brandweek*, November 13, 2000, p. 10; Peter J. Danaher and Terence W. Beed, "A Coincidental Survey of People Meter Panelists: Comparing What People Say with What They Do," *Journal of Advertising Research*, January/February 1993, p. 86.

19. "Marketing Research on a Shoestring," *Fortune*, May 29, 2005; "Listen Up: Your Customers Are Talking about You Online," MarketingProfs.com, May 24, 2005; "Why Market Research Matters," *Fortune*, August 31, 2004; "On Target," *Entrepreneur*, August 2004; "Borrowing from the Big Boys," MarketingProfs.com, June 17, 2003.

20. For more detail on data analysis techniques, see Joe Hair, Rolph Anderson, Ron Tatham, and William Black, *Multivariate Data Analysis* (New York: Prentice Hall, 2005) or other marketing research texts. See also "Ice Cream Shop Gets Scoop on Locales," *Investor's Business Daily*, February 17, 2006, p. A4; "Is Your Business in the Right Spot?" *Business 2.0*, May 2004, pp. 76–77; "Merry Maids Clean Up Territories with MapInfo System," *Investor's Business Daily*, February 20, 2001, p. A8; Michael D. Johnson and Elania J. Hudson, "On the Perceived Usefulness of Scaling Techniques in Market Analysis," *Psychology & Marketing*, October 1996, p. 653; Milton D. Rosenau, "Graphing Statistics and Data: Creating Better Charts," *Journal of Product Innovation Management*, March 1997, p. 144.

21. For a discussion of ethical issues in marketing research, see "Name, Please: Surveyor Quietly Sells Student Information to Youth Marketer," *Wall Street Journal*, December 13, 2001, p. A1; "How 'Tactical Research' Muddied Diaper Debate: a Case," *Wall Street Journal*, May 17, 1994, p. B1. See also Rita Marie Cain, "Supreme Court Expands Federal Power to Regulate the Availability and Use of Data," *Journal of the Academy of Marketing Science*, Fall 2001, p. 425; Malcolm Kirkup and Marylyn Carrigan, "Video Surveillance Research in Retailing: Ethical Issues," *International Journal of Retail & Distribution Management*, no. 11 (2002), p. 470; Brian Carroll, "Price of Privacy: Selling Consumer Databases in Bankruptcy," *Journal of Interactive Marketing*, Summer 2002, p. 47; Eve M. Caudill and Patrick E. Murphy, "Consumer Online Privacy: Legal and Ethical Issues," *Journal of Public Policy & Marketing*, Spring 2000, p. 7; John R. Sparks and Shelby D. Hunt, "Marketing Researcher Ethical Sensitivity: Conceptualization, Measurement, and Exploratory Investigation," *Journal of Marketing*, April 1998, p. 92; Naresh K. Malhotra and Gina L. Miller, "An Integrated Model for Ethical Decisions in Marketing Research," *Journal of Business Ethics*, February 1998, p. 263.

22. "More Companies Are Offshoring R&D," *Investor's Business Daily*, November 21, 2005, p. A10ff; "Chinese Puzzle: Spotty Consumer Data," *Wall Street Journal*, October 15, 2003, p. B1. See also Thomas Tsu Wee Tan and Tan Jee Lui, "Globalization and Trends in International Marketing Research in Asia," *Journal of Business Research*, October 2002, p. 799; Masaaki Kotabe, "Using Euromonitor Database in International Marketing Research," *Journal of the Academy of Marketing Science*, Spring 2002, p. 172.

CHAPTER 8

1. See www.citysegwaytours.com and www.segway.com; "What the Recall Reveals about Segway," www.time.com, September 14, 2006; "Reinventing the Wheel, Slowly," *BusinessWeek Online*, September 11, 2006; "The Segway Riddle," *Time.com*, August 13, 2006; "Segway Rolls with Garmin," *PR Newswire*, October 19, 2005; "Scoot on by in Florida," *The News and Observer*, October 9, 2005, p. H1; "Touring

Washington the Seg-Way," *Cox News Service*, June 10, 2005; "Segway Conference in Chicago Lures Device's Die-Hard Fans," *Investor's Business Daily*, September 2, 2003, p. A6; "President's Tumble Off a Segway Seems a Tiny Bit Suspicious," *USA Today*, June 18, 2003, p. 3B; "Watch Your Step: Segways Ahead," *USA Today*, June 17, 2003, p. 1A; "A Costly Segway," *Fortune*, April 28, 2003, p. 42; "Segway Gives an Easy Ride, but It's Best on City Sidewalks," *Wall Street Journal*, April 10, 2003, p. B1; "A Glint in Detroit's Eyes," *Business 2.0*, February 2003, p. 44; "Is Segway Going Anywhere?" *Business Week*, January 27, 2003, p. 42; "Smoothing the Way for Segway," *Business Week*, April 15, 2002, p. 10.

2. R. Kenneth Teas and Sanjeev Agarwal, "The Effects of Extrinsic Product Cues on Consumers' Perceptions of Quality, Sacrifice, and Value," *Journal of the Academy of Marketing Science*, Spring 2000, p. 278; Amna Kirmani and Akshay R. Rao, "No Pain, No Gain: A Critical Review of the Literature on Signaling Unobservable Product Quality," *Journal of Marketing*, April 2000, p. 66; Neil A. Morgan and Douglas W. Vorhies, "Product Quality Alignment and Business Unit Performance," *Journal of Product Innovation Management*, November 2001, p. 396; Joseph M. Juran, "Made in U.S.A.: A Renaissance in Quality," *Harvard Business Review*, July–August 1993, p. 42.

3. Example inspired by other case studies: Robert Solomon and Kathleen Higgins, "Case Study: Cement for Sale," Center for the Study of Ethics, Utah Valley State College; C.B. Fledderman, "Denver Runway Concrete," *Engineering Ethics* (Englewood Cliffs, NJ: Prentice Hall, 1999).

4. For more on service expectations, see Chapter 5, footnote 12. For more on service quality, see *2005 Annual Report*, MCI; *2005 Annual Report*, Merrill Lynch. For an excellent example on Avis, see "The Payoff for Trying Harder," *Business 2.0*, July 2002, p. 84; "Avis to Try Even Harder with Ads Touting High Quality of Service," *Wall Street Journal*, February 18, 2000, p. B9. For more on air service, see "Paved Paradise: The New Airport Parking Lots," *Wall Street Journal*, November 12, 2003, p. D1; "Flat-Out Winners," *Business Week*, October 27, 2003, p. 132. See also Neeli Bendapudi and Robert P. Leone, "Psychological Implications of Customer Participation in Co-Production," *Journal of Marketing*, January 2003, p. 14; Leonard L. Berry, Kathleen Seiders, and Dhruv Grewal, "Understanding Service Convenience," *Journal of Marketing*, July 2002, p. 1; Valarie A. Zeithaml, A. Parasuraman, and Arvind Malhotra, "Service Quality Delivery through Web Sites: A Critical Review of Extant Knowledge," *Journal of the Academy of Marketing Science*, Fall 2002, p. 362; James L. Thomas, Scott J. Vitell, Faye W. Gilbert, and Gregory M. Rose, "The Impact of Ethical Cues on Customer Satisfaction with Service," *Journal of Retailing*, Fall 2002, p. 167; Valerie S. Folkes and Vanessa M. Patrick, "The Positivity Effect in Perceptions of Services: Seen One, Seen Them All?" *Journal of Consumer Research*, June 2003, p. 125; Dwayne D. Gremler, "Discovering the Soul of Service: The Nine Drivers of Sustainable Business Success," *Journal of the Academy of Marketing Science*, Spring 2000, p. 311; James Reardon, Chip Miller, Ronald Hasty, and Blaise J. Waguespack, "A Comparison of Alternative Theories of Services Marketing," *Journal of Marketing Theory & Practice*, Fall 1996, p. 61; James C. Anderson and James A. Narus, "Capturing the Value of Supplementary Services," *Harvard Business Review*, January–February 1995, p. 75; Matthew L. Meuter, Mary Jo Bitner, Amy L. Ostrom, and Stephen W. Brown, "Choosing among Alternative Service Delivery Modes: An Investigation of Customer Trial of Self-Service Technologies," *Journal of Marketing*, April 2005, p. 61; D. Todd Donavan, Tom J. Brown, and John C. Mowen, "Internal Benefits of Service-Worker Customer Orientation: Job Satisfaction, Commitment, and Organizational Citizenship Behaviors," *Journal of Marketing*, January 2004, p. 128; Stephen L. Vargo and Robert F. Lusch, "Evolving to a New Dominant Logic for Marketing," *Journal of Marketing*, January 2004, p. 1; Ruth N. Bolton, George S. Day, John Deighton, Das Narayandas, Evert Gummesson, Shelby D. Hunt, C. K. Prahalad, Roland T. Rust, and Steven M. Shugan, "Invited Commentaries on 'Evolving to a New Dominant Logic for Marketing,'" *Journal of Marketing*, January 2004, p. 18; Robert D. Winsor, Jagdish N. Sheth, and Chris Manolis,

"Differentiating Goods, and Services Retailing Using Form and Possession Utilities," *Journal of Business Research*, March 2004, p. 249; Jeffrey F. Rayport, Bernard J. Jaworski, and Ellie J. Kyung, "Best Face Forward: Improving Companies' Service Interfaces with Customers," *Journal of Interactive Marketing*, Autumn 2005, p. 67; Michel Laroche, Linda C. Ueltschy, Shuzo Abe, Mark Cleveland, and Peter P. Yannopoulos, "Service Quality Perceptions and Customer Satisfaction: Evaluating the Role of Culture," *Journal of International Marketing*, 2004, p. 58; Dawn Jing Lei, Roger Pruppers, Hans Ouwersloot, and Jos Lemmink, "Service Intensiveness and Brand Extension Evaluations," *Journal of Service Research*, February 2004, p. 243; Tom DeWitt and Michael K. Brady, "Rethinking Service Recovery Strategies," *Journal of Service Research*, November 2003, p. 193; Leonard L. Berry, Venkatesh Shankar, Janet Turner Parish, Susan Cadwallader, and Thomas Dotzel, "Creating New Markets through Service Innovation," *MIT Sloan Management Review*, Winter 2006, p. 56.

5. For example, see "Russian Maneuvers Are Making Palladium Ever More Precious," *Wall Street Journal*, March 6, 2000, p. A1. See also William S. Bishop, John L. Graham, and Michael H. Jones, "Volatility of Derived Demand in Industrial Markets and Its Management Implications," *Journal of Marketing*, Fall 1984, p. 95.

6. Edward M. Tauber, "Why Do People Shop?" *Journal of Marketing*, October 1972, p. 46; Christopher H. Lovelock, "Classifying Services to Gain Strategic Marketing Insights," *Journal of Marketing*, Summer 1983, p. 9; Tom Boyt and Michael Harvey, "Classification of Industrial Services," *Industrial Marketing Management*, July 1997, p. 291.

7. Dennis W. Rook, "The Buying Impulse," *Journal of Consumer Research*, September 1987, p. 189; Cathy J. Cobb and Wayne D. Hoyer, "Planned Versus Impulse Purchase Behavior," *Journal of Retailing*, Winter 1986, p. 384.

8. William B. Wagner and Patricia K. Hall, "Equipment Lease Accounting in Industrial Marketing Strategy," *Industrial Marketing Management* 20, no. 4 (1991), p. 305; Robert S. Eckley, "Caterpillar's Ordeal: Foreign Competition in Capital Goods," *Business Horizons*, March/April 1989, p. 80; M. Manley, "To Buy or Not to Buy," *Inc.*, November 1987, p. 189.

9. P. Matthyssens and W. Faes, "OEM Buying Process for New Components: Purchasing and Marketing Implications," *Industrial Marketing Management*, August 1985, p. 145; Paul A. Herbig and Frederick Palumbo, "Serving the Aftermarket in Japan and the United States," *Industrial Marketing Management*, November 1993, p. 339.

10. Ruth H. Krieger and Jack R. Meredith, "Emergency and Routine MRO Part Buying," *Industrial Marketing Management*, November 1985, p. 277; Warren A. French et al., "MRO Parts Service in the Machine Tool Industry," *Industrial Marketing Management*, November 1985, p. 283. See also "The Web's New Plumbers," *Ecompany*, March 2001, p. 126.

11. For more on Listerine PocketPaks, see "The Strip Club," *Business 2.0*, June 2003, p. 36; "Marketer of the Year: PocketPaks, a Breath of Minty Fresh Air," *Brandweek*, October 14, 2002, pp. M42–M46. For more on brand extensions, see Franziska Vlckner and Henrik Sattler, "Drivers of Brand Extension Success," *Journal of Marketing*, April 2006, p. 18; Chris Pullig, Carolyn J. Simmons, and Richard G. Netemeyer, "Brand Dilution: When Do New Brands Hurt Existing Brands?," *Journal of Marketing*, April 2006, p. 52; Tülin Erdem, Joffre Swait, and Ana Valenzuela, "Brands as Signals: A Cross-Country Validation Study," *Journal of Marketing*, January 2006, p. 34; Eric Yorkston and Geeta Menon, "A Sound Idea: Phonetic Effects of Brand Names on Consumer Judgments," *Journal of Consumer Research*, June 2004, p. 43; Mike Bendixen, Kalala A. Bukasa, and Russell Abratt, "Brand Equity in the Business-to-Business Market," *Industrial Marketing Management*, July 2004, p. 371; Pamela W. Henderson, Joseph A. Cote, Siew Meng Leong, and Bernd Schmitt, "Building Strong Brands in Asia: Selecting the Visual Components of Image to Maximize Brand Strength," *International Journal of Research in Marketing*, December 2003, p. 297; Yih Hwai Lee and Kim Soon Ang, "Brand Name Suggestiveness: A Chinese Language Perspective," *International Journal of Research in Marketing*, December 2003, p. 323; Thomas J. Madden, Frank Fehle, and Susan Fournier, "Brands Matter: An Empirical Demonstration of the Creation of Shareholder Value through Branding," *Journal of the Academy of Marketing Science*, Spring 2006, p. 224; Thomas J. Reynolds and Carol B. Phillips, "In Search of True Brand Equity Metrics: All Market Share Ain't Created Equal," *Journal of Advertising Research*, June 2005, p. 171; Girish N. Punj and Clayton L. Hillyer, "A Cognitive Model of Customer-Based Brand Equity for Frequently Purchased Products: Conceptual Framework and Empirical Results," *Journal of Consumer Psychology*, 2004, p. 124; Richard G. Netemeyer, Balaji Krishnan, Chris Pullig, Guangping Wang, Mehmet Yagci, Dwane Dean, Joe Ricks, and Ferdinand Wirth, "Developing and Validating Measures of Facets of Customer-Based Brand Equity," *Journal of Business Research*, February 2004, p. 209. For more on brand equity and brand value, see "Ranking Corporate Reputations," *Wall Street Journal*, December 6, 2005, p. B1ff.; "Hershey's Trumps Donald, McDonald's, and Martha," *Brandweek*, November 28, 2005, p. 15; "High Tech = High Loyalty," *Brandweek*, October 31, 2005, pp. 22–24; "Welch's Juices Equity with Fresh-Fruit Line," *Brandweek*, August 22, 2005, p. 9; "Mattress Maker Spreads the Word through Aggressive Marketing," *Investor's Business Daily*, July 1, 2005, p. A5; Mega Brands," *Advertising Age*, July 2005, pp. S1–S5; "Sharp Pursues Big-Screen Ambitions," *Wall Street Journal*, June 9, 2005, p. B10; "Hard Lesson Learned: Premium and No-Frills Don't Mix," *Wall Street Journal*, November 3, 2003, p. B1; "Nonprofits Can Provide a Brand Name That Sells," *Wall Street Journal*, September 23, 2003, p. B11. For more on brand naming, see "New Names for Old Companies," *Business 2.0*, November 2005, pp. 74–76; "Lost Verizon: Survey Urges Brand Names to Get Real," *Brandweek*, September 5, 2005, p. 11; "Tech Sector Ponders: What's in a Name?" *Advertising Age*, May 9, 2005, p. 20; "The New Science of Naming," *Business 2.0*, December 2004, pp. 53–55; "New ABCs of Branding," *Wall Street Journal*, August 26, 2002, p. B1. See also Arjun Chaudhuri and Morris B. Holbrook, "The Chain of Effects from Brand Trust and Brand Affect to Brand Performance: The Role of Brand Loyalty," *Journal of Marketing*, April 2001, p. 81; Zeynep Gurhan-Canli, "The Effect of Expected Variability of Product Quality and Attribute Uniqueness on Family Brand Evaluations," *Journal of Consumer Research*, June 2003, p. 105; Russell Casey, "Designing Brand Identity: A Complete Guide to Creating, Building, and Maintaining Strong Brands," *Journal of the Academy of Marketing Science*, Winter 2004, p. 100; Subramanian Balachander and Sanjoy Ghose, "Reciprocal Spillover Effects: a Strategic Benefit of Brand Extensions," *Journal of Marketing*, January 2003, p. 1; Elizabeth S. Moore, William L. Wilkie, and Richard J. Lutz, "Passing the Torch: Intergenerational Influences as a Source of Brand Equity," *Journal of Marketing*, April 2002, p. 17; Kevin P. Gwinner and John Eaton, "Building Brand Image through Event Sponsorship: The Role of Image Transfer," *Journal of Advertising*, Winter 1999, p. 47; Susan Mudambi, "Branding Importance in Business-to-Business Markets: Three Buyer Clusters," *Industrial Marketing Management*, September 2002, p. 525; John A. Quelch and David Kenny, "Extend Profits, Not Product Lines," *Harvard Business Review*, September–October 1994, p. 153; Linda B. Samuels and Jeffrey M. Samuels, "Famous Marks Now Federally Protected against Dilution," *Journal of Public Policy & Marketing*, Fall 1996, p. 307; Pamela W. Henderson and Joseph A. Cote, "Guidelines for Selecting or Modifying Logos," *Journal of Marketing*, April 1998, p. 14; Erich Joachimsthaler and David A. Aaker, "Building Brands without Mass Media," *Harvard Business Review*, January–February 1997, p. 39.

12. Peter Lawrence and Leigh McAllister, "Marketing Meets Design: Core Necessities for Successful New Product Development," *Journal of Product Innovation Management*, March 2005, p. 107; Helen Perks, Rachel Cooper, and Cassie Jones, "Characterizing the Role of Design in New Product Development: An Empirically Derived Taxonomy," *Journal of Product Innovation Management*, March 2005, p. 111;

K. Scott Swan, Masaaki Kotabe, and Brent B. Allred, "Exploring Robust Design Capabilities, Their Role in Creating Global Products, and Their Relationship to Firm Performance," *Journal of Product Innovation Management*, March 2005, p. 144; Lan Luo, P. K. Kannan, Babak Besharati, and Shapour Azarm, "Design of Robust New Products under Variability: Marketing Meets Design," *Journal of Product Innovation Management*, March 2005, p. 177; Julie H. Hertenstein, Marjorie B. Platt and Robert W. Veryzer, "The Impact of Industrial Design Effectiveness on Corporate Financial Performance," *Journal of Product Innovation Management*, January 2005, p. 3; Mariëlle E. H. Creusen and Jan P. L. Schoormans, "The Different Roles of Product Appearance in Consumer Choice," *Journal of Product Innovation Management*, January 2005, p. 63. See also "A Robot That Could Hit a Wall," *BusinessWeek Online*, September 5, 2005; "The Best Product Design of 2005 Winners," *Business Week*, July 4, 2005, pp. 62–72; "Masters of Design," *Fast Company*, June 2004, p. 61; Artemis March, "Usability: The New Dimension of Product Design," *Harvard Business Review*, September–October 1994, pp. 145–149.

13. "Lost in Translation," *Business 2.0*, August 2004, pp. 68–70; "Global Products Require Name-Finders," *Wall Street Journal*, April 11, 1996, p. B8; Martin S. Roth, "Effects of Global Market Conditions on Brand Image Customization and Brand Performance," *Journal of Advertising*, Winter 1995, p. 55.

14. See www.yahoo.com. See also "Nielsen//NetRatings Reports The Fastest Growing Web Sites Year-over-Year among Top Internet Properties: Apple, Google, and Amazon Take the Lead," Nielsen//NetRatings press release, December 20, 2005; "Yahoo: Exporting an *Uber*-Brand," *BusinessWeek Online*, April 4, 2005; "Coterie of Early Hires Made Yahoo! A Hit but an Insular Place," *Wall Street Journal*, March 9, 2001, p. A1; "Voulez-vous Yahoo Avec Moi?" *Fortune*, October 16, 2000, p. 245; "The Two Grown-Ups behind Yahoo!'s Surge," *Wall Street Journal*, April 10, 1998, p. B1.

15. "TiVo's Time Ticks Away, DirecTV Programs Attack," *Brandweek*, October 10, 2005, p. 5; "Road to Foreign Franchises Is Paved with New Problems," *Wall Street Journal*, May 14, 2001, p. B10; "Tiger Fight Sees Kellogg, ExxonMobil Clash in Court," *Ad Age Global*, November 2000; "Wrestling, Wildlife Fund Battle over WWF Site," *USA Today*, October 25, 2000, p. 1A; "More Firms Flash New Badge," *USA Today*, October 4, 2000, p. 3B; "Name Lawsuit Prompts Apple-Soup to Become Flycode," *USA Today*, September 11, 2000, p. 6B. See also Karen Gantt, "Revisiting the Scope of Lanham Act Protection," *Journal of the Academy of Marketing Science*, Winter 2004, p. 102; Maureen Morrin and Jacob Jacoby, "Trademark Dilution: Empirical Measures for an Elusive Concept," *Journal of Public Policy & Marketing*, Fall 2000, p. 265; F. C. Hong, Anthony Pecotich and Clifford J. Schultz II, "Brand Name Translation: Language Constraints, Product Attributes, and Consumer Perceptions in East and Southeast Asia," *Journal of International Marketing*, no. 2 (2002), p. 29; Lee B. Burgunder, "Trademark Protection of Product Characteristics: A Predictive Model," *Journal of Public Policy & Marketing*, Fall 1997, p. 277.

16. For more on piracy, see Ashutosh Prasad and Vijay Mahajan, "How Many Pirates Should a Software Firm Tolerate? An Analysis of Piracy Protection on the Diffusion of Software," *International Journal of Research in Marketing*, December 2003, p. 337; "Holograms Tell Fake from Fendi," *Wall Street Journal*, February 22, 2006, p. B1ff.; "Bagging Fakers and Sellers," *Wall Street Journal*, January 31, 2006, p. B1ff.; "As Luxury Industry Goes Global, Knock-Off Merchants Follow," *Wall Street Journal*, January 31, 2006, p. A1ff.; "As Pfizer Battles Fakes in China, Nation's Police Are Uneasy Allies," *Wall Street Journal*, January 24, 2006, p. A1ff.; "Pirated DVDs among Hottest Items on Shelves in Iraq," *USA Today*, January 20, 2006, p. 12A; "Software Shift to Subscriptions, Services Helps to Deter Piracy," *Investor's Business Daily*, December 5, 2005, p. A1ff.; "Firestorm Rages over Lockdown on Digital Music," *USA Today*, November 14, 2005, p. 1Bff.; "Cybercrime," *USA Today*, November 3, 2005, Sect. A&B; "Bootlegs Go Corporate," *Wall Street Journal*, September 27, 2005, p. D1ff.; "Newest Export from China: Pirated Pay TV," *Wall Street Journal*, September 2, 2005, p. B1ff.;

"Now, Complaints of Brand Name Piracy Go Both Ways," *Wall Street Journal*, July 11, 2005, p. B1ff.; "Companies Fight Hard vs. Fakes but Problems Are Getting Worse," *Investor's Business Daily*, July 7, 2005, p. A1ff.; "Fakes!" *Business Week*, February 7, 2005, pp. 54–64. See also Laurence Jacobs, A. Coskun Samli, and Tom Jedlik, "The Nightmare of International Product Piracy: Exploring Defensive Strategies," *Industrial Marketing Management*, August 2001, p. 499; Janeen E. Olsen and Kent L. Granzin, "Using Channels Constructs to Explain Dealers' Willingness to Help Manufacturers Combat Counterfeiting," *Journal of Business Research*, June 1993, p. 147; Alexander Nill and Clifford J. Schultz II, "The Scourge of Global Counterfeiting," *Business Horizons*, November/December 1996, p. 37.

17. For more on licensing, see "Food Marketers Hope Veggies Look Fun to Kids," *USA Today*, July 15, 2005, p. 5B; "Testing Limits of Licensing: SpongeBob-Motif Holiday Inn," *Wall Street Journal*, October 9, 2003, p. B1ff.; "Making Tracks beyond Tires," *Brandweek*, September 15, 2003, p. 16; "Candy Cosmetics: Licensing's Sweet Spot," *DSN Retailing Today*, August 4, 2003, p. 24; "The Creative License," *Brandweek*, June 9, 2003, p. 36; "Procter & Gamble Deals License Several Brand Names," *USA Today*, April 18, 2003, p. 3B.

18. For more on branding organic products, see "Private Food Labels also Seeking Organic Growth," *Brandweek*, November 7, 2005, p. 5; "Soap Can Proudly Display Certified 'Organic' Label," *USA Today*, August 25, 2005, p. 5B; "Health-Food Maker Hain Faces Rivals," *Wall Street Journal*, August 13, 2003, p. B5B; "Big Brand Logos Pop Up in Organic Aisle," *Wall Street Journal*, July 29, 2003, p. B1; "USDA Enters Debate on Organic Label Law," *New York Times*, February 26, 2003, p. D1; "Food Industry Gags at Proposed Label Rule for Trans Fat," *Wall Street Journal*, December 27, 2002, p. B1; "Curbs Are Eased on Food Makers' Health Claims," *Wall Street Journal*, December 19, 2002, p. D4. See also Amitabh Mungale, "Managing Product Families," *Journal of Product Innovation Management*, January 1998, p. 102; Gloria Barczak, "Product Management," *Journal of Product Innovation Management*, September 1997, p. 425.

19. S. Chan Choi and Anne T. Coughlan, "Private Label Positioning: Quality versus Feature Differentiation from the National Brand," *Journal of Retailing*, June 2006, p. 79; David E. Sprott and Terence A. Shimp, "Using Product Sampling to Augment the Perceived Quality of Store Brands," *Journal of Retailing*, Winter 2004, p. 305.

20. "Here's Mr. Macy," *Fortune*, November 28, 2005, pp. 138–42; "Private Label Brands Expand Public Image," *Brandweek*, February 2, 2004, p. 4; "Brand Killers," *Fortune*, August 11, 2003, p. 88; "And the Coolest New PC Is Made by . . . Best Buy?" *Business 2.0*, pp. 47–49; "Going Private (Label)," *Wall Street Journal*, June 12, 2003, p. B1; "7-Eleven Cracks Open a Private-Label Brew," *Wall Street Journal*, May 2, 2003, p. B1; "White Clouds Could Bring Rain on P&G," *Advertising Age*, July 2, 2001, p. 4. See also Rajeev Batra and Indrajit Sinha, "Consumer-Level Factors Moderating the Success of Private Label Brands," *Journal of Retailing*, Summer 2000, p. 175; John Low and Keith Blois, "The Evolution of Generic Brands in Industrial Markets: the Challenges to Owners of Brand Equity," *Industrial Marketing Management*, August 2002, p. 385; Judith A. Garretson, Dan Fisher, and Scot Burton, "Antecedents of Private Label Attitude and National Brand Promotion Attitude: Similarities and Differences," *Journal of Retailing*, Summer 2002, p. 91; R. Sethuraman and J. Mittelstaedt, "Coupons and Private Labels: A Cross-Category Analysis of Grocery Products," *Psychology & Marketing*, November/December 1992, p. 487; John A. Quelch and David Harding, "Brands versus Private Labels: Fighting to Win," *Harvard Business Review*, January–February 1996, p. 99; Piyush Kumar, "The Impact of Cobranding on Customer Evaluation of Brand Counterextensions," *Journal of Marketing*, July 2005, p. 1; Anders Bengtsson and Per Servais, "Co-Branding on Industrial Markets," *Industrial Marketing Management*, October 2005, p. 706.

21. For more on SoupatHand, see "Demand for Convenient Foods Continues to Rise," *Brandweek*, November 18, 2002, p. 8. For another example, milk packaging, see "Dean Foods: Dairy Processor Looks to Milk Other Products," *Investor's Business Daily*, March 28, 2003, p. A6; "Dean Foods: Dairy Firm Milks New Products for Growth, though Cows Still Account for Most Sales," *Investor's Business Daily*, September 18, 2002, p. A8; "Milk Chug Sweetens Double Chocolate Push," *Brandweek*, February 25, 2002, p. 9; "Many-Flavored Milk Competes with Sodas," *USA Today*, January 26, 2001, p. 1D.

22. "Cure for the Common Cold in the Beverage Aisles?" *Brandweek*, October 3, 2005, p. 12; "Thinking Outside of the Clamshell," *Business 2.0*, July 2005, p. 58; "Packaging as Entertainment," *Business 2.0*, June 2005, p. 73; "Going Home with the Customers," *Newsweek*, May 23, 2005, p. 66; "Put Some Pizzazz in Your Packaging," *Brandweek*, January 17, 2005, p. 17; "Beef's New Bag," *USA Today*, June 21, 2004, p. 6D; "Handles Help Paper Grocery Bags Hold On," *Wall Street Journal*, March 16, 2004, p. B1ff.; "Thinking Outside the Can," *Brandweek*, October 13, 2003, p. 13; "Are Your Competitors Packing?" *Business 2.0*, July 2003, p. 52; "Salad in Sealed Bags Isn't So Simple, It Seems," *New York Times*, January 14, 2003, p. A1; "Finger Food: Marketers Push Individual Portions and Families Bite," *Wall Street Journal*, July 23, 2002, p. A1. See also Brian Wansink and Koert van Ittersum, "Bottoms Up! The Influence of Elongation on Pouring and Consumption Volume," *Journal of Consumer Research*, December 2003, p. 455.

23. For more on food labeling, see "The Whole Truth about Whole Grain," *Wall Street Journal*, February 16, 2006, p. D1ff.; "Major Changes Set for Food Labels," *Wall Street Journal*, December 28, 2005, p. D1ff.; "FDA Says Food Labels Can Tout Tomatoes' Benefits on Cancer," *Wall Street Journal*, November 10, 2005, p. D6; "Read It and Weep? Big Mac Wrapper to Show Fat, Calories," *Wall Street Journal*, October 26, 2005, p. B1ff.; "How Much Soy Lecithin Is in That Cookie?" *Wall Street Journal*, October 13, 2005, p. D1ff.; "FDA ReExamines 'Serving Sizes,' May Change Misleading Labels," *Wall Street Journal*, November 20, 2003, p. A1; "A 'Fat-Free' Product That's 100% Fat: How Food Labels Legally Mislead," *Wall Street Journal*, July 15, 2003, p. D1. See also Siva K. Balasubramanian and Catherine Cole, "Consumers' Search and Use of Nutrition Information: the Challenge and Promise of the Nutrition Labeling and Education Act," *Journal of Marketing*, July 2002, p. 112; Bruce A. Silverglade, "The Nutrition Labeling and Education Act—Progress to Date and Challenges for the Future," *Journal of Public Policy & Marketing*, Spring 1996, p. 148; Sandra J. Burke, Sandra J. Milberg, and Wendy W. Moe, "Displaying Common but Previously Neglected Health Claims on Product Labels: Understanding Competitive Advantages, Deception, and Education," *Journal of Public Policy & Marketing*, Fall 1997, p. 242; Christine Moorman, "A Quasi Experiment to Assess the Consumer and Informational Determinants of Nutrition Information Processing Activities: The Case of the Nutrition Labeling and Education Act," *Journal of Public Policy & Marketing*, Spring 1996, p. 28.

24. "Open at Your Own Risk," *USA Today*, July 13, 2001, p. 1A; "Pushing Paper in a Plastic World," *Wall Street Journal*, February 24, 1998, p. B1; "Record Makers Giving Retailers the Blues," *Wall Street Journal*, March 16, 1992, p. B1; "New Packaging That's Thriftier! Niftier! and Cooks Your Food!" *Fortune*, September 5, 1994, p. 109.

25. "Do Food Claims Help Consumers or Baffle Them?" *Wall Street Journal*, May 27, 2005, p. B1ff.; Paula Fitzgerald, Bone Corey, and Robert J. Corey, "Ethical Dilemmas in Packaging: Beliefs of Packaging Professionals," *Journal of Macromarketing*, Spring 1992, p. 45. For more on package volume, see "Pay the Same, Get Less as Package Volume Falls," *USA Today*, March 17, 2003, p. 3B; "Taking the Value Out of Value-Sized," *Wall Street Journal*, August 14, 2002, p. D1; "Critics Call Cuts in Package Size Deceptive Move," *Wall Street Journal*, February 5, 1991, p. B1; "Disposing of the Green Myth," *Adweek's Marketing Week*, April 13, 1992, p. 20; "The Waste Land," *Adweek*, November 11, 1991, p. 26.

26. For more on Hyundai warranty, see "BMW, Mercedes—and Hyundai?" *Business Week*, December 5, 2005, p. 52; "Hyundai Makes Safety a Primary Selling Point," *Advertising Age*, May 2, 2005, p. 53;

"Extended Warranty Heats Up Auto Sales," *Advertising Age*, November 1, 2004, p. 12. For more on warranties and service guarantees, see "Little Tikes Proves Durable with Low-Tech Plastic Toys," *USA Today*, December 15, 2005, p. 1Bff.; "Faulty Chip Mars Many Camera Models," *Wall Street Journal*, October 27, 2005, p. D1ff.; "Or Your Money Back," *Inc. Magazine*, September 2005, p. 46; "Building a Luxury Retail Business on the Web," *Wall Street Journal*, July 12, 2005, p. B4; "Certified Used Cars Come under Fire," *Wall Street Journal*, July 12, 2005, p. D1ff.; "Wal-Mart Expands Warranty Business to Its Stores," *Wall Street Journal*, October 29, 2005, p. A3; "Sheraton Plans to Pay Guests for Bad Service," *Wall Street Journal*, September 6, 2002, p. B1; "Guaranteed to Last a Whole 90 Days," *Wall Street Journal*, July 16, 2002, p. D1; "Best Buy Co.: Retailer's 'Guaranteed' Strategy for Growth," *Investor's Business Daily*, May 21, 2002, p. A10. See also Jennifer Hamilton and Ross D. Petty, "The European Union's Consumer Guarantees Directive," *Journal of Public Policy & Marketing*, Fall 2001, p. 289; M. E. Blair and Daniel E. Innis, "The Effects of Product Knowledge on the Evaluation of Warranted Brands," *Psychology & Marketing*, August 1996, p. 445; Ellen M. Moore and F. Kelly Shuptrine, "Warranties: Continued Readability Problems after the 1975 Magnuson-Moss Warranty Act," *Journal of Consumer Affairs*, Summer 1993, p. 23.

CHAPTER 9

1. "Under Armour: Thrown for a Loss," *Business Week*, February 1, 2007; "Under Armour's," *Apparel Magazine*, February 2007, pp. 12–15; "Motion Commotion," *Time*, September 11, 2006, see www.time.com/time/magazine/articles; "Perspiration Inspiration," *Business Week*, June 5, 2006, p. 64; "Rag Trade Rivalry," *Forbes*, June 5, 2006; "Under Armour, A Brawny Tee House? No Sweat," *BusinessWeek Online*, May 25, 2006; "Under Armour Hits the Ground Running," *SGB*, May 2006, p. 10; "Under Armour Finds Sports Shoe Fits Its Philosophy," *USA Today*, April 14, 2006, p. 4B; "Hot and Cool," *Government Executive*, October 15, 2005, p. 30; "Protect This House," *Fast Company*, August 2005, p. 70; "Under Armour Shows Feminine Side," *Women's Wear Daily*, February 24, 2005, p. 12; "Under Armour's Apparel Appeal," *Brandweek*, February 21, 2005; *2005 Annual Report*, Under Armour; *2005 Annual Report*, Army and Air Force Exchange Service; "Kevin Plank," *Brandweek*, April 12, 2004, p. 33; "Tight Skivvies," *Time*, January 5, 2003, see www.time.com/time/magazine/articles.

2. Shih Chuan-Fong and Alladi Venkatesh, "Beyond Adoption: Development and Application of a Use-Diffusion Model," *Journal of Marketing*, January 2004, p. 59; Darren W. Dahl and Steve Hoeffler, "Visualizing the Self: Exploring the Potential Benefits and Drawbacks for New Product Evaluation," *Journal of Product Innovation Management*, July 2004, p. 259; Youngme Moon, "Break Free from the Product Life Cycle," *Harvard Business Review*, May 2005, p. 86; Alina B. Sorescu, Rajesh K. Chandy, and Jaideep C. Prabhu, "Sources and Financial Consequences of Radical Innovation: Insights from Pharmaceuticals," *Journal of Marketing*, October 2003, p. 82; Ulrike de Brentani, "Innovative versus Incremental New Business Services: Different Keys for Achieving Success," *Journal of Product Innovation Management*, May 2001, p. 169; Barry L. Bayus, "The Languages of Edison's Light," *Journal of Product Innovation Management*, May 2000, p. 254; Marion Debruyne, Rudy Moenaert, Abbie Griffin, Susan Hart et al. "The Impact of New Product Launch Strategies on Competitive Reaction in Industrial Markets," *Journal of Product Innovation Management*, March 2002, p. 159; X. Michael Song, C. Anthony Di Benedetto, and Lisa Z. Song, "Pioneering Advantage in New Service Development: A Multi-Country Study of Managerial Perceptions," *Journal of Product Innovation Management*, September 2000, p. 378; Christopher M. McDermott and Gina Colarelli O'Connor, "Managing Radical Innovation: An Overview of Emergent Strategy Issues," *Journal of Product Innovation Management*, November 2002, p. 424; Ronald W. Niedrich and Scott D. Swain, "The Influence of Pioneer Status and Experience Order on Consumer Brand Preference: A Mediated-Effects Model," *Journal of the Academy of Marketing Science*, Fall 2003, p. 468; Rajesh K. Chandy and Gerard J. Tellis, "The Incumbent's Curse? Incumbency, Size, and Radical Product Innovation," *Journal of Marketing*, July 2000, p. 1; Robert W. Veryzer, "Key Factors Affecting Customer Evaluation of Discontinuous New Products," *Journal of Product Innovation Management*, March 1998, p. 136; Neil A. Morgan, "Managing Imitation Strategies: How Later Entrants Seize Market Share from Pioneers," *Journal of Marketing*, October 1995, p. 104; David M. Szymanski, Lisa C. Troy, and Sundar G. Bharadwaj, "Order of Entry and Business Performance: An Empirical Synthesis and Reexamination," *Journal of Marketing*, October 1995, p. 17; George Day, "The Product Life Cycle: Analysis and Applications Issues," *Journal of Marketing*, Fall 1981, p. 60; Igal Ayal, "International Product Life Cycle: A Reassessment and Product Policy Implications," *Journal of Marketing*, Fall 1981, p. 91.

3. "Countering Tech Copycats," *Investor's Business Daily*, October 31, 2005, p. A10; "Behind TiVo, iPod, and Xbox: An Industry Struggles for Profits," *Wall Street Journal*, October 14, 2004, p. A1ff.; "Flash Memory Firms, Disk Drive Industry in Escalating Rivalry," *Investor's Business Daily*, October 13, 2005, p. A6. See also Jorge Alberto Sousa De Vasconcellos, "Key Success Factors in Marketing Mature Products," *Industrial Marketing Management* 20, no. 4 (1991), p. 263; Paul C.N. Michell, Peter Quinn, and Edward Percival, "Marketing Strategies for Mature Industrial Products," *Industrial Marketing Management* 20, no. 3 (1991), p. 201; Peter N. Golder and Gerard J. Tellis, "Pioneer Advantage: Marketing Logic or Marketing Legend?" *Journal of Marketing Research*, May 1993, p. 158.

4. For more on Xbox, see Chapter 4, endnote 8.

5. "Milk Industry's Pitch in Asia: Try the Ginger or Rose Flavor," *Wall Street Journal*, August 9, 2005.

6. "Video Slips as DVD Market Matures," *USA Today*, January 4, 2006, p. 1D; "DVD's Success Steals the Show," *USA Today*, January 8, 2004, p. 1Aff.; "DVD: It Pays to Spend a Little More," *USA Today*, December 3, 2003, p. 10D; "Backseat Movies: Car DVD Entertainment Systems . . .," *Business Week*, May 26, 2003, p. 108; "High-Definition Discs Aim to Outshine DVDs," *Investor's Business Daily*, May 6, 2003, p. A6; "Safe at Home and All Plugged In," *USA Today*, January 8, 2002, p. 1D; "Blockbuster Tests Postvideo Future," *Wall Street Journal*, June 18, 2001, p. B1; "Sales of DVD Players Boom, but Makers Record Little Profit," *Investor's Business Daily*, January 22, 2001, p. A6.

7. For more on EV1, see "An Electric Car Propelled by Star Power?" *Business Week*, December 9, 1996, p. 40; "GM Energizes EV1 Launch with $8 Mil Ad Blitz," *Advertising Age*, December 2, 1996, p. 12; "A Big Charge for Electric Vehicles," *Business Week*, November 18, 1996, p. 102. For more on Toyota and Honda hybrids, see Chapter 4, endnote 25. For another example involving the portable digital music market, see "Late Starts Can Be Great Starts," *Investor's Business Daily*, February 13, 2006, p. A10; "An iPod Casualty: The Rio Digital-Music Player," *Wall Street Journal*, September 1, 2005, p. B3; "When Being First Doesn't Make You No. 1," *Wall Street Journal*, August 12, 2004, p. B1ff. See also Sungwook Min, Manohar U. Kalwani, and William T. Robinson, "Market Pioneer and Early Follower Survival Risks: A Contingency Analysis of Really New versus Incrementally New Product-Markets," *Journal of Marketing*, January 2006, p. 15.

8. "A New Stretch for Fashion," *Wall Street Journal*, February 23, 2006, p. B1ff.; "Uggs Again? What Last Year's 'It' Gift Does for an Encore," *Wall Street Journal*, December 9, 2005, p. B1ff.; "Nice (Horizontal) Pants!" *Business 2.0*, December 2005, p. 68; "Men Say Bling It On," *Wall Street Journal*, November 30, 2005, p. B1ff.; "Escaping the Fashion Trap," *Wall Street Journal*, October 15, 2005, pp. P6–P7; "Thinking Outside the Shoe Box," *Business 2.0*, September 2005, p. 68; "Brace Yourself: Wristbands . . .," *USA Today*, July 8, 2005, p. 1Cff.; "Mattel Creates a Living Barbie to Revive Sales," *Wall Street Journal*, June 22, 2005, p. B1ff.; "Reshaping Boomer Fashion," *Wall Street Journal*, April 15, 2005, p. B1ff.; "Making Washer-Dryers a Fashion Statement," *Wall Street Journal*, January 13, 2005, p. D1ff.; "Back to Lean

Jeans," *Wall Street Journal*, March 12, 2004, p. B1ff.; "UGG Boots a Fashion Kick," *USA Today*, December 11, 2003, p. 3B; "Fashion Tip: Get Online," *Wall Street Journal*, October 31, 2003, p. B1; "The Skinny on the Mini," *Wall Street Journal*, February 4, 2003, p. B1; "Nothing Comes between Teens and Their Jeans—Not Even Cost," *USA Today*, September 5, 2002, p. 1D; "Fashion Marketing," *Advertising Age*, August 22, 1994, p. 23. See also Craig J. Thompson and Diana L. Haytko, "Speaking of Fashion: Consumers' Uses of Fashion Discourses and the Appropriation of Countervailing Cultural Meanings," *Journal of Consumer Research*, June 1997, p. 15.

9. For more on Zara, see "At Gucci, Mr. Polet's New Design Upends Rules for High Fashion," *Wall Street Journal*, August 9, 2005, p. A1ff.; "Making Fashion Faster," *Wall Street Journal*, February 24, 2004, p. B1ff.; "Just-in-Time Fashion," *Wall Street Journal*, May 18, 2001, p. B1; "Zara Has a Made-to-Order Plan for Success," *Fortune*, September 4, 2000, p.80.

10. "DVD Acceptance Picks Up Pace," *Discount Store News*, August 9, 1999, p. 29; "DVD and Conquer: Why One Technology Prevailed," *Business Week*, July 5, 1999, p. 34; "Divx: The Video Technology That Geeks Love to Hate," *Fortune*, June 21, 1999, p. 177; "Circuit City Pulls the Plug on Its Divx Videodisk Venture," *Wall Street Journal*, June 17, 1999, p. B10; "8-Tracks, Betamax—and Divx?" *Business Week*, November 9, 1998, p. 108. For more on the current battle between Blu-Ray and HD-DVD, see "The Beta-VHS Battle Offers Some Insights into Coming DVD War," *Wall Street Journal*, January 25, 2006, p. B1; "High-Def in a Format Showdown," *USA Today*, January 10, 2006, p. 3D.; "DVD Tug of War," *Fortune*, December 12, 2005, p. 32.

11. "Big Brands (Small Companies)," *Business Week Small Biz*, August 13, 2001, p. 13.

12. *2005 Annual Report*, RJR Nabisco; "Oreo, Ritz Join Nabisco's Low-Fat Feast," *Advertising Age*, April 4, 1994, p. 3; "They're Not Crying in Their Crackers at Nabisco," *Business Week*, August 30, 1993, p. 61; "Nabisco Unleashes a New Batch of Teddies," *Adweek's Marketing Week*, September 24, 1990, p.18.

13. For more on Tide, see *2005 Annual Report*, Procter & Gamble; "The Endurance Test," *Advertising Age*, November 14, 2005, pp. 3, 38–39; "Testing New-Style Stain Removers," *Wall Street Journal*, July 5, 2005, p. D5; "Life on the Go Means Eating on the Run, and a Lot of Spilling," *Wall Street Journal*, June 7, 2005, p. A1ff.; "Detergent Tablets of the '70s Make a Comeback," *USA Today*, July 27, 2000, p. 9B; "Boom in Liquid Detergents Has P&G Scrambling," *Wall Street Journal*, September 25, 1997, p. B1; "Ultra-Clean—Retail Cheers Still More P&G Concentrates," *Advertising Age*, August 22, 1994, p. 1; "Detergent Industry Spins into New Cycle," *Wall Street Journal*, January 5, 1993, p. B1; "P&G Unleashes Flood of New Tide Products," *Advertising Age*, June 16, 1986, p. 3. See also "The Hard Life of Orphan Brands," *Wall Street Journal*, April 13, 2001, p. B1; "Orphan Relief," *Advertising Age*, March 19, 2001, p. 3.

14. "Making Old Brands New," *American Demographics*, December 1997, p. 53; "Classic Roller Skates Return as Safety Fears Dull Blades," *Wall Street Journal*, October 24, 1997, p. B1; "Dusting Off the Britannica," *Business Week*, October 20, 1997, p. 143; "At Du Pont, Time to Both Sow and Reap," *Business Week*, September 29, 1997, p. 107; "A Boring Brand Can Be Beautiful," *Fortune*, November 18, 1991, p. 169; "Teflon Is 50 Years Old, but Du Pont Is Still Finding New Uses for Invention," *Wall Street Journal*, April 7, 1988, p. 34; Stephen W. Miller, "Managing Imitation Strategies: How Later Entrants Seize Markets from Pioneers," *Journal of the Academy of Marketing Science*, Summer 1996, p. 277; Regina Fazio Maruca and Amy L. Halliday, "When New Products and Customer Loyalty Collide," *Harvard Business Review*, November–December 1993, p. 22.

15. For more on Logitech, see "Logitech, Mobility Electronics Riding High Thanks to PCs," *Investor's Business Daily*, September 2, 2005, p. A4; "The Fastest-Growing Technology Companies," *Business 2.0*, October 2002, p. 81. For more on Gatorade, see "Gatorade Gallon Goes Rectangular," *Packaging Digest*, June 2003, p. 2; "Latest Gatorade Bottle Edges toward Ergonomics," *Packaging Digest*, November 1999, p. 15.

16. "Reposition: Simplifying the Customer's Brandscape," *Brandweek*, October 2, 2000, p. 36; "Consumers to GM: You Talking to Me?" *Business Week*, June 19, 2000, p. 213; "How Growth Destroys Differentiation," *Brandweek*, April 24, 2000, p. 42; "P&G, Seeing Shoppers Were Being Confused, Overhauls Marketing," *Wall Street Journal*, January 15, 1997, p. A1; "Make It Simple," *Business Week*, September 9, 1996, p.96; "Diaper Firms Fight to Stay on the Bottom," *Wall Street Journal*, March 23, 1993, p. B1.

17. "Ignore the Consumer," *Point*, September 2005, pp. 15–19; "Too Many Choices," *Wall Street Journal*, April 20, 2001, p. B1; "New Products," *Ad Age International*, April 13, 1998, p. 17; "The Ghastliest Product Launches," *Fortune*, March 16, 1998, p. 44; "Flops: Too Many New Products Fail. Here's Why—and How to Do Better," *Business Week*, August 16, 1993, p. 76; Brian D. Ottum and William L. Moore, "The Role of Market Information in New Product Success/Failure," *Journal of Product Innovation Management*, July 1997, p. 258.

18. "Makers of Chicken Tonight Find Many Cooks Say, 'Not Tonight,'" *Wall Street Journal*, May 17, 1994, p. B1; "Failure of Its Oven Lovin' Cookie Dough Shows Pillsbury Pitfalls of New Products," *Wall Street Journal*, June 17, 1993, p. B1; Sharad Sarin and Gour M. Kapur, "Lessons from New Product Failures: Five Case Studies," *Industrial Marketing Management*, November 1990, p. 301.

19. "Design Software Helps Give Life to ZMP's Robots," *Investor's Business Daily*, August 9, 2005, p. A4; "This Is Not a BMW Plant," *Fortune*, April 18, 2005, pp. 207C–L; "Helping Designers Go Digital," *Investor's Business Daily*, January 24, 2005, p. A22; "Not Your Grandfather's Assembly Line," *Fortune*, July 12, 2004, pp. 136C–H; "Design Tools Move into the Fast Lane," *Business Week*, June 2, 2003, pp. 84B–84C; "Digital Workflow Speeds Time to Shelf," *Brand Packaging*, March/April 2001, p. 24; "How Fast Can This Baby Go?" *Business Week*, April 10, 2000, p. 38. See also Muammer Ozer, "Process Implications of the Use of the Internet in New Product Development: a Conceptual Analysis," *Industrial Marketing Management*, August 2003, p. 517; J. Daniel Sherman, William E. Souder, and Svenn A. Jenssen, "Differential Effects of the Primary Forms of Cross Functional Integration on Product Development Cycle Time," *Journal of Product Innovation Management*, July 2000, p. 257; Daniel J. Flint, "Compressing New Product Success-to-Success Cycle Time: Deep Customer Value Understanding and Idea Generation," *Industrial Marketing Management*, July 2002, p. 305; Cornelia Droge, Jayanth Jayaram, and Shawnee K. Vickery, "The Ability to Minimize the Timing of New Product Development and Introduction: An Examination of Antecedent Factors in the North American Automobile Supplier Industry," *Journal of Product Innovation Management*, January 2000, p. 24; Kathleen M. Eisenhardt and Shona L. Brown, "Time Pacing: Competing in Markets That Won't Stand Still," *Harvard Business Review*, March–April 1998, p. 59. For more on P&G's efforts to bring products to market faster, see "Brands in a Bind," *Business Week*, August 28, 2000, p. 234; "Warm and Fuzzy Won't Save Procter & Gamble," *Business Week*, June 26, 2000, p. 48.

20. "Why the Kids Are Dissing Leapfrog," *Business 2.0*, November 2005, pp. 80–81; "LED Technology," *NecDigest*, August 2005, pp. 10, 48–53; "Let There Be L.E.D.s," *New York Times*, January 8, 2004, p. E1ff.; "Building a Better R&D Mousetrap," *Business 2.0*, September 2003, p. 50; "Critical Curds: At Kraft, Making Cheese Fun Is Serious Business," *Wall Street Journal*, May 31, 2002, p. A1; "Stuck on You: P&G's New Outlast Lipstick Is Nothing to Pout About," *Wall Street Journal*, May 9, 2002, p. B1; "Bleeding Cash: Pfizer Youth Pill Ate Up $71 Million before It Flopped," *Wall Street Journal*, May 2, 2002, p. A1; "How Burger King Got Burned in Quest to Make the Perfect Fry," *Wall Street Journal*, January 16, 2001, p. A1. See also Ashish Sood and Gerard J. Tellis, "Technological Evolution and Radical Innovation," *Journal of Marketing*, July 2005, p. 152; Debra Zahay, Abbie Griffin, and Elisa Fredericks, "Sources, Uses, and Forms of Data in the New Product Development Process," *Industrial Marketing Management*, October 2004, p. 658; Janice Griffiths-Hemans and Rajiv Grover, "Setting the Stage for Creative New Products: Investingating the Idea

Fruition Process," *Journal of the Academy of Marketing Science*, Winter 2006, p. 27; John E. Ettlie and Mohan Subramaniam, "Changing Strategies and Tactics for New Product Development," *Journal of Product Innovation Management*, March 2004, p. 95; Lisa C. Troy, David M. Szymanski, and P. Rajan Varadarajan, "Generating New Product Ideas: An Initial Investigation of the Role of Market Information and Organizational Characteristics," *Journal of the Academy of Marketing Science*, Winter 2001, p. 89; Rajesh Sethi, "New Product Quality and Product Development Teams," *Journal of Marketing*, April 2000, p. 1; Mark A. A. M. Leenders and Berend Wierenga, "The Effectiveness of Different Mechanisms for Integrating Marketing and R&D," *Journal of Product Innovation Management*, July 2002, p. 305; George J. Avlonitis, Susan J. Hart, and Nikolaos X. Tzokas, "An Analysis of Product Deletion Scenarios," *Journal of Product Innovation Management*, January 2000, p. 41; Elliot Maltz, William E. Souder, and Ajith Kumar, "Influencing R&D/Marketing Integration and the Use of Market Information by R&D Managers: Intended and Unintended Effects of Managerial Actions," *Journal of Business Research*, April 2001, p. 69; Robert Polk, Richard E. Plank, and David A. Reid, "Technical Risk and New Product Success: An Empirical Test in High Technology Business Markets," *Industrial Marketing Management*, November 1996, p. 531; Jeffrey B. Schmidt and Roger J. Calantone, "Are Really New Product Development Projects Harder to Shut Down?" *Journal of Product Innovation Management*, March 1998, p. 111; Cheryl Nakata and K. Sivakumar, "National Culture and New Product Development: An Integrative Review," *Journal of Marketing*, January 1996, p. 61; Gary S. Lynn, Joseph G. Morone, and Albert S. Paulson, "Marketing and Discontinuous Innovation: The Probe and Learn Process," *California Management Review*, Spring 1996, p. 8; X. M. Song and Mitzi M. Montoya-Weiss, "Critical Development Activities for Really New versus Incremental Products," *Journal of Product Innovation Management*, March 1998, p. 124.

21. "Mosh Pits of Creativity," *Business Week*, November 7, 2005, pp. 98–100; "Employers See Gold Mining Employees for Ideas," *Brandweek*, October 10, 2005, p. 16; "Managing Google's Idea Factory," *Business Week*, October 3, 2005, pp. 88–90; "Staples Lets Customers Do the Designing," *Fortune*, April 18, 2005, p. 48; "Outsourcing Innovation," *Business Week*, March 21, 2005, pp. 84–94; "This Volvo Is Not a Guy Thing," *Business Week*, March 15, 2004, pp. 84–86; "Pickups Get Women's Touch," *USA Today*, June 13, 2001 p. 1B; "Where Great Ideas Come From," *Inc.*, April 1998, p. 76. See also Edward F. McDonough III, Kenneth B. Kahn, and Gloria Barczak, "An Investigation of the Use of Global, Virtual, and Colocated New Product Development Teams," *Journal of Product Innovation Management*, March 2001, p. 110; Ari-Pekka Hameri and Jukka Nihtila, "Distributed New Product Development Project Based on Internet and World-Wide Web: A Case Study," *Journal of Product Innovation Management*, March 1997, p. 77.

22. "It Was a Hit in Buenos Aires—So Why Not Boise?" *Business Week*, September 7, 1998, p. 56. See also Rudy K. Moenaert, Filip Caeldries, Annouk Lievens, and Elke Wauters, "Communication Flows in International Product Innovation Teams," *Journal of Product Innovation Management*, September 2000, p. 360; Vittorio Chiesa, "Global R&D Project Management and Organization: A Taxonomy," *Journal of Product Innovation Management*, September 2000, p. 341; John J. Cristiano, Jeffrey K. Liker, and Chelsea C. White III, "Customer-Driven Product Development through Quality Function Deployment in the U.S. and Japan," *Journal of Product Innovation Management*, July 2000, p. 286.

23. Erik L. Olson and Geir Bakke, "Implementing the Lead User Method in a High Technology Firm: A Longitudinal Study of Intentions versus Actions," *Journal of Product Innovation Management*, November 2001, p. 388; Eric von Hippel, *The Sources of Innovation* (New York: Oxford University Press, 1988).

24. "Shielding the Shield Makers," *Wall Street Journal*, November 26, 2003, p. B1; "Gun Makers to Push Use of Gun Locks," *Wall Street Journal*, May 9, 2001, p. B12; "U.S. Recalls Millions of Evenflo

'Joyride' Infant Seats, Carriers," *Wall Street Journal*, May 2, 2001, p. B6; "Stand Up and Fight," *Business Week*, September 11, 2000, p. 54; "Why One Jury Dealt a Big Blow to Chrysler in Minivan-Latch Case," *Wall Street Journal*, November 19, 1997, p. A1; "How a Jury Decided that a Coffee Spill Is Worth $2.9 Million," *Wall Street Journal*, September 1, 1994, p. A1; Jennifer J. Argo and Kelley J. Main, "Meta-Analyses of the Effectiveness of Warning Labels," *Journal of Public Policy & Marketing*, Fall 2004, p. 193; Paul A. Herbig and James E. Golden, "Innovation and Product Liability," *Industrial Marketing Management*, July 1994, p. 245; Robert N. Mayer and Debra L. Scammon, "Caution: Weak Product Warnings May Be Hazardous to Corporate Health," *Journal of Business Research*, June 1992, p. 347.

25. "Want Shelf Space at the Supermarket? Ante Up," *Business Week*, August 7, 1989, p. 60; "Grocer 'Fee' Hampers New-Product Launches," *Advertising Age*, August 3, 1987, p. 1.

26. Susumu Ogawa and Frank T. Piller, "Reducing the Risks of New Product Development," *MIT Sloan Management Review*, Winter 2006, p. 65; Joseph M. Bonner, Robert W. Ruekert, and Orville C. Walker, Jr. "Upper Management Control of New Product Development Projects and Project Performance," *Journal of Product Innovation Management*, May 2002, p. 233; Harold Z. Daniel, Donald J. Hempel, and Narasimhan Srinivasan, "A Model of Value Assessment in Collaborative R&D Programs," *Industrial Marketing Management*, November 2002, p. 653; Sundar Bharadwaj and Anil Menon, "Making Innovations Happen in Organizations: Individual Creativity Mechanisms, Organizational Creativity Mechanisms or Both?" *Journal of Product Innovation Management*, November 2000, p. 424; Preston G. Smith, "Mastering Virtual Teams: Strategies, Tools, and Techniques That Succeed," *Journal of Product Innovation Management*, March 2001, p. 127; Gregory D. Githens, "Customer Centered Products: Creating Successful Products through Smart Requirements Management," *Journal of Product Innovation Management*, September 2001, p. 350; Keith Goffin, "Evaluating Customer Support During New Product Development—An Exploratory Study," *Journal of Product Innovation Management*, January 1998, p. 42; Paul S. Adler, Avi Mandelbaum, Vien Nguyen, and Elizabeth Schwerer, "Getting the Most Out of Your Product Development Process," *Harvard Business Review*, March–April 1996, p. 134.

27. "Torture Testing," *Fortune*, October 2, 2000, pp. 244B–X; "Industry's Amazing New Instant Prototypes," *Fortune*, January 12, 1998, pp. 120E–L; "Secrets of Product Testing," *Fortune*, November 28, 1994, p. 166; "A Smarter Way to Manufacture," *Business Week*, April 30, 1990, p. 110.

28. "Oops! Marketers Blunder their Way through the 'Herb Decade,'" *Advertising Age*, February 13, 1989, p. 3.

29. Eyal Biyalogorsky, William Boulding, and Richard Staelin, "Stuck in the Past: Why Managers Persist with New Product Failures," *Journal of Marketing*, April 2006, p. 108; Shankar Ganesan, Alan J. Malter, and Aric Rindfleisch, "Does Distance Still Matter? Geographic Proximity and New Product Development," *Journal of Marketing*, October 2005, p. 44; Subin Im and John P. Workman, Jr., "Market Orientation, Creativity, and New Product Performance in High-Technology Firms," *Journal of Marketing*, April 2004, p. 114; Steven C. Michael and Tracy Pun Palandjian, "Organizational Learning and New Product Introductions," *Journal of Product Innovation Management*, July 2004, p. 268; Erwin Danneels and Elko J. Kleinschmidt, "Product Innovativeness from the Firm's Perspective: Its Dimensions and Their Relation with Project Selection and Performance," *Journal of Product Innovation Management*, November 2001, p. 357; R. Jeffrey Thieme, Michael Song, and Geon-Cheol Shin, "Project Management Characteristics and New Product Survival," *Journal of Product Innovation Management*, March 2003, p. 104; William E. Souder, David Buisson, and Tony Garrett, "Success through Customer-Driven New Product Development: A Comparison of U.S. and New Zealand Small Entrepreneurial High Technology Firms," *Journal of Product Innovation Management*, November 1997, p. 459; Artemis March, "Usability: The New Dimension of Product

Design," *Harvard Business Review*, September–October 1994, p. 144; Peter H. Bloch, "Seeking the Ideal Form: Product Design and Consumer Response," *Journal of Marketing*, July 1995, p. 16; Alan Flaschner, "Technology Fountainheads: The Management Challenge of R&D Consortia," *Journal of Product Innovation Management*, July 1997, p. 309; John P. Workman, Jr., "Marketing's Limited Role in New Product Development in One Computer Systems Firm," *Journal of Marketing Research*, November 1993, p. 405.

30. "Care, Feeding, and Building of a Billion-Dollar Brand," *Advertising Age*, February 23, 2004, p. 26; "Brands at Work," *Brandweek*, April 13, 1998, p. 27; "Auto Marketing & Brand Management," *Advertising Age*, April 6, 1998, p. S1; "P&G Redefines the Brand Manager," *Advertising Age*, October 13, 1997, p. 1. See also Sanjay K. Dhar, Stephen J. Hoch, and Nanda Kumar, "Effective Category Management Depends on the Role of the Category," *Journal of Retailing*, Summer 2001, p. 165; Don Frey, "Learning the Ropes: My Life as a Product Champion," *Harvard Business Review*, September–October 1991, p. 46; Stephen K. Markham, "New Products Management," *Journal of Product Innovation Management*, July 1997, p. 312.

31. See www.3m.com; *2005 Annual Report*, 3M; "Pushing Past Post-Its by Allowing Top Scientists to Peek over Horizon . . .," *Business 2.0*, November 2005, pp. 54–56; "3M: Reading between the Lines," *Business Week Online*, August 1, 2005; "3M Aims to Make 'Vikuiti' a Household Name," in TV Screens," *Minneapolis Star Tribune*, July 18, 2005; "3M Innovation Will Juice Power Lines," *Wall Street Journal*, October 6, 2004, p. B2A; "3M's Rising Star," *Business Week*, April 12, 2004, pp. 62–74; "How Leader at 3M Got His Employees to Back Big Changes," *Wall Street Journal*, April 23, 2002, p. B1; "3M: A Lab for Growth?" *Business Week*, January 21, 2002, p. 50; "How 3M, by Tiptoeing into Foreign Markets, Became a Big Exporter," *Wall Street Journal*, March 29, 1991, p. A1. See also Ali E. Akgün, Gary S. Lynn, and John C. Byrne, "Antecedents and Consequences of Unlearning in New Product Development Teams," *Journal of Product Innovation Management*, January 2006, p. 73.

32. The restaurant case is adapted from Marie Gaudard, Roland Coates, and Liz Freeman, "Accelerating Improvement," *Quality Progress*, October 1991, p. 81. For more on quality management and control, see "By Focusing on Customers, Firms Can Boost Shareholder Value," *Investor's Business Daily*, October 11, 2002, p. A3; "Quality Isn't Just for Widgets," *Business Week*, July 22, 2002, p. 72; "Nicknamed 'Nag,' She's Just Doing Her Job," *Wall Street Journal*, May 14, 2002, p. B1; "The Net as a Lifeline," *Business Week E.Biz*, October 29, 2001, p. EB16; "The Lure of Six Sigma Quality: It Gets Everyone Thinking Alike," *Investor's Business Daily*, November 7, 2001, p. A1; "How to Bring Out Better Products Faster," *Fortune*, November 23, 1998, p. 238B; Roland T. Rust, Anthony J. Zahorik, and Timothy L. Keiningham, "Return on Quality (ROQ): Making Service Quality Financially Accountable," *Journal of Marketing*, April 1995, p. 58. See also Mark R. Colgate and Peter J. Danaher, "Implementing a Customer Relationship Strategy: The Asymetric Impact of Poor versus Excellent Execution," *Journal of the Academy of Marketing Science*, Summer 2000, p. 374; Jagdip Singh, "Performance Productivity and Quality of Frontline Employees in Service Organizations," *Journal of Marketing*, April 2000, p. 15; Simon J. Bell and Bulent Menguc, "The Employee-Organization Relationship, Organizational Citizenship Behaviors, and Superior Service Quality," *Journal of Retailing*, Summer 2002, p. 131; Roland T. Rust, Christine Moorman, and Peter R. Dickson, "Getting Return on Quality: Revenue Expansion, Cost Reduction, or Both?" *Journal of Marketing*, October 2002, p. 7; Pratibha A. Dabholkar, C. David Shepherd, and Dayle I. Thorpe, "A Comprehensive Framework for Service Quality: An Investigation of Critical Conceptual and Measurement Issues through a Longitudinal Study," *Journal of Retailing*, Summer 2000, p. 139; Scott S. Elliott, "Managing by Measuring: How to Improve Your Organization's Performance through Effective Benchmarking," *Journal of Product Innovation Management*, July 2000, p. 321; William B. Locander and Daniel J. Goebel, "The Quality Train Is Leaving and Marketers Are Nodding

Off in the Club Car," *Journal of Marketing Theory & Practice*, Summer 1996, p. 1; William C. LaFief, "Total Quality Marketing: The Key to Regaining Market Shares," *Journal of the Academy of Marketing Science*, Fall 1996, p. 377; David W. Finn, Julie Baker, Greg W. Marshall, and Roy Anderson, "Total Quality Management and Internal Customers: Measuring Internal Service Quality," *Journal of Marketing Theory & Practice*, Summer 1996, p. 36; Robert F. Hurley, Melissa T. Gropper, and Gianpaolo Roma, "The Role of TQM in Advertising: A Conceptualization and a Framework for Application," *Journal of Marketing Theory & Practice*, Summer 1996, p. 11; Teresa A. Swartz, "Why TQM Fails and What to Do about It," *Journal of the Academy of Marketing Science*, Fall 1996, p. 380; Iris Mohr-Jackson, "Managing a Total Quality Orientation: Factors Affecting Customer Satisfaction," *Industrial Marketing Management*, March 1998, p. 109; Cengiz Haksever, "Total Quality Management in the Small Business Environment," *Business Horizons*, March–April 1996, p. 33; Michael P. Bigwood, "Total Quality Management at Work: Development of an Effective Competitive Analysis Process," *Industrial Marketing Management*, September 1997, p. 459.

33. For Whole Foods example of empowerment, see Chapter 2, endnote 4. See also "Companies Give Front-Line Employees More Power," *USA Today*, June 27, 2005, p. 1; "Thinking Outside the Cereal Box," *Business Week*, July 28, 2003, p. 74; "Pentair Fixes Its Own Mess," *Fortune*, September 30, 2002, p. 156C; "Glass Act: How a Window Maker Rebuilt Itself," *Fortune*, November 13, 2000, p. 384B. See also Douglas W. Vorhies and Neil A. Morgan, "Benchmarking Marketing Capabilities for Sustainable Competitive Advantage," *Journal of Marketing*, January 2005, p. 80; Roland T. Rust, Tim Ambler, Gregory S. Carpenter, V. Kumar, and Rajendra K. Srivastava, "Measuring Marketing Productivity: Current Knowledge and Future Directions," *Journal of Marketing*, October 2004, p. 76; Anthony J. Capraro and Robert D. Yearout, "Selecting Quality Initiatives to Pursue: Integrating Demand Effects into the Evaluation and Selection of Potential Quality Initiatives," *Journal of Marketing Theory & Practice*, Summer 2004, p. 1; Frederick E. Webster, Jr., Alan J. Malter, and Shankar Ganesan, "The Decline and Dispersion of Marketing Competence," *MIT Sloan Management Review*, Summer 2005, p. 35; Dawn R. Deeter-Schmelz and Rosemary P. Ramsey, "An Investigation of Team Information Processing in Service Teams: Exploring the Link between Teams and Customers," *Journal of the Academy of Marketing Science*, Fall 2003, p. 409; Emin Babakus, Ugur Yavas, Osman M. Karatepe, and Turgay Avci, "The Effect of Management Commitment to Service Quality on Employees' Affective and Performance Outcomes," *Journal of the Academy of Marketing Science*, Summer 2003, p. 272; Roland T. Rust, Anthony J. Zahorik, and Timothy L. Keiningham, *Return on Quality* (Chicago: Probus, 1994); Timothy L. Keiningham, Roland T. Rust, and M. Marshall Weems, "The Bottom Line on Quality," *Financial Executive*, September/October 1994, p. 50; Warren S. Martin and Wendy K. Martin, "The Application of Benchmarking to Marketing," *Journal of Marketing Theory & Practice*, Summer 1996, p. 52; J. J. Cronin and Steven A. Taylor, "SERVPERF versus SERVQUAL: Reconciling Performance-Based and Perceptions-Minus-Expectations Measurement of Service Quality," *Journal of Marketing*, January 1994, p. 125; Timothy C. Johnston and Molly A. Hewa, "Fixing Service Failures," *Industrial Marketing Management*, September 1997, p. 467; Shirley Taylor, "Waiting for Service: The Relationship between Delays and Evaluations of Service," *Journal of Marketing*, April 1994, p. 56; Mary J. Bitner, Bernard H. Booms, and Lois A. Mohr, "Critical Service Encounters: The Employee's Viewpoint," *Journal of Marketing*, October 1994, p. 95; G. T. M. Hult, "Service Quality: New Directions in Theory and Practice," *Journal of the Academy of Marketing Science*, Summer 1997, p. 264; Scott W. Kelley, Timothy Longfellow, and Jack Malehorn, "Organizational Determinants of Service Employees' Exercise of Routine, Creative, and Deviant Discretion," *Journal of Retailing*, Summer 1996, p. 135; Pierre Filiatrault, Jean Harvey, and Jean-Charles Chebat, "Service Quality and Service Productivity Management Practices," *Industrial Marketing Management*, May 1996,

p. 243; Robert Simons, "Control in an Age of Empowerment," *Harvard Business Review*, March–April 1995, p. 80.

CHAPTER 10

1. See www.gamestop.com, www.ebgames.com, www.bn.com, and www.amazon.com; "New GameStop/EB Entity to Control 25% of Market," *DSN Retailing Today*, May 9, 2005, pp. 4, 41; "Game-Stop Buys Rival in $1.4B Deal," *USA Today*, April 19, 2005, p. 3B; *2005 Annual Report*, GameStop; *2004 Annual Report*, GameStop; "Barnes & Noble Pares GameStop," *Wall Street Journal*, October 5, 2004, p. B6; "To Compete with Book Chains, Some Think Big," *Wall Street Journal*, August 24, 2004, p. A1ff.; "Ingram Book Group and Valley Media Partner," *Nashville Business Journal*, May 29, 2001; "Why the Bookstore Wars Are Good," *Fortune*, October 27, 1997, p. 50; "Book Superstores Bring Hollywood-Like Risks to Publishing Business," *Wall Street Journal*, May 29, 1997, p. A1; "Superstores, Megabooks—and Humongous Headaches," *Business Week*, April 14, 1997, p. 92.

2. *2005 Annual Report*, Colgate-Palmolive; *2005 Annual Report*, Procter & Gamble; "PetSmart Thinks Outside the Big Box," *USA Today*, December 5, 2005, p. 4B; "Pets Are People, Too, You Know . . . P&G's Iams Treats Them That Way . . .," *Business Week*, November 28, 2005, p. 114; "Licensing Goes to the Dogs," *Brandweek*, June 13, 2005, pp. 20–26; "Pampered Pooches Nestle in Lap of Luxury," *USA Today*, February 11, 2005, p. 1Aff.; "For Petco, Success Is a Bitch," *Business 2.0*, November 2003, p. 54; "P&G Is Set to Unleash Dental Adult-Pet Food," *Wall Street Journal*, December 12, 2002, p. B4; "P&G Is Out to Fetch Distribution Gains for Iams Pet Food," *Wall Street Journal*, January 6, 2000, p. A6; "Big Pet-Supply Retailers Try to Tame the Competition," *Wall Street Journal*, August 20, 1999, p. B4. See also Daniel Corsten and Nirmalya Kumar, "Do Suppliers Benefit from Collaborative Relationships with Large Retailers? An Empirical Investigation of Efficient Consumer Response Adoption," *Journal of Marketing*, July 2005, p. 80.

3. For more on Apple, see "Nokia Plans Its Own Stores to Build Brand Loyalty," *Wall Street Journal*, February 23, 2006, p. B1ff.; "The iPod People Have Invaded Apple's Stores!" *Fortune*, December 13, 2004, p. 79; "Microsoft, Gateway, Sony Heed the Call of the Mall," *Brandweek*, December 6, 2004, p. 16; "Apple Reboots into Retailing," *USA Today*, November 22, 2004, p. 1Bff.; "As Sony Expands Chain of Stores, Retailers Fret about Competition," *Investor's Business Daily*, October 19, 2004, p. A6; "Have Your Tried to Get Tech Support Lately?," *USA Today*, August 27, 2004, p. 1Bff. For more on Glaceau, see "Move Over, Coke: How a Small Beverage Maker Managed to Win Shelf Space . . .," *Wall Street Journal Reports*, January 30, 2006, p. R1ff.; "Pepsi Picks Water Fight with Surging Glaceau," *Advertising Age*, October 17, 2005, p. 3ff.

4. S. Chan Choi, "Expanding to Direct Channel: Market Coverages as Entry Barrier," *Journal of Interactive Marketing*, Winter 2003, p. 25; David Shipley, Colin Egan, and Scott Edgett, "Meeting Source Selection Criteria: Direct versus Distributor Channels," *Industrial Marketing Management* 20, no. 4 (1991), p. 297.

5. Edward L. Nash, *Direct Marketing* (New York: McGraw-Hill, 1986).

6. For an example of a Levi Strauss' new indirect channels via discount stores, see "Levi's Signature Spreads Its Wings," *DSN Retailing Today*, April 25, 2005, p. 39; "Levi's Officially Goes Mass as Signature Lands at Kmart," *DSN Retailing Today*, August 16, 2004, p. 1ff.; "Jean Therapy, $23 a Pop," *Business Week*, June 28, 2004, pp. 91–93; "In Bow to Retailers' New Clout, Levi Strauss Makes Alterations," *Wall Street Journal*, June 17, 2004, p. A1ff.; "Lessons from a Faded Levi Strauss," *Business Week*, December 15, 2003, p. 44; "At Levi Strauss, Trouble Comes from All Angles," *Wall Street Journal*, October 13, 2003, p. B1; "Wal-Mart Adds Touch of Hip to Fashion Choices," *USA Today*, July 22, 2003, p. 3B; "Levi's Won't Fly Signature Ads," *Brandweek*, June 16, 2003, p. 18; "Mass Levi's, Class Levi's," *Wall*

Street Journal, October 31, 2002, p. B1. For two examples of unsuccessful attempts at indirect channels, see "Ovens Are Cooling at Krispy Kreme as Woes Multiply," *Wall Street Journal*, September 3, 2004, p. A1ff.; and "A Deal with Target Put Lid on Revival at Tupperware," *Wall Street Journal*, February 14, 2004, p. A1ff. For a discussion of indirect channel systems, see Richard Parker and G. R. Funkhouser, "The Consumer as an Active Member of the Channel: Implications for Relationship Marketing," *Journal of Marketing Theory & Practice*, Spring 1997, p. 72; Lou E. Pelton, David Strutton, and James R. Lumpkin, *Marketing Channels: A Relationship Management Approach* (Burr Ridge, IL: Irwin/McGraw-Hill, 2002). See also Bert Rosenbloom and Trina L. Larsen, "How Foreign Firms View Their U.S. Distributors," *Industrial Marketing Management*, May 1992, p. 93; Frank Lynn, "The Changing Economics of Industrial Distribution," *Industrial Marketing Management*, November 1992, p. 355. For more on intermediaries and their functions, see Richard Greene, "Wholesaling," *Forbes*, January 2, 1984, p. 226; W. Benoy et al., "How Industrial Distributors View Distributor-Supplier Partnership Arrangements," *Industrial Marketing Management*, January 1995, p. 27.

7. For a classic discussion of the discrepancy concepts, see Wroe Alderson, "Factors Governing the Development of Marketing Channels," in *Marketing Channels for Manufactured Goods*, ed. Richard M. Clewett (Homewood, IL: Richard D. Irwin, 1954), p. 7.

8. For some examples of how channels change to adjust discrepancies, see "Selling Literature like Dog Food Gives Club Buyer Real Bite," *Wall Street Journal*, April 10, 2002, p. A1. See also Robert Tamilia, Sylvain Senecal, and Gilles Corriveau, "Conventional Channels of Distribution and Electronic Intermediaries: A Functional Analysis," *Journal of Marketing Channels*, no 3/4 (2002), p. 27; Robert A. Mittel-staedt and Robert E. Stassen, "Structural Changes in the Phonograph Record Industry and Its Channels of Distribution, 1946–1966," *Journal of Macromarketing*, Spring 1994, p. 31; Arun Sharma and Luis V. Dominguez, "Channel Evolution: A Framework for Analysis," *Journal of the Academy of Marketing Science*, Winter 1992, p. 1.

9. Arne Nygaard and Robert Dahlstrom, "Role Stress and Effectiveness in Horizontal Alliances," *Journal of Marketing*, April 2002, p. 61; M. B. Sarkar, Raj Echambadi, S. Tamer Cavusgil, and Preet S. Aulakh, "The Influence of Complementarity, Compatibility, and Relationship Capital on Alliance Performance," *Journal of the Academy of Marketing Science*, Fall 2001, p. 358; Jakki J. Mohr, Robert J. Fisher, and John R. Nevin, "Collaborative Communication in Interfirm Relationships: Moderating Effects of Integration and Control," *Journal of Marketing*, July 1996, p. 103; Joseph P. Cannon, "Contracts, Norms, and Plural Form Governance," *Journal of the Academy of Marketing Science*, Spring 2000, p. 180.

10. "What's Wrong with Selling Used CDs?" *Business Week*, July 26, 1993, p. 38.

11. Nirmalya Kumar, "Living with Channel Conflict," *CMO*, October 2004.

12. "Bottlers Stand Up to Retail's Call for Change," *Financial Times*, March 22, 2006; "Channel Conflict on the Internet," www. grandgo.com/conflict.html; Gregory M. Rose and Aviv Shoham, "Interorganizational Task and Emotional Conflict with International Channels of Distribution," *Journal of Business Research*, September 2004, p. 942.

13. "Get Great Results from Salespeople by Finding What Really Moves Them," *Investor's Business Daily*, July 2, 2001, p. A1.

14. Kenneth H. Wathne and Jan B. Heide, "Relationship Governance in a Supply Chain Network," *Journal of Marketing*, January 2004, p. 73; David I. Gilliland, "Designing Channel Incentives to Overcome Reseller Rejection," *Industrial Marketing Management*, February 2004, p. 87; James R. Brown, Anthony T. Cobb, and Robert F. Lusch, "The Roles Played by Interorganizational Contracts and Justice in Marketing Channel Relationships," *Journal of Business Research*, February 2006, p. 166; Keysuk Kim and Changho Oh, "On Distributor Commitment in Marketing Channels for Industrial Products: Contrast between the United States and Japan," *Journal of*

International Marketing, no 1 (2002), p. 72; Pierre Berthon, Leyland F. Pitt, Michael T. Ewing, and Gunnar Bakkeland, "Norms and Power in Marketing Relationships: Alternative Theories and Empirical Evidence," *Journal of Business Research,* September 2003, p. 699; Rajiv Mehta, Alan J. Dubinsky, and Rolph E. Anderson, "Marketing Channel Management and the Sales Manager," *Industrial Marketing Management,* August 2002, p. 429; Donald V. Fites, "Make Your Dealers Your Partners," *Harvard Business Review,* March–April 1996, p. 84; John F. Tanner, Rick E. Ridnour, and Stephen B. Castleberry, "Types of Vertical Exchange Relationships: An Empirical Re-Examination of the Cadre/Hired-Hand Distinction," *Journal of Marketing Theory & Practice,* Summer 1997, p. 109; Zhan G. Li and Rajiv P. Dant, "An Exploratory Study of Exclusive Dealing in Channel Relationships," *Journal of the Academy of Marketing Science,* Summer 1997, p. 201.

15. See Janice M. Payan and Richard G. McFarland, "Decomposing Influence Strategies: Argument Structure and Dependence as Determinants of the Effectiveness of Influence Strategies in Gaining Channel Member Compliance," *Journal of Marketing,* July 2005, p. 66; G. Peter Dapiran and Sandra Hogarth-Scott, "Are Co-operation and Trust Being Confused with Power? An Analysis of Food Retailing in Australia and the UK," *International Journal of Retail & Distribution Management,* no. 4 (2003), p. 256; David I. Gilliland and Daniel C. Bello, "Two Sides to Attitudinal Commitment: The Effect of Calculative and Loyalty Commitment on Enforcement Mechanisms in Distribution Channels," *Journal of the Academy of Marketing Science,* Winter 2002, p. 24; "Making the Middleman an Endangered Species," *Business Week,* June 6, 1994, p. 114; Jule B. Gassenheimer et al., "Models of Channel Maintenance: What Is the Weaker Party to Do?" *Journal of Business Research,* July 1994, p. 225; Gregory T. Gundlach, Ravi S. Achrol, and John T. Mentzer, "The Structure of Commitment in Exchange," *Journal of Marketing,* January 1995, p. 78; Jan B. Heide, "Interorganizational Governance in Marketing Channels," *Journal of Marketing,* January 1994, p. 71; Jean L. Johnson et al., "The Exercise of Interfirm Power and Its Repercussions in U.S.-Japanese Channel Relationships," *Journal of Marketing,* April 1993, p. 1.

16. For some examples of vertical integration, see "Mothers Work: Oh Baby, Business at This Retailer Is Booming," *Investor's Business Daily,* December 2, 2002, p. A10; "Mothers Work: Giving the Lady What She Wants," *Fortune,* October 30, 2000, pp. T208BB–HH; "Moving On Up: Agricultural Firms Are Looking for New Growth Model . . . Vertical Integration," *Wall Street Journal Reports,* October 25, 2004, p. R6ff.; "Tiger's New Threads," *Wall Street Journal,* March 26, 2004, p. B1ff.

17. "Kimberly-Clark Keeps Costco in Diapers, Absorbing Costs Itself," *Wall Street Journal,* September 7, 2000, p. A1. For another example, see "Made to Measure: Invisible Supplier Has Penney's Shirts All Buttoned Up," *Wall Street Journal,* September 11, 2003, p. A1.

18. "Netflix to Rent High-Def DVDs Pronto," *Investor's Business Daily,* February 27, 2006, p. A6; "Multiplex under Seige," *Wall Street Journal,* December 24, 2005, p. P1ff.; "Wal-Mart Gives Up Online DVD Rentals, Will Promote Netflix," *Investor's Business Daily,* May 20, 2005, p. A1ff.; "Blockbuster Takes on the Entire Block," *Fortune,* March 21, 2005, pp. 30–34; "Showtime for Netflix," *Business 2.0,* March 2005, pp. 36–38; "Blockbuster Erases Its Late Fees—Sort of," *Advertising Age,* January 17, 2005, p. 6; "TiVo Strikes Deal with Netflix for Online Delivery of Movies," *Wall Street Journal,* October 1, 2004, p. B4; "Blockbuster Jabs Back at Its Rivals . . . Tries New Services," *USA Today,* June 22, 2004, p. 1Bff.

19. Kevin L. Webb, "Managing Channels of Distribution in the Age of Electronic Commerce," *Industrial Marketing Management,* February 2002, p. 95; Charles A. Ingene and Mark E. Parry, "Is Channel Coordination All It Is Cracked up to Be?" *Journal of Retailing,* Winter 2000, p. 511; Kenneth H. Wathne and Jan B. Heide, "Opportunism in Interfirm Relationships: Forms, Outcomes, and Solutions," *Journal of Marketing,* October 2000, p. 36; Kersi D. Antia and Gary L. Frazier, "The Severity of Contract Enforcement in Interfirm Channel Relationships," *Journal of Marketing,* October 2001, p. 67; Ravi S. Achrol, "Changes in the Theory of Interorganizational Relations in Marketing: Toward a Network Paradigm," *Journal of the Academy of Marketing Science,* Winter 1997, p. 56; Aric Rindfleisch and Jan B. Heide, "Transaction Cost Analysis: Past, Present, and Future Applications," *Journal of Marketing,* October 1997, p. 30.

20. "Partners," *Business Week,* October 25, 1999, p. 106.

21. "A Talk with the Man Who Got Rayovac All Charged Up," *Business Week,* February 21, 2000, p. 32F.

22. See www.esprit.com; "Esprit, a 1980s Fashion Icon, Struggles to Find a U.S. Fit," *Wall Street Journal,* October 28, 2005, p. B1ff.; "Esprit in the Spirit for Retail Expansion," *Brandweek,* June 20, 2005, p. 14; "Esprit Tries to Shed Its Youth Image," *Wall Street Journal,* September 3, 2004, p. A9; "Can Esprit Be Hip Again?" *Wall Street Journal,* June 17, 2002, p. B1. See also Carol J. Johnson, Robert E. Krapfel, Jr., and Curtis M. Grimm, "A Contingency Model of Supplier-Reseller Satisfaction Perceptions in Distribution Channels," *Journal of Marketing Channels,* no. 1/2 (2001), p. 65; Inge Geyskens and Jan-Benedict E. M. Steenkamp, "Economic and Social Satisfaction: Measurement and Relevance to Marketing Channel Relationships," *Journal of Retailing,* Spring 2000, p. 11; Gary L. Frazier and Walfried M. Lassar, "Determinants of Distribution Intensity," *Journal of Marketing,* October 1996, p. 39.

23. "Antitrust Issues and Marketing Channel Strategy" and "Case 1—Continental T.V., Inc., et al. v. GTE Sylvania, Inc.," in Louis W. Stern and Thomas L. Eovaldi, *Legal Aspects of Marketing Strategy* (Englewood Cliffs, NJ: Prentice Hall, 1984), p. 300. See also Debra M. Desrochers, Gregory T. Gundlach, and Albert A. Foer, "Analysis of Antitrust Challenges to Category Captain Arrangements," *Journal of Public Policy & Marketing,* Fall 2003, p. 201. For some examples of exclusive deals, see "Blue Nile: Online Jewelry Seller Looks to Be a Cut above the Competition," *Investor's Business Daily,* December 15, 2005, p. A6; "When Exclusivity Means Illegality," *Wall Street Journal,* January 6, 2005, p. A11ff.; "Bringing Chic to Sheets," *Wall Street Journal,* September 8, 2004, p. B1ff.

24. For more on Reebok, see *2005 Annual Report,* Reebok; "Reebok's Direct Sales Spark a Retail Revolt," *Adweek's Marketing Week,* December 2, 1991, p. 7. See also Jacquelyn S. Thomas and Ursula Y. Sullivan, "Managing Marketing Communications with Multichannel Customers," *Journal of Marketing,* October 2005, p. 239; David W. Wallace, Joan L. Giese, and Jean L. Johnson, "Customer Retailer Loyalty in the Context of Multiple Channel Strategies," *Journal of Retailing,* Winter 2004, p. 249; Stephanie M. Noble, David A. Griffith, and Marc G. Weinberger, "Consumer Derived Utilitarian Value and Channel Utilization in a Multi-Channel Retail Context," *Journal of Business Research,* December 2005, p. 1643; Venkatesh Shankar and Russell S. Winer, "Interactive Marketing Goes Multichannel," *Journal of Interactive Marketing,* Spring 2005, p. 2; Sridhar Balasubramanian, Rajagopal Raghunathan, and Vijay Mahajan, "Consumers in a Multichannel Environment: Product Utility, Process Utility, and Channel Choice," *Journal of Interactive Marketing,* Spring 2005, p. 12; Ruby Roy Dholakia, Miao Zhao, and Nikhilesh Dholakia, "Multichannel Retailing: A Case Study of Early Experiences," *Journal of Interactive Marketing,* Spring 2005, p. 63; Debra L. Scammon and Mary Jane Sheffet, "Legal Issues in Channels Modification Decisions: The Question of Refusals to Deal," *Journal of Public Policy and Marketing* 5 (1986), p. 82.

25. Gregory T. Gundlach and Patrick E. Murphy, "Ethical and Legal Foundations of Relational Marketing Exchanges," *Journal of Marketing,* October 1993, p. 35; Craig B. Barkacs, "Multilevel Marketing and Antifraud Statutes: Legal Enterprises or Pyramid Schemes?" *Journal of the Academy of Marketing Science,* Spring 1997, p. 176; Robert A. Robicheaux and James E. Coleman, "The Structure of Marketing Channel Relationships," *Journal of the Academy of Marketing Science,* Winter 1994, p. 38; Brett A. Boyle and F. Robert Dwyer, "Power, Bureaucracy, Influence and Performance: Their Relationships in Industrial Distribution Channels," *Journal of Business Research,* March 1995, p. 189.

26. R. Glenn Richey, Haozhe Chen, Stefan E. Genchev, and Patricia J. Daugherty, "Developing Effective Reverse Logistics Programs," *Industrial Marketing Management*, November 2005, p. 830; Joseph D. Blackburn, V. Daniel R. Guide, Jr., Gilvan C. Souza, and Luk N. Van Wassenhove, "Reverse Supply Chains for Commercial Returns," *California Management Review*, Winter 2004, p. 6; Roland Geyer and Tim Jackson, "Supply Loops and Their Constraints: The Industrial Ecology of Recycling and Reuse," *California Management Review*, Winter 2004, p. 55; H. Scott Matthews, "Thinking Outside 'the Box': Designing a Packaging Take-Back System," *California Management Review*, Winter 2004, p. 105. For more on online return policies, see "I Ordered That? Web Retailers Make It Easier to Return Goods," *Wall Street Journal*, September 4, 2003, p. D1; "Happy Returns," *Business Week Small Biz*, October 8, 2001, p. 12. For more on in-store return policies, see "Stores Toughen Return Policies," *USA Today*, December 27, 2005, p. 3B; "Taking Back That Bathrobe Gets Harder," *Wall Street Journal*, December 15, 2005, p. D1ff.; "New Return Policy: Retailers Say No to Serial Exchangers," *Wall Street Journal*, November 29, 2004, p. B1ff. See also Andy A. Tsay, "Risk Sensitivity in Distribution Channel Partnerships: Implications for Manufacturer Return Policies," *Journal of Retailing*, Summer 2002, p. 147; Sara Lonn and Julie Ann Stuart, "Increasing Service through Aggressive Dealer Inventory Return Policies," *International Journal of Physical Distribution & Logistics Management*, no. 6 (2003), p. 519.

27. See, for example, "P&G to Stores: Keep the Dented Crisco Cans," *Wall Street Journal*, March 21, 1997, p. B1. See also "Recycling E-Waste," *Wall Street Journal*, September 23, 2004, p. B1ff.; "Cellphone Makers Connect for Recycling Program," *USA Today*, October 22, 2003, p. 6B; "The Information Age's Toxic Garbage," *Business Week*, October 6, 2003, p. 54. See also Rene B. M. de Koster, Marisa P. de Brito, and Masja A. van de Vendel, "Return Handling: An Exploratory Study with Nine Retailer Warehouses," *International Journal of Retail & Distribution Management*, no. 8 (2002), p. 407; Ronald S. Tibben-Lembke, "Life after Death: Reverse Logistics and the Product Life Cycle," *International Journal of Physical Distribution & Logistics Management*, no. 3 (2002), p. 223; Chad W. Autry, Patricia J. Daugherty, and R. Glenn Richey, "The Challenge of Reverse Logistics in Catalog Retailing," *International Journal of Physical Distribution & Logistics Management*, no. 1 (2001), p. 26; Dale S. Rogers and Ronald Tibben-Lembke, "An Examination of Reverse Logistics Practices," *Journal of Business Logistics*, no. 2 (2001), p. 129.

CHAPTER 11

1. "So Many New Soft Drinks, So Little Time," *USA Today*, March 14, 2007, p. 3B; "Coke, Pepsi Continue to Lose Their Fizz," *Wall Street Journal*, March 9, 2007, p. B3; "Look Who's Calling Itself Sparkling," *Advertising Age*, February 19, 2007, p. 4ff.; "Smaller Brands Hitch Ride with Coke Distributors," *Wall Street Journal*, January 29, 2007, p. B1ff.; "Queen of Pop," *Business Week*, August 7, 2006, pp. 44–53; "Thirsting for More Variety," *Investor's Business Daily*, April 24, 2006, p. A8; "Killer Coke or Innocent Abroad?" *Business Week*, January 23, 2006, pp. 46–48; "Coke Poured Out 1,000 New Products in 2005," *USA Today*, December 8, 2005, p. 5B; "Afghan Coke a Taste of Things to Come," *Financial Times*, December 6, 2005, "Coke Bottler in Mexico Threatens to Cut Marketing," *Wall Street Journal*, November 1, 2005, p. B5; "Coke Gets Real: The World's Most Valuable Brand Wakes Up to a Waning Thirst for Cola," *Financial Times*, September 22, 2005; "EU Limits Coke's Sales Tactics in Settlement of Antitrust Case," *Wall Street Journal*, June 23, 2005, p. B6; "To Pitch New Soda, Coke Wants the World to Sing—Again," *Wall Street Journal*, June 13, 2005, p. B1ff.; "How a Global Web of Activists Gives Coke Problems in India," *Wall Street Journal*, June 7, 2005, p. A1ff.; "The Soda with Buzz," *Forbes*, March 28, 2005; "A Cold Shoulder for Coca-Cola . . . in Germany," *Business Week*, May 2, 2005, p. 52; "Parade of Drinks May Clog Channel," *Brandweek*, February 7, 2005, p. 4; "Hansen Natural," *BusinessWeek Online*, June 6, 2005; www.hansens.com; "Gone Flat," *Business Week*, December 20, 2004, pp. 76–82; "Coke to Alter Sales Methods," *USA Today*, October 20, 2004, p. 3B; "The Real Story," *Fortune*, May 31, 2004, pp. 84–98; "A Low-Budget Cola Shakes Up Markets South of the Border," *Wall Street Journal*, October 27, 2003, p. A1ff.; "Dial-a-Coke Is Slaking Thirsts in Australia," *Wall Street Journal Reports*, October 20, 2003, p. R3; "Into the Fryer: How Coke Officials Beefed Up Results of Marketing Tests," *Wall Street Journal*, August 20, 2003, p. A1; "Mooove Over, Milkman," *Wall Street Journal*, June 9, 2003, p. B1; "Fountain Dispenses Problems," *USA Today*, May 28, 2003, p. 1B; "Soft-Drink Suppliers Bottle a New Strategy," *Investor's Business Daily*, March 11, 2003, p. A10; "Cracking China's Market," *Wall Street Journal*, January 9, 2003, p. B1; "No Bull: Coke Targets Clubs," *Advertising Age*, December 9, 2002, p. 3; "Coke Works Harder at Being the Real Thing in Hinterland," *Wall Street Journal*, November 26, 2002, p. B1; "Coke Is B2B Success Story," *Investor's Business Daily*, February 21, 2002, p. A13; "Guess Who's Winning the Cola Wars," *Fortune*, April 2, 2001, p. 164; "Repairing the Coke Machine," *Business Week*, March 19, 2001, p. 86; "For Coke, Local Is It," *Business Week*, July 3, 2000, p. 122; "To Fix Coca-Cola, Daft Sets Out to Get Relationships Right," *Wall Street Journal*, June 23, 2000, p. A1; "I'd Like the World to Buy a Coke," *Business Week*, April 13, 1998, p. 70; "Coke Pours into Asia," *Business Week*, October 28, 1996, p. 72; "Coke's Soda Fountain for Offices Fizzles, Dashing High Hopes," *Wall Street Journal*, June 14, 1993, p. A1.

2. See www.transora.com and www.fmi.org/media/bg/ecr1; "How to Make a Frozen Lasagna (with Just $250 Million)," *Fortune*, April 30, 2001, p. 149; "Delivering the Goods," *Fortune*, November 28, 1994, p. 64; "Making the Middleman an Endangered Species," *Business Week*, June 6, 1994, p. 114; "The Nitty-Gritty of ECR Systems: How One Company Makes It Pay," *Advertising Age*, May 2, 1994, p. S1; "Behind the Tumult at P&G," *Fortune*, March 7, 1994, p. 74. See also Stefan Borchert, "Implementation Hurdles of ECR Partnerships—the German Food Sector as an ECR Case Study," *International Journal of Retail & Distribution Management*, no. 6 (2002), p. 354.

3. "Compaq Stumbles as PCs Weather New Blow," *Wall Street Journal*, March 9, 1998, p. B1; "At What Profit Price?" *Brandweek*, June 23, 1997, p. 24; "Delivering the Goods," *Fortune*, November 28, 1994, p. 64. See also Kofi Q. Dadzie, Cristian Chelariu, and Evelyn Winston, "Customer Service in the Internet-Enabled Logistics Supply Chain: Website Design Antecedents and Loyalty Effects," *Journal of Business Logistics*, 2005, p. 53; John C. Taylor, Stanley E. Fawcett, and George C. Jackson, "Catalog Retailer in-Stock Performance: An Assessment of Customer Service Levels," *Journal of Business Logistics*, 2004, p. 119; Elliot Rabinovich and Philip T. Evers, "Product Fulfillment in Supply Chains Supporting Internet-Retailing Operations," *Journal of Business Logistics*, 2003, p. 205; Daniel Corsten and Thomas Gruen, "Stock-Outs Cause Walkouts," *Harvard Business Review*, May 2004, p. 26; Theodore P. Stank, Thomas J. Goldsby, Shawnee K. Vickery, and Katrina Savitskie, "Logistics Service Performance: Estimating its Influence on Market Share," *Journal of Business Logistics*, no. 1 (2003), p. 27; Katia Campo, Els Gijsbrechts, and Patricia Nisol, "Towards Understanding Consumer Response to Stock-Outs," *Journal of Retailing*, Summer 2000, p. 219; Chris Dubelaar, Garland Chow, and Paul D. Larson, "Relationships between Inventory, Sales and Service in a Retail Chain Store Operation," *International Journal of Physical Distribution & Logistics Management*, no. 2 (2001), p. 96; Lloyd M. Rinehart, M. Bixby Cooper, and George D. Wagenheim, "Furthering the Integration of Marketing and Logistics through Customer Service in the Channel," *Journal of the Academy of Marketing Science*, Winter 1989, p. 63; Edward A. Morash and John Ozment, "Toward Management of Transportation Service Quality," *Logistics and Transportation Review*, June 1994, p. 115; William D. Perreault, Jr., and Frederick A. Russ, "Physical Distribution Service in Industrial Purchase Decisions," *Journal of Marketing*, April 1976, p. 3.

4. "Wal-Mart's H-P Elves," *Wall Street Journal*, December 15, 2005, p. B1ff.; "A More Profitable Harvest," *Business 2.0*, May 2005, pp. 66–67; "66,207,896 Bottles of Beer on the Wall," *Business 2.0*, January/February, 2004, pp. 47–49; "Logistics Gets a Little Respect," *Business Week E.Biz*, November 20, 2000, p. EB112; "One Smart Cookie," *Business Week E.Biz*, November 20, 2000, p. EB120; "A Cereal Maker Hitches Its Wagons to the Web," *Business Week E.Biz*, September 18, 2000, p. EB80; "Costs Too High? Bring in the Logistics Experts," *Fortune*, November 10, 1997, p.200C. See also Thierry Sauvage, "The Relationship between Technology and Logistics Third-Party Providers," *International Journal of Physical Distribution & Logistics Management*, no. 3 (2003), p. 236; Donald J. Bowersox, David J. Closs, and Theodore P. Stank, "Ten Mega-Trends That Will Revolutionize Supply Chain Logistics," *Journal of Business Logistics*, no. 2 (2000), p. 1; James R. Stock, "Marketing Myopia Revisited: Lessons for Logistics," *International Journal of Physical Distribution & Logistics Management*, no. 1 (2002), p. 12; Mark Goh and Charlene Ling, "Logistics Development in China," *International Journal of Physical Distribution & Logistics Management*, no. 9 (2003), p. 886; James H. Bookbinder and Chris S. Tan, "Comparison of Asian and European Logistics Systems," *International Journal of Physical Distribution & Logistics Management*, no. 1 (2003), p. 36; Carol J. Emerson and Curtis M. Grimm, "The Relative Importance of Logistics and Marketing Customer Service: A Strategic Perspective," *Journal of Business Logistics*, 1998, p. 17.

5. For more on Clorox, see www.clorox.com; *2005 Annual Report*, Clorox; "The Web @ Work/Clorox Co.," *Wall Street Journal*, October 9, 2000, p. B21. See also Forrest E. Harding, "Logistics Service Provider Quality: Private Measurement, Evaluation, and Improvement," *Journal of Business Logistics*, 1998, p. 103; Carol C. Bienstock, John T. Mentzer, and Monroe M. Bird, "Measuring Physical Distribution Service Quality," *Journal of the Academy of Marketing Science*, Winter 1997, p. 31; G. T. M. Hult, "Measuring Cycle Time of the Global Procurement Process," *Industrial Marketing Management*, September 1997, p. 403.

6. Mikko Karkkainen, Timo Ala-Risku, and Jan Holmstrom, "Increasing Customer Value and Decreasing Distribution Costs with Merge-In-Transit," *International Journal of Physical Distribution & Logistics Management*, no. 1 (2003), p. 132; Marc J. Schniederjans and Qing Cao, "An Alternative Analysis of Inventory Costs of JIT and EOQ Purchasing," *International Journal of Physical Distribution & Logistics Management*, no. 2 (2001), p. 109; Amy Z. Zeng and Christian Rossetti, "Developing a Framework for Evaluating the Logistics Costs in Global Sourcing Processes: an Implementation and Insights," *International Journal of Physical Distribution & Logistics Management*, no. 9 (2003), p. 785; Scott R. Swenseth and Michael R. Godfrey, "Estimating Freight Rates for Logistics Decisions," *Journal of Business Logistics*, 1996, p. 213; Philip T. Evers, "The Impact of Transshipments on Safety Stock Requirements," *Journal of Business Logistics*, 1996, p. 109.

7. For more on JIT, see "Retailers Rely More on Fast Deliveries," *Wall Street Journal*, January 14, 2004, p. B2B; "Uncertain Economy Hinders Highly Precise Supply System," *New York Times*, March 15, 2003, p. B1; "Port Tie-Up Shows Vulnerability," *USA Today*, October 9, 2002, p. 1B; "Deadline Scramble: A New Hazard for Recovery, Last-Minute Pace of Orders," *Wall Street Journal*, June 25, 2002, p. A1; "Parts Shortages Hamper Electronics Makers," *Wall Street Journal*, July 7, 2000, p. B5. See also Keely L. Croxton and Walter Zinn, "Inventory Considerations in Network Design," *Journal of Business Logistics*, 2005, p. 149; Ronald H. Ballou and Apostolos Burnetas, "Planning Multiple Location Inventories," *Journal of Business Logistics*, 2003, p. 65; Leroy B. Schwarz and Z. Kevin Weng, "The Design of a JIT Supply Chain: The Effect of Leadtime Uncertainty on Safety Stock," *Journal of Business Logistics*, no. 2 (2000), p. 231; Richard E. White and John N. Pearson, "JIT, System Integration and Customer Service," *International Journal of Physical Distribution & Logistics Management*, no. 5 (2001), p. 313; Richard Germain, Cornelia Droge, and Nancy Spears, "The Implications of Just-in-Time for Logistics Organization Management and Performance," *Journal of Business Logistics*, 1996, p. 19; Faye W. Gilbert, Joyce A. Young, and Charles R. O'Neal, "Buyer-Seller Relationships in Just-in-Time Purchasing Environments," *Journal of Business Research*, February 1994, p.111.

8. "Good Logistics Offer Better Relief," Financial Times, December 16, 2005; "Disasters Demand Supply Chain Software, Research Shows," eWeek, October 5, 2005; "The Only Lifeline Was the Wal-Mart," Fortune, October 3, 2005, pp. 74–80; "For FedEx, It Was Time to Deliver," Fortune, October 3, 2005, pp. 83–84; "Can Wal-Mart Wear a White Hat?" BusinessWeek Online, September 22, 2005; "They Don't Teach This in B-School," Business Week, September 19, 2005, pp. 46–48: "At Wal-Mart, Emergency Plan Has Big Payoff," Wall Street Journal, September 12, 2005, p. B1ff.; "Wal-Mart Praised for Hurricane Katrina Response Efforts," www.newsmax.com, September 6, 2005; "A Logistics Nightmare," Traffic World, January 10, 2005; "How to Deliver on the Promises," Financial Times, January 7, 2005, p. 9; "Geography and Logistics Confound Relief," MSNBC.com, January 3, 2005; Logistics and the Effective Delivery of Humanitarian Relief (The Fritz Institute, 2005); "Emergency Relief Logistics—A Faster Way across the Global Divide," Logistics Quarterly, Summer 2001.

9. Available online at http://silmaril.smeal.psu.edu/misc/supply_chain; Martin Christopher and John Gattorna, "Supply Chain Cost Management and Value-Based Pricing," *Industrial Marketing Management*, February 2005, p. 115; G. Tomas M. Hult, "Global Supply Chain Management: An Integration of Scholarly Thoughts," *Industrial Marketing Management*, January 2004, p. 3; David J. Closs and Diane A. Mollenkopf, "A Global Supply Chain Framework," *Industrial Marketing Management*, January 2004, p. 37; Daniel J. Flint, "Strategic Marketing in Global Supply Chains: Four Challenges," *Industrial Marketing Management*, January 2004, p. 45; Daniel C. Bello, Ritu Lohtia, and Vinita Sangtani, "An Institutional Analysis of Supply Chain Innovations in Global Marketing Channels," *Industrial Marketing Management*, January 2004, p. 57; Daekwan Kim, S. Tamer Cavusgil, and Roger J. Calantone, "Information System Innovations and Supply Chain Management: Channel Relationships and Firm Performance," *Journal of the Academy of Marketing Science*, Winter 2006, p. 40; Brian J. Gibson, John T. Mentzer, and Robert L. Cook, "Supply Chain Management: The Pursuit of a Consensus Definition," *Journal of Business Logistics*, 2005, p. 17; Theodore P. Stank, Beth R. Davis, and Brian S. Fugate, "A Strategic Framework for Supply Chain Oriented Logistics," *Journal of Business Logistics*, 2005, p. 27; Terry L. Esper, Thomas D. Jensen, Fernanda L. Turnipseed, and Scot Burton, "The Last Mile: An Examination of Effects of Online Retail Delivery Strategies on Consumers," *Journal of Business Logistics*, 2003, p. 177; Dale S. Rogers and Rudolf Leuschner, "Supply Chain Management: Retrospective and Prospective," *Journal of Marketing Theory & Practice*, Fall 2004, p. 60; Taylor R. Randall, Ruskin M. Morgan, and Alysse R. Morton, "Efficient versus Responsive Supply Chain Choice: An Empirical Examination of Influential Factors," *Journal of Product Innovation Management*, November 2003, p. 430; Christopher R. Moberg and Thomas W. Speh, "Evaluating the Relationship between Questionable Business Practices and the Strength of Supply Chain Relationships," *Journal of Business Logistics*, no. 2 (2003), p. 1; Subroto Roy, K. Sivakumar, and Ian F. Wilkinson, "Innovation Generation in Supply Chain Relationships: a Conceptual Model and Research Propositions," *Journal of the Academy of Marketing Science*, Winter 2004, p. 61; W. Lemoine and Lars Dagnaes, "Globalisation Strategies and Business of Organisation of a Network of Logistics Service Providers," *International Journal of Physical Distribution & Logistics Management*, no. 3 (2003), p. 209; Katarina Kempainen and Ari P. J. Vepsalainen, "Trends in Industrial Supply Chains and Networks," *International Journal of Physical Distribution & Logistics Management*, no. 8 (2003), p. 701; Rakesh Niraj, "Customer Profitability in a Supply Chain," *Journal of Marketing*, July 2001, p. 1.

10. For an excellent example of EDI, see "To Sell Goods to Wal-Mart, Get on the Net," *Wall Street Journal*, November 21, 2003, p. B1. See also Cornelia Droge and Richard Germain, "The Relationship of Electronic Data Interchange with Inventory and Financial Performance," *Journal of Business Logistics*, no. 2 (2000), p. 209; Lisa R. Williams, Avril Nibbs, Dimples Irby, and Terence Finley, "Logistics Integration:

The Effect of Information Technology, Team Composition, and Corporate Competitve Positioning," *Journal of Business Logistics*, 1997, p. 31; Paul R. Murphy and James M. Daley, "International Freight Forwarder Perspectives on Electronic Data Interchange and Information Management Issues," *Journal of Business Logistics*, 1996, p. 63.

11. "A Smart Cookie at Pepperidge," *Fortune*, December 22, 1986, p. 67.

12. "A New Push against Sweatshops," *Time*, October 7, 2005; "Cops of the Global Village, *Fortune*, June 27, 2005, pp. 158–66; "Stamping Out Sweatshops," *BusinessWeek Online*, May 23, 2005; "Nike Opens Its Books on Sweatshop Audits," *BusinessWeek Online*, April 27, 2000; "Nike Names Names," *BusinessWeek Online*, April 13, 2005; "Corporate Social Responsibility—Companies in the News Nike," see www.mallenbaker.net/csr/CSRfiles/nike.html.

13. Douglas Lambert, James R. Stock, and Lisa M. Ellram, *Fundamentals of Logistics* (Burr Ridge, IL: Irwin/McGraw-Hill, 1998).

14. For more on transportation security, see "Technology Roots Out Cargo Risks," *Investor's Business Daily*, October 4, 2005, p. A4; "Keeping Cargo Safe from Terror," *Wall Street Journal*, July 29, 2005, p. B1ff.; "In Terrorism Fight, Government Finds a Surprising Ally: FedEx," *Wall Street Journal*, May 26, 2005, p. A1ff.; "Sensors on Containers May Offer Safer Shipping," *Wall Street Journal*, March 31, 2005, p. B4; "Protecting America's Ports," *Fortune*, November 10, 2003, p. T198C; "FedEx Takes Direct Approach to Terrorism," *Wall Street Journal*, October 9, 2003, p. A4; "Safe Harbors?" *Wall Street Journal*, April 21, 2003, p. B1; "Companies Must Add Rising Security Costs to Bottom Line," *USA Today*, March 28, 2003, p.1B; "Shippers Get Caught in Customs' Net," *Business Week*, March 24, 2003, p. 76B; "The Friction Economy," *Fortune*, February 18, 2002, p. 104. For more on deregulation of transportation, see Paul D. Larson, "Transportation Deregulation, JIT, and Inventory Levels," *Logistics and Transportation Review*, June 1991, p. 99; James C. Nelson, "Politics and Economics in Transport Regulation and Deregulation—A Century Perspective of the ICC's Role," *Logistics and Transportation Review*, March, 1987, p. 5.

15. For a more detailed comparison of mode characteristics, see Robert Dahlstrom, Kevin M. McNeilly, and Thomas W. Speh, "Buyer-Seller Relationships in the Procurement of Logistical Services," *Journal of the Academy of Marketing Science*, Spring 1996, p. 110; Roger Dale Abshire and Shane R. Premeaux, "Motor Carriers' and Shippers' Perceptions of the Carrier Choice Decision," *Logistics and Transportation Review*, December 1991, p. 351; Brian J. Gibson, Harry L. Sink, and Ray A. Mundy, "Shipper-Carrier Relationships and Carrier Selection Criteria," *Logistics and Transportation Review*, December 1993, p. 371.

16. "Next Stop: The 21st Century," *Business 2.0*, September 2003, p. 152; "Back on Track: Left for Dead, Railroads Revive by Watching Clock," *Wall Street Journal*, July 25, 2003, p. A1; "Trains: Industry Report," *Investor's Business Daily*, May 7, 2001, p. B6; "America's Railroads Struggle to Recapture Their Former Glory," *Wall Street Journal*, December 5, 1997, p. A1; "The Rails: Trouble Behind, Trouble Ahead," *Business Week*, November 24, 1997, p. 40.

17. "Costs of Trucking Seen Rising under New Safety Rules," *Wall Street Journal*, November 12, 2003, p. A1; "Trucker Rewards Customers for Good Behavior," *Wall Street Journal*, September 9, 2003, p. B4; "Trucking: Rig and Roll," *Wall Street Journal*, October 23, 2000, p. R51; "Trucking Gets Sophisticated," *Fortune*, July 24, 2000, p. T270B; "Forward Air Corp.: Hauler Gets Freight from Jets to Businesses," *Investor's Business Daily*, June 6, 2000, p. A14; "Making Sure Big Rigs Have Something to Carry," *Business Week*, June 12, 2000, p.168F; "Trucking Finds the Internet," *Heavy Duty Trucking*, October 1999, p. 116; "Riding the Data Highway," *Newsweek*, March 21, 1994, p. 54; "E-Commerce's Newest Portals: Truck Drivers," *Wall Street Journal*, January 3, 2000, p. A11; "Getting the Goods," *Wall Street Journal*, November 22, 1999, p. R39.

18. For more on overnight carriers, see "Why FedEx Is Gaining Ground," *Business 2.0*, October 2003, p. 56; "FedEx Recasts Itself on the Ground," *Wall Street Journal*, September 4, 2003, p. B7; "UPS, FedEx Wage Handheld Combat," *Investor's Business Daily*, May 19, 2003, p. A6; "Shipping Firms' Web Sites Help You Track Items," *Investor's Business Daily*, July 6, 2001, p. A6; "UPS Puts Its Back into It," *Business Week*, October 27, 1997, p. 50. For an international example, see "More Green from Green Beans," *Business 2.0*, August, 2004, pp. 64–66.

19. K. Raguraman and Claire Chan, "The Development of SeaAir Intermodal Transportation: An Assessment of Global Trends," *Logistics and Transportation Review*, December 1994, p. 379; "Yule Log Jam," *Fortune*, December 13, 2004, pp. 162–70; "Monsters of the High Seas," *Business Week*, October 13, 2003, p. 58; "Cargo That Phones Home," *Fortune*, November 15, 1993, p. 143.

20. *2005 Annual Report*, Du Pont; *2005 Annual Report*, Matlack; *2005 Annual Report*, Shell; *2005 Annual Report*, FedEx; *2005 Annual Report*, UPS; "FedEx and Brown Are Going Green," *Business Week*, August 11, 2003, p. 60; "Conservation Power," *Business Week*, September 16, 1991, p. 86. See also Lawrence Christensen, "The Environment and Its Impact on the Supply Chain," *International Journal of Retail & Distribution Management*, no. 11 (2002), p. 571.

21. For more on Tostitos Gold example, see "Buyers Seek Hard-to-Find Tostitos Gold," *USA Today*, February 9, 2003, p. 1B; "Relevance Is Operative Word in Catfight or Chip-Dip Ads," *Advertising Age*, January 27, 2003, p. 20; "Frito-Lay Leverages National Championship Game as Major Marketing Platform for New Tostitos Gold Tortilla Chips," *PR Newswire*, December 30, 2002; Anita Haley, "Brand Revolution," www.fmi.org. For more on Rice Krispies Treats example, see "Brands in Demand," *Advertising Age*, February 7, 1994, p. S1; "Kellogg to Consumers: Please Bear with Us," *Advertising Age*, March 29, 1993, p. 44. See also J. Mahajan et al., "An Exploratory Investigation of the Interdependence between Marketing and Operations Functions in Service Firms," *International Journal of Research in Marketing*, January 1994, p. 1; Edward U. Bond III, Beth A. Walker, Michael D. Hutt, and Peter H. Reingen, "Reputational Effectiveness in Cross-Functional Working Relationships," *Journal of Product Innovation Management*, January 2004, p. 44.

22. "Hospital Cost Cutters Push Use of Scanners to Track Inventories," *Wall Street Journal*, June 10, 1997, p. A1. See also Charu Chandra and Sameer Kumar, "Taxonomy of Inventory Policies for Supply-Chain Effectiveness," *International Journal of Retail & Distribution Management*, no. 4 (2001), p. 164; Walter Zinn, John T. Mentzer, and Keely L. Croxton, "Customer-Based Measures of Inventory Availability," *Journal of Business Logistics*, no. 2 (2002), p. 19; Timothy L. Urban, "The Interdependence of Inventory Management and Retail Shelf Management," *International Journal of Physical Distribution & Logistics Management*, no. 1 (2002), p. 41; Matthew B. Myers, Patricia J. Daugherty, and Chad W. Autry, "The Effectiveness of Automatic Inventory Replenishment in Supply Chain Operations: Antecedents and Outcomes," *Journal of Retailing*, Winter 2000, p. 455; Paul Zinszer, "Supply Chain Strategies for Managing Excess Inventories," *Journal of Marketing Theory & Practice*, Spring 1996, p. 55.

23. "The Supersizing of Warehouses," *New York Times*, February 4, 2004, p. C5; "New Warehouses Take on a Luxe Look," *Wall Street Journal*, June 18, 2003, p. B6; Chad W. Autry, Stanley E. Griffis, Thomas J. Goldsby, and L. Michelle Bobbitt, "Warehouse Management Systems: Resource Commitment, Capabilities, and Organizational Performance," *Journal of Business Logistics*, 2005, p. 165; Arnold B. Maltz, "Outsourcing the Warehousing Function: Economics and Strategic Considerations," *Logistics and Transportation Review*, September 1994, p. 245.

24. "Wireless Grapes," *Fortune*, March 6, 2006, pp. 158B–D; "RFID Technology Getting Static in New Hampshire," *Brandweek*, January 23, 2006, p. 13; "LoJack Steals Street's Heart with Crime-Busting Devices," *Investor's Business Daily*, September 7, 2005, p. B3; "IBM, Smart Tags Helping Toyota Customize Its Cars," *Investor's Business Daily*, August 15, 2005, p. A4; "Who Made My Cheese? Tags

Track Parmesan's Age, Origin," *Wall Street Journal*, July 7, 2005, p. B1ff.; "Frequency of the Future," *DSN Retailing Today*, 1Q, 2005, pp. 18–23; "Electronic Tags Should Help Drug Makers Identify Fakes," *Investor's Business Daily*, November 29, 2004, p. A9; "Suppliers Struggle with Wal-Mart ID-Tag Plan," *Wall Street Journal*, November 18, 2004, pp. B4ff.; "RFID: Robot for Infinite Decluttering?" *USA Today*, October 6, 2004, p. 10B; "What's So Great about RFID Tags," *Investor's Business Daily*, August 16, 2004, p. A9; "Down, but Far from Out: RFID Technology Is Off to a Disappointing Start, but Retailers Are Convinced," *Wall Street Journal Reports*, January 12, 2004, p. R5; "Wal-Mart Keeps the Change," *Fortune*, November 10, 2003, p. 46; "Sensor Revolution: Bugging the World," *Business Week*, August 25, 2003, p. 100; "Cutting Navy Hospital Paperwork," *Investor's Business Daily*, May 22, 2003, p. A7; "Bar Codes Better Watch Their Backs," *Business Week*, July 14, 2003, p. 42; "Radio ID Tags Take on Bar Codes," *Investor's Business Daily*, March 13, 2003, p. A7; "A Radio Chip in Every Consumer Product," *New York Times*, February 25, 2003, p. C1.

25. "Wal-Mart's Need for Speed," *Wall Street Journal*, September 26, 2005, p. B4. See also Kum Khiong Yang, "Managing a Single Warehouse, Multiple Retailer Distribution Center," *Journal of Business Logistics*, no. 2 (2000), p. 161; Chin Chia Jane, "Storage Location Assignment in a Distribution Center," *International Journal of Physical Distribution & Logistics Management*, no. 1 (2000), p. 55; "Distribution Center Doubles Output with Paperless System," *Modern Materials Handling/Scan Tech News*, September 1994, p. S17.

CHAPTER 12

1. "Best Buy, Wal-Mart Take on RadioShack in Cell Phone Retail," *Investor's Business Daily*, April 5, 2007, p. A4; "Best Buy Gets in Touch with Its Feminine Side," *USA Today*, December 21, 2006, p. 1Bff.; "Best Buy Looking beyond Big Digital TV-Driven Growth," *Investor's Business Daily*, September 14, 2006, p. A4; "Talking Shop," *Fortune*, August 21, 2006, pp. 76–80; "Can Best Buy Get Geekier?" *Business 2.0*, June 2006, p. 30; "Best Buy's Giant Gamble," *Fortune*, April 3, 2006, pp. 68–75; "Geek Squad Is Popular at Best Buy," *Wall Street Journal*, December 14, 2005, p. B3A; "Best Buy Launches Six Niche Sites," *Advertising Age*, November 28, 2005, p. 39; "Best Buy Sees Growth by Studying Shoppers," *Investor's Business Daily*, July 5, 2005, p. A18; "Best Buy Taps Rapp to Weed Out Angels, Devils," *Advertising Age*, May 16, 2005, p. 8; "Slimming Down Stores: Big-Box Retailer Best Buy Experiments with Boutiques," *Wall Street Journal*, April 29, 2005, p. B1ff.; "Customer-Centric Model Future Focus at Best Buy," *DSN Retailing Today*, April 25, 2005, p. 4ff.; "Anchors Away! Store Closings that Follow Federated-May Combination May Be a Boon to Some Malls," *Wall Street Journal*, March 1, 2005, p. B1ff.; "Why Some Marketers Turn Away Customers," *Advertising Age*, February 14, 2005, p. 1ff.; "Electronics Retailers Woo Women," *Advertising Age*, November 15, 2004, p. 16; "Minding the Store: Analyzing Customers, Best Buy Decides Not All Are Welcome," *Wall Street Journal*, November 8, 2004, p. A1ff.; "5 Rules for Finding the Next Dell," *Fortune*, July 12, 2004, pp. 102–107; "Best Buy's Selling Machine," *Business 2.0*, July 2004, pp. 92–102; "Big Firms, Big Growth," *Fortune*, May 31, 2004, p. 180–84; "New Retail Offering: Geeks on Call," *Wall Street Journal*, May 20, 2004, p. D1ff.; "The Unprofitable Customer," *Wall Street Journal*, October 28, 2003, p. R7.

2. See www.census.gov/mrts/www/data/html/nsal05.html; U.S. Bureau of the Census, *Statistical Abstract of the United States 2006* (Washington, DC: U.S. Government Printing Office, 2005); *2002 Economic Census – Retail Trade, Subject Series, Establishment and Firm Size* (Washington, DC: U.S. Government Printing Office, 2005); "Where Consumer Shop Changes, but When They Do It Stays the Same," *Advertising Age*, November 21, 2005, p. 19; "Retail: Upscale Experience, Downscale Prices," *Wall Street Journal Reports*, November 21, 2005, p. R3; "Annual Industry Report, Top 150," *DSN Retailing Today*, July, 2005; "A Store Made for Right Now: You Shop until It's Dropped," *New York Times*, February 17, 2004, p. A1ff.; "Just Take the Money!" *Time* (Inside Business Bonus Section), July 2003; "Paying Less for Prada," *Wall Street Journal*, April 29, 2003, p. D1; "Point-of-Sale Technology Is Changing the Retailing Industry," *Investor's Business Daily*, February 25, 2003, p. A4; "Islands in the Mall: Pushcarts as Revenue Streams," *New York Times*, January 22, 2003, p. C6; "The 40 People and Events That Have Shaped Mass Market Retailing," *DSN Retailing Today*, August 2002; "Retail Reckoning," *Business Week*, December 10, 2001, p. 72; Velitchka D. Kaltcheva and Barton A. Weitz, "When Should a Retailer Create an Exciting Store Environment?" *Journal of Marketing*, January 2006, p. 107; Kathleen Seiders, Glenn B. Voss, Dhruv Grewal, and Andrea L. Godfrey, "Do Satisfied Customers Buy More? Examining Moderating Influences in a Retailing Context," *Journal of Marketing*, October 2005, p. 26; Charles M. Brooks, Patrick J. Kaufmann, and Donald R. Lichtenstein, "Travel Configuration on Consumer Trip-Chained Store Choice," *Journal of Consumer Research*, September 2004, p. 241; Ruth N. Bolton and Venkatesh Shankar, "An Empirically Derived Taxonomy of Retailer Pricing and Promotion Strategies," *Journal of Retailing*, Winter 2003, p. 213; Arthur W. Allaway, David Berkowitz and Giles D'Souza, "Spatial Diffusion of a New Loyalty Program through a Retail Market," *Journal of Retailing*, Fall 2003, p. 137; Katherine B. Hartman and Rosann L. Spiro, "Recapturing Store Image in Customer-Based Store Equity: A Construct Conceptualization," *Journal of Business Research*, August 2005, p. 1112; Mark J. Arnold, Kristy E. Reynolds, Nicole Ponder, and Jason E. Lueg, "Customer Delight in a Retail Context: Investigating Delightful and Terrible Shopping Experiences," *Journal of Business Research*, August 2005, p. 1132; Sevgin A. Eroglu, Karen Machleit, and Terri Feldman Barr, "Perceived Retail Crowding and Shopping Satisfaction: The Role of Shopping Values," *Journal of Business Research*, August 2005, p. 1146; Kiran Karande and John R. Lombardb, "Location Strategies of Broad-Line Retailers: An Empirical Investigation," *Journal of Business Research*, May 2005, p. 687; Elliot Bendoly, James D. Blocher, Kurt M. Bretthauer, Shanker Krishnan, and M. A. Venkataramanan, "Online/In-Store Integration and Customer Retention," *Journal of Service Research*, May 2005, p. 313.

3. For more on discount (dollar) stores, see "Can the Dollar Stores Rebound?" *Wall Street Journal*, September 21, 2005, p. C1ff.; "Behind the Dollar-Store Boom: A Nation of Bargain Hunters," *Wall Street Journal*, December 13, 2004, p. A1ff.; "Out-Discounting the Discounter," *Business Week*, May 10, 2004, pp. 78–79; "Family Dollar Stores: Growth Means Respect for Discount Retailer," *Investor's Business Daily*, February 22, 2002, p. A8; "Cheap Thrills for Shoppers," *Newsweek*, April 16, 2001, p. 45; "Beyond the Database: Sales and Service on a First-Name Basis," *Colloguy*, No. 1, 1997, p. 8; "Neiman Marcus, Saks Wage Expensive Battle for Upscale Shoppers," *Wall Street Journal*, November 21, 1996, p. A1. See also Kristy E. Reynolds and Mark J. Arnold, "Customer Loyalty to the Salesperson and the Store: Examining Relationship Customers in an Upscale Retail Context," *Journal of Personal Selling & Sales Management*, Spring 2000, p. 89; Alain d'Astous, "Irritating Aspects of the Shopping Environment," *Journal of Business Research*, August 2000, p. 149; Eric R. Spangenberg, Ayn E. Crowley, and Pamela W. Henderson, "Improving the Store Environment: Do Olfactory Cues Affect Evaluations and Behaviors?" *Journal of Marketing*, April 1996, p. 67.

4. "As Malls Think Small, Boutiques Get Their Big Chance," *Wall Street Journal*, June 24, 2005, p. B1ff.; "Urban Rarity: Stores Offering Spiffy Service," *Wall Street Journal*, July 25, 1996, p. B1; "Airports: New Destination for Specialty Retailers," *USA Today*, January 11, 1996, p. 5B; Sharon E. Beatty, Morris Mayer, James E. Coleman, Kristy E. Reynolds, and Jungki Lee, "Customer-Sales Associate Retail Relationships," *Journal of Retailing*, Fall 1996, p. 223.

5. See www.census.gov; U.S. Bureau of the Census, *2002 Economic Census - Retail Trade, Subject Series, Establishment and Firm Size*. For more on department stores, see "Changes in Store for Department Stores?" *USA Today*, January 21, 2005, p. 1Bff.; "The Department

Store Rises Again," *Business 2.0*, August 2004, pp. 56–57; "It's Not Your Mom's Department Store," *Business Week*, December 1, 2003, p. 98; "Idle Aisles: Department Stores Fight an Uphill Battle Just to Stay Relevant," *Wall Street Journal*, March 12, 2002, p. A1; "Department Stores and Designer Tenants Jockey Over Real Estate," *Wall Street Journal*, October 31, 2000, p. A1.

6. David Appel, "The Supermarket: Early Development of an Institutional Innovation," *Journal of Retailing*, Spring 1972, p. 39.

7. See www.census.gov and www.fmi.org/food/superfact; "Inventory Management 2002: Data, Detail, & Discipline in Supermarkets," *Chain Store Age*, December 2002, p. 17; "Grocery Shoppers Can Be Own Cashiers," *USA Today*, March 9, 1998, p. 6B; "The Taste of the Nation," *USA Today*, March 9, 1998, p. 1D. See also Brian T. Ratchford, "Has the Productivity of Retail Food Stores Really Declined?" *Journal of Retailing*, Fall 2003, p. 171; Mohammed A. Al-Sudairy and N.K.H. Tang, "Information Technology in Saudi Arabia's Supermarket Chains," *International Journal of Retail & Distribution Management*, no. 8 (2000), p. 341; Nobukaza Azuma and John Fernie, "Retail Marketing Strategies and Logistical Operations at a Japanese Grocery Supermarket Chain—Case Study of Summit Inc.," *International Journal of Retail & Distribution Management*, no. 6 (2001), p. 284.

8. For more on Wal-Mart's Neighborhood Markets, see "Neighborhood Market Caps Year with Round of New Market Entries," *DSN Retailing Today*, January 27, 2003, p. 1; "For America's Big Retailers, Small Is Beautiful, Sometimes," *New York Times*, January 22, 2003, p. C1; "Wal-Mart Is Eating Everyone's Lunch," *Business Week*, April 15, 2002, p. 43.

9. For more on Wal-Mart as mass-merchandiser, see Chapter 17, endnote 1. For more on Target as mass-merchandiser, see "Target Applies GM Merchandising to Food," *Food Retailing Today*, November 10, 2003, p. 1; "Target: The Challenges and Rewards of Being the No. 2 Discount Retailer," *DSN Retailing Today*, April 7, 2003, p.28; "Is Target's Wardrobe in Wal-Mart's Sights?" *AM Apparel Merchandising*, April 7, 2003, p. 1; "Target: The Cool Factor Fizzles," *Business Week*, February 24, 2003, p. 42; "Marketer of the Year: On Target," *Advertising Age*, December 11, 2000, p. 1.

10. For more on supercenters, see "Wal-Mart, the Category King," *DSN Retailing Today*, June 9, 2003, p. 65; "Price War in Aisle 3," *Wall Street Journal*, May 27, 2003, p. B1; "Supershoppers," *American Demographics*, May 2003, p. 17; "Wal-Mart, Target Gain Supercenter Share," *Food Retailing Today*, February 24, 2003, p. 4; "Supercenters Take Lead in Food Retailing," *Food Retailing Today*, May 6, 2002, p. 8. "How Grocers Are Fighting Giant Rivals," *Wall Street Journal*, March 27, 1997, p.B1.

11. For more on warehouse clubs, see "Warehouses Go Luxe," *Wall Street Journal*, November 11, 2005, p B1ff.; "Small Business Focus Pays Off for Sam's," *Food Retailing Today*, October 11, 2004, p. F1ff.; "Costco Wins Loyalty with Bulky Bargains," *USA Today*, September 24, 2004, p. 1Bff.; "Rising Sales, Falling Prices: Wal-Mart and Warehouse Clubs Claim Bulk of Discounters' Revenue," *Investor's Business Daily*, September 13, 2004, p. A13; "Costco: Retailer Sets Itself Apart from the Crowd," *Investor's Business Daily*, July 21, 2004, p. A8; "The Only Company Wal-Mart Fears," *Fortune*, November 24, 2003, p. 158; "Clubs Expand Despite Each Other," *Food Retailing Today*, July 21, 2003, p. 6; "Warehouse Stores Aren't Just for Those Pinching Pennies," *USA Today*, June 20, 2003, p. 1B; "Retailers Try New Venues to Boost Sales," *USA Today*, May 13, 2003, p. 3B; "Out of the Box Thinking," *Newsweek*, May 12, 2003, p. 40; "Sam's Club: Back to Business," *DSN Retailing Today*, April 2003.

12. For more on category killers, see "Big-Box Stores Squeeze into Big Apple: Home Depot, Others . . . ," *USA Today*, October 19, 2004, p. 3B; "Office Depot Shifts Store Expansion to M2 Format," *DSN Retailing Today*, July 19, 2004, pp. 4, 21; "Toys 'R' Us: Taking the Family of Brands to New Heights," *DSN Retailing Today*, October 2003; "Category Killers Go from Lethal to Lame in the Space of a Decade," *Wall Street Journal*, March 9, 2000, p. A1; "U.S. Superstores Find Japanese Are a Hard Sell," *Wall Street Journal*, February 14, 2000,

p. B1; "Office-Supply Superstores Find Bounty in the Boonies," *Wall Street Journal*, September 1, 1998, p. B1; "Health-Care Superstores Experience Growing Pains," *Wall Street Journal*, May 12, 1997, p. B1; "New Sneaker Superstores Aim to Step on Their Competition," *Wall Street Journal*, March 19, 1997, p. B1; "Bridal Superstores Woo Couples with Miles of Gowns and Tuxes," *Wall Street Journal*, February 14, 1996, p. B1.

13. For more on 7-Eleven in the U.S., see "Know What Customers Want," *Inc.*, August 2005, pp. 22–24; "7-Eleven Getting Boost from Wal-Mart's Rise," *Investor's Business Daily*, June 20, 2005, p. A20; "Convenience Stores Change Gears," *USA Today*, June 13, 2005, p. 7B; "It's a Wrap: 7-Eleven Delivers Freshness," *DSN Retailing Today*, April 11, 2005, p. 29; "At 7-Eleven, Fresh-Food Fix Is Focus," *Wall Street Journal*, August 21, 2002, p.B3B; "7-Eleven Cracks the Code on Elusive Sugar-Free Slurpee," *Wall Street Journal*, October 29, 2001, p. B9. For more on 7-Eleven in Japan, see "From Convenience Store to Online Behemoth?" *Business Week*, April 10, 2000, p. 64; "Japan Goes Web Crazy," *Fortune*, February 7, 2000, p. 115.

14. For more on vending and wireless, see "Buying an iPod from a Vending Machine," *Wall Street Journal*, September 1, 2005, p. D1ff; "Getting Your Drugs from a Vending Machine," *Wall Street Journal*, June 21, 2005; "Want a Soda? Call the Machine," *Investor's Business Daily*, November 13, 2002, p.A4; "Speedpass Use Shows Demand for Wireless Payments," *Investor's Business Daily*, April 19, 2002, p. A6.

15. "New QVC Catalog Is a Beauty," *DM News*, September 19, 2005, p. 18; "Catalog Sellers Also E-Tailers," *Investor's Business Daily*, September 12, 2005, p. A17; "Mail Order Survives, Thrives," *Investor's Business Daily*, February 22, 2005, p. A11; "Major Retailers to Stuff Mailboxes with Catalogs," *USA Today*, November 11, 2003, p. 6B; "New Page in E-Retailing: Catalogs," *Wall Street Journal*, November 30, 2000, p. B1; "Catalogers Expand in Asia," *USA Today*, October 18, 1996, p. 4B. See also Charla Mathwick, Naresh K. Malhotra, and Edward Rigdon, "The Effect of Dynamic Retail Experiences on Experiential Perceptions of Value: An Internet and Catalog Comparison," *Journal of Retailing*, Spring 2002, p. 51; C.R. Jasper and P.N.R. Lan, "Apparel Catalog Patronage: Demographic, Lifestyle, and Motivational Factors," *Psychology & Marketing*, July/August 1992, p. 275.

16. "A Sales Channel They Can't Resist," *Business 2.0*, September 2005, pp. 90–96; "Getting Ready for Prime Time," *Inc.*, November 2003, p. 17; "Is There a Future for the TV Mall?" *Brandweek*, March 25, 1996, p. 24; "QVC Draws Wares from Everywhere," *USA Today*, November 1, 1994, p. 1D; "Battling for Buck$," *Profiles*, November 1994, p. 49.

17. "Retailing: What's Working Online," *The McKinsey Quarterly*, #3, 2005; "Very Merry Holidays for Online Retailers," *Investor's Business Daily*, December 30, 2005, p. A4; "Target Finds Way to Beat Wal-Mart: Online," *Advertising Age*, November 14, 2005, p. 12; "Online Stores Keep Delivery Fees Low," *Wall Street Journal*, October 26, 2005, p. B4C; "Networks Hope Remote-Control Shopping Clicks," *USA Today*, May 25, 2005, p. 1Bff.; "A Wider Net Catches Shoppers," *Investor's Business Daily*, May 24, 2005, p. A14; "Target: Fine-Tuning the Right Formula for Success," *DSN Retailing Today*, April 11, 2005, pp. 31–45; "E-Biz Strikes Again," *Business Week*, May 10, 2004, pp. 80–90; "Lands' End Is an Ultimate Online Model," *USA Today*, December 3, 2004, p. 1Bff.; "Web Shopping Gains Popularity," *USA Today*, November 26, 2003, p. 3B; "Online Comparison Shopping's on a Spree," *Investor's Business Daily*, October 22, 2003, p. A4; "He Turned Website in the Rough into Online Jewel," *USA Today*, October 20, 2003, p. 5B; "Online Shoppers Still Fear Security Issues," *Investor's Business Daily*, June 3, 2003, p.A4; "Can You Really Buy a Couch Online?" *Wall Street Journal Reports*, April 28, 2003, p. R9; "Cruising the Online Mall," *Time (Inside Edition Bonus Section)*, April 2003; "Net vs. Not: Which Offers Better Shopping?" *USA Today*, March 10, 2003, p. 3B; "An Internet Model That Works," *Inc.*, May 2001, p. 25; "Battle-Tested Rules of Online Retail," *Ecompany*, April 2001, p. 72; "Rethinking the Internet," *Business Week*, March 26, 2001, p. 117; "Bricks vs. Clicks," *Wall Street Journal*, December

11, 2000, p. R10. See also Ann E. Schlosser, Tiffany Barnett White, and Susan M. Lloyd, "Converting Web Site Visitors into Buyers: How Web Site Investment Increases Consumer Trusting Beliefs and Online Purchase Intentions," *Journal of Marketing*, April 2006, p. 133; Yakov Bart, Venkatesh Shankar, Fareena Sultan, and Glen L. Urban, "Are the Drivers and Role of Online Trust the Same for All Web Sites and Consumers? A Large-Scale Exploratory Empirical Study," *Journal of Marketing*, October 2005, p. 133; Fabio Ancarani and Venkates Shankar, "Price Levels and Price Dispersion within and across Multiple Retailer Types: Further Evidence and Extension," *Journal of the Academy of Marketing Science*, Spring 2004, p. 176; Michael Lewis, "The Effect of Shipping Fees on Customer Acquisition, Customer Retention, and Purchase Quantities," *Journal of Retailing*, March 2006, p. 13; Manjit S. Yadav and P. Rajan Varadarajan, "Understanding Product Migration to the Electronic Marketplace: A Conceptual Framework," *Journal of Retailing*, 2005, p. 125; Heiner Evanschitzkya, Gopalkrishnan R. Iyer, Josef Hessea, and Dieter Ahlerta, "E-Satisfaction: A Re-Examination," *Journal of Retailing*, Fall 2004, p. 239; Khai Sheang Lee and Soo Jiuan Tan, "E-Retailing versus Physical Retailing: A Theoretical Model and Empirical Test of Consumer Choice," *Journal of Business Research*, November 2003, p. 877; Alka Varma Citrin, Donald E. Stem, Jr., Eric R. Spangenberg, and Michael J. Clark, "Consumer Need for Tactile Input: An Internet Retailing Challenge," *Journal of Business Research*, November 2003, p. 915; Dwayne D. Sijun Wang, Sharon E. Beatty, and William Foxx, "Signaling the Trustworthiness of Small Online Retailers," *Journal of Interactive Marketing*, Winter 2004, p. 53; Fang-Fang Tang and Xiaolin Xing, "Will the Growth of Multi-Channel Retailing Diminish the Pricing Efficiency of the Web?" *Journal of Retailing*, Fall 2001, p. 319.

18. "The Big Guns' Next Target: eBay," *Business 2.0*, January/February 2006, pp. 21–22; "FT MONEY: eBay," *Financial Times*, December 31, 2005; "Who'll Give Me $50 for This Purse from Nana?" *Wall Street Journal*, December 28, 2005, p. D1ff.; "Skype Plus eBay Equals Conversational Markets," *Financial Times*, September 21, 2005; "EBay Bidding to Give Voice to Customers," *Investor's Business Daily*, September 13, 2005, p. A6; "Buyers Kick Virtual Tires on eBay Motors Auction Site," *USA Today*, August 26, 2005, p. 1Bff; "Why eBay Must Win In China," *Time Asia*, August 22, 2005; "In a Challenging China Market, EBay Confronts a Big New Rival," *Wall Street Journal*, August 12, 2005, p. A1ff.; "Threatening eBay's Dominance, More Online Sellers Go It Alone," *Wall Street Journal*, June 22, 2005, p. A1; "10 Years Ago, eBay Changed the World, Sort of by Accident," *USA Today*, March 22, 2005, p. 1Bff.; "The World According to eBay," *Business 2.0*, January/February 2005, pp. 76–84; "eBay's Secret," *Fortune*, October 18, 2004, pp. 160–78; "Middlemen Emerge for Sellers on EBay," *Investor's Business Daily*, October 4, 2004, p. A5; "Hitching a Ride on eBay," *Wall Street Journal Reports*, October 20, 2003, p. R4. See also Matthew J. C. Walley and David R. Fortin, "Behavioral Outcomes from Online Auctions: Reserve Price, Reserve Disclosure, and Initial Bidding Influences in the Decision Process," *Journal of Business Research*, October 2004, p. 1409.

19. Chip E. Miller, "The Effects of Competition on Retail Structure: an Examination of Intratype, Intertype, and Intercategory Competition," *Journal of Marketing*, October 1999, p. 107; "New Options for Saving at the Pump," *Wall Street Journal*, August 16, 2005, p. D1ff.; "Your New Banker?" *Business Week*, February 7, 2005, pp. 28–31; "Snak 'n' Shop," *Wall Street Journal*, July 13, 2004, p. B1ff.; "A Quart of Milk, a Dozen Eggs, and a 2.6-GHz Laptop," *Business 2.0*, October 2003, p. 58; "Jordan's Puts Imax in Its Furniture Picture," *Wall Street Journal*, October 4, 2002, p. B6; "Latest Supermarket Special— Gasoline," *Wall Street Journal*, April 30, 2001, p. B1; "Levi's Doesn't Fancy Selling with Cukes," *Wall Street Journal*, April 10, 2001, p. B10; "Barnes & Noble Finds Grinch Effect in Games Strategy," *Wall Street Journal*, December 20, 2000, p. B4; "Savoring Chocolate," *Advertising Age*, September 4, 2000, p. 24; "In Aisle 10, Soup, Tea—and Bikinis?" *Wall Street Journal*, June 28, 2000, p. B1; Jack M. Cadeaux, "In-

dustry Product Volatility and Retailer Assortments," *Journal of Macromarketing*, Fall 1992, p. 28; Ronald Savitt, "The 'Wheel of Retailing' and Retail Product Management," *European Journal of Marketing* 18, no. 6/7 (1984), p. 43.

20. "How Did Sears Blow This Gasket?" *Business Week*, June 29, 1992, p. 38; "An Open Letter to Sears Customers," *USA Today*, June 25, 1992, p. 8A; see also John Paul Fraedrich, "The Ethical Behavior of Retail Managers," *Journal of Business Ethics*, March 1993, p. 207.

21. "What Price Virtue? At Some Retailers, 'Fair Trade' Carries a Very High Cost," *Wall Street Journal*, June 8, 2004, p. A1ff.

22. See www.census.gov; U.S. Bureau of the Census, "Table 1: Sales Size of Establishments for the United States: 2002," *2002 Economic Census - Retail Trade, Subject Series, Establishment and Firm Size*; "Retailers Grab Power, Control Marketplace," *Marketing News*, January 16, 1989, p. 1. See also Kusum L. Ailawadi, "The Retail Power Performance Conundrum: What Have We Learned?" *Journal of Retailing*, Fall 2001, p. 299; Dale D. Achabal, John M. Heineke, and Shelby H. McIntyre, "Issues and Perspectives on Retail Productivity," *Journal of Retailing*, Fall 1984, p. 107; Charles A. Ingene, "Scale Economies in American Retailing: A Cross-Industry Comparison," *Journal of Macromarketing* 4, no. 2 (1984), p. 49.

23. For an excellent example of AutoZone as successful chain, see "Rallying the Troops to Get Back in the Profit Zone," *DSN Retailing Today*, September 6, 2004, p. 56; "An Auto-Parts Store Your Mother Could Love," *Fortune*, November 10, 2003, p. 163; "Auto Accessories Still in the Fast Lane," *DSN Retailing Today*, May 5, 2003, p. 32; "AutoZone: The Hottest Growth Concept in Retailing," *DSN Retailing Today*, November 11, 2002; "In Corporate America It's Clean Up Time," *Fortune*, September 16, 2002, p. 62. See also "European Inns Take the Hilton Route," *Wall Street Journal*, April 23, 2001, p. B1; "Forging Ahead with Custom Contracts," *Foodservice Equipment & Supplies Specialist*, June 1994, p. 52; "CLOUT! More and More, Retail Giants Rule the Marketplace," *Business Week*, December 21, 1992, p. 66. See also Gary K. Rhoads, William R. Swinyard, Michael D. Geurts, and William D. Price, "Retailing as a Career: A Comparative Study of Marketers," *Journal of Retailing*, Spring 2002, p. 71; Marilyn Lavin, ""Not in My Neighborhood": Resistance to Chain Drug-Stores," *International Journal of Retail & Distribution Management*, no. 6 (2003), p. 321.

24. "Do You Have What It Takes? *Wall Street Journal Reports*, September 19, 2005, p. R11; "How to Grow a Chain That's Already Everywhere," *Business 2.0*, March 2005, p. 52; "When Franchisees Lose Part of Their Independence," *New York Times*, February 3, 2005, p. C6; "Why Subway Is 'The Biggest Problem in Franchising,'" *Fortune*, March 16, 1998, p. 126; "Fast-Food Fight," *Business Week*, June 2, 1997, p. 34; "Rattling the Chains," *Brandweek*, April 21, 1997, p. 28. See also Surinder Tikoo, "Franchiser Influence Strategy Use and Franchisee Experience and Dependence," *Journal of Retailing*, Fall 2002, p. 183; Mika Tuunanen, "An Ounce of Prevention Is Worth a Pound of Cure: Findings from National Franchisee (Dis-)Satisfaction Study," *Journal of Marketing Channels*, no. 2 (2002), p. 57; Patrick J. Kaufmann and Rajiv P. Dant, "The Pricing of Franchise Rights," *Journal of Retailing*, Winter 2001, p. 537; Madhav Pappu and David Strutton, "Toward an Understanding of Strategic Inter-Organizational Relationships in Franchise Channels," *Journal of Marketing Channels*, no. 1/2 (2001), p. 111; Rajiv P. Dant and Patrick J. Kaufmann, "Structural and Strategic Dynamics in Franchising," *Journal of Retailing*, no. 2 (2003), p. 63; Robert Dahlstom, "Franchising: Contemporary Issues and Research," *Journal of Public Policy & Marketing*, Spring 1996, p. 159; Roger D. Blair and Jill B. Herndon, "Franchise Supply Agreements: Quality Control or Illegal Tying?" *Journal of the Academy of Marketing Science*, Spring 1997, p. 177.

25. "How China Eats a Sandwich: Opening Subway Franchises . . .," *Fortune*, March 21, 2005, pp. F210B-D; "Tesco: California Dreaming?" *Business Week*, February 27, 2006, p. 38; "Tesco Jumps the Pond," *Wall Street Journal*, February 10, 2006, p. B2; "China's New Entrepreneurs: McDonald's and KFC Race to Recruit More

Franchisees . . .," *Wall Street Journal*, January 25, 2005, p. B1ff.; "China: Let the Retail Wars Begin," *Business Week*, January 17, 2005, pp. 44–45; "Carrefour Chief Gets Ultimatum," *Wall Street Journal*, July 9, 2004, p. C1ff.; "Global Retailing," *DSN Retailing Today*, July 5, 2004, p. 16; "Bare-Bones Shopping . . . Germany," *Wall Street Journal Reports*, May 10, 2004, p. R6; "The Next Wal-Mart?" *Business Week*, April 26, 2004, pp. 60–62; "China's Rush to Convenience," *Wall Street Journal*, November 3, 2003, p. A13; "Making the Cuts," *Wall Street Journal Reports*, September 22, 2003, p. R3; "Big German Retailer Metro AG Brings Superstores to Vietnam," *Wall Street Journal*, August 13, 2002, p. B3B; "Western Stores Woo Chinese Wallets," *Wall Street Journal*, November 26, 2002, p. B1; "To Russia, with Love: The Multinationals' Song," *Business Week*, September 16, 2002, p. 44; "U.S. Superstores Find Japanese Are a Hard Sell," *Wall Street Journal*, February 14, 2000, p. B1. See also T. Wing-Chun Lo, Ho-Fuk Lau, and Gong-Shi Lin, "Problems and Prospects of Supermarket Development in China," *International Journal of Retail & Distribution Management*, no. 2 (2001), p. 66; Paul T. McGurr, "The Largest Retail Firms: a Comparison of Asia-, Europe- and US-based Retailers," *International Journal of Retail & Distribution Management*, no. 2 (2002), p. 145; Barry Quinn and Nicholas Alexander, "International Retail Franchising: a Conceptual Framework," *International Journal of Retail & Distribution Management*, no. 5 (2002), p. 264; Marieke de Mooij and Geert Hofstede, "Convergence and Divergence in Consumer Behavior: Implications for International Retailing," *Journal of Retailing*, Spring 2002, p. 61; Valerie Severin, Jordan J. Louviere, and Adam Finn, "The Stability of Retail Shopping Choices over Time and across Countries," *Journal of Retailing*, Summer 2001, p. 185; Jozefina Simova, Colin M. Clarke-Hill, and Terry Robinson, "A Longitudinal Study of Changes in Retail Formats and Merchandise Assortment in Clothing Retailing in the Czech Republic in the Period 1994–1999," *International Journal of Retail & Distribution Management*, no. 6 (2003), p. 352; Arieh Goldman, "The Transfer of Retail Formats into Developing Economies: the Example of China," *Journal of Retailing*, Summer 2001, p. 221; Nicholas Alexander and Marcelo de Lira e Silva "Emerging Markets and the Internationalisation of Retailing: The Brazilian Experience," *International Journal of Retail & Distribution Management*, no. 6 (2002), p. 300.

26. See www.friedas.com.; "How Lower-Tech Gear Beat Web 'Exchanges' at Their Own Game," *Wall Street Journal*, March 16, 2001, p. A1; "Family Firms Confront Calamities of Transfer," *USA Today*, August 29, 2000, p. 1B; "Business, Too Close to Home," *Time*, July 17, 2000, pp. B24–B27; "The Kiwi to My Success," *Hemispheres*, July 1999; "Searching for the Next Kiwi: Frieda's Branded Produce," *Brandweek*, May 2, 1994, p. 46; "Strange Fruits," *Inc.*, November 1989, p. 80; "The Produce Marketer," *Savvy*, June 1988, p. 26.

27. "Why the Web Can't Kill the Middleman," *Ecompany*, April 2001, p. 75; "Not Dead Yet," *Inc. Tech*, No. 1, 2001, p. 58; "Electronics Distributors Are Reporting Record Profits," *Wall Street Journal*, July 13, 2000, p. B4; "Chow (On)Line," *Business Week E.Biz*, June 5, 2000, p. EB84; "Why Online Distributors—Once Written Off—May Thrive," *Fortune*, September 6, 1999, p. 270. See also Susan Mudambi and Raj Aggarwal, "Industrial Distributors: Can They Survive in the New Economy?" *Industrial Marketing Management*, May 2003, p. 317; Das Narayandas, Mary Caravella, and John Deighton, "The Impact of Internet Exchanges on Business-to-Business Distribution," *Journal of the Academy of Marketing Science*, Fall 2002, p. 500; Amrik S. Sohal, Damien J. Power, and Mile Terziovski, "Integrated Supply Chain Management from the Wholesaler's Perspective: Two Australian Case Studies," *International Journal of Physical Distribution & Logistics Management*, no. 1 (2002), p. 96.

28. "Cold War: Amana Refrigeration Fights Tiny Distributor," *Wall Street Journal*, February 26, 1992, p. B2. For another example, see "Quickie-Divorce Curbs Sought by Manufacturers' Distributors," *Wall Street Journal*, July 13, 1987, p. 27; "Merger of Two Bakers Teaches Distributors a Costly Lesson (3 parts)," *Wall Street Journal*, September 14, 1987, p. 29; October 19, 1987, p. 35; November 11, 1987, p. 33.

29. See www.census.gov; U.S. Bureau of the Census, "Table 1a: Summary Statistics for the United States: 2002," *2002 Economic Census - Wholesale Trade, Geographic Area Series, United States* (Washington, DC: U.S. Government Printing Office, 2005).

30. See www.fastenal.com; "Fastenal: Need to Fix Up a Building? This Firm's Got Your One-Stop Shop," *Investor's Business Daily*, November 28, 2005, p. A7; "Fastenal: In This Sluggish Market, You Gotta Have Faith," *Investor's Business Daily*, August 13, 2001, p. A12.

31. "Revolution in Japanese Retailing," *Fortune*, February 7, 1994, p. 143; Arieh Goldman, "Evaluating the Performance of the Japanese Distribution System," *Journal of Retailing*, Spring 1992, p. 11; "Japan Begins to Open the Door to Foreigners, a Little," *Brandweek*, August 2, 1993, p. 14.

32. See www.rell.com; "Richardson Electronics Ltd.: Maker of Ancient Tech Finds a Way to Prosper," *Investor's Business Daily*, June 27, 2000, p. A12; *2005 Richardson Electronics*.

33. See www.inmac.com and www.grainger.com; "B2B: Yesterday's Darling," *Wall Street Journal*, October 23, 2000, p. R8; "W.W. Grainger's Web Investments: Money Well Spent? Don't Ask Street," *Investor's Business Daily*, September 19, 2000, p. A1.

34. For more on manufacturers' agents being squeezed, see "Philips to End Long Relations with North American Reps—Will Build Internal Sales Force Instead," *EBN*, November 10, 2003, p. 8; "Wal-Mart Draws Fire: Reps, Brokers Protest Being Shut Out by New Policy," *Advertising Age*, January 13, 1992, p. 3; Daniel H. McQuiston, "A Conceptual Model for Building and Maintaining Relationships Between Manufacturers' Representatives and Their Principals," *Industrial Marketing Management*, February 2001, p. 165; Patrick R. Mehr, "Identifying Independent Reps," *Industrial Marketing Management*, November 1992, p. 319. For more discussion on wholesaling abroad, see "Japan Rises to P&G's No. 3 Market," *Advertising Age*, December 10, 1990, p. 42; "Papa-Mama Stores in Japan Wield Power to Hold Back Imports," *Wall Street Journal*, November 14, 1988, p. 1. See also Yoo S. Yang, Robert P. Leone, and Dana L. Alden, "A Market Expansion Ability Approach to Identify Potential Exporters," *Journal of Marketing*, January 1992, p. 84; Daniel C. Bello and Ritu Lohtia, "The Export Channel Design: The Use of Foreign Distributors and Agents," *Journal of the Academy of Marketing Science*, Spring 1995, p. 83; D. Steven White, "Behind the Success and Failure of U.S. Export Intermediaries: Transactions, Agents and Resources," *Journal of the Academy of Marketing Science*, Summer 2001, p. 18.

35. "Keep the Excess Moving," *Business Week E.Biz*, November 20, 2000, p. EB78; "Good-Bye to Fixed Pricing?" *Business Week*, May 4, 1998, p. 71; "Sales Are Clicking on Manufacturing's Internet Mart," *Fortune*, July 7, 1997, p. 136C.

36. "Will That Be Cash, Credit—or Fingertip?" *USA Today*, December 2, 2005, p. 1Bff.; "A Speedier Superstore," *Business 2.0*, December 2005, p. 38; "Putting a Finger on Biometrics," *Convenience Store Decisions*, August 2005, pp. 28–30; "The Grocery Store of the Future," *Business 2.0*, March 2005, p. 28; "The World of Business in 2020," *Business 2.0*, April 2004, pp. 119–26; "Delivering the Goods," *Wall Street Journal Reports*, February 11, 2002, p. R14; "What's Ahead for Retailing," *Wall Street Journal*, June 25, 2001, p. R16; "Digital ID Cards," *Wall Street Journal*, June 25, 2001, p. R16; "Leave It in the Box," *Business Week E.Biz*, December 11, 2000, p. EB82. See also Enrico Colla, "International Expansion and Strategies of Discount Grocery Retailers: The Winning Models," *International Journal of Retail & Distribution Management*, no. 1 (2003), p. 55; Robert A. Peterson and Sridhar Balasubramanian, "Retailing in the 21st Century: Reflections and Prologue to Research," *Journal of Retailing*, Spring 2002, p. 9; Elliot Rabinovich and Philip T. Evers, "Product Fulfillment in Supply Chains Supporting Internet-Retailing Operations," *Journal of Business Logistics*, no. 2 (2003), p. 205; Alan C. McKinnon and Deepak Tallam, "Unattended Delivery to the Home: an Assessment of the Security Implications," *International Journal of Retail & Distribution Management*, no. 1 (2003), p. 30; Hannu Yrjola, "Physical Distribution Considerations for Electronic Grocery Shopping," *International Journal of*

Physical Distribution & Logistics Management, no. 9 (2001), p. 746; Stacy L. Wood, "Future Fantasies: a Social Change Perspective of Retailing in the 21st Century," *Journal of Retailing*, Spring 2002, p. 77.

CHAPTER 13

1. See www.mini-cooper.com; "For Your Eyes Only," *Business Week*, July 31, 2006, p. 66; "Getting Creative with Mad Ave.," *Business Week*, February 6, 2006, pp. 80–81; "Car without a Hot Tin Roof," *Wall Street Journal*, January 21, 2005, p. W9C; "Soft Top, Hard Sell," *Advertising Age*, August 23, 2004, pp. 1, 34; "Dare-Devils: The Ad World's Most Buzzed-About Agency . . .," *Business 2.0*, April 2004, pp. 111–16; "A Skewed View of Advertising: CP+B . . .," *USA Today*, March 24, 2004, p. 1Bff.; "What to Expect when You're Expecting a Mini-Cooper," *New York Times*, January 25, 2004, Sect. 3, p. 7; "Hot Off the Lot," *Wall Street Journal*, September 10, 2003, p. D4; "Mini's Wild Ride," *Adweek*, June 2, 2003, p. 24; "What Went Right," *Fortune*, December 30, 2002, p. 164; "Creating Max Buzz for New BMW Mini," *Advertising Age*, June 17, 2002, p. 12; "Most Innovative Campaign," *Business 2.0*, May 2002, p. 98; "Big Enough to Turn Heads," *Business Week*, April 22, 2002, p. 100; "BMW 'Mini' Campaign: Odd to the Max," *Wall Street Journal*, March 1, 2002, p. B5.

2. "How Southwest Airlines Sold $1.5 Million in Tickets by Posting Four Press Releases Online," *Marketing Sherpa*, October 27, 2004.

3. "Old-Fashioned PR Gives General Mills Advertising Bargains," *Wall Street Journal*, March 20, 1997, p. A1. See also "How a Small Boutique Gets $25 Moccasins on Celebrities' Feet," *Wall Street Journal*, November 19, 2004, p. A1ff.; "Aflac Duck's Paddle to Stardom: Creativity on the Cheap," *Wall Street Journal*, July 30, 2004, p. B1ff.; "Name That Chintz! How Shelter Magazines Boost Brands," *Wall Street Journal*, March 14, 1997, p. B1; "Rosie and 'Friends' Make Drake's Cakes a Star," *Wall Street Journal*, February 10, 1997, p. B1; "Toy Story: How Shrewd Marketing Made Elmo a Hit," *Wall Street Journal*, December 16, 1996, p. B1; "PR Shouldn't Mean 'Poor Relations,'" *Industry Week*, February 3, 1992, p. 51; Siva K. Balasubramanian, "Beyond Advertising and Publicity: Hybrid Messages and Public Policy Issues," *Journal of Advertising*, December 1994, p. 29; Thomas H. Bivins, "Ethical Implications of the Relationship of Purpose to Role and Function in Public Relations," *Journal of Business Ethics*, January 1989, p. 65.

4. "President's Tumble Off a Segway Seems a Tiny Bit Suspicious," *USA Today*, June 18, 2003, p. 3B; "Watch Your Step: Segways Ahead," *USA Today*, June 17, 2003, p. 1A; "Segway Book: Inventor No 'Deep Throat,'" *Investor's Business Daily*, June 13, 2003, p. A4.

5. "How Companies Pay TV Experts for On-Air Product Mentions," *Wall Street Journal*, April 19, 2005, A1ff.

6. "Nortel Tests Virtual Tradeshow (Instead of Webinar): Tactics & Results," *Marketing Sherpa*, January 18, 2006; www.nortel.com.

7. For example of integrated campaign, see "Tylenol Hits the Gym for Launch," *Advertising Age*, May 26, 2003, p. 30. See also David A. Griffith, Aruna Chandra, and John K. Ryans, Jr., "Examining the Intricacies of Promotion Standardization: Factors Influencing Advertising Message and Packaging," *Journal of International Marketing*, no. 3 (2003), p. 30; Kim Bartel Sheehan and Caitlin Doherty, "Re-Weaving the Web: Integrating Print and Online Communications," *Journal of Interactive Marketing*, Spring 2001, p. 47; J. R. Shannon, "The New Promotions Mix: A Proposed Paradigm, Process, and Application," *Journal of Marketing Theory & Practice*, Winter 1996, p. 56; Kathleen J. Kelly, "Integrated Marketing Communication: Putting It Together & Making It Work," *Journal of the Academy of Marketing Science*, Winter 1997, p. 83.

8. "Reckitt Thrives in an Unloved Niche," *Wall Street Journal*, May 24, 2005, B5.

9. "In a Shift, Marketers Beef Up Ad Spending Inside Stores," *Wall Street Journal*, September 21, 2005, A1.

10. "Wi-Fis, PDAs, Blogs, Smart Phones, PVRs, Hmm . . . Overload?" *Investor's Business Daily*, November 7, 2005, p. A4; "Survey Shows Consumers Befuddled by Technology," *Advertising Age*, July 12, 2004, p. 8; "Ever Heard of a DVD Recorder? Many Americans Haven't, a New Survey Shows," *Investor's Business Daily*, May 4, 2004, p. A5; "High-Tech Branding: Pushing Digital PCS," *Brandweek*, August 4, 1997, p. 30; "Brand Builders: Delivery Guy Chic," *Brandweek*, June 30, 1997, p. 18; "Eye-Catching Logos All Too Often Leave Fuzzy Images in Minds of Consumers," *Wall Street Journal*, December 5, 1991, p. B1. See also George S. Low and Jakki J. Mohr, "Factors Affecting the Use of Information in the Evaluation of Marketing Communications Productivity," *Journal of the Academy of Marketing Science*, Winter 2001, p. 70; David I. Gilliland and Wesley J. Johnston, "Toward a Model of Business-to-Business Marketing Communications Effects," *Industrial Marketing Management*, January 1997, p. 15; Michel T. Pham and Gita V. Johar, "Contingent Processes of Source Identification," *Journal of Consumer Research*, December 1997, p. 249; Louisa Ha and Barry R. Litman, "Does Advertising Clutter Have Diminishing and Negative Returns?" *Journal of Advertising*, Spring 1997, p. 31; Barbara B. Stern, "A Revised Communication Model for Advertising: Multiple Dimensions of the Source, the Message, and the Recipient," *Journal of Advertising*, June 1994, p. 5; Ronald E. Dulek, John S. Fielden, and John S. Hill, "International Communication: An Executive Primer," *Business Horizons*, January/February 1991, p. 20; Richard F. Beltramini and Edwin R. Stafford, "Comprehension and Perceived Believability of Seals of Approval Information in Advertising," *Journal of Advertising*, September 1993, p. 3.

11. "Capturing a Piece of the Global Market," *Brandweek*, June 20, 2005, p. 20; "Global Branding: Same, but Different," *Brandweek*, April 9, 2001, p. 25; "When You Translate 'Got Milk' for Latinos, What Do You Get?" *Wall Street Journal*, June 3, 1999, p. A1; "Cash, Cache, Cachet: All 3 Seem to Matter When You Buy a PC," *Wall Street Journal*, December 18, 1998, p. A1; "Hey, #!@*% Amigo, Can You Translate the Word 'Gaffe'?" *Wall Street Journal*, July 8, 1996, p. B2; "Lost in Translation: How to 'Empower Women' in Chinese," *Wall Street Journal*, September 13, 1994, p. A1.

12. For more on video publicity releases, see "The Corruption of TV Health News," *Business Week*, February 28, 2000, p. 66; "Collagen Corp.'s Video Uses News Format," *Wall Street Journal*," March 29, 1994, p. B8; Thomas H. Bivins, "Public Relations, Professionalism, and the Public Interest," *Journal of Business Ethics*, February 1993, p. 117; Siva K. Balasubramanian, "Beyond Advertising and Publicity: Hybrid Messages and Public Policy Issues," *Journal of Advertising*, December 1994, p. 47. For more on celebrity endorsements, see "Culture of Celebrity," *Advertising Age*, February 20, 2006, pp. S1–S4; "Nike Relaunches Kobe Bryant after Two Years of Prep Work," *Wall Street Journal*, November 11, 2005, p. B1ff.; "Michelle Wie Wins a Deal Helping Nike Target Women Golfers," *Wall Street Journal*, October 5, 2005, p. B1ff.; "Playing the Hip-Hop Name Drop," *Brandweek*, July 25, 2005, pp. 24–27; "Athletes on the Outs in Ads," *USA Today*, July 5, 2005, p. 1Cff.; "Nascar Courts Minorities," *Wall Street Journal*, March 3, 2005, p. B1ff.; "Wow! Yao!" *Business Week*, October 25, 2004, pp. 86–90; "Dale Jr. Zooms to Front of Pack in Endorsements," *USA Today*, February 13, 2004, p. 1Bff. See also Therese A. Louie and Carl Obermiller, "Consumer Response to a Firm's Endorser (Dis)association Decisions," *Journal of Advertising*, Winter 2002, p. 41; Marla Royne Stafford, Thomas F. Stafford, and Ellen Day, "A Contingency Approach: The Effects of Spokesperson Type and Service Type on Service Advertising Perceptions," *Journal of Advertising*, Summer 2002, p. 17; Dwane Hal Dean and Abhijit Biswas, "Third-Party Organization Endorsement of Products: An Advertising Cue Affecting Consumer Prepurchase Evaluation of Goods and Services," *Journal of Advertising*, Winter 2001, p. 41; Ronald E. Goldsmith, Barbara A. Lafferty, and Stephen J. Newell, "The Impact of Corporate Credibility and Celebrity Credibility on Consumer Reaction to Advertisements and Brands," *Journal of Advertising*, Fall 2000, p. 43; Ron Coulter, "High Visibility: The Making and Marketing of Professionals into Celebrities," *Journal of the Academy of Marketing Science*, Winter 2001, p. 105.

13. "Depending on Direct: Discipline Grows to $161B," *Advertising Age*, October 24, 2005, p. 6; "Direct Gets Respect: Budgets Swell as Marketers Seek Accountability," *Advertising Age*, August 30, 2004, pp. 1, 21; "Direct Marketing," *BtoB*, October 13, 2003, p. 24; "DMA Benchmarks Response Rates," *BtoB*, July 14, 2003, p. 13; "Direct Marketing Gets Cannes Do Spirit," *USA Today*, June 17, 2002, p. 4B; "Escalade Got Game," *Advertising Age*, June 11, 2001, p. 42. For an electronic direct-mail example, see "Web Slice," *Brandweek*, May 26, 1997, p. 22. See also Sally J. McMillan and Jang-Sun Hwang, "Measures of Perceived Interactivity: An Exploration of the Role of Direction of Communication, User Control, and Time in Shaping Perceptions of Interactivity," *Journal of Advertising*, Fall 2002, p. 29; Carrie M. Heilman, Frederick Kaefer, and Samuel D. Ramenofsky, "Determining the Appropriate Amount of Data for Classifying Consumers for Direct Marketing Purposes," *Journal of Interactive Marketing*, Summer 2003, p. 5; Mark J. Arnold and Shelley R. Tapp, "The Effects of Direct Marketing Techniques on Performance: An Application to Arts Organizations," *Journal of Interactive Marketing*, Summer 2001, p. 41; Patrick Barwise and Colin Strong, "Permission-Based Mobile Advertising," *Journal of Interactive Marketing*, Winter 2002, p. 14; Charles R. Taylor, George R. Franke, and Michael L. Maynard, "Attitudes toward Direct Marketing and Its Regulation: A Comparison of the United States and Japan," *Journal of Public Policy & Marketing*, Fall 2000, p. 228; Jennifer Rowley and Frances Slack, "Kiosks in Retailing: The Quiet Revolution," *International Journal of Retail & Distribution Management*, no. 6 (2003), p. 329; Yuping Liu and L. J. Shrum, "What Is Interactivity and Is It Always Such a Good Thing? Implications of Definition, Person, and Situation for the Influence of Interactivity on Advertising Effectiveness," *Journal of Advertising*, Winter 2002, p. 53; Judy F. Davis, "Maintaining Customer Relationships through Effective Database Marketing: A Perspective for Small Retailers," *Journal of Marketing Theory & Practice*, Spring 1997, p. 31; Kapil Bawa, "Influences on Consumer Response to Direct Mail Coupons: An Integrative Review," *Psychology & Marketing*, March 1996, p. 129; William J. Carner, "Direct Marketing through Broadcast Media: TV, Radio, Cable, Infomercials, Home Shopping, and More," *Journal of the Academy of Marketing Science*, Winter 1997, p. 86.

14. "Behind-the-Scenes Discoveries from HP's Email Segmentation Tests," *Marketing Sherpa*, September 29, 2005; "Personal Touch Opens Up Hewlett-Packard's Portal Strategy," *inside 1to1*, July 11, 2005; "HP Continues Cost Savings with Vertical E-Newsletters," *BtoB*, July 1, 2004.

15. "54% of Permission E-mailers Are Filtered as Spammers: Including AOL News, Wal-Mart, IBM, and the Feds," *Marketing Sherpa*, June 9, 2005.

16. For more on privacy, see Chapter 18, endnote 11. For more on regulation of spam, junk mail, and telemarketing calls, see "Paper War," *Time*, January 2006, p. A11; "Record Fine Levied against Telemarketer," *Wall Street Journal*, December 14, 2005, p. D1ff.; "Splogs Roil Web, and Some Blame Google," *Wall Street Journal*, October 19, 2005, p. B1ff.; "A New Battle over No-Call Lists," *Wall Street Journal*, September 28, 2005, p. D1ff.; "The Taming of the Internet," *Business Week*, December 15, 2003, p. 78; "Telemarketing after Do Not Call," *Inc.*, November 2003, p. 32; "Silence of the Spams," *Brandweek*, October 20, 2003, p. 14; "America Hangs Up on Telemarketers," *Fortune*, October 13, 2003, p. 58; "FTC Told to Enforce Do-Not-Call List," *USA Today*, October 8, 2003, p. 1B; "A Stab at Stemming Spam," *Business Week*, October 6, 2003, p. 115; "The Do-Not-Call Law Won't Stop the Calls," *Business Week*, September 29, 2003, p. 89.

17. Monica Perry and Charles D. Bodkin, "Fortune 500 Manufacturer Websites: Innovative Marketing Strategies or Cyberbrochures?" *Industrial Marketing Management*, February 2002, p. 133; Nicole Coviello, Roger Milley, and Barbara Marcolin, "Understanding IT-Enabled Interactivity in Contemporary Marketing," *Journal of Interactive Marketing*, Autumn 2001, p. 18; Donna L. Hoffman and Thomas P. Novak, "Marketing in Hypermedia Computer-Mediated Environments: Conceptual Foundations," *Journal of Marketing*, July 1996, p. 50.

18. For more on direct-to-consumer drug advertising, see "Under Scrutiny, Drug Makers Rethink Ad Campaigns," *Investor's Business Daily*, October 24, 2005, p. A12; "Being Bold at Bristol-Myers Squibb," *Point*, October 2005, pp. 18–19; "PR Seems to Be the Rx to Get Around DTC Rules," *Advertising Age*, September 26, 2005, p. 6; "Big Pharma Finds Way into Doctors' Pockets," *Advertising Age*, September 19, 2005, pp. 4, 52; "Drugmakers Are Changing Channels," *Business Week*, August 15, 2005, pp. 44–45; "FDA to Review Drug Marketing to Consumers," *Wall Street Journal*, August 2, 2005, p. B1ff.; "To Sell Their Drugs, Companies Increasingly Rely on Doctors," *Wall Street Journal*, July 15, 2005, p. A1ff.; "Direct-to-Consumer Advertising Takes Direct Hit from FDA," *Investor's Business Daily*, May 31, 2005, p. A12; "Code Red for DTC," *Advertising Age*, January 3, 2005, pp. 1, 22. See also Steven W. Kopp and Mary J. Sheffet, "The Effect of Direct-to-Consumer Advertising of Prescription Drugs on Retail Gross Margins: Empirical Evidence and Public Policy Implications," *Journal of Public Policy & Marketing*, Fall 1997, p. 270; Mary C. Gilly and Mary Wolfinbarger, "Advertising's Internal Audience," *Journal of Marketing*, January 1998, p. 69; S. A. Erdem and L. J. Harrison-Walker, "Managing Channel Relationships: Toward an Identification of Effective Promotional Strategies in Vertical Marketing Systems," *Journal of Marketing Theory & Practice*, Spring 1997, p. 80.

19. "Decker Scores with Sweepstakes to Promote Days Inn," *USA Today*, November 6, 1997, p. B10; "Biore: The Nose Knew at Lilith Fair," *Brandweek*, September 15, 1997, p. 28; "Brand Builders: Progresso Warriors," *Brandweek*, June 23, 1997, p. 20; "Advertisers Often Cheer the Loudest," *USA Today*, March 27, 1997, p. 1A; "Crossing the Border," *Brandweek*, December 16, 1996, p. 17; "Brand Builders: Pie in the Sky," *Brandweek*, December 16, 1996, p. 23; "Tractor Dealers Get Down in the Dirt Promoting Machines," *Wall Street Journal*, July 16, 1996, p. A1; "Pepsi Cancels an Ad Campaign as Customers Clamor for Stuff," *Wall Street Journal*, June 27, 1996, p. B1.

20. "Compensation and Expenses," *Sales & Marketing Management*, June 28, 1993, p. 65; "The Cost of Selling Is Going Up," *Boardroom Reports*, December 15, 1991, p. 15; "An In-House Sales School," *Inc.*, May 1991, p. 85.

21. *Retail Customer Dissatisfaction Study – 2006*, Verde Group—Baker Retail Initiative at Wharton, 2006.

22. For more on Bzz-Agent, see "BzzAgent Seeks to Turn Word of Mouth into a Saleable Medium," *Advertising Age*, February 13, 2006, p. 12; "Small Firms Turn to Marketing Buzz Agents," *Wall Street Journal*, December 27, 2005, p. A14.

23. For more on Pontiac, see "A Car Is Born," *Newsweek*, September 27, 2004, pp. 40–41; "Pontiac Gets Major Mileage Out of $8 Million Oprah Deal," *Advertising Age*, September 20, 2004, p. 12. For more on opinion leaders, word-of-mouth publicity, buzz marketing, see Chapter 5, endnote 22. See also "Rules of the Game," *Point*, December 2005, pp. 22–23; "Buzz Tactics . . . :Play to Passions of Adults, Use Events, Experts Urge," *Advertising Age*, November 28, 2005, p. 33; "Leader of the Packs," *Business Week*, October 31, 2005, pp. 56–58; "What's in a Word?" *Brandweek*, October 24, 2005, pp. 30–31; "Mitsubishi Zips Past the Scrap Heap," *Business Week*, October 24, 2005, p. 56; "The Selling of a Geisha," *Wall Street Journal*, October 21, 2005, p. B1ff.; "JWT Tries to Build Buzz at Beer Convention," *Wall Street Journal*, October 10, 2005, p. B9; "Mellow Yellow Raises Glasses," *Brandweek*, September 19, 2005, pp. 16–17; "Gap Deploys Viral Online Promotion to Pump Up Sales," *Wall Street Journal*, August 10, 2005, p. B1ff.; "Advertising of, by, and for the People," *Business Week*, July 25, 2005, pp. 63–64; "What's the Buzz? If You're Smart, It's about Your Product," *USA Today*, July 25, 2005, p. 5B; "From a Whisper to a Scream," *Investor's Business Daily*, June 13, 2005, p. A13; "Word-of-Mouth Marketing Gets People Buzzing," *BtoB*, June 13, 2005, pp. 3, 62; "Word on the Street," *Adweek*, May 16, 2005, pp. 26–30; "Marketers of the Next Generation: Microsoft's Gamer Shrouded Halo 2 . . .," *Brandweek*, April 11, 2005, p. 32; "Fresh Off Oscar Boost, Everlast Set to Wring Big Buzz from Contender," *Advertising Age*, March 7, 2005, pp. 4, 53; "Getting Buzz Marketers to Fess Up," *Wall*

Street Journal, February 9, 2005, p. B9; "Clif Bar's Solo Climb," *Business 2.0*, December 2004, pp. 150–54; "Tall Tales," *Adweek*, October 11, 2004, pp. 28–29, 34; "The Rebirth of Cool," *Business 2.0*, September 2004, pp. 108–14; "Buzz Giant Poster Boy," *American Demographics*, June 2004, pp. 12–16; "At Dental Gear Maker, Word of Mouth Rules," *Investor's Business Daily*, January 6, 2004, p. A8. For an example of TiVo's targeting innovators and early adopters, see "New TV Ratings Will Produce Ad-Price Fight," *Wall Street Journal*, December 22, 2005, p. B1ff.; "TiVo and Other DVRs Gradually Catching On," *Investor's Business Daily*, December 9, 2005, p. A4; "TiVo Adds Movie Tickets, Photos to Offerings," *USA Today*, December 1, 2005, p. 1B; "DirecTV Poised to Take on TiVo," *USA Today*, August 24, 2005, p. 3B; "Marketers Seek New Approach as DVRs' Popularity Increases," *Wall Street Journal*, July 29, 2005, p. B3. For more on Toyota's marketing of the Scion, see "Scion Play Hip-Hop Impresario to Impress Young Drivers," *Wall Street Journal*, October 5, 2004, p. B1ff.; "Toyota Goes Guerilla to Roll Scion," *Advertising Age*, August 11, 2003, p. 4; "Toyota's Gen Y Gamble," *Wall Street Journal*, July 30, 2003, p. B1. See also Jyh-Shen Chiou and Cathy Cheng, "Should a Company Have Message Boards on Its Web Sites?" *Journal of Interactive Marketing*, Summer 2003, p. 50; Raji Srinivasan, Gary L. Lilien, and Arvind Rangaswamy, "Technological Opportunism and Radical Technology Adoption: An Application to E-Business," *Journal of Marketing*, July 2002, p. 47; Suman Basuroy, Subimal Chatterjee, and S. Abraham Ravid, "How Critical Are Critical Reviews? The Box Office Effects of Film Critics, Star Power, and Budgets," *Journal of Marketing*, October 2003, p. 103; Jeffrey G. Blodgett, Donald H. Granbois, and Rockney G. Walters, "The Effects of Perceived Justice on Complainants' Negative Word-of-Mouth Behavior and Repatronage Intentions," *Journal of Retailing*, Winter 1993, p. 399; Paula Fitzgerald Bone, "Word-of-Mouth Effects on Short-Term and Long-Term Product Judgments," *Journal of Business Research*, March 1995, p. 213.

24. Hokey Min and William P. Galle, "E-Purchasing: Profiles of Adopters and Nonadopters," *Industrial Marketing Management*, April 2003, p. 227; Yikuan Lee and Gina Colarelli O'Connor, "The Impact of Communication Strategy on Launching New Products: The Moderating Role of Product Innovativeness," *Journal of Product Innovation Management*, January 2003, p. 4; David R. Fell, Eric N. Hansen, and Boris W. Becker, "Measuring Innovativeness for the Adoption of Industrial Products," *Industrial Marketing Management*, May 2003, p. 347; Subin Im, Barry, L. Bayus, and Charlotte H. Mason, "An Empirical Study of Innate Consumer Innovativeness, Personal Characteristics, and New-Product Adoption Behavior," *Journal of the Academy of Marketing Science*, Winter 2003, p. 61; Eric Waarts, Yvonne M. van Everdingen, and Jos van Hillegersberg, "Dynamics of Factors Affecting the Adoption of Innovations," *Journal of Product Innovation Management*, November 2002, p. 412; S. Ram and Hyung-Shik Jung, "Innovativeness in Product Usage: A Comparison of Early Adopters and Early Majority," *Psychology & Marketing*, January/February 1994, p. 57; Robert J. Fisher and Linda L. Price, "An Investigation into the Social Context of Early Adoption Behavior," *Journal of Consumer Research*, December 1992, p. 477; Everett M. Rogers and F. Floyd Shoemaker, *Communication of Innovations: A Cross-Cultural Approach* (New York: Free Press, 1971), p. 203.

25. "Blogs in Business," *Marketing* (UK), March 1, 2006, pp. 35–36; "The Blog in the Corporate Machine," *Economist*, February 11, 2006, pp. 55–56; "When Blogs Go Bad," *Inc.*, November 2005, pp. 44–45; "Slowly, Marketers Learn How to Let Go and Let Blog; Losing Some Control of the Brand Starts to Pay Off," *Advertising Age*, October 31, 2005, p. 1ff.; "Get Connected: Leverage Blogs as Biz Tool," *Marketing News*, September 1, 2005, p. 7; "Blogging Becomes a Corporate Job; Digital 'Handshake'?" *Wall Street Journal*, May 31, 2005, p. B1ff; "Six Tips for Corporate Bloggers," *Business Week Online*, May 2, 2005; "Blogs Will Change Your Business," *Business Week*, May 2, 2005, pp. 57–67; "Want Truth in Advertising? Try a Blog," *Fortune*, January 14, 2005; "Why There's No Escaping the Blog," *Fortune*, January 10, 2005, pp. 44–50; "The Business of Blogging," *Business Week*, December 13, 2004, pp. 117–19.

26. "All-in-One Dinner Kits Gain Popularity," *Food Retailing Today*, May 5, 2003, p. 12; "Marketers of the Year: This One's a Stove Topper," *Brandweek*, October 14, 2002, pp. M30–M34.

27. Kusum L. Ailawadi, Paul W. Farris, and Mark E. Parry, "Share and Growth Are Not Good Predictors of the Advertising and Promotion/Sales Ratio," *Journal of Marketing*, January 1994, p. 86.

28. Kissan Joseph and Vernon J. Richardson, "Free Cash Flow, Agency Costs, and the Affordability Method of Advertising Budgeting," *Journal of Marketing*, January 2002, p. 94; John A. Weber, "Managing the Marketing Budget in a Cost-Constrained Environment," *Industrial Marketing Management*, November 2002, p. 705; Deborah Utter, "Marketing on a Budget," *Journal of the Academy of Marketing Science*, Summer 2000, p. 441; Kim P. Corfman and Donald R. Lehmann, "The Prisoner's Dilemma and the Role of Information in Setting Advertising Budgets," *Journal of Advertising*, June 1994, p. 35; C.L. Hung and Douglas West, "Advertising Budgeting Methods in Canada, the UK and the USA," *International Journal of Advertising* 10, no. 3 (1991), p. 239; Pierre Filiatrault and Jean-Charles Chebat, "How Service Firms Set Their Marketing Budgets," *Industrial Marketing Management*, February 1990, p. 63; James E. Lynch and Graham J. Hooley, "Industrial Advertising Budget Approaches in the U.K.," *Industrial Marketing Management* 18, no. 4 (1989), p. 265; Douglas J. Dalrymple and Hans B. Thorelli, "Sales Force Budgeting," *Business Horizons*, July/August 1984, p. 31; Peter J. Danaher and Roland T. Rust, "Determining the Optimal Level of Media Spending," *Journal of Advertising Research*, January/February 1994, p. 28.

CHAPTER 14

1. Based on author interviews with Ferguson management. See also www.ferguson.com; "Customer Focused," *US Business Review*, May 2005, pp. 3–16.

2. "Why the Chinese Hate to Use Voice Mail," *Wall Street Journal*, December 1, 2005, p. B1ff.; "Mind Your Manners," *Inc.*, September 2005, p. 50; "Avoid Costly Missteps in Overseas Business," *Investor's Business Daily*, June 27, 2005, pp. A10–A11; "The Seoul Answer to Selling," *Going Global* (supplement to *Inc.*), March 1994; "AIG Sells Insurance in Shanghai, Testing Service Firms' Role," *Wall Street Journal*, July 21, 1993, p.A1; "Hungarians Seeking to Find a New Way Find Instead Amway," *Wall Street Journal*, January 15, 1993, p. A1; "The Secret to Northern's Japanese Success: When in Tokyo . . .," *Business Week*, July 27, 1992, p. 57; Paul A. Herbig and Hugh E. Kramer, "Do's and Don'ts of Cross-Cultural Negotiations," *Industrial Marketing Management*, November 1992, p. 287; Alan J. Dubinsky et al., "Differences in Motivational Perceptions among U.S., Japanese, and Korean Sales Personnel," *Journal of Business Research*, June 1994, p. 175; Carl R. Ruthstrom and Ken Matejka, "The Meanings of 'YES' in the Far East," *Industrial Marketing Management*, August 1990, p. 191.

3. "Shhh!" *Forbes*, November 24, 2003, p. 84; "Deliver More Value to Earn Loyalty," *Selling*, May 2003; "Hush: Improving NVH through Improved Material," *Automotive Design and Production*, July 2003, p. 42.

4. Judy A. Siguaw, Sheryl E. Kimes, and Jule B. Gassenheimer, "B2B Sales Force Productivity: Applications of Revenue Management Strategies to Sales Management," *Industrial Marketing Management*, October 2003, p. 539; William C. Moncrief, Greg W. Marshall, and Felicia G. Lassk, "A Contemporary Taxonomy of Sales Positions," *Journal of Personal Selling & Sales Management*, Winter 2006, p. 55; Eli Jones, Steven P. Brown, Andris A. Zoltners, and Barton A. Weitz, "The Changing Environment of Selling and Sales Management," *Journal of Personal Selling & Sales Management*, Spring 2005, p. 105; Simon J. Bell and James A. Luddington, "Coping with Customer Complaints," *Journal of Service Research*, February 2006, p. 221; Julie T. Johnson, Hiram C. Barksdale, Jr., and James S. Boles, "The Strategic Role of the Salesperson in Reducing Customer Defection in

Business Relationships," *Journal of Personal Selling & Sales Management,* Spring 2001, p. 123; Sandy D. Jap, "The Strategic Role of the Salesforce in Developing Customer Satisfaction across the Relationship Lifecycle," *Journal of Personal Selling & Sales Management,* Spring 2001, p. 95; John E. Swan, Cathy Goodwin, Michael A. Mayo, and Lynne D. Richardson, "Customer Identities: Customers as Commercial Friends, Customer Coworkers or Business Acquaintances," *Journal of Personal Selling & Sales Management,* Winter 2001, p. 29; Michael J. Dorsch, Les Carlson, Mary Anne Raymond, and Robert Ranson, "Customer Equity Management and Strategic Choices for Sales Managers," *Journal of Personal Selling & Sales Management,* Spring 2001, p. 157; Thomas W. Leigh, Ellen Bolman Pullins, and Lucette B. Comer, "The Top Ten Sales Articles of the 20th Century," *Journal of Personal Selling & Sales Management,* Summer 2001, p. 217; Thomas Tellefsen and Nermin Eyuboglu, "The Impact of a Salesperson's In-House Conflicts and Influence Attempts on Buyer Commitment," *Journal of Personal Selling & Sales Management,* November 2002, p. 157; William M. Strahle, Rosann L. Spiro, and Frank Acito, "Marketing and Sales: Strategic Alignment and Functional Implementation," *Journal of Personal Selling & Sales Management,* Winter 1996, p. 1; Jerome A. Colletti and Lawrence B. Chonko, "Change Management Initiatives: Moving Sales Organizations from Obsolescence to High Performance," *Journal of Personal Selling & Sales Management,* Spring 1997, p.1; Douglas M. Lambert, Howard Marmorstein, and Arun Sharma, "Industrial Salespeople as a Source of Market Information," *Industrial Marketing Management,* May 1990, p. 141.

5. "Bank of (Middle) America," *Fast Company,* March 2003, p. 104; "A French Bank Hits the Road," *Business Week,* November 17, 2003, p. 20; "NationsBank Asks Tellers to Branch Out," *Raleigh News & Observer,* September 12, 1993, p. 1F. See also "Forget 'May I Help You?'" *Wall Street Journal,* July 8, 2003, p. B1; "Service—with a Side of Sales," *Wall Street Journal Reports,* October 29, 2001, p. R13; Rita Marie Cain, "Federal Do Not Call Registry Is Here Stay: What's Next for Direct Marketing Regulation?" *Journal of Interactive Marketing,* Winter 2005, p. 54.

6. Glen Urban and John Hauser, "Now Is the Time to Advocate for Your Customers," *Listening In to Find Unmet Customer Needs and Solutions,* Center for eBusiness@MIT, MIT Sloan School of Management; "The Man Who Wanted a Live Operator," *Inc.,* February 2006, p. 30; "Finding the Best Cell Phone Service Requires a Bit of Research," *Investor's Business Daily,* December 6, 2005, p. A8; "T-Mobile's Novel Sell: Great Cell Service," *Advertising Age,* November 28, 2005, p. 12; "Service with a Smile. Really. How Technology Ruined Customer Service . . .," *Inc.,* October 2005, pp. 75–76; "For Happier Customers, Call HR," *Fortune,* November 28, 2005, p. 272; "Help (May Be) on the Way," *Wall Street Journal Reports,* March 21, 2005, p. R13ff.; "Customer Service via Machine," *Investor's Business Daily,* February 14, 2005, p. A10; "They're Off to See the Wizards," *New York Times,* January 27, 2005, p. E1ff.; "This Call Is Being Monitored," *Business 2.0,* July 2004, p. 63; "Pop-Up Sales Clerks: Web Sites Try the Hard Sell," *Wall Street Journal,* April 15, 2004, p. D1ff.; "Giving Buyers Better Information," *Investor's Business Daily,* February 2, 2004, p. A11; "Whatever Happened to Customer Service?" *USA Today,* September 26, 2003, p. 1Aff.; "Where the Customer Service Rep Is King," *Business 2.0,* June 2003, pp. 70–72; "The Annoying New Face of Customer Service," *Wall Street Journal,* January 21, 2003, p. D1ff.; "Specialized Training Can Improve Sales Force Focus," *Investor's Business Daily,* January 16, 2003, p. A7; "Joe Galli's Army," *Fortune,* December 30, 2002, p. 134; "Operator, I Demand an Automated Menu," *Wall Street Journal,* July 30, 2002, p. D1ff.; "Best Call Centers Stress Training, Track Results to Gauge Success," *Investor's Business Daily,* October 17, 2001, p. A1; Michael G. Harvey, Milorad M. Novicevic, Thomas Hench, and Matthew Myers, "Global Account Management: A Supply-Side Managerial View," *Industrial Marketing Management,* October 2003, p. 563; Roberta J. Schultz and Kenneth R. Evans, "Strategic Collaborative Communication by Key Account

Representatives," *Journal of Personal Selling & Sales Management,* Winter 2002, p. 23; Jim Blythe, "Using Trade Fairs in Key Account Management," *Industrial Marketing Management,* October 2002, p. 627; Sanjit Sengupta, Robert E. Krapfel, and Michael A. Pusateri, "An Empirical Investigation of Key Account Salesperson Effectiveness," *Journal of Personal Selling & Sales Management,* Fall 2000, p. 253; Catherine Pardo, "Key Account Management in the Business to Business Field: The Key Account's Point of View," *Journal of Personal Selling & Sales Management,* Fall 1997, p. 17; Sanjit Sengupta, Robert E. Krapfel, and Michael A. Pusateri, "Switching Costs in Key Account Relationships," *Journal of Personal Selling & Sales Management,* Fall 1997, p. 9; Mark A. Moon and Susan F. Gupta, "Examining the Formation of Selling Centers: A Conceptual Framework," *Journal of Personal Selling & Sales Management,* Spring 1997, p. 31.

7. "How to Remake Your Sales Force," *Fortune,* May 4, 1992, p. 98; "Apparel Makers Play Bigger Part on Sales Floor," *Wall Street Journal,* March 2, 1988, p. 31.

8. "The Task at Hand," *Beverage World,* December 15, 2003, p. 46; "Sales Force Effectiveness through E-Learning," *Pharmaceutical Executive,* October 2003, p. 106; "The Biggest Mouth in Silicon Valley," *Business 2.0,* September 2003, p. 107; "Software That's Actually Useful," *Sales & Marketing Management,* August 2003, p. 25; Scott M. Widmier, Donald W. Jackson, Jr., and Deborah Brown McCabe, "Infusing Technology into Personal Selling," *Journal of Personal Selling & Sales Management,* November 2002, p. 189; "Salespeople Say Automation Software Still Lacking," *Investor's Business Daily,* January 18, 2001, p. A4; "MarketSoft Tailors Products to Solve Problems," *Wall Street Journal,* November 30, 2000, p. B8; "New Software's Payoff? Happier Salespeople," *Investor's Business Daily,* May 23, 2000, p. A8; "Making the Sale," *Wall Street Journal,* November 15, 1999, p. R16; "Offices Goin' Mobile," *USA Today,* May 17, 1999, p. 3B.

9. Earl D. Honeycutt, Jr., Tanya Thelen, Shawn T. Thelen, and Sharon K. Hodge, "Impediments to Sales Force Automation," *Industrial Marketing Management,* May 2005, p. 313; Niels Schillewaert, Michael J. Ahearne, Ruud T. Frambach, and Rudy K. Moenaert, "The Adoption of Information Technology in the Sales Force," *Industrial Marketing Management,* May 2005, p. 323; Stephan F. Gohmann, Jian Guan, Robert M. Barker, and David J. Faulds, "Perceptions of Sales Force Automation: Differences between Sales Force and Management," *Industrial Marketing Management,* May 2005, p. 337; Deva Rangarajan, Eli Jones, and Wynne Chin, "Impact of Sales Force Automation on Technology-Related Stress, Effort, and Technology Usage among Salespeople," *Industrial Marketing Management,* May 2005, p. 345; George J. Avlonitis and Nikolaos G. Panagopoulos, "Antecedents and Consequences of CRM Technology Acceptance in the Sales Force," *Industrial Marketing Management,* May 2005, p. 355; Alan J. Bush, Jarvis B. Moore, and Rich Rocco, "Understanding Sales Force Automation Outcomes: A Managerial Perspective," *Industrial Marketing Management,* May 2005, p. 369; Richard E. Buehrer, Sylvain Senecal, and Ellen Bolman Pullins, "Sales Force Technology Usage—Reasons, Barriers, and Support: An Exploratory Investigation," *Industrial Marketing Management,* May 2005, p. 389; Leroy Robinson, Jr., Greg W. Marshall, and Miriam B. Stamps, "An Empirical Investigation of Technology Acceptance in a Field Sales Force Setting," *Industrial Marketing Management,* May 2005, p. 407; Devon S. Johnson and Sundar Bharadwaj, "Digitization of Selling Activity and Sales Force Performance: An Empirical Investigation," *Journal of the Academy of Marketing Science,* Winter 2005, p. 3; Thomas G. Brashear, Danny N. Bellenger, James S. Boles, and Hiram C. Barksdale, Jr., "An Exploratory Study of the Relative Effectiveness of Different Types of Sales Force Mentors," *Journal of Personal Selling & Sales Management,* Winter 2006, p. 7; Gary L. Hunter, "Information Overload: Guidance for Identifying When Information Becomes Detrimental to Sales Force Performance," *Journal of Personal Selling & Sales Management,* Spring 2004, p. 91; Amy J. Morgan and Scott A. Inks, "Technology and the Sales Force: Increasing Acceptance of Sales Force Automation," *Industrial Marketing Management,* July

2001, p. 463; Mary E. Shoemaker, "A Framework for Examining IT-Enabled Market Relationships," *Journal of Personal Selling & Sales Management*, Spring 2001, p. 177; Robert C. Erffmeyer and Dale A. Johnson, "An Exploratory Study of Sales Force Automation Practices: Expectations and Realities," *Journal of Personal Selling & Sales Management*, Spring 2001, p. 167; Cheri Speier and Viswanath Venkatesh, "The Hidden Minefields in the Adoption of Sales Force Automation Technologies," *Journal of Marketing*, July 2002, p. 98; Eli Jones, Suresh Sundaram, and Wynne Chin, "Factors Leading to Sales Force Automation Use: a Longitudinal Analysis," *Journal of Personal Selling & Sales Management*, November 2002, p. 145.

10. "Selling Salesmanship," *Business 2.0*, December 2002, p. 66; "The Art of the Sale," *Wall Street Journal*, January 11, 2001, p. B1.

11. See www.achievement.com/sales; M. Asri Jantan, Earl D. Honeycutt, Shawn T. Thelen, and ashraf M. Atria, "Managerial Perceptions of Sales Training and Performance," *Industrial Marketing Management*, October 2004, p. 667; Karen E. Flaherty and James M. Pappas, "Job Selection among Salespeople: A Bounded Rationality Perspective," *Industrial Marketing Management*, May 2004, p. 325; Anand Krishnamoorthy, Sanjog Misra, and Ashutosh Prasad, "Scheduling Sales Force Training: Theory and Evidence," *International Journal of Research in Marketing*, December 2005, p. 427; Ashraf M. Attia, Earl D. Honeycutt, Jr., and Mark P. Leach, "A Three-Stage Model for Assessing and Improving Sales Force Training and Development," *Journal of Personal Selling & Sales Management*, Summer 2005, p. 253; Mark P. Leach, Annie H. Liu, and Wesley J. Johnston, "The Role of Self-Regulation Training in Developing the Motivation Management Capabilities of Salespeople," *Journal of Personal Selling & Sales Management*, Summer 2005, p. 269; William L. Cron, Greg W. Marshall, Jagdip Singh, Rosann L. Spiro, and Harish Sujan, "Salesperson Selection, Training, and Development: Trends, Implications, and Research Opportunities," *Journal of Personal Selling & Sales Management*, Spring 2005, p. 123; G. Martin Izzo and Scott J. Vitell, "Exploring the Effects of Professional Education on Salespeople: The Case of Autonomous Agents," *Journal of Marketing Theory & Practice*, Fall 2003, p. 26; Brian P. Matthews and Tom Redman, "Recruiting the Wrong Salespeople: Are the Job Ads to Blame?" *Industrial Marketing Management*, October 2001, p. 541; R. Edward Bashaw, Thomas N. Ingram, and Bruce D. Keillor, "Improving Sales Training Cycle Times for New Trainees: An Exploratory Study," *Industrial Marketing Management*, July 2002, p. 329; Ellen Bolman Pullins and Leslie M. Fine, "How the Performance of Mentoring Activities Affects the Mentor's Job Outcomes," *Journal of Personal Selling & Sales Management*, Fall 2002, p. 259; Phillip H. Wilson, David Strutton, and M. Theodore Farris II, "Investigating the Perceptual Aspect of Sales Training," *Journal of Personal Selling & Sales Management*, Spring 2002, p. 77; Earl D. Honeycutt, Jr., Kiran Karande, Ashraf Attia, and Steven D. Maurer, "An Utility Based Framework for Evaluating the Financial Impact of Sales Force Training Programs," *Journal of Personal Selling & Sales Management*, Summer 2001, p. 229; Ellen B. Pullins, Leslie M. Fine, and Wendy L. Warren, "Identifying Peer Mentors in the Sales Force: An Exploratory Investigation of Willingness and Ability," *Journal of the Academy of Marketing Science*, Spring 1996, p. 125.

12. William H. Murphy, Peter A. Dacin, and Neil M. Ford, "Sales Contest Effectiveness: An Examination of Sales Contest Design Preferences of Field Sales Forces," *Journal of the Academy of Marketing Science*, Spring 2004, p. 127; Steven P. Brown, Kenneth R. Evans, Murali K. Mantrala, and Goutam Challagalla, "Adapting Motivation, Control, and Compensation Research to a New Environment," *Journal of Personal Selling & Sales Management*, Spring 2005, p. 156; Charles H. Schwepker, Jr., and David J. Good, "Marketing Control and Sales Force Customer Orientation," *Journal of Personal Selling & Sales Management*, Summer 2004, p. 167; Jeong Eun Park and George D. Deitz, "The Effect of Working Relationship Quality on Salesperson Performance and Job Satisfaction: Adaptive Selling Behavior in Korean Automobile Sales Representatives," *Journal of Business Research*, February 2006, p. 204; J. K. Sager, H. D. Strutton, and D. A. Johnson,

"Core Self-Evaluations and Salespeople," *Psychology & Marketing*, February 2006, p. 95; Ken Grant, David W. Cravens, George S. Low, and William C. Moncrief, "The Role of Satisfaction with Territory Design on the Motivation, Attitudes, and Work Outcomes of Salespeople," *Journal of the Academy of Marketing Science*, Spring 2001, p. 165; Balaji C. Krishnan, Richard G. Netemeyer, and James S. Boles, "Self-Efficacy, Competitiveness, and Efforts as Antecedents of Salesperson Performance," *Journal of Personal Selling & Sales Management*, Fall 2002, p. 285; Guangping Wang and Richard G. Netemeyer, "The Effects of Job Autonomy, Customer Demandingness, and Trait Competitiveness on Salesperson Learning, Self-Efficacy, and Performance," *Journal of the Academy of Marketing Science*, Summer 2002, p. 217; Joseph O. Rentz, C. David Shepherd, Armen Tashchian, Pratibha A. Dabholkar, and Robert T. Ladd, "A Measure of Selling Skill: Scale Development and Validation," *Journal of Personal Selling & Sales Management*, Winter 2002, p. 13.

13. Sridhar N. Ramaswami and Jagdip Singh, "Antecedents and Consequences of Merit Pay Fairness for Industrial Salespeople," *Journal of Marketing*, October 2003, p. 46; Sunil Erevelles, Indranil Dutta, and Carolyn Galantine, "Sales Force Compensation Plans Incorporating Multidimensional Sales Effort and Salesperson Efficiency," *Journal of Personal Selling & Sales Management*, Spring 2004, p. 101; "The Sales Commission Dilemma," *Inc.*, May 2003, p. 49; "Creating Incentives Down in Ranks: Marriott Ties Pay to Guest Replies," *Investor's Business Daily*, July 6, 2001, p. A1; "Get Great Results from Salespeople by Finding What Really Moves Them," *Investor's Business Daily*, July 2, 2001, p. A1; "Medical Gear Sales Force Works on Commission," *Investor's Business Daily*, July 25, 2000, p. A14; R. Venkatesh, Goutam Challagalla, and Ajay K. Kohli, "Heterogeneity in Sales Districts: Beyond Individual-Level Predictors of Satisfaction and Performance," *Journal of the Academy of Marketing Science*, Summer 2001, p. 238; Ellen Bolman Pullins, "An Exploratory Investigation of the Relationship of Sales Force Compensation and Intrinsic Motivation," *Industrial Marketing Management*, July 2001, p. 403; Sridhar N. Ramaswami and Jagdip Singh, "Antecedents and Consequences of Merit Pay Fairness for Industrial Salespeople," *Journal of Marketing*, October 2003, p. 46; Goutam Ghallagalla, "Supervisory Orientations and Salesperson Work Outcomes: The Moderating Effect of Salesperson Location," *Journal of Personal Selling & Sales Management*, Summer 2000, p. 161; Kissan Joseph and Manohar U. Kalwani, "The Role of Bonus Pay in Salesforce Compensation Plans," *Industrial Marketing Management*, March 1998, p. 147.

14. "New Software's Payoff? Happier Salespeople," *Investor's Business Daily*, May 23, 2000, p. A8.

15. Eric G. Harris, John C. Mowen, and Tom J. Brown, "Re-examining Salesperson Goal Orientations: Personal Influencers, Customer Orientation, and Work Satisfaction," *Journal of the Academy of Marketing Science*, Winter 2005, p. 19; Dominique Rouziès, Erin Anderson, Ajay K. Kohli, Ronald E. Michaels, Barton A. Weitz, and Andris A. Zoltners, "Sales and Marketing Integration: A Proposed Framework," *Journal of Personal Selling & Sales Management*, Spring 2005, p. 113; Eric Fang, Kenneth R. Evans, and Shaoming Zou, "The Moderating Effect of Goal-Setting Characteristics on the Sales Control Systems-Job Performance Relationship," *Journal of Business Research*, September 2005, p. 1214; Kenneth B. Kahn, Richard C. Reizenstein, and Joseph O. Rentz, "Sales-Distribution Interfunctional Climate and Relationship Effectiveness," *Journal of Business Research*, October 2004, p. 1085; Rolph E. Anderson and Wen-yeh Huang, "Empowering Salespeople: Personal, Managerial, and Organizational Perspectives," *Psychology & Marketing*, February 2006, p. 139; Thomas G. Brashear, James S. Boles, Danny N. Bellenger, and Charles M. Brooks, "An Empirical Test of Trust-Building Processes and Outcomes in Sales Manager-Salesperson Relationships," *Journal of the Academy of Marketing Science*, Spring 2003, p. 189; Andrea L. Dixon, Rosann L. Spiro, and Lukas P. Forbes, "Attributions and Behavioral Intentions of Inexperienced Salespersons to Failure: An Empirical Investigation," *Journal of the Academy of Marketing Science*, Fall 2003, p. 459; Mark C.

Johlke, Dale F. Duhan, Roy D. Howell, and Robert W. Wilkes, "An Integrated Model of Sales Managers' Communication Practices," *Journal of the Academy of Marketing Science*, Spring 2000, p. 263; Dominique Rouzies and Anne Macquin, "An Exploratory Investigation of the Impact of Culture on Sales Force Management Control Systems in Europe," *Journal of Personal Selling & Sales Management*, Winter 2002–2003, p. 61; Scott B. MacKenzie, Philip M. Podsakoff, and Gregory A. Rich, "Transformational and Transactional Leadership and Salesperson Performance," *Journal of the Academy of Marketing Science*, Spring 2001, p. 115; Cengiz Yilmaz and Shelby D. Hunt, "Salesperson Cooperation: The Influence of Relational, Task, Organizational, and Personal Factors," *Journal of the Academy of Marketing Science*, Fall 2001, p. 335; Richard L. Oliver and Erin Anderson, "An Empirical Test of the Consequences of Behavior- and Outcome-Based Sales Control Systems," *Journal of Marketing*, October 1994, p. 53; Steven P. Brown and Robert A. Peterson, "The Effect of Effort on Sales Performance and Job Satisfaction," *Journal of Marketing*, April 1994, p. 70; Frederick A. Russ, Kevin M. McNeilly, and James M. Comer, "Leadership, Decision Making and Performance of Sales Managers: A Multi-Level Approach," *Journal of Personal Selling & Sales Management*, Summer 1996, p. 1; Douglas N. Behrman and William D. Perreault, Jr., "A Role Stress Model of the Performance and Satisfaction of Industrial Salespersons," *Journal of Marketing*, Fall 1984, p. 9.

16. "Chief Executives Are Increasingly Chief Salesmen," *Wall Street Journal*, August 6, 1991, p. B1; Joe F. Alexander, Patrick L. Schul, and Emin Babakus, "Analyzing Interpersonal Communications in Industrial Marketing Negotiations," *Journal of the Academy of Marketing Science*, Spring 1991, p. 129.

17. Michael G. Harvey, Milorad M. Novicevic, Thomas Hench, and Matthew Myers, "Global Account Management: A Supply-Side Managerial View," *Industrial Marketing Management*, October 2003, p. 563; Eli Jones, Andrea L. Dixon, Lawrence B. Chonko, and Joseph P. Cannon, "Key Accounts and Team Selling: A Review, Framework, and Research Agenda," *Journal of Personal Selling & Sales Management*, Spring 2005, p. 182; Dennis B. Arnett, Barry A. Macy, and James B. Wilcox, "The Role of Core Selling Teams in Supplier-Buyer Relationships," *Journal of Personal Selling & Sales Management*, Winter 2005, p. 27; Kirk Smith, Eli Jones, and Edward Blair, "Managing Salesperson Motivation in a Territory Realignment," *Journal of Personal Selling & Sales Management*, Fall 2000, p. 215; Andris A. Zoltners, "Sales Territory Alignment: An Overlooked Productivity Tool," *Journal of Personal Selling & Sales Management*, Summer 2000, p. 139; Ken Grant, "The Role of Satisfaction with Territory Design on the Motivation, Attitudes, and Work Outcomes of Salespeople," *Journal of the Academy of Marketing Science*, Spring 2001, p. 165.

18. "How to Get Your Company Where You Want It," *The American Salesman*, December 2003, p. 12; "When Should I Give Up on a Sales Prospect?" *Inc.*, May 1998, p. 129. See also Sean Dwyer, John Hill, and Warren Martin, "An Empirical Investigation of Critical Success Factors in the Personal Selling Process for Homogenous Goods," *Journal of Personal Selling & Sales Management*, Summer 2000, p. 151; Doris C. Van Doren and Thomas A. Stickney, "How to Develop a Database for Sales Leads," *Industrial Marketing Management*, August 1990, p. 201.

19. "Novartis' Marketing Doctor," *Business Week*, March 5, 2001, p. 56.

20. For more on sales presentation approaches, see "Firing Up Your Cold Calls," *Business 2.0*, December 2005, pp. 60–65; "Trapped in the Sales Presentation from Hell," *Information Week*, November 10, 2003, p. 122; "Advise and Conquer," *Brandweek*, May 14, 2001, p. 1; "Rick Francolini, TV Guide," *Brandweek*, October 25, 1999, p. 22; "The 60-Second Sales Pitch," *Inc.*, October 1994, p. 87. See also Daniel M. Eveleth and Linda Morris, "Adaptive Selling in a Call Center Environment: A Qualitative Investigation," *Journal of Interactive Marketing*, Winter 2002, p. 25; Thomas W. Leigh and John O. Summers, "An Initial Evaluation of Industrial Buyers' Impressions of Salespersons' Nonverbal Cues," *Journal of Personal Selling & Sales Management*, Winter 2002, p. 41; Kalyani Menon and Laurette Dube, "Ensuring Greater Satisfaction by Engineering Salesperson Response to Customer Emotions," *Journal of Retailing*, Fall 2000, p. 285; Susan K. DelVecchio, James E. Zemanek, Roger P. McIntyre, and Reid P. Claxton, "Buyers' Perceptions of Salesperson Tactical Approaches," *Journal of Personal Selling & Sales Management*, Winter 2002–2003, p. 39; Alfred M. Pelham, "An Exploratory Model and Initial Test of the Influence of Firm Level Consulting-Oriented Sales Force Programs on Sales Force Performance," *Journal of Personal Selling & Sales Management*, Spring 2002, p. 97; Annie H. Liu and Mark P. Leach, "Developing Loyal Customers with a Value-Adding Sales Force: Examining Customer Satisfaction and the Perceived Credibility of Consultative Salespeople," *Journal of Personal Selling & Sales Management*, Spring 2001, p. 147; Richard S. Jacobs, Kenneth R. Evans, Robert E. Kleine III, and Timothy D. Landry, "Disclosure and Its Reciprocity as Predictors of Key Outcomes of an Initial Sales Encounter," *Journal of Personal Selling & Sales Management*, Winter 2001, p. 51; Gary L. Frankwick, Stephen S. Porter, and Lawrence A. Crosby, "Dynamics of Relationship Selling: A Longitudinal Examination of Changes in Salesperson-Customer Relationship Status," *Journal of Personal Selling & Sales Management*, Spring 2001, p. 135; Willemijn van Dolen, Jos Lemmink, Ko de Ruyter, and Ad de Jong, "Customer-Sales Employee Encounters: A Dyadic Perspective," *Journal of Retailing*, Winter 2002, p. 265; Nancy M. Puccinelli, "Putting Your Best Face Forward: The Impact of Customer Mood on Salesperson Evaluation," *Journal of Consumer Psychology*, 2006, p. 156; Thomas E. DeCarlo, "The Effects of Sales Message and Suspicion of Ulterior Motives on Salesperson Evaluation," *Journal of Consumer Psychology*, 2005, p. 238; Amy Sallee and Karen Flaherty, "Enhancing Salesperson Trust: An Examination of Managerial Values, Empowerment, and the Moderating Influence of SBU Strategy," *Journal of Personal Selling & Sales Management*, Fall 2003, p. 299; Geok Theng Lau and Hsueh Wei Chin, "Trustworthiness of Salespeople in the Business-to-Business Market: The Five C's," *Journal of Business-to-Business Marketing*, 2003, p. 1; Tará Burnthorne, Jon Carr, Brian T. Gregory, and Sean Dwyer, "The Influence of Psychological Climate on the Salesperson Customer Orientation-Salesperson Performance Relationship," *Journal of Marketing Theory & Practice*, Spring 2005, p. 59; J. David Lichtenthal and Stephen A. Goodwin, "Product Attributes for Business Markets: Implications for Selling and Sales Management," *Psychology & Marketing*, March 2006, p. 225; C. David Shepherd, Sarah F. Gardial, Michael G. Johnson, and Joseph O. Rentz, "Cognitive Insights into the Highly Skilled or Expert Salesperson," *Psychology & Marketing*, February 2006, p. 115.

21. For more on pharmaceutical company selling tactics, see "Side Effects: As Drug-Sales Teams Multiply, Doctors Start to Tune Them Out," *Wall Street Journal*, June 13, 2003, p. A1; "New Prescription: Its Rivals in Funk, Novartis Finds a Way to Thrive," *Wall Street Journal*, August 23, 2002, p. A1; "Swallow This: How Drug Makers Use Pharmacies to Push Pricey Pills," *Wall Street Journal*, May 1, 2002, p. A1; "Sorry, Doc, No Dinners-to-Go," *Wall Street Journal*, April 23, 2002, p. D4; "More than Ads, Drug Makers Rely on Sales Reps," *Wall Street Journal*, March 14, 2002, p. B1; "Pushing Pills: Drug Firms' Incentives to Pharmacists in India Fuel Mounting Abuse," *Wall Street Journal*, August 16, 2001, p. A1; "Doctors Step Out; Drug Salesmen Step In," *USA Today*, July 5, 2001, p. 11A; "Sales Pitch: Drug Firms Use Perks to Push Pills," *USA Today*, May 16, 2001, p. 1B. For more on Oracle's selling tactics, see "Learning to Be a Great Host," *Business 2.0*, May 2003, p. 70; "Oracle Puts Priority on Customer Service," *Wall Street Journal*, January 21, 2003, p. B5; "Out of Control," *Business 2.0*, August 2002, p. 38. See also Jay Prakash Mulki, Fernando Jaramillo, and William B. Locander, "Effects of Ethical Climate and Supervisory Trust on Salesperson's Job Attitudes and Intentions to Quit," *Journal of Personal Selling & Sales Management*, Winter 2006, p. 19; Terry W. Loe and William A. Weeks, "An Experimental Investigation of Efforts to Improve Sales Students' Moral Reasoning,"

Journal of Personal Selling & Sales Management, Fall 2000, p. 243; Lawrence B. Chonko, Thomas R. Wotruba, and Terry W. Loe, "Direct Selling Ethics at the Top: an Industry Audit and Status Report," *Journal of Personal Selling & Sales Management*, Spring 2002, p. 87; Eugene Sivadas, Susan Bardi Kleiser, James Kellaris, and Robert Dahlstrom, "Moral Philosophy, Ethical Evaluations, and Sales Manager Hiring Intentions," *Journal of Personal Selling & Sales Management*, Winter 2002–2003, p. 7; John Cherry and John Fraedrich, "Perceived Risk, Moral Philosophy and Marketing Ethics: Mediating Influences on Sales Managers' Ethical Decision-Making," *Journal of Business Research*, December 2002, p. 951; Bulent Menguc, "Organizational Consequences, Marketing Ethics and Salesforce Supervision: Further Empirical Evidence," *Journal of Business Ethics*, March 1998, p. 333; David Strutton, J. B. I. Hamilton, and James R. Lumpkin, "An Essay on When to Fully Disclose in Sales Relationships: Applying Two Practical Guidelines for Addressing Truth-Telling Problems," *Journal of Business Ethics*, April 1997, p. 545; Lawrence B. Chonko, John F. Tanner, and William A. Weeks, "Ethics in Salesperson Decision Making: A Synthesis of Research Approaches and an Extension of the Scenario Method," *Journal of Personal Selling & Sales Management*, Winter 1996, p. 35.

CHAPTER 15

1. "Subway Corporate Grabs for Advertising Control: Franchisees Wary of Power Play," April 24, 2006, at www.adage.com; "Subway Teams with Discovery Kids to Reach Children," *Nation's Restaurant News*, January 9, 2006, p. 12; "It's Lunchtime and Jared from Subway Is on the Phone," Associated Press State & Local Wire, December 27, 2005; "Subway Announces 3-Year Little League Baseball and Softball Sponsorship, Reflects Chain's Dual Focus on Good Nutrition and Physical Activity," *PR Newswire US*, August 20, 2005; "Subway Targets Teen Appetites," *Connecticut Post*, May 17, 2005; "Subway Lets Local Tastes Guide New Products," *Advertising Age*, May 16, 2005, p. 14; "Subway Will Shed Fallon Worldwide," *Wall Street Journal*, May 25, 2004, p. B4; "Subway to Sell Kids Pak Meal That Focuses on Health," *USA Today*, September 26, 2003, p. 1B; "Subway Orders Weightier Campaign," *Wall Street Journal*, August 21, 2003, p. B6; "Creative: Ordinary People," *Adweek*, August 11, 2003, p. 24; "Fast-Food Firms' Big Budgets Don't Buy Consumer Loyalty," *Wall Street Journal*, July 24, 2003, p. B4; "Fallon Takes Home Subway after All-Star Shootout," *Adweek*, July 21, 2003, p. 7; "Marketers of the Year: Subway, in Search of Fresh Ideas," *Brandweek*, October 15, 2001, pp. M54–M63.

2. See Carolyn A. Lin, "Cultural Values Reflected in Chinese and American Television Advertising," *Journal of Advertising*, Winter 2001, p. 83; Christophe Collard, Michael Pustay, Christophe Roquilly, and Asghar Zardkoohi, "Competitive Cross-Couponing: A Comparison of French and U.S. Perspectives," *Journal of Public Policy & Marketing*, Spring 2001, p. 64; Charles R. Taylor, Gordon E. Miracle, and R. D. Wilson, "The Impact of Information Level on the Effectiveness of U.S. and Korean Television Commercials," *Journal of Advertising*, Spring 1997, p. 1; Ann M. Barry, "Advertising and Culture: Theoretical Perspectives," *Journal of the Academy of Marketing Science*, Winter 1998, p. 67; Ronald E. Taylor, Mariea G. Hoy, and Eric Haley, "How French Advertising Professionals Develop Creative Strategy," *Journal of Advertising*, Spring 1996, p. 1; Nan Zhou and Mervin Y. T. Chen, "A Content Analysis of Men and Women in Canadian Consumer Magazine Advertising: Today's Portrayal, Yesterday's Image?" *Journal of Business Ethics*, April 1997, p. 485; Yong Zhang and Betsy D. Gelb, "Matching Advertising Appeals to Culture: The Influence of Products' Use Conditions," *Journal of Advertising*, Fall 1996, p. 29; John L. Graham, Michael A. Kamins, and Djoko S. Oetomo, "Content Analysis of German and Japanese Advertising in Print Media from Indonesia, Spain, and the United States," *Journal of Advertising*, June 1993, p. 5.

3. See "Global Marketing," *Advertising Age* (special issue), November 14, 2005, at www.adage.com.

4. For more on advertising to sales ratios, see "2005 Advertising to Sales Ratios for 200 Largest Ad Spending Industries," from Schonfeld & Associates, Inc., *Advertising Ratios & Budgets*, 29th edition, at www.adage.com. For more on spending by top advertisers, see "2006 Fact Pack," *Advertising Age*, February 27, 2006, p. 10; "Top 100 Global Marketers," *Advertising Age*, November 14, 2005, pp. 4, 29; "100 Leading National Advertisers," *Advertising Age*, June 27, 2005, p. 4 (all at www.adage.com).

5. "2006 Fact Pack," *Advertising Age*, February 27, 2006, p. 10; and various "Insider's Reports" by Robert Coen of Universal McCann.

6. Exact data on this industry are elusive, but see U.S. Bureau of the Census, *Statistical Abstract of the United States 2006* (Washington, DC: U.S. Government Printing Office, 2005), p. 418. See also "Boom and Gloom: End May Be Near," *Advertising Age*, July 4, 2005, p. 1ff.; "My Job Search," *Adweek*, January 12, 2004, p. 34; "Despite Slump, Students Flock to Ad Schools," *Wall Street Journal*, October 14, 2003, p. B1; "Ads Rebound, but Jobs Don't," *Advertising Age*, August 4, 2003, p. 1.

7. "Viral Hall of Fame 2006: #1: Peerflix Paparazzi," *Marketing Sherpa*, http://marketingsherpa.com/vas2006/1.html. See also www.tacobell.com.

8. For more on Dryel, see "Putting Home Dry-Cleaning Products to the Test," *Wall Street Journal*, January 12, 2006, p. D5; "The Dirt on At-Home Dry Cleaning," *Wall Street Journal*, September 15, 2000, p. W14. See also "Industry Wrestles with Comparative Ads," *Advertising Age*, October 27, 2003, p.10; "Sour Dough: Pizza Hut v. Papa John's," *Brandweek*, May 21, 2001, p. 26; "Irate Firms Take Comparisons to Court," *Wall Street Journal*, December 22, 1999, p. B8; "Survey: Comparative Ads Can Dent Car's Credibility," *Advertising Age*, May 4, 1998, p. 26. For more on AT&T, MCI, and Sprint's comparative ads, see "Best Phone Discounts Go to Hardest Bargainers," *Wall Street Journal*, February 13, 1997, p. B1; "Fighting for Customers Gets Louder," *USA Today*, January 9, 1995, p. 1B. For other examples of comparative advertising, see "Allergy Drugs Wage a Bitter War of the Noses," *Wall Street Journal*, May 23, 1996, p. B1; "New Drug Ads Give Doctors Heartburn," *Wall Street Journal*, April 25, 1996, p. B9. See also Debora Viana Thompson and Rebecca W. Hamilton, "The Effects of Information Processing Mode on Consumers' Responses to Comparative Advertising," *Journal of Consumer Research*, March 2006, p. 530; Robert D. Jewell, H. Rao Unnava, David Glen Mick, and Merrie L. Brucks, "When Competitive Interference Can Be Beneficial," *Journal of Consumer Research*, September 2003, p. 283; Michael J. Barone, Kay M. Palan, and Paul W. Miniard, "Brand Usage and Gender as Moderators of the Potential Deception Associated with Partial Comparative Advertising," *Journal of Advertising*, Spring 2004, p. 19; Gerd Bohner, Sabine Einwiller, Hans-Peter Herb, and Frank Siebler, "When Small Means Comfortable: Relations between Product Attributes in Two-Sided Advertising," *Journal of Consumer Psychology*, 2003, p. 454; Paschalina Ziamou and S. Ratneshwar, "Innovations in Product Functionality: When and Why Are Explicit Comparisons Effective?" *Journal of Marketing*, April 2003, p. 49; Patrick Meirick, "Cognitive Responses to Negative and Comparitive Political Advertising," *Journal of Advertising*, Spring 2002, p. 49; Bruce E. Pinkleton, Nam-Hyun Um, and Erica Weintraub Austin, "An Exploration of the Effects of Negative Political Advertising on Political Decision Making," *Journal of Advertising*, Spring 2002, p. 13; Diana L. Haytko, "Great Advertising Campaigns: Goals and Accomplishments," *Journal of Marketing*, April 1995, p. 113; Carolyn Tripp, "Services Advertising: An Overview and Summary of Research, 1980–1995," *Journal of Advertising*, Winter 1997, p. 21; Thomas E. Barry, "Comparative Advertising: What Have We Learned in Two Decades?" *Journal of Advertising Research*, March/April 1993, p. 19.

9. "Feature: Cause Marketing," *Advertising Age*, June 13, 2005, pp. 31–35; "The Selling of Breast Cancer," *Business 2.0*, February 2003, p. 88; "Seeking Cause and Effect," *Brandweek*, November 11, 2002, p. 18; "Brands Step Up to Battle Breast Cancer," *USA Today*, September 5, 2001, p. 3B; "Spiffing up the Corporate Image," *For-*

tune, July 21, 1986, p. 68. See also Amitav Chakravarti and Chris Janiszewski, "The Influence of Generic Advertising on Brand Preferences," *Journal of Consumer Research*, March 2004, p. 487; T. Bettina Cornwell, Donald P. Roy, and Edward A. Steinard II, "Exploring Managers' Perceptions of the Impact of Sponsorship on Brand Equity," *Journal of Advertising*, Summer 2001, p. 41; Michael J. Barone, Anthony D. Miyazaki, and Kimberly A. Taylor, "The Influence of Cause-Related Marketing on Consumer Choice: Does One Good Turn Deserve Another?" *Journal of the Academy of Marketing Science*, Spring 2000, p. 248; Minette E. Drumwright, "Company Advertising With a Social Dimension: The Role of Noneconomic Criteria," *Journal of Marketing*, October 1996, p. 71; Eric Haley, "Exploring the Construct of Organization as Source: Consumer's Understandings of Organizational Sponsorship of Advocacy Advertising," *Journal of Advertising*, Summer 1996, p. 19.

10. For more on Got Milk campaign (and others), see "Got Milk? (Got Mess)," *Brandweek*, April 19, 2004, pp. 36–43. For more on Wendy's, see "The Year in 2003—Review," *Nation's Restaurant News*, December 22, 2003, p. 51. For more on Cadillac, see "Cadillac Steers Dealers toward Unified Messages," *Brandweek*, October 6, 2003, p. 77. For more on Benetton, see "Store Owners Rip into Benetton," *Advertising Age*, February 6, 1995, p. 1; "Benetton, German Retailers Squabble," *Advertising Age*, February 6, 1995, p. 46. For more on Intel, see "Intel Inside at 10," *Advertising Age*, April 30, 2001, p. 4; "Coop Crossroads," *Advertising Age*, November 15, 1999, p. 1. For more on GM, see "Still Pulling the Strings, but Locally, Too," *Brandweek*, April 17, 2000, p. 34; "GM Dealers Rebel against Local Ad Structure," *Advertising Age*, January 24, 2000, p. 3. See also Steffen Jorgensen, Simon Pierre Sigue, and Georges Zaccour, "Dynamic Cooperative Advertising in a Channel," *Journal of Retailing*, Spring 2000, p. 71.

11. For more on co-op ads, see "Nestlé Warns Stores: Prove It or Lose Out," *Advertising Age*, September 13, 2004, pp. 1, 52; "Appeals Court Rules against Pork Council," *Advertising Age*, October 27, 2003, p. 4; "Big Blue Offers Solutions with $60 Mil Co-op Effort," *Advertising Age*, April 30, 2001, p. 8; "Revlon Plans Another Makeover," *Wall Street Journal*, November 21, 2000, p. B1; "Joint Marketing with Retailers Spreads," *Wall Street Journal*, October 24, 1996, p. B6; "H&R Block, Excedrin Discover Joint Promotions Can Be Painless," *Wall Street Journal*, February 28, 1991, p. B3; John P. Murry and Jan B. Heide, "Managing Promotion Program Participation Within Manufacturer-Retailer Relationships," *Journal of Marketing*, January 1998, p. 58.

12. "Brands in the 'Hood," *Point*, December 2005, pp. 19–21; "TV's New Parallel Universe," *Business Week*, November 14, 2005, pp. 72–74; "As Podcasts Boom, Big Media Rushes to Stake a Claim," *Wall Street Journal*, October 10, 2005, p. A1ff.; "Advertisers Forced to Think Way Outside the Box," *USA Today*, June 20, 2005, p. 5B: "Non-Traditional Media Gain Ground, Consumers," *USA Today*, March 14, 2005, p. 3D;" "The Vanishing Mass Market," *Business Week*, July 12, 2004, pp. 60–72; "Nightmare on Madison Avenue," *Fortune*, June 28, 2004, pp. 92–108. For more on videogame medium, see "Guess What's Hiding in Your Videogame," *Wall Street Journal*, July 265, 2005, p. D1ff.; "Online Gaming," *Adweek*, May 16, 2005, pp. SR30–SR40; "Videogame Makers Borrow TV's Tactics for Selling Ads," *Wall Street Journal*, October 18, 2004, p. B5; "Ads in Videogames Pose a New Threat to Media Industry," *Wall Street Journal*, July 28, 2004, p. A1ff. For more on cell phone medium, see "Commercials by Cellphone," *Wall Street Journal*, August 22, 2005, p. B1ff.; "Your Favorite TV Show Is Calling," *Business Week*, January 17, 2005, p. 37. For more on in-store medium, see "In a Shift, Marketers Beef Up Ad Spending inside Stores," *Wall Street Journal*, September 21, 2005, p. A1ff.; "Is Wal-Mart TV a Smart Buy or a Defensive One?" *Advertising Age*, September 19, 2005, pp. 3, 49; For more on the Yellow Pages medium, see "Print Yellow Pages Are Still Profitable," *Wall Street Journal*, May 22, 2000, p. B16; Gerald L. Lohse and Dennis L. Rosen, "Signaling Quality and Credibility in Yellow Pages Advertising: The

Influence of Color and Graphics on Choice," *Journal of Advertising*, Summer 2001, p. 73. For more on the outdoor medium, see "Going Outside, Beyond the Billboard," *Wall Street Journal*, July 21, 2005, p. B3; "Outdoor Looks to the Age of Electronic Billboards," *Adweek*, May 9, 2005, p. 12; "The Signs They Are A-Changin'," *Business Week*, September 20, 2004, p. 60. See also Charles R. Taylor and John C. Taylor, "Regulatory Issues in Ourdoor Advertising: A Content Analysis of Billboards," *Journal of Public Policy & Marketing*, Spring 1994, p. 97. For more on the radio medium, see "The New Radio Revolution: From Satellite to Podcasts . . .," *Business Week*, March 14, 2005, pp. 32–35; "Sending Fans a Clear Signal," *Brandweek*, January 31, 2005, pp. 20–24. For more on the newspaper medium, see "Special Report: Newspapers," *Advertising Age*, April 29, 2002, pp. S1–S7; "How Newspaper Overcame Loss of Big Advertisers," *Wall Street Journal*, January 25, 2002, p. A13. See also Srini S. Srinivasan, Robert P. Leone, and Francis J. Mulhern, "The Advertising Exposure Effect of Free Standing Inserts," *Journal of Advertising*, Spring 1995, p. 29; Karen W. King, Leonard N. Reid, and Margaret Morrison, "Large-Agency Media Specialists' Opinions on Newspaper Advertising for National Accounts," *Journal of Advertising*, Summer 1997, p. 1. For more on the magazine medium, see "Magazine Editors Buck Marketers," *Wall Street Journal*, October 17, 2005, p. B3; "Blurring the Line," *Wall Street Journal*, August 9, 2004, p. B1ff.; "Adweek Magazines Special Report," *Adweek*, October 13, 2003, pp. SR1–SR22. For more on the television and cable medium, see "TV Ad Rules Are Challenged by Pod Busters," *Wall Street Journal*, November 21, 2005, p. B1ff.; "How to Watch TV," *Wall Street Journal*, November 9, 2005, p. D1ff.; "Hey, Advertisers, TiVo Is Your Friend," *Business Week*, October 17, 2005, pp. 97–98; "New Ways to Drive Home the Message," *Newsweek*, May 30, 2005, pp. 56–58; "Cable's Big Bet on Hyper-Targeting," *Business Week*, July 4, 2005, pp. 58–59; "Pay Per View Comes Full Circle," *Wall Street Journal*, April 1, 2005, p. B3; "The Man Who Can Save Advertising," *Business 2.0*, November 2004, pp. 119–28; "Can Mad Ave. Make Zap-Proof Ads?" *Business Week*, February 2, 2004; "Special Report: Cable TV," *Advertising Age*, June 9, 2003, pp. S1–S14; Ali M. Kanso and Richard Alan Nelson, "Internet and Magazine Advertising: Integrated Partnerships or Not?" *Journal of Advertising Research*, December 2004, p. 317; Yuhmiin Chang and Esther Thorson, "Television and Web Advertising Synergies," *Journal of Advertising*, Summer 2004, p. 75; Fareena Sultan and Andrew Rohm, "The Coming Era of Brand in the Hand Marketing," *MIT Sloan Management Review*, Fall 2005, p. 83; James R. Coyle and Esther Thorson, "The Effects of Progressive Levels of Interactivity and Vividness in Web Marketing Sites," *Journal of Advertising*, Fall 2001, p. 65; Mandeep Singh, Siva K. Balasubramanian, and Goutam Chakraborty, "A Comparative Analysis of Three Communication Formats: Advertising, Infomercial, and Direct Experience," *Journal of Advertising*, Winter 2000, p. 59.

13. "Staid U.S. Marketers Try Racier Ads," *Wall Street Journal*, July 31, 2003, p. B6; "A Leap for Advertising," *Adweek*, June 16, 2003, p. 28; "Sex-Themed Ads Often Don't Travel Well," *Wall Street Journal*, March 31, 2000, p. B7; "Underwear Ads Caught in Bind over Sex Appeal," *Advertising Age*, July 8, 1996, p. 27.

14. "Looking for Mr. Plumber," *MediaWeek*, June 27, 1994, p. 7; "Those Really Big Shows Are Often Disappointing to Those Who Advertise," *Wall Street Journal*, June 14, 1994, p. B1.

15. V. Kumar, Rajkumar Venkatesan, and Werner Reinartz, "Knowing What to Sell, When, and to Whom," *Harvard Business Review*, March 2006, pp. 1–9; Jacquelyn S. Thomas, Werner Reinartz, and V. Kumar, "Getting the Most Out of All Your Customers," *Harvard Business Review*, July–August, 2004, pp. 1–9.

16. For more on ATM ads, see "Ads on Automated Teller Machines Multiply as Technology Improves," *Investor's Business Daily*, October 5, 2000, p. A6. For more on Nascar ads, see "America's Fastest Growing Sport," *Fortune*, September 5, 2005, pp. 48–63; "Sponsored by . . . SomethingAde," *Business 2.0*, October 2004, p. 162; "Hotel Rides with Race Fans," *USA Today*, November 4, 2003, p. 3B;

"The Changing Face of Nascar," *USA Today* (Bonus Section E), August 29, 2003; "Space for Rent," *Brandweek*, June 2, 2003, p. 30. See also Stephen W. Pruitt, T. Bettina Cornwell, and John M. Clark, "The NASCAR Phenomenon: Auto Racing Sponsorships and Shareholder Wealth," *Journal of Advertising Research*, September 2004, p. 281; Nora J. Rifon, Sejung Marina Choi, Carrie S. Trimble, and Hairong Li, "Congruence Effects in Sponsorship," *Journal of Advertising*, Spring 2004, p. 29; Shelly Rodgers, "The Effects of Sponsor Relevance on Consumer Reactions to Internet Sponsorships," *Journal of Advertising*, Winter 2004, p. 67.

17. "Pet Sounds: Purina Hopes to Boost Its Brand Loyalty with Podcasts, *Wall Street Journal*, June 29, 2005, B2A; "Cell Phone Ads that Consumers Love," *Harvard Business School Working Knowledge*, February 28, 2005; Rama Yelkur, Chuck Tomkovick, and Patty Traczyk, "Super Bowl Advertising Effectiveness: Hollywood Finds the Games Golden," *Journal of Advertising Research*, March 2004, p. 143.

18. "10 Rules to Make Ads Magical," *USA Today*, February 3, 2006, p. 1Bff.; "Media Outlook 2006," *Adweek*, September 26, 2005, p. SR4; "Loving Raymond to the Tune of $1.3M: Fox Asks $1.2M for Spot in Idol Finale," *Advertising Age*, April 18, 2005, p. 1ff.

19. "Rated M for Mad Ave," *Business Week Online*, February 27, 2006; "Ads, Ads, Everywhere." *ABC News Online*, January 19, 2006; "Advertisers Find a Captive Audience: Travelers on Planes," Wall Street Journal, December 20, 2005, p. B1ff.; "Film Fans Can Expect More Advertising on Big Screen," USA Today, December 6, 2005, p. 1Bff.; "Subject: Email Ads Grow Up," *Wall Street Journal*, November 23, 2005, p. B1ff.; "Advertising: Anywhere, Anytime," *Wall Street Journal*, November 21, 2005, p. R6; "Art Meets Ads: Can Sculpture Sell Moisturizer?" *Wall Street Journal*, October 25, 2005, p. B7; "Best Appliance in a Supporting Role . . .," *Wall Street Journal*, September 22, 2005, p. B1ff.; "Tired of On-Air Promos? Nets Fan out to Gain Buzz," *Advertising Age*, September 19, 2005, p. S2; "PepsiCo's Mountain Dew Backs Film," *Wall Street Journal*, September 12, 2005, p. B4; "Product Placement Grows as Nets Worry about Glut," *Adweek*, August 22, 2005, p. 9; "With Ads Everywhere, U.S. Culture Is Reshaped," *Detroit News*, May 8, 2005; www.detnews.com and www.keyad.com; "Advertising on Truck Mud Flaps Comes to an Interstate near You," *PR Newswire*, January 6, 2005; "Get Me Rewrite! Miller Calls the TV Shots," *Wall Street Journal*, October 13, 2004, p. B1ff.; "The Robot Wore Converses," *Wall Street Journal*, September 2, 2004, p. B1ff.; "Trump to Brands: You're Hired," *Wall Street Journal*, September 2, 2004, p. B1ff.; "Water Works: How Fiji Brand Got Hip to Sip," *Wall Street Journal*, August 16, 2004, p. B1ff.; "Also Starring (Your Product Name Here)," *USA Today*, August 12, 2004, p. 1Bff.; "Too Much of a Good Thing?" *Brandweek*, August 9, 2004, pp. 21–24; "For More Advertisers, the Medium Is the Text Message," *Wall Street Journal*, August 2, 2004, p. B1ff.; "Hubcap Ads Put New Spin on Marketing," USA Today, July 19, 2004.

20. "Behind the Curtain: How Google Determines the Ranks and Rates of Its Sponsored Links," www.sfgate.com, March 5, 2006; "Internet's Ad Gains Bringing Bad News to Newspapers, TV," *Investor's Business Daily*, November 18, 2005, p. A1ff.; "Car Makers Hone Their Pitch Online," *Wall Street Journal*, October 14, 2005, p. B4; "BBC, Diet Coke Test RSS as Advertising Medium," *Brandweek*, September 19, 2005, p. 17; "Online Crisis Looms as Ad Demand Surges," *Advertising Age*, September 12, 2005, pp. 1, 53; "No More Free-for-All Online," *Investor's Business Daily*, August 8, 2005, p. A18; "Innovation: The Future of Advertising," *Fortune*, August 8, 2005, pp. 40–60; "I-Intelligence," *Advertising Age*, July 11, 2005, pp. S1–S7; "Measuring Up," *Brandweek*, June 6, 2005, pp. 32–34; "In Click Fraud, Web Outfits Have a Costly Problem," *Wall Street Journal*, April 6, 2005, p. A1ff.; "Web Search Sites See Clicks Add Up to Big Ad Dollars," *New York Times*, February 4, 2005, p. A1ff. See also Kelli S. Burns and Richard J. Lutz, "The Function of Format: Consumer Responses to Six On-line Advertising Formats," *Journal of Advertising*, Spring 2006, p. 53; Robert S. Moore, Claire Allison Stammerjohan, and Robin A. Coulter, "Banner Advertiser-Web Site Context Con-

gruity and Color Effects on Attention and Attitudes," *Journal of Advertising*, Summer 2005, p. 71; Nigel Hollis, "Ten Years of Learning on How Online Advertising Builds Brands," *Journal of Advertising Research*, June 2005, p. 255; Ritu Lohtia, Naveen Donthu, and Edmund K. Hershberger, "The Impact of Content and Design Elements on Banner Advertising Click-through Rates," *Journal of Advertising Research*, December 2003, p. 410; David R. Fortin and Ruby Roy Dholakia, "Interactivity and Vividness Effects on Social Presence and Involvement with a Web-Based Advertisement," *Journal of Business Research*, March 2005, p. 387; Chan Yun Yoo and Kihan Kim, "Processing of Animation in Online Banner Advertising: The Roles of Cognitive and Emotional Responses," *Journal of Interactive Marketing*, Autumn 2005, p. 18; Kim Bartel Sheehan, "Re-Weaving the Web: Integrating Print and Online Communications," *Journal of Interactive Marketing*, Spring 2001, p. 47; Lee Sherman, "Banner Advertising: Measuring Effectiveness and Optimizing Placement," *Journal of Interactive Marketing*, Spring 2001, p. 60; Satya Menon and Dilip Soman, "Managing the Power of Curiosity for Effective Web Advertising Strategies," *Journal of Advertising*, Fall 2002, p. 1; Steven M. Edwards, Hairong Li, and Joo-Hyun Lee, "Forced Exposure and Psychological Reactance: Antecedents and Consequences of the Perceived Intrusiveness of Pop-Up Ads," *Journal of Advertising*, Fall 2002, p. 83; Xavier Dreze and Francois-Xavier Hussherr, "Internet Advertising: Is Anybody Watching?" *Journal of Interactive Marketing*, Autumn 2003, p. 8; Erik L. Olson and Robert E. Widing II, "Are Interactive Decision Aids Better than Passive Decision Aids? A Comparison with Implications for Information Providers on the Internet," *Journal of Interactive Marketing*, Spring 2002, p. 22.

21. "Flowers That Pop," *Fortune*, December 3, 2003.

22. For an example of creative campaign, see Burger King's Subservient Chicken at www.subservientchicken.com; "Keepers of the Flame: A BK Roundtable," *Brandweek*, March 28, 2005, pp. 28–32; "Agency of the Year, Crispin Ups Ante," *Advertising Age*, January 10, 2005, pp. S1–S12; "Burger King Tastes Like Chicken, Smells Like Guerrilla Marketing," *Brandweek*, November 22, 2004, p. 27; "Creative: Chicken Rings," *Adweek*, October 18, 2004, pp. 34–35. For some creative and controversial ads, see "Marketers of the Year," *Brandweek*, October 20, 2003; "How to Sell a Strange Idea," *Adweek*, July 14, 2003, p. 22; "Downloading the Future of TV Advertising," *Business 2.0*, July 2003, p. 46; "Cheers and Jeers," *Adweek*, June 30, 2003, p. 20; "Ikea's 'Lamp' Wins Cannes," *Advertising Age*, June 23, 2003, p. 1; "A Leap for Advertising," *Adweek*, June 16, 2003, p. 28; "The Lowest Moments in Advertising," *Adweek*, June 9, 2003, p. 38; "Best Awards," *Advertising Age*, May 26, 2003, pp. S1–S6. See also Josephine L. C. M. Woltman Elpers, Ashesh Mukherjee, and Wayne D. Hoyer, "Humor in Television Advertising: A Moment-to-Moment Analysis," *Journal of Consumer Research*, December 2004, p. 592; Anand Kumar and Shanker Krishnan, "Memory Interference in Advertising: A Replication and Extension," *Journal of Consumer Research*, March 2004, p. 602; Pamela Miles Homer, "Relationships among Ad-Induced Affect, Beliefs, and Attitudes: Another Look," *Journal of Advertising*, Spring 2006, p. 35; Carl Obermiller, Eric Spangenberg, and Douglas L. MacLachlan, "Ad Skepticism," *Journal of Advertising*, Fall 2005 p. 7; Edward F. McQuarrie and Barbara J. Phillips, "Indirect Persuasion in Advertising," *Journal of Advertising*, Summer 2005, p. 7; Kathryn A. Braun-LaTour, Michael S. LaTour, Jacqueline E. Pickrell, and Elizabeth F. Loftus, "How and When Advertising Can Influence Memory for Consumer Experience," *Journal of Advertising*, Winter 2004, p. 7; Darrel D. Muehling and David E. Sprott, "The Power of Reflection," *Journal of Advertising*, Fall 2004, p. 25; William E. Baker, Heather Honea, and Cristel Antonia Russell, "Do Not Wait to Reveal the Brand Name," *Journal of Advertising*, Fall 2004, p. 77; Brett A. S. Martin, Bodo Lang, and Stephanie Wong, "Conclusion Explicitness in Advertising," *Journal of Advertising*, Winter 2004, p. 57; Thomas W. Cline, Moses B. Altsech, and James J. Kellaris, "When Does Humor Enhance or Inhibit Ad Responses?" *Journal of Advertising*, Fall 2003, p. 31; Zakary L. Tormala and Richard E. Petty, "Source

Credibility and Attitude Certainty: A Metacognitive Analysis of Resistance to Persuasion," *Journal of Consumer Psychology*, 2004, p. 427; Joan Meyers-Levy and Durairaj Maheswaran, "Exploring Message Framing Outcomes When Systematic, Heuristic, or Both Types of Processing Occur," *Journal of Consumer Psychology*, no. 1 (2004), p. 159; David W. Stewart and Ingrid M. Martin, "Advertising Disclosures: Clear and Conspicuous or Understood and Used?," *Journal of Public Policy & Marketing*, Fall 2004, p. 183; Mark I. Alpert, Judy I. Alpert, and Elliot N. Maltz, "Purchase Occasion Influence on the Role of Music in Advertising," *Journal of Business Research*, March 2005, p. 367; Barbara J. Phillips and Edward F. McQuarrie, "The Development, Change, and Transformation of Rhetorical Style in Magazine Advertisements 1954–1999," *Journal of Advertising*, Winter 2002, p. 1.

23. "One Size Doesn't Fit All," *Wall Street Journal*, October 1, 2003, p. B1; "Exxon Centralizes New Global Campaign," *Wall Street Journal*, July 11, 2001, p. B6; "McCann Finds Global a Tough Sell in Japan," *Wall Street Journal*, June 19, 1997, p. B2. See also Fahad S. Al-Olayan, "A Content Analysis of Magazine Advertisements from the United States and the Arab World," *Journal of Advertising*, Fall 2000, p. 69; Bongjin Cho, Up Kwon, James W. Gentry, Sunkyu Jun, and Fredric Kropp, "Cultural Values Reflected in Theme and Execution: a Comparative Study of U.S. and Korean Television Commercials," *Journal of Advertising*, Winter 1999, p. 59; Theodore Levitt, "The Globalization of Markets," *Harvard Business Review*, May–June 1983, p.92; Kamran Kashani, "Beware the Pitfalls of Global Marketing," *Harvard Business Review*, September–October 1989, p. 91.

24. "Madison Ave. Lights Up," *Fortune*, December 12, 2005, pp. 51–52; "Ending Advertising's Spiral," *Business 2.0*, September 2005, pp. 42–44; "Agencies Are from Mars, Clients Are from Venus," *Point*, July 2005, pp. 22–23; "The Fall of a Madison Avenue Icon," *Adweek*, July 25, 2005, pp. 27–41; "The Big Four Holding On," *Point*, July 2005, pp. 8–17; "How You Size Up the Competition," *Adweek*, May 2, 2005, pp. 25–30; "Bigger and Bigger," *Fortune*, November 29, 2004, pp. 146–55; "China's Edgy Advertising," *Wall Street Journal*, October 27, 2003, p. B1; "How Tiny German Shop Landed McDonald's," *Wall Street Journal*, August 6, 2003, p. B1; "Still in the Hunt," *Business Week*, July 7, 2003, p. 42; "WPP's Sorrell Bests Publicis in Cordiant Bid," *Wall Street Journal*, June 18, 2003, p. B1; "Are Holding Companies Obsolete?" *Adweek*, June 9, 2003, p. 30; "Integrated Agencies," *Advertising Age*, May 19, 2003, pp. S1–S5; "Agency Report: Top 100 National Agencies," *Adweek*, April 7, 2003; "The Rise of the Superagency," *Advertising Age*, January 28, 2002, p. 1; "Will Ad Agencies Survive Slowdown?" *Investor's Business Daily*, May 8, 2001, p. A1; "A Chill Hits Madison Avenue," *Wall Street Journal*, March 19, 2001, p. B1; "Culture Shock," *Advertising Age*, January 8, 2001, p. 1. See also Gerard Prendergast, Yizheng Shi, and Douglas West, "Organizational Buying and Advertising Agency-Client Relationships in China," *Journal of Advertising*, Summer 2001, p. 61; George C. Hozier, Jr. and John D. Schatzberg, "Advertising Agency Terminations and Reviews: Stock Returns and Firm Performance," *Journal of Business Research*, November 2000, p. 169; Douglas West and John Ford, "Advertising Agency Philosphies and Employee Risking Taking," *Journal of Advertising*, Spring 2001, p. 77; Mark Davies and Mel Prince, "Examining the Longevity of New Agency Accounts: a Comparative Study of U.S. and U.K. Advertising Experiences," *Journal of Advertising*, Winter 1999, p. 75.

25. "Ad-Industry Secret Comes to Light," *Wall Street Journal*, September 23, 2005, p. B5; "It's Pretty Grim (Hint) over There," *Advertising Age*, September 19, 2005, pp. 1, 52; "The Scramble on Mad. Ave," *Fortune*, August 8, 2005, pp. 63–64; "Taken for a Ride," *Brandweek*, November 1, 2004, pp. 24–32; "Agencies Face New Accountability," *Wall Street Journal*, October 2, 2003, p. B4; "Interpublic May Become More Open," *Wall Street Journal*, September 10, 2003, p. B4; "Kraft Rethinks Agency Pay, Brand Duties," *Adweek*, August 18, 2003, p. 6; "GM Overhauls Compensation," *Advertising Age*, March 17, 2003, p. 1; "Up Close and Personal," *Adweek*, March 17, 2003,

p. 26; "Adweek Adspend Survey: What Clients Think," *Adweek*, December 16, 2002, p. 21; "Nestlé Move on Fees Will Rattle Agencies," *Wall Street Journal*, October 8, 2001, p. A21; "Unilever Reviews the Way It Pays for Ads," *Wall Street Journal*, April 27, 2001, p. B6; "Performance Pays," *Advertising Age*, February 28, 2000, pp. S14–S16. See also Hao Zhao, "Incentive-Based Compensation to Advertising Agencies: A Principal-Agent Approach," *International Journal of Research in Marketing*, September 2005, p. 255; Diana L. Haytko, "Firm-to-Firm and Interpersonal Relationships: Perspectives from Advertising Agency Account Managers," *Journal of the Academy of Marketing Science*, Summer 2004, p. 312; John Sutherland, Lisa Duke, and Avery Abernethy, "A Model of Marketing Information Flow," *Journal of Advertising*, Winter 2004, p. 39; Judy Harris and Kimberly A. Taylor, "The Case for Greater Agency Involvement in Strategic Partnerships," *Journal of Advertising Research*, December 2003, p. 346; Mukund S. Kulkarni, Premal P. Vora, and Terence A. Brown, "Firing Advertising Agencies," *Journal of Advertising*, Fall 2003, p. 77.

26. "So Few Choices for Clients, So Many Account Conflicts," *Adweek*, June 6, 2005, p. 12; "Media Agencies Struggle to Manage Client Conflicts," *Advertising Age*, April 12, 2004, p. 16; "GM to Publicis: Loyalty Matters," *Advertising Age*, May 26, 2003, p. 16; "Foote Cone Loses Two Accounts from Coke in Wake of Pepsi Suit," *Wall Street Journal*, November 12, 2001, p. B3; "The Rise of the Superagency," *Advertising Age*, January 28, 2002, p. 1; "Commercial Break: An Ad Mega-Agency Faces Harsh Realities of a Shaken Industry," *Wall Street Journal*, October 31, 2001, p. A1; "Can An Agency Be Guilty of Malpractice?" *Advertising Age*, January 31, 2000, p. 24; see also Minette E. Drumwright and Patrick E. Murphy, "How Advertising Practitioners View Ethics," *Journal of Advertising*, Summer 2004, p. 7.

27. "Econometrics Buzzes Ad World as a Way of Measuring Results," *Wall Street Journal*, August 16, 2005, p. B8; "Putting a Value on Marketing Dollars," *Wall Street Journal*, July 27, 2005, p. B2; "Call to Action Ads Give Clients Results They Can Measure," *Wall Street Journal*, March 22, 2005, p. B1ff.; "How to Measure Product Placement," *Adweek*, January 17, 2005, pp. 18–20; "Making Marketing Measure Up," *Business Week*, December 13, 2004, pp. 112–13; "At Last a Way to Measure Ads," *Wall Street Journal Reports*, June 16, 2003, p. R4; "The Top 5 Rules of the Ad Game," *Business Week*, January 20, 2003, p. 72; "Consumers May Notice the Ads, but Will They Buy the Product?" *Investor's Business Daily*, December 19, 2002, p. A4; "Does Creativity Count?" *Brandweek*, December 11, 2000, p. 32. See also John E. Hogan, Katherine N. Lemon, and Barak Libai, "Quantifying the Ripple: Word-of-Mouth and Advertising Effectiveness," *Journal of Advertising Research*, September 2004, p. 271; Margaret H. Blair and Allan R. Kuse, "Better Practices in Advertising Can Change a Cost of Doing Business to Wise Investments in the Business," *Journal of Advertising Research*, March 2004, p. 71; Subodh Bhat, Michael Bevans, and Sanjit Sengupta, "Measuring Users' Web Activity to Evaluate and Enhance Advertising Effectiveness," *Journal of Advertising*, Fall 2002, p. 97; Ann Marie Barry, "How Advertising Works: The Role of Research," *Journal of the Academy of Marketing Science*, Winter 2001, p. 103; Els Gijsbrechts, Katia Campo, and Tom Goossens, "The Impact of Store Flyers on Store Traffic and Store Sales: A Geo-Marketing Approach," *Journal of Retailing*, no. 1 (2003), p. 1; Fuyuan Shen, "Banner Advertisement Pricing, Measurement, and Pretesting Practices: Perspectives from Interactive Agencies," *Journal of Advertising*, Fall 2002, p. 59; DeAnna S. Kempf and Russell N. Laczniak, "Advertising's Influence on Subsequent Product Trial Processing," *Journal of Advertising*, Fall 2001, p. 27; Gerald J. Tellis and Doyle L. Weiss, "Does TV Advertising Really Affect Sales? The Role of Measures, Models, and Data Aggregation," *Journal of Advertising*, Fall 1995, p. 1; John H. Holmes, "When Ads Work," *Journal of the Academy of Marketing Science*, Winter 1997, p. 88; Karen Whitehill King, John D. Pehrson, and Leonard N. Reid, "Pretesting TV Commercials: Methods, Measures, and Changing Agency Roles," *Journal of Advertising*, September 1993, p.85; Erik du Plessis, "Recognition versus Recall," *Journal of Advertising Research*, May/June 1994, p. 75.

28. "China Blocks News Corp. Plan for TV Channel," *Wall Street Journal*, August 25, 2005, p. B1ff.; "China Demands Concrete Proof of Ad Claims," *Wall Street Journal*, July 8, 2005, p. B1ff.; "India's Brewers Cleverly Dodge Alcohol-Ad Ban," *Wall Street Journal*, June 15, 2005, p. B1ff.; "New Star on Chinese TV: Product Placements," *Wall Street Journal*, June 2, 2004, p. B1ff.; "China Takes Aim at Racy, Violent TV Shows," *Wall Street Journal*, May 24, 2004, p. B1ff.; China Cracks Down on Commercials," *Wall Street Journal*, February 19, 2004, p. B1ff; "Treaty May Stub Out Cigarette Ads in China," *Wall Street Journal*, December 2, 2003, p. B1ff.; "U.K. TV Can Pose Tricky Hurdles," *Wall Street Journal*, June 27, 2003, p. B7; "McDonald's Arches Outlawed in Beijing," *USA Today*, March 5, 2002, p. 7B: "Chinese Officials Force Magazines to Go without Famous Names," *Wall Street Journal*, February 2, 2000, p. B1. See also Young Sook Moon and George R. Franke, "Cultural Influences on Agency Practitioners' Ethical Perceptions: A Comparison of Korea and the U.S.," *Journal of Advertising*, Spring 2000, p. 51; Kim Bartel Sheehan, "Balancing Acts: An Analysis of Food and Drug Administration Letters about Direct-to-Consumer Advertising Violations," *Journal of Public Policy & Marketing*, Fall 2003, p. 159; J. Howard Beales III, "The Federal Trade Commission's Use of Unfairness Authority: Its Rise, Fall, and Resurrection," *Journal of Public Policy & Marketing*, Fall 2003, p. 192; Alexander Simonson, "The Impact of Advertising Law on Business and Public Policy," *Journal of Marketing*, October 1994, p. 123; Ross D. Petty, "Advertising Law in the United States and European Union," *Journal of Public Policy & Marketing*, Spring 1997, p. 2; Steve Lysonski and Michael F. Duffy, "The New Zealand Fair Trading Act of 1986: Deceptive Advertising," *Journal of Consumer Affairs*, Summer 1992, p. 177.

29. For more on KFC, see "Hey, Fast Food: We Love You Just the Way You Are," *Brandweek*, November 24, 2003, p. 30; "FTC Examines Health Claims in KFC's Ads," *Wall Street Journal*, November 19, 2003, p. B1; "Garfield's Ad Review: KFC Serves Big, Fat Bucket of Nonsense in 'Healthy' Spots," *Advertising Age*, November 3, 2003, p. 61. See also "Regulators Take Another Look at Product Placement," *Brandweek*, October 10, 2005, p. 15; "Splenda Suit Points Up Dangers of Ad Claim Cases," *Adweek*, August 1, 2005, p. 9; "As 'Safer Smokes' Multiply, States Probe Marketing Claims," *Wall Street Journal*, May 18, 2004, p. B1ff.; "P&G Is Settling Disputes on Ads as Suits Pile Up," *Wall Street Journal*, November 26, 2003, p. B1; "Watchdog Group Hits TV Product Placement," *Advertising Age*, October 6, 2003, p. 12. See also Boris W. Becker, "The Tangled Web They Weave: Truth, Falsity, & Advertisers," *Journal of Advertising*, Summer 1996, p. 83; Elizabeth K. LaFleur, R. E. Reidenbach, Donald P. Robin, and P. J. Forrest, "An Exploration of Rule Configuration Effects on the Ethical Decision Processes of Advertising Professionals," *Journal of the Academy of Marketing Science*, Winter 1996, p. 66; Barbara B. Stern, "'Crafty Advertisers': Literary versus Literal Deceptiveness," *Journal of Public Policy & Marketing*, Spring 1992, p. 72; Joel J. Davis, "Ethics in Advertising Decisionmaking: Implications for Reducing the Incidence of Deceptive Advertising," *Journal of Consumer Affairs*, Winter 1994, p. 380. For more on advertising to kids, see "CARU's Medicine Hard to Swallow," *Advertising Age*, November 28, 2005, pp. 3, 45; "FCC, Kids' Networks Playing for Keeps," *Brandweek*, October 10, 2005, p. 4; "Divided, Companies Fight for Right to Plug Kids' Food," *Wall Street Journal*, January 26, 2005, p. B1ff.; "Curbing Their Appetite," *Brandweek*, December 6, 2004, pp. 24–28; "Seals and Deals," *Wall Street Journal*, July 20, 2004, p. B1ff.; "Junk-Food Games," *Wall Street Journal*, May 3, 2004, p. B1ff.; "Is Marketing to Kids Ethical?" *Brandweek*, April 5, 2004, pp. 44–48; "Coming Up Next . . . Calls for Tighter Restrictions on Kids' Ads . . .," *Wall Street Journal*, March 15, 2004, p. B1ff.; "Lawsuit Alleges Alcohol Industry Targets Underage Drinkers," *Wall Street Journal*, November 28, 2003, p. B1; "Beer Ads on TV, College Sports: Explosive Mix?" *Wall Street Journal*, November 12, 2003, p. B1; "Coors Slammed for Targeting Kids," *Advertising Age*, November 3, 2003, p. 1; "Alcohol Advertisers Agree to Raise Standards to Help Keep Their Messages Away from Kids," *USA Today*, September 10, 2003, p. 5B.

30. Kathy R. Fitzpatrick, "The Legal Challenge of Integrated Marketing Communication (IMC)," *Journal of Advertising*, Winter 2005, p. 93; Ivan L. Preston, "Regulatory Positions toward Advertising Puffery of the Uniform Commercial Code and the Federal Trade Commission," *Journal of Public Policy & Marketing*, Fall 1997, p. 336; Claude R. Martin, Jr., "Ethical Advertising Research Standards: Three Case Studies," *Journal of Advertising*, September 1994, p. 17; William K. Darley and Robert E. Smith, "Advertising Claim Objectivity: Antecedents and Effects," *Journal of Marketing*, October 1993, p. 100; George M. Zinkhan, "Advertising Ethics: Emerging Methods and Trends," *Journal of Advertising*, September 1994, p. 1.

31. "The Goody-Bag Game," *Wall Street Journal*, December 7, 2005, p. B1ff.; "High Noon in Aisle Five," *Inc.*, January 2004, pp. 88–95; "P&G Breaks Out of Its Slump," *USA Today*, October 14, 2003, p. 3B; "Ads Mmm, Junk Mail," *Newsweek*, August 18, 2003, p. 12; "Road Shows Take Brands to the People," *Wall Street Journal*, May 14, 2003, p. A10; "Offbeat Marketing Sells," *Investor's Business Daily*, March 27, 2002, p. A4.

32. "Too Many Choices," *Wall Street Journal*, April 20, 2001, p. B1; "Reposition: Simplifying the Customer's Brandscape," *Brandweek*, October 2, 2000, p. 36. See also Page Moreau, Aradhna Krishna, and Bari Harlam, "The Manufacturer-Retailer-Consumer Triad: Differing Perceptions Regarding Price Promotions," *Journal of Retailing*, Winter 2001, p. 547.

33. For more on Pampers example, see "P&G Promotion Is Too Successful, Angering Buyers," *Wall Street Journal*, April 2, 2002, p. B1. For another example, see "Shopper Turns Lots of Pudding into Free Miles," *Wall Street Journal*, January 24, 2000, p. B1; "The Pudding Guy Flies Again (and Again) Over Latin America," *Wall Street Journal*, March 16, 2000, p. B1.

34. George E. Belch and Michael E. Belch, *Advertising and Promotion, an Integrated Marketing Communication Perspective* (Burr Ridge, IL: McGraw-Hill, 2004). Priya Raghubir, J. Jeffrey Inman, and Hans Grande, "The Three Faces of Consumer Promotions," *California Management Review*, Summer 2004, p. 23.

35. "Cut It Out: U.S. Stores May Kill Coupon Clutter," *Advertising Age*, November 7, 2005, pp. 4, 57; "Designated Shopper," *Brandweek*, February 4, 2002, p. 34; "Cybercoupons," *Discount Store News*, March 9, 1998, p. 18; "The Scoop on Coupons," *Brandweek*, March 17, 1997, p. 34; "Many Companies Are Starting to Wean Shoppers Off Coupons," *Wall Street Journal*, January 22, 1997, p. B1; "Internet Coupons Offer H.O.T! Deals," *USA Today*, December 13, 1996, p. 17D.

36. "The Show Goes On: Online Trade Shows," *Wall Street Journal Reports*, April 28, 2003, p. R4; "The Cyber-Show Must Go On," *Trade Media*, May 7, 2001, p. SR3; "Getting the Most from a Trade-Show Booth," *Investor's Business Daily*, April 25, 2000, p. 1. See also Li Ling-yee, "Relationship Learning at Trade Shows: Its Antecedents and Consequences," *Industrial Marketing Management*, February 2006, p. 166; Timothy M. Smith, Srinath Gopalakrishna, and Paul M. Smith, "The Complementary Effect of Trade Shows on Personal Selling," *International Journal of Research in Marketing*, March 2004, p. 61; Marnik G. Dekimpe, Pierre Francois, Srinath Gopalakrishna, Gary L. Lilien, and Christophe Van den Bulte, "Generalizing about Trade Show Effectiveness: A Cross-National Comparison," *Journal of Marketing*, October 1997, p. 55; Scott Barlass, "How to Get the Most Out of Trade Shows," *Journal of Product Innovation Management*, September 1997, p. 423; Srinath Gopalakrishna, Gary L. Lilien, Jerome D. Williams, and Ian K. Sequeira, "Do Trade Shows Pay Off?" *Journal of Marketing*, July 1995, p. 75; "Trade Promotion Rises," *Advertising Age*, April 3, 2000, p. 24.

37. "Creating Incentives Down in Ranks: Marriott Ties Pay to Guest Replies," *Investor's Business Daily*, July 6, 2001, p. A1; "Get Great Results from Salespeople by Finding What Really Moves Them," *Investor's Business Daily*, July 2, 2001, p. A1.

CHAPTER 16

1. "Church & Dwight Agrees to Purchase SpinBrush Toothbrush Business from Procter & Gamble," *Business Wire*, September 14, 2005; "Lafley on P&G's Gadget Evolution," *Business Week Online*, January 31, 2005; "If the Pros Use a Tool or a Toothbrush, It Will Sell," *USA Today*, December 17, 2003, p. 1A; "Power Brushes a Hit at Every Level," *Advertising Age*, May 26, 2003, p. 10; "Less Power to You," *Newsweek*, January 27, 2003, p. 73; "Toothbrush Wars: Group's Findings Spark Another Battle," *Wall Street Journal*, January 14, 2003, p. D4; "New SpinBrush Line Backed by $30 Mil," *Advertising Age*, September 9, 2002, p. 3; "Why P&G's Smile Is So Bright," *Business Week*, August 12, 2002, p. 58; "SpinBrush Cost P&G a Hefty $475 Million," *Advertising Age*, May 13, 2002, p. 4; "Colgate Adds Motion to Brush Market," *Marketing Magazine*, April 8, 2002, p. 2; "Think Small: Procter & Gamble Takes a New Approach to Tackling the Competition," *Advertising Age*, January 21, 2002, p. 1; "What's Hot: Powered-Up Toothbrushes," *DSN Retailing Today*, April 16, 2001, p. 35.

2. "Car Makers Cut Free Maintenance," *Wall Street Journal*, July 7, 2005, p. D1ff.; "Detroit's Latest Offer: Pay More, Get Less," *Wall Street Journal*, July 24, 2002, p. D1; "Did You Overpay for Your Car? States Sue Dealers over Fees," *Wall Street Journal*, June 20, 2002, p. D1; "Sticker Shock: Detroit's Hidden Price Hikes," *Wall Street Journal*, April 10, 2002, p. D1; "Adding Options Helps Car Firms Increase Prices," *Wall Street Journal*, December 27, 1993, p. 9; "Car Makers Seek to Mask Price Increases," *Wall Street Journal*, August 16, 1989, p. B1. For another example involving the cruise industry, see "A Sea of Extra Charges," *USA Today*, March 14, 2003, p. 1Bff.; "All Your Onboard Fun Is Included*," *Wall Street Journal*, December 27, 2001, p. B1ff. For another example involving the car rental industry, see "Car-Rental Agencies Talk of Realistic Total Pricing," *New York Times*, February 10, 2004, p. C7; see also Hope Jensen Schau, Michael F. Smith, and Per Ivar Schau, "The Healthcare Network Economy: The Role of Internet Information Transfer and Implications for Pricing," *Industrial Marketing Management*, February 2005, p. 147; Ashutosh Dixit, Karin Braunsberger, George M. Zinkhan, and Yue Pan, "Information Technology—Enhanced Pricing Strategies: Managerial and Public Policy Implications," *Journal of Business Research*, September 2005, p. 1169; Robert M. Schindler, Maureen Morrin, and Nada Nasr Bechwati, "Shipping Charges and Shipping-Charge Skepticism: Implications for Direct Marketers' Pricing Formats," *Journal of Interactive Marketing*, Winter 2005, p. 41; Sandy D. Jap and Prasad A. Naik, "Introduction to the Special Issue on Online Pricing," *Journal of Interactive Marketing*, Autumn 2004, p. 4; Rajneesh Suri, Srinivasan Swaminathan, and Kent B. Monroe, "Price Communications in Online and Print Coupons: An Empirical Investigation," *Journal of Interactive Marketing*, Autumn 2004, p. 74; Michael R. Baye, John Morgan, and Patrick Scholten, "Temporal Price Dispersion: Evidence from an Online Consumer Electronics Market," *Journal of Interactive Marketing*, Autumn 2004, p. 101; Xing Pan, Brian T. Ratchford, and Venkatesh Shankar, "Price Dispersion on the Internet: A Review and Directions for Future Research," *Journal of Interactive Marketing*, Autumn 2004, p. 116.

3. Alfred Rappaport, "Executive Incentives versus Corporate Growth," *Harvard Business Review*, July–August 1978, p. 81; David M. Szymanski, Sundar G. Bharadwaj, and P. Rajan Varadarajan, "An Analysis of the Market Share-Profitability Relationship," *Journal of Marketing*, July 1993, p. 1.

4. "Decision on Lipitor Sets Express Scripts Apart from Its Field," *Investor's Business Daily*, November 7, 2005, p. A9; "EU Court Backs Resale of Drugs," *Wall Street Journal*, April 2, 2004, p. B3; "The Telecom Follies," *Wall Street Journal*, March 26, 2004, p. A8; "It's Time to Look at Rx Pricing," *Modern Healthcare*, March 15, 2004, p. 18; "The New Drug War," *Fortune*, March 8, 2004, p. 144; "Rethinking Restructuring," *Public Utilities Fortnightly*, February 2004, p. 12; "The Economy: Steel Prices Jump, Spurring Protests from Customers," *Wall Street Journal*, January 23, 2004, p. A2.

5. "Tiny Storage Makes Big Impact," *Investor's Business Daily*, October 4, 2001, p. A6.; see also Sushil Vachani and N. Craig Smith, "Socially Responsible Pricing: Lessons from the Pricing of AIDS Drugs in Developing Countries," *California Management Review*, Fall 2004, p. 117.

6. For more on the dot-com bust, see "Applying Old Pricing Lessons to a New Investing World," *Wall Street Journal*, May 21, 2001, p. C1; Stephen E. Frank, *Net Worth* (2001); "E-Assets for Sale," *Business Week E.Biz*, May 14, 2001, p. EB20; "Last Guys Finish First," *Ecompany*, May 2001, p. 93; "After the Wild Ride," *Business Week E.Biz*, April 16, 2001, p.EB29; "Study: Net Start-Ups Ignored Economics 101," *Investor's Business Daily*, March 2, 2001, p. A8; "12 Months When the Dot Turned into a Dark Period," *Investor's Business Daily*, January 2, 2001, p. A6; "We're Heading into Something Big—but What?" *USA Today*, December 29, 2000, p. 1B; "What Detonated Dot-Bombs?" *USA Today*, December 4, 2000, p. 1B; "Dot-Bombs," *Brandweek*, November 27, 2000, p.IQ16; see also Lan Xia, Kent B. Monroe, and Jennifer L. Cox, "The Price Is Unfair! A Conceptual Framework of Price Fairness Perceptions," *Journal of Marketing*, October 2004, p. 1; K. Sivakumar, "Price-Tier Competition: Distinguishing Between Intertier Competition and Intratier Competition," *Journal of Business Research*, December 2003, p. 947.

7. For more on Taurus, see "How Detroit Is Ruining Your Car's Value," *Wall Street Journal*, October 8, 2002, p. D1. For more on GM's (and others) attempts to add market share with employee discounts, see "Car Sales Suffer from Employee-Discount Program Hangover," *USA Today*, November 2, 2005, p. 4B; "Steve Hill, GM Exec Gives Everyone Employee Discount," *Point*, October 2005, pp. 22–23; "How GM Made Us All Feel like Family," *Business 2.0*, October 2005, p. 62; "Car Dealers Pile on Extra Discounts: New Deals Go Far Beyond Employee-Pricing Offers . . .," *Wall Street Journal*, September 15, 2005, p. D1ff.; "Employee Discounts Move Beyond Cars," *Wall Street Journal*, August 24, 2005, p. D1ff.; "Big 3 Continue Discount Offer after Big July," *Investor's Business Daily*, August 3, 2005, p. A1. See also Robert Jacobson and David A. Aaker, "Is Market Share All That It's Cracked Up to Be?" *Journal of Marketing*, Fall 1985, p. 11; Carolyn Y. Woo, "Market-Share Leadership—Not Always So Good," *Harvard Business Review*, January–February 1984, p. 50; "Reichhold Chemicals: Now the Emphasis Is on Profits Rather than Volume," *Business Week*, June 20, 1983, p. 178.

8. "E-Tailing Comes of Age," *Wall Street Journal*, December 8, 2003, p. B1; "Deck the Halls with High Speed Access," *Business Week*, December 8, 2003, p. 54; "What Are Price Wars Good For? Absolutely Nothing," *Fortune*, May 12, 1997, p. 156; "Price Wars," *Adweek's Marketing Week*, June 8, 1992, p. 18; "A Remarkable Gamble in an Industry Slump Pays Off Fast for Agco," *Wall Street Journal*, August 19, 1997, p. A1; "Why the Price Wars Never End," *Fortune*, March 23, 1992, p. 68.

9. "Aluminum Firms Offer Wider Discounts but Price Cuts Stop at Some Distributors," *Wall Street Journal*, November 16, 1984, p. 50. For another example of administered pricing, see "Why a Grand Plan to Cut CD Prices Went off the Track," *Wall Street Journal*, June 4, 2004, p. A1ff.

10. Moritz Fleischmann, Joseph M. Hall, and David F. Pyke, "Smart Pricing," *MIT Sloan Management Review*, Winter 2004, p. 9; ManMohan S. Sodhi and Navdeep S. Sodhi, "Six Sigma Pricing," *Harvard Business Review*, May 2005, p. 135; Eric Anderson and Duncan Simester, "Mind Your Pricing Cues," *Harvard Business Review*, September 2003, p. 96; Kissan Joseph, "On the Optimality of Delegating Pricing Authority to the Sales Force," *Journal of Marketing*, January 2001, p. 62; Michael V. Marn and Robert L. Rosiello, "Managing Price, Gaining Profit," *Harvard Business Review*, September–October 1992, p. 84; Subhash C. Jain and Michael B. Laric, "A Framework for Strategic Industrial Pricing," *Industrial Marketing Management* 8 (1979), p. 75; Peter R. Dickson and Joel E. Urbany, "Retailer Reactions to Competitive Price Changes," *Journal of Retailing*, Spring 1994, p. 1; Mary Karr, "The Case of the Pricing Predicament," *Har-*

vard Business Review, March–April, 1988, p. 10; Gerard J. Tellis, "Beyond the Many Faces of Price: An Integration of Pricing Strategies," Journal of Marketing, October 1986, p. 146.

11. For more on Priceline, see "Priceline Offers Two Approaches to Distinguish Itself from Herd," Investor's Business Daily, May 27, 2005, p. A4; "A Humbler, Happier Priceline," Business Week, August 11, 2003, p. 34; "Inside Jay Walker's House of Cards," Fortune, November 13, 2000, p. 127; "Letting the Masses Name Their Price," Business Week E.Biz, September 18, 2000, p. EB44. See also "The Discount Cards That Don't Save You Money," Wall Street Journal, January 21, 2003, p. D1; "Beating Retailers at the Discount Game," Wall Street Journal, November 27, 2002, p. D1; "Lessons from a Grocer," Investor's Business Daily, April 3, 2002, p. A4. For more on other online travel sites, see "Discount Travel Web Sites Offering Last-Minute Deals," Investor's Business Daily, December 21, 2005, p. A5; "Meet the Aggregators: A New Bread of Online Travel Web Sites . . .," Brandweek, May 30, 2005, pp. 25–32; "Scoring a Travel Discount Gets Easier," Wall Street Journal, November 4, 2003, p. D1; "The Travel Agent Bosses Love," Business Week, October 27, 2003, p. 134. See also Sucharita Chandran and Vicki G. Morwitz, "Effects of Participative Pricing on Consumers' Cognitions and Actions: A Goal Theoretic Perspective," Journal of Consumer Research, September 2005, p. 249.

12. For more on eBay and its flexible pricing, see Chapter 12, endnote 18. See also "Will Auction Frenzy Cool?" Business Week E. Biz, September 18, 2000, p. EB140; "Going, Going, Gone," Business Week, April 12, 1999, p. 30; "Good-Bye to Fixed Pricing," Business Week, May 4, 1998, p. 71; "One-Price Deals Save Time, Hassles, but Not Money," USA Today, March 11, 1998, p.1B. See also Markus Voeth and Uta Herbst, "Supply-Chain Pricing: A New Perspective on Pricing in Industrial Markets," Industrial Marketing Management, January 2006, p. 83; Howard Forman and James M. Hunt, "Managing the Influence of Internal and External Determinants on International Industrial Pricing Strategies," Industrial Marketing Management, February 2005, p. 133; Eric Matson, "Customizing Prices," Harvard Business Review, November–December 1995, p. 13; Sanjay K. Dhar and Stephen J. Hoch, "Price Discrimination Using In-Store Merchandising," Journal of Marketing, January 1996, p. 17; Michael H. Morris, "Separate Prices as a Marketing Tool," Industrial Marketing Management, May 1987, p. 79; P. Ronald Stephenson, William L. Cron, and Gary L. Frazier, "Delegating Pricing Authority to the Sales Force: The Effects on Sales and Profit Performance," Journal of Marketing, Spring 1979, p. 21.

13. "Online Stores Charge Different Prices Based on Shoppers' Surfing Habits," USA Today, June 2, 2005, p. 4B; "No-Haggle Pricing Climbs Higher, Finds Fans among Affluent, Educated," Advertising Age, August 1, 2005, p. 23. For more on Amazon offering different prices to different customers, see "Price? For You, $2; For the Rich Guy, $5," Investor's Business Daily, September 29, 2000, p. A8. For more on Winn-Dixie example, see "Squeezin' the Charmin," Fortune, January 16, 1989, p. 11; "Grocers Join Winn-Dixie," Advertising Age, November 7, 1988, p. 3; "Grocery Chains Pressure Suppliers for Uniform Prices," Wall Street Journal, October 21, 1988, p. B1. For more on car haggling, see "CarMax: Psst, Wanna Buy a Used Car, Hassle-Free?" Investor's Business Daily, January 30, 2002, p. A9. See also "Pay-as-You-Go M.D.: The Doctor Is In, but Insurance Is Out," Wall Street Journal, November 6, 2003, p. A1; "Medical Care: Can We Talk Price?" Wall Street Journal, February 8, 2002, p. W1.

14. "What's a Fair Price for Drugs?" Business Week, April 30, 2001, p. 105; "AIDS Gaffes in Africa Come Back to Haunt Drug Industry at Home," Wall Street Journal, April 23, 2001, p. A1; "Vaccine's Price Drives a Debate about Its Use," Wall Street Journal, February 16, 2000, p. B1. See also Richard A. Spinello, "Ethics, Pricing and the Pharmaceutical Industry," Journal of Business Ethics, August 1992, p. 617; Nicholas H. Lurie and Joydeep Srivastava, "Price-Matching Guarantees and Consumer Evaluations of Price Information," Journal of Consumer Psychology, 2005, p. 149; Bruce McWilliams and Eitan Gerstner, "Offering Low Price Guarantees to Improve Customer Retention," Journal of Retailing, June 2006, p. 105; Sujay Dutta and Abhijit Biswas, "Effects of Low Price Guarantees on Consumer Post-Purchase Search Intention: The Moderating Roles of Value Consciousness and Penalty Level," Journal of Retailing, 2005, p. 283.

15. "Wave of Price Cutting Hits Flat-Panel TV Sets: Sales Are Seen Doubling," Wall Street Journal, December 29, 2005, p. B3; "War of the Screens," Business Week, September 12, 2005, pp. 62–63; "Passing the Screen Test . . . Turned Sharp into Japan's Most Profitable," Business 2.0, August 2005, pp. 38–40; "Next Showdown: Plasma or LCD?" Investor's Business Daily, July 28, 2005, p. A4; "Flat-Panel TVs You Can Afford," Wall Street Journal, June 1, 2005, p. D1ff.; "Your Next TV," Business Week, April 4, 2005, pp. 33–36; "Cheaper Flat-Panel TVs—from PC Makers," Wall Street Journal, December 23, 2004, p. D1ff.; "Texas Instruments Inside?" Business Week, December 6, 2004, p. 48; "Flat TV Prices Are Falling, but . . . Not Low Enough . . . Blame Retailers' Margins," Wall Street Journal, November 3, 2004, p. B1ff.; "Once a Footnote, Flat Screens Grow into Huge Industry," Wall Street Journal, August 30, 2004, p. A1ff.; "I Want My Flat TV. Now! . . . Supply Shortfall," Wall Street Journal, May 27, 2004, p. B1f.; "Flat-Panel Sets Enhance Visibility of Samsung," New York Times, January 8, 2004, p. C1ff.; "In a Sleek Flat Set, Plasma's Price Plunges," New York Times, January 8, 2004, p. E3; "For Digital TVs, the Future Is Now," USA Today, December 3, 2003, p. 10D; "The Skinny on Flat Screens," Wall Street Journal, November 26, 2003, p. D1.

16. See www.palm.com; "Palm Fronds Diverge: One Business Excels, the Other Founders," Investor's Business Daily, December 1, 2004, p. A4ff.; "Stiff Competition, New Technology Mean Great Gadget Deals," USA Today, November 10, 2003, p. 3B; "Palm Reaches Out for a Hand," Business Week, November 3, 2003, p. 74; "Palm Hopes Breaking in Two Will Juice Its Sluggish Sales," Wall Street Journal, October 28, 2003, p. B1; "Hand-Helds' New Frontier," Wall Street Journal, August 8, 2003, p.B1; "Fewer Buyers Giving the Big Thumbs-Up to Handheld PC Gear," Investor's Business Daily, November 27, 2002, p. A5; "New Palms Offer Something for Every Pocketbook," USA Today, November 13, 2002, p.5D.; "An Address Book That Shoots Movies," Wall Street Journal, October 2, 2002, p. D1; "Palm, Seeking Business Clients, Targets Corporate Executives," Wall Street Journal, May 13, 2002, p. B6; "Start-Up Joins Hand-Held-Device Battle," Wall Street Journal, May 9, 2002, p.B5; "Price Wars Hit PDAs: Is It Time to Buy One Yet?" Wall Street Journal, May 9, 2002, p. D1; "Pilot Error: How Palm Tumbled from Star of Tech to Target of Microsoft," Wall Street Journal, September 7, 2001, p. A1; "Palm Slips to No. 2 in Revenue as iPaq Grabs the Top Spot," Investor's Business Daily, June 19, 2001, p. A6; "Palm Shares Sink as One-Time Star Says Sales Fading," Investor's Business Daily, May 21, 2001, p. A6; "HandEra's Hand-Held Puts Some New Twists on the Usual Formula," Wall Street Journal, May 10, 2001, p. B1.

17. Check out foreign exchange rates at www.imf.org, www.federalreserve.gov, and www.x-rates.com. See also "Trade Winds," Inc., November 2003, p. 36; "Same Cars Can Cost Oodles Less in Canada," USA Today, May 6, 2003, p. 1B; "Ship Those Boxes; Check the Euro!" Wall Street Journal, February 7, 2003, p. C1; "Revealing Price Disparities, the Euro Aids Bargain-Hunters," Wall Street Journal, January 30, 2002, p. A15; "One Dollar Is Worth One Dollar, but That Wasn't Always So," Wall Street Journal, January 13, 1998, p. A1. See also Ashok K. Lalwani and Kent B. Monroe, "A Reexamination of Frequency-Depth Effects in Consumer Price Judgments," Journal of Consumer Research, December 2005, p. 480; Luc Wathieu, A. V. Muthukrishnan, and Bart J. Bronnenberg, "The Asymmetric Effect of Discount Retraction on Subsequent Choice," Journal of Consumer Research, December 2004, p. 652; Chris Janiszewski and Marcus Cunha, Jr., "The Influence of Price Discount Framing on the Evaluation of a Product Bundle," Journal of Consumer Research, March 2004, p. 534; Keith S. Coulter and Robin A. Coulter, "Size Does Matter: The Effects of Magnitude Representation Congruency on Price Perceptions and Purchase Likelihood," Journal of Consumer Psychology, 2005,

p. 64; V. Kumar, Vibhas Madan, and Srini S. Srinivasan, "Price Discounts or Coupon Promotions: Does It Matter?" *Journal of Business Research*, September 2004, p. 933; David Smagalla, "Does Promotional Pricing Grow Future Business?" *MIT Sloan Management Review*, Summer 2004, p. 9; Priya Raghubir and Joydeep Srivastava, "Effect of Face Value on Product Valuation in Foreign Currencies," *Journal of Consumer Research*, December 2002, p. 335; Matthew B. Myers and Michael Harvey, "The Value of Pricing Control in Export Channels: a Governance Perspective," *Journal of International Marketing*, no. 4 (2001), p. 1.

18. "Now Hoarding: Airlines Are Giving Frequent Fliers More Ways to Cash In," *Wall Street Journal*, December 9, 2005, p. W1ff.; "Who Really Reaps Mileage Rewards?" *Advertising Age*, June 20, 2005, p. 12; "Why Your Free Trip to Maui Is Hobbling the Airline Industry," *Wall Street Journal*, February 4, 2004, p. D1ff.; "Fliers' Dilemma: Save Now or Later?" *Business Week*, October 13, 2003, p. 138. See also "Search Engines Start Rewards Programs," *Wall Street Journal*, February 23, 2006, p. D1ff. "A New Wrinkle in Rewards Programs," *Wall Street Journal*, March 2, 2005, p. D1ff.; "Pizza Hut Adds Videos, Loyalty Cards to Recipe," *Brandweek*, September 29, 2003, p. 9; "Plastic's New Pitch: Something for Nothing," *Wall Street Journal*, July 31 2003, p. D1; "Frequent Flier to Rental Driver Has Its Price," *New York Times*, January 14, 2003, p. C4; "The Holy Grail: Getting Miles for Your Mortgage," *Wall Street Journal*, December 5, 2002, p. D1. See also Andy A. Tsay, "Managing Retail Channel Overstock: Markdown Money and Return Policies," *Journal of Retailing*, Winter 2001, p. 457; David E. Sprott, Kenneth C. Manning, and Anthony D. Miyazaki, "Grocery Price Setting and Quantity Surcharges," *Journal of Marketing*, July 2003, p. 34; Douglas D. Davis and Charles A. Holt, "List Prices and Discounts: The Interrelationship between Consumer Shopping Patterns and Profitable Marketing Strategies," *Psychology & Marketing*, July 1996, p. 341; David W. Arnesen, C. P. Fleenor, and Rex S. Toh, "The Ethical Dimensions of Airline Frequent Flier Programs," *Business Horizons*, January/February 1997, p. 47; K.J. Blois, "Discounts in Business Marketing Management," *Industrial Marketing Management*, April 1994, p. 93; James B. Wilcox et al., "Price Quantity Discounts: Some Implications for Buyers and Sellers," *Journal of Marketing*, July 1987, p. 60; Mark T. Spriggs and John R. Nevin, "The Legal Status of Trade and Functional Price Discounts," *Journal of Public Policy & Marketing*, Spring 1994, p. 61.

19. "Grocery Stores Cut Out the Weekly Special," *Wall Street Journal*, July 20, 2005, p. D1ff. For more on P&G's everyday low pricing, see "P&G, Others Try New Uses for Coupon-Heavy Media," *Advertising Age*, September 22, 1997, p. 20; "Move to Drop Coupons Puts Procter & Gamble in Sticky PR Situation," *Wall Street Journal*, April 17, 1997, p. A1; "Zeroing In on Zero Coupons," *Brandweek*, June 3, 1996, p. 30; "Company Makes Big Cuts to Stay Fit," *USA Today*, July 16, 1993, p. 1B. See also Kusum L. Ailawadi, Donald R. Lehmann, and Scott A. Neslin, "Market Response to a Major Policy Change in the Marketing Mix: Learning from Procter & Gamble's Value Pricing Strategy," *Journal of Marketing*, January 2001, p. 44; Monika Kukar-Kinney and Rockney G. Walters, "Consumer Perceptions of Refund Depth and Competitive Scope in Price-Matching Guarantees: Effects on Store Patronage," *Journal of Retailing*, Fall 2003, p. 153.

20. For more on slotting fees, see "Kraft Speeds New Product Launch Times," *Advertising Age*, November 18, 2002, p. 1; "The Hidden Cost of Shelf Space," *Business Week*, April 15, 2002, p. 103. See also Ramarao Desiraju, "New Product Introductions, Slotting Allowances, and Retailer Discretion," *Journal of Retailing*, Fall 2001, p. 335; David Balto, "Recent Legal and Regulatory Developments in Slotting Allowances and Category Management," *Journal of Public Policy & Marketing*, Fall 2002, p. 289; William L. Wilkie, Debra M. Desrochers, and Gregory T. Gundlach, "Marketing Research and Public Policy: the Case of Slotting Fees," *Journal of Public Policy & Marketing*, Fall 2002, p. 275.

21. "The Real Problem with Rebates," *Primedia*, January 11, 2006; "The Great Rebate Runaround," *Business Week*, December 5, 2005; "Would You Like Some E-Mail with That Pizza? Papa John's, Blackberry Tie-in," *Advertising Age*, July 11, 2005, pp. 3, 37; "Many Consumers Never Cash in Rebates," *Newsday*, January 23, 2005; "Use Them or Lose Them: Rebates Key to Driving Tech Sales," *Business Wire*, December 27, 2004; "Retailers Simplify the Rebate Process," *Boston Globe*, November 7, 2004, p. C1; "Livewire: When Rebates Yield Headaches Instead of Cash," *Forbes*, June 25, 2003; "Let's Make a (Tough) Deal," *Newsweek*, June 23, 2003, p. 48; "Ford Tames the Rebate Monster," *Business Week*, May 5, 2003, p. 38; "Rejected! Rebates Get Harder to Collect," *Wall Street Journal*, June 11, 2002, p. D1.

22. For more on coupons, see "Clipped Profits?" *Wall Street Journal Reports*, December 13, 2004, p. R11; "The Latest Craze in Coupon-Clipping: Free Trial Offers for Prescription Drugs," *Wall Street Journal*, April 16, 2002, p. D1; "Penny-Pinchers' Paradise," *Business Week E.Biz*, January 22, 2001, p. EB12; "E-Tailers Missing the Mark with Flood of Web Coupons," *Advertising Age*, September 25, 2000, p. 104; Gail Ayala Taylor, "Coupon Response in Services," *Journal of Retailing*, Spring 2001, p.139.

23. "Easy Does It All," *Business 2.0*, August 2005, pp. 68–74; "America's Pricing Paradox," *Wall Street Journal*, May 16, 2003, p. B1; "Ideas + Innovations: How to Thrive When Prices Fall," *Fortune*, May 12, 2003, p. 130; "Why Some Companies Can Levy Premium Prices and Others Not," *Investor's Business Daily*, April 15, 2003, p. A1; "Survival Strategies: After Cost Cutting, Companies Turn toward Price Rises," *Wall Street Journal*, September 18, 2002, p. A1; "Stepping Up: Middle Market Shrinks as Americans Migrate toward the High End," *Wall Street Journal*, March 29, 2002, p. A1; "Two-Tier Marketing," *Business Week*, March 17, 1997, p. 82; "Value Marketing," *Business Week*, November 11, 1991, p. 132.

24. "Freeze-Dried Berries Heat Up Cereal Duel," *Wall Street Journal*, May 15, 2003, p. B2; "Garfield's AdReview: A Few Spoons of Truth Tossed into Special K Red Berries Spot," *Advertising Age*, May 12, 2003, p. 65.

25. For an excellent discussion of laws related to pricing, see Louis W. Stern and Thomas L. Eovaldi, *Legal Aspects of Marketing Strategy: Antitrust and Consumer Protection Issues* (Englewood Cliffs, NJ: Prentice Hall, 1984); Joseph P. Guiltinan and Gregory T. Gundlach, "Aggressive and Predatory Pricing: A Framework for Analysis," *Journal of Marketing*, July 1996, p. 87.

26. For more on steel tariff, see "Steel Bends but Doesn't Break," *Investor's Business Daily*, May 3, 2004, p. A11; "Administration Weighs New Protection for Steel," *New York Times*, December 12, 2003, p. C7; "The Genie Is Out of the Bottle," *Wall Street Journal*, December 8, 2003, p. A14; "US-China Trade Tensions Rise," *Christian Science Monitor*, December 2, 2003, p. 1; "The Steel Tariff's Costs," *Wall Street Journal*, February 25, 2003, p. A14. For more on China dumping, see "How China Will Change Your Business," *Inc.*, March 2005, pp. 70–84; "The China Price," *Business Week*, December 6, 2004, pp. 102–12; "Dumping: China Strikes Back," *Business Week*, July 5, 2004, p. 58; "Wielding a Heavy Weapon against China," *Business Week*, June 21, 2004, pp. 56–57; "Chinese Furniture Faces U.S. Tariffs," *Wall Street Journal*, June 17, 2004, p. A2ff.

27. Patrick J. Kaufmann, N. Craig Smith, and Gwendolyn K. Ortmeyer, "Deception in Retailer High-Low Pricing: A 'Rule of Reason' Approach," *Journal of Retailing*, Summer 1994, p. 115.

28. For more on airline pricing, see "Is American-United Rivalry Too Friendly?" *USA Today*, June 27, 2001, p. 1B; "Predatory Pricing: Cleared for Takeoff," *Business Week*, May 14, 2001, p. 50; "American Airlines Secures Antitrust Win," *Wall Street Journal*, April 30, 2001, p. A3; "Caveat Predator?" *Business Week*, May 22, 2000, p. 116. For more on credit card pricing, see "House of Cards?" *Time*, October 23, 2000, pp. B10–B11; "Breaking Up the Old Card Game," *Business Week*, June 12, 2000, p. 98; "Antitrust Suit Targeting MasterCard and Visa Puts the Pair at Odds," *Wall Street Journal*, June 12, 2000, p. B1. For more on CD pricing, see "Prices of CDs Likely to Drop, Thanks to FTC," *Wall Street Journal*, May 11, 2000, p. B1. For more on De Beers, see "De Beers to Pay $10 Million Fine, Ending 10-Year, Price-Fixing Suit," *Wall Street Journal*, July 14, 2004, p. A3; "De Beers Is in Talks to Settle Price-Fixing Charge . . . Could Finally Give Cartel a Retail Presence in U.S.," *Wall Street Journal*, February 24, 2004, p. B1ff. For more on ADM, see "Questions Linger on Price of Seeds," *New York Times*, January 6, 2004, p. A1ff.; "In Archer-Daniels Saga, Now the Executives Face Trial," *Wall Street Journal*, July 9, 1998, p. B10; "The ADM Scandal: Betrayal," *Fortune*, February 3, 1997, p. 82. See also "In FCC Auctions of Airwaves, Gabelli Was behind the Scenes," *Wall Street Journal*, December 27, 2005, p. A1ff.; "Samsung Fined $300 Million in Price Fix Case," *Investor's Business Daily*, October 14, 2005, p. A4; "Sweet Deals or Strong-Arm Tactics? AMD Allege that Intel Gave Customers Discounts to Keep Rivals Out . . .," *Business Week*, July 11, 2005, p. 40; Probing Price Tags," *Wall Street Journal*, May 13, 2005, p. B1ff.; "How Driving Prices Lower Can Violate Antitrust Statutes," *Wall Street Journal*, January 27, 2004, p. A1ff.; "Online Booksellers Abound in Japan, but Legal Price Fixing Poses Challenge," *Wall Street Journal*, July 31, 2000, p. B8; "P&G Calls the Cops as It Strives to Expand Sales in Latin America," *Wall Street Journal*, March 20, 1998, p. A1; "Independent Bookstores Are Suing Borders Group and Barnes & Noble," *Wall Street Journal*, March 19, 1998, p. B10; "Cargill Agrees to Pay $24 Million to Settle Price-Fixing Suit," *Wall Street Journal*, March 11, 2004, p. 8. See also Alexander James Nicholls, "Strategic Options in Fair Trade Retailing," *International Journal of Retail & Distribution Management*, no. 1 (2002), p. 6.

29. Richard L. Pinkerton and Deborah J. Kemp, "The Industrial Buyer and the Robinson-Patman Act," *International Journal of Purchasing & Materials Management*, Winter 1996, p. 29.

30. "Firms Must Prove Injury from Price Bias to Qualify for Damages, High Court Says," *Wall Street Journal*, May 19, 1981, p. 8.

31. "Booksellers Say Five Publishers Play Favorites," *Wall Street Journal*, May 27, 1994, p. B1; Joseph P. Vaccaro and Derek W. F. Coward, "Managerial and Legal Implications of Price Haggling: A Sales Manager's Dilemma," *Journal of Personal Selling & Sales Management*, Summer 1993, p. 79; John R. Davidson, "FTC, Robinson-Patman and Cooperative Promotion Activities," *Journal of Marketing*, January 1968, p. 14; L. X. Tarpey, Sr., "Buyer Liability under the Robinson-Patman Act: A Current Appraisal," *Journal of Marketing*, January 1972, p. 38.

CHAPTER 17

1. For more on Wal-Mart in the U.S., see www.walmart.com; "Gauging the Wal-Mart Effect," *Wall Street Journal*, December 3, 2005, p. A9; "Watch Out, Best Buy and Circuit City," *Business Week Online*, November 10, 2005; "In-Store Television Is Paying Off," *Digital Media*, November 2005, pp. 12–13; "Can Wal-Mart Fit into a White Hat?" *Business Week*, October 3, 2005, pp. 94–96; "Wal-Mart Pursues the Upscale Customer," *VM+SD*, October 2005, pp. 14–16; "Wal-Mart Sets Out to Prove It; in Vogue," *Wall Street Journal*, August 25, 2005, p. B1ff.; "Wal-Mart Set Sights on Target while Keeping Core Customers," *USA Today*, August 5, 2005, p. 1Bff.; "How to Beat Wal-Mart," *Business 2.0*, May 2005, pp. 108–14; "Is Mighty Wal-Mart Vulnerable?" *Advertising Age*, December 13, 2004, pp. 1, 35; "Wal-Mart's Next Victims," *Forbes*, November 10, 2004; "Working with Wal-Mart: America's Most Powerful Partnership," *DSN Retailing Today* (supplement), June 2004, pp. 1–30; "Bringing Big-Ticket Technology into the Fold—Wal-Mart—Merchandising: CE & Entertainment—Consumer Electronics," *DSN Retailing Today*, January 26, 2004; "Wal-Mart Tunes in to Music Downloads," *DSN Retailing Today*, January 5, 2004, pp. 1, 28; "Wal-Mart Weans Suppliers," *Advertising Age*, December 1, 2003, pp. 1, 33; "Wal*Mart, Retailer of the Century," *Discount Store News*, October 1999; p. 1ff. For more on Wal-Mart International, see "The Great Wal-Mart of China," *Fortune*, July 25, 2005, pp. 104–16; "Germany: Wal-Mart, Local Pipsqueak," *Business Week*, April 11, 2005, p. 54; "Wal-Marts in Germany Redefine the Term Checkout Aisle," *Wall Street Journal*, November 9,

2004, p. B1ff.; "Pacific Aisles: Wal-Mart's Foray into Japan Spurs a Retail Upheaval," *Wall Street Journal*, September 19, 2003, p. A1; "Wal-Mart Adds to Global Reach with Tokyo Supermarket Stake," *Investor's Business Daily*, March 15, 2002, p. A1; Angela da Rocha and Luis Antonio Dib, "The Entry of Wal-Mart in Brazil and the Competitive Responses of Multinational and Domestic Firms," *International Journal of Retail & Distribution Management*, no. 1 (2002), p. 61; John Fernie and Stephen J. Arnold, "Wal-Mart in Europe: Prospects for Germany, the UK and France," *International Journal of Retail & Distribution Management*, no. 2 (2002), p. 92.

2. Kusum L. Ailawadi and Bari Harlam, "An Empirical Analysis of the Determinants of Retail Margins: The Role of Store-Brand Share," *Journal of Marketing*, January 2004, p. 147; Ritu Lohtia, Ramesh Subramaniam, and Rati Lohtia, "Are Pricing Practices in Japanese Channels of Distribution Finally Changing?" *Journal of Marketing Channels*, no. 1/2 (2001), p. 5; Marvin A. Jolson, "A Diagrammatic Model for Merchandising Calculations," *Journal of Retailing*, Summer 1975, p. 3; C. Davis Fogg and Kent H. Kohnken, "Price-Cost Planning," *Journal of Marketing*, April 1978, p. 97.

3. See www.coach.com; *2005 Annual Report*, Coach; *2004 Annual Report*, Coach; "Coach's Split Personality," *Business Week*, November 7, 2005, pp. 60–62; "Why Some Brands Can Stand Alone," *Business 2.0*, October, 2005, pp. 49–51; "Coach, Inc.," *Datamonitor*, April 2005; "How Coach Pulled into Luxury's Fast Lane," *Financial Times*, June 30, 2004, p. 12; Michael J. Silverstein and Neil Fiske, *Trading Up: The New American Luxury* (New York: Penguin, 2003); "What Makes Coach a Winner? A Sharply Focused Game Plan," *Business and Industry*, January 3, 2003.

4. "The Little Extras That Count (Up)," *Wall Street Journal*, July 12, 2001, p. B1; "Battle-Tested Rules of Online Retail," *Ecompany*, April 2001; "The Return of Pricing Power," *Business Week*, May 8, 2000, p. 50; "The Power of Smart Pricing," *Business Week*, April 10, 2000, p. 160. See also Mary L. Hatten, "Don't Get Caught with Your Prices Down: Pricing in Inflationary Times," *Business Horizons*, March 1982, p. 23; Douglas G. Brooks, "Cost Oriented Pricing: A Realistic Solution to a Complicated Problem," *Journal of Marketing*, April 1975, p. 72; Steven M. Shugan, "Retail Product-Line Pricing Strategy When Costs and Products Change," *Journal of Retailing*, Spring 2001, Vol. 77, 1, p. 17.

5. G. Dean Kortge, "Inverted Breakeven Analysis for Profitable Marketing Decisions," *Industrial Marketing Management*, October 1984, p. 219; Thomas L. Powers, "Breakeven Analysis with Semifixed Costs," *Industrial Marketing Management*, February 1987, p. 35.

6. Approaches for estimating price-quantity relationships are reviewed in Kent B. Monroe, *Pricing: Making Profitable Decisions* (New York: McGraw-Hill, 2003). For specific examples see Gordon A. Wyner, Lois H. Benedetti, and Bart M. Trapp, "Measuring the Quantity and Mix of Product Demand," *Journal of Marketing*, Winter 1984, p. 101. See also Michael F. Smith and Indrajit Sinha, "The Impact of Price and Extra Product Promotions on Store Preference," *International Journal of Retail & Distribution Management*, no. 2 (2000), p. 83; Michael H. Morris and Mary L. Joyce, "How Marketers Evaluate Price Sensitivity," *Industrial Marketing Management*, May, 1988, p. 169. David E. Griffith and Roland T. Rust, "The Price of Competitiveness in Competitive Pricing," *Journal of the Academy of Marketing Science*, Spring 1997, p. 109; Frank D. Jones, "A Survey Technique to Measure Demand under Various Pricing Strategies," *Journal of Marketing*, July 1975, p. 75; Robert J. Dolan, "How Do You Know When the Price Is Right?" *Harvard Business Review*, September–October 1995, p. 174; S. C. Choi, "Price Competition in a Duopoly Common Retailer Channel," *Journal of Retailing*, Summer 1996, p. 117.

7. "Getting Skewered by Shrimp Prices," *Wall Street Journal*, October 16, 2003, p. D1; "Secret in the Dairy Aisle: Milk Is a Cash Cow," *Wall Street Journal*, July 28, 2003, p. B1; "New Status Symbol: Overpaying for Your Minivan," *Wall Street Journal*, July 23, 2003, p. D1; "No More Free Lunch . . . Please?" *Wall Street Journal Reports*, September 24, 2001, p. R13; "Who Really Needs a Pentium

4?" *Fortune*, January 8, 2001, p. 217; "Marriott International: A Hotel That Clicks with Guests," *Business Week E.Biz*, September 18, 2000, p. EB58; "The Paradox of Value," *Brandweek*, June 5, 2000, p. 40; Watts Wacker and Jim Taylor, *The Visionary's Handbook: Nine Paradoxes That Will Shape the Future of Your Business* (New York: HarperCollins, 2000). See also Kirk L. Wakefield and J. Jeffrey Inman, "Situational Price Sensitivity: The Role of Consumption Occasion, Social Context and Income," *Journal of Retailing*, Winter 2003, p. 199; Kristin Diehl, Laura J. Kornish, and John G. Lynch, Jr., "Smart Agents: When Lower Search Costs for Quality Information Increase Price Sensitivity," *Journal of Consumer Research*, Jun 2003, p. 56; Amir Heiman, Bruce McWilliams, Jinhua Zhao, and David Zilberman, "Valuation and Management of Money-Back Guarantee Options," *Journal of Retailing*, Fall 2002, p. 193; Dhruv Grewal, Kent B. Monroe, and R. Krishnan, "The Effects of Price-Comparison Advertising on Buyers' Perceptions of Acquisition Value, Transaction Value, and Behavioral Intentions," *Journal of Marketing*, April 1998, p. 46; John T. Gourville, "Pennies-a-Day: The Effect of Temporal Reframing on Transaction Evaluation," *Journal of Consumer Research*, March 1998, p. 395; Joel E. Urbany, Rosemary Kalapurakal, and Peter R. Dickson, "Price Search in the Retail Grocery Market," *Journal of Marketing*, April 1996, p. 91; Venkatesh Shankar and Lakshman Krishnamurthi, "Relating Price Sensitivity to Retailer Promotional Variables and Pricing Policy: An Empirical Analysis," *Journal of Retailing*, Fall 1996, p. 249; Chakravarthi Narasimhan, Scott A. Neslin, and Subrata K. Sen, "Promotional Elasticities and Category Characteristics," *Journal of Marketing*, April 1996, p. 17; K. Sivakumar and S. P. Raj, "Quality Tier Competition: How Price Change Influences Brand Choice and Category Choice," *Journal of Marketing*, July 1997, p. 71.

8. Thomas T. Nagle and Reed R. Holder, *The Strategy and Tactics of Pricing* (Englewood Cliffs, NJ: Prentice Hall, 2002); "Fram Pays Up Now," *Brandweek*, July 20, 1998, p. 16; "New Long-Life Bulbs May Lose Brilliance in a Crowded Market," *Wall Street Journal*, June 2, 1992, p. B4; Andreas Hinterhuber, "Towards Value-Based Pricing— An Integrative Framework for Decision Making," *Industrial Marketing Management*, November 2004, p. 765; Benson P. Shapiro and Barbara P. Jackson, "Industrial Pricing to Meet Customer Needs," *Harvard Business Review*, November–December 1978, p. 119; "The Race to the $10 Light Bulb," *Business Week*, May 19, 1980, p. 124; see also Michael H. Morris and Donald A. Fuller, "Pricing an Industrial Service," *Industrial Marketing Management*, May 1989, p. 139.

9. For more on eBay, see Chapter 12, endnote 18. See also "Copart: Auctioneer's Web Move Puts It in Fast Lane," *Investor's Business Daily*, June 16, 2004, p. A6; "Renaissance in Cyberspace," *Wall Street Journal*, November 20, 2003, p. B1; "Sold! to Save the Farm," *Wall Street Journal*, August 29, 2003, p. B1; "Online Liquidators Help Firm Shed Unsold Goods," *Investor's Business Daily*, August 13, 2002, p. A5; "Good-Bye to Fixed Pricing?" *Business Week*, May 4, 1998, p. 71. See also Larry R. Smeltzer and Amelia S. Carr, "Electronic Reverse Auctions: Promises, Risks and Conditions for Success," *Industrial Marketing Management*, August 2003, p. 481; Sandy D. Jap, "An Exploratory Study of the Introduction of Online Reverse Auctions," *Journal of Marketing*, July 2003, p. 96.

10. "The Price Is Really Right," *Business Week*, March 31, 2003, p. 62; "New Software Manages Price Cuts," *Investor's Business Daily*, March 31, 2003, p. A4; "The Power of Optimal Pricing," *Business 2.0*, September 2002, p. 68; "Priced to Move: Retailers Try to Get Leg Up on Markdowns with New Software," *Wall Street Journal*, August 7, 2001, p. A1; "The Price Is Right," *Inc.*, July 2001, p. 40. See also Tridib Mazumdar, S. P. Raj, and Indrajit Sinha, "Reference Price Research: Review and Propositions," *Journal of Marketing*, October 2005, p. 84; Michael J. Barone, Kenneth C. Manning, and Paul W. Miniard, "Consumer Response to Retailers' Use of Partially Comparative Pricing," *Journal of Marketing*, July 2004, p. 37; Chezy Ofir, "Reexamining Latitude of Price Acceptability and Price Thresholds: Predicting Basic Consumer Reaction to Price," *Journal of Consumer Research*, March 2004, p. 612; Aradhna Krishna, Mary Wagner, Carolyn Yoon, and

Rashmi Adaval, "Effects of Extreme-Priced Products on Consumer Reservation Prices," *Journal of Consumer Psychology*, 2006, p. 176; Sangkil Moon, Gary J. Russell, and Sri Devi Duvvuri, "Profiling the Reference Price Consumer," *Journal of Retailing*, March 2006, p. 1; John T. Gourville and Youngme Moon, "Managing Price Expectations through Product Overlap," *Journal of Retailing*, Spring 2004, p. 23; Marc Vanhuele and Xavier Dreze, "Measuring the Price Knowledge Shoppers Bring to the Store," *Journal of Marketing*, October 2002, p. 72; Rashmi Adaval and Kent B. Monroe, "Automatic Construction and Use of Contextual Information for Product and Price Evaluations," *Journal of Consumer Research*, March 2002, p. 572; Sangman Han, Sunil Gupta, and Donald R. Lehmann, "Consumer Price Sensitivity and Price Thresholds," *Journal of Retailing*, Winter 2001, p. 435; David Ackerman and Gerard Tellis, "Can Culture Affect Prices? A Cross-Cultural Study of Shopping and Retail Prices," *Journal of Retailing*, Spring 2001, p. 57; David M. Hardesty and William O. Bearden, "Consumer Evaluations of Different Promotion Types and Price Presentations: The Moderating Role of Promotional Benefit Level," *Journal of Retailing*, no. 1 (2003), p. 17; Rajesh Chandrashekaran and Dhruv Grewal, "Assimilation of Advertised Reference Prices: the Moderating Role of Involvement," *Journal of Retailing*, no. 1 (2003), p. 53; Thomas Jensen, Jeremy Kees, Scot Burton, and Fernanda Lucarelli Turnipseed, "Advertised Reference Prices in an Internet Environment: Effects on Consumer Price Perceptions and Channel Search Intentions," *Journal of Interactive Marketing*, Spring 2003, p. 20; Joel E. Urbany, Peter R. Dickson, and Alan G. Sawyer, "Insights into Cross- and Within-Store Price Search: Retailer Estimates vs. Consumer Self-Reports," *Journal of Retailing*, Summer 2000, p. 243; Merrie Brucks, Valarie A. Zeithaml, and Gillian Naylor, "Price and Brand Name as Indicators of Quality Dimensions for Consumer Durables," *Journal of the Academy of Marketing Science*, Summer 2000, p. 359; Joydeep Srivastava and Nicholas Lurie, "A Consumer Perspective on Price-Matching Refund Policies: Effect on Price Perceptions and Search Behavior," *Journal of Consumer Research*, September 2001, p. 296; Ronald W. Niedrich, Subhash Sharma, and Douglas H. Wedell, "Reference Price and Price Perceptions: A Comparison of Alternative Models," *Journal of Consumer Research*, December 2001, p. 339; Erica Mina Okada, "Trade-Ins, Mental Accounting, and Product Replacement Decisions," *Journal of Consumer Research*, March 2001, p. 433; Aradhna Krishna, Richard Briesch, Donald R. Lehmann, and Hong Yuan, "A Meta-Analysis of the Impact of Price Presentation on Perceived Savings," *Journal of Retailing*, Summer 2002, p. 101; Valerie A. Taylor and William O. Bearden, "The Effects of Price on Brand Extension Evaluations: The Moderating Role of Extension Similarity," *Journal of the Academy of Marketing Science*, Spring 2002, p. 131; James K. Binkley and John Bejnarowicz, "Consumer Price Awareness in Food Shopping: The Case of Quantity Surcharges," *Journal of Retailing*, no. 1 (2003), p. 27; Lesa E. Bolton, Luk Warlop, and Joseph W. Alba, "Consumer Perceptions of Price (Un)fairness," *Journal of Consumer Research*, March 2003, p. 474; Amir Heiman, Bruce McWilliams, and David Zilberman, "Demonstrations and Money-Back Guarantees: Market Mechanisms to Reduce Uncertainty," *Journal of Business Research*, October 2001, p. 71; Edward A. Blair, Judy Harris, and Kent B. Monroe, "Effects of Shopping Information on Consumers' Responses to Comparative Price Claims," *Journal of Retailing*, Fall 2002, p. 175; Hooman Estelami, "The Impact of Research Design on Consumer Price Recall Accuracy: An Integrative Review," *Journal of the Academy of Marketing Science*, Winter 2001, p. 36; Richard A. Briesch, Lakshman Krishnamurthi, Tridib Mazumdar, and S. P. Raj, "A Comparative Analysis of Reference Price Models," *Journal of Consumer Research*, September 1997, p. 202.

11. For a classic example applied to a high-price item, see "Sale of Mink Coats Strays a Fur Piece from the Expected," *Wall Street Journal*, March 21, 1980, p. 30.

12. K. Douglas Hoffman, L. W. Turley, and Scott W. Kelley, "Pricing Retail Services," *Journal of Business Research*, December

2002, p. 1015; Steven M. Shugan and Ramarao Desiraju, "Retail Product-Line Pricing Strategy When Costs and Products Change," *Journal of Retailing*, Spring 2001, p. 17; Noel M. Noel and Nessim Hanna, "Benchmarking Consumer Perceptions of Product Quality With Price: An Exploration," *Psychology & Marketing*, September 1996, p. 591; Niraj Dawar and Philip Parker, "Marketing Universals: Consumers' Use of Brand Name, Price, Physical Appearance, and Retailer Reputation as Signals of Product Quality," *Journal of Marketing*, April 1994, p. 81; Tung-Zong Chang and Albert R. Wildt, "Impact of Product Information on the Use of Price as a Quality Cue," *Psychology & Marketing*, January 1996, p. 55; B. P. Shapiro, "The Psychology of Pricing," *Harvard Business Review*, July–August 1968, p. 14; Lutz Hildebrandt, "The Analysis of Price Competition between Corporate Brands," *International Journal of Research in Marketing*, June 2001, p. 139.

13. Lee C. Simmons and Robert M. Schindler, "Cultural Superstitions and the Price Endings Used in Chinese Advertising," *Journal of International Marketing*, no. 2 (2003), p. 101; Robert M. Schindler and Thomas M. Kibarian, "Image Communicated by the Use of 99 Endings in Advertised Prices," *Journal of Advertising*, Winter 2001, p. 95; Robert M. Schindler and Patrick N. Kirby, "Patterns of Rightmost Digits Used in Advertised Prices: Implications for Nine-Ending Effects," *Journal of Consumer Research*, September 1997, p. 192; Mark Stiving and Russell S. Winer, "An Empirical Analysis of Price Endings with Scanner Data," *Journal of Consumer Research*, June 1997, p. 57; Robert M. Schindler and Alan R. Wiman, "Effects of Odd Pricing on Price Recall," *Journal of Business Research*, November 1989, p. 165.

14. "For Landlords, Jewelry Stores Are Big Gems," *Wall Street Journal*, May 20, 2005, p. B1ff.; "Diamond Store in the Rough: Opening of De Beers Boutique . . .," *Wall Street Journal*, May 20, 2005, p. B1ff.; "Reaching Out to Younger Crowd Works for Tiffany," *USA Today*, February 26, 2004, p. 5B; "Tiffany & Co. Branches Out under an Alias," *Wall Street Journal*, July 23, 2003, p. B1; "The Cocoon Cracks Open," *Brandweek*, April 28, 2003, p. 32; "Goodbye, Mr. Goodbar: Chocolate Gets Snob Appeal," *Wall Street Journal*, February 13, 2003, p. D1; "Luxury Marketing," *Advertising Age*, March 11, 2002, pp. S1–S10; "Keeping the Cachet," *Wall Street Journal*, April 23, 2001, p. R28; "Luxury Sites Get Scrappy," *Wall Street Journal*, December 4, 2000, p. B1; "Online Luxury Has Limits," *Business Week E.Biz*, September 18, 2000, p. EB24; "Luxury Marketing," *Advertising Age*, August 14, 2000, p. S1; "The Galloping Gourmet Chocolate," *Brandweek*, July 31, 2000, p. 32. See also Xing Pan, Brian T. Ratchford, and Venkatesh Shankar, "Can Price Dispersion in Online Markets Be Explained by Differences in E-Tailer Service Quality?" *Journal of the Academy of Marketing Science*, Fall 2002, p. 433; Kusum L. Ailawadi, Donald R. Lehmann, and Scott A. Neslin, "Revenue Premium as an Outcome Measure of Brand Equity," *Journal of Marketing*, October 2003, p. 1; "Life on Easy Street," *American Demographics*, April 1997, p. 33; G. Dean Kortge and Patrick A. Okonkwo, "Perceived Value Approach to Pricing," *Industrial Marketing Management*, May 1993, p. 133.

15. For more on Gillette's complementary pricing, see "How Many Blades Is Enough?" *Fortune*, October 31, 2005, p. 40; "Gillette's Smooth Bet: Mean Will Pay More for Five-Blade Razor," *Wall Street Journal*, September 15, 2005, p. B1ff.; "Can Gillette Regain Its Edge?" *Business Week*, January 26, 2004, p. 46; See also "Google, Sun Agree to Bundle Programs," *Investor's Business Daily*, October 5, 2005, p. A6; "Adobe Turns Page with New Software Line," *Investor's Business Daily*, November 13, 2003, p. A4; "The Allure of Bundling," *Wall Street Journal*, October 7, 2003, p. B1; "Computer Deals Hit New Lows," *Wall Street Journal*, August 13, 2003, p. D1. For more on phone bundling, see "Internet Phone Calls Could Squeeze Prices," *Investor's Business Daily*, December 12, 2003, p. A1; "Circuit Breaker: Battered Telecoms Face New Challenge: Internet Calling," *Wall Street Journal*, October 9, 2003, p. A1; "BellSouth Hooks Up with DirecTV," *Wall Street Journal*, August 27, 2003, p. B7; "Honey, I Shrunk the Phone Bill," *Business Week*, June 9, 2003, p. 132; "Cellphone Giveaways Get an Upgrade," *Wall Street Journal*, May 20, 2003, p. D1; "A Nickel Here, a Buck There Add Up to Big Local Bills," *USA Today*, February 28, 2003, p. 1B; "Phone, Cable Cos. Use Bundling to Keep Users from Switching," *Investor's Business Daily*, December 13, 2002, p. A1. For more on airline food unbundling, see "Dining Out at 32,000 Feet," *Wall Street Journal*, June 3, 2003, p. D1; "Food Flights," *USA Today*, January 17, 2003, p. 1D. See also R. Venkatesh and Rabikar Chatterjee, "Bundling, Unbundling, and Pricing of Multiform Products: The Case of Magazine Content," *Journal of Interactive Marketing*, Spring 2006, p. 21; Andrea Ovans, "Make a Bundle Bundling," *Harvard Business Review*, November–December 1997, p. 18; Preyas S. Desai and Kannan Srinivasan, "Aggregate versus Product-Specific Pricing: Implications for Franchise and Traditional Channels," *Journal of Retailing*, Winter 1996, p. 357; Manjit S. Yadav and Kent B. Monroe, "How Buyers Perceive Savings in a Bundle Price: An Examination of a Bundle's Transaction Value," *Journal of Marketing Research*, August 1993, p. 350; Dorothy Paun, "When to Bundle or Unbundle Products," *Industrial Marketing Management*, February 1993, p. 29.

16. Mary Anne Raymond, John F. Tanner, Jr., and Jonghoon Kim, "Cost Complexity of Pricing Decisions for Exporters in Developing and Emerging Markets," *Journal of International Marketing*, no. 3 (2001), p. 19; Peter E. Connor and Robert K. Hopkins, "Cost Plus What? The Importance of Accurate Profit Calculations in Cost-Plus Agreements," *International Journal of Purchasing & Materials Management*, Spring 1997, p. 35; Daniel T. Ostas, "Ethics of Contract Pricing," *Journal of Business Ethics*, February 1992, p. 137; J. Steve Davis, "Ethical Problems in Competitive Bidding: The Paradyne Case," *Business and Professional Ethics Journal* 7, no. 2 (1988), p. 3; David T. Levy, "Guaranteed Pricing in Industrial Purchases: Making Use of Markets in Contractual Relations," *Industrial Marketing Management*, October 1994, p. 307; Akintola Akintoye and Martin Skitmore, "Pricing Approaches in the Construction Industry," *Industrial Marketing Management*, November 1992, p. 311.

CHAPTER 18

1. For more on consumer choice, see Ross D. Petty, "Limiting Product Choice: Innovation, Market Evolution, and Antitrust," *Journal of Public Policy & Marketing*, Fall 2002, p. 269; Mitch Griffin, Barry J. Babin, and Doan Modianos, "Shopping Values of Russian Consumers: The Impact of Habituation in a Developing Economy," *Journal of Retailing*, Spring 2000, p. 33; Suk-ching Ho, "The Emergence of Consumer Power in China," *Business Horizons*, September–October 1997, p. 15; Matthew B. Myers, "New and Improved: The Story of Mass Marketing in America," *Journal of the Academy of Marketing Science*, Summer 1997, p. 258; Terry Clark, "Moving Mountains to Market: Reflections on Restructuring the Russian Economy," *Business Horizons*, March–April 1994, p. 16. See also "From Sour Grapes to Online Whine," *USA Today*, April 7, 2000, p. 1B; "Service with a What?" *Business Week*, September 8, 1997, pp. 130F–H; "Oh, What a Feeling," *Newsweek*, July 28, 1997, p. 51; "Attention, Wal-Mart Shoppers: You Want Fries with That?" *Wall Street Journal*, July 25, 1997, p. B6; "Buyers Get No Satisfaction," *USA Today*, July 22, 1997, p. 1B. For more on Tesco, see "Teaching the Big Box New Tricks," *Fortune*, November 14, 2005, pp. 208B-F; "With Help of Clever Trolley, Tesco Speeds Online Orders," *Investor's Business Daily*, December 8, 2004, p. A6; "British Supermarket Giant Cooks Up Plans to Go Global," *Wall Street Journal*, July 5, 2001, p. A9; "British Grocer Tesco Thrives Filling Web Orders from Its Stores' Aisles," *Wall Street Journal*, October 16, 2000, p. B1; "Tesco: A Fresh Approach to Online Groceries," *Business Week E.Biz*, September 18, 2000, p. EB79. For more on online shopping for groceries in the U.S., see "Click Here for Groceries," *Health*, October 2005, pp. 170–73; "FreshDirect Cooks Up New Web Retail Angle," *DSN Retailing Today*, October 11, 2004, p. F5; "Online Grocers: Ready to Deliver?" *Brandweek*, May 3, 2004, pp. 26–30; "The Big Cheese of Online Grocers," *Business 2.0*, January/February 2004, pp. 60–61; "Virtual Bounty: Groceries to Go," *Brandweek*, November 24, 2003, p. 19; "Services: Online Grocers," *Newsweek*, August 4, 2003, p. 60; "Amazon, Mail-Order Retailers Reheat Online Food Sales," *Wall Street Journal*, June 23, 2003, p. B1; "What's for Dinner?" *Time*, May 19, 2003, p. 85; "Online Grocers: Finally Delivering the Lettuce," *Business Week*, April 28, 2003, p. 67; "Back from the Dead: Buying Groceries Online," *Wall Street Journal*, February 25, 2003, p. D1; "Webvan May Be Long Gone, but the Concept's Living On," *Investor's Business Daily*, November 5, 2001, p. A9. For more on Webvan's failed effort, see "Traditional Grocers Feel Vindicated by Webvan's Failure," *Wall Street Journal*, July 11, 2001, p. B4. See also "Information Gridlock: Fate, Fortune Ride on Flow of Critical Data," *USA Today*, July 2, 1996, p. 1B; Michael B. Mazis, "Marketing and Public Policy: Prospects for the Future," *Journal of Public Policy & Marketing*, Spring 1997, p. 139; Cornelia Droge et al., "The Consumption Culture and Its Critiques: A Framework for Analysis," *Journal of Macromarketing*, Fall 1993, p. 32. For more on obesity concerns, see "Helping Your Kids Slim Down," *Business Week*, January 9, 2006, pp. 86–87; "Tony the Tiger on Death Row?" *Advertising Age*, December 12, 2005, pp. 1, 30; "Panel Faults Food Packaging for Kid Obesity," *Wall Street Journal*, December 7, 2005, p. B1ff.; "Why Kraft Decided to Ban Some Food Ads to Children," *Wall Street Journal*, October 31, 2005, p. A1ff.; "You Want Nutrition Info with That?" *USA Today*, October 26, 2005, p. 1Aff.; "Slimmer Kids, Fatter Profits," *Business Week*, September 5, 2005, pp. 72–73; "Food Fight's New Fronts: Viral Marketing, Games," *Advertising Age*, July 18, 2005, pp. 3, 35; "Food Makers Propose Tougher Guidelines for Children's Ads," *Wall Street Journal*, July 13, 2005, p. B1f.; "Obesity Surges among Affluent," *USA Today*, May 3, 2005, p. 1A; "For the Health-Unconscious, Era of Mammoth Burger Is Here," *Wall Street Journal*, January 27, 2005, p. B1ff; "New Obesity Boom in Arab Countries Has Old Ancestry," *Wall Street Journal*, December 29, 2004, p. A1ff.; "Let Them Eat Cake—If They Want To," *Business Week*, February 23, 2004, pp. 110–11; "Downsize This!" *Wall Street Journal*, January 27, 2004, p. B1ff.; "Why We're Losing the War against Obesity," *American Demographics*, January 2004, pp. 24–31; "Today's Kids Are Helping Themselves," *USA Today*, November 20, 2003, p. 1D; "Junk Food Super-Sizing Europeans," *USA Today*, November 18, 2003, p. 13A; "The Dining Hall Diet," *Wall Street Journal*, November 7, 2003, p. W1; "Dieters' Taboo Foods Not So Bad, Ads Claim," *USA Today*, November 3, 2003, p. 4B; "Pizza Hut to Serve Up Slices of Healthier Pie," *USA Today*, October 15, 2003, p. 1B; "Americans Start to Shape Up, Eat Healthier," *Wall Street Journal*, October 14, 2003, p. B1; "Obesity Predicted for 40% of America," *USA Today*, October 14, 2003, p. 7D; "A Real Food Fight Breaks Out in Schools," *Investor's Business Daily*, September 22, 2003, p. A8; "Guess What F Is For? Fat," *Time*, September 15, 2003, p. 68; "Obesity Suit against McDonald's Is Dismissed by Federal Judge," *Wall Street Journal*, September 5, 2003, p. B4; "Fast Foods: Back in Court," *Time* (Inside Edition Bonus Section), September 2003; "Saving Mickey D's Bacon," *Business Week*, August 25, 2003, p. 46; "Obesity Goes Global," *Time*, August 25, 2003, p. 53; "Frito-Lay Puts Smart-Snack Label on Baked Chips," *Wall Street Journal*, August 6, 2003, p. D3; "Judge Drops Lawsuit against McDonald's," *USA Today*, January 23, 2003, p. 2B; "That Veggie Wrap You Just Chowed Down Is More Fattening than a Ham Sandwich," *Wall Street Journal*, January 14, 2003, p. D1; "Obesity: A World-Wide Woe," *Wall Street Journal*, July 1, 2002, p. B1; "Is Food the Next Tobacco?" *Wall Street Journal*, June 13, 2002, p. B1; Stephanie Dellande, Mary C. Gilly, and John L. Graham, "Gaining Compliance and Losing Weight: The Role of the Service Provider in Health Care Services," *Journal of Marketing*, July 2004, p. 78; Rosellina Ferraro, Baba shiv Shiv, James R. Bettman, Dawn Iacobucci, and Barbara Kahn, "Let Us Eat and Drink, for Tomorrow We Shall Die: Effects of Mortality Salience and Self-Esteem on Self-Regulation in Consumer Choice," *Journal of Consumer Research*, June 2005, p. 65; Melissa Grills Robinson, Paul N. Bloom, and Nicholas H. Lurie, "Combating Obesity in the Courts: Will Lawsuits against McDonald's Work?," *Journal of Public Policy & Marketing*, Fall 2005, p. 299; Kathleen Seiders and Ross D. Petty, "Obesity and the Role of Food Marketing: A Policy Analysis of Issues and Remedies," *Journal of Public Policy & Marketing*, Fall 2004, p. 153; Brian Wansink and Mike Huckabee, "De-Marketing Obesity," *California Management Review*, Summer 2005, p. 6.

2. *The American Customer Satisfaction Index*, www.theacsi.org, and "Now Are You Satisfied? The 1998 American Customer Satisfaction Index," *Fortune*, February 16, 1998, p. 161. See also Terrence H. Witkowski and Mary F. Wolfinbarger, "Comparative Service Quality: German and American Ratings across Service Settings," *Journal of Business Research*, November 2002, p. 875; Eugene W. Anderson and Linda Court Salisbury, "The Formation of Market-Level Expectations and Its Covariates," *Journal of Consumer Research*, Jun 2003, p. 115; Claes Fornell, Michael D. Johnson, Eugene W. Anderson, Jaesung Cha, and Barbara E. Bryant, "The American Customer Satisfaction Index: Nature, Purpose, and Findings," *Journal of Marketing*, October 1996, p. 7; Eugene W. Anderson, Claes Fornell, and Donald R. Lehmann, "Customer Satisfaction, Market Share, and Profitability: Findings from Sweden," *Journal of Marketing*, July 1994, p. 53; John F. Gaski and Michael J. Etzel, "The Index of Consumer Sentiment toward Marketing," *Journal of Marketing*, July 1986, p. 71; "The Limits of Customer Satisfaction," *Brandweek*, March 3, 1997, p. 17; Hiram C. Barksdale et al., "A Cross-National Survey of Consumer Attitudes toward Marketing Practices, Consumerism, and Government Regulations," *Columbia Journal of World Business*, Summer 1982, p. 71; Hiram C. Barksdale and William D. Perreault, Jr., "Can Consumers Be Satisfied?" *MSU Business Topics*, Spring 1980, p. 19.

3. "Expanding J.D.'s Power," *Business Week*, November 22, 2004, pp. 158–60; "Consumer Complaints Soared in 2002," *Wall Street Journal*, November 25, 2003, p. D2; "Will Jeff Immelt's New Push Pay Off for GE?" *Business Week*, October 13, 2003, p. 94; "Whatever Happened to Customer Service?" *USA Today*, September 26, 2003, p. 1A; "Ma'am, Please: Never Call Us Again," *Brandweek*, September 22, 2003, p. 38; "J.D. Power for the People," *USA Today*, August 28, 2003, p. 3B; "Web-Portal Satisfaction Rises," *Wall Street Journal*, August 20, 2003, p. D2; "My Cookies Are Crumbled; the Art of Consumer Griping," *Wall Street Journal*, August 27, 2002, p. D1. See also Judy Strauss and Donna J. Hill, "Consumer Complaints by E-Mail: an Exploratory Investigation of Corporate Responses and Customer Reactions," *Journal of Interactive Marketing*, Winter 2001, p. 63; James G. Maxham III and Richard G. Netemeyer, "Modeling Customer Perceptions of Complaint Handling over Time: the Effects of Perceived Justice on Satisfaction and Intent," *Journal of Retailing*, Winter 2002, p. 239; James G. Maxham III and Richard G. Netemeyer, "A Longitudinal Study of Complaining Customers' Evaluations of Multiple Service Failures and Recovery Efforts," *Journal of Marketing*, October 2002, p. 57; James G. Maxham III and Richard G. Netemeyer, "Firms Reap What They Sow: The Effects of Shared Values and Perceived Organizational Justice on Customers' Evaluations of Complaint Handling," *Journal of Marketing*, January 2003, p. 46; Roger Bougie, Rik Pieters, and Marcel Zeelenberg, "Angry Customers Don't Come Back, They Get Back: The Experience and Behavioral Implications of Anger and Dissatisfaction in Services," *Journal of the Academy of Marketing Science*, Fall 2003, p. 377; Amy K. Smith and Ruth N. Bolton, "The Effect of Customers' Emotional Responses to Service Failures on Their Recovery Effort Evaluations and Satisfaction Judgments," *Journal of the Academy of Marketing Science*, Winter 2002, p. 5; Michael Brady, "Improving Your Measurement of Customer Satisfaction: A Guide to Creating, Conducting, Analyzing, and Reporting Customer Satisfaction Measurement Programs," *Journal of the Academy of Marketing Science*, Spring 2000, p. 315; David M. Szymanski, "Customer Satisfaction: A Meta-Analysis of the Empirical Evidence," *Journal of the Academy of Marketing Science*, Winter 2001, p. 16; Thorsten Hennig-Thurau and Alexander Klee, "The Impact of Customer Satisfaction and Relationship Quality on Customer Retention: A Critical Reassessment and Model Development," *Psychology & Marketing*, December 1997, p. 737; Scott W. Hansen, Thomas L. Powers, and John E. Swan, "Modeling Industrial Buyer Complaints: Implications for Satisfying and Saving Customers," *Journal of Marketing Theory & Practice*, Fall 1997, p. 12; Paul G. Patterson, Lester W. Johnson, and Richard A. Spreng, "Modeling the Determinants of Customer Satisfaction for Business-to-Business Professional Services," *Journal of the Academy of Marketing Science*, Winter 1997, p. 4; Stephen S. Tax, Stephen W. Brown, and Murali Chandrashekaran, "Customer Evaluations of Service Complaint Experiences: Implications for Relationship Marketing," *Journal of Marketing*, April 1998, p. 60; F. Gouillart and F. Sturdivant, "Spend a Day in the Life of Your Customers," *Harvard Business Review*, January–February 1994, p. 116.

4. Claes Fornell, Sunil Mithas, Forrest V. Morgeson III, and M. S. Krishnan, "Customer Satisfaction and Stock Prices: High Returns, Low Risk," *Journal of Marketing*, January 2006, p. 3; Neil A. Morgan, Eugene W. Anderson, and Vikas Mittal, "Understanding Firms' Customer Satisfaction Information Usage," *Journal of Marketing*, July 2005, p. 131; Eugene W. Anderson, Claes Fornell, and Sanal K. Mazvancheryl, "Customer Satisfaction and Shareholder Value," *Journal of Marketing*, October 2004, p. 172; Michael Tsirod, Vikas Mittal, and Willam T. Ross, Jr., "The Role of Attributions in Customer Satisfaction: A Reexamination," *Journal of Consumer Research*, September 2004, p. 476; Scott R. Colwell, "The Future of Marketing: Practical Strategies for Marketers in the Post-Internet Age," *Journal of the Academy of Marketing Science*, Winter 2003, p. 95; Kevin J. Clancy and Robert S. Shulman, *Marketing Myths That Are Killing Business: The Cure for Death Wish Marketing* (New York: McGraw-Hill, 1994); Regina E. Herzlinger, "Can Public Trust in Nonprofits and Governments Be Restored?" *Harvard Business Review*, March–April 1996, p. 97; Michael S. Minor, "Relentless: The Japanese Way of Marketing," *Journal of the Academy of Marketing Science*, Spring 1998, p. 160; Charles C. Snow, "Twenty-First-Century Organizations: Implications for a New Marketing Paradigm," *Journal of the Academy of Marketing Science*, Winter 1997, p. 72; Frederick F. Reichheld, "Learning from Customer Defections," *Harvard Business Review*, March–April 1996, p. 56. For a classic discussion of the problem and mechanics of measuring the efficiency of marketing, see Reavis Cox, *Distribution in a High-Level Economy* (Englewood Cliffs, NJ: Prentice Hall, 1965).

5. For more on criticisms of advertising, see David C. Vladeck, "Truth and Consequences: the Perils of Half-Truths and Unsubstantiated Health Claims for Dietary Supplements," *Journal of Public Policy & Marketing*, Spring 2000, p. 132; Barbara J. Phillips, "In Defense of Advertising: A Social Perspective," *Journal of Business Ethics*, February 1997, p. 109; Charles Trappey, "A Meta-Analysis of Consumer Choice and Subliminal Advertising," *Psychology & Marketing*, August 1996, p. 517; Karl A. Boedecker, Fred W. Morgan, and Linda B. Wright, "The Evolution of First Amendment Protection for Commercial Speech," *Journal of Marketing*, January 1995, p. 38; Thomas C. O'Guinn and L. J. Shrum, "The Role of Television in the Construction of Consumer Reality," *Journal of Consumer Research*, March 1997, p. 278; see also Robert B. Archibald, Clyde A. Haulman, and Carlisle E. Moody, Jr., "Quality, Price, Advertising, and Published Quality Ratings," *Journal of Consumer Research*, March 1983, p. 347.

6. Thomas O. Jones and W. E. Sasser, "Why Satisfied Customers Defect," *Harvard Business Review*, November–December 1995, p. 88; "The Satisfaction Trap," *Harvard Business Review*, March–April 1996, p. 58.

7. "Angry NFL Slams ABC's 'Desperate Housewives' Promo," *Wall Street Journal*, November 17, 2004, p. B1ff.; "FDA Tells Pfizer to Pull Viagra Ads about 'Wild Thing,'" *Wall Street Journal*, November 16, 2004, p. B1ff.; "First, FCC Scrutiny, Are Ad Probes Next?" *Brandweek*, March 1, 2004, pp. 4–8; "Can Money Buy Happiness?" *Adweek*, February 3, 2003, p. 26; James E. Burroughs and Aric Rindfleisch, "Materialism and Well-Being: A Conflicting Values Perspective," *Journal of Consumer Research*, December 2002, p. 348; John Watson, Steven Lysonski, Tamara Gillan, and Leslie Raymore, "Cultural Values and Important Processions: A Cross-Cultural Analysis," *Journal of Business Research*, November 2002, p. 923; Roy F. Baumeister, "Yielding to Temptation: Self-Control Failure, Impulsive Purchasing, and Consumer Behavior," *Journal of Consumer Research*, March 2002, p. 670; Donald F. Dixon, "The Economics of Conspicuous Consumption: Theory and Thought since 1700," *Journal of Macromarketing*, 21, no. 1 (June 2001), p. 101; Guliz Ger, "Human Development and Humane Consumption: Well-Being beyond the 'Good Life,'" *Journal of Public Policy & Marketing*, Spring 1997, p. 110; Ronald P. Hill and Sandi Macan, "Consumer Survival on Welfare with an Emphasis on Medicaid and the Food Stamp Program," *Journal of Public Policy & Marketing*, Spring 1996, p. 118; Dennis J. Cahill, "The Refinement of America: Persons, Houses, Cities," *Journal of Marketing*, October 1994, p. 121. See also Michael J. Barone, Randall L. Rose, Kenneth C. Manning, and Paul W. Miniard, "Another Look at the Impact of Reference Information on Consumer Impressions of Nutrition Information," *Journal of Public Policy & Marketing*, Spring 1996, p. 55; Thomas A. Hemphill, "Legislating Corporate Social Responsibility," *Business Horizons*, March/April 1997, p. 53; Priscilla A. La Barbera and Zeynep Gurhan, "The Role of Materialism, Religiosity, and Demographics in Subjective Well-Being," *Psychology & Marketing*, January 1997, p. 71; Dennis J. Cahill, "Consumption and the World of Goods," *Journal of Marketing*, April 1994, p. 131; Jacqueline K. Eastman, Bill Fredenberger, David Campbell, and Stephen Calvert, "The Relationship between Status Consumption and Materialism: A Cross-Cultural Comparison of Chinese, Mexican and American Students," *Journal of Marketing Theory & Practice*, Winter 1997, p. 52; James A. Muncy and Jacqueline K. Eastman, "Materialism and Consumer Ethics: An Exploratory Study," *Journal of Business Ethics*, January 1998, p. 137; Donald P. Robin and R. Eric Reidenbach, "Identifying Critical Problems for Mutual Cooperation Between the Public and Private Sectors: A Marketing Perspective," *Journal of the Academy of Marketing Science*, Fall 1986, p. 1. See also Terrence H. Witkowski, "The Early American Style: A History of Marketing and Consumer Values," *Psychology & Marketing*, March 1998, p. 125; Arnold J. Toynbee, *America and World Revolution* (New York: Oxford University Press, 1966), p. 144; John Kenneth Galbraith, *Economics and the Public Purpose* (Boston: Houghton Mifflin, 1973), p. 144.

8. Peter R. Dickson, Paul W. Farris, and Willem J. M. I. Verbeke, "Dynamic Strategic Thinking," *Journal of the Academy of Marketing Science*, Summer 2001, p. 216; Gloria Barczak, "Analysis for Marketing Planning," *Journal of Product Innovation Management*, September 1997, p. 424; William A. Sahlman, "How to Write a Great Business Plan," *Harvard Business Review*, July–August 1997, p. 98; Paul Boughton, "The 1-Day Marketing Plan: Organizing and Completing the Plan That Works," *Journal of the Academy of Marketing Science*, Summer 1996, p. 275; William Sandy, "Avoid the Breakdowns between Planning and Implementation," *Journal of Business Strategy*, September/October 1991, p. 30; Michael MacInnis and Louise A. Heslop, "Market Planning in a High-Tech Environment," *Industrial Marketing Management*, May 1990, p. 107; David Strutton, "Marketing Strategies: New Approaches, New Techniques," *Journal of the Academy of Marketing Science*, Summer 1997, p. 261; Rita G. McGrath and Ian C. MacMillan, "Discovery-Driven Planning," *Harvard Business Review*, July–August 1995, p. 44; Jeffrey Elton and Justin Roe, "Bringing Discipline to Project Management," *Harvard Business Review*, March–April 1998, p. 153; Andrew Campbell and Marcus Alexander, "What's Wrong with Strategy?" *Harvard Business Review*, November–December 1997, p. 42.

9. For more on global social responsibility, see Chapter 1, endnote 10. See also J. Craig Andrews, Richard G. Netemeyer, Scot Burton, D. Paul Moberg, and Ann Christiansen, "Understanding Adolescent Intentions to Smoke: An Examination of Relationships Among Social Influence, Prior Trial Behavior, and Antitobacco Campaign Advertising," *Journal of Marketing*, July 2004, p. 110; Jill Gabrielle Klein, N. Craig Smith, and Andrew John, "Why We Boycott: Consumer Motivations for Boycott Participation," *Journal of Marketing*, July 2004, p. 92; Robert V. Kozinets and Jay M. Handelman, "Adversaries of Consumption: Consumer Movements, Activism, and Ideology," *Journal of Consumer Research*, December 2004, p. 691; Eric

J. Arnould and Jakki J. Mohr, "Dynamic Transformations for Base-of-the-Pyramid Market Clusters," *Journal of the Academy of Marketing Science*, Summer 2005, p. 254; Jagdip Singh, Jean E. Kilgore, Rama K. Jayanti, Kokil Agarwal, and Ramadesikan R. Gandarvakottai, "What Goes Around Comes Around: Understanding Trust—Value Dilemmas of Market Relationships," *Journal of Public Policy & Marketing*, Spring 2005, p. 38; Julie M. Donohue and Ernst R. Berndt, "Effects of Direct-to-Consumer Advertising on Medication Choice: The Case of Antidepressants," *Journal of Public Policy & Marketing*, Fall 2004, p. 115; Ajit M. Menon, Aparna D. Deshpande, Matthew Perri III, and George M. Zinkhan, "Consumers' Attention to the Brief Summary in Print Direct-to-Consumer Advertisements: Perceived Usefulness in Patient—Physician Discussions," *Journal of Public Policy & Marketing*, Fall 2003, p. 181; Donald A. Fuller and Jacquelyn A. Ottman, "Moderating Unintended Pollution: The Role of Sustainable Product Design," *Journal of Business Research*, November 2004, p. 1231; Marie-Louise Fry and Michael Jay Polonsky, "Examining the Unintended Consequences of Marketing," *Journal of Business Research*, November 2004, p. 1303; Joann Peck and Barbara Loken, "When Will Larger-Sized Female Models in Advertisements Be Viewed Positively? The Moderating Effects of Instructional Frame, Gender, and Need for Cognition," *Psychology & Marketing*, June 2004, p. 425; Renato J. Orsato, "Competitive Environmental Strategies: When Does It Pay to be Green?" *California Management Review*, Winter 2006, p. 127; Jill Meredith Ginsberg and Paul N. Bloom, "Choosing the Right Green Marketing Strategy," *MIT Sloan Management Review*, Fall 2004, p. 79.

10. For other environmental issues, see "War on the Water Front," *Time*, December 19, 2005, p. 60; "Whole Fuels," *Business 2.0*, December 2005, p. 78; "Is It Too Easy Being Green?" *Wall Street Journal*, October 19, 2005, p. B1ff.; "Turning Waste into Watts," *Business 2.0*, October 2005, p. 126; "Getting More Miles to the Gallon—Fast," *Business Week*, September 26, 2005, pp. 40–41; "It's Easier Being Green," *Business Week*, September 19, 2005, pp. 50–51; "Automakers Jack Up MPG PDG," *USA Today*, September 16, 2005, p. 1Bff.; "New Incentives for Being Green," *Wall Street Journal*, August 4, 2005, p. D1ff.; "The Great Windfall," *Business 2.0*, August 2005, pp. 86–90; "China: Wasteful Ways," *Business Week*, April 11, 2005, pp. 50–51; "Eco Trends," *Business Week*, March 21, 2005, p. 14; "Beyond Recycling: Manufacturers Embrace C2C Design," *Wall Street Journal*, March 3, 2005, p. B1ff.; "Old Cellphones Pile Up by the Millions," *Wall Street Journal*, September 23, 2004, p. B1ff.; "The Race to Save a Rainforest," *Business Week*, November 24, 2003, p. 125; "Cellphone Makers Connect for Recycling Program," *USA Today*, October 22, 2003, p. 6B; "The Information Age's Toxic Garbage," *Business Week*, October 6, 2003, p. 54; "Offsetting Environmental Damage by Planes," *New York Times*, February 18, 2003, p. C6; "Behind Roses' Beauty, Poor and Ill Workers," *New York Times*, February 13, 2003, p. A1; "Industrial Evolution," *Business Week*, April 8, 2002, p. 70; "Green Sales Pitch Isn't Moving Many Products," *Wall Street Journal*, March 6, 2002, p. B1; "Brazilian Mahogany: Too Much in Demand," *Wall Street Journal*, November 14, 2001, p. B1; "How Much Power Do You Use?" *Wall Street Journal*, August 16, 2001, p. B1; "Choice of Evils: As a Tropical Scourge Makes a Comeback, So, Too, Does DDT," *Wall Street Journal*, July 26, 2001, p. A1; "It May Be Time to Toss Old Ideas on Recycling," *USA Today*, July 2, 2001, p. 7D; "As BP Goes Green, the Fur Is Flying," *Wall Street Journal*, April 16, 2001, p. A10; "Once Is Not Enough," *Business Week*, April 16, 2001, p. 128B; "EarthShell Saw Big Macs and Big Bucks—Got Big Woes," *Wall Street Journal*, April 10, 2001, p. B2; "Recycling Redefined," *Wall Street Journal*, March 6, 2001, p. B1; "More Gas-Powered Autos on 'Green' List," *USA Today*, February 9, 2001, p. 3B; "Nonprofits—and Landfills—Deluged with Old PCs," *Investor's Business Daily*, November 27, 2000, p. A6; "Conservation: Been There, Doing That," *Business Week*, November 27, 2000, p. 194F; "Recycler's Nightmare: Beer in Plastic," *Wall Street Journal*, November 16, 1999, p. B1; "As Old Pallets Pile Up, Critics Hammer Them as a New Eco-Menace," *Wall Street Journal*, April 1, 1998, p. A1. See also Lynette Knowles Mathur and Ike

Mathur, "An Analysis of the Wealth Effects of Green Marketing Strategies," *Journal of Business Research*, November 2000, p. 193; Subhabrata Bobby Banerjee, Easwar S. Iyer, and Rajiv K. Kashyap, "Corporate Environmentalism: Antecedents and Influence of Industry Type," *Journal of Marketing*, April 2003, p. 106; Anil Menon and Ajay Menon, "Enviropreneurial Marketing Strategy: The Emergence of Corporate Environmentalism as Market Strategy," *Journal of Marketing*, January 1997, p. 51; William E. Kilbourne, "Green Advertising: Salvation or Oxymoron?" *Journal of Advertising*, Summer 1995, p. 7.

11. For more on privacy, see Chapter 13, endnote 16. See also "Company to Offer Tracking by Phone," *Investor's Business Daily*, November 16, 2005, p. A5; "Security's New World Order," *Investor's Business Daily*, November 7, 2005, p. A12; "'Working Late' Won't Work Anymore," *Business Week*, October 31, 2005, p. 40; "New Services Guard against ID Theft," *Wall Street Journal*, October 6, 2005, p. D1ff.; "Prying Eyes Are Everywhere," *USA Today*, April 14, 2005, p. 1Dff.; "America Online, RSA Wage Token Effort to Improve Security," *Investor's Business Daily*, September 22, 2004, p. A6; "You're on Candid Cellphone!" *Wall Street Journal*, September 30, 2003, p. B1; "Stalk Market: New Battlefront in Web Privacy War, Ads That Snoop," *Wall Street Journal*, August 27, 2003, p. A1; "Online Shopper Still Fear Security Issues," *Investor's Business Daily*, June 3, 2003, p. A4; "Privacy in an Age of Terror," *Business Week*, November 5, 2001, p. 83; "Internet Insecurity," *Time*, July 2, 2001, p. 44; "Privacy Options Are a Blur," *USA Today*, April 10, 2001, p. 3D; "The Battle over Web Privacy," *Wall Street Journal*, March 21, 2001, p. B1. See also George R. Milne and Mary J. Culnan, "Strategies for Reducing Online Privacy Risks: Why Consumers Read (or Don't Read) Online Privacy Notices," *Journal of Interactive Marketing*, Summer 2004, p. 15; Curt J. Dommeyer and Barbara L. Gross, "What Consumers Know and What They Do: An Investigation of Consumer Knowledge, Awareness, and Use of Privacy Protection Strategies," *Journal of Interactive Marketing*, Spring 2003, p. 34; John A. McCarty, "Data Privacy in the Information Age," *Journal of Public Policy & Marketing*, Fall 2002, p. 336; George R. Milne and Andrew J. Rohm, "Consumer Privacy and Name Removal across Direct Marketing Channels: Exploring Opt-In and Opt-Out Alternatives," *Journal of Public Policy & Marketing*, Fall 2000, p. 238; Joseph E. Phelps, Giles D'Souza, and Glen J. Nowak, "Antecedents and Consequences of Consumer Privacy Concerns: An Empirical Investigation," *Journal of Interactive Marketing*, Autumn 2001, p. 2; Ellen R. Foxman and Paula Kilcoyne, "Information Technology, Marketing Practice, and Consumer Privacy: Ethical Issues," *Journal of Public Policy & Marketing*, Spring 1993, p. 106; Robert E. Thomas and Virginia G. Maurer, "Database Marketing Practice: Protecting Consumer Privacy," *Journal of Public Policy & Marketing*, Spring 1997, p. 147; Marren J. Roy, "Regulation of Automatic Dialing and Announcing Devices Upheld," *Journal of the Academy of Marketing Science*, Summer 1997, p. 269.

12. "Advertisers Catch the School Bus," *USA Today*, December 27, 2005, p. 3A; "MealPay Tracks Kids' Eating," *USA Today*, October 4, 2005, p. 8D; "McDonald's Kicks Off School PE Program," *USA Today*, September 13, 2005, p. 7D; "Fast Food Surrounds Metropolitan Schools," *USA Today*, August 24, 2005, p. 5D; "Health Movement Has School Cafeterias in a Food Fight," *USA Today*, August 22, 2005, p. 1Aff.; "Soda Marketers Will Cut Back Sales to Schools," *Wall Street Journal*, August 17, 2005, p. B1ff.; "Got Bottles? Schools Sell More Milk Outside Box," *Wall Street Journal*, December 29, 2004, p. D4; "Stonyfield Heads Back to School," *Advertising Age*, September 20, 2004, p. 8; "A Lesson in Selling Healthy Snacks," *Investor's Business Daily*, May 24, 2004, p. A12; "How Young Is Too Young?" *Brandweek*, April 5, 2004, pp. 44–48; "The Good News: No More Coke in School. The Bad News: Snapple Is Replacing It," *Wall Street Journal*, January 13, 2004, p. D1; "Coke's Guidelines for Soft Drinks in Schools Faces Some Criticism," *Wall Street Journal*, November 17, 2003, p. A6; "New in School Vending Machines: Yogurt, Soy," *Wall Street Journal*, October 15, 2003, p. B1; "A Real Food Fight Breaks Out in Schools,"

Investor's Business Daily, September 22, 2003, p. A8; "Head of the Class: Don't Spare the Brand," *Brandweek*, March 10, 2003, p. 20; "Cafeteria Food Fight," *Wall Street Journal*, June 14, 2002, p. B1; "Coke Finds Its Exclusive School Contracts Aren't So Easily Given Up," *Wall Street Journal*, June 26, 2001, p. B1; "Web-Filter Data from Schools Put Up for Sale," *Wall Street Journal*, January 26, 2001, p. B1; "On Many Campuses, Big Brewers Play a Role in New Alcohol Policies," *Wall Street Journal*, November 2, 2000, p. A1; "Pepsi Hits High Note with Schools," *Advertising Age*, October 9, 2000, p. 30; "If It's Marketing, Can It Also Be Education?" *Fortune*, October 2, 2000, p. 274; "AOL to Announce This Week the Launch of Free Online Service Aimed at Schools," *Wall Street Journal*, May 16, 2000, p. B6; "Mouse-Trapping the Student Market," *American Demographics*, May 2000, p. 30; "Grad Students Match Wits in Marketing Competition," *Wall Street Journal*, February 9, 2000, p. S1; "Pitching Saturns to Your Classmates—for Credit," *Wall Street Journal*, January 31, 2000, p. B1; "Marketers on Campus: A New Bag of Tricks," *Wall Street Journal*, January 31, 2000, p. B1; "Tobacco Money Sparks a New Fight," *Wall Street Journal*, December 10, 1999, p. B1; "Schools for Sale," *Advertising Age*, October 25, 1999, p. 22; "Big Cards on Campus," *Business Week*, September 20, 1999, p. 138; "Cola Contracts Lose Fizz in Schools," *USA Today*, August 18, 1999, p. 9D; "Ads in Schools: Lesson in Failure?" *Advertising Age*, June 7, 1999, p. 26; "Classrooms for Sale," *Time*, April 19, 1999, p. 44; "Big Car on Campus?" *Business Week*, August 31, 1998, p. 32; "Are We Selling Our Students?" *Raleigh News & Observer*, August 2, 1998, p. 25A; "This School Was Sponsored by . . .," *Parenting*, March 1998, p. 23; "Channel One Taps Principals as Promoters," *Wall Street Journal*, September 15, 1997, p. B1; "School's Back, and So Are the Marketers," *Wall Street Journal*, September 15, 1997, p. B1; "Hey Kid, Buy This!" *Business Week*, June 30, 1997, p. 62; "This Class Brought to You by . . .," *USA Today*, January 3, 1997, p. 3A; "New Ad Vehicles: Police Car, School Bus, Garbage Truck," *Wall Street Journal*, February 20, 1996, p. B1. See also Judith A. Garretson and Scot Burton, "The Role of Spokescharacters as Advertisement and Package Cues in Integrated Marketing Communications," *Journal of Marketing*, October 2005, p. 118; Sabrina M. Neeley and David W. Schumann, "Using Animated Spokes-Characters in Advertising to Young Children," *Journal of Advertising*, Fall 2004, p. 7.

13. For more on online fraud, see "At Online Stores, Sniffing Out Crooks Is a Matter of Survival," *Wall Street Journal*, August 4, 2005, p. A1ff.; "Problem for Cops on eBay Beat: Crooks Keep Getting Smarter," *Wall Street Journal*, August 3, 2004, p. A1ff.; "Scammed! Web Merchants Use New Tools to Keep Buyers from Ripping Them Off," *Wall Street Journal Reports*, January 27, 2003, p. R6; "E-Commerce Report: Crime Is Soaring in Cyberspace," *New York Times*, January 27, 2003, p. C4; "Credit-Card Scams Bedevil E-Stores," *Wall Street Journal*, September 19, 2000, p. B1; "Fraud on the Internet," *Business Week E.Biz*, April 3, 2000, p. EB58; "Online Scambusters," *Business Week E.Biz*, April 3, 2000, p. EB66; "Card Sharps," *Business Week E.Biz*, April 3, 2000, p.EB68. For more on in-store fraud, see "Stores Battle Employee Theft," *Raleigh News & Observer*, October 15, 2000, p. 1E; "As Thievery by Insiders Overtakes Shoplifting, Retailers Crack Down," *Wall Street Journal*, September 8, 2000, p. A1; "Electronic Tags Are Beeping Everywhere," *Wall Street Journal*, April 20, 1998, p. B1; "A Time to Steal," *Brandweek*, February 16, 1998, p. 24.

14. For more on socially responsible and ethical behavior, see "Alcohol Makers Tread Tricky Path in Marketing to College Students," *USA Today*, November 17, 2005, p. 1Bff.; "Rx from Marlboro Man: Device That Delivers Drugs, Not Smoke," *Wall Street Journal*, October 27, 2005, p. A1ff.; "The Debate over Doing Good," *Business Week*, August 15, 2005, pp. 76–78; "Cops of the Global Village," *Fortune*, June 27, 2005, pp. 158–66; "At Some Retailers, 'Fair Trade' Carries a Very High Cost," *Wall Street Journal*, June 8, 2004, p. A1ff.; "Drug Ills? Follow the Money," *Brandweek*, February 7, 2005, pp. 24–28; "Car Seats for Eight-Year-Olds," *Wall Street Journal*, January 27, 2005, p. D1ff.; "Money and Morals at GE," *Fortune*, November 15, 2004, pp. 176–82; "Nestlé Markets Baby Formula to Hispanic Mothers in U.S.," *Wall Street Journal*, March 4, 2004, p. B1ff.; "Teaching the Wrong Lesson," *Business 2.0*, November 2003, p. 60; "Food Sellers Push Animal Welfare," *USA Today*, August 13, 2003, p. 1D; "In the Name of Responsibility," *Brandweek*, May 12, 2003, p. 32; "For MBAs, Soul-Searching 101," *Business Week*, September 16, 2002, p. 64; "Wanted: Ethical Employer," *Wall Street Journal*, July 9, 2002, p. B1; "I Take Thee . . . Back to the Store," *Wall Street Journal*, May 30, 2002, p. D1. See also John C. Kozup, Elizabeth H. Creyer, and Scot Burton, "Making Healthful Food Choices: The Influence of Health Claims and Nutrition Information on Consumers' Evaluations of Packaged Food Products and Restaurant Menu Items," *Journal of Marketing*, April 2003, p. 19; Sankar Sen, Zeynep Gurhan-Canli, and Vicki Morwitz, "Withholding Consumption: A Social Dilemma Perspective on Consumer Boycotts," *Journal of Consumer Research*, December 2001, p. 399; Steve Hoeffler and Kevin Lane Keller, "Building Brand Equity through Corporate Societal Marketing," *Journal of Public Policy & Marketing*, Spring 2002, p. 78; Dwane Hal Dean, "Associating the Cooperation with a Charitable Event Through Sponsorship: Measuring the Effects on Corporate Community Relations," *Journal of Advertising*, Winter 2002, p. 77; Richard Pearce and Maria Hansson, "Retailing and Risk Society: Genetically Modified Food," *International Journal of Retail & Distribution Management*, no. 11 (2000), p. 450; W. P. Cunningham, "The Golden Rule as Universal Ethical Norm," *Journal of Business Ethics*, January 1998, p. 105; "'Ethnic Pricing' Means Unfair Air Fares," *Wall Street Journal*, December 5, 1997, p. B1; William P. Cordeiro, "Suggested Management Responses to Ethical Issues Raised by Technological Change," *Journal of Business Ethics*, September 1997, p. 1393; Eli P. I. Cox, Michael S. Wogalter, Sara L. Stokes, and Elizabeth J. T. Murff, "Do Product Warnings Increase Safe Behavior? A Meta-Analysis," *Journal of Public Policy & Marketing*, Fall 1997, p. 195; "On the Net, Anything Goes," *Newsweek*, July 7, 1997, p. 28; "'Levi's as Ye Sew, So Shall Ye Reap," *Fortune*, May 12, 1997, p. 104; "48% of Workers Admit to Unethical or Illegal Acts," *USA Today*, April 4, 1997, p. 1A; H. R. Dodge, Elizabeth A. Edwards, and Sam Fullerton, "Consumer Transgressions in the Marketplace: Consumers' Perspectives," *Psychology & Marketing*, December 1996, p. 821; David W. Stewart, "Internet Marketing, Business Models, and Public Policy," *Journal of Public Policy & Marketing*, Fall 2000, p. 287; Albert A. Foer, "E-commerce Meets Antitrust: A Primer," *Journal of Public Policy & Marketing*, Spring 2001, p. 51; "Ethics for Hire," *Business Week*, July 15, 1996, p. 26; "How a Drug Firm Paid for University Study, Then Undermined It," *Wall Street Journal*, April 25, 1996, p. A1; James A. Roberts, "Will the Real Socially Responsible Consumer Please Step Forward?" *Business Horizons*, January/February 1996, p. 79; John Priddle, "Marketing Ethics, Macromarketing, and the Managerial Perspective Reconsidered," *Journal of Macromarketing*, Fall 1994, p. 47; Bernard Avishai, "What Is Business's Social Compact?" *Harvard Business Review*, January–February 1994, p. 38; Paul N. Bloom, George R. Milne, and Robert Adler, "Avoiding Misuse of New Information Technologies: Legal and Societal Considerations," *Journal of Marketing*, January 1994, p. 98; James A. Muncy and Scott J. Vitell, "Consumer Ethics: An Investigation of the Ethical Beliefs of the Final Consumer," *Journal of Business Research*, June 1992, p. 297; Gene R. Laczniak and Patrick E. Murphy, "Fostering Ethical Marketing Decisions," *Journal of Business Ethics*, April 1991, p. 259.

Illustration Credits

CHAPTER 1

Exhibits: Exhibit 1-1, adapted from William McInnes, "A Conceptual Approach to Marketing," in *Theory in Marketing*, 2d ser., ed. Reavis Cox, Wroe Alderson, and Stanley J. Shapiro (Homewood, IL: Richard D. Irwin, 1964), pp. 51–67. Exhibit 1-2, model suggested by Professor A. A. Brogowicz, Western Michigan University. Exhibit 1-4, adapted from R. F. Vizza, T. E. Chambers, and E. J. Cook, *Adoption of the Marketing Concept—Fact or Fiction* (New York: Sales Executive Club, Inc., 1967), pp. 13–15. Exhibit 1-5, this exhibit is different from, but stimulated by, a graph that appears on the Satisfaction Management Systems, Inc., website, www.satmansys.com. Exhibit 1-7, adapted from discussions of an American Marketing Association Strategic Planning Committee.

Photos/ads: Pg. 3, ©William D. Perreault, Jr. Ph.D. Pg. 4, Jeff Maloney/Getty Images. Pg. 5, *No credit.* Pg. 8, AP Photo/Kent Gibert. Pg. 8, ©Evans Vestal Ward. Pg. 11, These materials have been reproduced with the permission of eBay, Inc. COPYRIGHT ©2006 EBAY INC. ALL RIGHTS RESERVED. Pg. 11, Courtesy CarQuest Corporation. Pg. 16, Courtesy SAP AG. Pg. 16, Courtesy ACCION International. Pg. 21, Courtesy L.L.Bean. Pg. 22, ©William D. Perreault, Jr. Ph.D. Pg. 22, CLOROX® is a registered trademark of The Clorox Company. Used with permission. ©1994 The Clorox Company. Reprinted with permission. Pg. 22, ©Air Products and Chemicals, Inc. 2003. Pg. 25, ©Yahoo, Inc.

CHAPTER 2

Exhibits: Exhibit 2-10, Copernicus: The Marketing Investment Strategy Group, Inc., 450 Lexington Street, Auburndale, MA 02166. Exhibit 2-11, Igor Ansoff, *Corporate Strategy* (New York; McGraw-Hill, 1965).

Photos/ads: Pg. 31, Courtesy Cirque du Soleil. Pg. 36, ZIPLOC® brand containers is a registered trademark of S.C. Johnson Home Storage, Inc. Used with permission. Pg. 36, Courtesy of Lufthansa. Pg. 38, *Both* Courtesy Toddler University. Pg. 41, *All* Courtesy of Campbell Soup Company. Pg. 42, ©William D. Perreault, Jr. Ph.D. Pg. 46, Courtesy Timex Corporation. Pg. 48, *No credit.* Pg. 50, Courtesy Duracell. Pg. 50, Courtesy of Workrite Uniform Company, Oxnard, CA. Pg. 51, ©William D. Perreault, Jr. Ph.D. Pg. 53, Courtesy of Zippo Manufacturing Company, Inc. Pg. 53, Courtesy Sara Lee Bakery Group. Pg. 53, Courtesy Unilever P.L.C. Pg. 53, ©Barry Lewis.

CHAPTER 3

Exhibits: Exhibit 3-11, Russell I. Haley, "Benefit Segmentation: A Decision-Oriented Research Tool," *Journal of Marketing*, July 1968, p. 33.

Photos/ads: Pg. 50, ©Bob Riha. Pg. 62, Courtesy Glaces Thiriet SAS. Pg. 62, Courtesy Kahala Management LLC; Blimpie Franchise Systems. Pg. 64, Courtesy Nestlé S.A. Pg. 67, Reproduced by permission of The PSNE Group.com. All Rights Reserved. Pg. 67, Designed by Locomotion Creative/Nashville, TN. For VF Imagewear, Inc. Pg. 69, ©William D. Perreault, Jr. Ph.D. Pg. 70, Photographer: Steven Bonini. Pg. 74, ©William D. Perreault, Jr. Ph.D. Pg. 76, Courtesy Audi of Norway; Agency: Bates Reklamebyra/Oslo.

CHAPTER 4

Exhibits: Exhibit 4-5, table based on U.S. Census "International Data Base" available online at http://www.census.gov/ipc/www/idbsum. html and other U.S. Census data including, Global Population Profile: 2002 (WP/02) and Global Population at a Glance: 2002 and Beyond, WP/02-1 and An Aging World: 2001, P95/01-1 (Washington, DC: Government Printing Office). Also based on World Bank data available online at http://www.worldbank.org/data/dataquery.html and other World Bank data including, World Development Report 2006: Equity and Development and World Development Indicators: 2005 (Washington, DC: International Bank for Reconstruction and Development/The World Bank). Also based on Population Reference Bureau data available online at http://www.prb.org/pubs/wpds2005 and other PRB data including 2005 World Population Data Sheet (Washington, DC: Population Reference Bureau). Also based on Central Intelligence Agency data available online at http://www.odci. gov/cia/publications/factbook. Also based on GlobalEDGE data from Michigan State University available online at http://globaledge.msu. edu. Exhibit 4-6, map developed by the authors based on U.S. Census data including U.S. Bureau of the Census, Statistical Abstract of the United States 2006 (Washington, DC: U.S. Government Printing Office), p. 21 and p.23 and available online at http://www.census.gov/ statab. Exhibit 4-7, graph developed by the authors based on U.S. Census data: including U.S. Bureau of the Census, Statistical Abstract of the United States 2006 (Washington, DC: U.S. Government Printing Office), p. 14 (for 2020 figures) and p. 17 (for 2010 figures) and p. 16 (for 2000 figures) and available online at http://www.census.gov/ statab. Exhibit 4-10, adapted from M. G. Allen, "Strategic Problems Facing Today's Corporate Planner," speech given at the Academy of Management, 36th Annual Meeting, Kansas City, Missouri, 1976.

Photos/ads: Pg. 83, ©Blaise Hayward Studio. Pg. 86, Courtesy Universidad de Palermo, Prof. Orlando C. Aprile; Copywriter: Kalmus Mariano. Pg. 88, Courtesy Unilever U.S., Inc. Pg. 89, Reprinted with permission from the Minwax Company/Upper Saddle River, N.J. ©2006 Minwax Company. All Rights Reserved. Pg. 89, Courtesy Royal Appliance Mfg. Co. Pg. 94, Courtesy Young & Rubicam. Pg. 95, Courtesy Adero, Inc. Pg. 98, Courtesy adidas America; Photo by: Bob Allen. Pg. 101, Huang Jinguo/ImagineChina. Pg. 105, Use of Ad reproduced courtesy of Unilever. Pg. 105, Courtesy International Networks/AZN TELEVISION. Pg. 105, ©2006 MTV Networks, A Division of Viacom International Incorporated. Pg. 109, Con Agra Foods Specialty Potato Products; Agency: Strahan Advertising. Pg. 109, Courtesy Click2Asia.

CHAPTER 5

Exhibits: Exhibit 5-2, graph developed by the authors based on U.S. Census data including "Table F-1. Income Limits for Each Fifth and Top 5 Percent of Families (All Races): 1947 to 2004" and available online at http:// www.census.gov/hhes/income/histinc/f01ar.html; "Table F-2. Share of Aggregate Income Received by Each Fifth and Top 5 Percent of Families (All Races): 1947 to 2004" and available online at http://www.census.gov/hhes/income/histinc/f02ar.html. Exhibit 5-4, adapted from C. Glenn Walters, *Consumer Behavior*, 3d ed. (Homewood, IL: Richard D. Irwin, 1979). Exhibit 5-7, Joseph T. Plummer, "The Concept and Application of Life-Style Segmentation," *Journal of Marketing*, January 1974, pp. 33–37. Exhibit 5-8, adapted from Patrick E. Murphy and William A. Staples, "A Modern Family Life Cycle," Journal of Consumer Research, June 1979, p. 17.

Photos/ads: Pg. 115, Courtesy Apple Computer. Pg. 118, Courtesy of CBS Television Network. Pg. 120, Courtesy GEICO. Pg. 120, Courtesy of ConAgra Foods. Pg. 122, Courtesy Young & Laramore Advertising/

Indianapolis. Pg. 123, Courtesy General Mills, Inc. Pg. 127, Courtesy Carmichael Lynch/Minneapolis. Pg. 128, ©Matthew Staver. Pg.129, ©2000 Jockey International, Inc. Pg. 131, Courtesy Univision Communications, Inc. Pg. 135, Courtesy Columbia Sportwear Company. Pg. 136, AP Photo/Christopher Morris VII. Pg. 136, AP Photo.

CHAPTER 6

Exhibits: Exhibit 6-4, adapted from Rowland T. Moriarty, Jr., and Robert E. Spekman, "An Empirical Investigation of the Information Sources Used during the Industrial Buying Process, *Journal of Marketing Research*, May 1984, pp. 137–47. Exhibit 6-6, graph developed by the authors based on U. S. Census data including "Table 5: Industry Statistics for Subsectors by Employment Size: 2002" from *2002 Economic Census—Manufacturing, Subject Series, General Summary* (Washington, DC: U.S. Government Printing Office, 2005) and available online at http://www.census.gov. Exhibit 6-7, available online at http://www.naics.com.

Photos/ads: Pg. 141, ©William D. Perreault, Jr. Ph.D. Pg. 144, Courtesy Arlington Industries, Inc. Pg. 144, Courtesy Sharp Electronics Corporation. Pg. 146, *Both* ©Roger Ball. Pg. 147, Courtesy Yellow Freight Systems, Inc. Pg. 147, Courtesy Canon USA, Inc. Pg. 150, Courtesy Liberty Mutual. Pg. 150, Courtesy Rockwell International Corporation. Pg. 154, These materials have been reproduced with the permission of eBay, Inc. COPYRIGHT ©2006 EBAY INC. ALL RIGHTS RESERVED. Pg. 155, Courtesy The California Department of Transportation. Pg. 156, Reprinted with permission from BtoB Magazine, 2006 Copyright, Crain Communications, Inc. Pg. 160, *All* Courtesy of Alcoa. Pg. 161, Courtesy Shell Oil Company; Photographer: John Roe/Roe Photo. Pg. 162, Reprinted with permission of Cargill Salt Ó. Pg. 162, Courtesy Haier America. Pg. 163, Courtesy Caterpillar Inc. Pg. 163, Courtesy Eye Safety Systems, Inc.

CHAPTER 7

Exhibits: Exhibit 7-6, adapted from Paul E. Green, Frank J. Carmone, and David P. Wachpress, "On the Analysis of Qualitative Data in Marketing Research," *Journal of Marketing Research*, February 1977, pp. 52–59.

Photos/ads: Pg. 169, ©The Procter & Gamble Company. Used by permission. Pg. 172, Courtesy of MapInfo. Pg. 172, Reprinted with permission from Northern Light Technology, Inc. Copyright 1999. Pg. 174, Courtesy Find/SVP; Created by Sonnenberg, Haviland & Partners, Ridgewood, N.J. Pg. 174, Courtesy JRP Marketing Research Services. Pg. 179, Courtesy Abacus B2B/A Division of DoubleClick, Inc. Pg. 179, Courtesy Catalina Marketing. Pg. 182, Courtesy Focus Vision Worldwide, ™Inc. Pg. 182, Courtesy Focus World International. Pg. 183, Courtesy Greenfield Online. Pg. 184, Courtesy Zero Knowledge Systems, Inc. Pg. 185, ©2005 Ocean Spray Cranberries, Inc. Pg. 188, Courtesy Energizer Holdings, Inc. Pg. 188, Courtesy Survey Sampling, Inc. Pg. 190, Courtesy P. Robert & Partners. Pg. 190, Courtesy Quality Controlled Services/St. Louis, MO.

CHAPTER 8

Exhibits: Exhibit 8-5, Timberland logo reprinted with the permission of The Timberland Company. Timberland and   are trademarks or registered trademarks of The Timberland Company; Courtesy Starbucks Corporation; Courtesy Volkswagen of America; Michelin and the Tire Man logo are registered trademarks of Michelin North America, Inc. and are used here by permission; Courtesy AT&T; Created by Larry Ewing and The Gimp; Courtesy Yahoo! Inc; [eBay Mark] is a trademark of eBay Inc; Courtesy Intel Corporation; Courtesy Boys & Girls Clubs of America; Courtesy Dole Food Company, Inc; ©2006 Hertz System, Inc. and Hertz is registered service mark and trademark of Hertz System, Inc; Courtesy Nestlé Waters North America, Inc.

Photos/ads: Pg. 195, Courtesy Michael Coburn/Electric Rentals, Inc. Pg. 198, Courtesy Garrity Industries. Pg. 198, Courtesy The Hertz Corporation. Pg. 200, Courtesy Allen Edmonds Shoe Corporation. Pg. 200, Courtesy 3M. Pg. 203, Courtesy Weber Shandwick Worldwide. Pg. 203, Courtesy BSH Home Appliances Corporation. Pg. 204, *Both* Courtesy Bush Brothers & Company. Pg. 208, Courtesy Unilever, United States, Inc. Pg. 208, Courtesy Johnson & Johnson. Pg. 210, Courtesy Chiquita Brands International Inc. Pg. 210, Courtesy Del Monte Fresh Produce N.A., Inc. Pg. 212, ©William D. Perreault, Jr. Ph.D. Pg. 212, ©William D. Perreault, Jr. Ph.D. Pg. 212, Courtesy Societe Alimentaire de Guidel/France. Pg. 214, ©William D. Perreault, Jr. Ph.D. Pg. 215, Courtesy Stonyfield Farm. Pg. 216, Courtesy Bristol-Myers Squibb Co. Pg. 216, Courtesy LensCrafters, Inc.

CHAPTER 9

Exhibits: Exhibit 9-4, adapted from Frank R. Bacon, Jr., and Thomas W. Butler, *Planned Innovation* (Ann Arbor: University of Michigan Institute of Science and Technology, 1980). Exhibit 9-5, adapted from Philip Kotler, "What Consumerism Means for Marketers," *Harvard Business Review*, May–June 1972, pp. 55–56. Exhibit 9-7, Marie Gaudard, Roland Coates, and Liz Freeman, "Accelerating Improvement," *Quality Progress*, October 1991, pp. 81–88. Exhibit, 9-8, Marie Gaudard, Roland Coates, and Liz Freeman, "Accelerating Improvement," *Quality Progress*, October 1991, pp. 81–88.

Photos/ads: Pg. 221, Courtesy Brendan Mattingly Photography, Inc. Pg. 225, Courtesy Garmin International. Pg. 225, Courtesy AK Steel Corporation. Pg. 226, *Both* Courtesy Nestlé S.A. Pg. 227, Courtesy Braun, Inc. Pg. 228, Courtesy Zara International, Inc. Pg. 231, Courtesy DuPont Textiles & Interiors' LYCRA®; Agency: Saatchi & Saatchi/Zurich. Pg. 232, ©The Procter & Gamble Company. Used by permission. Pg. 232, Courtesy Bic Corporation. Pg. 234, Courtesy Greenfield Online, Inc. Pg. 234, Courtesy Sauder Woodworking Company. Pg. 237, Courtesy CSA International. Pg. 237, ©American Honda Motor Co., Inc. Pg. 239, Courtesy Microsoft Corporation. Pg. 241, Courtesy of Nabisco Brands, Inc. Pg. 242, Courtesy Toyota Motor Company. Pg. 246, Courtesy Plastic Services & Products, Inc.

CHAPTER 10

Exhibits: Exhibit 10-2, adapted from D. J. Bowersox and E. J. McCarthy, "Strategic Development of Planned Vertical Marketing Systems," in *Vertical Marketing Systems*, ed. Louis Bucklin (Glenview, IL: Scott, Foresman, 1970).

Photos/ads: Pg. 251, ©William D. Perrerault Jr., Ph.D. Pg. 254, ©The Procter & Gamble Company. Used by permission. Pg. 254, Courtesy Colgate-Palmolive Company. Pg. 255, Courtesy Oakley United States of America. Pg. 255, Courtesy Energy Brands, Inc. Pg. 256, *All* Courtesy Unilever, P.L.C. Pg. 257, ©William D. Perreault, Jr. Ph.D. Pg. 258, AP Photo/Scott Sady. Pg. 259, Ann Ryan/Polaris Images. Pg. 260, Courtesy Peterson Manufacturing Company. Pg. 265, Courtesy Mother Work, Inc. Pg. 266, Courtesy Stihl Incorporated. Pg. 270, Courtesy Office Depot, Inc.

CHAPTER 11

Exhibits: Exhibit 11-5, adapted from B. J. LaLonde and P. H. Zinzer, *Customer Service: Meaning and Measurement* (Chicago: National Council of Physical Distribution Management, 1976); and D. Phillip Locklin, *Transportation for Management* (Homewood, IL: Richard D. Irwin, 1972). Exhibit 11-8, adapted from Louis W. Stern and Adel I. El-Ansary, *Marketing Channels* (Englewood Cliffs, NJ: Prentice Hall, 1977), p. 150.

Photos/ads: Pg. 275, McGraw-Hill Education Digital Asset Library. Pg. 279, Courtesy Fahlgren Advertising; Mike Sanford/Copywriter, Dave Rogers/Art Director. Pg. 280, Courtesy Sauder

Woodworking Company. Pg. 280, Reprinted with permission of Sage Software. Pg. 284, AP Photo/Greg Baker. Pg. 285, ©Allan Hunter Shoemaker Photography, Inc. Pg. 285, ©Steve Smith. Pg. 288, Courtesy Copexeu. Pg. 288, Courtesy AMR Corporation. Pg. 288, AP Photo/Luis E. Ascui. Pg. 289, ©The Procter & Gamble Company. Used by permission. Pg. 289, Courtesy U.S. Environmental Protection Agency. Pg. 290, ©William D. Perreault, Jr. Ph.D. Pg. 290, Courtesy Great Plains Software, Inc. Pg. 293, Courtesy RFID Journal.

CHAPTER 12

Exhibits: Exhibit 12-5 graph developed by the authors based on U. S. Census data including, "Table 1a: Summary Statistics for the United States 2002," from *2002 Economic Census—Wholesale Trade Geographic Area Series, United States* (Washington, DC: U.S. Government Printing Office, 2005) and available online at http://www.census.gov.

Photos/ads: Pg. 297, Photo by Tim Boyle/Getty Images. Pg. 302, *Both* 2003 ©Lands' End, Inc. Used with permission. Pg. 304-305, Courtesy of Office Depot. Pg. 306, Greg Wood/AFP/Getty Images. Pg. 306, Reproduced courtesy of Exxon Mobil Corp. Pg. 309, Courtesy GlaxoSmithKline. Pg. 309, Courtesy 1-800-PetMeds. Pg. 310, Courtesy Best Buy. Pg. 310, Courtesy www.htd.com Home Theater Direct, Inc. Pg. 313, Courtesy Lowe's Companies, Inc. Pg. 313, Courtesy Ace Hardware. Pg. 315, Photo: Karen Capland; Courtesy Frieda's, Inc. Pg. 318, Artwork provided by A.L. Lightech, Inc. Pg. 319, ©Steve Niedorf. Pg. 320, Courtesy The Orchard Network Ltd. Pg. 321, These materials have been reproduced with the permission of eBay, Inc. COPYRIGHT ©2006 EBAY INC. ALL RIGHTS RESERVED.

CHAPTER 13

Photos/ads: Pg. 327, Courtesy MINI USA. Pg. 330, *No credit.* Pg. 333, *All* Courtesy Stanley Works. Pg. 337, Courtesy of Davis Wright Tremaine LLP. Pg. 338, *No credit.* Pg. 339, Courtesy Google. Pg. 342, Both Courtesy Sara Lee Corporation. Pg. 344, ©LivePerson, Inc. All rights reserved. Pg. 346, Courtesy The Hearst Corporation. Pg. 347, Courtesy Johnson & Johnson. Pg. 347, Courtesy Alice/Paris. Pg. 349, ©2000 Network Solutions, Inc. Pg. 349, Courtesy Tierney Communications.

CHAPTER 14

Exhibits: Exhibit 14-3, exhibit suggested by Professor A. A. Brogowicz, Western Michigan University.

Photos/ads: Pg. 355, ©William D. Perreault, Jr. Ph.D. Pg. 358, Courtesy Prudential Financial, Inc. Pg. 358, Courtesy Boise Cascade Office Products. Pg. 359, ©2004. The Charles Schwab Corporation. Pg. 360, Courtesy General Electric Company; Photo by: Brownie Harris. Pg. 362, Courtesy Hobart Corporation. Pg. 364, CLOROX® is a registered trademark of The Clorox Company. Used with permission. ©The Clorox Company. Reprinted with permission. Pg. 367, Courtesy Hass Avocado Board. Pg. 368, Courtesy Salesforce.com., Inc. Pg. 370, Digital Vision/Getty Images. Pg. 371, Courtesy Caliper. Pg. 372, Robert Wahrenburg, Rental Advertising Manager; Caterpillar, Inc. Pg. 376, Vince Bitel, Lisa Johnson, Tech Target 2006. Pg. 379, Courtesy Keebler.

CHAPTER 15

Exhibits: Exhibit 15-2, "2005 Advertising to Sales Ratios for 200 Largest Ad Spending Industries," from Schonfeld & Associates, Inc., *Advertising Rations & Budgets, 29th edition,* and available online at http://www.adage.com. Exhibit 15-5, spending and percent growth data are a compilation by the authors from, "2006 Fact Pack," *Adver-*

tising Age (supplement), February 27, 2006, p. 10; "100 Leading National Advertisers," *Advertising Age* (special issue), June 27, 2005, p.4; both available online at http://www.adage.com. Additional data available online at http://www.tns-mi.com. Earlier 2002 data compiled from "2004 Fact Pack," *Advertising Age* (supplement), February 2004, "Ad Industry Looks Ahead with Cautious Optimism,: *Advertising Age,* December 16, 2002, p. 4; and various "Insider's Reports" by Robert Coen of Universal McCann, and available online at http://www.adage.com.

Photos/ads: Pg. 383, Courtesy Subway Restaurants/Doctor's Associates, Inc. Pg. 386, Procter & Gamble Rejoice 'Giant Comb' Courtesy: Leo Burnett Bangkok; Executive Creative Director: Chris Chiu. Pg. 386, ©The Procter & Gamble Company. Used by permission. Pg. 390, Courtesy General Mills. Pg. 390, Courtesy Philips Electronics North America. Pg. 391, Courtesy E! Entertainment Television, Inc. Pg. 391, Courtesy SiTV, Inc. Pg. 393, David Taylor/Allsport. Pg. 396, *No credit.* Pg. 397, *Both* Courtesy Lowe Pirella/Milan. Pg. 398, Courtesy Biano Danmark A/S. Pg. 400, Courtesy WonderGroup. Pg. 400, Courtesy FLOORgraphics, Inc. Pg. 401, Courtesy Bates USA South/Miami. Pg. 401, Courtesy Greenfield Online, Inc. Pg. 405, *All* ©The Procter & Gamble Company. Used by permission. Pg. 406, The McGraw-Hill Companies, Inc./Christopher Kerrigan, Photographer.

CHAPTER 16

Exhibits: Exhibit 16-6, exchange rate data is available from the Federal Reserve Bank; see also International Monetary Fund data available online at http://www.imf.org/external/np/tre/sdr/drates and Universal Currency Converter available online at http://www.x-rates.com.

Photos/ads: Pg. 411, Redux Pictures/Mark Leong. Pg. 412, Courtesy Clarke Goward Agency. Pg. 416, Courtesy Merck Co., Inc. Pg. 418, Courtesy Trico Products Corporation. Pg. 418, Courtesy Carnival Corporation. Pg. 421, Courtesy Dupont Surfaces. Pg. 421, All rights reserved, Palm, Inc. Pg. 422, Courtesy 8 in 1 Pet Products, Inc. Pg. 422, Courtesy Nestle U.S.A. – Prepared Foods. Pg. 424, Courtesy The Richards Group; Copywriter: Chris Smith; Art Director: Warren Lewis. Pg. 424, *No credit.* Pg. 425, These materials have been reproduced with the permission of eBay, Inc. COPYRIGHT ©2006 EBAY INC. ALL RIGHTS RESERVED. Pg. 426, Courtesy Con Agra Foods, Inc. – Grocery Products Division. Pg. 429, Courtesy Transamerican Wholesale. Pg. 429, ©The Procter & Gamble Company. Used by permission. Pg. 430, *No credit.* Pg. 431, Courtesy CNET. Pg. 432, ©William D. Perreault, Jr. Ph.D. Pg. 433, Mike Williams/Mercury. Pg. 434, ©William D. Perreault, Jr. Ph.D.

CHAPTER 17

Exhibits: Exhibit 17-11, this exhibit is different from, but stimulated by, a graph that appears on the Satisfaction Management Systems, Inc., website at http://www.satmansys.com.

Photos/ads: Pg. 439, Photo by Tim Boyle/Getty Images. Pg. 442, Courtesy Kohler, Co. Pg. 442, Courtesy Dr. Pepper/7-UP Bottling Group, Inc. Pg. 442, ©William D. Perreault, Jr. Ph.D. Pg. 445, Courtesy Cargill. Pg. 451, Mark Henley/Impact. Pg. 454, ©The Procter & Gamble Company. Used by permission. Pg. 455, PORSCHE, BOXSTER, the Porsche Crest area registered trademarks and the distinctive shapes of Porsche automobiles are trademarks of Dr. Ing. h.c. F. Porsche AG. Used with permission of Porsche Cars North America, Inc. All rights reserved. Do not copy without the permission of Porsche Cars North America, Inc. Pg. 456, Courtesy The Grasshopper Company. Pg. 457, Courtesy eCampus.com; Agency: Devito-Verdi Advertising. Pg. 457, Courtesy Hallmark Cards, Inc.; Agency: Leo Burnett/Chicago, IL. Pg. 458, Courtesy Affordable Furniture.

Pg. 459, Courtesy Rolex Watch U.S.A., Inc. Pg. 459, Courtesy Audio Stream. Pg. 461, Courtesy Worldbid.com. Pg. 461, Courtesy Jaffe Software Systems.

CHAPTER 18

Exhibits: Exhibit 18-5, adapted and updated from discussions of an American Marketing Association Strategic Planning Committee.

Photos/ads: Pg. 465, Guang Niu/Reuters. Pg. 466, Courtesy Sprint Nextel Corporation. Pg. 468, Courtesy Planetfeedback. Pg. 468, Courtesy Carlson Hospitality Worldwide. Pg. 470, Courtesy New Product Works. Pg. 472, Courtesy Sara Lee Bakery Group. Pg. 472, Courtesy Marie's Brand. Pg. 473, Courtesy of GoDaddy.com, Inc. Pg. 474, ©2006 Swagelok Company. Pg. 475, Courtesy Trief USA, Inc. Pg. 475, Courtesy Rubin Postaer & Assoc.; Photography: Stock. Pg. 482, Courtesy Waste Management, Inc. Pg. 482, Courtesy Shell Oil Company. Pg. 484, Photo by: Bob Wolter & Associates. Pg. 485, Courtesy Your Credit Card Companies. Pg. 485, Courtesy Zippo Manufacturing Company, Inc.

APPENDIX B

Exhibits: Exhibit B-4, "2003 Survey of Buying Power," *Sales & Marketing Management*, Supplement, 2003.

Photos/ads: Pg. 513, Courtesy SunLite Casual Furniture. Pg. 513, Courtesy of Third Wave Research Group, Ltd. Pg. 516, ©2006 Kellogg North America Company. Pg. 516, Courtesy Greenfield Online, Inc. Pg. 517, ©William D. Perreault, Jr., Ph.d.

APPENDIX C

Photos/ads: Pg. 531, *Both* Courtesy Monster.

Author Index

I-11

Author Index

Company Index

Subject Index

Glossary

Accessories Short-lived capital items—tools and equipment used in production or office activities.

Accumulating Collecting products from many small producers.

Administered channel systems Various channel members informally agree to cooperate with each other.

Administered prices Consciously set prices aimed at reaching the firm's objectives.

Adoption curve Shows when different groups accept ideas.

Adoption process The steps individuals go through on the way to accepting or rejecting a new idea.

Advertising Any *paid* form of nonpersonal presentation of ideas, goods, or services by an identified sponsor.

Advertising agencies Specialists in planning and handling mass-selling details for advertisers.

Advertising allowances Price reductions to firms in the channel to encourage them to advertise or otherwise promote the firm's products locally.

Advertising managers Managers of their company's mass-selling effort in television, newspapers, magazines, and other media.

Agent middlemen Wholesalers who do not own (take title to) the products they sell.

AIDA model Consists of four promotion jobs: (1) to get *Attention*, (2) to hold *Interest*, (3) to arouse *Desire*, and (4) to obtain *Action*.

Allowance (accounting term) Occurs when a customer is not satisfied with a purchase for some reason and the seller gives a price reduction on the original invoice (bill), but the customer keeps the goods or services.

Allowances Reductions in price given to final consumers, customers, or channel members for doing something or accepting less of something.

Assorting Putting together a variety of products to give a target market what it wants.

Attitude A person's point of view toward something.

Auction companies Agent middlemen that provide a place where buyers and sellers can come together and complete a transaction.

Automatic vending Selling and delivering products through vending machines.

Average cost (per unit) The total cost divided by the related quantity.

Average-cost pricing Adding a reasonable markup to the average cost of a product.

Average fixed cost (per unit) The total fixed cost divided by the related quantity.

Average variable cost (per unit) The total variable cost divided by the related quantity.

Bait pricing Setting some very low prices to attract customers but trying to sell more expensive models or brands once the customer is in the store.

Balance sheet An accounting statement that shows a company's assets, liabilities, and net worth.

Basic list prices The prices that final customers or users are normally asked to pay for products.

Basic sales tasks *Order-getting, order-taking,* and *supporting.*

Battle of the brands The competition between dealer brands and manufacturer brands.

Belief A person's opinion about something.

Benchmarking Picking a basis of comparison for evaluating how well a job is being done.

Bid pricing Offering a specific price for each possible job rather than setting a price that applies for all customers.

Brand equity The value of a brand's overall strength in the market.

Brand familiarity How well customers recognize and accept a company's brand.

Brand insistence Customers insist on a firm's branded product and are willing to search for it.

Brand managers Manage specific products, often taking over the jobs formerly handled by an advertising manager—sometimes called *product managers.*

Brand name A word, letter, or a group of words or letters.

Brand nonrecognition Final customers don't recognize a brand at all—even though middlemen may use the brand name for identification and inventory control.

Brand preference Target customers usually choose the brand over other brands, perhaps because of habit or favorable past experience.

Brand recognition Customers remember the brand.

Brand rejection Potential customers won't buy a brand—unless its image is changed.

Branding The use of a name, term, symbol, or design—or a combination of these—to identify a product.

Break-even analysis An approach to determine whether the firm will be able to break even—that is, cover all its costs—with a particular price.

Break-even point (BEP) The sales quantity where the firm's total cost will just equal its total revenue.

Breakthrough opportunities Opportunities that help innovators develop hard-to-copy marketing strategies that will be very profitable for a long time.

Brokers Agent middlemen who specialize in bringing buyers and sellers together.

Bulk-breaking Dividing larger quantities into smaller quantities as products get closer to the final market.

Business and organizational customers Any buyers who buy for resale or to produce other goods and services.

Business products Products meant for use in producing other products.

Buying center All the people who participate in or influence a purchase.

Buying function Looking for and evaluating goods and services.

Capital item A long-lasting product that can be used and depreciated for many years.

Cash-and-carry wholesalers Like service wholesalers, except that the customer must pay cash.

Cash discounts Reductions in the price to encourage buyers to pay their bills quickly.

Catalog wholesalers Sell out of catalogs that may be distributed widely to smaller industrial customers or retailers that might not be called on by other middlemen.

Channel captain A manager who helps direct the activities of a whole channel and tries to avoid, or resolve, channel conflicts.

Channel of distribution Any series of firms or individuals who participate in the flow of products from producer to final user or consumer.

Close The salesperson's request for an order.

Clustering techniques Approaches used to try to find similar patterns within sets of data.

Collaborators Firms that provide one or more of the marketing functions other than buying or selling.

Combination export manager A blend of manufacturers' agent and selling agent—handling the entire export function for several producers of similar but noncompeting lines.

Combined target market approach Combining two or more submarkets into one larger target market as a basis for one strategy.

Combiners Firms that try to increase the size of their target markets by combining two or more segments.

Command economy Government officials decide what and how much is to be produced and distributed by whom, when, to whom, and why.

Communication process A source trying to reach a receiver with a message.

Comparative advertising Advertising that makes specific brand comparisons using actual product names.

Competitive advantage A firm has a marketing mix that the target market sees as better than a competitor's mix.

Competitive advertising Advertising that tries to develop selective demand for a specific brand rather than a product category.

Competitive barriers The conditions that may make it difficult, or even impossible, for a firm to compete in a market.

Competitive bids Terms of sale offered by different suppliers in response to the buyer's purchase specifications.

Competitive environment The number and types of competitors the marketing manager must face, and how they may behave.

Competitive rivals A firm's closest competitors.

Competitor analysis An organized approach for evaluating the strengths and weaknesses of current or potential competitors' marketing strategies.

Complementary product pricing Setting prices on several related products as a group.

Components Processed expense items that become part of a finished product.

Concept testing Getting reactions from customers about how well a new-product idea fits their needs.

Consultative selling approach A type of sales presentation in which the salesperson develops a good understanding of the individual customer's needs before trying to close the sale.

Consumer panel A group of consumers who provide information on a continuing basis.

Consumer Product Safety Act A 1972 law that set up the Consumer Product Safety Commission to encourage more awareness of safety in product design and better quality control.

Consumer products Products meant for the final consumer.

Consumer surplus The difference to consumers between the value of a purchase and the price they pay.

Consumerism A social movement that seeks to increase the rights and powers of consumers.

Containerization Grouping individual items into an economical shipping quantity and sealing them in protective containers for transit to the final destination.

Continuous improvement A commitment to constantly make things better one step at a time.

Contractual channel systems Various channel members agree by contract to cooperate with each other.

Convenience (food) stores A convenience-oriented variation of the conventional limited-line food stores.

Convenience products Products a consumer needs but isn't willing to spend much time or effort shopping for.

Cooperative advertising Middlemen and producers sharing in the cost of ads.

Cooperative chains Retailer-sponsored groups formed by independent retailers to run their own buying organizations and conduct joint promotion efforts.

Copy thrust What the words and illustrations of an ad should communicate.

Corporate chain A firm that owns and manages more than one store—and often it's many.

Corporate channel systems Corporate ownership all along the channel.

Corrective advertising Ads to correct deceptive advertising.

Cost of sales Total value (at cost) of the sales during the period.

Cues Products, signs, ads, and other stimuli in the environment.

Cultural and social environment Affects how and why people live and behave as they do.

Culture The whole set of beliefs, attitudes, and ways of doing things of a reasonably homogeneous set of people.

Cumulative quantity discounts Reductions in price for larger purchases over a given period, such as a year.

Customer equity The expected earnings stream (profitability) of a firm's current and prospective customers over some period of time.

Customer relationship management (CRM) An approach where the seller fine-tunes the marketing effort with information from a detailed customer database.

Customer satisfaction The extent to which a firm fulfills a consumer's needs, desires, and expectations.

Customer service A personal communication between a seller and a customer who wants the seller to resolve a problem with a purchase; often the key to building repeat business.

Customer service level How rapidly and dependably a firm can deliver what customers want.

Customer service reps Supporting salespeople who work with customers to resolve problems that arise with a purchase, usually after the purchase has been made.

Customer value The difference between the benefits a customer sees from a market offering and the costs of obtaining those benefits.

Data warehouse A place where databases are stored so that they are available when needed.

Dealer brands Brands created by middlemen—sometimes referred to as *private brands*.

Decision support system (DSS) A computer program that makes it easy for marketing managers to get and use information *as they are making decisions*.

Decoding The receiver in the communication process translating the message.

Demand-backward pricing Setting an acceptable final consumer price and working backward to what a producer can charge.

Demand curve A graph of the relationship between price and quantity demanded in a market, assuming all other things stay the same.

Department stores Larger stores that are organized into many separate departments and offer many product lines.

Derived demand Demand for business products derives from the demand for final consumer products.

Determining dimensions The dimensions that actually affect the customer's purchase of a *specific* product or brand in a *product-market*.

Differentiation The marketing mix is distinct from and better than what's available from a competitor.

Direct marketing Direct communication between a seller and an individual customer using a promotion method other than face-to-face personal selling.

Direct type advertising Competitive advertising that aims for immediate buying action.

Discount houses Stores that sell hard goods (cameras, TVs, appliances) at substantial price cuts to customers who go to discounter's low-rent store, pay cash, and take care of any service or repair problems themselves.

Discounts Reductions from list price given by a seller to buyers, who either give up some marketing function or provide the function themselves.

Discrepancy of assortment The difference between the lines a typical producer makes and the assortment final consumers or users want.

Discrepancy of quantity The difference between the quantity of products it is economical for a producer to make and the quantity final consumers or users normally want.

Discretionary income Income that is left after paying taxes and paying for necessities.

Dissonance Tension caused by uncertainty about the rightness of a decision.

Distribution center A special kind of warehouse designed to speed the flow of goods and avoid unnecessary storing costs.

Diversification Moving into totally different lines of business—perhaps entirely unfamiliar products, markets, or even levels in the production-marketing system.

Door-to-door selling Going directly to the consumer's home.

Drive A strong stimulus that encourages action to reduce a need.

Drop-shippers Wholesalers that own (take title to) the products they sell but do not actually handle, stock, or deliver them.

Dual distribution When a producer uses several competing channels to reach the same target market—perhaps using several middlemen in addition to selling directly (sometimes called *multichannel distribution*).

Dumping Pricing a product sold in a foreign market below the cost of producing it or at a price lower than in its domestic market.

Early adopters The second group in the adoption curve to adopt a new product; these people are usually well respected by their peers and often are opinion leaders.

Early majority A group in the adoption curve that avoids risk and waits to consider a new idea until many early adopters try it and like it.

E-commerce Exchanges between individuals or organizations—and activities that facilitate those exchanges—based on applications of information technology.

Economic and technological environment Affects the way firms, and the whole economy, use resources.

Economic buyers People who know all the facts and logically compare choices to get the greatest satisfaction from spending their time and money.

Economic needs Needs concerned with making the best use of a consumer's time and money—as the consumer judges it.

Economic system The way an economy organizes to use scarce resources to produce goods and services and distribute them for consumption by various people and groups in the society.

Economies of scale As a company produces larger numbers of a particular product, the cost for each of these products goes down.

Elastic demand If prices are dropped, the quantity demanded will stretch enough to increase total revenue.

Elastic supply The quantity supplied does stretch more if the price is raised.

Electronic data interchange (EDI) An approach that puts information in a standardized format easily shared between different computer systems.

Emergency products Products that are purchased immediately when the need is great.

Empowerment Giving employees the authority to correct a problem without first checking with management.

Empty nesters People whose children are grown and who are now able to spend their money in other ways.

Encoding The source in the communication process deciding what it wants to say and translating it into words or symbols that will have the same meaning to the receiver.

Equilibrium point The quantity and the price sellers are willing to offer are equal to the quantity and price that buyers are willing to accept.

Everyday low pricing Setting a low list price rather than relying on frequent sales, discounts, or allowances.

Exclusive distribution Selling through only one middleman in a particular geographic area.

Expectation An outcome or event that a person anticipates or looks forward to.

Expense item A product whose total cost is treated as a business expense in the period it's purchased.

Expenses All the remaining costs that are subtracted from the gross margin to get the net profit.

Experimental method A research approach in which researchers compare the responses of two or more groups that are similar except on the characteristic being tested.

Export agents Manufacturers' agents who specialize in export trade.

Export brokers Brokers who specialize in bringing together buyers and sellers from different countries.

Extensive problem solving The type of problem solving consumers use for a completely new or important need—when they put much effort into deciding how to satisfy it.

Factor A variable that shows the relation of some other variable to the item being forecast.

Factor method An approach to forecast sales by finding a relation between the company's sales and some other factor (or factors).

Family brand A brand name that is used for several products.

Farm products Products grown by farmers, such as oranges, sugar cane, and cattle.

Fashion Currently accepted or popular style.

Federal Fair Packaging and Labeling Act A 1966 law requiring that consumer goods be clearly labeled in easy-to-understand terms.

Federal Trade Commission (FTC) Federal government agency that polices antimonopoly laws.

Financing Provides the necessary cash and credit to produce, transport, store, promote, sell, and buy products.

Fishbone diagram A visual aid that helps organize cause and effect relationships for "things gone wrong."

Fixed-cost (FC) contribution per unit The selling price per unit minus the variable cost per unit.

Flexible-price policy Offering the same product and quantities to different customers at different prices.

F.O.B. A transportation term meaning free on board some vehicle at some point.

Focus group interview An interview of 6 to 10 people in an informal group setting.

Foreign Corrupt Practices Act A law passed by the U.S. Congress in 1977 that prohibits U.S. firms from paying bribes to foreign officials.

Franchise operation A franchisor develops a good marketing strategy, and the retail franchise holders carry out the strategy in their own units.

Freight-absorption pricing Absorbing freight cost so that a firm's delivered price meets that of the nearest competitor.

Full-line pricing Setting prices for a whole line of products.

General merchandise wholesalers Service wholesalers that carry a wide variety of nonperishable items such as hardware, electrical supplies, furniture, drugs, cosmetics, and automobile equipment.

General stores Early retailers who carried anything they could sell in reasonable volume.

Generic market A market with *broadly* similar needs—and sellers offering various and *often diverse* ways of satisfying those needs.

Generic products Products that have no brand at all other than identification of their contents and the manufacturer or middleman.

Gross domestic product (GDP) The total market value of all goods and services provided in a country's economy in a year by both residents and nonresidents of that country.

Gross margin (gross profit) The money left to cover the expenses of selling the products and operating the business.

Gross sales The total amount charged to all customers during some time period.

Heterogeneous shopping products Shopping products the customer sees as different and wants to inspect for quality and suitability.

Homogeneous shopping products Shopping products the customer sees as basically the same and wants at the lowest price.

Hypermarkets Very large stores that try to carry not only food and drug items but all goods and services that the consumer purchases *routinely* (also called *supercenters*).

Hypotheses Educated guesses about the relationships between things or about what will happen in the future.

Ideal market exposure When a product is available widely enough to satisfy target customers' needs but not exceed them.

Implementation Putting marketing plans into operation.

Import agents Manufacturers' agents who specialize in import trade.

Import brokers Brokers who specialize in bringing together buyers and sellers from different countries.

Impulse products Products that are bought quickly as *unplanned* purchases because of a strongly felt need.

Indirect type advertising Competitive advertising that points out product advantages—to affect future buying decisions.

Individual brands Separate brand names used for each product.

Individual product A particular product within a product line.

Inelastic demand Although the quantity demanded increases if the price is decreased, the quantity demanded will not stretch enough to avoid a decrease in total revenue.

Inelastic supply The quantity supplied does not stretch much (if at all) if the price is raised.

Innovation The development and spread of new ideas, goods, and services.

Innovators The first group to adopt new products.

Installations Important capital items such as buildings, land rights, and major equipment.

Institutional advertising Advertising that tries to promote an organization's image, reputation, or ideas rather than a specific product.

Integrated marketing communications The intentional coordination of every communication from a firm to a target customer to convey a consistent and complete message.

Intensive distribution Selling a product through all responsible and suitable wholesalers or retailers who will stock or sell the product.

Intermediary Someone who specializes in trade rather than production, sometimes called a *middleman*.

Internet A system for linking computers around the world.

Intranet A system for linking computers within a company.

Introductory price dealing Temporary price cuts to speed new products into a market and get customers to try them.

Inventory The amount of goods being stored.

ISO 9000 A way for a supplier to document its quality procedures according to internationally recognized standards.

Job description A written statement of what a salesperson is expected to do.

Jury of executive opinion Forecasting by combining the opinions of experienced executives, perhaps from marketing, production, finance, purchasing, and top management.

Just-in-time delivery Reliably getting products there *just* before the customer needs them.

Laggards Prefer to do things the way they have been done in the past and are very suspicious of new ideas; sometimes called *nonadopters*—see *adoption curve*.

Lanham Act A 1946 law that spells out what kinds of marks (including brand names) can be protected and the exact method of protecting them.

Late majority A group of adopters who are cautious about new ideas—see *adoption curve*.

Law of diminishing demand If the price of a product is raised, a smaller quantity will be demanded—and if the price of a product is lowered, a greater quantity will be demanded.

Leader pricing Setting some very low prices—real bargains—to get customers into retail stores.

Learning A change in a person's thought processes caused by prior experience.

Licensed brand A well-known brand that sellers pay a fee to use.

Lifestyle analysis The analysis of a person's day-to-day pattern of living as expressed in that person's Activities, Interests, and Opinions—sometimes referred to as *AIOs* or *psychographics*.

Limited-function wholesalers Merchant wholesalers that provide only *some* wholesaling functions.

Limited-line stores Stores that specialize in certain lines of related products rather than a wide assortment—sometimes called *single-line stores*.

Limited problem solving When a consumer is willing to put *some* effort into deciding the best way to satisfy a need.

Logistics The transporting, storing, and handling of goods in ways that match target customers' needs with a firm's marketing mix—both within individual firms and along a channel of distribution (i.e., another name for *physical distribution*).

Low-involvement purchases Purchases that have little importance or relevance for the customer.

Macro-marketing A social process that directs an economy's flow of goods and services from producers to consumers in a way that effectively matches supply and demand and accomplishes the objectives of society.

Magnuson-Moss Act A 1975 law requiring that producers provide a clearly written warranty if they choose to offer any warranty.

Major accounts sales force Salespeople who sell directly to large accounts such as major retail chain stores.

Manufacturer brands Brands created by producers.

Manufacturers' agents Agent middlemen who sell similar products for several noncompeting producers for a commission on what is actually sold.

Manufacturers' sales branches Separate warehouses that producers set up away from their factories.

Marginal analysis Evaluating the change in total revenue and total cost from selling one more unit to find the most profitable price and quantity.

Markdown A retail price reduction that is required because customers won't buy some item at the originally marked-up price.

Markdown ratio A tool used by many retailers to measure the efficiency of various departments and their whole business.

Market A group of potential customers with similar needs who are willing to exchange something of value with sellers offering various goods or services—that is, ways of satisfying those needs.

Market development Trying to increase sales by selling present products in new markets.

Market-directed economy The individual decisions of the many producers and consumers make the macro-level decisions for the whole economy.

Market growth A stage of the product life cycle when industry sales grow fast—but industry profits rise and then start falling.

Market information function The collection, analysis, and distribution of all the information needed to plan, carry out, and control marketing activities.

Market introduction A stage of the product life cycle when sales are low as a new idea is first introduced to a market.

Market maturity A stage of the product life cycle when industry sales level off and competition gets tougher.

Market penetration Trying to increase sales of a firm's present products in its present markets—probably through a more aggressive marketing mix.

Market potential What a whole market segment might buy.

Market segment A relatively homogeneous group of customers who will respond to a marketing mix in a similar way.

Market segmentation A two-step process of (1) *naming* broad product-markets and (2) *segmenting* those broad product-markets in order to select target markets and develop suitable marketing mixes.

Marketing The performance of activities that seek to accomplish an organization's objectives by anticipating customer or client needs and directing a flow of need-satisfying goods and services from producer to customer or client.

Marketing company era A time when, in addition to short-run marketing planning, marketing people develop long-range plans—sometimes five or more years ahead—and the whole company effort is guided by the marketing concept.

Marketing concept The idea that an organization should aim *all* its efforts at satisfying its *customers*—at a *profit*.

Marketing department era A time when all marketing activities are brought under the control of one department to improve short-run policy planning and to try to integrate the firm's activities.

Marketing ethics The moral standards that guide marketing decisions and actions.

Marketing information system (MIS) An organized way of continually gathering, accessing, and analyzing information that marketing managers need to make ongoing decisions.

Marketing management process The process of (1) *planning* marketing activities, (2) directing the *implementation* of the plans, and (3) *controlling* these plans.

Marketing mix The controllable variables that the company puts together to satisfy a target group.

Marketing model A statement of relationships among marketing variables.

Marketing orientation Trying to carry out the marketing concept.

Marketing plan A written statement of a marketing strategy *and* the time-related details for carrying out the strategy.

Marketing program Blends all of the firm's marketing plans into one big plan.

Marketing research Procedures to develop and analyze new information to help marketing managers make decisions.

Marketing research process A five-step application of the scientific method that includes (1) defining the problem, (2) analyzing the situation, (3) getting problem-specific data, (4) interpreting the data, and (5) solving the problem.

Marketing strategy Specifies a target market and a related marketing mix.

Markup A dollar amount added to the cost of products to get the selling price.

Markup chain The sequence of markups firms use at different levels in a channel—determining the price structure in the whole channel.

Markup (percent) The percentage of selling price that is added to the cost to get the selling price.

Mass marketing The typical production-oriented approach that vaguely aims at everyone with the same marketing mix.

Mass-merchandisers Large, self-service stores with many departments that emphasize soft goods (housewares, clothing, and fabrics) and staples (like health and beauty aids) and selling on lower margins to get faster turnover.

Mass-merchandising concept The idea that retailers should offer low prices to get faster turnover and greater sales volume by appealing to larger numbers.

Mass selling Communicating with large numbers of potential customers at the same time.

Merchant wholesalers Wholesalers who own (take title to) the products they sell.

Message channel The carrier of the message.

Metropolitan Statistical Area (MSA) An integrated economic and social unit with a large population nucleus.

Micro-macro dilemma What is good for some producers and consumers may not be good for society as a whole.

Middleman An intermediary.

Mission statement Sets out the organization's basic purpose for being.

Missionary salespeople Supporting salespeople who work for producers by calling on their middlemen and their customers.

Modified rebuy The in-between process where some review of the buying situation is done—though not as much as in new-task buying or as little as in straight rebuys.

Monopolistic competition A market situation that develops when a market has (1) different (heterogeneous) products and (2) sellers who feel they do have some competition in this market.

Multichannel distribution When a producer uses several competing channels to reach the same target market—perhaps using several middlemen in addition to selling directly (sometimes called *dual distribution*).

Multiple buying influence Several people share in making a purchase decision—perhaps even top management.

Multiple target market approach Segmenting the market and choosing two or more segments, then treating each as a separate target market needing a different marketing mix.

Nationalism An emphasis on a country's interests before everything else.

Natural products Products that occur in nature—such as timber, iron ore, oil, and coal.

Needs The basic forces that motivate a person to do something.

Negotiated contract buying Agreeing to a contract that allows for changes in the purchase arrangements.

Negotiated price A price that is set based on bargaining between the buyer and seller.

Net An invoice term meaning that payment for the face value of the invoice is due immediately—also see *cash discounts*.

Net profit What the company earns from its operations during a particular period.

Net sales The actual sales dollars the company receives.

New product A product that is new *in any way* for the company concerned.

New-task buying When an organization has a new need and the buyer wants a great deal of information.

New unsought products Products offering really new ideas that potential customers don't yet know about.

Noise Any distraction that reduces the effectiveness of the communication process.

Nonadopters Prefer to do things the way they have been done in the past and are very suspicious of new ideas; sometimes called *laggards*—see *adoption curve*.

Noncumulative quantity discounts Reductions in price when a customer purchases a larger quantity on an *individual order*.

Nonprice competition Aggressive action on one or more of the Ps other than Price.

North American Free Trade Agreement (NAFTA) Lays out a plan to reshape the rules of trade among the U.S., Canada, and Mexico.

North American Industry Classification System (NAICS) codes Codes used to identify groups of firms in similar lines of business.

Odd-even pricing Setting prices that end in certain numbers.

Oligopoly A special market situation that develops when a market has (1) essentially homogeneous products, (2) relatively few sellers, and (3) fairly inelastic industry demand curves.

One-price policy Offering the same price to all customers who purchase products under essentially the same conditions and in the same quantities.

Open to buy A buyer has budgeted funds that he can spend during the current time period.

Operating ratios Ratios of items on the operating statement to net sales.

Operating statement A simple summary of the financial results of a company's operations over a specified period of time.

Operational decisions Short-run decisions to help implement strategies.

Opinion leader A person who influences others.

Order getters Salespeople concerned with establishing relationships with new customers and developing new business.

Order-getting Seeking possible buyers with a well-organized sales presentation designed to sell a good, service, or idea.

Order takers Salespeople who sell to regular or established customers, complete most sales transactions, and maintain relationships with their customers.

Order-taking The routine completion of sales made regularly to target customers.

Outsource When the buying organization chooses to contract with an outside firm to produce goods or services rather than producing them internally.

Packaging Promoting, protecting, and enhancing the product.

Pareto chart A graph that shows the number of times a problem cause occurs, with problem causes ordered from most frequent to least frequent.

Penetration pricing policy Trying to sell the whole market at one low price.

Perception How we gather and interpret information from the world around us.

Personal needs An individual's need for personal satisfaction unrelated to what others think or do.

Personal selling Direct spoken communication between sellers and potential customers, usually in person but sometimes over the telephone or even via a video conference over the Internet.

Phony list prices Misleading prices that customers are shown to suggest that the price they are to pay has been discounted from list.

Physical distribution (PD) The transporting, storing, and handling of goods in ways that match target customers' needs with a firm's marketing mix—both within individual firms and along a channel of distribution (i.e., another name for *logistics*).

Physical distribution (PD) concept All transporting, storing, and product-handling activities of a business and a whole channel system should be coordinated as one system that seeks to minimize the cost of distribution for a given customer service level.

Physiological needs Biological needs such as the need for food, drink, rest, and sex.

Piggyback service Loading truck trailers or flatbed trailers carrying containers on railcars to provide both speed and flexibility.

Pioneering advertising Advertising that tries to develop primary demand for a product category rather than demand for a specific brand.

Place Making goods and services available in the right quantities and locations—when customers want them.

Population In marketing research, the total group you are interested in.

Positioning An approach that refers to how customers think about proposed or present brands in a market.

Prepared sales presentation A memorized presentation that is not adapted to each individual customer.

Prestige pricing Setting a rather high price to suggest high quality or high status.

Price The amount of money that is charged for "something" of value.

Price discrimination Injuring competition by selling the same products to different buyers at different prices.

Price fixing Competitors illegally getting together to raise, lower, or stabilize prices.

Price lining Setting a few price levels for a product line and then marking all items at these prices.

Primary data Information specifically collected to solve a current problem.

Primary demand Demand for the general product idea, not just the company's own brand.

Private brands Brands created by middlemen—sometimes referred to as *dealer brands*.

Private warehouses Storing facilities owned or leased by companies for their own use.

Product The need-satisfying offering of a firm.

Product advertising Advertising that tries to sell a specific product.

Product assortment The set of all product lines and individual products that a firm sells.

Product-bundle pricing Setting one price for a set of products.

Product development Offering new or improved products for present markets.

Product liability The legal obligation of sellers to pay damages to individuals who are injured by defective or unsafe products.

Product life cycle The stages a new product idea goes through from beginning to end.

Product line A set of individual products that are closely related.

Product managers Manage specific products, often taking over the jobs formerly handled by an advertising manager—sometimes called *brand managers*.

Product-market A market with *very* similar needs—and sellers offering various *close substitute* ways of satisfying those needs.

Production Actually *making* goods or *performing* services.

Production era A time when a company focuses on production of a few specific products—perhaps because few of these products are available in the market.

Production orientation Making whatever products are easy to produce and *then* trying to sell them.

Professional services Specialized services that support a firm's operations.

Profit maximization objective An objective to get as much profit as possible.

Promotion Communicating information between seller and potential buyer or others in the channel to influence attitudes and behavior.

Prospecting Following all the leads in the target market to identify potential customers.

Psychographics The analysis of a person's day-to-day pattern of living as expressed in that person's Activities, Interests, and Opinions—sometimes referred to as *AIOs* or *lifestyle analysis*.

Psychological pricing Setting prices that have special appeal to target customers.

Public relations Communication with noncustomers—including labor, public interest groups, stockholders, and the government.

Public warehouses Independent storing facilities.

Publicity Any *unpaid* form of nonpersonal presentation of ideas, goods, or services.

Pulling Using promotion to get consumers to ask middlemen for the product.

Purchase discount A reduction of the original invoice amount for some business reason.

Purchasing managers Buying specialists for their employers.

Purchasing specifications A written (or electronic) description of what the firm wants to buy.

Pure competition A market situation that develops when a market has (1) homogeneous (similar) products, (2) many buyers and sellers who have full knowledge of the market, and (3) ease of entry for buyers and sellers.

Pure subsistence economy Each family unit produces everything it consumes.

Push money (or prize money) allowances Allowances (sometimes called *PMs* or *spiffs*) given to retailers by manufacturers or wholesalers to pass on to the retailers' salesclerks for aggressively selling certain items.

Pushing Using normal promotion effort—personal selling, advertising, and sales promotion—to help sell the whole marketing mix to possible channel members.

Qualifying dimensions The dimensions that are relevant to including a customer type in a product-market.

Qualitative research Seeks in-depth, open-ended responses, not yes or no answers.

Quality A product's ability to satisfy a customer's needs or requirements.

Quantitative research Seeks structured responses that can be summarized in numbers—like percentages, averages, or other statistics.

Quantity discounts Discounts offered to encourage customers to buy in larger amounts.

Rack jobbers Merchant wholesalers that specialize in hard-to-handle assortments of products that a retailer doesn't want to manage—and they often display the products on their own wire racks.

Raw materials Unprocessed expense items—such as logs, iron ore, and wheat—that are moved to the next production process with little handling.

Rebates Refunds to consumers after a purchase.

Receiver The target of a message in the communication process, usually a potential customer.

Reference group The people to whom an individual looks when forming attitudes about a particular topic.

Reference price The price a consumer expects to pay.

Regrouping activities Adjusting the quantities or assortments of products handled at each level in a channel of distribution.

Regularly unsought products Products that stay unsought but not unbought forever.

Reinforcement Occurs in the learning process when the consumer's response is followed by satisfaction—that is, reduction in the drive.

Reminder advertising Advertising to keep the product's name before the public.

Requisition A request to buy something.

Research proposal A plan that specifies what marketing research information will be obtained and how.

Resident buyers Independent buying agents who work in central markets for several retailer or wholesaler customers based in outlying areas or other countries.

Response An effort to satisfy a drive.

Response rate The percent of people contacted in a research sample who complete the questionnaire.

Retailing All of the activities involved in the sale of products to final consumers.

Return When a customer sends back purchased products.

Return on assets (ROA) The ratio of net profit (after taxes) to the assets used to make the net profit—multiplied by 100 to get rid of decimals.

Return on investment (ROI) Ratio of net profit (after taxes) to the investment used to make the net profit—multiplied by 100 to get rid of decimals.

Reverse channels Channels used to retrieve products that customers no longer want.

Risk taking Bearing the uncertainties that are part of the marketing process.

Robinson-Patman Act A 1936 law that makes illegal any price discrimination if it injures competition.

Routinized response behavior When consumers regularly select a particular way of satisfying a need when it occurs.

Safety needs Needs concerned with protection and physical well-being.

Sale price A temporary discount from the list price.

Sales analysis A detailed breakdown of a company's sales records.

Sales decline A stage of the product life cycle when new products replace the old.

Sales era A time when a company emphasizes selling because of increased competition.

Sales forecast An estimate of how much an industry or firm hopes to sell to a market segment.

Sales managers Managers concerned with managing personal selling.

Sales-oriented objective An objective to get some level of unit sales, dollar sales, or share of market—without referring to profit.

Sales presentation A salesperson's effort to make a sale or address a customer's problem.

Sales promotion Those promotion activities—other than advertising, publicity, and personal selling—that stimulate interest, trial, or purchase by final customers or others in the channel.

Sales promotion managers Managers of their company's sales promotion effort.

Sales quota The specific sales or profit objective a salesperson is expected to achieve.

Sales territory A geographic area that is the responsibility of one salesperson or several working together.

Sample A part of the relevant population.

Scientific method A decision-making approach that focuses on being objective and orderly in *testing* ideas before accepting them.

Scrambled merchandising Retailers carrying any product lines that they think they can sell profitably.

Search engine A computer program that helps a marketing manager find information that is needed.

Seasonal discounts Discounts offered to encourage buyers to buy earlier than present demand requires.

Secondary data Information that has been collected or published already.

Segmenters Aim at one or more homogeneous segments and try to develop a different marketing mix for each segment.

Segmenting An aggregating process that clusters people with similar needs into a market segment.

Selective demand Demand for a company's own brand rather than a product category.

Selective distribution Selling through only those middlemen who will give the product special attention.

Selective exposure Our eyes and minds seek out and notice only information that interests us.

Selective perception People screen out or modify ideas, messages, and information that conflict with previously learned attitudes and beliefs.

Selective retention People remember only what they want to remember.

Selling agents Agent middlemen who take over the whole marketing job of producers, not just the selling function.

Selling formula approach A sales presentation that starts with a prepared presentation outline—much like the prepared approach—and leads the customer through some logical steps to a final close.

Selling function Promoting the product.

Senior citizen group People over 65.

Service A deed performed by one party for another.

Service mark Those words, symbols, or marks that are legally registered for use by a single company to refer to a service offering.

Service wholesalers Merchant wholesalers that provide all the wholesaling functions.

Shopping products Products that a customer feels are worth the time and effort to compare with competing products.

Simple trade era A time when families traded or sold their surplus output to local middlemen who resold these goods to other consumers or distant middlemen.

Single-line (or general-line) wholesalers Service wholesalers that carry a narrower line of merchandise than general merchandise wholesalers.

Single-line stores Stores that specialize in certain lines of related products rather than a wide assortment—sometimes called *limited-line stores*.

Single target market approach Segmenting the market and picking one of the homogeneous segments as the firm's target market.

Situation analysis An informal study of what information is already available in the problem area.

Skimming price policy Trying to sell the top of the market—the top of the demand curve—at a high price before aiming at more price-sensitive customers.

Social class A group of people who have approximately equal social position as viewed by others in the society.

Social needs Needs concerned with love, friendship, status, and esteem—things that involve a person's interaction with others.

Social responsibility A firm's obligation to improve its positive effects on society and reduce its negative effects.

Sorting Separating products into grades and qualities desired by different target markets.

Source The sender of a message.

Specialty products Consumer products that the customer really wants and makes a special effort to find.

Specialty shop A type of conventional limited-line store—usually small and with a distinct personality.

Specialty wholesalers Service wholesalers that carry a very narrow range of products and offer more information and service than other service wholesalers.

Standardization and grading Sorting products according to size and quality.

Staples Products that are bought often, routinely, and without much thought.

Statistical packages Easy-to-use computer programs that analyze data.

Status quo objectives "Don't-rock-the-*pricing*-boat" objectives.

Stocking allowances Allowances given to middlemen to get shelf space for a product—sometimes called *slotting allowances*.

Stockturn rate The number of times the average inventory is sold during a year.

Storing The marketing function of holding goods.

Storing function Holding goods until customers need them.

Straight rebuy A routine repurchase that may have been made many times before.

Strategic business unit (SBU) An organizational unit (within a larger company) that focuses its efforts on some product-markets and is treated as a separate profit center.

Strategic (management) planning The managerial process of developing and maintaining a match between an organization's resources and its market opportunities.

Substitutes Products that offer the buyer a choice.

Supercenters Very large stores that try to carry not only food and drug items, but all goods and services that the consumer purchases routinely (also called *hypermarkets*).

Supermarkets Large stores specializing in groceries—with self-service and wide assortments.

Supplies Expense items that do not become part of a finished product.

Supply chain The complete set of firms and facilities and logistics activities that are involved in procuring materials, transforming them into intermediate and finished products, and distributing them to customers.

Supply curve The quantity of products that will be supplied at various possible prices.

Supporting salespeople Salespeople who help the order-oriented salespeople but don't try to get orders themselves.

S.W.O.T. analysis Identifies and lists the firm's strengths and weaknesses and its opportunities and threats.

Target market A fairly homogeneous (similar) group of customers to whom a company wishes to appeal.

Target marketing A marketing mix is tailored to fit some specific target customers.

Target return objective A specific level of profit as an objective.

Task method An approach to developing a budget—basing the budget on the job to be done.

Team selling Different sales reps working together on a specific account.

Technical specialists Supporting salespeople who provide technical assistance to order-oriented salespeople.

Technology The application of science to convert an economy's resources to output.

Telemarketing Using the telephone to call on customers or prospects.

Telephone and direct-mail retailing Allows consumers to shop at home—usually placing orders by mail or via a toll-free long-distance telephone call and charging the purchase to a credit card.

Total cost The sum of total fixed and total variable costs.

Total cost approach Evaluating each possible PD system and identifying *all* of the costs of each alternative.

Total fixed cost The sum of those costs that are fixed in total—no matter how much is produced.

Total quality management (TQM) The philosophy that everyone in the organization is concerned about quality, throughout all of the firm's activities, to better serve customer needs.

Total variable cost The sum of those changing expenses that are closely related to output—such as expenses for parts, wages, packaging materials, outgoing freight, and sales commissions.

Trade (functional) discount A list price reduction given to channel members for the job they are going to do.

Trade-in allowance A price reduction given for used products when similar new products are bought.

Trademark Those words, symbols, or marks that are legally registered for use by a single company.

Traditional channel systems A channel in which the various channel members make little or no effort to cooperate with each other.

Transporting The marketing function of moving goods.

Transporting function The movement of goods from one place to another.

Trend extension Extends past experience to predict the future.

Truck wholesalers Wholesalers that specialize in delivering products that they stock in their own trucks.

2/10, net 30 Allows a 2 percent discount off the face value of the invoice if the invoice is paid within 10 days.

Unfair trade practice acts Put a lower limit on prices, especially at the wholesale and retail levels.

Uniform delivered pricing Making an average freight charge applicable to all buyers.

Universal functions of marketing Buying, selling, transporting, storing, standardizing and grading, financing, risk taking, and market information.

Unsought products Products that potential customers don't yet want or know they can buy.

Validity The extent to which data measures what it is intended to measure.

Value in use pricing Setting prices that will capture some of what customers will save by substituting the firm's product for the one currently being used.

Value pricing Setting a fair price level for a marketing mix that really gives the target market superior customer value.

Vendor analysis Formal rating of suppliers on all relevant areas of performance.

Vertical integration Acquiring firms at different levels of channel activity.

Vertical marketing systems Channel systems in which the whole channel focuses on the same target market at the end of the channel.

Voluntary chains Wholesaler-sponsored groups that work with independent retailers.

Wants Needs that are learned during a person's life.

Warranty What the seller promises about its product.

Wheel of retailing theory New types of retailers enter the market as low-status, low-margin, low-price operators and then, if successful, evolve into more conventional retailers offering more services with higher operating costs and higher prices.

Wheeler Lea Amendment Law that bans unfair or deceptive acts in commerce.

Wholesalers Firms whose main function is providing *wholesaling activities*.

Wholesaling The *activities* of those persons or establishments that sell to retailers and other merchants, or to industrial, institutional, and commercial users, but who do not sell in large amounts to final consumers.

Zone pricing Making an average freight charge applicable to all buyers within specific geographic areas.